D0187904

military		
music		
noun		
nautical		
oneself		
pejorative		
photography	*Photo*	fotografía
plural	*pl*	plural
politics	*Pol*	política
possessive	*poss*	posesivo
past participle	*pp*	participio pasado
preposition	*prep*	preposición
present participle	*pres p*	participio de presente
pronoun	*pron*	pronombre
past tense	*pt*	tiempo pasado
railroad	*Rail*	ferrocarril
religion	*Relig*	religión
school	*Schol*	enseñanza
singular	*sing*	singular
someone	*s. o.*	alguien
something	*sth*	algo
technical	*Tec*	técnico
university	*Univ*	universidad
verb	*vb*	verbo
intransitive verb	*vi*	verbo intransitivo
pronominal verb	*vpr*	verbo pronominal
transitive verb	*vt*	verbo transitivo
transitive & intransitive verb	*vti*	verbo transitivo e intransitivo

Oxford Spanish Mini Dictionary
Diccionario Oxford Mini

Spanish–English • English–Spanish
español-inglés • inglés-español

Diccionario Oxford Mini

CUARTA EDICIÓN

español–inglés
inglés–español

OXFORD
UNIVERSITY PRESS

Oxford
Spanish
Mini Dictionary

FOURTH EDITION

Spanish–English
English–Spanish

OXFORD
UNIVERSITY PRESS

OXFORD

UNIVERSITY PRESS

Great Clarendon Street, Oxford OX2 6DP

Oxford University Press is a department of the University of Oxford.
It furthers the University's objective of excellence in research, scholarship,
and education by publishing worldwide in

Oxford New York

Auckland Cape Town Dar es Salaam Hong Kong Karachi Kuala Lumpur
Madrid Melbourne Mexico City Nairobi New Delhi Shanghai Taipei
Toronto

With offices in

Argentina Austria Brazil Chile Czech Republic France Greece
Guatemala Hungary Italy Japan South Korea Poland Portugal
Singapore Switzerland Thailand Turkey Ukraine Vietnam

Oxford is a registered trade mark of Oxford University Press
in the UK and in certain other countries

Published in the United States
by Oxford University Press Inc., New York

British Library Cataloguing in Publication Data
Data available

Library of Congress Cataloging in Publication Data
Data available

ISBN 978-0-19-953435-7
ISBN 978-0-19-954126-3 (US edition)
ISBN 978-0-19-953490-6 (Spanish cover edition)

10 9 8 7 6 5 4 3

Typeset by Interactive Sciences Ltd, Gloucester
Printed and bound in Italy by
L.E.G.O. S.p.A., Lavis (TN)

Contents/Índice

Proprietary terms

This dictionary includes some words which have, or are asserted to have, proprietary status as trademarks. Their inclusion does not imply that they have acquired for legal purposes a non-proprietary or general significance, nor any other judgement concerning their legal status. In cases where the editorial staff have some evidence that a word has proprietary status this is indicated in the entry for that word by the symbol ®, but no judgement concerning the legal status of such words is made or implied thereby.

Marcas registradas

Este diccionario incluye algunas palabras que son o pretenden ser marcas registradas. Cuando al editor le consta que una palabra es una marca registrada, esto se indica por medio del símbolo ®. No debe atribuirse ningún valor jurídico ni a la presencia ni a la ausencia de tal designación.

Contributors/Colaboradores

Fourth Edition/Cuarta edición

Editors/Editores
Joanna Rubery
Nicholas Rollin

Phrasefinder/Frases útiles
Pablo Pérez D'Ors
Carol Styles Carvajal
Oriana Orellana Jordán

Data input/Entrada de datos
Susan Wilkin

Third Edition/Tercera edición

Nicholas Rollin
Carol Styles Carvajal

Second Edition/Segunda edición

Editors/Editores
Carol Styles Carvajal
Michael Britton
Jane Horwood

Phrasefinder/Frases útiles
Idoia Noble
Neil and Roswitha Morris

Data input/Entrada de datos
Susan Wilkin

First Edition/Primera edición

Editor/Editora
Christine Lea

Introduction

This new edition of the *Oxford Spanish Mini Dictionary* is designed as an effective and practical reference tool for the student, adult learner, traveller, and business professional.

The wordlist has been revised and updated to reflect recent additions to both languages. The *Phrasefinder* section has been expanded. It aims to provide the user with the confidence to communicate in the most commonly encountered social situations such as travel, shopping, eating out, and organizing leisure activities.

Another valuable feature of the dictionary is the special status given to more complex grammatical words which provide the basic structure of both languages. Boxed entries in the text for these *function words* provide extended treatment, including notes to warn of possible pitfalls.

The dictionary has an easy-to-use, streamlined layout. Bullets separate each new part of speech within an entry. Nuances of sense or usage are pinpointed by indicators or by typical collocates with which the word frequently occurs. Extra help is given in the form of symbols to mark the register of words and phrases. An exclamation mark 🛈 indicates colloquial language, and a cross ✖ indicates slang.

Each English headword is followed by its phonetic transcription between slashes. The symbols used are those of the International Phonetic Alphabet. Pronunciation is also shown for derivatives and compounds where it is not easily deduced from that of a headword. The rules for the pronunciation of Spanish are given on pages xii–xiii.

The swung dash (∼) is used to represent a headword or that part of a headword preceding the vertical bar (|).

In both English and Spanish only irregular plurals are given. Normally Spanish nouns and adjectives ending in an unstressed vowel form the plural by adding s (e.g. *libro, libros*). Nouns and adjectives ending in a stressed vowel or a consonant add es (e.g. *rubí, rubíes, pared, paredes*). An accent on the final syllable is not required when es is added (e.g. *nación, naciones*). Final *z* becomes *ces* (e.g. *vez, veces*).

Spanish nouns and adjectives ending in o form the feminine by changing the final *o* to *a* (e.g. *hermano, hermana*). Most Spanish nouns and adjectives ending in anything other than final *o* do not have a separate feminine form, with the exception of those denoting nationality etc.; these add a to the masculine singular form (e.g. *español, española*). An accent on the penultimate syllable is then not required (e.g. *inglés, inglesa*). Adjectives ending in *án, ón*, or *or* behave like those denoting nationality, with the following exceptions: *inferior, mayor, mejor, menor, peor, superior*, where the feminine has the same form as the masculine. Spanish verb tables will be found at the end of the book.

The Spanish alphabet

In Spanish ñ is considered a separate letter and in the Spanish–English section, therefore, is alphabetized after *ny*.

Introducción

Esta nueva edición del *Diccionario Oxford Mini* ha sido concebida a fin de proporcionar una herramienta de referencia práctica y eficaz al estudiante, joven y adulto, al viajero y a la persona de negocios.

Se ha revisado la lista de palabras con el objeto de incorporar nuevos términos en ambos idiomas. La sección central contiene una lista de *Frases útiles*, que se ha ampliado, destinada a que el usuario adquiera la confianza necesaria para comunicarse en las situaciones más normales de la vida diaria, como las que se encuentran al viajar, hacer compras, comer fuera y organizar actividades recreativas.

Otro valioso aspecto del diccionario es la importancia especial que se da a palabras con una función más compleja dentro de la gramática y que proveen la estructura básica de ambos idiomas. Estos *vocablos clave* están contenidos en recuadros dentro del texto, donde se les da un tratamiento amplio y se incluyen notas para advertir sobre posibles escollos.

El diccionario tiene una presentación clara y es fácil de usar. Símbolos distintivos separan las diferentes categorías gramaticales dentro de cada entrada. Los matices de sentido y de uso se muestran con precisión mediante indicadores o por colocaciones típicas con las que la palabra se usa frecuentemente. Se encuentra ayuda adicional en los signos que indican el registro idiomático de las palabras y frases. Un signo de exclamación ▣ señala el uso coloquial y una cruz ▣ el uso argot.

Cada palabra cabeza de artículo en inglés va seguida de su transcripción fonética entre barras oblicuas. Los símbolos que se usan son los del Alfabeto Fonético Internacional. También aparece la pronunciación de derivados y nombres compuestos cuando no es posible deducirla de la palabra cabeza de artículo. Las reglas sobre pronunciación inglesa se encuentran en la página xiv.

La tilde (~) se emplea para sustituir la palabra cabeza de artículo o aquella parte de tal palabra que precede a la barra vertical (|).

Tanto en inglés como en español se dan los plurales solamente si son irregulares. Para formar el plural regular en inglés se añade la letra s al sustantivo singular, pero es cuando se trata de una palabra que termina en *ch*, *sh*, *s*, *ss*, *us*, *x*, *o*, *z* (p.ej. *sash*, *sashes*). En el caso de una palabra que termine en *y* precedida por una consonante, la *y* se transforma en *ies* (p.ej. *baby*, *babies*). Para formar el tiempo pasado y el participio pasado se añade *ed* al infinitivo de los verbos regulares ingleses (p.ej. *last*, *lasted*). En el caso de los verbos ingleses que terminan en e muda se añade sólo la *d* (p.ej. *move*, *moved*). En el caso de los verbos ingleses que terminan en *y*, se debe cambiar la *y* por *ied* (p.ej. *carry*, *carried*). Los verbos irregulares se encuentran en el diccionario por orden alfabético remitidos al infinitivo, y también en la lista que aparece en las últimas páginas del diccionario.

Pronunciation of Spanish

Vowels

a between pronunciation of *a* in English *cat* and *arm*

e like *e* in English *bed*

i like *ee* in English *see* but a little shorter

o like *o* in English *hot* but a little longer

u like *oo* in English *too*

y when a vowel is as Spanish **i**

Consonants

b (1) in initial position or after a nasal consonant is like English *b*
    (2) in other positions is between English *b* and English *v*

c (1) before **e** or **i** is like *th* in English *thin*. In Latin American Spanish is like English *s*.
    (2) in other positions is like *c* in English *cat*

ch like *ch* in English *chip*

d (1) in initial position, after nasal consonants and after **l** is like English *d*
    (2) in other positions is like *th* in English *this*

f like English *f*

g (1) before **e** or **i** is like *ch* in Scottish *loch*
    (2) in initial position is like *g* in English *get*
    (3) in other positions is like (2) but a little softer

j	like *ch* in Scottish *loch*
k	like English *k*
l	like English *l* but see also **ll**
ll	like *lli* in English *million*
m	like English *m*
n	like English *n*
ñ	like *ni* in English *opinion*
p	like English *p*
q	like English *k*
r	rolled or trilled
s	like *s* in English *sit*
t	like English *t*
v	(1) in initial position or after a nasal consonant is like English *b*
	(2) in other positions is between English *b* and English *v*
w	like Spanish **b** or **v**
x	like English *x*
y	like English *y*
z	like *th* in English *thin*

Pronunciación inglesa

Símbolos fonéticos

Vocales y diptongos

iː	see	ɔː	saw	eɪ	page	ɔɪ	join
ɪ	sit	ʊ	put	əʊ	home	ɪə	near
e	ten	uː	too	aɪ	five	eə	hair
æ	hat	ʌ	cup	aɪə	fire	ʊə	poor
ɑː	arm	ɜː	fur	aʊ	now		
ɒ	got	ə	ago	aʊə	flour		

Consonantes

p	pen	tʃ	chin	s	so	n	no
b	bad	dʒ	June	z	zoo	ŋ	sing
t	tea	f	fall	ʃ	she	l	leg
d	dip	v	voice	ʒ	measure	r	red
k	cat	θ	thin	h	how	j	yes
g	got	ð	then	m	man	w	wet

El símbolo ' precede a la sílaba sobre la cual recae el acento tónico.

Aa

a *preposición*

> Note that **a** followed by **el** becomes **al**, e.g. vamos al cine

····▸ (*dirección*) to. fui a México I went to Mexico. muévete a la derecha move to the right

····▸ (*posición*) se sentaron a la mesa they sat at the table. al lado del banco next to the bank. a orillas del río on the banks of the river

····▸ (*distancia*) queda a 5 km it's 5 km away. a pocos metros de aquí a few meters from here

····▸ (*fecha*) hoy estamos a 5 today is the 5th. ¿a cuánto estamos?, (*LAm*) ¿a cómo estamos? what's the date?

····▸ (*hora, momento*) at. a las 2 at 2 o'clock. a fin de mes at the end of the month. a los 21 años at the age of 21; (*después de*) after 21 years

····▸ (*precio*) ¿a cómo están las peras? how much are the pears? están a 3 euros el kilo they're 3 euros a kilo. salen a 15 euros cada uno they work out at 15 euros each.

····▸ (*medio, modo*) fuimos a pie we went on foot. hecho a mano hand made. pollo al horno (*LAm*) roast chicken

····▸ (*cuando precede al objeto directo de persona*) no se traduce. conocí a Juan I met Juan. quieren mucho a sus hijos they love their children very much

····▸ (*con objeto indirecto*) to. se lo di a Juan I gave it to Juan. le vendí el coche a mi amigo I sold my friend the car, I sold the car to my friend. se lo compré a mi madre I bought it from my mother; (*para*) I bought it for my mother

> ➡ Cuando la preposición **a** se emplea precedida de ciertos verbos como **empezar, faltar, ir, llegar** etc., ver bajo el respectivo verbo

ábaco *m* abacus

abadejo *m* pollack

abadía *f* abbey

abajo *adv* (*down*) below; (*dirección*) down(wards); (*en casa*) downstairs. ● *int* down with. ~ **de** (*LAm*) under(neath). **calle** ~ down the street. **escaleras** ~ down the stairs. **la parte de** ~ the bottom (part). **más** ~ further down

abalanzarse 10 *vpr* rush (*hacia towards*)

abanderado *m* standard-bearer; (*Mex, en fútbol*) linesman

abandon|ado *adj* abandoned; (*descuidado*) neglected; (*persona*) untidy. **~ar** *vt* leave (*un lugar*); abandon (*persona, cosa*). ● *vi* give up. ~**arse** *vpr* give in; (*descuidarse*) let o.s. go. ~**o** *m* abandonment; (*estado*) neglect

abani|car 🔟 *vt* fan. ~**co** *m* fan

abaratar *vt* reduce

abarcar 🔟 *vt* put one's arms around, embrace; (*comprender*) embrace

abarrotar *vt* overfill, pack full

abarrotes *mpl* (*LAm*) groceries; (*tienda*) grocer's shop

abast|ecer 🔢 *vt* supply. ~**ecimiento** *m* supply; (*acción*) supplying. ~**o** *m* supply. no dar ~**o** be unable to cope (con with)

abati|do *adj* depressed. ~**miento** *m* depression

abdicar 🔟 *vt* give up. • *vi* abdicate

abdom|en *m* abdomen. ~**inal** *adj* abdominal

abec|é *m* 🔟 alphabet, ABC. ~**edario** *m* alphabet

abedul *m* birch (tree)

abej|a *f* bee. ~**orro** *m* bumblebee

aberración *f* aberration

abertura *f* opening

abeto *m* fir (tree)

abierto *pp véase* **ABRIR** • *adj* open

abism|al *adj* abysmal; (*profundo*) deep. ~**ar** *vt* throw into an abyss; (*fig, abatir*) humble. ~**arse** *vpr* be absorbed (en in), be lost (en in). ~**o** *m* abyss; (*fig, diferencia*) world of difference

ablandar *vt* soften.~**se** *vpr* soften

abnega|ción *f* self-sacrifice. ~**do** *adj* self-sacrificing

abochornar *vt* embarrass. ~**se** *vpr* feel embarrassed

abofetear *vt* slap

aboga|cía *f* law. ~**do** *m* lawyer, solicitor; (*ante tribunal superior*) barrister (*Brit*), attorney (*Amer*)

abolengo *m* ancestry

aboli|ción *f* abolition. ~**cionismo** *m* abolitionism. ~**cionista** *m & f* abolitionist. ~**r** 🔢 *vt* abolish

abolla|dura *f* dent. ~**r** *vt* dent

abolsado *adj* baggy

abomba|do *adj* convex; (*LAm, atontado*) dopey. ~**r** *vt* make convex. ~**rse** *vpr* (*LAm, descomponerse*) go bad

abominable *adj* abominable

abona|ble *adj* payable. ~**do** *adj* paid. •*m* subscriber. ~**r** *vt* pay; (*en agricultura*) fertilize. ~**rse** *vpr* subscribe.

abono *m* payment; (*estiércol*) fertilizer; (*a un periódico*) subscription

aborda|ble *adj* reasonable; (*persona*) approachable. ~**je** *m* boarding. ~**r** *vt* tackle (un asunto); approach (una persona); (*Naut*) come alongside; (*Mex, Aviac*) board

aborigen *adj & m* native

aborrec|er 🔢 *vt* loathe. ~**ible** *adj* loathsome. ~**ido** *adj* loathed. ~**imiento** *m* loathing

abort|ar *vi* have a miscarriage. ~**ivo** *adj* abortive. ~**o** *m* miscarriage; (*voluntario*) abortion. **hacerse un** ~ have an abortion

abotonar *vt* button (up). ~**se** *vpr* button (up)

abovedado *adj* vaulted

abrasa|dor *adj* burning. ~**r** *vt* burn. ~**rse** *vpr* burn

abraz|ar *vt* 🔟 embrace. ~**arse** *vpr* embrace. ~**o** *m* hug. **un fuerte** ~**o** (*en una carta*) with best wishes from

abre|botellas *m invar* bottle-opener. **~cartas** m invar paper-knife. **~latas** m invar tin opener (Brit), can opener

abrevia|ción f abbreviation; (texto abreviado) abridged text. **~do** adj brief; (texto) abridged. **~r** vt abbreviate; abridge (texto); cut short (viaje etc). ● vi be brief. **~tura** f abbreviation

abriga|do adj (lugar) sheltered; (persona) well wrapped up. **~ador** adj (Mex, ropa) warm. **~r** vt shelter; cherish (esperanza); harbour (duda, sospecha). **~rse** vpr (take) shelter; (con ropa) wrap up. **~o** m (over)coat; (lugar) shelter

abril m April. **~eño** adj April

abrillantar vt polish

abrir (pp abierto) vt/i open. **~se** vpr open; (extenderse) open out; (el tiempo) clear

abrochar vt do up; (con botones) button up

abruma|dor adj overwhelming. **~r** vt overwhelm

abrupto adj steep; (áspero) harsh

abrutado adj brutish

absentismo m absenteeism

absolución f (Relig) absolution; (Jurid) acquittal

absolut|amente adv absolutely, completely. **~o** adj absolute. en **~o** (not) at all. **~orio** adj of acquittal

absolver 2 (pp absuelto) vt (Relig) absolve; (Jurid) acquit

absor|bente adj absorbent; (fig, interesante) absorbing. **~ber** vt absorb. **~ción** f absorption. **~to** adj absorbed

abstemio adj teetotal. ● m teetotaller

absten|ción f abstention. **~erse** 40 vpr abstain, refrain (de from)

abstinencia f abstinence

abstra|cción f abstraction. **~cto** adj abstract. **~er** 41 vt abstract. **~erse** vpr be lost in thought. **~ído** adj absent-minded

absuelto adj (Relig) absolved; (Jurid) acquitted

absurdo adj absurd. ● m absurd thing

abuchea|r vt boo. **~o** m booing

abuel|a f grandmother. **~o** m grandfather. **~os** mpl grandparents

abu|lia f apathy. **~úlico** adj apathetic

abulta|do adj bulky. **~r** vt (fig, exagerar) exaggerate. ● vi be bulky

abunda|ncia f abundance. nadar en la **~ncia** be rolling in money. **~nte** adj abundant, plentiful. **~r** vi be plentiful

aburguesarse vpr become middle-class

aburri|do adj (con estar) bored; (con ser) boring. **~dor** adj (LAm) boring. **~miento** m boredom; (cosa pesada) bore. **~r** vt bore. **~rse** vpr get bored

abus|ar vi take advantage. **~ar de la bebida** drink too much. **~ivo** adj excessive. **~o** m abuse

acá adv here. **~ y allá** here and there. **de ~ para allá** to and fro. **de ayer ~** since yesterday. **más ~** nearer

acaba|do adj finished; (perfecto) perfect. ● m finish. **~r** vt/i finish. **~rse** vpr finish; (agotarse) run out; (morirse) die. **~r con** put an end to. **~r de** (+ infinitivo) have just (+ pp). **~ de llegar** he has just arrived. **~r por** (+ infinitivo) end up (+ gerundio). **¡se acabó!** that's it!

acabóse m. ser el **~** be the end, be the limit

a **acad|emia** f academy. **~émico** adj academic

acallar vt silence

acalora|do adj heated; (persona) hot. **~rse** vpr get hot; (fig, excitarse) get excited

acampar vi camp

acantilado m cliff

acapara|r vt hoard; (monopolizar) monopolize. **~miento** m hoarding; (monopolio) monopolizing

acariciar vt caress; (animal) stroke; (idea) nurture

ácaro m mite

acarre|ar vt transport; (desgracias etc) cause. **~o** m transport

acartona|do adj (piel) wizened. **~rse** vpr (ponerse rígido) go stiff; (piel) become wizened

acaso adv maybe, perhaps. ● m chance. **~ llueva mañana** perhaps it will rain tomorrow. **por si ~** (just) in case

acata|miento m compliance (de with). **~r** vt comply with

acatarrarse vpr catch a cold, get a cold

acaudalado adj well off

acceder vi agree; (tener acceso) have access

acces|ible adj accessible; (persona) approachable. **~o** m access, entry; (Med, ataque) attack

accesorio adj & m accessory

accident|ado adj (terreno) uneven; (agitado) troubled; (persona) injured. **~al** adj accidental. **~arse** vpr have an accident. **~e** m accident

acci|ón f (incl Jurid) action; (hecho) deed; (Com) share. **~onar** vt work. ● vi gesticulate. **~onista** m & f shareholder

acebo m holly (tree)

acech|ar vt lie in wait for. **~o** m spying. **al ~o** on the look-out

aceit|ar vt oil; (Culin) add oil to. **~e** m oil. **~e de oliva** olive oil. **~e de ricino** castor oil. **~era** f cruet; (para engrasar) oilcan. **~ero** adj oil. **~oso** adj oily

aceitun|a f olive. **~ado** adj olive. **~o** m olive tree

acelera|dor m accelerator. **~r** vt accelerate; (fig) speed up, quicken

acelga f chard

acent|o m accent; (énfasis) stress. **~uación** f accentuation. **~uar** [21] vt stress; (fig) emphasize. **~uarse** vpr become noticeable

acepción f meaning, sense

acepta|ble adj acceptable. **~ción** f acceptance; (éxito) success. **~r** vt accept

acequia f irrigation channel

acera f pavement (Brit), sidewalk (Amer)

acerca de prep about

acerca|miento m approach; (fig) reconciliation. **~r** [7] vt bring near. **~rse** vpr approach

acero m steel. **~ inoxidable** stainless steel

acérrimo adj (fig) staunch

acert|ado adj right, correct; (apropiado) appropriate. **~ar** [1] vt (adivinar) get right, guess. ● vi get right; (en el blanco) hit. **~ar a** happen to. **~ar con** hit on. **~ijo** m riddle

achacar [7] vt attribute

achacoso adj sickly

achaque m ailment

achatar vt flatten

achicar [7] vt make smaller; (fig, fam, empequeñecer) belittle; (Naut)

bale out. **~se** *vpr* become smaller; (*humillarse*) be intimidated

achicharra|r *vt* burn; (*fig*) pester. **~rse** *vpr* burn

achichincle *m & f* (*Mex*) hanger-on

achicopalado *adj* (*Mex*) depressed

achicoria *f* chicory

achiote *m* (*LAm*) annatto

achispa|do *adj* tipsy. **~rse** *vpr* get tipsy

achulado *adj* cocky

acicala|do *adj* dressed up. **~r** *vt* dress up. **~rse** *vpr* get dressed up

acicate *m* spur

acidez *f* acidity; (*Med*) heartburn

ácido *adj* sour. ● *m* acid

acierto *m* success; (*idea*) good idea; (*habilidad*) skill

aclama|ción *f* acclaim; (*aplausos*) applause. **~r** *vt* acclaim; (*aplaudir*) applaud

aclara|ción *f* explanation. **~r** *vt* lighten (*colores*); (*explicar*) clarify; (*enjuagar*) rinse. ● *vi* (*el tiempo*) brighten up. **~rse** *vpr* become clear. **~torio** *adj* explanatory

aclimata|ción *f* acclimatization, acclimation (*Amer*). **~r** *vt* acclimatize, acclimate (*Amer*). **~rse** *vpr* become acclimatized, become acclimated (*Amer*)

acné *m* acne

acobardar *vt* intimidate. **~se** *vpr* lose one's nerve

acocil *m* (*Mex*) freshwater shrimp

acoge|dor *adj* welcoming; (*ambiente*) friendly. **~r** 14 *vt* welcome; (*proteger*) shelter; (*recibir*) receive. **~rse** *vpr* take refuge. **~ida** *f* welcome; (*refugio*) refuge

acolcha|do *adj* quilted. **~r** *vt*

quilt, pad

acomedido *adj* (*Mex*) obliging

acomet|er *vt* attack; (*emprender*) undertake. **~ida** *f* attack

acomod|ado *adj* well off. **~ador** *m* usher. **~adora** *f* usherette. **~ar** *vt* arrange; (*adaptar*) adjust. ● *vi* be suitable. **~arse** *vpr* settle down; (*adaptarse*) conform

acompaña|miento *m* accompaniment. **~nte** *m & f* companion; (*Mus*) accompanist. **~r** *vt* go with; (*hacer compañía*) keep company; (*adjuntar*) enclose

acondicionar *vt* fit out; (*preparar*) prepare

aconseja|ble *adj* advisable. **~do** *adj* advised. **~r** *vt* advise. **~rse** *vpr*. **~rse con** consult

acontec|er 11 *vi* happen. **~imiento** *m* event

acopla|miento *m* coupling; (*Elec*) connection. **~r** *vt* fit; (*Elec*) connect; (*Rail*) couple

acorazado *adj* armour-plated. ● *m* battleship

acord|ar 2 *vt* agree (upon); (*decidir*) decide; (*recordar*) remind. **~arse** *vpr* remember. ● *adj* in agreement; (*Mus*) harmonious. ● *m* chord

acorde|ón *m* accordion. **~onista** *m & f* accordionist

acordona|do *adj* (*lugar*) cordoned off; (*zapatos*) lace-up. **~r** *vt* lace (up); (*rodear*) cordon off

acorralar *vt* round up (*animales*); corner (*personas*)

acortar *vt* shorten; cut short (*permanencia*). **~se** *vpr* get shorter

acos|ar *vt* hound; (*fig*) pester. **~o** *m* pursuit; (*fig*) pestering

acostar 2 *vt* put to bed; (*Naut*) bring alongside. ● *vi* (*Naut*) reach land. **~se** vpr go to bed; (*echarse*) lie down. **~se con** (*fig*) sleep with

acostumbra|do adj (*habitual*) usual. **~do a** used to. **~r** vt get used. **me ha ~do a levantarme por la noche** he's got me used to getting up at night. ● vi. **~r** be accustomed to. **acostumbro a comer a la una** I usually have lunch at one o'clock. **~rse** vpr become accustomed, get used

acota|ción f (*nota*) margin note (*en el teatro*) stage direction; (*cota*) elevation mark. **~miento** m (*Mex*) hard shoulder

acrecentar 1 vt increase. **~se** vpr increase

acredita|do adj reputable; (*Pol*) accredited. **~r** vt prove; accredit (*diplomático*); (*garantizar*) guarantee; (*autorizar*) authorize. **~rse** vpr make one's name

acreedor adj worthy (de of). ● m creditor

acribillar vt (a balazos) riddle (a with); (a picotazos) cover (a with); (fig, a preguntas etc) bombard (a with)

acr|obacia f acrobatics. **~obacias aéreas** aerobatics. **~óbata** m & f acrobat. **~obático** adj acrobatic

acta f minutes; (*certificado*) certificate

actitud f posture, position; (*fig*) attitude, position

activ|ar vt activate; (*acelerar*) speed up. **~idad** f activity. **~o** adj active. ● m assets

acto m act; (*ceremonia*) ceremony. **en el ~** immediately

act|or m actor. **~riz** f actress

actuación f action; (*conducta*) behaviour; (*Theat*) performance

actual adj present; (*asunto*) top-

ical. **~idad** f present; (de asunto) topicality. **en la ~idad** (en este momento) currently; (hoy en día) nowadays. **~idades** fpl current affairs. **~ización** f modernization. **~izar** 10 vt modernize. **~mente** adv now, at the present time

actuar 21 vi act. **~ como** de act as

acuarel|a f watercolour. **~ista** m & f watercolourist

acuario m aquarium. **A~** Aquarius

acuartelar vt quarter, billet; (*mantener en cuartel*) confine to barracks

acuático adj aquatic

acuchillar vt slash; stab (*persona*)

acuci|ante adj urgent. **~ar** vt urge on; (dar prisa a) hasten. **~oso** adj keen

acudir vi. **~ a** go to; (*asistir*) attend; turn up for (a una cita); (en auxilio) go to help

acueducto m aqueduct

acuerdo m agreement. ● vb véase **ACORDAR. ¡de ~!** OK! **de ~ con** in accordance with. **estar de ~** agree. **ponerse de ~** agree

acuesto vb véase **ACOSTAR**

acumula|dor m accumulator. **~r** vt accumulate. **~rse** vpr accumulate

acunar vt rock

acuñar vt mint, coin

acupuntura f acupuncture

acurrucarse 7 vpr curl up

acusa|do adj accused; (*destacado*) marked. ● m accused. **~r** vt accuse; (*mostrar*) show; (*denunciar*) denounce; acknowledge (*recibo*)

acuse m. **~ de recibo** acknowledgement of receipt

acus|ica m & f 1 telltale. **~ón** m

① telltale

acústic|a f acoustics. **~o** adj acoustic

adapta|ble adj adaptable. **~ción** f adaptation. **~dor** m adapter. **~r** vt adapt; (ajustar) fit. **~rse** vpr adapt o.s.

adecua|do adj suitable. **~r** vt adapt, make suitable

adelant|ado adj advanced; (niño) precocious; (reloj) fast. **por ~ado** in advance.. **~amiento** m advance(ment); (Auto) overtaking. **~ar** vt advance, move forward; (acelerar) speed up; put forward (reloj). ● vi advance, go forward; (reloj) gain, be fast. **~arse** vpr advance, move forward; (reloj) gain; (Auto) overtake. **~e** adv forward. ● int come in!; (¡siga!) carry on! **más ~e** (lugar) further on; (tiempo) later on. **~o** m advance; (progreso) progress

adelgaza|miento m slimming. **~r** ⑩ vt make thin; lose (kilos). ● vi lose weight; (adrede) slim. **~rse** vpr lose weight; (adrede) slim

ademán m gesture. **en ~ de** as if to. **ademanes** mpl (modales) manners.

además adv besides; (también) also; (lo que es más) what's more. **~ de** besides

adentr|arse vpr. **~arse en** penetrate into; study thoroughly (tema etc). **~o** adv in(side). **~ de** (LAm) in(side). **mar ~o** out at sea. **tierra ~o** inland

adepto m supporter

aderez|ar ⑩ vt flavour (bebidas); (condimentar) season; dress (ensalada). **~o** m flavouring; (con condimentos) seasoning; (para ensalada) dressing

adeud|ar vt owe. **~o** m debit

adhe|rir ④ vt/i stick. **~rirse** vpr stick; (fig) follow. **~sión** f adhesion; (fig) support. **~sivo** adj & m adhesive

adici|ón f addition. **~onal** adj additional. **~onar** vt add

adicto adj addicted. ● m addict; (seguidor) follower

adiestra|do adj trained. **~miento** m training. **~r** vt train. **~rse** vpr practise

adinerado adj wealthy

adiós int goodbye!; (al cruzarse con alguien) hello!

adit|amento m addition; (accesorio) accessory. **~ivo** m additive

adivin|anza f riddle. **~ar** vt foretell; (acertar) guess. **~o** m fortune-teller

adjetivo adj adjectival. ● m adjective

adjudica|ción f award. **~r** ⑦ vt award. **~rse** vpr appropriate. **~tario** m winner of an award

adjunt|ar vt enclose. **~o** adj enclosed; (auxiliar) assistant. ● m assistant

administra|ción f administration; (gestión) management. **~dor** m administrator; (gerente) manager. **~dora** f administrator; manageress. **~r** vt administer. **~tivo** adj administrative

admira|ble adj admirable. **~ción** f admiration. **~dor** m admirer. **~r** vt admire; (sorprender) amaze. **~rse** vpr be amazed

admi|sibilidad f admissibility. **~sible** adj acceptable. **~sión** f admission; (aceptación) acceptance. **~tir** vt admit; (aceptar) accept

adobar vt (Culin) pickle; (condimentar) marinade

a

adobe *m* sun-dried brick

adobo *m* pickle; (*condimento*) marinade

adoctrinar *vt* indoctrinate

adolecer 🔟 *vi*. ~ de suffer from

adolescen|cia *f* adolescence. ~**te** *adj* adolescent. ● *m & f* teenager, adolescent

adonde *adv* where

adónde *adv* where?

adop|ción *f* adoption. ~**tar** *vt* adopt. ~**tivo** *adj* adoptive; (hijo) adopted; (patria) of adoption

adoqu|ín *m* paving stone; (*imbécil*) idiot. ~**inado** *m* paving. ~**inar** *vt* pave

adora|ción *f* adoration. ~**r** *vt* adore

adormec|er 🔟 *vt* send to sleep; (*fig, calmar*) calm, soothe. ~**erse** *vpr* fall asleep; (un miembro) go to sleep. ~**ido** *adj* sleepy; (un miembro) numb

adormilarse *vpr* doze

adorn|ar *vt* adorn (con, de with). ~**o** *m* decoration

adosar *vt* lean (a against); (*Mex, adjuntar*) to enclose

adqui|rir 🔟 *vt* acquire; (*comprar*) purchase. ~**sición** *f* acquisition; (*compra*) purchase. ~**sitivo** *adj* purchasing

adrede *adv* on purpose

adrenalina *f* adrenalin

aduan|a *f* customs. ~**ero** *adj* customs. ● *m* customs officer

aducir 🔟 *vt* allege

adueñarse *vpr* take possession

adul|ación *f* flattery. ~**ador** *adj* flattering. ● *m* flatterer. ~**ar** *vt* flatter

ad|ulterar *vt* adulterate. ~**ulterio** *m* adultery

adulto *adj & m* adult, grown-up

advenedizo *adj & m* upstart

advenimiento *m* advent, arrival; (*subida al trono*) accession

adverbio *m* adverb

advers|ario *m* adversary. ~**idad** *f* adversity. ~**o** *adj* adverse, unfavourable

advert|encia *f* warning. ~**ir** 🔟 *vt* warn; (*notar*) notice

adviento *m* Advent

adyacente *adj* adjacent

aéreo *adj* air; (foto) aerial; (ferrocarril) overhead

aeróbico *adj* aerobic

aerodeslizador *m* hovercraft

aero|ligero *m* microlight. ~**lito** *m* meteorite. ~**moza** *f* (*LAm*) flight attendant. ~**puerto** *m* airport. ~**sol** *m* aerosol

afab|ilidad *f* affability. ~**le** *adj* affable

afamado *adj* famous

af|án *m* hard work; (*deseo*) desire. ~**anador** *m* (*Mex*) cleaner. ~**anar** *vt* 🅧 pinch 🔟. ~**anarse** *vpr* strive (en, por to)

afear *vt* disfigure, make ugly; (*censurar*) censure

afecta|ción *f* affectation. ~**do** *adj* affected. ~**r** *vt* affect

afect|ivo *adj* sensitive. ~**o** *m* (*cariño*) affection. ● *a*. ~**o** a attached to. ~**uoso** *adj* affectionate. con un ~**uoso** saludo (*en cartas*) with kind regards. suyo ~**ísimo** (*en cartas*) yours sincerely

afeita|do *m* shave. ~**dora** *f* electric razor. ~**r** *vt* shave. ~**rse** *vpr* shave, have a shave

afeminado *adj* effeminate. ● *m* effeminate person

aferrar *vt* grasp. ~**se** *vpr* to

cling (a to)

afianza|miento m (refuerzo) strengthening; (garantía) guarantee. **~rse** 🔟 vpr become established

afiche m (LAm) poster

afici|ón f liking; (conjunto de aficionados) fans. **por ~ón** as a hobby. **~onado** adj keen (a on), fond (a of). ● m fan. **~onar** vt make fond. **~onarse** vpr take a liking to

afila|do adj sharp. **~dor** m knifegrinder. **~r** vt sharpen

afilia|ción f affiliation. **~do** adj affiliated. **~rse** vpr become a member (a of)

afín adj similar; (contiguo) adjacent; (personas) related

afina|ción f (Auto, Mus) tuning. **~do** adj (Mus) in tune. **~dor** m tuner. **~r** vt (afilar) sharpen; (Auto, Mus) tune. **~rse** vpr become thinner

afincarse 🔟 vpr settle

afinidad f affinity; (parentesco) relationship by marriage

afirma|ción f affirmation. **~r** vt make firm; (asentir) affirm. **~rse** vpr steady o.s. **~tivo** adj affirmative

aflicción f affliction

afligi|do adj distressed. **~r** 🔢 vt distress. **~rse** vpr distress o.s.

aflojar vt loosen; (relajar) ease. ● vi let up. **~se** vpr loosen

aflu|encia f flow. **~ente** adj flowing. ● m tributary. **~ir** 🔢 vi flow (a into)

afónico adj hoarse

aforismo m aphorism

aforo m capacity

afortunado adj fortunate, lucky

afrancesado adj Frenchified

afrenta f insult; (vergüenza) disgrace

África f Africa. **~ del Sur** South Africa

africano adj & m African

afrodisíaco adj & m aphrodisiac

afrontar vt bring face to face; (enfrentar) face, confront

afuera adv out(side) **¡~!** out of the way! **~ de** (LAm) outside. **~s** fpl outskirts

agachar vt lower. **~se** vpr bend over

agalla f (de los peces) gill. **~s** fpl (fig) guts

agarradera f (LAm) handle

agarr|ado adj (fig, fam) mean. **~ar** vt grasp; (esp LAm) take; (LAm, pillar) catch. **~arse** vpr hold on; (fam, reñirse) have a fight. **~ón** m tug; (LAm, riña) row

agarrotar vt tie tightly; (el frío) stiffen; garotte (un reo). **~se** vpr go stiff; (Auto) seize up

agasaj|ado m guest of honour. **~ar** vt look after well. **~o** m good treatment

agazaparse vpr crouch

agencia f agency. **~ de viajes** travel agency. **~ inmobiliaria** estate agency (Brit), real estate agency (Amer). **~rse** vpr find (out) for o.s.

agenda f diary (Brit), appointment book (Amer); (programa) agenda

agente m agent; (de policía) policeman. ● f agent; (de policía) policewoman. **~ de aduanas** customs officer. **~ de bolsa** stockbroker

ágil adj agile

agili|dad f agility. **~zación** f speeding up. **~zar** vt speed up

agita|ción f waving; (de un lí-

a

quido) stirring; (*intranquilidad*) agitation. **~do** *adj* (el mar) rough; (*fig*) agitated. **~dor** *m* (*Pol*) agitator

agitar *vt* wave; shake (botellas etc); stir (líquidos); (*fig*) stir up. **~se** *vpr* wave; (el mar) get rough; (*fig*) get excited

aglomera|ción *f* agglomeration; (*de tráfico*) traffic jam. **~r** *vt* amass. **~rse** *vpr* form a crowd

agnóstico *adj & m* agnostic

agobi|ante *adj* (trabajo) exhausting; (calor) oppressive. **~ar** *vt* weigh down; (*fig, abrumar*) overwhelm. **~o** *m* weight; (cansancio) exhaustion; (opresión) oppression

agolparse *vpr* crowd together

agon|ía *f* death throes; (*fig*) agony. **~izante** *adj* dying; (luz) failing. **~izar** 10 *vi* be dying

agosto *m* August. hacer su **~** feather one's nest

agota|do *adj* exhausted; (todo vendido) sold out; (libro) out of print. **~dor** *adj* exhausting. **~miento** *m* exhaustion. **~r** *vt* exhaust. **~rse** *vpr* be exhausted; (existencias) sell out; (libro) go out of print

agracia|do *adj* attractive; (que tiene suerte) lucky. **~r** *vt* make attractive

agrada|ble *adj* pleasant, nice. **~r** *vt/i* please. esto me **~** I like this

agradec|er 11 *vt* thank (persona); be grateful for (cosa). **~ido** *adj* grateful. ¡muy **~ido**! thanks a lot! **~imiento** *m* gratitude

agrado *m* pleasure; (amabilidad) friendliness

agrandar *vt* enlarge; (*fig*) exaggerate. **~se** *vpr* get bigger

agrario *adj* agrarian, land; (política) agricultural

agrava|nte *adj* aggravating. ● *f* additional problem. **~r** *vt* aggravate; (aumentar el peso) make heavier. **~rse** *vpr* get worse

agravi|ar *vt* offend; (perjudicar) wrong. **~o** *m* offence

agredir 24 *vt* attack. **~ de palabra** insult

agrega|do *m* aggregate; (diplomático) attaché. **~r** 12 *vt* add; appoint (persona). **~rse** *vpr* to join

agres|ión *f* aggression; (ataque) attack. **~ividad** *f* aggressiveness. **~ivo** *adj* aggressive. **~or** *m* aggressor

agreste *adj* country; (terreno) rough

agri|ar regular, o raramente 20 *vt* sour. **~se** *vpr* turn sour; (*fig*) become embittered

agr|ícola *adj* agricultural. **~icultor** *m* farmer. **~icultura** *f* agriculture, farming

agridulce *adj* bitter-sweet; (*Culin*) sweet-and-sour

agrietar *vt* crack. **~se** *vpr* crack; (piel) chap

agrio *adj* sour. **~s** *mpl* citrus fruits

agro|nomía *f* agronomy. **~pecuario** *adj* farming

agrupa|ción *f* group; (acción) grouping. **~r** *vt* group. **~rse** *vpr* form a group

agruras *fpl* (*Mex*) heartburn

agua *f* water; (lluvia) rain; (marea) tide; (vertiente del tejado) slope. **~ abajo** downstream. **~ arriba** upstream. **~ o** *m* offence bendita holy water. **~ corriente** running water. **~ de colonia** eau de cologne. **~ dulce** fresh water. **~ mineral con gas** fizzy mineral water. **~ mineral sin gas** still mineral water. **~ potable**

drinking water. ~ **salada** salt water. **hacer** ~ (Naut) leak. **se me hizo** ~ **la boca** (LAm) my mouth watered

aguacate m avocado pear; (árbol) avocado pear tree

aguacero m downpour, heavy shower

aguado adj watery; (Mex, aburrido) boring

agua|fiestas m & f invar spoilsport, wet blanket. ~**mala** f (Mex), ~**mar** m jellyfish. ~**marina** f aquamarine

aguant|ar vt put up with, bear; (sostener) support. ● vi hold out. ~**arse** vpr restrain o.s. ~**e** m patience; (resistencia) endurance

aguar [15] vt water down

aguardar vt wait for. ● vi wait

agua|rdiente m (cheap) brandy. ~**rrás** m turpentine, turps [1]

agud|eza f sharpness; (fig, perspicacia) insight; (fig, ingenio) wit. ~**izar** [10] vt sharpen. ~**izarse** vpr (enfermedad) get worse. ~**o** adj sharp; (ángulo, enfermedad) acute; (voz) high-pitched

agüero m omen. **ser de mal** ~ be a bad omen

aguijón m sting; (vara) goad

águila f eagle; (persona perspicaz) astute person; (Mex, de moneda) heads. ¿~ **o sol?** heads or tails?

aguileño adj aquiline

aguinaldo m Christmas box; (LAm, paga) Christmas bonus

aguja f needle; (del reloj) hand; (de torre) steeple. ~**s** fpl (Rail) points

aguj|ear vt make holes in. ~**o** m hole

agujetas fpl stiffness; (Mex, de zapatos) shoe laces. **tener** ~ be stiff

aguzado adj sharp

ah int ah!, oh!

ahí adv there. ~ **nomás** (LAm) just there. **de** ~ **que** that is why. **por** ~ that way; (aproximadamente) thereabouts

ahija|da f god-daughter, godchild. ~**do** m godson, godchild. ~**dos** mpl godchildren

ahínco m enthusiasm; (empeño) insistence

ahog|ado adj (en el agua) drowned; (asfixiado) suffocated. ~**ar** [12] vt (en el agua) drown; (asfixiar) suffocate; put out (fuego). ~**arse** vpr (en el agua) drown; (asfixiarse) suffocate. ~**o** m breathlessness; (fig, angustia) distress

ahondar vt deepen. ● vi go deep. ~ **en** (fig) examine in depth. ~**se** vpr get deeper

ahora adv now; (hace muy poco) just now; (dentro de poco) very soon. ~ **bien** however. ~ **mismo** right now. **de** ~ **en adelante** from now on, in future. **por** ~ for the time being

ahorcar [7] vt hang. ~**se** vpr hang o.s.

ahorita adv (esp LAm fam) now. ~ **mismo** right now

ahorr|ador adj thrifty. ~**ar** vt save. ~**arse** vpr save o.s. ~**o** m saving. ~**os** mpl savings

ahuecar [7] vt hollow; fluff up (colchón); deepen (la voz)

ahuizote m (Mex) scourge

ahuma|do adj (Culin) smoked; (de colores) smoky. ~**r** vt (Culin) smoke; (llenar de humo) fill with smoke. ● vi smoke. ~**rse** vpr become smoky; (comida) acquire a smoky taste

ahuyentar vt drive away; banish (pensamientos etc)

aimará adj & m Aymara. ● m & f Aymara indian

airado adj annoyed

aire m air; (viento) breeze; (corriente) draught; (aspecto) appearance; (Mus) tune, air. ~ acondicionado air-conditioning. al ~ libre outdoors. darse ~s give o.s. airs. ~ar vt air; (ventilar) ventilate; (fig, publicar) make public. ~arse vpr. salir para ~arse go out for some fresh air

airoso adj graceful; (exitoso) successful

aisla|do adj isolated; (Elec) insulated. ~dor adj (Elec) insulating. ~nte adj insulating. ~r 🔢 vt isolate; (Elec) insulate

ajar vt crumple; (estropear) spoil

ajedre|cista m & f chess-player. ~z m chess

ajeno adj (de otro) someone else's; (de otros) other people's; (extraño) alien

ajetre|ado adj hectic, busy. ~o m bustle

ají m (LAm) chilli; (salsa) chilli sauce

aj|illo m garlic. al ~illo cooked with garlic. ~o m garlic. ~onjoli m sesame

ajuar m furnishings; (de novia) trousseau; (de bebé) layette

ajust|ado adj right; (vestido) tight. ~ar vt fit; (adaptar) adapt; (acordar) agree; settle (una cuenta); (apretar) tighten. ● vi fit. ~arse vpr fit; (adaptarse) adapt o.s.; (acordarse) come to an agreement. ~e m fitting; (adaptación) adjustment; (acuerdo) agreement; (de una cuenta) settlement

al = a + el

ala f wing; (de sombrero) brim. ● m & f (deportes) winger

alaba|nza f praise. ~r vt praise

alacena f cupboard (Brit), closet (Amer)

alacrán m scorpion

alambr|ada f wire fence. ~ado m (LAm) wire fence. ~e m wire. ~e de púas barbed wire

alameda f avenue; (plantío de álamos) poplar grove

álamo m poplar. ~ temblón aspen

alarde m show. hacer ~ de boast of

alarga|do adj long. ~dor m extension. ~r 🔢 vt lengthen; stretch out (mano etc); (dar) give, pass. ~rse vpr get longer

alarido m shriek

alarm|a f alarm. ~ante adj alarming. ~ar vt alarm, frighten. ~arse vpr be alarmed. ~ista m & f alarmist

alba f dawn

albacea m & f executor

albahaca f basil

albanés adj & m Albanian

Albania f Albania

albañil m builder; (que coloca ladrillos) bricklayer

albarán m delivery note

albaricoque m apricot. ~ro m apricot tree

albedrío m will. libre ~ free will

alberca f tank, reservoir; (Mex, piscina) swimming pool

alberg|ar 🔢 vt (alojar) put up; (vivienda) house; (dar refugio) shelter. ~arse vpr stay; (refugiarse) shelter. ~ue m accommodation; (refugio) shelter. ~ue de juventud youth hostel

albino adj & m albino

albóndiga f meatball, rissole

albornoz m bathrobe

alborot|ado adj excited; (aturdido) hasty. **~ador** adj rowdy. ● m trouble-maker. **~ar** vt disturb, upset. ● vi make a racket. **~arse** vpr get excited; (el mar) get rough. **~o** m row, uproar

álbum m (pl **~es** o **~s**) album

alcachofa f artichoke

alcald|e m mayor. **~esa** f mayoress. **~ía** f mayoralty; (oficina) mayor's office

alcance m reach; (de arma, telescopio etc) range; (déficit) deficit

alcancía f money-box; (LAm, de niño) piggy bank

alcantarilla f sewer; (boca) drain

alcanzar 🔟 vt (llegar a) catch up; (coger) reach; catch (un autobús); (bala etc) strike, hit. ● vi reach; (ser suficiente) be enough. **~ a** manage

alcaparra f caper

alcázar m fortress

alcoba f bedroom

alcoh|ol m alcohol. **~ol desnaturalizado** methylated spirits, meths. **~ólico** adj & m alcoholic. **~olímetro** m Breathalyser . **~olismo** m alcoholism

alcornoque m cork-oak; (persona torpe) idiot

aldaba f door-knocker

aldea f village. **~no** adj village. ● m villager

alea|ción f alloy. **~r** vt alloy

aleatorio adj uncertain

aleccionar vt instruct

aledaños mpl outskirts

alega|ción f allegation; (LAm, disputa) argument. **~r** 🔢 vt claim; (Jurid) plead. ● vi (LAm) argue. **~ta** f (Mex) argument. **~to** m plea

alegoría f allegory

alegr|ar vt make happy; (avivar) brighten up. **~arse** vpr be happy; (emborracharse) get merry. **~e** adj happy; (achispado) merry, tight. **~ía** f happiness

aleja|do adj distant. **~miento** m removal; (entre personas) estrangement; (distancia) distance. **~r** vt remove; (ahuyentar) get rid of; (fig, apartar) separate. **~rse** vpr move away

alemán adj & m German

Alemania f Germany. **~ Occidental** (historia) West Germany. **~ Oriental** (historia) East Germany

alenta|dor adj encouraging. **~r** 🔢 vt encourage. ● vi breathe

alerce m larch

al|ergia f allergy. **~érgico** adj allergic

alero m (del tejado) eaves

alerta adj alert. ¡**~**! look out! **estar ~** be alert; (en guardia) be on the alert. **~r** vt alert

aleta f wing; (de pez) fin

aletarga|do adj lethargic. **~r** 🔢 vt make lethargic. **~rse** vpr become lethargic

alet|azo m (de un ave) flap of the wings; (de un pez) flick of the fin. **~ear** vi flap its wings, flutter

alevosía f treachery

alfab|ético adj alphabetical. **~etizar** 🔟 vt alphabetize; teach to read and write. **~eto** m alphabet. **~eto Morse** Morse code

alfalfa f alfalfa

alfar|ería m pottery. **~ero** m potter

alféizar m (window)sill

alférez m second lieutenant

alfil m (en ajedrez) bishop

alfile|r m pin. ~**tero** m pincushion; (*estuche*) pin-case

alfombr|a f (*grande*) carpet; (*pequeña*) rug, mat. ~**ado** adj (LAm) carpeted. ~**ar** vt carpet. ~**illa** f rug, mat; (*Med*) type of measles

alforja f saddle-bag

algarabía f hubbub

algas fpl seaweed

álgebra f algebra

álgido adj (*fig*) decisive

algo pron something; (*en frases interrogativas, condicionales*) anything. ● adv rather. ¿~ más? anything else? ¿quieres tomar ~? would you like a drink?; (*de comer*) would you like something to eat?

algod|ón m cotton. ~**ón de azúcar** candy floss (*Brit*), cotton candy (*Amer*). ~**ón hidrófilo** cotton wool. ~**onero** adj cotton. ● m cotton plant

alguacil m bailiff

alguien pron someone, somebody; (*en frases interrogativas, condicionales*) anyone, anybody

algún *véase* ALGUNO

alguno adj (*delante de nombres masculinos en singular* algún) some; (*en frases interrogativas, condicionales*) any; (*pospuesto al nombre en frases negativas*) at all. **no tiene idea alguna** he hasn't any idea at all. **alguna que otra vez** from time to time. **algunas veces, alguna vez** sometimes. ● pron one; (*en plural*) some; (*alguien*) someone

alhaja f piece of jewellery; (*fig*) treasure. ~**s** fpl jewellery

alharaca f fuss

alhelí m wallflower

alia|do adj allied. ● m ally. ~**nza** f alliance; (*anillo*) wedding ring. ~**r**

🔟 vt combine. ~**rse** vpr be combined; (*formar una alianza*) form an alliance

alias adv & m alias

alicaído adj (*fig, débil*) weak; (*fig, abatido*) depressed

alicates mpl pliers

aliciente m incentive; (*de un lugar*) attraction

alienado adj mentally ill

aliento m breath; (*ánimo*) courage

aligerar vt make lighter; (*aliviar*) alleviate, ease; (*apresurar*) quicken

alijo m (*de contrabando*) consignment

alimaña f pest. ~**s** fpl vermin

aliment|ación f diet; (*acción*) feeding. ~**ar** vt feed; (*nutrir*) nourish. ● vi be nourishing. ~**arse** vpr feed (con, de on). ~**icio** adj nourishing. **productos** ~**icios** foodstuffs. ~**o** m food. ~**os** mpl (*Jurid*) alimony

alinea|ción f alignment; (*en deportes*) line-up. ~**r** vt align, line up

aliñ|ar vt (*Culin*) season; dress (*ensalada*). ~**o** m seasoning; (*para ensalada*) dressing

alioli m garlic mayonnaise

alisar vt smooth

alistar vt put on a list; (*Mil*) enlist. ~**se** vpr enrol; (*Mil*) enlist; (*LAm, prepararse*) get ready

alivi|ar vt lighten; relieve (*dolor, etc*); (*arg, hurtar*) steal, pinch 🔠. ~**arse** vpr (*dolor*) diminish; (*persona*) get better. ~**o** m relief

aljibe m tank

allá adv (*over*) there. **i~ él!** that's his business! **i~ fuera** out there. **~ por 1970** back in 1970. **el más ~** the beyond. **más ~** further on. **más ~ de** beyond. **por ~** that way

allana|miento *m.* ~miento (de morada) breaking and entering; (*LAm, por la autoridad*) raid. ~r *vt* level; remove (obstáculos). *(fig)* iron out (dificultades etc); break into (una casa), (*LAm, por la autoridad*) raid

allega|do *adj* close. ● *m* close friend; (*pariente*) close relative. ~r 🔢 *vt* collect

allí *adv* there; (*tiempo*) then. ~ fuera out there. por ~ that way

alma *f* soul; (*habitante*) inhabitant

almac|én *m* warehouse; (*LAm, tienda*) grocer's shop; (de un arma) magazine. ~enes *mpl* department store. ~enaje *m* storage; (*derechos*) storage charges. ~enar *vt* store; stock up with (provisiones)

almanaque *m* almanac

almeja *f* clam

almendr|a *f* almond. ~ado *adj* almond-shaped. ~o *m* almond tree

alm|íbar *m* syrup. ~ibarar *vt* cover in syrup

almid|ón *m* starch. ~onado *adj* starched; (*fig, estirado*) starchy

almirante *m* admiral

almizcle *m* musk. ~ra *f* muskrat

almohad|a *f* pillow. consultar con la ~a sleep on it. ~illa *f* small cushion. ~ón *m* large pillow, bolster

almorranas *fpl* haemorrhoids, piles

alm|orzar 🔢 & 🔟 *vt* (a mediodía) have for lunch; (*desayunar*) have for breakfast. ● *vi* (a mediodía) have lunch; (*desayunar*) have breakfast. ~uerzo *m* (a mediodía) lunch; (*desayuno*) breakfast

alocado *adj* scatter-brained

aloja|miento *m* accommoda-

tion. ~r *vt* put up. ~rse *vpr* stay

alondra *f* lark

alpaca *f* alpaca

alpargata *f* canvas shoe, espadrille

alpin|ismo *m* mountaineering, climbing. ~ista *m & f* mountaineer, climber. ~o *adj* Alpine

alpiste *m* birdseed

alqui|lar *vt* (tomar en alquiler) hire (vehículo), rent (piso, casa); (dar en alquiler) hire (out) (vehículo), rent (out) (piso, casa). se alquila to let (Brit), for rent (Amer.) ~er *m* (acción — de alquilar un piso etc) renting; (— de alquilar un vehículo) hiring; (precio — por el que se alquila un piso etc) rent; (— por el que se alquila un vehículo) hire charge. de ~er for hire

alquimi|a *f* alchemy. ~sta *m* alchemist

alquitrán *m* tar

alrededor *adv* around. ~ de around; (con números) about. ~es *mpl* surroundings; (de una ciudad) outskirts

alta *f* discharge

altaner|ía *f* (arrogancia) arrogance. ~o *adj* arrogant, haughty

altar *m* altar

altavoz *m* loudspeaker

altera|ble *adj* changeable. ~ción *f* change, alteration. ~r *vt* change, alter; (perturbar) disturb; (enfadar) anger, irritate. ~rse *vpr* change, alter; (agitarse) get upset; (enfadarse) get angry; (comida) go off

altercado *m* argument

altern|ar *vt/i* alternate. ~arse *vpr* take turns. ~ativa *f* alternative. ~ativo *adj* alternating. ~o *adj* alternate; (Elec) alternating

Alteza *f* (título) Highness

a **altibajos** *mpl* (*de terreno*) uneven-
ness; (*fig*) ups and downs

altiplanicie *f*, **altiplano** *m* high
plateau

altisonante *adj* pompous

altitud *f* altitude

altiv|ez *f* arrogance. ∼**o** *adj* arro-
gant

alto *adj* high; (*persona, edificio*)
tall; (*voz*) loud; (*fig, elevado*) lofty;
(*Mus*) (*nota*) high(-pitched); (*Mus*)
(*voz, instrumento*) alto; (*horas*)
early. ● *m* height; (*de sonidos*)
loud(ly). ● *m* height; (*de un edifi-
cio*) top floor; (*viola*) viola; (*voz*)
alto; (*parada*) stop. ● *int* halt!,
stop! **en lo ∼ de** on the top of.
tiene 3 metros de ∼ it is 3
metres high

altoparlante *m* (*esp LAm*) loud-
speaker

altruis|mo *m* altruism. ∼**ta** *adj*
altruistic. ● *m & f* altruist

altura *f* height; (*Aviac, Geog*) alti-
tude; (*de agua*) depth; (*fig, cielo*)
sky. **a estas ∼s** at this stage.
tiene 3 metros de ∼ it is 3
metres high

alubia *f* (haricot) bean

alucinación *f* hallucination

alud *m* avalanche

aludi|do *adj* in question. **darse
por ∼do** take it personally. **no
darse por ∼do** turn a deaf ear.
∼**r** *vi* mention

alumbra|do *adj* lit. ● *m* lighting.
∼**miento** *m* lighting; (*parto*) child-
birth. ∼**r** *vt* light

aluminio *m* aluminium (*Brit*), alu-
minum (*Amer*)

alumno *m* pupil; (*Univ*) student

aluniza|je *m* landing on the
moon. ∼**r** ⑩ *vi* land on the moon

alusión *f* allusion. ∼**vo** *adj*

allusive

alza *f* rise. ∼**da** *f* (*de caballo*)
height; (*Jurid*) appeal. ∼**do** *adj*
raised; (*Mex, soberbio*) vain; (*pre-
cio*) fixed. ∼**miento** *m* (*Pol*) upris-
ing. ∼**r** ⑩ *vt* raise, lift (up); raise
(*precios*). ∼**rse** *vpr* (*Pol*) rise up

ama *f* lady of the house. ∼ **de
casa** housewife. ∼ **de cría** wet-
nurse. ∼ **de llaves** housekeeper

amab|ilidad *f* kindness. ∼**le** *adj*
kind; (*simpático*) nice

amaestra|do *adj* trained. ∼**r** *vt*
train

amag|ar ⑫ *vt* (*mostrar intención
de*) make as if to; (*Mex, amenazar*)
threaten. ● *vi* threaten; (*algo
bueno*) be in the offing. ∼**o** *m*
threat; (*señal*) sign; (*Med*) symptom

amainar *vt* let up

amalgama *f* amalgam. ∼**r** *vt*
amalgamate

amamantar *vt/i* breast-feed;
(*animal*) to suckle

amanecer *m* dawn. ● *vi* dawn;
(*persona*) wake up. **al ∼** at dawn,
at daybreak. ∼**se** *vpr* (*Mex*) stay up
all night

amanera|do *adj* affected. ∼**rse**
vpr become affected

amansar *vt* tame; break in (*un
caballo*); soothe (*dolor* etc). ∼**se**
vpr calm down

amante *adj* fond. ● *m & f* lover

amapola *f* poppy

amar *vt* love

amara|je *m* landing on water; (*de
astronave*) splash-down. ∼**r** *vi* land
on water; (*astronave*) splash down

amarg|ado *adj* embittered. ∼**ar**
⑫ *vt* make bitter; embitter (*per-
sona*). ∼**arse** *vpr* become bitter.
∼**o** *adj* bitter. ∼**ura** *f* bitterness

amariconado *adj* ① effeminate

amarill|ento *adj* yellowish; (*tez*) sallow. **∼o** *adj & m* yellow

amarra|s *fpl.* soltar las **∼s** cast off. **∼do** *adj* (*LAm*) mean. **∼r** *vt* moor; (*esp LAm*, *atar*) tie. **∼rse** *vpr LAm* tie up

amas|ar *vt* knead; (*acumular*) to amass. **∼ijo** *m* dough; (*acción*) kneading; (*fig, fam, mezcla*) hotchpotch

amate *m* (*Mex*) fig tree

amateur *adj & m & f* amateur

amazona *f* Amazon; (*jinete*) horsewoman

ámbar *m* amber

ambici|ón *f* ambition. **∼onar** *vt* aspire to. **∼onar ser** have an ambition to be. **∼oso** *adj* ambitious. ● *m* ambitious person

ambidextro *adj* ambidextrous. ● *m* ambidextrous person

ambient|ar *vt* give an atmosphere to. **∼arse** *vpr* adapt o.s. **∼e** *m* atmosphere; (*entorno*) environment

ambig|üedad *f* ambiguity. **∼uo** *adj* ambiguous

ámbito *m* sphere; (*alcance*) scope

ambos *adj & pron* both

ambulancia *f* ambulance

ambulante *adj* travelling

ambulatorio *m* out-patients' department

amedrentar *vt* frighten, scare. **∼se** *vpr* be frightened

amén *m* amen. ● *int* amen! en un decir **∼** in an instant

amenaza *f* threat. **∼r** 🔟 *vt* threaten

amen|idad *f* pleasantness. **∼izar** 🔟 *vt* brighten up. **∼o** *adj* pleasant

América *f* America. **∼ Central**

Central America. **∼ del Norte** North America. **∼ del Sur** South America. **∼ Latina** Latin America

american|a *f* jacket. **∼ismo** *m* Americanism. **∼o** *adj* American

amerita|do *adj* (*LAm*) meritorious. **∼r** *vt* (*LAm*) deserve

amerizaje *m véase* **AMARAJE**

ametralla|dora *f* machine-gun. **∼r** *vt* machine-gun

amianto *m* asbestos

amig|a *f* friend; (*novia*) girl-friend; (*amante*) lover. **∼able** *adj* friendly. **∼ablemente** *adv* amicably

am|ígdala *f* tonsil. **∼igdalitis** *f* tonsillitis

amigo *adj* friendly. ● *m* friend; (*novio*) boyfriend; (*amante*) lover. **ser ∼ de** be fond of. **ser muy ∼s** be close friends

amilanar *vt* daunt. **∼se** *vpr* be daunted

aminorar *vt* lessen; reduce (*velocidad*)

amist|ad *f* friendship. **∼ades** *fpl* friends. **∼oso** *adj* friendly

amn|esia *f* amnesia. **∼ésico** *adj* amnesiac

amnist|ía *f* amnesty. **∼iar** 🔟 *vt* grant an amnesty to

amo *m* master; (*dueño*) owner

amodorrarse *vpr* feel sleepy

amoldar *vt* mould; (*adaptar*) adapt; (*acomodar*) fit. **∼se** *vpr* adapt

amonestar *vt* rebuke, reprimand; (*anunciar la boda*) publish the banns

amoniaco, amoníaco *m* ammonia

amontonar *vt* pile up; (*fig, acumular*) accumulate. **∼se** *vpr* pile up; (*gente*) crowd together

a

amor *m* love. **~es** *mpl* (*relaciones amorosas*) love affairs. **~ propio** pride. **con mil ~es, de mil ~es** with (the greatest of) pleasure. **hacer el ~** make love. **por (el) ~ de Dios** for God's sake

amoratado *adj* purple; (*de frío*) blue

amordazar 🔟 *vt* gag; (*fig*) silence

amorfo *adj* amorphous, shapeless

amor|ío *m* affair. **~oso** *adj* loving; (*cartas*) love; (*LAm*), *encantador*) cute

amortajar *vt* shroud

amortigua|dor *adj* deadening. • *m* (*Auto*) shock absorber. **~r** 🔟 *vt* deaden (*ruido*); dim (*luz*); cushion (*golpe*); tone down (*color*)

amortiza|ble *adj* redeemable. **~ción** *f* (*de una deuda*) repayment; (*de bono etc*) redemption. **~r** 🔟 *vt* repay (*una deuda*)

amotinar *vt* incite to riot. **~se** *vpr* rebel; (*Mil*) mutiny

ampar|ar *vt* help; (*proteger*) protect. **~arse** *vpr* seek protection; (*de la lluvia*) shelter. **~o** *m* protection; (*de la lluvia*) shelter. **al ~o de** under the protection of

amperio *m* ampere, amp 🅰

amplia|ción *f* extension; (*photo*) enlargement. **~r** 🔟 *vt* enlarge, extend; (*photo*) enlarge

amplifica|ción *f* amplification. **~dor** *m* amplifier. **~r** 🔽 *vt* amplify

ampli|o *adj* wide; (*espacioso*) spacious; (*ropa*) loose-fitting. **~tud** *f* extent; (*espaciosidad*) spaciousness; (*espacio*) space

ampolla *f* (*Med*) blister; (*de medicamento*) ampoule, phial

ampuloso *adj* pompous

amputar *vt* amputate; (*fig*) delete

amueblar *vt* furnish

amuleto *m* charm, amulet

amuralla|do *adj* walled. **~r** *vt* build a wall around

anacr|ónico *adj* anachronistic. **~onismo** *m* anachronism

anales *mpl* annals

analfabet|ismo *m* illiteracy. **~o** *adj* & *m* illiterate

analgésico *adj* analgesic. • *m* painkiller

an|álisis *m invar* analysis. **~álisis de sangre** blood test. **~alista** *m* & *f* analyst. **~alítico** *adj* analytical. **~alizar** 🔟 *vt* analyze

an|alogía *f* analogy. **~álogo** *adj* analogous

ananarranjado *adj* orangey

an|arquía *f* anarchy. **~árquico** *adj* anarchic. **~arquismo** *m* anarchism. **~arquista** *adj* anarchistic. • *m* & *f* anarchist

anat|omía *f* anatomy. **~ómico** *adj* anatomical

anca *f* haunch; (*parte superior*) rump; (*fam, nalgas*) bottom. **en ~s** (*LAm*) on the crupper

ancestro *m* ancestor

ancho *adj* wide; (*ropa*) loose-fitting; (*fig*) relieved; (*demasiado grande*) too big; (*ufano*) smug. • *m* width; (*Rail*) gauge. **~ de banda** bandwidth. **tiene 3 metros de ~** it is 3 metres wide

anchoa *f* anchovy

anchura *f* width; (*medida*) measurement

ancian|o *adj* elderly, old. • *m* elderly man, old man. **~a** *f* elderly woman, old woman. **los ~os** old people

ancla *f* anchor. **echar ~s** drop anchor. **levar ~s** weigh anchor. **~r** *vi* anchor

andad|eras fpl (Mex) baby-walker. **~or** m baby-walker

Andalucía f Andalusia

andaluz adj & m Andalusian

andamio m platform. **~s** mpl scaffolding

and|anzas fpl adventures. **~ar** 25 vt (recorrer) cover, go. ● vi walk; (máquina) go, work; (estar) be; (moverse) move. **~ar a caballo** (LAm) ride a horse. **~ar en bicicleta** (LAm) ride a bicycle. ¡**anda! go on!, come on! **~ar por** be about. **~arse** vpr (LAm, en imperativo) ¡**andate!** go away! **~ariego** adj fond of walking

andén m platform

Andes mpl. **los ~** the Andes

andin|o adj Andean. **~ismo** m (LAm) mountaineering, climbing. **~ista** m & f (LAm) mountaineer, climber

andrajo m rag. **~so** adj ragged

anduve vb véase ANDAR

anécdota f anecdote

anecdótico adj anecdotal

anegar 12 vt flood. **~se** vpr be flooded, flood

anejo adj véase ANEXO

an|emia f anaemia. **~émico** adj anaemic

anest|esia f anaesthesia; (droga) anaesthetic. **~esiar** vt anaesthetize. **~ésico** adj & m anaesthetic. **~esista** m & f anaesthetist

anex|ar vt annex. **~o** adj attached. ● m annexe

anfibio adj amphibious. ● m amphibian

anfiteatro m amphitheatre; (en un teatro) upper circle

anfitri|ón m host. **~ona** f hostess

ángel m angel; (encanto) charm

angelical adj, **angélico** adj angelic

angina f. **~ de pecho** angina (pectoris). **tener ~s** have tonsillitis

anglicano adj & m Anglican

angl|icismo m Anglicism. **~ófilo** adj & m Anglophile. **~ohispánico** adj Anglo-Spanish. **~osajón** adj & m Anglo-Saxon

angosto adj narrow

angu|ila f eel. **~la** f elver, baby eel

ángulo m angle; (rincón, esquina) corner; (curva) bend

angusti|a f anguish. **~ar** vt distress; (inquietar) worry. **~arse** vpr get distressed; (inquietarse) get worried. **~oso** adj anguished; (que causa angustia) distressing

anhel|ar vt (+ nombre) long for; (+ verbo) long to. **~o** m (fig) yearning

anidar vi nest

anill|a f ring. **~o** m ring. **~o de boda** wedding ring

ánima f soul

anima|ción f (de personas) life; (de cosas) liveliness; (bullicio) bustle; (en el cine) animation. **~do** adj lively; (sitio etc) busy. **~dor** m host. **~dora** f hostess; (de un equipo) cheerleader

animadversión f ill will

animal adj animal; (fig, fam, torpe) stupid. ● m animal; (fig, fam, idiota) idiot; (fig, fam, bruto) brute

animar vt give life to; (dar ánimo) encourage; (dar vivacidad) liven up. **~se** vpr (decidirse) decide; (ponerse alegre) cheer up. **¿te animas a ir al cine?** do you feel like going to the cinema?

ánimo m soul; (mente) mind; (valor) courage; (intención) intention. ¡~! come on!, cheer up! dar ~s encourage

animos|idad f animosity. ~o adj brave; (*resuelto*) determined

aniquilar vt annihilate; (*acabar con*) ruin

anís m aniseed; (*licor*) anisette

aniversario m anniversary

anoche adv last night, yesterday evening

anochecer [11] vi get dark. anocheció en Madrid I was in Madrid at dusk. ● m nightfall, dusk. al ~ at nightfall

anodino adj bland

an|omalía f anomaly. ~ómalo adj anomalous

an|onimato m anonymity. ~ónimo adj anonymous; (*sociedad*) limited. ● m (*carta*) anonymous letter

anormal adj abnormal. ● m & f [1] idiot. ~idad f abnormality

anota|ción f (*nota*) note; (*acción de poner notas*) annotation. ~r vt (*poner nota*) annotate; (*apuntar*) make a note of; (*LAm*) score (un gol)

anquilosa|miento m (*fig*) paralysis. ~rse vpr become paralyzed

ansi|a f anxiety, worry; (*anhelo*) yearning. ~ar [20] vt long for. ~edad f anxiety. ~oso adj anxious; (*deseoso*) eager

antag|ónico adj antagonistic. ~onismo m antagonism. ~onista m & f antagonist

antaño adv in days gone by

antártico adj & m Antarctic

ante prep in front of, before; (*frente a*) in the face of; (*en vista de*) in view of. ● m elk; (*piel*) suede. ~anoche adv the night before last. ~ayer adv the day before

yesterday. ~brazo m forearm

antece|dente adj previous. ● m antecedent. ~dentes mpl history, background. ~dentes penales criminal record. ~der vt precede. ~sor m predecessor; (*antepasado*) ancestor

antelación f (*advance*) notice. con ~ in advance

antemano adv. de ~ beforehand

antena f antenna; (*radio, TV*) aerial

antenoche adv (*LAm*) the night before last

anteoj|eras fpl blinkers. ~o m telescope. ~os mpl binoculars; (*LAm, gafas*) glasses, spectacles. ~os de sol sunglasses

ante|pasados mpl forebears, ancestors. ~poner [34] vt put in front (a of); (*fig*) put before, prefer. ~proyecto m preliminary sketch; (*fig*) blueprint

anterior adj previous; (*delantero*) front. ~idad f. con ~idad previously. con ~idad a prior to

antes adv before; (*antiguamente*) in the past; (*mejor*) rather; (*primero*) first. ~ de before. ~ de ayer the day before yesterday. ~ de que + subjuntivo before. ~ de que llegue before he arrives. cuanto ~, lo ~ posible as soon as possible

anti|aéreo adj anti-aircraft. ~biótico adj & m antibiotic. ~ciclón m anticyclone

anticip|ación f. con ~ación in advance. con media hora de ~ación half an hour early. ~ado adj advance. por ~ado in advance. ~ar vt bring forward; advance (dinero). ~arse vpr be early. ~o m (*dinero*) advance; (*fig*) foretaste

anti|conceptivo adj & m contraceptive. ~ **de emergencia** morning-after pill. **~congelante** *m* antifreeze

anticua|do *adj* old-fashioned. **~rio** *m* antique dealer

anticuerpo *m* antibody

antídoto *m* antidote

anti|estético *adj* ugly. **~faz** *m* mask

antig|ualla *f* old relic. **~uamente** *adv* formerly; (*hace mucho tiempo*) long ago. **~üedad** *f* antiquity; (*objeto*) antique; (*en un empleo*) length of service. **~uo** *adj* old; (*ruinas*) ancient; (*mueble*) antique

Antillas *fpl.* las ~ the West Indies

antílope *m* antelope

antinatural *adj* unnatural

antip|atía *f* dislike; (*cualidad de antipático*) unpleasantness. **~ático** *adj* unpleasant, unfriendly

anti|semita *m & f* anti-Semite. **~séptico** *adj* & *m* antiseptic. **~social** *adj* antisocial

antítesis *f invar* antithesis

antoj|adizo *adj* capricious. **~arse** *vpr* fancy. se le ~a un caramelo he fancies a sweet. **~itos** *mpl* (*Mex*) snacks bought at street stands. **~o** *m* whim; (*de embarazada*) craving

antología *f* anthology

antorcha *f* torch

ántrax *m* anthrax

antro *m* (*fig*) dump, hole. ~ **de perversión** den of iniquity

antrop|ología *f* anthropology. **~ólogo** *m* anthropologist

anua|l *adj* annual. **~lidad** *f* annuity. **~lmente** *adv* yearly. **~rio** *m* yearbook

anudar *vt* tie, knot. **~se** *vpr* tie

anula|ción *f* annulment, cancellation. **~r** *vt* annul, cancel. ● *adj* (*dedo*) ring. ● *m* ring finger

anunci|ante *m & f* advertiser. **~ar** *vt* announce; advertise (*producto comercial*); (*presagiar*) be a sign of. **~o** *m* announcement; (*para vender algo*) advertisement, advert ①; (*cartel*) poster

anzuelo *m* (fish)hook; (*fig*) bait. **tragar el** ~ swallow the bait

añadi|dura *f* addition. **por ~dura** in addition. **~r** *vt* add

añejo *adj* (*vino*) mature

añicos *mpl.* **hacer(se)** ~ smash to pieces

año *m* year. ~ **bisiesto** leap year. ~ **nuevo** new year. **al** ~ per year, a year. **¿cuántos** ~s **tiene?** how old is he? **tiene 5** ~s he's 5 (years old). **el** ~ **pasado** last year. **el** ~ **que viene** next year. **entrado en** ~s elderly. **los** ~s **60** the sixties

añora|nza *f* nostalgia. **~r** *vt* miss

apabulla|nte *adj* overwhelming. **~r** *vt* overwhelm

apacible *adj* gentle; (*clima*) mild

apacigua|r ⑮ *vt* pacify; (*calmar*) calm; relieve (*dolor etc*). **~rse** *vpr* calm down

apadrinar *vt* sponsor; be godfather to (*a un niño*)

apag|ado *adj* extinguished; (*color*) dull; (*aparato eléctrico, luz*) off; (*persona*) lifeless; (*sonido*) muffled. **~ar** ⑫ *vt* put out (*fuego, incendio*); turn off, switch off (*aparato eléctrico, luz*); quench (*sed*); muffle (*sonido*). **~arse** *vpr* (*fuego, luz*) go out; (*sonido*) die away. **~ón** *m* blackout

apalabrar *vt* make a verbal agreement; (*contratar*) engage

apalear *vt* winnow (*grano*); beat

(alfombra, frutos, persona)

apantallar vt (Mex) impress

apañar vt (arreglar) fix; (remendar) mend; (agarrar) grasp, take hold of. **~se** vpr get along, manage

apapachar vt (Mex) cuddle

aparador m sideboard; (Mex, de tienda) shop window

aparato m apparatus; (máquina) machine; (doméstico) appliance; (teléfono) telephone; (radio, TV) set; (ostentación) show, pomp. **~so** adj showy, ostentatious; (caída) spectacular

aparca|miento m car park (Brit), parking lot (Amer). **~r** 7 vt/i park

aparea|miento m mate (animales).**~se** vpr mate

aparecer 11 vi appear. **~se** vpr appear

apareja|do adj. llevar **~ado**, traer **~ado** mean, entail. **~o** m (avíos) equipment; (de caballo) tack; (de pesca) tackle

aparent|ar vt (afectar) feign; (parecer) look. ● vi show off. **~a** 20 años se he looks like she's 20. **~e** adj apparent

apari|ción f appearance; (visión) apparition. **~encia** f appearance; (fig) show. guardar las **~encias** keep up appearances

apartado adj separated; (aislado) isolated. ● m (de un texto) section. **~** (de correos) post-office box, PO box

apartamento m apartment, flat (Brit)

apart|ar vt separate; (alejar) move away; (quitar) remove; (guardar) set aside. **~arse** vpr leave; (quitarse de en medio) get out of the way; (aislarse) cut o.s. off. **~e** adv apart; (por separado) separately; (además)

besides. ● m aside; (párrafo) new paragraph. **~e de** apart from. dejar **~e** leave aside. eso **~e** apart from that

apasiona|do adj passionate; (entusiasta) enthusiastic; (falto de objetividad) biased. ● m. **~do de** lover. **~miento** m passion. **~r** vt excite. **~rse** vpr be mad (por about); (ser parcial) become biased

ap|atía f apathy. **~ático** adj apathetic

apea|dero m (Rail) halt. **~rse** vpr get off

apechugar 12 vi. 11 **~ con** put up with

apedrear vt stone

apeg|ado adj attached (a to). **~o** m 11 attachment. tener **~o a** be fond of

apela|ción f appeal. **~r** vi appeal; (recurrir) resort (a to). ● vt (apodar) call. **~tivo** m (nick)name

apellid|ar vt call. **~arse** vpr be called. ¿cómo te apellidas? what's your surname? **~o** m surname

apelmazarse vpr (lana) get matted

apenar vt sadden; (LAm, avergonzar) embarrass. **~se** vpr be sad; (LAm, avergonzarse) be embarrassed

apenas adv hardly, scarcely; (Mex, sólo) only. ● conj (esp LAm, en cuanto) as soon as. **~ si** 11 hardly

ap|éndice m appendix. **~endicitis** f appendicitis

apergaminado adj (piel) wrinkled

aperitivo m (bebida) aperitif; (comida) appetizer

aperos mpl implements; (de labranza) agricultural equipment; (LAm, de un caballo) tack

apertura f opening

apesadumbrar vt upset. **~se** vpr sadden

apestar vt infect. ● vi stink (a of)

apet|ecer 11 vi. ¿te **~ece una copa?** do you fancy a drink? do you feel like a drink?. **no me ~ece** I don't feel like it. **~ecible** adj attractive. **~ito** m appetite; (fig) desire. **~itoso** adj appetizing

apiadarse vpr feel sorry (de for)

ápice m (nada, en frases negativas) anything. **no ceder un ~** not give an inch

apilar vt pile up

apiñar vt pack in. **~se** vpr (personas) crowd together; (cosas) be packed tight

apio m celery

aplacar 7 vt placate; soothe (dolor)

aplanar vt level. **~ calles** (LAm fam) loaf around

aplasta|nte adj overwhelming. **~r** vt crush. **~rse** vpr flatten o.s.

aplau|dir vt clap, applaud; (fig) applaud. **~so** m applause; (fig) praise

aplaza|miento m postponement. **~r** 10 vt postpone; defer (pago)

aplica|ble adj applicable. **~ción** f application. **~do** adj (persona) diligent. **~r** 7 vt apply. ● vi (LAm, a un puesto) apply (for). **~rse** vpr apply o.s.

aplom|ado adj composed. **~o** m composure

apocado adj timid

apocar 7 vt belittle (persona). **~se** vpr feel small

apodar vt nickname

apodera|do m representative.

~rse vpr seize

apodo m nickname

apogeo m (fig) height

apolilla|do adj moth-eaten. **~rse** vpr get moth-eaten

apolítico adj non-political

apología f defence

apoltronarse vpr settle o.s. down

apoplejía f stroke

aporrear vt hit, thump; beat up (persona)

aport|ación f contribution. **~ar** vt contribute. **~e** m (LAm) contribution

aposta adv on purpose

apostar[^1] 2 vt/i bet

apostar[^2] vt station. **~se** vpr station o.s.

apóstol m apostle

apóstrofo m apostrophe

apoy|ar vt lean (en against); (descansar) rest; (asentar) base; (reforzar) support. **~arse** vpr lean, rest. **~o** m support

apreci|able adj appreciable; (digno de estima) worthy. **~ación** f appreciation; (valoración) appraisal. **~ar** vt value; (estimar) appreciate. **~o** m appraisal; (fig) esteem

apremi|ante adj urgent, pressing. **~ar** vt urge; (obligar) compel; (dar prisa a) hurry up. ● vi be urgent. **~o** m urgency; (obligación) obligation

aprender vt/i learn. **~se** vpr learn

aprendiz m apprentice. **~aje** m learning; (período) apprenticeship

aprensi|ón f apprehension; (miedo) fear. **~vo** adj apprehensive, fearful

apresar vt seize; (capturar) capture

aprestar vt prepare. ~**se** vpr prepare

apresura|do adj in a hurry; (*hecho con prisa*) hurried. ~**r** vt hurry. ~**rse** vpr hurry up

apret|ado adj tight; (*difícil*) difficult; (*tacaño*) stingy, mean. ~**ar** 🔳 vt tighten; press (botón); squeeze (persona); (*comprimir*) press down. ● vi be too tight. ~**arse** vpr crowd together. ~**ón** m squeeze. ~**ón de manos** handshake

aprieto m difficulty. **verse en un ~** be in a tight spot

aprisa adv quickly

aprisionar vt trap

aproba|ción f approval. ~**r** 🔳 vt approve (of); pass (examen). ● vi pass

apropia|ción f appropriation. ~**do** adj appropriate. ~**rse** vpr. ~**rse de** appropriate, take

aprovecha|ble adj usable. ~**do** adj (*aplicado*) diligent; (*ingenioso*) resourceful; (*oportunista*) opportunist. **bien ~do** well spent. ~**miento** m advantage; (*uso*) use. ~**r** vt take advantage of; (*utilizar*) make use of. ● vi make the most of it. **¡que aproveche!** enjoy your meal! ~**rse** vpr. ~**rse de** take advantage of

aprovisionar vt provision (con, de with). ~**se** vpr stock up

aproxima|ción f approximation; (*proximidad*) closeness; (*en la lotería*) consolation prize. ~**damente** adv roughly, approximately. ~**do** adj approximate, rough. ~**r** vt bring near; (*fig*) bring together (personas). ~**rse** vpr come closer, approach

apt|itud f suitability; (*capacidad*) ability. ~**o** adj (*capaz*) capable;

(*adecuado*) suitable

apuesta f bet

apuesto m handsome. ● vb véase **APOSTAR** ¹

apuntalar vt shore up

apunt|ar vt aim (arma); (*señalar*) point at; (*anotar*) make a note of, note down; (*inscribir*) enrol; (*en el teatro*) prompt. ● vi (*con un arma*) to aim (a at). ~**arse** vpr put one's name down; score (triunfo, tanto etc). ~**e** m note; (*bosquejo*) sketch. **tomar ~s** take notes

apuñalar vt stab

apur|ado adj difficult; (*sin dinero*) hard up; (*LAm, con prisa*) in a hurry. ~**ar** vt (*acabar*) finish; drain (vaso etc); (*causar vergüenza*) embarrass; (*LAm, apresurar*) hurry. ~**arse** vpr worry; (*LAm, apresurarse*) hurry up. ~**o** m tight spot, difficult situation; (*vergüenza*) embarrassment; (*estrechez*) hardship, want; (*LAm, prisa*) hurry

aquejar vt afflict

aquel adj (*f* **aquella**, *mpl* **aquellos**, *fpl* **aquellas**) that; (*en plural*) those

aquél pron (*f* **aquélla**, *mpl* **aquéllos**, *fpl* **aquéllas**) that one; (*en plural*) those

aquello pron that; (*asunto*) that business

aquí adv here. **de ~** from here. **de ~ a 15 días** in a fortnight's time. **~ mismo** right here. **de ~ para allá** to and fro. **de ~ que** that is why. **hasta ~** until now. **por ~** around here

aquietar vt calm (down)

árabe adj & m & f Arab; (*lengua*) Arabic

Arabia f Arabia. **~ Saudita**, **~ Saudí** Saudi Arabia

arado m plough. ~**r** m ploughman

arancel m tariff; (*impuesto*) duty. ~**ario** adj tariff

arándano m blueberry

arandela f washer

araña f spider; (*lámpara*) chandelier. ~**r** vt scratch

arar vt plough

arbitra|je m arbitration; (*en deportes*) refereeing. ~**r** vt/i arbitrate; (*en fútbol etc*) referee; (*en tenis etc*) umpire

arbitr|ariedad f arbitrariness. ~**ario** adj arbitrary. ~**io** m (*free*) will

árbitro m arbitrator; (*en fútbol etc*) referee; (*en tenis etc*) umpire

árbol m tree; (*eje*) axle; (*palo*) mast. ~ **genealógico** family tree. ~ **de Navidad** Christmas tree

arbol|ado m trees. ~**eda** f wood

arbusto m bush

arca f (*caja*) chest. ~ **de Noé** Noah's ark

arcada f arcade; (*de un puente*) arch; (*náuseas*) retching

arcaico adj archaic

arce m maple (tree)

arcén m (*de autopista*) hard shoulder; (*de carretera*) verge

archipiélago m archipelago

archiv|ador m filing cabinet. ~**ar** vt file (*ánvay*). ~**o** m file; (*de documentos históricos*) archives. ~**o adjunto** (*email*) attachment

arcilla f clay

arco m arch; (*Elec, Mat*) arc; (*Mus, arma*) bow; (*LAm, en fútbol*) goal. ~ **iris** rainbow

arder vi burn; (*LAm, escocer*) sting; (*fig, de ira*) seethe. **estar que arde** be very tense

ardid m trick, scheme

ardiente adj burning

ardilla f squirrel

ardor m heat; (*fig*) ardour; (*LAm, escozor*) smarting. ~ **de estómago** heartburn

arduo adj arduous

área f area

arena f sand; (*en deportes*) arena; (*en los toros*) (bull)ring. ~ **movediza** quicksand

arenoso adj sandy

arenque m herring. ~ **ahumado** kipper

arete m (*LAm*) earring

Argel m Algiers. ~**ia** f Algeria

Argentina f Argentina

argentino adj Argentinian, Argentine. ● m Argentinian

argolla f ring. ~ **de matrimonio** (*LAm*) wedding ring

arg|ot m slang. ~**ótico** adj slang

argucia f cunning argument

argüir 19 vt (*probar*) prove, show; (*argumentar*) argue. ● vi argue

argument|ación f argument. ~**ar** vt/i argue. ~**o** m argument; (*de libro, película etc*) story, plot

aria f aria

aridez f aridity, dryness

árido adj dry. ~**s** mpl dry goods

Aries m Aries

arisco adj unfriendly

arist|ocracia f aristocracy. ~**ócrata** m & f aristocrat. ~**ocrático** adj aristocratic

aritmética f arithmetic

arma f arm, weapon; (*sección*) section. ~ **de fuego** firearm, ~**s de destrucción masiva** weapons of mass destruction. ~**da** f navy; (*flota*) fleet. ~**do** adj armed (**de** with). ~**dura** f armour; (*de gafas etc*) frame; (*Tec*) framework. ~**mentismo** m build up of arms.

a

~mento m arms, armaments; (acción de armar) armament. **~r** vt arm (de with); (montar) put together. **~r un lío** kick up a fuss

armario m cupboard; (para ropa) wardrobe (Brit), closet (Amer)

armatoste m huge great thing

armazón m & f frame(work)

armiño m ermine

armisticio m armistice

armonía f harmony

armónica f harmonica, mouth organ

armoni|oso adj harmonious. **~zar** 🔟 vt harmonize. ● vi harmonize; (personas) get on well (con with); (colores) go well (con with)

arn|és m armour. **~eses** mpl harness

aro m ring, hoop

arom|a m aroma; (de flores) scent; (de vino) bouquet. **~ático** adj aromatic

arpa f harp

arpía f harpy; (fig) hag

arpillera f sackcloth, sacking

arpón m harpoon

arquear vt arch, bend. **~se** vpr arch, bend

arque|ología f archaeology. **~ológico** adj archaeological. **~ólogo** m archaeologist

arquero m archer; (LAm, en fútbol) goalkeeper

arquitect|o m architect. **~ónico** adj architectural. **~ura** f architecture

arrabal m suburb; (barrio pobre) poor area. **~es** mpl outskirts. **~ero** adj suburban; (de modales groseros) common

arraiga|do adj deeply rooted. **~r**

🔢 vi take root. **~rse** vpr take root; (fig) settle

arran|car 🔽 vt pull up (planta); pull out (diente); (arrebatar) snatch; (Auto) start. ● vi start. **~carse** vpr pull out. **~que** m sudden start; (Auto) start; (fig) outburst

arras fpl security; (en boda) coins

arrasar vt level, smooth; raze to the ground (edificio etc); (llenar) fill to the brim. ● vi (en deportes) sweep to victory; (en política) win a landslide victory

arrastr|ar vt pull; (por el suelo) drag (along); give rise to (consecuencias). ● vi trail on the ground. **~arse** vpr crawl; (humillarse) grovel. **~e** m dragging; (transporte) haulage. **estar para el ~e** 🔢 be done in

arre int gee up! **~ar** vt urge on

arrebat|ado adj (irreflexivo) impetuous. **~ar** vt snatch (away); (fig) win (over); captivate (corazón etc). **~arse** vpr get carried away. **~o** m (de cólera etc) fit; (éxtasis) ecstasy

arrech|ar vt (LAm fam, enfurecer) to infuriate. **~arse** vpr get furious. **~o** adj furious

arrecife m reef

arregl|ado adj neat; (bien vestido) well-dressed; (LAm, amañado) fixed. **~ar** vt arrange; (poner en orden) tidy up; sort out (asunto, problema etc); (reparar) mend. **~arse** vpr (solucionarse) get sorted out; (prepararse) get ready; (apañarse) manage, make do; (ponerse de acuerdo) come to an agreement. **~árselas** manage, get by. **~o** m (incl Mus) arrangement; (acción de reparar) repair; (acuerdo) agreement; (solución) solution. **con**

~o a according to

arrellanarse *vpr* settle o.s. (en into)

arremangar 🔢 *vt* roll up (mangas); tuck up (falda). ~se *vpr* roll up one's sleeves

arremeter *vi* charge (contra at); (atacar) attack

arremolinarse *vpr* mill about; (el agua) to swirl

arrenda|dor *m* landlord. ~dora *f* landlady. ~miento *m* renting; (contrato) lease; (precio) rent. ~r 🔢 *vt* (dar casa en alquiler) let; (dar cosa en alquiler) hire out; (tomar en alquiler) rent. ~tario *m* tenant

arreos *mpl* tack

arrepenti|miento *m* repentance, regret. ~rse 🔢 *vpr* (retractarse) to change one's mind; (lamentarse) be sorry. ~rse de regret; repent of (pecados)

arrest|ar *vt* arrest, detain; (encarcelar) imprison. ~o *m* arrest; (encarcelamiento) imprisonment

arriar 🔢 *vt* lower (bandera, vela)

arriba *adv* up; (dirección) up(wards); (en casa) upstairs. • *int* up with; (¡levántate!) up you get!; (¡ánimo!) come on! | ~ España! long live Spain! ~ de (LAm) on top of. ~ mencionado aforementioned. calle ~ up the street. de ~ abajo from top to bottom. de 10 euros para ~ over 10 euros. escaleras ~ upstairs. la parte de ~ the top part. los de ~ those at the top. más ~ higher up

arrib|ar *vi* (barco) reach port; (esp LAm, llegar) arrive. ~ista *m & f* social climber. ~o *m* (esp LAm) arrival

arriero *m* muleteer

arriesga|do *adj* risky; (person) daring. ~r 🔢 *vt* risk; (aventurar)

venture. ~rse *vpr* take a risk

arrim|ar *vt* bring close(r). ~arse *vpr* come closer, approach

arrincona|do *adj* forgotten; (acorralado) cornered. ~r *vt* put in a corner; (perseguir) corner (arrumbar) put aside. ~rse *vpr* become a recluse

arroba *f* (Internet) at (@); measure of weight

arrocero *adj* rice

arrodillarse *vpr* kneel (down)

arrogan|cia *f* arrogance; (orgullo) pride. ~te *adj* arrogant; (orgulloso) proud

arroj|ar *vt* throw; (emitir) give off, throw out; (producir) produce. • *vi* (esp LAm, vomitar) throw up. ~arse *vpr* throw o.s. ~o *m* courage

arrollar *vt* roll (up); (atropellar) run over; (vencer) crush

arropar *vt* wrap up; (en la cama) tuck up. ~se *vpr* wrap (o.s.) up

arroyo *m* stream; (de una calle) gutter. ~uelo *m* small stream

arroz *m* rice. ~ con leche rice pudding. ~al *m* rice field

arruga *f* (en la piel) wrinkle, line; (en tela) crease. ~r 🔢 *vt* wrinkle; crumple (papel); crease (tela). ~rse *vpr* (la piel) become wrinkled; (tela) get creased

arruinar *vt* ruin; (destruir) destroy. ~se *vpr* (persona) be ruined

arrullar *vt* lull to sleep. • *vi* (palomas) coo

arrumbar *vt* put aside

arsenal *m* (astillero) shipyard; (de armas) arsenal; (fig) mine

arsénico *m* arsenic

arte *m* (f en plural) art; (habilidad) skill; (astucia) cunning. bellas ~s fine arts. con ~ skilfully. malas a

~s trickery. **por amor al** ~ for the fun of it

artefacto *m* device

arteria *f* artery; (*fig, calle*) main road

artesan|al *adj* craft. ~**ía** *f* handicrafts. **objeto de** ~**ía** traditional craft object. ~**o** *m* artisan, craftsman

ártico *adj* Arctic. Á~ *m*. **el** Á~ the Arctic

articula|ción *f* joint; (*pronunciación*) articulation. ~**do** *adj* articulated; (*lenguaje*) articulate. ~**r** *vt* articulate

artículo *m* article. ~**s** *mpl* (*géneros*) goods. ~ **de exportación** export product. ~ **de fondo** editorial, leader

artifice *m & f* artist; (*creador*) architect

artificil|al *adj* artificial. ~**o** *m* (*habilidad*) skill; (*dispositivo*) device; (*engaño*) trick

artiller|ía *f* artillery. ~**o** *m* artilleryman, gunner

artilugio *m* gadget

artimaña *f* trick

art|ista *m & f* artist. ~**ístico** *adj* artistic

artritis *f* arthritis

arveja *f* (*LAm*) pea

arzobispo *m* archbishop

as *m* ace

asa *f* handle

asado *adj* roast(ed). ● *m* roast (meat), joint; (*LAm, reunión*) barbecue. ~**o a la parrilla** grilled meat; (*LAm*) barbecued meat

asalariado *adj* salaried. ● *m* employee

asalt|ante *m* attacker; (*de un banco*) robber. ~**ar** *vt* storm (forta-

leza); attack (persona); raid (banco etc); (*fig*) (duda) assail; (*fig*) (idea etc) cross one's mind. ~**o** *m* attack; (*robo*) robbery; (*en boxeo*) round

asamblea *f* assembly; (*reunión*) meeting

asar *vt* roast. ~**se** *vpr* be very hot. ~ **a la parrilla** grill; (*LAm*) barbecue. ~ **al horno** (*sin grasa*) bake; (*con grasa*) roast

asbesto *m* asbestos

ascend|encia *f* descent; (*LAm, influencia*) influence. ~**ente** *adj* ascending. ~**er** **1** *vt* promote. ● *vi* go up, ascend; (*cuenta etc*) come to, amount to; (*ser ascendido*) be promoted. ~**iente** *m & f* ancestor; (*influencia*) influence

ascens|ión *f* ascent; (*de grado*) promotion. **día** *m* **de la** A~**ión** Ascension Day. ~**o** *m* ascent; (*de grado*) promotion

ascensor *m* lift (*Brit*), elevator (*Amer*). ~**ista** *m & f* lift attendant (*Brit*), elevator operator (*Amer*)

asco *m* disgust. **dar** ~ be disgusting; (*fig, causar enfado*) be infuriating. **estar hecho un** ~ be disgusting. **me da** ~ it makes me feel sick. **¡qué** ~! how disgusting! **ser un** ~ be disgusting

ascua *f* ember. **estar en** ~**s** be on tenterhooks

asea|do *adj* clean; (*arreglado*) neat. ~**r** *vt* (*lavar*) wash; (*limpiar*) clean; (*arreglar*) tidy up

asedi|ar *vt* besiege; (*fig*) pester. ~**o** *m* siege

asegura|do *adj & m* insured. ~**dor** *m* insurer. ~**r** *vt* secure, make safe; (*decir*) assure; (*concertar un seguro*) insure; (*preservar*) safeguard. ~**rse** *vpr* make sure

asemejarse *vpr* be alike

asenta|do *adj* situated; (*arraigado*) established. **~r 1** *vt* place; (*asegurar*) settle; (*anotar*) note down; (*Mex, afirmar*) state. **~rse** *vpr* settle; (*estar situado*) be situated; (*esp LAm, sentar cabeza*) settle down

asentir 4 *vi* agree (a to). **~ con la cabeza** nod

aseo *m* cleanliness. **~s** *mpl* toilets

asequible *adj* obtainable; (*precio*) reasonable; (*persona*) approachable

asesin|ar *vt* murder; (*Pol*) assassinate. **~ato** *m* murder; (*Pol*) assassination. **~o** *m* murderer; (*Pol*) assassin

asesor *m* adviser, consultant. **~ar** *vt* advise. **~arse** *vpr*. **~arse con** consult. **~ía** *f* consultancy; (*oficina*) consultant's office

asfalt|ado *adj* asphalt. **~ar** *vt* asphalt. **~o** *m* asphalt

asfixia *f* suffocation. **~nte** *adj* suffocating. **~r** *vt* suffocate. **~rse** *vpr* suffocate

así *adv* (*de esta manera*) like this, like that. ● *adj* such. **~ como** so-so. **~ como** just as. **~ ... como** as, (*LAm*) **~ nomás** just like that. **~ ... como** both ... and. **~ pues** so. **~ que** so; (*en cuanto*) as soon as. **~ sea** so be it. **~ y todo** even so. **aun ~** even so. **¿no es ~?** isn't that right? **si es ~** if that is the case. **y ~ (sucesivamente)** and so on

Asia *f* Asia

asiático *adj & m* Asian

asidero *m* handle; (*fig, pretexto*) excuse

asidu|amente *adv* regularly. **~o** *adj & m* regular

asiento *m* seat; (*en contabilidad*)

entry. **~ delantero** front seat. **~ trasero** back seat

asignar *vt* assign; allot (*porción, tiempo etc*)

asignatura *f* subject. **~ pendiente** (*en enseñanza*) failed subject; (*fig*) matter still to be resolved

asil|ado *m* inmate; (*Pol*) refugee. **~o** *m* asylum; (*fig*) shelter; (*de ancianos etc*) home. **pedir ~o político** ask for political asylum

asimétrico *adj* asymmetrical

asimila|ción *f* assimilation. **~r** *vt* assimilate

asimismo *adv* also; (*igualmente*) in the same way, likewise

asir 45 *vt* grasp

asist|encia *f* attendance; (*gente*) people (present); (*en un teatro etc*) audience; (*ayuda*) assistance. **~encia médica** medical care. **~enta** *f* (*mujer de la limpieza*) charwoman. **~ente** *m & f* assistant. **~ente social** social worker. **~ido** *adj* assisted. **~ir** *vt* assist, help. ● *vi*. **~ir a** attend, be present at

asma *f* asthma. **~ático** *adj & m* asthmatic

asno *m* donkey; (*fig*) ass

asocia|ción *f* association; (*Com*) partnership. **~do** *adj* associated; (*socio*) associate. ● *m* associate. **~r** *vt* associate; (*Com*) take into partnership. **~rse** *vpr* associate; (*Com*) become a partner

asolar 1 *vt* devastate

asomar *vt* show. ● *vi* appear, show. **~se** *vpr* (*persona*) lean out (a, por of); (*cosa*) appear

asombr|ar *vt* (*pasmar*) amaze; (*sorprender*) surprise. **~arse** *vpr* be amazed; (*sorprenderse*) be surprised. **~o** *m* amazement, surprise.

a ~**oso** adj amazing, astonishing

asomo m sign. **ni por** ~ by no means

aspa f cross, X-shape; (de molino) (windmill) sail. **en** ~ X-shaped

aspaviento m show, fuss. ~**s** mpl gestures. **hacer** ~**s** make a big fuss

aspecto m look, appearance; (fig) aspect

aspereza f roughness; (de sabor etc) sourness

áspero adj rough; (sabor etc) bitter

aspersión f sprinkling

aspiración f breath; (deseo) ambition

aspirador m, **aspiradora** f vacuum cleaner

aspira|nte m & f candidate. ~**r** vt breathe in; (máquina) suck up. ● vi breathe in; (máquina) suck. ~**r a** aspire to

aspirina f aspirin

asquear vt sicken. ● vi be sickening. ~**se** vpr be disgusted

asqueroso adj disgusting

asta f spear; (de la bandera) flagpole; (cuerno) horn. **a media** ~ at half-mast. ~**bandera** f (Mex) flagpole

asterisco m asterisk

astilla f splinter. ~**s** fpl firewood

astillero m shipyard

astringente adj & m astringent

astr|o m star. ~**ología** f astrology. ~**ólogo** m astrologer. ~**onauta** m & f astronaut. ~**onave** f spaceship. ~**onomía** f astronomy. ~**ónomo** m astronomer

astu|cia f cleverness; (ardid) cunning trick. ~**to** adj astute; (taimado) cunning

asumir vt assume

asunción f assumption. **la A**~ the Assumption

asunto m (cuestión) matter; (de una novela) plot; (negocio) business. ~**s** mpl **exteriores** foreign affairs. **el** ~ **es que** the fact is that

asusta|dizo adj easily frightened. ~**r** vt frighten. ~**rse** vpr be frightened

ataca|nte m & f attacker. ~**r** 7 vt attack

atad|o adj tied. ●**m** bundle. ~**ura** f tie

ataj|ar vi take a short cut; (Mex, en tenis) pick up the balls. ●**vt** (LAm, agarrar) catch. ~**o** m short cut

atañer 22 vt concern

ataque m attack; (Med) fit, attack. ~ **al corazón** heart attack. ~ **de nervios** fit of hysterics

atar vt tie. ~**se** vpr tie up

atarantar vt (LAm) fluster. ~**se** vpr (LAm) get flustered

atardecer 11 vi get dark. ● m dusk. **al** ~ at dusk

atareado adj busy

atasc|ar 7 vt block; (fig) hinder. ~**arse** vpr get stuck; (tubo etc) block. ~**o** m blockage; (Auto) traffic jam

ataúd m coffin

atav|iar 20 vt dress up. ~**iarse** vpr dress up, get dressed up. ~**io** m dress, attire

atemorizar 10 vt frighten. ~**se** vpr be frightened

atención f attention; (cortesía) courtesy, kindness; (interés) interest. **¡**~**!** look out!. **llamar la** ~ attract attention, catch the eye; **prestar** ~ pay attention

atender 1 vt attend to; (cuidar) look after. ● vi pay attention

atenerse 40 *vpr* abide (a by)

atentado *m* (*ataque*) attack; (*afrenta*) affront (**contra** to). ~ **contra la vida de uno** attempt on s.o.'s life

atentamente *adv* attentively; (*con cortesía*) politely; (*con amabilidad*) kindly. **lo saluda** ~ (*en cartas*) yours faithfully

atentar *vi*. ~ **contra** threaten. ~ **contra la vida de uno** make an attempt on s.o.'s life

atento *adj* attentive; (*cortés*) polite; (*amable*) kind

atenua|nte *adj* extenuating. ● *f* extenuating circumstance. ~**r** 21 *vt* attenuate; (*hacer menor*) diminish, lessen

ateo *adj* atheistic. ● *m* atheist

aterciopelado *adj* velvety

aterra|dor *adj* terrifying. ~**r** *vt* terrify

aterriza|je *m* landing. ~**je forzoso** emergency landing. ~**r** 10 *vt* land

aterrorizar 10 *vt* terrify

atesorar *vt* hoard; amass (*fortuna*)

atesta|do *adj* packed, full up. ● *m* sworn statement. ~**r** *vt* fill up, pack; (*Jurid*) testify

atestiguar 15 *vt* testify to; (*fig*) prove

atiborrar *vt* fill, stuff. ~**se** *vpr* stuff o.s.

ático *m* attic

atina|do *adj* right; (*juicioso*) wise, sensible. ~**r** *vt/i* hit upon; (*acertar*) guess right

atizar 10 *vt* poke; (*fig*) stir up

atlántico *adj* Atlantic. **el (océano) A**~ the Atlantic (Ocean)

atlas *m* atlas

atl|eta *m & f* athlete. ~**ético** *adj* athletic. ~**etismo** *m* athletics

atmósfera *f* atmosphere

atole *m* (*LAm*) boiled maize drink

atolladero *m* bog; (*fig*) tight corner

atolondra|do *adj* scatterbrained; (*aturdido*) stunned. ~**r** *vt* fluster; (*pasmar*) stun. ~**rse** *vpr* get flustered

at|ómico *adj* atomic. ~**omizador** *m* spray, atomizer

átomo *m* atom

atónito *m* amazed

atonta|do *adj* stunned; (*tonto*) stupid. ~**r** *vt* stun. ~**rse** *vpr* get confused

atorar *vt* (*esp LAm*) to block; (*Mex, sujetar*) secure. ~**se** *vpr* (*esp LAm, atragantarse*) choke; (*atascarse*) get blocked; (*puerta*) get jammed

atormentar *vt* torture. ~**se** *vpr* worry, torment o.s.

atornillar *vt* screw on

atosigar 12 *vt* pester

atraca|dor *m* mugger; (*de banco*) bank robber. ~**r** 7 *vt* dock; (*arrimar*) bring alongside; hold up (*banco*); mug (*persona*). ● *vi* (*barco*) dock

atracci|ón *f* attraction. ~**ones** *fpl* entertainment, amusements

atrac|o *m* hold-up, robbery. ~**ón** *m*. **darse un** ~**ón** stuff o.s. (**de** with)

atractivo *adj* attractive. ● *m* attraction; (*encanto*) charm

atraer 41 *vt* attract

atragantarse *vpr* choke (**con** on). **la historia se me atraganta** I can't stand history

atrancar 7 *vt* bolt (*puerta*). ~**se**

a *vpr* get stuck

atrapar *vt* catch; (*encerrar*) trap

atrás *adv* back; (*tiempo*) previously, before. años ~ years ago. ~ de (*LAm*) behind. dar un paso ~ step backwards. hacia ~, para ~ backwards

atras|ado *adj* behind; (*reloj*) slow; (*con deudas*) in arrears; (*país*) backward. llegar ~ado (*esp LAm*) arrive late. ~ar *vt* put back (*reloj*); (*demorar*) delay, postpone. ● *vi* (*reloj*) be slow. ~arse *vpr* be late; (*reloj*) be slow; (*quedarse atrás*) fall behind. ~o *m* delay; (*de un reloj*) slowness; (*de un país*) backwardness. ~os *mpl* (*Com*) arrears

atravesa|do *adj* lying across. ~r **1** *vt* cross; (*traspasar*) go through (*poner transversalmente*) lay across. ~rse *vpr* lie across; (*en la garganta*) get stuck, stick

atrayente *adj* attractive

atrev|erse *vpr* dare. ~erse con tackle. ~ido *adj* daring; (*insolente*) insolent. ~imiento *m* daring; (*descaro*) insolence

atribu|ción *f* attribution. ~ciones *fpl* authority. ~uir **17** *vt* attribute; confer (*función*). ~irse *vpr* claim

atribulado *adj* afflicted

atributo *m* attribute

atril *m* lectern; (*Mus*) music stand

atrocidad *f* atrocity. ¡qué ~! how awful!

atrofiarse *vpr* atrophy

atropell|ado *adj* hasty. ~ar *vt* knock down; (*por encima*) run over; (*empujar*) push aside; (*fig*) outrage, insult. ~arse *vpr* rush. ~o *m* (*Auto*) accident; (*fig*) outrage

atroz *adj* appalling; (*fig*) atrocious

atuendo *m* dress, attire

atún *m* tuna (fish)

aturdi|do *adj* bewildered; (*por golpe*) stunned. ~r *vt* bewilder; (*golpe*) stun; (*ruido*) deafen

auda|cia *f* boldness, audacity. ~z *adj* bold

audi|ble *adj* audible. ~ción *f* hearing; (*prueba*) audition. ~encia *f* audience; (*tribunal*) court; (*sesión*) hearing

auditor *m* auditor. ~io *m* audience; (*sala*) auditorium

auge *m* peak; (*Com*) boom

augur|ar *vt* predict; (*cosas*) augur. ~io *m* prediction. con nuestros mejores ~ios para with our best wishes for. mal ~ bad omen

aula *f* class-room; (*Univ*) lecture room

aull|ar **23** *vi* howl. ~ido *m* howl

aument|ar *vt* increase; magnify (*imagen*). ● *vi* increase. ~o *m* increase; (*de sueldo*) rise

aun *adv* even. ~ así even so. ~ cuando although. más ~ even more. ni ~ not even

aún *adv* still, yet. ~ no ha llegado it still hasn't arrived, it hasn't arrived yet

aunar **23** *vt* join. ~se *vpr* join together

aunque *conj* although, (even) though

aúpa *int* up! de ~ wonderful

aureola *f* halo

auricular *m* (*de teléfono*) receiver. ~es *mpl* headphones

aurora *f* dawn

ausen|cia *f* absence. en ~cia de in the absence of. ~tarse *vpr* leave. ~te *adj* absent. ● *m & f* ab-

sentee; (Jurid) missing person.
~tismo m (LAm) absenteeism

auspici|ador m sponsor. ~**ar** vt
sponsor. ~**o** m sponsorship; (signo)
omen. **bajo los** ~**s de** sponsored by

auster|idad f austerity. ~**o** adj
austere

austral adj southern

Australia f Australia

australiano adj & m Australian

Austria f Austria

austriaco, austríaco adj & m Austrian

aut|enticar 7 authenticate.
~**enticidad** f authenticity. ~**éntico** adj authentic

auto m (Jurid) decision; (orden)
order; (Auto, fam) car. ~**s** mpl proceedings

auto|abastecimiento m self-sufficiency. ~**biografía** f autobiography

autobús m bus. **en** ~ by bus

autocar m (long-distance) bus,
coach (Brit)

autocontrol m self-control

autóctono adj indigenous

auto|determinación f self-determination. ~**didacta** adj self-taught. ● m & f self-taught person. ~**escuela** f driving school. ~**financiamiento** m self-financing

autógrafo m autograph

autómata m robot

autom|ático adj automatic. ● m
press-stud. ~**atización** f automation

automotor m diesel train

autom|óvil adj motor. ● m car.
~**ovilismo** m motoring. ~**ovilista** m & f driver, motorist

aut|onomía f autonomy. ~**onómico** adj, ~**ónomo** adj autonomous

autopista f motorway (Brit), freeway (Amer)

autopsia f autopsy

autor m author. ~**a** f author(ess)

autori|dad f authority. ~**tario** adj authoritarian

autoriza|ción f authorization.
~**do** adj authorized, official; (opinión etc) authoritative. ~**r** 10 vt authorize

auto|rretrato m self-portrait.
~**servicio** m self-service restaurant. ~**stop** m hitch-hiking. **hacer** ~**stop** hitch-hike

autosuficiente adj self-sufficient

autovía f dual carriageway

auxili|ar adj auxiliary; (profesor)
assistant. ● m & f assistant. ● vt
help. ~**o** m help. ¡~**o**! help! **en**
~**o de** in aid of. **pedir** ~**o** shout
for help. **primeros** ~**os** first aid

Av. abrev (**Avenida**) Ave

aval m guarantee

avalancha f avalanche

avalar vt guarantee

aval|uar vt 21 (LAm) value. ~**úo** m
valuation

avance m advance; (en el cine)
trailer. **avances** mpl (Mex) trailer

avanzar 10 vt move forward. ~
la pantalla scroll up. ● vi advance

avar|icia f avarice. ~**icioso** adj,
~**iento** adj greedy; (tacaño)
miserly. ~**o** adj miserly. ● m miser

avasallar vt dominate

Avda. abrev (**Avenida**) Ave

ave f bird. ~ **de paso** (incl fig) bird
of passage. ~ **de rapiña** bird of
prey

AVE - Alta Velocidad Española *i* A high-speed train service linking Madrid, Seville and Huelva via Cadiz, established in 1992 in time for the international exhibition, Expo 92 in Seville. Lines under construction include: Madrid-Barcelona, with an extension to France, and Barcelona-Valencia. An Ave service linking Madrid and Galicia is planned.

avecinarse *vpr* approach

avejentar *vt* age

avellana *f* hazelnut. **~o** *m* hazel (tree)

avemaría *f* Hail Mary

avena *f* oats

avenida *f* (*calle*) avenue

avenir 53 *vt* reconcile. **~se** *vpr* come to an agreement; (*entenderse*) get on well (con with)

aventajado *adj* outstanding. **~r** *vt* be ahead of; (*superar*) surpass

aventar 1 *vt* fan; winnow (grano etc); (*Mex, lanzar*) throw; (*Mex, empujar*) push. **~arse** *vpr* (*Mex*) throw o.s.; (*atreverse*) dare. **~ón** *m* (*Mex*) ride, lift (*Brit*)

aventura *f* adventure. **~a amorosa** love affair. **~ado** *adj* risky. **~ero** *adj* adventurous. ● *m* adventurer

avergonzar 10 & 18 *vt* shame; (*abochornar*) embarrass. **~se** *vpr* be ashamed; (*abochornarse*) be embarrassed

avería *f* (*Auto*) breakdown; (*en máquina*) failure. **~iado** *adj* broken down. **~iarse** 20 *vpr* break down

averiguación *f* inquiry; (*disputa*) argument. **~r** 15 *vt* find out. ● *vi* (*Mex*) argue

aversión *f* aversion (a, hacia,

por to)

avestruz *m* ostrich

aviación *f* aviation; (*Mil*) air force. **~dor** *m* (*piloto*) pilot

avícola *adj* poultry. **~icultura** *f* poultry farming

avidez *f* eagerness, greed

ávido *adj* eager, greedy

avinagrado *adj* sour. **~rse** *vpr* go sour; (*fig*) become embittered

avión *m* aeroplane (*Brit*), airplane (*Amer*); (*Mex, juego*) hopscotch. **~onazo** *m* (*Mex*) plane crash

avisar *vt* warn; (*informar*) notify, inform; call (médico etc). **~o** *m* warning; (*comunicación*) notice; (*LAm, anuncio, cartel*) advertisement; (*en televisión*) commercial. **estar sobre ~o** be on the alert. **sin previo ~o** without prior warning

avispa *f* wasp. **~ado** *adj* sharp. **~ero** *m* wasps' nest; (*fig*) mess. **~ón** *m* hornet

avistar *vt* catch sight of

avivar *vt* stoke up (fuego); brighten up (color); arouse (interés, pasión); intensify (dolor). **~se** *vpr* revive; (*animarse*) cheer up; (*LAm, despabilarse*) wise up

axila *f* armpit, axilla

axioma *m* axiom

ay *int* (*de dolor*) ouch!; (*de susto*) oh!; (*de pena*) oh dear! **¡~ de ti!** poor you!

aya *f* governess, child's nurse

ayer *adv* yesterday. ● *m* past. **antes de ~** the day before yesterday. **~ por la mañana**, (*LAm*) **en la mañana** yesterday morning

ayuda *f* help, aid. **~ de cámara** valet. **~nta** *f*, **~nte** *m* assistant; (*Mil*) adjutant. **~r** *vt* help

ayunar *vi* fast. **~as** *fpl*. **estar en**

~as have had nothing to eat or drink; (*fig, fam*) be in the dark. **~o** *m* fasting

ayuntamiento *m* town council, city council; (*edificio*) town hall

azabache *m* jet

azad|a *f* hoe. **~ón** *m* (large) hoe

azafata *f* air hostess

azafate *m* (*LAm*) tray

azafrán *m* saffron

azahar *m* orange blossom; (*del limonero*) lemon blossom

azar *m* chance; (*desgracia*) misfortune. **al ~** at random. **por ~** by chance. **~es** *mpl* ups and downs

azaros|amente *adv* hazardously. **~o** *adj* hazardous, risky; (*vida*) eventful

azorar *vt* embarrass. **~rse** *vpr* be embarrassed

Azores *fpl.* **las ~** the Azores

azotador *m* (*Mex*) caterpillar

azot|ar *vt* whip, beat; (*Mex, puerta*) slam. **~e** *m* whip; (*golpe*) smack; (*fig, calamidad*) calamity

azotea *f* flat roof

azteca *adj & m & f* Aztec

Aztecas A Náhuatl-speaking people who in the fourteenth century established a brilliant and tyrannical civilization in central and southern Mexico. Its capital was Tenochtitlán, built on reclaimed marshland, and which became Mexico City. The Aztec empire collapsed in 1521 after defeat by the Spaniards led by Hernán Cortés.

az|úcar *m & f* sugar. **~ucarado** *adj* sweet, sugary. **~ucarar** *vt* sweeten. **~ucarero** *m* sugar bowl

azucena *f* (white) lily

azufre *m* sulphur

azul *adj & m* blue. **~ado** *adj* bluish. **~ marino** navy blue

azulejo *m* tile

azuzar Ⓒ *vt* urge on, incite

Año Nuevo See ▷**Nochevieja**

Bb

bab|a *f* spittle. **~ear** *vi* drool, slobber; (*niño*) dribble. **caérsele la ~a** a uno be delighted. **~eo** *m* drooling; (*de un niño*) dribbling. **~ero** *m* bib

babor *m* port. **a ~** to port, on the port side

babosa *f* slug

babosada *f* (*Mex*) drivel

babos|ear *vt* slobber over; (*niño*) dribble over. ●*vi* (*Mex*) day dream. **~o** *adj* slimy; (*LAm, tonto*) silly

babucha *f* slipper

baca *f* luggage rack

bacalao *m* cod

bache *m* pothole; (*fig*) bad patch

bachillerato *m* school-leaving examination

bacteria *f* bacterium

bagaje *m.* **~ cultural** cultural knowledge; (*de un pueblo*) cultural heritage

bahía *f* bay

bail|able *adj* dance. **~aor** *m* Flamenco dancer. **~ar** *vt/i* dance. **ir a ~ar** go dancing. **~arín** *m* dancer.

~arina f dancer; (de ballet) ballerina. **~e** m dance; (actividad) dancing. **~e de etiqueta** ball

baja f drop, fall; (Mil) casualty. **~ por maternidad** maternity leave. **darse de ~** take sick leave. **~da** f slope; (acto de bajar) descent; (camino) way down. **~r** vt lower; (llevar abajo) get down; go down (escalera); bow (la cabeza). ● vi go down; (temperatura, precio) fall. **~rse** vpr pull down (pantalones). **~r(se) de** get out of (coche); get off (autobús, caballo, tren, bicicleta)

bajeza f vile deed

bajío m shallows; (de arena) sandbank; (LAm, terreno bajo) low-lying area

bajo adj low; (de estatura) short, small; (cabeza, ojos) lowered; (humilde) humble, low; (vil) vile, low; (voz) low; (Mus) deep. ● m lowland; (Mus) bass. ● adv quietly; (volar) low. ● prep under. **~ cero** below zero. **~ la lluvia** in the rain. **los ~s** (LAm) ground floor (Brit), first floor (Amer); **los ~s fondos** the underworld

bajón m sharp drop; (de salud) sudden decline

bala f bullet; (de algodón etc) bale. (LAm, en atletismo) shot. **como una ~** like a shot. **lanzamiento de ~** (LAm) shot put

balada f ballad

balan|ce m balance; (documento) balance sheet; (resultado) outcome. **~cear** vt balance. **~cearse** vpr swing. **~ceo** m swinging. **~cín** m rocking chair; (de niños) seesaw. **~za** f scales; (Com) balance

balar vi bleat

balazo m (disparo) shot; (herida) bullet wound

balboa f (unidad monetaria panameña) balboa

balbuc|ear vt/i stammer; (niño) babble. **~eo** m stammering; (de niño) babbling. **~ir** 24 vt/i stammer; (niño) babble

balcón m balcony

balda f shelf

balde m bucket. **de ~** free (of charge). **en ~** in vain

baldío adj (terreno) waste

baldosa f (floor) tile; (losa) flagstone

bale|ar adj Balearic. ● **las (Islas) B~ares** the Balearics, the Balearic Islands. ● vt (LAm) to shoot. **~o** m (LAm, tiroteo) shooting

balero m (Mex) cup and ball toy; (rodamiento) bearing

balido m bleat; (varios sonidos) bleating

balística f ballistics

baliza f (Naut) buoy; (Aviac) beacon

ballena f whale

ballet /ba'le/ (pl ~s) m ballet

balneario m spa; (con playa) seaside resort

balompié m soccer, football (Brit)

bal|ón m ball. **~oncesto** m basketball. **~onmano** m handball. **~onvolea** m volleyball

balotaje m (LAm) voting

balsa f (de agua) pool; (plataforma flotante) raft

bálsamo m balsam; (fig) balm

---

balseros The name given to illegal immigrants who try to enter a country in small boats or on rafts. It applies particularly to Cubans who try to enter the US by sailing to *i*

Florida and to immigrants attempting to enter Spain by crossing the Straits of Gibraltar.

baluarte m (incl fig) bastion

bambalina f drop curtain. entre ∼s behind the scenes

bambole|ar vi sway. ∼arse vpr sway; (mesa etc) wobble; (barco) rock. ∼o m swaying; (de mesa etc) wobbling; (de barco) rocking

bambú m (pl ∼es) bamboo

banal adj banal. ∼idad f banality

banan|a f (esp LAm) banana. ∼ero adj banana. ∼o m (LAm) banana tree

banc|a f banking; (conjunto de bancos) banks; (en juegos) bank; (LAm, asiento) bench. ∼ario adj bank, banking. ∼arrota f bankruptcy. hacer ∼arrota, ir a la ∼arrota go bankrupt. ∼o m (asiento) bench; (Com) bank; (bajío) sandbank; (de peces) shoal

banda f (incl Mus, Radio) band; (Mex, para el pelo) hair band; (raya ancha) stripe; (cinta ancha) sash; (grupo) gang, group. ∼ acha broadband. ∼ sonora sound-track. ∼da f (de pájaros) flock; (de peces) shoal

bandeja f tray

bandejón m (Mex) central reservation (Brit), median strip (Amer)

bander|a f flag. ∼illa f banderilla. ∼ear vt stick the banderillas in ∼ero m banderillero. ∼ín m pennant, small flag

bandido m bandit

bando m edict, proclamation; (facción) camp, side. ∼s mpl banns. pasarse al otro ∼ go over to the other side

bandolero m bandit

bandoneón m large accordion

banjo m banjo

banquero m banker

banquete m banquet; (de boda) wedding reception

banquillo m bench; (Jurid) dock; (taburete) footstool

bañ|ador m (de mujer) swimming costume; (de hombre) swimming trunks. ∼ar vt bath (niño); (Culin, recubrir) coat. ∼arse vpr go swimming, have a swim; (en casa) have a bath. ∼era f bath (tub). ∼ista m & f bather. ∼o m bath; (en piscina, mar etc) swim; (cuarto) bathroom; (LAm, wáter) toilet; (bañera) bath-(tub); (capa) coat(ing)

baqueano (LAm), **baquiano** m guide

bar m bar

baraja f pack of cards. ∼r vt shuffle; juggle (cifras etc); consider (posibilidades); (Mex, explicar) explain

baranda, barandilla f rail; (de escalera) banisters

barat|a f (Mex) sale. ∼ija f trinket. ∼illo m junk shop; (géneros) cheap goods. ∼o adj cheap. ● adv cheap(ly)

barba f chin; (pelo) beard

barbacoa f barbecue; (carne) barbecued meat

barbari|dad f atrocity; (fam, mucho) awful lot 🔲. ¡qué ∼dad! how awful! ∼e f barbarity; (fig) ignorance. ∼smo m barbarism

bárbaro adj barbaric, cruel; (bruto) uncouth; (fam, estupendo) terrific 🔲. ● m barbarian. ¡qué ∼! how marvellous!

barbear vt (Mex, lisonjear) suck up to

barbecho m. en ∼ fallow

barber|ía f barber's (shop). ∼o m

barber; (*Mex, adulador*) creep

barbilla *f* chin

barbitúrico *m* barbiturate

barbudo *adj* bearded

barca *f* (*small*) boat. ~ de pasaje ferry. ~za *f* barge

barcelonés *adj* of Barcelona, from Barcelona. ● *m* native of Barcelona

barco *m* boat; (*navío*) ship. ~ cisterna tanker. ~ de vapor steamer. ~ de vela sailing boat. ir en ~ go by boat

barda *f* (*Mex*) wall; (*de madera*) fence

barítono *adj & m* baritone

barman *m* (*pl* ~s) barman

barniz *m* varnish; (*para loza etc*) glaze; (*fig*) veneer. ~ar 🔟 *vt* varnish; glaze (*loza etc*)

barómetro *m* barometer

bar|ón *m* baron. ~onesa *f* baroness

barquero *m* boatman

barquillo *m* wafer; (*Mex, de helado*) ice-cream cone

barra *f* bar; (*pan*) loaf of French bread; (*palanca*) lever; (*de arena*) sandbank; (*LAm, de hinchas*) supporters. ~ de labios lipstick

barrabasada *f* mischief, prank

barraca *f* hut; (*vivienda pobre*) shack, shanty

barranco *m* ravine, gully; (*despeñadero*) cliff, precipice

barrer *vt* sweep; thrash (*rival*)

barrera *f* barrier. ~ del sonido sound barrier

barriada *f* district; (*LAm, barrio marginal*) slum

barrial *m* (*LAm*) quagmire

barrida *f* sweep; (*LAm, redada*) police raid

barrig|a *f* belly. ~ón *adj*, ~udo *adj* pot-bellied

barril *m* barrel

barrio *m* district, area. ~s bajos poor quarter, poor area. el otro ~ (*fig, fam*) the other world. ~bajero *adj* vulgar, common

barro *m* mud; (*arcilla*) clay; (*arcilla cocida*) earthenware

barroco *adj* Baroque. ● *m* Baroque style

barrote *m* bar

bartola *f*. tirarse a la ~ take it easy

bártulos *mpl* things. liar los ~ pack one's bags

barullo *m* racket; (*confusión*) confusion. a ~ galore

basar *vt* base. ~se *vpr*. ~se en be based on

báscula *f* scales

base *f* base; (*fig*) basis, foundation. a ~ de thanks to; (*mediante*) by means of; (*en una receta*) mainly consisting of. ~ de datos database. partiendo de la ~ de, tomando como ~ on the basis of

básico *adj* basic

basílica *f* basilica

básquetbol, basquetbol *m* (*LAm*) basketball

---

bastante

● *adjetivo/pronombre*

····▶ (*suficiente*) enough. ¿hay ~s sillas? are there enough chairs? ya tengo ~ I have enough already

····▶ (*mucho*) quite a lot. vino ~ gente quite a lot of people came. tiene ~s amigos he has quite a lot of friends ¿te gusta?- sí, ~ do you like it?

— yes, quite a lot
● **adverbio**

····▸ (*suficientemente*) enough. no has estudiado ~ you haven't studied enough. no es lo ~ inteligente he's not clever enough (como para to)

····▸ **bastante** + *adjetivo/adverbio* (*modificando la intensidad*) quite, fairly. parece ~ simpático he looks quite friendly. es ~ fácil de hacer it's quite easy to do. canta ~ bien he sings quite well

····▸ **bastante** con verbo (*considerablemente*) quite a lot. el lugar ha cambiado ~ the place has changed quite a lot

bastar *vi* be enough. ¡basta! that's enough! basta con decir que suffice it to say that. basta y sobra that's more than enough

bastardilla *f* italics

bastardo *adj & m* bastard

bastidor *m* frame; (*Auto*) chassis. ~**es** *mpl* (*en el teatro*) wings. entre ~**es** behind the scenes

basto *adj* coarse. ~**s** *mpl* (*naipes*) clubs

bast|ón *m* walking stick; (*de esquí*) ski pole. ~**onazo** *m* blow with a stick; (*de mando*) staff of office

basur|a *f* rubbish, garbage (*Amer*); (*en la calle*) litter. ~**al** *m* (*LAm, lugar*) rubbish dump. ~**ero** *m* dustman (*Brit*), garbage collector (*Amer*); (*sitio*) rubbish dump; (*Mex, recipiente*) dustbin (*Brit*), garbage can (*Amer*)

bata *f* dressing-gown; (*de médico etc*) white coat; (*esp LAm, de baño*) bathrobe

batahola *f* (*LAm*) pandemonium

batall|a *f* battle. ~**a campal** pitched battle. de ~**a** everyday. ~**ador** *adj* fighting. ● *m* fighter. ~**ar** *vi* battle, fight. ~**ón** *m* battalion

batata *f* sweet potato

bate *m* bat. ~**ador** *m* batter; (*cricket*) batsman. ~**ar** *vi* bat

batería *f* battery; (*Mus*) drums. ● *m & f* drummer. ~ **de cocina** kitchen utensils, pots and pans

baterista *m & f* drummer

batido *adj* beaten; (*nata*) whipped. ● *m* batter; (*bebida*) milk shake. ~**ra** *f* (*food*) mixer

batir *vt* beat; break (*récord*); whip (*nata*). ~ **palmas** clap. ~**se** *vpr* fight

batuta *f* baton. llevar la ~ be in command, be the boss

baúl *m* trunk

bauti|smal *adj* baptismal. ~**smo** *m* baptism, christening. ~**zar** [10] *vt* baptize, christen. ~**zo** *m* christening

baya *f* berry

bayeta *f* cloth

bayoneta *f* bayonet

baza *f* (*naipes*) trick; (*fig*) advantage. meter ~ interfere

bazar *m* bazaar

bazofia *f* revolting food; (*fig*) rubbish

beato *adj* blessed; (*piadoso*) devout; (*pey*) overpious

bebé *m* baby

beb|edero *m* drinking trough; (*sitio*) watering place. ~**edizo** *m* potion; (*veneno*) poison. ~**edor** *m* heavy drinker. ~ *er vt/i* drink. ~**ida** *f* drink. ~**ido** *adj* drunk

beca *f* grant, scholarship. ~**do** *m* (*LAm*) scholarship holder, scholar.

~r 7 *vt* give a scholarship to. **~rio** *m* scholarship holder, scholar

b **beige** /beis, beʒ/ *adj & m* beige

béisbol *m*, (*Mex*) **beisbol** *m* baseball

belén *m* crib, nativity scene

belga *adj & m & f* Belgian

Bélgica *f* Belgium

bélico *adj*, **belicoso** *adj* warlike

bell|eza *f* beauty. **~o** *adj* beautiful. **~as artes** *fpl* fine arts

bellota *f* acorn

bemol *m* flat. tener (muchos) **~es** be difficult

bend|ecir 46 (*pero imperativo* bendice, *futuro, condicional y pp regulares*) *vt* bless. **~ición** *f* blessing. **~ito** *adj* blessed; (*que tiene suerte*) lucky; (*feliz*) happy

benefactor *m* benefactor

benefic|encia *f* charity. de **~encia** charitable. **~iar** *vt* benefit. **~iarse** *vpr* benefit. **~iario** *m* beneficiary; (*de un cheque etc*) payee. **~io** *m* benefit; (*ventaja*) advantage; (*ganancia*) profit, gain. **~ioso** *adj* beneficial

benéfico *adj* beneficial; (*de beneficencia*) charitable

ben|evolencia *f* benevolence. **~évolo** *adj* benevolent

bengala *f* flare. luz *f* de **~** flare

benigno *adj* kind; (*moderado*) gentle, mild; (*tumor*) benign

berberecho *m* cockle

berenjena *f* aubergine (*Brit*), eggplant (*Amer*)

berr|ear *vi* (*animales*) bellow; (*niño*) bawl. **~ido** *m* bellow; (*de niño*) bawling

berrinche *m* temper; (*de un niño*) tantrum

berro *m* watercress

besamel(a) *f* white sauce

bes|ar *vt* kiss. **~arse** *vpr* kiss (each other). **~o** *m* kiss

bestia *f* beast; (*bruto*) brute; (*idiota*) idiot. **~ de carga** beast of burden. **~l** *adj* bestial, animal; (*fig, fam*) terrific. **~lidad** *f* (*acción brutal*) horrid thing; (*insensatez*) stupidity

besugo *m* red bream

besuquear *vt* cover with kisses

betabel *f* (*Mex*) beetroot

betún *m* (*para el calzado*) shoe polish

biberón *m* feeding-bottle

Biblia *f* Bible

bibliografía *f* bibliography

biblioteca *f* library; (*mueble*) bookcase. **~ de consulta** reference library. **~rio** *m* librarian

bicarbonato *m* bicarbonate

bicho *m* insect, bug; (*animal*) small animal, creature. **~ raro** odd sort

bici *f* 1 bike. **~cleta** *f* bicycle. ir en **~cleta** cycle. **~moto** (*LAm*) moped

bidé, bidet /biˈðeɪ/ *m* bidet

bidón *m* drum, can

bien *adv* well; (*muy*) very, quite; (*correctamente*) right; (*de buena gana*) willingly. ● *m* good; (*efectos*) property. ¡**~**! fine!, OK!, good! **~...** (o) ... either... or. ¡está **~**! fine!, alright!; (*basta*) that is enough!. más **~** rather. ¡muy **~**! good! no **~** as soon as. ¡qué **~**! marvellous!, great! 1. si **~** although

bienal *adj* biennial

bien|aventurado *adj* fortunate. **~estar** *m* well-being. **~hablado** *adj* well-spoken. **~hechor** *m* benefactor. **~intencionado** *adj* well-meaning

bienio *m* two year-period

bienvenid|a *f* welcome. dar la ∼a a uno welcome s.o. ∼o *adj* welcome. ¡∼o! welcome!

bifurca|ción *f* junction. ∼rse **7** *vpr* fork; (*rail*) branch off

b|igamia *f* bigamy. ∼ígamo *adj* bigamous. ● *m* bigamist

bigot|e *m* moustache. ∼ón *adj* (*Mex*), ∼udo *adj* with a big moustache

bikini *m* bikini

bilingüe *adj* bilingual

billar *m* billiards

billete *m* ticket; (*de banco*) (bank) note (*Brit*), bill (*Amer*). ∼ de ida y vuelta return ticket (*Brit*), round-trip ticket (*Amer*). ∼ sencillo single ticket (*Brit*), one-way ticket (*Amer*). ∼ra *f*, ∼ro *m* wallet, billfold (*Amer*)

billón *m* billion (*Brit*), trillion (*Amer*)

bi|mensual *adj* fortnightly, twice-monthly. ∼mestral *adj* two-monthly. ∼mestre two-month period. ∼motor *adj* twin-engined. ● *m* twin-engined plane

binoculares *mpl* binoculars

biocarburante *m* biofuel

bi|ografía *f* biography. ∼ográfico *adj* biographical

bi|ología *f* biology. ∼ológico *adj* biological. ∼ólogo *m* biologist

biombo *m* folding screen

biopsia *f* biopsy

bioterrorismo *m* bioterrorism

biplaza *m* two-seater

biquini *m* bikini

birlar *vt* ① steal, pinch ①

bis *m* encore. ¡∼! encore! vivo en el 3 ∼ I live at 3A

bisabuel|a *f* great-grandmother. ∼o *m* great-grandfather. ∼os *mpl* great-grandparents

bisagra *f* hinge

bisiesto *adj.* año *m* ∼ leap year

bisniet|a *f* great-granddaughter. ∼o *m* great-grandson. ∼os *mpl* great-grandchildren

bisonte *m* bison

bisoño *adj* inexperienced

bisté, bistec *m* steak

bisturí *m* scalpel

bisutería *f* costume jewellery

bitácora *f* binnacle

bizco *adj* cross-eyed

bizcocho *m* sponge (cake)

bizquear *vi* squint

blanc|a *f* white woman; (*Mus*) minim. ∼o *adj* white; (*tez*) fair. ● *m* white; (*persona*) white man; (*espacio*) blank; (*objetivo*) target. dar en el ∼o hit the mark. dejar en ∼o leave blank. pasar la noche en ∼o have a sleepless night. ∼ura *f* whiteness

blandir **24** *vt* brandish

bland|o *adj* soft; (*carácter*) weak; (*cobarde*) cowardly; (*carne*) tender. ∼ura *f* softness; (*de la carne*) tenderness

blanque|ar *vt* whiten; whitewash (*paredes*); bleach (*tela*); launder (*dinero*). ● *vi* turn white. ∼o *m* whitening; (*de dinero*) laundering

blasón *m* coat of arms

bledo *m.* me importa un ∼ I couldn't care less

blinda|je *m* armour (plating). ∼r *vt* armour(-plate)

bloc *m* (*pl* ∼s) pad

bloque *m* block; (*Pol*) bloc. en ∼ en bloc. ∼ar *vt* block; (*Mil*) blockade; (*Com*) freeze. ∼o *m* blockade; (*Com*) freezing

blusa *f* blouse

bob|ada f silly thing. decir ∼adas talk nonsense. ∼**eria** f silly thing

bobina f reel; (Elec) coil

bobo adj silly, stupid. ● m idiot, fool

boca f mouth; (fig, entrada) entrance; (de buzón) slot; (de cañón) muzzle. ∼ abajo face down. ∼ arriba face up

bocacalle f junction. la primera ∼ a la derecha the first turning on the right

bocad|illo m (filled) roll; (fam, comida ligera) snack. ∼**o** m mouthful; (mordisco) bite; (de caballo) bit

boca|jarro. a ∼**jarro** point-blank. ∼**manga** f cuff

bocanada f puff; (de vino etc) mouthful; (ráfaga) gust

bocata f sandwich

bocatería f sandwich bar

bocaza m & f invar big-mouth

boceto m sketch; (de proyecto) outline

bochinche m row; (alboroto) racket. ∼**ro** adj (LAm) rowdy

bochorno m sultry weather; (fig, vergüenza) embarrassment. ¡qué ∼! how embarrassing!. ∼**so** adj oppressive; (fig) embarrassing

bocina f horn; (LAm, auricular) receiver. tocar la ∼ sound one's horn. ∼**zo** m toot

boda f wedding

bodeg|a f cellar; (de vino) wine cellar; (LAm, almacén) warehouse; (de un barco) hold. ∼**ón** m cheap restaurant; (pintura) still life

bodoque m & f (fam, tonto) thick-head; (Mex, niño) kid

bofes mpl lights. echar los ∼ slog away

bofet|ada f slap; (fig) blow. ∼**ón** m punch

boga f (moda) fashion. estar en ∼ be in fashion, be in vogue. ∼**r** [12] vt row. ∼**vante** m (crustáceo) lobster

Bogotá f Bogotá

bogotano adj from Bogotá. ● m native of Bogotá

bohemio adj & m Bohemian

bohío m (LAm) hut

boicot m (pl ∼s) boycott. ∼**ear** vt boycott. ∼**eo** m boycott. hacer un ∼ boycott

boina f beret

bola f ball; (canica) marble; (mentira) fib; (Mex, reunión desordenada) rowdy party; (Mex, montón) una ∼ de a bunch of; (Mex, revolución) revolution; (Mex, brillo) shine

boleadoras (LAm) fpl bolas

bolear vt (Mex) polish, shine

bolera f bowling alley

bolero m (baile, chaquetilla) bolero; (fig, fam, mentiroso) liar; (Mex, limpiabotas) bootblack

bole|ta f (LAm, de rifa) ticket; (Mex, de notas) (school) report; (Mex, electoral) ballot paper. ∼**taje** m (Mex) tickets. ∼**tería** f (LAm) ticket office; (de teatro, cine) box office. ∼**tero** m (LAm) ticket-seller

boletín m bulletin; (publicación periódica) journal; (de notas) report

boleto m (esp LAm) ticket; (Mex, de avión) (air) ticket. ∼ de ida y vuelta, (Mex) ∼ redondo return ticket (Brit), round-trip ticket (Amer). ∼ sencillo single ticket (Brit), one-way ticket (Amer)

boli m [1] Biro (P), ball-point pen

boliche m (juego) bowls; (bolera) bowling alley

bolígrafo m Biro (P), ball-point pen

bolillo m bobbin; (Mex, pan) (bread) roll

bolívar m (unidad monetaria venezolana) bolívar

Bolivia f Bolivia

boliviano adj Bolivian. ●m Bolivian; (unidad monetaria de Bolivia) boliviano

boll|ería f baker's shop. ~o m roll; (con azúcar) bun

bolo m skittle; (Mex, en bautizo) coins. ~s mpl (juego) bowling

bols|a f bag; (Mex, bolsillo) pocket; (Mex, de mujer) handbag; (Com) stock exchange; (cavidad) cavity. ~a de agua caliente hot-water bottle. ~illo m pocket. ~o m (de mujer) handbag. ~o de mano, ~o de viaje (overnight) bag

bomba f bomb; (máquina) pump; (noticia) bombshell. ~ de aceite (Auto) oil pump. ~ de agua (Auto) water pump. pasarlo ~ have a marvellous time

bombachos mpl baggy trousers, baggy pants (Amer)

bombarde|ar vt bombard; (desde avión) bomb. ~o m bombardment; (desde avión) bombing. ~ro m (avión) bomber

bombazo m explosion

bombear vt pump

bombero m fireman. cuerpo de ~s fire brigade (Brit), fire department (Amer)

bombilla f (light) bulb; (LAm, para mate) pipe for drinking maté

bombín m pump; (fam, sombrero) bowler (hat) (Brit), derby (Amer)

bombo m (tambor) bass drum. a ~ y platillos with a lot of fuss

bomb|ón m chocolate; (Mex, malvavisco) marshmallow. ~ona f gas

cylinder

bonachón adj easygoing; (bueno) good-natured

bonaerense adj from Buenos Aires. ●m native of Buenos Aires

bondad f goodness; (amabilidad) kindness; (del clima) mildness. tenga la ~ de would you be kind enough to. ~oso adj kind

boniato m sweet potato

bonito adj nice; (mono) pretty. ¡muy ~!, ¡qué ~! that's nice!, very nice!. ●m bonito

bono m voucher; (título) bond. ~ del Tesoro government bond

boñiga f dung

boqueada f gasp. dar la última ~ be dying

boquerón m anchovy

boquete m hole; (brecha) breach

boquiabierto adj openmouthed; (fig) amazed, dumbfounded. quedarse ~ be amazed

boquilla f mouthpiece; (para cigarillos) cigarette-holder; (filtro de cigarillo) tip

borbotón m. hablar a borbotones gabble. salir a borbotones gush out

borda|do adj embroidered. ● m embroidery. ~r vt embroider

bord|e m edge; (de carretera) side; (de plato etc) rim; (de un vestido) hem. al ~e de on the edge of; (fig) on the brink of. ●adj (Esp fam) stroppy. ~ear vt go round; (fig) border on. ~illo m kerb (Brit), curb (esp Amer)

bordo. a ~ on board

borla f tassel

borrach|era f drunkenness. pegarse una ~era get drunk. ~ín m drunk; (habitual) drunkard. ~o adj drunk. ● m drunkard. estar ~o be drunk. ser ~o be a drunkard

borrador m rough draft; (de contrato) draft; (para la pizarra) (black)board rubber; (goma) eraser

borrar vt rub out; (tachar) cross out; delete (información)

borrasc|a f depression; (tormenta) storm. ~**oso** adj stormy

borrego m year-old lamb; (Mex, noticia falsa) canard

borrico m donkey; (fig, fam) ass

borrón m smudge; (de tinta) inkblot. ~ y cuenta nueva let's forget about it!

borroso adj blurred; (fig) vague

bos|coso adj wooded. ~**que** f wood, forest

bosquej|ar vt sketch; outline (plan). ~**o** m sketch; (de plan) outline

bosta f dung

bostez|ar 10 vi yawn. ~**o** m yawn

bota f boot; (recipiente) wineskin

botana f (Mex) snack, appetizer

botánic|a f botany. ~**o** adj botanical. ● m botanist

botar vt launch; bounce (pelota); (esp LAm, tirar) throw away. ● vi bounce

botarate m irresponsible person; (esp LAm, derrochador) spendthrift

bote m boat; (de una pelota) bounce; (lata) tin, can; (vasija) jar. ~ de la basura (Mex) rubbish bin (Brit), trash can (Amer). ~ salvavidas lifeboat. de ~ en ~ packed

botella f bottle

botica f chemist's (shop) (Brit), drugstore (Amer). ~**rio** m chemist (Brit), druggist (Amer)

botijo m earthenware jug

botín m half boot; (de guerra) booty; (de ladrones) haul

botiquín m medicine chest; (de primeros auxilios) first aid kit

bot|ón m button; (yema) bud; (LAm, insignia) badge. ~**ones** m invar bellboy (Brit), bellhop (Amer)

bóveda f vault

boxe|ador m boxer. ~**ar** vi box. ~**o** m boxing

boya f buoy; (corcho) float. ~**nte** adj buoyant

bozal m (de perro etc) muzzle; (de caballo) halter

bracear vi wave one's arms; (nadar) swim, crawl

bracero m seasonal farm labourer

braga(s) f(pl) panties, knickers (Brit)

bragueta f flies

bram|ar vi bellow. ~**ido** m bellowing

branquia f gill

bras|a f ember. a la ~**a** grilled. ~**ero** m brazier

brasier m (Mex) bra

Brasil m. (el) ~ Brazil

brasile|ño adj & m Brazilian. ~**ro** adj & m (LAm) Brazilian

bravío adj wild

brav|o adj fierce; (valeroso) brave; (mar) rough. ¡~! int well done! bravo! ~**ura** f ferocity; (valor) bravery

braz|a f fathom. nadar a ~**a** swim breast-stroke. ~**ada** f (en natación) stroke. ~**alete** m bracelet; (brazal) arm-band. ~**o** m arm; (de caballo) foreleg; (rama) branch. ~**o** derecho right-hand man. del ~**o** arm in arm

brea f tar, pitch

brebaje m potion; (pej) concoction

brecha f opening; (Mil) breach; (Med) gash. ~ **generacional** generation gap. **estar en la** ~ be in the thick of it

brega f struggle. **andar a la** ~ work hard

breva f early fig

breve adj short. **en** ~ soon, shortly. **en** ~**s momentos** soon. ~**dad** f shortness

brib|ón m rogue, rascal. ~**onada** f dirty trick

brida f bridle

brigad|a f squad; (Mil) brigade. ~**ier** m brigadier (Brit), brigadier-general (Amer)

brill|ante adj bright; (lustroso) shiny; (persona) brilliant. ● m diamond. ~**ar** vi shine; (centellear) sparkle. ~**o** m shine; (brillantez) brilliance; (centelleo) sparkle. **sacar** ~**o** polish. ~**oso** adj (LAm) shiny

brinc|ar 7 vi jump up and down. ~**o** m jump. **dar un** ~**o, pegar un** ~**o** jump

brind|ar vt offer. ● vi. ~**ar por** toast, drink a toast to. ~**is** m toast

br|ío m energy; (decisión) determination. ~**ioso** adj spirited; (garboso) elegant

brisa f breeze

británico adj British. ● m Briton, British person

brocha f paintbrush; (para afeitarse) shaving-brush

broche m clasp, fastener; (joya) brooch; (Mex, para el pelo) hairslide (Brit), barrete (Amer)

brocheta f skewer; (plato) kebab

brócoli m broccoli

brom|a f joke. ~**a pesada** practical joke. **en** ~**a** in fun. **ni de** ~**a** no way. ~**ear** vi joke. ~**ista** adj

fond of joking. ● m & f joker

bronca f row; (reprensión) telling-off; (LAm, rabia) foul mood. **dar** ~ **a uno** bug s.o.

bronce m bronze; (LAm) brass. ~**ado** adj bronze; (por el sol) tanned. ~**ar** vt tan (piel). ~**arse** vpr get a suntan

bronquitis f bronchitis

brot|ar vi (plantas) sprout; (Med) break out; (líquido) gush forth; (lágrimas) well up. ~**e** m shoot; (Med) outbreak

bruces: de ~ face down(wards). **caer de** ~ fall flat on one's face

bruj|a f witch. ~**ería** f witchcraft. ~**o** m wizard, magician. ● adj (Mex) broke

brújula f compass

brum|a f mist; (fig) confusion. ~**oso** adj misty, foggy

brusco adj (repentino) sudden; (persona) brusque

Bruselas f Brussels

brusquedad f roughness; (de movimiento) abruptness

brut|al adj brutal. ~**alidad** f brutality; (estupidez) stupidity. ~**o** adj ignorant; (tosco) rough; (peso, sueldo) gross

bucal adj oral; (lesión) mouth

buce|ar vi dive; (nadar) swim under water. ~**o** m diving; (natación) underwater swimming

bucle m ringlet

budín m pudding

budis|mo m Buddhism. ~**ta** m & f Buddhist

buen véase BUENO

buenaventura f good luck; (adivinación) fortune

bueno adj (delante de nombre masculino en *singular* buen) good; (*agradable*) nice; (*tiempo*) fine. ●*int* well!; (*de acuerdo*) OK!, very well! ¡buena la has hecho! you've gone and done it now! ¡buenas noches! good night! ¡buenas tardes! (*antes del atardecer*) good afternoon!; (*después del atardecer*) good evening! ¡~s días! good morning! estar de buenas be in a good mood. por las buenas willingly. ¡qué bueno! (*LAm*) great!

Buenos Aires *m* Buenos Aires

buey *m* ox

búfalo *m* buffalo

bufanda *f* scarf

bufar *vi* snort

bufete *m* (*mesa*) writing-desk; (*despacho*) lawyer's office

buf|o *adj* comic. **~ón** *adj* comical. ● *m* buffoon; (*Historia*) jester

buhardilla *f* attic; (*ventana*) dormer window

búho *m* owl

buhonero *m* pedlar

buitre *m* vulture

bujía *f* (*Auto*) spark plug

bulbo *m* bulb

bulevar *m* avenue, boulevard

Bulgaria *f* Bulgaria

búlgaro *adj & m* Bulgarian

bull|a *f* noise. **~icio** *m* hubbub; (*movimiento*) bustle. **~icioso** *adj* bustling; (*ruidoso*) noisy

bullir 22 *vi* boil; (*burbujear*) bubble; (*fig*) bustle

bulto *m* (*volumen*) bulk; (*forma*) shape; (*paquete*) package; (*maleta etc*) piece of luggage; (*protuberancia*) lump

buñuelo *m* fritter

BUP *abrev* (**Bachillerato Unificado**

Polivalente) secondary school education

buque *m* ship, boat

burbuj|a *f* bubble. **~ear** *vi* bubble; (*vino*) sparkle

burdel *m* brothel

burdo *adj* rough, coarse; (*excusa*) clumsy

burgu|és *adj* middle-class, bourgeois. ● *m* middle-class person. **~esía** *f* middle class, bourgeoisie

burla *f* taunt; (*broma*) joke; (*engaño*) trick. **~r** *vt* evade. **~rse** *vpr*. **~rse de** mock, make fun of

burlesco *adj* (*en literatura*) burlesque

burlón *adj* mocking

bur|ocracia *f* bureaucracy; (*Mex*, *funcionariado*) civil service. **~ócrata** *m & f* bureaucrat; (*Mex*, *funcionario*) civil servant. **~ocrático** *adj* bureaucratic; (*Mex*) (*empleado*) government

burro *adj* stupid; (*obstinado*) pig-headed. ●*m* donkey; (*fig*) ass

bursátil *adj* stock-exchange

bus *m* bus

busca *f* search. **a la ~ de** in search of. ●*m* beeper

buscador *m* search engine

buscapleitos *m & f invar* (*LAm*) trouble-maker

buscar 7 *vt* look for. ●*vi* look. buscársela ask for it; ir a ~ a uno fetch s.o.

búsqueda *f* search

busto *m* bust

butaca *f* armchair; (*en el teatro etc*) seat

buzo *m* diver

buzón *m* postbox (*Brit*), mailbox (*Amer*)

Cc

C/ abrev (**Calle**) St, Rd

cabal adj exact; (completo) complete. **no estar en sus ~es** not be in one's right mind

cabalga|dura f mount, horse. **~r** 12 vt ride. ● vi ride, go riding. **~ta** f ride; (desfile) procession

caballa f mackerel

caballerango m (Mex) groom

caballeresco adj gentlemanly. **literatura** f **caballeresca** books of chivalry

caballer|ía f mount, horse. **~iza** f stable. **~izo** m groom

caballero m gentleman; (de orden de caballería) knight; (tratamiento) sir. **~so** adj gentlemanly

caballete m (del tejado) ridge; (para mesa) trestle; (de pintor) easel

caballito m pony. **~ del diablo** dragonfly. **~ de mar** sea-horse. **~s** mpl (carrusel) merry-go-round

caballo m horse; (del ajedrez) knight; (de la baraja española) queen; (de fuerza) horsepower. **a ~** on horseback

cabaña f hut

cabaret /kaba're/ m (pl **~s**) night-club

cabecear vi nod off; (en fútbol) head the ball; (caballo) toss its head

cabecera f (de la cama) headboard; (de la mesa) head; (en un impreso) heading

cabecilla m ringleader

cabello m hair. **~s** mpl hair

caber 28 vi fit (en into). **no cabe duda** there's no doubt

cabestr|illo m sling. **~o** m halter

cabeza f head; (fig, inteligencia) intelligence. **andar de ~** have a lot to do. **~da** f nod. **dar una ~da** nod off. **~zo** m butt; (en fútbol) header

cabida f capacity; (extensión) area; (espacio) room. **dar ~ a** have room for, accommodate

cabina f (de pasajeros) cabin; (de pilotos) cockpit; (electoral) booth; (de camión) cab. **~ telefónica** telephone box (Brit), telephone booth (Amer)

cabizbajo adj crestfallen

cable m cable

cabo m end; (trozo) bit; (Mil) corporal; (mango) handle; (en geografía) cape; (Naut) rope. **al ~ de** after. **de ~ a rabo** from beginning to end. **llevar a ~** carry out

cabr|a f goat. **~iola** f jump, skip. **~itilla** f kid. **~ito** m kid

cábula f (Mex) crook

cacahuate, (Mex) **cacahuete** m peanut

cacalote m (Mex) crow

cacao m (planta y semillas) cacao; (polvo) cocoa; (fig) confusion

cacarear vt boast about. ● vi (gallo) crow; (gallina) cluck

cacería f hunt. **ir de ~** go hunting

cacerola f saucepan, casserole

cacharro m (earthenware) pot; (coche estropeado) wreck; (cosa inútil) piece of junk; (chisme) thing. **~s** mpl pots and pans

cachear vt frisk

cachemir m, **cachemira** f cashmere

cacheo m frisking

cachetada f (LAm) slap

cache|te m slap; (esp LAm, mejilla) cheek. ~**tear** vt (LAm) slap. ~**tón** adj (LAm) chubby-cheeked

cachimba f pipe

cachiporra f club, truncheon

cachivache m piece of junk. ~**s** mpl junk

cacho m bit, piece; (LAm, cuerno) horn

cachondeo m 🗓 joking, joke

cachorro m (perrito) puppy; (de león, tigre) cub

cachucha f (Mex) cup

caciqu|e m cacique, chief; (Pol) local political boss; (hombre poderoso) tyrant. ~**il** adj despotic. ~**ismo** m despotism

caco m thief

cacofonía f cacophony

cacto m, **cactus** m invar cactus

cada adj invar each, every. ~ uno each one, everyone. uno de ~ cinco one in five. ~ vez más more and more

cadáver m corpse

cadena f chain; (TV) channel. ~ de fabricación production line. ~ de montañas mountain range. ~ perpetua life imprisonment

cadera f hip

cadete m cadet

caduc|ar 🗓 vi expire. ~**idad** f. fecha f de ~**idad** sell-by date. ~**o** adj outdated

cae|r 🗓 vi fall. dejar ~**r** drop. este vestido no me ~ bien this dress doesn't suit me. hacer ~**r** knock over. Juan me ~ bien I like Juan. su cumpleaños cayó en martes his birthday fell on a Tuesday. ~**rse** vpr fall (over). se le

cayó he dropped it

café m coffee; (cafetería) café; (Mex, marrón) brown. ● adj color ~ coffee-coloured. ~ con leche white coffee. ~ cortado coffee with a little milk. ~ negro (LAm) expresso. ~ solo black coffee

cafe|ína f caffeine. ~**tal** m coffee plantation. ~**tera** f coffee-pot. ~**tería** f café. ~**tero** adj coffee

caíd|a f fall; (disminución) drop; (pendiente) slope. ~**o** adj fallen

caigo vb véase **CAER**

caimán m cayman, alligator

caj|a f box; (de botellas) case; (ataúd) coffin; (en tienda) cash desk; (en supermercado) check-out; (en banco) cashier's desk. ~**a** de ahorros savings bank. ~**a** de cambios gearbox. ~**a** de caudales, ~**a** fuerte safe. ~**a** negra black box. ~**a** registradora till. ~**ero** m cashier. ~**ero** automático cash dispenser. ~**etilla** f packet. ~**ita** f small box. ~**ón** m (de mueble) drawer; (caja grande) crate; (LAm, ataúd) coffin; (Mex, en estacionamiento) parking space. ser de ~**ón** be obvious. ~**uela** f (Mex) boot (Brit), trunk (Amer)

cal m lime

cala f cove

calaba|cín m, |**cita** f (Mex) courgette (Brit), zucchini (Amer). ~**za** f pumpkin; (fig, fam, idiota) idiot.

dar ～zas a uno give s.o. the brush-off

calabozo m prison; (celda) cell

calado adj soaked. estar ～ hasta los huesos be soaked to the skin. ● m (Naut) draught

calamar m squid

calambre m cramp

calami|dad f calamity, disaster. ～toso adj calamitous

calaña f sort

calar vt soak; (penetrar) pierce; (fig, penetrar) see through; rumble (persona); sample (fruta). ～se vpr get soaked; (zapatos) leak; (Auto) stall

calavera f skull; (Mex, Auto) tail light

calcar 🔢 vt trace; (fig) copy

calcet|a f. hacer ～ knit. ～ín m sock

calcetín m sock

calcinar vt burn

calcio m calcium

calcomanía f transfer

calcula|dor adj calculating. ～dora f calculator. ～r vt calculate; (suponer) reckon, think; (imaginar) imagine

cálculo m calculation; (Med) stone

caldear vt heat, warm. ～se vpr get hot

caldera f boiler

calderilla f small change

caldo m stock; (sopa) clear soup, broth

calefacción f heating. ～ central central heating

caleidoscopio m kaleidoscope

calendario m calendar; (programa) schedule

calenta|dor m heater. ～miento m warming; (en depor-

tes) warm-up. ～ar 🔢 vt heat; (templar) warm. ～arse vpr get hot; (templarse) warm up; (LAm, enojarse) get mad. ～ura f fever, (high) temperature. ～uriento adj feverish

calibr|ar vt calibrate; (fig) weigh up. ～e m calibre; (diámetro) diameter; (fig) importance

calidad f quality; (condición) capacity. en ～ de as

calidez f (LAm) warmth

cálido adj warm

caliente adj hot; (habitación, ropa) warm; (LAm, enojado) angry

califica|ción f qualification; (evaluación) assessment; (nota) mark. ～do adj (esp LAm) qualified; (mano de obra) skilled. ～r 🔢 vt qualify; (evaluar) assess; mark (examen etc). ～r de describe as, label

cáliz m chalice; (en botánica) calyx

caliz|a f limestone. ～o adj lime

calla|do adj quiet. ～r vt silence; keep (secreto); hush up (asunto). ● vi be quiet, keep quiet, shut up 🔢. ～rse vpr be quiet, keep quiet, shut up 🔢. ¡cállate! be quiet!, shut up! 🔢

calle f street, road; (en deportes, autopista) lane. ～ de dirección única one-way street. ～ mayor high street, main street. de ～ everyday. ～ja f narrow street. ～jear vi hang out on the streets. ～jero adj street. ● m street plan. ～jón m alley. ～jón sin salida dead end. ～juela f back street, side street

call|ista m & f chiropodist. ～o m corn, callus. ～os mpl tripe. ～osidad f callus

calm|a f calm. ¡～a! calm down!. en ～a calm. perder la ～a lose one's composure. ~ante *m* tranquilizer; (*para el dolor*) painkiller. ~ar *vt* calm; (*aliviar*) soothe. ● *vi* (*viento*) abate. ~arse *vpr* calm down; (*viento*) abate. ~o *adj* calm. ~oso *adj* calm; (*fam, flemático*) slow

calor *m* heat; (*afecto*) warmth. hace ~ it's hot. tener ~ be hot. ~ía *f* calorie. ~ífero *adj* heat-producing. ~ífico *adj* calorific

calumni|a *f* calumny; (*oral*) slander; (*escrita*) libel. ~ar *vt* slander; (*por escrito*) libel. ~oso *adj* slanderous; (*cosa escrita*) libellous

caluroso *adj* warm; (*clima*) hot

calv|a *f* bald head; (*parte sin pelo*) bald patch. ~icie *f* baldness. ~o *adj* bald

calza *f* wedge

calzada *f* road; (*en autopista*) carriageway

calza|do *adj* wearing shoes. ● *m* footwear, shoe. ~dor *m* shoehorn. ~r 🔟 *vt* put shoes on; (*llevar*) wear. ¿qué número calza Vd? what size shoe do you take? ● *vi* wear shoes. ~rse *vpr* put on

calz|ón *m* shorts. ~ones *mpl* shorts; (*LAm, ropa interior*) panties. ~oncillos *mpl* underpants

cama *f* bed. ~ de matrimonio double bed. ~ individual single bed. guardar ~ stay in bed

camada *f* litter

camafeo *m* cameo

camaleón *m* chameleon

cámara *f* (*aposento*) chamber; (*fotográfica*) camera. ~ fotográfica camera. a ~ lenta in slow motion

camarad|a *m & f* colleague; (*de colegio*) schoolfriend; (*Pol*) comrade. ~ería *f* camaraderie

camarer|a *f* chambermaid; (*de*

restaurante etc) waitress. ~o *m* waiter

camarógrafo *m* cameraman

camarón *m* shrimp

camarote *m* cabin

cambi|able *adj* changeable; (*Com etc*) exchangeable. ~ante *adj* variable; (*persona*) moody. ~ar *vt* change; (*trocar*) exchange. ● *vi* change. ~ar de idea change one's mind. ~arse *vpr* change. ~o *m* change; (*Com*) exchange rate; (*moneda menuda*) (small) change; (*Auto*) gear. ~o climático climate change. en ~o on the other hand

camello *m* camel

camellón *m* (*Mex*) traffic island

camerino *m* dressing room

camilla *f* stretcher

camin|ante *m* traveller. ~ar *vt/i* walk. ~ata *f* long walk. ~o *m* road; (*sendero*) path, track; (*dirección, ruta*) way. ~o de towards, on the way to. abrir ~o make way. a medio ~o, a la mitad del ~o half-way. de ~o on the way

cami|ón *m* truck, lorry; (*Mex, autobús*) bus. ~onero *m* lorry-driver; (*Mex, de autobús*) bus driver. ~oneta *f* van; (*LAm, coche familiar*) estate car

> **Camino de Santiago** A *i*
> pilgrimage route since the
> Middle Ages across north-western
> Spain to Santiago de Compostela
> in Galicia. The city was founded
> at a place where a shepherd is
> said to have discovered the tomb
> of St James the Apostle, and its
> cathedral reputedly houses the
> saint's relics.

camis|a *f* shirt. ~a de fuerza strait-jacket. ~ería *f* shirtmaker's.

~eta f T-shirt; (*ropa interior*) vest. ~ón m nightdress

camorra f 1 row. buscar ~ look for a fight

camote m (*LAm*) sweet potato

campamento m camp. **de ~** adj camping

campan|a f bell. ~**ada** f stroke. ~**ario** m bell tower, belfry. ~**illa** f bell

campaña f campaign

campe|ón adj & m champion. ~**onato** m championship

campes|ino adj country. ● m peasant. ~**tre** adj country

camping /'kampiŋ/ m (pl ~s) camping; (*lugar*) campsite. hacer ~ go camping

camp|iña f countryside. ~**o** m country; (*agricultura, fig*) field; (*de fútbol*) pitch; (*de golf*) course. ~**osanto** m cemetery

camufla|je m camouflage. ~**r** vt camouflage

cana f grey hair, white hair. peinar ~s be getting old

Canadá m. **el ~** Canada

canadiense adj & m & f Canadian

canal m (*incl TV*) channel; (*artificial*) canal; (*del tejado*) gutter. ~ de la Mancha English Channel. ~ de Panamá Panama Canal. ~**ón** m (*horizontal*) gutter; (*vertical*) drainpipe

canalla f rabble. ● m (*fig, fam*) swine. ~**da** f dirty trick

canapé m sofa, couch; (*Culin*) canapé

Canarias fpl. **las (islas) ~** the Canary Islands, the Canaries

canario adj of the Canary Islands. ● m native of the Canary Islands; (*pájaro*) canary

canast|a f (large) basket ~**illa** f small basket; (*para un bebé*) layette. ~**illo** m small basket. ~**o** m (large) basket

cancela|ción f cancellation. ~**r** vt cancel; write off (*deuda*)

cáncer m cancer. **C~** Cancer

cancha f court; (*LAm, de fútbol, rugby*) pitch, ground

canciller m chancellor; (*LAm, ministro*) Minister of Foreign Affairs

canci|ón f song. ~**ón de cuna** lullaby. ~**onero** m song-book

candado m padlock

candel|a f candle. ~**abro** m candelabra. ~**ero** m candlestick

candente adj (*rojo*) red-hot; (*fig*) burning

candidato m candidate

candidez f innocence; (*ingenuidad*) naivety

cándido adj naive

candil m oil lamp. ~**ejas** fpl footlights

candor m innocence; (*ingenuidad*) naivety

canela f cinnamon

cangrejo m crab. ~ de río crayfish

canguro m kangaroo. ●m & f (*persona*) baby-sitter

caníbal adj & m & f cannibal

canica f marble

canijo adj weak; (*Mex, terco*) stubborn; (*Mex, intenso*) incredible

canilla f (*LAm*) shinbone

canino adj canine. ● m canine (tooth)

canje m exchange. ~**ar** vt exchange

cano adj grey. **de pelo ~** greyhaired

canoa f canoe

can|ónigo m canon. **~onizar** 🔟 vt canonize

canoso adj grey-haired

cansa|do adj tired; (que cansa) tiring. **~dor** (LAm) tiring. **~ncio** m tiredness. **~r** vt tire; (aburrir) bore. ● vi be tiring; (aburrir) get boring. **~rse** vpr get tired

canta|nte adj singing. ● m & f singer. **~or** m Flamenco singer. **~r** vt/i sing. **~rlas claras** speak frankly. ● m singing; (poema) poem

cántaro m pitcher. **llover a ~s** pour down

cante m folk song. **~ flamenco**, **~ jondo** Flamenco singing

cantera f quarry

cantidad f quantity; (número) number; (de dinero) sum. **una ~ de** lots of

cantimplora f water-bottle

cantina f canteen; (Rail) buffet; (LAm, bar) bar

cant|inela f song. **~o** m singing; (canción) chant; (borde) edge; (de un cuchillo) blunt edge. **~o rodado** boulder; (guijarro) pebble. **de ~o** on edge

canturre|ar vt/i hum. **~o** m humming

canuto m tube

caña f (planta) reed; (del trigo) stalk; (del bambú) cane; (de pescar) rod; (de la bota) leg; (vaso) glass. **~ de azúcar** sugar-cane. **~da** f ravine; (camino) track; (LAm, arroyo) stream

cáñamo m hemp. **~ indio** cannabis

cañ|ería f pipe; (tubería) piping. **~o** m pipe, tube; (de fuente) jet. **~ón** m (de pluma) quill; (de artillería) cannon; (de arma de fuego)

barrel; (desfiladero) canyon. **~onera** f gunboat

caoba f mahogany

ca|os m chaos. **~ótico** adj chaotic

capa f layer; (de pintura) coat; (Culin) coating; (prenda) cloak; (más corta) cape; (en geología) stratum

capaci|dad f capacity; (fig) ability. **~tar** vt qualify, enable; (instruir) train

caparazón m shell

capataz m foreman

capaz adj capable, able

capcioso adj sly, insidious

capellán m chaplain

caperuza f hood; (de bolígrafo) cap

capilla f chapel

capital adj capital, very important. ● m (dinero) capital. ● f (ciudad) capital. **~ de provincia** county town. **~ino** adj (LAm) of/from the capital. **~ismo** m capitalism. **~ista** adj & m & f capitalist. **~izar** 🔟 vt capitalize

capit|án m captain; (de pesquero) skipper. **~anear** vt lead, command; skipper (pesquero); captain (un equipo)

capitel m (de columna) capital

capitulaci|ón f surrender. **~ones** fpl marriage contract

capítulo m chapter; (de serie) episode

capó m bonnet (Brit), hood (Amer)

capón m (pollo) capon

caporal m (Mex) foreman

capot|a f (de mujer) bonnet; (Auto) folding top; (de cochecito) hood. **~e** m (Mex, de coche) bonnet (Brit), hood (Amer)

capricho m whim. **~so** adj capricious, whimsical

Capricornio *m* Capricorn

cápsula *f* capsule

captar *vt* harness (agua); grasp (sentido); capture (atención); win (confianza); (radio) pick up

captura *f* capture. **~r** *vt* capture

capucha *f* hood

capullo *m* bud; (de insecto) cocoon

caqui *m* khaki

cara *f* face; (de una moneda) heads; (de un objeto) side; (aspecto) look, appearance; (descaro) cheek. **~ a** facing. **~ a ~** face to face. **~ dura** véase **CARADURA**. **~ o cruz** heads or tails. **dar la ~ a** face up to. **hacer ~ a** face. **tener mala ~** look ill. **volver la ~** look the other way

carabela *f* caravel

carabina *f* carbine; (fig, fam, señora) chaperone

caracol *m* snail; (de mar) winkle; (LAm, concha) conch; (de pelo) curl. **¡~es!** Good Heavens!. **~a** *f* conch

carácter *m* (pl caracteres) character; (índole) nature. **con ~ de** as

característic|a *f* characteristic. **~o** *adj* characteristic, typical

caracteriza|do *adj* characterized; (prestigioso) distinguished. **~r** *vt* characterize

caradura *f* cheek, nerve. ● *m & f* cheeky person

caramba *int* good heavens!

carambola *f* (en billar) cannon; (Mex, choque múltiple) pile-up. **de ~** by pure chance

caramelo *m* sweet (Brit), candy (Amer); (azúcar fundido) caramel

caraqueño *adj* from Caracas

carátula *f* (de disco) sleeve (Brit), jacket (Amer); (de vídeo) case; (de

libro) cover; (Mex, del reloj) face

caravana *f* caravan; (de vehículos) convoy; (Auto) long line, traffic jam; (remolque) caravan (Brit), trailer (Amer); (Mex, reverencia) bow

caray *int* ① good heavens!

carb|ón *m* coal; (para dibujar) charcoal. **~ de leña** charcoal. **~oncillo** *m* charcoal. **~onero** *adj* coal. ● *m* coal-merchant. **~onizar** ⑩ *vt* (fig) burn (to a cinder). **~ono** *m* carbon

carbura|dor *m* carburettor. **~nte** *m* fuel

carcajada *f* guffaw. **reírse a ~s** roar with laughter. **soltar una ~** burst out laughing

cárcel *f* prison, jail

carcelero *m* jailer

carcom|er *vt* eat away; (fig) undermine. **~erse** *vpr* be eaten away; (fig) waste away

cardenal *m* cardinal; (contusión) bruise

cardiaco, cardíaco *adj* cardiac, heart

cardinal *adj* cardinal

cardo *m* thistle

carear *vt* bring face to face (personas); compare (cosas)

care|cer ⑪ *vi*. **~cer de** lack. **~cer de sentido** not to make sense. **~ncia** *f* lack. **~nte** *adj* lacking

care|ro *adj* pricey. **~stía** *f* (elevado) high cost

careta *f* mask

carey *m* tortoiseshell

carga *f* load; (fig) burden; (acción) loading; (de barco, avión) cargo; (de tren) freight; (de arma) charge; (Elec, ataque) charge; (obligación) obligation. **llevar la ~ de algo** be responsible for sth. **~da** *f* (Mex,

Pol) supporters. **~do** *adj* loaded; *(fig)* burdened; *(atmósfera)* heavy; *(café)* strong; *(pila)* charged. **~mento** *m* load; *(acción)* loading; *(de un barco)* cargo. **~r** 12 *vt* load; *(fig)* burden; *(Elec, atacar)* charge; fill *(pluma etc)*. ● *vi* load. **~r** *con* carry. **~rse** *vpr (pila)* charge. **~rse de** to load s.o. down with

cargo *m (puesto)* post; *(acusación)* charge. a **~** de in the charge of. hacerse **~** de take responsibility for. tener a su **~** be in charge of

carguero *m (Naut)* cargo ship

caria|do *adj* decayed. **~rse** *vpr* decay

caribeño *adj* Caribbean

caricatura *f* caricature

caricia *f* caress; *(a animal)* stroke

caridad *f* charity. ¡por **~**! for goodness sake!

caries *f invar* tooth decay; *(lesión)* cavity

cariño *m* affection; *(caricia)* caress. **~** mío my darling. con mucho **~** *(en carta)* with love from. tener **~** a be fond of. tomar **~** a become fond of. **~so** *adj* affectionate

carisma *m* charisma

caritativo *adj* charitable

cariz *m* look

carmesí *adj & m* crimson

carmín *m (de labios)* lipstick; *(color)* red

carnal *adj* carnal. primo **~** first cousin

carnaval *m* carnival. **~esco** *adj* carnival

carne *f* meat; *(Anat, de frutos, pescado)* flesh. **~** de cerdo pork. **~** de cordero lamb. **~** de gallina goose pimples. **~** molida *(LAm)*, **~** picada *(Brit)* mince, ground beef *(Amer)*. **~** de ternera veal. **~** de

vaca beef. me pone la **~** de gallina it gives me the creeps. ser de **~** y hueso be only human

carné, carnet *m* card. **~** de conducir driving licence *(Brit)*, driver's license *(Amer)* **~** de identidad identity card. **~** de manejar *(LAm)* driving license *(Brit)*, driver's license *(Amer)*. **~** de socio membership card

carnero *m* ram

carnicer|ía *f* butcher's (shop); *(fig)* massacre. **~o** *adj* carnivorous. ● *m* butcher

carnívoro *adj* carnivorous. ● *m* carnivore

carnoso *adj* fleshy; *(pollo)* meaty

caro *adj* expensive. ● *adv* dear, dearly. costar **~** a uno cost s.o. dear.

carpa *f* carp; *(LAm, tienda)* tent

carpeta *f* folder, file. **~zo** *m.* dar **~zo** a shelve

carpinter|ía *f* carpentry. **~o** *m* carpenter, joiner

carraspe|ar *vi* clear one's throat. **~ra** *f.* tener **~ra** have a frog in one's throat

carrera *f* run; *(prisa)* rush; *(concurso)* race; *(estudios)* degree course; *(profesión)* career; *(de taxi)* journey

carreta *f* cart. **~da** *f* cartload

carrete *m* reel; *(película)* film

carretear *vi (LAm)* taxi

carretera *f* road. **~** de circunvalación bypass, ring road. **~** nacional A road *(Brit)*, highway *(Amer)*

carretilla *f* wheelbarrow

carril *m* lane; *(Rail)* rail

carrito *m (en supermercado, para equipaje)* trolley *(Brit)*, cart *(Amer)*

carro *m* cart; *(LAm, coche)* car;

(Mex, vagón) coach. **~ de combate** tank. **~cería** f (Auto) bodywork

carroña f carrion

carroza f coach, carriage; (en desfile de fiesta) float

carruaje m carriage

carrusel m merry-go-round

cart|a f letter; (lista de platos) menu; (lista de vinos) list; (mapa) map; (naipe) card. **~a blanca** free hand. **~a de crédito** letter of credit. **~a verde** green card. **~earse** vpr correspond

cartel m poster; (letrero) sign. **~era** f hoarding; (en periódico) listings; (LAm en escuela, oficina) notice board (Brit); bulletin board (Amer). **de ~** celebrated

carter|a f wallet; (de colegial) satchel; (para documentos) briefcase; (LAm, de mujer) handbag (Brit), purse (Amer). **~ista** m & f pickpocket

cartero m postman, mailman (Amer)

cartílago m cartilage

cartilla f first reading book. **~ de ahorros** savings book. **leerle la ~ a uno** tell s.o. off

cartón m cardboard

cartucho m cartridge

cartulina f card

casa f house; (hogar) home; (empresa) firm. **~ de huéspedes** boarding-house. **~ de socorro** first aid post. **ir a ~** go home. **salir de ~** go out

casaca f jacket

casado adj married. **los recién ~s** the newly-weds

casa|mentero m matchmaker. **~miento** m marriage; (ceremonia) wedding. **~r** vt marry. **~rse** vpr get married

cascabel m small bell; (de serpiente) rattle

cascada f waterfall

casca|nueces m invar nutcrackers. **~r 7** vt crack (nuez, huevo); (pegar) beat. **~rse** vpr crack

cáscara f (de huevo, nuez) shell; (de naranja) peel; (de plátano) skin

cascarrabias adj invar grumpy

casco m helmet; (de cerámica etc) piece, fragment; (de cabeza) scalp; (de barco) hull; (envase) empty bottle; (de caballo) hoof; (de una ciudad) part, area

cascote m piece of rubble. **~s** mpl rubble

caserío m country house; (poblado) hamlet

casero adj home-made; (doméstico) domestic; (amante del hogar) home-loving; (reunión) family. ● m owner; (vigilante) caretaker

caseta f hut; (puesto) stand. **~ de baño** bathing hut

casete m & f cassette

casi adv almost, nearly; (en frases negativas) hardly. **~ ~** very nearly. **~ nada** hardly any. **¡~ nada!** is that all? **~ nunca** hardly ever

casill|a f hut; (en ajedrez etc) square; (en formulario) box; (compartimento) pigeonhole. **~a electrónica** e-mail address. **~ero** m pigeonholes; (compartimento) pigeonhole

casino m casino; (club social) club

caso m case. **el ~ es que** the fact is that. **en ~ de** in the event of. **en cualquier ~** in any case, whatever happens. **en ese ~** in that case. **en todo ~** in any case. **en último ~** as a last resort. **hacer ~ de** take notice of. **poner por ~** suppose

caspa f dandruff

casquivana f flirt

cassette m & f cassette

casta f (de animal) breed; (de persona) descent; (grupo social) caste

castaña f chestnut

castañetear vi (dientes) chatter

castaño adj chestnut; (ojos) brown. ● m chestnut (tree)

castañuela f castanet

castellano adj Castilian. ● m (persona) Castilian; (lengua) Castilian, Spanish. ~parlante adj Castilian-speaking, Spanish-speaking. ¿habla Vd ~? do you speak Spanish?

> **castellano** In Spain the
> term *castellano*, rather
> than *español*, refers to the Spanish language as opposed to Catalan, Basque etc. The choice of word has political overtones; *castellano* has separatist connotations and *español* is considered neutral. In Latin America *castellano* is another term for Spanish.

castidad f chastity

castigar 12 vt punish; (en deportes) penalize. ~o m punishment; (en deportes) penalty

castillo m castle

castizo adj traditional; (puro) pure. ~o adj chaste

castor m beaver

castrar vt castrate

castrense m military

casual adj chance, accidental. ~idad f chance, coincidence. dar la ~idad happen. de ~idad, por ~idad by chance. ¡qué ~idad! what a coincidence!. ~mente adv by chance; (precisamente) actually

cataclismo m cataclysm

catador m taster

catalán adj & m Catalan

catalizador m catalyst

catalogar 12 vt catalogue; (fig) classify. ~álogo m catalogue

Cataluña f Catalonia

catamarán m catamaran

catapulta f catapult

catar vt taste, try

catarata f waterfall, falls; (Med) cataract

catarro m cold

catástrofe m catastrophe. ~astrófico adj catastrophic

catecismo m catechism

cátedra f (en universidad) professorship, chair; (en colegio) post of head of department

catedral f cathedral

catedrático m professor; (de colegio) teacher, head of department

categoría f category; (clase) class. de ~oría important. de primera ~oría first-class. ~órico adj categorical

catolicismo m catholicism. ~ólico adj (Roman) Catholic ● m (Roman) Catholic

catorce adj & m fourteen

cauce m river bed; (fig, artificial) channel

caucho m rubber

caudal m (de río) volume of flow; (riqueza) wealth. ~oso adj (río) large

caudillo m leader

causa f cause; (motivo) reason; (Jurid) trial. a ~ de, por ~ de because of. ~r vt cause

cautela f caution. ~oso adj cautious, wary

cauterizar 10 vt cauterize

cautivar | cenar

cautiv|ar vt capture; (*fig, fascinar*) captivate. **~erio** m, **~idad** f captivity. **~o** adj & m captive

cauto adj cautious

cavar vt/i dig

caverna f cave, cavern

caviar m caviare

cavidad f cavity

caza f hunting; (*con fusil*) shooting; (*animales*) game. ● m fighter. andar a la) ~ de be in search of. ~ mayor game hunting. dar ~ chase, go after. ir de ~ go hunting/shooting. **~dor** m hunter. **~dora** f jacket. **~r 10** vt hunt; (*con fusil*) shoot; (*fig*) track down; (*obtener*) catch, get

caz|o m saucepan; (*cucharón*) ladle. **~oleta** f (small) saucepan. **~uela** f casserole

cebada f barley

ceb|ar vt fatten (up); bait (anzuelo); prime (arma de fuego). **~o** m bait; (*de arma de fuego*) charge

ceboll|a f onion. **~eta** f spring onion (*Brit*), scallion (*Amer*). **~ino** m chive

cebra f zebra

cece|ar vi lisp. **~o** m lisp

cedazo m sieve

ceder vt give up; (*transferir*) transfer. ● vi give in; (*disminuir*) ease off; (*romperse*) give way, collapse. ceda el paso give way (*Brit*), yield (*Amer*)

cedro m cedar

cédula f bond. ~ de identidad identity card

CE(E) abrev (**Comunidad (Económica) Europea**) E(E)C

ceg|ador adj blinding. **~ar 1 & 12** vt blind; (*tapar*) block up. **~arse** vpr be blinded (de by). **~uera** f blindness

ceja f eyebrow

cejar vi give way

celada f ambush; (*fig*) trap

cela|dor m (de cárcel) prison warder; (de museo etc) security guard. **~r** vt watch

celda f cell

celebra|ción f celebration. **~r** vt celebrate; (*alabar*) praise. **~rse** vpr take place

célebre adj famous

celebridad f fame; (*persona*) celebrity

celest|e adj heavenly; (*vestido*) pale blue. azul **~e** sky-blue. **~ial** adj heavenly

celibato m celibacy

célibe adj celibate

celo m zeal; (*de las hembras*) heat; (*de los machos*) rut; (*cinta adhesiva*) Sellotape (P) (*Brit*), Scotch (P) tape (*Amer*). **~s** mpl jealousy. dar **~s** make jealous. tener **~s** be jealous

celofán m cellophane

celoso adj conscientious; (*que tiene celos*) jealous

celta adj & m (*lengua*) Celtic. ● m & f Celt

célula f cell

celular adj cellular. ● m (*LAm*) mobile, cellphone

celulosa f cellulose

cementerio m cemetery

cemento m cement; (*hormigón*) concrete; (*LAm, cola*) glue

cena f dinner; (*comida ligera*) supper

cenag|al m marsh, bog; (*fig*) tight spot. **~oso** adj boggy

cenar vt have for dinner; (*en cena ligera*) have for supper. ● vi have dinner; (*tomar cena ligera*) have supper

cenicero m ashtray

ceniza f ash

censo m census. ~ **electoral**
electoral roll

censura f censure; (de prensa etc)
censorship. ~**r** vt censure; **censor**
(prensa etc)

centavo adj & m hundredth; (moneda) centavo

centell|a f flash; (chispa) spark.
~**ar**, ~**ear** vi sparkle

centena f hundred. ~**r** m hundred. **a** ~**res** by the hundred. ~**rio**
adj centenarian. ● m centenary;
(persona) centenarian

centeno m rye

centésim|a f hundredth. ~**o** adj
hundredth

cent|ígrado adj centigrade, Celsius. ~**igramo** m centigram.
~**ilitro** m centilitre.
~**imetro** m centimetre

céntimo adj hundredth. ● m cent

centinela f sentry

centolla f, **centollo** m spider crab

central adj central. ● f head office. ~ **de correos** general post
office. ~ **eléctrica** power station.
~ **nuclear** nuclear power station.
~ **telefónica** telephone exchange.
~**ita** f switchboard

centraliza|ción f centralization.
~**r** vt centralize

centrar vt centre

céntrico adj central

centrífugo adj centrifugal

centro m centre. ~ **comercial**
shopping centre (Brit), shopping
mall (Amer). ~ **de llamadas** call
centre

Centroamérica f Central America

centroamericano adj & m Central American

ceñi|do adj tight. ~**r** vt
take (corona); (vestido) cling to.
~**rse** vpr limit o.s. (a to)

ceñ|o m frown. **fruncir el** ~**o**
frown. ~**udo** adj frowning

cepill|ar vt brush; (en carpintería)
plane. ~**o** m brush; (en carpintería)
plane. ~**o de dientes** toothbrush

cera f wax

cerámic|a f ceramics; (materia)
pottery; (objeto) piece of pottery.
~**o** adj ceramic

cerca f fence; (de piedra) wall. ● adv
near, close. ~ **de** prep close to,
close up, closely

cercan|ía f nearness, proximity.
~**ías** fpl vicinity. **tren m de** ~**ías**
local train. ~**o** adj near, close.

cercar vt fence in, enclose;
(gente) surround; (asediar) besiege

cerciorar vt convince. ~**se** vpr
make sure

cerco m (asedio) siege; (círculo)
ring; (LAm, valla) fence; (LAm, seto)
hedge

cerdo m pig; (carne) pork

cereal m cereal

cerebr|al adj cerebral. ~**o** m
brain; (persona) brains

ceremoni|a f ceremony. ~**al** adj
ceremonial. ~**oso** adj ceremonious

cerez|a f cherry. ~**o** m cherry tree

cerill|a f match. ~**o** m (Mex)
match

cern|er vt sieve. ~**erse** vpr
hover. ~**idor** m sieve

cero m nought, zero; (fútbol) nil
(Brit), zero (Amer); (tenis) love; (persona) nonentity

cerquillo m (LAm, flequillo) fringe
(Brit), bangs (Amer)

cerra|do adj shut, closed; (espa-

cio) shut in, enclosed; (*cielo*) overcast; (*curva*) sharp. ~**dura** *f* lock; (*acción de cerrar*) shutting, closing. ~**jero** *m* locksmith. ~**r 1** *vt* shut, close; (*con llave*) lock; (*cercar*) enclose; turn off (*grifo*); block up (*agujero* etc). ● *vi* shut, close. ~**rse** *vpr* shut, close; (*herida*) heal. ~**r con llave** lock

cerro *m* hill

cerrojo *m* bolt. **echar el** ~ bolt

certamen *m* competition, contest

certero *adj* accurate

certeza, **certidumbre** *f* certainty

certifica|do *adj* (*carta* etc) registered. ● *m* certificate. ~**r 7** *vt* certify

certitud *f* certainty

cervatillo, **cervato** *m* fawn

cerve|cería *f* beerhouse, bar; (*fábrica*) brewery. ~**za** *f* beer. ~**za de barril** draught beer. ~**za rubia** lager

cesa|ción *f* cessation, suspension. ~**nte** *adj* redundant. ~**r** *vt* stop. ● *vi* stop, cease; (*dejar un empleo*) resign. **sin** ~**r** incessantly

cesárea *f* caesarian (section)

cese *m* cessation; (*de un empleo*) dismissal. ~ **del fuego** (*LAm*) ceasefire

césped *m* grass, lawn

cest|a *f* basket. ~**o** *m* basket. ~**o de los papeles** waste-paper basket

chabacano *adj* common; (*chiste* etc) vulgar. ● *m* (*Mex*, *albaricoque*) apricot

chabola *f* shack. ~**s** *fpl* shanty town

cháchara *f* 🔢 chatter; (*Mex*, *objetos sin valor*) junk

chacharear *vt* (*Mex*) sell. ● *vi* 🔢 chatter

chacra *f* (*LAm*) farm

chal *m* shawl

chalado *adj* 🔢 crazy

chalé *m* house (with a garden), villa

chaleco *m* waistcoat, vest (*Amer*). ~ **salvavidas** life-jacket

chalet *m* (*pl* ~**s**) house (with a garden), villa

chalote *m* shallot

chamac|a *f* (*esp Mex*) girl. ~**o** *m* (*esp Mex*) boy

chamarra *f* sheepskin jacket; (*Mex*, *chaqueta corta*) jacket

chamb|a *f* (*Mex*, *trabajo*) work. **por** ~**a** by fluke. ~**ear** *vi* (*Mex*, *fam*) work

champán *m*, **champaña** *m & f* champagne

champiñón *m* mushroom

champú *m* (*pl* ~**es** o ~**s**) shampoo

chamuscar 7 *vt* scorch

chance *m* (*esp LAm*) chance

chancho *m* (*LAm*) pig

chanchullo *m* 🔢 swindle, fiddle 🔢

chanclo *m* clog; (*de caucho*) rubber overshoe

chándal *m* (*pl* ~**s**) tracksuit

chantaje *m* blackmail. ~**ar** *vt* blackmail

chanza *f* joke

chapa *f* plate, sheet; (*de madera*) plywood; (*de botella*) metal top; (*carrocería*) bodywork; (*LAm cerradura*) lock. ~**do** *adj* plated. ~**do a la antigua** old-fashioned. ~**do en oro** gold-plated

chaparro *adj* (*LAm*) short, squat

chaparrón *m* downpour

chapopote *m* (*Mex*) tar

chapotear *vi* splash

chapucero adj (persona) slapdash; (trabajo) shoddy

chapulín m (Mex) locust; (saltamontes) grasshopper

chapurrar, **chapurrear** vt have a smattering of, speak a little

chapuza f botched job; (trabajo ocasional) odd job

chaquet|a f jacket. **cambiar de** ~**a** change sides. ~**ón** m three-quarter length coat

charc|a f pond, pool. ~**o** m puddle, pool

charcutería f delicatessen

charla f chat; (conferencia) talk. ~**dor** adj talkative. ~**r** vi 🔟 chat. ~**tán** adj talkative. ● m chatterbox; (vendedor) cunning hawker; (curandero) charlatan

charol m varnish; (cuero) patent leather. ~**a** f (Mex) tray

charr|a f (Mex) horsewoman, cowgirl. ~**o** m (Mex) horseman, cowboy

chascar 🔽 vt crack (látigo); click (lengua); snap (dedos). ● vi (madera) creak. ~ **con la lengua** click one's tongue

chasco m disappointment

chasis m (Auto) chassis

chasqu|ear vt crack (látigo); click (lengua); snap (dedos). ● vi (madera) creak. ~ **con la lengua** click one's tongue. ~**ido** m crack; (de la lengua) click; (de los dedos) snap

chatarra f scrap iron; (fig) scrap

chato adj (nariz) snub; (objetos) flat. ● m wine glass

chav|a f (Mex) girl, lass. ~**al** m 🔟 boy, lad. ~**o** m (Mex) boy, lad.

checa|da f (Mex) check; (Mex, Med) checkup. ~**r** 🔽 vt (Mex) check; (vigilar) check up on. ~**r tarjeta** clock in

checo adj & m Czech. ~**slovaco** adj & m (History) Czechoslovak

chelín m shilling

chelo m cello

cheque m cheque. ~ **de viaje** traveller's cheque. ~**ar** vt check; (Lam) check in (equipaje). ~**o** m check; (Med) checkup. ~**ra** f cheque-book

chévere adj (LAm) great

chica f girl; (criada) maid, servant

chicano adj & m Chicano, Mexican-American

> **Chicano** Chicanos are 🛈
> Mexican Americans, descendants of Mexican immigrants living in US. For long looked down by Americans of European descent, Chicanos have found a new pride in their origins and culture. There are numerous Chicano radio stations and many universities and colleges now offer courses in Chicano studies.

---

chícharo m (Mex) pea

chicharra f cicada; (timbre) buzzer

chichón m bump

chicle m chewing-gum

chico adj 🔟 small; (esp LAm, de edad) young. ● m boy. ~**s** mpl children

chicoria f chicory

chifla|do adj 🔟 crazy, daft. ~**r** vt whistle at, boo. ● vi (LAm) whistle; (🔟, gustar mucho) **me chifla el chocolate** I'm mad about chocolate. ~**rse** vpr be mad (por about)

chilango adj (Mex) from Mexico City

chile m chilli

Chile m Chile

chileno adj & m Chilean

chill|ar vi scream, shriek; (ratón) squeak; (cerdo) squeal. ~**ido** m scream, screech. ~**ón** adj noisy; (colores) loud; (sonido) shrill

chimenea f chimney; (hogar) fireplace

chimpancé m chimpanzee

china f Chinese (woman)

China f China

chinche m drawing-pin (Brit), thumbtack (Amer); (insecto) bedbug; (fig) nuisance. ~**eta** f drawing-pin (Brit), thumbtack (Amer)

chinela f slipper

chino adj Chinese; (Mex rizado) curly. ● m Chinese (man); (Mex, de pelo rizado) curly-haired person

chipriota adj & m & f Cypriot

chiquero m pen; (LAm, pocilga) pigsty (Brit), pigpen (Amer)

chiquillo adj childish. ● m child, kid 🔢

chirimoya f custard apple

chiripa f fluke

chirri|ar 🔢 vi creak; (frenos) screech; (pájaro) chirp. ~**do** m creaking; (de frenos) screech; (de pájaros) chirping

chis int sh!, hush!; (fam, para llamar a uno) hey!, psst!

chism|e m gadget, thingumajig 🔢; (chismorreo) piece of gossip. ~**es** mpl things, bits and pieces. ~**orreo** m gossip. ~**oso** adj gossipy.● m gossip

chisp|a f spark; (pizca) drop; (gracia) wit; (fig) sparkle. estar que echa ~**a(s)** be furious. ~**eante** adj sparkling. ~**ear** vi spark; (lloviznar) drizzle; (fig) sparkle. ~**orrotear** vt throw out sparks; (fuego) crackle.

(aceite) spit

chistar vi. ni chistó he didn't say a word. sin ~ without saying a word

chiste m joke, funny story. tener ~ be funny

chistera f top hat

chistoso adj funny

chiva|rse vpr tip-off; (niño) tell. ~**tazo** m tip-off. ~**to** m informer; (niño) telltale

chivo m kid; (LAm, macho cabrío) billy goat

choca|nte adj shocking; (Mex desagradable) unpleasant. ~**r** 🔢 vt clink (vasos); (LAm) crash (vehículo). ¡chócala! give me five! ● vi collide, hit. ~**r con**, ~**r contra** crash into

choch|ear vi be gaga. ~**o** adj gaga; (fig) soft

choclo m (LAm) corn on the cob

chocolate m chocolate. tableta f de ~ bar of chocolate

chófer, (LAm) **chofer** m chauffeur; (conductor) driver

cholo adj & m (LAm) half-breed

chopo m poplar

choque m collision; (fig) clash; (eléctrico) shock; (Auto, Rail etc) crash, accident; (sacudida) jolt

chorizo m chorizo

chorro m jet, stream; (caudal pequeño) trickle; (fig) stream. a ~ (avión) jet. a ~**s** (fig) in abundance

chovinista adj chauvinistic. ● m & f chauvinist

choza f hut

chubas|co m shower. ~**quero** m raincoat, anorak

chuchería f trinket

chueco adj (LAm) crooked

c

chufa f tiger nut

chuleta f chop

chulo adj cocky; (bonito) lovely (Brit), neat (Amer); (Mex, atractivo) cute. ● m tough guy; (proxeneta) pimp

chup|ada f suck; (al helado) lick; (al cigarro) puff. ~ado adj skinny; (fam, fácil) very easy. ~ar vt suck; puff at (cigarro etc); (absorber) absorb. ~ete m dummy (Brit), pacifier (Amer). ~ón m sucker; (LAm) dummy (Brit), pacifier (Amer); (Mex, del biberón) teat

churrasco m barbecued steak

churro m fritter; 🔲 mess

chut|ar vi shoot. ~e m shot

cianuro m cyanide

cibernética f cybernetics

cicatriz f scar. ~ar 🔟 vt/i heal. ~arse vpr heal

cíclico adj cyclic(al)

ciclis|mo m cycling. ~ta adj cycle. ● m & f cyclist

ciclo m cycle; (de películas, conciertos) season; (de conferencias) series

ciclomotor m moped

ciclón m cyclone

ciego adj blind. ● m blind man, blind person. a ciegas in the dark

cielo m sky; (Relig) heaven; (persona) darling. ¡~s! good heavens!, goodness me!

ciempiés m invar centipede

cien adj a hundred. ~ por ~ one hundred per cent

ciénaga f bog, swamp

ciencia f science; (fig) knowledge. ~s fpl (Univ etc) science. ~s empresariales business studies. a ~ cierta for certain

cieno m mud

científico adj scientific. ● m scientist

ciento adj & m a hundred, one hundred. ~s de hundreds of. por ~ per cent

cierre m fastener; (acción de cerrar) shutting, closing; (LAm, cremallera) zip, zipper (Amer)

cierto adj certain; (verdad) true. estar en lo ~ be right. lo ~ es que the fact is that. no es ~ that's not true. ¿no es ~? isn't that right? por ~ by the way. si bien es ~ que although

ciervo m deer

cifra f figure, number; (cantidad) sum. en ~ coded, in code. ~do adj coded. ~r vt code; place (esperanzas)

cigala f crayfish

cigarra f cicada

cigarr|illera f cigarette box; (de bolsillo) cigarette case. ~illo m cigarette. ~o m (cigarrillo) cigarette; (puro) cigar

cigüeña f stork

cilantro m coriander

cil|índrico adj cylindrical. ~indro m cylinder

cima f top; (fig) summit

cimbr|ear vt shake. ~earse vpr sway. ~onada f, ~onazo m (LAm) jolt; (de explosión) blast

cimentar 🔳 vt lay the foundations of; (fig, reforzar) strengthen

cimientos mpl foundations

cinc m zinc

cincel m chisel. ~ar vt chisel

cinco adj & m five; (en fechas) fifth

cincuent|a adj & m fifty; (quincuagésimo) fiftieth. ~ón adj in his fifties

cine m cinema; (local) cinema (Brit), movie theater (Amer). ~asta m & f

film maker (*Brit*), **movie maker** (*Amer*). ~**matográfico** *adj* film (*Brit*), movie (*Amer*)

cínico *adj* cynical. • *m* cynic

cinismo *m* cynicism

cinta *f* ribbon; (*película*) film (*Brit*), movie (*Amer*); (*para grabar, en carreras*) tape. ~ **aislante** insulating tape. ~ **métrica** tape measure. ~ **virgen** blank tape

cintur|a *f* waist. ~**ón** *m* belt. ~**ón de seguridad** safety belt. ~**ón salvavidas** lifebelt

ciprés *m* cypress (tree)

circo *m* circus

circuito *m* circuit; (*viaje*) tour. ~ **cerrado** closed circuit. **corto** ~ short circuit

circula|ción *f* circulation; (*vehículos*) traffic. ~**r** *adj* circular. • *vi* circulate; (*líquidos*) flow; (*conducir*) drive; (*caminar*) walk; (*autobús*) run

círculo *m* circle. ~ **vicioso** vicious circle. **en** ~ in a circle

circunci|dar *vt* circumcise. ~**sión** *f* circumcision

circunferencia *f* circumference

circunflejo *m* circumflex

circunscri|bir (*pp* **circunscrito**) *vt* confine. ~**birse** *vpr* confine o.s. (**a** to). ~**pción** *f* (*distrito*) district. ~**pción electoral** constituency

circunspecto *adj* circumspect

circunstancia *f* circumstance

circunv|alar *vt* bypass. ~**olar** *vt* ❷ circle

cirio *m* candle

ciruela *f* plum. ~ **pasa** prune

ciru|gía *f* surgery. ~**jano** *m* surgeon

cisne *m* swan

cisterna *f* tank, cistern

cita *f* appointment; (*entre chico y chica*) date; (*referencia*) quotation. ~ **a ciegas** blind date. ~ **flash** speed dating. ~**ción** *f* quotation; (*Jurid*) summons. ~**do** *adj* aforementioned. ~**r** *vt* make an appointment with; (*mencionar*) quote; (*Jurid*) summons. ~**rse** *vpr* arrange to meet

cítara *f* zither

ciudad *f* town; (*grande*) city. ~ **balneario** (*LAm*) coastal resort. ~ **perdida** (*Mex*) shanty town. ~ **universitaria** university campus. ~**anía** *f* citizenship; (*habitantes*) citizens. ~**ano** *adj* civic. • *m* citizen, inhabitant

cívico *adj* civic

civil *adj* civil. • *m & f* civil guard; (*persona no militar*) civilian

civiliza|ción *f* civilization. ~**r** ❿ *vt* civilize. ~**rse** *vpr* become civilized

civismo *m* community spirit

clam|ar *vi* cry out, clamour. ~**or** *m* clamour; (*protesta*) outcry. ~**oroso** *adj* noisy; (*éxito*) resounding

clandestino *adj* clandestine, secret; (*periódico*) underground

clara *f* (*de huevo*) egg white

claraboya *f* skylight

clarear *vi* dawn; (*aclarar*) brighten up

clarete *m* rosé

claridad *f* clarity; (*luz*) light

clarifica|ción *f* clarification. ~**r** ❼ *vt* clarify

clar|ín *m* bugle. ~**inete** *m* clarinet. ~**inetista** *m & f* clarinettist

clarividen|cia *f* clairvoyance; (*fig*) far-sightedness. ~**te** *adj* clairvoyant; (*fig*) far-sighted

claro *adj* clear; (*luminoso*) bright;

(colores) light; (líquido) thin. ● m (en bosque etc) clearing; (espacio) gap. ● adv clearly. ● int of course! ¡~ que sí! yes, of course! ¡~ que no! of course not!

clase f class; (tipo) kind, sort; (aula) classroom. ~ **media** middle class. ~ **obrera** working class. ~ **social** social class. **dar** ~ teach

clásico adj classical; (típico) classic. ● m classic

clasifica|ción f classification; (deportes) league. ~**r 7** vt classify

claustro m cloister; (Univ) staff

claustrof|obia f claustrophobia. ~**óbico** adj claustrophobic

cláusula f clause

clausura f closure

clava|do adj fixed; (con clavo) nailed. **es** ~**do a su padre** he's the spitting image of his father. ● m (LAm) dive. ~**r** vt knock in (clavo); stick in (cuchillo); (fijar) fix; (juntar) nail together

clave f key; (Mus) clef; (instrumento) harpsichord. ~**cín** m harpsichord

clavel m carnation

clavícula f collarbone, clavicle

clav|ija f peg; (Elec) plug. ~**o** m nail; (Culin) clove

claxon /ˈklakson/ m (pl ~**s**) horn

clemencia f clemency, mercy

clementina f tangerine

cleptómano m kleptomaniac

clerical adj clerical

clérigo m priest

clero m clergy

clic m: **hacer** ~ **en** to click on

cliché m cliché; (Foto) negative

cliente m customer; (de médico) patient; (de abogado) client. ~**la** f

clientele, customers; (de médico) patients

clim|a m climate; (ambiente) atmosphere. ~**ático** adj climatic. ~**atizado** adj air-conditioned

clínic|a f clinic. ~**o** adj clinical

cloaca f drain, sewer

clon m clone

cloro m chlorine

club m (pl ~**s** o ~**es**) club

coacci|ón f coercion. ~**onar** vt coerce

coagular vt coagulate; clot (sangre); curdle (leche). ~**se** vpr coagulate; (sangre) clot; (leche) curdle

coalición f coalition

coarta|da f alibi. ~**r** vt hinder; restrict (libertad etc)

cobarde adj cowardly. ● m coward. ~**ía** f cowardice

cobert|izo m shed. ~**ura** f covering; (en radio, TV) coverage

cobij|a f (Mex, manta) blanket. ~**as** fpl (LAm, ropa de cama) bedclothes. ~**ar** vt shelter. ~**arse** vpr (take) shelter. ~**o** m shelter

cobra f cobra

cobra|dor m collector; (de autobús) conductor. ~**r** vt collect; (ganar) earn; charge (precio); cash (cheque); (recuperar) recover. ● vi be paid

cobr|e m copper. ~**izo** adj coppery

cobro m collection; (de cheque) cashing; (pago) payment. **presentar al** ~ cash

coca|ína f cocaine. ~**lero** adj (of) coca farming. ●n coca farmer

cocción f cooking; (Tec) firing

coc|er 2 & 9 vt/i cook; (hervir) boil; (Tec) fire. ~**ido** m stew

coche m car, automobile (Amer); (de tren) coach, carriage; (de bebé) pram (Brit), baby carriage (Amer). ~-cama sleeper. ~ fúnebre hearse. ~ restaurante dining-car. ~s de choque dodgems. ~ra f garage; (de autobuses) depot

cochin|ada f dirty thing. ~o adj dirty, filthy. • m pig

cociente m quotient. ~ intelectual intelligence quotient, IQ

cocin|a f kitchen; (arte) cookery, cuisine; (aparato) cooker. ~a de gas gas cooker. ~a eléctrica electric cooker. ~ar vt/i cook. ~ero m cook

coco m coconut; (árbol) coconut palm; (cabeza) head; (que mete miedo) bogeyman. **comerse el ~** think hard

cocoa f (LAm) cocoa

cocodrilo m crocodile

cocotero m coconut palm

cóctel m (pl ~s o ~es) cocktail

cod|azo m nudge (with one's elbow). ~ear vt/i elbow, nudge. ~earse vpr rub shoulders (con with)

codici|a f greed. ~ado adj coveted, sought after. ~ar vt covet. ~oso adj greedy

código m code. ~ de la circulación Highway Code

codo m elbow; (dobladura) bend. ~ a ~ side by side. hablar (hasta) por los ~s talk too much

codorniz m quail

coeficiente m coefficient. ~ intelectual intelligence quotient, IQ

coerción f constraint

coetáneo adj & m contemporary

coexist|encia f coexistence. ~ir vi coexist

cofradía f brotherhood

cofre m chest; (Mex, capó) bonnet (Brit), hood (Amer)

coger 🔟 vt (esp Esp) take; catch (tren, autobús, pelota, catarro); (agarrar) take hold of; (del suelo) pick up; pick (frutos etc); (LAm, vulgar) to screw. ~se vpr trap, catch; (agarrarse) hold on

cogollo m (de lechuga etc) heart; (brote) bud

cogote m nape; (LAm, cuello) neck

cohech|ar vt bribe. ~o m bribery

cohe|rente adj coherent. ~sión f cohesion

cohete m rocket

cohibi|do adj shy; (inhibido) awkward; (incómodo) awkward. ~r vt inhibit; (incomodar) make s.o. feel embarrassed. ~rse vpr feel inhibited

coima f (LAm) bribe

coincid|encia f coincidence. **dar la ~encia** happen. ~ir vt coincide

coje|ar vi limp; (mueble) wobble. ~ra f lameness

cojín m cushion. ~inete m small cushion

cojo adj lame; (mueble) wobbly. • m lame person

col f cabbage. ~es de Bruselas Brussel sprouts

cola f tail; (fila) queue; (para pegar) glue. a la ~ at the end. **hacer ~** queue (up) (Brit), line up (Amer)

colabora|ción f collaboration. ~dor m collaborator. ~r vi collaborate

colada f washing. **hacer la ~** do the washing

colador m strainer

colapso m collapse; (fig) standstill

colar 2 vt strain; pass (moneda falsa etc). ● vi (líquido) seep through; (fig) be believed. ~**se** vpr slip; (en una cola) jump the queue; (en fiesta) gatecrash

colch|a f bedspread. ~**ón** m mattress. ~**oneta** f air bed; (en gimnasio) mat

colear vi wag its tail; (asunto) not be resolved. vivito y coleando alive and kicking

colecci|ón f collection. ~**onar** vt collect. ~**onista** m & f collector

colecta f collection

colectivo adj collective

colega m & f colleague

colegi|al m schoolboy. ~**ala** f schoolgirl. ~**o** m school; (de ciertas profesiones) college. ~**o mayor** hall of residence

cólera m cholera. ● f anger, fury. montar en ~ fly into a rage

colérico adj furious, irate

colesterol m cholesterol

coleta f pigtail

colga|nte adj hanging. ● m pendant. ~**r** 2 & 12 vt hang; hang (ropa lavada); hang up (abrigo etc); put down (teléfono). ● vi hang; (teléfono) hang up. ~**rse** vpr hang o.s. dejar a uno ~**do** let s.o. down

colibrí m hummingbird

cólico m colic

coliflor f cauliflower

colilla f cigarette end

colina f hill

colinda|nte adj adjoining. ~**r** vt border (con on)

colisión f collision, crash; (fig) clash

collar m necklace; (de perro) collar

colmar vt fill to the brim; try (paciencia); (fig) fulfill. ~ **a uno de atenciones** lavish attention on s.o.

colmena f beehive, hive

colmillo m eye tooth, canine (tooth); (de elefante) tusk; (de carnívoro) fang

colmo m height. ser el ~ be the limit, be the last straw

coloca|ción f positioning; (empleo) job, position. ~**r** 7 vt put, place; (invertir) invest. ~**rse** vpr find work for. ~**rse** vpr find a job

Colombia f Colombia

colombiano adj & m Colombian

colon m colon

colón m (unidad monetaria de Costa Rica y El Salvador) colon

coloni|a f colony; (comunidad) community; (agua de colonia) cologne; (Mex, barrio) residential suburb. ~**ia de verano** holiday camp. ~**iaje** m (LAm) colonial period. ~**ial** adj colonial. ~**ialista** m & f colonialist. ~**ización** f colonization. ~**izar** 10 colonize. ~**o** m colonist, settler; (labrador) tenant farmer

coloqui|al adj colloquial. ~**o** m conversation; (congreso) conference

color m colour. de ~ colour. en ~(es) (fotos, película) colour. ~**ado** adj (rojo) red. ~**ante** m colouring. ~**ear** vt/i colour. ~**ete** m blusher. ~**ido** m colour

colosal adj colossal; (fig, fam, magnífico) terrific

columna f column; (en anatomía) spine. ~ **vertebral** spinal column; (fig) backbone

columpi|ar vt swing. ~**arse** vpr swing. ~**o** m swing

coma f comma; (Mat) point. ● m

(Med) coma

comadre f (madrina) godmother; (amiga) friend. **~ar** vi gossip

comadreja f weasel

comadrona f midwife

comal m (Mex) griddle

comand|ancia f command. **~ante** m & f commander; (Mil, soldado) commando; (de terroristas) cell

comarca f area, region

comba f bend; (juguete) skipping-rope; (de viga) sag. **saltar a la ~** skip. **~rse** vpr bend; (viga) sag

combat|e m combat; (pelea) fight. **~iente** m fighter. **~ir** vt/i fight

combina|ción f combination; (enlace) connection; (prenda) slip. **~r** vt combine; put together (colores)

combustible m fuel

comedia f comedy; (cualquier obra de teatro) play; (LAm, telenovela) soap (opera)

comedi|do adj restrained; (LAm, atento) obliging. **~rse 5** vpr show restraint

comedor m dining-room; (restaurante) restaurant

comensal m fellow diner

comentar vt comment on; discuss (tema); (mencionar) mention. **~io** m commentary; (observación) comment. **~ios** mpl gossip. **~ista** m & f commentator

comenzar 1 & 10 vt/i begin, start

comer vt eat; (a mediodía) have for lunch; (esp LAm, cenar) have for dinner; (corroer) eat away; (en ajedrez) take. ● vi eat; (a mediodía) have lunch; (esp LAm, cenar) have

dinner. **dar de ~** a feed. **~se** vpr eat (up)

comerci|al adj commercial; (ruta) trade; (nombre, trato) business. ● m (LAm) commercial, ad. **~ante** m trader; (de tienda) shopkeeper. **~ar** vi trade (con with, en in); (con otra persona) do business. **~o** m commerce; (actividad) trade; (tienda) shop; (negocios) business. **~o justo** fair trade

comestible adj edible. **~s** mpl food. **tienda de ~s** grocer's (shop) (Brit), grocery (Amer)

cometa m comet. ● f kite

comet|er vt commit; make (falta). **~ido** m task

comezón m itch

comicios mpl elections

cómico adj comic; (gracioso) funny. ● m comic actor; (humorista) comedian

comida f food; (a mediodía) lunch; (esp LAm, cena) dinner; (acto) meal

comidilla f. **ser la ~ del pueblo** be the talk of the town

comienzo m beginning, start

comillas fpl inverted commas

comil|ón adj greedy. **~ona** f feast

comino m cumin. **(no) me importa un ~** I couldn't care less

comisar|ía f police station. **~io** m commissioner; (deportes) steward

comisión f assignment; (organismo) commission, committee; (Com) commission

comisura f corner. **~ de los labios** corner of the mouth

comité m committee

como prep as; (comparación) like. ● adv about. ● conj as. **~ quieras** as you like. **~ si** as if

cómo *adverbio*

····▸ how. ¿~ se llega? how do you get there? ¿~ es de alto? how tall is it? sé ~ pasó I know it happened

! Cuando **cómo** va seguido del verbo **llamar** se traduce por *what*, p. ej. ¿~ **te llamas?** what's your name?

····▸ cómo + ser (*sugiriendo descripción*) ¿~ es su marido? what's her husband like?; (*físicamente*) what does her husband look like? no sé ~ es la comida I don't know what the food's like

····▸ (*por qué*) why. ¿~ no actuaron antes? why didn't they act sooner?

····▸ (*pidiendo que se repita*) sorry?, pardon? ¿~? no te escuché sorry? I didn't hear you

····▸ (*en exclamaciones*) ¡~ llueve! it's really pouring! ¡~! ¿que no lo sabes? what! you mean you don't know? ¡~ no! of course!

cómoda *f* chest of drawers

comodidad *f* comfort. a su ~ at your convenience

cómodo *adj* comfortable; (*conveniente*) convenient

comoquiera *conj.* ~ que sea however it may be

compacto *adj* compact; (*denso*) dense; (*líneas etc*) close

compadecer [11] *vt* feel sorry for. ~se *vpr.* ~se de feel sorry for

compadre *m* godfather; (*amigo*) friend

compañ|ero *m* companion; (*de trabajo*) colleague; (*de clase*) class-

mate; (*pareja*) partner. ~ía *f* company. en ~ía de with

compara|ble *adj* comparable. ~ción *f* comparison. ~r *vt* compare. ~tivo *adj & m* comparative

comparecer [11] *vi* appear

comparsa *f* group. ●*m & f* (*en el teatro*) extra

compartim(i)ento *m* compartment

compartir *vt* share

compás *m* (*instrumento*) (pair of) compasses; (*ritmo*) rhythm; (*división*) bar (*Brit*), measure (*Amer*); (*Naut*) compass. a ~ in time

compasi|ón *f* compassion, pity. tener ~ón de feel sorry for. ~vo *adj* compassionate

compatib|ilidad *f* compatibility. ~le *adj* compatible

compatriota *m & f* compatriot

compendio *m* summary

compensa|ción *f* compensation. ~ción por despido redundancy payment. ~r *vt* compensate

competen|cia *f* competition; (*capacidad*) competence; (*poder*) authority; (*incumbencia*) jurisdiction. ~te *adj* competent

competi|ción *f* competition. ~dor *m* competitor. ~r [5] *vi* compete

compinche *m* accomplice; (*fam, amigo*) friend, mate [1]

complac|er [32] *vt* please. ~erse *vpr* be pleased. ~iente *adj* obliging; (*marido*) complaisant

complej|idad *f* complexity. ~o *adj & m* complex

complement|ario *adj* complementary. ~o *m* complement; (*Gram*) object, complement

completar *vt* complete. ~o *adj* complete; (*lleno*) full; (*exhaustivo*) comprehensive

complexión f build

complica|ción f complication; (esp AmL, implicación) involvement. ~**r** [7] vt implicate; involve (persona). ~**rse** vpr become complicated; (implicarse) get involved

cómplice m & f accomplice

complot m (pl ~s) plot

compon|ente adj component. ● m component; (miembro) member. ~**er** [34] vt make up; (Mus, Literatura etc) write, compose; (esp LAm, reparar) mend; (LAm) set (hueso); (estómago) settle. ~**erse** vpr be made up; (arreglarse) get better. ~**érselas** manage

comporta|miento m behaviour. ~**rse** vpr behave. ~**rse mal** misbehave

composi|ción f composition. ~**tor** m composer

compostura f composure; (LAm, arreglo) repair

compota f stewed fruit

compra f purchase. ~ **a plazos** hire purchase. **hacer la(s)** ~**(s)** do the shopping. **ir de** ~**s** go shopping. ~**dor** m buyer. ~**r** vt buy. ~**venta** f buying and selling; (Jurid) sale and purchase contract. **negocio** m **de** ~**venta** second-hand shop

compren|der vt understand; (incluir) include. ~**sión** f understanding. ~**sivo** adj understanding

compresa f compress; (de mujer) sanitary towel

compr|esión f compression. ~**imido** adj compressed. ● m pill, tablet. ~**imir** vt compress

comproba|nte m proof; (recibo) receipt. ~**r** vt check; (demostrar) prove

comprom|eter vt compromise; (arriesgar) jeopardize. ~**eterse** vpr compromise o.s.; (obligarse) agree to; (novios) get engaged. ~**etido** adj (situación) awkward, delicate; (autor) politically committed. ~**iso** m obligation; (apuro) predicament; (cita) appointment; (acuerdo) agreement. **sin** ~**iso** without obligation

compuesto adj compound; (persona) smart. ● m compound

computa|ción f (esp LAm) computing. **curso** m **de** ~**ción** computer course. ~**dor** m, computadora f computer. ~**r** vt calculate. ~**rizar, computerizar** [10] vt computerize

cómputo m calculation

comulgar [12] vi take Communion

común adj common; (compartido) joint. ● m el ~ de most

comunal adj communal

comunica|ción f communication. ~**do** m communiqué. ~**do de prensa** press release. ~**r** [7] vt communicate; (informar) inform; (LAm, por teléfono) put through. **está** ~**ndo** (teléfono) it's engaged. ~**rse** vpr communicate; (ponerse en contacto) get in touch. ~**tivo** adj communicative

comunidad f community. ~ **de vecinos** residents' association. C~ (Económica) Europea European (Economic) Community. **en** ~ together

---

Comunidad Autónoma [i]
In 1978 Spain was divided into comunidades autónomas or autonomías, which have far greater powers than the old

regiones. The *comunidades autónomas* are: Andalusia, Aragon, Asturias, Balearic Islands, the Basque Country, Canary Islands, Cantabria, Castilla y León, Castilla-La Mancha, Catalonia, Extremadura, Galicia, Madrid, Murcia, Navarre, La Rioja, Valencia and the North African enclaves of Ceuta and Melilla.

comunión f communion; (*Relig*) (Holy) Communion

comunis|mo m communism. **~ta** adj & m & f communist

con prep with; (+ *infinitivo*) by. **~** decir la verdad by telling the truth. **~** que so. **~** tal que as long as

concebir 5 vt/i conceive

conceder vt concede, grant; award (*premio*); (*admitir*) admit

concej|al m councillor. **~ero** m (*LAm*) councillor. **~o** m council

concentra|ción f concentration; (*Pol*) rally. **~r** vt concentrate; assemble (*personas*). **~rse** vpr concentrate

concep|ción f conception. **~to** m concept; (*opinión*) opinion. bajo ningún **~to** in no way

concerniente adj. en lo **~** a with regard to

concertar 1 vt arrange; agree (upon) (*plan*)

concesión f concession

concha f shell; (*carey*) tortoiseshell

conciencia f conscience; (*conocimiento*) awareness. **~** limpia clear conscience. **~** sucia guilty conscience. a **~** de que fully aware that. en **~** honestly. tener **~** de be aware of. tomar **~** de become aware of. **~r** vt make aware. **~rse**

vpr become aware

concientizar 10 vt (*esp LAm*) make aware. **~se** vpr become aware

concienzudo adj conscientious

concierto m concert; (*acuerdo*) agreement; (*Mus, composición*) concerto

concilia|ción f reconciliation. **~r** vt reconcile. **~r el sueño** get to sleep. **~rse** vpr gain

concilio m council

conciso m concise

conclu|ir 17 vt finish; (*deducir*) conclude. **•** vi finish, end. **~sión** f conclusion. **~yente** adj conclusive

concord|ancia f agreement. **~ar** 2 vt reconcile. **•** vi agree. **~e** adj in agreement. **~ia** f harmony

concret|amente adv specifically, to be exact. **•** **~ar** vt make specific. **~arse** vpr become definite; (*limitarse*) confine o.s. **~o** adj concrete; (*determinado*) specific, particular. en **~o** definite; (*concretamente*) to be exact; (*en resumen*) in short. **•** m (*LAm, hormigón*) concrete

concurr|encia f concurrence; (*reunión*) audience. **~ido** adj crowded, busy. **~ir** vi meet; ; (*coincidir*) agree. **~** a (*asistir a*) attend

concurs|ante m & f competitor, contestant. **~ar** vi compete, take part. **~o** m competition; (*ayuda*) help

cond|ado m county. **~e** m earl, count

condena f sentence. **~ción** f condemnation. **~do** m convicted person. **~r** vt condemn; (*Jurid*) convict

condensa|ción f condensation.

~r vt condense

condesa f countess

condescende|ncia f condescension; (tolerancia) indulgence. ~r **1** vi agree; (dignarse) condescend

condici|ón f condition. a ~ón de (que) on condition that. ~onal adj conditional. ~onar vt condition

condiment|ar vt season. ~o m seasoning

condolencia f condolence

condominio m joint ownership; (LAm, edificio) block of flats (Brit), condominium (esp Amer)

condón m condom

condonar vt (perdonar) reprieve; cancel (deuda)

conducir **47** vt drive (vehículo); carry (electricidad, gas, agua). ● vi drive; (fig, llevar) lead. ¿a qué conduce? what's the point? ~se vpr behave

conducta f behaviour

conducto m pipe, tube; (en anatomía) duct. por ~ de through. ~r m driver; (jefe) leader; (Elec) conductor

conduzco vb véase CONDUCIR

conectar vt/i connect

conejo m rabbit

conexión f connection

confabularse vpr plot

confecci|ón f (de trajes) tailoring; (de vestidos) dressmaking. ~ones fpl clothing, clothes. de ~ón ready-to-wear. ~onar vt make

confederación f confederation

conferencia f (al teléfono) long-distance call; (Univ) lecture. ~ en la cima, ~ (en la) cumbre summit conference. ~nte m & f lecturer

conferir **4** vt confer; award (premio)

confes|ar **1** vt/i confess. ~arse vpr confess. ~ión f confession. ~ionario m confessional. ~or m confessor

confeti m confetti

confia|do adj trusting; (seguro de sí mismo) confident. ~nza f trust; (en sí mismo) confidence; (intimidad) familiarity. ~r **20** vt entrust. ● vi. ~r en trust

confiden|cia f confidence, secret. ~cial adj confidential. ~te m confidant. ● f confidante

configur|ación f configuration. ~ar vt to configure

conf|ín m border. ~ines mpl outermost parts. ~inar vt confine; (desterrar) banish

confirma|ción f confirmation. ~r vt confirm

confiscar **7** vt confiscate

confit|ería f sweet-shop (Brit), candy store (Amer). ~ura f jam

conflict|ivo adj difficult; (época) troubled; (polémico) controversial. ~o m conflict

confluencia f confluence

conform|ación f conformation, shape. ~ar vt (acomodar) adjust. ● vi agree. ~arse vpr conform. ~e adj in agreement; (contento) happy, satisfied; (según) according (con to). ~e a in accordance with, according to a. ● conj as. ● int OK!. ~idad f agreement; (tolerancia) resignation. ~ista m & f conformist

conforta|ble adj comfortable. ~nte adj comforting. ~r vt comfort

confronta|ción f confrontation. ~r vt confront

confu|ndir vt (equivocar) mistake,

confuse; (*mezclar*) mix up, confuse; (*turbar*) embarrass. **~ndirse** *vpr* become confused; (*equivocarse*) make a mistake. **~sión** *f* confusion; (*vergüenza*) embarrassment. **~so** *adj* confused; (*borroso*) blurred

congela|do *adj* frozen. **~dor** *m* freezer. **~r** *vt* freeze

congeniar *vi* get on

congesti|ón *f* congestion. **~onado** *adj* congested. **~onarse** *vpr* become congested

congoja *f* distress; (*pena*) grief

congraciarse *vpr* ingratiate o.s.

congratular *vt* congratulate

congrega|ción *f* gathering; (*Relig*) congregation. **~rse** 🄬 *vpr* gather, assemble

congres|ista *m & f* delegate, member of a congress. **~o** *m* congress, conference. C~o Parliament. C~o de los Diputados Chamber of Deputies

cónico *adj* conical

conifer|a *f* conifer. **~o** *adj* coniferous

conjetura *f* conjecture, guess. **~r** *vt* conjecture, guess

conjuga|ción *f* conjugation. **~r** 🄬 *vt* conjugate

conjunción *f* conjunction

conjunto *adj* joint. • *m* collection; (*Mus*) band; (*ropa*) suit, outfit. en ~ altogether

conjurar *vt* exorcise; avert (*peligro*). • *vi* plot, conspire

conllevar *vt* to entail

conmemora|ción *f* commemoration. **~r** *vt* commemorate

conmigo *pron* with me

conmo|ción *f* shock; (*tumulto*) upheaval. **~ción** cerebral concussion. **~cionar** *vt* shock. **~ver** 🄬 *vt*

shake; (*emocionar*) move

conmuta|dor *m* switch; (*LAm, de teléfonos*) switchboard. **~r** *vt* exchange

connota|ción *f* connotation. **~do** *adj* (*LAm, destacado*) distinguished. **~r** *vt* connote

cono *m* cone

conoc|edor *adj & m* expert. **~er** 🄫 *vt* know; (*por primera vez*) meet; (*reconocer*) recognize, know. se conoce que apparently. dar a **~er** make known. **~erse** *vpr* know o.s.; (*dos personas*) know each other; (*notarse*) be obvious. **~ido** *adj* well-known. • *m* acquaintance. **~imiento** *m* knowledge; (*sentido*) consciousness. sin **~imiento** unconscious. tener **~imiento** de know about

conozco *vb* véase **CONOCER**

conque *conj* so

conquista *f* conquest. **~dor** *adj* conquering. • *m* conqueror; (*de América*) conquistador. **~r** *vt* conquer, win

consabido *adj* usual, habitual

> **Conquistadores** The collective term for the succession of explorers, soldiers and adventurers who, from the sixteenth century onward led the settlement and exploitation of Spain's Latin American colonies. *i*

---

consagra|ción *f* consecration. **~r** *vt* consecrate; (*fig*) devote. **~rse** *vpr* devote o.s.

consanguíneo *m* blood relation

consciente *adj* conscious

consecuen|cia *f* consequence; (*coherencia*) consistency. a **~cia** de as a result of. **~te** *adj* consistent

consecutivo adj consecutive

conseguir 5 & 13 vt get, obtain; (*lograr*) manage; achieve (*objetivo*)

consej|ero m adviser; (*miembro de consejo*) member. **~o** m piece of advice; (*Pol*) council. **~o de ministros** cabinet

consenso m assent, consent

consenti|do adj (*niño*) spoilt. **~miento** m consent. **~r** 4 vt allow; spoil (*niño*). ● vi consent

conserje m porter, caretaker. **~ría** f porter's office

conserva f (*mermelada*) preserve; (*en lata*) tinned food. **en ~** tinned (*Brit*), canned. **~ción** f conservation; (*de alimentos*) preservation

conservador adj & m (*Pol*) conservative

conservar vt keep; preserve (*alimentos*). **~se** vpr keep; (*costumbre*) survive

conservatorio m conservatory

considera|ble adj considerable. **~ción** f consideration; (*respeto*) respect. **de ~ción** serious. **de mi ~ción** (*LAm, en cartas*) Dear Sir. **~do** adj considerate; (*respetado*) respected. **~r** vt consider; (*respetar*) respect

consigna f order; (*para equipaje*) left luggage office (*Brit*), baggage room (*Amer*); (*eslogan*) slogan

consigo pron (*él*) with him; (*ella*) with her; (*Ud, Uds*) with you; (*uno mismo*) with o.s.

consiguiente adj consequent. **por ~** consequently

consist|encia f consistency. **~ente** adj consisting (*en of*); (*firme*) solid; (*LAm, congruente*) consistent. **~ir** vi. **~ en** consist of; (*radicar en*) be due to

consola|ción f consolation. **~r**

2 vt console, comfort. **~rse** vpr console o.s.

consolidar vt consolidate. **~se** vpr consolidate

consomé m clear soup, consommé

consonante adj consonant. ● f consonant

consorcio m consortium

conspira|ción f conspiracy. **~dor** m conspirator. **~r** vi conspire

consta|ncia f constancy; (*prueba*) proof; (*LAm, documento*) written evidence. **~nte** adj constant. **~r** vi be clear; (*figurar*) appear, figure; (*componerse*) consist. **hacer ~r** state; (*por escrito*) put on record. **me ~ que** I'm sure that. **que conste que** believe me

constatar vt check; (*confirmar*) confirm

constipa|do m cold. ● adj. **estar ~do** have a cold; (*LAm, estreñido*) be constipated. **~rse** vpr catch a cold

constitu|ción f constitution; (*establecimiento*) setting up. **~cional** adj constitutional. **~ir** 17 vt constitute; (*formar*) form; (*crear*) set up, establish. **~irse** vpr set o.s. up (*en* as). **~tivo** adj, **~yente** adj constituent

constru|cción f construction. **~ctor** m builder. **~ir** 17 vt construct; build (*edificio*)

consuelo m consolation

consuetudinario adj customary

cónsul m & f consul

consulado m consulate

consult|a f consultation. **horas** fpl **de ~a** surgery hours. **obra** f **de ~a** reference book. **~ar** vt consult. **~orio** m surgery

consumar vt complete; commit (crimen); carry out (robo); consummate (matrimonio)

consum|ición f consumption; (bebida) drink; (comida) food. ~ición mínima minimum charge. ~ido adj (persona) skinny, wasted. ~idor m consumer. ~ir vt consume. ~irse vpr (persona) waste away; (vela, cigarillo) burn down; (líquido) dry up. ~ismo m consumerism. ~o m consumption; (LAm, en restaurante etc) (bebida) drink; (comida) food. ~o mínimo minimum charge

contab|ilidad f book-keeping; (profesión) accountancy. ~le m & f accountant

contacto m contact. ponerse en ~ con get in touch with

conta|do adj. al ~ cash. ~s adj pl few. tiene los días ~s his days are numbered. ~dor m meter; (LAm, persona) accountant

contagi|ar vt infect (persona); pass on (enfermedad); (fig) contaminate. ~o m infection; (directo) contagion. ~oso adj infectious; (por contacto directo) contagious

contamina|ción f contamination, pollution. ~r vt contaminate, pollute

contante adj. dinero m ~ cash

contar [2] vt count; tell (relato). se cuenta que it's said that. ● vi count. ~ con rely on, count on. ~se vpr be included (entre among)

contempla|ción f contemplation. sin ~ciones unceremoniously. ~r vt look at; (fig) contemplate

contemporáneo adj & m contemporary

conten|er [40] vt contain; hold (respiración). ~erse vpr contain o.s. ~ido adj contained. ● m contents

content|ar vt please. ~arse vpr. ~arse con be satisfied with, be pleased with. ~o adj (alegre) happy; (satisfecho) pleased

contesta|ción f answer. ~dor m. ~ automático answering machine. ~r vt/i answer; (replicar) answer back

contexto m context

contienda f conflict; (lucha) contest

contigo pron with you

contiguo adj adjacent

continen|tal adj continental. ~te m continent

continu|ación f continuation. a ~ación immediately after. ~ar [21] vt continue, resume. ● vi continue. ~idad f continuity. ~o adj continuous; (frecuente) continual. corriente f ~a direct current

contorno m outline; (de árbol) girth; (de caderas) measurement. ~s mpl surrounding area

contorsión f contortion

contra prep against. en ~ against. ● m cons. ● f snag. llevar la ~ contradict

contraata|car [7] vt/i counterattack. ~que m counter-attack

contrabaj|ista m & f double-bass player. ~o m double-bass; (persona) double-bass player

contraband|ista m & f smuggler. ~o m contraband

contracción f contraction

contrad|ecir [46] vt contradict. ~icción f contradiction. ~ictorio adj contradictory

contraer [41] vt contract. ~ matrimonio marry. **~se** vpr contract

contralto m counter tenor. ● f contralto

contra|mano. a **~** in the wrong direction. **~partida** f compensation. **~pelo**. a **~** the wrong way

contrapes|ar vt counterweight. **~o** m counterweight

contraproducente adj counter-productive

contrari|a f. llevar la **~a** contradict. **~ado** adj upset; (enojado) annoyed. **~ar** 20 vt upset; (enojar) annoy. **~edad** f setback; (disgusto) annoyance. **~o** adj contrary (a to); (dirección) opposite. al **~o** on the contrary. al **~o** de contrary to. de lo **~o** otherwise. por el **~o** on the contrary. ser **~o** a be opposed to, be against

contrarrestar vt counteract

contrasentido m contradiction

contraseña f (palabra) password; (en cine) stub

contrast|ar vt check, verify. ● vi contrast. **~e** m contrast; (en oro, plata) hallmark

contratar vt contract (servicio); hire, take on (empleados); sign up (jugador)

contratiempo m setback; (accidente) mishap

contrat|ista m & f contractor. **~o** m contract

contraven|ción f contravention. **~ir** 53 vt contravene

contraventana f shutter

contribu|ción f contribution; (tributo) tax. **~ir** 17 vt/i contribute. **~yente** m & f contributor; (que paga impuestos) taxpayer

contrincante m rival, opponent

control m control; (vigilancia) check; (lugar) checkpoint. **~ar** vt control; (vigilar) check. **~arse** vpr control s.o.

controversia f controversy

contundente adj (arma) blunt; (argumento) convincing

contusión f bruise

convalec|encia f convalescence. **~er** 11 vi convalesce. **~iente** adj & m & f convalescent

convalidar vt recognize (título)

convenc|er 9 vt convince. **~imiento** m conviction

convenci|ón f convention. **~onal** adj conventional

conveni|encia f convenience; (aptitud) suitability. **~ente** adj suitable; (aconsejable) advisable; (provechoso) useful. **~o** m agreement. **~r** 53 vt agree. ● vi agree (en on); (ser conveniente) be convenient for, suit; (ser aconsejable) be advisable

convento m (de monjes) monastery; (de monjas) convent

conversa|ción f conversation. **~ciones** fpl talks. **~r** vi converse, talk

conver|sión f conversion. **~so** adj converted. ● m convert. **~tible** adj convertible. ● m (LAm) convertible. **~tir** 4 vt convert. **~tirse** vpr. **~tirse** en turn into; (Relig) convert

convic|ción f conviction. **~to** adj convicted

convida|do m guest. **~r** vt invite

convincente adj convincing

conviv|encia f coexistence; (de parejas) life together. **~ir** vi live together; (coexistir) coexist

convocar 7 vt call (huelga, elecciones); convene (reunión); summon (personas)

convulsión f convulsion

conyugal adj marital, conjugal; (vida) married

cónyuge m spouse. **~s** mpl married couple

coñac m (pl ~s) brandy

coopera|ción f cooperation. **~r** vi cooperate. **~nte** m & f voluntary aid worker. **~tiva** f cooperative. **~tivo** adj cooperative

coordinar vt coordinate

copa f glass; (deportes, fig) cup; (de árbol) top. **~s** fpl (naipes) hearts. tomar una ~ have a drink

copia f copy. ~ en limpio fair copy. sacar una ~ make a copy. **~r** vt copy

copioso adj copious; (lluvia, nevada etc) heavy

copla f verse; (canción) folksong

copo m flake. ~ de nieve snowflake. **~s** de maíz cornflakes

coquet|a f flirt; (mueble) dressing-table. **~ear** vi flirt. **~o** adj flirtatious

coraje m courage; (rabia) anger

coral adj choral. ● m coral; (Mus) chorale

coraza f cuirass; (Naut) armour-plating; (de tortuga) shell

coraz|ón m heart; (persona) darling. sin ~ón heartless. tener buen ~ón be good-hearted. **~onada** f hunch; (impulso) impulse

corbata f tie, necktie (esp Amer). ~ de lazo bow tie

corche|a f quaver. **~te** m fastener, hook and eye; (gancho) hook; (paréntesis) square bracket

corcho m cork. **~lata** f (Mex) (crown) cap

corcova f hump

cordel m cord, string

cordero m lamb

cordial adj cordial, friendly. ● m

tonic. **~idad** f cordiality, warmth

cordillera f mountain range

córdoba m (unidad monetaria de Nicaragua) córdoba

cordón m string; (de zapatos) lace; (cable) cord; (fig) cordon. ~ umbilical umbilical cord

coreografía f choreography

corista f (bailarina) chorus girl

cornet|a f bugle; (Mex, de coche) horn. **~ín** m cornet

coro m (Mus) choir; (en teatro) chorus

corona f crown; (de flores) wreath, garland. **~ción** f coronation. **~r** vt crown

coronel m colonel

coronilla f crown. estar hasta la ~ be fed up

corpora|ción f corporation. **~l** adj (castigo) corporal; (trabajo) physical

corpulento adj stout

corral m farmyard. aves fpl de ~ poultry

correa f strap; (de perro) lead; (cinturón) belt

correc|ción f correction; (cortesía) good manners. **~to** adj correct; (cortés) polite

corrector ortográfico m spell checker

corre|dizo adj running. nudo m **~dizo** slip knot. puerta f **~diza** sliding door. **~dor** m runner; (pasillo) corridor; (agente) agent, broker. **~dor de coches** racing driver

corregir 🖪 & 🔟 vt correct

correlación f correlation

correo m post, mail; (persona) courier; (LAm, oficina) post office. **~s** mpl post office. ~ electrónico e-mail. echar al ~ post

correr vt run; (mover) move; draw (cortinas). ●vi run; (agua, electricidad etc) flow; (tiempo) pass. ~se vpr (apartarse) move along; (colores) run

correspond|encia f correspondence. ~er vi correspond; (ser adecuado) be fitting; (contestar) reply; (pertenecer) belong; (incumbir) fall to. ~erse vpr (amarse) love one another. ~iente adj corresponding

corresponsal m correspondent

corrid|a f run. ~a de toros bullfight. de ~a from memory. ~o adj (continuo) continuous

corriente adj (agua) running; (monedas, publicación, cuenta, año) current; (ordinario) ordinary. ●f current; (de aire) draught; (fig) tendency. ●m current month. al ~ (al día) up-to-date; (enterado) aware

corr|illo m small group. ~o m circle

corroborar vt corroborate

corroer 24 & 37 vt corrode; (en geología) erode; (fig) eat away

corromper vt corrupt, rot (materia). ~se vpr become corrupted; (materia) rot; (alimentos) go bad

corrosi|ón f corrosion. ~vo adj corrosive

corrupción f corruption; (de materia etc) rot

corsé m corset

corta|do adj cut; (carretera) closed; (leche) curdled; (avergonzado) embarrassed; (confuso) confused. ●m coffee with a little milk. ~dura f cut. ~nte adj sharp; (viento) biting; (frío) bitter. ~r vt cut; (recortar) cut out; (aislar, separar, interrumpir) cut off. ●vi cut; (novios) break up. ~rse vpr cut o.s.; (leche etc) curdle; (fig) be embarrassed. ~rse el pelo have one's hair cut. ~rse las uñas cut one's nails. ~uñas m invar nail-clippers

corte m cut; (de tela) length. ~ de luz power cut. ~ y confección dressmaking. ~ f court; (LAm, tribunal) Court of Appeal. hacer la ~ court. las C~s the Spanish parliament. la C~ Suprema the Supreme Court

cortej|ar vt court. ~o m (de rey etc) entourage. ~o fúnebre cortège, funeral procession

cortés adj polite

cortesía f courtesy

corteza f bark; (de queso) rind; (de pan) crust

cortijo m farm; (casa) farmhouse

cortina f curtain

corto adj short; (apocado) shy. ~ de short of. ~ de alcances dim, thick. ~ de vista short-sighted. a la corta o a la larga sooner or later. quedarse ~ fall short; (subestimar) underestimate. ~circuito m short circuit.

Coruña f. La ~ Corunna

cosa f thing; (asunto) business; (idea) idea. como si tal ~ just like that; (como si no hubiera pasado nada) as if nothing had happened. decirle a uno cuatro ~s tell s.o. a thing or two

cosecha f harvest; (de vino) vintage. ~r vt harvest

coser vt sew; sew on (botón); stitch (herida). ●vi sew. ~se vpr stick to s.o.

cosmético adj & m cosmetic

cósmico adj cosmic

cosmo|polita adj & m & f cosmo-

politan. ~s m cosmos
cosquillas fpl. dar ~ tickle.
hacer ~ tickle. tener ~ be tick-
lish
costa f coast. a ~ de at the ex-
pense of. a toda ~ at any cost
costado m side
costal m sack
costar 2 vt cost. ● vi cost; (*resul-
tar difícil*) to be hard. ~ caro be
expensive. cueste lo que cueste at
any cost
costarricense adj & m, costarri-
queño adj & m Costa Rican
cost|as fpl (*Jurid*) costs. ~e m cost.
~ear vt pay for; (*Naut*) sail along
the coast
costero adj coastal
costilla f rib; (*chuleta*) chop
costo m cost. ~so adj expensive
costumbre f custom; (*de per-
sona*) habit. de ~ usual; (*como
adv*) usually
costur|a f sewing; (*línea*) seam;
(*confección*) dressmaking. ~era f
dressmaker. ~ero m sewing box
cotejar vt compare
cotidiano adj daily
cotille|ar vt gossip. ~o m gossip
cotiza|ción f quotation, price.
~r 10 vt (*en la bolsa*) quote. ● vi
pay contributions. ~rse vpr fetch;
(*en la bolsa*) stand at; (*fig*) be val-
ued
coto m enclosure; (*de caza*) pre-
serve. ~ de caza game preserve
cotorr|a f parrot; (*fig*) chatterbox.
~ear vi chatter
coyuntura f joint
coz f kick
cráneo m skull
cráter m crater
crea|ción f creation. ~dor adj

creative. ● m creator. ~r vt create
crec|er 11 vi grow; (*aumentar*) in-
crease; (*río*) rise. ~ida f (*de río*)
flood. ~ido adj (*persona*) grown-
up; (*número*) large, considerable;
(*plantas*) fully-grown. ~iente adj
growing; (*luna*) crescent.
~imiento m growth
credencial f document. ● adj.
cartas fpl ~es credentials
credibilidad f credibility
crédito m credit; (*préstamo*) loan.
digno de ~ reliable
credo m creed
crédulo adj credulous
cre|encia f belief. ~er 18 vt/i be-
lieve; (*pensar*) think. ~o que no I
don't think so, I think not. ~o que
sí I think so. no ~o I should think so!.
¡ya lo ~o! I should think so!.
~erse vpr consider o.s. no me lo
~o I don't believe it. ~ible adj
credible
crema f cream; (*Culin*) custard;
(*LAm, de la leche*) cream. ~ batida
(*LAm*) whipped cream. ~ broncea-
dora sun-tan cream
cremallera f zip (*Brit*), zipper
(*Amer*)
crematorio m crematorium
crepitar vi crackle
crepúsculo m twilight
crespo adj frizzy; (*LAm, rizado*)
curly. ● m (*LAm*) curl
cresta f crest; (*de gallo*) comb
creyente m believer
cría f breeding; (*animal*) baby ani-
mal. las ~s the young
cria|da f maid, servant. ~dero m
(*de pollos etc*) farm; (*de ostras*) bed;
(*de plantas*) nursery. ● m servant.
~dor m breeder. ~nza f breeding.
~r 20 vt suckle; grow (*plantas*);
breed (*animales*); (*educar*) bring up

(Brit), raise (esp Amer). **~rse** vpr grow up

criatura f creature; (niño) baby

crim|en m (serious) crime; (asesinato) murder; (fig) crime. **~inal** adj & m & f criminal

crin f mane

crío m child

criollo adj Creole; (LAm, música, comida) traditional. ● m Creole; (LAm, nativo) Peruvian, Chilean etc

crisantemo m chrysanthemum

crisis f invar crisis

crispar vt twitch; (fam, irritar) annoy. **~le los nervios a uno** get on s.o.'s nerves

cristal m crystal; (Esp, vidrio) glass; (Esp, de una ventana) pane of glass. **limpiar los ~es** (Esp) clean the windows. **~ino** adj crystalline; (fig) crystal-clear. **~izar** 10 crystallize. **~izarse** vpr crystallize

cristian|dad f Christendom. **~ismo** m Christianity. **~o** adj Christian. **ser ~o** be a Christian. ● m Christian

cristo m crucifix

Cristo m Christ

criterio m criterion; (discernimiento) judgement; (opinión) opinion

cr|ítica f criticism; (reseña) review. **~iticar** 7 vt criticize. **~ítico** adj critical. ● m critic

croar vi croak

crom|ado adj chromium-plated. **~o** m chromium, chrome

crónic|a f chronicle; (de radio, TV) report; (de periódico) feature. **~a deportiva** sport section. **~o** adj chronic

cronista m & f reporter

crono|grama m schedule, time-

table. **~logía** f chronology

cron|ometrar vt time. **~ómetro** m (en deportes) stop-watch

croqueta f croquette

cruce m crossing; (de calles, carreteras) crossroads; (de peatones) (pedestrian) crossing

crucial adj crucial

crucifi|car 7 vt crucify. **~jo** m crucifix

crucigrama m crossword (puzzle)

crudo adj raw; (fig) harsh. ● m crude (oil)

cruel adj cruel. **~dad** f cruelty

cruji|do m (de seda, de hojas secas) rustle; (de muebles) creak. **~r** vi (seda, hojas secas) rustle; (muebles) creak

cruz f cross; (de moneda) tails. **~ gamada** swastika. **la C~ Roja** the Red Cross

cruza|da f crusade. **~r** 10 vt cross; exchange (palabras). **~rse** vpr cross; (pasar en la calle) pass each other. **~rse con** pass

cuaderno m exercise book; (para apuntes) notebook

cuadra f (caballeriza) stable; (LAm, distancia) block

cuadrado adj & m square

cuadragésimo adj fortieth

cuadr|ar vt square. ● vi suit; (cuentas) tally. **~arse** vpr (Mil) stand to attention; (fig) dig one's heels in. **~ilátero** m quadrilateral; (Boxeo) ring

cuadrilla f group; (pandilla) gang

cuadro m square; (pintura) painting; (Teatro) scene; (de números) table; (de mando etc) panel; (conjunto del personal) staff. **~ de distribución** switchboard. **a ~s, de ~s** check. **¡qué ~!, ¡vaya un ~!**

what a sight!

cuadrúpedo *m* quadruped

cuádruple *adj & m* quadruple

cuajar *vt* congeal (sangre); curdle (leche); (llenar) fill up. ● *vi* (nieve) settle; (fig, fam) work out. cua- jado de full of. ~se *vpr* coagulate; (sangre) clot; (leche) curdle

cual *pron*. el ~, la ~ etc (animales y cosas) that, which; (personas, sujeto) who, that; (personas, objeto) whom. ● *adj* (LAm, qué) what. ~ si as if. cada ~ everyone. lo ~ which. por lo ~ because of which. sea ~ sea whatever

cuál *pron* which; (LAm, qué) what

cualidad *f* quality

cualquiera *adj* (delante de nom- bres cualquier, pl cualesquiera) any. ● *pron* (pl cualesquiera) any- one, anybody; (cosas) whatever, whichever. un ~ a nobody. una ~ a slut

cuando *adv* when. ● *conj* when; (si) if. ~ más at the most. ~ menos at the least. aun ~ even if. de ~ en ~ from time to time

cuándo *adv & conj* when. ¿de ~ acá?, ¿desde ~? since when? ¡~ no! (LAm) as usuall, typical!

cuant|ía *f* quantity; (extensión) ex- tent. ~ioso *adj* abundant. ~o *adj* as much ... as, as many ... as. ● *pron* as much as, as many as. ● *adv* as much as. ~o antes as soon as possible. en ~o as soon as. en ~o a as for. por ~o since. unos ~os a few, some

cuánto *adj* (interrogativo) how much?; (interrogativo en plural) how many?; (exclamativo) what a lot of! ● *pron* how much?; (en plu- ral) how many? ● *adv* how much.

¿~ mides? how tall are you? ¿~ tiempo? how long? ¡~ tiempo sin verte! it's been a long time! ¿a ~s estamos? what's the date today? un Sr. no sé ~s Mr So-and-So

cuáquero *m* Quaker

cuarent|a *adj & m* forty; (cuadra- gésimo) fortieth. ~ena *f* (Med) quarantine. ~ón *adj* about forty

cuaresma *f* Lent

cuarta *f* (palmo) span

cuartel *m* (Mil) barracks. ~ gene- ral headquarters

cuarteto *m* quartet

cuarto *adj* fourth. ● *m* quarter; (habitación) room. ~ de baño bathroom. ~ de estar living room. ~ de hora quarter of an hour. estar sin un ~ be broke. y ~ (a) quarter past

cuarzo *m* quartz

cuate *m* (Mex) twin; (amigo) friend; (⸚, tipo) guy

cuatro *adj & m* four. ~cientos *adj & m* four hundred

Cuba *f* Cuba

cuba|libre *m* rum and Coke (P). ~no *adj & m* Cuban

cúbico *adj* cubic

cubículo *m* cubicle

cubiert|a *f* cover; (neumático) tyre; (Naut) deck. ~o *adj* covered; (cielo) overcast. ● *m* place setting, piece of cutlery; (en restaurante) cover charge. a ~o under cover

cubilete *m* bowl; (molde) mould; (para los dados) cup

cubis|mo *m* cubism. ~ta *adj & m & f* cubist

cubo *m* bucket; (Mat) cube

cubrecama *m* bedspread

cubrir (pp cubierto) *vt* cover; fill

(vacante). ~se *vpr* cover o.s.; (*ponerse el sombrero*) put on one's hat; (*el cielo*) cloud over, become overcast

cucaracha *f* cockroach

cuchar|**a** *f* spoon. ~**ada** *f* spoonful. ~**adita** *f* teaspoonful. ~**illa**, ~**ita** *f* teaspoon. ~**ón** *m* ladle

cuchichear *vi* whisper

cuchill|**a** *f* large knife; (*de carnicero*) cleaver; (*hoja de afeitar*) razor blade. ~**ada** *f* stab; (*herida*) knife wound. ~**o** *m* knife

cuchitril *m* (*fig*) hovel

cuclillas: en ~ *adv* squatting

cuco *adj* shrewd; (*mono*) pretty, nice. ● *m* cuckoo

cucurucho *m* cornet

cuello *m* neck; (*de camisa*) collar. cortar(le) el ~ a uno cut s.o.'s throat

cuenc|**a** *f* (*del ojo*) (eye) socket; (*de río*) basin. ~**o** *m* hollow; (*vasija*) bowl

cuenta *f* count; (*acción de contar*) counting; (*cálculo*) calculation; (*factura*) bill; (*en banco, relato*) account; (*de collar*) bead. ~ **corriente** current account, checking account (*Amer*). dar ~ de give an account of. darse ~ de realize. en resumidas ~s in short. por mi propia ~ on my own account. tener en ~ bear in mind

cuentakilómetros *m invar* milometer

cuent|**ista** *m & f* story-writer; (*de mentiras*) fibber. ~**o** *m* story; (*mentira*) fib, tall story; (*cuento*). ~ **de hadas** fairy tale. ● *vb véase* CONTAR

cuerda *f* rope; (*más fina*) string; (*Mus*) string. ~ **floja** tightrope. dar ~ a wind up (un reloj)

cuerdo *adj* (*persona*) sane; (*ac-*

ción) sensible

cuerno *m* horn

cuero *m* leather; (*piel*) skin; (*del grifo*) washer. ~ **cabelludo** scalp. en ~s (*vivos*) stark naked

cuerpo *m* body

cuervo *m* crow

cuesta *f* slope, hill. ~ **abajo** downhill. ~ **arriba** uphill. a ~s on one's back

cuestión *f* matter; (*problema*) problem; (*cosa*) thing

cueva *f* cave

cuida|**do** *m* care; (*preocupación*) worry. i~**do!** *int* watch out! tener ~**do** be careful. ~**doso** *adj* careful. ~**r** *vt* look after. ● *vi*. ~**r de** look after. ~**rse** *vpr* look after o.s. ~**rse de** be careful to

culata *f* (*de revólver, fusil*) butt. ~**zo** *m* recoil

culebr|**a** *f* snake. ~**ón** *m* soap opera

culinario *adj* culinary

culminar *vi* culminate

culo *m* 🄸 bottom; (*LAm vulg*) arse (*Brit vulg*), ass (*Amer vulg*)

culp|**a** *f* fault. echar la ~ blame. por ~ de because of. tener la ~ be to blame (de for). ~**abilidad** *f* guilt. ~**able** *adj* guilty. ● *m & f* culprit. ~**r** *vt* blame (de for)

cultiv|**ar** *vt* farm; grow (*plantas*); (*fig*) cultivate. ~**o** *m* farming; (*de plantas*) growing

cult|**o** *adj* (*persona*) educated. ● *m* cult; (*homenaje*) worship. ~**ura** *f* culture. ~**ural** *adj* cultural

culturismo *m* body-building

cumbre *f* summit

cumpleaños *m invar* birthday

cumplido *adj* perfect; (*cortés*) polite. ● *m* compliment. **de ~** cour-

tesy. por ~ out of a sense of duty.
~r *adj* reliable

cumpli|miento *m* fulfilment; (*de ley*) observance; (*de orden*) carrying out. ~r *vt* carry out; observe (*ley*); serve (*condena*); reach (*años*); keep (*promesa*). hoy cumple 3 años he's 3 (years old) today. ● *vi* do one's duty. por ~r as a mere formality. ~rse *vpr* expire; (*realizarse*) be fulfilled

cuna *f* cradle; (*fig, nacimiento*) birthplace

cundir *vi* spread; (*rendir*) go a long way

cuneta *f* ditch

cuña *f* wedge

cuñad|a *f* sister-in-law. ~o *m* brother-in-law

cuño *m* stamp. de nuevo ~ new

cuota *f* quota; (*de sociedad etc*) membership, fee; (*LAm, plazo*) instalment; (*Mex, peaje*) toll

cupe *vb véase* CABER

cupo *m* cuota; (*LAm, capacidad*) room; (*Mex, plaza*) place

cupón *m* coupon

cúpula *f* dome

cura *f* (*tratamiento*) treatment. ●*m* priest. ~ción *f* healing. ~ndero *m* faith-healer. ~r *vt* (*incl Culin*) cure; dress (*herida*); (*tratar*) treat; (*fig*) remedy; tan (*pieles*). ~rse *vpr* recover

curios|ear *vi* pry; (*mirar*) browse. ~idad *f* curiosity. ~o *adj* curious; (*raro*) odd, unusual ●*m* onlooker; (*fisgón*) busybody

curita *f* (*LAm*) (sticking) plaster

curriculum (vitae) *m* curriculum vitae, CV

cursar *vt* issue; (*estudiar*) study

cursi *adj* pretentious, showy

cursillo *m* short course

cursiva *f* italics

curso *m* course; (*Univ etc*) year. en ~ under way; (*año etc*) current

cursor *m* cursor

curtir *vt* tan; (*fig*) harden. ~se *vpr* become tanned; (*fig*) become hardened

curv|a *f* curve; (*de carretera*) bend. ~ar *vt* bend; bow (*estante*). ~arse *vpr* bend; (*estante*) bow; (*madera*) warp. ~ilíneo *adj* curvilinear; (*mujer*) curvaceous. ~o *adj* curved

cúspide *f* top; (*fig*) pinnacle

custodi|a *f* safe-keeping; (*Jurid*) custody. ~ar *vt* guard; (*guardar*) look after. ~o *m* guardian

cutáneo *adj* skin

cutis *m* skin, complexion

cuyo *pron* (*de persona*) whose, of whom; (*de cosa*) whose, of which. en ~ caso in which case

Dd

dactilógrafo *m* typist

dado *m* dice. ● *adj* given. ~ que since, given that

daltónico *adj* colour-blind

dama *f* lady. ~ de honor bridesmaid. ~s *fpl* draughts (*Brit*), checkers (*Amer*)

damasco *m* damask; (*LAm, fruta*) apricot

danés *adj* Danish. ● *m* Dane; (*idioma*) Danish

danza *f* dance; (*acción*) dancing. ~r 🔟 *vt/i* dance

dañar *vt* damage. ~se *vpr* get

damaged. ~ino *adj* harmful. ~o *m* damage; (*a una persona*) harm. ~os y perjuicios damages. hacer ~o a harm, hurt. hacerse ~o hurt o.s.

dar 26 *vt* give; bear (frutos); give out (calor); strike (la hora). ● *vi* give. da igual it doesn't matter. ¡dale! go on! da lo mismo it doesn't matter. ~ a (ventana) look on to; (edificio) face. ~ a luz give birth. ~ con meet (persona); find (cosa). ¿qué más da? it doesn't matter! ~se *vpr* have (baño). dárselas de make o.s. out to be. ~se por consider o.s.

dardo *m* dart

datar *vi*. ~ de date from

dátil *m* date

dato *m* piece of information. ~s *mpl* data, information. ~s personales personal details

---

de *preposición*

Note that **de** before **el** becomes **del**, e.g. es del norte

····▸ (*contenido, material*) of. un vaso de agua a glass of water. es de madera it's made of wood (*pertenencia*) el coche de Juan Juan's car. es de ella it's hers. es de María it's María's. las llaves del coche the car keys (*procedencia, origen, época*) from. soy de Madrid I'm from Madrid. una llamada de Lima a call from Lima. es del siglo V it's from the 5th century (*causa, modo*) se murió de cáncer he died of cancer. temblar de miedo to tremble with fear. de dos en dos two by two

····▸ (*parte del día, hora*) de noche at night. de madrugada early in the morning. las diez de la mañana ten (o'clock) in the morning. de 9 a 12 from 9 to 12

····▸ (*en oraciones pasivas*) by. rodeado de agua surrounded by water. va seguido de coma it's followed by a comma. es de Mozart it's by Mozart

····▸ (*al especificar*) el cajón de arriba the top drawer. la clase de inglés the English lesson. la chica de verde the girl in green. el de debajo the one underneath

····▸ (*en calidad de*) as. trabaja de oficinista he works as a clerk. vino de chaperón he came as a chaperon

····▸ (*en comparaciones*) than. pesa más de un kilo it weighs more than a kilo

····▸ (*con superlativo*) el más alto del mundo the tallest in the world. el mejor de todos the best of all

····▸ (*sentido condicional*) if. de haberlo sabido if I had known. de continuar así if this goes on

➡ Cuando la preposición **de** se emplea como parte de expresiones como **de prisa, de acuerdo** etc., y de nombres compuestos como **hombre de negocios, saco de dormir** etc., ver bajo el respectivo nombre

deambular *vi* roam (por about)
debajo *adv* underneath. ~ de under(neath). el de ~ the one

underneath. por ~ underneath.
por ~ de below

debat|e m debate. **~ir** vt debate

deber vt owe. ● verbo auxiliar have
to, must; (en condicional) should.
debo marcharme I must go, I
have to go. ● m duty. **~es** mpl
homework. **~se** vpr. **~se a** be
due to

debido adj due; (correcto) proper.
~ a due to. como es ~ as is
proper

débil adj weak; (sonido) faint; (luz)
dim

debili|dad f weakness. **~tar** vt
weaken. **~tarse** vpr weaken, get
weak

débito m debit. ~ **bancario** (LAm)
direct debit

debut m debut

debutar vi make one's debut

década f decade

deca|dencia f decline. **~dente**
adj decadent. **~er** 29 vi decline;
(debilitarse) weaken. **~ído** adj in
low spirits. **~imiento** m decline,
weakening

decano m dean; (miembro más an-
tiguo) senior member

decapitar vt behead

decena f ten. una ~ de about
ten

decencia f decency

decenio m decade

decente adj decent; (decoroso) re-
spectable; (limpio) clean, tidy

decepci|ón f disappointment.
~onar vt disappoint

decidi|do adj decided; (persona)
determined, resolute. **~r** vt decide;
settle (cuestión etc). ● vi decide.
~rse vpr make up one's mind

decimal adj & m decimal

décimo adj & m tenth. ● m (de lo-
tería) tenth part of a lottery ticket

decir 46 vt say; (contar) tell. ● m
saying. ~ que no say no. ~ que
sí say yes. dicho de otro modo in
other words. dicho y hecho no
sooner said than done. ¿digame?
can I help you? ¡dígame! (al telé-
fono) hello! digamos let's say. es
~ that is to say. mejor dicho ra-
ther. ¡no me digas! you don't say!,
really! por así ~, por ~lo así so
to speak, as it were. querer ~
mean. se dice que it is said that,
they say that

decisi|ón f decision. **~vo** adj de-
cisive

declara|ción f declaration; (a au-
toridad, prensa) statement. **~ción
de renta** income tax return. **~r**
vt/i declare. **~rse** vpr declare o.s.;
(epidemia etc) break out

declinar vt turn down; (Gram) de-
cline

declive m slope; (fig) decline. en
~ sloping

decola|je m (LAm) take-off. **~r** vi
(LAm) take off

decolorarse vpr become discol-
oured, fade

decora|ción f decoration. **~do**
m (en el teatro) set. **~r** vt decorate.
~tivo adj decorative

decoro m decorum. **~so** adj de-
cent, respectable

decrépito adj decrepit

decret|ar vt decree. **~o** m decree

dedal m thimble

dedica|ción f dedication. **~r** 7
vt dedicate; devote (tiempo). **~rse**
vpr. **~rse a** devote o.s. to. ¿a qué
se dedica? what does he do?
~toria f dedication

dedo m finger; (del pie) toe. ~

anular ring finger. **~ corazón** middle finger. **~ gordo** thumb; (*del pie*) big toe. **~ índice** index finger. **~ meñique** little finger. **~ pulgar** thumb

deduc|ción *f* deduction. **~ir** 47 *vt* deduce; (*descontar*) deduct

defect|o *m* fault, defect. **~uoso** *adj* defective

defen|der 1 *vt* defend. **~sa** *f* defence. **~derse** *vpr* defend o.s. **~sivo** *adj* defensive. **~sor** *m* defender. **abogado** *m* **~sor** defence counsel

defeño *m* (*Mex*) person from the Federal District

deficien|cia *f* deficiency. **~cia mental** mental handicap. **~te** *adj* poor, deficient. ● *m & f* **~te mental** mentally handicapped person

déficit *m invar* deficit

defini|ción *f* definition. **~do** *adj* defined. **~r** *vt* define. **~tivo** *adj* definitive. **en ~tiva** all in all

deform|ación *f* deformation; (*de imagen etc*) distortion. **~ar** *vt* deform; distort (*imagen, metal*). **~arse** *vpr* go out of shape. **~e** *adj* deformed

defraudar *vt* defraud; (*decepcionar*) disappoint

defunción *f* death

degenera|ción *f* degeneration; (*cualidad*) degeneracy. **~do** *adj* degenerate. **~r** *vi* degenerate

degollar 16 *vt* cut s.o.'s throat

degradar *vt* degrade; (*Mil*) demote. **~se** *vpr* demean o.s..

degusta|ción *f* tasting. **~r** *vt* taste

dehesa *f* pasture

deja|dez *f* slovenliness; (*pereza*) laziness. **~do** *adj* slovenly; (*descuidado*) slack, negligent. **~r** *vt* leave;

(*abandonar*) abandon; give up (*estudios*); (*prestar*) lend; (*permitir*) let. **~r a un lado** leave aside. **~r de** stop

dejo *m* aftertaste; (*tonillo*) slight accent; (*toque*) touch

del = **de + el**

delantal *m* apron

delante *adv* in front. **~ de** in front of. **de ~** front. **~ra** *f* front; (*de teatro etc*) front row; (*ventaja*) lead; (*de equipo*) forward line. **llevar la ~ra** be in the lead. **~ro** *adj* front. ● *m* forward

delat|ar *vt* denounce. **~or** *m* informer

delega|ción *f* delegation; (*oficina*) regional office; (*Mex, comisaría*) police station. **~do** *m* delegate; (*Com*) agent, representative. **~r** 12 *vt* delegate

deleit|ar *vt* delight. **~e** *m* delight

deletrear *vt* spell (out)

delfín *m* dolphin

delgad|ez *f* thinness. **~o** *adj* thin; (*esbelto*) slim. **~ucho** *adj* skinny

delibera|ción *f* deliberation. **~do** *adj* deliberate. **~r** *vi* deliberate (*sobre on*)

delicad|eza *f* gentleness; (*fragilidad*) frailty; (*tacto*) tact. **falta de ~eza** tactlessness. **tener la ~ de** have the courtesy to. **~o** *adj* delicate; (*refinado*) refined; (*sensible*) sensitive

delici|a *f* delight. **~oso** *adj* delightful; (*sabor etc*) delicious

delimitar *vt* delimit

delincuen|cia *f* delinquency. **~te** *m & f* criminal, delinquent

delinquir 8 *vi* commit a criminal offence

delir|ante *adj* delirious. **~ar** *vi* be delirious; (*fig*) talk nonsense. **~io**

m delirium; (*fig*) frenzy

delito *m* crime, offence

demacrado *adj* haggard

demagogo *m* demagogue

demanda *f* demand; (*en plural*) lawsuit. ~**do** *m* defendant. ~**nte** *m* & *f* (*Jurid*) plaintiff. ~**r** *vt* (*Jurid*) sue; (*LAm, requerir*) require

demarcación *f* demarcation

demás *adj* rest of the, the other. ● *pron* rest, others. lo ~ the rest. por ~ extremely. por lo ~ otherwise

demas|ía *f*. en ~ía in excess. ~**iado** *adj* too much; (*en plural*) too many. ● *adv* too much; (*con adjetivo*) too

demen|cia *f* madness. ~**te** *adj* demented, mad

dem|ocracia *f* democracy. ~**ócrata** *m* & *f* democrat. ~**ocrático** *adj* democratic

demol|er **2** *vt* demolish. ~**ición** *f* demolition

demonio *m* devil, demon. ¡~s! hell! ¿cómo ~s? how the hell? ¡qué ~s! what the hell!

demora *f* delay. ~**r** *vt* delay. ● *vi* stay on. ~**rse** *vpr* be too long; (*LAm, cierto tiempo*). se ~ una hora en llegar it takes him an hour to get there

demostra|ción *f* demonstration, show. ~**r** **2** *vt* demonstrate; (*mostrar*) show; (*probar*) prove. ~**tivo** *adj* demonstrative

dengue *m* dengue fever

denigrar *vt* denigrate

denominado *adj* named; (*supuesto*) so-called

dens|idad *f* density. ~**o** *adj* dense, thick

denta|dura *f* teeth. ~**dura** postiza dentures, false teeth. ~**l** *adj*

dental

dent|era *f*. darle ~**era** a uno set s.o.'s teeth on edge. ~**ífrico** *m* toothpaste. ~**ista** *m* & *f* dentist

dentro *adv* inside; (*de un edificio*) indoors. ~ de in. ~ de poco soon. por ~ inside

denuncia *f* report; (*acusación*) accusation. ~**r** *vt* report; (*periódico etc*) denounce

departamento *m* department; (*LAm, apartamento*) flat (*Brit*), apartment (*Amer*)

depend|encia *f* dependence; (*sección*) section; (*oficina*) office. ~**encias** *fpl* buildings. ~**er** *vi* depend (de on). ~**ienta** *f* shop assistant. ~**iente** *adj* dependent (de on). ● *m* shop assistant

depila|r *vt* depilate. ~**torio** *adj* depilatory

deplora|ble *adj* deplorable. ~**r** *vt* deplore, regret

deponer **34** *vt* remove from office; depose (*rey*); lay down (*armas*). ● *vi* give evidence

deporta|ción *f* deportation. ~**r** *vt* deport

deport|e *m* sport. hacer ~**e** take part in sports. ~**ista** *m* sportsman. ● *f* sportswoman. ~**ivo** *adj* sports. ● *m* sports car

dep|ositante *m* & *f* depositor. ~**ositar** *vt* deposit; (*poner*) put, place. ~**ósito** *m* deposit; (*almacén*) warehouse; (*Mil*) depot; (*de líquidos*) tank

depravado *adj* depraved

deprecia|ción *f* depreciation. ~**r** *vt* depreciate. ~**rse** *vpr* depreciate

depr|esión *f* depression. ~**imido** *adj* depressed. ~**imir** *vt* depress. ~**imirse** *vpr* get depressed

depura|ción f purification. ~**do** adj refined. ~**r** vt purify; (Pol) purge; refine (estilo)

derech|a f (mano) right hand; (lado) right. **a la ~a** on the right; (hacia el lado derecho) to the right. ~**ista** adj right-wing. ● m & f right-winger. ~**o** adj right; (vertical) upright; (recto) straight. ● adv straight. **todo ~o** straight on. ● m right; (Jurid) law; (lado) right side. ~**os** mpl dues. ~**os de autor** royalties

deriva f drift. **a la ~** drifting, adrift

deriva|do adj derived. ● m derivative, by-product. ~**r** vt divert. ● vi. ~**r** de derive from. be derived from. ~**rse** vpr. ~**rse de** be derived from

derram|amiento m spilling. ~**amiento de sangre** bloodshed. ~**ar** vt spill; shed (lágrimas). ~**arse** vpr spill. ● **e** m spilling; (pérdida) leakage; (Med) discharge; (Med, de sangre) haemorrhage

derretir 5 vt melt

derribar vt knock down; bring down, overthrow (gobierno etc)

derrocar 7 vt bring down, overthrow (gobierno etc)

derroch|ar vt squander. ● **e** m waste

derrot|a f defeat. ~**ar** vt defeat. ~**ado** adj defeated. ~**ero** m course

derrumba|r vt knock down. ~**rse** vpr collapse; (persona) go to pieces

desabotonar vt unbutton, undo. ~**se** vpr come undone; (persona) undo

desabrido adj tasteless; (persona)

surly; (LAm) dull

desabrochar vt undo. ~**se** vpr come undone; (persona) undo

desacato m defiance; (Jurid) contempt of court

desac|ertado adj ill-advised; (erróneo) wrong. ~**ierto** m mistake

desacreditar vt discredit

desactivar vt defuse

desacuerdo m disagreement

desafiar 20 vt challenge; (afrontar) defy

desafina|do adj out of tune. ~**r** vi be out of tune. ~**rse** vpr go out of tune

desafio m challenge; (a la muerte) defiance; (combate) duel

desafortunada|mente adv unfortunately. ~**o** adj unfortunate

desagrada|ble adj unpleasant. ~**r** vt displease. ● vi be unpleasant. **me ~ el sabor** I don't like the taste

desagradecido adj ungrateful

desagrado m displeasure. **con ~** unwillingly

desagüe m drain; (acción) drainage. **tubo m de ~** drain-pipe

desahog|ado adj roomy; (acomodado) comfortable. ~**ar** 12 vt vent. ~**arse** vpr let off steam. ~**o** m comfort; (alivio) relief

desahuci|ar vt declare terminally ill (enfermo); evict (inquilino). ~**o** m eviction

desair|ar vt snub. ● **e** m snub

desajuste m maladjustment; (desequilibrio) imbalance

desala|dora f desalination plant. ~**r** vt to desalinate

desal|entador adj disheartening. ~**entar** 1 vt discourage. ~**iento** m discouragement

desaliñado adj slovenly

desalmado adj heartless

desalojar vt (ocupantes) evacuate; (policía) to clear; (LAm) evict (inquilino)

d **desampar|ado** adj helpless; (lugar) unprotected. **~ar** vt abandon. **~o** m helplessness; (abandono) lack of protection

desangrar vt bleed. **~se** vpr bleed

desanima|do adj down-hearted. **~r** vt discourage. **~rse** vpr lose heart

desapar|ecer 11 vi disappear; (efecto) wear off. **~ecido** adj missing. **~ m** missing person. **~ición** f disappearance

desapego m indifference

desapercibido adj. pasar **~** go unnoticed

desaprobar 2 vt disapprove of

desarm|able adj collapsible; (estante) easy to dismantle. **~ar** vt disarm; (desmontar) dismantle; take apart; (LAm) take down (carpa). **~e** m disarmament

desarraig|ado adj rootless. **~ar** 12 vt uproot. **~o** m uprooting

desarregl|ado adj mess up; (alterar) disrupt. **~o** m disorder

desarroll|ar vt develop. **~arse** vpr (incl Foto) develop; (suceso) take place. **~o** m development

desaseado adj dirty; (desordenado) untidy

desasosiego m anxiety; (intranquilidad) restlessness

desastr|ado adj scruffy. **~e** m disaster. **~oso** adj disastrous

desatar vt untie; (fig, soltar) unleash. **~se** vpr come undone; to undo (zapatos)

desatascar 7 vt unblock

desaten|der 1 vt not pay attention to; neglect (deber etc). **~to** adj inattentive; (descortés) discourteous

desatin|ado adj silly. **~o** m silliness; (error) mistake

desatornillar vt unscrew

desautorizar 10 vt declare unauthorized; discredit (persona); (desmentir) deny

desavenencia f disagreement

desayun|ar vt have for breakfast. **•** vi have breakfast. **~o** m breakfast

desazón m (fig) unease

desbandarse vpr (Mil) disband; (dispersarse) disperse

desbarajust|ar vt mess up. **~e** m mess

desbaratar vt spoil; (Mex) mess up (papeles)

desbloquear vt clear; release (mecanismo); unfreeze (cuenta)

desbocado adj (caballo) runaway; (escote) wide

desbordarse vpr overflow; (río) burst its banks

descabellado adj crazy

descafeinado adj decaffeinated. **•** m decaffeinated coffee

descalabro m disaster

descalificar 7 vt disqualify; (desacreditar) discredit

descalz|ar 10 vt take off (zapatos). **~o** adj barefoot

descampado m open ground. al **~** (LAm) in the open air

descans|ado adj rested; (trabajo) easy. **~ar** vt/i rest. **~illo** m landing. **~o** m rest; (del trabajo) break; (LAm, rellano) landing; (en deportes) half-time; (en el teatro etc) interval

descapotable adj convertible

descarado adj cheeky; (sin vergüenza) shameless

descarg|a f unloading; (Mil, Elec) discharge. ~**ar 12** vt unload; (Mil, Elec) discharge; (Informática) download. ~**o** m (recibo) receipt; (Jurid) evidence

descaro m cheek, nerve

descarriarse 20 vpr go the wrong way; (res) stray; (fig) go astray

descarrila|miento m derailment. ~**r** vi be derailed. ~**rse** vpr (LAm) be derailed

descartar vt rule out

descascararse vpr (pintura) peel; (taza) chip

descen|dencia f descent; (personas) descendants. ~**der 1** vt go down (escalera etc). ● vi go down; (temperatura) fall, drop; (provenir) be descended (de from). ~**diente** m & f descendant. ~**so** m descent; (de temperatura, fiebre etc) fall, drop

descifrar vt decipher; decode (clave)

descolgar 2 & 12 vt take down; pick up (el teléfono). ~**se** vpr lower o.s.

descolor|ar vt discolour, fade. ~**ido** adj discoloured, faded; (persona) pale

descomp|oner 34 vt break down; decompose (materia); upset (estómago); (esp LAm, estropear) break; (esp LAm, desarreglar) mess up. ~**onerse** vpr decompose; (esp LAm, estropearse) break down; (persona) feel sick. ~**ostura** f (esp LAm, de máquina) breakdown; (esp LAm, náuseas) sickness; (esp LAm, diarrea) diarrhoea; (LAm, falla) fault. ~**uesto** adj decomposed; (encoleri-

zado) angry; (esp LAm, estropeado) broken. **estar** ~**uesto** (del estómago) have diarrhoea

descomunal adj enormous

desconc|ertante adj disconcerting. ~**ertar 1** vt disconcert; (dejar perplejo) puzzle. ~**ertarse** vpr be put out, be disconcerted

desconectar vt disconnect

desconfia|do adj distrustful. ~**nza** f distrust, suspicion. ~**r 20** vi. ~**r de** mistrust; (no creer) doubt

descongelar vt defrost; (Com) unfreeze

desconoc|er 11 vt not know, not recognize. ~**ido** adj unknown; (cambiado) unrecognizable. ● m stranger. ~**imiento** m ignorance

desconsidera|ción f lack of consideration. ~**do** adj inconsiderate

descons|olado adj distressed. ~**uelo** m distress; (tristeza) sadness

desconta|do adj. **dar por** ~**do** (que) take for granted (that). ~**r 2** vt discount; deduct (impuestos etc)

descontento adj unhappy (con with), dissatisfied (con with). ● m\ discontent

descorazonar vt discourage. ~**se** vpr lose heart

descorchar vt uncork

descorrer vt draw (cortina). ~ **el cerrojo** unbolt the door

descort|és adj rude, discourteous. ~**esía** f rudeness

descos|er vt unpick. ~**erse** vpr come undone. ~**ido** adj unstitched

descrédito m disrepute. **ir en** ~ de damage the reputation of

descremado adj skimmed

descri|bir (pp descrito) vt describe. ~**pción** f description

descuartizar ⑩ vt cut up

descubierto adj discovered; (no cubierto) uncovered; (vehículo) open-top; (piscina) open-air; (cielo) clear; (cabeza) bare. ● m overdraft. poner al ~ expose

descubri|miento m discovery. ~r (pp descubierto) vt discover; (destapar) uncover; (revelar) reveal; unveil (estatua). ~rse vpr (quitarse el sombrero) take off one's hat

descuento m discount; (del sueldo) deduction; (en deportes) injury time

descuid|ado adj careless; (aspecto etc) untidy; (desprevenido) unprepared. ~ar vt neglect. ● vi not worry. ¡~a! don't worry. ~arse vpr be careless ~o m carelessness; (negligencia) negligence

desde prep (lugar etc) from; (tiempo) since, from. ~ ahora from now on. ~ hace un mes for a month. ~ luego of course. ~ Madrid hasta Barcelona from Madrid to Barcelona. ~ niño since childhood

desdecirse ㊻ vpr. ~ de take back (palabras etc); go back on (promesa)

desd|én m scorn. ~eñable adj insignificant. nada ~eñable significant. ~eñar vt scorn

desdicha f misfortune. por ~ unfortunately. ~do adj unfortunate

desdoblar vt (desplegar) unfold

desear vt want; wish (suerte etc). le deseo un buen viaje I hope you have a good journey. ¿qué desea Vd? can I help you?

desech|able adj disposable. ~ar vt throw out; (rechazar) reject. ~o m waste

desembalar vt unpack

desembarcar �7 vt unload. ● vi disembark

desemboca|dura f (de río) mouth; (de calle) opening. ~r �7 vi. ~r en (río) flow into; (calle) lead to

desembolso m payment

desembragar ⑫ vi declutch

desempaquetar vt unwrap

desempat|ar vi break a tie. ~e m tie-breaker

desempeñ|ar vt redeem; play (papel); hold (cargo); perform, carry out (deber etc). ~arse vpr (LAm) perform. ~arse bien manage well. ~o m redemption; (de un deber, una función) discharge; (LAm, actuación) performance

desemple|ado adj unemployed. ● m unemployed person. los ~ados the unemployed. ~o m unemployment

desencadenar vt unchain (preso); unleash (perro); (causar) trigger. ~se vpr be triggered off; (guerra etc) break out

desencajar vt dislocate; (desconectar) disconnect. ~se vpr become dislocated

desenchufar vt unplug

desenfad|ado adj uninhibited; (desenvuelto) self-assured. ~o m lack of inhibition; (desenvoltura) self-assurance

desenfocado adj out of focus

desenfren|ado adj unrestrained. ~o m licentiousness

desenganchar vt unhook; uncouple (vagón)

desengañ|ar vt disillusion. ~arse vpr become disillusioned; (darse cuenta) realize. ~o m disillusionment, disappointment

desenlace m outcome

desenmascarar vt unmask
desenredar vt untangle. **~se** vpr untangle
desenro||llar vt unroll, unwind. **~scar** 7 vt unscrew
desentend|erse 1 vpr want nothing to do with. **~ido** m. hacerse el **~ido** (fingir no oír) pretend not to hear; (fingir ignorancia) pretend not to know
desenterrar 1 vt exhume; (fig) unearth
desentonar vi be out of tune; (colores) clash
desenvoltura f ease; (falta de timidez) confidence
desenvolver 2 (pp desenvuelto) vt unwrap; expound (idea etc). **~se** vpr perform; (manejarse) manage
deseo m wish, desire. **~so** adj eager. estar **~so** de be eager to
desequilibr|ado adj unbalanced. **~io** m imbalance
des|ertar vt desert; (Pol) defect. **~értico** adj desert-like. **~ertor** m deserter; (Pol) defector
desespera|ción f despair. **~do** adj desperate. **~nte** adj infuriating. **~r** vt drive to despair. **~rse** vpr despair
desestimar vt (rechazar) reject
desfachat|ado adj brazen, shameless. **~ez** f nerve, cheek
desfallec|er 11 vt weaken. ● vi become weak; (desmayarse) faint. **~imiento** m weakness; (desmayo) faint
desfasado adj out of phase; (idea) outdated; (persona) out of touch
desfavorable adj unfavourable
desfil|adero m narrow mountain pass; (cañón) narrow gorge. **~ar** vi

march (past). **~e** m procession, parade. **~e de modelos** fashion show
desgana f, (LAm) **desgano** m (falta de apetito) lack of appetite; (Med) weakness, faintness; (fig) unwillingness
desgarr|ador adj heart-rending. **~ar** vt tear; (fig) break (corazón). **~o** m tear, rip
desgast|ar vt wear away; wear out (ropa). **~arse** vpr wear away; (ropa) be worn out; (persona) wear o.s. out. **~e** m wear
desgracia f misfortune; (accidente) accident; por **~** unfortunately. ¡qué **~**! what a shame! **~do** adj unlucky; (pobre) poor. ● m unfortunate person, poor devil 1
desgranar vt shell (habas etc)
desgreñado adj ruffled, dishevelled
deshabitado adj uninhabited; (edificio) unoccupied
deshacer 31 vt undo; strip (cama); unpack (maleta); (desmontar) take to pieces; break (trato); (derretir) melt; (disolver) dissolve. **~se** vpr come undone; (disolverse) dissolve; (derretirse) melt. **~se de algo** get rid of sth. **~se en lágrimas** dissolve into tears. **~se por hacer algo** go out of one's way to do sth
desheredar vt disinherit
deshidratarse vpr become dehydrated
deshielo m thaw
deshilachado adj frayed
deshincha|do adj (neumático) flat. **~r** vt deflate; (Med) reduce the swelling in. **~rse** vpr go down
deshollinador m chimney sweep

d

deshon|esto *adj* dishonest; (*obsceno*) indecent. **~ra** *f* disgrace. **~rar** *vt* dishonour

deshora *f*. a ~ out of hours. comer a ~ eat between meals

deshuesar *vt* bone (*carne*); stone (*fruta*)

desidia *f* slackness; (*pereza*) laziness

desierto *adj* deserted. ● *m* desert

designar *vt* designate; (*fijar*) fix

desigual *adj* unequal; (*terreno*) uneven; (*distinto*) different. **~dad** *f* inequality

desilusi|ón *f* disappointment; (*pérdida de ilusiones*) disillusionment. **~onar** *vt* disappoint; (*quitar las ilusiones*) disillusion. **~onarse** *vpr* be disappointed; (*perder las ilusiones*) become disillusioned

desinfecta|nte *m* disinfectant. **~r** *vt* disinfect

desinflar *vt* deflate. **~se** *vpr* go down

desinhibido *adj* uninhibited

desintegrar *vt* disintegrate. **~se** *vpr* disintegrate

desinter|és *m* lack of interest; (*generosidad*) unselfishness. **~esado** *adj* uninterested; (*liberal*) unselfish

desistir *vi*. ~ de give up

desleal *adj* disloyal. **~tad** *f* disloyalty

desligar 🄓 *vt* untie; (*separar*) separate; (*fig, librar*) free. **~se** *vpr* break away; (*de un compromiso*) free o.s. (de from)

desliza|dor *m* (*Mex*) hang glider. **~r** 🔟 *vt* slide, slip. **~se** *vpr* slide, slip; (*patinador*) glide; (*tiempo*) slip by, pass; (*fluir*) flow

deslucido *adj* tarnished; (*gastado*) worn out; (*fig*) undistinguished

deslumbrar *vt* dazzle

desmadr|arse *vpr* get out of control. **~e** *m* excess

desmán *m* outrage

desmanchar *vt* (*LAm*) remove the stains from

desmantelar *vt* dismantle; (*despojar*) strip

desmaquillador *m* make-up remover

desmay|ado *adj* unconscious. **~arse** *vpr* faint. **~o** *m* faint

desmedido *adj* excessive

desmemoriado *adj* forgetful

desmenti|do *m* denial. **~r** 🄌 *vt* deny; (*contradecir*) contradict

desmenuzar 🔟 *vt* crumble; shred (*carne etc*)

desmerecer 🄌 *vi*. no ~ de compare favourably with

desmesurado *adj* excessive; (*enorme*) enormous

desmonta|ble *adj* collapsible; (*armario*) easy to dismantle; (*separable*) removable. **~r** *vt* (*quitar*) remove; (*desarmar*) dismantle, take apart. ● *vi* dismount

desmoralizar 🔟 *vt* demoralize

desmoronarse *vpr* crumble; (*edificio*) collapse

desnatado *adj* skimmed

desnivel *m* unevenness; (*fig*) difference, inequality

desnud|ar *vt* strip; undress, strip (*persona*). **~arse** *vpr* undress. **~ez** *f* nudity. **~o** *adj* naked; (*fig*) bare. ● *m* nude

desnutri|ción *f* malnutrition. **~do** *adj* undernourished

desobed|ecer 🄌 *vt* disobey. **~iencia** *f* disobedience

desocupa|do *adj* (*asiento etc*) vacant, free; (*sin trabajo*) unemployed; (*ocioso*) idle. **~r** *vt* vacate; (*vaciar*) empty; (*desalojar*) clear

desodorante *m* deodorant

desolado *adj* desolate; (*persona*) sorry, sad

desorbitante *adj* excessive

desorden *m* disorder, untidiness; (*confusión*) confusion. **~ado** *adj* untidy. **~ar** *vt* disarrange, make a mess of

desorganizar ⑩ *vt* disorganize; (*trastornar*) disturb

desorienta|do *adj* confused. **~r** *vt* disorientate. **~rse** *vpr* lose one's bearings

despabila|do *adj* wide awake; (*listo*) quick. **~r** *vt* (*despertar*) wake up; (*avivar*) wise up. **~rse** *vpr* wake up; (*avivarse*) wise up

despach|ar *vt* finish; (*tratar con*) deal with; (*atender*) serve; (*vender*) sell; (*enviar*) send; (*despedir*) fire. **~o** *m* dispatch; (*oficina*) office; (*venta*) sale; (*de localidades*) box-office

despacio *adv* slowly

despampanante *adj* stunning

desparpajo *m* confidence; (*descaro*) impudence

desparramar *vt* scatter; spill (*líquidos*)

despavorido *adj* terrified

despecho *m* spite. **a ~ de** in spite of. **por ~** out of spite

despectivo *adj* contemptuous; (*sentido etc*) pejorative

despedazar ⑩ *vt* tear to pieces

despedi|da *f* goodbye, farewell. **~da de soltero** stag-party. **~r** ⑤ *vt* say goodbye to, see off; dismiss (*empleado*); evict (*inquilino*); (*arrojar*) throw; give off (*olor etc*). **~rse** *vpr* say goodbye (**de** to)

despeg|ar ⑫ *vt* unstick. ● *vi*

(*avión*) take off. **~ue** *m* take-off

despeinar *vt* ruffle the hair of

despeja|do *adj* clear; (*persona*) wide awake. **~r** *vt* clear; (*aclarar*) clarify. ● *vi* clear. **~rse** *vpr* (*aclararse*) become clear; (*tiempo*) clear up

despellejar *vt* skin

despenalizar *vt* decriminalize

despensa *f* pantry, larder

despeñadero *m* cliff

desperdici|ar *vt* waste. **~o** *m* waste. **~os** *mpl* rubbish

desperta|dor *m* alarm clock. **~r** ① *vt* wake (up); (*fig*) awaken. **~rse** *vpr* wake up

despiadado *adj* merciless

despido *m* dismissal

despierto *adj* awake; (*listo*) bright

despilfarr|ar *vt* waste. **~o** *m* squandering

despintarse *vpr* (*Mex*) run

despista|do *adj* (*con estar*) confused; (*con ser*) absent-minded. **~r** *vt* throw off the scent; (*fig*) mislead. **~rse** *vpr* (*fig*) get confused

despiste *m* mistake; (*confusión*) muddle

desplaza|miento *m* displacement; (*de opinión etc*) swing, shift. **~r** ⑩ *vt* displace. **~rse** *vpr* travel

desplegar ① & ⑫ *vt* open out; spread (*alas*); (*fig*) show

desplomarse *vpr* collapse

despoblado *m* deserted area

despoj|ar *vt* deprive (*persona*); strip (*cosa*). **~os** *mpl* remains; (*de res*) offal; (*de ave*) giblets

despreci|able *adj* despicable; (*cantidad*) negligible. **~ar** *vt* despise; (*rechazar*) scorn. **~o** *m* contempt; (*desaire*) snub

desprender *vt* remove; give off

(olor). ∼**se** *vpr* fall off; (*fig*) part with; (*deducirse*) follow

despreocupa|do *adj* unconcerned; (*descuidado*) careless. ∼**rse** *vpr* not worry

desprestigiar *vt* discredit

desprevenido *adj* unprepared. **pillar a uno** ∼ catch s.o. unawares

desproporcionado *adj* disproportionate

desprovisto *adj*. ∼ **de** lacking in, without

después *adv* after, afterwards; (*más tarde*) later; (*a continuación*) then. ∼ **de** after. ∼ **de comer** after eating. ∼ **de todo** after all. ∼ (**de**) **que** after. **poco** ∼ soon after

desquit|arse *vpr* get even (de with). ∼**e** *m* revenge

destaca|do *adj* outstanding. ∼**r** **7** *vt* emphasize. ● *vi* stand out. ∼**rse** *vpr* stand out. ∼**rse en** excel at

destajo *m*. **trabajar a** ∼ do piece-work

destap|ar *vt* uncover; open (botella). ∼**arse** *vpr* reveal one's true self. ∼**e** *m* (*fig*) permissiveness

destartalado *adj* (coche) clapped-out; (casa) ramshackle

destello *m* sparkle; (*de estrella*) twinkle; (*fig*) glimmer

destemplado *adj* discordant; (nervios) frayed

desteñir **5** & **22** *vt* fade. ● *vi* fade; (color) run. ∼**se** *vpr* fade; (color) run

desterra|do *m* exile. ∼**r** **1** *vt* banish

destetar *vt* wean

destiempo *m*. **a** ∼ at the wrong moment; (*Mus*) out of time

destierro *m* exile

destil|ar *vt* distil. ∼**ería** *f* distillery

destin|ar *vt* destine; (*nombrar*) post. ∼**atario** *m* addressee. ∼**o** *m* (*uso*) use, function; (*lugar*) destination; (*suerte*) destiny. **con** ∼**o a** (going) to

destituir **17** *vt* dismiss

destornilla|dor *m* screwdriver. ∼**r** *vt* unscrew

destreza *f* skill

destroz|ar **10** *vt* destroy; (*fig*) shatter. ∼**os** *mpl* destruction, damage

destru|cción *f* destruction. ∼**ir** **17** *vt* destroy

desus|ado *adj* old-fashioned; (*insólito*) unusual. ∼**o** *m* disuse. **caer en** ∼**o** fall into disuse

desvalido *adj* needy, destitute

desvalijar *vt* rob; ransack (casa)

desvalorizar **10** *vt* devalue

desván *m* loft

desvanec|er **11** *vt* make disappear; (*borrar*) blur; (*fig*) dispel. ∼**erse** *vpr* disappear; (*desmayarse*) faint. ∼**imiento** *m* (*Med*) faint

desvariar **20** *vi* be delirious; (*fig*) talk nonsense

desvel|ar *vt* keep awake. ∼**arse** *vpr* stay awake, have a sleepless night. ∼**o** *m* sleeplessness

desvencijado *adj* (mueble) rickety

desventaja *f* disadvantage

desventura *f* misfortune. ∼**do** *adj* unfortunate

desverg|onzado *adj* impudent, cheeky. ∼**üenza** *f* impudence, cheek

desvestirse **5** *vpr* undress

desv|iación *f* deviation; (*Auto*) diversion. ∼**iar** **20** *vt* divert; deflect (pelota). ∼**iarse** *vpr* (carretera) branch off; (del camino) make a detour; (del tren) stray. **~io** m diversion

desvivirse vpr. **~se** por be completely devoted to; (esforzarse) go out of one's way to

detall|ar vt relate in detail. **~e** m detail; (fig) gesture. al **~e** retail. entrar en **~es** go into detail. ¡qué **~e!** how thoughtful! **~ista** m & f retailer

detect|ar vt detect. **~ive** m detective

deten|ción f stopping; (Jurid) arrest; (en la cárcel) detention. **~er** 🗓 vt stop; (Jurid) arrest; (encarcelar) detain; (retrasar) delay. **~erse** vpr stop; (entretenerse) spend a lot of time. **~idamente** adv at length. **~ido** adj (Jurid) under arrest. ● m prisoner

detergente adj & m detergent

deterior|ar vt damage, spoil. **~arse** vpr deteriorate. **~o** m deterioration

determina|ción f determination; (decisión) decison. **~nte** adj decisive. **~r** vt determine; (decidir) decide

detestar vt detest

detrás adv behind; (en la parte posterior) on the back. **~ de** behind. por **~** at the back; (por la espalda) from behind

detrimento m detriment. en **~** de to the detriment of

deud|a f debt. **~or** m debtor

devalua|ción f devaluation. **~r** 🗓 vt devalue. **~se** vpr depreciate

devastador adj devastating

devoción f devotion

devol|ución f return; (Com) repayment, refund. **~ver** 🗓 (pp devuelto) vt return; (Com) repay, re-

fund. ● vi be sick

devorar vt devour

devoto adj devout; (amigo etc) devoted. ● m admirer

di vb véase **DAR, DECIR**

día m day. **~ de fiesta** (public) holiday. **~ del santo** saint's day. **~ feriado** (LAm), **~ festivo** (public) holiday. al **~** up to date. al **~ siguiente** (on) the following day. ¡buenos **~s!** good morning! de **~** by day. el **~ de hoy** today. el **~ de mañana** tomorrow. un **~ sí** y otro no every other day. vivir al **~** live from hand to mouth

Día de la raza In Latin America, the anniversary of Columbus's discovery of America, October 12. In Spain it is known as *Día de la Hispanidad*. It is a celebration of the cultural ties shared by Spanish-speaking countries.

diab|etes f diabetes. **~ético** adj diabetic

diab|lo m devil. **~lura** f mischief. **~ólico** adj diabolical

diadema f diadem

diáfano adj diaphanous; (cielo) clear

diafragma m diaphragm

diagn|osis f diagnosis. **~osticar** 🗓 vt diagnose. **~óstico** m diagnosis

diagonal adj & f diagonal

diagrama m diagram

dialecto m dialect

dial|ogar 🗓 vi talk. **~ogo** m dialogue; (Pol) talks

diamante m diamond

diámetro m diameter

diana f reveille; (blanco) bull's-eye

diapositiva f slide, transparency

diario adj daily. ● m newspaper; (libro) diary. a ~o daily. de ~o everyday, ordinary

diarrea f diarrhoea

dibuj|ante m draughtsman. ● f draughtswoman. ~ar vt draw. ~o m drawing. ~os animados cartoons

diccionario m dictionary

dich|a f happiness. por ~a fortunately. ~o adj said; (tal) such. ● m saying. y hecho no sooner said than done. mejor ~o rather. propiamente ~o strictly speaking. ~oso adj happy; (afortunado) fortunate

diciembre m December

dicta|do m dictation. ~dor m dictator. ~dura f dictatorship. ~men m opinion; (informe) report. ~r vt dictate; pronounce (sentencia etc); (LAm) give (clase)

didáctico adj didactic

dieci|nueve adj & m nineteen. ~ocho adj & m eighteen. ~séis adj & m sixteen. ~siete adj & m seventeen

diente m tooth; (de tenedor) prong; (de ajo) clove. ~ de león dandelion. hablar entre ~s mumble

diestro adj right-handed; (hábil) skillful

dieta f diet

diez adj & m ten

diezmar vt decimate

difamación f (con palabras) slander; (por escrito) libel

diferen|cia f difference; (desacuerdo) disagreement. ~ciar vt differentiate between. ~ciarse vpr differ. ~te adj different; (diversos) various

diferido adj (TV etc) en ~ recorded

dif|ícil adj difficult; (poco probable) unlikely. ~icultad f difficulty. ~icultar vt make difficult

difteria f diphtheria

difundir vt spread; (TV etc) broadcast

difunto adj late, deceased. ● m deceased

difusión f spreading

dige|rir 4 vt digest. ~stión f digestion. ~stivo adj digestive

digital adj digital; (de los dedos) finger

dign|arse vpr deign to. ~atario m dignitary. ~idad f dignity. ~o adj honourable; (decoroso) decent; (merecedor) worthy (de of). ~ de elogio praiseworthy

digo vb véase DECIR

dije vb véase DECIR

dilatar vt expand; (Med) dilate; (prolongar) prolong. ~se vpr expand; (Med) dilate; (extenderse) extend; (Mex, demorarse) be late

dilema m dilemma

diligen|cia f diligence; (gestión) job; (carruaje) stagecoach. ~te adj diligent

dilucidar vt clarify; solve (misterio)

diluir 17 vt dilute

diluvio m flood

dimensión f dimension; (tamaño) size

diminut|ivo adj & m diminutive. ~o adj minute

dimitir vt/i resign

Dinamarca f Denmark

dinamarqués adj Danish. ● m Dane

dinámic|a f dynamics. ~o adj

dynamic

dinamita f dynamite

dínamo m dynamo

dinastía f dynasty

diner|al m fortune. **~o** m money. **~o efectivo** cash. **~o suelto** change

dinosaurio m dinosaur

dios m god. **~a** f goddess. **¡D~ mío!** good heavens! **¡gracias a D~!** thank God!

diplom|a m diploma. **~acia** f diplomacy. **~ado** adj qualified. **~arse** vpr (LAm) graduate. **~ático** adj diplomatic. • m diplomat

diptongo m diphthong

diputa|ción f delegation. **~ción provincial** county council. **~do** m deputy; (Pol, en España) member of the Cortes; (Pol, en Inglaterra) Member of Parliament; (Pol, en Estados Unidos) congressman

dique m dike

direc|ción f direction; (señas) address; (los que dirigen) management; (Pol) leadership; (Auto) steering. **~ción prohibida** no entry. **~ción única** one-way. **~ta** f (Auto) top gear. **~tiva** f board; (Pol) executive committee. **~tivas** fpl guidelines. **~to** adj direct; (línea) straight; (tren) through. **en ~to** (TV etc) live. **~tor** m director; (Mus) conductor; (de escuela) headmaster; (de periódico) editor; (gerente) manager. **~tora** f (de escuela etc) headmistress. **~torio** m board of directors; (LAm, de teléfonos) telephone directory

dirig|ente adj ruling. • m & f leader; (de empresa) manager. **~ir** 🄳 vt direct; (Mus) conduct; run (empresa etc); address (carta etc). **~irse** vpr make one's way; (hablar)

---

address

disciplina f discipline. **~r** vt discipline. **~rio** adj disciplinary

discípulo m disciple; (alumno) pupil

disco m disc; (Mus) record; (deportes) discus; (de teléfono) dial; (de tráfico) sign; (Rail) signal. **~ duro** hard disk. **~ flexible** floppy disk

disconforme adj not in agreement

discord|e adj discordant. **~ia** f discord

discoteca f discothèque, disco 🅃; (colección de discos) record collection

discreción f discretion

discrepa|ncia f discrepancy; (desacuerdo) disagreement. **~r** vi differ

discreto adj discreet; (moderado) moderate

discrimina|ción f discrimination. **~r** vt (distinguir) discriminate between; (tratar injustamente) discriminate against

disculpa f apology; (excusa) excuse. **pedir ~s** apologize. **~r** vt excuse, forgive. **~rse** vpr apologize

discurs|ar vi speak (sobre about). **~o** m speech

discusión f discussion; (riña) argument

discuti|ble adj debatable. **~r** vt discuss; (contradecir) contradict. • vi argue (por about)

disecar 🄷 vt stuff; (cortar) dissect

diseminar vt disseminate, spread

disentir 🄴 vi disagree (de with, en on)

diseñ|ador m designer. **~ar** vt design. **~o** m design; (fig) sketch

disertación f dissertation

disfraz m fancy dress; (para engañar) disguise. **~ar** 🔟 vt dress up; (para engañar) disguise. **~arse** vpr. **~arse** de dress up as; (para engañar) disguise o.s. as.

disfrutar vt enjoy. • vi enjoy o.s. **~ de** enjoy

disgust|ar vt displease; (molestar) annoy. **~arse** vpr get annoyed, get upset; (dos personas) fall out. **~o** m annoyance; (problema) trouble; (riña) quarrel; (dolor) sorrow, grief

disidente adj & m & f dissident

disimular vt conceal. • vi pretend

disipar vt dissipate; (derrochar) squander

dislocarse 🔁 vpr dislocate

disminu|ción f decrease. **~ir** 🔟 vi diminish

disolver ② (pp disuelto) vt dissolve. **~se** vpr dissolve

dispar adj different

disparar vt fire; (Mex, pagar) buy. • vi shoot (contra at)

disparate m silly thing; (error) mistake. decir **~s** talk nonsense. ¡qué **~**! how ridiculous!

disparidad f disparity

disparo m (acción) firing; (tiro) shot

dispensar vt give; (eximir) exempt. • vi. ¡Vd dispense! forgive me

dispers|ar vt scatter, disperse. **~arse** vpr scatter, disperse. **~ión** f dispersion. **~o** adj scattered

dispon|er 🔢 vt arrange; (Jurid) order. • vi. **~er de** have; (vender etc) dispose of. **~erse** vpr prepare (a to). **~ibilidad** f availability. **~ible** adj available

disposición f arrangement; (aptitud) talent; (disponibilidad) dis

posal; (Jurid) order, decree. **~ de ánimo** frame of mind. **a la ~ de** at the disposal of. **a su ~** at your service

dispositivo m device

dispuesto adj ready; (persona) disposed (a to); (servicial) helpful

disputa f dispute; (pelea) argument

disquete m diskette, floppy disk

dista|ncia f distance. **a ~ncia** from a distance. guardar las **~ncias** keep one's distance. **~nciar** vt space out; distance (amigos). **~nciarse** vpr (dos personas) fall out. **~nte** adj distant. **~r** vi be away; (fig) be far. **~ 5 kilómetros** it's 5 kilometres away

distin|ción f distinction; (honor) award. **~guido** adj distinguished. **~guir** 🔢 vt/i distinguish. **~guirse** vpr distinguish o.s.; (diferenciarse) differ. **~tivo** adj distinctive. • m badge. **~to** adj different, distinct

distra|cción f amusement; (descuido) absent-mindedness, inattention. **~er** 🔢 vt distract; (divertir) amuse. **~erse** vpr amuse o.s.; (descuidarse) not pay attention. **~ído** adj (desatento) absent-minded

distribu|ción f distribution. **~idor** m distributor. **~ir** 🔟 vt distribute

distrito m district

disturbio m disturbance

disuadir vt deter, dissuade

diurno adj daytime

divagar 🔢 vi digress; (hablar sin sentido) ramble

diván m settee, sofa

diversi|dad f diversity. **~ficar** 🔁 vt diversify

diversión f amusement, entertainment; (pasatiempo) pastime

diverso *adj* different

diverti|do *adj* amusing; *(que tiene gracia)* funny. **~r** ④ *vt* amuse, entertain. **~rse** *vpr* enjoy o.s.

dividir *vt* divide; *(repartir)* share out

divino *adj* divine

divisa *f* emblem. **~s** *fpl* currency

divisar *vt* make out

división *f* division

divorci|ado *adj* divorced. ● *m* divorcee. **~ar** *vt* divorce. **~arse** *vpr* get divorced. **~o** *m* divorce

divulgar ⑫ *vt* spread; divulge *(secreto)*

dizque *adv* (LAm) apparently; *(supuestamente)* supposedly

do *m* C; *(solfa)* doh

DNI - Documento Nacional de Identidad See ▷DOCUMENTO DE IDENTIDAD

dobl|adillo *m* hem; *(de pantalón)* turn-up *(Brit)*, cuff *(Amer)*. **~ar** *vt* double; *(plegar)* fold; *(torcer)* bend; turn *(esquina)*; dub *(película)*. ● *vi* turn; *(campana)* toll. **~arse** *vpr* double; *(curvarse)* bend. **~e** *adj* double. ● *m* double. **el ~e** twice as much (de, que as). **~egar** ⑫ *vt* *(fig)* force to give in. **~egarse** *vpr* give in

doce *adj* & *m* twelve. **~na** *f* dozen

docente *adj* teaching. ● *m* & *f* teacher

dócil *adj* obedient

doctor *m* doctor. **~ado** *m* doctorate

doctrina *f* doctrine

document|ación *f* documentation, papers. **~al** *adj* & *m* documentary. **~o** *m* document. D**~o** Nacional de Identidad identity

card

documento de identidad An identity card that all residents over a certain age in Spain and Latin America must carry at all times. Holders must quote their identity card number on most official forms. The card is also known as *carné de identidad*, and in Spain as the *DNI (Documento Nacional de Identidad)*.

dólar *m* dollar

dolarizar *vt* dollarize

dol|er ② *vi* hurt, ache; *(fig)* grieve. **me duele la cabeza** I have a headache. **le duele el estómago** he has (a) stomach-ache. **~or** *m* pain; *(sordo)* ache; *(fig)* sorrow. **~or de cabeza** headache. **~or de muelas** toothache. **~oroso** *adj* painful

domar *vt* tame; break in *(caballo)*

dom|esticar ⑦ *vt* domesticate. **~éstico** *adj* domestic

domicili|ar *vt*. **~ar los pagos** pay by direct debit. **~o** *m* address. **~o particular** home address. **reparto a ~** home delivery service

domina|nte *adj* dominant; *(persona)* domineering. **~r** *vt* dominate; *(contener)* control; *(conocer)* have a good command of. ● *vi* dominate. **~rse** *vpr* control o.s.

domingo *m* Sunday

dominio *m* authority; *(territorio)* domain; *(fig)* command

dominó *m* *(pl ~s)* dominoes; *(ficha)* domino

don *m* talent, gift; *(en un sobre)* Mr. **~** Pedro Pedro

donación *f* donation

donaire *m* grace, charm

dona|nte *m & f* (*de sangre*) donor. **~r** *vt* donate

doncella *f* maiden; (*criada*) maid

donde *adv* where

dónde *adv* where?; (*LAm, cómo*) how; ¿hasta ~? how far? ¿por ~? whereabouts?; (*por qué camino?*) which way? ¿a ~ vas? where are you going? ¿de ~ eres? where are you from?

dondequiera *adv.* ~ que wherever. por ~ everywhere

doña *f* (*en un sobre*) Mrs. ~ María María

dora|do *adj* golden; (*cubierto de oro*) gilt. **~r** *vt* gilt; (*Culin*) brown

dormi|do *adj* asleep. quedarse ~do fall asleep; (*no despertar*) oversleep. **~r** 6 *vt* send to sleep. ● *vi* sleep. **~rse** *vpr* fall asleep. **~r la siesta** have an afternoon nap, have a siesta. **~tar** *vi* doze. **~torio** *m* bedroom

dors|al *adj* back. ● *m* (*en deportes*) number. **~o** *m* back. nadar de ~ (*Mex*) do (the) backstroke

dos *adj & m* two. de ~ en ~ in twos, in pairs. los ~, las ~ both (of them). **~cientos** *adj & m* two hundred

dosi|ficar 7 *vt* dose; (*fig*) measure out. **~s** *f invar* dose

dot|ado *adj* gifted. **~ar** *vt* give a dowry; (*proveer*) provide (de with). **~e** *m* dowry

doy *vb véase* DAR

dragar 12 *vt* dredge

drama *m* drama; (*obra de teatro*) play. **~turgo** *m* playwright

drástico *adj* drastic

droga *f* drug. **~dicto** **~dicto** *m* drug addict. **~do** *m* drug addict. **~r** 12 *vt* drug. **~rse** *vpr* take drugs

droguería *f* hardware store

ducha *f* shower. **~rse** *vpr* have a shower

dud|a *f* doubt. poner en ~a question. sin ~a (*alguna*) without a doubt. **~ar** *vt/i* doubt. **~oso** *adj* doubtful; (*sospechoso*) dubious

duelo *m* duel; (*luto*) mourning

duende *m* imp

dueñ|a *f* owner, proprietress; (*de una pensión*) landlady. **~o** *m* owner, proprietor; (*de una pensión*) landlord

duermo *vb véase* DORMIR

dul|ce *adj* sweet; (*agua*) fresh; (*suave*) soft, gentle. ● *m* (*LAm*) sweet. **~zura** *f* sweetness; (*fig*) gentleness

duna *f* dune

dúo *m* duet, duo

duplica|do *adj* duplicated. por ~ in duplicate. ● *m* duplicate. **~r** 7 *vt* duplicate. **~rse** *vpr* double

duque *m* duke. **~sa** *f* duchess

dura|ción *f* duration, length. **~dero** *adj* lasting. **~nte** *prep* during; (*medida de tiempo*) for. ~ todo el año all year round. **~r** *vi* last

durazno *m* (*LAm, fruta*) peach

dureza *f* hardness; (*Culin*) toughness; (*fig*) harshness

duro *adj* hard; (*Culin*) tough; (*fig*) harsh. ● *adv* (*esp LAm*) hard

DVD *m* (**Disco Versátil Digital**) DVD. **~teca** *f* DVD library

Ee

e *conj* and
Ébola *m* ebola
ebrio *adj* drunk
ebullición *f* boiling
eccema *m* eczema
echar *vt* throw; post (carta); give off (olor); pour (líquido); (*expulsar*) expel; (*de recinto*) throw out; fire (empleado); (*poner*) put on; get (gasolina); put out (raíces); show (película). ~ a start. ~ a perder spoil. ~ de menos miss. ~se atrás (*fig*) back down. echárselas de feign. ~se *vpr* throw o.s.; (*tumbarse*) lie down
eclesiástico *adj* ecclesiastical
eclipse *m* eclipse
eco *m* echo. hacerse ~ de echo
ecología *f* ecology. ~ista *m & f* ecologist
economato *m* cooperative store
economía *f* economy; (*ciencia*) economics. ~ómico *adj* economic; (*no caro*) inexpensive. ~omista *m & f* economist. ~omizar 🔟 *vt/i* economize
ecoturismo *m* ecotourism
ecuación *f* equation
ecuador *m* equator. el E~ the Equator. E~ (*país*) Ecuador
ecuánime *adj* level-headed; (*imparcial*) impartial
ecuatoriano *adj & m* Ecuadorian
ecuestre *adj* equestrian
edad *f* age. ~ avanzada old age. E~ de Piedra Stone Age. E~ Media Middle Ages. ¿qué ~ tiene? how old is he?

edición *f* edition; (*publicación*) publication
edicto *m* edict
edificación *f* building. ~ante *adj* edifying. ~ar 🔽 *vt* build; (*fig*) edify. ~io *m* building; (*fig*) structure
editar *vt* edit; (*publicar*) publish. ~or *adj* publishing. ● *m* editor; (*que publica*) publisher. ~orial *adj* editorial. ● *m* leading article. ● *f* publishing house
edredón *m* duvet
educación *f* upbringing; (*modales*) (good) manners; (*enseñanza*) education. falta de ~ción rudeness, bad manners. ~do *adj* polite. bien ~do polite. mal ~do rude. ~r 🔽 *vt* bring up; (*enseñar*) educate. ~tivo *adj* educational
edulcorante *m* sweetener
EE.UU. *abrev* (**Estados Unidos**) USA
efectivamente *adv* really; (*por supuesto*) indeed. ~ivo *adj* effective; (*auténtico*) real. ● *m* cash. ~o *m* effect; (*impresión*) impression. en ~o really; (*como respuesta*) indeed. ~os *mpl* belongings; (*Com*) goods. ~uar �ʻ21ʼ *vt* carry out; make (viaje, compras etc)
efervescente *adj* effervescent; (*bebidas*) fizzy
eficacia *f* effectiveness; (*de persona*) efficiency. ~z *adj* effective; (*persona*) efficient
eficiencia *f* efficiency. ~te *adj* efficient
efímero *adj* ephemeral
efusividad *f* effusiveness. ~vo *adj* effusive; (*persona*) demonstrative
egipcio *adj & m* Egyptian
Egipto *m* Egypt

ego|ísmo m selfishness, egotism. **~ista** adj selfish

egresar vi (LAm) graduate; (de colegio) leave school, graduate (Amer)

eje m axis; (Tec) axle

ejecu|ción f execution; (Mus) performance. **~tar** vt carry out; (Mus) perform; (matar) execute. **~tivo** m executive

ejempl|ar adj exemplary; (ideal) model. ● m specimen; (libro) copy; (revista) issue, number. **~ificar** 🔢 vt exemplify. **~o** m example. dar (el) **~o** set an example. por **~o** for example

ejerc|er 🔟 vt exercise; practise (profesión); exert (influencia). ● vi practise. **~icio** m exercise; (de profesión) practice. hacer **~icios** exercise. **~itar** vt exercise

ejército m army

ejido m (Mex) cooperative

ejote m (Mex) green bean

---

el *artículo definido masculino* (*pl* **los**)

The masculine article **el** is also used before feminine nouns which begin with stressed **a** or **ha**, e.g. **el ala derecha, el hada madrina**. Also, **de** followed by **el** becomes **del** and **el** preceded by **a** becomes **al**

····▸ the. **el** tren de las seis the six o'clock train. **el** vecino de al lado the next-door neighbour. cerca **del** hospital near the hospital

····▸ *No se traduce en los siguientes casos:* (con nombre abstracto, genérico) **el** tiempo vuela time flies. odio **el** queso l

---

hate cheese. **el** hilo es muy durable linen is very durable

····▸ (con colores, días de la semana) **el** rojo está de moda red is in fashion. **el** lunes es fiesta Monday is a holiday

····▸ (con algunas instituciones) termino **el** colegio mañana l finish school tomorrow. lo ingresaron en **el** hospital he was admitted to hospital

····▸ (con nombres propios) **el** Sr. Díaz Mr Díaz. **el** doctor Lara Doctor Lara

····▸ (antes de infinitivo) es muy cuidadosa en **el** vestir she takes great care in the way she dresses. me di cuenta al verlo l realized when l saw him

····▸ (con partes del cuerpo, artículos personales) *se traduce por un posesivo*. apretó **el** puño he clenched his fist. tienes **el** zapato desatado your shoe is undone

····▸ **el** + **de**. es **el de** Pedro it's Pedro's. **el del** sombrero the one with the hat

····▸ **el** + **que** (*persona*) **el** que me atendió the one who served me. (*cosa*) **el** que se rompió the one that broke.

····▸ **el** + **que** + *subjuntivo* (quienquiera) whoever. **el** que gane la lotería whoever wins the lottery. (cualquiera) whichever. compra **el** que sea más barato buy whichever is cheaper

---

él pron (*persona*) he; (*persona con prep*) him; (*cosa*) it. es de **~** it's his

elabora|ción f elaboration; (*fabricación*) manufacture. **~r** vt elaborate; manufacture (producto);

(*producir*) produce

el|asticidad *f* elasticity. **~ástico** *adj & m* elastic

elec|ción *f* choice; (*de político etc*) election. **~ciones** *fpl* (Pol) election. **~tor** *m* voter. **~torado** *m* electorate. **~toral** *adj* electoral; (*campaña*) election

electrici|dad *f* electricity. **~sta** *m & f* electrician

eléctrico *adj* electric; (*aparato*) electrical

electri|ficar 🔳 *vt* electrify. **~zar** 🔳 *vt* electrify

electrocutar *vt* electrocute. **~se** *vpr* be electrocuted

electrodoméstico *adj* electrical appliance

electrónic|a *f* electronics. **~o** *adj* electronic

elefante *m* elephant

elegan|cia *f* elegance. **~te** *adj* elegant

elegía *f* elegy

elegi|ble *adj* eligible. **~do** *adj* chosen. **~r** 🔳 & 🔳 *vt* choose; (*por votación*) elect

element|al *adj* elementary; (*esencial*) fundamental. **~o** *m* element; (*persona*) person, bloke (*Brit, fam*). **~os** *mpl* (*nociones*) basic principles

elenco *m* (*en el teatro*) cast

eleva|ción *f* elevation; (*de precios*) rise, increase; (*acción*) raising. **~dor** *m* (Mex) lift (Brit), elevator (Amer). **~r** *vt* raise; (*promover*) promote

elimina|ción *f* elimination. **~r** *vt* eliminate; (*Informática*) delete. **~toria** *f* preliminary heat

élite /e'lit, e'lite/ *f* elite

ella *pron* (*persona*) she; (*persona con prep*) her; (*cosa*) it. es de **~s** it's theirs. **~s** *pron pl* they; (con

prep) them. es de **~** it's hers

ello *pron* it

ellos *pron pl* they; (*con prep*) them. es de **~** it's theirs

elocuen|cia *f* eloquence. **~te** *adj* eloquent

elogi|ar *vt* praise. **~o** *m* praise

elote *m* (Mex) corncob; (*Culin*) corn on the cob

eludir *vt* avoid, elude

emanar *vi* emanate (de from); (*originarse*) originate (de from, in)

emancipa|ción *f* emancipation. **~r** *vt* emancipate. **~rse** *vpr* become emancipated

embadurnar *vt* smear

embajad|a *f* embassy. **~or** *m* ambassador

embalar *vt* pack

embaldosar *vt* tile

embalsamar *vt* embalm

embalse *m* reservoir

embaraz|ada *adj* pregnant. ● *f* pregnant woman. **~ar** 🔳 *vt* get pregnant. **~o** *m* pregnancy; (*apuro*) embarrassment; (*estorbo*) hindrance. **~oso** *adj* awkward, embarrassing

embar|cación *f* vessel. **~cadero** *m* jetty, pier. **~car** 🔳 *vt* load (*mercancías* etc). **~carse** *vpr* board. **~carse en** (*fig*) embark upon

embargo *m* embargo; (*Jurid*) seizure. sin **~** however

embarque *m* loading; (*de pasajeros*) boarding

embaucar 🔳 *vt* trick

embelesar *vt* captivate

embellecer 🔳 *vt* make beautiful

embesti|da *f* charge. **~r** 🔳 *vt/i* charge

emblema *m* emblem

embolsarse *vpr* pocket

embonar *vt* (Mex) fit

emborrachar *vt* get drunk. ~se *vpr* get drunk

emboscada *f* ambush

embotar *vt* dull

embotella|miento *m* (de vehículos) traffic jam. ~r *vt* bottle

embrague *m* clutch

embriag|arse 12 *vpr* get drunk. ~uez *f* drunkenness

embrión *m* embryo

embroll|ar *vt* mix up; involve (persona); ~arse *vpr* get into a muddle; (en un asunto) get involved. ~o *m* tangle; (fig) muddle

embruj|ado *adj* bewitched; (casa) haunted. ~ar *vt* bewitch. ~o *m* spell

embrutecer 11 *vt* brutalize

embudo *m* funnel

embuste *m* lie. ~ro *adj* deceitful. • *m* liar

embuti|do *m* (Culin) sausage. ~r *vt* stuff

emergencia *f* emergency

emerger 14 *vi* appear, emerge

emigra|ción *f* emigration. ~nte *adj & m & f* emigrant. ~r *vi* emigrate

eminen|cia *f* eminence. ~te *adj* eminent

emisario *m* emissary

emi|sión *f* emission; (de dinero) issue; (TV etc) broadcast. ~sor *adj* issuing; (TV etc) broadcasting. ~sora *f* radio station. ~tir *vt* emit, give out; (TV etc) broadcast; cast (voto); (poner en circulación) issue

emoci|ón *f* emotion; (excitación) excitement. ¡qué ~ón! how exciting!. ~onado *adj* moved.

~onante *adj* exciting; (conmovedor) moving. ~onar *vt* move. ~onarse *vpr* get excited; (conmoverse) be moved

emotivo *adj* emotional; (conmovedor) moving

empacar 7 *vt* (LAm) pack

empacho *m* indigestion

empadronar *vt* register. ~se *vpr* register

empalagoso *adj* sickly; (persona) cloying

empalizada *f* fence

empalm|ar *vt* connect, join. • *vi* meet. ~e *m* junction; (de trenes) connection

empan|ada *f* (savoury) pie; (LAm, individual) pasty. ~adilla *f* pasty

empantanarse *vpr* become swamped; (coche) get bogged down

empañar *vt* steam up; (fig) tarnish. ~se *vpr* steam up

empapar *vt* soak. ~se *vpr* get soaked

empapela|do *m* wallpaper. ~r *vt* wallpaper

empaquetar *vt* package

emparedado *m* sandwich

emparentado *adj* related

empast|ar *vt* fill (muela). ~e *m* filling

empat|ar *vi* draw. ~e *m* draw

empedernido *adj* confirmed; (bebedor) inveterate

empedrar 1 *vt* pave

empeine *m* instep

empeñ|ado *adj* in debt; (decidido) determined (en to). ~ar *vt* pawn; pledge (palabra). ~arse *vpr* get into debt; (estar decidido a) be determined (en to). ~o *m* pledge; (resolución) determination. casa *f* de ~s pawnshop. ~**oso** adj (LAm) hardworking

empeorar vt make worse. ● vi get worse. ~**se** vpr get worse

empequeñecer 🔟 vt become smaller; (fig) belittle

empera|dor m emperor. ~**triz** f empress

empezar 🔟 & 🔟 vt/i start, begin. **para** ~ to begin with

empina|do adj (cuesta) steep. ~**r** vt raise. ~**rse** vpr (persona) stand on tiptoe

empírico adj empirical

emplasto m plaster

emplaza|miento m (Jurid) summons; (lugar) site. ~**r** 🔟 vt summon; (situar) site

emple|ada f employee; (doméstica) maid. ~**ado** m employee. ~**ar** vt use; employ (persona); spend (tiempo). ~**arse** vpr get a job. ~**o** m use; (trabajo) employment; (puesto) job

empobrecer 🔟 vt impoverish. ~**se** vpr become poor

empoll|ar vt incubate (huevos); (arg, estudiar) cram 🇬🇧. ● vi (ave) sit; (estudiante) 🇬🇧 cram. ~**ón** m 🇬🇧 swot (Brit, fam), grind (Amer, fam)

empolvarse vpr powder

empotra|do adj built-in, fitted. ~**r** vt fit

emprende|dor adj enterprising. ~**r** vt undertake; set out on (viaje). ~**rla con uno** pick a fight with s.o.

empresa f undertaking; (Com) company, firm. ~ **puntocom** dotcom company. ~**rio** m businessman; (patrón) employer; (de teatro etc) impresario

empuj|ar vt push. ~**e** m (fig) drive. ~**ón** m push, shove

empuña|dura f handle

emular vt emulate

en prep in; (sobre) on; (dentro) inside, in; (medio de transporte) by. ~ **casa** at home. ~ **coche** by car. ~ **10 días** in 10 days. **de pueblo** ~ **pueblo** from town to town

enagua f petticoat

enajena|ción f alienation. ~**ción mental** insanity. ~**r** vt alienate; (volver loco) derange

enamora|do adj in love. ● m lover. ~**r** vt win the love of. ~**rse** vpr fall in love (**de** with)

enano adj & m dwarf

enardecer 🔟 vt inflame. ~**se** vpr get excited (**por** about)

encabeza|do m (Mex) headline. ~**miento** m heading; (de periódico) headline. ~**r** 🔟 vt head; lead (revolución etc)

encabritarse vpr rear up

encadenar vt chain; (fig) tie down

encaj|ar vt fit; fit together (varias piezas). ● vi fit; (cuadrar) tally. ~**arse** vpr put on. ~**e** m lace; (Com) reserve

encaminar vt direct. ~**se** vpr make one's way

encandilar vt dazzle; (estimular) stimulate

encant|ado adj enchanted; (persona) delighted. **¡~ado!** pleased to meet you! ~**ador** adj charming. ~**amiento** m spell. ~**ar** vt bewitch; (fig) charm, delight. **me ~a la leche** I love milk. ~**o** m spell; (fig) delight

encapricharse vpr. ~ **con** take a fancy to

encarar vt face; (LAm) stand up to (persona). ~**se** vpr. ~**se con** stand up to

e

encarcelar vt imprison

encarecer 11 vt put up the price of. **~se** vpr become more expensive

encarg|ado adj in charge. ● m manager, person in charge. **~ar** 12 vt entrust; (*pedir*) order. **~arse** vpr take charge (de of). **~o** m job; (Com) order; (*recado*) errand. **hecho de ~o** made to measure

encariñarse vpr. **~ con** take to, become fond of

encarna|ción f incarnation. **~do** adj incarnate; (*rojo*) red; (*uña*) ingrowing. ● m red

encarnizado adj bitter

encarpetar vt file; (LAm, dar carpetazo) shelve

encarrilar vt put back on the rails; (*fig*) direct, put on the right track

encasillar vt classify; (*fig*) pigeonhole

encauzar 10 vt channel

enceguecer 11 (LAm) blind

encend|edor m lighter. **~er** 1 vt light; switch on, turn on (aparato eléctrico); start (motor); (*fig*) arouse. **~erse** vpr light; (aparato eléctrico) come on; (*excitarse*) get excited; (*ruborizarse*) blush. **~ido** adj lit; (aparato eléctrico) on; (*rojo*) bright red. ● m (Auto) ignition

encera|do adj waxed. ● m (*pizarra*) blackboard. **~r** vt wax

encerr|ar 1 vt shut in; (con llave) lock up; (*fig, contener*) contain. **~ona** f trap

enchilar vt (Mex) add chili to

enchinar vt (Mex) perm

enchuf|ado adj switched on. **~ar** vt plug in; fit together (tubos etc). **~e** m socket; (*clavija*) plug; (de tubos etc) joint; (*fam, influen-*

cia) contact. **tener ~e** have friends in the right places

encía f gum

enciclopedia f encyclopaedia

encierro m confinement; (*cárcel*) prison

encim|a adv on top; (*arriba*) above. **~ de** on, on top of; (*sobre*) over; (*además de*) besides, as well as. **por ~** on top; (*adj ligera*) superficially. **por ~ de todo** above all. **~ar** vt (Mex) stack up. **~era** f worktop

encina f holm oak

encinta adj pregnant

enclenque adj weak; (*enfermizo*) sickly

encoger 14 vt shrink; (*contraer*) contract. **~se** vpr shrink. **~erse de hombros** shrug one's shoulders

encolar vt glue; (*pegar*) stick

encolerizar 10 vt make angry. **~se** vpr get furious

encomendar 1 vt entrust

encomi|ar vt praise. **~o** m praise. **~oso** adj (LAm) complimentary

encono m bitterness, ill will

encontra|do adj contrary, conflicting. **~r** 2 vt find; (*tropezar con*) meet. **~rse** vpr meet; (*hallarse*) be. **no ~rse** feel uncomfortable

encorvar vt hunch. **~se** vpr stoop

encrespa|do adj (pelo) curly; (mar) rough. **~r** vt curl (pelo); make rough (mar)

encrucijada f crossroads

encuaderna|ción f binding. **~dor** m bookbinder. **~r** vt bind

encub|ierto adj hidden. **~rir** (pp encubierto) vt hide, conceal; cover up (delito); shelter (delincuente)

encuentro m meeting; (*en depor-*

tes) match; (*Mil*) encounter

encuesta *f* survey; (*investigación*) inquiry

encumbrado *adj* eminent; (*alto*) high

encurtidos *mpl* pickles

endeble *adj* weak

endemoniado *adj* possessed; (*muy malo*) wretched

enderezar 10 *vt* straighten out; (*poner vertical*) put upright; (*fig, arreglar*) put right, sort out; (*dirigir*) direct. **~se** *vpr* straighten out

endeudarse *vpr* get into debt

endiablado *adj* possessed; (*malo*) terrible; (*difícil*) difficult

endosar *vt* endorse (*cheque*)

endulzar 10 *vt* sweeten; (*fig*) soften

endurecer 11 *vt* harden. **~se** *vpr* harden

enemi|go *adj* enemy. ● *m* enemy. **~stad** *f* enmity. **~star** *vt* make an enemy of. **~starse** *vpr* fall out (*con with*)

en|ergía *f* energy. **~érgico** *adj* (*persona*) lively; (*decisión*) forceful

energúmeno *m* madman

enero *m* January

enésimo *adj* nth, umpteenth [T]

enfad|ado *adj* angry; (*molesto*) annoyed. **~ar** *vt* make cross, anger; (*molestar*) annoy. **~arse** *vpr* get angry; (*molestarse*) get annoyed. **~o** *m* anger; (*molestia*) annoyance

énfasis *m invar* emphasis, stress. poner **~** stress, emphasize

enfático *adj* emphatic

enferm|ar *vi* fall ill. **~arse** *vpr* (*LAm*) fall ill. **~edad** *f* illness. **~era** *f* nurse. **~ería** *f* sick bay; (*carrera*) nursing. **~ero** *m* (*male*) nurse

~izo *adj* sickly. **~o** *adj* ill. ● *m* patient

enflaquecer 11 *vt* make thin. ● *vi* lose weight

enfo|car 7 *vt* shine on; focus (*lente*); (*fig*) approach. **~que** *m* focus; (*fig*) approach

enfrentar *vt* face, confront; (*poner frente a frente*) bring face to face. **~se** *vpr*. **~se con** confront; (*en deportes*) meet

enfrente *adv* opposite. **~** de opposite. de **~** opposite

enfria|miento *m* cooling; (*catarro*) cold. **~r** 20 *vt* cool (down); (*fig*) cool down. **~rse** *vpr* go cold; (*fig*) cool off

enfurecer 11 *vt* infuriate. **~se** *vpr* get furious

engalanar *vt* adorn. **~se** *vpr* dress up

enganchar *vt* hook; hang up (*ropa*). **~se** *vpr* get caught; (*Mil*) enlist

engañ|ar *vt* deceive, trick; (*ser infiel*) be unfaithful. **~arse** *vpr* be wrong, be mistaken; (*no admitir la verdad*) deceive o.s. **~o** *m* deceit, trickery; (*error*) mistake. **~oso** *adj* deceptive; (*persona*) deceitful

engarzar 10 *vt* string (*cuentas*); set (*joyas*)

engatusar *vt* [T] coax

engendr|ar *vt* father; (*fig*) breed. **~o** *m* (*monstruo*) monster; (*fig*) brainchild

englobar *vt* include

engomar *vt* glue

engordar *vt* fatten, gain (*kilo*). ● *vi* get fatter, put on weight

engorro *m* nuisance

engranaje *m* (*Auto*) gear

engrandecer 11 *vt* (*enaltecer*) exalt, raise

engrasar vt grease; (con aceite) oil; (ensuciar) get grease on

engreído adj arrogant

engullir 22 vt gulp down

enhebrar vt thread

enhorabuena f congratulations. dar la ~ congratulate

enigm|a m enigma. ~ático adj enigmatic

enjabonar vt soap. ~se vpr to soap o.s.

enjambre m swarm

enjaular vt put in a cage

enjuag|ar 12 vt rinse. ~ue m rinsing; (para la boca) mouthwash

enjugar 12 vt wipe (away)

enjuiciar vt pass judgement on

enjuto adj (persona) skinny

enlace m connection; (matrimonial) wedding

enlatar vt tin, can

enlazar 10 vt link; tie together (cintas); (Mex, casar) marry

enlodar vt, **enlodazar** 10 vt cover in mud

enloquecer 11 vt drive mad. ● vi go mad. ~se vpr go mad

enlosar vt (con losas) pave; (con baldosas) tile

enmarañar vt tangle (up), entangle; (confundir) confuse. ~se vpr get into a tangle; (confundirse) get confused

enmarcar 7 vt frame

enm|endar vt correct. ~endarse vpr mend one's way. ~ienda f correction; (de ley etc) amendment

enmohecerse 11 vpr (con óxido) go rusty; (con hongos) go mouldy

enmudecer 11 vi be dumbstruck; (callar) fall silent

ennegrecer 11 vt blacken

ennoblecer 11 vt ennoble; (fig) add style to

enoj|adizo adj irritable. ~ado adj angry; (molesto) annoyed. ~ar vt anger; (molestar) annoy. ~arse vpr get angry; (molestarse) get annoyed. ~o m anger; (molestia) annoyance. ~oso adj annoying

enorgullecerse 11 vpr be proud

enorm|e adj huge, enormous. ~emente adv enormously. ~idad f immensity; (de crimen) enormity

enraizado adj deeply rooted

enrarecido adj rarefied

enred|adera f creeper. ~ar vt tangle (up), entangle; (confundir) confuse; (involucrar) involve. ~arse vpr get tangled; (confundirse) get confused; (persona) get involved (con with). ~o m tangle; (fig) muddle, mess

enrejado m bars

enriquecer 11 vt make rich; (fig) enrich. ~se vpr get rich

enrojecerse 11 vpr (persona) go red, blush

enrolar vt enlist

enrollar vt roll (up), wind (hilo etc)

enroscar 7 vt coil; (atornillar) screw in

ensalad|a f salad. armar una ~a make a mess. ~era f salad bowl. ~illa f Russian salad

ensalzar 10 vt praise; (enaltecer) exalt

ensambla|dura f, **ensamblaje** m (acción) assembling; (efecto) joint. ~r vt join

ensanch|ar vt widen; (agrandar) enlarge. ~arse vpr get wider. ~e m widening

ensangrentar 1 vt stain with blood

ensañarse | entraña

ensañarse *vpr.* ~ **con** treat cruelly

ensartar *vt* string (cuentas etc)

ensay|ar *vt* test; rehearse (obra de teatro etc). ~**o** *m* test, trial; (*composición literaria*) essay

enseguida *adv* at once, immediately

ensenada *f* inlet, cove

enseña|nza *f* education; (*acción de enseñar*) teaching. ~**nza media** secondary education. ~**r** *vt* teach; (*mostrar*) show

enseres *mpl* equipment

ensillar *vt* saddle

ensimismarse *vpr* be lost in thought

ensombrecer 🔢 *vt* darken

ensordecer 🔢 *vt* deafen. ● *vi* go deaf

ensuciar *vt* dirty. ~**se** *vpr* get dirty

ensueño *m* dream

entablar *vt* (*empezar*) start

entablillar *vt* put in a splint

entallar *vt* tailor (un vestido). ● *vi* fit

entarimado *m* parquet; (*plataforma*) platform

ente *m* entity, being; (*fam, persona rara*) weirdo; (*Com*) firm, company

entend|er 🔢 *vt* understand; (*opinar*) believe, think. ● *vi* understand. ~**er** de know about. **a mi** ~**er** in my opinion. **dar a** ~**er** hint. **darse a** ~**er** (*LAm*) make o.s. understood ~**erse** *vpr* make o.s. understood; (*comprenderse*) be understood. ~**erse con** get on with. ~**ido** adj understood; (*enterado*) well-informed. **no darse por** ~**ido** pretend not to understand. ● *interj* agreed!, OK! 🔢. ~**imiento** *m* understanding

entera|do *adj* well-informed; (*que sabe*) aware. **darse por** ~**do** take the hint. ● ~**r** *vt* inform (**de** of). ~**rse** *vpr.* ~**rse de** find out about, hear of. **¡entérate!** listen! **¿te** ~**s?** do you understand?

entereza *f* (*carácter*) strength of character

enternecer 🔢 *vt* (*fig*) move, touch. ~**se** *vpr* be moved, be touched

entero *adj* entire, whole. **por** ~ entirely, completely

enterra|dor *m* gravedigger. ~**r** 🔢 *vt* bury

entibiar *vt* (*enfriar*) cool; (*calentar*) warm (up). ~**se** *vpr* (*enfriarse*) cool down; (*fig*) cool; (*calentarse*) get warm

entidad *f* entity; (*organización*) organization; (*Com*) company; (*importancia*) significance

entierro *m* burial; (*ceremonia*) funeral

entona|ción *f* intonation. ~**r** *vt* intone; sing (nota). ● *vi* (*Mus*) be in tune; (*colores*) match. ~**rse** *vpr* (*emborracharse*) get tipsy

entonces *adv* then. **en aquel** ~ at that time, then

entorn|ado *adj* (*puerta*) ajar; (*ventana*) slightly open. ~**o** *m* environment; (*en literatura*) setting

entorpecer 🔢 *vt* dull; slow down (*tráfico*); (*dificultar*) hinder

entra|da *f* entrance; (*incorporación*) admission, entry; (*para cine* etc) ticket; (*de datos, Tec*) input; (*de una comida*) starter. **de** ~**da** right away. ~**do** *adj.* ~**do en años** elderly. **ya** ~**da la noche** late at night. ~**nte** *adj* next, coming

entraña *f* (*fig*) heart. ~**s** *fpl* entrails; (*fig*) heart. ~**ble** *adj* (*cariño*) deep; (amigo) close. ~r vt involve

entrar vt (traer) bring in; (llevar) take in. ● vi go in, enter; (venir) come in, enter; (empezar) start, begin; (incorporarse) join. ~ en, (LAm) ~ a go into

entre prep (dos personas o cosas) between; (más de dos) among(st)

entre|abierto adj half-open. ~abrir (pp entreabierto) vt half open. ~acto m interval. ~cejo m forehead. fruncir el ~cejo frown. ~cerrar **1** vt (LAm) half close. ~cortado adj (voz) faltering; (respiración) laboured. ~cruzar **10** vt intertwine

entrega f handing over; (de mercancías etc) delivery; (de novela etc) instalment. (dedicación) commitment. ~r **12** vt deliver; (dar) give; hand in (deberes); hand over (poder). ~rse vpr surrender, give o.s. up; (dedicarse) devote o.s. (a to)

entre|lazar **10** vt intertwine. ~més m hors-d'oeuvre; (en el teatro) short comedy. ~mezclar vt intermingle

entrena|dor m trainer. ~miento m training. ~r vt train. ~rse vpr train

entre|pierna f crotch; medida inside leg measurement. ~piso m (LAm) mezzanine. ~sacar **7** pick out; (peluquería) thin out ~suelo m mezzanine; (de cine) dress circle ~tanto adv meanwhile, in the meantime ~tejer vt weave; (entrelazar) interweave

entreten|ción f (LAm) entertainment. ~er **40** vt entertain, amuse; (detener) delay, keep. ~erse vpr amuse o.s.; (tardar) delay, linger. ~ido adj (con ser) entertaining;

(con estar) busy. ~imiento m entertainment

entrever **43** vt make out, glimpse

entrevista f interview; (reunión) meeting. ~rse vpr have an interview

entristecer **11** vt sadden, make sad. ~se vpr grow sad

entromet|erse vpr interfere. ~ido adj interfering

entumec|erse **11** vpr go numb. ~ido adj numb

enturbiar vt cloud

entusi|asmar vt fill with enthusiasm; (gustar mucho) delight. ~asmarse vpr. ~asmarse con get enthusiastic about. ~asmo m enthusiasm. ~asta adj enthusiastic. ● m & f enthusiast

enumerar vt enumerate

envalentonar vt encourage. ~se vpr become bolder

envas|ado m packaging; (en latas) canning; (en botellas) bottling. ~ar vt package; (en latas) tin, can; (en botellas) bottle. ~e m packing; (lata) tin, can; (botella) bottle

envejec|er **11** vt make (look) older. ● vi age, grow old. ~erse vpr age, grow old

envenenar vt poison

envergadura f importance

envia|do m envoy; (de la prensa) correspondent. ~r **20** vt send

enviciarse vpr become addicted (con to)

envidi|a f envy; (celos) jealousy. ~ar vt envy, be envious of. ~oso adj envious; (celoso) jealous. tener ~a a envy

envío m sending, dispatch; (de

mercancías) consignment; (de dinero) remittance. ~ contra reembolso cash on delivery. gastos mpl de ~ postage and packing (costs)

enviudar vi be widowed

env|oltura f wrapping. **~olver** 2 (pp envuelto) vt wrap; (cubrir) cover; (rodear) surround; (fig, enredar) involve. **~uelto** adj wrapped (up)

enyesar vt plaster; (Med) put in plaster

épica f epic

épico adj epic

epid|emia f epidemic. **~émico** adj epidemic

epil|epsia f epilepsy. **~éptico** adj epileptic

epílogo m epilogue

episodio m episode

epístola f epistle

epitafio m epitaph

época f age; (período) period. hacer ~ make history, be epoch-making

equidad f equity

equilibr|ado adj (well-)balanced. **~ar** vt balance. **~io** m balance; (de balanza) equilibrium. **~ista** m & f tightrope walker

equinoccio m equinox

equipaje m luggage (esp Brit), baggage (esp Amer)

equipar vt equip; (de ropa) fit out

equiparar vt make equal; (comparar) compare

equipo m equipment; (de personas) team

equitación f riding

equivale|nte adj equivalent. **~r** 42 vi be equivalent; (significar) mean

equivoca|ción f mistake, error.

~do adj wrong. **~rse** vpr make a mistake; (estar en error) be wrong, be mistaken. **~rse de** be wrong about. **~rse de número** dial the wrong number. si no me equivoco if I'm not mistaken

equívoco adj equivocal; (sospechoso) suspicious ● m misunderstanding; (error) mistake

era f era. ● vb véase SER

erario m treasury

erección f erection

eres vb véase SER

erguir 48 vt raise. **~se** vpr raise

erigir 14 vt erect. **~se** vpr ~se en set o.s. up as; (llegar a ser) become

eriza|do adj prickly. **~rse** 10 vpr stand on end; (LAm) (persona) get goose pimples

erizo m hedgehog; (de mar) sea urchin. ~ de mar sea urchin

ermita f hermitage. **~ño** m hermit

erosi|ón f erosion. **~onar** vt erode

er|ótico adj erotic. **~otismo** m eroticism

err|ar 1 (la i inicial pasa a ser y) vt miss. ● vi wander; (equivocarse) make a mistake, be wrong. **~ata** f misprint. **~óneo** adj erroneous, wrong. **~or** m error, mistake. estar en un **~or** be wrong, be mistaken

eruct|ar vi belch. **~o** m belch

erudi|ción f learning, erudition. **~to** adj learned; (palabra) erudite

erupción f eruption; (Med) rash

es vb véase SER

esa adj véase ESE

ésa pron véase ÉSE

esbelto adj slender, slim

esboz|ar 10 vt sketch, outline. **~o**

e

m sketch, outline

escabeche *m* brine. en ~ pickled

escabroso *adj* (terreno) rough; (asunto) difficult; (atrevido) crude

escabullirse 22 *vpr* slip away

escafandra *f* diving-suit

escala *f* scale; (escalera de mano) ladder; (Aviac) stopover. hacer ~ en stop at. vuelo sin ~s non-stop flight. ~da *f* climbing; (Pol) escalation. ~r *vt* climb; break into (una casa). • *vi* climb, go climbing

escaldar *vt* scald

escalera *f* staircase, stairs; (de mano) ladder. ~ de caracol spiral staircase. ~ de incendios fire escape. ~ de tijera step-ladder. ~ mecánica escalator

escalfa|do *adj* poached. ~r *vt* poach

escalinata *f* flight of steps

escalofrío *m* shiver. tener ~s be shivering

escalón *m* step, stair; (de escala) rung

escalope *m* escalope

escam|a *f* scale; (de jabón, de la piel) flake. ~oso *adj* scaly; (piel) flaky

escamotear *vt* make disappear; (robar) steal, pinch

escampar *vt* stop raining

esc|andalizar 10 *vt* scandalize, shock. ~andalizarse *vpr* be shocked. ~ándalo *m* scandal; (alboroto) commotion, racket. armar un ~ make a scene. ~andaloso *adj* scandalous; (alborotador) noisy

escandinavo *adj & m* Scandinavian

escaño *m* bench; (Pol) seat

escapa|da *f* escape; (visita) flying visit. ~r *vi* escape. dejar ~r let

out ~rse *vpr* escape; (líquido, gas) leak

escaparate *m* (shop) window

escap|atoria *f* (fig) way out. ~e *m* (de gas, de líquido) leak; (fuga) escape; (Auto) exhaust

escarabajo *m* beetle

escaramuza *f* skirmish

escarbar *vt* scratch; pick (dientes, herida); (fig, escudriñar) pry (en into). ~se *vpr* pick

escarcha *f* frost. ~do *adj* (fruta) crystallized

escarlat|a *adj invar* scarlet. ~ina *f* scarlet fever

escarm|entar 1 *vt* teach a lesson to. • *vi* learn one's lesson. ~iento *m* punishment; (lección) lesson

escarola *f* endive

escarpado *adj* steep

escas|ear *vi* be scarce. ~ez *f* scarcity, shortage; (pobreza) poverty. ~o *adj* scarce; (poco) little; (muy justo) barely. ~o de short of

escatimar *vt* be sparing with

escayola *f* plaster

esc|ena *f* scene; (escenario) stage. ~enario *m* stage; (fig) scene. ~énico *adj* stage. ~enografía *f* set design

esc|epticismo *m* scepticism. ~éptico *adj* sceptical. • *m* sceptic

esclarecer 11 *vt* (fig) throw light on, clarify

esclav|itud *f* slavery. ~izar 10 *vt* enslave. ~o *m* slave

esclusa *f* lock; (de presa) floodgate

escoba *f* broom

escocer 2 & 9 *vi* sting

escocés *adj* Scottish. • *m* Scot

Escocia *f* Scotland

escog|er 🔟 vt choose. **~ido** adj chosen; (mercancía) choice; (clientela) select

escolar adj school. ● m schoolboy. ● f schoolgirl

escolta f escort

escombros mpl rubble

escond|er vt hide. **~erse** vpr hide. **~idas** fpl (LAm, juego) hide-and-seek. a **~idas** secretly. **~ite** m hiding place; (juego) hide-and-seek. **~rijo** m hiding place

escopeta f shotgun

escoria f slag; (fig) dregs

escorpión m scorpion

Escorpión m Scorpio

escot|ado adj low-cut. **~e** m low neckline. pagar a **~e** share the expenses

escozor m stinging

escri|bano m clerk. **~bir** (pp escrito) vt/i write. **~bir a máquina** type. ¿cómo se escribe...? how do you spell...? **~birse** vpr write to each other. **~to** adj written. por **~to** in writing. ● m document. **~tor** m writer. **~torio** m desk; (oficina) office; (LAm, en una casa) study. **~tura** f (hand)writing; (Jurid) deed

escr|úpulo m scruple. **~upuloso** adj scrupulous

escrut|ar vt scrutinize; count (votos). **~inio** m count

escuadr|a f (instrumento) square; (Mil) squad; (Naut) fleet. **~ón** m squadron

escuálido adj skinny

escuchar vt listen to; (esp LAm, oír) hear. ● vi listen

escudo m shield. **~ de armas** coat of arms

escudriñar vt examine

escuela f school. **~ normal** teachers' training college

escueto adj simple

escuincle m (Mex fam) kid 🔟

escul|pir vt sculpture. **~tor** m sculptor. **~tora** f sculptress. **~tura** f sculpture

escupir vt/i spit

escurr|eplatos m invar plate rack. **~idizo** adj slippery. **~ir** vt drain; wring out (ropa). ● vi drain; (ropa) drip. **~irse** vpr slip

ese adj (f esa) that; (mpl esos, fpl esas) those

ése pron (f ésa) that one; (mpl ésos, fpl ésas) those; (primero de dos) the former

esencia f essence. **~l** adj essential. lo **~l** the main thing

esf|era f sphere; (de reloj) face. **~érico** adj spherical

esf|orzarse 🔽 & 🔟 vpr make an effort. **~uerzo** m effort

esfumarse vpr fade away; (persona) vanish

esgrim|a f fencing. **~ir** vt brandish; (fig) use

esguince m sprain

eslabón m link

eslavo adj Slavic, Slavonic

eslogan m slogan

esmalt|ar vt enamel. **~e** m enamel. **~e de uñas** nail polish

esmerado adj careful; (persona) painstaking

esmeralda f emerald

esmer|arse vpr take care (en over).

esmero m care

esmoquin (pl esmóquines) m dinner jacket, tuxedo (Amer)

esnob adj invar snobbish. ● m & f (pl **~s**) snob. **~ismo** m snobbery

e

esnórkel *m* snorkel
eso *pron* that. ¡~ es! that's it! ~ mismo exactly. a ~ de about. en ~ at that moment. ¿no es ~? isn't that right? por ~ that's why. y ~ que even though
esos *adj pl véase* ESE
ésos *pron pl véase* ESE
espabila|do *adj* bright; (*despierto*) awake. ~**r** *vt* (*avivar*) brighten up; (*despertar*) wake up. ~**rse** *vpr* wake up; (*avivarse*) wise up; (*apresurarse*) hurry up
espaci|al *adj* space. ~**ar** *vt* space out. ~**o** *m* space. ~**oso** *adj* spacious
espada *f* sword. ~**s** *fpl* (*en naipes*) spades
espaguetis *mpl* spaghetti
espald|a *f* back. a ~**s de** uno behind s.o.'s back. **volver la(s)** ~**a(s)** a uno give s.o. the cold shoulder. ~ **mojada** wetback. ~**illa** *f* shoulder-blade
espant|ajo *m*, ~**apájaros** *m invar* scarecrow. ~**ar** *vt* frighten; (*ahuyentar*) frighten away. ~**arse** *vpr* be frightened; (*ahuyentarse*) be frightened away. ~**o** *m* terror; (*horror*) horror. ¡qué ~**o!** how awful! ~**oso** *adj* horrific; (*terrible*) terrible
España *f* Spain
español *adj* Spanish. ● *m* (*persona*) Spaniard; (*lengua*) Spanish. **los** ~**es** the Spanish
esparadrapo *m* (sticking) plaster
esparcir ⑨ *vt* scatter; (*difundir*) spread. ~**rse** *vpr* be scattered; (*difundirse*) spread; (*divertirse*) enjoy o.s.
espárrago *m* asparagus
espasm|o *m* spasm. ~**ódico** *adj* spasmodic
espátula *f* spatula; (*en pintura*)

palette knife
especia *f* spice
especial *adj* special. **en** ~ especially. ~**idad** *f* speciality (*Brit*), specialty (*Amer*). ~**ista** *adj* & *m* & *f* specialist. ~**ización** *f* specialization. ~**izarse** ⑩ *vpr* specialize. ~**mente** *adv* especially
especie *f* kind, sort; (*en biología*) species. **en** ~ in kind
especifica|ción *f* specification. ~**r** ⑦ *vt* specify
específico *adj* specific
espect|áculo *m* sight; (*de circo etc*) show. ~**acular** *adj* spectacular. ~**ador** *m* & *f* spectator
espectro *m* spectre; (*en física*) spectrum
especula|dor *m* speculator. ~**r** *vi* speculate
espej|ismo *m* mirage. ~**o** *m* mirror. ~**o retrovisor** (*Auto*) rear-view mirror
espeluznante *adj* horrifying
espera *f* wait. **a la** ~ waiting (de for). ~**nza** *f* hope. ~**r** *vt* hope; (*aguardar*) wait for; expect (vista, carta, bebé). **espero que no** I hope not. **espero que sí** I hope so. ● *vi* (*aguardar*) wait. ~**rse** *vpr* hang on; (*prever*) expect
esperma *f* sperm
esperpento *m* fright
espes|ar *vt/i* thicken. ~**arse** *vpr* thicken. ~**o** *adj* thick. ~**or** *m* thickness
espetón *m* spit
esp|ía *f* spy. ~**iar** ⑳ *vt* spy on. ● *vi* spy
espiga *f* (*de trigo etc*) ear
espina *f* thorn; (*de pez*) bone; (*en anatomía*) spine. ~ **dorsal** spine
espinaca *f* spinach

espinazo *m* spine

espinilla *f* shin; (*Med*) blackhead; (*LAm, grano*) spot

espino *m* hawthorn. ~**so** *adj* thorny; (*fig*) difficult

espionaje *m* espionage

espiral *adj & f* spiral

esp|iritista *m & f* spiritualist. ~**íritu** *m* spirit; (*mente*) mind. ~**íritual** *adj* spiritual

espl|éndido *adj* splendid; (*persona*) generous. ~**endor** *m* splendour

espolear *vt* spur (on)

espolvorear *vt* sprinkle

esponj|a *f* sponge. ~**oso** *adj* spongy

espont|aneidad *f* spontaneity. ~**áneo** *adj* spontaneous

esporádico *adj* sporadic

espos|a *f* wife. ~**as** *fpl* handcuffs. ~**ar** *vt* handcuff. ~**o** *m* husband

espuela *f* spur; (*fig*) incentive

espum|a *f* foam; (*en bebidas*) froth; (*de jabón*) lather; (*de las olas*) surf. **echar** ~**a** foam, froth. ~**oso** *adj* (*vino*) sparkling

esqueleto *m* skeleton; (*estructura*) framework

esquema *m* outline

esqu|í *m* (*pl* ~**is**, ~**íes**) ski; (*deporte*) skiing. ~**iar** 20 *vi* ski

esquilar *vt* shear

esquimal *adj & m* Eskimo

esquina *f* corner

esquiv|ar *vt* avoid; dodge (*golpe*). ~**o** *adj* elusive

esquizofrénico *adj & m* schizophrenic

esta *adj véase* ESTE

ésta *pron véase* ÉSTE

estab|ilidad *f* stability. ~**le** *adj* stable

establec|er 11 *vt* establish. ~**erse** *vpr* settle; (*Com*) set up. ~**imiento** *m* establishment

establo *m* cattleshed

estaca *f* stake

estación *f* station; (*del año*) season. ~ **de invierno** winter (sports) resort. ~ **de servicio** service station

estaciona|miento *m* parking; (*LAm, lugar*) car park (*Brit*), parking lot (*Amer*). ~**r** *vt* station; (*Auto*) park. ~**rio** *adj* stationary

estadía *f* (*LAm*) stay

estadio *m* stadium; (*fase*) stage

estadista *m* statesman. ● *f* stateswoman

estadístic|a *f* statistics; (*cifra*) statistic. ~**o** *adj* statistical

estado *m* state; (*Med*) condition. ~ **civil** marital status. ~ **de ánimo** frame of mind. ~ **de cuenta** bank statement. ~ **mayor** (*Mil*) staff. **en buen** ~ in good condition

Estados Unidos *mpl* United States

estadounidense *adj* American, United States. ● *m & f* American

estafa *f* swindle. ~**r** *vt* swindle

estafeta *f* (*oficina de correos*) (sub-)post office

estala|ctita *f* stalactite. ~**gmita** *f* stalagmite

estall|ar *vi* explode; (*olas*) break; (*guerra etc*) break out; (*fig*) burst. ~**ar en llanto** burst into tears. ~**ar de risa** burst out laughing. ~**ido** *m* explosion; (*de guerra etc*) outbreak

estamp|a *f* print; (*aspecto*) appearance. ~**ado** *adj* printed. ●*m* printing; (*motivo*) pattern; (*tela*) cotton print. ~**ar** *vt* stamp;

(*imprimir*) print

estampido m bang

estampilla f (*LAm, de correos*) (postage) stamp

estanca|do adj stagnant. ~r **7** vt stem. ~rse vpr stagnate

estancia f stay; (*cuarto*) large room

estanco adj watertight. ● m tobacconist's (shop)

> **estanco** In Spain, an establishment selling tobacco, stamps, bus and metro passes and other products whose sale is restricted. Cigarettes etc are sold in bars and cafés but at higher prices. *Estancos* also sell stationery and sometimes papers.

estandarte m standard, banner

estanque m pond; (*depósito de agua*) (water) tank

estanquero m tobacconist

estante m shelf. ~ría f shelves; (*para libros*) bookcase

estaño m tin

estar 27

● *verbo intransitivo*

····▸ to be ¿cómo estás? how are you?. estoy enfermo I'm ill. está muy cerca it's very near. ¿está Pedro? is Pedro in? ¿cómo está el tiempo? what's the weather like? ya estamos en invierno it's winter already

····▸ (*quedarse*) to stay. sólo ~é una semana I'll only be staying for a week. estoy en un hotel I'm staying in a hotel

····▸ (*con fecha*) ¿a cuánto estamos? what's the date today?

estamos a 8 de mayo it's the 8th of May.

····▸ (*en locuciones*) ¿estamos? all right? ¡ahí está! that's it! ~ por (*apoyar a*) to support; (*LAm, encontrarse a punto de*) to be about to; (*quedar por*) eso está por verse that remains to be seen. son cuentas que están por pagar they're bills still to be paid

● *verbo auxiliar*

····▸ (*con gerundio*) estaba estudiando I was studying

····▸ (*con participio*) está condenado a muerte he's been sentenced to death. está mal traducido it's wrongly translated.

estarse *verbo pronominal* to stay. no se está quieto he won't stay still

➡ Cuando el verbo **estar** forma parte de expresiones como **estar de acuerdo, estar a la vista, estar constipado,** etc., ver bajo el respectivo nombre o adjetivo

estatal adj state

estático adj static

estatua f statue

estatura f height

estatuto m statute; (*norma*) rule

este adj (*región*) eastern; (*viento, lado*) east. ● m east. ● adj (*f esta*) this; (*mpl estos, fpl estas*) these. ● int (*LAm*) well, er

éste pron (*f ésta*) this one; (*mpl éstos, fpl éstas*) these; (*segundo de dos*) the latter

estela f wake; (*de avión*) trail; (*lápida*) carved stone

estera f mat; (*tejido*) matting

est|éreo adj stereo. ~ereofónico adj stereo, stereophonic

estereotipo m stereotype

estéril adj sterile; (terreno) barren

esterilla f mat

esterlina adj. libra f ~ pound sterling

estético adj aesthetic

estiércol m dung; (abono) manure

estigma m stigma. ~s mpl (Relig) stigmata

estil|arse vpr be used. ~o m style; (en natación) stroke. ~ mariposa butterfly. ~ pecho (LAm) breaststroke. por el ~o of that sort

estilográfica f fountain pen

estima f esteem. ~do adj (amigo, colega) valued. ~do señor (en cartas) Dear Sir. ~r vt esteem; have great respect for (persona); (valorar) value; (juzgar) consider

est|imulante adj stimulating. • m stimulant. ~imular vt stimulate; (incitar) incite. ~imulo m stimulus

estir|ado adj stretched; (persona) haughty. ~ar vt stretch; (fig) stretch out. ~ón m pull, tug; (crecimiento) sudden growth

estirpe m stock

esto pron neutro this; (este asunto) this business. en ~ at this point. en ~ de in this business of. por ~ therefore

estofa|do adj stewed. • m stew. ~r vt stew

estómago m stomach. dolor de ~ stomach ache

estorb|ar vt obstruct; (molestar) bother. • vi be in the way. ~o m hindrance; (molestia) nuisance

estornud|ar vi sneeze. ~o m sneeze

estos adj mpl véase ESTE

éstos pron mpl véase ÉSTE

estoy vb véase ESTAR

estrabismo m squint

estrado m stage; (Mus) bandstand

estrafalario adj eccentric; (ropa) outlandish

estrago m devastation. hacer ~os devastate

estragón m tarragon

estrambótico adj eccentric; (ropa) outlandish

estrangula|dor m strangler; (Auto) choke. ~r vt strangle

estratagema f stratagem

estrat|ega m & f strategist. ~egia f strategy. ~égico adj strategic

estrato m stratum

estrech|ar vt make narrower; take in (vestido); embrace (persona). ~ar la mano a uno shake hands with s.o. ~arse vpr become narrower; (abrazarse) embrace. ~ez f narrowness. ~eces fpl financial difficulties. ~o adj narrow; (vestido etc) tight; (fig, íntimo) close. ~o de miras narrow-minded. • m strait(s)

estrella f star. ~ de mar starfish. ~ado adj starry

estrellar vt smash; crash (coche). ~se vpr crash (contra into)

estremec|er 🔢 vt shake. ~erse vpr shake; (de emoción etc) tremble (with). ~imiento m shaking

estren|ar vt wear for the first time (vestido etc); show for the first time (película). ~arse vpr make one's début. ~o m (de película) première; (de obra de teatro) first night; (de persona) debut

estreñi|do adj constipated. ~miento m constipation

estrés m stress

estria f groove; (de la piel) stretch mark

estribillo m (incl Mus) refrain

estribo m stirrup; (de coche) step. perder los ~s lose one's temper

estribor m starboard

estricto adj strict

estridente adj strident, raucous

estrofa f stanza, verse

estropajo m scourer

estropear vt damage; (plan) spoil; ruin (ropa). ~se vpr be damaged; (averiarse) break down; (ropa) get ruined; (fruta etc) go bad; (fracasar) fail

estructura f structure. ~l adj structural

estruendo m roar; (de mucha gente) uproar

estrujar vt squeeze; wring (out) (ropa); (fig) drain

estuario m estuary

estuche m case

estudi|ante m & f student. ~antil adj student. ~ar vt study. ~o m study; (de artista) studio. ~oso adj studious

estufa f heater; (Mex, cocina) cooker

estupefac|iente m narcotic. ~to adj astonished

estupendo adj marvellous; (persona) fantastic; ¡~! that's great!

est|upidez f stupidity; (acto) stupid thing. ~úpido adj stupid

estupor m amazement

estuve vb véase ESTAR

etapa f stage. por ~s in stages

etéreo adj ethereal

etern|idad f eternity. ~o adj eternal

étic|a f ethics. ~o adj ethical

etimología f etymology

etiqueta f ticket, tag; (ceremonial) etiquette. de ~ formal

étnico adj ethnic

eucalipto m eucalyptus

eufemismo m euphemism

euforia f euphoria

euro m euro. ~escéptico adj & m Eurosceptic

Europa f Europe

euro|peo adj & m European. ~zona f eurozone

eutanasia f euthanasia

evacua|ción f evacuation. ~r 21 vt evacuate

evadir vt avoid; evade (impuestos). ~se vpr escape

evalua|ción f evaluation. ~r 21 vt assess; evaluate (datos)

evangeli|o m gospel. ~sta m & f evangelist; (Mex, escribiente) scribe

evapora|ción f evaporation. ~rse vpr evaporate; (fig) disappear

evasi|ón f evasion; (fuga) escape. ~vo adj evasive

evento m event; (caso) case

eventual adj possible. ~idad f eventuality

eviden|cia f evidence. poner en ~cia a uno show s.o. up. ~ciar vt show. ~ciarse vpr be obvious. ~te adj obvious. ~temente adv obviously

evitar vt avoid; (ahorrar) spare; (prevenir) prevent

evocar 7 vt evoke

evolu|ción f evolution. ~onar vi evolve; (Mil) manoeuvre

ex prefijo ex-, former

exacerbar vt exacerbate

exact|amente adv exactly. ~itud f exactness. ~o adj exact; (preciso) accurate; (puntual) punctual. ¡~! exactly!

exagera|ción f exaggeration. ~do adj exaggerated. ~r vt/i exaggerate

exalta|do adj exalted; (excitado) (over)excited; (fanático) hotheaded. ~r vt exalt. ~rse vpr get excited

exam|en m exam, examination. ~inar vt examine. ~inarse vpr take an exam

exasperar vt exasperate. ~se vpr get exasperated

excarcela|ción f release (from prison). ~r vt release

excava|ción f excavation. ~dora f digger. ~r vt excavate

excede|ncia f leave of absence. ~nte adj & m surplus. ~r vi exceed. ~rse vpr go too far

excelen|cia f excellence; (tratamiento) Excellency. ~te adj excellent

exc|entricidad f eccentricity. ~éntrico adj & m eccentric

excepci|ón f exception. ~onal adj exceptional. a ~ón de, con ~ón de except (for)

except|o prep except (for). ~uar [21] vt except

exces|ivo adj excessive. ~o m excess. ~o de equipaje excess luggage (esp Brit), excess baggage (esp Amer)

excita|ción f excitement. ~r vt excite; (incitar) incite. ~rse vpr get excited

exclama|ción f exclamation. ~r vi exclaim

exclu|ir [17] vt exclude. ~sión f exclusion. ~siva f sole right; (reportaje) exclusive (story). ~sivo adj exclusive

excomu|lgar [12] vt excommuni-

cate. ~nión f excommunication

excremento m excrement

excursi|ón f excursion, outing. ~onista m & f day-tripper

excusa f excuse; (disculpa) apology. presentar sus ~s apologize. ~r vt excuse

exento adj exempt; (libre) free

exhalar vt exhale, breath out; give off (olor etc)

exhaust|ivo adj exhaustive. ~o adj exhausted

exhibi|ción f exhibition; (demostración) display. ~cionista m & f exhibitionist. ~r vt exhibit ~rse vpr show o.s.; (hacerse notar) draw attention to o.s.

exhumar vt exhume; (fig) dig up

exig|encia f demand. ~ente adj demanding. ~ir [14] vt demand

exiguo adj meagre

exil|(i)ado adj exiled. ●m exile. ~(i)arse vpr go into exile. ~io m exile

exim|ente m reason for exemption; (Jurid) grounds for acquittal. ~ir vt exempt

existencia f existence. ~s fpl stock. ~lismo m existentialism

exist|ente adj existing. ~ir vi exist

éxito m success. no tener ~ fail. tener ~ be successful

exitoso adj successful

éxodo m exodus

exonerar vt exonerate

exorbitante adj exorbitant

exorci|smo m exorcism. ~zar [10] vt exorcise

exótico adj exotic

expan|dir vt expand; (fig) spread. ~dirse vpr expand. ~sión f expansion. **~sivo** adj expansive

expatria|do adj & m expatriate. **~rse** vpr emigrate; (exiliarse) go into exile

expectativa f prospect; (esperanza) expectation. estar a la ~ be waiting

expedi|ción f expedition; (de documento) issue; (de mercancías) dispatch. **~ente** m record, file; (Jurid) proceedings. **~r 5** vt issue; (enviar) dispatch, send. **~to** adj clear; (LAm, fácil) easy

expeler vt expel

expend|edor m dealer. **~edor automático** vending machine. **~io** m (LAm) shop; (venta) sale

expensas fpl (Jurid) costs. a ~ de at the expense of. a mis ~ at my expense

experiencia f experience

experiment|al adj experimental. **~ar** vt test, experiment with; (sentir) experience. **~o** m experiment

experto adj & m expert

expiar 20 vt atone for

expirar vi expire

explanada f levelled area; (paseo) esplanade

explayarse vpr speak at length; (desahogarse) unburden o.s. (con to)

explica|ción f explanation. **~r 7** vt explain. **~rse** vpr understand; (hacerse comprender) explain o.s. no me lo explico I can't understand it

explícito adj explicit

explora|ción f exploration. **~dor** m explorer; (muchacho) boy scout. **~r** vt explore

explosi|ón f explosion; (fig) outburst. **~onar** vt blow up. **~vo**

adj & m explosive

explota|ción f working; (abuso) exploitation. **~r** vt work (mina); farm (tierra); (abusar) exploit. ● vi explode

expone|nte m exponent. **~r 34** vt expose; display (mercancías); present (tema); set out (hechos); exhibit (cuadros etc); (arriesgar) risk. ● vi exhibit. **~rse** vpr. **~se a** que run the risk of

exporta|ción f export. **~dor** m exporter. **~r** vt export

exposición f exposure; (de cuadros etc) exhibition; (de hechos) exposition

expres|ar vt express. **~arse** vpr express o.s. **~ión** f expression. **~ivo** adj expressive; (cariñoso) affectionate

expreso adj express. ● m express; (café) expresso

exprimi|dor m squeezer. **~r** vt squeeze

expropiar vt expropriate

expuesto adj on display; (lugar etc) exposed; (peligroso) dangerous. estar ~ a be exposed to

expuls|ar vt expel; throw out (persona); send off (jugador). **~ión** f expulsion

exquisito adj exquisite; (de sabor) delicious

éxtasis m invar ecstasy

extend|er 1 vt spread (out); (ampliar) extend; issue (documento). **~erse** vpr spread; (paisaje etc) extend, stretch. **~ido** adj spread out; (generalizado) widespread; (brazos) outstretched

extens|amente adv widely; (detalladamente) in full. **~ión** f extension; (área) expanse; (largo) length.

~o adj extensive

extenuar 🔢 vt exhaust

exterior adj external, exterior; (del extranjero) foreign; (aspecto etc) outward. ● m outside, exterior; (países extranjeros) abroad

extermin|ación f extermination. **~ar** vt exterminate. **~io** m extermination

externo adj external; (signo etc) outward. ● m day pupil

extin|ción f extinction. **~guidor** m (LAm) fire extinguisher. **~guir** 🔢 vt extinguish. **~guirse** vpr die out; (fuego) go out. **~to** adj (raza etc) extinct. **~tor** m fire extinguisher

extirpar vt eradicate; remove (tumor)

extorsión f extortion

extra adj invar extra; (de buena calidad) good-quality; (huevos) large. paga f ~ bonus

extracto m extract

extradición f extradition

extraer 🔢 vt extract

extranjer|ía f (Esp) la ley de ~ immigration law. **~o** adj foreign. ● m foreigner; (países) foreign countries. del ~ from abroad. en el ~, por el ~ abroad

extrañar vt surprise; (encontrar extraño) find strange; (LAm, echar de menos) miss. **~arse** vpr be surprised (de at). **~eza** f strangeness; (asombro) surprise. **~o** adj strange. ● m stranger

extraoficial adj unofficial

extraordinario adj extraordinary

extrarradio m outlying districts

extraterrestre adj extraterrestrial. ● m alien

extravagan|cia f oddness, ec-

centricity. **~te** adj odd, eccentric

extrav|iado adj lost. **~iar** 🔢 vt lose. **~iarse** vpr get lost; (objetos) go missing. **~ío** m loss

extremar vt take extra (precauciones); tighten up (vigilancia). **~se** vpr make every effort

extremeño adj from Extremadura

extrem|idad f end. **~idades** fpl extremities. **~ista** adj & m & f extremist. **~o** adj extreme. ● m end; (colmo) extreme. en ~ extremely. en último ~o as a last resort

extrovertido adj & m extrovert

exuberan|cia f exuberance. **~te** adj exuberant

eyacular vt/i ejaculate

••••••••••••••••••••••••••••••••••

Ff

••••••••••••••••••••••••••••••••••

fa m F; (solfa) fah

fabada f bean and pork stew

fábrica f factory. marca f de ~ trade mark

fabrica|ción f manufacture. **~ción en serie** mass production. **~nte** m & f manufacturer. **~r** 🔢 vt manufacture

fábula f fable; (mentira) fabrication

fabuloso adj fabulous

facci|ón f faction. **~ones** fpl (de la cara) features

faceta f facet

facha f (fam, aspecto) look. **~da** f façade

fácil adj easy; (probable) likely

facili|dad f ease; (disposición) aptitude. **~dades** fpl facilities. **~tar** vt facilitate; (proporcionar) provide

factible adj feasible

factor m factor

factura f bill, invoice. **~r** vt (hacer la factura) invoice; (al embarcar) check in

faculta|d f faculty; (capacidad) ability; (poder) power. **~tivo** adj optional

faena f job. **~s domésticas** housework

faisán m pheasant

faja f (de la cintura) strip; (corsé) corset; (Mil etc) sash

fajo m bundle; (de billetes) wad

falda f skirt; (de montaña) side

falla f fault; (defecto) flaw. **~ humana** (LAm) human error. **~r** vi fail. **me falló** he let me down. **sin ~r** without fail. ● vt (errar) miss

fallec|er 🔟 vi die. **~ido** m deceased

fallido adj vain; (fracasado) unsuccessful

fallo m (defecto) fault; (error) mistake. **~ humano** human error; (en certamen) decision; (Jurid) ruling

falluca f (Mex) smuggled goods

fals|ear vt falsify, distort. **~ificación** f forgery. **~ificador** m forger. **~ificar** 🔟 vt forge. **~o** adj false; (falsificado) forged; (joya) fake

falt|a f (ausencia) absence; (escasez) shortage; (defecto) fault, defect; (culpa) fault; (error) mistake; (en fútbol etc) foul; (en tenis) fault. **a ~a de** for lack of. **echar en ~a** miss. **hacer ~a** be necessary. **me hace ~** I need. **sacar ~as** find fault. **~o** adj lacking (de in)

---

faltar verbo intransitivo

❗ cuando el verbo **faltar** va precedido del complemento indirecto **le** (o **les, nos** etc) el sujeto en español pasa a ser el objeto en inglés p.ej: **les falta experiencia** they lack experience

····▸ (no estar) to be missing **¿quién falta?** who's missing? **falta una de las chicas** one of the girls is missing. **al abrigo le faltan 3 botones** the coat has three buttons missing. **~ a algo** (no asistir) to be absent from sth; (no acudir) to miss sth

····▸ (no haber suficiente) **va a ~ leche** there won't be enough milk. **nos faltó tiempo** we didn't have enough time

····▸ (no tener) **le falta cariño** he lacks affection

····▸ (hacer falta) **le falta sal** it needs more salt. **¡es lo que nos faltaba!** that's all we needed!

····▸ (quedar) **¿te falta mucho?** are you going to be much longer? **falta poco para Navidad** it's not long until Christmas. **aún falta mucho** (distancia) there's a long way to go yet **¡no faltaba más!** of course!

---

fama f fame; (reputación) reputation

famélico adj starving

familia f family; (hijos) children. **~ numerosa** large family. **~r** adj familiar; (de la familia) family; (sin ceremonia) informal; (lenguaje) colloquial. ● m & f relative. **~ridad** f familiarity. **~rizarse** 🔟 vpr become familiar (con with)

famoso adj famous

fanático adj fanatical. ● m fanatic

fanfarr|ón m boastful. ● m braggart. **~onear** vi show off

fango m mud. **~so** adj muddy

fantasía f fantasy. de **~** fancy; (joya) imitation

fantasma m ghost

fantástico adj fantastic

fardo m bundle

faringe f pharynx

farmac|éutico m chemist (Brit), pharmacist, druggist (Amer). **~ia** f (ciencia) pharmacy; (tienda) chemist's (shop) (Brit), pharmacy

faro m lighthouse; (Aviac) beacon; (Auto) headlight

farol m lantern; (de la calle) street lamp. **~a** f street lamp

farr|a f partying. **~ear** vi (LAm) go out partying

farsa f farce. **~nte** m & f fraud

fascículo m instalment

fascinar vt fascinate

fasci|smo m fascism

fase f phase

fastidi|ar vt annoy; (estropear) spoil. **~arse** vpr (máquina) break down; hurt (pierna); (LAm, molestarse) get annoyed. ¡para que te **~es**! so there!. **~o** m nuisance; (aburrimiento) boredom. **~oso** adj annoying

fatal adj fateful; (mortal) fatal; (fam, pésimo) terrible. **~idad** f fate; (desgracia) misfortune

fatig|a f fatigue. **~ar** 🔢 vt tire. **~arse** vpr get tired. **~oso** adj tiring

fauna f fauna

favor m favour. a **~** de, en **~** de in favour of. haga el **~** de would

you be so kind as to, please. por **~** please

favorec|er 🔢 vt favour; (vestido, peinado etc) suit. **~ido** adj favoured

favorito adj & m favourite

fax m fax

faxear vt fax

faz f face

fe f faith. dar **~** de certify. de buena **~** in good faith

febrero m February

febril adj feverish

fecha f date. a estas **~s** now; (todavía) still. hasta la **~** so far. poner la **~** date. **~r** vt date

fecund|ación f fertilization. **~ación** artificial artificial insemination. **~ar** vt fertilize. **~o** adj fertile; (fig) prolific

federa|ción f federation. **~l** adj federal

felici|dad f happiness. **~dades** fpl best wishes; (congratulaciones) congratulations. **~tación** f letter of congratulation. ¡**~taciones**! (LAm) congratulations! **~tar** vt congratulate

feligrés m parishioner

feliz adj happy; (afortunado) lucky. ¡Felices Pascuas! Happy Christmas! ¡F**~** Año Nuevo! Happy New Year!

felpudo m doormat

fem|enil adj (Mex) women's. **~enino** adj feminine; (equipo) women's; (en biología) female. ● m feminine. **~inista** adj & m & f feminist.

fen|omenal adj phenomenal. **~ómeno** m phenomenon; (monstruo) freak

feo adj ugly; (desagradable) nasty. ● adv (LAm) (mal) bad

feria f fair; (*verbena*) carnival; (*Mex, cambio*) small change. **~do** m (*LAm*) public holiday
ferment|ar vt/i ferment. **~o** m ferment
fero|cidad f ferocity. **~z** adj fierce
férreo adj iron; (*disciplina*) strict
ferreter|ía f hardware store, iron-monger's (*Brit*). **~o** m hardware dealer, ironmonger (*Brit*)
ferro|carril m railway (*Brit*), rail-road (*Amer*). **~viario** adj rail. ● m railwayman (*Brit*), railroader (*Amer*)
fértil adj fertile
fertili|dad f fertility. **~zante** m fertilizer. **~zar** 🔟 vt fertilize
ferv|iente adj fervent. **~or** m fervour
festej|ar vt celebrate; entertain (*persona*). **~o** m celebration
festiv|al m festival. **~idad** f festivity. **~o** adj festive. ● m public holiday
fétido adj stinking
feto m foetus
fiable adj reliable
fiado m. al **~** on credit. **~r** m (*Jurid*) guarantor
fiambre m cold meat. **~ría** f (*LAm*) delicatessen
fianza f (*dinero*) deposit; (*objeto*) surety. bajo **~** on bail
fiar 🔟 vt (*vender*) sell on credit; (*confiar*) confide. ● vi give credit. **~se** vpr. **~se de** trust
fibra f fibre. **~ de vidrio** fibreglass
ficción f fiction
fich|a f token; (*tarjeta*) index card; (*en juegos*) counter. **~ar** vt open a file on. estar **~ado** have a (police) record. **~ero** m card index; (*en informática*) file
fidedigno adj reliable

fidelidad f faithfulness
fideos mpl noodles
fiebre f fever. **~ aftosa** foot-and-mouth disease. **~ del heno** hay fever. **~ porcina** swine fever. tener **~** have a temperature
fiel adj faithful; (*memoria, relato etc*) reliable. ● m believer
fieltro m felt
fier|a f wild animal. **~o** adj fierce
fierro m (*LAm*) metal bar; (*hierro*) iron
fiesta f party; (*día festivo*) holiday. **~s** fpl celebrations

> **fiestas** A *fiesta* in Spain can be a day of local cele- *i* brations, a larger event for a town or city, or a national holiday to commemorate a saint's day or a historical event. Famous Span-ish *fiestas* include The *Fallas* in Valencia, the *Sanfermines* in Pam-plona, and the *Feria de Sevilla*. In Latin America *fiestas patrias* are a period of one or more days when each country celebrates its inde-pendence. There are usually mili-tary parades, firework displays, and cultural events typical of the country.

figura f figure; (*forma*) shape. **~r** vi appear; (*destacar*) show off. **~rse** vpr imagine. ¡figúrate! just imagine!
fij|ación f fixing; (*obsesión*) fix-ation. **~ar** vt fix; establish (*residencia*). **~arse** vpr (*poner atención*) pay attention; (*percatarse*) notice. ¡fíjate! just imagine! **~o** adj fixed; (*firme*) stable; (*permanente*) per-manent. ● adv. mirar **~o** stare
fila f line; (*de soldados etc*) file; (*en el teatro, cine etc*) row; (*cola*)

queue. **ponerse en** ∿ line up

filántropo m philanthropist

filat|elia f stamp collecting, philately. ∿**élico** adj philatelic. • m stamp collector, philatelist

filete m fillet

filial adj filial. • f subsidiary

Filipinas fpl. **las (islas)** ∿ the Philippines

filipino adj Philippine, Filipino

filmar vt film; shoot (película)

filo m edge; (de hoja) cutting edge. **al** ∿ **de las doce** at exactly twelve o'clock. **sacar** ∿ **a** sharpen

filología f philology

filón m vein; (fig) gold-mine

fil|osofía f philosophy. ∿**ósofo** m philosopher

filtr|ar vt filter. ∿**arse** vpr filter; (dinero) disappear; (noticia) leak. ∿**o** m filter; (bebida) philtre. ∿ **solar** sunscreen

fin m end; (objetivo) aim. ∿ **de semana** weekend. **a** ∿ **de** in order to. **a** ∿ **de cuentas** at the end of the day. **a** ∿ **de que** in order that. **a** ∿**es de** at the end of. **al** ∿ **finally. al** ∿ **y al cabo** after all. dar ∿ **a** end. **en** ∿ in short. **por** ∿ finally. **sin** ∿ endless

final adj final. • m end. • f final. ∿**idad** f aim. ∿**ista** m & f finalist. ∿**izar** [10] vt finish. • vi end

financi|ación f financing; (fondos) funds; (facilidades) credit facilities. ∿**ar** vt finance. ∿**ero** adj financial. • m financier

finca f property; (tierras) estate; (rural) farm; (de recreo) country house

fingir [14] vt feign; (simular) simulate. • vi pretend. ∿**se** vpr pretend to be

finlandés adj Finnish. • m (per-

sona) Finn; (lengua) Finnish

Finlandia f Finland

fino adj fine; (delgado) thin; (oído) acute; (de modales) refined; (sutil) subtle

firma f signature; (acto) signing; (empresa) firm

firmar vt/i sign

firme adj firm; (estable) stable, steady; (color) fast. • m (pavimento) (road) surface. • adv hard. ∿**za** f firmness

fisc|al adj fiscal, tax. • m & f public prosecutor. ∿**o** m treasury

fisg|ar [12] vi snoop (around). ∿**ón** adj nosy. • m snooper

físic|a f physics. ∿**o** adj physical. • m physique; (persona) physicist

fisonomista m & f. **ser buen** ∿ be good at remembering faces

fistol m (Mex) tiepin

flaco adj thin, skinny; (débil) weak

flagelo m scourge

flagrante adj flagrant. **en** ∿ redhanded

flama f (Mex) flame

flamante adj splendid; (nuevo) brand-new

flamear vi flame; (bandera etc) flap

flamenco adj flamenco; (de Flandes) Flemish. • m (ave) flamingo; (música etc) flamenco; (idioma) Flemish

> **ⓘ** **flamenco** Flamenco is performed in three forms: guitar, singing and dancing. Originally a gypsy art form, it also has Arabic and North African influences. Modern flamenco blends traditional forms with rock, jazz

and salsa. In its pure form the music and lyrics are improvised, but tourists are more likely to see rehearsed performances.

flan m crème caramel

flaqueza f thinness; (*debilidad*) weakness

flauta f flute

flecha f arrow. **~zo** m love at first sight

fleco m fringe; (*Mex, en el pelo*) fringe (*Brit*), bangs (*Amer*)

flem|a f phlegm. **~ático** adj phlegmatic

flequillo m fringe (*Brit*), bangs (*Amer*)

fletar vt charter; (*LAm, transportar*) transport

flexible adj flexible

flirte|ar vi flirt. **~o** m flirting

floj|ear vi flag; (*holgazanear*) laze around. **~o** adj loose; (*poco fuerte*) weak; (*perezoso*) lazy

flor f flower. la **~ y** nata the cream. **~a** f flora. **~ecer** 11 vi flower, bloom; (*fig*) flourish. **~eciente** adj (*fig*) flourishing. **~ero** m flower vase. **~ista** m & f florist

flot|a f fleet. **~ador** m float; (*de niño*) rubber band. **~ar** vi float. **~e. a ~e** afloat

fluctua|ción f fluctuation. **~r** 21 vi fluctuate

flu|idez f fluidity; (*fig*) fluency. **~ido** adj fluid; (*fig*) fluent. ● m fluid. **~ir** 17 vi flow

fluoruro m fluoride

fluvial adj river

fobia f phobia

foca f seal

foco m focus; (*lámpara*) floodlight;

(*LAm, de coche*) (head)light; (*Mex, bombilla*) light bulb

fogón m cooker; (*LAm, fogata*) bonfire

folio m sheet

folklórico adj folk

follaje m foliage

follet|ín m newspaper serial. **~o** m pamphlet

follón m 1 mess; (*alboroto*) row; (*problema*) trouble

fomentar vt promote; boost (*ahorro*); stir up (*odio*)

fonda f (*pensión*) boarding-house; (*LAm, restaurant*) cheap restaurant

fondo m bottom; (*de calle, pasillo*) end; (*de sala etc*) back; (*de escenario, pintura etc*) background. **~ de reptiles** slush fund. **~s** mpl funds, money. **a ~** thoroughly

fonétic|a f phonetics. **~o** adj phonetic

fontanero m plumber

footing /'futin/ m jogging

forastero m stranger

forcejear vi struggle

forense adj forensic. ● m & f forensic scientist

forj|ar vt forge. **~se** vpr forge; build up (*ilusiones*)

forma f form; (*contorno*) shape; (*modo*) way; (*Mex, formulario*) form. **~s** fpl conventions. **de todas ~s** anyway. **estar en ~** be in good form. **~ción** f formation; (*educación*) training. **~l** adj formal; (*de fiar*) reliable; (*serio*) serious. **~lidad** f formality; (*fiabilidad*) reliability; (*seriedad*) seriousness. **~r** vt form; (*componer*) make up; (*enseñar*) train. **~rse** vpr form; (*desarrollarse*) develop; (*educarse*) to be educated. **~to** m format

formidable adj formidable; (*muy*

grande) enormous

fórmula *f* formula; (*sistema*) way. **~ de cortesía** polite expression

formular *vt* formulate; make (queja etc). **~io** *m* form

fornido *adj* well-built

forr|ar *vt* (*en el interior*) line; (*en el exterior*) cover. **~o** *m* lining; (*cubierta*) cover

fortale|cer 11 *vt* strengthen. **~za** *f* strength; (*Mil*) fortress; (*fuerza moral*) fortitude

fortuito *adj* fortuitous; (*encuentro*) chance

fortuna *f* fortune; (*suerte*) luck

forz|ar 2 & 10 *vt* force; strain (*vista*). **~osamente** *adv* necessarily. **~oso** *adj* necessary

fosa *f* ditch; (*tumba*) grave. **~s** *fpl* **nasales** nostrils

fósforo *m* phosphorus; (*cerilla*) match

fósil *adj* & *m* fossil

foso *m* ditch; (*en castillo*) moat; (*de teatro*) pit

foto *f* photo. **sacar ~s** take photos

fotocopia *f* photocopy. **~dora** *f* photocopier. **~r** *vt* photocopy

fotogénico *adj* photogenic

fot|ografía *f* photography; (*Foto*) photograph. **~ografiar** 20 *vt* photograph. **~ógrafo** *m* photographer

foul /faul/ *m* (*pl* **~s**) (*LAm*) foul

frac *m* (*pl* **~s** o **fraques**) tails

fracas|ar *vi* fail. **~o** *m* failure

fracción *f* fraction; (*Pol*) faction

fractura *f* fracture. **~r** *vt* fracture. **~rse** *vpr* fracture

fragan|cia *f* fragrance. **~te** *adj* fragrant

frágil *adj* fragile

fragmento *m* fragment; (*de canción etc*) extract

fragua *f* forge. **~r** 15 *vt* forge; (*fig*) concoct. • *vi* set

fraile *m* friar; (*monje*) monk

frambuesa *f* raspberry

franc|és *adj* French. • *m* (*persona*) Frenchman; (*lengua*) French. **~esa** *f* Frenchwoman

Francia *f* France

franco *adj* frank; (*evidente*) marked; (*Com*) free. • *m* (*moneda*) franc

francotirador *m* sniper

franela *f* flannel

franja *f* border; (*banda*) stripe; (*de terreno*) strip

franque|ar *vt* clear; (*atravesar*) cross; pay the postage on (*carta*). **~o** *m* postage

franqueza *f* frankness

frasco *m* bottle; (*de mermelada etc*) jar

frase *f* phrase; (*oración*) sentence. **~ hecha** set phrase

fratern|al *adj* fraternal. **~idad** *f* fraternity

fraud|e *m* fraud. **~ulento** *adj* fraudulent

fray *m* brother, friar

frecuen|cia *f* frequency. **con ~cia** frequently. **~tar** *vt* frequent. **~te** *adj* frequent

frega|dero *m* sink. **~r** 1 & 12 scrub; wash (los platos); mop (el suelo); (*LAm, fam, molestar*) annoy

freír 51 (*pp* **frito**) *vt* fry. **~se** *vpr* fry; (*persona*) roast

frenar *vt* brake; (*fig*) check

frenético *adj* frenzied; (*furioso*) furious

freno *m* (*de caballería*) bit; (*Auto*)

brake; (*fig*) check

frente *m* front. ~ a opposite. ~ a
~ face to face. al ~ at the head;
(*hacia delante*) forward. chocar de
~ crash head on. de ~ a (*LAm*) fa-
cing. hacer a ~ (*cosa*); stand
up to (*persona*). ● *f* forehead. arru-
gar la ~ frown

fresa *f* strawberry

fresc|o *adj* (*frío*) cool; (*reciente*)
fresh; (*descarado*) cheeky. ● *m* fresh
air; (*frescor*) coolness; (*mural*)
fresco; (*persona*) impudent person.
al ~o in the open air. hacer ~o to
be cool. tomar el ~o get some
fresh air. ~or *m* coolness. ~ura *f*
freshness; (*frío*) coolness; (*descaro*)
cheek

frialdad *f* coldness; (*fig*) indiffer-
ence

fricci|ón *f* rubbing; (*fig, Tec*) fric-
tion; (*masaje*) massage. ~onar *vt*
rub

frigidez *f* frigidity

frígido *adj* frigid

frigorífico *m* fridge, refrigerator

frijol *m* (*LAm*) bean. ~es refritos
(*Mex*) fried purée of beans

frío *adj* & *m* cold. tomar ~ catch
cold. hacer ~ be cold. tener ~ be
cold

frito *adj* fried; (fam, *harto*) fed up.
me tiene ~ I'm sick of him

fr|ivolidad *f* frivolity. ~ívolo *adj*
frivolous

fronter|a *f* border, frontier. ~izo
adj border; (*país*) bordering

frontón *m* pelota court; (*pared*)
fronton

frotar *vt* rub; strike (*cerilla*)

fructífero *adj* fruitful

fruncir 🔟 *vt* gather (*tela*). ~ el
ceño frown

frustra|ción *f* frustration. ~r *vt*
frustrate. ~rse *vpr* (*fracasar*) fail.
quedar ~do be disappointed

frut|a *f* fruit. ~al *adj* fruit. ~ería *f*
fruit shop. ~ero *m* fruit seller; (*re-
cipiente*) fruit bowl. ~icultura *f*
fruit-growing. ~o *m* fruit

fucsia *f* fuchsia. ● *m* fuchsia

fuego *m* fire. ~s artificiales fire-
works. a ~ lento on a low heat.
tener ~ have a light

fuente *f* fountain; (*manantial*)
spring; (*plato*) serving dish; (*fig*)
source

fuera *adv* out; (*al exterior*) outside;
(*en otra parte*) away; (*en el extran-
jero*) abroad. ~ de outside; (*ex-
cepto*) except for, besides. por ~
on the outside. ● *vb véase* IR *y* SER

fuerte *adj* strong; (*color*) bright;
(*sonido*) loud; (*dolor*) severe;
(*duro*) hard; (*grande*) large; (*lluvia,
nevada*) heavy. ● *m* fort; (*fig*)
strong point. ● *adv* hard; (*con ha-
blar etc*) loudly; (*llover*) heavily;
(*mucho*) a lot

fuerza *f* strength; (*poder*) power;
(*en física*) force; (*Mil*) forces. ~ de
voluntad will-power. a ~ de by
(*dint of*). a la ~ by necessity. por
~ by force; (*por necesidad*) by ne-
cessity. tener ~s para have the
strength to

fuese *vb véase* IR *y* SER

fug|a *f* flight, escape; (*de gas etc*)
leak; (*Mus*) fugue. ~arse 🔟 *vpr*
flee, escape. ~az *adj* fleeting.
~itivo *adj* & *m* fugitive

fui *vb véase* IR, SER

fulano *m* so-and-so. ~, mengano
y zutano every Tom, Dick and
Harry

fulminar *vt* (*fig, con mirada*) look
daggers at

fuma|dor adj smoking. • m smoker. ~r vt/i smoke. ~r en pipa smoke a pipe. ~rse vpr smoke. ~rada f puff of smoke

funci|ón f function; (de un cargo etc) duty; (de teatro) show, performance. ~onal adj functional. ~onar vi work, function. no ~ona out of order. ~onario m civil servant

funda f cover. ~ de almohada pillowcase

funda|ción f foundation. ~mental adj fundamental. ~mentar vt base (en on). ~mento m foundation. ~r vt found; (fig) base. ~rse vpr be based

fundi|ción f melting; (de metales) smelting; (taller) foundry. ~r vt melt; smelt (metales); cast (objeto); blend (colores); (fusionar) merge; (Elec) blow; (LAm) seize up (motor). ~rse vpr melt; (unirse) merge

fúnebre adj funeral; (sombrío) gloomy

funeral adj funeral. • m funeral. ~es mpl funeral

funicular adj & m funicular

furg|ón m van. ~oneta f van

fur|ia f fury; (violencia) violence. ~ibundo adj furious. ~ioso adj furious. ~or m fury

furtivo adj furtive. cazador ~ poacher

furúnculo m boil

fusible m fuse

fusil m rifle. ~ar vt shoot

fusión f melting; (unión) fusion; (Com) merger

fútbol m, (Mex) **futbol** m football

futbolista m & f footballer

futur|ista adj futuristic. • m & f futurist. ~o adj & m future

Gg

gabardina f raincoat

gabinete m (Pol) cabinet; (en museo etc) room; (de dentista, médico etc) consulting room

gaceta f gazette

gafa f hook. ~s fpl glasses, spectacles. ~s de sol sunglasses

gaf|ar vt 🔢 bring bad luck to. ~e m jinx

gaita f bagpipes

gajo m segment

gala f gala. ~s fpl finery, best clothes. estar de ~ be dressed up. hacer ~ de show off

galán m (en el teatro) (romantic) hero; (enamorado) lover

galante adj gallant. ~ar vt court. ~ría f gallantry

galápago m turtle

galardón m award

galaxia f galaxy

galera f galley

galer|ía f gallery. ~ía comercial (shopping) arcade. ~ón m (Mex) hall

Gales m Wales. país de ~ Wales

gal|és adj Welsh. • m Welshman; (lengua) Welsh. ~esa f Welshwoman

galgo m greyhound

Galicia f Galicia

galimatías m invar gibberish

gallard|ía f elegance. ~o adj elegant

gallego adj & m Galician

galleta f biscuit (Brit), cookie (Amer)

gall|ina f hen, chicken; (fig, fam) coward. ~o m cock

galón m gallon; (cinta) braid; (Mil) stripe

galop|ar vi gallop. ~e m gallop

gama f scale; (fig) range

gamba f prawn (Brit), shrimp (Amer)

gamberro m hooligan

gamuza f (piel) chamois leather; (de otro animal) suede

gana f wish, desire; (apetito) appetite. de buena ~ willingly. de mala ~ reluctantly. no me da la ~ I don't like it. tener ~s de (+ infinitivo) feel like (+ gerundio)

ganad|ería f cattle raising; (ganado) livestock. ~o m livestock. ~o lanar sheep. ~o porcino pigs. ~o vacuno cattle

gana|dor adj winning. ● m winner. ~ncia f gain; (Com) profit. ~r vt earn; (en concurso, juego etc) win; (alcanzar) reach. ● vi (vencer) win; (mejorar) improve. ~rle a uno beat s.o. ~rse la vida earn a living. salir ~ndo come out better off

ganch|illo m crochet. hacer ~illo crochet. ~o m hook; (LAm, colgador) hanger. tener ~o be very attractive

ganga f bargain

ganso m goose

garabat|ear vt/i scribble. ~o m scribble

garaje m garage

garant|e m & f guarantor. ~ía f guarantee. ~izar **10** vt guarantee

garapiña f (Mex) pineapple

squash. ~do adj. almendras fpl ~das sugared almonds

garbanzo m chick-pea

garbo m poise; (de escrito) style. ~so adj elegant

garganta f throat; (valle) gorge

gárgaras fpl. hacer ~ gargle

garita f hut; (de centinela) sentry box

garra f (de animal) claw; (de ave) talon

garrafa f carafe

garrafal adj huge

garrapata f tick

garrapat|ear vi scribble. ~o m scribble

garrote m club, cudgel; (tormento) garrotte

gar|úa f (LAm) drizzle. ~uar vi **21** (LAm) drizzle

garza f heron

gas m gas. con ~ fizzy. sin ~ still

gasa f gauze

gaseosa f fizzy drink

gas|óleo m diesel. ~olina f petrol (Brit), gasoline (Amer), gas (Amer). ~olinera f petrol station (Brit), gas station (Amer)

gast|ado adj spent; (vestido etc) worn out. ~ador m spendthrift. ~ar vt spend; (consumir) use; (malgastar) waste; (desgastar) wear out; wear (vestido etc); crack (broma). ~arse vpr wear out. ~o m expense; (acción de gastar) spending

gastronomía f gastronomy

gat|a f cat. a ~as on all fours. ~ear vi crawl

gatillo m trigger

gat|ito m kitten. ~o m cat. dar ~o por liebre take s.o. in

gaucho m Gaucho

gaucho A peasant of the pampas of Argentina, Uruguay and Brazil. Modern gauchos work as foremen on farms and ranches and take part in rodeos. Traditionally, a gaucho's outfit was characterized by its baggy trousers, leather chaps, and *chiripá*, a waist-high garment. They also used *boleadoras* for catching cattle.

gaveta f drawer

gaviota f seagull

gazpacho m gazpacho

gelatina f gelatine; (*jalea*) jelly

gema f gem

gemelo m twin. ~**s** mpl (*anteojos*) binoculars; (*de camisa*) cuff-links

gemido m groan

Géminis m Gemini

gemir 5 vi moan; (*animal*) whine, howl

gen m, **gene** m gene

geneal|ogía f genealogy. ~**ógico** adj genealogical. **árbol** m ~**ógico** family tree

generaci|ón f generation. ~**onal** adj generational

general adj general. **en** ~ in general. **por lo** ~ generally. ●m general. ~**izar** 10 vt/i generalize. ~**mente** adv generally

generar vt generate

género m type, sort; (*en biología*) genus; (*Gram*) gender; (*en literatura etc*) genre; (*producto*) product; (*tela*) material. ~**s de punto** knitwear. ~ **humano** mankind

generos|idad f generosity. ~**o** adj generous

genétic|a f genetics. ~**o** adj genetic

geni|al adj brilliant; (*divertido*) funny. ~**o** m temper; (*carácter*) nature; (*talento, persona*) genius

genital adj genital. ~**es** mpl genitals

genoma m genome

gente f people; (*nación*) nation; (*fam, familia*) family, folks; (*Mex, persona*) person. ●adj (*LAm*) respectable; (*amable*) kind

gentil adj charming. ~**eza** f kindness. **tener la** ~**eza de** be kind enough to

gentío m crowd

genuflexión f genuflection

genuino adj genuine

ge|ografía f geography. ~**ográfico** adj geographical

ge|ología f geology. ~**ólogo** m geologist

geom|etría f geometry. ~**étrico** adj geometrical

geranio m geranium

geren|cia f management. ~**ciar** vt (*LAm*) manage. ~**te** m & f manager

germen m germ

germinar vi germinate

gestación f gestation

gesticula|ción f gesticulation. ~**r** vi gesticulate

gesti|ón f step; (*administración*) management. ~**onar** vt take steps to arrange; (*dirigir*) manage

gesto m expression; (*ademán*) gesture; (*mueca*) grimace

gibraltareño adj & m Gibraltarian

gigante adj gigantic. ● m giant. ~**sco** adj gigantic

gimn|asia f gymnastics. ~**asio** m gymnasium, gym 1. ~**asta** m & f gymnast. ~**ástic** adj gymnastic

gimotear vi whine

ginebra f gin

ginec|ólogo m gynaecologist

gira f tour. ~r vt spin; draw (cheque); transfer (dinero). ● vi rotate, go round; (en camino) turn

girasol m sunflower

gir|atorio adj revolving. ~o m turn; (Com) draft; (locución) expression. ~o postal money order

gitano adj & m gypsy

glacia|l adj icy. ~r m glacier

glándula f gland

glasear vt glaze; (Culin) ice

glob|al adj global; (fig) overall. ~alización f globalization. ~o m globe; (juguete) balloon

glóbulo m globule

gloria f glory; (placer) delight. ~rse vi boast (de about)

glorieta f square; (Auto) roundabout (Brit), (traffic) circle (Amer)

glorificar 7 vt glorify

glorioso adj glorious

glotón adj gluttonous. ● m glutton

gnomo /'nomo/ m gnome

gob|ernación f government. Ministerio m de la G~ernación Home Office (Brit), Department of the Interior (Amer). ~ernador adj governing. ● m governor. ~ernante adj governing. ● m & f leader. ~ernar 1 vt govern. ~ierno m government

goce m enjoyment

gol m goal

golf m golf

golfo m gulf; (niño) urchin; (holgazán) layabout

golondrina f swallow

golos|ina f titbit; (dulce) sweet. ~o adj fond of sweets

golpe m blow; (puñetazo) punch;

(choque) bump; (de emoción) shock; (arg, atraco) job 🔟; (en golf, en tenis, de remo) stroke. ~ de estado coup d'etat. ~ de fortuna stroke of luck. ~ de vista glance. ~ militar military coup. de ~ suddenly. de un ~ in one go. ~ar vt hit; (dar varios golpes) beat; (con mucho ruido) bang; (con el puño) punch. ● vi knock

goma f rubber; (para pegar) glue; (banda) rubber band; (de borrar) eraser. ~ de mascar chewing gum. ~ espuma foam rubber

googlear ® vt/i 🔟 to google

gord|a f (Mex) small thick tortilla. ~o adj (persona) (con ser) fat; (con estar) have put on weight; (carne) fatty; (grueso) thick; (grande) large, big. ~ m first prize. ~ura f fatness; (grasa) fat

gorila f gorilla

gorje|ar vi chirp. ~o m chirping

gorra f cap. ~ de baño (LAm) bathing cap

gorrión m sparrow

gorro m cap; (de niño) bonnet. ~ de baño bathing cap

got|a f drop; (Med) gout. ni ~a nothing. ~ear vi drip. ~era f leak

gozar 🔟 vt enjoy. ● vi. ~ de enjoy

gozne m hinge

gozo m pleasure; (alegría) joy. ~so adj delighted

graba|ción f recording. ~do m engraving, print; (en libro) illustration. ~dora f tape-recorder. ~r vt engrave; record (discos etc)

graci|a f grace; (favor) favour; (humor) wit. ~as fpl thanks. ¡~as! thank you!, thanks! dar las ~as thank. hacer ~a amuse; (gustar) please. ¡muchas ~as! thank you very much! tener ~a be funny. ~**oso** adj funny. • m fool, comic character

grad|a f step. ~**as** fpl stand(s). ~**ación** f gradation. ~**o** m degree; (en enseñanza) year (Brit), grade (Amer). de buen ~**o** willingly

gradua|ción f graduation; (de alcohol) proof. ~**do** m graduate. ~**l** adj gradual. ~**r** 21 vt graduate; (regular) adjust. ~**rse** vpr graduate

gráfic|a f graph. ~**o** adj graphic. • m graph

gram|ática f grammar. ~**atical** adj grammatical

gramo m gram, gramme (Brit)

gran adj véase GRANDE

grana f (color) deep red

granada f pomegranate; (Mil) grenade

granate m (color) maroon

Gran Bretaña f Great Britain

grande adj (delante de nombre en singular **gran**) big, large; (alto) tall; (fig) great; (LAm, de edad) grown up. ~**za** f greatness

grandioso adj magnificent

granel m. a ~ in bulk; (suelto) loose; (fig) in abundance

granero m barn

granito m granite; (grano) small grain

graniz|ado m iced drink. ~**ar** 10 vi hail. ~**o** m hail

granj|a f farm. ~**ero** m farmer

grano m grain; (semilla) seed; (de café) bean; (Med) spot. ~**s** mpl cereals

granuja m & f rogue

grapa f staple. ~**r** vt staple

gras|a f grease; (Culin) fat. ~**iento** adj greasy

gratifica|ción f (de sueldo)

bonus (recompensa) reward. ~**r** 7 vt reward

grat|is adv free. ~**itud** f gratitude. ~**o** adj pleasant ~**uito** adj free; (fig) uncalled for

grava|men m tax; (carga) burden; (sobre inmueble) encumbrance. ~**r** vt tax; (cargar) burden

grave adj serious; (voz) deep; (sonido) low; (acento) grave. ~**dad** f gravity

gravilla f gravel

gravitar vi gravitate; (apoyarse) rest (sobre on); (peligro) hang (sobre over)

gravoso adj costly

graznar vi (cuervo) caw; (pato) quack; honk (ganso)

Grecia f Greece

gremio m union

greña f mop of hair

gresca f rumpus; (riña) quarrel

griego adj & m Greek

grieta f crack

grifo m tap, faucet (Amer)

grilletes mpl shackles

grillo m cricket. ~**s** mpl shackles

gringo m (LAm) foreigner; (norteamericano) Yankee 🄸

gripe f flu

gris adj grey. • m grey; (fam, policía) policeman

grit|ar vi shout. ~**ería** f, ~**erío** m uproar. ~**o** m shout; (de dolor, sorpresa) cry; (chillido) scream. dar ~**s** shout

grosell|a f redcurrant. ~ **negra** blackcurrant

groser|ía f rudeness; (ordinariez) coarseness; (comentario etc) coarse remark; (palabra) swearword. ~**o** adj coarse; (descortés) rude

grosor m thickness

grotesco adj grotesque

grúa f crane

grueso adj thick; (persona) fat, stout. • m thickness; (fig) main body

grumo m lump

gruñi|do m grunt; (de perro) growl. ~**r** [22] vi grunt; (perro) growl

grupa f hindquarters

grupo m group

gruta f grotto

guacamole m guacamole

guadaña f scythe

guaje m (Mex) gourd

guajolote m (Mex) turkey

guante m glove

guapo adj good-looking; (chica) pretty; (elegante) smart

guarda m & f guard; (de parque etc) keeper. ~**barros** m invar mudguard. ~**bosque** m gamekeeper. ~**costas** m invar coastguard vessel. ~**espaldas** m invar bodyguard. ~**meta** m goalkeeper. ~**r** vt keep; (proteger) protect; (en un lugar) put away; (reservar) save, keep. ~**rse** vpr. ~**rse de** (+ infinitivo) avoid (+ gerundio). ~**rropa** m wardrobe; (en local público) cloakroom. ~**vallas** m invar (LAm) goalkeeper

guardería f nursery

guardia f guard; (policía) policewoman; (de médico) shift. G~ **Civil** Civil Guard. ~ **municipal** municipal police. **estar de** ~ be on duty. **estar en** ~ be on one's guard. **montar la** ~ mount guard. • m policeman. ~ **jurado** m & f security guard. ~ **de tráfico** m traffic policeman. •f traffic policewoman

guardián m guardian; (de parque etc) keeper; (de edificio) security guard

guar|ecer [11] vt (albergar) give shelter to. ~**ecerse** vpr take shelter. ~**ida** f den, lair; (de personas) hideout

guarn|ecer [11] vt (adornar) adorn; (Culin) garnish. ~**ición** f adornment; (de caballo) harness; (Culin) garnish; (Mil) garrison; (de piedra preciosa) setting

guas|a f joke. ~**ón** adj humorous. • m joker

Guatemala f Guatemala

guatemalteco adj & m Guatemalan

guateque m party, bash

guayab|a f guava; (dulce) guava jelly. ~**era** f lightweight jacket

gubernatura f (Mex) government

güero adj (Mex) fair

guerr|a f war; (método) warfare. **dar** ~**a** annoy. ~**ero** adj warlike; (belicoso) fighting. • m warrior. ~**illa** f band of guerrillas. ~**illero** m guerrilla

guía m & f guide. • f guidebook; (de teléfonos) directory

guiar [20] vt guide; (llevar) lead; (Auto) drive. ~**se** vpr be guided (por by)

guijarro m pebble

guillotina f guillotine

guind|a f morello cherry. ~**illa** f chilli

guiñapo m rag; (fig, persona) wreck

guiñ|ar vt/i wink. ~**o** m wink. **hacer** ~**os** wink

guión m hyphen, dash; (de película etc) script. ~**onista** m & f scriptwriter

guirnalda f garland

guisado m stew

guisante m pea. ~ de olor sweet pea

guis|ar vt/i cook. ~o m stew

guitarr|a f guitar. ~ista m & f guitarist

gula f gluttony

gusano m worm; (larva de mosca) maggot

---

gustar

● verbo intransitivo

> ❗ Cuando el verbo **gustar** va precedido del complemento indirecto **le** (o **les, nos** etc), el sujeto en español pasa a ser el objeto en inglés. **me gusta mucho la música** I like music very much. **le gustan los helados** he likes ice cream. **a Juan no le gusta** Juan doesn't like it (or her etc)

····➤ gustar + infinitivo. les gusta ver televisión they like watching television

····➤ gustar que + subjuntivo. me ~ía que vinieras I'd like you to come. no le gusta que lo corrijan he doesn't like being corrected. ¿te ~ía que te lo comprara? would you like me to buy it for you?

····➤ gustar de algo to like sth. gustan de las fiestas they like parties

····➤ (tener acogida) to go down well. ese tipo de cosas que siempre gusta those sort of things always go down well. el libro no gustó the book didn't go down well

····➤ (en frases de cortesía) to wish. como guste as you

wish. cuando gustes whenever you wish

● verbo transitivo

····➤ (LAm, querer) ¿gusta un café? would you like a coffee? ¿gustan pasar? would you like to come in? **gustarse** verbo pronominal to like each other

gusto m taste; (placer) pleasure. a ~ comfortable. a mí ~ to my liking. buen ~ good taste. con mucho ~ with pleasure. dar ~ please. mucho ~ pleased to meet you. ~so adj tasty; (de buen grado) willingly

gutural adj guttural

Hh

ha vb véase **HABER**

haba f broad bean

Habana f La ~ Havana

habano m (puro) Havana

haber verbo auxiliar **30** have. ● v impersonal (presente s & pl **hay**, imperfecto s & pl **había**, pretérito s & pl **hubo**). hay una carta para ti there's a letter for you. hay 5 bancos en la plaza there are 5 banks in the square. hay que hacerlo it must be done, you have to do it. he aquí here is, here are. no hay de qué don't mention it, not at all. ¿qué hay? (¿qué pasa?) what's the matter?; (¿qué tal?) how are you?

habichuela f bean

hábil adj skilful; (listo) clever; (día) working; (Jurid) competent

habili|dad f skill; (astucia) clever-

ness; (*Jurid*) competence. ∼**tar** *vt*
qualify

habita|ción *f* room; (*dormitorio*)
bedroom; (*en biología*) habitat.
∼**ción de matrimonio**, ∼**ción
doble** double room. ∼**ción indi-
dual**, ∼**ción sencilla** single room.
∼**do** *adj* inhabited. ∼**nte** *m* inhab-
itant. ∼**r** *vi* live in. ● *vi* live

hábito *m* habit

habitua|l *adj* usual, habitual;
(*cliente*) regular. ∼**r** 21 *vt* accus-
tom. ∼**rse** *vpr.* ∼**rse a** get used to

habla *f* speech; (*idioma*) language;
(*dialecto*) dialect. **al** ∼ (*al teléfono*)
speaking. **ponerse al** ∼ **con** get in
touch with. ∼**dor** *adj* talkative. ● *m*
chatterbox. ∼**duria** *f* rumour.
∼**durías** (*f pl*) gossip. ∼**nte** *adj*
speaking. ● *m & f* speaker. ∼**r** *vt*
speak. ● *vi* speak, talk (con to);
(*Mex, por teléfono*) call. **¡ni** ∼**r!** out
of the question! **se** ∼ **español**
Spanish spoken

hacend|ado *m* landowner; (*LAm*)
farmer. ∼**oso** *adj* hard-working

hacer 31

● *verbo transitivo*

····▸ to do. **¿qué haces?** what are
you doing? ∼ **los deberes** to
do one's homework. **no sé qué**
∼ I don't know what to do.
hazme un favor can you do
me a favour?

····▸ (*fabricar, preparar, producir*)
to make. **me hizo un vestido**
she made me a dress. ∼ **un
café** to make a (cup of) coffee.
no hagas tanto ruido don't
make so much noise

····▸ (*construir*) to build (casa,
puente)

····▸ **hacer que uno haga algo** to

make s.o. do sth. **haz que se
vaya** make him leave. **hizo
que se equivocara** he made
her go wrong

····▸ **hacer hacer algo** to have
sth done. **hizo arreglar el
techo** he had the roof repaired

➡ Cuando el verbo **hacer**
se emplea en expresiones
como **hacer una pregunta,
hacer trampa** etc., ver bajo el
respectivo nombre

● *verbo intransitivo*

····▸ (*actuar, obrar*) to do. **hi-
ciste bien en llamar** you did
the right thing to call **¿cómo
haces para parecer tan
joven?** what do you do to
look so young?

····▸ (*fingir, simular*) **hacer
como que** to pretend. **hizo
como que no me conocía** he
pretended not to know me.
haz como que estás dormido
pretend you're asleep

····▸ **hacer de** (*en teatro*) to play
the part of; (*ejercer la función
de*) to act as

····▸ (*LAm, sentar*) **tanta sal
hace mal** so much salt is not
good for you. **dormir le hizo
bien** the sleep did him good.
el pepino me hace mal cu-
cumber doesn't agree with me

● *verbo impersonal*

····▸ (*hablando del tiempo atmos-
férico*) to be. **hace sol** it's
sunny. **hace 3 grados** it's 3
degrees

····▸ (*con expresiones temporales*)
hace una hora que espero
I've been waiting for an hour.

hacha | hecho

llegó hace 3 días he arrived 3 days ago. hace mucho tiempo a long time ago. hasta hace poco until re-cently

● **hacerse** *verbo pronominal*

····▶ (*para sí*) to make o.s. (falda, café)

····▶ (*hacer que otro haga*) se hizo la permanente she had her hair permed. me hice una pis-cina I had a pool built

····▶ (*convertirse en*) to become. se hicieron amigos they be-came friends

····▶ (*acostumbrarse*) ~se a algo to get used to sth

····▶ (*fingirse*) to pretend. ~se el enfermo to pretend to be ill

····▶ (*moverse*) to move. hazte para atrás move back

····▶ **hacerse de** (*LAm*) to make (amigo, dinero)

hacha *f* axe; (*antorcha*) torch

hacia *prep* towards; (*cerca de*) near; (*con tiempo*) at about. ~ **abajo** downwards. ~ **arriba** upwards. ~ **atrás** backwards. ~ **las dos** (at) about two o'clock

hacienda *f* country estate; (*en LAm*) ranch; **la ~ pública** the Treasury. **Ministerio** *m* **de H~** Ministry of Finance; (*en Gran Bretaña*) Exchequer; (*en Estados Unidos*) Treasury

hada *f* fairy. **el ~ madrina** the fairy godmother

hago *vb véase* HACER

Haití *m* Haiti

halag|ar 12 *vt* flatter. ~**üeño** *adj* flattering; (*esperanzador*) promising

halcón *m* falcon

hallar *vt* find; (*descubrir*) discover.

~**rse** *vpr* be. ~**zgo** *m* discovery

hamaca *f* hammock; (*asiento*) deck-chair

hambr|e *f* hunger; (*de muchos*) famine. **tener ~e** be hungry. ~**iento** *adj* starving

hamburguesa *f* hamburger

haragán *adj* lazy, idle. ● *m* lay-about. ~**anear** *vi* laze around

harap|iento *adj* in rags. ~**o** *m* rag

harina *f* flour

hart|ar *vt* (*fastidiar*) annoy. me estás ~**ando** you're annoying me. ~**arse** (*llenarse*) gorge o.s. (de on); (*cansarse*) get fed up (de with). ~**o** *adj* full; (*cansado*) tired; (*fastidiado*) fed up (de with). ● *adv* (*LAm*) (*muy*) very; (*mucho*) a lot

hasta *prep* as far as; (*en el tiempo*) until, till; (*Mex*) not until. ● *adv* even. ¡~ **la vista!** goodbye!, see you! ① ¡~ **luego!** see you later! ¡~ **mañana!** see you tomorrow! ¡~ **pronto!** see you soon!

hast|iar 20 *vt* (*cansar*) weary, tire; (*aburrir*) bore. ~**iarse** *vpr* get fed up (de with). ~**io** *m* weariness; (*aburrimiento*) boredom

haya *f* beech (tree). ● *vb véase* HABER

hazaña *f* exploit

hazmerreír *m* laughing stock

he *vb véase* HABER

hebilla *f* buckle

hebra *f* thread; (*fibra*) fibre

hebreo *adj* & *m* Hebrew

hechi|cería *f* witchcraft. ~**cero** *m* wizard. ~**zar** 10 *vt* cast a spell on; (*fig*) captivate. ~**zo** *m* spell; (*fig*) charm

hecho *pp de* hacer. ● *adj* (*manu-facturado*) made; (*terminado*) done; (*vestidos etc*) ready-made; (*fig*) (Culin) done. ● *m* fact; (*acto*) deed; (*cuestión*) matter; (*suceso*) event. de ∼o in fact. ∼ura *f* making; (*forma*) form; (*del cuerpo*) build; (*calidad de fabricación*) workmanship

hed|er **1** *vi* stink. ∼iondez *f* stench. ∼iondo *adj* stinking, smelly. ∼or *m* stench

hela|da *f* frost. ∼dera *f* (*LAm*) fridge, refrigerator. ∼dería *f* ice-cream shop. ∼do *adj* freezing; (*congelado*) frozen; (*LAm, bebida*) chilled. ● *m* ice-cream. ∼r **1** *vt/i* freeze. anoche heló there was a frost last night. ∼rse *vpr* freeze

helecho *m* fern

hélice *f* propeller

helicóptero *m* helicopter

hembra *f* female; (*mujer*) woman

hemorr|agia *f* haemorrhage. ∼oides *fpl* haemorrhoids

hendidura *f* crack, split; (*en geología*) fissure

heno *m* hay

heráldica *f* heraldry

hered|ar *vt/i* inherit. ∼era *f* heiress. ∼ero *m* heir. ∼itario *adj* hereditary

hereje *m* heretic. ∼ía *f* heresy

herencia *f* inheritance; (*fig*) heritage

heri|da *f* injury; (*con arma*) wound. ∼do *adj* injured; (*con arma*) wounded; (*fig*) hurt. ● *m* injured person. ∼r **4** *vt* injure; (*con arma*) wound; (*fig*) hurt. ∼rse *vpr* hurt o.s.

herman|a *f* sister. ∼a política sister-in-law. ∼astra *f* stepsister. ∼astro *m* stepbrother. ∼o *m* brother. ∼o político brother-in-law. ∼os *mpl* brothers; (*chicos y chicas*) brothers and sisters. ∼os gemelos twins

hermético *adj* hermetic; (*fig*) watertight

hermos|o *adj* beautiful; (*espléndido*) splendid. ∼ura *f* beauty

héroe *m* hero

hero|ico *adj* heroic. ∼ína *f* heroine; (*droga*) heroin. ∼ismo *m* heroism

herr|adura *f* horseshoe. ∼amienta *f* tool. ∼ero *m* blacksmith

herv|idero *m* (*fig*) hotbed; (*multitud*) throng. ∼ir **4** *vt/i* boil. ∼or *m* (*fig*) ardour. romper el ∼ come to the boil

hiberna|ción *f* hibernation. ∼r *vi* hibernate

híbrido *adj & m* hybrid

hice *vb véase* HACER

hidalgo *m* nobleman

hidrata|nte *adj* moisturizing. ∼r *vt* hydrate; (*crema etc*) moisturize

hidráulico *adj* hydraulic

hidr|oavión *m* seaplane. ∼oeléctrico *adj* hydroelectric. ∼ofobia *f* rabies. ∼ófobo *adj* rabid. ∼ógeno *m* hydrogen

hiedra *f* ivy

hielo *m* ice

hiena *f* hyena

hierba *f* grass; (*Culin, Med*) herb mala ∼ weed. ∼buena *f* mint.

hierro *m* iron

hígado *m* liver

higi|ene *f* hygiene. ∼énico *adj* hygienic

hig|o *m* fig. ∼uera *f* fig tree

hij|a *f* daughter. ∼astra *f* stepdaughter. ∼astro *m* stepson. ∼o *m* son. ∼os *mpl* sons; (*chicos y chicas*) children

hilar *vt* spin. ∼ delgado split hairs

hilera *f* row; (*Mil*) file

hilo *m* thread; (*Elec*) wire; (*de líquido*) trickle; (*lino*) linen

hilv|án *m* tacking. **~anar** *vt* tack; (*fig*) put together

himno *m* hymn. **~ nacional** anthem

hincapié *m.* hacer **~ en** stress, insist on

hincar **7** *vt* drive (estaca) (en into). **~se** *vpr.* **~se de rodillas** kneel down

hincha *f* **1** grudge. ● *m & f* (*fam, aficionado*) fan

hincha|do *adj* inflated; (*Med*) swollen. **~r** *vt* inflate, blow up. **~rse** *vpr* swell up; (*fig, fam, comer mucho*) gorge o.s. **~zón** *f* swelling

hinojo *m* fennel

hiper|mercado *m* hypermarket. **~sensible** *adj* hypersensitive. **~tensión** *f* high blood pressure

hípic|a *f* horse racing. **~o** *adj* horse

hipn|osis *f* hypnosis. **~otismo** *m* hypnotism. **~otizar** **10** *vt* hypnotize

hipo *m* hiccup. tener **~** have hiccups

hipo|alérgeno *adj* hypoallergenic. **~condríaco** *adj & m* hypochondriac

hip|ocresía *f* hypocrisy. **~ócrita** *adj* hypocritical. ● *m & f* hypocrite

hipódromo *m* racecourse

hipopótamo *m* hippopotamus

hipoteca *f* mortgage. **~r** **7** *vt* mortgage

hip|ótesis *f invar* hypothesis. **~otético** *adj* hypothetical

hiriente *adj* offensive, wounding

hirsuto *adj* (barba) bristly; (pelo) wiry

hispánico *adj* Hispanic

Hispanidad - Día de la
See ▷**DÍA DE LA RAZA**

Hispanoamérica *f* Spanish America

hispano|americano *adj* Spanish American. **~hablante** *adj* Spanish-speaking

hist|eria *f* hysteria. **~érico** *adj* hysterical

hist|oria *f* history; (*relato*) story; (*excusa*) tale, excuse. **pasar a la ~oria** go down in history. **~oriador** *m* historian. **~órico** *adj* historical. **~orieta** *f* tale; (*con dibujos*) strip cartoon

hito *m* milestone

hizo *vb véase* HACER

hocico *m* snout

hockey /'(x)oki/ *m* hockey. **~ sobre hielo** ice hockey

hogar *m* home; (*chimenea*) hearth. **~eño** *adj* domestic; (*persona*) home-loving

hoguera *f* bonfire

hoja *f* leaf; (*de papel, metal etc*) sheet; (*de cuchillo, espada etc*) blade. **~ de afeitar** razor blade. **~lata** *f* tin

hojaldre *m* puff pastry

hojear *vt* leaf through

hola *int* hello!

Holanda *f* Holland

holand|és *adj* Dutch. ● *m* Dutchman; (*lengua*) Dutch. **~esa** *f* Dutchwoman. **los ~eses** the Dutch

holg|ado *adj* loose; (*fig*) comfortable. **~ar** **2** & **12** *vi.* **huelga decir que** needless to say. **~azán** *adj* lazy. ● *m* idler. **~ura** *f* looseness; (*fig*) comfort

hollín *m* soot

hombre m man; *(especie humana)* man(kind). ● *int* Good Heavens!; *(de duda)* well. ~ **de negocios** businessman. ~ **rana** frogman

hombr|era f shoulder pad. ~**o** m shoulder

homenaje m homage, tribute. **rendir** ~ **a** pay tribute to

home|ópata m homoeopath. ~**opatía** f homoeopathy. ~**opático** adj homoeopathic

homicid|a adj murderous. ● m & f murderer. ~**io** m murder

homosexual adj & m & f homosexual. ~**idad** f homosexuality

hond|o adj deep. ~**onada** f hollow

Honduras f Honduras

hondureño adj & m Honduran

honest|idad f honesty. ~**o** adj honest

hongo m fungus; *(LAm, Culin)* mushroom; *(venenoso)* toadstool

hon|or m honour. ~**orable** adj honourable. ~**orario** adj honorary. ~**orarios** mpl fees. ~**ra** f honour; *(buena fama)* good name. ~**radez** f honesty. ~**rado** adj honest. ~**rar** vt honour

hora f hour; *(momento puntual)* time; *(cita)* appointment. ~ **pico,** ~ **punta** rush hour. ~**s** fpl **de trabajo** working hours. ~**s** fpl **extraordinarias** overtime. ~**s** fpl **libres** free time. **a estas** ~**s** now. **¿a qué** ~? (at) what time? **a última** ~ **at the last moment. de última** ~ **last-minute. en buena** ~ **at the right time. media** ~ **half an hour. pedir** ~ **to make an appointment. ¿qué** ~ **es?** what time is it?

horario adj hourly. ● m timetable. ~ **de trabajo** working hours

horca f gallows

horcajadas fpl. **a** ~ astride

horchata f tiger-nut milk

horizont|al adj & f horizontal. ~**e** m horizon

horma f mould; *(para fabricar calzado)* last; *(para conservar su forma)* shoe-tree. **de** ~ **ancha** broad-fitting

hormiga f ant

hormigón m concrete

hormigue|ar vi tingle; *(bullir)* swarm. **me** ~ **a la mano** I've got pins and needles in my hand. ~**o** m tingling; *(fig)* anxiety

hormiguero m anthill; *(de gente)* swarm

hormona f hormone

horn|ada f batch. ~**illa** f *(LAm)* burner. ~**illo** m burner; *(cocina portátil)* portable electric cooker. ~**o** m oven; *(para cerámica etc)* kiln; *(Tec)* furnace

horóscopo m horoscope

horquilla f pitchfork; *(para el pelo)* hairpin

horr|endo adj awful. ~**ible** adj horrible. ~**ipilante** adj terrifying. ~**or** m horror; *(atrocidad)* atrocity. **¡qué** ~**or!** how awful. ~**orizar** 🔟 vt horrify. ~**orizarse** vpr be horrified. ~**oroso** adj horrifying

hort|aliza f vegetable. ~**elano** m market gardener

hosco adj surly

hospeda|je m accommodation. ~**r** vt put up. ~**rse** vpr stay

hospital m hospital. ~**ario** adj hospitable. ~**idad** f hospitality

hostal m boarding-house

hostería f inn

hostia f *(Relig)* host

hostigar 🔢 vt whip; *(fig, molestar)* pester

hostil adj hostile. ~**idad** f hostility

hotel m hotel. ~**ero** adj hotel. • m hotelier

hoy adv today. ~ (en) día nowadays. ~ **por** ~ at the present time. de ~ **en adelante** from now on

hoy|o m hole. ~**uelo** m dimple

hoz f sickle

hube vb véase **HABER**

hucha f money box

hueco adj hollow; (palabras) empty; (voz) resonant; (persona) superficial. • m hollow; (espacio) space; (vacío) gap

huelg|a f strike. ~**a de brazos caídos** sit-down strike. ~**a de hambre** hunger strike. **declararse en** ~**a** come out on strike. ~**uista** m & f striker

huella f footprint; (de animal etc) track. ~ **de carbono** carbon footprint. ~ **digital** fingerprint

huelo vb véase **OLER**

huérfano adj orphaned. • m orphan. ~ **de** without

huert|a f market garden (Brit), truck farm (Amer); (terreno de regadío) irrigated plain. ~**o** m vegetable garden; (de árboles frutales) orchard

hueso m bone; (de fruta) stone

huésped m guest; (que paga) lodger

huesudo adj bony

huev|a f roe. ~**o** m egg. ~**o duro** hard-boiled egg. ~**o escalfado** poached egg. ~**o estrellado**, ~**o frito** fried egg. ~**o pasado por agua** boiled egg. ~**os revueltos** scrambled eggs. ~**o tibio** (Mex) boiled egg

hui|da f flight, escape. ~**dizo** adj (tímido) shy; (esquivo) elusive

huipil m (Mex) traditional embroidered smock

> ℹ️ **huipil** A traditional garment worn by Indian and mestizo women in Mexico and Central America. Huipiles are generally made of richly embroidered cotton. They are very wide and low-cut, and are either waist- or thigh-length.

---

huir vi ⑰ flee, run away; (evitar). ~ **de** avoid. **me huye** he avoids me

huitlacoche m (Mex) edible black fungus

hule m oilcloth; (Mex, goma) rubber

human|idad f mankind; (fig) humanity. ~**itario** adj humanitarian. ~**o** adj human; (benévolo) humane

humareda f cloud of smoke

humed|ad f dampness; (en meteorología) humidity; (gotitas de agua) moisture. ~**ecer** ⑪ vt moisten. ~**ecerse** vpr become moist

húmedo adj damp; (clima) humid; (labios) moist; (mojado) wet

humi|ldad f humility. ~**lde** adj humble. ~**llación** f humiliation. ~**llar** vt humiliate. ~**llarse** vpr lower o.s.

humo m smoke; (vapor) steam; (gas nocivo) fumes. ~**s** mpl airs

humor m mood, temper; (gracia) humour. **estar de mal** ~ be in a bad mood. ~**ista** m & f humorist. ~**ístico** adj humorous

hundi|miento m sinking. ~**r** vt sink; destroy (persona). ~**rse** vpr sink; (edificio) collapse

húngaro adj & m Hungarian

Hungría f Hungary

huracán m hurricane

huraño *adj* unsociable

hurgar 12 *vi* rummage (en through). ~**se** *vpr.* ~**se la nariz** pick one's nose

hurra *int* hurray!

hurtadillas *fpl.* **a** ~ stealthily

hurt|ar *vt* steal. ~**o** *m* theft; (*cosa robada*) stolen object

husmear *vt* sniff out; (*fig*) pry into

huyo *vb véase* **HUIR**

Ii

iba *véase* **IR**

ibérico *adj* Iberian

iberoamericano *adj & m* Latin American

iceberg /iθ'ber/ *m* (*pl* ~s) iceberg

ictericia *f* jaundice

ida *f* outward journey; (*partida*) departure. **de** ~ **y vuelta** (*billete*) return (*Brit*), round-trip (*Amer*); (*viaje*) round

idea *f* idea; (*opinión*) opinion. **cambiar de** ~ change one's mind. **no tener la más remota** ~, **no tener la menor** ~ not have the slightest idea, not have a clue 1

ideal *adj & m* ideal. ~**ista** *m & f* idealist. ~**izar** 10 *vt* idealize

idear *vt* think up, conceive; (*inventar*) invent

ídem *pron & adv* the same

idéntico *adj* identical

identi|dad *f* identity. ~**ficación** *f* identification. ~**ficar** 7 *vt* identify. ~**ficarse** *vpr* identify o.s. ~**ficarse con** identify with

ideolo|gía *f* ideology. ~**ógico** *adj* ideological

idílico *adj* idyllic

idilio *m* idyll

idiom|a *m* language. ~**ático** *adj* idiomatic

idiosincrasia *f* idiosyncrasy

idiot|a *adj* idiotic. ● *m & f* idiot. ~**ez** *f* stupidity

idolatrar *vt* worship; (*fig*) idolize

ídolo *m* idol

idóneo *adj* suitable (para for)

iglesia *f* church

iglú *m* igloo

ignora|ncia *f* ignorance. ~**nte** *adj* ignorant. ● *m* ignoramus. ~**r** *vt* not know, be unaware of; (*no hacer caso de*) ignore

igual *adj* equal; (*mismo*) the same; (*similar*) like; (*llano*) even; (*liso*) smooth. ● *adv* the same. ● *m* equal. ~ **que** (the same) as. **al** ~ **que** the same as. **da** ~, **es** ~ it doesn't matter. **sin** ~ unequalled

igual|ar *vt* make equal; (*éxito*, *récord*); (*allanar*) level. ~**arse** *vpr* be equal. ~**dad** *f* equality. ~**mente** *adv* equally; (*también*) also, likewise; (*respuesta de cortesía*) the same to you

ilegal *adj* illegal

ilegible *adj* illegible

ilegítimo *adj* illegitimate

ileso *adj* unhurt

ilícito *adj* illicit

ilimitado *adj* unlimited

ilógico *adj* illogical

ilumina|ción *f* illumination; (*alumbrado*) lighting. ~**r** *vt* light (up). ~**rse** *vpr* light up

ilusi|ón *f* illusion; (*sueño*) dream; (*alegría*) joy. **hacerse** ~**ones** build up one's hopes. **me hace** ~**ón** I'm thrilled; I'm looking forward to (algo en el futuro). **~onado** adj excited. **~onar** vt give false hope. **~onarse** vpr have false hopes

ilusionis|mo m conjuring. **~ta** m & f conjurer

iluso adj naive. ● m dreamer. **~rio** adj illusory

ilustra|ción f learning; (dibujo) illustration. **~do** adj learned; (con dibujos) illustrated. **~r** vt explain; (instruir) instruct; (añadir dibujos etc) illustrate. **~rse** vpr acquire knowledge. **~tivo** adj illustrative

ilustre adj illustrious

imagen f image; (TV etc) picture

imagina|ble adj imaginable. **~ción** f imagination. **~r** vt imagine. **~rse** vpr imagine. **~rio** m imaginary. **~tivo** adj imaginative

imán m magnet

imbécil adj stupid. ● m & f idiot

imborrable adj indelible; (recuerdo etc) unforgettable

imita|ción f imitation. **~r** vt imitate

impacien|cia f impatience. **~tarse** vpr lose one's patience. **~te** adj impatient

impacto m impact; (huella) mark. **~ de bala** bullet hole

impar adj odd

imparcial adj impartial. **~idad** f impartiality

impartir vt impart, give

impasible adj impassive

impávido adj fearless; (impasible) impassive

impecable adj impeccable

impedi|do adj disabled. **~mento** m impediment. **~r** 5 vt prevent; (obstruir) hinder

impenetrable adj impenetrable

impensa|ble adj unthinkable. **~do** adj unexpected

impera|r vi prevail. **~tivo** adj imperative; (necesidad) urgent

imperceptible adj imperceptible

imperdible m safety pin

imperdonable adj unforgivable

imperfec|ción f imperfection. **~to** adj imperfect

imperi|al adj imperial. **~alismo** m imperialism. **~o** m empire; (poder) rule. **~oso** adj imperious

impermeable adj waterproof. ● m raincoat

impersonal adj impersonal

impertinen|cia f impertinence. **~te** adj impertinent

imperturbable adj imperturbable

ímpetu m impetus; (impulso) impulse; (violencia) force

impetuos|idad f impetuosity. **~o** adj impetuous

implacable adj implacable

implantar vt introduce

implementación f implementation

implica|ción f implication. **~r** 7 vt implicate; (significar) imply

implícito adj implicit

implorar vt implore

impon|ente adj imposing; 1 terrific. **~er** 34 vt impose; (requerir) demand; deposit (dinero). **~erse** vpr (hacerse obedecer) assert o.s.; (hacerse respetar) command respect; (prevalecer) prevail. **~ible** adj taxable

importa|ción f importation; (artículo) import. **~ciones** fpl imports. **~dor** adj importing. ● m importer

importa|ncia f importance.

∼**nte** adj important; (en cantidad) considerable. ∼**r** vt import; (ascender a) amount to. ● vi be important, matter. ¿le ∼**ría**...? would you mind...? no ∼ it doesn't matter

importe m price; (total) amount

importun|ar vt bother. ∼**o** adj troublesome; (inoportuno) inopportune

imposib|ilidad f impossibility. ∼**le** adj impossible. hacer lo ∼**le** para do all one can to

imposición f imposition; (impuesto) tax

impostor m impostor

impoten|cia f impotence. ∼**te** adj impotent

impracticable adj impracticable; (intransitable) unpassable

impreci|sión f vagueness; (error) inaccuracy. ∼**o** adj imprecise

impregnar vt impregnate; (empapar) soak

imprenta f printing; (taller) printing house, printer's

imprescindible adj indispensable, essential

impresi|ón f impression; (acción de imprimir) printing; (tirada) edition; (huella) imprint. ∼**onable** adj impressionable. ∼**onante** adj impressive; (espantoso) frightening. ∼**onar** vt impress; (negativamente) shock; (conmover) move; (Foto) expose. ∼**onarse** vpr be impressed; (negativamente) be shocked; (conmover) be moved

impresionis|mo m impressionism. ∼**ta** adj & m & f impressionist

impreso adj printed. ● m form. ∼**s** mpl printed matter. ∼**ra** f printer

imprevis|ible adj unforeseeable;

∼**to** adj unforeseen

imprimir (pp impreso) vt print (libro etc)

improbab|ilidad f improbability. ∼**le** adj unlikely, improbable

improcedente adj inadmissible; (conducta) improper; (despido) unfair

improductivo adj unproductive

improperio m insult. ∼**s** mpl abuse

impropio adj improper

improvis|ación f improvisation. ∼**ado** adj improvised. ∼**ar** vt improvise. ∼**o** adj. de ∼**o** unexpectedly

impruden|cia f imprudence. ∼**te** adj imprudent

imp|udicia f indecency; (desvergüenza) shamelessness. ∼**údico** adj indecent; (desvergonzado) shameless. ∼**udor** m indecency; (desvergüenza) shamelessness

impuesto adj imposed. ● m tax. ∼ a la renta income tax. ∼ sobre el valor agregado (LAm), ∼ sobre el valor añadido VAT, value added tax

impuls|ar vt propel; drive (persona); boost (producción etc). ∼**ividad** f impulsiveness. ∼**ivo** adj impulsive. ∼**o** m impulse

impun|e adj unpunished. ∼**idad** f impunity

impur|eza f impurity. ∼**o** adj impure

imputa|ción f charge. ∼**r** vt attribute; (acusar) charge

inaccesible adj inaccessible

inaceptable adj unacceptable

inactiv|idad f inactivity. ∼**o** adj inactive

inadaptado adj maladjusted

inadecuado *adj* inadequate; *(inapropiado)* unsuitable

inadmisible *adj* inadmissible; *(inaceptable)* unacceptable

inadvertido *adj* distracted. pasar ~ go unnoticed

inagotable *adj* inexhaustible

inaguantable *adj* unbearable

inaltera|ble *adj* impassive; *(color)* fast; *(convicción)* unalterable. ~**do** *adj* unchanged

inapreciable *adj* invaluable; *(imperceptible)* imperceptible

inapropiado *adj* inappropriate

inasequible *adj* out of reach

inaudito *adj* unprecedented

inaugura|ción *f* inauguration. ~**l** *adj* inaugural. ~**r** *vt* inaugurate

inca *adj & m & f* Inca. ~**ico** *adj* Inca

Incas Founded in the twelfth century, the Andean empire of the Quechua-speaking Incas grew and extended from southern Colombia to Argentina and central Chile. Its capital was Cuzco. The Incas built an extensive road network and impressive buildings, including Machu Picchu. The empire collapsed in 1533 after defeat by the Spaniards led by Francisco Pizarro.   *i*

---

incalculable *adj* incalculable

incandescente *adj* incandescent

incansable *adj* tireless

incapa|cidad *f* incapacity; *(física)* disability. ~**citado** *adj* disabled. ~**citar** *vt* incapacitate. ~**z** *adj* incapable

incauto *adj* unwary; *(fácil de engañar)* gullible

incendi|ar *vt* set fire to. ~**arse**

vpr catch fire. ~**ario** *adj* incendiary. ● *m* arsonist. ~**o** *m* fire

incentivo *m* incentive

incertidumbre *f* uncertainty

incesante *adj* incessant

incest|o *m* incest. ~**uoso** *adj* incestuous

inciden|cia *f* incidence; *(efecto)* impact; *(incidente)* incident. ~**tal** *adj* incidental. ~**te** *m* incident

incidir *vi* fall (en into); *(influir)* influence

incienso *m* incense

incierto *adj* uncertain

incinera|dor *m* incinerator. ~**r** *vt* incinerate; cremate *(cadáver)*

incipiente *adj* incipient

incisi|ón *f* incision. ~**vo** *adj* incisive. ● *m* incisor

incitar *vt* incite

inclemen|cia *f* harshness. ~**te** *adj* harsh

inclina|ción *f* slope; *(de la cabeza)* nod; *(fig)* inclination. ~**r** *vt* tilt; *(inducir)* incline. ~**rse** *vpr* lean; *(en saludo)* bow; *(tender)* be inclined (a to)

inclu|ido *adj* included; *(precio)* inclusive. ~**ir** 🟦 *vt* include; *(en cartas)* enclose. ~**sión** *f* inclusion. ~**sive** *adv* inclusive. hasta el lunes ~**sive** up to and including Monday. ~**so** *adv* even

incógnito *adj* unknown. de ~ incognito

incoheren|cia *f* incoherence. ~**te** *adj* incoherent

incoloro *adj* colourless

incomestible *adj*, **incomible** *adj* uneatable, inedible

incomodar *vt* inconvenience; *(causar vergüenza)* make feel uncomfortable. ~**se** *vpr* feel uncomfortable; (*enojarse*) get angry

incómodo *adj* uncomfortable; (*inconveniente*) inconvenient

incomparable *adj* incomparable

incompatib|ilidad *f* incompatibility. ~le *adj* incompatible

incompeten|cia *f* incompetence. ~te *adj* & *m* & *f* incompetent

incompleto *adj* incomplete

incompren|dido *adj* misunderstood. ~sible *adj* incomprehensible. ~sión *f* incomprehension

incomunicado *adj* cut off; (*preso*) in solitary confinement

inconcebible *adj* inconceivable

inconcluso *adj* unfinished

incondicional *adj* unconditional

inconfundible *adj* unmistakable

incongruente *adj* incoherent; (*contradictorio*) inconsistent

inconmensurable *adj* immeasurable

inconscien|cia *f* unconsciousness; (*irreflexión*) recklessness. ~te *adj* unconscious; (*irreflexivo*) reckless

inconsecuente *adj* inconsistent

inconsistente *adj* flimsy

inconsolable *adj* unconsolable

inconstan|cia *f* lack of perseverance. ~te *adj* changeable; (*persona*) lacking in perseverance; (*voluble*) fickle

incontable *adj* countless

incontenible *adj* irrepressible

incontinen|cia *f* incontinence. ~te *adj* incontinent

inconvenien|cia *f* inconvenience. ~te *adj* inconvenient; (*inapropiado*) inappropriate; (*incorrecto*) improper. ● *m* problem; (*desventaja*) drawback

incorpora|ción *f* incorporation.

~r *vt* incorporate; (*Culin*) add. ~rse *vpr* sit up; join (*sociedad, regimiento* etc)

incorrecto *adj* incorrect; (*descortés*) discourteous

incorregible *adj* incorrigible

incorruptible *adj* incorruptible

incrédulo *adj* sceptical; (*mirada, gesto*) incredulous

increíble *adj* incredible

increment|ar *vt* increase. ~o *m* increase

incriminar *vt* incriminate

incrustar *vt* encrust

incuba|ción *f* incubation. ~dora *f* incubator. ~r *vt* incubate; (*fig*) hatch

incuestionable *adj* unquestionable

inculcar ⁊ *vt* inculcate

inculpar *vt* accuse

inculto *adj* uneducated

incumplimiento *m* non-fulfilment; (*de un contrato*) breach

incurable *adj* incurable

incurrir *vi.* ~ en incur (*gasto*); fall into (*error*); commit (*crimen*)

incursión *f* raid

indagar ⒓ *vt* investigate

indebido *adj* unjust; (*uso*) improper

indecen|cia *f* indecency. ~te *adj* indecent

indecible *adj* indescribable

indecis|ión *f* indecision. ~o *adj* (*con ser*) indecisive; (*con estar*) undecided

indefenso *adj* defenceless

indefini|ble *adj* indefinable. ~do *adj* indefinite; (*impreciso*) undefined

indemnizar ⒑ *vt* compensate

independ|encia *f* independ-

ence. ~**lente** *adj* independent.
~**izarse** 🔟 *vpr* become independent

indes|cifrable *adj* indecipherable. ~**criptible** *adj* indescribable
indeseable *adj* undesirable
indestructible *adj* indestructible
indetermina|ble *adj* indeterminable. ~**do** *adj* indeterminate; (tiempo) indefinite
India *f.* la ~ India
indica|ción *f* indication; (señal) signal. ~**ciones** *fpl* directions. ~**dor** *m* indicator; (Tec) gauge. ~**r** 🔟 *vt* show, indicate; (apuntar) point at; (hacer saber) point out; (aconsejar) advise. ~**tivo** *adj* indicative. ● *m* indicative; (al teléfono) dialling code
índice *m* index; (dedo) index finger; (catálogo) catalogue; (indicación) indication; (aguja) pointer
indicio *m* indication, sign; (vestigio) trace
indiferen|cia *f* indifference. ~**te** *adj* indifferent. me es ~**te** it's all the same to me
indígena *adj* indigenous. ● *m & f* native
indigen|cia *f* poverty. ~**te** *adj* needy
indigest|ión *f* indigestion. ~**o** *adj* indigestible
indign|ación *f* indignation. ~**ado** *adj* indignant. ~**ar** *vt* make indignant. ~**arse** *vpr* become indignant. ~**o** *adj* unworthy; (despreciable) contemptible
indio *adj & m* Indian
indirect|a *f* hint. ~**o** *adj* indirect
indisciplinado *adj* undisciplined
indiscre|ción *f* indiscretion. ~**to** *adj* indiscreet
indiscutible *adj* unquestionable

indisoluble *adj* indissoluble
indispensable *adj* indispensable
indisp|oner 🟥 *vt* (enemistar) set against. ~**onerse** *vpr* fall out; (ponerse enfermo) fall ill. ~**osición** *f* indisposition. ~**uesto** *adj* indisposed
individu|al *adj* individual; (cama) single. ● *m* (en tenis etc) singles. ~**alidad** *f* individuality. ~**alista** *m & f* individualist. ~**alizar** 🔟 *vt* individualize. ~**o** *m* individual
indocumentado *m* person without identity papers; (inmigrante) illegal immigrant
índole *f* nature; (clase) type
indolen|cia *f* indolence. ~**te** *adj* indolent
indoloro *adj* painless
indomable *adj* untameable
inducir 🟦 *vt* induce. ~ **a error** be misleading
indudable *adj* undoubted
indulgen|cia *f* indulgence. ~**te** *adj* indulgent
indult|ar *vt* pardon. ~**o** *m* pardon
industria *f* industry. ~**l** *adj* industrial. ● *m & f* industrialist. ~**lización** *f* industrialization. ~**lizar** 🔟 *vt* industrialize
inédito *adj* unpublished; (fig) unknown
inefable *adj* indescribable
ineficaz *adj* ineffective; (sistema etc) inefficient
ineficiente *adj* inefficient
ineludible *adj* inescapable, unavoidable
inept|itud *f* ineptitude. ~**o** *adj* inept
inequívoco *adj* unequivocal
inercia *f* inertia
inerte *adj* inert; (sin vida) lifeless

inesperado adj unexpected

inestable adj unstable

inestimable adj inestimable

inevitable adj inevitable

inexistente adj non-existent

inexorable adj inexorable

inexper|iencia f inexperience. ~to adj inexperienced

inexplicable adj inexplicable

infalible adj infallible

infam|ar vt defame. ~atorio adj defamatory. ~e adj infamous; (fig, fam, muy malo) awful. ~ia f infamy

infancia f infancy

infant|a f infanta, princess. ~e m infante, prince. ~ería f infantry. ~il adj children's; (población) child; (actitud etc) childish, infantile

infarto m heart attack

infec|ción f infection. ~cioso adj infectious. ~tar vt infect. ~tarse vpr become infected. ~to adj infected; [!] disgusting

infeli|cidad f unhappiness. ~z adj unhappy

inferior adj inferior. ● m & f inferior. ~idad f inferiority

infernal adj infernal, hellish

infestar vt infest; (fig) inundate

infi|delidad f unfaithfulness. ~el adj unfaithful

infierno m hell

infiltra|ción f infiltration. ~rse vpr infiltrate

ínfimo adj lowest; (calidad) very poor

infini|dad f infinity. ~tivo m infinitive. ~to adj infinite. ● m. el ~to the infinite; (en matemáticas) infinity. ~dad de countless

inflación f inflation

inflama|ble adj (in)flammable.

~ción f inflammation. ~r vt set on fire; (fig, Med) inflame. ~rse vpr catch fire; (Med) become inflamed

inflar vt inflate; blow up (globo); (fig, exagerar) exaggerate

inflexi|ble adj inflexible. ~ón f inflexion

influ|encia f influence (en on). ~ir [17] vt influence. ● vi. ~ en influence. ~jo m influence. ~yente adj influential

informa|ción f information; (noticias) news; (en aeropuerto etc) information desk; (de teléfonos) directory enquiries. ~dor m informant

informal adj informal; (persona) unreliable

inform|ante m & f informant. ~ar vt/i inform. ~arse vpr find out. ~ática f information technology, computing. ~ativo adj informative; (programa) news. ~atizar [10] vt computerize

informe adj shapeless. ● m report. ~s fpl references, information

infracción f infringement. ~ de tráfico traffic offence

infraestructura f infrastructure

infranqueable adj impassable; (fig) insuperable

infrarrojo adj infrared

infringir [14] vt infringe

infructuoso adj fruitless

ínfulas fpl. darse ~ give o.s. airs. tener ~ de fancy o.s. as

infundado adj unfounded

infu|ndir vt instil. ~sión f infusion

ingeni|ar vt invent. ~árselas para find a way to

ingenier|ía f engineering. ~o m engineer

ingenio m ingenuity; (*agudeza*) wit; (*LAm, de azúcar*) refinery. **~so** adj ingenious

ingenu|idad f naivety. **~o** adj naive

Inglaterra f England

ingl|és adj English. ● m Englishman; (*lengua*) English. **~esa** f Englishwoman. **los ~eses** the English

ingrat|itud f ingratitude. **~o** adj ungrateful; (*desagradable*) thankless

ingrediente m ingredient

ingres|ar vt deposit. ● vi. **~ar en** come in, enter; join (sociedad). **~o** m entrance; (*de dinero*) deposit; (*en sociedad, hospital*) admission. **~os** mpl income

inh|ábil adj unskilful; (*no apto*) unfit. **~abilidad** f unskilfulness; (*para cargo*) ineligibility

inhabitable adj uninhabitable

inhala|dor m inhaler. **~r** vt inhale

inherente adj inherent

inhibi|ción f inhibition. **~r** vt inhibit

inhóspito adj inhospitable

inhumano adj inhuman

inici|ación f beginning. **~al** adj & f initial. **~ar** vt initiate; (*comenzar*) begin, start. **~ativa** f initiative. **~o** m beginning

inigualado adj unequalled

ininterrumpido adj uninterrupted

injert|ar vt graft. **~to** m graft

injuri|a f insult. **~ar** vt insult. **~oso** adj insulting

injust|icia f injustice. **~o** adj unjust, unfair

inmaculado adj immaculate

inmaduro adj unripe; (*persona*) immature

inmediaciones fpl. **las ~** the vicinity, the surrounding area

inmediat|amente adv immediately. **~o** adj immediate; (*contiguo*) next. **de ~o** immediately

inmejorable adj excellent

inmemorable adj immemorial

inmens|idad f immensity. **~o** adj immense

inmersión f immersion

inmigra|ción f immigration. **~nte** adj & m & f immigrant. **~r** vt immigrate

inminen|cia f imminence. **~te** adj imminent

inmiscuirse 17 vpr interfere

inmobiliario adj property

inmolar vt sacrifice

inmoral adj immoral. **~idad** f immorality

inmortal adj immortal. **~izar** 10 vt immortalize

inmóvil adj immobile

inmovilizador m immobilizer

inmueble adj. **bienes ~s** property

inmund|icia f filth. **~o** adj filthy

inmun|e adj immune. **~idad** f immunity. **~ización** f immunization. **~izar** 10 vt immunize

inmuta|ble adj unchangeable. **~rse** vpr be perturbed. **sin ~rse** unperturbed

innato adj innate

innecesario adj unnecessary

innegable adj undeniable

innova|ción f innovation. **~r** vi innovate. ● vt make innovations in

innumerable adj innumerable

inocen|cia f innocence. **~tada** f practical joke. **~te** adj innocent. **~tón** adj naïve

inocuo adj innocuous

inodoro adj odourless. • m toilet

inofensivo adj inoffensive

inolvidable adj unforgettable

inoperable adj inoperable

inoportuno adj untimely; (comentario) ill-timed

inoxidable adj stainless

inquiet|ar f worry. ~**arse** vpr get worried. ~**o** adj worried; (agitado) restless. ~**ud** f anxiety

inquilino m tenant

inquirir 4 vt enquire into, investigate

insaciable adj insatiable

insalubre adj unhealthy

insatisfecho adj unsatisfied; (descontento) dissatisfied

inscri|bir (pp inscrito) vt (en registro) register; (en curso) enrol; (grabar) inscribe. ~**birse** vpr register. ~**pción** f inscription; (registro) registration

insect|icida m insecticide. ~**o** m insect

insegur|idad f insecurity. ~**o** adj insecure; (ciudad) unsafe, dangerous

insemina|ción f insemination. ~**r** vt inseminate

insensato adj foolish

insensible adj insensitive

inseparable adj inseparable

insertar vt insert

insidi|a f malice. ~**oso** adj insidious

insigne adj famous

insignia f badge; (bandera) flag

insignificante adj insignificant

insinu|ación f insinuation. ~**ante** adj insinuating. ~**ar** 21 vt imply; insinuate (algo ofensivo). ~**arse** vpr. ~**ársele a** make a pass at

insípido adj insipid

insist|encia f insistence. ~**ente** adj insistent. ~**ir** vi insist; (hacer hincapié) stress

insolación f sunstroke

insolen|cia f rudeness, insolence. ~**te** adj rude, insolent

insólito adj unusual

insolven|cia f insolvency. ~**te** adj & m & f insolvent

insomn|e adj sleepless. • m & f insomniac. ~**io** m insomnia

insondable adj unfathomable

insoportable adj unbearable

insospechado adj unexpected

insostenible adj untenable

inspec|ción f inspection. ~**cionar** vt inspect. ~**tor** m inspector

inspira|ción f inspiration. ~**r** vt inspire. ~**rse** vpr be inspired

instala|ción f installation. ~**r** vt install. ~**rse** vpr settle

instancia f request. en última ~ as a last resort

instant|ánea f snapshot. ~**áneo** adj instantaneous; (café etc) instant. ~**e** m instant. a cada ~**e** constantly. al ~**e** immediately

instaura|ción f establishment. ~**r** vt establish

instiga|ción f instigation. ~**dor** m instigator. ~**r** 12 vt instigate; (incitar) incite

instint|ivo adj instinctive. ~**o** m instinct

institu|ción f institution. ~**cional** adj institutional. ~**ir** 17 vt establish. ~**to** m institute; (en enseñanza) (secondary) school. ~**triz** f governess

instru|cción f education; (Mil) training. ~**cciones** fpl instruction. ~**ctivo** adj instructive; (película etc) educational. **~ctor** m instructor. **~ir** [17] vt instruct, teach; (Mil) train

instrument|ación f instrumentation. **~al** adj instrumental. **~o** m instrument; (herramienta) tool

insubordina|ción f insubordination. **~r** vt stir up. **~rse** vpr rebel

insuficien|cia f insufficiency; (inadecuación) inadequacy. **~te** adj insufficient

insufrible adj insufferable

insular adj insular

insulina f insulin

insulso adj tasteless; (fig) insipid

insult|ar vt insult. **~o** m insult

insuperable adj insuperable; (inmejorable) unbeatable

insurgente adj insurgent

insurrec|ción f insurrection. **~to** adj insurgent

intachable adj irreproachable

intacto adj intact

intangible adj intangible

integra|ción f integration. **~l** adj integral; (completo) complete; (incorporado) built-in; (pan) wholemeal (Brit), wholewheat (Amer). **~r** vt make up

integridad f integrity; (entereza) wholeness

íntegro adj complete; (fig) upright

intelect|o m intellect. **~ual** adj & m & f intellectual

inteligen|cia f intelligence. **~te** adj intelligent

inteligible adj intelligible

intemperie f. a la **~** in the open

intempestivo adj untimely

intenci|ón f intention. con doble **~ón** implying sth else. **~onado** adj deliberate. bien **~onado** well-meaning. mal **~onado** malicious.

~onal adj intentional

intens|idad f intensity. **~ificar** [7] vt intensify. **~ivo** adj intensive. **~o** adj intense

intent|ar vt try. **~o** m attempt; (Mex, propósito) intention

inter|calar vt insert. **~cambio** m exchange. **~ceder** vt intercede

interceptar vt intercept

interdicto m ban

inter|és m interest; (egoísmo) self-interest. **~esado** adj interested; (parcial) biassed; (egoísta) selfish. **~esante** adj interesting. **~esar** vt interest; (afectar) concern. **~vi** be of interest. **~esarse** vpr take an interest (por in)

interfaz m & f interface

interfer|encia f interference. **~ir** [4] vi interfere

interfono m intercom

interino adj temporary; (persona) acting. ● m stand-in

interior adj interior; (comercio etc) domestic. ● m inside. Ministerio del I**~** Interior Ministry

interjección f interjection

inter|locutor m speaker. **~mediario** adj & m intermediary. **~medio** adj intermediate. ● m interval

interminable adj interminable

intermitente adj intermittent. ● m indicator

internacional adj international

intern|ado m (Escol) boarding-school. **~ar** vt (en manicomio) commit; (en hospital) admit. **~arse** vpr penetrate

internauta m & f netsurfer

Internet m Internet

interno adj internal; (en enseñanza) boarding. ● m boarder

interponer 34 vt interpose. ~**se** vpr intervene

int|erpretación f interpretation. ~**erpretar** vt interpret; (*Mús etc*) play. ~**érprete** m interpreter; (*Mus*) performer

interroga|ción f interrogation; (*signo*) question mark. ~**r** 12 vt question. ~**tivo** adj interrogative

interru|mpir vt interrupt; cut off (suministro); cut short (viaje etc); block (tráfico). ~**pción** f interruption. ~**ptor** m switch

inter|sección f intersection. ~**urbano** adj inter-city; (llamada) long-distance

intervalo m interval; (*espacio*) space. a ~**s** at intervals

interven|ir 53 vt control; (*Med*) operate on. ● vi intervene; (*participar*) take part. ~**tor** m inspector; (*Com*) auditor

intestino m intestine

intim|ar vi become friendly. ~**idad** f intimacy

intimidar vt intimidate

íntimo adj intimate; (*amigo*) close. ● m close friend

intolera|ble adj intolerable. ~**nte** adj intolerant

intoxicar 7 vt poison

intranquilo adj worried

intransigente adj intransigent

intransitable adj impassable

intransitivo adj intransitive

intratable adj impossible

intrépido adj intrepid

intriga f intrigue. ~**nte** adj intriguing. ~**r** 12 vt intrigue

intrincado adj intricate

intrínseco adj intrinsic

introduc|ción f introduction. ~**ir** 47 vt introduce; (*meter*) insert.

~**irse** vpr get into

intromisión f interference

introvertido adj introverted. ● m introvert

intruso m intruder

intui|ción f intuition. ~**r** 17 vt sense. ~**tivo** adj intuitive

inunda|ción f flooding. ~**r** vt flood

inusitado adj unusual

in|útil adj useless; (*vano*) futile. ~**utilidad** f uselessness

invadir vt invade

inv|alidez f invalidity; (*Med*) disability. ~**álido** adj & m invalid

invariable adj invariable

invas|ión f invasion. ~**or** adj invading. ● m invader

invencible adj invincible

inven|ción f invention. ~**tar** vt invent

inventario m inventory

invent|iva f inventiveness. ~**ivo** adj inventive. ~**or** m inventor

invernadero m greenhouse

invernal adj winter

inverosímil adj implausible

inver|sión f inversion; (*Com*) investment. ~**sionista** m & f investor

inverso adj inverse; (*contrario*) opposite. a la inversa the other way round. a la inversa de contrary to

inversor m investor

invertir 4 vt reverse; (*Com*) invest; put in (tiempo)

investidura f investiture

investiga|ción f investigation; (*Univ*) research. ~**dor** m investigator; (*Univ*) researcher. ~**r** 12 vt investigate; (*Univ*) research

investir 5 vt invest

invicto adj unbeaten

invierno *m* winter

inviolable *adj* inviolate

invisible *adj* invisible

invita|ción *f* invitation. **~do** *m* guest. **~r** *vt* invite. te invito a una copa I'll buy you a drink

invocar 7 *vt* invoke

involuntario *adj* involuntary

invulnerable *adj* invulnerable

inyec|ción *f* injection. **~tar** *vt* inject

---

ir 49

● *verbo intransitivo*

····▸ to go. fui a verla I went to see her. ir a pie to go on foot. ir en coche to go by car. vamos a casa let's go home. fue (a) por el pan he went to get some bread

> ! Cuando la acción del verbo **ir** significa trasladarse hacia o con el interlocutor la traducción es *to come*, p.ej: **¡ya voy!** I'm coming! **yo voy contigo** I'll come with you

····▸ (*estar*) to be. iba con su novio she was with her boyfriend. ¿cómo te va? how are you?

····▸ (*sentar*) to suit. ese color no le va that colour doesn't suit her. no me va ni me viene I don't mind at all

····▸ (*Méx, apoyar*) irle a to support. le va al equipo local he supports the local team

····▸ (*en exclamaciones*) ¡vamos! come on! ¡vaya! what a surprise!; (*contrariedad*) oh, dear! ¡vaya noche! what a night!

¡qué va! nonsense!

> ➡ Cuando el verbo intransitivo se emplea con expresiones como **ir de paseo, ir de compras, ir tirando** etc., ver bajo el respectivo nombre, verbo etc.

● *verbo auxiliar*

····▸ ir a + *infinitivo* (*para expresar futuro, propósito*) to be going to + *infinitive*; (*al prevenir*) no te vayas a caer be careful you don't fall. no vaya a ser que llueva in case it rains; (*en sugerencias*) vamos a dormir let's go to sleep. vamos a ver let's see

····▸ ir + *gerundio*. ve arreglándote start getting ready. el tiempo va mejorando the weather is gradually getting better.

● *irse* *verbo pronominal*

····▸ to go. se ha ido a casa he's gone home

····▸ (*marcharse*) to leave. se fue sin despedirse he left without saying goodbye. se fue de casa she left home

ira *f* anger. **~cundo** *adj* irascible

Irak *m* Iraq

Irán *m* Iran

iraní *adj & m & f* Iranian

iraquí *adj & m & f* Iraqi

iris *m* (*del ojo*) iris

Irlanda *f* Ireland

irland|és *adj* Irish. ● *m* Irishman; (*lengua*) Irish. **~esa** *f* Irishwoman. los **~eses** the Irish

ir|onía *f* irony. **~ónico** *adj* ironic

irracional *adj* irrational

irradiar vt radiate
irreal adj unreal. ~**idad** f unreality
irrealizable adj unattainable
irreconciliable adj irreconcilable
irreconocible adj unrecognizable
irrecuperable adj irretrievable
irreflexión f impetuosity
irregular adj irregular. ~**idad** f irregularity
irreparable adj irreparable
irreprimible adj irrepressible
irreprochable adj irreproachable
irresistible adj irresistible
irrespetuoso adj disrespectful
irresponsable adj irresponsible
irriga|ción f irrigation. ~**r** 12 vt irrigate
irrisorio adj derisory
irrita|ble adj irritable. ~**ción** f irritation. ~**r** vt irritate. ~**rse** vpr get annoyed
irrumpir vi burst (en in)
isla f island. las I~s Británicas the British Isles
islámico adj Islamic
islandés adj Icelandic. ● m Icelander; (lengua) Icelandic
Islandia f Iceland
isleño adj island. ● m islander
Israel m Israel
israelí adj & m Israeli
Italia f Italy
italiano adj & m Italian
itinerario adj itinerary
IVA abrev (**impuesto sobre el valor agregado** (LAm), **impuesto sobre el valor añadido**) VAT
izar 10 vt hoist
izquierd|a f. la ~**a** the left hand; (Pol) left. a la ~**a** on the left; (con movimiento) to the left. de ~**a**

left-wing. ~**ista** m & f leftist. ~**o** adj left

Jj

ja int ha!
jabalí m (pl ~**es**) wild boar
jabalina f javelin
jab|ón m soap. ~**onar** vt soap. ~**onoso** adj soapy
jaca f pony
jacinto m hyacinth
jactarse vpr boast
jadea|nte adj panting. ~**r** vi pant
jaguar m jaguar
jaiba f (LAm) crab
jalar vt (LAm) pull
jalea f jelly
jaleo m row, uproar. armar un ~ kick up a fuss
jalón m (LAm, tirón) pull; (Mex fam, trago) drink; (Mex, tramo) stretch
jamás adv never. nunca ~ never ever
jamelgo m nag
jamón m ham. ~ **de York** boiled ham. ~ **serrano** cured ham
Japón m. el ~ Japan
japonés adj & m Japanese
jaque m check. ~ **mate** checkmate
jaqueca f migraine
jarabe m syrup
jardín m garden. ~ **de la infancia**, (Mex) ~ **de niños** kindergarten, nursery school
jardiner|ía f gardening. ~**o** m gardener

jarr|a f jug. **en ~as** with hands on hips. **~o** m jug. **caer como un ~o de agua fría** come as a shock. **~ón** m vase

jaula f cage

jauría f pack of hounds

jazmín m jasmine

jef|a f boss. **~atura** f leadership; (*sede*) headquarters. **~e** m boss; (*Pol etc*) leader. **~e de camareros** head waiter. **~e de estación** station-master. **~e de ventas** sales manager

jengibre m ginger

jer|arquía f hierarchy. **~árquico** adj hierarchical

jerez m sherry. **al ~** with sherry

---

i **jerez** Sherry is produced in an area around Jerez de la Frontera near Cádiz. Sherries are drunk worldwide as an aperitif, and in Spain as an accompaniment to tapas. The main types are: the pale *fino* and *manzanilla* and the darker *oloroso* and *amontillado*. It is from *Jerez* that sherry takes its English name.

---

jerga f coarse cloth; (*argot*) jargon

jerigonza f jargon; (*galimatías*) gibberish

jeringa f syringe; (*LAm fam, molestia*) nuisance. **~r** 12 vt (*fig, fam, molestar*) annoy

jeroglífico m hieroglyph(ic)

jersey m (*pl* ~s) jersey

Jesucristo m Jesus Christ. **antes de ~** BC, before Christ

jesuita adj & m Jesuit

Jesús m Jesus. ● int good heavens!; (*al estornudar*) bless you!

jícara f (*Mex*) gourd

jilguero m goldfinch

jinete m & f rider

jipijapa m panama hat

jirafa f giraffe

jirón m shred, tatter

jitomate m (*Mex*) tomato

jorna|da f working day; (*viaje*) journey; (*etapa*) stage. **~l** m day's wage. **~lero** m day labourer

joroba f hump. **~do** adj hunchbacked. ● m hunchback. **~r** vt 1 annoy

jota f letter J; (*danza*) jota, popular dance. **ni ~** nothing

joven (*pl* jóvenes) adj young. ● m young man. ● f young woman

jovial adj jovial

joy|a f jewel. **~as** fpl jewellery. **~ería** f jeweller's (shop). **~ero** m jeweller; (*estuche*) jewellery box

juanete m bunion

jubil|ación f retirement. **~ado** adj retired. **~ar** vt pension off. **~arse** vpr retire. **~eo** m jubilee

júbilo m joy

judaísmo m Judaism

judía f Jewish woman; (*alubia*) bean. **~ blanca** haricot bean. **~ escarlata** runner bean. **~ verde** French bean

judicial adj judicial

judío adj Jewish. ● m Jewish man

judo m judo

juego m play; (*de mesa, niños*) game; (*de azar*) gambling; (*conjunto*) set. **estar en ~** be at stake. **estar fuera de ~** be offside. **hacer ~** match. **~s malabares** juggling. **~s** mpl **Olímpicos** Olympic Games. ● vb *véase* JUGAR

juerga f spree

jueves m invar Thursday

juez m judge. **~ de instrucción** examining magistrate. **~ de línea**

linesman

juga|dor *m* player; (*habitual, por dinero*) gambler. **~r 3** *vt* play. ● *vi* play; (*apostar fuerte*) gamble. **~rse** *vpr* risk. **~r al fútbol,** (*LAm*) **~r fútbol** play football

juglar *m* minstrel

jugo *m* juice; (*de carne*) gravy; (*fig*) substance. **~so** *adj* juicy; (*fig*) substantial

juguet|e *m* toy. **~ear** *vi* play. **~ón** *adj* playful

juicio *m* judgement; (*opinión*) opinion; (*razón*) reason. **a mi ~** in my opinion. **~so** *adj* wise

juliana *f* vegetable soup

julio *m* July

junco *m* rush, reed

jungla *f* jungle

junio *m* June

junt|a *f* meeting; (*consejo*) board, committee; (*Pol*) junta; (*Tec*) joint. **~ar** *vt* join; (*reunir*) collect. **~arse** *vpr* (*gente*) meet. **~o** *adj* joined; (*en plural*) together. **~o a** next to. **~ura** *f* joint

jura|do *adj* sworn. ● *m* jury; (*miembro de jurado*) juror. **~mento** *m* oath. **prestar ~mento** take an oath. **~r** *vt/i* swear. **~r en falso** commit perjury. **jurárselas a uno** have it in for s.o.

jurel *m* (type of) mackerel

jurídico *adj* legal

juris|dicción *f* jurisdiction. **~prudencia** *f* jurisprudence

justamente *adj* exactly; (*con justicia*) fairly

justicia *f* justice

justifica|ción *f* justification. **~r 7** *vt* justify

justo *adj* fair, just; (*exacto*) exact;

(*ropa*) tight. ● *adv* just. **~ a tiempo** just in time

juven|il *adj* youthful. **~tud** *f* youth; (*gente joven*) young people

juzga|do *m* (*tribunal*) court. **~r 12** *vt* judge. **a ~r por** judging by

---

K k

---

kilo *m,* **kilogramo** *m* kilo, kilogram

kil|ometraje *m* distance in kilometres, mileage. **~ométrico** *adj* 1 endless. **~ómetro** *m* kilometre. **~ómetro cuadrado** square kilometre

kilovatio *m* kilowatt

kiosco *m* kiosk

L l

---

la *artículo definido femenino* (*pl* **las**)

····▶ the. **la flor azul** the blue flower. **la casa de al lado** the house next door. **cerca de la iglesia** near the church *No se traduce en los siguientes casos:*

····▶ (*con nombre abstracto, genérico*) **la paciencia es una virtud** patience is a virtue. **odio la leche** I hate milk. **la madera es muy versátil** wood is very versatile

····▶ (*con algunas instituciones*)

termino la universidad mañana I finish university tomorrow. no va nunca a la iglesia he never goes to church. está en la cárcel he's in jail

····▶ (con nombres propios) la Sra. Díaz Mrs Díaz. la doctora Lara doctor Lara

····▶ (con partes del cuerpo, artículos personales) se traduce por un posesivo. apretó la mano he clenched his fist. tienes la camisa desabrochada your shirt is undone

····▶ la + de. es la de Ana it's Ana's. la del sombrero the one with the hat

····▶ la + que (persona) la que me atendió the one who served me. (cosa) la que se rompió the one that broke

····▶ la + que + subjuntivo (quienquiera) la que gane pasará a la final whoever wins will go to the final. (cualquiera) whichever. compra la que sea más barata buy whichever is cheaper

laberinto m labyrinth, maze
labia f gift of the gab
labio m lip
labor f work. ~es de aguja needlework. ~es de ganchillo crochet. ~es de punto knitting. ~es domésticas housework. ~able adj working. ~ar vi work
laboratorio m laboratory
laborioso adj laborious
laborista adj Labour. ● m & f member of the Labour Party
labra|do adj worked; (madera) carved; (metal) wrought; (tierra)

ploughed. ~dor m farmer; (obrero) farm labourer. ~nza f farming. ~r vt work; carve (madera); cut (piedra); till (la tierra). ~rse vpr. ~rse un porvenir carve out a future for o.s.
labriego m peasant
laca f lacquer
lacayo m lackey
lacio adj straight; (flojo) limp
lacón m shoulder of pork
lacónico adj laconic
lacr|ar vt seal. ~e m sealing wax
lactante adj (niño) still on milk
lácteo adj milky. productos mpl ~s dairy products
ladear vt tilt. ~se vpr lean
ladera f slope
ladino adj astute
lado m side. al ~ near. al ~ de next to, beside. de ~ sideways. en todos ~s everywhere. los de al ~ the next door neighbours. por otro ~ on the other hand. por todos ~s everywhere. por un ~ on the one hand
ladr|ar vi bark. ~ido m bark
ladrillo m brick
ladrón m thief, robber; (de casas) burglar
lagart|ija f (small) lizard. ~o m lizard
lago m lake
lágrima f tear
lagrimoso adj tearful
laguna f small lake; (fig, omisión) gap
laico adj lay
lament|able adj deplorable; (que da pena) pitiful; (pérdida) sad. ~ar vt be sorry about. ~arse vpr lament; (quejarse) complain. ~o m moan

lamer vt lick

lámina f sheet; (ilustración) plate; (estampa) picture card

lamina|do adj laminated. **~r** vt laminate

lámpara f lamp. **~** de pie standard lamp

lamparón m stain

lampiño adj beardless; (cuerpo) hairless

lana f wool. de **~** wool(len)

lanceta f lancet

lancha f boat. **~** motora motor boat. **~** salvavidas lifeboat

langost|a f (de mar) lobster; (insecto) locust. **~ino** m king prawn

languide|cer 11 vi languish. **~z** f languor

lánguido adj languid; (decaído) listless

lanilla f nap; (tela fina) flannel

lanudo adj woolly; (perro) shaggy

lanza f lance, spear

lanza|llamas m invar flamethrower. **~miento** m throw; (acción de lanzar) throwing; (de proyectil, de producto) launch. **~miento** de peso, (LAm) **~miento** de bala shot put. **~r** 10 vt throw; (de un avión) drop; launch (proyectil, producto). **~rse** vpr throw o.s.

lapicero m (propelling) pencil

lápida f tombstone; (placa conmemorativa) memorial tablet

lapidar vt stone

lápiz m pencil. **~** de labios lipstick. a **~** in pencil

lapso m lapse

laptop m laptop

larg|a f. a la **~a** in the long run. dar **~as** put off. **~ar** 12 vt (Naut) let out; (fam, dar) give; 11 deal

(bofetada etc). **~arse** vpr 11 beat it 11. **~o** adj long. ● m length. ¡**~o**! go away! a lo **~o** lengthwise. a lo **~o** de along. tener 100 metros de **~o** be 100 metres long

laring|e f larynx. **~itis** f laryngitis

larva f larva

las artículo definido fpl the. véase tb **LA**. ● pron them. **~** de those, the ones. **~** de Vd your ones, yours. **~** que whoever, the ones

láser m laser

lástima f pity; (queja) complaint. da **~** ver lo it's sad to see him like that. ella me da **~** I feel sorry for her. ¡qué **~**! what a pity!

lastim|ado adj hurt. **~ar** vt hurt. **~arse** vpr hurt o.s. **~ero** adj doleful. **~oso** adj pitiful

lastre m ballast; (fig) burden

lata f tinplate; (envase) tin (esp Brit), can; (fam, molestia) nuisance. dar la **~** be a nuisance. ¡qué **~**! what a nuisance!

latente adj latent

lateral adj side, lateral

latido m beating; (cada golpe) beat

latifundio m large estate

latigazo m (golpe) lash; (chasquido) crack

látigo m whip

latín m Latin. saber **~** 11 know what's what 11

latino adj Latin. **L~américa** f Latin America. **~americano** adj & m Latin American

latir vi beat; (herida) throb

latitud f latitude

latón m brass

latoso adj annoying; (pesado) boring

laúd m lute

laureado adj honoured; (premiado) prize-winning

laurel m laurel; (Culin) bay

lava f lava

lava|ble adj washable. ~**bo** m wash-basin; (retrete) toilet. ~**dero** m sink. ~**do** m washing. ~**do de cerebro** brainwashing. ●m (Mex, fregadero) sink. ~**dora** f washing machine. ~**ndería** f laundry. ~**ndería automática** launderette, laundromat (esp Amer). ~**platos** m & f invar dishwasher; (Mex, fregadero) sink. ~**r** vt wash. ~**r en seco** dry-cleaning. ~**rse** vpr have a wash. ~**rse las manos** (incl fig) wash one's hands. ~**tiva** f enema. ~**vajillas** m invar dishwasher; (detergente) washing-up liquid (Brit), dishwashing liquid (Amer)

laxante adj & m laxative

lazada f bow

lazarillo m guide for a blind person

lazo m knot; (lazada) bow; (fig, vínculo) tie; (con nudo corredizo) lasso; (Mex, cuerda) rope

le pron (acusativo, él) him; (acusativo, Vd) you; (dativo, él) (to) him; (dativo, ella) (to) her; (dativo, cosa) (to) it; (dativo, Vd) (to) you

leal adj loyal; (fiel) faithful. ~**tad** f loyalty; (fidelidad) faithfulness

lección f lesson

leche f milk; (golpe) bash. ~ **condensada** condensed milk. ~ **desnatada** skimmed milk. ~ **en polvo** powdered milk. ~ **sin desnatar** whole milk. **tener mala** ~ be spiteful. ~**ra** f (vasija) milk jug. ~**ría** f dairy. ~**ro** adj milk, dairy. ●m milkman

lecho m (en literatura) bed. ~ **de río** river bed

lechoso adj milky

lechuga f lettuce

lechuza f owl

lector m reader; (Univ) language assistant. ~**ura** f reading

leer 18 vt/i read

legación f legation

legado m legacy; (enviado) legate

legajo m bundle, file

legal adj legal. ~**idad** f legality. ~**izar** 10 vt legalize; (certificar) authenticate. ~**mente** adv legally

legar 12 vt bequeath

legible adj legible

legi|ón f legion. ~**onario** m legionary. ~**onella** f legionnaire's disease

legisla|ción f legislation. ~**dor** m legislator. ~**r** vi legislate. ~**tura** f term (of office); (año parlamentario) session; (LAm, cuerpo) legislature

legitimidad f legitimacy. ~**ítimo** adj legitimate; (verdadero) real

lego adj lay; (ignorante) ignorant. ●m layman

legua f league

legumbre f vegetable

lejan|ía f distance. ~**o** adj distant

lejía f bleach

lejos adv far. ~ **de** far from. **a lo** ~ in the distance. **desde** ~ from a distance, from afar

lema m motto

lencería f linen; (de mujer) lingerie

lengua f tongue; (idioma) language. **irse de la** ~ talk too much. **morderse la** ~ hold one's tongue

lenguas cooficiales The *i* regional languages of Spain, *catalán*, *euskera* and *gallego*, which now have equal status with Castilian in the regions where they are spoken. Banned under Franco, they continued to be spoken privately. They are now more widely used in public life, education, the media, cinema and literature.

lenguado *m* sole

lenguaje *m* language

lengüeta *f* (*de zapato*) tongue. **~da** *f*, **~zo** *m* lick

lente *f* lens. **~s** *mpl* glasses. **~s de contacto** contact lenses

lentej|a *f* lentil. **~uela** *f* sequin

lentilla *f* contact lens

lent|itud *f* slowness. **~o** *adj* slow

leñ|a *f* firewood. **~ador** *m* woodcutter. **~o** *m* log

Leo *m* Leo

le|ón *m* lion. **~ona** *f* lioness

leopardo *m* leopard

leotardo *m* thick tights

lepr|a *f* leprosy. **~oso** *m* leper

lerdo *adj* dim; (*torpe*) clumsy

les *pron* (*acusativo*) them; (*acusativo, Vds*) you; (*dativo*) (to) them; (*dativo, Vds*) (to) you

lesbiana *f* lesbian

lesi|ón *f* wound. **~onado** *adj* injured. **~onar** *vt* injure; (*dañar*) damage

letal *adj* lethal

let|árgico *adj* lethargic. **~argo** *m* lethargy

letr|a *f* letter; (*escritura*) handwriting; (*de una canción*) words, lyrics. **~a de cambio** bill of exchange. **~a de imprenta** print. **~ado** *adj*

learned. **~ero** *m* notice; (*cartel*) poster

letrina *f* latrine

leucemia *f* leukaemia

levadura *f* yeast. **~ en polvo** baking powder

levanta|miento *m* lifting; (*sublevación*) uprising. **~r** *vt* raise, lift; (*construir*) build; (*recoger*) pick up. **~rse** *vpr* get up; (*ponerse de pie*) stand up; (*erguirse, sublevarse*) rise up

levante *m* east; (*viento*) east wind

levar *vt*. **~ anclas** weigh anchor

leve *adj* light; (*sospecha etc*) slight; (*enfermedad*) mild; (*de poca importancia*) trivial. **~dad** *f* lightness; (*fig*) slightness

léxico *m* vocabulary

lexicografía *f* lexicography

ley *f* law; (*parlamentaria*) act

leyenda *f* legend

liar [20] *vt* tie; (*envolver*) wrap up; roll (*cigarrillo*); (*fig, confundir*) confuse; (*fig, enredar*) involve. **~se** *vpr* get involved

libanés *adj* & *m* Lebanese

libelo *m* (*escrito*) libellous article; (*Jurid*) petition

libélula *f* dragonfly

libera|ción *f* liberation. **~dor** *adj* liberating. ● *m* liberator

liberal *adj* & *m* & *f* liberal. **~idad** *f* liberality

liber|ar *vt* free. **~tad** *f* freedom. **~tad de cultos** freedom of worship. **~tad de imprenta** freedom of the press. **~tad provisional** bail. **en ~tad** free. **~tador** *m* liberator. **~tar** *vt* free

libertino *m* libertine

libido *f* libido

libio *adj* & *m* Libyan

libra f pound. ~ **esterlina** pound sterling

Libra m Libra

libra|dor m (Com) drawer. ~r vt free; (de un peligro) save. ~rse vpr free o.s. ~rse de get rid of

libre adj free. **estilo** ~ (en natación) freestyle. ~ **de impuestos** tax-free

librea f livery

libr|ería f bookshop (Brit), bookstore (Amer); (mueble) bookcase. ~**ero** m bookseller; (Mex, mueble) bookcase. ~**eta** f notebook. ~**o** m book. ~**o de bolsillo** paperback. ~**o de ejercicios** exercise book. ~**o de reclamaciones** complaints book

licencia f permission; (documento) licence. ~**do** m graduate; (Mex, abogado) lawyer. ~ **para manejar** (Mex) driving licence. ~**r** vt (Mil) discharge; (echar) dismiss. ~**tura** f degree

licencioso adj licentious

licitar vt bid for

lícito adj legal; (permisible) permissible

licor m liquor; (dulce) liqueur

licua|dora f blender. ~**r** 21 liquefy; (Culin) blend

lid f fight. ~**es** fpl matters

líder m leader

liderato m, **liderazgo** m leadership

lidia f bullfighting; (lucha) fight. ~**r** vt/i fight

liebre f hare

lienzo m linen; (del pintor) canvas; (muro, pared) wall

liga f garter; (alianza) league; (LAm, gomita) rubber band. ~**dura** f bond; (Mus) slur; (Med) ligature.

~**mento** m ligament. ~**r** 12 vt bind; (atar) tie; (Mus) slur. ~ vi mix. ~**r con** (fig) pick up. ~**rse** vpr (fig) commit o.s.

liger|eza f lightness; (agilidad) agility; (rapidez) swiftness; (de carácter) fickleness. ~**o** adj light; (rápido) quick; (ágil) agile; (superficial) superficial; (de poca importancia) slight. ● adv quickly. **a la** ~**a** lightly, superficially

liguero m suspender belt

lija f dogfish; (papel de lija) sandpaper. ~**r** vt sand

lila f lilac. ● m (color) lilac

lima f file; (fruta) lime. ~**duras** fpl filings. ~**r** vt file (down)

limita|ción f limitation. ~**do** adj limited. ~**r** vt limit. ~**r con** border on. ~**tivo** adj limiting

límite m limit. ~ **de velocidad** speed limit

limítrofe adj bordering

lim|ón m lemon; (Mex) lime. ~**onada** f lemonade

limosn|a f alms. **pedir** ~**a** beg. ~**ear** vi beg

limpia|botas m invar bootblack. ~**parabrisas** m invar windscreen wiper (Brit), windshield wiper (Amer). ~**pipas** m invar pipe-cleaner. ~**r** vt clean; (enjugar) wipe. ~**vidrios** m invar (LAm) window cleaner

limpi|eza f cleanliness; (acción de limpiar) cleaning. ~**eza en seco** dry-cleaning. ~**o** adj clean; (cielo) clear; (fig, honrado) honest; (neto) net. **pasar a** ~**o**, (LAm) **pasar en** ~**o** make a fair copy. ● adv fairly. **jugar** ~**o** play fair

linaje m lineage; (fig, clase) kind

lince m lynx

linchar vt lynch

lind|ar vi border (con on). ● f

boundary. **~ero** m border

lindo adj pretty, lovely. **de lo ~** [1] a lot

línea f line. **en ~** online. **en ~s generales** broadly speaking. **guardar la ~** watch one's figure

lingote m ingot

lingü|ista m & f linguist. **~ística** f linguistics. **~ístico** adj linguistic

lino m flax; (tela) linen

linterna f lantern; (de bolsillo) torch, flashlight (Amer)

lío m bundle; (jaleo) fuss; (embrollo) muddle; (amorío) affair

liquida|ción f liquidation; (venta especial) sale. **~r** vt liquify; (Com) liquidate; settle (cuenta)

líquido adj liquid; (Com) net. ● m liquid; (Com) cash

lira f lyre; (moneda italiana) lira

liric|a f lyric poetry. **~o** adj lyric(al)

lirio m iris

lirón m dormouse; (fig) sleepyhead. **dormir como un ~** sleep like a log

lisiado adj crippled

liso adj smooth; (pelo) straight; (tierra) flat; (sencillo) plain

lisonj|a f flattery. **~eador** adj flattering. ● m flatterer. **~ear** vt flatter. **~ero** adj flattering

lista f stripe; (enumeración) list. **~ de correos** poste restante. **a ~s** striped. **pasar ~** take the register. **~do** adj striped

listo adj clever; (preparado) ready

listón m strip; (en saltos) bar; (Mex, cinta) ribbon

litera f (en barco, tren) berth; (en habitación) bunk bed

literal adj literal

litera|rio adj literary. **~tura** f literature

litig|ar [12] vi dispute; (Jurid) litigate. **~io** m dispute; (Jurid) litigation

litografía f (arte) lithography; (cuadro) lithograph

litoral adj coastal. ● m coast

litro m litre

lituano adj & m Lithuanian

liturgia f liturgy

liviano adj fickle; (LAm, de poco peso) light

lívido adj livid

llaga f wound; (úlcera) ulcer

llama f flame; (animal) llama

llamada f call

llama|do adj called. ● m (LAm) call. **~miento** m call. **~r** vt call; (por teléfono) phone. ● vi call; (golpear en la puerta) knock; (tocar el timbre) ring. **~r por teléfono** phone, telephone. **~rse** vpr be called. **¿cómo te ~s?** what's your name?

llamarada f sudden blaze; (fig, de pasión etc) outburst

llamativo adj flashy; (color) loud; (persona) striking

llamear vi blaze

llano adj flat, level; (persona) natural; (sencillo) plain. ● m plain

llanta f (Auto) (wheel) rim; (LAm, neumático) tyre

llanto m crying

llanura f plain

llave f key; (para tuercas) spanner; (LAm, del baño etc) tap (Brit), faucet (Amer); (Elec) switch. **~ inglesa** monkey wrench. **cerrar con ~** lock. **echar la ~** lock up. **~ro** m key-ring

llega|da f arrival. **~r** [12] vi arrive, come; (alcanzar) reach; (bastar) be enough. **~r a** (conseguir) manage to. ~r a saber find out. ~r a ser become. ~r hasta go as far as

llen|ar vt fill (up); (rellenar) fill in; (cubrir) cover (de with). ~o adj full. ● m (en el teatro etc) full house. de ~ entirely

lleva|dero adj tolerable. ~r vt carry; (inducir, conducir) lead; (acompañar) take; wear (ropa). ¿cuánto tiempo ~s aquí? how long have you been here? llevo 3 años estudiando inglés I've been studying English for 3 years. ~rse vpr take away; win (premio etc); (comprar) take. ~rse bien get on well together

llor|ar vi cry; (ojos) water. ~iquear vi whine. ~iqueo m whining. ●o m crying. ~ón adj whining. ● m cry-baby. ~oso adj tearful

llov|er 2 vi rain. ~izna f drizzle. ~iznar vi drizzle

llueve vb véase **LLOVER**

lluvi|a f rain; (fig) shower. ~oso adj rainy; (clima) wet

lo artículo definido neutro. ~ importante what is important, the important thing. ● pron (él) him; (cosa) it. ~ que what, that which

loa f praise. ~ble adj praiseworthy. ~r vt praise

lobo m wolf

lóbrego adj gloomy

lóbulo m lobe

local adj local. ● m premises. ~idad f locality; (de un espectáculo) seat; (entrada) ticket. ~izador m pager; (de reserva) booking reference. ~izar 10 vt find, locate

loción f lotion

loco adj mad, crazy. ● m lunatic. ~ de alegría mad with joy. estar ~ por be crazy about. volverse ~

go mad

locomo|ción f locomotion. ~tora f locomotive

locuaz adj talkative

locución f expression

locura f madness; (acto) crazy thing. con ~ madly

locutor m broadcaster

lod|azal m quagmire. ~o m mud

lógic|a f logic. ~o adj logical

logr|ar vt get; (premio). ~ hacer manage to do. ~o m achievement; (de premio) winning; (éxito) success

loma f small hill

lombriz f worm

lomo m back; (de libro) spine. ~ de cerdo loin of pork

lona f canvas

loncha f slice; (de tocino) rasher

londinense adj from London. ● m Londoner

Londres m London

loneta f thin canvas

longaniza f sausage

longev|idad f longevity. ~o adj long-lived

longitud f length; (en geografía) longitude

lonja f slice; (de tocino) rasher; (Com) market

loro m parrot

los artículo definido mpl the. véase tb **EL**. ● pron them. ~ de Antonio's. ~ que whoever, the ones

losa f (baldosa) flagstone. ~ sepulcral tombstone

lote m share; (de productos) batch; (terreno) plot (Brit), lot (Amer)

lotería f lottery

loto m lotus

loza f crockery; (fina) china

lozano adj fresh; (vegetación) lush; (persona) healthy-looking

lubina f sea bass

lubrica|nte adj lubricating. ● m lubricant. ~r **7** vt lubricate

lucero m bright star. ~ del alba morning star

lucha f fight; (fig) struggle. ~dor m fighter. ~r vi fight; (fig) struggle

lucid|ez f lucidity. ~o adj splendid

lúcido adj lucid

luciérnaga f glow-worm

lucimiento m brilliance

lucio m pike

lucir 11 vt (fig) show off. ● vi shine; (joya) sparkle; (LAm, mostrarse) look. ~se vpr (fig) shine, excel; (presumir) show off

lucr|ativo adj lucrative. ~o m gain

luego adv then; (más tarde) later (on); (Mex, pronto) soon. ● conj therefore. ~ que as soon as. desde ~ of course

lugar m place; (espacio libre) room. ~ común cliché. dar ~ a give rise to. en ~ de instead of. en primer ~ first. hacer ~ make room. tener ~ take place. ~eño adj local, village

lugarteniente m deputy

lúgubre adj gloomy

lujo m luxury. ~so adj luxurious. de ~ luxury

lumbago m lumbago

lumbre f fire; (luz) light

luminoso adj luminous; (fig) bright; (letrero) illuminated

luna f moon; (espejo) mirror. ~ de miel honeymoon. claro de ~ moonlight. estar en la ~ be miles away. ~r adj lunar. ● m mole;

(en tela) spot

lunes m invar Monday

lupa f magnifying glass

lustr|abotas m invar (LAm) bootblack. ~ar vt shine, polish. ~e m shine; (fig, esplendor) splendour. dar ~e a, sacar ~e a polish. ~oso adj shining

luto m mourning. estar de ~ be in mourning

luz f light; (electricidad) electricity. luces altas (LAm) headlights on full beam. luces bajas (LAm) dipped headlights. luces cortas dipped headlights. luces antiniebla fog light. luces largas headlights on full beam. a la ~ de in the light of. a todas luces obviously. dar a ~ give birth. hacer la ~ sobre shed light on. sacar a la ~ bring to light

••••••••••••••••••••••••••••

Mm

••••••••••••••••••••••••••••

macabro adj macabre

macaco m macaque (monkey)

macanudo adj **1** great **1**

macarrones mpl macaroni

macerar vt macerate (fruta); marinade (carne etc)

maceta f mallet; (tiesto) flowerpot

machacar 7 vt crush. ● vi go on (sobre about)

machamartillo. a ~ adj ardent; (como adv) firmly

machet|azo m blow with a machete; (herida) wound from a machete. ~e m machete

mach|ista m male chauvinist. ~o adj male; (varonil) macho

machu|car 🔲 *vt* bruise; (*aplastar*) crush. **~cón** *m* (*LAm*) bruise

macizo *adj* solid. ● *m* mass; (*de plantas*) bed

madeja *f* skein

madera *m* (*vino*) Madeira. ● *f* wood; (*naturaleza*) nature. **~ble** *adj* yielding timber. **~men** *m* woodwork

madero *m* log; (*de construcción*) timber

madona *f* Madonna

madr|astra *f* stepmother. **~e** *f* mother. **~eperla** *f* mother-of-pearl. **~eselva** *f* honeysuckle

madrigal *m* madrigal

madriguera *f* den; (*de conejo*) burrow

madrileño *adj* of Madrid. ● *m* person from Madrid

madrina *f* godmother; (*en una boda*) matron of honour

madrug|ada *f* dawn. de **~ada** at dawn. **~ador** *adj* who gets up early. ● *m* early riser. **~ar** 🔲 *vi* get up early

madur|ación *f* maturing; (*de fruta*) ripening. **~ar** *vt/i* mature; (*fruta*) ripen. **~ez** *f* maturity; (*de fruta*) ripeness. **~o** *adj* mature; (*fruta*) ripe

maestr|ía *f* skill; (*Univ*) master's degree. **~o** *m* master; (*de escuela*) schoolteacher

mafia *f* mafia

magdalena *f* fairy cake (*Brit*), cup cake (*Amer*)

magia *f* magic

mágico *adj* magic; (*maravilloso*) magical

magist|erio *m* teaching (profession); (*conjunto de maestros*) teachers. **~rado** *m* magistrate; (*juez*) judge. **~ral** *adj* teaching; (*bien*

hecho) masterly. **~ratura** *f* magistracy

magn|animidad *f* magnanimity. **~ánimo** *adj* magnanimous. **~ate** *m* magnate, tycoon

magnavoz *m* (*Mex*) megaphone

magnético *adj* magnetic

magneti|smo *m* magnetism. **~zar** 🔟 *vt* magnetize

magn|ificar *vt* extol; (*LAm*) magnify (*objeto*). **~ificencia** *f* magnificence. **~ífico** *adj* magnificent. **~itud** *f* magnitude

magnolia *f* magnolia

mago *m* magician; (*en cuentos*) wizard

magro *adj* lean; (*tierra*) poor

magulla|dura *f* bruise. **~r** *vt* bruise. **~rse** *vpr* bruise

mahometano *adj* Islamic

maíz *m* maize, corn (*Amer*)

majada *f* sheepfold; (*estiércol*) manure; (*LAm*) flock of sheep

majader|ía *f* silly thing. **~o** *m* idiot. ● *adj* stupid

majest|ad *f* majesty. **~uoso** *adj* majestic

majo *adj* nice

mal *adv* badly; (*poco*) poorly; (*difícilmente*) hardly; (*equivocadamente*) wrongly; (*desagradablemente*) bad. ● *adj*. estar **~** be ill; (*anímicamente*) be in a bad way; (*incorrecto*) be wrong. estar **~** de (*escaso de*) be short of. *véase tb* MALO. ● *m* evil; (*daño*) harm; (*enfermedad*) illness. **~** que **~** somehow (or other). de **~** en peor from bad to worse. hacer **~** en be wrong to. ¡menos **~**! thank goodness!

malabaris|mo *m* juggling. **~ta** *m* & *f* juggler

mala|consejado *adj* ill-advised.

~costumbrado adj spoilt.
~crianza (LAm) rudeness. **~gra·decido** adj ungrateful
malagueño adj of Málaga. ● m person from Málaga
malaria f malaria
Malasia f Malaysia
malavenido adj incompatible
malaventura adj unfortunate
malayo adj Malay(an)
malbaratar vt sell off cheap; (malgastar) squander
malcarado adj nasty looking
malcriado adj (niño) spoilt
maldad f evil; (acción) wicked thing
maldecir 46 (pero imperativo maldice, futuro y condicional regulares, pp maldecido o maldito) vt curse. ● vi curse; speak ill (de of)
maldi|ciente adj backbiting; (que blasfema) foul-mouthed. **~ción** f curse. **~to** adj damned. ¡~to sea! damn (it)!
maleab|ilidad f malleability. **~le** adj malleable
malea|nte m criminal. **~r** vt damage; (pervertir) corrupt. **~rse** vpr be spoilt; (pervertirse) be corrupted
malecón m breakwater; (embarcadero) jetty; (Rail) embankment; (LAm, paseo marítimo) seafront
maledicencia f slander
mal|eficio m curse. **~éfico** adj evil
malestar m discomfort; (fig) uneasiness
malet|a f (suit)case. hacer la **~a** pack (one's case). **~ero** m porter; (Auto) boot, trunk (Amer). **~ín** m small case; (para documentos) briefcase

mal|evolencia f malevolence. **~évolo** adj malevolent
maleza f weeds; (matorral) undergrowth
mal|gastar vt waste. **~hablado** adj foul-mouthed. **~hechor** m criminal. **~humorado** adj bad-tempered
malici|a f malice; (picardía) mischief. **~arse** vpr suspect. **~oso** adj malicious; (pícaro) mischievous
maligno adj malignant; (persona) evil
malintencionado adj malicious
malla f mesh; (de armadura) mail; (de gimnasia) leotard
Mallorca f Majorca
mallorquín adj & m Majorcan
malmirado adj (con estar) frowned upon
malo adj (delante de nombre masculino en singular mal) bad; (enfermo) ill. **~** de difficult to. estar de malas (malhumorado) be in a bad mood; (LAm, con mala suerte) be out of luck. lo **~** es que the trouble is that. por las malas by force
malogr|ar vt waste; (estropear) spoil. **~arse** vpr fall through
maloliente adj smelly
malpensado adj nasty, malicious
malsano adj unhealthy
malsonante adj ill-sounding; (grosero) offensive
malt|a f malt. **~eada** f (LAm) milk shake. **~ear** vt malt
maltr|atar vt ill-treat; (pegar) batter; mistreat (juguete etc). **~echo** adj battered
malucho adj 1 under the weather
malva f mallow. (color de) **~** adj invar mauve

malvado adj wicked

malvavisco m marshmallow

malversa|ción f embezzlement. ~**dor** adj embezzling. ● m embezzler. ~**r** vt embezzle

Malvinas fpl. las (islas) ~ the Falklands, the Falkland Islands

mama f mammary gland; (de mujer) breast

mamá f mum; (usado por niños) mummy

mama|da f sucking. ~**r** vt suck; (fig) grow up with. ● vi (bebé) feed; (animal) suckle. dar de ~ breastfeed

mamario adj mammary

mamarracho m clown; (cosa ridícula) (ridiculous) sight; (cosa mal hecha) botch; (cosa fea) mess. ir hecho un ~ look a sight

mameluco m (LAm) overalls; (de niño) rompers

mamífero adj mammalian. ● m mammal

mamila f (Mex) feeding bottle

mamotreto m (libro) hefty volume; (armatoste) huge thing

mampara f screen

mampostería f masonry

mamut m mammoth

manada f herd; (de lobos) pack; (de leones) pride. en ~ in crowds

mana|ntial m spring; (fig) source. ~**r** vi flow; (fig) abound. ● vt drip with

manaza f big hand

mancha f stain; (en la piel) blotch. ~**do** adj stained; (sucio) dirty; (animal) spotted. ~**r** vt stain; (ensuciar) dirty. ~**rse** vpr get stained; (ensuciarse) get dirty

manchego adj of la Mancha. ● m person from la Mancha

manchón m large stain

mancilla f blemish. ~**r** vt stain

manco adj (de una mano) one-handed; (de las dos manos) handless; (de un brazo) one-armed; (de los dos brazos) armless

mancomun|adamente adv jointly. ~**ar** vt unite; (Jurid) make jointly liable. ~**arse** vpr unite. ~**idad** f union

manda f (Mex) religious offering

manda|dero m messenger. ~**do** m (LAm) shopping; (diligencia) errand. hacer los ~**dos** (LAm) do the shopping. ~**miento** m order; (Relig) commandment. ~**r** vt order; (enviar) send; (gobernar) rule. ● vi be in command. ¿**mande**? (Mex) pardon?

mandarin|a f (naranja) mandarin (orange). ~**o** m mandarin tree

mandat|ario m attorney; (Pol) head of state. ~**o** m mandate; (Pol) term of office

mandíbula f jaw

mando m command. ~ a distancia remote control. al ~ de in charge of. altos ~**s** mpl high-ranking officers

mandolina f mandolin

mandón adj bossy

manducar 7 vt 1 stuff oneself with

manecilla f hand

manej|able adj manageable. ~**ar** vt use; handle (asunto etc); (fig) manage; (LAm, conducir) drive. ~**arse** vpr get by. ~**o** m handling. ~**os** mpl scheming

manera f way. ~**s** fpl manners. de alguna ~ somehow. de ~ que so (that). de ninguna ~ by no means. de otra ~ otherwise. de todas ~**s** anyway

m

manga f sleeve; (tubo de goma) hose; (red) net; (para colar) filter; (LAm, de langostas) swarm

mango m handle; (fruta) mango. ~**near** vi boss about. ● vi (entrometerse) interfere

manguera f hose(pipe)

manguito m muff

maní m (pl ~es) (LAm) peanut

manía f mania; (antipatía) dislike. **tener la** ~ **de** have an obsession with

maniaco adj, **maníaco** adj maniac(al). ● m maniac

maniatar vt tie s.o.'s hands

maniático adj maniac(al); (obsesivo) obsessive; (loco) crazy; (delicado) finicky

manicomio m lunatic asylum

manicura f manicure; (mujer) manicurist

manido adj stale

manifesta|ción f manifestation, sign; (Pol) demonstration. ~**nte** m demonstrator. ~**r 1** vt show; (Pol) state. ~**rse** vpr show; (Pol) demonstrate

manifiesto adj clear; (error) obvious; (verdad) manifest. ● m manifesto

manilargo adj light-fingered

manilla f (de cajón etc) handle; (de reloj) hand. ~**r** m handlebar(s)

maniobra f manoeuvre. ~**r** vt operate; (Rail) shunt. ● vt/i manoeuvre. ~**s** fpl (Mil) manoeuvres

manipula|ción f manipulation. ~**r** vt manipulate

maniquí m dummy. ● m & f model

manirroto adj & m spendthrift. ~**ta** f, (LAm) ~**to** m little hand

manivela f crank

manjar m delicacy

mano f hand; (de animales) front foot; (de perros, gatos) front paw. ~ **de obra** work force. ¡~**s arriba!** hands up! a ~ by hand; (próximo) handy. a ~ **derecha** on the right. **de segunda** ~ second hand. **echar una** ~ lend a hand. **tener buena** ~ **para** be good at. ● m (LAm, fam) mate (Brit), buddy (Amer)

manojo m bunch

manose|ar vt handle. ~**o** m handling

manotada f, **manotazo** m slap

manote|ar vi gesticulate. ~**o** m gesticulation

mansalva: a ~ adv without risk

mansarda f attic

mansión f mansion. ~ **señorial** stately home

manso adj gentle; (animal) tame

manta f blanket

manteca f fat. ~**oso** adj greasy

mantel m tablecloth; (del altar) altar cloth. ~**ería** f table linen

mant|ener 40 vt support; (conservar) keep; (sostener) maintain. ~**erse** vpr support o.s.; (permanecer) remain. ~**se de/con** live off. ~**imiento** m maintenance

mantequ|era f butter churn. ~**illa** f butter

mant|illa f mantilla. ~**o** m cloak. ~**ón** m shawl

manual adj & m manual

manubrio m crank; (LAm, de bicicleta) handlebars

manufactura f manufacture. ~**r** vt manufacture, make

manuscrito adj handwritten. ● m manuscript

manutención f maintenance

manzana f apple; (de edificios)

block. **~r** m (apple) orchard. **~ de Adán** (LAm) Adam's apple

manzan|illa f camomile tea. ● m manzanilla, pale dry sherry. **~o** m apple tree

maña f skill. **~s** fpl cunning

mañan|a f morning. **~a por la ~a** tomorrow morning. **pasado ~a** the day after tomorrow. **en la ~a** (LAm), **por la ~a** in the morning. ● m future. **~a** adv tomorrow. **~ero** adj who gets up early. ● m early riser

mañoso adj clever; (astuto) crafty; (LAm, caprichoso) difficult

mapa m map

mapache m racoon

maqueta f scale model

maquiladora f (Mex) cross-border assembly plant

maquilla|je m make-up. **~r** vt make up. **~rse** vpr make up

máquina f machine; (Rail) engine. **~ de afeitar** shaver. **~ de escribir** typewriter. **~ fotográfica** camera

maquin|ación f machination. **~al** adj mechanical. **~aria** f machinery. **~ista** m & f operator; (Rail) engine driver

mar m & f sea. **alta ~** high seas. **la ~ de** 🔢 lots of

maraña f thicket; (enredo) tangle; (embrollo) muddle

maratón m & f marathon

maravill|a f wonder. **a las mil ~as**, **de ~as** marvellously. **contar/decir ~as de** speak wonderfully of. **hacer ~as** work wonders. **~ar** vt astonish. **~arse** vpr be astonished (de at). **~oso** adj marvellous, wonderful

marca f mark; (de coches etc) make; (de alimentos, cosméticos)

brand; (Deportes) record. **~ de fábrica** trade mark. **de ~** brand name; (fig) excellent. **de mayor ~** 🔢 absolute. **~do** adj marked. **~dor** m marker; (Deportes) scoreboard. **~r** vt mark; (señalar) show; score (un gol); dial (número de teléfono). ● vi score

marcha f (incl Mus) march; (Auto) gear; (desarrollo) course; (partida) departure. **a toda ~** at full speed. **dar/hacer ~ atrás** put into reverse. **poner en ~** start; (fig) set in motion

marchante m (f marchanta) art dealer; (Mex, en mercado) stall holder

marchar vi go; (funcionar) work, go; (Mil) march. **~se** vpr leave

marchit|ar vt wither. **~arse** vpr wither. **~o** adj withered

marcial adj martial

marciano adj & m Martian

marco m frame; (moneda alemana) mark; (deportes) goal-posts

marea f tide. **~do** adj sick; (en el mar) seasick; (aturdido) dizzy; (borracho) drunk. **~r** vt make feel sick; (aturdir) make feel dizzy; (confundir) confuse. **~rse** vpr feel sick; (en un barco) get seasick; (estar aturdido) feel dizzy; (irse la cabeza) feel faint; (emborracharse) get slightly drunk; (confundirse) get confused

marejada f swell; (fig) wave

mareo m sickness; (en el mar) seasickness; (aturdimiento) dizziness; (confusión) muddle

marfil m ivory

margarina f margarine

margarita f daisy; (cóctel) margarita

marg|en m margin; (de un ca-

mino) side. ● *f (de un río*) bank. ~**inado** *adj* excluded. ● *m* outcast. **al ~en** *(fig*) outside. ~**inal** *adj* marginal. ~**inar** *vt (excluir*) exclude; *(fijar márgenes*) set margins

mariachi *m (Mex) (música popular de Jalisco*) Mariachi music; *(conjunto*) Mariachi band; *(músico*) Mariachi musician

---

mariachi The word can mean the traditional Mexican musical ensemble, the musicians and the lively mestizo music they play. *Mariachis* wearing costumes based on those worn by *charros* can be seen in the Plaza Garibaldi, in Mexico City, where they are hired for parties, or to sing *mañanitas* or serenades.

i

---

maric|a *m* ⓘ sissy ⓘ. ~**ón** *m* ⓘ homosexual, queer ⓘ; *(LAm, cobarde*) wimp

marido *m* husband

mariguana *f*, **marihuana** *f* marijuana

marimacho *f* mannish woman

marimba *f (type of) drum (LAm, especie de xilofón*) marimba

marin|a *f* navy; *(barcos*) fleet; *(cuadro*) seascape. **~a de guerra** navy. **~a mercante** merchant navy. **~ería** *f* seamanship; *(marineros*) sailors. **~ero** *adj* marine; *(barco*) seaworthy. ● *m* sailor. **a la ~era** in tomato and garlic sauce. **~o** *adj* marine

marioneta *f* puppet. **~s** *fpl* puppet show

maripos|a *f* butterfly. **~a nocturna** moth. **~ear** *vi* be fickle; *(galantear*) flirt. **~ón** *m* flirt

mariquita *f* ladybird *(Brit)*, ladybug *(Amer)*. ● *m* ⓘ sissy ⓘ

mariscador *m* shell-fisher

mariscal *m* marshal

maris|car *vt* fish for shellfish. **~co** *m* seafood, shellfish. **~quero** *m (pescador de mariscos*) seafood fisherman; *(vendedor de mariscos*) seafood seller

marital *adj* marital; *(vida*) married

marítimo *adj* maritime; *(ciudad etc*) coastal, seaside

marmita *f* cooking pot

mármol *m* marble

marmota *f* marmot

maroma *f* rope; *(Mex, voltereta*) somersault

marqu|és *m* marquess. **~esa** *f* marchioness. **~esina** *f* glass canopy; *(en estadio*) roof

marran|a *f* sow. **~ada** *f* filthy thing; *(cochinada*) dirty trick. **~o** *adj* filthy. ● *m* hog

marrón *adj & m* brown

marroqu|í *adj & m & f* Moroccan. ● *m (leather*) morocco. **~inería** *f* leather goods

Marruecos *m* Morocco

marsopa *f* porpoise

marsupial *adj & m* marsupial

marta *f* marten

martajar *vt (Mex*) crush *(maíz*)

Marte *m* Mars

martes *m invar* Tuesday. **~ de carnaval** Shrove Tuesday

martill|ar *vt* hammer. **~azo** *m* blow with a hammer. **~ear** *vt* hammer. **~eo** *m* hammering. **~o** *m* hammer

martín *m* **pescador** kingfisher

martinete *m (del piano*) hammer; *(ave*) heron

martingala *f (ardid*) trick

mártir *m & f* martyr

martir|io *m* martyrdom; *(fig*) torment. **∼izar** 10 *vt* martyr; (*fig*) torment, torture

marxis|mo *m* Marxism. **∼ta** *adj* & *m* & *f* Marxist

marzo *m* March

más *adv* & *adj* (*comparativo*) more; (*superlativo*) most. ∼ caro dearer. ∼ doloroso more painful. el ∼ caro the dearest, el ∼ caro (*de dos*) the dearer. el ∼ curioso the most curious; (*de dos*) the more curious. ● *prep* plus. ∼ o *m* plus (sign). ∼ bien rather. ∼ de (*cantidad indeterminada*) more than. ∼ o menos more or less. ∼ que more than. ∼ y ∼ more and more. a lo ∼ at (the) most. dos ∼ dos two plus two. de ∼ too many. es ∼ moreover. nadie ∼ nobody else. no ∼ no more

masa *f* mass; (*Culin*) dough. en ∼ en masse

masacre *f* massacre

masaj|e *m* massage. **∼ear** *vt* massage. **∼ista** *m* masseur. ● *f* masseuse

mascada *f* (*Mex*) scarf

mascar 7 *vt* chew

máscara *f* mask

mascar|ada *f* masquerade. **∼illa** *f* mask. **∼ón** *m* (*Naut*) figurehead

mascota *f* mascot

masculin|idad *f* masculinity. **∼o** *adj* masculine; (*sexo*) male. ● *m* masculine

mascullar 3 *vt* mumble

masilla *f* putty

masivo *adj* massive, large-scale

mas|ón *m* Freemason. **∼onería** *f* Freemasonry. **∼ónico** *adj* Masonic

masoquis|mo *m* masochism. **∼ta** *adj* masochistic. ● *m* & *f* masochist

mastica|ción *f* chewing. **∼r** 7

vt chew

mástil *m* (*Naut*) mast; (*de bandera*) flagpole; (*de guitarra, violín*) neck

mastín *m* mastiff

mastodonte *m* mastodon; (*fig*) giant

masturba|ción *f* masturbation. **∼rse** *vpr* masturbate

mata *f* (*arbusto*) bush; (*Lam, planta*) plant

matad|ero *m* slaughterhouse. **∼or** *adj* killing. ● *m* (*torero*) matador

matamoscas *m invar* fly swatter

mata|nza *f* killing. **∼r** *vt* kill (personas); slaughter (reses). **∼rife** *m* butcher. **∼rse** *vpr* kill o.s.; (*en un accidente*) be killed; (*Mex, para un examen*) cram. **∼rse trabajando** work like mad

mata|polillas *m invar* moth killer. **∼rratas** *m invar* rat poison

matasanos *m invar* quack

matasellos *m invar* postmark

mate *adj* matt. ● *m* (*ajedrez*) (check)mate (*Lam, bebida*) maté

matemátic|as *fpl* mathematics, maths (*Brit*), math (*Amer*). **∼o** *adj* mathematical. ● *m* mathematician

materia *f* matter; (*material*) material; (*Lam, asignatura*) subject. ∼ prima raw material. en ∼ de on the question of

material *adj* & *m* material. **∼idad** *f* material nature. **∼ismo** *m* materialism. **∼ista** *adj* materialistic. ● *m* & *f* materialist; (*Mex, constructor*) building contractor. **∼izar** 10 *vt* materialize. **∼izarse** *vpr* materialize. **∼mente** *adv* materially; (*absolutamente*) absolutely

matern|al *adj* maternal; (*amor*) motherly. **∼idad** *f* motherhood; (*hospital*) maternity hospital; (*sala*)

m

maternity ward. **~o** adj motherly; (lengua) mother

matin|al adj morning. **~ée** f matinée

matiz m shade; (fig) nuance. **~ación** f combination of colours. **~ar** [10] vt blend (colores); (introducir variedad) vary; (teñir) tinge (de with)

mat|ón m bully; (de barrio) thug. **~onismo** m bullying; (de barrio) thuggery

matorral m scrub; (conjunto de matas) thicket

matraca f rattle. dar **~** pester

matraz m flask

matriarca f matriarch. **~do** m matriarchy. **~l** adj matriarchal

matr|ícula f (lista) register, list; (inscripción) registration; (Auto) registration number; (placa) licence plate. **~icular** vt register. **~icularse** vpr enrol, register

matrimoni|al adj matrimonial. **~o** m marriage; (pareja) married couple

matriz f matrix; (molde) mould; (útero) womb, uterus

matrona f matron; (partera) midwife

matutino adj morning

maull|ar vi miaow. **~ido** m miaow

mausoleo m mausoleum

maxilar adj maxillary. **●** m jaw(bone)

máxim|a f maxim. **~e** adv especially. **~o** adj maximum; (punto) highest. **●** m maximum

maya f daisy. **●** adj Mayan. **●** m & f (persona) Maya

mayo m May

mayonesa f mayonnaise

mayor adj (más grande, comparativo) bigger; (más grande, superlativo) biggest; (de edad, comparativo) older; (de edad, superlativo) oldest; (adulto) grown-up; (principal) main, major; (Mus) major. **●** m & f (adulto) adult. al por **~** wholesale. **~al** m foreman. **~azgo** m entailed estate

mayordomo m butler

mayor|ía f majority. **~ista** m & f wholesaler. **~itario** adj majority; (socio) principal. **~mente** adv especially

mayúscul|a f capital (letter). **~o** adj capital; (fig, grande) big

mazacote m hard mass

mazapán m marzipan

mazmorra f dungeon

mazo m mallet; (manojo) bunch; (LAm, de naipes) pack (Brit), deck (Amer)

mazorca f cob. **~** de maíz corncob

me pron (acusativo) me; (dativo) (to) me; (reflexivo) (to) myself

mecánic|a f mechanics. **~o** adj mechanical. **●** m mechanic

mecani|smo m mechanism. **~zación** f mechanization. **~zar** [10] vt mechanize

mecanograf|ía f typing. **~iado** adj typed, typewritten. **~iar** [20] vt type

mecanógrafo m typist

mecate m (Mex) string; (más grueso) rope

mecedora f rocking chair

mecenas m & f invar patron

mecer [9] vt rock; swing (columpio). **~se** vpr rock; (en un columpio) swing

mecha f (de vela) wick; (de explosivo) fuse. **~s** fpl highlights

mechar vt stuff, lard

mechero m (cigarette) lighter

mechón m (de pelo) lock

medall|a f medal. ~**ón** m medallion; (relicario) locket

media f stocking; (promedio) average. a ~**s** half each

mediación f mediation

mediado adj half full; (a mitad de) halfway through. a ~**s de** marzo in mid-March

mediador m mediator

medialuna f (pl medialunas) croissant

median|amente adv fairly. ~**a** f (Auto) central reservation (Brit), median strip (Amer). ~**era** f party wall. ~**ero** m (muro) party. ~**o** adj medium; (mediocre) average, mediocre

medianoche f (pl medianoches) midnight; (Culin) type of roll

mediante prep through, by means of

mediar vi mediate; (llegar a la mitad) be halfway through; (interceder) intercede (por for)

medic|ación f medication. ~**amento** m medicine. ~**ina** f medicine. ~**inal** adj medicinal

medición f measurement

médico adj medical. ● m doctor. ~ **de cabecera** GP, general practitioner

medid|a f measurement; (unidad) measure; (disposición) measure, step; (prudencia) moderation. a la ~**a** made to measure. a ~**a que** as. en cierta ~**a** to a certain extent. ~**or** m (LAm) meter

medieval adj medieval. ~**ista** m & f medievalist

medio adj half (a); (mediano) average. **dos horas y media** two and a half hours. ~ **litro** half a litre. **las dos y media** half past two. ● m middle; (Math) half; (manera) means; (en deportes) half(-back). **en** ~ in the middle (de of). **por** ~ **de** through. ~ **ambiente** m environment

medioambiental adj environmental

mediocr|e adj mediocre. ~**idad** f mediocrity

mediodía m midday, noon; (sur) south

medioevo m Middle Ages

Medio Oriente m Middle East

medir 5 vt measure; weigh up (palabras etc). ● vi measure, be. ¿**cuánto mide de alto?** how tall is it? ~**se** vpr (moderarse) measure o.s.; (Mex, probarse) try on

medita|bundo adj thoughtful. ~**ción** f meditation. ~**r** vt think about. ● vi meditate

mediterráneo adj Mediterranean

Mediterráneo m Mediterranean

médium m & f medium

médula f marrow

medusa f jellyfish

megáfono m megaphone

megalómano m megalomaniac

mejicano adj & m Mexican

Méjico m Mexico

mejilla f cheek

mejillón m mussel

mejor adj & adv (comparativo) better; (superlativo) best. ~ **dicho** rather. **a lo** ~ perhaps. **tanto** ~ so much the better. **a** ~ f improvement. ~**able** adj improvable. ~**amiento** m improvement

mejorana f marjoram

mejorar vt improve, better. ● vi

get better. ~**se** *vpr* get better

mejunje *m* mixture

melancolía *f* melancholy.
~**ólico** *adj* melancholy

melaza *f* molasses

melena *f* long hair; (*de león*)
mane. ~**udo** *adj* long-haired

melindr|es *mpl* affectation. hacer
~**es con la comida** be picky
about food. ~**oso** *adj* affected

mellizo *adj* & *m* twin

melocot|ón *m* peach. ~**onero** *m*
peach tree

mel|odía *f* melody. ~**ódico** *adj*
melodic. ~**odioso** *adj* melodious

melodram|a *m* melodrama.
~**ático** *adj* melodramatic

melómano *m* music lover

melón *m* melon

meloso *adj* sickly-sweet; (*canción*)
slushy

membran|a *f* membrane. ~**oso**
adj membranous

membrete *m* letterhead

membrill|ero *m* quince tree.
~**o** *m* quince

memo *adj* stupid. ● *m* idiot

memorable *adj* memorable

memorando *m*, **memorándum**
m notebook; (*nota*) memorandum,
memo

memori|a *f* memory; (*informe*)
report; (*tesis*) thesis. ~**as** *fpl* (*auto-
biografía*) memoirs. **de** ~**a** by
heart; (*citar*) from memory. ~**al** *m*
memorial. ~**ón** *m* good memory.
~**zación** *f* memorizing. ~**zar** [10] *vt*
memorize

menaje *m* household goods. ~
de cocina kitchenware

menci|ón *f* mention. ~**onado** *adj*
aforementioned. ~**onar** *vt* men-
tion

mendi|cidad *f* begging. ~**gar**
[12] *vt* beg for. ● *vi* beg. ~**go** *m*
beggar

mendrugo *m* piece of stale
bread

mene|ar *vt* wag (*rabo*); shake (*ca-
beza*); wiggle (*caderas*). ~**arse** *vpr*
move; (*con inquietud*) fidget; (*ba-
lancearse*) swing. ~**o** *m* movement;
(*sacudida*) shake

menester *m* occupation. **ser** ~
be necessary. ~**oso** *adj* needy

menestra *f* vegetable stew

mengano *m* so-and-so

mengua *f* decrease; (*falta*) lack.
~**do** *adj* diminished. ~**nte** *adj*
(*luna*) waning; (*marea*) ebb. ~**r** [15]
vt/i decrease, diminish

meningitis *f* meningitis

menjurje *m* mixture

menopausia *f* menopause

menor *adj* (*más pequeño, compara-
tivo*) smaller; (*más pequeño, super-
lativo*) smallest; (*más joven, compa-
rativo*) younger; (*más joven,
superlativo*) youngest; (*Mus*) minor.
● *m* & *f* (*menor de edad*) minor. **al
por** ~ retail

menos *adj* (*comparativo*) less;
(*comparativo, con plural*) fewer;
(*superlativo*) least; (*superlativo, con
plural*) fewest. ● *adv* (*comparativo*)
less; (*superlativo*) least. ● *prep* ex-
cept. **al** ~ at least. **a** ~ **que** un-
less. **las dos** ~ **diez** ten to two. **ni
mucho** ~ far from it. **por lo** ~ at
least. ~**cabar** *vt* lessen; (*fig, estro-
pear*) damage. ~**cabo** *m* lessening.
~**preciable** *adj* contemptible.
~**preciar** *vt* despise. ~**precio** *m*
contempt

mensaje *m* message. ~**ro** *m*
messenger

menso *adj* (*LAm, fam*) stupid

menstru|ación f menstruation. **~al** adj menstrual. **~ar** 21 vi menstruate

mensual adj monthly. **~idad** f monthly pay; (*cuota*) monthly payment

mensurable adj measurable

menta f mint

mental adj mental. **~idad** f mentality. **~mente** adv mentally

mentar 1 vt mention, name

mente f mind

mentecato adj stupid. ● m idiot

mentir 4 vi lie. **~a** f lie. **~ijillas** fpl. de **~ijillas** for a joke. **~oso** adj lying. ● m liar

mentís m invar denial

mentor m mentor

menú m menu

menud|ear vi happen frequently; (*Mex, Com*) sell retail. **~encia** f trifle. **~encias** fpl (*LAm*) giblets. **~eo** m (*Mex*) retail trade. **~illos** mpl giblets. **~o** adj small; (*lluvia*) fine. a **~o** often. **~os** mpl giblets

meñique adj (*dedo*) little. ● m little finger

meollo m (*médula*) marrow; (*de tema etc*) heart

merca|chifle m hawker; (*fig*) profiteer. **~der** m merchant. **~dería** f (*LAm*) merchandise. **~do** m market. M**~do Común** Common Market. **~do negro** black market

mercan|cía(s) f(pl) goods, merchandise. **~te** adj merchant. ● m merchant ship. **~til** adj mercantile, commercial. **~tilismo** m mercantilism

merced f favour. su/vuestra **~** your honour

mercenario adj & m mercenary

mercer|ía f haberdashery (*Brit*), notions (*Amer*)

mercurial adj mercurial

mercurio m mercury

merec|edor adj worthy (de of). **~er** 11 vt deserve. **~erse** vpr deserve. **~idamente** adv deservedly. **~ido** adj well deserved. **~imiento** m (*mérito*) merit

merend|ar 1 vt have as an afternoon snack. ● vi have an afternoon snack. **~ero** m snack bar; (*lugar*) picnic area

merengue m meringue

meridi|ano adj midday; (*fig*) dazzling. ● m meridian. **~onal** adj southern. ● m southerner

merienda f afternoon snack

mérito m merit; (*valor*) worth

meritorio adj praiseworthy. ● m unpaid trainee

merluza f hake

merma f decrease. **~r** vt/i decrease, reduce

mermelada f jam

mero adj mere; (*Mex, verdadero*) real. ● adv (*Mex, precisamente*) exactly; (*Mex, casi*) nearly. ● m grouper

merode|ador m prowler. **~ar** vi prowl

mes m month

mesa f table; (*para escribir o estudiar*) desk. poner la **~** lay the table

mesarse vpr tear at one's hair

meser|a f (*LAm*) waitress. **~o** m (*LAm*) waiter

meseta f plateau; (*descansillo*) landing

Mesías m Messiah

mesilla f, **mesita** f small table. **~**

m

de noche bedside table

mesón m inn

mesoner|a f landlady. ~**o** m landlord

mestiz|aje m crossbreeding. ~**o** adj (persona) half-caste; (animal) cross-bred. ● m (persona) half-caste; (animal) cross-breed

mesura f moderation. ~**do** adj moderate

meta f goal; (de una carrera) finish

metabolismo m metabolism

metafísic|a f metaphysics. ~**o** adj metaphysical

met|áfora f metaphor. ~**afórico** adj metaphorical

met|al m metal; (de la voz) timbre. ~**ales** mpl (instrumentos de latón) brass. ~**álico** adj (objeto) metal; (sonido) metallic

metal|urgia f metallurgy. ~**úrgico** adj metallurgical

metamorfosis f invar metamorphosis

metedura de pata f blunder

mete|órico adj meteoric. ~**orito** m meteorite. ~**oro** m meteor. ~**orología** f meteorology. ~**orológico** adj meteorological. ~**oró-logo** m meteorologist

meter vt put; score (un gol); (enredar) involve; (causar) make. ~**se** vpr get involved (en in); (entrometerse) meddle. ~**se con uno** pick a quarrel with s.o.

meticulos|idad f meticulousness. ~**o** adj meticulous

metida de pata f (LAm) blunder

metido m reprimand. ● adj. ~ **en años** getting on. **estar** ~ be involved in sth. **estar muy** ~ **con uno** be in well in with s.o.

metódico adj methodical

metodis|mo m Methodism. ~**ta** adj & m & f Methodist

método m method

metodología f methodology

metraje m length. **de largo** ~ (película) feature

metrall|a f shrapnel. ~**eta** f sub-machine gun

métric|a f metrics. ~**o** adj metric; (verso) metrical

metro m metre; (tren) underground (Brit), subway (Amer). ~ **cuadrado** square metre

metrónomo m metronome

metr|ópoli f metropolis. ~**opolitano** adj metropolitan. ● m metropolitan; (tren) underground (Brit), subway (Amer)

mexicano adj & m Mexican

México m Mexico. ~ **D. F.** Mexico City

mezcal m (Mex) mescal

mezcl|a f (acción) mixing; (sustancia) mixture; (argamasa) mortar. ~**lador** m mixer. ~**lar** vt mix; shuffle (los naipes). ~**larse** vpr mix; (intervenir) interfere. ~**olanza** f mixture

mezquin|dad f meanness. ~**o** adj mean; (escaso) meagre. ● m mean person

mezquita f mosque

mi adj my. ● m (Mus) E; (solfa) mi

mí pron me

miau m miaow

mica f (silicato) mica

mico m (long-tailed) monkey

micro|bio m microbe. ~**biología** f microbiology. ~**cosmos** m invar microcosm. ~**film(e)** m microfilm

micrófono m microphone

microonda f microwave. ~**s** m invar microwave oven

microordenador m microcomputer

micros|cópico adj microscopic. **∼copio** m microscope. **∼urco** m long-playing record

miedo m fear (a for.). **dar ∼** frighten. **morirse de ∼** be scared to death. **tener ∼** be frightened. **∼so** adj fearful

miel f honey

miembro m limb; (persona) member

mientras conj while. ● adv meanwhile. **∼ que** whereas. **∼ tanto** in the meantime

miércoles m invar Wednesday. **∼ de ceniza** Ash Wednesday

mierda f (🔲) shit

mies f ripe, grain

miga f crumb; (fig, meollo) essence. **∼jas** fpl crumbs; (sobras) scraps. **∼r** 12 vt crumble

migra|ción f migration. **∼torio** adj migratory

mijo m millet

mil adj & m a/one thousand. **∼es de** thousands of. **∼ novecientos noventa y nueve** nineteen ninety-nine. **∼ euros** a thousand euros

milagro m miracle. **∼so** adj miraculous

milen|ario adj millenial. **∼io** m millennium

milésimo adj & m thousandth

mili f 🔳 military service. **∼cia** f soldiering; (gente armada) militia

mili|gramo m milligram. **∼litro** m millilitre

milímetro m millimetre

militante adj & m & f activist

militar adj military. ● m soldier. **∼ismo** m militarism. **∼ista** adj militaristic. ● m & f militarist.

∼izar 10 vt militarize

milla f mile

millar m thousand. **a ∼es** by the thousand

mill|ón m million. **un ∼ón de libros** a million books. **∼onada** f fortune. **∼onario** m millionaire. **∼onésimo** adj & m millionth

milonga f popular dance and music from the River Plate region

milpa f (Mex) maize field, cornfield (Amer)

milpies m invar woodlouse

mimar vt spoil

mimbre m & f wicker. **∼arse** vpr sway. **∼ra** f osier. **∼ral** m osierbed

mimetismo m mimicry

mímic|a f mime. **∼o** adj mimic

mimo m mime; (adj un niño) spoiling; (caricia) cuddle

mimosa f mimosa

mina f mine. **∼r** vt mine; (fig) undermine

minarete m minaret

mineral m mineral; (mena) ore. **∼ogia** f mineralogy. **∼ogista** m & f mineralogist

miner|ía f mining. **∼o** adj mining. ● m miner

miniatura f miniature

minifundio m smallholding

minimizar 10 vt minimize

mínim|o adj & m minimum. **como ∼** at least. **∼um** m minimum

minino m 🔳 cat, puss 🔳

minist|erial adj ministerial; (reunión) cabinet. **∼erio** m ministry. **∼ro** m minister

minor|ía f minority. **∼idad** f minority. **∼ista** m & f retailer

minuci|a f trifle. **∼osidad** f thoroughness. **∼oso** adj thorough; (de-

tallado) detailed

minúscul|a f lower case letter. **∼o** adj tiny

minuta f draft copy; (*de abogado*) bill

minut|ero m minute hand. **∼o** m minute

mío adj & pron mine. **un amigo ∼** a friend of mine

miop|e adj short-sighted. ● m & f short-sighted person. **∼ía** f short-sightedness

mira f sight; (*fig, intención*) aim. **a la ∼** on the lookout. **con ∼s a** with a view to. **∼da** f look. echar **una ∼da a** a glance at. **∼do** adj careful with money; (*comedido*) considerate. **bien ∼do** highly regarded. no estar **bien ∼do** be frowned upon. **∼dor** m viewpoint. **∼miento** m consideration. **∼r** vt look at; (*observar*) watch; (*considerar*) consider. **∼r fijamente** a stare at. ● vi look (*edificio etc*). **∼ hacia** face. **∼rse** vpr (*personas*) look at each other

mirilla f peephole

miriñaque m crinoline

mirlo m blackbird

mirón adj nosey. ● m nosey-parker; (*espectador*) onlooker

mirto m myrtle

misa f mass. **∼l** m missal

misántropo m misanthropist

miscelánea f miscellany; (*Mex, tienda*) corner shop (Brit), small general store (*Amer*)

miser|able adj very poor; (*lastimoso*) miserable; (*tacaño*) mean. **∼ia** f extreme poverty; (*suciedad*) squalor

misericordi|a f pity; (*piedad*) mercy. **∼oso** adj merciful

mísero adj miserable; (*tacaño*)

mean; (*malvado*) wicked

misil m missile

misi|ón f mission. **∼onero** m missionary

misiva f missive

mism|ísimo adj very same. **∼o** adj same; (*después de pronombre personal*) myself, yourself, himself, herself, itself, ourselves, yourselves, themselves; (*enfático*) very. ● adv. **ahora ∼** right now. **aquí ∼** right here. **lo ∼** the same

misterio m mystery. **∼so** adj mysterious

mística f mysticism. **∼o** adj mystical. ●m mystic

mistifica|ción f mystification. **∼r 7** vt mystify

mitad f half; (*centro*) middle. cortar algo por la **∼** cut sth in half

mitigar 12 vt mitigate; quench (*sed*); relieve (*dolor etc*)

mitin, mitin m meeting

mito m myth. **∼logía** f mythology. **∼lógico** adj mythological

mitón m mitten

mitote m (Mex) Aztec dance

mixt|o adj mixed. educación **mixta** coeducation

mobbing m harassment

mobiliario m furniture

moce|dad f youth. **∼río** m young people. **∼tón** m strapping lad. **∼tona** f strapping girl

mochales adj invar. estar **∼** be round the bend

mochila f rucksack

mocho adj blunt. ● m butt end

mochuelo m little owl

moción f motion

moco m mucus. limpiarse los **∼s** blow one's nose

moda f fashion. estar de **∼** be in

fashion. ∼l adj modal. ∼les mpl manners. ∼lidad f kind

model|ado m modelling. ∼ador m modeller. ∼ar vt model; (fig, configurar) form. ∼o m & f model

módem m modem

modera|ción f moderation. ∼do adj moderate. ∼r vt moderate; reduce (velocidad). ∼rse vpr control oneself

modern|idad f modernity. ∼ismo m modernism. ∼ista m & f modernist. ∼izar **10** vt modernize. ∼o adj modern; (a la moda) fashionable

modest|ia f modesty. ∼o adj modest

módico adj moderate

modifica|ción f modification. ∼r **7** vt modify

modismo m idiom

modista f dressmaker. ∼o m designer

modo m manner, way; (Gram) mood; (Mus) mode. ∼ de ser character. de ∼ que so that. de ningún ∼ certainly not. de todos ∼s anyhow. ni ∼ (LAm) no way

modorra f drowsiness

modula|ción f modulation. ∼dor m modulator. ∼r vt modulate

módulo m module

mofa f mockery. ∼rse vpr. ∼rse de make fun of

mofeta f skunk

moflet|e m chubby cheek. ∼udo adj with chubby cheeks

mohín m grimace. hacer un ∼ pull a face

moho m mould; (óxido) rust. ∼so adj mouldy; (metales) rusty

moisés m Moses basket

mojado adj wet

mojar vt wet; (empapar) soak; (humedecer) moisten, dampen

mojigat|ería f prudishness. ∼o m prude. ● adj prudish

mojón m boundary post; (señal) signpost

molar m molar

mold|e m mould; (aguja) knitting needle. ∼ear vt mould, shape; (fig) form. ∼ura f moulding

mole f mass, bulk. ● m (Mex, salsa) chili sauce with chocolate and sesame

mol|écula f molecule. ∼ecular adj molecular

mole|dor adj grinding. ● m grinder. ∼r **2** grind

molest|ar vt annoy; (incomodar) bother. ¿le ∼a que fume? do you mind if I smoke? ● vi be a nuisance. no ∼ar do not disturb. ∼arse vpr bother; (ofenderse) take offence. ∼ia f bother, nuisance; (inconveniente) inconvenience; (incomodidad) discomfort. ∼o adj annoying; (inconveniente) inconvenient; (ofendido) offended

molicie f softness; (excesiva comodidad) easy life

molido adj ground; (fig, muy cansado) worn out

molienda f grinding

molin|ero m miller. ∼ete m toy windmill. ∼illo m mill; (juguete) toy windmill. ∼o m mill. ∼ de agua watermill. ∼o de viento windmill

molleja f gizzard

mollera f (de la cabeza) crown; (fig, sesera) brains

molusco m mollusc

moment|áneamente adv momentarily. ∼áneo adj (breve) mo-

m

mentary; (*pasajero*) temporary. ~**o**
m moment; (*ocasión*) time. al ~**o**
at once. de ~**o** for the moment
momi|a *f* mummy. ~**ficar** 🔟 *vt*
mummify. ~**ficarse** *vpr* become
mummified
monacal *adj* monastic
monada *f* beautiful thing; (*niño
bonito*) cute kid; (*acción tonta*) silli-
ness
monaguillo *m* altar boy
mon|arca *m & f* monarch. ~**ar-
quía** *f* monarchy. ~**árquico** *adj*
monarchical
monasterio *m* monastery
mond|a *f* peeling; (*piel*) peel.
~**adientes** *m invar* toothpick.
~**adura** *f* peeling; (*piel*) peel. ~**ar**
vt peel (*fruta etc*). ~**o** *adj* (*sin pelo*)
bald
mondongo *m* innards
moned|a *f* coin; (*de un país*) cur-
rency. ~**ero** *m* purse (*Brit*), change
purse (*Amer*)
monetario *adj* monetary
mongolismo *m* Down's syn-
drome
monigote *m* weak character;
(*muñeco*) rag doll; (*dibujo*) doodle
monitor *m* monitor
monj|a *f* nun. ~**e** *m* monk. ~**il** *adj*
nun's; (*como de monja*) like a nun
mono *m* monkey; (*sobretodo*)
overalls. ● *adj* pretty
monocromo *adj & m* mono-
chrome
monóculo *m* monocle
mon|ogamia *f* monogamy.
~**ógamo** *adj* monogamous
monogra|fía *f* monograph.
~**ma** *m* monogram
mon|ologar 🔢 *vi* soliloquize.
~**ólogo** *m* monologue

monoplano *m* monoplane
monopoli|o *m* monopoly. ~**zar**
🔟 *vt* monopolize
monos|ilábico *adj* monosyllabic.
~**ílabo** *m* monosyllable
monoteís|mo *m* monotheism.
~**ta** *adj* monotheistic. ● *m & f*
monotheist
mon|otonía *f* monotony.
~**ótono** *adj* monotonous
monseñor *m* monsignor
monstruo *m* monster. ~**sidad** *f*
monstrosity; (*atrocidad*) atrocity.
~**so** *adj* monstrous
monta *f* mounting; (*valor*) total
value
montacargas *m invar* service lift
(*Brit*), service elevator (*Amer*)
monta|dor *m* fitter. ~**je** *m*
assembly; (*Cine*) montage; (*teatro*)
staging, production
montaña *f* mountain. ~**a rusa**
roller coaster. ~**ero** *adj* mountain-
eer. ~**és** *adj* mountain. ● *m* high-
lander. ~**ismo** *m* mountaineering.
~**oso** *adj* mountainous
montaplatos *m invar* dumb
waiter
montar *vt* ride; (*subirse a*) get on;
(*ensamblar*) assemble; cock (*arma*);
set up (*una casa, un negocio*). ● *vi*
ride; (*subirse*) mount. ~ **a caballo**
ride a horse
monte *m* (*montaña*) mountain;
(*terreno inculto*) scrub; (*bosque*)
woodland. ~ **de piedad** pawnshop
montepío *m* charitable fund for
dependents
montés *adj* wild
montevideano *adj & m*
Montevidean
montículo *m* hillock
montón *m* heap, pile. **a montó-
nes** in abundance. **un ~ de**

loads of

montura f mount; (silla) saddle

monument|al adj monumental; (fig, muy grande) enormous. **~o** m monument

monzón m & f monsoon

moña f ribbon. **~o** m bun; (LAm, lazo) bow

moque|o m runny nose. **~ro** m ① handkerchief

moqueta f fitted carpet

moquillo m distemper

mora f mulberry; (de zarzamora) blackberry; (Jurid) default

morada f dwelling

morado adj purple

morador m inhabitant

moral f mulberry tree. **•f** morals. **•** adj moral. **~eja** f moral. **~idad** f morality. **~ista** m & f moralist. **~izador** adj moralizing. **•** m moralist. **~izar** ⑩ vt moralize

morar vi live

moratoria f moratorium

mórbido adj soft; (malsano) morbid

morbo m illness. **~sidad** f morbidity. **~so** adj unhealthy

morcilla f black pudding

morda|cidad f sharpness. **~z** adj scathing

mordaza f gag

morde|dura f bite. **~r** ② vt bite; (Mex, exigir soborno a) extract a bribe from. **•** vi bite. **~rse** vpr bite o.s. **~rse las uñas** bite one's nails

mordi|da f (Mex) bribe. **~sco** m bite. **~squear** vt nibble (at)

moreno adj (con ser) dark; (de pelo obscuro) dark-haired; (de raza negra) dark-skinned; (con estar) brown, tanned

morera f white mulberry tree

moretón m bruise

morfema m morpheme

morfin|a f morphine. **~ómano** m morphine addict

morfolog|ía f morphology. **~ógico** adj morphological

moribundo adj dying

morir ⑥ (pp muerto) vi die; (fig, extinguirse) die away; (fig, terminar) end. **~ ahogado** drown. **~se** vpr die. **~se de hambre** starve to death; (fig) be starving. **se muere por una flauta** she's dying to have a flute

morisco adj Moorish. **•** m Moor

morm|ón m Mormon. **~ónico** adj Mormon. **~onismo** m Mormonism

moro adj Moorish. **•** m Moor

morral m (mochila) rucksack; (de cazador) gamebag; (para caballos) nosebag

morrillo m nape of the neck

morriña f homesickness

morro m snout

morrocotudo adj (①, tremendo) terrible; (estupendo) terrific ①

morsa f walrus

mortaja f shroud

mortal adj & m & f mortal. **~idad** f mortality. **~mente** adv mortally

mortandad f loss of life; (Mil) carnage

mortecino adj failing; (color) pale

mortero m mortar

mortífero adj deadly

mortifica|ción f mortification. **~r** ⑦ vt (atormentar) torment. **~rse** vpr distress o.s.

mortuorio adj death

mosaico m mosaic; (Mex, baldosa) floor tile

mosca f fly. **~rda** f blowfly. **~rdón** m botfly; (de cuerpo azul)

m

bluebottle

moscatel *adj* muscatel

moscón *m* botfly; (*mosca de cuerpo azul*) bluebottle

moscovita *adj & m & f* Muscovite

mosque|arse *vpr* get cross. **~o** *m* resentment

mosquete *m* musket. **~ro** *m* musketeer

mosquit|ero *m* mosquito net. **~o** *m* mosquito

mostacho *m* moustache

mostaza *f* mustard

mosto *m* must, grape juice

mostrador *m* counter

mostrar 2 *vt* show. **~se** *vpr* (show oneself to) be. se mostró muy amable he was very kind

mota *f* spot, speck

mote *m* nickname

motea|do *adj* speckled. **~r** *vt* speckle

motejar *vt* call

motel *m* motel

motete *m* motet

motín *m* riot; (*de tropas, tripulación*) mutiny

motiv|ación *f* motivation. **~ar** *vt* motivate. **~o** *m* reason. con **~o** de because of

motocicl|eta *f* motor cycle, motor bike 1. **~ista** *m & f* motorcyclist

motoneta *f* (*LAm*) (motor) scooter

motor *adj* motor. ● *m* motor, engine. **~ de arranque** starter motor. **~a** *f* motor boat. **~ismo** *m* motorcycling. **~ista** *m & f* motorist; (*de una moto*) motorcyclist. **~izar** 10 *vt* motorize

motriz *adj* motor

move|dizo *adj* movable; (*poco firme*) unstable; (*persona*) fickle. **~r** 2 *vt* move; shake (la cabeza); (*provocar*) cause. **~rse** *vpr* move; (*darse prisa*) hurry up

movi|ble *adj* movable. **~do** *adj* moved; (*Foto*) blurred

móvil *adj* mobile; (*Esp, teléfono*) mobile phone, cellphone. ● *m* motive

movili|dad *f* mobility. **~zación** *f* mobilization. **~zar** 10 *vt* mobilize

movimiento *m* movement, motion; (*agitación*) bustle

moza *f* young girl. **~lbete** *m* lad

mozárabe *adj* Mozarabic. ● *m & f* Mozarab

moz|o *m* young boy. **~uela** *f* young girl. **~uelo** *m* young boy/lad

mucam|a *f* (*LAm*) servant. **~o** *m* (*LAm*) servant

muchach|a *f* girl; (*sirvienta*) servant, maid. **~o** *m* boy, lad

muchedumbre *f* crowd

mucho *adj* a lot of; (*en negativas, preguntas*) much, a lot of. **~s** a lot of; (*en negativas, preguntas*) many, a lot of. ● *pron* a lot of; (*personas*) many (people). como **~** at the most. ni **~** menos by no means. por **~** que however much. ● *adv* a lot, very much; (*tiempo*) long, a long time

mucos|idad *f* mucus. **~o** *adj* mucous

muda *f* change of clothing; (*de animales*) shedding. **~ble** *adj* changeable; (*personas*) fickle. **~nza** *f* move, removal (*Brit*). **~r** *vt* change; shed (piel). **~rse** *vpr* (*de ropa*) change one's clothes; (*de casa*) move (house)

mudéjar *adj & m & f* Mudejar

mud|ez *f* dumbness. **~o** *adj*

dumb; (*callado*) silent

mueble *adj* movable. ● *m* piece of furniture. **~s** *mpl* furniture

mueca *f* grimace, face. hacer una ~ pull a face

muela *f* back tooth, molar; (*piedra de afilar*) grindstone; (*piedra de molino*) millstone. ~ **del juicio** wisdom tooth

muelle *adj* soft. ● *m* spring; (*Naut*) wharf; (*malecón*) jetty

muérdago *m* mistletoe

muero *vb véase* MORIR

muert|e *f* death; (*homicidio*) murder. ~**o** *adj* dead. ● *m* dead person

muesca *f* nick; (*ranura*) slot

muestra *f* sample; (*prueba*) proof; (*modelo*) model; (*señal*) sign. ~**rio** *m* collection of samples

muestro *vb véase* MOSTRAR

muevo *vb véase* MOVER

mugi|do *m* moo. ~**r** 14 *vi* moo

mugr|e *m* dirt. ~**iento** *adj* dirty, filthy

mugrón *m* sucker

mujer *f* woman; (*esposa*) wife. ● *int* my dear! ~**iego** *adj* fond of the women. ● *m* womanizer. ~**zuela** *f* prostitute

mula *f* mule. ~**da** *f* drove of mules

mulato *adj* of mixed race (*black and white*). ● *m* person of mixed race

mulero *m* muleteer

muleta *f* crutch; (*toreo*) stick with a red flag

mulli|do *adj* soft. ~**r** 22 *vt* soften

mulo *m* mule

multa *f* fine. ~**r** *vt* fine

multi|color *adj* multicoloured. ~**copista** *m* duplicator. ~**cultural** *adj* multicultural. ~**forme** *adj*

multiform. ~**lateral** *adj* multilateral. ~**lingüe** *adj* multilingual. ~**millonario** *m* multimillionaire

múltiple *adj* multiple

multiplic|ación *f* multiplication. ~**ar** 7 *vt* multiply. ~**arse** *vpr* multiply. ~**idad** *f* multiplicity

múltiplo *m* multiple

multitud *f* multitude, crowd. ~**inario** *adj* mass; (*concierto*) with mass audience

mund|ano *adj* wordly; (*de la sociedad elegante*) society. ~**ial** *adj* world-wide. la segunda guerra ~**ial** the Second World War. ~**illo** *m* world, circles. ~**o** *m* world. todo el ~**o** everybody

munición *f* ammunition; (*provisiones*) supplies

municip|al *adj* municipal. ~**alidad** *f* municipality. ~**io** *m* municipality; (*ayuntamiento*) town council

muñe|ca *f* (*en anatomía*) wrist; (*juguete*) doll; (*maniquí*) dummy. ~**co** *m* doll. ~**quera** *f* wristband

muñón *m* stump

mura|l *adj* mural, wall. ● *m* mural. ~**lla** *f* (*city*) wall. ~**r** *vt* wall

murciélago *m* bat

murga *f* street band

murmullo *m* (*incl fig*) murmur

murmura|ción *f* gossip. ~**dor** *adj* gossiping. ● *m* gossip. ~**r** *vi* murmur; (*criticar*) gossip

muro *m* wall

murria *f* depression

mus *m* card game

musa *f* muse

musaraña *f* shrew

muscula|r *adj* muscular. ~**tura** *f* muscles

músculo *m* muscle

musculoso *adj* muscular

muselina f muslin

museo m museum. ~ de arte art gallery

musgo m moss. ~so adj mossy

música f music

musical adj & m musical

músico adj musical. • m musician

music|ología f musicology. ~ólogo m musicologist

muslo m thigh

mustio adj (plantas) withered; (cosas) faded; (personas) gloomy; (Mex, hipócrita) two-faced

musulmán adj & m Muslim

muta|bilidad f mutability. ~ción f mutation

mutila|ción f mutilation. ~do adj crippled. • m cripple. ~r vt mutilate; maim (persona)

mutis m (en el teatro) exit. ~mo m silence

mutu|alidad f mutuality; (asociación) friendly society. ~amente adv mutually. ~o adj mutual

muy adv very; (demasiado) too

Nn

nabo m turnip

nácar m mother-of-pearl

nac|er 🔟 vi be born; (pollito) hatch out; (planta) sprout. ~ido adj born. recien ~ido newborn. ~iente adj (sol) rising. ~imiento m birth; (de río) source; (belén) crib. lugar m de ~imiento place of birth

nación f nation. ~onal adj national. ~onalidad f nationality.

~onalismo m nationalism. ~onalista m & f nationalist. ~onalizar 🔟 vt nationalize. ~onalizarse vpr become naturalized

nada pron nothing, not anything. • adv not at all. ¡~ de eso! nothing of the sort! antes que ~ first of all. ¡de ~! (después de gracias') don't mention it! para ~ (not) at all. por ~ del mundo for not anything in the world

nada|dor m swimmer. ~r vi swim. ~r de espalda(s) do (the) backstroke

nadería f trifle

nadie pron no one, nobody

nado m (Mex) swimming. • adv a ~ swimming

naipe m (playing) card. juegos mpl de ~s card games

nalga f buttock. ~s fpl bottom. ~da f (Mex) smack on the bottom

nana f lullaby

naran|ja f orange. ~ada f orangeade. ~al m orange grove. ~ero m orange tree

narcótico adj & m narcotic

nariz f nose. ¡narices! rubbish!

narra|ción f narration. ~dor m narrator. ~r vt tell. ~tivo adj narrative

nasal adj nasal

nata f cream

natación f swimming

natal adj native; (pueblo etc) home. ~idad f birth rate

natillas fpl custard

nativo adj & m native

nato adj born

natural adj natural. • m native. ~eza f nature. ~eza muerta still life. ~idad f naturalness. ~ista m & f naturalist. ~izar 🔟 vt natural-

ize. **~izarse** *vpr* become natural-
ized. **~mente** *adv* naturally. ● *int* of
course!

naufrag|ar 12 *vi* (barco) sink;
(persona) be shipwrecked; (*fig*) fail.
~io *m* shipwreck

náufrago *adj* shipwrecked. ● *m*
shipwrecked person

náuseas *fpl* nausea. dar **~s** a uno
make s.o. feel sick. sentir **~s** feel
sick

náutico *adj* nautical

navaja *f* penknife; (*de afeitar*)
razor. **~zo** *m* slash

naval *adj* naval

nave *f* ship; (*de iglesia*) nave. **~**
espacial spaceship. quemar las
~s burn one's boats

navega|ble *adj* navigable; (barco)
seaworthy. **~ción** *f* navigation;
(*tráfico*) shipping. **~dor** *m* (*Informá-
tica*) browser. **~nte** *m* & *f* navigator.
~r 12 *vi* sail; (*Informática*) browse

Navid|ad *f* Christmas. **~eño** *adj*
Christmas. en **~ades** at Christmas.
¡feliz **~ad!** Happy Christmas! por
~ad at Christmas

nazi *adj* & *m* & *f* Nazi. **~smo** *m* Naz-
ism

neblina *f* mist

nebuloso *adj* misty; (*fig*) vague

necedad *f* foolishness. decir **~es**
talk nonsense. hacer una **~** do
sth stupid

necesari|amente *adv* necessar-
ily. **~o** *adj* necessary

necesi|dad *f* need; (*cosa esencial*)
necessity; (*pobreza*) poverty.
~dades *fpl* hardships. no hay
~dad there's no need. por **~**
(out) of necessity. **~tado** *adj* in
need (de of). **~tar** *vt* need. ● *vi*.
~tar de need

necio *adj* silly. ● *m* idiot

néctar *m* nectar

nectarina *f* nectarine

nefasto *adj* unfortunate; (*conse-
cuencia*) disastrous; (*influencia*)
harmful

nega|ción *f* denial; (*Gram*) nega-
tive. **~do** *adj* useless. **~r** 1 & 12
vt deny; (*rehusar*) refuse. **~rse** *vpr*
refuse (a to). **~tiva** *f* (*acción*) de-
nial; (*acción de rehusar*) refusal.
~tivo *adj* & *m* negative

negligen|cia *f* negligence. **~te**
adj negligent

negoci|able *adj* negotiable.
~ación *f* negotiation. **~ante** *m* & *f*
dealer. **~ar** *vt/i* negotiate. **~ar en**
trade in. **~o** *m* business; (*Com,
trato*) deal. **~os** *mpl* business.
hombre de **~os** businessman

negr|a *f* black woman; (*Mus*) crot-
chet. **~o** *adj* black; (*ojos*) dark. ●
m (*color*) black; (*persona*) black
man. **~ura** *f* blackness. **~uzco** *adj*
blackish

nen|a *f* little girl. **~o** *m* little boy

nenúfar *m* water lily

neocelandés *adj* from New Zea-
land. ● *m* New Zealander

neón *m* neon

nepotismo *m* nepotism

nervio *m* nerve; (*tendón*) sinew;
(*en botánica*) vein. **~sidad** *f*,
~sismo *m* nervousness; (*impacien-
cia*) impatience. **~so** *adj* nervous;
(*de temperamento*) highly-strung.
ponerse **~so** get nervous

neto *adj* clear; (*verdad*) simple;
(*Com*) net

neumático *adj* pneumatic. ● *m*
tyre

neumonía *f* pneumonia

neur|algia *f* neuralgia. **~ología** *f*
neurology. **~ólogo** *m* neurologist.
~osis *f* neurosis. **~ótico** *adj*

neurotic

neutr|al adj neutral. **~alidad** f neutrality. **~alizar** [10] vt neutralize. **~o** adj neutral; (Gram) neuter

neva|da f snowfall. **~r** [1] vi snow. **~sca** f blizzard

nevera f refrigerator, fridge (Brit)

nevisca f light snowfall

nexo m link

ni conj. **~... ~** neither... nor. **~ aunque** not even if. **~ siquiera** not even. **sin...~** ... without ... or...

Nicaragua f Nicaragua

nicaragüense adj & m & f Nicaraguan

nicho m niche

nicotina f nicotine

nido m nest; (de ladrones) den

niebla f fog. **hay ~** it's foggy. **un día de ~** a foggy day

niet|a f granddaughter. **~o** m grandson. **~os** mpl grandchildren

nieve f snow; (Mex, helado) sorbet

niki m polo shirt

nimi|edad f triviality. **~o** adj insignificant

ninfa f nymph

ningún véase **NINGUNO**

ninguno adj (delante de nombre masculino en singular ningún) no; (con otro negativo) any. **de ninguna manera, de ningún modo** by no means. **en ninguna parte** nowhere. **sin ningún amigo** without any friends. ●pron (de dos) neither; (de más de dos) none; (nadie) no-one, nobody

niñ|a f (little) girl. **~era** f nanny. **~ería** f childish thing. **~ez** f childhood. **~o** adj childish. ● m (little) boy **de ~o** as a child. **desde ~o** from childhood

níquel m nickel

níspero m medlar

nitidez f clarity; (de foto, imagen) sharpness

nítido adj clear; (foto, imagen) sharp

nitrógeno m nitrogen

nivel m level; (fig) standard. **~ de vida** standard of living. **~ar** vt level. **~arse** vpr become level

no adv not; (como respuesta) no. **¿~?** isn't it? **¡a que ~!** I bet you don't! **¡cómo ~!** of course! **Felipe ~ tiene hijos** Felipe has no children. **¡que ~!** certainly not!

nob|iliario adj noble. **~le** adj & m & f noble. **~leza** f nobility

noche f night. **~ vieja** New Year's Eve. **de ~** at night. **hacerse de ~** get dark. **hacer ~** spend the night. **media ~** midnight. **en la ~** (LAm), **por la ~** at night

---

> **Nochevieja** In Spain and other Spanish-speaking countries, where it is known as Año Nuevo, it is customary to see the New Year in by eating twelve grapes for good luck, one on each chime of the clock at midnight.

Nochebuena f Christmas Eve

noción f notion. **nociones** fpl rudiments

nocivo adj harmful

nocturno adj nocturnal; (clase) evening; (tren etc) night. ● m nocturne

nodriza f wet nurse

nogal m walnut tree; (madera) walnut

nómada adj nomadic. ● m & f nomad

nombr|ado *adj* famous; *(susodicho)* aforementioned. **~amiento** *m* appointment. **~ar** *vt* appoint; *(citar)* mention. **~e** *m* name; *(Gram)* noun; *(fama)* renown. **~e de pila** Christian name. **en ~e de** in the name of. **no tener ~e** be unspeakable. **poner de ~e** call

nomeolvides *m invar* forget-me-not

nómina *f* payroll

nomina|l *adj* nominal. **~tivo** *adj & m* nominative. **~tivo a** *(cheque etc)* made out to

non *adj* odd. ● *m* odd number. **pares y ~es** odds and evens

nono *adj* ninth

nordeste *adj (región)* north-eastern; *(viento)* north-easterly. ●*m* northeast

nórdico *adj* Nordic. ● *m* Northern European

noria *f* water-wheel; *(en una feria)* big wheel *(Brit)*, Ferris wheel *(Amer)*

norma *f* rule

normal *adj* normal. ● *f* teachers' training college. **~idad** *f* normality *(Brit)*, normalcy *(Amer)*. **~izar** 🔟 *vt* normalize. **~mente** *adv* normally, usually

noroeste *adj (región)* north-western; *(viento)* north-westerly. ●*m* northwest

norte *adj (región)* northern; *(viento, lado)* north. ●*m* north; *(fig, meta)* aim

Norteamérica *f* (North) America

norteamericano *adj & m* (North) American

norteño *adj* northern. ● *m* northerner

Noruega *f* Norway

noruego *adj & m* Norwegian

nos *pron (acusativo)* us; *(dativo)* (to) us; *(reflexivo)* (to) ourselves; *(recíproco)* (to) each other

nosotros *pron* we; *(con prep)* us

nost|algia *f* nostalgia; *(de casa, de patria)* homesickness. **~álgico** *adj* nostalgic

nota *f* note; *(de examen etc)* mark. **de ~** famous. **de mala ~** notorious. **digno de ~** notable. **~ble** *adj* notable. **~ción** *f* notation. **~r** *vt* notice. **es de ~r** it should be noted. **hacerse ~r** stand out

notario *m* notary

notici|a *f* (piece of) news. **~as** *fpl* news. **atrasado de ~as** behind with the news. **tener ~as de** to hear from. **~ario**, *(LAm)* **~ero** *m* news

notifica|ción *f* notification. **~r** 🔽 *vt* notify

notori|edad *f* notoriety. **~o** *adj* well-known; *(evidente)* obvious; *(notable)* marked

novato *adj* inexperienced. ●*m* novice

novecientos *adj & m* nine hundred

noved|ad *f* newness; *(cosa nueva)* innovation; *(cambio)* change; *(moda)* latest fashion. **llegar sin ~ad** arrive safely. **~oso** *adj* novel

novel|a *f* novel. **~ista** *m & f* novelist

noveno *adj* ninth

noventa *adj & m* ninety; *(nonagésimo)* ninetieth

novia *f* girlfriend; *(prometida)* fiancée; *(en boda)* bride. **~r** *vi (LAm)* go out together. **~zgo** *m* engagement

novicio *m* novice

noviembre *m* November

novill|a *f* heifer. **~o** *m* bullock. **hacer ~os** play truant

n

novio m boyfriend; (*prometido*) fiancé; (*en boda*) bridegroom. los ~s the bride and groom

nub|arrón m large dark cloud. ~e f cloud; (*de insectos etc*) swarm. ~lado adj cloudy, overcast. • m cloud. ~lar vt cloud. ~larse vpr become cloudy, (*vista*) cloud over. ~oso adj cloudy

nuca f back of the neck

nuclear adj nuclear

núcleo m nucleus

nudillo m knuckle

nudis|mo m nudism. ~ta m & f nudist

nudo m knot; (*de asunto etc*) crux. tener un ~ en la garganta have a lump in one's throat. ~so adj knotty

nuera f daughter-in-law

nuestro adj our. • pron ours. ~ amigo our friend. un coche ~ a car of ours

nueva f (*piece of*) news. ~s fpl news. ~mente adv again

Nueva Zelanda f, (*LAm*) **Nueva Zelandia** f New Zealand

nueve adj & m nine

nuevo adj new. de ~ again. estar ~ be as good as new

nuez f walnut. ~ de Adán Adam's apple. ~ moscada nutmeg

nul|idad f nullity; (*fam, persona*) dead loss ⚴. ~o adj useless; (*Jurid*) null and void

num|eración f numbering. ~eral adj & m numeral. ~erar vt number. ~érico adj numerical

número m number; (*arábigo, romano*) numeral; (*de zapatos etc*) size; (*billete de lotería*) lottery ticket; (*de publicación*) issue. sin ~ countless

numeroso adj numerous

nunca adv never. ~ (ja)más never again. casi ~ hardly ever. como ~ like never before. más que ~ more than ever

nupcial adj nuptial. banquete ~ wedding breakfast

nutria f otter

nutri|ción f nutrition. ~do adj nourished, fed; (*fig*) large; (*aplausos*) loud; (*fuego*) heavy. ~r vt nourish, feed; (*fig*) feed. ~tivo adj nutritious. valor m ~tivo nutritional value

nylon m nylon

Ññ

ñapa f (*LAm*) extra goods given free

ñato adj (*LAm*) snub-nosed

ñoñ|ería f, ~ez f insipidity. ~o adj insipid; (*tímido*) bashful; (*quisquilloso*) prudish

Oo

o conj or. ~ bien rather. ~... ~ either ... or

oasis m invar oasis

obed|ecer vt/i obey. ~iencia f obedience. ~iente adj obedient

obes|idad f obesity. ~o adj obese

obispo m bishop

obje|ción f objection. ~**tar** vt/i object

objetivo adj objective. ● m objective; (foto etc) lens

objeto m object. ~**r** m objector. ~ **de conciencia** conscientious objector

oblicuo adj oblique

obliga|ción f obligation; (Com) bond. ~**do** adj obliged; (forzoso) obligatory; ~**r** 12 vt force, oblige. ~**rse** vpr. ~**rse a** undertake to. ~**torio** adj obligatory

oboe m oboe. ● m & f (músico) oboist

obra f work; (acción) deed; (de teatro) play; (construcción) building work. ~ **maestra** masterpiece. en ~**s** under construction. por ~ **de** thanks to. ~**r** vt do

obrero adj labour; (clase) working. ● m workman; (de fábrica, construcción) worker

obscen|idad f obscenity. ~**o** adj obscene

obscu... véase **oscu...**

obsequi|ar vt lavish attention on. ~**ar con** give, present with. ~**o** m gift, present; (agasajo) attention. ~**oso** adj obliging

observa|ción f observation. **hacer una ~ción** make a remark. ~**dor** m observer. ~**ncia** f observance. ~**r** vt observe; (notar) notice. ~**torio** m observatory

obsesi|ón f obsession. ~**ionar** vt obsess. ~**ivo** adj obsessive. ~**o** adj obsessed

obst|aculizar 10 vt hinder; hold up (tráfico). ~**áculo** m obstacle

obstante: no ~ adv however, nevertheless; (como prep) in spite of

obstar vi. eso no obsta para que vaya that should not prevent him

from going

obstina|do adj obstinate. ~**rse** vpr. ~**rse en** (+ infinitivo) insist on (+ gerundio)

obstru|cción f obstruction. ~**ir** 17 vt obstruct

obtener 40 vt get, obtain

obtura|dor m (Foto) shutter. ~**r** vt plug; fill (muela etc)

obvio adj obvious

oca f goose

ocasi|ón f occasion; (oportunidad) opportunity. **aprovechar la ~ón** take the opportunity. **con ~ón de** on the occasion of. **de ~ón** bargain; (usado) second-hand. **en ~ones** sometimes. **perder una ~ón** miss a chance. ~**onal** adj chance. ~**onar** vt cause

ocaso m sunset; (fig) decline

occident|al adj western. ● m & f westerner. ~**e** m west

océano m ocean

ochenta adj & m eighty

ocho adj & m eight. ~**cientos** adj & m eight hundred

ocio m idleness; (tiempo libre) leisure time. ~**sidad** f idleness. ~**so** adj idle; (inútil) pointless

oct|agonal adj octagonal. ~**ágono** m octagon

octano m octane

octav|a f octave. ~**o** adj & m eighth

octogenario adj & m octogenarian

octubre m October

ocular adj eye

oculista m & f ophthalmologist, ophthalmic optician

ocult|ar vt hide. ~**arse** vpr hide. ~**o** adj hidden; (secreto) secret

ocupa|ción f occupation. ~**do**

adj occupied; (persona) busy. estar ~do (asiento) be taken; (línea telefónica) be engaged (Brit), be busy (Amer). ~nte *m & f* occupant. ~r *vt* occupy, take up (espacio). ~rse *vpr* look after

ocurr|encia *f* occurrence, event; (idea) idea; (que tiene gracia) witty remark. ~ir *vi* happen. ¿qué ~e? what's the matter? ~irse *vpr* occur. se me ~e que it occurs to me that

oda *f* ode

odi|ar *vt* hate. ~o *m* hatred. ~oso *adj* hateful; (persona) horrible

oeste *adj* (región) western; (viento, lado) west. ● *m* west

ofen|der *vt* offend; (insultar) insult. ~derse *vpr* take offence. ~sa *f* offence. ~siva *f* offensive. ~sivo *adj* offensive

oferta *f* offer; (en subasta) bid. ~s de empleo situations vacant. en ~ on (special) offer

oficial *adj* official. ● *m* skilled worker; (Mil) officer

oficin|a *f* office. ~a de colocación employment office. ~a de turismo tourist office. horas *fpl* de ~a business hours. ~ista *m & f* office worker

oficio *m* trade. ~so *adj* (no oficial) unofficial

ofrec|er 🔟 *vt* offer; give (fiesta, banquete etc); (prometer) promise. ~erse *vpr* (persona) volunteer. ~imiento *m* offer

ofrenda *f* offering. ~r *vt* offer

ofuscar 🔽 *vt* blind; (confundir) confuse. ~se *vpr* get worked up

oí|ble *adj* audible. ~do *m* ear; (sentido) hearing. al ~do in one's ear. de ~das by hearsay. conocer

de ~das have heard of. de ~do by ear. duro de ~do hard of hearing

oigo *vb véase* **oír**

oír 🔟 *vt* hear. ¡oiga! listen!; (al teléfono) hello!

ojal *m* buttonhole

ojalá *int* I hope so! ● *conj* if only

oje|da *f* glance. dar una ~da a, echar una ~da a have a quick glance at. ~r *vt* have a look at

ojeras *fpl* rings under one's eyes

ojeriza *f* ill will. tener ~ a have a grudge against

ojo *m* eye; (de cerradura) keyhole; (de un puente) span. ¡~! careful!

ola *f* wave

olé *int* bravo!

olea|da *f* wave. ~je *m* swell

óleo *m* oil; (cuadro) oil painting

oleoducto *m* oil pipeline

oler 🔁 (las formas que empiecen por ue se escriben hue) *vt* smell. ● *vi* smell (a of). me huele mal (fig) it sounds fishy to me

olfat|ear *vt* sniff; scent (rastro). ~o *m* (sense of) smell; (fig) intuition

olimpiada *f*, **olimpíada** *f* Olympic games, Olympics

olímpico *adj* Olympic; (fig, fam) total

oliv|a *f* olive. ~ar *m* olive grove. ~o *m* olive tree

olla *f* pot, casserole. ~ a/de presión, ~ exprés pressure cooker

olmo *m* elm (tree)

olor *m* smell. ~oso *adj* sweet-smelling

olvid|adizo *adj* forgetful. ~ar *vt* forget. ~arse *vpr* forget. ~arse de forget. se me ~ó I forgot. ~o *m* oblivion; (acto) omission

ombligo m navel

omi|sión f omission. **~tir** vt omit

ómnibus adj omnibus

omnipotente adj omnipotent

omóplato m shoulder blade

once adj & m eleven

ond|a f wave. **~a corta** short wave. **~a larga** long wave. longitud f de **~a** wavelength. **~ear** vi wave; (agua) ripple. **~ulación** f undulation; (del pelo) wave. **~ular** vi wave

onomásti|co adj (índice) of names. ● m (LAm) saint's day

onomástica See ▸SANTO

ONU abrev (**Organización de las Naciones Unidas**) UN

OPA f take-over bid

opac|ar 7 (LAm) make opaque; (deslucir) mar; (anular) overshadow. **~o** adj opaque; (fig) dull

opci|ón f option. **~onal** adj optional

open-jaw m open jaws ticket

ópera f opera

opera|ción f operation; (Com) transaction; **~ retorno** (Esp) return to work (after the holidays). **~dor** m operator; (TV) cameraman; (Mex, obrero) machinist. **~r** vt operate on; work (milagro etc); (Mex) operate (máquina). ● vi operate; (Com) deal. **~rio** m machinist. **~rse** vpr take place; (Med) have an operation. **~torio** adj operative

opereta f operetta

opin|ar vi express one's opinion. ● vt think. **~ que** think that. ¿qué opinas? what do you think? **~ión** f opinion. la **~ión pública** public opinion

opio m opium

opone|nte adj opposing. ● m & f opponent. **~r** vt oppose; offer (resistencia); raise (objeción). **~rse** vpr be opposed; (dos personas) oppose each other

oporto m port (wine)

oportun|idad f opportunity; (cualidad de oportuno) timeliness; (LAm, ocasión) occasion. **~ista** m & f opportunist. **~o** adj opportune; (apropiado) suitable

oposi|ción f opposition. **~ciones** fpl public examination. **~tor** m candidate; (Pol) opponent

opres|ión f oppression; (ahogo) difficulty in breathing. **~ivo** adj oppressive. **~or** m oppressor

oprimir vt squeeze; press (botón etc); (ropa) be too tight for; (fig) oppress

optar vi choose. **~ por** opt for

ópti|ca f optics; (tienda) optician's (shop). **~o** adj optic(al). ● m optician

optimis|mo m optimism. **~ta** adj optimistic. ● m & f optimist

óptimo adj ideal; (condiciones) perfect

opuesto adj opposite; (opiniones) conflicting

opulen|cia f opulence. **~to** adj opulent

oración f prayer; (Gram) sentence

ora|dor m speaker. **~l** adj oral

órale int (Mex) come on!; (de acuerdo) OK!

orar vi pray (por for)

órbita f orbit

orden f order. **~ del día** agenda. órdenes fpl sagradas Holy Orders. **a sus órdenes** (esp Mex) can I help you? **~ de arresto** arrest warrant. **en ~** in order. **por ~** in turn.

~ado adj tidy

ordenador m computer

ordena|nza f ordinance. ● m (Mil) orderly. **~r** vt put in order; (mandar) order; (Relig) ordain; (LAm, en restaurante) order

ordeñar vt milk

ordinario adj ordinary; (grosero) common; (de mala calidad) poor-quality

orear vt air

orégano m oregano

oreja f ear

orfanato m orphanage

orfebre m goldsmith, silversmith

orfeón m choral society

orgánico adj organic

organillo m barrel-organ

organismo m organism

organista m & f organist

organiza|ción f organization. **~dor** m organizer. **~r** 10 vt organize. **~rse** vpr get organized

órgano m organ

orgasmo m orgasm

orgía f orgy

orgullo m pride. **~so** adj proud

orientación f orientation; (guía) guidance; (Archit) aspect

oriental adj & m & f oriental

orientar vt position; advise; (persona). **~se** vpr point; (persona) find one's bearings

oriente m east

orificio m hole

orig|en m origin. dar **~en** a give rise to. **~inal** adj original; (excéntrico) odd. **~inalidad** f originality. **~inar** vt give rise to. **~inario** adj original; (nativo) native. ser **~ina-rio de** come from. **~inarse** vpr originate; (incendio) start

orilla f (del mar) shore; (de río) bank; (borde) edge. a **~s del** by the sea

orina f urine. **~l** m chamber-pot. **~r** vi urinate

oriundo adj native. ser **~ de** (persona) come from; (especie etc) native to

ornamental adj ornamental

ornitología f ornithology

oro m gold. **~s** mpl Spanish card suit. **~ de ley** 9 carat gold. hacerse de **~** make a fortune. prometer el **~ y el moro** promise the moon

orquesta f orchestra. **~l** adj orchestral. **~r** vt orchestrate

orquídea f orchid

ortiga f nettle

ortodoxo adj orthodox

ortografía f spelling

ortopédico adj orthopaedic

oruga f caterpillar

orzuelo m sty

os pron (acusativo) you; (dativo) (to) you; (reflexivo) (to) yourselves; (recíproco) (to) each other

osad|ía f boldness. **~o** adj bold

oscila|ción f swinging; (de precios) fluctuation; (Tec) oscillation. **~r** vi swing; (precio) fluctuate; (Tec) oscillate

oscur|ecer 11 vi get dark. ● vt darken; (fig) obscure. **~ecerse** vpr grow dark; (nublarse) cloud over. **~idad** f darkness; (fig) obscurity. **~o** adj dark; (fig) obscure. a **~as** in the dark

óseo adj bone

oso m bear. **~ de felpa**, **~ de peluche** teddy bear

ostensible adj obvious

ostent|ación f ostentation. **~ar**

vt show off; (*mostrar*) show. **~oso**
adj ostentatious

osteópata *m & f* osteopath

ostión *m* (*esp Mex*) oyster

ostra *f* oyster

ostracismo *m* ostracism

Otan *abrev* (**Organización del Tra-
tado del Atlántico Norte**) NATO,
North Atlantic Treaty Organization

otitis *f* inflammation of the ear

otoño *m* autumn (*Brit*), fall (*Amer*)

otorga|miento *m* granting. **~r**
⬛ *vt* give; grant (*préstamo*); (*Jurid*)
draw up (*testamento*)

otorrinolaringólogo *m* ear,
nose and throat specialist

---

otro, otra

● *adjetivo*

····▸ another; (*con artículo, pose-
sivo*) other. **come ~ pedazo**
have another piece. **el ~ día**
the other day. **mi ~ coche** my
other car. **otra cosa** something
else. **otra persona** somebody
else. **otra vez** again

····▸ (*en plural*) other; (*con nume-
ral*) another. **en otras ocasio-
nes** on other occasions. **~s 3
vasos** another 3 glasses

····▸ (*siguiente*) next. **al ~ día** the
next day. **me bajo en la otra
estación** I get off at the next
station

● *pronombre*

····▸ (*cosa*) another one. **lo cam-
bié por ~** I changed it for an-
other one

····▸ (*persona*) someone else. **in-
vitó a ~** she invited someone
else

····▸ (*en plural*) (some) others.
tengo ~s en casa I have

(some) others at home. **~s
piensan lo contrario** others
think the opposite

····▸ (*con artículo*) **el ~** the other
one. **los ~s** the others. **uno
detrás del ~** one after the
other. **los ~s no vinieron** the
others didn't come. **esta se-
mana no, la otra** not this
week, next week. **de un día
para el ~** from one day to the
next

➡ Para usos complementa-
rios ver **uno, tanto**

---

ovación *f* ovation

oval *adj*, **ovalado** *adj* oval

óvalo *m* oval

ovario *m* ovary

oveja *f* sheep; (*hembra*) ewe

overol *m* (*LAm*) overalls

ovillo *m* ball. **hacerse un ~**
curl up

OVNI *abrev* (**objeto volante no
identificado**) UFO

ovulación *f* ovulation

óxida|ción *f* rusting. **~r** *vi* rust.
~rse *vpr* go rusty

óxido *m* rust; (*en química*) oxide

oxígeno *m* oxygen

oye *vb véase* OÍR

oyente *adj* listening. ● *m & f* lis-
tener; (*Univ*) occasional student

ozono *m* ozone

Pp

pabellón m pavilion; (en jardín) summerhouse; (en hospital) block; (de instrumento) bell; (bandera) flag

pacer ⓫ vi graze

pachucho adj (fruta) overripe; (persona) poorly

pacien|cia f patience. perder la ~cia lose patience. ~te adj & m & f patient

pacificar ⓱ vt pacify. ~se vpr calm down

pacífico adj peaceful. el (Océano) P~ the Pacific (Ocean)

pacifis|mo m pacifism. ~ta adj & m & f pacifist

pact|ar vi agree, make a pact. ~o m pact, agreement

padec|er ⓫ vt/i suffer (de from); (soportar) bear. ~er del corazón have heart trouble. ~imiento m suffering

padrastro m stepfather

padre adj ⓵ terrible; (Mex, estupendo) great. ● m father. ~s mpl parents

padrino m godfather; (en boda) man who gives away the bride

padrón m register. ~ electoral (LAm) electoral roll

paella f paella

paga f payment; (sueldo) pay. ~dero adj payable

pagano adj & m pagan

pagar ⓬ vt pay; pay for (compras). ● vi pay. ~é m IOU

página f page

pago m payment

país m country; (ciudadanos) na-

tion. ~ natal native land. el P~ Vasco the Basque Country. los P~es Bajos the Low Countries

paisaje m landscape, scenery

paisano m compatriot

paja f straw; (en texto) padding

pájaro m bird. ~ carpintero woodpecker

paje m page

pala f shovel; (para cavar) spade; (para basura) dustpan; (de pimpón) bat

palabr|a f word; (habla) speech. pedir la ~a ask to speak. tomar la ~a take the floor. ~ota f swear-word. decir ~otas swear

palacio m palace

paladar m palate

palanca f lever; (fig) influence. ~ de cambio (de velocidades) gear lever (Brit), gear shift (Amer)

palangana f washbasin (Brit), washbowl (Amer)

palco m (en el teatro) box

palestino adj & m Palestinian

paleta f (de pintor) palette; (de albañil) trowel

paleto m yokel

paliativo adj & m palliative

palide|cer ⓫ vi turn pale. ~z f paleness

pálido adj pale. ponerse ~ turn pale

palillo m (de dientes) toothpick; (para comer) chopstick

paliza f beating

palma f (de la mano) palm; (árbol) palm (tree); (de dátiles) date palm. dar ~s clap. ~da f pat; (LAm) slap. ~das fpl applause

palmera f palm tree

palmo m span; (fig) few inches. ~ a ~ inch by inch

palmote|ar *vi* clap. **~o** *m* clapping, applause

palo *m* stick; (*de valla*) post; (*de golf*) club; (*golpe*) blow; (*de naipes*) suit; (*mástil*) mast

paloma *f* pigeon; (*blanca, símbolo*) dove

palomitas *fpl* popcorn

palpar *vt* feel

palpita|ción *f* palpitation. **~nte** *adj* throbbing. **~r** *vi* beat; (*latir con fuerza*) pound; (*vena, sien*) throb

palta *f* (*LAm*) avocado (pear)

paludismo *m* malaria

pamela *f* (woman's) broad-brimmed dress hat

pamp|a *f* pampas. **~ero** *adj* of the pampas

pan *m* bread; (*barra*) loaf. **~ integral** wholewheat bread, wholemeal bread (*Brit*). **~ tostado** toast. **~ rallado** breadcrumbs. **ganarse el ~** earn one's living

pana *f* corduroy

panader|ía *f* bakery; (*tienda*) baker's (shop). **~o** *m* baker

panal *m* honeycomb

panameño *adj* & *m* Panamanian

pancarta *f* banner, placard

panda *m* panda

pander|eta *f* (small) tambourine. **~o** *m* tambourine

pandilla *f* gang

panecillo *m* (bread) roll

panel *m* panel

panfleto *m* pamphlet

pánico *m* panic. **tener ~** be terrified (a of)

panor|ama *m* panorama. **~ámico** *adj* panoramic

panque *m* (*Mex*) sponge cake

pantaletas *fpl* (*Mex*) panties, knickers (*Brit*)

pantalla *f* screen; (*de lámpara*) (lamp)shade

pantalón *m*, **pantalones** *mpl* trousers. **~ a la cadera** bumsters

pantano *m* marsh; (*embalse*) reservoir. **~so** *adj* marshy

pantera *f* panther

panti *m*, (*Mex*) **pantimedias** *fpl* tights (*Brit*), pantyhose (*Amer*)

pantomima *f* pantomime

pantorrilla *f* calf

pantufla *f* slipper

panz|a *f* belly. **~udo** *adj* pot-bellied

pañal *m* nappy (*Brit*), diaper (*Amer*)

paño *m* material; (*de lana*) woollen cloth; (*trapo*) cloth. **~ de cocina** dishcloth; (*para secar*) tea towel. **~ higiénico** sanitary towel. **en ~s menores** in one's underclothes

pañuelo *m* handkerchief; (*de cabeza*) scarf

papa *m* pope. **•** *f* (*LAm*) potato. **~s fritas** (*LAm*) chips (*Brit*), French fries (*Amer*); (*de paquete*) crisps (*Brit*), chips (*Amer*)

papá *m* dad(dy). **~s** *mpl* parents. **P~ Noel** Father Christmas

papada *f* (*de persona*) double chin

papagayo *m* parrot

papalote *m* (*Mex*) kite

papanatas *m invar* simpleton

paparrucha *f* (*tontería*) silly thing

papaya *f* papaya, pawpaw

papel *m* paper; (*en el teatro etc*) role. **~ carbón** carbon paper. **~ de calcar** tracing paper. **~ de envolver** wrapping paper. **~ de plata** silver paper. **~ higiénico** toi-

P

let paper. ~ **pintado** wallpaper. ~
secante blotting paper. ● **eo** m
paperwork. ~**era** f waste-paper
basket. ~**ería** f stationer's (shop).
~**eta** f (para votar) (ballot) paper

paperas fpl mumps

paquete m packet; (bulto) parcel;
(LAm, de papas fritas) bag; (Mex,
problema) headache. ~ **postal** par-
cel

Paquistán m Pakistan

paquistaní adj & m Pakistani

par adj (número) even. ● m couple;
(dos cosas iguales) pair. a ~**es** two
by two. de ~ **en** ~ wide open.
~**es y nones** odds and evens. sin
~ without equal. ● f par. **a la** ~
(Com) at par. **a la** ~ **que** at the
same time

para preposición

····▸ for. **es** ~ **ti** it's for you. ~
siempre for ever. **¿**~ **qué?**
what for? ~ **mi cumpleaños**
for my birthday

····▸ (con infinitivo) to. **es muy
tarde** ~ **llamar** it's too late to
call. **salió** ~ **divertirse** he went
out to have fun. **lo hago** ~
ahorrar I do it (in order) to
save money

····▸ (dirección) **iba** ~ **la oficina**
he was going to the office. **em-
pújalo** ~ **atrás** push it back.
¿vas ~ **casa?** are you going
home?

····▸ (tiempo) by. **debe estar listo**
~ **el 5** it must be ready by the
5th. ~ **entonces** by then

····▸ (LAm, hora) to. **son 5** ~ **la
una** it's 5 to one

····▸ ~ **que** so (that). **grité**
que me oyera I shouted so

(that) he could hear me.

Note that **para que** is always
followed by a verb in the sub-
junctive

parabienes mpl congratulations

parábola f (narración) parable

parabólica f satellite dish

para|brisas m invar windscreen
(Brit), windshield (Amer). ~**caídas** m
invar parachute. ~**caidista** m & f
parachutist; (Mil) paratrooper.
~**choques** m invar bumper (Brit),
fender (Amer) (Rail) buffer

parad|a f (acción) stop; (lugar) bus
stop; (de taxis) rank; (Mil) parade.
~**ero** m whereabouts; (LAm, lugar)
bus stop. ~**o** adj stationary; (des-
empleado) unemployed. **estar** ~
(LAm, de pie) be standing

paradoja f paradox

parador m state-owned hotel

**parador (nacional de
turismo)** A national chain _i_
of hotels in Spain. They are
often converted castles, palaces and
monasteries. They provide a high
standard of accommodation but
are relatively inexpensive and
often act as showcases for local
craftsmanship and cooking.

parafina f paraffin

paraguas m invar umbrella

Paraguay m Paraguay

paraguayo adj & m Paraguayan

paraíso m paradise; (en el teatro)
gallery

paralel|a f parallel (line). ~**as** fpl
parallel bars. ~**o** adj & m parallel

par|álisis f invar paralysis. ~**alí-
tico** adj paralytic. ~**alizar** **10** vt

paralyse

parámetro m parameter

paramilitar adj paramilitary

páramo m bleak upland

parangón m comparison

paraninfo m main hall

paranoi|a f paranoia. **~co** adj paranoiac

parar vt/i stop. **sin ~** continuously. **~se** vpr stop; (LAm, ponerse de pie) stand

pararrayos m invar lightning conductor

parásito adj parasitic. ● m parasite

parcela f plot. **~r** vt divide into plots

parche m patch

parcial adj partial. **a tiempo ~** part-time. **~idad** f prejudice

parco adj laconic; (sobrio) frugal

parear vt put into pairs

parec|er m opinion. **al ~er** apparently. **a mi ~er** in my opinion. ● vi 🔢 seem; (asemejarse) look like; (tener aspecto de) look. **me ~e l** I think. **~e fácil** it looks easy. **¿qué te ~e?** what do you think? **según ~e** apparently. **~erse** vpr look like. **~ido** adj similar. **bien ~ido** good-looking. ● m similarity

pared f wall. **~ por medio** next door. **~ón** m (de fusilamiento) wall. **llevar al ~ón** shoot

parej|a f pair; (hombre y mujer) couple; (compañero) partner. **~a de hecho** legalised partnership of unmarried couple. **~o** adj the same; (LAm, sin desniveles) even; (LAm, liso) smooth; (Mex, equitativo) equal. ● adv (LAm) evenly

parente|la f relations. **~sco** m relationship

paréntesis m invar parenthesis, bracket (Brit); (intervalo) break. **entre ~** in brackets (Brit), in parenthesis; (fig) by the way

paria m & f outcast

paridad f equality; (Com) parity

pariente m & f relation, relative

parir vt give birth to. ● vi give birth

parisiense adj & m & f, **parisino** adj & m Parisian

parking /'parkin/ m car park (Brit), parking lot (Amer)

parlament|ar vi talk. **~ario** adj parliamentary. ● m member of parliament (Brit), congressman (Amer). **~o** m parliament

parlanchín adj talkative. ● m chatterbox

parlante m (LAm) loudspeaker

paro m stoppage; (desempleo) unemployment; (subsidio) unemployment benefit; (LAm, huelga) strike. **~ cardiaco** cardiac arrest

parodia f parody

parpadear vi blink; (luz) flicker

párpado m eyelid

parque m park. **~ de atracciones** funfair. **~ eólico** wind farm. **~ infantil** playground. **~ zoológico** zoo, zoological gardens

parquímetro m parking meter

parra f grapevine

párrafo m paragraph

parrilla f grill; (LAm, Auto) luggage rack. **a la ~** grilled. **~da** f grill

párroco m parish priest

parroquia f parish; (iglesia) parish church. **~no** m parishioner

parte m (informe) report. **dar ~** report. **de mi ~** for me ● f part; (porción) share; (Jurid) party; (Mex,

repuesto) spare (part). de ~ de
from. ¿de ~ de quién? *(al telé-
fono)* who's speaking? en cual-
quier ~ anywhere. en parte ~
largely. en ~ partly. en todas ~s
everywhere. la mayor ~ the ma-
jority. la ~ superior the top. nin-
guna ~ nowhere. por otra ~ on
the other hand. por todas ~s
everywhere

partera f midwife

partición f division; *(Pol)* parti-
tion

participa|ción f participation;
(noticia) announcement; *(de lotería)*
share. ~nte adj participating. ● m
& f participant. ~r vt announce. ●
vi take part

participio m participle

particular adj particular; *(clase)*
private. nada de ~ nothing spe-
cial. ●m private individual.

partida f departure; *(en registro)*
entry; *(documento)* certificate; *(de
mercancías)* consignment; *(juego)*
game; *(de gente)* group

partidario adj & m partisan. ~ de
in favour of

parti|do m *(Pol)* party; *(encuentro)*
match, game; *(LAm, de ajedrez)*
game. ~r vt cut; *(romper)* break;
crack *(nueces).* ● vi leave. a ~r de
from. ~ de start from. ~rse vpr
(romperse) break; *(dividirse)* split

partitura f *(Mus)* score

parto m labour. estar de ~ be in
labour

parvulario m kindergarten, nur-
sery school *(Brit)*

pasa f raisin. ~ de Corinto cur-
rant

pasa|da f passing; *(de puntos)*
row. de ~da in passing. ~dero
adj passable. ~dizo m passage.

~do adj past; *(día, mes etc)* last;
(anticuado) old-fashioned; *(comida)*
bad, off. ~do mañana the day
after tomorrow. ~dos tres días
after three days. ~dor m bolt; *(de
pelo)* hair-slide

pasaje m passage; *(pasajeros)* pas-
sengers; *(LAm, de avión etc)* ticket.
~ro adj passing. ● m passenger

pasamano(s) m handrail; *(baran-
dilla de escalera)* banister('s)

pasamontañas m invar balaclava

pasaporte m passport

pasar vt pass; *(atravesar)* go
through; *(filtrar)* strain; spend
(tiempo); show *(película)*; *(tolerar)*
tolerate; give *(mensaje, enferme-
dad).* ● vi pass; *(suceder)* happen;
(ir) go; *(venir)* come; *(tiempo)* go
by. ~ de have no interest in. ~lo
bien have a good time. ~ frío be
cold. ~ la aspiradora vacuum. ~
por alto leave out. lo que pasa es
que the fact is that. pase lo que
pase whatever happens. ¡pase Vd!
come in!, go in! ¡que lo pases
bien! have a good time! ¿qué
pasa? what's the matter?, what's
happening? ~se vpr pass; *(dolor)*
go away; *(flores)* wither; *(comida)*
go bad; spend *(tiempo)*; *(exce-
derse)* go too far

pasarela f footbridge; *(Naut)*
gangway

pasatiempo m hobby, pastime

Pascua f *(fiesta de los hebreos)*
Passover; *(de Resurrección)* Easter;
(Navidad) Christmas. ~s fpl Christ-
mas

pase m pass

pase|ante m & f passer-by. ~ar vt
walk *(perro)*; *(exhibir)* show off. ●
vi walk. ir a ~ar, salir a ~ar walk.
~arse vpr walk. ~o m walk; *(en
coche etc)* ride; *(calle)* avenue. ~o

maritimo promenade. **dar un** ∼**o**, **ir de** ∼ go for a walk. **¡vete a** ∼**o!** Ⓣ get lost!

pasillo m corridor; (*de cine, avión*) aisle

pasión f passion

pasivo adj passive

pasm|ar vt astonish. ∼**arse** vpr be astonished

paso m step; (*acción de pasar*) passing; (*camino*) way; (*entre montañas*) pass; (*estrecho*) strait(s). ∼ **a nivel** level crossing (*Brit*), grade crossing (*Amer*). ∼ **de cebra** zebra crossing. ∼ **de peatones** pedestrian crossing. ∼ **elevado** flyover (*Brit*), overpass (*Amer*). **a cada** ∼ at every turn. **a dos** ∼**s** very near. **de** ∼ in passing. **de** ∼ **por** just passing through. **oír** ∼ hear footsteps. **prohibido el** ∼ no entry

pasota m & f drop-out

pasta f paste; (*masa*) dough; (*sl, dinero*) dough Ⓧ. ∼**s** fpl pasta; (*pasteles*) pastries. ∼ **de dientes**, ∼ **dentífrica** toothpaste

pastel m cake; (*empanada*) pie; (*lápiz*) pastel. ∼**ería** f cake shop

pasteurizado adj pasteurized

pastilla f pastille; (*de jabón*) bar; (*de chocolate*) piece

pasto m pasture; (*hierba*) grass; (*LAm, césped*) lawn. ∼**r** m shepherd; (*Relig*) minister. ∼**ra** f shepherdess

pata f leg; (*pie de perro, gato*) paw; (*de ave*) foot. ∼**s arriba** upside down. **a cuatro** ∼**s** on all fours. **meter la** ∼ put one's foot in it. **tener mala** ∼ have bad luck. ∼**da** f kick. ∼**lear** vi stamp one's feet; (*niño*) kick

patata f potato. ∼**s fritas** chips (*Brit*), French fries (*Amer*); (*de bolsa*) (potato) crisps (*Brit*), (potato) chips (*Amer*)

patente adj obvious. ● f licence

patern|al adj paternal; (*cariño etc*) fatherly. ∼**idad** f paternity. ∼**o** adj paternal; (*cariño etc*) fatherly

patético adj moving

patillas fpl sideburns

patín m skate; (*con ruedas*) roller skate. **patines en línea** Rollerblades (P)

patina|dor m skater. ∼**je** m skating. ∼**r** vi skate; (*resbalar*) slide; (*coche*) skid

patio m patio. ∼ **de butacas** stalls (*Brit*), orchestra (*Amer*)

pato m duck

patológico adj pathological

patoso adj clumsy

patraña f hoax

patria f homeland

patriarca m patriarch

patrimonio m patrimony; (*fig*) heritage

patri|ota adj patriotic. ● m & f patriot. ∼**otismo** m patriotism

patrocin|ar vt sponsor. ∼**io** m sponsorship

patrón m (*jefe*) boss; (*de pensión etc*) landlord; (*en costura*) pattern

patrulla f patrol; (*fig, cuadrilla*) group. ∼**r** vt/i patrol

pausa f pause. ∼**do** adj slow

pauta f guideline

paviment|ar vt pave. ∼**o** m pavement

pavo m turkey. ∼ **real** peacock

pavor m terror

payas|ada f buffoonery. ∼**o** m clown

paz f peace

peaje m toll

peatón m pedestrian

peca f freckle

peca|do m sin; (*defecto*) fault. ~**dor** m sinner. ~**minoso** adj sinful. ~**r** 🔢 vi sin

pech|o m chest; (*de mujer*) breast; (*fig, corazón*) heart. dar el ~o a un niño breast-feed a child. tomar a ~o take to heart. ~**uga** f breast

pecoso adj freckled

peculiar adj peculiar, particular. ~**idad** f peculiarity

pedal m pedal. ~**ear** vi pedal

pedante adj pedantic

pedazo m piece, bit. a ~s in pieces. hacer(se) ~s smash

pediatra m & f paediatrician

pedicuro m chiropodist

pedi|do m order; (*LAm, solicitud*) request. ~**r** 🔢 vt ask for; (*Com, en restaurante*) order. ● vi ask. ~**r prestado** borrow

pega|dizo adj catchy. ~**joso** adj sticky

pega|mento m glue. ~**r** 🔢 vt stick (on); (*coser*) sew on; give (*enfermedad etc*); (*juntar*) join; (*golpear*) hit; (*dar*) give. ~**r fuego a** set fire to. ● vi stick. ~**rse** vpr stick; (*pelearse*) hit each other. ~**tina** f sticker

pein|ado m hairstyle. ~**ar** vt comb. ~**arse** vpr comb one's hair. ~**e** m comb. ~**eta** f ornamental comb

p.ej. abrev (**por ejemplo**) e.g.

pelado adj (*fruta*) peeled; (*cabeza*) bald; (*terreno*) bare

pela|je m (*de animal*) fur; (*fig, aspecto*) appearance. ~**mbre** m (*de animal*) fur; (*de persona*) thick hair

pelar vt peel; shell (*habas*); skin (*tomates*); pluck (*ave*)

peldaño m step; (*de escalera de mano*) rung

pelea f fight; (*discusión*) quarrel. ~**r** vi fight; (*discutir*) quarrel. ~**rse** vpr fight; (*discutir*) quarrel

peletería f fur shop

peliagudo adj difficult, tricky

pelícano m pelican

película f film (*esp Brit*), movie (*esp Amer*). ~ **de dibujos animados** cartoon (film)

peligro m danger; (*riesgo*) hazard, risk. poner en ~ endanger. ~**so** adj dangerous

pelirrojo adj red-haired

pellejo m skin

pellizc|ar 🔢 vt pinch. ~**o** m pinch

pelma m & f, **pelmazo** m bore, nuisance

pelo m hair. no tener ~s en la lengua be outspoken. tomar el ~ a uno pull s.o.'s leg

pelota f ball. ~ **vasca** pelota. hacer la ~ a uno suck up to s.o.

pelotera f squabble

peluca f wig

peludo adj hairy

peluquer|ía f hairdresser's. ~**o** m hairdresser

pelusa f down

pena f sadness; (*lástima*) pity; (*LAm, vergüenza*) embarrassment; (*Jurid*) sentence. ~ **de muerte** death penalty. a duras ~s with difficulty. da ~ que it's a pity that. me da ~ it makes me sad. merecer la ~ be worthwhile. pasar ~s suffer hardship. ¡qué ~! what a pity! valer la ~ be worthwhile

penal adj penal; (*derecho*) criminal. ● m prison; (*LAm, penalty*)

penalty. **~idad** f suffering; (*Jurid*) penalty. **~ty** m penalty

pendiente adj hanging; (*cuenta*) outstanding; (*asunto etc*) pending. ● m earring. ● f slope

péndulo m pendulum

pene m penis

penetra|nte adj penetrating; (*sonido*) piercing; (*viento*) bitter. **~r** vt penetrate; (*fig*) pierce. ● vi. **~r en** penetrate; (*entrar*) go into

penicilina f penicillin

pen|ínsula f peninsula. **~insular** adj peninsular

penique m penny

penitencia f penitence; (*castigo*) penance

penoso adj painful; (*difícil*) difficult; (*LAm, tímido*) shy; (*LAm, embarazoso*) embarrassing

pensa|do adj. **bien ~do** all things considered. **menos ~do** least expected. **~dor** m thinker. **~miento** m thought. **~r 🔢** vt think; (*considerar*) consider. **cuando menos se piensa** when least expected. **¡ni ~rlo!** no way! **pienso que sí** I think so. ● vi think. **~r en** think about. **~tivo** adj thoughtful

pensi|ón f pension; (*casa de huéspedes*) guest-house. **~ón completa** full board. **~onista** m & f pensioner; (*huésped*) lodger

penúltimo adj & m penultimate, last but one

penumbra f half-light

penuria f shortage. **pasar ~s** suffer hardship

peña f rock; (*de amigos*) group; (*LAm, club*) folk club. **~ón** m rock. **el P~ón de Gibraltar** The Rock (of Gibraltar)

peón m labourer; (*en ajedrez*)

pawn; (*en damas*) piece

peonza f (*spinning*) top

peor adj (*comparativo*) worse; (*superlativo*) worst. ● adv worse. **de mal en ~** from bad to worse. **lo ~** the worst thing. **tanto ~** so much the worse

pepin|illo m gherkin. **~o** m cucumber. (**no**) **me importa un ~o** I couldn't care less

pepita f pip; (*de oro*) nugget

pequeñ|ez f smallness; (*minucia*) trifle. **~o** adj small, little; (*de edad*) young; (*menor*) younger. ● m little one. **es el ~o** he's the youngest

pera f (*fruta*) pear. **~l** m pear (tree)

percance m mishap

percatarse vpr. **~ de** notice

perc|epción f perception. **~ibir** vt perceive; earn (*dinero*)

percha f hanger; (*de aves*) perch

percusión f percussion

perde|dor adj losing. ● m loser. **~r 🔢** vt lose; (*malgastar*) waste; miss (*tren etc*). ● vi lose. **~rse** vpr get lost; (*desaparecer*) disappear; (*desperdiciarse*) be wasted; (*estropearse*) be spoilt. **echar(se) a ~r** spoil

pérdida f loss; (*de líquido*) leak; (*de tiempo*) waste

perdido adj lost

perdiz f partridge

perd|ón m pardon, forgiveness. **pedir ~ón** apologize. ● int sorry! **~onar** vt excuse, forgive; (*Jurid*) pardon. **¡~one (Vd)!** sorry!

perdura|ble adj lasting. **~r** vi last

perece|dero adj perishable. **~r 🔢** vi perish

peregrin|ación f pilgrimage.

~o adj strange. ● m pilgrim
perejil m parsley
perengano m so-and-so
perenne adj everlasting; (planta) perennial
perez|a f laziness. **~oso** adj lazy
perfec|ción f perfection. a la **~ción** perfectly, to perfection. **~cionar** vt perfect; (mejorar) improve. **~cionista** m & f perfectionist. **~to** adj perfect; (completo) complete
perfil m profile; (contorno) outline. **~ado** adj well-shaped
perfora|ción f perforation. **~dora** f punch. **~r** vt pierce, perforate; punch (papel, tarjeta etc)
perfum|ar vt perfume. **~arse** vpr put perfume on. ● m perfume, scent. **~ería** f perfumery
pericia f skill
perif|eria f (de ciudad) outskirts. **~érico** adj (barrio) outlying. ● m (Mex, carretera) ring road
perilla f (barba) goatee
perímetro m perimeter
periódico adj periodic(al). ● m newspaper
periodis|mo m journalism. **~ta** m & f journalist
período m, **periodo** m period
periquito m budgerigar
periscopio m periscope
perito adj & m expert
perju|dicar 🔟 vt damage; (desfavorecer) not suit. **~dicial** adj damaging. **~icio** m damage. en **~icio** de to the detriment of
perla f pearl. de **~s** adv very well
permane|cer 🔟 vi remain. **~ncia** f permanence; (estancia) stay. **~nte** adj permanent. ● f perm. ● m (Mex) perm

permi|sivo adj permissive. **~so** m permission; (documento) licence; (Mil etc) leave. **~so de conducir** driving licence (Brit), driver's license (Amer). con **~so** excuse me. **~tir** vt allow, permit. ¿me **~te?** may I? **~tirse** vpr allow s.o.
pernicioso adj pernicious; (persona) wicked
perno m bolt
pero conj but. ● m fault; (objeción) objection
perogrullada f platitude
perpendicular adj & f perpendicular
perpetrar vt perpetrate
perpetu|ar 🔟 vt perpetuate. **~o** adj perpetual
perplejo adj perplexed
perr|a f (animal) bitch; (moneda) coin, penny (Brit), cent (Amer); (rabieta) tantrum. estar sin una **~a** be broke. **~era** f dog pound; (vehículo) dog catcher's van. **~o** adj awful. ● m dog. **~o galgo** greyhound. de **~os** awful
persa adj & m & f Persian
perse|cución f pursuit; (política etc) persecution. **~guir** 🔟 & 🔟 vt pursue; (por ideología etc) persecute
persevera|nte adj persevering. **~r** vi persevere
persiana f blind; (LAm, contraventana) shutter
persignarse vpr cross o.s.
persist|ente adj persistent. **~ir** vi persist
person|a f person. **~as** fpl people. **~aje** m (persona importante) important figure; (de obra literaria) character. **~al** adj personal. ● m staff. **~alidad** f personality. **~arse** vpr appear in person. **~ifi-**

car 7 *vt* personify

perspectiva *f* perspective

perspica|cia *f* shrewdness; (*de vista*) keen eyesight. ~z *adj* shrewd; (*vista*) keen

persua|dir *vt* persuade. ~sión *f* persuasion. ~sivo *adj* persuasive

pertenecer 11 *vi* belong

pértiga *f* pole. salto *m* con ~ pole vault

pertinente *adj* relevant

perturba|ción *f* disturbance. ~ción del orden público breach of the peace. ~r *vt* disturb; disrupt (*orden*)

Perú *m*. el ~ Peru

peruano *adj* & *m* Peruvian

perver|so *adj* evil. ● *m* evil person. ~tir 4 *vt* pervert

pesa *f* weight. ~dez *f* weight; (*de cabeza etc*) heaviness; (*lentitud*) sluggishness; (*cualidad de fastidioso*) tediousness; (*cosa fastidiosa*) bore, nuisance

pesadilla *f* nightmare

pesado *adj* heavy; (*sueño*) deep; (*viaje*) tiring; (*duro*) hard; (*aburrido*) boring, tedious

pésame *m* sympathy, condolences

pesar *vt* weigh. ● *vi* be heavy. ● *m* sorrow; (*remordimiento*) regret. a ~ de (que) in spite of. pese a (que) in spite of

pesca *f* fishing; (*peces*) fish; (*pescado*) catch. ir de ~ go fishing. ~da *f* hake. ~dería *f* fish shop. ~dilla *f* whiting. ~do *m* fish. ~dor *adj* fishing. ~ *m* fisherman. ~r 7 *vt* catch. ● *vi* fish

pescuezo *m* neck

pesebre *m* manger

pesero *m* (*Mex*) minibus

peseta *f* peseta

pesimista *adj* pessimistic. ● *m & f* pessimist

pésimo *adj* very bad, awful

peso *m* weight; (*moneda*) peso. ~ bruto gross weight. ~ neto net weight. al ~ by weight. de ~ influential

pesquero *adj* fishing

pestaña *f* eyelash. ~ear *vi* blink

peste *f* plague; (*hedor*) stench. ~icida *m* pesticide

pestillo *m* bolt; (*de cerradura*) latch

petaca *f* cigarette case; (*Mex, maleta*) suitcase

pétalo *m* petal

petardo *m* firecracker

petición *f* request; (*escrito*) petition

petirrojo *m* robin

petrificar 7 *vt* petrify

petr|óleo *m* oil. ~olero *adj* oil. ● *m* oil tanker

petulante *adj* smug

peyorativo *adj* pejorative

pez *f* fish; (*substancia negruzca*) pitch. ~ espada swordfish

pezón *m* nipple

pezuña *f* hoof

piadoso *adj* compassionate; (*devoto*) devout

pian|ista *m & f* pianist. ~o *m* piano. ~o de cola grand piano

piar 20 *vi* chirp

picad|a *f*. caer en ~a (*LAm*) nosedive. ~o *adj* perforated; (*carne*) minced (*Brit*), ground (*Amer*); (*ofendido*) offended; (*mar*) choppy; (*diente*) bad. ● *m*. caer en ~o nosedive. ~ura *f* bite, sting; (*de polilla*) moth hole

picaflor *m* (*LAm*) hummingbird

p

picante adj hot; (chiste etc) risqué

picaporte m door-handle; (aldaba) knocker

picar 🗷 vt (ave) peck; (insecto, pez) bite; (abeja, avispa) sting; (comer poco) pick at; mince (Brit), grind (Amer) (carne); chop (up) (cebolla etc); (Mex, pinchar) prick. • vi itch; (ave) peck; (insecto, pez) bite; (sol) scorch; (comida) be hot

picardía f craftiness; (travesura) naughty thing

pícaro adj crafty; (niño) mischievous. • m rogue

picazón f itch

pichón m pigeon; (Mex, novato) beginner

pico m beak; (punta) corner; (herramienta) pickaxe; (cima) peak. y ~ (con tiempo) a little after; (con cantidad) a little more than. ~**tear** vt peck; (fam, comer) pick at

picudo adj pointed

pido vb véase **PEDIR**

pie m foot; (Bot, de vaso) stem. ~ cuadrado square foot. a cuatro ~s on all fours. al ~ de la letra literally. a ~ on foot. a ~(s) juntillas (fig) firmly. buscarle tres ~s al gato split hairs. de ~ standing (up). de ~s a cabeza from head to toe. en ~ standing (up). ponerse de ~ stand up

piedad f pity; (Relig) piety

piedra f stone; (de mechero) flint

piel f skin; (cuero) leather

pienso vb véase **PENSAR**

pierdo vb véase **PERDER**

pierna f leg

pieza f piece; (parte) part; (obra teatral) play; (moneda) coin; (habitación) room. ~ de recambio spare part

pijama m pyjamas

pila f (montón) pile; (recipiente) basin; (eléctrica) battery. ~ bautismal font. ~r m pillar

píldora f pill

pilla|je m pillage. ~r vt catch

pillo adj wicked. • m rogue

pilot|ar vt pilot. ~o m pilot

pim|entero m (vasija) pepperpot. ~**entón** m paprika; (LAm, fruto) pepper. ~**ienta** f pepper. grano m de ~ienta peppercorn. ~**iento** m pepper

pináculo m pinnacle

pinar m pine forest

pincel m paintbrush. ~**ada** f brush-stroke. la última ~ada (fig) the finishing touch

pinch|ar vt pierce, prick; puncture (neumático); (fig, incitar) push; (Med, fam) give an injection to. ~**azo** m prick; (en neumático) puncture. ~**itos** mpl kebab(s); (tapas) savoury snacks. ~**o** m point

ping-pong m table tennis, ping-pong

pingüino m penguin

pino m pine (tree)

pint|a f spot; (fig, aspecto) appearance. tener ~a de look like. ~**ada** f graffiti. ~**ar** vt paint. no ~a nada (fig) it doesn't count. ~**arse** vpr put on make-up. ~**or** m painter. ~**oresco** adj picturesque. ~**ura** f painting; (material) paint

pinza f (clothes-)peg (Brit), clothespin (Amer); (de cangrejo etc) claw. ~s fpl tweezers

piña f pine cone; (fruta) pineapple. ~**ón** m (semilla) pine nut

pío adj pious. • m chirp. no decir ni ~ not say a word

piojo m louse

pionero m pioneer

pipa f pipe; (semilla) seed; (de girasol) sunflower seed

pique m resentment; (rivalidad) rivalry. **irse a ~** sink

piquete m picket; (Mex, herida) prick; (Mex, de insecto) sting

piragua f canoe

pirámide f pyramid

pirata adj invar pirate. ● m & f pirate

Pirineos mpl. los **~**the Pyrenees

piropo m flattering comment

pirueta f pirouette

pirulí m lollipop

pisa|da f footstep; (huella) footprint. **~papeles** m invar paperweight. **~r** vt tread on. ● vi tread

piscina f swimming pool

Piscis m Pisces

piso m floor; (vivienda) flat (Brit), apartment (Amer); (de autobús) deck

pisotear vt trample (on)

pista f track; (fig, indicio) clue. **~ de aterrizaje** runway. **~ de baile** dance floor. **~ de carreras** racing track. **~ de hielo** ice-rink. **~ de tenis** tennis court

pisto|la f pistol. **~era** f holster. **~ero** m gunman

pistón m piston

pit|ar, (LAm) **~ear** vt whistle at; (conductor) hoot at; award (falta). ● vi blow a whistle; (Auto) sound one's horn. **~ido** m whistle

pitill|era f cigarette case. **~o** m cigarette

pito m whistle; (Auto) horn

pitón m python

pitorre|arse vpr. **~arse de** make fun of. **~o** m teasing

pitorro m spout

piyama m (LAm) pyjamas

pizarr|a f slate; (en aula) blackboard. **~ón** m (LAm) blackboard

pizca f (fam) tiny piece; (de sal) pinch. **ni ~** not at all

placa f plate; (con inscripción) plaque; (distintivo) badge. **~ de matrícula** number plate

place|ntero adj pleasant. **~r** 32 vi. haz lo que te plazca do as you please. me **~** hacerlo I'm pleased to do it. ● m pleasure

plácido adj placid

plaga f (also fig) plague. **~do** adj. **~do de** filled with

plagio m plagiarism

plan m plan. **en ~ de** as

plana f page. **en primera ~** on the front page

plancha f iron; (lámina) sheet. a la **~** grilled. tirarse una **~** put one's foot in it. **~do** m ironing. **~r** vt iron. ● vi do the ironing

planeador m glider

planear vt plan. ● vi glide

planeta m planet

planicie f plain

planifica|ción f planning. **~r** 7 vt plan

planilla f (LAm) payroll; (personal) staff

plano adj flat. ● m plane; (de edificio) plan; (de ciudad) street plan. **primer ~** foreground; (Foto) close-up

planta f (del pie) sole; (en botánica, fábrica) plant; (plano) ground plan; (piso) floor. **~ baja** ground floor (Brit), first floor (Amer)

planta|ción f plantation. **~r** vt plant; deal (golpe). **~r en la calle** throw out. **~rse** vpr stand; (fig) stand firm

plantear vt (exponer) expound; (causar) create; raise (cuestión)

plantilla f insole; (nómina) payroll; (personal) personnel

plaqué m plating. de ~ plated

plástico adj & m plastic

plata f silver; (fig, fam, dinero) money. ~ de ley hallmarked silver

plataforma f platform

plátano m plane (tree); (fruta) banana. **platanero** m banana tree

platea f stalls (Brit), orchestra (Amer)

plateado adj silver-plated; (color de plata) silver

pl|ática f talk. **~aticar** 🔟 vi (Mex) talk. ●vt (Mex) tell

platija f plaice

platillo m saucer; (Mus) cymbal. ~ volador (LAm), ~ volante flying saucer

platino m platinum. ~s mpl (Auto) points

plato m plate; (comida) dish; (parte de una comida) course

platónico adj platonic

playa f beach; (fig) seaside

plaza f square; (mercado) market (place); (sitio) place; (empleo) job. ~ de toros bullring

plazco vb véase PLACER

plazo m period; (pago) instalment; (fecha) date. comprar a ~s buy on hire purchase (Brit), buy on the installment plan (Amer)

plazuela f little square

pleamar f high tide

pleb|e f common people. **~eyo** adj & m plebeian. **~iscito** m plebiscite

plega|ble adj pliable; (silla) folding. **~r** 🔳 & 🔢 vt fold. **~rse** vpr

bend; (fig) yield

pleito m (court) case; (fig) dispute

plenilunio m full moon

plen|itud f fullness; (fig) height. **~o** adj full. en ~o día in broad daylight. en ~o verano at the height of the summer

plieg|o m sheet. **~ue** m fold; (en ropa) pleat

plisar vt pleat

plom|ero m (LAm) plumber. **~o** m lead; (Elec) fuse. con ~o leaded. sin ~o unleaded

pluma f feather; (para escribir) pen. ~ atómica (Mex) ballpoint pen. ~ estilográfica fountain pen. **~je** m plumage

plum|ero m feather duster; (para plumas, lápices etc) pencil-case. **~ón** m down; (edredón) down-filled quilt

plural adj & m plural. en ~ in the plural

pluri|empleo m having more than one job. **~partidismo** m multi-party system. **~étnico** adj multiethnic

plus m bonus

pluscuamperfecto m pluperfect

plusvalía f capital gain

pluvial adj rain

pobla|ción f population; (ciudad) city, town; (pueblo) village. **~do** adj populated. ●m village. **~r** 🖪 vt populate; (habitar) inhabit. **~rse** vpr get crowded

pobre adj poor. ● m & f poor person; (fig) poor thing. **¡~cito!** poor (little) thing! **¡~ de mí!** poor (old) me! **~za** f poverty

pocilga f pigsty

poción f potion

poco

● **adjetivo/pronombre**

····► poco, poca little, not much. tiene poca paciencia he has little patience. ¿cuánta leche queda? - poca how much milk is there left? - not much

····► pocos, pocas few. muy ∼s días very few days. unos ∼s dólares a few dollars. compré unos ∼s I bought a few. aceptaron a muy ∼s very few (people) were accepted

····► a ∼ de llegar soon after he arrived. ¡a ∼ ! (Mex) really? dentro de ∼ soon. a ∼ ∼, (LAm) de a ∼ gradually, little by little. hace ∼ recently, not long ago. por ∼ nearly. un ∼ (cantidad) a little; (tiempo) a while. un ∼ de a (little) bit of, a little, some

● **adverbio**

····► (con verbo) not much. lee muy ∼ he doesn't read very much

····► (con adjetivo) un lugar ∼ conocido a little known place. es ∼ inteligente he's not very intelligent

❗ Cuando **poco** modifica a un adjetivo, muchas veces el inglés prefiere el uso del prefijo un-, p. ej. **poco amistoso** unfriendly. **poco agradecido** ungrateful

podar vt prune

poder 33 verbo auxiliar be able to. no voy a ∼ terminar I won't be able to finish. no pudo venir he couldn't come. ¿puedo hacer algo? can I do anything? ¿puedo pasar? may I come in? no ∼ con not be able to cope with; (no aguantar) not be able to stand. no ∼ más be exhausted; (estar harto de algo) not be able to manage any more. no ∼ menos que have no alternative but. puede que it is possible that. puede ser it is possible. ¿se puede ...? may I...? ● m power. en el ∼ in power. ∼es públicos authorities. ∼oso adj powerful

podrido adj rotten

po|ema m poem. ∼esía f poetry; (poema) poem. ∼eta m & f poet. ∼ético adj poetic

polaco adj Polish. ● m Pole; (lengua) Polish

polar adj polar. **estrella** ∼ polestar

polea f pulley

pol|émica f controversy. ∼emizar 10 vi argue

polen m pollen

policía f police (force); (persona) policewoman. ● m policeman. ∼co adj police; (novela etc) detective

policromo adj, **policromo** adj polychrome

polideportivo m sports centre

polietileno m polythene

poligamia f polygamy

polígono m polygon

polilla f moth

polio(mielitis) f polio(myelitis)

polític|a f politics; (postura) policy; (mujer) politician. ∼ **interior** domestic policy. ∼o adj political. **familia** ∼a in-laws. ● m politician

póliza f (de seguros) policy

poll|o m chicken; (gallo joven) chick. ∼uelo m chick

polo m pole; (helado) ice lolly (Brit),

Popsicle (P) (*Amer*); (*juego*) polo.
P∼ norte North Pole

Polonia *f* Poland

poltrona *f* armchair

polución *f* pollution

polv|areda *f* dust cloud; (*fig, escándalo*) uproar. ∼**era** *f* compact. ∼**o** *m* powder; (*suciedad*) dust. ∼**os** *mpl* powder. en ∼**o** powdered. estar hecho ∼**o** be exhausted. quitar el ∼**o** dust

pólvora *f* gunpowder; (*fuegos artificiales*) fireworks

polvoriento *adj* dusty

pomada *f* ointment

pomelo *m* grapefruit

pómez *adj*. piedra *f* ∼ pumice stone

pomp|a *f* bubble; (*esplendor*) pomp. ∼**as fúnebres** funeral. ∼**oso** *adj* pompous; (*espléndido*) splendid

pómulo *m* cheekbone

ponchar *vt* (*Mex*) puncture

ponche *m* punch

poncho *m* poncho

ponderar *vt* (*alabar*) speak highly of

poner 34 *vt* put; put on (*ropa, obra de teatro, TV etc*); lay (*la mesa, un huevo*); set (*examen, deberes*); (*contribuir*) contribute; give (*nombre*); make (*nervioso*); pay (*atención*); show (*película, interés*); open (*una tienda*); equip (*una casa*). ∼ con (*al teléfono*) put through to. ∼ **por escrito** put into writing. ∼ **una multa** fine. pongamos let's suppose. ● *vi* lay. ∼**se** *vpr* put o.s.; (*volverse*) get; put on (*ropa*); (*sol*) set. ∼**se a** start to. ∼**se a mal con uno** fall out with s.o.

pongo *vb* véase **PONER**

poniente *m* west; (*viento*) west wind

pont|ificar 7 *vi* pontificate. ∼**ifice** *m* pontiff

popa *f* stern

popote *m* (*Mex*) (drinking) straw

popul|acho *m* masses. ∼**ar** *adj* popular; (*costumbre*) traditional; (*lenguaje*) colloquial. ∼**aridad** *f* popularity. ∼**arizar** 10 *vt* popularize.

póquer *m* poker

poquito *m*. un ∼ **a** little bit. ● *adv* a little

---

por *preposición*

·····▸ for. es ∼ **tu bien** it's for your own good. lo compró por 5 dólares he bought it for 5 dollars. si no fuera por ti if it weren't for you. vino por una semana he came for a week

➡ Para expresiones como **por la mañana, por la noche** etc., ver bajo el respectivo nombre

·····▸ (*causa*) because of. se retrasó ∼ **la lluvia** he was late because of the rain. no hay trenes ∼ **la huelga** there aren't any trains because of the strike

·····▸ (*medio, agente*) by. lo envié ∼ **correo** I sent it by post. fue destruida ∼ **las bombas** it was destroyed by the bombs

·····▸ (*a través de*) through. entró ∼ **la ventana** he got in through the window. me enteré ∼ **un amigo** I found out through a friend. ∼ **todo el** país throughout the country

····▸ (a lo largo de) along. caminar ∼ la playa to walk along the beach. cortar ∼ la línea de puntos cut along the dotted line

····▸ (proporción) per. cobra 30 dólares ∼ hora he charges 30 dollars per hour. uno ∼ persona one per person. 10 ∼ ciento 10 per cent

····▸ (Mat) times. dos ∼ dos (son) cuatro two times two is four

····▸ (modo) in. ∼ escrito in writing. pagar ∼ adelantado to pay in advance

➡ Para expresiones como **por dentro, por fuera** etc., ver bajo el respectivo adverbio

····▸ (en locuciones) ∼ más que no matter how much. ¿∼ qué? why? ∼ si in case. ∼ supuesto of course

porcelana f china

porcentaje m percentage

porcino adj pig

porción f portion; (de chocolate) piece

pordiosero m beggar

porfía|do adj stubborn. ∼r 20 vi insist

pormenor m detail

pornogr|afía f pornography. ∼áfico adj pornographic

poro m pore; (Mex, puerro) leek. ∼so adj porous

porque conj because; (para que) so that

porqué m reason

porquería f filth; (basura) rubbish; (grosería) dirty trick

porra f club

porrón m wine jug (with a long spout)

portaaviones m invar aircraft carrier

portada f (de libro) title page; (de revista) cover

portadocumentos m invar (LAm) briefcase

portador m bearer

portaequipaje(s) m invar boot (Brit), trunk (Amer); (encima del coche) roof-rack

portal m hall; (puerta principal) main entrance. ∼es mpl arcade

porta|ligas m invar suspender belt. ∼monedas m invar purse

portarse vpr behave

portátil adj portable. ● m portable computer, laptop

portavoz m spokesman. ● f spokeswoman

portazo m bang. dar un ∼ slam the door

porte m transport; (precio) carriage; (LAm, tamaño) size. ∼ador m carrier

portento m marvel

porteño adj from Buenos Aires

porter|ía f porter's lodge; (en deportes) goal. ∼o m caretaker, porter; (en deportes) goalkeeper. ∼o automático entryphone

pórtico m portico

portorriqueño adj & m Puerto Rican

Portugal m Portugal

portugués adj & m Portuguese

porvenir m future

posada f inn. dar ∼ give shelter

posar vt put. ● vi pose. ∼se vpr

P

(pájaro) perch; (avión) land

posdata f postscript

pose|dor m owner; (de récord, billete, etc) holder. **~er** 18 vt own; hold (récord) have (conocimientos). **~sión** f possession. **~sionarse** vpr. **~sionarse de** take possession of. **~sivo** adj possessive

posgraduado adj & m postgraduate

posguerra f post-war years

posib|ilidad f possibility. **~le** adj possible. **de ser ~le** if possible. **en lo ~le** as far as possible. **si es ~le** if possible

posición f position; (en sociedad) social standing

positivo adj positive

poso m sediment

posponer 34 vt put after; (diferir) postpone

posta f. **a ~** on purpose

postal adj postal. ● f postcard

poste m pole; (de valla) post

póster m (pl ~s) poster

postergar 12 vt pass over; (diferir) postpone

posteri|dad f posterity. **~or** adj back; (años) later; (capítulos) subsequent. **~ormente** adv later

postigo m door; (contraventana) shutter

postizo adj false, artificial. ● m hairpiece

postrarse vpr prostrate o.s.

postre m dessert, pudding (Brit)

postular vt postulate; (LAm) nominate (candidato)

póstumo adj posthumous

postura f position, stance

potable adj drinkable; (agua) drinking

potaje m vegetable stew

potasio m potassium

pote m pot

poten|cia f power. **~cial** adj & m potential. **~te** adj powerful

potro m colt; (en gimnasia) horse

pozo m well; (hoyo seco) pit; (de mina) shaft; (fondo común) pool

práctica f practice. **en la ~** in practice

practica|nte m & f nurse. **~r** 7 vt practise; play (deportes); (ejecutar) carry out

práctico adj practical; (conveniente, útil) handy. ● m practitioner

prad|era f meadow; (terreno grande) prairie. **~o** m meadow

pragmático adj pragmatic

preámbulo m preamble

precario adj precarious; (medios) scarce

precaución f precaution; (cautela) caution. **con ~** cautiously

precaverse vpr take precautions

prece|dencia f precedence; (prioridad) priority. **~nte** adj preceding. ● m precedent. **~r** vt/i precede

precepto m precept. **~r** m tutor

precia|do adj valued; (don) valuable. **~rse** vpr. **~rse de** pride o.s. on

precio m price. **~ de venta al público** retail price. **al ~ de** at the cost of. **no tener ~** be priceless. **¿qué ~ tiene?** how much is it?

precios|idad f (cosa preciosa) beautiful thing. **¡es una ~idad!** it's beautiful! **~o** adj precious; (bonito) beautiful

precipicio m precipice

precipita|ción f precipitation; (prisa) rush. **~damente** adv hastily. **~do** adj hasty. **~r** vt (apre-

surar) hasten; (*arrojar*) hurl. ~**rse**
vpr throw o.s.; (*correr*) rush; (*actuar
sin reflexionar*) act rashly

precis|amente *adj* exactly. ~**ar**
vt require; (*determinar*) determine.
~**ión** *f* precision. ~**o** *adj* precise;
(*necesario*) necessary. **si es** ~**o** if
necessary

preconcebido *adj* preconceived

precoz *adj* early; (*niño*) precocious

precursor *m* forerunner

predecesor *m* predecessor

predecir 46. (*pero imperativo* pre-
dice, *futuro y condicional regulares*) *vt*
foretell

predestinado *adj* predestined

prédica *f* sermon

predicar 7 *vt/i* preach

predicción *f* prediction; (*del
tiempo*) forecast

predilec|ción *f* predilection.
~**to** *adj* favourite

predisponer 34 *vt* predispose

predomin|ante *adj* predomin-
ant. ~**ar** *vi* predominate. ~**io** *m*
predominance

preeminente *adj* pre-eminent

prefabricado *adj* prefabricated

prefacio *m* preface

prefer|encia *f* preference; (*Auto*)
right of way. **de** ~**encia** prefer-
ably. ~**ente** *adj* preferential. ~**ible**
adj preferable. ~**ido** *adj* favourite.
~**ir** 4 *vt* prefer

prefijo *m* prefix; (*telefónico*) dial-
ling code

pregonar *vt* announce

pregunta *f* question. **hacer una**
~ ask a question. ~**r** *vt/i* ask (*por*
about). ~**rse** *vpr* wonder

prehistórico *adj* prehistoric

preju|icio *m* prejudice. ~**zgar** 12
vt prejudge

preliminar *adj & m* preliminary

preludio *m* prelude

premarital *adj*, **prematrimonial**
adj premarital

prematuro *adj* premature

premedita|ción *f* premedita-
tion. ~**r** *vt* premeditate

premi|ar *vt* give a prize to; (*re-
compensar*) reward. ~**o** *m* prize;
(*recompensa*) reward. ~**o gordo**
jackpot

premonición *f* premonition

prenatal *adj* antenatal

prenda *f* garment; (*garantía*)
surety; (*en juegos*) forfeit. **en** ~ **de**
as a token of. ~**r** *vt* captivate.
~**rse** *vpr* fall in love (*de* with)

prende|dor *m* brooch. ~**r** *vt*
capture; (*sujetar*) fasten; light (*ci-
garrillo*); (*LAm*) turn on (gas, radio,
etc). ● *vt* catch; (*arraigar*) take
root. ~**rse** *vpr* (*encenderse*) catch
fire

prensa *f* press. ~**r** *vt* press

preñado *adj* pregnant; (*fig*) full

preocupa|ción *f* worry. ~**do** *adj*
worried. ~**r** *vt* worry. ~**rse** *vpr*
worry. ~**rse de** look after

prepara|ción *f* preparation.
~**do** *adj* prepared. ● *m* prepar-
ation. ~**r** *vt* prepare. ~**rse** *vpr* get
ready. ~**tivos** *mpl* preparations.
~**torio** *adj* preparatory

preposición *f* preposition

prepotente *adj* arrogant; (*acti-
tud*) high-handed

prerrogativa *f* prerogative

presa *f* (*cosa*) prey; (*embalse*) dam

presagi|ar *vt* presage. ~**o** *m*
omen

presb|iteriano *adj & m* Presby-
terian. ~**ítero** *m* priest

prescindir *vi.* ~ **de** do without;

(*deshacerse de*) dispense with

prescri|bir (pp prescrito) vt prescribe. ~**pción** f prescription

presencia f presence; (*aspecto*) appearance. en ~ de in the presence of. ~**r** vt be present at; (*ver*) witness

presenta|ble adj presentable. ~**ción** f presentation; (*de una persona a otra*) introduction. ~**dor** m presenter. ~**r** vt present; (*ofrecer*) offer; (*entregar*) hand in; (*hacer conocer*) introduce; show (película). ~**rse** vpr present o.s.; (*hacerse conocer*) introduce o.s.; (*aparecer*) turn up

presente adj present; (*actual*) this. • m present. los ~**s** those present. tener ~ remember

presenti|miento m premonition. ~**r** 4 vt have a feeling (que that)

preserva|r vt preserve. ~**tivo** m condom

presiden|cia f presidency; (*de asamblea*) chairmanship. ~**cial** adj presidential. ~**ta** f (woman) president. ~**te** m president; (*de asamblea*) chairman. ~**te del gobierno** prime minister

presidi|ario m convict. ~**o** m prison

presidir vt be president of; preside over (tribunal); chair (reunión, comité)

presi|ón f pressure. a ~**ón** under pressure. hacer ~**ón** press. ~**onar** vt press; (*fig*) put pressure on

preso adj. estar ~ be in prison. llevarse ~ a uno take s.o. away under arrest. • m prisoner

presta|do adj (de uno) lent; (a uno) borrowed. pedir ~**do** bor-

row. ~**mista** m & f moneylender

préstamo m loan; (*acción de pedir prestado*) borrowing; (*acción de prestar*) lending

prestar vt lend; give (ayuda etc); pay (atención). ~**se** vpr. ~**se a** be open to; (*ser apto*) be suitable (para for)

prestidigita|ción f conjuring. ~**dor** m conjurer

prestigio m prestige. ~**so** adj prestigious

presu|mido adj conceited. ~**mir** vi show off; boast (de about). ~**nción** f conceit; (*suposición*) presumption. ~**nto** adj alleged. ~**ntuoso** adj conceited

presup|oner 34 vt presuppose. ~**uesto** m budget; (*precio estimado*) estimate

preten|cioso adj pretentious. ~**der** vt try to; (*afirmar*) claim; (*solicitar*) apply for; (*cortejar*) court. ~**diente** m pretender; (*a una mujer*) suitor. ~**sión** f pretension; (*aspiración*) aspiration

pretérito m preterite, past

pretexto m pretext. con el ~ de on the pretext of

prevalecer 11 vi prevail (sobre over)

preven|ción f prevention; (*prejuicio*) prejudice. ~**ido** adj ready; (*precavido*) cautious. ~**ir** 53 vt prevent; (*advertir*) warn. ~**tiva** f (Mex) amber light. ~**tivo** adj preventive

prever 43 vt foresee; (*planear*) plan

previo adj previous

previs|ible adj predictable. ~**ión** f forecast; (*prudencia*) precaution

prima f (*pariente*) cousin; (*cantidad*) bonus

primario adj primary

primavera f spring. ∼l adj spring

primer adj véase PRIMERO. ∼a f (Auto) first (gear); (en tren etc) first class. ∼o adj (delante de nombre masculino en singular primer) first; (mejor) best; (principal) leading. la ∼a fila the front row. lo ∼o es the most important thing is. ∼a enseñanza primary education. a ∼os de at the beginning of. de ∼a first-class. ● n (the) first. ● adv first

primitivo adj primitive

primo m cousin; ⊞ fool. hacer el ∼ be taken for a ride

primogénito adj & m first-born, eldest

primor m delicacy; (cosa) beautiful thing

primordial adj fundamental; (interés) paramount

princesa f princess

principal adj main. lo ∼ es que the main thing is that

príncipe m prince

principi|ante m & f beginner. ∼o m beginning; (moral, idea) principle; (origen) origin. al ∼o at first. a ∼o(s) de at the beginning of. desde el ∼o from the start. en ∼o in principle. ∼os mpl (nociones) rudiments

prión m prion

prioridad f priority

prisa f hurry, haste. darse ∼ hurry (up). de ∼ quickly. tener ∼ be in a hurry

prisi|ón f prison; (encarcelamiento) imprisonment. ∼onero m prisoner

prismáticos mpl binoculars

priva|ción f deprivation. ∼da f (Mex) private road. ∼do adj (particular) private. ∼r vt deprive (de of). ∼tivo adj exclusive (de to)

privilegi|ado adj privileged; (muy bueno) exceptional. ∼o m privilege

pro prep. en ∼ de for, in favour of. ● m advantage. los ∼s y los contras the pros and cons

proa f bow

probab|ilidad f probability. ∼le adj probable, likely. ∼lemente adv probably

proba|dor m fitting-room. ∼r ② vt try; try on (ropa); (demostrar) prove. ● vi try. ∼rse vpr try on

probeta f test-tube

problema m problem. hacerse ∼as (LAm) worry

procaz adj indecent

proced|encia f origin. ∼ente adj (razonable) reasonable. ∼ente de (coming) from. ∼er m conduct. ● vi proceed. ∼er contra start legal proceedings against. ∼er de come from. ∼imiento m procedure; (sistema) process; (Jurid) proceedings

proces|ador m. ∼ de textos word processor. ∼al adj procedural. costas ∼ales legal costs. ∼amiento m processing; (Jurid) prosecution. ∼amiento de textos word-processing.. ∼ar vt process; (Jurid) prosecute

procesión f procession

proceso m process; (Jurid) trial; (transcurso) course

proclamar vt proclaim

procrea|ción f procreation. ∼r vt procreate

procura|dor m attorney, solicitor; (asistente) clerk (Brit), paralegal (Amer). ∼r vt try; (obtener) obtain

prodigar ⑫ vt lavish

prodigio m prodigy; (maravilla) wonder; (milagro) miracle. ∼so adj prodigious

P

pródigo *adj* prodigal

produc|ción *f* production. **~ir**
47 *vt* produce; (*causar*) cause.
~irse *vpr* (*suceder*) happen. **~tivo**
adj productive. **~to** *m* product.
~tos agrícolas farm produce.
~tos alimenticios foodstuffs.
~tos de belleza cosmetics. **~tos**
de consumo consumer goods.
~tor *m* producer.

proeza *f* exploit

profan|ación *f* desecration. **~ar**
vt desecrate. **~o** *adj* profane

profecía *f* prophecy

proferir **4** *vt* utter; hurl (*insultos*
etc)

profes|ión *f* profession. **~ional**
adj professional. **~or** *m* teacher;
(*en universidad*) lecturer. **~orado**
m teaching profession; (*conjunto de*
profesores) staff

prof|eta *m* prophet. **~etizar** **10**
vt/i prophesize

prófugo *adj* & *m* fugitive

profund|idad *f* depth. **~o** *adj*
deep; (*fig*) profound. **poco ~o**
shallow

progenitor *m* ancestor

programa *m* programme; (*de es-*
tudios) syllabus. **~ concurso** quiz
show. **~ de entrevistas** chat
show. **~ción** *f* programming; (*TV*
etc) programmes; (*en periódico*) TV
guide. **~r** *vt* programme. **~dor** *m*
computer programmer

progres|ar *vi* (make) progress.
~ión *f* progression. **~ista** *adj* pro-
gressive. **~ivo** *adj* progressive. **~o**
m progress. **hacer ~os** make pro-
gress

prohibi|ción *f* prohibition. **~do**
adj forbidden. **prohibido fumar** no
smoking. **~r** *vt* forbid. **~tivo** *adj*
prohibitive

prójimo *m* fellow man

prole *f* offspring

proletari|ado *m* proletariat. **~o**
adj & *m* proletarian

prol|iferación *f* proliferation.
~iferar *vi* proliferate. **~ífico** *adj*
prolific

prolijo *adj* long-winded

prólogo *m* prologue

prolongar **12** *vt* prolong; (*alar-*
gar) lengthen. **~se** *vpr* go on

promedio *m* average. **como ~**
on average

prome|sa *f* promise. **~ter** *vt*
promise. ● *vi* show promise.
~terse *vpr* (*novios*) get engaged.
~tida *f* fiancée. **~tido** *adj* prom-
ised; (*novios*) engaged. ● *m* fiancé

prominente *f* prominence

promiscu|idad *f* promiscuity.
~o *adj* promiscuous

promo|ción *f* promotion. **~tor**
m promoter. **~ver** **2** *vt* promote;
(*causar*) cause

promulgar **12** *vt* promulgate

pronombre *m* pronoun

pron|osticar **7** *vt* predict; fore-
cast (*tiempo*). **~óstico** *m* predic-
tion; (*del tiempo*) forecast; (*Med*)
prognosis

pront|itud *f* promptness. **~o** *adj*
quick. ● *adv* quickly; (*dentro de*
poco) soon; (*temprano*) early. **de**
~o suddenly. **por lo ~o** for the
time being. **tan ~o como** as
soon as

pronuncia|ción *f* pronunciation.
~miento *m* revolt. **~r** *vt* pro-
nounce; deliver (*discurso*). **~rse**
vpr (*declararse*) declare o.s.; (*suble-*
varse) rise up

propagación *f* propagation

propaganda *f* propaganda;

(*anuncios*) advertising

propagar 12 *vt/i* propagate. ~**se** *vpr* spread

propasarse *vpr* go too far

propens|ión *f* inclination. ~**o** *adj* inclined

propici|ar *vt* favour; (*provocar*) bring about. ~**o** *adj* favourable

propie|dad *f* property. ~**tario** *m* owner

propina *f* tip

propio *adj* own; (*característico*) typical; (*natural*) natural; (*apropiado*) proper. **el ~ médico** the doctor himself

proponer 34 *vt* propose; put forward (*persona*). ~**se** *vpr.* ~**se hacer** intend to do

proporci|ón *f* proportion. ~**onado** *adj* proportioned. ~**onal** *adj* proportional. ~**onar** *vt* provide

proposición *f* proposition

propósito *m* intention. **a ~** (*adrede*) on purpose; (*de paso*) by the way. **a ~ de** with regard to

propuesta *f* proposal

propuls|ar *vt* propel; (*fig*) promote. ~**ión** *f* propulsion. ~**ión a chorro** jet propulsion

prórroga *f* extension

prorrogar 12 *vt* extend

prosa *f* prose. ~**ico** *adj* prosaic

proscri|bir (*pp* proscrito) *vt* exile; (*prohibir*) ban. ~**to** *adj* banned. ● *m* exile; (*bandido*) outlaw

proseguir 5 & 13 *vt/i* continue

prospecto *m* prospectus; (*de fármaco*) directions for use

prosper|ar *vi* prosper; (*persona*) do well. ~**idad** *f* prosperity

próspero *adj* prosperous. **¡P~**

Año Nuevo! Happy New Year!

prostit|ución *f* prostitution. ~**uta** *f* prostitute

protagonista *m & f* protagonist

prote|cción *f* protection. ~**ctor** *adj* protective. ● *m* protector; (*benefactor*) patron. ~**ger** 14 *vt* protect. ~**gida** *f* protégée. ~**gido** *adj* protected. ● *m* protegé

proteína *f* protein

protesta *f* protest; (*manifestación*) demonstration; (*Mex, promesa*) promise; (*Mex, juramento*) oath

protestante *adj & m & f* Protestant

protestar *vt/i* protest

protocolo *m* protocol

provecho *m* benefit. **¡buen ~!** enjoy your meal! **de ~** useful. **en ~ de** to the benefit of. **sacar ~ de** benefit from

proveer 18 (*pp* proveído *y* provisto) *vt* supply, provide

provenir 53 *vi* come (**de** from)

proverbi|al *adj* proverbial. ~**o** *m* proverb

provincia *f* province. ~**l** *adj*, ~**no** *adj* provincial

provisional *adj* provisional

provisto *adj* provided (**de** with)

provoca|ción *f* provocation. ~**r** 7 *vt* provoke; (*causar*) cause. ~**tivo** *adj* provocative

proximidad *f* proximity

próximo *adj* next; (*cerca*) near

proyec|ción *f* projection. ~**tar** *vt* hurl; cast (*luz*); show (*película*). ~**til** *m* missile. ~**to** *m* plan. ~**to de ley** bill. **en ~to** planned. ~**tor** *m* projector

pruden|cia *f* prudence; (*cuidado*) caution. ~**te** *adj* prudent, sensible

prueba f proof; (examen) test; (de ropa) fitting. a ~ on trial. a ~ de proof against. a ~ de agua waterproof. poner a ~ test

pruebo vb véase **PROBAR**

psicoan|álisis f psychoanalysis. ~**alista** m & f psychoanalyst. ~**alizar** 10 vt psychoanalyse

psic|ología f psychology. ~**ológico** adj psychological. ~**ólogo** m psychologist. ~**ópata** m & f psychopath. ~**osis** f invar psychosis

psiqu|e f psyche. ~**iatra** m & f psychiatrist. ~**iátrico** adj psychiatric

psíquico adj psychic

ptas, pts abrev (pesetas) pesetas

púa f sharp point; (espina) thorn; (de erizo) quill; (de peine) tooth; (Mus) plectrum

pubertad f puberty

publica|ción f publication. ~**r** 7 vt publish

publici|dad f publicity; (Com) advertising. ~**tario** adj advertising

público adj public. ● m public; (de espectáculo etc) audience

puchero m cooking pot; (guisado) stew. hacer ~s (fig, fam) pout

pude vb véase **PODER**

pudor m modesty. ~**oso** adj modest

pudrir (pp podrido) vt rot; (fig, molestar) annoy. ~**se** vpr rot

puebl|ecito m small village. ~**erino** m country bumpkin. ~**o** m town; (aldea) village; (nación) nation, people

puedo vb véase **PODER**

puente m bridge; (fig, fam) long weekend. ~ **colgante** suspension bridge. ~ **levadizo** drawbridge. hacer ~ 11 have a long weekend

puente Puentes are very important in Spain and Latin America. Hacer Puente means that when a working day falls between two public holidays, it too is taken as a holiday. [i]

puerco adj filthy; (grosero) coarse. ● m pig. ~ **espín** porcupine

puerro m leek

puerta f door; (en deportes) goal; (de ciudad, en jardín) gate. ~ **principal** main entrance. a ~ **cerrada** behind closed doors

puerto m port; (fig, refugio) refuge; (entre montañas) pass. ~ **franco** free port

puertorriqueño adj & m Puerto Rican

pues adv (entonces) then; (bueno) well. ● conj since

puest|a f setting; (en juegos) bet. ~**a de sol** sunset. ~**a en escena** staging. ~**a en marcha** starting. ~**o** put; (vestido) dressed. ● m place; (empleo) position, job; (en mercado etc) stall. ● conj. ~**o que** since

pugna f struggle. ~**r** vi. ~**r por** strive to

puja f struggle (por to); (en subasta) bid. ~**r** vt struggle; (en subasta) bid

pulcro adj neat

pulga f flea. tener malas ~s be bad-tempered

pulga|da f inch. ~**r** m thumb; (del pie) big toe

puli|do adj polished; (modales) refined. ~**r** vt polish; (suavizar) smooth

pulla f gibe

pulm|ón m lung. ~**onar** adj pulmonary. ~**onía** f pneumonia

pulpa f pulp

pulpería f (LAm) grocer's shop (Brit), grocery store (Amer)

púlpito m pulpit

pulpo m octopus

pulque m (Mex) pulque, alcoholic Mexican drink. ~**ría** f bar

pulsa|ción f pulsation. ~**dor** m button. ~**r** vt press; (Mus) pluck

pulsera f bracelet

pulso m pulse; (firmeza) steady hand. echar un ~ arm wrestle. tomar el ~ a uno take s.o.'s pulse

pulular vi teem with

puma m puma

puna f puna, high plateau

punitivo adj punitive

punta f point; (extremo) tip. estar de ~ be in a bad mood. ponerse de ~ con uno fall out with s.o. sacar ~ a sharpen

puntada f stitch

puntaje m (LAm) score

puntal m prop, support

puntapié m kick

puntear vt mark; (Mus) pluck; (LAm, en deportes) lead

puntería f aim; (destreza) markmanship

puntiagudo adj pointed; (afilado) sharp

puntilla f (encaje) lace. en ~s (LAm), de ~s on tiptoe

punto m point; (señal, trazo) dot; (de examen) mark; (lugar) spot, place; (de taxis) stand; (momento) moment; (punto final) full stop (Brit), period (Amer); (puntada) stitch. ~ de vista point of view. ~ com dot-com. ~ final full stop (Brit), period (Amer). ~ muerto (Auto) neutral (gear). ~ y aparte full stop, new paragraph (Brit),

period, new paragraph (Amer). ~ y coma semicolon. a ~ on time; (listo) ready. a ~ de on the point of. de ~ knitted. dos ~s colon. en ~ exactly. hacer ~ knit. hasta cierto ~ to a certain extent

puntuación f punctuation; (en deportes, acción) scoring; (en deportes, número de puntos) score

puntual adj punctual; (exacto) accurate. ~**idad** f punctuality; (exactitud) accuracy

puntuar 🟦 vt punctuate; mark (Brit), grade (Amer) (examen). ● vi score (points)

punza|da f sharp pain; (fig) pang. ~**nte** adj sharp. ~**r** 🔟 vt prick

puñado m handful. a ~s by the handful

puñal m dagger. ~**ada** f stab

puñ|etazo m punch. ~**o** m fist; (de ropa) cuff; (mango) handle. de su ~**o** (y letra) in his own handwriting

pupa f (fam, en los labios) cold sore

pupila f pupil

pupitre m desk

puré m purée; (sopa) thick soup. ~ de papas (LAm), ~ de patatas mashed potatoes

pureza f purity

purga f purge. ~**torio** m purgatory

puri|ficación f purification. ~**ficar** 🟨 vt purify. ~**sta** m & f purist. ~**tano** adj puritanical. ● m puritan

puro adj pure; (cielo) clear. de pura casualidad by sheer chance. de ~ tonto out of sheer stupidity. ● m cigar

púrpura f purple

pus m pus

puse vb véase PONER

pusilánime adj fainthearted
puta f (vulg) whore

....

Qq

....

que pron rel (personas, sujeto) who;
(personas, complemento) whom;
(cosas) which, that. ● conj that. ¡~
tengan Vds buen viaje! have a
good journey! ¡~ venga! let him
come! ~ venga o no venga
whether he comes or not. creo ~
tiene razón I think (that) he is
right. más ~ more than. lo ~
what. yo ~ tú if I were you

qué adj (con sustantivo) what; (con
a o adv) how. ● pron what. ¡~ bo-
nito! how nice!. ¿en ~ piensas?
what are you thinking about?

quebra|da f gorge; (paso) pass.
~dizo adj fragile. ~do adj broken;
(Com) bankrupt. ● m (Math) frac-
tion. ~ntar vt break; disturb (paz).
~nto m (pérdida) loss; (daño)
damage. ~r **1** vt break. ● vi
break; (Com) go bankrupt. ~rse vpr
break

quechua adj Quechua. ● m & f
Quechuan. ● m (lengua) Quechua

quedar vi stay, remain; (estar) be;
(haber todavía) be left. ~ bien
come off well. ~se vpr stay. ~
con arrange to meet. ~ en agree
to. ~ en nada come to nothing.
~ por (+ infinitivo) remain to be (+
pp)

quehacer m work. ~es domésti-
cos household chores

queja| f complaint; (de dolor)
moan. ~arse vpr complain (de

about); (gemir) moan. ~ido m
moan

quema|do adj burnt; (LAm, bron-
ceado) tanned; (fig) annoyed.
~dor m burner. ~dura f burn. ~r
vt/i burn. ~rse vpr burn o.s.; (con-
sumirse) burn up; (con el sol) get
sunburnt. ~rropa adv. a ~rropa
point-blank

quena f Indian flute

quepo vb véase CABER

querella f (riña) quarrel, dispute;
(Jurid) criminal action

quer|er **35** vt want; (amar) love;
(necesitar) need. ~ decir mean.
● m love; (amante) lover. como
quiera que however. cuando
quiera whenever. donde
quiera wherever. ¿quieres darme
ese libro? would you pass me that
book? ¿quieres un helado? would
you like an ice-cream? quisiera ir
a la playa I'd like to go to the
beach. sin ~er without meaning
to. ~ido adj dear; (amado) loved

querosén m, **queroseno** m kero-
sene

querubín m cherub

ques|adilla f (Mex) tortilla filled
with cheese. ~o m cheese

quetzal m (unidad monetaria ecua-
toriana) quetzal

quicio m frame. sacar de ~ a
uno infuriate s.o.

quiebra f (Com) bankruptcy

quien pron rel (sujeto) who; (com-
plemento) whom

quién pron interrogativo (sujeto) who;
(tras preposición) ¿con ~? who
with?, to whom? ¿de ~ son
estos libros? whose are these
books?

quienquiera pron whoever

quiero vb véase QUERER

quiet|o *adj* still; (*inmóvil*) motionless; (*carácter etc*) calm. **~ud** *f* stillness

quijada *f* jaw

quilate *m* carat

quilla *f* keel

quimera *f* (*fig*) illusion

químic|a *f* chemistry. **~o** *adj* chemical. • *m* chemist

quince *adj* & *m* fifteen. **~** días *a* fortnight. **~na** *f* fortnight. **~nal** *adj* fortnightly

quincuagésimo *adj* fiftieth

quiniela *f* pools coupon. **~s** *fpl* (football) pools

quinientos *adj* & *m* five hundred

quinquenio *m* (period of) five years

quinta *f* (*casa*) villa

quintal *m* a hundred kilograms

quinteto *m* quintet

quinto *adj* & *m* fifth

quiosco *m* kiosk; (*en jardín*) summerhouse; (*en parque etc*) bandstand

quirúrgico *adj* surgical

quise *vb* *véase* QUERER

quisquill|a *f* trifle; (*camarón*) shrimp. **~oso** *adj* irritable; (*exigente*) fussy

quita|esmalte *m* nail polish remover. **~manchas** *m invar* stain remover. **~nieves** *m invar* snow plough. **~r** *vt* remove, take away; take off (*ropa*); (*robar*) steal. **~ndo** (*fam, a excepción de*) apart from. **~rse** *vpr* get rid of (*dolor*); take off (*ropa*). **~rse de** (*no hacerlo más*) stop. **~rse de en medio** get out of the way. **~sol** *m* sunshade

quizá(s) *adv* perhaps

quórum *m* quorum

Rr

rábano *m* radish. **~** picante horseradish. me importa un **~** I couldn't care less

rabi|a *f* rabies; (*fig*) rage. **~ar** *vi* (*de dolor*) be in great pain; (*estar enfadado*) be furious. dar **~a** infuriate. **~eta** *f* tantrum

rabino *m* rabbi

rabioso *adj* rabid; (*furioso*) furious

rabo *m* tail

racha *f* gust of wind; (*fig*) spate. pasar por una mala **~** go through a bad patch

racial *adj* racial

racimo *m* bunch

ración *f* share, ration; (*de comida*) portion

racional *adj* rational. **~lizar** 🔟 *vt* rationalize. **~r** *vt* (*limitar*) ration; (*repartir*) ration out

racis|mo *m* racism. **~ta** *adj* racist

radar *m* radar

radiación *f* radiation

radiactiv|idad *f* radioactivity. **~o** *adj* radioactive

radiador *m* radiator

radiante *adj* radiant; (*brillante*) brilliant

radical *adj* & *m* & *f* radical

radicar 🔟 *vi* lie (en in). **~se** *vpr* settle

radio *m* radius; (*de rueda*) spoke; (*LAm*) radio. • *f* radio. **~actividad** *f* radioactivity. **~activo** *adj* radioactive. **~difusión** *f* broadcasting. **~emisora** *f* radio station. **~escucha** *m* & *f* listener. **~grafia** *f* radiography

radi|ólogo m radiologist. ~ote- **rapia** f radiotherapy

radioyente m & f listener

raer 38 vt scrape; (quitar) scrape off

ráfaga f (de viento) gust; (de ametralladora) burst

rafia f raffia

raído adj threadbare

raíz f root. a ~ de as a result of. echar raices (fig) settle

raja f split; (Culin) slice. ~r vt split. ~rse vpr split; (fig) back out

rajatabla. a ~ rigorously

ralea f sort

ralla|dor m grater. ~r vt grate

ralo adj (pelo) thin

rama f branch. ~je m branches. ~l m branch

rambla f watercourse; (avenida) avenue

ramera f prostitute

ramifica|ción f ramification. ~rse 7 vpr branch out

ram|illete m bunch. ~o m branch; (de flores) bunch, bouquet

rampa f ramp, slope

rana f frog

ranch|era f (Mex) folk song. ~ero m cook; (Mex, hacendado) rancher. ~o m (LAm, choza) hut; (LAm, casucha) shanty; (Mex, hacienda) ranch

rancio adj rancid; (vino) old; (fig) ancient

rango m rank

ranúnculo m buttercup

ranura f groove; (para moneda) slot

rapar vt shave; crop (pelo)

rapaz adj rapacious; (ave) of prey

rape m monkfish

rapidez f speed

rápido adj fast, quick. ● adv quickly. ● m (tren) express. ~s mpl rapids

rapiña f robbery. ave f de ~ bird of prey

rapsodia f rhapsody

rapt|ar vt kidnap. ~o m kidnapping; (de ira etc) fit

raqueta f racquet

rar|eza f rarity; (cosa rara) oddity. ~o adj rare; (extraño) odd. es ~o que it is strange that. ¡qué ~o! how strange!

ras. a ~ de level with

rasca|cielos m invar skyscraper. ~r 7 vt scratch; (raspar) scrape

rasgar 12 vt tear

rasgo m characteristic; (gesto) gesture; (de pincel) stroke. ~s mpl (facciones) features

rasguear vt strum

rasguñ|ar vt scratch. ~o m scratch

raso adj (cucharada etc) level; (vuelo etc) low. al ~ in the open air. ● m satin

raspa|dura f scratch; (acción) scratching. ~r vt scratch; (rozar) scrape

rastr|a. a ~as dragging. ~ear vt track. ~ero adj creeping. ~illar vt rake. ~illo m rake. ~o m track; (señal) sign. ni ~o not a trace

rata f rat

ratero m petty thief

ratifica|ción f ratification. ~r 7 vt ratify

rato m moment, short time. ~s libres spare time. a ~s at times. a cada ~ (LAm) always. hace un ~ a moment ago. pasar un mal ~ have a rough time

rat|ón m mouse. ~onera f

mousetrap; (*madriguera*) mouse hole

raudal *m* torrent. a ~**les** in abundance

raya *f* line; (*lista*) stripe; (*de pelo*) parting. a ~**s** striped. pasarse de la ~ go too far. ~**r** *vt* scratch. ~**r** en border on

rayo *m* ray; (*descarga eléctrica*) lightning. ~ de luna moonbeam. ~ láser laser beam. ~**s** X X-rays

raza *f* race; (*de animal*) breed. de ~ (*caballo*) thoroughbred; (*perro*) pedigree

raz|ón *f* reason. a ~**ón** de at the rate of. tener ~ to be right. ~**onable** *adj* reasonable. ~**onar** *vt* reason out. ● *vi* reason

RDSI *abrev* (**Red Digital de Servicios Integrados**) ISDN

re *m* D; (*solfa*) re

reac|ción *f* reaction; (*LAm, Pol*) right wing. ~**ción en cadena** chain reaction. ~**cionario** *adj & m* reactionary. ~**tor** *m* reactor; (*avión*) jet

real *adj* real; (*de rey etc*) royal; (*hecho*) true. ● *m* real, old Spanish coin

realidad *f* reality; (*verdad*) truth. en ~ in fact. hacerse ~ come true

realis|mo *m* realism. ~**ta** *adj* realistic. ● *m & f* realist

realiza|ción *f* fulfilment. ~**r** 🔟 *vt* carry out; make (*viaje*); fulfil (*ilusión*); (*vender*) sell. ~**rse** *vpr* (*sueño, predicción etc*) come true; (*persona*) fulfil o.s.

realzar 🔟 *vt* (*fig*) enhance

reanimar *vt* revive. ~**se** *vpr* revive

reanudar *vt* resume; renew (*amistad*)

reavivar *vt* revive

rebaja *f* reduction. en ~**s** in the sale. ~**do** *adj* (*precio*) reduced. ~**r** *vt* lower; lose (*peso*)

rebanada *f* slice

rebaño *m* herd; (*de ovejas*) flock

rebasar *vt* exceed; (*dejar atrás*) leave behind; (*Mex, Auto*) overtake

rebatir *vt* refute

rebel|arse *vpr* rebel. ~**de** *adj* rebellious; (*grupo*) rebel. ● *m* rebel. ~**día** *f* rebelliousness. ~**ión** *f* rebellion

rebosa|nte *adj* brimming (de with). ~**r** *vi* overflow; (*abundar*) abound

rebot|ar *vt* bounce; (*rechazar*) repel. ● *vi* bounce; (*bala*) ricochet. ~**e** *m* bounce, rebound. de ~**e** on the rebound

reboz|ar 🔟 *vt* wrap up; (*Culin*) coat in batter. ~**o** *m* (*LAm*) shawl

rebusca|do *adj* affected; (*complicado*) over-elaborate. ~**r** 🔽 *vt* search through

rebuznar *vi* bray

recado *m* errand; (*mensaje*) message

reca|er 🔞 *vi* fall back; (*Med*) relapse; (*fig*) fall. ~**ída** *f* relapse

recalcar 🔽 *vt* stress

recalcitrante *adj* recalcitrant

recalentar 🔟 *vt* reheat; (*demasiado*) overheat

recámara *f* small room; (*de arma de fuego*) chamber; (*Mex, dormitorio*) bedroom

recambio *m* (*Mec*) spare (part); (*de pluma etc*) refill. de ~ spare

recapitular *vt* sum up

recarg|ar 🔃 *vt* overload; (*aumentar*) increase; recharge (*batería*); top up (*móvil*). ~**o** *m* increase

recat|ado adj modest. ∼**o** m prudence; (*modestia*) modesty. **sin** ∼**o** openly

recauda|ción f (*cantidad*) takings. ∼**dor** m tax collector. ∼**r** vt collect

recel|ar vt suspect. ● vi be suspicious (**de** of). ∼**o** m distrust; (*temor*) fear. ∼**oso** adj suspicious

recepci|ón f reception. ∼**onista** m & f receptionist

receptáculo m receptacle

receptor m receiver

recesión f recession

receta f (*Culin*) recipe; (*Med*) prescription

rechaz|ar [10] vt reject; defeat (*moción*); repel (*ataque*); (*no aceptar*) turn down. ∼**o** m rejection

rechifla f booing

rechinar vi squeak. **le rechinan los dientes** he grinds his teeth

rechoncho adj stout

recib|imiento m (*acogida*) welcome. ∼**ir** vt receive; (*acoger*) welcome ● vi entertain. ∼**irse** vpr graduate. ∼**o** m receipt. **acusar** ∼**o** acknowledge receipt

reci|én adv recently, (*LAm*, *hace poco*) just. ∼ **casado** newly married. ∼ **nacido** newborn. ∼**ente** adj recent; (*Culin*) fresh

recinto m enclosure; (*local*) premises

recio adj strong; (*voz*) loud. ● adv hard; (*en voz alta*) loudly

recipiente m receptacle. ●m & f recipient

recíproco adj reciprocal; (*sentimiento*) mutual

recita|l m recital; (*de poesías*) reading. ∼**r** vt recite

reclama|ción f claim; (*queja*) complaint. ● vi appeal

réclame m (*LAm*) advertisement

reclamo m (*LAm*) complaint

reclinar vi lean. ∼**se** vpr lean

reclus|ión f imprisonment. ∼**o** m prisoner

recluta m & f recruit. ∼**miento** m recruitment. ∼**r** vt recruit

recobrar vt recover. ∼**se** vpr recover

recodo m bend

recog|er [14] vt collect; pick up (*cosa caída*); (*cosechar*) harvest. ∼**erse** vpr withdraw; (*ir a casa*) go home; (*acostarse*) go to bed. ∼**ida** f collection; (*cosecha*) harvest

recomenda|ción f recommendation. ∼**r** [1] vt recommend; (*encomendar*) entrust

recomenzar [1] & [10] vt/i start again

recompensa f reward. ∼**r** vt reward

reconcilia|ción f reconciliation. ∼**r** vt reconcile. ∼**rse** vpr be reconciled

reconoc|er [11] vt recognize; (*admitir*) acknowledge; (*examinar*) examine. ∼**imiento** m recognition; (*admisión*) acknowledgement; (*agradecimiento*) gratitude; (*examen*) examination

reconozco vb véase RECONOCER

reconquista f reconquest. ∼**r** vt reconquer; (*fig*) win back

Reconquista *i* The period in Spain's history during which the Christian kingdoms slowly recovered the territories occupied by the Moslem Moors of North Africa. The Moorish invasion began in 711 AD and was halted in 718. The expulsion of the last Moorish ruler of Granada in 1492 completed the *Reconquista*.

reconsiderar *vt* reconsider

reconstruir 🔟 *vt* reconstruct

récord /'rekor/ *m* (*pl* ~s) record

recordar ② *vt* remember; (*hacer acordar*) remind. ● *vi* remember. **que yo recuerde** as far as I remember. **si mal no recuerdo** if I remember rightly

recorr|er *vt* tour (*país*); go round (*zona, museo*); cover (*distancia*). ~ **mundo** travel all around the world. ~**ido** *m* journey; (*trayecto*) route

recort|ar *vt* cut (out). ~**e** *m* cutting (out); (*de periódico etc*) cutting

recostar ② *vt* lean. ~**se** *vpr* lie down

recoveco *m* bend; (*rincón*) nook

recre|ación *f* recreation. ~**ar** *vt* recreate; (*divertir*) entertain. ~**arse** *vpr* amuse o.s. ~**ativo** *adj* recreational. ~**o** *m* recreation; (*en escuela*) break

recrudecer 🕠 *vi* intensify

recta *f* straight line. ~ **final** home stretch

rect|angular *adj* rectangular. ~**ángulo** *adj* rectangular; (*triángulo*) right-angled. ●*m* rectangle

rectifica|ción *f* rectification. ~**r** 🟨 *vt* rectify

rect|itud *f* straightness; (*fig*) honesty. ~**o** *adj* straight; (*fig, justo*) fair; (*fig, honrado*) honest. **todo** ~**o** straight on. ● *m* rectum

rector *adj* governing. ● *m* rector

recubrir (*pp* recubierto) *vt* cover (**con**, de with)

recuerdo *m* memory; (*regalo*) souvenir. ~**s** *mpl* (*saludos*) regards. ●*vb véase* **RECORDAR**

recupera|ción *f* recovery. ~**r** *vt* recover. ~**r el tiempo perdido** make up for lost time. ~**rse** *vpr* recover

recur|rir *vi.* ~**rir a** a resort to (*cosa*); turn to (*persona*). ~**so** *m* resort; (*medio*) resource; (*Jurid*) appeal. ~**sos** *mpl* resources

red *f* network; (*malla*) net; (*para equipaje*) luggage rack; (*Com*) chain; (*Elec, gas*) mains. **la R**~ the Net

redac|ción *f* writing; (*lenguaje*) wording; (*conjunto de redactores*) editorial staff; (*oficina*) editorial office; (*Escol, Univ*) essay. ~**tar** *vt* write. ~**tor** *m* writer; (*de periódico*) editor

redada *f* catch; (*de policía*) raid

redecilla *f* small net; (*para el pelo*) hairnet

redentor *adj* redeeming

redimir *vt* redeem

redoblar *vt* redouble; step up (*vigilancia*)

redomado *adj* utter

redond|a *f* (*de imprenta*) roman (type); (*Mus*) semibreve (*Brit*), whole note (*Amer*). **a la** ~**a** around. ~**ear** *vt* round off. ~**el** *m* circle; (*de plaza de toros*) arena. ~**o** *adj* round; (*completo*) complete; (*Mex, boleto*) return, round-trip (*Amer*). **en** ~**o** round; (*categóricamente*) flatly

reduc|ción *f* reduction. ~**ido** *adj* reduced; (*limitado*) limited; (*pequeño*) small; (*precio*) low. ~**ir** 🠲 *vt* reduce. ~**irse** *vpr* be reduced; (*fig*) amount

reduje *vb véase* **REDUCIR**

redundan|cia *f* redundancy. ~**te** *adj* redundant

reduzco *vb véase* **REDUCIR**

reembols|ar vt reimburse. ~**o** m repayment. **contra** ~**o** cash on delivery

reemplaz|ar 10 vt replace. ~**o** m replacement

refacci|ón f (LAm) refurbishment; (Mex, Mec) spare part. ~**onar** vt (LAm) refurbish. ~**onaria** f (Mex) repair shop

referencia f reference; (información) report. **con** ~ **a** with reference to. **hacer** ~ **a** refer to

referéndum m (pl ~**s**) referendum

referir 4 vt tell; (remitir) refer. ~**se** vpr refer. **por lo que se refiere a** as regards

refiero vb véase **REFERIR**

refilón. **de** ~ obliquely

refin|amiento m refinement. ~**ar** vt refine. ~**ería** f refinery

reflector m reflector; (proyector) searchlight

reflej|ar vt reflect. ~**o** adj reflex. ● m reflection; (Med) reflex; (en el pelo) highlights

reflexi|ón f reflection. **sin** ~**ón** without thinking. ~**onar** vi reflect. ~**vo** adj (persona) thoughtful; (Gram) reflexive

reforma f reform. ~**s** fpl (reparaciones) repairs. ~**r** vt reform. ~**rse** vpr reform

reforzar 2 & 10 vt reinforce

refrac|ción f refraction. ~**tario** adj heat-resistant

refrán m saying

refregar 1 & 12 vt scrub

refresc|ar 7 vt refresh; (enfriar) cool. ● vi get cooler. ~**arse** vpr refresh o.s. ~**o** m cold drink. ~**os** mpl refreshments

refrigera|ción f refrigeration; (aire acondicionado) air-conditioning; (de motor) cooling. ~**r** vt refrigerate; air-condition (lugar); cool (motor). ~**dor** m refrigerator

refuerzo m reinforcement

refugi|ado m refugee. ~**arse** vpr take refuge. ~**o** m refuge, shelter

refunfuñar vi grumble

refutar vt refute

regadera f watering-can; (Mex, ducha) shower

regala|do adj as a present, free; (cómodo) comfortable. ~**r** vt give

regalo m present, gift

regañ|adientes. **a** ~**adientes** reluctantly. ~**ar** vt scold. ● vi moan; (dos personas) quarrel. ~**o** m (reprensión) scolding

regar 1 & 12 vt water

regata f boat race; (serie) regatta

regate|ar vt haggle over; (economizar) economize on. ● vi haggle; (en deportes) dribble. ~**o** m haggling; (en deportes) dribbling

regazo m lap

regenerar vt regenerate

régimen m (pl **regímenes**) regime; (Med) diet; (de lluvias) pattern

regimiento m regiment

regi|ón f region. ~**onal** adj regional

regir 5 & 14 vt govern. ● vi apply, be in force

registr|ado adj registered. ~**ar** vt register; (Mex) check in (equipaje); (grabar) record; (examinar) search. ~**arse** vpr (darse) be reported. ~**o** m (padrón de registro) registration; (libro) register; (cosa anotada) entry; (inspección) search. ~**o civil** (oficina) registry office

regla f ruler; (norma) rule; (mens-

truación) period. en ~ in order.
por ~ general as a rule. **~mentación** f regulation. **~mentar** vt
regulate. **~mentario** adj regulation; (horario) set. **~mento** m regulations

regocij|arse vpr be delighted.
~o m delight

regode|arse vpr (+ gerundio) delight in (+ gerund). ~o m delight

regordete adj chubby

regres|ar vi return; (LAm) send
back (persona). ~ar vt (LAm)
return. **~ivo** adj backward. **~o** m
return

regula|ble adj adjustable. **~dor**
m control. **~r** adj regular; (mediano) average; (no bueno) so-so.
● vt regulate; adjust (volumen
etc). **~ridad** f regularity. con
~ridad regularly

rehabilita|ción f rehabilitation;
(en empleo etc) reinstatement. **~r**
vt rehabilitate; (en cargo) reinstate

rehacer 31 vt redo; (repetir) repeat; rebuild (vida). **~se** vpr recover

rehén m hostage

rehogar 12 vt sauté

rehuir 17 vt avoid

rehusar vt/i refuse

reimpr|esión f reprinting.
~imir (pp reimpreso) vt reprint

reina f queen. **~do** m reign.
~nte adj ruling; (fig) prevailing.
~r vi reign; (fig) prevail

reincidir vi (Jurid) reoffend

reino m kingdom. R~ Unido
United Kingdom

reintegr|ar vt reinstate (persona); refund (cantidad). **~arse** vpr
return. **~o** m refund

reír 51 vi laugh. **~se** vpr laugh.
~se de laugh at. echarse a ~

burst out laughing

reivindica|ción f claim. **~r** 7
vt claim; (rehabilitar) restore

reja f grille; (verja) railing. entre
~as behind bars. **~illa** f grille,
grating; (red) luggage rack

rejuvenecer 11 vt/i rejuvenate.
~se vpr be rejuvenated

relaci|ón f connection; (trato) relation(ship); (relato) account; (lista)
list. con ~ a, en ~ a in a relation to. **~onado** adj related. bien
~onado well-connected. **~onar** vt
relate (con to). **~onarse** vpr be
connected; (tratar) mix (con with)

relaja|ción f relaxation; (aflojamiento) slackening. **~do** adj relaxed. **~r** vt relax; (aflojar) slacken.
~rse vpr relax

relamerse vpr lick one's lips

relámpago m (flash of) lightning

relatar vt tell, relate

relativ|idad f relativity. **~o** adj
relative

relato m tale; (relación) account

relegar 12 vt relegate. ~ al olvido consign to oblivion

relev|ante adj outstanding. **~ar**
vt relieve; (substituir) replace. **~o** m
relief. carrera f de ~os relay race

relieve m relief; (fig) importance.
de ~ important. poner de ~ emphasize

religi|ón f religion. **~osa** f nun.
~oso adj religious. ● m monk

relinch|ar vi neigh. **~o** m neigh

reliquia f relic

rellano m landing

rellen|ar vt refill; (Culin) stuff; fill
in (formulario). **~o** adj full up;
(Culin) stuffed. ● m filling; (Culin)
stuffing

reloj m clock; (de bolsillo o pulsera)

r

watch. ~ de caja grandfather clock. ~ de pulsera wrist-watch. ~ de sol sundial. ~ despertador alarm clock. ~ería f watchmaker's (shop). ~ero m watchmaker

reluci|ente adj shining. ~r **11** vi shine; (destellar) sparkle

relumbrar vi shine

remach|ar vt rivet. ~e m rivet

remangar **12** vt roll up

remar vi row

remat|ado adj (total) complete. ~ar vt finish off; (agotar) use up; (Com) sell off cheap; (LAm, subasta) auction; (en tenis) smash. ~e m end; (fig) finishing touch; (LAm, subastar) auction; (en tenis) smash. de ~e completely

remedar vt imitate

remedi|ar vt remedy; repair (daño); (fig, resolver) solve. no lo pude ~ar I couldn't help it. ~o m remedy; (fig) solution; (LAm, medicamento) medicine. como último ~o as a last resort. no hay más ~o there's no other way. no tener más ~o have no choice

remedo m poor imitation

rem|endar **11** vt repair. ~iendo m patch

remilg|ado adj fussy; (afectado) affected. ~o m fussiness; (afectación) affectation. ~oso adj (Mex) fussy

reminiscencia f reminiscence

remisión f remission; (envío) sending; (referencia) reference

remit|e m sender's name and address. ~ente m sender. ~ir vt send; (referir) refer ● vi diminish

remo m oar

remoj|ar vt soak; (fig, fam) celebrate. ~o m soaking. poner a ~o soak

remolacha f beetroot. ~ azucarera sugar beet

remolcar **7** vt tow

remolino m swirl; (de aire etc) whirl

remolque m towing; (cabo) towrope; (vehículo) trailer. a ~ on tow. dar ~ a tow

remontar vt overcome. ~ el vuelo soar up; (avión) gain height. ~se vpr soar up; (en el tiempo) go back to

remord|er **2** vi. eso le remuerde he feels guilty for it. me remuerde la conciencia I have a guilty conscience. ~imiento m remorse. tener ~imientos feel remorse

remoto adj remote; (época) distant

remover **2** vt stir (líquido); turn over (tierra); (quitar) remove; (fig, activar) revive

remunera|ción f remuneration. ~r vt remunerate

renac|er **11** vi be reborn; (fig) revive. ~imiento m rebirth. R~imiento Renaissance

renacuajo m tadpole; (fig) tiddler

rencilla f quarrel

rencor m bitterness. guardar ~ a have a grudge against. ~oso adj resentful

rendi|ción f surrender. ~do adj submissive; (agotado) exhausted

rendija f crack

rendi|miento m performance; (Com) yield. ~r **5** vt yield; (agotar) exhaust; pay (homenaje); present (informe). ~ vi pay; (producir) produce. ~rse vpr surrender

renegar **1** & **12** vt deny. ● vi grumble. ~ de renounce (fe etc); disown (personas)

renglón m line; (*Com*) item. a ~ seguido straight away

reno m reindeer

renombr|ado adj renowned. ~e m renown

renova|ción f renewal; (*de edificio*) renovation; (*de mobiliario*) complete change. ~r vt renew; renovate (edificio); change (mobiliario)

rent|a f income; (*Mex, alquiler*) rent. ~a vitalicia (life) annuity. ~able adj profitable. ~ar vt yield; (*Mex, alquilar*) rent, hire. ~ista m & f person of independent means

renuncia f renunciation; (*dimisión*) resignation. ~r vi. ~r a renounce, give up; (*dimitir*) resign

reñi|do adj hard-fought. estar ~do con be incompatible with (cosa); be on bad terms with (persona). ~r 5 & 22 vt scold. • vi quarrel

reo m & f (*Jurid*) accused; (*condenado*) convicted offender; (*pez*) sea trout

reojo. mirar de ~ look out of the corner of one's eye at

reorganizar 10 vt reorganize

repar|ación f repair; (*acción*) repairing (*fig, compensación*) reparation. ~ar vt repair; (*fig*) make amends for; (*notar*) notice. • vi. ~ar en notice; (*hacer caso de*) pay attention to. ~o m fault; (*objeción*) objection. poner ~os raise objections

repart|ición f distribution. ~idor m delivery man. ~imiento m distribution. ~ir vt distribute, share out; deliver (cartas, leche etc); hand out (folleto, premio). ~o m distribution; (*de cartas, leche* etc) delivery; (*actores*) cast

repas|ar vt go over; check (cuenta); revise (texto); (*leer a la ligera*) glance through; (*coser*) mend. • vi revise. ~o m revision; (*de ropa*) mending. dar un ~o look through

repatria|ción f repatriation. ~r vt repatriate

repel|ente adj repulsive. • m insect repellent. ~r vt repel

repent|e. de ~ suddenly. ~ino adj sudden

repercu|sión f repercussion. ~tir vi reverberate; (*fig*) have repercussions (en on)

repertorio m repertoire

repeti|ción f repetition; (*de programa*) repeat. ~damente adv repeatedly. ~r 5 vt repeat; have a second helping of (plato); (*imitar*) copy. • vi have a second helping of

repi|car vt ring (campanas). ~que m peal

repisa f shelf. ~ de chimenea mantlepiece

repito vb véase **REPETIR**

replegarse 1 & 12 vpr withdraw

repleto adj full up. ~ de gente packed with people

réplica adj reply; (*copia*) replica

replicar 7 vi reply

repollo m cabbage

reponer 34 vt replace; revive (obra de teatro); (*contestar*) reply. ~se vpr recover

report|aje m report; (*LAm, entrevista*) interview. ~ar vt yield; (*LAm, denunciar*) report. ~e m (*Mex, informe*) report; (*Mex, queja*) complaint. ~ero m reporter

repos|ado adj quiet; (*sin prisa*) unhurried. ~ar vt rest; (*líquido*) settle. ~o m rest

repostar vt replenish. • vi (avión)

refuel; (Auto) fill up. **~ería** f pastrymaking

reprender vt reprimand

represalia f reprisal. **tomar ~s** retaliate

representa|ción f representation; (en el teatro) performance. **en ~ción de** representing. **~nte** m representative. **~r** vt represent; perform (obra de teatro); play (papel); (aparentar) look. **~rse** vpr imagine. **~tivo** adj representative

represi|ón f repression. **~vo** adj repressive

reprimenda f reprimand

reprimir vt supress. **~se** vpr control o.s.

reprobar 2 vt condemn; (LAm, Univ, etc) fail

reproch|ar vt reproach. **~e** m reproach

reproduc|ción f reproduction. **~ir** 47 vt reproduce. **~tor** adj reproductive; (animal) breeding

reptil m reptile

rep|ública f republic. **~ublicano** adj & m republican

repudiar vt condemn; (Jurid) repudiate

repuesto m (Mec) spare (part). **de ~** spare

repugna|ncia f disgust. **~nte** adj repugnant; (olor) disgusting. **~r** vt disgust

repuls|a f rebuff. **~ión** f repulsion. **~ivo** adj repulsive

reputa|ción f reputation. **~do** adj reputable. **~r** vt consider

requeri|miento m request; (necesidad) requirement. **~r** 4 vt require; summons (persona)

requesón m curd cheese

requete... prefijo (fam) extremely

requis|a f requisition; (confiscación) seizure; (inspección) inspection; (Mil) requisition. **~ar** vt requisition; (confiscar) seize; (inspeccionar) inspect. **~ito** m requirement

res f animal. **~ lanar** sheep. **~ vacuna** (vaca) cow; (toro) bull; (buey) ox. **carne de ~** (Mex) beef

resabido adj well-known; (persona) pedantic

resaca f undercurrent; (después de beber) hangover

resaltar vi stand out. **hacer ~** emphasize

resarcir 9 vt repay; (compensar) compensate. **~se** vpr make up for

resbal|adilla f (Mex) slide. **~adizo** adj slippery. **~ar** vi slip; (Auto) skid; (líquido) trickle. **~arse** vpr slip; (Auto) skid; (líquido) trickle. **~ón** m slip; (de vehículo) skid. **~oso** adj (LAm) slippery

rescat|ar vt rescue; (fig) recover. **~e** m ransom; (recuperación) recovery; (salvamento) rescue

rescoldo m embers

resecar 7 vt dry up. **~se** vpr dry up

resenti|do adj resentful. **~miento** m resentment. **~rse** vpr feel the effects; (debilitarse) be weakened; (ofenderse) take offence (de at)

reseña f summary; (de persona) description; (en periódico) report, review. **~r** vt describe; (en periódico) report on, review

reserva f reservation; (provisión) reserve(s). **de ~** in reserve. **~ción** f (LAm) reservation. **~do** adj reserved. **~r** vt reserve; (guardar) keep, save. **~rse** vpr save o.s.

resfria|do m cold. **~rse** vpr catch

a cold

resguard|ar vt protect. **~arse** vpr protect o.s.; (fig) take care. **~o** m protection; (garantía) guarantee; (recibo) receipt

resid|encia f residence; (Univ) hall of residence (Brit), dormitory (Amer); (de ancianos etc) home. **~encial** adj residential. **~ente** adj & m & f resident. **~ir** vi reside; (fig) lie (en in)

residu|al adj residual. **~o** m residue. **~os** mpl waste

resigna|ción f resignation. **~rse** vpr resign o.s. (a to)

resist|encia f resistance. **~ente** adj resistent. **~ir** vt resist; (soportar) bear. ● vi resist. ya no resisto más I can't take it any more

resol|ución f resolution; (solución) solution; (decisión) decision. **~ver** 2 (pp resuelto) resolve; solve (problema etc). **~verse** vpr resolve itself; (resultar bien) work out; (decidir) decide

reson|ancia f resonance. tener **~ncia** cause a stir. **~nte** adj resonant; (fig) resounding. **~r** 2 vi resound

resorte m spring; (Mex, elástico) elastic. tocar (todos los) **~s** (fig) pull strings

respald|ar vt back; (escribir) endorse. **~arse** vpr lean back. **~o** m backing; (de asiento) back

respect|ar vi. en lo que **~a** a with regard to. en lo que a mí **~a** as far as I'm concerned. **~ivo** adj respective. **~o** m respect. al **~o** on this matter. (con) **~o** a with regard to

respet|able adj respectable. ● m audience. **~ar** vt respect. **~o** m respect. faltar al **~o** a be disres-

pectful to. **~uoso** adj respectful

respir|ación f breathing; (ventilación) ventilation. **~ar** vi breathe; (fig) breathe a sigh of relief. **~o** m breathing; (fig) rest

respland|ecer 11 vi shine. **~eciente** adj shining. **~or** m brilliance; (de llamas) glow

responder vi answer; (replicar) answer back; (reaccionar) respond. **~** de be responsible for. **~ por** uno vouch for s.o.

responsab|ilidad f responsibility. **~le** adj responsible

respuesta f reply, answer

resquebrajar vt crack. **~se** vpr crack

resquemor m (fig) uneasiness

resquicio m crack; (fig) possibility

resta f subtraction

restablecer 11 vt restore. **~se** vpr recover

rest|ante adj remaining. lo **~nte** the rest. **~ar** vt take away; (substraer) subtract. ● vi be left

restaura|ción f restoration. **~nte** m restaurant. **~r** vt restore

restitu|ción f restitution. **~ir** 17 vt return; (restaurar) restore

resto m rest, remainder; (en matemática) remainder. **~s** mpl remains; (de comida) leftovers

restorán m restaurant

restregar 1 & 12 vt rub

restri|cción f restriction. **~ngir** 14 vt restrict, limit

resucitar vt resuscitate; (fig) revive. ● vi return to life

resuello m breath; (respiración) heavy breathing

resuelto adj resolute

resulta|do m result (en in). **~r** vi result; (salir) turn out; (dar resul-

tado) work; (*ser*) be; (*costar*) come to

resum|en *m* summary. **en ~en** in short. **~ir** *vt* summarize; (*recapitular*) sum up

resur|gir 14 *vi* reemerge; (*fig*) revive. **~gimiento** *m* resurgence. **~rección** *f* resurrection

retaguardia *f* (*Mil*) rearguard

retahíla *f* string

retar *vt* challenge

retardar *vt* slow down; (*demorar*) delay

retazo *m* remnant; (*fig*) piece, bit

reten|ción *f* retention. **~er** 40 *vt* keep; (*en la memoria*) retain; (*no dar*) withhold

reticencia *f* insinuation; (*reserva*) reluctance

retina *f* retina

retir|ada *f* withdrawal. **~ado** *adj* remote; (*vida*) secluded; (*jubilado*) retired. **~ar** *vt* move away; (*quitar*) remove; withdraw (*dinero*); (*jubilar*) pension off. **~arse** *vpr* draw back; (*Mil*) withdraw; (*jubilarse*) retire; (*acostarse*) go to bed. **~o** *m* retirement; (*pensión*) pension; (*lugar apartado*) retreat; (*LAm, de apoyo, fondos*) withdrawal

reto *m* challenge

retocar 7 *vt* retouch

retoño *m* shoot; (*fig*) kid

retoque *m* (*acción*) retouching; (*efecto*) finishing touch

retorc|er 2 & 9 *vt* twist; wring (*ropa*). **~erse** *vpr* get twisted up; (*de dolor*) writhe. **~ijón** *m* (*LAm*) stomach cramp

retóric|a *f* rhetoric; (*grandilocuencia*) grandiloquence. **~o** *m* rhetorical

retorn|ar *vt/i* return. **~o** *m* return

retortijón *m* twist; (*de tripas*) stomach cramp

retractarse *vpr* retract. **~ de lo dicho** withdraw what one said

retransmitir *vt* repeat; (*radio, TV*) broadcast. **~ en directo** broadcast live

retras|ado *adj* (*con ser*) mentally handicapped; (*con estar*) behind; (*reloj*) slow; (*poco desarrollado*) backward; (*anticuado*) old-fashioned. **~ar** *vt* delay; put back (*reloj*); (*retardar*) slow down; (*posponer*) postpone. • *vi* (*reloj*) be slow. **~arse** *vpr* be late; (*reloj*) be slow. **~o** *m* delay; (*poco desarrollo*) backwardness; (*de reloj*) slowness. **traer ~o** be late. **~os** *mpl* arrears

retrato *m* portrait; (*fig, descripción*) description. **ser el vivo ~ de** be the living image of

retrete *m* toilet

retribu|ción *f* payment; (*recompensa*) reward. **~ir** 17 *vt* pay; (*recompensar*) reward; (*LAm*) return (*favor*)

retroce|der *vi* move back; (*fig*) back down. **~so** *m* backward movement; (*de arma de fuego*) recoil; (*Med*) relapse

retrógrado *adj & m* (*Pol*) reactionary

retrospectivo *adj* retrospective

retrovisor *m* rear-view mirror

retumbar *vt* echo; (*trueno etc*) boom

reum|a *m*, **reúma** *m* rheumatism. **~ático** *adj* rheumatic. **~atismo** *m* rheumatism

reuni|ón *f* meeting; (*entre amigos*) reunion. **~ir** 23 *vt* join together; (*recoger*) gather (together); raise (*fondos*). **~rse** *vpr* meet; (*amigos etc*) get together

revalidar vt confirm; (Mex, estudios) validate

revalorizar 🔟 vt, (LAm) **revaluar** 🟤 vt revalue; increase (pensiones). **~se** vpr appreciate

revancha f revenge; (en deportes) return match. **tomar la ~** get one's own back

revela|ción f revelation. **~do** m developing. **~dor** adj revealing. **~r** vt reveal; (Foto) develop

revent|ar 🟦 vi burst; (tener ganas) be dying to. **~arse** vpr burst. **~ón** m burst; (Auto) blow out; (Mex, fiesta) party

reveren|cia f reverence; (de hombre, niño) bow; (de mujer) curtsy. **~ciar** vt revere. **~do** adj (Relig) reverend. **~te** adj reverent

revers|ible adj reversible. **~o** m reverse; (de papel) back

revertir 🟦 vi revert (a to)

revés m wrong side; (de prenda) inside; (contratiempo) setback; (en deportes) backhand. **al ~** the other way round; (con lo de arriba abajo) upside down; (con lo de dentro fuera) inside out

revesti|miento m coating. **~r** 🟦 vt cover

revis|ar vt check; overhaul (mecanismo); service (coche etc); (LAm, equipaje) search. **~ión** f check(ing); (Med) checkup; (de coche etc) service; (LAm, de equipaje) inspection. **~or** m inspector

revista f magazine; (inspección) inspection; (artículo) review; (espectáculo) revue. **pasar ~ a** inspect

revivir vt revive

revolcar 🟦 & 🟦 vt knock over. **~se** vpr roll around

revolotear vi flutter

revoltijo m, **revoltillo** m mess

revoltoso adj rebellious; (niño) naughty

revoluci|ón f revolution. **~onar** vt revolutionize. **~onario** adj & m revolutionary

revolver 🟦 (pp **revuelto**) vt mix; stir (líquido); (desordenar) mess up

revólver m revolver

revuelo m fluttering; (fig) stir

revuelt|a f revolt; (conmoción) disturbance. **~o** adj mixed up; (líquido) cloudy; (mar) rough; (tiempo) unsettled; (huevos) scrambled

rey m king. **los ~es** the king and queen. **los R~es Magos** the Three Wise Men

reyerta f brawl

rezagarse 🟦 vpr fall behind

rez|ar 🔟 vt say. ● vi pray; (decir) say. **~o** m praying; (oración) prayer

rezongar 🟦 vi grumble

ría f estuary

riachuelo m stream

riada f flood

ribera f bank

ribete m border; (fig) embellishment

rico adj rich; (Culin, fam) good, nice. ● m rich person

ridículo adj ridiculous. **~iculizar** 🔟 vt ridicule

riego m watering; (irrigación) irrigation

riel m rail

rienda f rein

riesgo m risk. **correr (el) ~ de** run the risk of

rifa f raffle. **~r** vt raffle

rifle m rifle

rigidez f rigidity; (fig) inflexibility

rígido adj rigid; (fig) inflexible

rig|or *m* strictness; (*exactitud*) exactness; (*de clima*) severity. **de ~or** compulsory. **en ~or** strictly speaking. **~uroso** *adj* rigorous

rima *f* rhyme. **~r** *vt/i* rhyme

rimbombante *adj* resounding; (*lenguaje*) pompous; (*fig, ostentoso*) showy

rímel *m* mascara

rin *m* (Mex) rim

rincón *m* corner

rinoceronte *m* rhinoceros

riña *f* quarrel; (*pelea*) fight

riñón *m* kidney

río *m* river; (*fig*) stream. **~ abajo** downstream. **~ arriba** upstream.
• *vb véase* REÍR

riqueza *f* wealth; (*fig*) richness. **~s** *fpl* riches

ris|a *f* laugh. **desternillarse de ~a** split one's sides laughing. **la ~a** laughter. **~otada** *f* guffaw. **~ueño** *adj* smiling; (*fig*) cheerful

rítmico *adj* rhythmic(al)

ritmo *m* rhythm; (*fig*) rate

rit|o *m* rite; (*fig*) ritual. **~ual** *adj* & *m* ritual

rival *adj* & *m* & *f* rival. **~idad** *f* rivalry. **~izar** 10 *vi* rival

riz|ado *adj* curly. **~ar** 10 *vt* curl; ripple (agua). **~o** *m* curl; (*en agua*) ripple

róbalo *m* bass

robar *vt* steal (cosa); rob (banco); (*raptar*) kidnap

roble *m* oak (tree)

robo *m* theft; (*de banco, museo*) robbery; (*en vivienda*) burglary

robusto *adj* robust

roca *f* rock

roce *m* rubbing; (*señal*) mark; (*fig, entre personas*) regular contact; (*Pol*) friction. **tener un ~ con uno**

have a brush with s.o.

rociar 20 *vt* spray

rocín *m* nag

rocío *m* dew

rodaballo *m* turbot

rodaja *f* slice. **en ~s** sliced

roda|je *m* (*de película*) shooting; (*de coche*) running in. **~r** 2 *vt* shoot (película); run in (coche). • *vi* roll; (*coche*) run; (*hacer una película*) shoot

rode|ar *vt* surround; (LAm) round up (ganado). **~arse** *vpr* surround o.s. (**de** with). **~o** *m* detour; (*de ganado*) round-up. **andar con ~os** beat about the bush. **sin ~os** plainly

rodill|a *f* knee. **ponerse de ~as** kneel down. **~era** *f* knee-pad

rodillo *m* roller; (Culin) rolling-pin

roe|dor *m* rodent. **~r** 37 *vt* gnaw

rogar 2 & 12 *vt/i* beg; (*Relig*) pray; **se ruega a los Sres. pasajeros...** passengers are requested.... **se ruega no fumar** please do not smoke

roj|izo *adj* reddish. **~o** *adj* & *m* red. **ponerse ~o** blush

roll|izo *adj* plump; (*bebé*) chubby. **~o** *m* roll; (*de cuerda*) coil; (Culin, *rodillo*) rolling-pin; (*fig, fam, pesadez*) bore

romance *adj* Romance. • *m* (*idilio*) romance; (*poema*) ballad

roman|o *adj* & *m* Roman. **a la ~a** (Culin) (deep-)fried in batter

rom|anticismo *m* romanticism. **~ántico** *adj* romantic

romería *f* pilgrimage; (LAm, *multitud*) mass

romero *m* rosemary

romo *adj* blunt; (*nariz*) snub

rompe|cabezas *m invar* puzzle;

(de piezas) jigsaw (puzzle). **∼olas** m invar breakwater

romp|er (pp **roto**) vt break; tear (hoja, camisa etc); break off (relaciones etc). ● vi break; (novios) break up. **∼er a** burst out. **∼erse** vpr break

ron m rum

ronc|ar 🇻 vi snore. **∼o** adj hoarse

roncha f lump; (por alergia) rash

ronda f round; (patrulla) patrol; (serenata) serenade. **∼r** vt patrol. ● vi be on patrol; (merodear) hang around

ronqu|era f hoarseness. **∼ido** m snore

ronronear vi purr

roñ|a f (suciedad) grime. **∼oso** adj dirty; (oxidado) rusty; (tacaño) mean

rop|a f clothes, clothing. **∼a blanca** linen, underwear. **∼a de cama** bedclothes. **∼a interior** underwear. **∼aje** m robes; (excesivo) heavy clothing. **∼ero** m wardrobe

ros|a adj invar pink. ● f rose. ● m pink. **∼áceo** adj pinkish. **∼ado** adj pink; (mejillas) rosy. ● m (vino) rosé. **∼al** m rose-bush

rosario m rosary; (fig) series

ros|ca f (de tornillo) thread; (de pan) roll; (bollo) type of doughnut. **∼co** m roll. **∼quilla** f type of doughnut

rostro m face

rota|ción f rotation. **∼r** vt/i rotate. **∼rse** vpr take turns. **∼tivo** adj rotary

roto adj broken

rótula f kneecap

rotulador m felt-tip pen

rótulo m sign; (etiqueta) label; (logotipo) logo

rotundo adj categorical

rotura f tear; (grieta) crack

rozadura f scratch

rozagante adj (LAm) healthy

rozar 🔟 vt rub against; (ligeramente) brush against; (raspar) graze. **∼se** vpr rub; (con otras personas) mix

Rte. abrev (**Remite(nte)**) sender

rubéola f German measles

rubí m ruby

rubicundo adj ruddy

rubio adj (pelo) fair; (persona) fair-haired; (tabaco) Virginia

rubor m blush; (Mex, cosmético) blusher. **∼izarse** 🔟 vpr blush

rúbrica f (de firma) flourish; (firma) signature; (título) heading

rudeza f roughness

rudiment|ario adj rudimentary. **∼os** mpl rudiments

rueca f distaff

rueda f wheel; (de mueble) castor; (de personas) ring; (Culin) slice. **∼ de prensa** press conference

ruedo m edge; (redondel) bullring

ruego m request; (súplica) entreaty. ● vb véase **ROGAR**

rufián m pimp; (granuja) rogue

rugby m rugby

rugi|do m roar. **∼r** 🔢 vi roar

ruibarbo m rhubarb

ruido m noise. **∼so** adj noisy; (fig) sensational

ruin adj despicable; (tacaño) mean

ruin|a f ruin; (colapso) collapse. **∼oso** adj ruinous

ruiseñor m nightingale

ruleta f roulette

rulo m curler

rumano adj & m Romanian

rumbo m direction; (fig) course;

r

(*fig, esplendidez*) lavishness. con ~
a in the direction of. ~**so** *adj* lavish

rumia|nte *adj & m* ruminant. ~**r**
vt chew; (*fig*) brood over. • *vi* ru-
minate

rumor *m* rumour; (*ruido*) murmur.
~**earse** *vpr se* ~**ea que** rumour
has it that. ~**oso** *adj* murmuring

runrún *m* (*de voces*) murmur; (*de
motor*) whirr

ruptura *f* breakup; (*de relaciones
etc*) breaking off; (*de contrato*)
breach

rural *adj* rural

ruso *adj & m* Russian

rústico *adj* rural; (*de carácter*)
coarse. **en rústica** paperback

ruta *f* route; (*fig*) course

rutina *f* routine. ~**rio** *adj* routine;
(*trabajo*) monotonous

· ·

Ss

S.A. *abrev* (**Sociedad Anónima**)
Ltd, plc, Inc (*Amer*)

sábado *m* Saturday

sábana *f* sheet

sabañón *m* chilblain

sabático *adj* sabbatical

sabelotodo *m & f invar* know-all
1. ~**er 38** *vt* know; (*ser capaz de*)
be able to, know how to; (*enterarse
de*) find out. • *vi* know. ~**er** a
taste of. **hacer** ~**er** let know. **¡qué
sé yo!** how should I know? **que yo
sepa** as far as I know. **¿**~**es
nadar?** can you swim? **un no sé
qué** a certain sth. **¡yo qué sé!** how
should I know? **¡vete a ~er!** who

knows? ~**er** *m* knowledge. ~**ido**
adj well-known. ~**iduría** *f* wisdom;
(*conocimientos*) knowledge

sabi|endas. a ~ knowingly; (*a
propósito*) on purpose. ~**hondo** *m*
know-all. ~**o** *adj* learned; (*pru-
dente*) wise

sabor *m* taste, flavour; (*fig*) fla-
vour. ~**ear** *vt* taste; (*fig*) savour

sabot|aje *m* sabotage. ~**eador** *m*
saboteur. ~**ear** *vt* sabotage

sabroso *adj* tasty; (*chisme*) juicy;
(*LAm, agradable*) pleasant

sabueso *m* (*perro*) bloodhound;
(*fig, detective*) detective

saca|corchos *m invar* corkscrew.
~**puntas** *m invar* pencil-sharpener

sacar 7 *vt* take out; put out
(*parte del cuerpo*); (*quitar*) remove;
take (*foto*); win (*premio*); get (*bi-
llete, entrada*); withdraw (*dinero*);
reach (*solución*); draw (*conclu-
sión*); make (*copia*). ~ **adelante**
bring up (*niño*); carry on (*negocio*)

sacarina *f* saccharin

sacerdo|cio *m* priesthood. ~**te**
m priest

saciar *vt* satisfy; quench (*sed*)

saco *m* sack; (*LAm, chaqueta*)
jacket. ~ **de dormir** sleeping-bag

sacramento *m* sacrament

sacrific|ar 7 *vt* sacrifice; slaugh-
ter (*res*); put to sleep (*perro, gato*).
~**arse** *vpr* sacrifice o.s. ~**io** *m* sac-
rifice; (*de res*) slaughter

sacr|ilegio *m* sacrilege. ~**ílego**
adj sacrilegious

sacudi|da *f* shake; (*movimiento
brusco*) jolt, jerk; (*fig*) shock. ~**da
eléctrica** electric shock. ~**r** *vt*
shake; (*golpear*) beat. ~**rse** *vpr*
shake off; (*fig*) get rid of

sádico *adj* sadistic. • *m* sadist

sadismo *m* sadism

safari *m* safari

sagaz *adj* shrewd

Sagitario *m* Sagittarius

sagrado *adj* (*lugar*) holy, sacred; (*altar, escrituras*) holy; (*fig*) sacred

sal *f* salt. ● *vb véase* **SALIR**

sala *f* room; (*en casa*) living room; (*en hospital*) ward; (*para reuniones etc*) hall; (*en teatro*) house; (*Jurid*) courtroom. ~ **de embarque** departure lounge. ~ **de espera** waiting room. ~ **de estar** living room. ~ **de fiestas** nightclub

salado *adj* salty; (*agua del mar*) salt; (*no dulce*) savoury; (*fig*) witty

salario *m* wage

salchich|a *f* (*pork*) sausage. ~**ón** *m* salami

sald|ar *vt* settle (*cuenta*); (*vender*) sell off. ~**o** *m* balance. ~**os** *mpl* sales. **venta de** ~**os** clearance sale

salero *m* salt-cellar

salgo *vb véase* **SALIR**

sali|da *f* departure; (*puerta*) exit, way out; (*de gas, de líquido*) leak; (*de astro*) rising; (*Com, venta*) sale; (*chiste*) witty remark; (*fig*) way out; ~**da de emergencia** emergency exit. ~**ente** *adj* (*Archit*) projecting; (*pómulo etc*) prominent. ~**r** 52 *vi* leave; (*ir afuera*) go out; (*Informática*) exit; (*revista etc*) be published; (*resultar*) turn out; (*astro*) rise; (*aparecer*) appear. ~**r adelante** get by. ~**rse** *vpr* leave; (*recipiente, líquido etc*) leak. ~**rse con la suya** get one's own way

saliva *f* saliva

salmo *m* psalm

salm|ón *m* salmon. ~**onete** *m* red mullet

salón *m* living-room, lounge. ~ **de**

actos assembly hall. ~ **de clases** classroom. ~ **de fiestas** dancehall

salpica|dera *f* (*Mex*) mudguard. ~**dero** *m* (*Auto*) dashboard. ~**dura** *f* splash; (*acción*) splashing. ~**r** 7 *vt* splash; (*fig*) sprinkle

salsa *f* sauce; (*para carne asada*) gravy; (*Mus*) salsa. ~**a verde** parsley sauce. ~**era** *f* sauce-boat

salt|amontes *m invar* grasshopper. ~**ar** *vt* jump (over); (*fig*) miss out. ● *vi* jump; (*romperse*) break; (*líquido*) spurt out; (*desprenderse*) come off; (*pelota*) bounce; (*estallar*) explode. ~**eador** *m* highwayman. ~**ear** *vt* (*Culin*) sauté

salt|o *m* jump; (*al agua*) dive. ~**o de agua** waterfall. ~ **mortal** somersault. **de un** ~**o** with one jump. ~**ón** *adj* (*ojos*) bulging

salud *f* health. ● *int* cheers!; (*LAm, al estornudar*) bless you! ~**able** *adj* healthy

salud|ar *vt* greet, say hello to; (*Mil*) salute. **lo** ~**a atentamente** (*en cartas*) yours faithfully. ~ **con la mano** wave. ~**o** *m* greeting; (*Mil*) salute. ~**os** *mpl* best wishes

salva *f* salvo. **una** ~ **de aplausos** a burst of applause

salvación *f* salvation

salvado *m* bran

salvaguardia *f* safeguard

salvaje *adj* (*planta, animal*) wild; (*primitivo*) savage. ● *m & f* savage

salva|mento *m* rescue. ~**r** *vt* save, rescue; (*atravesar*) cross (*recorrer*) travel; (*fig*) overcome. ~**rse** *vpr* save o.s. ~**vidas** *m & f invar* lifeguard. ● *m* lifebelt. **chaleco** *m* ~**vidas** life-jacket

salvo *adj* safe. ● *adv & prep* except (for). **a** ~ out of danger. **poner a** ~ put in a safe place. ~ **que un-**

less. **~conducto** m safe-conduct.

San adj Saint, St. **~ Miguel** St Michael

sana|r vt cure. ● vi recover; heal (herida). **~torio** m sanatorium

sanci|ón f sanction. **~onar** vt sanction

sandalia f sandal

sandía f watermelon

sándwich /'sæŋgwitʃ/ m (pl **~s**, **~es**) sandwich

sangr|ante adj bleeding; (fig) flagrant. **~ar** vt/i bleed. **~e** f blood. **a ~e fría** in cold blood

sangría f (bebida) sangria

sangriento adj bloody

sangu|ijuela f leech. **~íneo** adj blood

san|idad f health. **~itario** adj sanitary. ● m (Mex) toilet. **~o** adj healthy; (mente) sound. **~o y salvo** safe and sound. **cortar por lo ~o** settle things once and for all

santiamén m. **en un ~** in an instant

sant|idad f sanctity. **~ificar** 🔽 vt sanctify. **~iguarse** 🔟 vpr cross o.s. **~o** adj holy; (delante de nombre) Saint, St. ● m saint; (día) saint's day, name day. **~uario** m sanctuary. **~urrón** adj sanctimonious

> **santo** Most first names in Spanish-speaking countries are those of saints. A person's *santo* (also known as *onomástico* in Latin America and *onomástica* in Spain) is the saint's day of the saint they are named after. As well as celebrating their calendar birthday many people also celebrate their *santo*.

saña f viciousness. **con ~** viciously

sapo m toad

saque m (en tenis) service; (inicial en fútbol) kick-off. **~ de banda** throw-in; (en rugby) line-out. **~ de esquina** corner (kick)

saque|ar vt loot. **~o** m looting

sarampión m measles

sarape m (Mex) colourful blanket

sarc|asmo m sarcasm. **~ástico** adj sarcastic

sardina f sardine

sargento m sergeant

sarpullido m rash

sartén f or m frying-pan (Brit), frypan (Amer)

sastre m tailor. **~ría** f tailoring; (tienda) tailor's (shop)

Sat|anás m Satan. **~ánico** adj satanic

satélite m satellite

satinado adj shiny

sátira f satire

satírico adj satirical. ● m satirist

satisf|acción f satisfaction. **~acer** 🔢 vt satisfy; (pagar) pay; (gustar) please; meet (gastos, requisitos). **~acerse** vpr satisfy o.s.; (vengarse) take revenge. **~actorio** adj satisfactory. **~echo** adj satisfied. **~echo de sí mismo** smug

satura|ción f saturation. **~r** vt saturate

Saturno m Saturn

sauce m willow. **~ llorón** weeping willow

sauna f, (LAm) **sauna** m sauna

saxofón m, **saxófono** m saxophone

sazona|do adj ripe; (Culin) seasoned. **~r** vt ripen; (Culin) season

se *pronombre*

● (*en lugar de le, les*) **se lo di** (*a él*) I gave it to him; (*a ella*) I gave it to her; (*a usted, ustedes*) I gave it to you; (*a ellos, ellas*) I gave it to them. **se lo compré** I bought it for him (*or her etc*). **se lo quité** I took it away from him (*or her etc*). **se lo dije** I told him (*or her etc*)

····▶ (*reflexivo*) **se secó** (*él*) he dried himself; (*ella*) she dried herself; (*usted*) you dried yourself. (*sujeto no humano*) it dried itself. **se secaron** (*ellos, ellas*) they dried themselves. (*ustedes*) you dried yourselves. (*con partes del cuerpo*) **se lavó la cara** (*él*) he washed his face; (*con efectos personales*) **se limpian los zapatos** they clean their shoes

····▶ (*recíproco*) each other, one another. **se ayudan mucho** they help each other a lot. **no se hablan** they don't speak to each other

····▶ (*cuando otro hace la acción*) **va a operarse** she's going to have an operation. **se cortó el pelo** he had his hair cut

····▶ (*enfático*) **se bebió el café** he drank his coffee. **se subió al tren** he got on the train

➡ **se** also forms part of certain pronominal verbs such as **equivocarse**, **arrepentirse**, **caerse** etc., which are treated under the respective entries

····▶ (*voz pasiva*) **se construyeron muchas casas** many houses were built. **se vendió**

rápidamente it was sold very quickly

····▶ (*impersonal*) **antes se escuchaba más radio** people used to listen to the radio more in the past. **no se puede entrar** you can't get in. **se está bien aquí** it's very nice here

····▶ (*en instrucciones*) **sírvase frío** serve cold

sé *vb véase* SABER *y* SER

sea *vb véase* SER

seca|dor *m* drier; (*de pelo*) hairdrier. **~nte** *adj* drying. ● *m* blotting-paper. **~r** **7** *vt* dry. **~rse** *vpr* dry; (*río etc*) dry up; (*persona*) dry o.s.

sección *f* section

seco *adj* dry; (*frutos, flores*) dried; (*flaco*) thin; (*respuesta*) curt. **a secas** just. **en ~** (*bruscamente*) suddenly. **lavar en ~** dry-clean

secretar|ía *f* secretariat; (*Mex, ministerio*) ministry. **~io** *m* secretary; (*Mex, Pol*) minister

secreto *adj & m* secret

secta *f* sect. **~rio** *adj* sectarian

sector *m* sector

secuela *f* consequence

secuencia *f* sequence

secuestr|ar *vt* confiscate; kidnap (*persona*); hijack (*avión*). **~o** *m* seizure; (*de persona*) kidnapping; (*de avión*) hijack(ing)

secundar *vt* second, help. **~io** *adj* secondary

sed *f* thirst. ● *vb véase* SER. **tener ~** be thirsty. **tener ~ de** (*fig*) be hungry for

seda *f* silk. **~ dental** dental floss

sedante *adj & m* sedative

sede *f* seat; (*Relig*) see; (*de organismo*) headquarters; (*de congreso,* *juegos etc*) venue

sedentario *adj* sedentary

sedici|ón *f* sedition. ∼**oso** *adj* seditious

sediento *adj* thirsty

seduc|ción *f* seduction. ∼**ir** 47 *vt* seduce; (*atraer*) attract. ∼**tor** *adj* seductive. ● *m* seducer

seglar *adj* secular. ● *m* layman

segrega|ción *f* segregation. ∼**r** 12 *vt* segregate

segui|da *f*. en ∼**da** immediately. ∼**do** *adj* continuous; (*en plural*) consecutive. ∼ de followed by. ● *adv* straight; (*LAm, a menudo*) often. **todo** ∼**do** straight ahead. ∼**dor** *m* follower; (*en deportes*) supporter. ∼**r** 5 & 13 *vt* follow. ● *vi* (*continuar*) continue; (*por un camino*) go on. ∼**r adelante** carry on

según *prep* according to. ● *adv* it depends; (*a medida que*) as

segund|a *f* (*Auto*) second gear; (*en tren, avión etc*) second class. ∼**o** *adj* & *m* second

segur|amente *adv* certainly; (*muy probablemente*) surely. ∼**o** *f* security; (*ausencia de peligro*) safety; (*certeza*) certainty; (*aplomo*) confidence. ∼**idad en sí mismo** self-confidence. ∼**idad social** social security. ∼**o** *adj* safe; (*cierto*) certain, sure; (*estable*) secure; (*de fiar*) reliable. ● *adv* for certain. ● *m* insurance; (*dispositivo de seguridad*) safety device. ∼**o de sí mismo** self-confident. ∼**o contra terceros** third-party insurance

seis *adj* & *m* six. ∼**cientos** *adj* & *m* six hundred

seísmo *m* earthquake

selec|ción *f* selection. ∼**cionar** *vt* select, choose. ∼**tivo** *adj* selective.

∼**to** *adj* selected; (*fig*) choice

sell|ar *vt* stamp; (*cerrar*) seal. ∼**o** *m* stamp; (*precinto*) seal; (*fig, distintivo*) hallmark; (*LAm, en moneda*) reverse

selva *f* forest; (*jungla*) jungle

semáforo *m* (*Auto*) traffic lights; (*Rail*) signal; (*Naut*) semaphore

semana *f* week. **S∼** Santa Holy Week. ∼**l** *adj* weekly. ∼**rio** *adj* & *m* weekly

---

Semana Santa The most *i* famous Holy Week celebrations in the Spanish-speaking world are held in Sevilla between Palm Sunday and Easter Sunday. Lay brotherhoods, *cofradías*, process through the city in huge parades. During the processions they sing *saetas*, flamenco verses mourning Christ's passion.

---

semántic|a *f* semantics. ∼**o** *adj* semantic

semblante *m* face; (*fig*) look

sembrar 1 *vt* sow; (*fig*) scatter

semeja|nte *adj* similar; (*tal*) such. ● *m* fellow man. ∼**nza** *f* similarity. a ∼**nza de** like. ∼**r** *vi*. ∼**r a** resemble

semen *m* semen. ∼**tal** *adj* stud. ● *m* stud animal

semestr|al *adj* half-yearly. ∼**e** *m* six months

semi|circular *adj* semicircular. ∼**círculo** *m* semicircle. ∼**final** *f* semifinal

semill|a *f* seed. ∼**ero** *m* seedbed; (*fig*) hotbed

seminario *m* (*Univ*) seminar; (*Relig*) seminary

sémola *f* semolina

senado *m* senate. ∼**r** *m* senator

sencill|ez *f* simplicity. **~o** *adj* simple; (*para viajar*) single ticket; (*disco*) single; (*LAm, dinero suelto*) change

senda *f*, **sendero** *m* path

sendos *adj pl* each

seno *m* bosom. **~ materno** womb

sensaci|ón *f* sensation; (*percepción, impresión*) feeling. **~onal** *adj* sensational

sensat|ez *f* good sense. **~o** *adj* sensible

sensi|bilidad *f* sensibility. **~ble** *adj* sensitive; (*notable*) notable; (*lamentable*) lamentable. **~tivo** *adj* (*órgano*) sense

sensual *adj* sensual. **~idad** *f* sensuality

senta|do *adj* sitting (down); **dar algo por ~do** take something for granted. **~dor** *adj* (*LAm*) flattering. **~r 1** *vt* sit; (*establecer*) establish. ● *vi* suit; (*de medidas*) fit; (*comida*) agree with. **~rse** *vpr* sit (down)

sentencia *f* (*Jurid*) sentence. **~r** *vt* sentence (a to)

sentido *adj* heartfelt; (*sensible*) sensitive. ● *m* sense; (*dirección*) direction; (*conocimiento*) consciousness. **~ común** common sense. **~ del humor** sense of humour. **~ único** one-way. **doble ~** double meaning. **no tener ~** not make sense. **perder el ~** faint. **sin ~** senseless

sentim|ental *adj* sentimental. **~iento** *m* feeling; (*sentido*) sense; (*pesar*) regret

sentir 4 *vt* feel; (*oír*) hear; (*lamentar*) be sorry for. **lo siento mucho** I'm really sorry. ● *m* (*opinión*) opinion. **~se** *vpr* feel; (*Mex, ofenderse*) be offended

seña *f* sign. **~s** *fpl* (*dirección*) address; (*descripción*) description. **dar ~s de** show signs of

señal *f* signal; (*letrero, aviso*) sign; (*telefónica*) tone; (*Com*) deposit. **dar ~es de** show signs of. **en ~ de** as a token of. **~ado** *adj* (*hora, día*) appointed. **~ar** *vt* signal; (*poner señales en*) mark; (*apuntar*) point out; (*manecilla, aguja*) point to; (*determinar*) fix. **~arse** *vpr* stand out

señor *m* man, gentleman; (*delante de nombre propio*) Mr; (*tratamiento directo*) sir. **~a** *f* lady, woman; (*delante de nombre propio*) Mrs; (*esposa*) wife; (*tratamiento directo*) madam. **el ~** Mr. **muy ~ mío** Dear Sir. **¡no ~!** certainly not!. **~ial** *adj* (*casa*) stately. **~ita** *f* young lady; (*delante de nombre propio*) Miss; (*tratamiento directo*) miss. **~ito** *m* young gentleman

señuelo *m* lure

sepa *vb véase* SABER

separa|ción *f* separation. **~do** *adj* separate. **por ~do** separately. **~r** *vt* separate; (*de empleo*) dismiss. **~rse** *vpr* separate; (*amigos*) part. **~tista** *adj & m & f* separatist

septentrional *adj* north(ern)

septiembre *m* September

séptimo *adj* seventh

sepulcro *m* sepulchre

sepult|ar *vt* bury. **~ura** *f* burial; (*tumba*) grave. **~urero** *m* gravedigger

sequ|edad *f* dryness. **~ía** *f* drought

séquito *m* entourage; (*fig*) train

---

ser 39

● *verbo intransitivo*

⸻⸻► to be. **es bajo** he's short. **es abogado** he's a lawyer.

S

serenar | seta   240

ábreme, soy yo open up, it's me. ¿cómo es? (*como persona*) what's he like?; (*físicamente*) what does he look like? era invierno it was winter

....➤ **ser de** (*indicando composición*) to be made of. **es de hierro** it's made of iron. (*provenir de*) to be from. **es de México** he's from Mexico. (*pertenecer a*) to belong to. **el coche es de Juan** the car belongs to Juan, it's Juan's car

....➤ (*sumar*) ¿cuánto es todo? how much is that altogether? **son 40 dólares** that's 40 dollars. **somos 10** there are 10 of us

....➤ (*con la hora*) **son las 3** it's 3 o'clock. **tuvo que ser la una** it must have been one o'clock

....➤ (*tener lugar*) to be held. **será en la iglesia** it will be held in the church

....➤ (*ocurrir*) to happen ¿dónde fue el accidente? where did the accident happen? **me contó cómo fue** he told me how it happened

....➤ (*en locuciones*) **a no ~ que** unless. **como sea** no matter what. **cuando sea** whenever. **donde sea** wherever. **¡eso es!** that's it! **es que** the thing is. **lo que sea** anything. **no sea que, no vaya a ~ que** in case. **o sea** in other words. **sea ... sea ... either ... or ... sea como sea** at all costs

● *nombre masculino* being; (*persona*) person. **el ~ humano** the human being. **un ~ amargado**

a bitter person. **los ~es queridos** the loved ones

seren|ar *vt* calm down. **~arse** *vpr* calm down. **~ata** *f* serenade. **~idad** *f* serenity. **~o** *adj* serene; (*cielo*) clear; (*mar*) calm

seri|al *m* serial. **~e** *f* series. **fuera de ~e** (*fig*) out of this world. **producción** *f* **en ~e** mass production

seri|edad *f* seriousness. **~o** *adj* serious; (*confiable*) reliable; **en ~o** seriously. **poco ~o** frivolous

sermón *m* sermon; (*fig*) lecture

serp|enteante *adj* winding. **~entear** *vi* wind. **~iente** *f* snake. **~iente de cascabel** rattlesnake

serr|ar ❶ *vt* saw. **~ín** *m* sawdust. **~uchar** *vt* (*LAm*) saw. **~ucho** *m* (hand)saw

servi|cial *adj* helpful. **~cio** *m* service; (*conjunto*) set; (*aseo*) toilet; **~cio a domicilio** delivery service. **~dor** *m* servant. **su (seguro) ~dor** (*en cartas*) yours faithfully. **~dumbre** *f* servitude; (*criados*) servants, staff. **~l** *adj* servile

servidor *m* server; (*criado*) servant

servilleta *f* napkin, serviette

servir ❺ *vt* serve; (*en restaurante*) wait on. ● *vi* serve; (*ser útil*) be of use. **~se** *vpr* help o.s. **~se de** use. **no ~ de nada** be useless. **para ~le** at your service. **sírvase sentarse** please sit down

sesent|a *adj* & *m* sixty. **~ón** *adj* & *m* sixty-year-old

seseo *m* pronunciation of the Spanish *c* as an *s*

sesión *f* session; (*en el cine, teatro*) performance

seso *m* brain

seta *f* mushroom

sete|cientos adj & m seven hundred. **~nta** adj & m seventy. **~ntón** adj & m seventy-year-old

setiembre m September

seto m fence; (de plantas) hedge. **~ vivo** hedge

seudónimo m pseudonym

sever|idad f severity; (de profesor etc) strictness. **~o** adj severe; (profesor etc) strict

sevillan|as fpl popular dance from Seville. **~o** m person from Seville

sexo m sex

sext|eto m sextet. **~o** adj sixth

sexual adj sexual. **~idad** f sexuality

si m (Mus) B; (solfa) te. ● conj if; (dubitativo) whether; **~ no** otherwise. **por ~ (acaso)** in case

sí[1] pron reflexivo (él) himself; (ella) herself; (de cosa) itself; (uno) oneself; (Vd) yourself; (ellos, ellas) themselves; (Vds) yourselves; (recíproco) each other

sí[2] adv yes. ● m consent

sida m Aids

sidra f cider

siembra f sowing; (época) sowing time

siempre adv always; (LAm, todavía) still; (Mex, por fin) after all. **~ que** if; (cada vez) whenever. **como ~** as usual. **de ~** (acostumbrado) usual. **lo de ~** the usual thing. **para ~** for ever

sien f temple

siento vb véase SENTAR y SENTIR

sierra f saw; (cordillera) mountain range

siesta f nap, siesta

siete adj & m seven

sífilis f syphilis

---

sifón m U-bend; (de soda) syphon

sigilo m stealth; (fig) secrecy

sigla f abbreviation

siglo m century; (época) age. **hace ~s que no escribe** he hasn't written for ages

significa|ción f significance. **~do** adj (conocido) well-known. ● m meaning; (importancia) significance. **~r** [7] vt mean; (expresar) express. **~tivo** adj meaningful; (importante) significant

signo m sign. **~ de admiración** exclamation mark. **~ de interrogación** question mark

sigo vb véase SEGUIR

siguiente adj following, next. **lo ~** the following

sílaba f syllable

silb|ar vt/i whistle. **~ato** m, **~ido** m whistle

silenci|ador m silencer. **~ar** vt hush up. **~o** m silence. **~oso** adj silent

sill|a f chair; (de montar) saddle (Relig) see **~a de ruedas** wheelchair. **~ín** m saddle. **~ón** m armchair

silueta f silhouette; (dibujo) outline

silvestre adj wild

simb|ólico adj symbolic(al). **~olismo** m symbolism. **~olizar** [10] vt symbolize

símbolo m symbol

sim|etría f symmetry. **~étrico** adj symmetric(al)

similar adj similar (a to)

simp|atía f friendliness; (cariño) affection. **~ático** adj nice, likeable; (ambiente) pleasant. **~atizante** m & f sympathizer. **~atizar** [10] vi get on (well together)

s

simpl|e adj simple; (mero) mere. ~**eza** f simplicity; (tontería) stupid thing; (insignificancia) trifle. ~**icidad** f simplicity. ~**ificar 7** vt simplify. ~**ista** adj simplistic. ~**ón** m simpleton

simula|ción f simulation. ~**r** vt simulate; (fingir) feign

simultáneo adj simultaneous

sin prep without. ~ **saber** without knowing. ~ **querer** accidentally

sinagoga f synagogue

sincer|idad f sincerity. ~**o** adj sincere

sincronizar 10 vt synchronize

sindica|l adj (trade-)union. ~**lista** m & f trade-unionist. ~**to** m trade union

síndrome m syndrome

sinfín m endless number (de of)

sinfonía f symphony

singular adj singular; (excepcional) exceptional. ~**izarse** vpr stand out

siniestro adj sinister. ● m disaster; (accidente) accident

sinnúmero m endless number (de of)

sino m fate. ● conj but

sinónimo adj synonymous. ● m synonym (de for)

sintaxis f syntax

síntesis f invar synthesis; (resumen) summary

sint|ético adj synthetic. ~**etizar 10** vt synthesize; (resumir) summarize

síntoma f symptom

sintomático adj symptomatic

sinton|ía f tuning; (Mus) signature tune. ~**izar 10** vt (con la radio) tune (in) to

sinvergüenza m & f crook

siquiera conj even if. ● adv at least. **ni** ~ not even

sirena f siren; (en cuentos) mermaid

sirio adj & m Syrian

sirvient|a f maid. ~**e** m servant

sirvo vb véase **SERVIR**

sísmico adj seismic

sismo m earthquake

sistem|a m system. por ~**a** as a rule. ~**ático** adj systematic

sitiar vt besiege; (fig) surround

sitio m place; (espacio) space; (Mil) siege; (Mex, parada de taxi) taxi rank. en cualquier ~ anywhere. ~ **web** website

situa|ción f situation; (estado, condición) position. ~**r 21** vt place, put; locate (edificio). ~**rse** vpr be successful, establish o.s.

slip /es'lip/ m (pl ~s) underpants, briefs

smoking /es'mokin/ m (pl ~s) dinner jacket (Brit), tuxedo (Amer)

sobaco m armpit

sobar vt handle; knead (masa)

soberan|ía f sovereignty. ~**o** adj sovereign; (fig) supreme. ● m sovereign

soberbi|a f pride; (altanería) arrogance. ~**o** adj proud; (altivo) arrogant

soborn|ar vt bribe. ~**o** m bribe

sobra f surplus. de ~ more than enough. ~**s** fpl leftovers. **de ~** more than enough. ~**nte** adj surplus. ~**r** vi be left over; (estorbar) be in the way

sobre prep on; (encima de) on top of; (más o menos) about; (por encima de) above; (sin tocar) over. ~ **todo** above all, especially. ● m envelope. ~**cargar 12** vt overload. ~**coger 14** vt startle; (conmover) move. ~**cubierta** f dustcover. ~**dosis** f invar overdose. ~**entender** ◼ vt understand, infer. ~**girar** vt (LAm) overdraw. ~**giro** m (LAm) overdraft. ~**humano** adj superhuman. ~**llevar** vt bear. ~**mesa** f de ~**mesa** after-dinner. ~**natural** adj supernatural. ~**nombre** m nickname. ~**pasar** vt exceed. ~**peso** m (LAm) excess baggage. ~**poner** ◼ vt superimpose. ~**ponerse** vpr overcome. ~**saliente** adj (fig) outstanding. ● m excellent mark. ~**salir** ◼ vi stick out; (fig) stand out. ~**saltar** vt startle. ~**salto** m fright. ~**sueldo** m bonus. ~**todo** m overcoat. ~**venir** ◼ vi happen. ~**viviente** adj surviving. ● m & f survivor. ~**vivir** vi survive. ~**volar** vt fly over

sobriedad f moderation; (de estilo) simplicity

sobrin|a f niece. ~**o** m nephew. ~**os** (varones) nephews; (varones y mujeres) nieces and nephews

sobrio adj moderate, sober

socavar vt undermine

soci|able adj sociable. ~**al** adj social. ~**aldemócrata** m & f social democrat. ~**alismo** m socialism. ~**alista** adj & m & f socialist. ~**edad** f society; (Com) company. ~**edad anónima** limited company. ~**o** m member; (Com) partner. ~**ología** f sociology. ~**ólogo** m sociologist

socorr|er vt help. ~**o** m help

soda f (bebida) soda (water)

sodio m sodium

sofá m sofa, settee

sofistica|ción f sophistication. ~**do** adj sophisticated

sofo|cante adj suffocating; (fig) stifling. ~**car** ◼ vt smother

(fuego); (fig) stifle. ~**carse** vpr get upset

soga f rope

soja f soya (bean)

sojuzgar ◼ vt subdue

sol m sun; (luz) sunlight; (Mus) G; (solfa) soh. al ~ in the sun. día de ~ sunny day. hace ~, hay ~ it is sunny. tomar el ~ sunbathe

solamente adv only

solapa f lapel; (de bolsillo etc) flap. ~**do** adj sly

solar adj solar. ● m plot

solariego adj (casa) ancestral

soldado m soldier. ~ **raso** private

solda|dor m welder; (utensilio) soldering iron. ~**r** ◼ vt weld, solder

soleado adj sunny

soledad f solitude; (aislamiento) loneliness

solemn|e adj solemn. ~**idad** f solemnity

soler ◼ vi be in the habit of. suele despertarse a las 6 he usually wakes up at 6 o'clock

sol|icitante m applicant. ~ **de asilo** asylum seeker. ~**icitar** vt request, ask for; apply for (empleo). ~**ícito** adj solicitous. ~**icitud** f request; (para un puesto) application; (formulario) application form; (preocupación) concern

solidaridad f solidarity

solid|ez f solidity; (de argumento etc) soundness. ~**ificarse** ◼ vpr solidify

sólido adj solid; (argumento etc) sound. ● m solid

soliloquio m soliloquy

solista m & f soloist

solitario adj solitary; (aislado) lonely. ● m loner; (juego, diamante) solitaire

solloz|ar 🔟 *vi* sob. **~o** *m* sob

solo *adj* (*sin compañía*) alone; (*aislado*) lonely; (*sin ayuda*) by oneself; (*único*) only; (*Mus*) solo; (*café*) black. ● *m* solo; (*juego*) solitaire. a solas alone

sólo *adv* only. **~** que except that. no **~...** sino también not only... but also.... tan **~** only

solomillo *m* sirloin

soltar 🔢 *vt* let go of; (*dejar ir*) release; (*dejar caer*) drop; (*dejar salir, decir*) let out; give (*golpe etc*). **~se** *vpr* come undone; (*librarse*) break loose

solter|a *f* single woman. **~o** *adj* single. ● *m* bachelor

soltura *f* looseness; (*fig*) ease, fluency

solu|ble *adj* soluble. **~ción** *f* solution. **~cionar** *vt* solve; settle (*huelga, asunto*)

solvente *adj* & *m* solvent

sombr|a *f* shadow; (*lugar sin sol*) shade. a la **~** in the shade. **~eado** *adj* shady

sombrero *m* hat. **~** hongo bowler hat

sombrío *adj* sombre

somero *adj* superficial

someter *vt* subdue; subject (*persona*); (*presentar*) submit. **~se** *vpr* give in

somn|oliento *adj* sleepy. **~ífero** *m* sleeping-pill

somos *vb véase* SER

son *m* sound. ● *vb véase* SER

sonámbulo *m* sleepwalker. ser **~** walk in one's sleep

sonar 🔢 *vt* blow; ring (*timbre*). ● *vi* sound; (*timbre, teléfono etc*) ring; (*despertador*) go off; (*Mus*) play; (*fig, ser conocido*) be familiar. **~** a sound like. **~se** *vpr* blow

one's nose

sonde|ar *vt* sound out; explore (*espacio*); (*Naut*) sound. **~o** *m* poll; (*Naut*) sounding

soneto *m* sonnet

sonido *m* sound

sonoro *adj* sonorous; (*ruidoso*) loud

sonr|eír 🔢 *vi* smile. **~eírse** *vpr* smile. **~isa** *f* smile

sonroj|arse *vpr* blush. **~o** *m* blush

sonrosado *adj* rosy, pink

sonsacar 🔢 *vt* wheedle out

soñ|ado *adj* dream. **~ador** *m* dreamer. **~ar** 🔢 *vi* dream (con of). ¡ni **~arlo**! not likely!

sopa *f* soup

sopesar *vt* (*fig*) weigh up

sopl|ar *vt* blow; blow out (*vela*); blow off (*polvo*); (*inflar*) blow up. ● *vi* blow. **~ete** *m* blowlamp. **~o** *m* puff

soport|al *m* porch. **~ales** *mpl* arcade. **~ar** *vt* support; (*fig*) bear, put up with. **~e** *m* support

soprano *f* soprano

sor *f* sister

sorb|er *vt* sip; (*con ruido*) slurp; (*absorber*) absorb. **~** por la nariz sniff. **~ete** *m* sorbet, water-ice. **~o** *m* (*pequeña cantidad*) sip; (*trago grande*) gulp

sordera *f* deafness

sórdido *adj* squalid; (*asunto*) sordid

sordo *adj* deaf; (*ruido etc*) dull. ● *m* deaf person. hacerse el **~** turn a deaf ear. **~mudo** *adj* deaf and dumb

soroche *m* (*LAm*) mountain sickness

sorpre|ndente *adj* surprising. ●

~nder vt surprise. ~nderse vpr be surprised. ~sa f surprise

sorte|ar vt draw lots for; (*fig*) avoid. ~o m draw. por ~o by drawing lots

sortija f ring; (*de pelo*) ringlet

sortilegio m sorcery; (*embrujo*) spell

sos|egar **1** & **12** vt calm. ~iego m calmness

soslayo. de ~ sideways

soso adj tasteless; (*fig*) dull

sospech|a f suspicion. ~ar vt suspect. ● vi. ~ de suspect. ~oso adj suspicious. ● m suspect

sost|én m support; (*prenda femenina*) bra **11**, brassière. ~ener **40** vt support; bear (*peso*); (*sujetar*) hold; (*sustentar*) maintain; (*alimentar*) sustain. ~enerse vpr support o.s.; (*continuar*) remain. ~enido adj sustained; (*Mus*) sharp. ● m (*Mus*) sharp

sota f (*de naipes*) jack

sótano m basement

soviético adj (*Historia*) Soviet

soy vb véase SER

Sr. abrev (Señor) Mr. ~a. abrev (Señora) Mrs. ~ta. abrev (Señorita) Miss

su adj (*de él*) his; (*de ella*) her; (*de animal, objeto*) its; (*de uno*) one's; (*de Vd*) your; (*de ellos, de ellas*) their; (*de Vds*) your

suav|e adj smooth; (*fig*) gentle; (*color, sonido*) soft; (*tabaco, sedante*) mild. ~idad f smoothness, softness. ~izante m conditioner; (*para ropa*) softener. ~izar **10** vt smooth, soften

subalimentado adj underfed

subarrendar **1** vt sublet

subasta f auction. ~r vt auction

sub|campeón m runner-up. ~consciencia f subconscious. ~consciente adj & m subconscious. ~continente m subcontinent. ~desarrollado adj underdeveloped. ~director m assistant manager

súbdito m subject

sub|dividir vt subdivide. ~estimar vt underestimate

subi|da f rise; (*a montaña*) ascent; (*pendiente*) slope. ~do adj (*color*) intense. ~r vt go up; climb (*montaña*); (*llevar*) take up; (*aumentar*) raise; turn up (*radio, calefacción*). ● vi go up. ~r a get into (*coche*); get on (*autobús, avión, barco, tren*); (*aumentar*) rise. ~ a pie walk up. ~rse vpr climb up. ~rse a get on (*tren etc*)

súbito adj sudden. de ~ suddenly

subjetivo adj subjective

subjuntivo adj & m subjunctive

subleva|ción f uprising. ~rse vpr rebel

sublim|ar vt sublimate. ~e adj sublime

submarino adj underwater. ● m submarine

subordinado adj & m subordinate

subrayar vt underline

subsanar vt rectify; overcome (*dificultad*); make up for (*carencia*)

subscri|bir vt (*pp* subscrito) sign. ~birse vpr subscribe (a to). ~pción f subscription

subsidi|ario adj subsidiary. ~o m subsidy. ~o de desempleo, ~o de paro unemployment benefit

subsiguiente adj subsequent

subsist|encia f subsistence. ~ir vi subsist; (*perdurar*) survive

substraer **41** vt take away

subterráneo adj underground

subtítulo m subtitle

suburb|ano adj suburban. **~io** m suburb; (barrio pobre) depressed area

subvenci|ón f subsidy. **~onar** vt subsidize

subver|sión f subversion. **~sivo** adj subversive. **~tir** 4 vt subvert

succi|ón f suction. **~onar** vt suck

suce|der vi happen; (seguir) ~ a follow. ● vt (substituir) succeed. lo que ~ de es que the trouble is that. ¿qué ~ de? what's the matter? **~sión** f succession. **~sivo** adj successive; (consecutivo) consecutive. en lo **~sivo** in future. **~so** m event; (incidente) incident. **~sor** m successor

suciedad f dirt; (estado) dirtiness

sucinto adj concise; (prenda) scanty

sucio adj dirty; (conciencia) guilty. en ~ in rough

sucre m (unidad monetaria del Ecuador) sucre

suculento adj succulent

sucumbir vi succumb (a to)

sucursal f branch (office)

Sudáfrica f South Africa

sudafricano adj & m South African

Sudamérica f South America

sudamericano adj & m South American

sudar vi sweat

sud|este m south-east. **~oeste** m south-west

sudor m sweat

Suecia f Sweden

sueco adj Swedish. ● m (persona) Swede; (lengua) Swedish. hacerse el ~ pretend not to hear

suegr|a f mother-in-law. **~o** m father-in-law. **mis ~os** my in-laws

suela f sole

sueldo m salary

suelo m ground; (dentro de edificio) floor; (territorio) soil; (en la calle etc) road surface. ● vb véase **SOLER**

suelto adj loose; (cordones) undone; (sin pareja) odd; (lenguaje) fluent. **con el pelo ~** with one's hair down. ● m change

sueño m sleep; (lo soñado, ilusión) dream. **tener ~** be sleepy

suerte f luck; (destino) fate; (azar) chance. **de otra ~** otherwise. **de ~ que** so. **echar ~s** draw lots. **por ~** fortunately. **tener ~** be lucky

suéter m sweater, jersey

suficien|cia f (aptitud) aptitude; (presunción) smugness. **~te** adj enough, sufficient; (presumido) smug. **~temente** adv sufficiently

sufijo m suffix

sufragio m (voto) vote

sufri|miento m suffering. **~r** vt suffer; undergo (cambio); have (accident). ● vi suffer

suge|rencia f suggestion. **~rir** 4 vt suggest. **~stión** f (en psicología) suggestion. **es pura ~stión** it's all in one's mind. **~stionable** adj impressionable. **~stionar** vt influence. **~stivo** adj (estimulante) stimulating; (atractivo) sexy

suicid|a adj suicidal. ● m & f suicide victim; (fig) maniac. **~arse** vpr commit suicide. **~io** m suicide

Suiza f Switzerland

suizo adj & m Swiss

suje|ción f subjection. **con ~ a** in accordance with. **~tador** m bra ⑪, brassière. **~tapapeles** m invar paper-clip. **~tar** vt fasten; (agarrar) hold. **~tarse** vpr. **~se a** hold on to; (someterse) abide by. **~to** fastened; (susceptible) subject (a to). ● m individual; (Gram) subject.

suma f sum; (Math) addition; (combinación) combination. **en ~** in short. **~mente** adv extremely. **~r** vt add (up); (totalizar) add up to. ● vi add up. **~rse** vpr. **~rse a** join in

sumario adj brief; (Jurid) summary. ● m table of contents; (Jurid) pre-trial proceedings

sumergi|ble adj submersible. **~r** 14 vt submerge

suministr|ar vt supply. **~o** m supply; (acción) supplying

sumir vt sink; (fig) plunge

sumis|ión f submission. **~o** adj submissive

sumo adj great; (supremo) supreme. **a lo ~** at the most

suntuoso adj sumptuous

supe vb véase SABER

superar vt surpass; (vencer) overcome; beat (marca); (dejar atrás) get over. **~se** vpr better o.s.

superchería f swindle

superfici|al adj superficial. **~e** f surface; (extensión) area. **de ~e** surface

superfluo adj superfluous

superior adj superior; (más alto) higher; (mejor) better; (piso) upper. ● m superior. **~idad** f superiority

superlativo adj & m superlative

supermercado m supermarket

superstici|ón f superstition. **~oso** adj superstitious

supervis|ar vt supervise. **~ión** f supervision. **~or** m supervisor

superviv|encia f survival. **~iente** adj surviving. ● m & f survivor

suplantar vt supplant

suplement|ario adj supplementary. **~o** m supplement

suplente adj & m & f substitute

súplica f entreaty; (Jurid) request

suplicar 7 vt beg

suplicio m torture

suplir vt make up for; (reemplazar) replace

supo|ner 34 vt suppose; (significar) mean; involve (gasto, trabajo). **~sición** f supposition

suprem|acía f supremacy. **~o** adj supreme

supr|esión f suppression; (de impuesto) abolition; (de restricción) lifting. **~imir** vt suppress; abolish (impuesto); lift (restricción); delete (párrafo)

supuesto adj supposed; (falso) false; (denominado) so-called. ● m assumption. **¡por ~!** of course!

sur m south; (viento) south wind

surc|ar 7 vt plough; cut through (agua). **~o** m furrow; (de rueda) rut

surfear vi (Informática) surf

surgir 14 vi spring up; (elevarse) loom up; (aparecer) appear; (dificultad, oportunidad) arise

surrealis|mo m surrealism. **~ta** adj & m & f surrealist

surti|do adj well-stocked; (variado) assorted. ● m assortment, selection. **~dor** m (de gasolina) petrol pump (Brit), gas pump (Amer). **~r** vt supply; have (efecto). **~rse** vpr provide o.s. (de with)

susceptib|ilidad f sensitivity. **~le** adj susceptible; (sensible) sensitive

suscitar vt provoke; arouse

s

(curiosidad, interés)

suscr... *véase* **SUBSCR...**

susodicho *adj* aforementioned

suspen|der *vt* suspend; stop (tratamiento); call off (viaje); (en examen) fail; (colgar) hang (de from). ~**se** *m* suspense. novela de ~**se** thriller. ~**sión** *f* suspension. ~**so** *m* fail; (LAm, en libro, película) suspense. en ~**so** suspended

suspir|ar *vi* sigh. ~**o** *m* sigh

sust... *véase* **SUBST...**

sustanci|a *f* substance. ~**al** *adj* substantial. ~**oso** *adj* substantial

sustantivo *m* noun

sustent|ación *f* support. ~**ar** *vt* support; (alimentar) sustain; (mantener) maintain. ~**o** *m* support; (alimento) sustenance

sustitu|ción *f* substitution; (permanente) replacement. ~**ir** 17 *vt* substitute, replace. ~**to** *m* substitute; (permanente) replacement

susto *m* fright

susurr|ar *vi* (persona) whisper; (agua) murmur; (hojas) rustle

sutil *adj* fine; (fig) subtle. ~**eza** *f* subtlety

suyo *adj & pron* (de él) his; (de ella) hers; (de animal) its; (de Vd) yours; (de ellos, de ellas) theirs; (de Vds) yours. un amigo ~ a friend of his, a friend of theirs, etc

Tt

tabac|alera *f* (state) tobacco monopoly. ~**o** *m* tobacco; (cigarrillos) cigarettes

tabern|a *f* bar. ~**ero** *m* barman; (dueño) landlord

tabique *m* partition wall; (Mex, ladrillo) brick

tabl|a *f* plank; (del suelo) floorboard; (de vestido) pleat; (índice) index; (gráfico, en matemática etc) table. hacer ~**as** (en ajedrez) draw. ~**a de surf** surfboard. ~**ado** *m* platform; (en el teatro) stage. ~**ao** *m* place where flamenco shows are held. ~**ero** *m* board. ~**ero de mandos** dashboard

tableta *f* tablet; (de chocolate) bar

tabl|illa *f* splint; (Mex, de chocolate) bar. ~**ón** *m* plank. ~**ón de anuncios** notice board (esp Brit), bulletin board (Amer)

tabú *m* (pl ~**es**, ~**s**) taboo

tabular *vt* tabulate

taburete *m* stool

tacaño *adj* mean

tacha *f* stain, blemish. sin ~ unblemished; (conducta) irreproachable. ~**r** *vt* (con raya) cross out; (Jurid) impeach. ~ **de** accuse of

tácito *adj* tacit

taciturno *adj* taciturn; (triste) glum

taco *m* plug; (LAm, tacón) heel; (de billar) cue; (de billetes) book; (fig, fam, lío) mess; (palabrota) swearword; (Mex, Culin) taco, filled tortilla

tacón *m* heel

táctic|a *f* tactics. ~**o** *adj* tactical

táctil adj tactile

tacto m touch; (fig) tact

tahúr m card-sharp

tailandés adj & m Thai

Tailandia f Thailand

taimado adj sly

taj|ada f slice. sacar ~ada profit. ~ante adj categorical; (tono) sharp. ~ear vt (LAm) slash. ~o m cut; (en mina) face

tal adj such. de ~ manera in such a way. un ~ someone called. ● pron. como ~ as such. y ~ and things like that. ● adv. con ~ de que as long as. ~ como the way. ~ para cual 🔟 two of a kind. ~ vez maybe. ¿qué ~? how are you? ¿qué ~ es ella? what's she like?

taladr|ar vt drill. ~o m drill

talante m mood. de buen ~ (estar) in a good mood; (ayudar) willingly

talar vt fell

talco m talcum powder

talega f, **talego** m sack

talento m talent; (fig) talented person

talismán m talisman

talla f carving; (de diamante etc) cutting; (estatura) height; (tamaño) size. ~do m carving; (de diamante etc) cutting. ~dor m carver; (cortador) cutter; (LAm, de naipes) dealer. ~r vt carve; sculpt (escultura); cut (diamante); (Mex, restregar) scrub. ~rse vpr (Mex) rub o.s.

tallarín m noodle

talle m waist; (figura) figure

taller m workshop; (de pintor etc) studio; (Auto) garage

tallo m stem, stalk

tal|ón m heel; (recibo) counterfoil; (cheque) cheque. ~onario m receipt book; (de cheques) cheque book

tamal m (LAm) tamale

tamaño adj such a. ● m size. de ~ natural life-size

tambalearse vpr (persona) stagger; (cosa) wobble

también adv also, too

tambor m drum. ~ del freno brake drum. ~ilear vi drum

tamiz m sieve. ~ar vt sieve

tampoco adv neither, nor, not either. yo ~ fui I didn't go either

tampón m tampon; (para entintar) ink-pad

tan adv so. ~... como as... as. ¿qué ~...? (LAm) how...?

tanda f group; (de obreros) shift

tang|ente adj & f tangent. ~ible adj tangible

tango m tango

tanque m tank

tante|ar vt estimate; sound up (persona); (ensayar) test; (fig) weigh up; (LAm, palpar) feel. ● vi (LAm) feel one's way. ~o m estimate; (prueba) test; (en deportes) score

tanto adj (en singular) so much; (en plural) so many; (comparación en singular) as much; (comparación en plural) as many. ● pron so much; (en plural) so many. ● adv so; (con verbo) so much. hace ~ tiempo it's been so long. ~... como both ...and. ¿qué ~...? (LAm) how much...? ~ como as well as; (cantidad) as much as. ~ más... cuanto que all the more ... because. ~ si... como si whether ... or. a ~s de sometime in. en ~, entre ~ meanwhile. en ~ que while. entre ~ meanwhile. hasta

~ que until. no es para ~ it's not as bad as all that. otro ~ the same; (el doble) as much again. por (lo) ~ therefore. ● m certain amount; (punto) point; (gol) goal. estar al ~ de be up to date with

tañer 22 vi peal

tapa f lid; (de botella) top; (de libro) cover. ~s fpl savoury snacks. ~dera f cover, lid; (fig) cover. ~r vt cover; (abrigar) wrap up; (obturar) plug. ~rrabo(s) m invar loincloth

> **tapas** In Spain these are small portions of food served in bars and cafés with a drink. There is a wide variety, including Spanish omelette, seafood, different kinds of cooked potatoes, cheese, ham, chorizo etc. The practice of going out for a drink and tapas is known as tapeo.

tapete m (de mesa) table cover; (Mex, alfombra) rug

tapia f wall. ~r vt enclose

tapi|cería f tapestry; (de muebles) upholstery. ~z m tapestry. ~zar 10 vt upholster (muebles)

tapón m stopper; (Tec) plug

taqui|grafía f shorthand

taquilla f ticket office; (fig, dinero) takings. ~ero m box-office

tara f (peso) tare; (defecto) defect

tarántula f tarantula

tararear vt/i hum

tarda|nza f delay. ~r vt take. ● vi (retrasarse) be late; (emplear mucho tiempo) take a long time. a más ~r at the latest. sin ~r without delay

tard|e adv late. ● f (antes del atardecer) afternoon; (después del atardecer) evening. en la ~e (LAm), por la ~e in the afternoon. ~ío adj late

tarea f task, job

tarifa f rate; (en transporte) fare; (lista de precios) tariff

tarima f dais

tarjeta f card. ~ de crédito credit card. ~ de fidelidad loyalty card. ~ postal postcard. T~ Sanitaria Europea European Health Insurance Card. t~ SIM SIM card. ~ telefónica telephone card

tarro m jar; (Mex, taza) mug

tarta f cake; (con base de masa) tart. ~ helada ice-cream gateau

tartamud|ear vi stammer. ~o adj. es ~o he stammers

tasa f valuation; (impuesto) tax; (índice) rate. ~r vt value; (limitar) ration

tasca f bar

tatarabuel|a f great-great-grandmother. ~o m great-great-grandfather. ~os mpl great-great-grandparents

tatua|je m (acción) tattooing; (dibujo) tattoo. ~r 21 vt tattoo

taurino adj bullfighting

Tauro m Taurus

tauromaquia f bullfighting

taxi m taxi. ~ista m & f taxi-driver

taz|a f cup. ~ón m bowl

te pron (acusativo) you; (dativo) (to) you; (reflexivo) (to) yourself

té m tea; (LAm, reunión) tea party

teatr|al adj theatre; (exagerado) theatrical. ~o m theatre; (literatura) drama

tebeo m comic

tech|ado m roof. ~ar vt roof. ~o m (interior) ceiling; (LAm, tejado) roof. ~umbre f roof

tecl|a f key. ~**ado** m keyboard. ~**ear** vt key in

técnica f technique

tecnicismo m technical nature; (*palabra*) technical term

técnico adj technical. • m technician; (*en deportes*) trainer

tecnol|ogía f technology. ~**ógico** adj technological

tecolote m (*Mex*) owl

teja f tile. ~**s** de pizarra slates. ~**do** m roof. a toca ~ cash

teje|dor m weaver. ~**r** vt weave; (*hacer punto*) knit

tejemaneje m 🗋 intrigue. ~**s** mpl scheming

tejido m material; (*Anat*) tissue. ~**s** mpl textiles

tejón m badger

tela f material, fabric; (*de araña*) web; (*en líquido*) skin

telar m loom. ~**es** mpl textile mill

telaraña f spider's web, cobweb

tele f 🗔 TV, telly

tele|banca f telephone banking. ~**comunicación** f telecommunication. ~**diario** m television news. ~**dirigido** adj remote-controlled; (*misil*) guided. ~**férico** m cable-car

tel|efonear vt/i telephone. ~**efónico** adj telephone. ~**efonista** m & f telephonist.

teléfono m telephone. ~ **celular** (*LAm*) mobile phone, cellular phone. ~ **móvil** (*Esp*) mobile phone, cellular phone. ~ **satélite** satphone

tel|egrafía f telegraphy. ~**égrafo** m telegraph. ~**egrama** m telegram

telenovela f television soap opera

teleobjetivo m telephoto lens

telep|atía f telepathy. ~**ático** adj telepathic

telesc|ópico adj telescopic. ~**opio** m telescope

telesilla m & f chair-lift

telespectador m viewer

telesquí m ski-lift

televi|dente m & f viewer. ~**sar** vt televise. ~**sión** f television. ~**sor** m television (set)

télex m invar telex

telón m curtain

tema m subject; (*Mus*) theme

tembl|ar 🚹 vi shake; (*de miedo*) tremble; (*de frío*) shiver. ~**or** m shaking; (*de miedo*) trembling; (*de frío*) shivering. ~**or** de tierra earth tremor. ~**oroso** adj trembling

tem|er vt be afraid (of). • vi be afraid. ~**erse** vpr be afraid. ~**erario** adj reckless. ~**eroso** adj frightened. ~**ible** adj fearsome. ~**or** m fear

témpano m floe

temperamento m temperament

temperatura f temperature

tempest|ad f storm. ~**uoso** adj stormy

templ|ado adj (*tibio*) warm; (*clima, tiempo*) mild; (*valiente*) courageous. ~**anza** f mildness. ~**ar** vt temper; (*calentar*) warm up. ~**e** m tempering; (*coraje*) courage; (*humor*) mood

templo m temple

tempora|da f season. ~**l** adj temporary. • m storm

tempran|ero adj (*frutos*) early. ser ~**ero** be an early riser. ~**o** adj & adv early

tenacidad f tenacity

tenacillas fpl tongs

tenaz *adj* tenacious

tenaza *f*, **tenazas** *fpl* pliers; (*de chimenea*, *Culin*) tongs; (*de cangrejo*) pincer

tende|ncia *f* tendency. **~nte** *adj*. **~nte a** aimed at. **~r 1** *vt* spread (out); hang out (ropa a secar); (*colocar*) lay. ● *vi* tend (a to). **~rse** *vpr* lie down

tender|ete *m* stall. **~o** *m* shopkeeper

tendido *adj* spread out; (ropa) hung out; (persona) lying down. ● *m* (*en plaza de toros*) front rows

tendón *m* tendon

tenebroso *adj* gloomy; (asunto) sinister

tenedor *m* fork; (*poseedor*) holder

---

tener 40

● *verbo transitivo*

! El presente del verbo **tener** admite dos traducciones: to have y to have got, este último de uso más extendido en el inglés británico

····▸ to have. ¿tienen hijos? do you have any children?, have you got any children? no tenemos coche we don't have a car, we haven't got a car. tiene gripe he has (the) flu, he's got (the) flu

····▸ to be. (dimensiones, edad) tiene 1 metro de largo it's 1 meter long. tengo 20 años I'm 20 (years old)

····▸ (sentir) tener + nombre to be + adjective. ~ celos to be jealous. ~ frío to be cold

····▸ (sujetar, sostener) to hold. tenme la escalera hold the ladder for me

····▸ (indicando estado) tiene las manos sucias his hands are dirty. me tiene preocupada I'm worried about him. me tuvo esperando he kept me waiting

····▸ (llevar puesto) to be wearing, to have on. ¡qué zapatos más elegantes tienes! those are very smart shoes you're wearing! tienes el suéter al revés you have your sweater on inside out

····▸ (considerar) ~ a uno por algo to think s.o. is sth. lo tenía por tímido I thought he was shy

● *verbo auxiliar*

····▸ ~ que hacer algo to have to do sth. tengo que irme I have to go

····▸ tener + participio pasado. tengo pensado comprarlo I'm thinking of buying it. tenía entendido otra cosa I understood something else

····▸ (LAm, con expresiones temporales) tienen 2 años de estar aquí they've been here for 2 months. tiene mucho tiempo sin verlo he hasn't seen him for a long time

····▸ (en locuciones) aquí tiene here you are. ¿qué tienes? what's the matter with you? ¿y eso qué tiene? (LAm) and what's wrong with that?

● *verbo pronominal*

tenerse *verbo pronominal*

····▸ (sostenerse) no podía ~se en pie (de cansancio) he was dead on his feet; (de borracho) he could hardly stand

···→ (*considerarse*) to consider o.s.
se tiene por afortunado he
considers himself lucky

tengo *vb véase* TENER

teniente *m* lieutenant

tenis *m* tennis. ~ **de mesa** table
tennis. ~**ta** *m & f* tennis player

tenor *m* sense; (*Mus*) tenor. **a** ~
de according to

tens|ión *f* tension; (*arterial*) blood
pressure; (*Elec*) voltage; (*estrés*)
strain. ~**o** *adj* tense

tentación *f* temptation

tentáculo *m* tentacle

tenta|dor *adj* tempting. ~**r** ① *vt*
tempt; (*palpar*) feel

tentativa *f* attempt

tenue *adj* thin; (*luz, voz*) faint;
(*color*) subdued

teñi|r ⑤ & ㉒ *vt* dye; (*fig*) tinge
(de with). ~**rse** *vpr* dye one's hair

teología *f* theology

te|oría *f* theory. ~**órico** *adj* theor-
etical

tequila *f* tequila

terap|euta *m & f* therapist. ~**éu-
tico** *adj* therapeutic. ~**ia** *f* therapy

terc|er *adj véase* TERCERO. ~**era** *f*
(*Auto*) third (gear). ~**ero** *adj* (*delante
de nombre masculino singular* tercer)
third. ● *m* third party. ~**io** *m* third

terciopelo *m* velvet

terco *adj* obstinate

tergiversar *vt* distort

termal *adj* thermal

térmico *adj* thermal

termina|ción *f* ending; (*conclu-
sión*) conclusion. ~**l** *adj & m* ter-
minal. ~**nte** *adj* categorical. ~**r** *vt*
finish, end. ~**r por** end up. ~**rse**
vpr come to an end

término *m* end; (*palabra*) term;

(*plazo*) period. ~ **medio** average.
dar ~ **a** finish off. **en primer** ~
first of all. **en último** ~ **as** a last
resort. **estar en buenos** ~**s con**
be on good terms with. **llevar a** ~
carry out

terminología *f* terminology

termita *f* termite

termo *m* Thermos (P) flask, flask

termómetro *m* thermometer

termo|nuclear *adj* thermo-
nuclear. ~**stato** *m* thermostat

terner|a *f* (*carne*) veal. ~**o** *m* calf

ternura *f* tenderness

terquedad *f* stubbornness

terrado *m* flat roof

terraplén *m* embankment

terrateniente *m & f* landowner

terraza *f* terrace; (*balcón*) bal-
cony; (*terrado*) flat roof

terremoto *m* earthquake

terre|no *adj* earthly. ● *m* land;
(*solar*) plot (*fig*) field. ~**stre** *adj*
land; (*Mil*) ground

terrible *adj* terrible. ~**mente** *adv*
awfully

territori|al *adj* territorial. ~**o** *m*
territory

terrón *m* (*de tierra*) clod; (*Culin*)
lump

terror *m* terror. ~**ífico** *adj* terrify-
ing. ~**ismo** *m* terrorism. ~**ista** *m
& f* terrorist

terso *adj* smooth

tertulia *f* gathering

tesina *f* dissertation

tesón *m* tenacity

tesor|ería *f* treasury. ~**ero** *m*
treasurer. ~**o** *m* treasure; (*tesore-
ría*) treasury; (*libro*) thesaurus

testaferro *m* figurehead

testa|mento *m* will. T~**mento**
(*Relig*) Testament. ~**r** *vi* make a will

testarudo adj stubborn

testículo m testicle

testi|ficar 7 vt/i testify. **~go** m witness. **~go ocular**, **~go presencial** eyewitness. **ser ~go de** witness. **~monio** m testimony

teta f tit (fam o vulg); (de biberón) teat

tétanos m tetanus

tetera f (para el té) teapot

tetilla f nipple; (de biberón) teat

tétrico adj gloomy

textil adj & m textile

text|o m text. **~ual** adj textual; (traducción) literal; (palabras) exact

textura f texture

tez f complexion

ti pron you

tía f aunt; 🔲 woman

tiara f tiara

tibio adj lukewarm

tiburón m shark

tiempo m time; (atmosférico) weather; (Mus) tempo; (Gram) tense; (en partido) half. **a su ~** in due course. **a ~** in time. **¿cuánto ~?** how long? **hace buen ~** the weather is fine. **hace ~** some time ago. **mucho ~** a long time. **perder el ~** waste time

tienda f shop (esp Brit), store (esp Amer); (de campaña) tent. **~ de comestibles**, **~ de ultramarinos** grocer's (shop) (Brit), grocery store (Amer)

tiene vb véase TENER

tienta. **andar a ~s** feel one's way

tierno adj tender; (joven) young

tierra f land; (planeta, Elec) earth; (suelo) ground; (en geología) soil, earth; (LAm, polvo) dust. **por ~** overland, by land

tieso adj stiff; (engreído) conceited

tiesto m flowerpot

tifón m typhoon

tifus m typhus; (fiebre tifoidea) typhoid (fever)

tigre m tiger. **~sa** f tigress

tijera f, **tijeras** fpl scissors; (de jardín) shears

tijeretear vt snip

tila f (infusión) lime tea

tild|ar vt. **~ar de** (fig) brand as. **~e** f tilde

tilo m lime(-tree)

timar vt swindle

timbal m kettledrum; (Culin) timbale, meat pie. **~es** mpl (Mus) timpani

timbr|ar vt stamp. **~e** m (sello) fiscal stamp; (Mex) postage stamp; (Elec) bell; (sonido) timbre

timidez f shyness

tímido adj shy

timo m swindle

timón m rudder; (rueda) wheel; (fig) helm

tímpano m eardrum

tina f tub. **~co m** (Mex) water tank. **~ja** f large earthenware jar

tinglado m mess; (asunto) racket

tinieblas fpl darkness; (fig) confusion

tino m good sense; (tacto) tact

tint|a f ink. **de buena ~a** on good authority. **~e** m dyeing; (color) dye; (fig) tinge. **~ero** m ink-well

tintinear vi tinkle; (vasos) chink, clink

tinto adj (vino) red

tintorería f dry cleaner's

tintura f dyeing; (color) dye

tío m uncle; 🔲 man. **~s** mpl uncle and aunt

tiovivo m merry-go-round

típico adj typical

tipo m type; (fam, persona) person; (figura de mujer) figure; (figura de hombre) build; (Com) rate

tip|ografía f typography. ~ográfico adj typographic(al)

tira f strip. la ~ de lots of

tirabuzón m corkscrew; (de pelo) ringlet

tirad|a f distance; (serie) series; (de periódico etc) print-run. de una ~a in one go. ~o adj (barato) very cheap; (fam, fácil) very easy. ~or m (asa) handle

tiran|ía f tyranny. ~izar 🔟 vt tyrannize. ~o adj tyrannical. ● m tyrant

tirante adj tight; (fig) tense; (relaciones) strained. ~s mpl strap. ~s mpl braces (esp Brit), suspenders (Amer)

tirar vt throw; (desechar) throw away; (derribar) knock over; drop (bomba); fire (cohete); (imprimir) print. ● vi (disparar) shoot. ~ a tend to (be); (parecerse a) resemble. ~ abajo knock down. ~ de pull. a todo ~ at the most. ir tirando get by. ~se vpr throw o.s.; (tumbarse) lie down

tirita f (sticking) plaster

tiritar vi shiver (de with)

tiro m throw; (disparo) shot. ~ libre free kick. a ~ within range. errar el ~ miss. pegarse un ~ shoot o.s.

tiroides m thyroid (gland)

tirón m tug. de un ~ in one go

tirote|ar vt shoot at. ~o m shooting

tisana f herb tea

tisú m (pl ~s, ~es) tissue

títere m puppet. ~s mpl puppet show

titilar vi (estrella) twinkle

titiritero m puppeteer; (acróbata) acrobat

titube|ante adj faltering; (fig) hesitant. ~ar vi falter. ~o m hesitation

titula|do adj (libro) entitled; (persona) qualified. ~r m headline; (persona) holder. ● vt call. ~rse vpr be called; (persona) graduate

título m title; (académico) qualification; (Univ) degree. a ~ de as, by way of

tiza f chalk

tiz|nar vt dirty. ~ne m soot

toall|a f towel. ~ero m towel-rail

tobillo m ankle

tobogán m slide; (para la nieve) toboggan

tocadiscos m invar record-player

toca|do adj touched 🔟. ● m headdress. ~dor m dressing-table. ~nte adj. en lo ~nte a with regard to. ~r 🗷 vt touch; (palpar) feel; (Mus) play; ring (timbre); (mencionar) touch on; (barco) stop at. ● vi ring; (corresponder a uno). te ~ a ti it's your turn. en lo que ~ a as for. ~rse vpr touch; (personas): touch each other

tocayo m namesake

tocino m bacon

tocólogo m obstetrician

todavía adv still; (con negativos) yet. ~ no not yet

---

todo, **toda**

● adjetivo

····▷ (la totalidad) all. ~ el vino all the wine. ~s los edificios all the buildings. ~ ese dinero all that money. ~ el mundo everyone. (como adv) está toda sucia it's all dirty

····▸ (entero) whole. ~ el día the whole day, all day. toda su familia his whole family. ~ el tiempo the whole time, all the time

····▸ (cada, cualquiera) every. ~ tipo de coche every type of car. ~ los días every day

····▸ (enfático) a toda velocidad at top speed. es ~ un caballero he's a real gentleman

····▸ (en locuciones) ante ~ above all. a ~ esto meanwhile. con ~ even so. del ~ lo contrario quite the opposite

➡ Para expresiones como **todo recto, todo seguido** etc., ver bajo el respectivo adjetivo

● pronombre

····▸ all; (todas las cosas) everything. eso es ~ that's all. lo perdieron ~ they lost everything. quiere comprar ~ he wants to buy everything

····▸ todos, todas all; (todo el mundo) everyone. los compró ~s he bought them all, he bought all of them. ~s queríamos ir we all wanted to go. vinieron ~s everyone came

● nombre masculino el/un ~ the/a whole

toldo m awning

tolera|ncia f tolerance. ~nte adj tolerant. ~r vt tolerate

toma f taking; (de universidad etc) occupation; (Med) dose; (de agua) intake; (Elec) socket; (LAm, acequia) irrigation channel. ● int well!, fancy

that! ~ de corriente power point. ~dura f. ~dura de pelo hoax. ~r vt take; catch (autobús, tren); occupy (universidad etc); (beber) drink, have; (comer) eat, have. ● vi take; (esp LAm, beber) drink; (LAm, dirigirse) go. ~r a bien take well. ~r a mal take badly. ~r en serio take seriously. ~rla con uno pick on s.o. ~r por take for. ~ y daca give and take. ¿qué va a ~r? what would you like? ~rse vpr take; (beber) drink, have; (comer) eat, have

tomate m tomato

tomillo m thyme

tomo m volume

ton: sin ~ ni son without rhyme or reason

tonad|a f tune; (canción) popular song; (LAm, acento) accent. ~illa f tune

tonel m barrel. ~ada f ton. ~aje m tonnage

tónic|a f trend; (bebida) tonic water. ~o adj tonic; (sílaba) stressed. ● m tonic

tonificar 7 vt invigorate

tono m tone; (Mus, modo) key; (color) shade

tont|ería f silliness; (cosa) silly thing; (dicho) silly remark. dejarse de ~erías stop fooling around. ~o adj silly. ● m fool, idiot; (payaso) clown. hacer el ~o act the fool. hacerse el ~o act dumb

topacio m topaz

topar vi ~ con run into

tope adj maximum. ● m end; (de tren) buffer; (Mex, Auto) speed bump. hasta los ~s crammed full. ir a ~ go flat out

tópico adj trite. de uso ~ (Med) for external use only. ● m cliché

topo m mole

topogr|afía f topography. ~**áfico** adj topographical

toque m touch; (sonido) sound; (de campana) peal; (de reloj) stroke. ~ de queda curfew. dar los últimos ~s put the finishing touches. ~**tear** vt fiddle with

toquilla f shawl

tórax m invar thorax

torcer 2 & 9 vt twist; (doblar) bend; wring out (ropa). • vi turn. ~**se** vpr twist

tordo adj dapple grey. • m thrush

tore|ar vt fight; (evitar) dodge. • vi fight (bulls). ~**o** m bullfighting. ~**ro** m bullfighter

torment|a f storm. ~**o** m torture. ~**oso** adj stormy

tornado m tornado

tornasolado adj iridescent

torneo m tournament

tornillo m screw

torniquete m (Med) tourniquet; (entrada) turnstile

torno m lathe; (de alfarero) wheel. en ~ a around

toro m bull. ~**s** mpl bullfighting. ir a los ~s go to a bullfight

---

(la fiesta de) los toros *i*
Bullfighting is popular in Spain and some Latin American countries. The season runs from March to October in Spain, from November to March in Latin America. The bullfighters who take part in a corrida gather in *cuadrillas*. The principal bullfighter or *matador* is assisted by *peones*.

---

toronja f (LAm) grapefruit

torpe adj clumsy; (estúpido) stupid

torpedo m torpedo

torpeza f clumsiness; (de inteligencia) slowness. una ~ a blunder

torre f tower; (en ajedrez) castle, rook; (Elec) pylon; (edificio) tower block (Brit), apartment block (Amer)

torren|cial adj torrential. ~**te** m torrent; (circulatorio) bloodstream; (fig) flood

tórrido adj torrid

torsión f twisting

torso m torso

torta f tart; (LAm, de verduras) pie; (golpe) slap, punch; (Mex, bocadillo) filled roll. **no entender ni** ~ not understand a thing. ~**zo** m slap, punch. **pegarse un** ~**zo** have a bad accident

tortícolis f stiff neck

tortilla f omelette; (Mex, de maíz) tortilla. ~ **española** potato omelette. ~ **francesa** plain omelette

tórtola f turtle-dove

tortuoso adj winding; (fig) devious

tortura f torture. ~**r** vt torture

tos f cough. ~ **ferina** whooping cough

tosco adj crude; (persona) coarse

toser vi cough

tost|ada f piece of toast. ~**adas** fpl toast; (Mex, de tortilla) fried tortillas. ~**ado** adj (pan) toasted; (café) roasted; (persona, color) tanned. ~**ar** vt toast (pan); roast (café); tan (piel)

total adj total. • adv after all. ~ **que** so, to cut a long story short. • m total; (totalidad) whole. ~**idad** f whole. ~**itario** adj totalitarian. ~**izar** 10 vt total

tóxico adj toxic

toxi|cómano m drug addict. ~**na** f toxin

tozudo adj stubborn

traba f catch; (fig, obstáculo) obstacle. poner ∼s a hinder

trabaj|ador adj hard-working. ● m worker. ∼ar vt work; knead (masa). ● vi work (de as); (actor) act. ¿en qué ∼as? what do you do? ∼o m work. costar ∼o be difficult. ∼oso adj hard

trabalenguas m invar tonguetwister

traba|r vt (sujetar) fasten; (unir) join; (entablar) strike up. ∼rse vpr get stuck. trabársele la lengua get tongue-tied

trácala m (Mex) cheat. ●f (Mex) trick

tracción f traction

tractor m tractor

tradici|ón f tradition. ∼onal adj traditional

traduc|ción f translation. ∼ir 47 vt translate (a into). ∼tor m translator

traer 41 vt bring; (llevar) carry; (causar) cause. traérselas be difficult

trafica|nte m & f dealer. ∼r 7 vi deal

tráfico m traffic; (Com) trade

traga|luz m skylight. ∼perras f invar slot-machine. ∼r 12 vt swallow; (comer mucho) devour; (soportar) put up with. no lo trago! I can't stand him. ∼rse vpr swallow; (fig) swallow up

tragedia f tragedy

trágico adj tragic. ● m tragedian

trag|o m swallow, gulp; (pequeña porción) sip; (fig, disgusto) blow; (LAm, bebida alcohólica) drink. echar(se) un ∼o have a drink. ∼ón adj greedy. ●m glutton

trai|ción f treachery; (Pol) treason. ∼cionar vt betray. ∼cionero adj treacherous. ∼dor adj treacherous. ● m traitor

traigo vb véase TRAER

traje m dress; (de hombre) suit. ∼ de baño swimming-costume. ∼ de etiqueta, ∼ de noche evening dress. ●vb véase TRAER

traj|ín m coming and going; (ajetreo) hustle and bustle. ∼inar vi bustle about

trama f weft; (fig, argumento) plot. ∼r vt weave; (fig) plot

tramitar vt negotiate

trámite m step. ∼s mpl procedure

tramo m (parte) section; (de escalera) flight

tramp|a f trap; (fig) trick. hacer ∼a cheat. ∼illa f trapdoor

trampolín m trampoline; (de piscina) springboard; (rígido) diving board

tramposo adj cheating. ● m cheat

tranca f bar. ∼r vt bar

trance m moment; (hipnótico etc) trance

tranco m stride

tranquil|idad f peace; (de espíritu) peace of mind. con ∼ calmly. ∼izar 10 vt calm down; (reconfortar) reassure. ∼o adj calm; (lugar) quiet; (conciencia) clear. estáte ∼o don't worry

transa|cción f transaction; (acuerdo) settlement. ∼r vi (LAm) compromise

transatlántico adj transatlantic. ● m (ocean) liner

transbord|ador m ferry. ∼ar vt transfer. ∼o m transfer. hacer ∼o change (en at)

transcri|bir (pp transcrito) vt transcribe. ∼pción f transcription

transcur|rir vi pass. **~so** m course

transeúnte m & f passer-by

transfer|encia f transfer. **~ir** 4 vt transfer

transforma|ción f transformation. **~dor** m transformer. **~r** vt transform

transfusión f transfusion

transgre|dir vt transgress. **~sión** f transgression

transición f transition

transigir 14 vi give in, compromise

transistor m transistor

transita|ble adj passable. **~r** vi go

transitivo adj transitive

tránsito m transit; (tráfico) traffic

transitorio adj transitory

transmi|sión f transmission; (radio, TV) broadcast. **~sor** m transmitter. **~sora** f broadcasting station. **~tir** vt transmit; (radio, TV) broadcast; (fig) pass on

transparen|cia f transparency. **~tar** vt show. **~te** adj transparent

transpira|ción f perspiration. **~r** vi transpire; (sudar) sweat

transport|ar vt transport. **~e** m transport. empresa f de **~es** removals company

transversal adj transverse. una calle **~** a la Gran Vía a street which crosses the Gran Vía

tranvía m tram

trapear vt (LAm) mop

trapecio m trapeze; (Math) trapezium

trapo m cloth. **~s** mpl rags; (🔲, ropa) clothes a todo **~** out of control

tráquea f windpipe, trachea

traquete|ar vt bang, rattle; (persona) rush around. **~o** m banging, rattle

tras prep after; (detrás) behind

trascende|ncia f significance; (alcance) implication. **~ntal** adj transcendental; (importante) important. **~r** 1 vi (saberse) become known; (extenderse) spread

trasero adj back, rear. • m (de persona) bottom

trasfondo m background

traslad|ar vt move; transfer (empleado etc); (aplazar) postpone. **~o** m transfer; (copia) copy. (mudanza) removal. dar **~o** notify

traslúcido adj translucent. **~ucirse** 11 vpr be translucent; (dejarse ver) show through; (fig, revelarse) be revealed. **~uz** m. al **~uz** against the light

trasmano. a **~** out of the way

trasnochar vt (acostarse tarde) go to bed late; (no acostarse) stay up all night; (no dormir) be unable to sleep

traspas|ar vt go through; (transferir) transfer; go beyond (límite). se **~a** for sale. **~o** m transfer

traspié m trip; (fig) slip. dar un **~** stumble; (fig) slip up

trasplant|ar vt transplant. **~e** m transplant

trastada f prank; (jugada) dirty trick

traste m fret. dar al **~** con ruin. ir al **~** fall through. **~s** mpl (Mex) junk

trastero m storeroom

trasto m piece of junk. • **~s** mpl junk

trastorn|ado adj mad. **~ar** vt upset; (volver loco) drive mad; (fig, fam, gustar mucho) delight. **~arse**

t

vpr get upset; (*volverse loco*) go
mad. **~o** *m* (*incl Med*) upset; (*Pol*)
disturbance; (*fig*) confusion

trat|able *adj* friendly; (*Med*) treat-
able. **~ado** *m* treatise; (*acuerdo*)
treaty. **~amiento** *m* treatment;
(*título*) title. **~ante** *m & f* dealer.
~ar *vt* (*incl Med*) treat; deal with
(*asunto etc*); (*manejar*) handle; (*de
tú, de Vd*) address (de as). ● *vi*
deal (with). **~ar con** have to do
with; (*Com*) deal in. **~ar de** be
about; (*intentar*) try. ¿de qué se
~a? what's it about? **~o** *m* treat-
ment; (*acuerdo*) agreement; (*título*)
title; (*relación*) relationship. ¡**~o**
hecho! agreed! **~os** *mpl* dealings

traum|a *m* trauma. **~ático** *adj*
traumatic

través: a **~ de** through; (*de lado
a lado*) crossways

travesaño *m* crossbeam; (*de por-
tería*) crossbar

travesía *f* crossing; (*calle*) side-
street

trav|esura *f* prank. **~ieso** *adj*
(*niño*) mischievous, naughty

trayecto *m* (*tramo*) stretch; (*ruta*)
route; (*viaje*) journey. **~ria** *f* trajec-
tory; (*fig*) course

traz|a *f* (*aspecto*) appearance. **~as**
fpl signs. **~ado** *m* plan. **~ar** 🔟 *vt*
draw; (*bosquejar*) sketch. **~o** *m*
stroke; (*línea*) line

trébol *m* clover. **~es** *mpl* (*en nai-
pes*) clubs

trece *adj & m* thirteen

trecho *m* stretch; (*distancia*) dis-
tance; (*tiempo*) while. a **~s** here
and there. de **~ en ~** at intervals

tregua *f* truce; (*fig*) respite

treinta *adj & m* thirty

tremendo *adj* terrible; (*extraordi-
nario*) terrific

tren *m* train. **~ de aterrizaje** land-
ing gear. **~ de vida** lifestyle

tren|cilla *f* braid. **~za** *f* braid; (*de
pelo*) plait. **~zar** 🔟 *vt* plait

trepa|dor *adj* climbing. **~dora** *f*
climber. **~r** *vt/i* climb. **~rse** *vpr*.
~rse a climb (*árbol*); climb onto
(*silla etc*)

tres *adj & m* three. **~cientos** *adj &
m* three hundred. **~illo** *m* three-
piece suite; (*Mus*) triplet

treta *f* trick

tri|angular *adj* triangular. **~án-
gulo** *m* triangle

trib|al *adj* tribal. **~u** *f* tribe

tribuna *f* platform; (*de espectado-
res*) stand. **~l** *m* court; (*de examen
etc*) board; (*fig*) tribunal

tribut|ar *vt* pay. **~o** *m* tribute;
(*impuesto*) tax

triciclo *m* tricycle

tricolor *adj* three-coloured

tricotar *vt/i* knit

tridimensional *adj* three-
dimensional

trig|al *m* wheat field. **~o** *m* wheat

trigésimo *adj* thirtieth

trigueño *adj* olive-skinned; (*pelo*)
dark blonde

trilla|do (*fig, manoseado*) trite;
(*fig, conocido*) well-known. **~r** *vt*
thresh

trilogía *f* trilogy

trimestr|al *adj* quarterly. **~e** *m*
quarter; (*en enseñanza*) term

trin|ar *vi* warble. **estar que trina**
be furious

trinchar *vt* carve

trinchera *f* ditch; (*Mil*) trench;
(*abrigo*) trench coat

trineo *m* sledge

trinidad *f* trinity

trino *m* warble

trío *m* trio

tripa *f* intestine; (*fig, vientre*) tummy, belly. **~s** *fpl* (*de máquina etc*) parts, workings. **revolver las ~s** turn one's stomach

triple *adj* triple. ● *m*. **el ~e (de)** three times as much (as). **~icado** *adj.* **por ~icado** in triplicate. **~icar 7** *vt* treble

tripula|ción *f* crew. **~nte** *m & f* member of the crew. **~r** *vt* man

tris *m*. **estar en un ~** be on the point of

triste *adj* sad; (*paisaje, tiempo etc*) gloomy; (*fig, insignificante*) miserable. **~za** *f* sadness

triturar *vt* crush

triunf|al *adj* triumphal. **~ante** *adj* triumphant. **~ar** *vi* triumph (**de**, **sobre** over). **~o** *m* triumph

trivial *adj* trivial. **~idad** *f* triviality

trizas. **hacer algo ~** smash sth to pieces. **hacerse ~** smash

trocear *vt* cut up, chop

trocha *f* narrow path; (*LAm, rail*) gauge

trofeo *m* trophy

tromba *f* whirlwind; (*marina*) waterspout. **~ de agua** heavy downpour

trombón *m* trombone

trombosis *f invar* thrombosis

trompa *f* horn; (*de orquesta*) French horn; (*de elefante*) trunk; (*hocico*) snout; (*en anatomía*) tube. **coger una ~ 1** get drunk. **~zo** *m* bump

trompet|a *f* trumpet; (*músico*) trumpet player; (*Mil*) trumpeter. **~illa** *f* ear-trumpet

trompo *m* (*juguete*) spinning top

tronar *vt* (*Mex*) shoot. ● *vi* thunder

tronchar *vt* bring down; (*fig*) cut short. **~se de risa** laugh a lot

tronco *m* trunk. **dormir como un ~** sleep like a log

trono *m* throne

trop|a *f* troops. **~el** *m* mob

tropez|ar 1 & 10 *vi* trip; (*fig*) slip up. **~ar con** run into. **~ón** *m* stumble; (*fig*) slip

tropical *adj* tropical

trópico *adj* tropical. ● *m* tropic

tropiezo *m* slip; (*desgracia*) hitch

trot|ar *vi* trot. **~e** *m* trot; (*fig*) toing and froing. **al ~e** at a trot; (*de prisa*) in a rush. **de mucho ~e** hard-wearing

trozo *m* piece, bit. **a ~s** in bits

trucha *f* trout

truco *m* trick. **coger el ~** get the knack

trueno *m* thunder; (*estampido*) bang

trueque *m* exchange; (*Com*) barter

trufa *f* truffle

truhán *m* rogue

truncar 7 *vt* truncate; (*fig*) cut short

tu *adj* your

tú *pron* you

tuba *f* tuba

tubérculo *m* tuber

tuberculosis *f* tuberculosis

tub|ería *f* pipes; (*oleoducto etc*) pipeline. **~o** *m* tube. **~o de ensayo** test tube. **~o de escape** (*Auto*) exhaust (pipe). **~ular** *adj* tubular

tuerca *f* nut

tuerto *adj* one-eyed, blind in one eye. ● *m* one-eyed person

tuétano *m* marrow; (*fig*) heart. **hasta los ~s** completely

tufo m stench

tugurio m hovel

tul m tulle

tulipán m tulip

tulli|do adj paralysed. **~r** 22 vt cripple

tumba f grave, tomb

tumb|ar vt knock over, knock down (estructura); (fig, fam, en examen) fail. **~arse** vpr lie down. **~o** m jolt. **dar un ~o** tumble. **~ona** f sun lounger.

tumor m tumour

tumulto m turmoil; (Pol) riot

tuna f prickly pear; (de estudiantes) student band

tunante m & f rogue

túnel m tunnel

túnica f tunic

tupé m toupee; (fig) nerve

tupido adj thick

turba f peat; (muchedumbre) mob

turbado adj upset

turbante m turban

turbar vt upset; (molestar) disturb. **~se** vpr be upset

turbina f turbine

turbi|o adj cloudy; (vista) blurred; (asunto etc) shady. **~ón** m squall

turbulen|cia f turbulence; (disturbio) disturbance. **~te** adj turbulent

turco adj Turkish. ● m Turk; (lengua) Turkish

tur|ismo m tourism; (coche) car. **hacer ~** travel around. **~ cultural** heritage tourism. **~ patrimonial** (LAm) heritage tourism. **~ista** m & f tourist. **~ístico** adj tourist

turn|arse vpr take turns (para to). **~o** m turn; (de trabajo) shift. **de ~** on duty

turquesa f turquoise

Turquía f Turkey

turrón m nougat

tutear vt address as tú. **~se** vpr be on familiar terms

tutela f (Jurid) guardianship; (fig) protection

tutor m guardian; (en enseñanza) form master

tuve vb véase TENER

tuyo adj & pron yours. **un amigo ~** a friend of yours

· · · · · · · · · · · · · · · · · · · ·

Uu

· · · · · · · · · · · · · · · · · · · ·

u conj or

ubic|ar vt (LAm) place; (localizar) find. **~arse** vpr (LAm) be situated; (orientarse) find one's way around

ubre f udder

Ud. abrev (Usted) you

UE abrev (Unión Europea) EU

uf int phew!; (de repugnancia) ugh!

ufan|arse vpr be proud (con, de of); (jactarse) boast (con, de about). **~o** adj proud

úlcera f ulcer

últimamente adv (recientemente) recently; (finalmente) finally

ultim|ar vt complete; (LAm, matar) kill. **~átum** m ultimatum

último adj last; (más reciente) latest; (más lejano) furthest; (más alto) top; (más bajo) bottom; (definitivo) final. ● m last one. **estar en las últimas** be on one's last legs; (sin dinero) be down to one's last penny. **por ~** finally. **vestido a la última** dressed in the latest fashion

ultra adj ultra, extreme
ultraj|ante adj offensive. ～**e** m insult, outrage
ultramar m. de ～ overseas; (productos) foreign. ～**inos** mpl groceries. **tienda de** ～**s** grocer's (shop) (Brit), grocery store (Amer)
ultranza. **a** ～ (con decisión) decisively; (extremo) out-and-out
ultravioleta adj invar ultraviolet
umbilical adj umbilical
umbral m threshold

---

un , una *artículo indefinido*

❗ The masculine article **un** is also used before feminine nouns which begin with stressed **a** or **ha**, e.g. **un alma piadosa, un hada madrina**

••••▶ (en sing) a; (antes de sonido vocálico) an. **un perro** a dog. **una hora** an hour

••••▶ unos, unas (cantidad incierta) some. **compré ～os libros** I bought some books. (cantidad cierta) **tiene ～os ojos preciosos** she has beautiful eyes. **tiene ～os hijos muy buenos** her children are very good. (en aproximaciones) about. **en ～as 3 horas** in about 3 hours

➡ For further information see **uno**

un|ánime adj unanimous. ～**animidad** f unanimity
undécimo adj eleventh
ungüento m ointment
únic|amente adv only. ～**o** adj only; (fig, incomparable) unique
unicornio m unicorn

---

unid|ad f unit; (cualidad) unity. ～**ad de disco** disk drive. ～**o** adj united
unifica|ción f unification. ～**r** 🔢 vt unite, unify
uniform|ar vt standardize. ～**e** adj & m uniform. ～**idad** f uniformity
unilateral adj unilateral
uni|ón f union; (cualidad) unity; (Tec) joint. ～**r** vt join; mix (líquidos). ～**rse** vpr join together; (caminos) converge; (compañías) merge
unísono m unison. **al** ～ in unison
univers|al adj universal. ～**idad** f university. ～**itario** adj university. ～**o** m universe

---

uno , una

● *adjetivo*

Note that **uno** becomes **un** before masculine nouns

one. **una peseta** one peseta. **un dólar** one dollar. **ni una persona** not one person, not a single person. **treinta y un años** thirty one years

● *pronombre*

••••▶ one. ～ **es mío** one (of them) is mine. **es la una** it's one o'clock. **se ayudan el** ～ **al otro** they help one another, they help each other. **lo que sienten el** ～ **por el otro** what they feel for each other

••••▶ (fam, alguien) someone. **le pregunté a** ～ I asked someone

••••▶ unos, unas some. **no tenía vasos así es que le presté** ～**s** she didn't have any glasses so I lent her some. **a** ～**s les** gusta, a otros no some like it, others don't. los ~s a los otros one another, each other ····▷ (impersonal) you. ~ no sabe qué decir you don't know what to say

untar vt grease; (cubrir) spread; (fig, fam, sobornar) bribe

uña f nail; (de animal) claw; (casco) hoof

uranio m uranium

Urano m Uranus

urban|idad f politeness. ~ismo m town planning. ~ización f development. ~izar 10 vt develop. ~o adj urban

urbe f big city

urdir vt (fig) plot

urg|encia f urgency; (emergencia) emergency. ~encias A & E, (Amer) emergency room. ~ente adj urgent; (carta) express. ~ir 14 vi be urgent.

urinario m urinal

urna f urn; (Pol) ballot box

urraca f magpie

URSS abrev (Historia) USSR

Uruguay m. el ~ Uruguay

uruguayo adj & m Uruguayan

us|ado adj (con estar) used; (ropa etc) worn; (con ser) secondhand. ~ar vt use; (llevar) wear. ~arse vpr (LAm) be in fashion. ~o m use; (costumbre) custom. al ~o de in the style of

usted pron you. ~es you

usual adj usual

usuario adj user

usur|a f usury. ~ero m usurer

usurpar vt usurp

utensilio m utensil; (herramienta) tool

útero m womb, uterus

útil adj useful. ~es mpl implements; (equipo) equipment

utili|dad f usefulness. ~dades fpl (LAm) profits. ~zación f use, utilization. ~zar 10 vt use, utilize

utopía f Utopia

uva f grape. ~ pasa raisin. mala ~ bad mood

Vv

vaca f cow. carne de ~ beef

vacaciones fpl holiday(s), vacation(s) (Amer). de ~ on holiday, on vacation (Amer)

vacante adj vacant. ● f vacancy

vaciar 20 vt empty; (ahuecar) hollow out; (en molde) cast

vacila|ción f hesitation. ~nte adj unsteady; (fig) hesitant. ~r vi hesitate (⚡, bromear) tease; (LAm, divertirse) have fun

vacío adj empty; (frívolo) frivolous. ● m empty space; (estado) emptiness; (en física) vacuum; (fig) void

vacuna f vaccine. ~ción f vaccination. ~r vt vaccinate

vacuno adj bovine

vad|ear vt ford. ~o m ford

vaga|bundear vi wander. ~bundo adj vagrant; (perro) stray. niño ~ m tramp, vagrant. ~ncia f vagrancy; (fig) laziness. ~r 12 vi wander (about)

vagina f vagina

vago adj vague; (holgazán) lazy. ● m layabout

vagón m coach, carriage; (de mercancías) wagon. ~ón restaurante dining-car. ~oneta f small freight wagon; (Mex, para pasajeros) van

vaho m breath; (vapor) steam. ~s mpl inhalation

vain|a f sheath; (de semillas) pod. ~illa f vanilla

vaivén m swinging; (de tren etc) rocking. ~enes mpl (fig, de suerte) swings

vajilla f dishes, crockery

vale m voucher; (pagaré) IOU. ~dero adj valid

valenciano adj from Valencia

valentía f bravery, courage

valer 42 vt be worth; (costar) cost; (fig, significar) mean. ● vi be worth; (costar) cost; (servir) be of use; (ser valedero) be valid; (estar permitido) be allowed. ~ la pena be worthwhile, be worth it. ¿cuánto vale? how much is it? no ~ para nada be useless. eso no me vale (Mex, fam) I don't give a damn about that. ¡vale! all right!, OK! 🔟

valeroso adj courageous

valgo vb véase VALER

valía f worth

validez f validity. dar ~ a validate

válido adj valid

valiente adj brave; (en sentido irónico) fine. ● m brave person

valija f suitcase. ~ diplomática diplomatic bag

valioso adj valuable

valla f fence; (en atletismo) hurdle

valle m valley

val|or m value, worth; (coraje) courage. objetos mpl de ~or valuables. sin ~or worthless. ~ores mpl securities. ~oración f valu-

ation. ~orar vt value

vals m invar waltz

válvula f valve

vampiro m vampire

vanagloriarse vpr boast

vandalismo m vandalism

vándalo m & f vandal

vanguardia f vanguard. de ~ (en arte, música etc) avant-garde

van|idad f vanity. ~idoso adj vain. ~o adj vain; (inútil) futile; (palabras) empty. en ~ in vain

vapor m steam, vapour; (Naut) steamer. al ~ (Culin) steamed. ~izador m vaporizer. ~izar 🔟 vaporize

vaquer|o m cowherd, cowboy. ~os mpl jeans

vara f stick; (de autoridad) staff (medida) yard

varar vi run aground

varia|ble adj & f variable. ~ción f variation. ~do adj varied. ~nte f variant; (Auto) by-pass. ~ntes fpl hors d'oeuvres. ~r 20 vt change; (dar variedad a) vary. ● vi vary; (cambiar) change

varicela f chickenpox

variedad f variety

varilla f stick; (de metal) rod

varios adj several

varita f wand

variz f (pl varices, (LAm) várices) varicose vein

var|ón adj male. ● m man; (niño) boy. ~onil adj manly

vasco adj & m Basque

vaselina f Vaseline (P), petroleum jelly

vasija f vessel, pot

vaso m glass; (en anatomía) vessel

vástago m shoot; (descendiente) descendant

v

vasto adj vast

vaticin|ar vt forecast. **~io** m prediction, forecast

vatio m watt

vaya vb véase **IR**

Vd. abrev (Usted) you

vecin|al adj local. **~dad** f neighbourhood; (vecinos) residents; (Mex, edificio) tenement house. **~dario** m neighbourhood; (vecinos) residents. **~o** adj neighbouring. ● m neighbour; (de barrio, edificio) resident

ve|da f close season. **~do** m reserve. **~do de caza** game reserve. **~r** vt prohibit

vega f fertile plain

vegeta|ción f vegetation. **~l** adj & m plant, vegetable. **~r** vi grow; (persona) vegetate. **~riano** adj & m vegetarian

vehemente adj vehement

vehículo m vehicle

veinte adj & m twenty

veinti|cinco adj & m twenty-five. **~cuatro** adj & m twenty-four. **~dós** adj & m twenty-two. **~nueve** adj & m twenty-nine. **~ocho** adj & m twenty-eight. **~séis** adj & m twenty-six. **~siete** adj & m twenty-seven. **~trés** adj & m twenty-three. **~uno** adj & m (delante de nombre masculino **veintiún**) twenty-one

vejación f humiliation

vejar vt ill-treat

veje|storio m old crock; (LAm, cosa) old relic. **~z** f old age

vejiga f bladder

vela f (Naut) sail; (de cera) candle; (vigilia) vigil. **pasar la noche en ~** have a sleepless night

velada f evening

vela|do adj veiled; (Foto) exposed.

~r vt watch over; hold a wake over (difunto); (encubrir) veil; (Foto) expose. ● vi stay awake. **~r por** look after. **~rse** vpr (Foto) get exposed

velero m sailing-ship

veleta f weather vane

vell|o m hair; (pelusa) down. **~ón** m fleece

velo m veil

veloc|idad f speed; (Auto, Mec) gear. **a toda ~idad** at full speed. **~ímetro** m speedometer. **~ista** m & f sprinter

velódromo m cycle-track

veloz adj fast, quick

vena f vein; (en madera) grain. **estar de/en ~** be in the mood

venado m deer; (Culin) venison

vencedor adj winning. ● m winner

venc|er 图 vt defeat; (superar) overcome. ● vi win; (pasaporte) expire. **~erse** vpr collapse; (LAm, pasaporte) expire. **~ido** adj beaten; (pasaporte) expired; (Com, atrasado) in arrears. **darse por ~ido** give up. **~imiento** m due date; (de pasaporte) expiry date

venda f bandage. **~je** m dressing. **~r** vt bandage

vendaval m gale

vende|dor adj selling. ● m seller; (en tienda) salesperson. **~dor ambulante** pedlar. **~r** vt sell. **se ~** for sale. **~rse** vpr (persona) sell out

vendimia f grape harvest

veneciano adj Venetian

veneno m poison; (malevolencia) venom. **~so** adj poisonous

venera|ble adj venerable. **~ción** f reverence. **~r** vt revere

venéreo adj venereal

venezolano *adj & m* Venezuelan

Venezuela *f* Venezuela

venga|nza *f* revenge. **~r** 12 *vt* avenge. **~rse** *vpr* take revenge (de, por for) (en on). **~tivo** *adj* vindictive

vengo *vb véase* **VENIR**

venia *f* (*permiso*) permission. **~l** *adj* venial

veni|da *f* arrival; (*vuelta*) return. **~dero** *adj* coming. **~r** 53 *vi* come. **~r bien** suit. **la semana que viene** next week. **¡venga!** come on!

venta *f* sale; (*posada*) inn. **en ~** for sale

ventaj|a *f* advantage. **~oso** *adj* advantageous

ventan|a *f* (*inc informática*) window; (*de la nariz*) nostril. **~illa** *f* window

ventarrón *m* 1 strong wind

ventila|ción *f* ventilation. **~dor** *m* fan. **~r** *vt* air

vent|isca *f* blizzard. **~olera** *f* gust of wind. **~osa** *f* sucker. **~osidad** *f* wind, flatulence. **~oso** *adj* windy

ventrílocuo *m* ventriloquist

ventur|a *f* happiness; (*suerte*) luck. **a la ~a** with no fixed plan. **echar la buena ~a a** uno tell s.o.'s fortune. **por ~** fortunately; (*acaso*) perhaps. **~oso** *adj* happy, lucky

Venus *m* Venus

ver 43 *vt* see; watch (television). **•vi** see. **a mi modo de ~** in my view. **a ~** let's see. **dejarse ~** show. **no lo puedo ~** I can't stand him. **no tener nada que ~ con** have nothing to do with. **vamos a ~** let's see. **ya lo veo** that's obvious. **ya ~emos** we'll see. **~se** *vpr*

see o.s.; (*encontrarse*) find o.s.; (*dos personas*) meet; (*LAm, parecer*) look

veran|eante *m & f* holidaymaker, vacationer (*Amer*). **~ear** *vi* spend one's summer holiday. **~eo** *m*. **ir de ~eo** spend one's summer holiday. **lugar** *m* **de ~eo** summer resort. **~iego** *adj* summer. **~o** *m* summer

vera|s. **de ~** really; (*verdadero*) real. **~z** *adj* truthful

verbal *adj* verbal

verbena *f* (*fiesta*) fair; (*baile*) dance

verbo *m* verb. **~so** *adj* verbose

verdad *f* truth. **¿~?** isn't it?, aren't they?, won't it? etc. **a decir ~** to tell the truth. **de ~** really. **~eramente** *adv* really. **~ero** *adj* true; (*fig*) real

verd|e *adj* green; (*fruta*) unripe; (*chiste*) dirty. **•m** green; (*hierba*) grass. **~or** *m* greenness

verdugo *m* executioner; (*fig*) tyrant

verdu|lería *f* greengrocer's (shop). **~lero** *m* greengrocer

vereda *f* path; (*LAm, acera*) pavement (*Brit*), sidewalk (*Amer*)

veredicto *m* verdict

verg|onzoso *adj* shameful; (*tímido*) shy. **~üenza** *f* shame; (*bochorno*) embarrassment. **¡es una ~üenza!** it's a disgrace! **me da ~üenza** I'm ashamed; (*cohibido*) embarrassed. **tener ~üenza** be ashamed/embarrassed

verídico *adj* true

verifica|ción *f* verification. **~r** 7 *vt* check. **~rse** *vpr* take place; (*resultar verdad*) come true

verja *f* (*cerca*) railings; (*puerta*) iron gate

vermú m, vermut m vermouth

verosímil adj likely; (relato) credible

verruga f wart

versa|do adj versed. ~r vi. ~ sobre deal with

versátil adj versatile; (fig) fickle

versión f version; (traducción) translation

verso m verse; (poema) poem

vértebra f vertebra

verte|dero m dump; (desagüe) drain ~r **1** vt pour; (derramar) spill ● vi flow

vertical adj & f vertical

vértice f vertex

vertiente f slope

vertiginoso adj dizzy

vértigo m (Med) vertigo. dar ~ make dizzy

vesícula f vesicle. ~ biliar gall bladder

vespertino adj evening

vestíbulo m hall; (de hotel, teatro) foyer

vestido m dress

vestigio m trace. ~s mpl remains

vest|imenta f clothes. ~ir **5** vt (llevar) wear; dress (niño etc). ● vi dress. ~ir de wear. ~irse vpr get dressed. ~irse de wear; (disfrazarse) dress up as. ~uario m wardrobe; (en gimnasio etc) changing room (Brit), locker room (Amer)

vetar vt veto

veterano adj veteran

veterinari|a f veterinary science. ~o adj veterinary. ● m vet **1**, veterinary surgeon (Brit), veterinarian (Amer)

veto m veto

vez f time; (turno) turn. a la ~ at the same time. alguna ~ some-

times; (en preguntas) ever. algunas veces sometimes. a su ~ in turn. a veces sometimes. cada ~ each time. cada ~ más more and more. de una ~ in one go. de una ~ para siempre once and for all. de ~ en cuando from time to time. dos veces twice. en ~ de instead of. érase una ~, había una ~ once upon a time there was. otra ~ again. pocas veces, rara ~ seldom. una ~ (que) once

vía f road; (Rail) line; (en anatomía) tract; (fig) way. ~ férrea railway (Brit), railroad (Amer). ~ rápida fast lane. estar en ~s de be in the process of. ● prep via. ~ aérea by air. ~ de comunicación means of communication.

viab|ilidad f viability. ~le adj viable

viaducto m viaduct

viaj|ante m & f commercial traveller. ~ar vi travel. ~e m journey; (corto) trip. ~e de novios honeymoon. ¡buen ~e! have a good journey!. estar de ~e be away. salir de ~e go on a trip. ~ero m traveller; (pasajero) passenger

víbora f viper

vibra|ción f vibration. ~nte adj vibrant. ~r vt/i vibrate

vicario m vicar

viceversa adv vice versa

vici|ado adj (texto) corrupt; (aire) stale. ~ar vt corrupt; (estropear) spoil. ~o m vice; (mala costumbre) bad habit. ~oso adj dissolute; (círculo) vicious

víctima f victim; (de un accidente) casualty

victori|a f victory. ~oso adj victorious

vid f vine

vida f life; (*duración*) lifetime. ¡~ mía! my darling! **de por ~** for life. **en mi ~** never (in my life). **estar con ~** be still alive

vídeo m, (*LAm*) **video** m video; (*cinta*) videotape; (*aparato*) video recorder

videojuego m video game

vidri|**era** f stained glass window; (*puerta*) glass door; (*LAm, escaparate*) shop window. **~ería** f glass works. **~ero** m glazier. **~o** m glass; (*LAm, en ventana*) window pane. **limpiar los ~os** clean the windows. **~oso** adj glassy

vieira f scallop

viejo adj old. ● m old person

viene vb véase VENIR

viento m wind. **hacer ~** be windy

vientre m stomach; (*cavidad*) abdomen; (*matriz*) womb; (*intestino*) bowels; (*de vasija etc*) belly

viernes m invar Friday. **V~ Santo** Good Friday

viga f beam; (*de metal*) girder

vigen|**cia** f validity. **~te** adj valid; (*ley*) in force. **entrar en ~cia** come into force

vigésimo adj twentieth

vigía f watch-tower. ● m & f (*persona*) lookout

vigil|**ancia** f vigilance. **~ante** adj vigilant. ● m & f security guard; (*nocturno*) watchman. **~ar** vt keep an eye on. ● vi be vigilant; (*vigía*) keep watch. **~ia** f vigil; (*Relig*) fasting

vigor m vigour; (*vigencia*) force. **entrar en ~** come into force. **~oso** adj vigorous

vil adj vile. **~eza** f vileness; (*acción*) vile deed

villa f (*casa*) villa; (*Historia*) town. **la V~** Madrid

villancico m (Christmas) carol

villano adj villanous; (*Historia*) peasant

vilo. **en ~** in the air

vinagre m vinegar. **~ra** f vinegar bottle. **~ras** fpl cruet. **~ta** f vinaigrette

vincular vt bind

vínculo m tie, bond

vindicar [7] vt (*rehabilitar*) vindicate

vine vb véase VENIR

vinicult|**or** m wine-grower. **~ura** f wine growing

vino m wine. **~ de la casa** house wine. **~ de mesa** table wine. **~ tinto** red wine

viña f vineyard. **~ atero** m (*LAm*) wine-grower. **~edo** m vineyard

viola f viola

viola|**ción** f violation; (*de una mujer*) rape. **~r** vt violate; break (*ley*); rape (*mujer*)

violen|**cia** f violence; (*fuerza*) force. **~tarse** vpr get embarrassed. **~to** adj violent; (*fig*) awkward

violeta adj invar & f violet

viol|**ín** m violin. ● m & f (*músico*) violinist. **~inista** m & f violinist. **~ón** m double bass. **~onc(h)elista** m & f cellist. **~onc(h)elo** m cello

vira|**je** m turn. **~r** vt turn. ● vi turn; (*fig*) change direction. **~r bruscamente** swerve

virg|**en** adj. **ser ~en** be a virgin. ● f virgin. **~inal** adj virginal. **~inidad** f virginity

Virgo m Virgo

viril adj virile. **~idad** f virility

virtu|**al** adj virtual. **~d** f virtue; (*capacidad*) power. **en ~ de** by virtue of. **~oso** adj virtuous. ● m

v

virtuoso

viruela f smallpox

virulento adj virulent

virus m invar virus

visa f (LAm) visa. **~ado** m visa. **~r** vt endorse

vísceras fpl entrails

viscoso adj viscous

visera f visor; (de gorra) peak

visib|ilidad f visibility. **~le** adj visible

visillo m (cortina) net curtain

visi|ón f vision; (vista) sight. **~onario** adj & m visionary

visita f visit; (visitante) visitor; (invitado) guest; (Internet) hit. **~nte** m & f visitor. **~r** vt visit

vislumbrar vt glimpse

viso m sheen; (aspecto) appearance

visón m mink

visor m viewfinder

víspera f day before, eve

vista f sight, vision; (aspecto, mirada) look; (panorama) view. apartar la ~ look away. a primera ~, a simple ~ at first sight. con ~s a with a view to. en ~ de in view of. estar a la ~ be obvious. hacer la ~ gorda turn a blind eye. perder la ~ lose one's sight. tener a la ~ have in front of one. volver la ~ atrás look back. **~zo** m glance. dar/echar un **~zo** a glance at

visto adj seen; (poco original) common (considerado) considered. ~ que since. bien ~ acceptable. está ~ que it's obvious that. mal ~ unacceptable. por lo ~ apparently. ●vb véase VESTIR ~ **bueno** m approval. **~so** adj colourful, bright

visual adj visual. **campo ~** field of vision

vital adj vital. **~icio** adj life; (cargo) held for life. **~idad** f vitality

vitamina f vitamin

viticult|or m wine-grower. **~ura** f wine growing

vitorear vt cheer

vítreo adj vitreous

vitrina f showcase; (en casa) glass cabinet; (LAm, escaparate) shop window

viud|a f widow. **~ez** f widowhood. **~o** adj widowed. ● m widower

viva m cheer. **~cidad** f liveliness. **~mente** adv vividly. **~z** adj lively

víveres mpl supplies

vivero m nursery; (de peces) hatchery; (de moluscos) bed

viveza f vividness; (de inteligencia) sharpness; (de carácter) liveliness

vívido adj vivid

vividor m pleasure seeker

vivienda f housing; (casa) house; (piso) flat (Brit), apartment (esp Amer). **sin ~** homeless

viviente adj living

vivificar 7 vt (animar) enliven

vivir vt live through. ●vi live; (estar vivo) be alive. ¡viva! hurray! ¡viva el rey! long live the king! ● m life. ~ de live on. de mal ~ dissolute

vivisección f vivisection

vivo adj alive; (viviente) living; (color) bright; (listo) clever, (fig) lively. ● m sharp operator

vocab|lo m word. **~ulario** m vocabulary

vocación f vocation

vocal adj vocal. ● f vowel. ● m & f member. **~ista** m & f vocalist

voce|ar vt call (mercancías); (fig)

271

proclaim; (*Mex*) page (persona). ●
vi shout. ~**río** m shouting. ~**ro**
(*LAm*) spokesperson

vociferar vi shout

vola|dor adj flying. ● m rocket.
~**ndas**. en ~**ndas** in the air.
~**nte** adj flying. ● m (*Auto*)
steering-wheel; (*nota*) note; (*rehi-
lete*) shuttlecock. ~**r** 🛈 vt blow up.
● vi fly; (*fam, desaparecer*) disap-
pear

volátil adj volatile

volcán m volcano. ~**ico** adj vol-
canic

volcar 🛈 & 🛈 vt knock over; (*va-
ciar*) empty out; turn over (molde).
● vi overturn. ~**se** vpr fall over; (*ve-
hículo*) overturn; (*fig*) do one's ut-
most. ~**se** en throw o.s. into

vóleibol m, (*Mex*) **volibol** m vol-
leyball

voltaje m voltage

volte|ar vt turn over; (*en el aire*)
toss; ring (campanas); (*LAm*) turn
over (colchón etc). ~**arse** vpr (*LAm*)
turn around; (*carro*) overturn.
~**reta** f somersault

voltio m volt

voluble adj (*fig*) fickle

volum|en m volume. ~**inoso** adj
voluminous

voluntad f will; (*fuerza de volun-
tad*) willpower; (*deseo*) wish; (*inten-
ción*) intention. **buena** ~ goodwill.
mala ~ ill will

voluntario adj voluntary. ● m
volunteer

voluptuoso adj voluptuous

volver 🛈 (*pp* vuelto) vt turn; (*de
arriba a abajo*) turn over; (*devolver*)
restore. ● vi return; (*fig*) revert. ~
a hacer algo do sth again. ~ **en
sí** come round. ~**se** vpr turn

round; (*hacerse*) become

vomit|ar vt bring up. ● vi be sick,
vomit. ~**ivo** adj disgusting

vómito m vomit; (*acción*) vomit-
ing

voraz adj voracious

vos pron (*LAm*) you. ~**otros** pron
you; (*reflexivo*) yourselves

vot|ación f voting; (*voto*) vote.
~**ante** m & f voter. ~**ar** vt vote for.
● vi vote (por for). ~**o** m vote;
(*Relig*) vow

voy vb véase **IR**

voz f voice; (*rumor*) rumour; (*pala-
bra*) word. ~ **pública** public opin-
ion. **a media** ~ softly. **a una** ~
unanimously. **dar voces** shout. **en**
~ **alta** loudly

vuelco m upset. **el corazón me
dio un** ~ my heart missed a beat

vuelo m flight; (*acción*) flying; (*de
ropa*) flare. **al** ~ in flight; (*fig*) in
passing

vuelta f turn; (*curva*) bend;
(*paseo*) walk; (*revolución*) revolu-
tion; (*regreso*) return; (*dinero*)
change. **a la** ~ on one's return. **a
la** ~ **de la esquina** round the cor-
ner. **dar la** ~ **al mundo** go round
the world. **dar una** ~ go for a
walk. **estar de** ~ be back

vuelvo vb véase **VOLVER**

vuestro adj your. ● pron yours. **un
amigo** ~ a friend of yours

vulg|ar adj vulgar; (*persona*) com-
mon. ~**aridad** f vulgarity. ~**ari-
zar** 🛈 vt popularize. ~**o** m com-
mon people

vulnerable adj vulnerable

Ww

wáter /'(g)water/ m toilet
Web m /'(g)web/. **el ~** the Web
whisky /'(g)wiski/ m whisky

Xx

xenofobia f xenophobia
xilófono m xylophone

Yy

y conj and
ya adv already; (ahora) now; (con negativos) any more; (para afirmar) yes, sure; (en seguida) immediately; (pronto) soon. **~ mismo** (LAm) right away. ● int of course! ● no **no longer. ~ que** since. **¡~!, ~! oh** sure!
yacaré m (LAm) alligator
yac|er 44 vi lie. **~imiento** m deposit; (de petróleo) oilfield
yanqui m & f American, Yank(ee)
yate m yacht
yegua f mare
yelmo m helmet
yema f (en botánica) bud; (de huevo) yolk; (golosina) sweet. **~ del dedo** fingertip

Zz

yerba f (LAm) grass; (Med) herb
yergo vb véase ERGUIR
yermo adj uninhabited; (no cultivable) barren. ● m wasteland
yerno m son-in-law
yerro m mistake. ● vb véase ERRAR
yeso m plaster; (mineral) gypsum
yo pron l. **~ mismo** myself. **¿quién, ~?** who, me? **soy ~** it's me
yodo m iodine
yoga m yoga
yogur m yog(h)urt
yuca f yucca
yugo m yoke
Yugoslavia f Yugoslavia
yugoslavo adj & m Yugoslav
yunque m anvil
yunta f yoke

zafarrancho m (confusión) mess; (riña) quarrel
zafarse vpr escape; get out of (obligación etc); (Mex, dislocarse) dislocate
zafiro m sapphire
zaga f rear; (en deportes) defence. **a la ~** behind
zaguán m hall
zaherir 4 vt hurt
zahorí m dowser
zaino adj (caballo) chestnut; (vaca) black
zalamer|ía f flattery. **~o** adj flattering. ● m flatterer
zamarra f (piel) sheepskin; (prenda) sheepskin jacket

zamarrear vt shake

zamba f South American dance

zambulli|da f dive; (baño) dip. **~rse** vpr dive

zamparse vpr gobble up

zanahoria f carrot

zancad|a f stride. **~illa** f trip. hacer una **~illa** a uno trip s.o. up

zanc|o m stilt. **~udo** adj long-legged; (ave) wading. ● m (LAm) mosquito

zanganear vi idle

zángano m drone. ● m & f (persona) idler

zangolotear vt shake. ● vi rattle; (persona) fidget

zanja f ditch; (para tuberías etc) trench. **~r** vt (fig) settle

zapat|ear vi tap with one's feet. **~ería** f shoe shop; (arte) shoe-making. **~ero** m shoemaker; (el que remienda zapatos) cobbler. **~illa** f slipper; (de deportes) trainer. **~illa de ballet** ballet shoe. **~o** m shoe

zarand|a f sieve. **~ear** vt (sacudir) shake

zarcillo m earring

zarpa f paw

zarpar vi set sail, weigh anchor

zarza f bramble. **~mora** f black-berry

zarzuela f Spanish operetta

zarzuela A musical drama consisting of alternating passages of dialogue, songs, choruses, and dancing that originated in Spain in the seventeenth century. Also popular in Latin America, its name derives from the Palacio de la Zarzuela, the Madrid palace where the Royal family now lives.

zigzag m zigzag. **~uear** vi zigzag

zinc m zinc

zócalo m skirting-board; (pedestal) plinth; (Mex, plaza) main square

zodiaco m, **zodíaco** m zodiac

zona f zone; (área) area

zoo m zoo. **~logía** f zoology. **~lógico** adj zoological

zoólogo m zoologist

zopenco adj stupid. ● m idiot

zoquete m blockhead

zorr|a f vixen. **~illo** m (LAm) skunk.. **~o** m fox

zorzal m thrush

zozobra f (fig) anxiety. **~r** vi founder

zueco m clog

zumb|ar vt ① give (golpe etc). ● vi buzz. **~ido** m buzzing

zumo m juice

zurci|do m darning. **~r** ⑨ vt darn

zurdo adj left-handed; (mano) left

zurrar vt (fig, fam, dar golpes) beat (up)

zutano m so-and-so

Phrasefinder/Frases útiles

Useful phrases · Expresiones útiles

yes, please/no, thank you	sí, por favor/no, gracias
sorry	perdone
excuse me	disculpe
I'm sorry, I don't understand	perdone, pero no le entiendo
you're welcome!	¡de nada!, ¡no hay de qué!

Meeting people · Saludos

hello/goodbye	hola/adiós
how are you?	¿cómo está usted?
nice to meet you	mucho gusto

Asking questions	**Preguntas**
do you speak English/Spanish?	¿habla usted inglés/español?
what's your name?	¿cómo se llama?
where are you from?	¿de dónde es?
how much is it?	¿cuánto es?
where is...?	¿dónde está...?
can I have...?	¿me da...?
would you like...?	¿quiere usted...?

About you	**Información personal**
my name is...	me llamo...
I'm American/I'm Mexican	soy americano/-a/mexicano/-a
I don't speak Spanish/English	no hablo español/inglés
I live near Seville/Chester	vivo cerca de Sevilla/Chester
I'm a student	soy estudiante
I work in an office	trabajo en una oficina

Emergencies	**Emergencias**
can you help me, please?	¿me ayuda, por favor?
I'm lost	me he perdido
I'm ill	no me encuentro bien
call an ambulance	llamen a una ambulancia

Reading signs	**Carteles y señales**
no entry	prohibido el paso
no smoking	prohibido fumar
fire exit	salida de emergencia
for sale	en venta
push	empujar
pull	tirar, (*LAm*) jalar
press	apretar, pulsar

Going Places/Viajes

By rail and underground | En tren y en metro

where can I buy a ticket?	¿dónde se sacan los billetes, (*LAm*) boletos?
what time is the next train to Barcelona/New York?	¿a qué hora sale el próximo tren para Barcelona/Nueva York?
do I have to change?	¿tengo que hacer algún transbordo?
can I take my bike on the train?	¿puedo llevar la bicicleta en el tren?
which platform for the train to San Sebastian/Bath?	¿de qué andén sale el tren para San Sebastián/Bath?
a single/return, (*Amer*) round trip to Baltimore/Valencia, please	un billete, (*LAm*) boleto de ida/ida y vuelta para Baltimore/Valencia, por favor
I'd like an all-day ticket	quiero un billete, (*LAm*) boleto que valga para todo el día
I'd like to reserve a seat	quisiera reservar una plaza
is there a student/senior citizen discount?	¿hacen descuentos para estudiantes/jubilados?
is this the train for Seville/Manchester?	¿éste es el tren para Sevilla/Manchester?
what time does the train arrive in Madrid/Washington?	¿a qué hora llega el tren a Madrid/Washington?
have I missed the train?	¿he perdido el tren?
which line do I need to take for the Prado/London Eye?	¿qué línea se coge, (*LAm*) toma para ir al Prado/London Eye?

el tren va a llegar al andén número 2	the train is arriving at platform 2
hay un tren que sale para Madrid a las 10	there's a train to Madrid at 10 o'clock
el tren llegará con retraso/puntual	the train is delayed/on time
la próxima parada es..., (LAm) el próximo paradero es...	the next stop is...
su billete, (LAm) boleto no es válido	your ticket isn't valid

MORE USEFUL WORDS:	MÁS PALABRAS ÚTILES:
underground station, (Amer) subway station	estación de metro
timetable	horario
connection	transbordo
seat reservation	reserva de plaza/asiento
express train	tren expreso
local train	tren de cercanías
high-speed train	tren de alta velocidad

DID YOU KNOW...?	¿SABÍAS QUE...?
In some of the larger Spanish train stations, you will need to take a ticket and wait for your number to be called before you can speak to a clerk.	En Inglaterra se puede ir del aeropuerto de Heathrow al centro de Londres en menos de veinte minutos gracias a un tren que se llama Heathrow Express.

At the airport — En el aeropuerto

when's the next flight to Paris/Rome?	¿cuándo sale el próximo vuelo para París/Roma?
what time do I have to check in?	¿a qué hora tengo que facturar, (*LAm*) chequear, (*Mex*) registrar el equipaje?
where do I check in?	¿dónde puedo facturar, (*LAm*) chequear, (*Mex*) registrar el equipaje?
I'd like to confirm my flight	quisiera confirmar mi vuelo
I'd like a window seat/an aisle seat	quisiera un asiento de ventanilla/pasillo
I want to change/cancel my reservation	quiero cambiar/cancelar mi reserva
can I carry this in my hand, (*Amer*) carry-on luggage?	¿puedo llevar ésto como equipaje de mano?
my luggage hasn't arrived	mi equipaje no ha llegado

YOU WILL HEAR:	OIRÁS:
el vuelo BA7057 saldrá con retraso/ha sido cancelado	flight BA7057 is delayed/cancelled
vaya a la puerta (de embarque), (*Mex*) sala de abordar 29	please go to gate 29
su tarjeta de embarque, (*Mex*) pase de abordar, por favor	your boarding card, please

MORE USEFUL WORDS:	MÁS PALABRAS ÚTILES:
arrivals	llegadas
departures	salidas
baggage claim	recogida de equipajes

Asking how to get there　Cómo llegar a los sitios

how do I get to the airport?	¿cómo se llega al aeropuerto?
how long will it take to get there?	¿cuánto tiempo se tarda en llegar?
how far is it from here?	¿a qué distancia está?
which bus do I take for the cathedral?	¿qué autobús debo coger, (*LAm*) tomar, para ir a la catedral?
where does this bus go?	¿a dónde va este autobús?
does this bus/train go to...?	¿éste autobús/tren va a ...?
where should I get off?	¿dónde me tengo que bajar?
how much is it to the town centre?	¿cuánto cuesta ir al centro de la ciudad?
what time is the last bus?	¿a qué hora sale el último autobús?
where's the nearest underground station, (*Amer*) subway station?	¿dónde está la estación de metro más cercana?
is this the turning for...?	¿es ésta la calle para...?
can you call me a taxi?	¿me puede pedir un taxi?

YOU WILL HEAR:	OIRÁS:
tome la primera (calle) a la derecha	take the first turning, (*Amer*) turn on the right
al llegar al semáforo/después de pasar la iglesia, gire a la izquierda	turn left at the traffic lights/ just past the church

Disabled travellers　Viajeros discapacitados

I'm disabled	soy minusválido
is there wheelchair access?	¿hay un acceso para sillas de ruedas?
are guide dogs permitted?	¿se permite la entrada de perros lazarillo?

On the road · Por carretera

where's the nearest petrol station, (*Amer*) gas station?	¿dónde está la gasolinera más cercana?
what's the best way to get there?	¿cuál es la mejor forma de llegar?
I've got a puncture, (*Amer*) flat tire	he tenido un pinchazo, (*Mex*) se nos ponchó una llanta
I'd like to hire, (*Amer*) rent a bike/car	quisiera alquilar, (*Mex*) rentar una bicicleta/un coche
where can I park around here?	¿dónde puedo aparcar por aquí?
there's been an accident	ha habido un accidente
my car's broken down	se me ha estropeado el coche, (*LAm*) se me descompuso el carro
the car won't start	el coche, (*LAm*) carro no arranca
where's the nearest garage?	¿dónde está el taller más cercano?
pump number six, please	surtidor, (*Andes*, *Ven*) bomba número seis, por favor
fill it up, please	llénelo, por favor
can I wash my car here?	¿tienen túnel de lavado?
can I park here?	¿aquí se puede aparcar, (*LAm*) estacionar, (*Col*) parquear?
there's a problem with the brakes/lights	les pasa algo a los frenos/los faros
the clutch/gearstick isn't working	no funciona el embrague/cambio de marchas, (*LAm*) la palanca de cambios, (*Mex*) de velocidades
take the third exit off the roundabout, (*Amer*) traffic circle	en la rotonda, vaya por la tercera salida
turn right at the next junction	gire a la derecha en el próximo cruce
slow down	vaya más despacio
I can't drink – I'm driving	tengo que conducir, (*LAm*) manejar así que no puedo beber, (*LAm*) tomar
can I buy a road map here?	¿venden mapas de carreteras?

YOU WILL HEAR:	OIRÁS:
enséñeme su carnet de conducir, (LAm) licencia, (Col) pase, (Chi) carné, (Ur) libreta de manejar, (Per) su brevete, (Arg) registro	can I see your driving licence?
tiene que rellenar un parte de accidente	you need to fill out an accident report
esta carretera es de un solo sentido	this road is one-way
está prohibido aparcar, (LAm) estacionar aquí	you can't park here

MORE USEFUL WORDS:	MÁS PALABRAS ÚTILES:
diesel	diésel
unleaded	sin plomo
motorway, (Amer) expressway	autopista
toll	peaje, (Mex) cuota
satnav, (Amer) GPS	navegación vía satélite
speed camera	radar de tráfico, (Chi) fotorradar
roundabout	rotonda, glorieta
crossroads	cruce
dual carriageway, (Amer) divided highway	vía de doble sentido
exit	salida
traffic lights	semáforo
driver	conductor, -ora, chofer (or esp Spain) chófer

DID YOU KNOW...? ¿SABÍAS QUE...?

The speed limits on Spanish roads are as follows: motorway 120 km/h (74 mph), open roads 90-100 km/h (56-62 mph), towns and villages 50 km/h (31 mph).

Para entrar en coche hasta el centro de Londres hay que pagar una tasa de circulación especial; hay un sistema electrónico para detectar a los infractores.

COMMON SPANISH ROAD SIGNS

Aparcamiento, (*LAm*) estacionamiento, (*Col*) parqueadero	Parking
Atención: Paso a nivel de tren	Beware: level crossing
Autopista	Motorway, (*Amer*) Expressway
Autovía	Dual carriageway, (*Amer*) Divided highway
Cambio de sentido, (*Mex*) retorno	Change of direction
Casco urbano	Urban area
Ceda el Paso	Give Way, (*Amer*) Yield
(*LAm*) Cuidado: Cruce de ferrocarril/vía férrea	Beware: level crossing
Desvío	Detour
Dirección Única, (*LAm*) calle de sentido único	One-way street
Obras	Roadworks, (*Amer*) Men working
Peligro	Danger
Vado permanente	No parking (at any time)
Zona de residentes	Parking only for people with resident cards
Zona peatonal	Pedestrian area

SEÑALES DE TRÁFICO CORRIENTES EN PAÍSES DE HABLA INGLESA

Cattle	Ganado
Contraflow	Carril en sentido contrario
Ford	Vado, (*LAm*) Acceso
Get in lane	Incorpórese al carril
Give way	Ceda el Paso
Keep clear	No estacionar
No overtaking, (*Amer*) Do not pass	Prohibido adelantar, (*Mex*) rebasar
Pedestrians crossing	Peatones cruzando
Red route – no stopping	Prohibido parar
Reduce speed now	Reduzca su velocidad
Stop	Stop, (*LAm*) pare

Keeping in touch/Comunicación

On the phone / Por teléfono

where can I buy a phone card?	¿dónde puedo comprar una tarjeta telefónica?
may I use your phone?	¿podría usar su teléfono?
do you have a mobile, (*Amer*) cell phone?	¿tiene usted un móvil, (*LAm*) un celular?
what is your phone number?	¿cuál es su número (de teléfono)?
what is the area code for Santiago/Cardiff?	¿cuál es el prefijo, (*LAm*) código de Santiago/Cardiff?
I want to make a phone call	quiero hacer una llamada
I'd like to reverse the charges, (*Amer*) call collect	quisiera hacer una llamada a cobro revertido, (*LAm*) una llamada por cobrar
the line's engaged/busy	está comunicando, (*LAm*) está ocupado
there's no answer	no contestan
hello, this is Natalia	hola, soy, (*esp LAm*) habla Natalia
is Juan there, please?	¿está Juan, por favor?
who's calling?	¿de parte de quién?
sorry, wrong number	perdone, se ha confundido
just a moment, please	un momentito, por favor
would you like to hold?	¿le importa esperar?
it's a business/personal call	es una llamada personal/de negocios
I'll put you through to him/her	le pongo (*or* le paso, comunico) con él/ella
s/he cannot come to the phone at the moment	en este momento está ocupado/-a
please tell him/her I called	dígale que he llamado, (*LAm*) que llamé, por favor
I'd like to leave a message for him/her	quisiera dejarle un mensaje

I'll try again later	volveré a llamar más tarde
please tell him/her that María called	dígale que ha llamado, (LAm) que llamó María, por favor
can he/she call me back?	¿le puede decir que me llame?
my home number is...	mi número de casa es...
my business number is...	mi número del trabajo es...
my fax number is...	mi número de fax es...
we were cut off	se ha cortado, (LAm) se cortó
I'll call you later	te llamaré más tarde
I need to top up my phone	tengo que recargar el saldo
the battery's run out	me he quedado sin batería
I'm running low on credit	se me está gastando el saldo
send me a text	mándame un mensaje
there's no signal here	aquí no hay cobertura
you're breaking up	te oigo fatal, (LAm) te escucho muy mal
could you speak a little louder?	¿podría hablar un poco más alto?

YOU WILL HEAR:	OIRÁS:
sí, diga, dígame, (LAm) aló, (Mex) bueno	hello
llámame al móvil, (LAm) al celular	call me on my mobile, (Amer) cell phone
¿quiere dejar un mensaje/recado?	would you like to leave a message?

MORE USEFUL WORDS:	MÁS PALABRAS ÚTILES:
text message	mensaje (de texto)/SMS
top-up card	tarjeta de saldo, (LAm) de prepago
phone box, (Amer) phone booth	cabina de teléfono
dial	marcar, (LAm) discar
directory enquiries	información de direcciones/guía

Writing   Por carta

what's your address?	¿cuál es su dirección?
where is the nearest post office?	¿dónde está la oficina de correos más cercana?, (*LAm*) ¿dónde está el correo más cercano?
could I have a stamp for Argentina/Italy, please?	¿me da un sello, (*LAm*) una estampilla, (*Mex*) un timbre para Argentina/Italia, por favor?
I'd like to send a parcel	quisiera mandar un paquete
where is the nearest postbox, (*Amer*) mailbox?	¿dónde está el buzón más cercano?
dear Isabel/Fred	querida/querido Isabel/Fred
dear Sir or Madam	muy señor mío
yours sincerely	atentamente
yours faithfully	le envía un cordial saludo
best wishes	un abrazo

YOU WILL HEAR:	OIRÁS:
¿Quiere mandarlo por envío urgente?	Would you like to send it first class?
¿Contiene objetos de valor?	Is it valuable?

MORE USEFUL WORDS:	MÁS PALABRAS ÚTILES:
letter	carta
postcode, (*Amer*) ZIP code	código postal
airmail	correo aéreo
postcard	postal
fragile	frágil
urgent	urgente
registered post, (*Amer*) mail	correo certificado

On line   En línea

are you on the Internet?	¿está conectado/-a a Internet?
what's your e-mail address?	¿cuál es su dirección de correo electrónico?
I'll e-mail it to you on Tuesday	se lo mandaré por correo electrónico el martes
I looked it up on the Internet	lo he buscado, (LAm) lo busqué en Internet
the information is on their website	la información está en su sitio web
my e-mail address is jane dot smith at new99 dot com	mi correo electrónico es jane punto smith arroba new99 punto com
can I check my e-mail here?	¿puedo mirar el correo (electrónico)?
I have broadband/dial-up	tengo banda ancha/ conexión por módem
do you have wireless internet access?	¿tienen wi-fi?
I'll send you the file as an attachment	le mandaré el archivo como (archivo) adjunto, (LAm also) anexo

YOU WILL SEE:	VERÁS:
buscar	search
hacer doble clic en el icono	double-click on the icon
abrir la aplicación	open (up) the application
descargar archivo	download file

MORE USEFUL WORDS:	MÁS PALABRAS ÚTILES:
subject (of an email)	asunto (de un email)
password	contraseña
social networking site	red de contacto en línea
search engine	buscador
mouse	ratón, (LAm also) mouse
keyboard	teclado

....

Meeting up Citas, encuentros

what shall we do this evening?	¿qué hacemos esta tarde?
do you want to go out tonight?	¿quieres que salgamos esta noche?
where shall we meet?	¿dónde quedamos, (LAm) nos encontramos?
I'll see you outside the café at 6 o'clock	nos vemos a las 6 a la puerta de la cafetería
see you later	hasta luego
I can't today, I'm busy	hoy no puedo, estoy ocupado/-a
I'm sorry, I've got something planned	lo siento, tengo otros planes
let's meet for a coffee in town	¿nos tomamos un café por ahí?
would you like to see a show/film (Amer) movie?	¿quieres que vayamos al teatro/cine?
what about next week instead?	¿qué tal si lo dejamos para la semana que viene?
shall we go for something to eat?	¿vamos a tomar, (LAm) comer algo?

YOU WILL HEAR:	OIRÁS:
encantado/-a	nice to meet you
¿te invito a una copa?	can I buy you a drink?

MORE USEFUL WORDS:	MÁS PALABRAS ÚTILES:
bar	bar
bar (serving counter in a bar/pub)	barra
meal	comida
snack	algo para picar
date	cita
cigarette	pitillo

Food and Drink/Comer y beber

Booking a restaurant | Reservar mesa en un restaurante

can you recommend a good restaurant?	¿me puede recomendar un buen restaurante?
I'd like to reserve a table for four	quisiera reservar una mesa para cuatro
a reservation for tomorrow evening at eight o'clock	una reserva para mañana a las ocho de la tarde

Ordering | Pedir la comida

could we see the menu/wine list, please?	¿nos enseña el menú/la carta de vinos, por favor?
do you have a vegetarian/children's menu?	¿tienen un menú especial para vegetarianos/niños?
as a starter... and to follow...	de primero.. y de segundo...
could we have some more bread?	¿nos puede traer más pan?
what would you recommend?	¿qué recomienda?
I'd like a white coffee	quisiera un café con leche
...black coffee	...café solo, (*LAm*) café negro
...a decaffeinated coffee	...un café descafeinado
could I have the bill, (*Amer*) check?	¿me trae la cuenta, por favor?

YOU WILL HEAR	OIRÁS
¿Ya han decidido lo que van a pedir?	Are you ready to order?
¿Quieren entrada/un aperitivo?	Would you like a starter/aperitif?
¿Qué van a pedir de segundo plato?	What will you have as main course?
¿Quieren postre/café?	Would you like a dessert/coffee?
¿Algo más?	Anything else?
¡Buen provecho!	Enjoy your meal!
El servicio (no) está incluido.	Service is (not) included.

15

The menu   La carta/El menú

starters	de primero	de primero	starters
hors d'oeuvres	entremeses, (Mex) botanas	entremeses, botanas (Mex)	hors d'oeuvres
omelette	omelette, tortilla	omelette, tortilla	omelette
soup	sopa	sopa	soup

fish	pescado	pescado	fish
bass	lubina	anguila	eel
cod	bacalao	arenque	herring
eel	anguila	atún	tuna
hake	merluza	bacalao	cod
herring	arenque	calamares	squid
monkfish	rape	camarones (LAm)	prawns, shrimps
mullet	mújol, (LAm) lisa	gambas	prawns, shrimps
mussels	mejillones	lenguado	sole
oyster	ostra, (Mex) ostión	lisa (LAm)	mullet
		lubina	bass
prawns	gambas	mejillones	mussels
salmon	salmón	merluza	hake
sardines	sardinas	mújol	mullet
shrimps	gambas	ostra, (Mex) ostión	oyster
sole	lenguado	rape	monkfish
squid	calamares	róbalo	bass
trout	trucha	rodaballo	turbot
tuna	atún	trucha	trout
turbot	rodaballo		

meat	carne	carne	meat
beef	carne de vaca	bistec, filete	steak
chicken	pollo	carne de vaca, de res (Mex)	beef
duck	pato		

16

goose	ganso	cerdo	pork
hare	liebre	codorniz	quail
ham	jamón	conejo	rabbit
kidneys	riñones	cordero	lamb
lamb	cordero	ganso	goose
liver	hígado	hígado	liver
pork	cerdo	jamón	ham
quail	codorniz	liebre	hare
rabbit	conejo	pato	duck
steak	bistec, filete	pollo	chicken
tenderloin	lomo	puerco (*Mex*)	pork
turkey	pavo	riñones	kidneys
veal	ternera	solomillo (*Esp*)	sirloin steak
venison	venado	ternera	veal
white meat	carne blanca	venado	venison

vegetables	**verduras**	**verduras**	**vegetables**
artichoke	alcachofa	alcachofa	artichoke
asparagus	ésparragos	arvejas (*LAm*)	peas
aubergine	berenjena	apio	celery
beans	frijoles	batata	sweet potato
carrots	zanahorias	berenjena	aubergine
cabbage	col, repollo	camote (*LAm*)	sweet potato
celery	apio	cebollas	onions
endive	endivia	champiñones	mushrooms
lettuce	lechuga	chícharos (*Mex*)	peas
mushrooms	champiñones	col, repollo	cabbage
peas	guisantes, (*LAm*) arvejas	coliflor	cauliflower
pepper	pimiento	ésparragos	asparagus
potatoes	patatas, (*LAm*) papas	frijoles	beans
		guisantes	peas
runner bean	habichuela	haba	broad bean

17

tomato	tomate, (*Mex*) jitomate	jitomate (*Mex*)	tomato
sweet potato	batata, camote (*LAm*)	papas	potatoes
		patatas	potatoes
zucchini	calabacines	pimiento	pepper
		zanahorias	carrots

the way it's cooked	cómo se prepara	cómo se prepara	the way it's cooked
boiled	cocido -da	a la parilla	grilled
roast	asado -da	a la plancha	griddled
fried	frito -ta	asado -da	roast
pureed	puré de	bien cocido	well done
grilled	a la parilla	bien hecho	well done
griddled	a la plancha	cocido -da	boiled
stewed	estofado -da, guisado -da	estofado -da	stewed
		guisado -da	stewed
rare	poco hecho	frito -ta	fried
well done	bien hecho	poco hecho	rare

deserts	postres	postres	deserts
ice cream	helados	fruta	fruit
fruits	fruta	helados	ice cream
pie	tarta, (*LAm*) pay	pastel, (*LAm*) pay	pie
tart	tarta	tarta	tart

other		otros	
bread	pan	aceite de oliva	olive oil
butter	mantequilla	ajo	garlic
cheese	queso	arroz	rice
cheeseboard	tabla de quesos	condimento	seasoning
garlic	ajo	mantequilla	butter
mayonnaise	mayonesa	mayonesa	mayonnaise
mustard	mostaza	mostaza	mustard
olive oil	aceite de oliva	pan	bread

pepper	pimienta	pimienta	pepper
rice	arroz	queso	cheese
salt	sal	sal	salt
sauce	salsa	salsa	sauce
seasoning	condimento	tabla de quesos	cheeseboard
vinegar	vinagre	vinagre	vinegar

drinks	**bebidas**	**bebidas**	**drinks**
beer	cerveza	agua mineral	mineral water
bottle	botella	bebida no alcohólica	soft drink
carbonated	con gas		
half-bottle	media botella	botella	botella
liqueur	licor	cerveza	beer
mineral water	agua mineral	con gas	carbonated
red wine	vino tinto	licor	liqueur
rosé	vino rosado	media botella	half-bottle
soft drink	bebida no alcohólica	sin gas	still
		vino	wine
still	sin gas	vino blanco	white wine
house wine	vino de la casa	vino de la casa	house wine
table wine	vino de mesa	vino de mesa	table wine
white wine	vino blanco	vino rosado	rosé
wine	vino	vino tinto	red wine

Places to stay/Alojamiento

Camping Campings

can we pitch our tent here?	¿podemos montar la tienda (de campaña) aquí?
can we park our caravan here?	¿podemos aparcar la caravana aquí?, (*LAm*) ¿podemos estacionar el tráiler aquí?
what are the facilities like?	¿cómo son las instalaciones?
how much is it per night?	¿cuánto cobran por (pasar la) noche?
where do we park the car?	¿dónde podemos aparcar, (esp *LAm*) estacionar?
we're looking for a campsite	estamos buscando un camping

At the hotel Hoteles ★★★

I'd like a double/single room with bath	quisiera una habitación individual/doble con baño
we have a reservation in the name of Morris	tenemos una reserva a nombre de Morris
we'll be staying three nights, from Friday to Sunday	nos quedaremos tres noches, de viernes a domingo
how much does the room cost?	¿cuánto cuesta la habitación?
I'd like to see the room	quisiera ver la habitación
what time is breakfast?	¿a qué hora se sirve el desayuno?
can I leave this in your safe?	¿puedo dejar esto en la caja fuerte?
bed and breakfast	(lugar donde dan) alojamiento y desayuno
we'd like to stay another night	nos gustaría quedarnos una noche más
please call me at 7:30	¿me podría despertar a las 7:30, por favor?
are there any messages for me?	¿hay algún mensaje para mí?

Hostels Albergues

could you tell me where the youth hostel is?	¿me podría indicar dónde está el albergue?
what time does the hostel close?	¿a qué hora cierra el albergue?
I'll be staying in a hostel	me alojaré en un albergue
the hostel we're staying in is great value	el albergue donde nos alojamos ofrece una buena relación calidad-precio
I know a really good hostel in Dublin	conozco un albergue estupendo en Dublín
I'd like to go backpacking in Australia	me gustaría irme a Australia con la mochila al hombro

Rooms to rent Alquiler de habitaciones

I'm looking for a room with a reasonable rent	quiero alquilar, (*Mex*) rentar una habitación que tenga un precio razonable
I'd like to rent an apartment for a few weeks	me gustaría alquilar, (*Mex*) rentar un apartamento para unas cuantas semanas
where do I find out about rooms to rent?	¿dónde me puedo informar sobre alquileres, (*Mex*) rentas de habitaciones?
what's the weekly rent?	¿cuánto cuesta el alquiler, (*Mex*) la renta semanal?
I'm staying with friends at the moment	en este momento estoy alojado en casa de unos amigos
I rent an apartment on the outskirts of town	vivo en un apartamento alquilado, (*Mex*) rentado en las afueras
the room's fine — I'll take it	la habitación está muy bien, me la quedo
the deposit is one month's rent in advance	como depósito, se paga un mes de alquiler, (*Mex*) renta por adelantado

Shopping/Las compras

At the bank · En el banco

I'd like to change some money	quisiera cambiar dinero
I want to change some dollars into euros	quisiera cambiar dólares a euros
do you take Eurocheques?	¿aceptan Eurocheques?
what's the exchange rate today?	¿a cuánto está hoy el cambio?
I prefer traveller's cheques, (*Amer*) traveler's checks to cash	prefiero cheques de viaje que dinero en metálico, (*esp LAm*) en efectivo
I'd like to transfer some money from my account	quisiera hacer una transferencia desde mi cuenta corriente
I'll get some money from the cash machine	sacaré dinero del cajero (automático)
I'm with another bank	no soy cliente/-a de este banco

Finding the right shop · Dar con la tienda adecuada

where's the main shopping district?	¿dónde está la zona de tiendas?
where can I buy batteries/postcards?	¿dónde puedo comprar unas pilas/postales?
where's the nearest pharmacy/bookshop?	¿dónde está la farmacia/librería más cercana?
is there a good food shop around here?	¿hay una buena tienda de comestibles por aquí?
what time do the shops open/close?	¿a qué hora abren/cierran las tiendas?
where did you get those?	¿dónde los/las ha comprado?
I'm looking for presents for my family	estoy buscando regalos para mi familia
we'll do our shopping on Saturday	(nosotros) haremos las compras el sábado
I love shopping	me encanta ir de compras

Are you being served? ¿Lo/La atienden?

how much does that cost?	¿cuánto cuesta?
can I try it on?	¿me lo puedo probar?
could you wrap it for me, please?	¿me lo envuelve, por favor?
can I pay by credit card/cheque, (Amer) check?	¿puedo pagar con tarjeta/cheque?
do you have this in another colour, (Amer) color?	¿tiene éste/-a en otro color?
could I have a bag, please?	¿me da una bolsa, por favor?
I'm just looking	sólo estoy mirando
I'll think about it	me lo voy a pensar
I'd like a receipt, please	¿me da el recibo, por favor?
I need a bigger/smaller size	necesito una talla más grande/más pequeña
I take a size 10/a medium	uso la talla 38/mediana
it doesn't suit me	no me queda bien
I'm sorry, I don't have any change/ anything smaller	perdone, pero no tengo cambio/ billetes más pequeños
that's all, thank you	nada más, gracias

Changing things Devoluciones

can I have a refund?	¿me podría devolver el dinero?
can you mend it for me?	¿me lo/la podrían arreglar?
can I speak to the manager?	quisiera hablar con el encargado/ la encargada
it doesn't work	no funciona
I'd like to change it, please	quisiera cambiarlo/-a, por favor
I bought this here yesterday	compré esto ayer

23

Currency Convertor		Convertidor de divisas	
€/$	**£/$**	**£/$**	**€/$**
0.25		0.25	
0.5		0.5	
0.75		0.75	
1		1	
1.5		1.5	
2		2	
3		3	
5		5	
10		10	
20		20	
30		30	
40		40	
50		50	
100		100	
200		200	
1000		1000	

Sports and leisure/Deportes y ocio

Keeping fit Mantenerse en forma

where can we play tennis/squash?	¿dónde se puede jugar al tenis/squash, (LAm) jugar tenis/squash?
where is the local sports centre, (Amer) center?	¿hay por aquí cerca un polideportivo?
what's the charge per day?	¿cuánto cobran (al día)?
is there a reduction for children/a student discount?	¿hacen descuentos a niños/estudiantes?
I'm looking for a swimming pool/tennis court	estoy buscando una piscina, (Mex) alberca/un club de tenis
are there any yoga/pilates classes here?	¿hay clases de yoga/pilates?
I want to do aerobics	quiero hacer aerobic
is there a hotel gym?	¿hay gimnasio en este hotel?
you have to be a member	(para entrar) hace falta ser socio
I would like to go fishing/riding	me gustaría ir a pescar/montar a caballo
I love swimming	me encanta nadar

Watching sport Ver espectáculos deportivos

is there a match, (Amer) game on Saturday?	¿hay un partido el sábado?
which teams are playing?	¿quién está jugando?
where can I get tickets?	¿dónde se compran las entradas?
I'd like to see a match	me gustaría ver un partido
my favourite, (Amer) favorite team is...	mi equipo favorito es el...
let's watch the match, (Amer) game on TV	veamos el partido por la tele
who's winning?	¿quién gana?
the reds are winning 3-1	los rojos van ganando 3 a 1

SPORTS AND PASTIMES

American football/football	fútbol americano
badminton	bádminton
basketball	baloncesto, (*LAm*) básquetbol
cycling	ciclismo
football/soccer	fútbol
golf	golf
hiking	montañismo
horse-riding	equitación
paddle tennis	pádel, (*LAm*) paddle
pelota	pelota
roller-blading	patinaje
running	correr
sailing	vela
surfing	surf
swimming	natación

DEPORTES Y PASATIEMPOS

bádminton	**badminton**
baloncesto, (*LAm*) básquetbol	**basketball**
ciclismo	**cycling**
correr	**running**
equitación	**horse-riding**
fútbol americano	**American football/football**
fútbol	**football/soccer**
golf	**golf**
montañismo	**hiking**
natación	**swimming**
pádel, (*LAm*) paddle	**paddle tennis**
patinaje	**roller-blading**
pelota	**pelota**
surf	**surfing**
vela	**sailing**

Movies/theatres/clubs — Cine/Teatro/Discotecas

what's on?	¿qué ponen, (esp LAm) dan (en el cine/teatro)?
when does the box office open/close?	¿a qué hora abren/cierran la taquilla, (LAm) boletería?
what time does the concert/performance start?	¿a qué hora empieza el concierto/la representación?
when does it finish?	¿a qué hora termina?
are there any seats left for tonight?	¿quedan entradas para esta noche?
how much are the tickets?	¿cuánto cuestan las entradas?
where can I get a programme, (Amer) program?	¿dónde puedo conseguir un programa?
I want to book tickets for tonight's performance	quiero reservar entradas para esta noche
I'll book seats in the circle	reservaré entradas de platea
I'd rather have seats in the stalls, (Amer) orchestra	prefiero el patio de butacas
somewhere in the middle, but not too far back	que sean centrales, pero no demasiado atrás
four, please	cuatro, por favor
for Saturday	para el sábado
we'd like to go to a club	nos gustaría ir a una discoteca

Hobbies — Aficiones y hobbies

what do you do at, (Amer) on weekends?	¿qué hace los fines de semana?
I like reading/listening to music/going out	me gusta leer/escuchar música/salir
do you like watching TV/shopping/travelling?	¿te gusta ver la tele/ir de compras/viajar?
I read a lot	leo mucho
I collect musical instruments	colecciono instrumentos musicales

Good timing/A tiempo

Telling the time La hora

what time is it?	¿qué hora es?
it's 2 o'clock	son las 2
at about 8 o'clock	hacia las 8
from 10 o'clock onwards	a partir de las 10
at 5 o'clock in the morning/afternoon	a las cinco de la mañana/tarde
it's five past/quarter past/half past one	es la una y cinco/y cuarto/y media
it's twenty-five to/quarter to one	es la una menos veinticinco/menos cuarto/(LAm) son veinticinco/un cuarto para la una
a quarter/three quarters of an hour	un cuarto/tres cuartos de hora

Days and dates Días y fechas

Sunday, Monday, Tuesday, Wednesday, Thursday, Friday, Saturday	domingo, lunes, martes, miércoles, jueves, viernes, sábado
January, February, March, April, May, June, July, August, September, October, November, December	enero, febrero, marzo, abril, mayo, junio, julio, agosto, septiembre, octubre, noviembre, diciembre
what's the date?	¿qué fecha es hoy?
it's the second of June	(es el) dos de junio
we meet up every Monday	nos vemos todos los lunes
we're going away in August	nos vamos fuera en agosto
on November 8th	el 8 de noviembre

Public holidays and special days / Fiestas y celebraciones especiales

Bank holiday	día festivo en el Reino Unido
Bank holiday Monday	lunes de puente
New Year's Day (Jan 1)	Año Nuevo (1 de enero)
Epiphany (Jan 6)	Reyes (6 de enero)
St Valentine's Day (Feb 14)	San Valentín (14 de febrero)
Shrove Tuesday/Pancake Day	Martes de Carnaval
Ash Wednesday	Miércoles de Ceniza
Holy Week	Semana Santa
Good Friday	Viernes Santo
Easter	Pascua (de Resurrección)
Easter Monday	lunes de Pascua
May Day (May 1)	1 de mayo, día del trabajador
Independence Day	4 de julio, fiesta de la independencia de los EEUU
Thanksgiving	día de Acción de Gracias, fiesta típica de EEUU y Canadá
Halloween (Oct 31)	Halloween (fiesta de fantasmas y brujas que se celebra la víspera de Todos los Santos)
All Saints' Day	Todos los Santos
Guy Fawkes Day/ Bonfire Night (Nov 5)	fiesta de Guy Fawkes (5 de noviembre: se celebra que el católico Guy Fawkes fracasó en su intento de incendiar el parlamento)
Remembrance Sunday	fiesta en recuerdo a los caídos en las dos guerras mundiales
St Nicholas' Day (Dec 6)	San Nicolás (6 de diciembre)
Christmas Eve (Dec 24)	Nochebuena (24 de diciembre)
Christmas Day (Dec 25)	Navidad (25 de diciembre)
Boxing Day (Dec 26)	día de fiesta que sigue al día de Navidad
New Year's Eve (Dec 31)	Nochevieja (31 de diciembre)

Health and Beauty/Salud y belleza

At the doctor's   En el médico

can I see a doctor?	¿podría verme un médico?
I don't feel well	no me encuentro, (*LAm*) no me siento bien
it hurts here	me duele aquí
I have a migraine/stomach ache	tengo migrañas/dolor de tripa, (*LAm*) de estómago
are there any side effects?	¿tiene efectos secundarios?
I have a sore ankle/wrist/knee	me he hecho daño, (*LAm*) me hice daño en el tobillo/la muñeca/la rodilla

YOU WILL HEAR: OIRÁS:

necesita pedir cita (*or* pedir hora)	you need to make an appointment
siéntese, por favor	please take a seat
¿tiene una Tarjeta Sanitaria Europea (TSE)?	do you have a European Health Insurance Card (EHIC)?
¿tiene seguro médico?	do you have Health Insurance?
tengo que tomarle la tensión, (*LAm*) presión	I need to take your blood pressure

MORE USEFUL WORDS: MÁS PALABRAS ÚTILES:

nurse	enfermera/-o
antibiotics	antibióticos
medicine	medicina
infection	infección
treatment	tratamiento
rest	reposo

At the pharmacy — En la farmacia

can I have some painkillers?	¿me puede dar un analgésico?
I have asthma/hay fever/eczema	tengo asma/alergia al polen/eccema
I've been stung by a wasp/bee	me ha picado una avispa/abeja
I've got a cold/cough/the flu	tengo catarro/tos/gripe
I need something for diarrhoea/stomachache	necesito algo para la diarrea/el dolor de estómago
I'm pregnant	estoy embarazada

YOU WILL HEAR: — OIRÁS:

¿lo ha tomado alguna vez?/¿ha tomado alguna vez este medicamento?	have you taken this/these before?/have you taken this medicine before?
su receta estará lista en diez minutos	your prescription will be ready in ten minutes
tómese con las comidas/tres veces al día	take at mealtimes/three times a day
¿tiene alguna alergia?	are you allergic to anything?
¿está tomando otros medicamentos?	are you taking any other medication?

MORE USEFUL WORDS: — MÁS PALABRAS ÚTILES:

plasters, (Amer) Band-Aid™	tiritas, (LAm) curitas
insect repellent	repelente contra insectos
contraception	anticonceptivos
sun cream	crema de sol
aftersun	loción aftersun, (LAm) para después de asolearse
dosage	dosis

At the hairdresser's/salon En la peluquería

I'd like a cut and blow dry	¿me puede cortar y secar?
just a trim please	corte nada más que las puntas, por favor
a grade 3 back and sides	lo quiero al 3 por detrás y por los lados
I'd like my hair washed first please	lavar y cortar, por favor
can I have a manicure/pedicure/facial?	¿hacen la manicura/la pedicura/tratamiento facial?
how much is a head/back massage?	¿cuánto cuesta el masaje de cabeza/espalda?
can I see a price list?	¿puedo ver la lista de precios?
do you offer reflexology/aromatherapy treatments?	¿hacen reflexología/aromaterapia?

YOU WILL HEAR: OIRÁS:

¿quiere que le seque el pelo?	would you like your hair blow-dried?
¿dónde quiere la raya, (Col, Ven) la carrera, (Chi) la partidura?	where is your parting, (Amer) part?
¿quiere que le corte a (LAm) en capas?	would you like your hair layered?

MORE USEFUL WORDS: MÁS PALABRAS ÚTILES:

dry/greasy/fine/flyaway/frizzy	seco/graso/fino/lacio/crespo
highlights	mechas, (Mex) luces, (Chi, Mex) rayitos, (Col) mechones, (RPl) claritos
extensions	extensiones
sunbed	solarium, (LAm also) cama solar
leg/arm/bikini wax	depilación a la cera en las piernas/los brazos/las ingles

At the dentist's — En el dentista

I have toothache	me duele un diente
I'd like an emergency appointment	necesito una cita de urgencia
I have cracked a tooth	se me ha roto, (LAm) se me rompió un diente
my gums are bleeding	me sangran las encías

YOU WILL HEAR: — OIRÁS:

abra la boca	open your mouth
necesita un empaste, (Chi, Mex) una tapadura, (RPl) una emplomadura, (Col) una calza	you need a filling
tenemos que hacer una radiografía	we need to take an X-ray
enjuáguese, por favor	please rinse

MORE USEFUL WORDS: — MÁS PALABRAS ÚTILES:

anaesthetic	anestesia
root canal treatment	endodoncia
injection	inyección
floss	hilo dental

DID YOU KNOW...? — ¿SABÍAS QUE...?

Spanish hairdressers will normally wash your hair before your haircut. If you don't want them to do so, you should tell them beforehand.

Antiguamente, las peluquerías se anunciaban con un poste pintado con bandas rojas y blancas en espiral.

Weights & measures/Pesos y medidas

Length/Longitud

inches/pulgadas	0.39	3.9	7.8	11.7	15.6	19.7	39
cm/centímetros	1	10	20	30	40	50	100

Distance/Distancia

miles/millas	0.62	6.2	12.4	18.6	24.9	31	62
km/km	1	10	20	30	40	50	100

Weight/Peso

pounds/libras	2.2	22	44	66	88	110	220
kg/kilos	1	10	20	30	40	50	100

Capacity/Capacidad

gallons/galones	0.22	2.2	4.4	6.6	8.8	11	22
litres/litros	1	10	20	30	40	50	100

Temperature/Temperatura

°C	0	5	10	15	20	25	30	37	38	40
°F	32	41	50	59	68	77	86	98.4	100	104

Clothing and shoe sizes/Tallas de ropa y calzado

Women's clothing sizes/Ropa de señora

UK	8	10	12	14	16	18
US	6	8	10	12	14	16
Continent	36	38	40	42	44	46

Men's clothing sizes/Ropa de caballero

UK/US	36	38	40	42	44	46
Continent	46	48	50	52	54	56

Men's and women's shoes/Calzado de señora y caballero

UK women	4	5	6	7	7.5	8			
UK men			6	7	8	9	10	11	
US	6.5	7.5	8.5	9.5	10.5	11.5	12.5	13.5	14.5
Continent	37	38	39	40	41	42	43	44	45

Aa

a /ə/, stressed form /eɪ/

before vowel sound or silent 'h' **an**

indefinite article

···▸ un (*m*), una (*f*). a problem un problema. an apple una manzana. have you got a pencil? ¿tienes un lápiz?

❗ Feminine singular nouns beginning with stressed or accented *a* or *ha* take the article *un* instead of *una*, e.g. *un águila, un hada*

···▸ (*when talking about prices and quantities*) por. 30 miles an hour 30 millas por hora. twice a week dos veces por semana, dos veces a la semana

❗ There are many cases in which *a* is not translated, such as when talking about people's professions, in exclamations, etc: she's a lawyer *es abogada.* what a beautiful day! ¡qué día más precioso!. have you got a car? ¿tienes coche? half a cup media taza

A & E /eɪənd'iː/ *n* urgencias *fpl*

aback /ə'bæk/ *adv.* be taken ∼ quedar desconcertado

abandon /ə'bændən/ *vt* abandonar. ● *n* abandono *m*, desenfado *m*. ∼ed *a* abandonado

abashed /ə'bæʃt/ *adj* confuso

abate /ə'beɪt/ *vi* disminuir; (storm etc) calmarse

abattoir /'æbətwɑː(r)/ *n* matadero *m*

abbess /'æbɪs/ *n* abadesa *f*

abbey /'æbɪ/ *n* abadía *f*

abbot /'æbət/ *n* abad *m*

abbreviat|e /ə'briːvɪeɪt/ *vt* abreviar. ∼ion /-'eɪʃn/ *n* abreviatura *f*; (*act*) abreviación *f*

abdicat|e /'æbdɪkeɪt/ *vt/i* abdicar. ∼ion /-'eɪʃn/ *n* abdicación *f*

abdom|en /'æbdəmən/ *n* abdomen *m*. ∼inal /-'dɒmɪnl/ *adj* abdominal

abduct /æb'dʌkt/ *vt* secuestrar. ∼ion /-ʃn/ *n* secuestro *m*

abhor /əb'hɔː(r)/ *vt* (*pt* abhorred) aborrecer. ∼rence /-'hɒrəns/ *n* aborrecimiento *m*. ∼rent /-'hɒrənt/ *adj* aborrecible

abide /ə'baɪd/ *vt* (*pt* abided) soportar. ● *vi* (old use, *pt* abode) morar. □ ∼ **by** *vt* atenerse a; cumplir (promise)

ability /ə'bɪlətɪ/ *n* capacidad *f*; (*cleverness*) habilidad *f*

abject /'æbdʒekt/ *adj* (*wretched*) miserable

ablaze /ə'bleɪz/ *adj* en llamas

able /'eɪbl/ *adj* (-er, -est) capaz. be ∼ poder; (*know how to*) saber. ∼-**bodied** /-'bɒdɪd/ *adj* sano, no discapacitado

ably /'eɪblɪ/ *adv* hábilmente

abnormal /æb'nɔːml/ *adj* anormal. ∼ity /-'mælətɪ/ *n* anormalia dad f

aboard /ə'bɔːd/ adv a bordo. ●prep a bordo de

abode /ə'bəʊd/ see ABIDE. ●n (old use) domicilio m

aboli|sh /ə'bɒlɪʃ/ vt abolir. ~tion /æbə'lɪʃn/ n abolición f

abominable /ə'bɒmɪnəbl/ adj abominable

aborigin|al /æbə'rɪdʒənl/ adj & n aborigen (m & f), indígena (m & f). ~es /-iːz/ npl aborígenes mpl

abort /ə'bɔːt/ vt hacer abortar. ~ion /-ʃn/ n aborto m provocado; (fig) aborto m. have an ~ion hacerse un aborto. ~ive adj fracasado

abound /ə'baʊnd/ vi abundar (in en)

about /ə'baʊt/ adv (approximately) alrededor de; (here and there) por todas partes; (in existence) por aquí. ~ here por aquí. be ~ to estar a punto de. ●prep sobre; (around) alrededor de; (somewhere in) en. talk ~ hablar de. ~-face, ~-turn n (fig) cambio m rotundo

above /ə'bʌv/ adv arriba. ●prep encima de; (more than) más de. ~ all sobre todo. ~ board adj legítimo. ●adv abiertamente. ~-mentioned adj susodicho

abrasi|on /ə'breɪʒn/ n abrasión f. ~ve /-sɪv/ adj abrasivo

abreast /ə'brest/ adv. march four ~ marchar en columna de cuatro en fondo. keep ~ of mantenerse al corriente de

abroad /ə'brɔːd/ adv (be) en el extranjero; (go) al extranjero; (far and wide) por todas partes

abrupt /ə'brʌpt/ adj brusco. ~ly adv (suddenly) repentinamente; (curtly) bruscamente

abscess /'æbsɪs/ n absceso m

abscond /əb'skɒnd/ vi fugarse

absen|ce /'æbsəns/ n ausencia f; (lack) falta f. ~t /'æbsənt/ adj ausente. ~t-minded /-'maɪndɪd/ adj distraído. ~t-mindedness n distracción f, despiste m. ~tee /-'tiː/ n ausente m & f. ~teeism n absentismo m, ausentismo m (LAm)

absolute /'æbsəluːt/ adj absoluto. ~ly adv absolutamente

absolve /əb'zɒlv/ vt (from sin) absolver; (from obligation) liberar

absor|b /əb'zɔːb/ vt absorber. ~bent /-bənt/ adj absorbente. ~bent cotton n (Amer) algodón m hidrófilo. ~ption /əb'zɔːpʃən/ n absorción f

abstain /əb'steɪn/ vi abstenerse (from de)

abstemious /əb'stiːmɪəs/ adj abstemio

abstention /əb'stenʃn/ n abstención f

abstract /'æbstrækt/ adj abstracto. ●n (summary) resumen m; (painting) cuadro m abstracto. ●/əb'strækt/ vt extraer; (summarize) resumir. ~ion /-ʃn/ n abstracción f

absurd /əb'sɜːd/ adj absurdo. ~ity n absurdo m, disparate m

abundan|ce /ə'bʌndəns/ n abundancia f. ~t adj abundante

abus|e /ə'bjuːz/ vt (misuse) abusar de; (ill-treat) maltratar; (insult) insultar. ●/ə'bjuːs/ n abuso m; (insults) insultos mpl. ~ive /ə'bjuːsɪv/ adj injurioso

abysmal /ə'bɪzməl/ adj ① pésimo

abyss /ə'bɪs/ n abismo m

academic /ækə'demɪk/ adj académico; (pej) teórico. ●n universitario *m*, catedrático *m*

academy /ə'kædəmi/ *n* academia *f*.

accelerat|e /æk'seləreɪt/ *vt* acelerar. ● *vi* acelerar; (Auto) apretar el acelerador. ~**ion** /-'reɪʃn/ *n* aceleración *f*. ~**or** *n* acelerador *m*

accent /'æksənt/ *n* acento *m*

accept /ək'sept/ *vt* aceptar. ~**able** *adj* aceptable. ~**ance** *n* aceptación *f*; (approval) aprobación *f*

access /'ækses/ *n* acceso *m*. ~**ible** /ək'sesəbl/ *adj* accesible; (person) tratable

accession /æk'seʃn/ *n* (to power, throne etc) ascenso *m*; (thing added) adquisición *f*

accessory /ək'sesərɪ/ *adj* accesorio. ● *n* accesorio *m*, complemento *m*; (Jurid) cómplice *m* & *f*

accident /'æksɪdənt/ *n* accidente *m*; (chance) casualidad *f*. by ~ sin querer; (by chance) por casualidad. ~**al** /-'dentl/ *adj* accidental, fortuito. ~**ally** /-'dentlɪ/ *adv* sin querer; (by chance) por casualidad. ~-**prone** *adj* propenso a los accidentes

acclaim /ə'kleɪm/ *vt* aclamar. ● *n* aclamación *f*

accolade /'ækəleɪd/ *n* (praise) encomio *m*

accommodat|e /ə'kɒmədeɪt/ *vt* (give hospitality to) alojar; (adapt) acomodar; (oblige) complacer. ~**ing** *adj* complaciente. ~**ion** /-'deɪʃn/ *n*, ~**ions** *npl* (Amer) alojamiento *m*

accompan|iment /ə'kʌmpənɪmənt/ *n* acompañamiento *m*. ~**ist** *n* acompañante *m* & *f*. ~**y** /ə'kʌmpənɪ/ *vt* acompañar

accomplice /ə'kʌmplɪs/ *n* cómplice *m* & *f*

accomplish /ə'kʌmplɪʃ/ *vt* (complete) acabar; (achieve) realizar; (carry out) llevar a cabo. ~**ed** *adj* consumado. ~**ment** *n* realización *f*; (ability) talento *m*; (thing achieved) triunfo *m*, logro *m*

accord /ə'kɔːd/ *vi* concordar. ● *vt* conceder. ● *n* acuerdo *m*; (harmony) armonía *f*. of one's own ~ espontáneamente. ~**ance** *n*. in ~**ance with** de acuerdo con. ~**ing** *adv*. ~**ing to** según. ~**ingly** *adv* en conformidad; (therefore) por consiguiente

accordion /ə'kɔːdɪən/ *n* acordeón *m*

accost /ə'kɒst/ *vt* abordar

account /ə'kaʊnt/ *n* cuenta *f*; (description) relato *m*. ~**s** *npl* (in business) contabilidad *f*. on ~ of a causa de. on no ~ de ninguna manera. on this ~ por eso. take into ~ tener en cuenta. ● *vt* considerar. □ ~ **for** *vt* dar cuenta de, explicar

accountan|cy /ə'kaʊntənsɪ/ *n* contabilidad *f*. ~**t** *n* contable *m* & *f*, contador *m* (LAm)

accumulat|e /ə'kjuːmjʊleɪt/ *vt* acumular. ● *vi* acumularse. ~**ion** /-'leɪʃn/ *n* acumulación *f*

accura|cy /'ækjərəsɪ/ *n* exactitud *f*, precisión *f*. ~**te** /-ət/ *adj* exacto, preciso

accus|ation /ækjuː'zeɪʃn/ *n* acusación *f*. ~**e** /ə'kjuːz/ *vt* acusar

accustom /ə'kʌstəm/ *vt* acostumbrar. ~**ed** *adj*. be ~**ed (to)** estar acostumbrado (a). get ~**ed (to)** acostumbrarse (a)

ace /eɪs/ *n* as *m*

ache /eɪk/ *n* dolor *m*. ● *vi* doler. my leg ~**s** me duele la pierna

achieve /ə'tʃiːv/ *vt* realizar; lograr

(success). **~ment** *n* realización *f*; (*feat*) proeza *f*; (*thing achieved*) logro *m*

acid /'æsɪd/ *adj* & *n* ácido (*m*). **~ic** /ə'sɪdɪk/ *adj* ácido. **~ rain** *n* lluvia *f* ácida

acknowledge /ək'nɒlɪdʒ/ *vt* reconocer. **~ receipt of** acusar recibo de. **~ment** *n* reconocimiento *m*; (*Com*) acuse *m* de recibo

acne /'ækni/ *n* acné *m*

acorn /'eɪkɔːn/ *n* bellota *f*

acoustic /ə'kuːstɪk/ *adj* acústico. **~s** *npl* acústica *f*

acquaint /ə'kweɪnt/ *vt*. **~ s.o. with** poner a uno al corriente de. **be ~ed with** conocer (*person*); saber (*fact*). **~ance** *n* conocimiento *m*; (*person*) conocido *m*

acquiesce /ækwɪ'es/ *vi* consentir (**in** en). **~nce** *n* aquiescencia *f*, consentimiento *m*

acqui|re /ə'kwaɪə(r)/ *vt* adquirir; aprender (*language*). **~re a taste for** tomar gusto a. **~sition** /ækwɪ'zɪʃn/ *n* adquisición *f*. **~sitive** /ə'kwɪzətɪv/ *adj* codicioso

acquit /ə'kwɪt/ *vt* (*pt* **acquitted**) absolver. **~tal** *n* absolución *f*

acre /'eɪkə(r)/ *n* acre *m*

acrid /'ækrɪd/ *adj* acre

acrimonious /ækrɪ'məʊnɪəs/ *adj* cáustico, mordaz

acrobat /'ækrəbæt/ *n* acróbata *m* & *f*. **~ic** /-'bætɪk/ *adj* acrobático. **~ics** *npl* acrobacia *f*

acronym /'ækrənɪm/ *n* acrónimo *m*, siglas *fpl*

across /ə'krɒs/ *adv* & *prep* (*side to side*) de un lado al otro; (*on other side*) al otro lado de; (*crosswise*) a través. **it is 20 metres ~** tiene 20 metros de ancho. **go** or **walk ~** atravesar, cruzar

act /ækt/ *n* acto *m*; (*action*) acción *f*; (*in variety show*) número *m*; (*decree*) decreto *m*. ● *vt* hacer (part, role). ● *vi* actuar; (*pretend*) fingir. **~ as** actuar de; (*object*) servir de. **~ for** representar. **~ing** *adj* interino. ● *n* (*of play*) representación *f*; (*by actor*) interpretación *f*; (*profession*) profesión *f* de actor

action /'ækʃn/ *n* acción *f*; (*Jurid*) demanda *f*; (*plot*) argumento *m*. **out of ~** no funciona. **put out of ~** inutilizar. **take ~** tomar medidas. **~ replay** *n* repetición *f* de la jugada

activate /'æktɪveɪt/ *vt* activar

activ|e /'æktɪv/ *adj* activo; (*energetic*) lleno de energía; (*volcano*) en actividad. **~ist** *n* activista *m* & *f*. **~ity** /-'tɪvətɪ/ *n* actividad *f*

act|or /'æktə(r)/ *n* actor *m*. **~ress** /-trɪs/ *n* actriz *f*

actual /'æktʃʊəl/ *adj* verdadero. **~ly** *adv* en realidad, efectivamente; (*even*) incluso

acute /ə'kjuːt/ *adj* agudo. **~ly** *adv* agudamente

ad /æd/ *n* 🄣 anuncio *m*, aviso *m* (*LAm*)

AD /eɪ'diː/ *abbr* (= **Anno Domini**) d. de J.C.

Adam's apple /ædəmz'æpl/ *n* nuez *f* de Adán

adapt /ə'dæpt/ *vt* adaptar. ● *vi* adaptarse. **~ability** /-ə'bɪlətɪ/ *n* adaptabilidad *f*. **~able** /-əbl/ *adj* adaptable. **~ation** /ædæp'teɪʃn/ *n* adaptación *f*; (*of book etc*) versión *f*. **~or** /ə'dæptə(r)/ *n* (*Elec*, *with several sockets*) enchufe *m* múltiple; (*Elec*, *for different sockets*) adaptador *m*

add /æd/ *vt* añadir. ● *vi* sumar. ◻ **~ up** *vt* sumar; (*fig*) tener sentido. **~**

up to equivaler a

adder /'ædə(r)/ n víbora f

addict /'ædɪkt/ n adicto m; (fig) entusiasta m & f. ~**ed** /ə'dɪktɪd/ adj. ~**ed to** adicto a; (fig) fanático de. ~**ion** /-ʃn/ n (Med) dependencia f; (fig) afición f. ~**ive** /ə'dɪktɪv/ adj que crea adicción; (fig) que crea hábito

addition /ə'dɪʃn/ n suma f. **in** ~ además. ~**al** adj suplementario

address /ə'dres/ n dirección f; (on form) domicilio m; (speech) discurso m. ● vt poner la dirección en; (speak to) dirigirse a. ~ **book** n libreta f de direcciones. ~**ee** /ædre'si:/ n destinatario m

adept /'ædept/ adj & n experto (m)

adequa|cy /'ædɪkwəsɪ/ n suficiencia f. ~**te** /-ət/ adj suficiente, adecuado. ~**tely** adv suficientemente, adecuadamente

adhere /əd'hɪə(r)/ vi adherirse (to a); observar (rule). ~**nce** /-rəns/ n adhesión f; (to rules) observancia f

adhes|ion /əd'hi:ʒn/ n adherencia f. ~**ve** /-sɪv/ adj & n adhesivo (m)

adjacent /ə'dʒeɪsnt/ adj contiguo

adjective /'ædʒɪktɪv/ n adjetivo m

adjourn /ə'dʒɜːn/ vt aplazar; suspender (meeting etc). ● vi suspenderse

adjust /ə'dʒʌst/ vt ajustar (machine); (arrange) arreglar. ● vi. ~ **(to)** adaptarse (a). ~**able** adj ajustable. ~**ment** n adaptación f; (Tec) ajuste m

administer /əd'mɪnɪstə(r)/ vt administrar

administrat|ion /ədmɪnɪ'streɪʃn/ n administración f. ~**ive** /əd'mɪnɪstrətɪv/ adj administrativo. ~**or** /əd'mɪnɪstreɪtə(r)/ n administrador m

admirable /'ædmərəbl/ adj admirable

admiral /'ædmərəl/ n almirante m

admir|ation /ædmə'reɪʃn/ n admiración f. ~**e** /əd'maɪə(r)/ vt admirar. ~**er** /əd'maɪərə(r)/ n admirador m

admission /əd'mɪʃn/ n admisión f; (entry) entrada f

admit /əd'mɪt/ vt (pt admitted) dejar entrar; (acknowledge) admitir, reconocer. ~ **to** confesar. be ~**ted** (to hospital etc) ingresar. ~**tance** n entrada f. ~**tedly** adv es verdad que

admonish /əd'mɒnɪʃ/ vt reprender; (advise) aconsejar

ado /ə'du:/ n alboroto m; (trouble) dificultad f. **without more** or **further** ~ en seguida, sin más

adolescen|ce /ædə'lesns/ n adolescencia f. ~**t** adj & n adolescente (m & f)

adopt /ə'dɒpt/ vt adoptar. ~**ed** adj (child) adoptivo. ~**ion** /-ʃn/ n adopción f

ador|able /ə'dɔːrəbl/ adj adorable. ~**ation** /ædə'reɪʃn/ n adoración f. ~**e** /ə'dɔː(r)/ vt adorar

adorn /ə'dɔːn/ vt adornar. ~**ment** n adorno m

adrift /ə'drɪft/ adj & adv a la deriva

adult /'ædʌlt/ adj & n adulto (m)

adulter|er /ə'dʌltərə(r)/ n adúltero m. ~**ess** /-ɪs/ n adúltera f. ~**y** n adulterio m

advance /əd'vɑːns/ vt adelantar. ● vi adelantarse. ● n adelanto m. **in** ~ con anticipación, por adelantado. ~**d** adj avanzado; (studies) superior

advantage /əd'vɑːntɪdʒ/ n ventaja f. **take** ~ **of** aprovecharse de; abusar de (person). ~**ous** /ædvən

'teɪdʒəs/ adj ventajoso

advent /'ædvənt/ n venida f. **A~**
n adviento m

adventure /əd'ventʃə(r)/ n
aventura f. **~er** n aventurero m.
~ous adj (person) aventurero;
(thing) arriesgado; (fig, bold)
audaz

adverb /'ædvз:b/ n adverbio m

adversary /'ædvəsəri/ n adversa-
rio m

adverse /ædvз:s/ adj adverso,
contrario, desfavorable. **~ity** /əd
'vз:səti/ n infortunio m

advert /'ædvз:t/ n 🇬🇧 anuncio m,
aviso m (LAm). **~ise** /'ædvətaɪz/ vt
anunciar. **~vi** hacer publicidad;
(seek, sell) poner un anuncio.
~isement /əd'vз:tɪsmənt/ n anun-
cio m, aviso m (LAm). **~iser**
/'ædvətaɪzə(r)/ n anunciante m & f

advice /əd'vaɪs/ n consejo m; (re-
port) informe m

advisable /əd'vaɪzəbl/ adj acon-
sejable. **~e** /əd'vaɪz/ vt aconsejar;
(inform) avisar. **~e against** acon-
sejar en contra de. **~er** n conse-
jero m; (consultant) asesor m. **~ory**
adj consultivo

advocate /'ædvəkət/ n defensor
m; (Jurid) abogado m. **•**/'ædvəkeɪt/
vt recomendar

aerial /'eərɪəl/ adj aéreo. **•**n an-
tena f

aerobics /eə'rəʊbɪks/ npl aeró-
bica f

aerodrome /'eərədrəʊm/ n aeró-
dromo m

aerodynamic /eərəʊdə'næmɪk/
adj aerodinámico

aeroplane /'eərəpleɪn/ n avión m

aerosol /'eərəsɒl/ n aerosol m

aesthetic /i:s'θetɪk/ adj estético

afar /ə'fɑ:(r)/ adv lejos

affable /'æfəbl/ adj afable

affair /ə'feə(r)/ n asunto m. (love)
~ aventura f, amorío m. **~s** npl
(business) negocios mpl

affect /ə'fekt/ vt afectar; (pretend)
fingir. **~ation** /æfek'teɪʃn/ n afec-
tación f. **~ed** adj afectado, amane-
rado

affection /ə'fekʃn/ n cariño m.
~ate /-ət/ adj cariñoso

affiliate /ə'fɪlɪeɪt/ vt afiliar

affirm /ə'fз:m/ vt afirmar. **~ative**
/-ətɪv/ adj afirmativo. **•**n respuesta
f afirmativa

afflict /ə'flɪkt/ vt afligir. **~ion**
/-ʃn/ n aflicción f, pena f

affluence /'æfluəns/ n riqueza f.
~t adj rico.

afford /ə'fɔ:d/ vt permitirse; (pro-
vide) dar. he can't **~** a car no le
alcanza el dinero para comprar un
coche

affront /ə'frʌnt/ n afrenta f,
ofensa f. **•**vt afrentar, ofender

afield /ə'fi:ld/ adv. far **~** muy lejos

afloat /ə'fləʊt/ adv a flote

afraid /ə'freɪd/ adj. be **~** tener
miedo (of a); (be sorry) sentir, la-
mentar

afresh /ə'freʃ/ adv de nuevo

Africa /'æfrɪkə/ n África f. **~n** adj
& n africano (m). **~n-American** adj
& n norteamericano (m) de origen
africano

after /'ɑ:ftə(r)/ adv después; (be-
hind) detrás. **•**prep después de; (be-
hind) detrás de. it's twenty **~**
four (Amer) son las cuatro y veinte.
be **~** (seek) andar en busca de.
•conj después de que. **•**adj poste-
rior. **~-effect** n consecuencia f,
efecto m secundario. **~math**
/'ɑ:ftəmæθ/ n secuelas fpl. **~noon**
/-'nu:n/ n tarde f. **~shave** n loción

f para después de afeitarse. **∼thought** *n* ocurrencia *f* tardía. **∼wards** /-wədz/ *adv* después

again /ə'gen/ *adv* otra vez; (*besides*) además. **do ∼** volver a hacer, hacer otra vez. **∼ and ∼** una y otra vez

against /ə'genst/ *prep* contra; (*in opposition to*) en contra de, contra

age /eɪdʒ/ *n* edad *f*. **at four years of ∼** a los cuatro años. **under ∼** menor de edad. **∼s** *npl* ① siglos *mpl.* **●vt/i** (*pres p* **ageing**) envejecer. **∼d** /'eɪdʒd/ *adj* de ... años. **∼d 10** de 10 años. **∼d** /'eɪdʒɪd/ *adj* viejo, anciano

agency /'eɪdʒənsɪ/ *n* agencia *f*; (*department*) organismo *m*

agenda /ə'dʒendə/ *n* orden *m* del día

agent /'eɪdʒənt/ *n* agente *m & f*; (*representative*) representante *m & f*

aggravat|e /'ægrəveɪt/ *vt* agravar; (*fam, irritate*) irritar. **∼ion** /-'veɪʃn/ *n* agravación *f*; (*fam, irritation*) irritación *f*

aggress|ion /ə'greʃn/ *n* agresión *f*. **∼ive** *adj* agresivo. **∼iveness** *n* agresividad *f*. **∼or** *n* agresor *m*

aggrieved /ə'griːvd/ *adj* apenado, ofendido

aghast /ə'gɑːst/ *adj* horrorizado

agil|e /'ædʒaɪl/ *adj* ágil. **∼ity** /ə'dʒɪlətɪ/ *n* agilidad *f*

aging /'eɪdʒɪŋ/ *adj* envejecido. **●n** envejecimiento *m*

agitat|e /'ædʒɪteɪt/ *vt* agitar. **∼ed** *adj* nervioso. **∼ion** /-'teɪʃn/ *n* agitación *f*, excitación *f*. **∼or** *n* agitador *m*

ago /ə'gəʊ/ *adv.* **a long time ∼** hace mucho tiempo. **3 days ∼** hace 3 días

agon|ize /'ægənaɪz/ *vi* atormen-

tarse. **∼izing** *adj* (*pain*) atroz; (*experience*) angustioso. **∼y** *n* dolor *m* (*agudo*); (*mental*) angustia *f*

agree /ə'griː/ *vt* acordar. **●vi** estar de acuerdo; (*of figures*) concordar; (*get on*) entenderse. □ **∼ on** *vt* acordar (*date, details*). □ **∼ with** *vt* (*of food etc*) sentarle bien a. **∼able** /ə'griːəbl/ *adj* agradable. **be ∼able** (*willing*) estar de acuerdo. **∼d** *adj* (*time, place*) convenido. **∼ment** /-mənt/ *n* acuerdo *m*. **in ∼ment** de acuerdo

agricultur|al /ægrɪ'kʌltʃərəl/ *adj* agrícola. **∼e** /'ægrɪkʌltʃə(r)/ *n* agricultura *f*

aground /ə'graʊnd/ *adv.* **run ∼** (*of ship*) varar, encallar

ahead /ə'hed/ *adv* delante; (*in time*) antes de tiempo. **be ∼** ir delante

aid /eɪd/ *vt* ayudar. **●n** ayuda *f*. **in ∼ of** a beneficio de

AIDS /eɪdz/ *n* sida *m*

ailment /'eɪlmənt/ *n* enfermedad *f*

aim /eɪm/ *vt* apuntar; (*fig*) dirigir. **●vi** apuntar; (*fig*) pretender. **●n** puntería *f*; (*fig*) objetivo *m*. **∼less** *adj.* **∼lessly** *adv* sin objeto, sin rumbo

air /eə(r)/ *n* aire *m*. **be on the ∼** (*Radio, TV*) estar en el aire. **put on ∼s** darse aires. **●vt** airear. **put on ∼ bag** *n* (*Auto*) bolsa *f* de aire. **∼ base** *n* base *f* aérea. **∼borne** *adj* en el aire; (*Mil*) aerotransportado. **∼-conditioned** *adj* climatizado, con aire acondicionado. **∼ conditioning** *n* aire *m* acondicionado. **∼craft** *n* (*pl invar*) avión *m*. **∼craft carrier** *n* portaaviones *m*. **∼field** *n* aeródromo *m*. **A∼ Force** *n* fuerzas *fpl* aéreas. **∼ freshener** *n* ambientador *m*. **∼gun** *n* escopeta *f* de aire comprimido. **∼ hostess** *n* aza-

fata f, aeromoza f (LAm). ~line n
línea f aérea. ~ mail n correo m
aéreo. ~plane n (Amer) avión m.
~port n aeropuerto m. ~sick adj
mareado (en un avión). ~tight adj
hermético. ~ traffic controller n
controlador m aéreo. ~y adj (-ier,
-iest) aireado; (manner) desenfa-
dado

aisle /aɪl/ n nave f lateral; (gang-
way) pasillo m

ajar /əˈdʒɑː(r)/ adj entreabierto

alarm /əˈlɑːm/ n alarma f. ● vt
asustar. ~ **clock** n despertador m.
~**ist** n alarmista m & f

Albania /ælˈbeɪnɪə/ n Albania f.
~**n** adj & n albanés (m)

albatross /ˈælbətrɒs/ n alba-
tros m

album /ˈælbəm/ n álbum m

alcohol /ˈælkəhɒl/ n alcohol m.
~**ic** /-ˈhɒlɪk/ adj & n alcohólico (m)

alcove /ˈælkəʊv/ n nicho m

ale /eɪl/ n cerveza f

alert /əˈlɜːt/ adj vivo; (watchful) vi-
gilante. ● n alerta f. on the ~
alerta. ● vt avisar

algebra /ˈældʒɪbrə/ n álgebra f

Algeria /ælˈdʒɪərɪə/ n Argelia f.
~**n** adj & n argelino (m)

alias /ˈeɪlɪəs/ n (pl -ases) alias m.
● adv alias

alibi /ˈælɪbaɪ/ n (pl -is) coartada f

alien /ˈeɪlɪən/ n extranjero m. ● adj
ajeno. ~**ate** /-eɪt/ vt enajenar.
~**ation** /-ˈneɪʃn/ n enajenación f

alienate|e /ˈeɪlɪəneɪt/ vt enajenar.
~**ion** /-ˈneɪʃn/ n enajenación f

alight /əˈlaɪt/ adj ardiendo; (light)
encendido

align /əˈlaɪn/ vt alinear. ~**ment** n
alineación f

alike /əˈlaɪk/ adj parecido, seme-

jante. **look** or **be** ~ parecerse.
● adv de la misma manera

alive /əˈlaɪv/ adj vivo. ~ **with**
lleno de

alkali /ˈælkəlaɪ/ n (pl -is) álcali m.
~**ne** adj alcalino

all /ɔːl/

● adjective todo, -da; (pl) todos,
-das. ~ day todo el día. ~ the
windows todas las ventanas. ~
four of us went fuimos los
cuatro

● pronoun

····▸ (everything) todo. that's ~
eso es todo. I did ~ I could to
persuade her hice todo lo que
pude para convencerla

····▸ (after pronoun) todo, -da;
(pl) todos, -das. he helped us
~ nos ayudó a todos

····▸ all of todo, -da, (pl) todos,
-das. ~ of the paintings todos
los cuadros. ~ of the milk
toda la leche

····▸ (in phrases) all in all en ge-
neral. not at all (in no way) de
ninguna manera; (after thanks)
de nada, no hay de qué. it's
not at ~ bad no está nada
mal. I don't like it at ~ no me
gusta nada

● adverb

····▸ (completely) completamente.
she was ~ alone estaba com-
pletamente sola. I got ~ dirty
me ensucié todo/toda. I don't
know him ~ that well no lo
conozco tan bien

····▸ (in scores) the score was
one ~ iban empatados uno a
uno

····▸ (in phrases) to be all for sth

estar completamente a favor de algo. **to be all in** 🔲 estar rendido

all-around /ɔːləˈraʊnd/ adj (Amer) completo

allay /əˈleɪ/ vt aliviar (pain); aquietar (fears etc)

all-clear /ɔːlˈklɪə(r)/ n fin m de (la) alarma; (permission) visto m bueno

alleg|ation /æləˈɡeɪʃn/ n alegato m. **~e** /əˈledʒ/ vt alegar. **~ed** adj presunto. **~edly** /-ɪdlɪ/ adv según se dice, supuestamente

allegiance /əˈliːdʒəns/ n lealtad f

allegory /ˈæləɡərɪ/ n alegoría f

allerg|ic /əˈlɜːdʒɪk/ adj alérgico (to a). **~y** /ˈælədʒɪ/ n alergia f

alleviate /əˈliːvɪeɪt/ vt aliviar

alley /ˈælɪ/ (pl -eys) n callejuela f

alliance /əˈlaɪəns/ n alianza f

alligator /ˈælɪɡeɪtə(r)/ n caimán m

allocat|e /ˈæləkeɪt/ vt asignar; (share out) repartir. **~ion** /-ˈkeɪʃn/ n asignación f; (distribution) reparto m

allot /əˈlɒt/ vt (pt allotted) asignar. **~ment** n asignación f; (land) parcela f

allow /əˈlaʊ/ vt permitir; (grant) conceder; (reckon on) prever; (agree) admitir. **□ ~ for** vt tener en cuenta. **~ance** /əˈlaʊəns/ n concesión f; (pension) pensión f; (Com) rebaja f. **make ~ances for** ser indulgente con (person); (take into account) tener en cuenta

alloy /ˈælɔɪ/ n aleación f

all: **~ right** adj & adv bien. ● int ¡vale!, ¡okey! (esp LAm), ¡órale! (Mex). **~-round** adj completo

allusion /əˈluːʒn/ n alusión f

ally /ˈælaɪ/ n aliado m. ● /əˈlaɪ/ vt. **~ o.s.** aliarse (with con)

almighty /ɔːlˈmaɪtɪ/ adj todopoderoso

almond /ˈɑːmənd/ n almendra f

almost /ˈɔːlməʊst/ adv casi

alone /əˈləʊn/ adj solo. ● adv sólo, solamente

along /əˈlɒŋ/ prep por, a lo largo de. ● adv. **~ with** junto con. **all ~** todo el tiempo. **come ~** venga. **~side** /-ˈsaɪd/ adv (Naut) al costado. ● prep al lado de

aloof /əˈluːf/ adv apartado. ● adj reservado

aloud /əˈlaʊd/ adv en voz alta

alphabet /ˈælfəbet/ n alfabeto m. **~ical** /-ˈbetɪkl/ adj alfabético

Alps /ælps/ npl. **the ~** los Alpes

already /ɔːlˈredɪ/ adv ya

Alsatian /ælˈseɪʃn/ n pastor m alemán

also /ˈɔːlsəʊ/ adv también; (moreover) además

altar /ˈɔːltə(r)/ n altar m

alter /ˈɔːltə(r)/ vt cambiar. ● vi cambiarse. **~ation** /-ˈreɪʃn/ n modificación f; (to garment) arreglo m

alternate /ɔːlˈtɜːnət/ adj alterno; (Amer) see **ALTERNATIVE**. ● /ˈɔːltəneɪt/ vi/t alternar. **~ly** /ɔːlˈtɜːnətlɪ/ adv alternativamente

alternative /ɔːlˈtɜːnətɪv/ adj alternativo. ● n alternativa f. **~ly** adv en cambio, por otra parte

although /ɔːlˈðəʊ/ conj aunque

altitude /ˈæltɪtjuːd/ n altitud f

altogether /ɔːltəˈɡeðə(r)/ adv completamente; (on the whole) en total

aluminium /æljʊˈmɪnɪəm/, **aluminum** /əˈluːmɪnəm/ (Amer) n aluminio m a

always /ˈɔːlweɪz/ adv siempre

am /æm/ see BE

a.m. abbr (= ante meridiem) de la mañana

amalgamate /əˈmælɡəmeɪt/ vt amalgamar. ●vi amalgamarse

amass /əˈmæs/ vt acumular

amateur /ˈæmətə(r)/ adj & n amateur (m & f). ~**ish** adj (pej) torpe, chapucero

amaz|e /əˈmeɪz/ vt asombrar. ~**ed** adj asombrado, estupefacto. be ~**ed** at quedarse asombrado de, asombrarse de. ~**ement** n asombro m. ~**ing** adj increíble

ambassador /æmˈbæsədə(r)/ n embajador m

ambigu|ity /æmbɪˈɡjuːətɪ/ n ambigüedad f. ~**ous** /æmˈbɪɡjʊəs/ adj ambiguo

ambiti|on /æmˈbɪʃn/ n ambición f. ~**ous** /-ʃəs/ adj ambicioso

ambivalent /æmˈbɪvələnt/ adj ambivalente

amble /ˈæmbl/ vi andar despacio, andar sin prisa

ambulance /ˈæmbjʊləns/ n ambulancia f

ambush /ˈæmbʊʃ/ n emboscada f. ●vt tender una emboscada a

amen /ɑːˈmen/ int amén

amend /əˈmend/ vt enmendar. ~**ment** n enmienda f. ~**s** npl. make ~**s** reparar

amenities /əˈmiːnətɪz/ npl servicios mpl; (of hotel, club) instalaciones fpl

America /əˈmerɪkə/ n (continent) América f; (North America) Estados mpl Unidos, Norteamérica f. ~**n** adj & n americano (m); (North American) estadounidense (m & f), norteamericano (m). ~**nism** n americanismo m

American dream El sueño americano se basa en la idea de que cualquier persona en los Estados Unidos puede prosperar mediante el trabajo duro. Para los inmigrantes y las minorías, el concepto abarca la libertad y la igualdad de derechos.

amiable /ˈeɪmɪəbl/ adj simpático

amicable /ˈæmɪkəbl/ adj amistoso

amid(st) /əˈmɪd(st)/ prep entre, en medio de

ammonia /əˈməʊnɪə/ n amoníaco m, amoniaco m

ammunition /æmjʊˈnɪʃn/ n municiones fpl

amnesty /ˈæmnəstɪ/ n amnistía f

amok /əˈmɒk/ adv. run ~ volverse loco

among(st) /əˈmʌŋ(st)/ prep entre

amount /əˈmaʊnt/ n cantidad f; (total) total m, suma f. □ ~ **to** vt sumar; (fig) equivaler a, significar

amp(ere) /ˈæmp(eə(r))/ n amperio m

amphibi|an /æmˈfɪbɪən/ n anfibio m. ~**ous** /-əs/ adj anfibio

amphitheatre /ˈæmfɪθɪətə(r)/ n anfiteatro m

ampl|e /ˈæmpl/ adj (-er, -est) amplio; (enough) suficiente; (plentiful) abundante. ~**y** adv ampliamente, bastante

amplif|ier /ˈæmplɪfaɪə(r)/ n amplificador m. ~**y** /ˈæmplɪfaɪ/ vt amplificar

amputat|e /ˈæmpjʊteɪt/ vt amputar. ~**ion** /-ˈteɪʃn/ n amputación f

amus|e /əˈmjuːz/ vt divertir. ~**ed** adj (expression) divertido. keep s.o. ~**ed** entretener a uno. ~**ement** n diversión f. ~**ing** adj divertido

an /ən, æn/ *see* A

anaemia /əˈniːmɪə/ n anemia f. **~c** *adj* anémico

anaesthetic /ænɪsˈθetɪk/ n anestésico m. **~tist** /əˈniːsθɪtɪst/ n anestesista m & f

anagram /ˈænəgræm/ n anagrama m

analogy /əˈnælədʒɪ/ n analogía f

analyse /ˈænəlaɪz/ vt analizar. **~sis** /əˈnæləsɪs/ n (pl -ses /-siːz/) n análisis m. **~st** /ˈænəlɪst/ n analista m & f. **~tic(al)** /ænəˈlɪtɪk(əl)/ adj analítico

anarchist /ˈænəkɪst/ n anarquista m & f. **~y** n anarquía f

anatomical /ænəˈtɒmɪkl/ adj anatómico. **~y** /əˈnætəmɪ/ n anatomía f

ancestor /ˈænsestə(r)/ n antepasado m. **~ral** /-ˈsestrəl/ adj ancestral. **~ry** /ˈænsestrɪ/ n ascendencia f

anchor /ˈæŋkə(r)/ n ancla f. ●vt anclar; (fig) sujetar. ●vi anclar. **~man** n (on TV) presentador m. **~woman** n (on TV) presentadora f.

ancient /ˈeɪnʃənt/ adj antiguo, viejo

ancillary /ænˈsɪlərɪ/ adj auxiliar

and /ænd, ənd/ conj y; (before i and hi-) e. bread ~ butter pan m con mantequilla. go ~ see him ve a verlo. more ~ more cada vez más. try ~ come trata de venir

anecdote /ˈænɪkdəʊt/ adj anecdótico. **~e** /ˈænɪkdəʊt/ n anécdota f

anew /əˈnjuː/ adv de nuevo

angel /ˈeɪndʒl/ n ángel m. **~ic** /ænˈdʒelɪk/ adj angélico

anger /ˈæŋgə(r)/ n ira f. ●vt enfa-

dar, (esp LAm) enojar

angle /ˈæŋgl/ n ángulo m; (fig) punto m de vista. **~r** /ˈæŋglə(r)/ n pescador m

Anglican /ˈæŋglɪkən/ adj & n anglicano (m)

angrily /ˈæŋgrɪlɪ/ adv con enfado, (esp LAm) con enojo. **~y** /ˈæŋgrɪ/ adj (-ier, -iest) enfadado, (esp LAm) enojado. get **~y** enfadarse, enojarse (esp LAm)

anguish /ˈæŋgwɪʃ/ n angustia f

animal /ˈænɪməl/ adj & n animal (m)

animate /ˈænɪmeɪt/ vt animar. **~ion** /-ˈmeɪʃn/ n animación f

animosity /ænɪˈmɒsətɪ/ n animosidad f

ankle /ˈæŋkl/ n tobillo m. **~ boot** botín m. **~ sock** calcetín m corto

annexe /ˈæneks/ n anexo m

annihilate /əˈnaɪəleɪt/ vt aniquilar. **~ion** /-ˈleɪʃn/ n aniquilación f

anniversary /ænɪˈvɜːsərɪ/ n aniversario m

announce /əˈnaʊns/ vt anunciar, comunicar. **~ment** n anuncio m; (official) comunicado m. **~r** n (Radio, TV) locutor m

annoy /əˈnɔɪ/ vt molestar. **~ance** n molestia f. **~ed** adj enfadado, enojado (LAm). **~ing** adj molesto

annual /ˈænjʊəl/ adj anual. ●n anuario m. **~ly** adv cada año

annul /əˈnʌl/ vt (pt annulled) anular. **~ment** n anulación f

anonymous /əˈnɒnɪməs/ adj anónimo

anorak /ˈænəræk/ n anorac m

another /əˈnʌðə(r)/ adj & pron otro. ~ 10 minutes 10 minutos más. in ~ way de otra manera. one ~ el uno al otro; (pl) unos a otros

answer /'ɑːnsə(r)/ n respuesta f; (solution) solución f. ● vt contestar; escuchar, oír (prayer). ~ **the door** abrir la puerta. ● vi contestar. □ ~ **back** vi contestar. □ ~ **for** vt ser responsable de. ~**able** adj responsable. ~**ing machine** n contestador m automático

ant /ænt/ n hormiga f

antagoni|sm /æn'tægənɪzəm/ n antagonismo m. ~**stic** /-'nɪstɪk/ adj antagónico, opuesto. ~**ze** /æn 'tægənaɪz/ vt provocar la enemistad de

Antarctic /æn'tɑːktɪk/ adj antártico. ● n the ~ la región antártica

antelope /'æntɪləʊp/ n antílope m

antenatal /'æntɪneɪtl/ adj prenatal

antenna /æn'tenə/ (pl -nae /-niː/) (of insect etc) n antena f; (pl -nas) (of radio, TV) antena f

anthem /'ænθəm/ n himno m

anthology /æn'θɒlədʒɪ/ n antología f

anthrax /'ænθræks/ n ántrax m

anthropolog|ist /ænθrə 'pɒlədʒɪst/ n antropólogo m. ~**y** n antropología f

anti-... /ænti/ pref anti... ~**aircraft** /-'eəkrɑːft/ adj antiaéreo

antibiotic /æntɪbaɪ'ɒtɪk/ adj & n antibiótico (m)

anticipat|e /æn'tɪsɪpeɪt/ vt anticiparse a; (foresee) prever; (forestall) prevenir. ~**ion** /-'peɪʃn/ n (foresight) previsión f; (expectation) expectativa f

anti: ~**climax** /-'klaɪmæks/ n decepción f. ~**clockwise** /-'klɒkwaɪz/ adv & adj en sentido contrario a las agujas del reloj

antidote /'æntɪdəʊt/ n antídoto m

antifreeze /'æntɪfriːz/ n anticongelante m

antiperspirant /ænti 'pɜːspɪrənt/ n antitranspirante m

antiquated /'æntɪkweɪtɪd/ adj anticuado

antique /æn'tiːk/ adj antiguo. ● n antigüedad f. ~ **dealer** anticuario m. ~ **shop** tienda f de antigüedades

antiquity /æn'tɪkwətɪ/ n antigüedad f

anti: ~**septic** /-'septɪk/ adj & n antiséptico (m). ~**social** /-'səʊʃl/ adj antisocial

antlers /'æntləz/ npl cornamenta f

anus /'eɪnəs/ n ano m

anvil /'ænvɪl/ n yunque m

anxi|ety /æŋ'zaɪətɪ/ n ansiedad f; (worry) inquietud f; (eagerness) anhelo m. ~**ous** /'æŋkʃəs/ adj inquieto; (eager) deseoso. ~**ously** adv con inquietud; (eagerly) con impaciencia

any /'enɪ/ adj algún; (negative) ningún m; (whatever) cualquier; (every) todo. at ~ moment en cualquier momento. have you ~ wine? ¿tienes vino? ● pron alguno; (negative) ninguno. have we ~? ¿tenemos algunos? not ~ ninguno. ● adv (a little) un poco, algo. is it ~ better? ¿está algo mejor?

anybody /'enɪbɒdɪ/ pron alguien; (after negative) nadie. ~ **can do it** cualquiera puede hacerlo

anyhow /'enɪhaʊ/ adv de todas formas; (in spite of all) a pesar de todo; (badly) de cualquier manera

anyone /'enɪwʌn/ pron see **ANYBODY**

anything /'enɪθɪŋ/ pron algo; (whatever) cualquier cosa; (after negative) nada. ~ **but** todo menos

anyway /'eniweı/ adv de todas formas

anywhere /'eniweə(r)/ adv en cualquier parte; (after negative) en ningún sitio. ~ else en cualquier otro lugar. ~ you go dondequiera que vayas

apart /ə'pɑːt/ adv aparte; (separated) separado. ~ from aparte de. come ~ romperse. take ~ desmontar

apartheid /ə'pɑːtheıt/ n apartheid m

apartment /ə'pɑːtmənt/ n (Amer) apartamento m, piso m. ~ **building** n (Amer) edificio m de apartamentos, casa f de pisos

apath|etic /æpə'θetık/ adj apático. ~**y** /'æpəθı/ n apatía f

ape /eıp/ n mono m. ● vt imitar

aperitif /ə'perətıf/ n aperitivo m

aperture /'æpətʃʊə(r)/ n abertura f

apex /'eıpeks/ n ápice m

aphrodisiac /æfrə'dızıæk/ adj & n afrodisíaco (m), afrodisiaco (m)

apolog|etic /əpɒlə'dʒetık/ adj lleno de disculpas. be ~**etic** disculparse. ~**ize** /ə'pɒlədʒaız/ vi disculparse (for de). ~**y** /ə'pɒlədʒı/ n disculpa f

apostle /ə'pɒsl/ n apóstol m

apostrophe /ə'pɒstrəfı/ n apóstrofo m

appal /ə'pɔːl/ vt (pt appalled) horrorizar. ~**ling** adj espantoso

apparatus /æpə'reıtəs/ n aparato m

apparel /ə'pærəl/ n (Amer) ropa f

apparent /ə'pærənt/ adj aparente; (clear) evidente. ~**ly** adv por lo visto

apparition /æpə'rıʃn/ n aparición f

appeal /ə'piːl/ vi apelar; (attract) atraer. ● n llamamiento m; (attraction) atractivo m; (Jurid) apelación f. ~**ing** adj atrayente

appear /ə'pıə(r)/ vi aparecer; (seem) parecer; (in court) comparecer. ~**ance** n aparición f; (aspect) aspecto m; (in court) comparecencia f

appease /ə'piːz/ vt aplacar; (pacify) apaciguar

append /ə'pend/ vt adjuntar

appendicitis /əpendı'saıtıs/ n apendicitis f

appendix /ə'pendıks/ n (pl -ices /-ısıːz/) (of book) apéndice m. (pl -ixes) (organ) apéndice m

appetite /'æpıtaıt/ n apetito m

applau|d /ə'plɔːd/ vt/i aplaudir. ~**se** /ə'plɔːz/ n aplausos mpl. round of ~se aplauso m

apple /'æpl/ n manzana f. ~ **tree** n manzano m

appliance /ə'plaıəns/ n aparato m. electrical ~ electrodoméstico m

applic|able /'æplıkəbl/ adj aplicable; (relevant) pertinente. ~**ant** /'æplıkənt/ n candidato m, solicitante m & f. ~**ation** /æplı'keıʃn/ n aplicación f; (request) solicitud f. ~**ation form** formulario m (de solicitud)

appl|ied /ə'plaıd/ adj aplicado. ~**y** /ə'plaı/ vt aplicar. ● vi aplicarse; (ask) presentar una solicitud. ~**y for** solicitar (job etc)

appoint /ə'pɔınt/ vt nombrar; (fix) señalar. ~**ment** n cita f

apprais|al /ə'preızl/ n evaluación f. ~**e** /ə'preız/ vt evaluar

appreciable /ə'priːʃəbl/ adj (considerable) considerable

appreciat|e /ə'priːʃıeıt/ vt (value)

a apreciar; (*understand*) comprender; (*be grateful for*) agradecer. ∼ion /-'eɪʃn/ n aprecio m; (*gratitude*) agradecimiento m. ∼ive /-ɪv/ adj /ə'priːʃɪətɪv/ adj agradecido

apprehen|sion /æprɪ'henʃn/ n (*fear*) recelo m. ∼sive adj aprensivo

apprentice /ə'prentɪs/ n aprendiz m. •vt. be ∼d to s.o. estar de aprendiz con uno. ∼ship n aprendizaje m

approach /ə'prəʊtʃ/ vt acercarse a. •vi acercarse. •n acercamiento m; (*to problem*) enfoque m; (*access*) acceso m

appropriate /ə'prəʊprɪət/ adj apropiado. •/ə'prəʊprɪeɪt/ vt apropiarse de. ∼ly /-ətlɪ/ adv apropiadamente

approv|al /ə'pruːvl/ n aprobación f. on ∼al a la prueba. ∼e /ə'pruːv/ vt/i aprobar. ∼ingly adv con aprobación

approximat|e /ə'prɒksɪmət/ adj aproximado. •/ə'prɒksɪmeɪt/ vt aproximarse a. ∼ely /-ətlɪ/ adv aproximadamente. ∼ion /-'meɪʃn/ n aproximación f

apricot /'eɪprɪkɒt/ n albaricoque m, chabacano m (Mex)

April /'eɪprəl/ n abril m. ∼ fool! ¡inocentón!

apron /'eɪprən/ n delantal m

apt /æpt/ adj apropiado. be ∼ to tener tendencia a. ∼itude /'æptɪtjuːd/ n aptitud f. ∼ly adv acertadamente

aquarium /ə'kweərɪəm/ n (pl -ums) acuario m

Aquarius /ə'kweərɪəs/ n Acuario m

aquatic /ə'kwætɪk/ adj acuático

aqueduct /'ækwɪdʌkt/ n acueducto m

Arab /'ærəb/ adj & n árabe (m & f). ∼ian /ə'reɪbɪən/ adj árabe. ∼ic /'ærəbɪk/ adj & n árabe (m). ∼ic numerals números mpl arábigos

arable /'ærəbl/ adj cultivable

arbitrary /'ɑːbɪtrərɪ/ adj arbitrario

arbitrat|e /'ɑːbɪtreɪt/ vi arbitrar. ∼ion /-'treɪʃn/ n arbitraje m. ∼or n árbitro m

arc /ɑːk/ n arco m

arcade /ɑː'keɪd/ n arcada f; (*around square*) soportales mpl; (*shops*) galería f

arch /ɑːtʃ/ n arco m. •vt arquear. •vi arquearse

archaeolog|ical /ɑːkɪə'lɒdʒɪkl/ adj arqueológico. ∼ist /ɑːkɪ'ɒlədʒɪst/ n arqueólogo m. ∼y /ɑːkɪ'ɒlədʒɪ/ n arqueología f

archaic /ɑː'keɪɪk/ adj arcaico

archbishop /ɑːtʃ'bɪʃəp/ n arzobispo m

archer /'ɑːtʃə(r)/ n arquero m. ∼y n tiro m con arco

architect /'ɑːkɪtekt/ n arquitecto m. ∼ure /-tʃə(r)/ n arquitectura f. ∼ural /-'tektʃərəl/ adj arquitectónico

archives /'ɑːkaɪvz/ npl archivo m

archway /'ɑːtʃweɪ/ n arco m

Arctic /'ɑːktɪk/ adj ártico. •n. the ∼ el Ártico

ard|ent /'ɑːdənt/ adj fervoroso; (*supporter, lover*) apasionado. ∼our /'ɑːdə(r)/ n fervor m; (*love*) pasión f

arduous /'ɑːdjʊəs/ adj arduo

are /ɑː(r)/ see BE

area /'eərɪə/ n (Math) superficie f; (*of country*) zona f; (*of city*) barrio m

arena /ə'riːnə/ n arena f; (*scene of activity*) ruedo m

aren't /ɑːnt/ = are not

Argentin|a /ɑːdʒənˈtiːnə/ n Argentina f. **∼ian** /-ˈtɪnɪən/ adj & n argentino (m)

argu|able /ˈɑːɡjʊəbl/ adj discutible. **∼e** /ˈɑːgjuː/ vi discutir; (reason) razonar. **∼ment** /ˈɑːɡjʊmənt/ n disputa f; (reasoning) argumento m. **∼mentative** /ɑːɡjʊˈmentətɪv/ adj discutidor

arid /ˈærɪd/ adj árido

Aries /ˈeəriːz/ n Aries m

arise /əˈraɪz/ vi (pt arose, pp arisen) surgir (from de)

aristocra|cy /ærɪˈstɒkrəsɪ/ n aristocracia f. **∼t** /ˈærɪstəkræt/ n aristócrata m & f. **∼tic** /-ˈkrætɪk/ adj aristocrático

arithmetic /əˈrɪθmətɪk/ n aritmética f

ark /ɑːk/ n (Relig) arca f

arm /ɑːm/ n brazo m; (of garment) manga f. **∼s** npl armas fpl. ●vt armar

armament /ˈɑːməmənt/ n armamento m

arm: **∼band** n brazalete m. **∼chair** n sillón m

armed /ɑːmd/ adj armado. **∼ robbery** n robo a mano armada

armful /ˈɑːmfʊl/ n brazada f

armour /ˈɑːmə(r)/ n armadura f. **∼ed** /-məd/ adj blindado. **∼y** /ˈɑːmərɪ/ n arsenal m

armpit /ˈɑːmpɪt/ n sobaco m, axila f

army /ˈɑːmɪ/ n ejército m

aroma /əˈrəʊmə/ n aroma m

arose /əˈrəʊz/ see ARISE

around /əˈraʊnd/ adv alrededor; (near) cerca. all **∼** por todas partes. ●prep alrededor de; (with time) a eso de

arouse /əˈraʊz/ vt despertar

arrange /əˈreɪndʒ/ vt arreglar;

(fix) fijar. **∼ment** n arreglo m; (agreement) acuerdo m. **∼ments** npl (plans) preparativos mpl

arrears /əˈrɪəz/ npl atrasos mpl. in **∼** atrasado en el pago (with de)

arrest /əˈrest/ vt detener. ●n detención f. **under ∼** detenido

arriv|al /əˈraɪvl/ n llegada f. new **∼al** recién llegado m. **∼e** /əˈraɪv/ vi llegar

arrogan|ce /ˈærəgəns/ n arrogancia f. **∼t** adj arrogante. **∼tly** adv con arrogancia

arrow /ˈærəʊ/ n flecha f

arse /ɑːs/ n (vulgar) culo m

arsenal /ˈɑːsənl/ n arsenal m

arsenic /ˈɑːsnɪk/ n arsénico m

arson /ˈɑːsn/ n incendio m provocado. **∼ist** n incendiario m

art /ɑːt/ n arte m. **A∼s** npl (Univ) Filosofía y Letras fpl. fine **∼s** bellas artes fpl

art² /ɑːt/ (old use, with thou) see ARE

artery /ˈɑːtərɪ/ n arteria f

art gallery n museo m de arte, pinacoteca f; (commercial) galería f de arte

arthritis /ɑːˈθraɪtɪs/ n artritis f

article /ˈɑːtɪkl/ n artículo m. **∼ of clothing** prenda f de vestir

articulat|e /ɑːˈtɪkjʊlət/ adj (utterance) articulado; (person) que sabe expresarse. **∼** /ɑːˈtɪkjʊleɪt/ vt/i articular. **∼ed lorry** n camión m articulado. **∼ion** /-ˈleɪʃn/ n articulación f

artificial /ɑːtɪˈfɪʃl/ adj artificial. **∼ respiration** respiración f artificial

artillery /ɑːˈtɪlərɪ/ n artillería f

artist /ˈɑːtɪst/ n artista m & f. **∼tic** /ɑːˈtɪstɪk/ adj artístico. **∼ry** /ˈɑːtɪstrɪ/ n arte m, habilidad f

as /æz, əz/ adv & conj como; (since) ya que; (while) mientras. **∼ big ∼**

tan grande como. ~ far ~ (*distance*) hasta; (*qualitative*) en cuanto a. ~ far ~ I know que yo sepa. ~ **if** como si. ~ **long** ~ mientras. ~ **much** ~ tanto como. ~ **soon** ~ tan pronto como. ~ **well** también

asbestos /æz'bestɒs/ n amianto m, asbesto m

ascen|d /ə'send/ vt/i subir. A~**sion** /ə'senʃn/ n. the A~**sion** la Ascensión. ~**t** /ə'sent/ n subida f

ascertain /æsə'teɪn/ vt averiguar

ash /æʃ/ n ceniza f. • n. ~ (tree) fresno m

ashamed /ə'ʃeɪmd/ adj avergonzado (of de). be ~ of s.o. avergonzarse de uno

ashore /ə'ʃɔː(r)/ adv a tierra. go ~ desembarcar

ash: ~tray n cenicero m. A~ **Wednesday** n Miércoles m de Ceniza

Asia /'eɪʃə/ n Asia f. ~**n** adj & n asiático m. ~**tic** /-ɪ'ætɪk/ adj asiático

aside /ə'saɪd/ adv a un lado. • n (in theatre) aparte m

ask /ɑːsk/ vt pedir; hacer (question); (invite) invitar. ~ **about** enterarse de. ~ s.o. to do something pedirle a uno que haga algo. □~ **after** vt preguntar por. □~ **for** vt. ~ **for help** pedir ayuda. ~ **for trouble** buscarse problemas. □~ **in** vt. ~ s.o. in invitar a uno a pasar

askew /ə'skjuː/ adv & adj torcido

asleep /ə'sliːp/ adv & adj dormido. **fall** ~ dormirse

asparagus /ə'spærəgəs/ n espárrago m

aspect /'æspekt/ n aspecto m

asphalt /'æsfælt/ n asfalto m. • vt

asfaltar

aspir|ation /æspə'reɪʃn/ n aspiración f. ~**e** /əs'paɪə(r)/ vi aspirar

aspirin /'æsprɪn/ n aspirina f

ass /æs/ n asno m; (fig, fam) imbécil m; (Amer vulgar) culo m

assassin /ə'sæsɪn/ n asesino m. ~**ate** /-eɪt/ vt asesinar. ~**ation** /-'eɪʃn/ n asesinato m

assault /ə'sɔːlt/ n (Mil) ataque m; (Jurid) asalto m. • vt asaltar

assembl|e /ə'sembl/ vt reunir; (Mec) montar. • vi reunirse. ~**y** n reunión f; (Pol etc) asamblea f. ~**y line** n línea f de montaje

assent /ə'sent/ n asentimiento m. • vi asentir

assert /ə'sɜːt/ vt afirmar; hacer valer (one's rights). ~**ion** /-ʃn/ n afirmación f. ~**ive** adj positivo, firme

assess /ə'ses/ vt evaluar; (determine) determinar; fijar (tax etc). ~**ment** n evaluación f

asset /'æset/ n (advantage) ventaja f. ~**s** npl (Com) bienes mpl

assign /ə'saɪn/ vt asignar; (appoint) nombrar. ~**ment** n asignación f; (mission) misión f; (task) función f; (for school) trabajo m

assimilate /ə'sɪmɪleɪt/ vt asimilar. • vi asimilarse

assist /ə'sɪst/ vt/i ayudar. ~**ance** n ayuda f. ~**ant** n ayudante m & f; (shop) dependienta f, dependiente m. • adj auxiliar, adjunto

associat|e /ə'səʊʃɪeɪt/ vt asociar. • vi asociarse. ~ /ə'səʊʃɪət/ adj asociado. • n colega m & f; (Com) socio m. ~**ion** /-'eɪʃn/ n asociación f.

assort|ed /ə'sɔːtɪd/ adj surtido. ~**ment** n surtido m

assum|e /ə'sjuːm/ vt suponer; tomar (power, attitude); asumir (role, burden). **~ption** /ə'sʌmpʃn/ n suposición f

assur|ance /ə'ʃʊərəns/ n seguridad f; (insurance) seguro m. **~e** /ə'ʃʊə(r)/ vt asegurar. **~ed** adj seguro

asterisk /'æstərɪsk/ n asterisco m

asthma /'æsmə/ n asma f. **~tic** /-'mætɪk/ adj & n asmático (m)

astonish /ə'stɒnɪʃ/ vt asombrar. **~ed** adj asombrado. **~ing** adj asombroso. **~ment** n asombro m

astound /ə'staʊnd/ vt asombrar. **~ed** adj atónito. **~ing** adj increíble

astray /ə'streɪ/ adv. go **~** extraviarse. lead **~** llevar por mal camino

astrology /ə'strɒlədʒɪ/ n astrología f

astronaut /'æstrənɔːt/ n astronauta m & f

astronom|er /ə'strɒnəmə(r)/ n astrónomo m. **~ical** /æstrə'nɒmɪkl/ adj astronómico. **~y** /ə'strɒnəmɪ/ n astronomía f

astute /ə'stjuːt/ adj astuto

asylum /ə'saɪləm/ n asilo m. lunatic **~** manicomio m. **~ seeker** n solicitante m & f de asilo

de. I'll be at Rachel's estaré en casa de Rachel

····➤ (Comput: @) arroba f

····➤ (talking about time) at 7 o'clock a las siete. at night por la noche, de noche, en la noche (LAm). at Christmas en Navidad

····➤ (talking about age) a. at six (years of age) a los seis años

····➤ (with measurements, numbers etc) a. at 60 miles an hour a 60 millas por hora. at a depth of a una profundidad de. three at a time de tres en tres

➡ For translations of phrasal verbs with at, such as look at, see entries for those verbs

ate /et/ see **EAT**

atheis|m /'eɪθɪɪzəm/ n ateísmo m. **~t** n ateo m

athlet|e /'æθliːt/ n atleta m & f. **~ic** /-'letɪk/ adj atlético. **~ics** npl atletismo m; (Amer, Sport) deportes mpl

Atlantic /ət'læntɪk/ adj atlántico. ● n. the **~** (Ocean) el (Océano) Atlántico

atlas /'ætləs/ n atlas m

ATM abbr (= automated teller machine) cajero m automático

atmospher|e /'ætməsfɪə(r)/ n atmósfera f; (fig) ambiente m. **~ic** /-'ferɪk/ adj atmosférico

atom /'ætəm/ n átomo m. **~ic** /ə'tɒmɪk/ adj atómico

atroci|ous /ə'trəʊʃəs/ adj atroz. **~ty** /ə'trɒsətɪ/ n atrocidad f

attach /ə'tætʃ/ vt sujetar; adjuntar (document etc). be **~ed to** (be fond of) tener cariño a. **~ment** n (affection) cariño m; (tool)

a

accesorio m; (to email) archivo m adjunto

attack /əˈtæk/ n ataque m. ● vt/i atacar. ~er n agresor m

attain /əˈteɪn/ vt conseguir. ~able adj alcanzable

attempt /əˈtempt/ vt intentar. ● n tentativa f; (attack) atentado m

attend /əˈtend/ vt asistir a; (escort) acompañar. ● vi prestar atención. □ ~ to vt (look after) ocuparse de. ~ance n asistencia f; (people present) concurrencia f.

atten|tion /əˈtenʃn/ n atención f. ~tion! (Mil) ¡firmes! pay ~tion prestar atención. ~tive adj atento

attic /ˈætɪk/ n desván m

attire /əˈtaɪə(r)/ n atavío m

attitude /ˈætɪtjuːd/ n postura f

attorney /əˈtɜːnɪ/ n (pl -eys) (Amer) abogado m

attract /əˈtrækt/ vt atraer. ~ion /-ʃn/ n atracción f; (charm) atractivo m. ~ive adj atractivo; (interesting) atrayente

attribute /əˈtrɪbjuːt/ vt atribuir. ● /ˈætrɪbjuːt/ n atributo m

aubergine /ˈəʊbəʒiːn/ n berenjena f

auction /ˈɔːkʃn/ n subasta f. ● vt subastar. ~eer /-ˈnɪə(r)/ n subastador m

audaci|ous /ɔːˈdeɪʃəs/ adj audaz. ~ty /ɔːˈdæsəti/ n audacia f

audible /ˈɔːdəbl/ adj audible

audience /ˈɔːdɪəns/ n (at play, film) público m; (TV) audiencia f; (interview) audiencia f

audiovisual /ɔːdɪəʊˈvɪʒʊəl/ adj audiovisual

audit /ˈɔːdɪt/ n revisión f de cuentas. ● vt revisar

audition /ɔːˈdɪʃn/ n audición f.

● vt hacerle una audición a. ● vi dar una audición (for para)

auditor /ˈɔːdɪtə(r)/ n interventor m de cuentas

auditorium /ɔːdɪˈtɔːrɪəm/ n (pl -riums or -ria /-rɪə/) n sala f, auditorio m

augment /ɔːgˈment/ vt aumentar

augur /ˈɔːgə(r)/ vt augurar. it ~s well es de buen agüero

August /ˈɔːgəst/ n agosto m

aunt /ɑːnt/ n tía f

au pair /əʊˈpeə(r)/ n chica f au pair

aura /ˈɔːrə/ n aura f, halo m

auster|e /ɔːˈstɪə(r)/ adj austero. ~ity /-ˈsterəti/ n austeridad f

Australia /ɒˈstreɪlɪə/ n Australia f. ~n adj & n australiano (m)

Austria /ˈɒstrɪə/ n Austria f. ~n adj & n austríaco m

authentic /ɔːˈθentɪk/ adj auténtico. ~ate /-keɪt/ vt autenticar. ~ity /-ənˈtɪsəti/ n autenticidad f

author /ˈɔːθə(r)/ n autor m. ~ess /-ɪs/ n autora f

authoritative /ɔːˈθɒrɪtətɪv/ adj autorizado; (manner) autoritario

authority /ɔːˈθɒrəti/ n autoridad f; (permission) autorización f

authoriz|ation /ɔːθəraɪˈzeɪʃn/ n autorización f. ~e /ˈɔːθəraɪz/ vt autorizar

autobiography /ɔːtəʊbaɪˈɒgrəfɪ/ n autobiografía f

autograph /ˈɔːtəgrɑːf/ n autógrafo m. ● vt firmar, autografiar

automat|e /ˈɔːtəmeɪt/ vt automatizar. ~ic /-ˈmætɪk/ adj automático. ~ion /-ˈmeɪʃn/ n automatización f. ~on /ɔːˈtɒmətən/ n (pl -tons or -ta /-tə/) autómata m

automobile /ˈɔːtəməbiːl/ n

(*Amer*) coche *m*, carro *m* (*LAm*), automóvil *m*

autonom|ous /ɔːˈtɒnəməs/ *adj* autónomo. ~**y** *n* autonomía *f*

autopsy /ˈɔːtɒpsɪ/ *n* autopsia *f*

autumn /ˈɔːtəm/ *n* otoño *m*. ~**al** /ɔːˈtʌmnəl/ *adj* otoñal

auxiliary /ɔːɡˈzɪlɪərɪ/ *adj & n* auxiliar (*m & f*)

avail /əˈveɪl/ *v*. to no ~ inútil

availab|ility /əveɪləˈbɪlɪtɪ/ *n* disponibilidad *f*. ~**le** /əˈveɪləbl/ *adj* disponible

avalanche /ˈævəlɑːnʃ/ *n* avalancha *f*

avaric|e /ˈævərɪs/ *n* avaricia *f*. ~**ious** /-ˈrɪʃəs/ *adj* avaro

avenue /ˈævənjuː/ *n* avenida *f*; (*fig*) vía *f*

average /ˈævərɪdʒ/ *n* promedio *m*. on ~ por término medio. ● *adj* medio

avers|e /əˈvɜːs/ *adj*. be ~e to ser reacio a. ~**ion** /-ʃn/ *n* repugnancia *f*

avert /əˈvɜːt/ *vt* (*turn away*) apartar; (*ward off*) desviar

aviation /eɪvɪˈeɪʃn/ *n* aviación *f*

avid /ˈævɪd/ *adj* ávido

avocado /ævəˈkɑːdəʊ/ *n* (*pl* -os) aguacate *m*

avoid /əˈvɔɪd/ *vt* evitar. ~**able** *adj* evitable. ~**ance** *n* el evitar

await /əˈweɪt/ *vt* esperar

awake /əˈweɪk/ *vt/i* (*pt* awoke, *pp* awoken) despertar. ● *adj* despierto. wide ~ completamente despierto; (*fig*) despabilado. ~**n** /əˈweɪkən/ *vt/i* despertar. ~**ning** *n* el despertar

award /əˈwɔːd/ *vt* otorgar; (*Jurid*) adjudicar. ● *n* premio *m*; (*Jurid*) adjudicación *f*; (*scholarship*) beca *f*

aware /əˈweə(r)/ *adj*. be ~ of sth ser consciente de algo, darse cuenta de algo. ~**ness** *n* conciencia *f*

awash /əˈwɒʃ/ *adj* inundado

away /əˈweɪ/ *adv* (*absent*) fuera. far ~ muy lejos. ● *adj* ~ match partido *m* fuera de casa

awe /ɔː/ *n* temor *m*. ~-**inspiring** *adj* impresionante. ~**some** /-səm/ *adj* imponente

awful /ˈɔːfʊl/ *adj* terrible, malísimo. feel ~ sentirse muy mal

awkward /ˈɔːkwəd/ *adj* difícil; (*inconvenient*) inoportuno; (*clumsy*) desmañado; (*embarrassed*) incómodo. ~**ness** *n* dificultad *f*; (*discomfort*) molestia *f*; (*clumsiness*) torpeza *f*

awning /ˈɔːnɪŋ/ *n* toldo *m*

awoke /əˈwəʊk/, **awoken** /əˈwəʊkən/ *see* AWAKE

axe /æks/ *n* hacha *f*. ● *vt* (*pres p* axing) cortar con hacha; (*fig*) recortar

axis /ˈæksɪs/ *n* (*pl* axes/-iːz/) eje *m*

axle /ˈæksl/ *n* eje *m*

Bb

BA /biːˈeɪ/ *abbr see* BACHELOR

babble /ˈbæbl/ *vi* balbucir; (*chatter*) parlotear; (*stream*) murmullar

baboon /bəˈbuːn/ *n* mandril *m*

baby /ˈbeɪbɪ/ *n* niño *m*, bebé *m*. ~ **buggy**, ~ **carriage** *n* (*Amer*) cochecito *m*. ~**ish** *adj* /ˈbeɪbɪɪʃ/ infantil. ~-**sit** *vi* cuidar a los niños, hacer de canguro. ~-**sitter** *n* baby sitter *m* & *f*, canguro *m* & *f*

bachelor /'bætʃələ(r)/ *n* soltero *m*. B~ of Arts (BA) licenciado *m* en filosofía y letras. B~ of Science (BSc) licenciado *m* en ciencias

back /bæk/ *n* espalda *f*; (*of car*) parte *f* trasera; (*of chair*) respaldo *m*; (*of cloth*) revés *m*; (*of house*) parte *f* de atrás; (*of animal, book*) lomo *m*; (*of hand, document*) dorso *m*; (*football*) defensa *m* & *f*. **in the ~ of beyond** en el quinto infierno. ●*adj* trasero. **the ~ door** la puerta trasera. ●*adv* atrás; (*returned*) de vuelta. ●*vt* apoyar; (*betting*) apostar a; dar marcha atrás a (car). ●*vi* retroceder; (car) dar marcha atrás. □~ **down** *vi* volverse atrás. □~ **out** *vi* retirarse. □~ **up** *vt* apoyar; (*Comp*) hacer una copia de seguridad de. **~ache** *n* dolor *m* de espalda. **~bone** *n* columna *f* vertebral; (*fig*) pilar *m*. **~date** /-'deɪt/ *vt* antedatar. **~er** *n* partidario *m*; (*Com*) financiador *m*. **~fire** /-'faɪə(r)/ *vi* (*Auto*) petardear; (*fig*) fallar. **his plan ~fired** on him le salió el tiro por la culata. **~ground** *n* fondo *m*; (*environment*) antecedentes *mpl*. **~hand** *n* (*Sport*) revés *m*. **~ing** *n* apoyo *m*. **~lash** *n* reacción *f*. **~log** *n* atrasos *mpl*. **~side** /-'saɪd/ *n* 🄵 trasero *m*. **~stage** /-'steɪdʒ/ *adj* de bastidores. ●*adv* entre bastidores. **~stroke** *n* (*tennis etc*) revés *m*; (*swimming*) estilo *m* espalda, estilo *m* dorso (*Mex*). **~-up** *n* apoyo *m*; (*Comp*) copia *f* de seguridad. **~ward** /-wəd/ *adj* (*step etc*) hacia atrás; (*retarded*) retrasado; (*undeveloped*) atrasado. ●*adv* (*Amer*) *see* BACKWARDS. **~wards** *adv* hacia atrás; (*fall*) de espaldas; (*back to front*) al revés. **go ~wards and forwards** ir de acá para allá. **~water** *n* agua *f* o estan-

cada; (*fig*) lugar *m* apartado

bacon /'beɪkən/ *n* tocino *m*

bacteria /bæk'tɪərɪə/ *npl* bacterias *fpl*

bad /bæd/ *adj* (**worse, worst**) malo; (*before masculine singular noun*) mal; (*serious*) grave; (*harmful*) nocivo; (*language*) indecente. **feel ~** sentirse mal

bade /beɪd/ *see* BID

badge /bædʒ/ *n* distintivo *m*, chapa *f*

badger /'bædʒə(r)/ *n* tejón *m*. ●*vt* acosar

bad: ~ly *adv* mal. **want ~ly** desear muchísimo. **~ly injured** gravemente herido. **~ly off** mal de dinero. **~-mannered** /-'mænəd/ *adj* mal educado

badminton /'bædmɪntən/ *n* bádminton *m*

bad-tempered /bæd'tempəd/ *adj* (*always*) de mal carácter; (*temporarily*) de mal humor

baffle /'bæfl/ *vt* desconcertar. **~d** *adj* perplejo

bag /bæg/ *n* bolsa *f*; (*handbag*) bolso *m*. ●*vt* (*pt* **bagged**) ensacar; (*take*) coger (*esp Spain*), agarrar (*LAm*). **~s** *npl* (*luggage*) equipaje *m*

baggage /'bægɪdʒ/ *n* equipaje *m*. **~ room** (*Amer*) consigna *f*

baggy /'bægɪ/ *adj* (*clothes*) holgado

bagpipes /'bægpaɪps/ *npl* gaita *f*

baguette /bæ'get/ *n* baguette *f*

bail¹ /beɪl/ *n* fianza *f*. ●*vt* poner en libertad bajo fianza. **~ s.o. out** pagar la fianza a uno

bail² *vt*. **~ out** (*Naut*) achicar

bait /beɪt/ *n* cebo *m*

bak|e /beɪk/ *vt* cocer al horno. ●*vi* cocerse. **~er** *n* panadero *m*. **~ery**

n panadería *f*

balance /ˈbæləns/ *n* equilibrio *m*; (Com) balance *m*; (sum) saldo *m*; (scales) balanza *f*; (remainder) resto *m*. ●*vt* equilibrar (load); mantener en equilibrio (object); nivelar (budget). ●*vi* equilibrarse; (Com) cuadrar. ~**d** *adj* equilibrado

balcony /ˈbælkənɪ/ *n* balcón *m*

bald /bɔːld/ *adj* (-er, -est) calvo, pelón (Mex)

bale /beɪl/ *n* bala *f*, fardo *m*. ●*vi*. ~ out lanzarse en paracaídas

Balearic /bælɪˈærɪk/ *adj*. the ~ Islands las Islas *fpl* Baleares

ball /bɔːl/ *n* bola *f*; (tennis etc) pelota *f*; (football etc) balón *m*, pelota *f* (esp LAm); (of yarn) ovillo *m*; (dance) baile *m*

ballad /ˈbæləd/ *n* balada *f*

ballast /ˈbæləst/ *n* lastre *m*

ball bearing *n* cojinete *m* de bolas

ballerina /bæləˈriːnə/ *n* bailarina *f*

ballet /ˈbæleɪ/ *n* ballet *m*. ~ **dancer** *n* bailarín *m* de ballet, bailarina *f* de ballet

balloon /bəˈluːn/ *n* globo *m*

ballot /ˈbælət/ *n* votación *f*. ~ **box** *n* urna *f*. ~ **paper** *n* papeleta *f*

ball: ~**point** *n*. ~**point (pen)** bolígrafo *m*, pluma *f* atómica (Mex). ~**room** *n* salón *m* de baile

bamboo /bæmˈbuː/ *n* bambú *m*

ban /bæn/ *vt* (pt banned) prohibir. ~ **s.o. from** sth prohibir que a uno. ●*n* prohibición *f*

banal /bəˈnɑːl/ *adj* banal. ~**ity** /bəˈnælətɪ/ *n* banalidad *f*

banana /bəˈnɑːnə/ *n* plátano *m*

band /bænd/ *n* (strip) banda *f*. ●*n* (Mus) orquesta *f*; (military, brass)

banda *f*. ▢~ **together** *vi* juntarse

bandage /ˈbændɪdʒ/ *n* venda *f*. ●*vt* vendar

Band-Aid /ˈbændeɪd/ *n* (Amer, ®) tirita *f*, curita *f* (LAm)

B & B /ˈbiːənbiː/ *abbr* (= bed and breakfast) cama *f* y desayuno; (place) pensión *f*

bandit /ˈbændɪt/ *n* bandido *m*

band: ~**stand** *n* quiosco *m* de música. ~**wagon** *n*. **jump on the** ~**wagon** (fig) subirse al carro

bandy /ˈbændɪ/ *adj* (-ier, -iest) patizambo

bang /bæŋ/ *n* (noise) ruido *m*; (blow) golpe *m*; (of gun) estampido *m*; (of door) golpe *m*. ●*vt* (strike) golpear. ~ **the door** dar un portazo. ●*adv* exactamente. ●*int* ¡pum! ~**s** *npl* (Amer) flequillo *m*, cerquillo *m* (LAm), fleco *m* (Mex)

banger /ˈbæŋə(r)/ *n* petardo *m*; (🚗, Culin) salchicha *f*

bangle /ˈbæŋgl/ *n* brazalete *m*

banish /ˈbænɪʃ/ *vt* desterrar

banisters /ˈbænɪstəz/ *npl* pasamanos *m*

banjo /ˈbændʒəʊ/ *n* (pl -os) banjo *m*

bank /bæŋk/ *n* (Com) banco *m*; (of river) orilla *f*. ●*vt* depositar. ●*vi* (in flying) ladearse. ▢~ **on** *vt* contar con. ▢~ **with** *vt* tener una cuenta con. ~ **card** *n* tarjeta *f* bancaria; (Amer) tarjeta *f* de crédito (expedida por un banco). ~**er** *n* banquero *m*. ~ **holiday** *n* día *m* festivo, día *m* feriado (LAm). ~**ing** *n* (Com) banca *f*. ~**note** *n* billete *m* de banco

bankrupt /ˈbæŋkrʌpt/ *adj* & *n* quebrado (m). go ~ quebrar. ●*vt* hacer quebrar. ~**cy** /-rʌpsɪ/ *n* bancarrota *f*, quiebra *f*

bank statement *n* estado *m*

de cuenta

banner /'bænə(r)/ n bandera f; (in demonstration) pancarta f

banquet /'bæŋkwɪt/ n banquete m

banter /'bæntə(r)/ n chanza f

bap /bæp/ n panecillo m blando

baptism /'bæptɪzəm/ n bautismo m; (act) bautizo m

Baptist /'bæptɪst/ n bautista m & f

baptize /bæp'taɪz/ vt bautizar

bar /bɑː(r)/ n barra f; (on window) reja f; (of chocolate) tableta f; (of soap) pastilla f; (pub) bar m; (Mus) compás f; (Jurid) abogacía f; (fig) obstáculo m. ● vt (pt barred) atrancar (door); (exclude) excluir; (prohibit) prohibir. ● prep excepto

barbar|ian /bɑː'beərɪən/ adj & n bárbaro (m). ~ic /bɑː'bærɪk/ adj bárbaro

barbecue /'bɑːbɪkjuː/ n barbacoa f. ● vt asar a la parrilla

barbed wire /bɑːbd 'waɪə(r)/ n alambre m de púas

barber /'bɑːbə(r)/ n peluquero m, barbero m

barbwire /'bɑːb'waɪə(r)/ n (Amer) see BARBED WIRE

bare /beə(r)/ adj (-er, -est) desnudo; (room) con pocos muebles; (mere) simple; (empty) vacío. ● vt desnudar; (uncover) descubrir. ~ one's teeth mostrar los dientes. ~back adv a pelo. ~faced adj descarado. ~foot adj descalzo. ~headed /-'hedɪd/ adj descubierto. ~ly adv apenas.

bargain /'bɑːgɪn/ n (agreement) pacto m; (good buy) ganga f. ● vi negociar; (haggle) regatear. □ ~ for vt esperar, contar con

barge /bɑːdʒ/ n barcaza f. ● vi. ~ in irrumpir

baritone /'bærɪtəʊn/ n barítono m

bark /bɑːk/ n (of dog) ladrido m; (of tree) corteza f. ● vi ladrar

barley /'bɑːlɪ/ n cebada f

bar: ~maid n camarera f. ~man /-mən/ n camarero m, barman m

barmy /'bɑːmɪ/ adj 🅇 chiflado

barn /bɑːn/ n granero m

barometer /bə'rɒmɪtə(r)/ n barómetro m

baron /'bærən/ n barón m. ~ess /-ɪs/ n baronesa f

barracks /'bærəks/ npl cuartel m

barrage /'bærɑːʒ/ n (Mil) barrera f; (dam) presa f. a ~ of questions un aluvión de preguntas

barrel /'bærəl/ n barril m; (of gun) cañón m

barren /'bærən/ adj estéril

barrette /bə'ret/ n (Amer) pasador m

barricade /bærɪ'keɪd/ n barricada f. ● vt cerrar con barricadas

barrier /'bærɪə(r)/ n barrera f

barrister /'bærɪstə(r)/ n abogado m

bartender /'bɑːtendə(r)/ n (Amer) (male) camarero m, barman m; (female) camarera f

barter /'bɑːtə(r)/ n trueque m. ● vt trocar

base /beɪs/ n base f. ● vt basar. ~ball n béisbol m, beisbol m (Mex)

basement /'beɪsmənt/ n sótano m

bash /bæʃ/ vt golpear. ● n golpe m. have a ~ 🅇 probar

bashful /'bæʃfl/ adj tímido

basic /'beɪsɪk/ adj básico, fundamental. ~ally adv fundamentalmente

basin /'beɪsn/ n (for washing) palangana f; (for food) cuenco m; (of river) cuenca f

basis /'beɪsɪs/ n (pl bases/-siːz/) base f

bask /bɑːsk/ vi asolearse; (fig) gozar (in de)

basket /'bɑːskɪt/ n cesta f; (big) cesto m. **~ball** n baloncesto m, básquetbol m (LAm)

bass[1] /beɪs/ adj bajo. ●n (Mus) bajo m

bass[2] /bæs/ n (fish) lubina f

bassoon /bə'suːn/ n fagot m

bastard /'bɑːstəd/ n bastardo m. you **~**! (vulgar) ¡cabrón! (vulgar)

bat /bæt/ n (for baseball, cricket) bate m; (for table tennis) raqueta f; (mammal) murciélago m. off one's own **~** por sí solo. ●vt (pt batted) golpear. without **~**ting an eyelid sin pestañear. ●vi batear

batch /bætʃ/ n (of people) grupo m; (of papers) pila f; (of goods) remesa f; (of bread) hornada f; (Comp) lote m

bated /'beɪtɪd/ adj. with **~** breath con aliento entrecortado

bath /bɑːθ/ n (pl -s /bɑːðz/) baño m; (tub) bañera f, tina f (LAm). **~s** npl (swimming pool) piscina f, alberca f (Mex). have a **~**, take a **~** (Amer) bañarse. ●vt bañar. ●vi bañarse

bathe /beɪð/ vt bañar. ●vi bañarse. ●n baño m. **~r** n bañista m & f

bathing /'beɪðɪŋ/ n baños mpl. **~ costume**, **~ suit** n traje m de baño

bathroom /'bɑːθrʊm/ n cuarto m de baño; (Amer, toilet) servicio m, baño m (LAm)

batsman /'bætsmən/ n (pl -men) bateador m

battalion /bə'tælɪən/ n batallón m

batter /'bætə(r)/ vt (beat) apalear; (cover with batter) rebozar. ●n batido m para rebozar; (Amer, for cake) masa f. **~ed** /'bætəd/ adj (car etc) estropeado; (wife etc) maltratado

battery /'bætərɪ/ n (Mil, Auto) batería f; (of torch, radio) pila f

battle /'bætl/ n batalla f; (fig) lucha f. ●vi luchar. **~field** n campo m de batalla. **~ship** n acorazado m

bawl /bɔːl/ vt/i gritar

bay /beɪ/ n (on coast) bahía f. keep at **~** mantener a raya

bayonet /'beɪənet/ n bayoneta f

bay window /beɪ 'wɪndəʊ/ n ventana f salediza

bazaar /bə'zɑː(r)/ n bazar m

BC abbr (= before Christ) a. de C., antes de Cristo

be /biː/

present am, are, is; past was, were; past participle been

● intransitive verb

❗ Spanish has two verbs meaning be, ser and estar. See these entries for further information about the differences between them.

····▸ (position, changed condition or state) estar. where is the library? ¿dónde está la biblioteca? she's tired está cansada. how are you? ¿cómo estás?

····▸ (identity, nature or permanent characteristics) ser. she's tall es alta. he's Scottish es escocés. I'm a journalist soy periodista. he's very kind es muy bondadoso

···▸ (feel) to be + adjective tener + sustantivo. to be cold/hot tener frío/calor. he's hungry/thirsty tiene hambre/sed

···▸ (age) he's thirty tiene treinta años

···▸ (weather) it's cold/hot hace frío/calor. it was 40 degrees hacía 40 grados

● auxiliary verb

···▸ (in tenses) estar. I'm working since trabajando. they were singing estaban cantando, cantaban

···▸ (in tag questions) it's a beautiful house, isn't it? es una casa preciosa, ¿verdad? or ¿no? or ¿no es cierto?

···▸ (in short answers) are you disappointed? – yes, I am ¿estás desilusionado? – sí (,lo estoy). I'm surprised, aren't you? estoy sorprendido, ¿tú no?

···▸ (in passive sentences) it was built in 1834 fue construido en 1834, se construyó en 1834. she was told that ... le dijeron que..., se le dijo que ...

❗ Note that passive sentences in English are often translated using the pronoun se or using the third person plural.

beach /biːtʃ/ n playa f

beacon /ˈbiːkən/ n faro m

bead /biːd/ n cuenta f; (of glass) abalorio m

beak /biːk/ n pico m

beaker /ˈbiːkə(r)/ n taza f (alta y sin asa)

beam /biːm/ n (of wood) viga f; (of light) rayo m; (Naut) bao m. ● vt emitir. ● vi irradiar; (smile) sonreír

bean /biːn/ n alubia f, frijol m (LAm); (broad bean) haba f; (of coffee) grano m

bear /beə(r)/ vt (pt bore, pp borne) llevar; parir (niño); (endure) soportar. ∼ **right** torcer a la derecha. ∼ **in mind** tener en cuenta. □ ∼ **with** vt tener paciencia con. ● n oso m. ∼**able** adj soportable

beard /bɪəd/ n barba f. ∼**ed** adj barbudo

bearer /ˈbeərə(r)/ n portador m; (of passport) titular m & f

bearing /ˈbeərɪŋ/ n comportamiento m; (relevance) relación f; (Mec) cojinete m. **get one's** ∼**s** orientarse. **lose one's** ∼**s** desorientarse

beast /biːst/ n bestia f; (person) bruto m. ∼**ly** adj (-ier, -iest) bestial; 🄳 horrible

beat /biːt/ vt (pt beat, pp beaten) (hit) pegar; (Culin) batir; (defeat) derrotar; (better) sobrepasar; batir (record); (baffle) dejar perplejo. ∼ **it** 🄳 largarse. ● vi (heart) latir. ● n latido m; (Mus) ritmo m; (of policeman) ronda f. □ ∼ **up** vt darle una paliza a; (Culin) batir. ∼ **up on** (Amer, fam) darle una paliza a. ∼**er** n batidor m. ∼**ing** n paliza f

beautician /bjuːˈtɪʃn/ n esteticista m & f

beautiful /ˈbjuːtɪfl/ adj hermoso. ∼**ly** adv maravillosamente

beauty /ˈbjuːtɪ/ n belleza f. ∼ **salon**, ∼ **shop** (Amer) n salón m de belleza. ∼ **spot** n (on face) lunar m; (site) lugar m pintoresco

beaver /ˈbiːvə(r)/ n castor m

became | being

became /bɪˈkeɪm/ see BECOME

because /bɪˈkɒz/ conj porque.
● adv. ~ of por, a causa de

beckon /ˈbekən/ vt/i. ~ (to) hacer señas (a)

become /bɪˈkʌm/ vi (pt became, pp become) hacerse, llegar a ser, volverse, convertirse en. what has ~ of her? ¿qué es de ella?

bed /bed/ n cama f; (layer) estrato m; (of sea, river) fondo m; (of flowers) macizo m. **go to** ~ acostarse. ● vi (pt bedded). ~ **and breakfast** (B & B) cama y desayuno; (place) pensión f. ~**bug** n chinche f. ~**clothes** npl, ~**ding** n ropa f de cama, cobijas fpl (LAm)

> **Bed and breakfast** Los bed & breakfast o B&B son casas privadas o pequeños hoteles que ofrecen alojamiento y desayuno a precios generalmente módicos. *i*

bed: ~**room** n dormitorio m, cuarto m, habitación f, recámara f (Mex). ~**sitter** /-ˈsɪtə(r)/ n habitación f con cama y uso de cocina y baño compartidos, estudio m. ~**spread** n colcha f. ~**time** n hora f de acostarse

bee /biː/ n abeja f; (Amer, social gathering) círculo m

beech /biːtʃ/ n haya f

beef /biːf/ n carne f de vaca, carne f de res (Mex). ● vi 🗙 quejarse. ~**burger** n hamburguesa f. ~**y** adj (-ier, -iest) musculoso

bee: ~**hive** n colmena f. ~**line** n. **make a** ~**line for** ir en línea recta hacia

been /biːn/ see BE

beer /bɪə(r)/ n cerveza f.

beet /biːt/ n (Amer) remolacha f,

betabel f (Mex)

beetle /ˈbiːtl/ n escarabajo m

beetroot /ˈbiːtruːt/ n invar remolacha f, betabel f (Mex)

befall /bɪˈfɔːl/ vt (pt befell, pp befallen) ocurrirle a. ● vi ocurrir

before /bɪˈfɔː(r)/ prep (time) antes de; (place) delante de. ~ **leaving** antes de marcharse. ● adv (place) delante; (time) antes. **a week** ~ una semana antes. **the week** ~ la semana anterior. ● conj (time) antes de que. ~ **he leaves** antes de que se vaya. ~**hand** adv de antemano

befriend /bɪˈfrend/ vt hacerse amigo de

beg /beg/ vt/i (pt begged) mendigar; (entreat) suplicar; (ask) pedir. ~ **s.o.'s pardon** pedir perdón a uno. **I** ~ **your pardon!** ¡perdóne Vd! **I** ~ **your pardon?** ¿cómo?

began /bɪˈɡæn/ see BEGIN

beggar /ˈbeɡə(r)/ n mendigo m

begin /bɪˈɡɪn/ vt/i (pt began, pp begun, pres p beginning) comenzar, empezar. ~**ner** n principiante m & f. ~**ning** n principio m

begrudge /bɪˈɡrʌdʒ/ vt envidiar; (give) dar de mala gana

begun /bɪˈɡʌn/ see BEGIN

behalf /bɪˈhɑːf/ n. **on** ~ **of, in** ~ **of** (Amer) de parte de, en nombre de

behav|e /bɪˈheɪv/ vi comportarse, portarse. ~**e (o.s.)** portarse bien. ~**iour** /bɪˈheɪvjə(r)/ n comportamiento m

behead /bɪˈhed/ vt decapitar

behind /bɪˈhaɪnd/ prep detrás de, atrás de (LAm). ● adv detrás; (late) atrasado. ● n 🗓 trasero m

beige /beɪʒ/ adj & n beige (m)

being /ˈbiːɪŋ/ n ser m. **come into** ~ nacer

belated /br'lertid/ adj tardío

belch /beltʃ/ vi eructar. □ ~ **out** vt arrojar (smoke)

belfry /'belfri/ n campanario m

Belgian /'beldʒən/ adj & n belga (m & f). ~**um** /'beldʒəm/ n Bélgica f

belie|f /br'li:f/ n (trust) fe f; (opinion) creencia f. ~**ve** /br'li:v/ vt/i creer. ~**ve in** creer en. make ~**ve** fingir

belittle /br'lɪtl/ vt menospreciar (achievements); denigrar (person)

bell /bel/ n campana f; (on door, bicycle) timbre m

belligerent /br'lɪdʒərənt/ adj beligerante

bellow /'beləʊ/ vt gritar. ● vi bramar. ~**s** npl fuelle m

bell pepper n (Amer) pimiento m

belly /'beli/ n barriga f

belong /br'lɒŋ/ vi pertenecer (to a); (club) ser socio (to de); (have as usual place) ir. ~**ings** /br'lɒŋɪŋz/ npl pertenencias fpl. personal ~**ings** efectos mpl personales

beloved /br'lʌvɪd/ adj querido

below /br'ləʊ/ prep debajo de, abajo de (LAm); (fig) inferior a. ● adv abajo

belt /belt/ n cinturón m; (area) zona f. ● vt (fig) rodear; (▣) darle una paliza a. ~**way** n (Amer) carretera f de circunvalación

bench /bentʃ/ n banco m

bend /bend/ n curva f. ● vt (pt & pp bent) doblar; torcer (arm, leg). ● vi doblarse; (road) torcerse. □ ~ **down** vi inclinarse □ ~ **over** vi agacharse

beneath /br'ni:θ/ prep debajo de; (fig) inferior a. ● adv abajo

beneficial /benɪ'fɪʃl/ adj provechoso

beneficiary /benɪ'fɪʃəri/ n beneficiario m

benefit /'benɪfɪt/ n provecho m, ventaja f; (allowance) prestación f; (for unemployed) subsidio m; (perk) beneficio m. ● vt (pt benefited, pres p benefiting) beneficiar. ● vi beneficiarse

benevolent /bə'nevələnt/ adj benévolo

benign /br'naɪn/ adj benigno

bent /bent/ see BEND. ● n inclinación f. ● adj torcido; (▣, corrupt) corrompido

bereave|d /br'ri:vd/ n. the ~**d** la familia del difunto. ~**ment** n pérdida f; (mourning) luto m

beret /'bereɪ/ n boina f

berry /'beri/ n baya f

berserk /bə'sɜ:k/ adj. go ~ volverse loco

berth /bɜ:θ/ n litera f; (anchorage) amarradero m. give a wide ~ to evitar. ● vt/i atracar

beside /br'saɪd/ prep al lado de. be ~ o.s. estar fuera de sí

besides /br'saɪdz/ prep además de; (except) excepto. ● adv además

besiege /br'si:dʒ/ vt sitiar, asediar; (fig) acosar

best /best/ adj (el) mejor. the ~ thing is to... lo mejor es... ● adv mejor. like ~ preferir. ● n lo mejor. at ~ a lo más. do one's ~ hacer todo lo posible. make the ~ of contentarse con. ~ **man** n padrino m (de boda)

bestow /br'stəʊ/ vt conceder

bestseller /best'selə(r)/ n éxito m de librería, bestseller m

bet /bet/ n apuesta f. ● vt/i (pt bet or betted) apostar

betray /br'treɪ/ vt traicionar. ~**al** n traición f

better /'betə(r)/ *adj & adv* mejor. ~ **off** en mejores condiciones; (*richer*) más rico. **get** ~ mejorar. **all the** ~ tanto mejor. **I'd** ~ **be off** me tengo que ir. **the** ~ **part of** la mayor parte de. ● *vt* mejorar; (*beat*) sobrepasar. ● **o.s.** superarse. ● **n** superior *m*. **get the** ~ **of** vencer a. **my** ~**s** mis superiores *mpl*

between /bɪ'twiːn/ *prep* entre. ● *adv* en medio

beverage /'bevərɪdʒ/ *n* bebida *f*

beware /bɪ'weə(r)/ *vi* tener cuidado. ● *int* ¡cuidado!

bewilder /bɪ'wɪldə(r)/ *vt* desconcertar. ~**ment** *n* aturdimiento *m*

bewitch /bɪ'wɪtʃ/ *vt* hechizar; (*delight*) cautivar

beyond /bɪ'jɒnd/ *prep* más allá de; (*fig*) fuera de. ~ **doubt** sin lugar a duda. ● *adv* más allá

bias /'baɪəs/ *n* tendencia *f*; (*prejudice*) prejuicio *m*. ● *vt* (*pt* **biased**) influir en. ~**ed** *adj* parcial

bib /bɪb/ *n* babero *m*

Bible /'baɪbl/ *n* Biblia *f*

biblical /'bɪblɪkl/ *adj* bíblico

bibliography /bɪblɪ'ɒgrəfɪ/ *n* bibliografía *f*

biceps /'baɪseps/ *n invar* bíceps *m*

bicker /'bɪkə(r)/ *vi* altercar

bicycle /'baɪsɪkl/ *n* bicicleta *f*

bid /bɪd/ *n* (*offer*) oferta *f*; (*attempt*) tentativa *f*. ● *vi* hacer una oferta. ● *vt* (*pt & pp* **bid**, *pres p* **bidding**) ofrecer; (*pt* **bid**, *pp* **bidden**, *pres p* **bidding**) mandar; dar (*welcome, good day etc*). ~**der** *n* postor *m*. ~**ding** *n* (*at auction*) ofertas *fpl*; (*order*) mandato *m*

bide /baɪd/ *vt*. ~ **one's time** esperar el momento oportuno

bifocals /baɪ'fəʊklz/ *npl* gafas *fpl*

bifocales, anteojos *mpl* bifocales (*LAm*)

big /bɪg/ *adj* (**bigger**, **biggest**) grande, (*before singular noun*) gran. ● *adv*. **talk** ~ fanfarronear

bigam|ist /'bɪgəmɪst/ *n* bígamo *m*. ~**ous** /'bɪgəməs/ *adj* bígamo. ~**y** *n* bigamia *f*

big-headed /-'hedɪd/ *adj* engreído

bigot /'bɪgət/ *n* fanático *m*. ~**ed** *adj* fanático

bike /baɪk/ *n* Ⓘ bici *f* Ⓘ

bikini /bɪ'kiːnɪ/ *n* (*pl* **-is**) bikini *m*

bile /baɪl/ *n* bilis *f*

bilingual /baɪ'lɪŋgwəl/ *adj* bilingüe

bill /bɪl/ *n* cuenta *f*; (*invoice*) factura *f*; (*notice*) cartel *m*; (*Amer, banknote*) billete *m*; (*Pol*) proyecto *m* de ley; (*of bird*) pico *m*

billet /'bɪlɪt/ *n* (*Mil*) alojamiento *m*. ● *vt* alojar

billfold /'bɪlfəʊld/ *n* (*Amer*) cartera *f*, billetera *f*

billiards /'bɪlɪədz/ *n* billar *m*

billion /'bɪlɪən/ *n* billón *m*; (*Amer*) mil millones *mpl*

bin /bɪn/ *n* recipiente *m*; (*for rubbish*) cubo *m* de basura, bote *m* de basura (*Mex*); (*for waste paper*) papelera *f*

bind /baɪnd/ *vt* (*pt* **bound**) atar; encuadernar (*book*); (*Jurid*) obligar. ● *n* Ⓘ lata *f*. ~**ing** *n* (*of books*) encuadernación *f*; (*braid*) ribete *m*

binge /bɪndʒ/ *n* Ⓘ, (*of food*) comilona *f*; (*of drink*) borrachera *f*. **go on a** ~ ir de juerga

bingo /'bɪŋgəʊ/ *n* bingo *m*

binoculars /bɪ'nɒkjʊləz/ *npl* gemelos *mpl*

biofuel /'baɪəʊfjuːəl/ *n* biocarburante *m*

biograph|er /baɪ'ɒgrəfə(r)/ *n*

b

biógrafo m. **~y** n biografía f

biolog|ical /baɪəˈlɒdʒɪkl/ adj biológico. **~ist** /baɪˈɒlədʒɪst/ n biólogo m. **~y** /baɪˈɒlədʒɪ/ n biología f

bioterrorism /baɪəʊˈterərɪzm/ n bioterrorismo m

birch /bɜːtʃ/ n (tree) abedul m

bird /bɜːd/ n ave f; (small) pájaro m; (sl, girl) chica f

Biro /ˈbaɪərəʊ/ n (pl -os) (®) bolígrafo m

birth /bɜːθ/ n nacimiento m. give ~ dar a luz. **~ certificate** n partida f de nacimiento. **~ control** n control m de la natalidad. **~day** n cumpleaños m. **~mark** n marca f de nacimiento. **~place** n lugar m de nacimiento. **~ rate** n natalidad f

biscuit /ˈbɪskɪt/ n galleta f

bisect /baɪˈsekt/ vt bisecar

bishop /ˈbɪʃəp/ n obispo m; (Chess) alfil m

bit /bɪt/ see BITE. ●n trozo m; (quantity) poco m; (of horse) bocado m; (Mec) broca f; (Comp) bit m

bitch /bɪtʃ/ n perra f; (fam, woman) bruja f 🛈

bit|e /baɪt/ vt/i (pt bit, pp bitten) morder; (insect) picar. **~e one's nails** morderse las uñas. ●n mordisco m; (mouthful) bocado m; (of insect etc) picadura f. **~ing** /ˈbaɪtɪŋ/ adj mordaz

bitter /ˈbɪtə(r)/ adj amargo; (of weather) glacial. ●n cerveza f amarga. **~ly** adv amargamente. it's **~ly** cold hace un frío glacial. **~ness** n amargor m; (resentment) amargura f

bizarre /bɪˈzɑː(r)/ adj extraño

black /blæk/ adj (-er, -est) negro. ~ **and blue** amoratado. ●n negro m; (coffee) solo, negro (LAm). ●vt

ennegrecer; limpiar (shoes). **~ out** vi desmayarse. **~ and white** n blanco y negro m. **~-and-white** adj en blanco y negro. **~berry** /-bərɪ/ n zarzamora f. **~bird** n mirlo m. **~board** n pizarra f. **~currant** /-ˈkʌrənt/ n grosella f negra. **~en** vt ennegrecer. ~ **eye** n ojo m morado. **~list** vt poner en la lista negra. **~mail** n chantaje m. ●vt chantajear. **~mailer** n chantajista m & f. **~out** n apagón m; (Med) desmayo m; (of news) censura f. **~smith** n herrero m

bladder /ˈblædə(r)/ n vejiga f

blade /bleɪd/ n (of knife, sword) hoja f. ~ **of grass** brizna f de hierba

blame /bleɪm/ vt echar la culpa a. be to ~ tener la culpa. ●n culpa f. **~less** adj inocente

bland /blænd/ adj (-er, -est) suave

blank /blæŋk/ adj (page, space) en blanco; (cassette) virgen; (cartridge) sin bala; (fig) vacío. ●n blanco m

blanket /ˈblæŋkɪt/ n manta f, cobija f (LAm), frazada f (LAm); (fig) capa f. ●vt (pt blanketed) (fig) cubrir (in, with de)

blare /bleə(r)/ vi sonar muy fuerte. ●n estrépito m

blasphem|e /blæsˈfiːm/ vt/i blasfemar. **~ous** /ˈblæsfəməs/ adj blasfemo. **~y** /ˈblæsfəmɪ/ n blasfemia f

blast /blɑːst/ n explosión f; (gust) ráfaga f; (sound) toque m. ●vt volar. **~ed** adj maldito. **~off** n (of missile) despegue m

blatant /ˈbleɪtnt/ adj patente; (shameless) descarado

blaze /bleɪz/ n llamarada f; (of light) resplandor m; (fig) arranque m. ●vi arder en llamas; (fig) brillar

blazer /'bleɪzə(r)/ n chaqueta f

bleach /bliːtʃ/ n lejía f, cloro m (LAm), blanqueador m (LAm). ● vt blanquear; decolorar (hair).

bleak /bliːk/ adj (-er, -est) desolado; (fig) sombrío

bleat /bliːt/ n balido m. ● vi balar

bleed /bliːd/ vt/i (pt bled /bled/) sangrar

bleep /bliːp/ n pitido m

blemish /'blemɪʃ/ n mancha f

blend /blend/ n mezcla f. ● vt mezclar. ● vi combinarse. **~er** n licuadora f

bless /bles/ vt bendecir. **~ you!** (on sneezing) ¡Jesús!, ¡salud! (Mex). **~ed** /'blesɪd/ adj bendito. **~ing** n bendición f; (advantage) ventaja f

blew /bluː/ see **BLOW**

blight /blaɪt/ n añublo m, tizón m; (fig) plaga f. ● vt añublar, atizonar; (fig) destrozar

blind /blaɪnd/ adj ciego. **~ alley** callejón m sin salida. (fig) pretexto m. ● vt dejar ciego; (dazzle) deslumbrar. **~fold** adj & adv con los ojos vendados. ● n venda f. ● vt vendar los ojos a. **~ly** adv a ciegas. **~ness** n ceguera f

blink /blɪŋk/ vi parpadear; (light) centellear. **~ers** npl (on horse) anteojeras fpl

bliss /blɪs/ n felicidad f. **~ful** adj feliz

blister /'blɪstə(r)/ n ampolla f

blizzard /'blɪzəd/ n ventisca f

bloated /'bləʊtɪd/ adj hinchado (with de)

blob /blɒb/ n (drip) gota f; (stain) mancha f

bloc /blɒk/ n (Pol) bloque m

block /blɒk/ n bloque m; (of wood) zoquete m; (of buildings)

manzana f, cuadra f (LAm). **in ~** letters en letra de imprenta. **~ of flats** edificio m de apartamentos, casa f de pisos. ● vt bloquear. **~ade** /blɒ'keɪd/ n bloqueo m. ● vt bloquear. **~age** /-ɪdʒ/ n obstrucción f. **~head** n 🖪 zopenco m

bloke /bləʊk/ n 🖪 tipo m, tío m 🖪

blond /blɒnd/ adj & n rubio (m), güero (m) (Mex fam). **~e** adj & n rubia (f), güera (f) (Mex fam)

blood /blʌd/ n sangre f. **~bath** n masacre m. **~-curdling** /-kɜːdlɪŋ/ adj horripilante. **~hound** n sabueso m. **~ pressure** n tensión f arterial. **high ~ pressure** hipertensión f. **~shed** n derramamiento m de sangre. **~shot** adj sanguinolento; (eye) inyectado de sangre. **~stream** n torrente m sanguíneo. **~thirsty** adj sanguinario. **~y** adj (-ier, -iest) sangriento; (stained) ensangrentado; 🖪 maldito

bloom /bluːm/ n flor f. ● vi florecer

blossom /'blɒsəm/ n flor f. ● vi florecer. **~ (out) into** (fig) llegar a ser

blot /blɒt/ n borrón m. ● vt (pt blotted) manchar; (dry) secar. □ **~ out** vt oscurecer

blotch /blɒtʃ/ n mancha f. **~y** adj lleno de manchas

blotting-paper /'blɒtɪŋ/ n papel m secante

blouse /blaʊz/ n blusa f

blow /bləʊ/ vt (pt blew, pp blown) soplar; fundir (fuse); tocar (trumpet). ● vi soplar; (fuse) fundirse; (sound) sonar. ● n golpe m. □ **~ down** vt derribar. □ **~ out** vi apagar (candle). □ **~ over** vi pasar. □ **~ up** vt inflar; (explode) volar;

(*Photo*) ampliar. vi (*explode*) estallar; (*burst*) reventar. ~**dry** vt secar con secador. ~**lamp** n soplete m. ~**out** n (*of tyre*) reventón m. ~**torch** n soplete m

blue /bluː/ adj (-er, -est) azul; (*joke*) verde. ● n azul m. out of the ~ totalmente inesperado. ~s npl. have the ~s tener tristeza. ~**bell** n campanilla f. ~**berry** n arándano m. ~**bottle** n moscarda f. ~**print** n plano m; (fig, plan) programa m

bluff /blʌf/ n (*poker*) farol m, bluff m (LAm), blof m (Mex). ● vt engañar. ● vi tirarse un farol, hacer un bluf (LAm), blofear (Mex)

blunder /ˈblʌndə(r)/ vi cometer un error. ● n metedura f de pata

blunt /blʌnt/ adj desafilado; (*person*) directo, abrupto. ● vt desafilar. ~**ly** adv francamente

blur /blɜː(r)/ n impresión f indistinta. ● vt (pt blurred) hacer borroso

blurb /blɜːb/ n resumen m publicitario

blurt /blɜːt/ vt. ~ out dejar escapar

blush /blʌʃ/ vi ruborizarse. ● n rubor m

boar /bɔː(r)/ n verraco m. wild ~ jabalí m

board /bɔːd/ n tabla f, tablero m; (for notices) tablón m de anuncios, tablero m de anuncios (LAm); (*blackboard*) pizarra f; (*food*) pensión f; (*of company*) junta f. full ~ and lodging casa y comida. full ~ pensión f completa. go by the ~ ser abandonado. ● vt alojar; ~ a ship embarcarse. ● vi alojarse (with en casa de); (at school) ser interno. ~**er** n huésped m & f; (*school*) interno m. ~**ing card** n tarjeta f de embarque. ~**ing**

house n casa f de huéspedes, pensión f. ~**ing pass** n see ~ING CARD. ~**ing school** n internado m

boast /bəʊst/ vt enorgullecerse de. ● vi jactarse. ● n jactancia f. ~**ful** adj jactancioso

boat /bəʊt/ n barco m; (*small*) bote m, barca f

bob /bɒb/ vi (pt bobbed) menearse, subir y bajar. □ ~ **up** vi presentarse súbitamente

bobbin /ˈbɒbɪn/ n carrete m; (in sewing machine) canilla f, bobina f

bobby pin /ˈbɒbɪ/ n (Amer) horquilla f, pasador m (Mex). ~ **sox** /sɒks/ npl (Amer) calcetines mpl cortos

bobsleigh /ˈbɒbsleɪ/ n bob (sleigh) m

bode /bəʊd/ vi. ~ well/ill ser de buen/mal agüero

bodice /ˈbɒdɪs/ n corpiño m

bodily /ˈbɒdɪlɪ/ adj físico, corporal. ● adv físicamente

body /ˈbɒdɪ/ n cuerpo m; (dead) cadáver m. ~**guard** n guardaespaldas m. ~ **part** n pedazo m de cuerpo. ~**work** n carrocería f

bog /bɒg/ n ciénaga f. □ ~ **down** vt (pt bogged). get ~ged down empantanarse

boggle /ˈbɒgl/ vi sobresaltarse. the mind ~s uno se queda atónito

bogus /ˈbəʊgəs/ adj falso

boil /bɔɪl/ vt/i hervir. be ~ing hot estar ardiendo; (weather) hacer mucho calor. ● n furúnculo m. □ ~ **away** vi evaporarse. □ ~ **down to** vt reducirse a. □ ~ **over** vi rebosar. ~**ed** adj hervido; (egg) pasado por agua. ~**er** n caldera f. ~ **suit** n mono m, overol m (LAm)

boisterous /ˈbɔɪstərəs/ adj ruidoso, bullicioso

bold /bəʊld/ adj (-er, -est) audaz. ~**ly** adv con audacia, audazmente

Bolivia /bə'lɪvɪə/ n Bolivia f. ~**n** adj & n boliviano (m)

bolster /'bəʊlstə(r)/ □ ~ **up** vt sostener

bolt /bəʊlt/ n (on door) cerrojo m; (for nut) perno m; (lightning) rayo m; (leap) fuga f. ● vt echar el cerrojo a (door); engullir (food). ● vi fugarse. ● adv. ~ **upright** rígido

bomb /bɒm/ n bomba f. ● vt bombardear. ~**ard** /bɒm'bɑːd/ vt bombardear ~**er** /'bɒmə(r)/ n (plane) bombardero m; (terrorist) terrorista m & f. ~**ing** /'bɒmɪŋ/ n bombardeo m. ~**shell** n bomba f

bond /bɒnd/ n (agreement) obligación f; (link) lazo m; (Com) bono m. ● vi (stick) adherirse. ~**age** /-ɪdʒ/ n esclavitud f

bone /bəʊn/ n hueso m; (of fish) espina f. ● vt deshuesar; quitar las espinas a (fish). ~**-dry** adj completamente seco. ~ **idle** adj holgazán

bonfire /'bɒnfaɪə(r)/ n hoguera f, fogata f

bonnet /'bɒnɪt/ n gorra f; (Auto) capó m, capote m (Mex)

bonus /'bəʊnəs/ n (payment) bonificación f; (fig) ventaja f

bony /'bəʊnɪ/ adj (-ier, -iest) huesudo; (fish) lleno de espinas

boo /buː/ int ¡bu! ● vt/i abuchear

boob /buːb/ n (fam, mistake) metedura f de pata. ● vi 🛈 meter la pata

book /bʊk/ n libro m; (of cheques etc) talonario m, chequera f; (notebook) libreta f; (exercise book) cuaderno m. ~**s** (mpl) (Com) cuentas fpl. ● vt (enter) registrar; (reserve) reservar. ● vi reservar. ~**case** n bi-

blioteca f, librería f, librero m (Mex). ~**ing** n reserva f, reservación f (LAm). ~**ing office** n (in theatre) taquilla f, boletería f (LAm). ~**keeping** n contabilidad f. ~**let** /'bʊklɪt/ n folleto m. ~**maker** n corredor de apuestas. ~**mark** n señal f. ~**seller** n librero m. ~**shop**, (Amer) ~**store** n librería f. ~**worm** n (fig) ratón m de biblioteca

boom /buːm/ vi retumbar; (fig) prosperar. ● n estampido m; (Com) boom m

boost /buːst/ vt estimular; reforzar (morale). ● n empuje m. ~**er** n (Med) revacunación f. ~**er cable** n (Amer) cable m de arranque

boot /buːt/ n bota f; (Auto) maletero m, cajuela f (Mex). □ ~ **up** vt (Comp) cargar

booth /buːð/ n cabina f; (at fair) puesto m

booze /buːz/ vi 🛈 beber mucho. ● n 🛈 alcohol m

border /'bɔːdə(r)/ n borde m; (frontier) frontera f; (in garden) arriate m. □ ~ **on** vi lindar con. ~**line** n línea f divisoria. ~**line case** n caso m dudoso

bor|e /bɔː(r)/ see **BEAR**. ● vt (annoy) aburrir; (Tec) taladrar. ● vi taladrar. ● n (person) pelmazo m; (thing) lata f. ● **ed** adj aburrido. be ~**ed** estar aburrido. get ~**ed** aburrirse. ~**edom** /'bɔːdəm/ n aburrimiento m. ~**ing** adj aburrido, pesado

born /bɔːn/ adj nato. be ~ nacer

borne /bɔːn/ see **BEAR**

borough /'bʌrə/ n municipio m

borrow /'bɒrəʊ/ vt pedir prestado

boss /bɒs/ n 🛈 jefe m. ● vt. ~ (about) 🛈 dar órdenes a. ~**y** adj mandón

botan|ical /bə'tænɪkl/ adj botánico. • **~ist** /'bɒtənɪst/ n botánico m. • **~y** /'bɒtənɪ/ n botánica f

both /bəʊθ/ adj & pron ambos (mpl), los dos (mpl). • adv al mismo tiempo, a la vez. **~ Ann and Brian came** tanto Ann como Bob vinieron.

bother /'bɒðə(r)/ vt (inconvenience) molestar; (worry) preocupar. • **~ it!** ¡caramba! • vi molestarse. **~ about** preocuparse de. **~ doing** tomarse la molestia de hacer. • n molestia f

bottle /'bɒtl/ n botella, mamila f (Mex); (for baby) biberón m. • vt embotellar. □ **~ up** vt (fig) reprimir. **~neck** n (traffic jam) embotellamiento m. **~ opener** n abrebotellas m, destapador m (LAm)

bottom /'bɒtəm/ n fondo m; (of hill) pie m; (buttocks) trasero m. • adj de más abajo; (price) más bajo; (lip, edge) inferior. **~less** adj sin fondo

bough /baʊ/ n rama f

bought /bɔːt/ see BUY

boulder /'bəʊldə(r)/ n canto m

bounce /baʊns/ vt hacer rebotar. • vi rebotar; (person) saltar; 🔲 (cheque) ser rechazado. • n rebote m

bound /baʊnd/ see BIND. • vi saltar. • n (jump) salto m. **~s** npl (limits) límites mpl. out of **~s** zona f prohibida. • adj. be **~ for** dirigirse a. **~ to** obligado a; (certain) seguro de

boundary /'baʊndərɪ/ n límite m

bouquet /bʊ'keɪ/ n ramo m; (of wine) buqué m, aroma m

bout /baʊt/ n período m; (Med) ataque m; (Sport) encuentro m

bow¹ /baʊ/ n (weapon, Mus) arco

m; (knot) lazo m, moño m (LAm)

bow² /baʊ/ n reverencia f; (Naut) proa f. • vi inclinarse. • vt inclinar

bowels /'baʊəlz/ npl intestinos mpl; (fig) entrañas fpl

bowl /bəʊl/ n (container) cuenco m; (for washing) palangana f; (ball) bola f. • vt (cricket) arrojar. • vi (cricket) arrojar la pelota. □ **~ over** vt derribar

bowl: **~er** n (cricket) lanzador m. **~er (hat)** sombrero m de hongo, bombín m. **~ing** n bolos mpl. **~ing alley** n bolera f

bow tie /baʊ 'taɪ/ n corbata f de lazo, pajarita f

box /bɒks/ n caja f; (for jewels etc) estuche m; (in theatre) palco m. • vt boxear contra. **~ s.o.'s ears** dar una manotada a uno. • vi boxear. **~er** n boxeador m. **~ing** n boxeo m. **B~ing Day** n el 26 de diciembre. **~ office** n taquilla f, boletería f (LAm). **~ room** n trastero m

boy /bɔɪ/ n chico m, muchacho m; (young) niño m

boy: **~ band** n grupo m pop de chicos. **~friend** n novio m. **~hood** n niñez f. **~ish** adj de muchacho; (childish) infantil

boycott /'bɔɪkɒt/ vt boicotear. • n boicoteo m

bra /brɑː/ n sostén m, sujetador m, brasier m (Mex)

brace /breɪs/ n abrazadera f. • vt asegurar. **~ o.s.** prepararse. **~s** npl tirantes mpl; (Amer, dental) aparato(s) m(pl)

bracelet /'breɪslɪt/ n pulsera f

bracken /'brækən/ n helecho m

bracket /'brækɪt/ n soporte m; (group) categoría f; (parenthesis) paréntesis m. **square ~s** corchetes mpl. • vt poner entre paréntesis;

(*join together*) agrupar

brag /bræg/ *vi* (*pt* bragged) jactarse (about de)

braid /breɪd/ *n* galón *m*; (*Amer, in hair*) trenza *f*

brain /breɪn/ *n* cerebro *m*. ● *vt* romper la cabeza a. ~**child** *n* invento *m*. ~**drain** *n* 🗍 fuga *f* de cerebros. ~**storm** *n* ataque *m* de locura; (*Amer, brainwave*) idea *f* genial. ~**wash** *vt* lavar el cerebro. ~**wave** *n* idea *f* genial. ~**y** *adj* (-ier, -iest) inteligente

brake /breɪk/ *n* freno *m*. ● *vt/i* frenar. ~ **fluid** *n* líquido *m* de freno. ~ **lights** *npl* luces *fpl* de freno.

bramble /'bræmbl/ *n* zarza *f*

bran /bræn/ *n* salvado *m*

branch /brɑːntʃ/ *n* rama *f*; (*of road*) bifurcación *f*; (*Com*) sucursal *m*; (*fig*) ramo *m*. □ ~ **off** *vi* bifurcarse. □ ~ **out** *vi* ramificarse

brand /brænd/ *n* marca *f*. ● *vt* marcar; (*label*) tildar de

brandish /'brændɪʃ/ *vt* blandir

brand: ~ **name:** ~ **name** *n* marca *f*. ~**-new** /-'nju:/ *adj* flamante

brandy /'brændɪ/ *n* coñac *m*

brash /bræʃ/ *adj* descarado

brass /brɑːs/ *n* latón *m*. **get down to** ~ **tacks** (*fig*) ir al grano. ~ **band** *n* banda *f* de música

brassière /'bræsjeə(r)/ *n see* BRA

brat /bræt/ *n* (*pej*) mocoso *m*

bravado /brə'vɑːdəʊ/ *n* bravata *f*

brave /breɪv/ *adj* (-er, -est) valiente. ● *n* (*North American Indian*) guerrero *m* indio. **the** ~ *npl* los valientes. ● *vt* afrontar. ~**ry** /-ərɪ/ *n* valentía *f*, valor *m*

brawl /brɔːl/ *n* alboroto *m*. ● *vi* pelearse

brazen /'breɪzn/ *adj* descarado

Brazil /brə'zɪl/ *n* Brasil *m*. ~**ian** /-jən/ *adj* & *n* brasileño (*m*)

breach /briːtʃ/ *n* infracción *f*, violación *f*; (*of contract*) incumplimiento *m*; (*gap*) brecha *f*. ~ **of the peace** alteración *f* del orden público. ● *vt* abrir una brecha en

bread /bred/ *n* pan *m*. **a loaf of** ~ un pan. ~**crumbs** *npl* migajas *fpl*; (*Culin*) pan *m* rallado, pan *m* molido (*Mex*)

breadth /bredθ/ *n* anchura *f*

breadwinner /'bredwɪnə(r)/ *n* sostén *m* de la familia

break /breɪk/ *vt* (*pt* broke, *pp* broken) romper; infringir, violar (law); batir (record); comunicar (news); interrumpir (journey). ● *vi* romperse; (news) divulgarse. ● *n* ruptura *f*; (*interval*) intervalo *m*; (*fam, chance*) oportunidad *f*; (in weather) cambio *m*. □ ~ **away** *vi* escapar. □ ~ **down** *vt* derribar; analizar (figures). *vi* estropearse, descomponerse (*LAm*), (*Auto*) averiarse; (*cry*) deshacerse en lágrimas. □ ~ **in** *vi* (intruder) entrar (*para robar*). □ ~ **into** *vt* entrar en (*para robar*) (house etc); (*start doing*) ponerse a. □ ~ **off** *vi* interrumpise. □ ~ **out** *vi* (war, disease) estallar; (*run away*) escaparse. □ ~ **up** *vi* romperse; (band, lovers) separarse; (schools) terminar. ~**able** *adj* frágil. ~**age** /-ɪdʒ/ *n* rotura *f*. ~**down** *n* (*Tec*) falla *f*; (*Med*) colapso *m*, crisis *f* nerviosa; (*of figures*) análisis *f*. ~**er** *n* (wave) ola *f* grande

breakfast /'brekfəst/ *n* desayuno *m*. **have** ~ desayunar

break: ~**through** *n* adelanto *m*. ~**water** *n* rompeolas *m*

breast /brest/ *n* pecho *m*; (*of chicken etc*) pechuga *f*. (estilo *m*)

~**stroke** n braza f, (estilo m) pecho m (LAm)

b **breath** /breθ/ n aliento m, respiración f. **be out of** ~ estar sin aliento. **hold one's** ~ aguantar la respiración. **under one's** ~ a media voz

breath|e /briːð/ vt/i respirar. ~**er** n descanso m, pausa f. ~**ing** n respiración f

breathtaking /'breθteɪkɪŋ/ adj impresionante

bred /bred/ see **BREED**

breed /briːd/ vt (pt bred) criar; (fig) engendrar. ● vi reproducirse. ● n raza f

breez|e /briːz/ n brisa f. ~**y** adj de mucho viento

brew /bruː/ vt hacer (beer); preparar (tea). ● vi hacer cerveza; (tea) reposar; (fig) prepararse. ● n infusión f. ~**er** n cervecero m. ~**ery** n cervecería f, fábrica f de cerveza

bribe /braɪb/ n soborno m. ● vt sobornar. ~**ry** /braɪbərɪ/ n soborno m

brick /brɪk/ n ladrillo m. ~**layer** n albañil m

bridal /'braɪdl/ adj nupcial

bride /braɪd/ m novia f. ~**groom** n novio m. ~**smaid** /'braɪdzmeɪd/ n dama f de honor

bridge /brɪdʒ/ n puente m; (of nose) caballete m; (Cards) bridge m. ● vt tender un puente sobre. ~ **a gap** llenar un vacío

bridle /'braɪdl/ n brida f. ~ **path** n camino m de herradura

brief /briːf/ adj (-er, -est) breve. ● n (Jurid) escrito m. ● vt dar instrucciones a. ~**case** n maletín m, portafolio(s) m (LAm). ~**ly** adv brevemente. ~**s** npl (man's) calzoncillos mpl; (woman's) bragas fpl, calzo-

nes mpl (LAm), pantaletas fpl (Mex)

brigade /brɪ'geɪd/ n brigada f

bright /braɪt/ adj (-er, -est) brillante, claro; (clever) listo; (cheerful) alegre. ~**en** vt aclarar; hacer más alegre (house etc). ● vi (weather) aclararse; (face) illuminarse

brillian|ce /'brɪljəns/ n brillantez f, brillo m. ~**t** adj brillante

brim /brɪm/ n borde m; (of hat) ala f. □ ~ **over** vi (pt brimmed) desbordarse

brine /braɪn/ n salmuera f

bring /brɪŋ/ vt (pt brought) traer; (lead) llevar. □ ~ **about** vt causar. □ ~ **back** vt devolver. □ ~ **down** vt derribar. □ ~ **off** vt lograr. □ ~ **on** vt causar. □ ~ **out** vt sacar; lanzar (product); publicar (book). □ ~ **round/to** vt hacer volver en sí. □ ~ **up** vt (Med) vomitar; educar (children); plantear (question)

brink /brɪŋk/ n borde m

brisk /brɪsk/ adj (-er, -est) enérgico, vivo

bristle /'brɪsl/ n cerda f. ● vi erizarse

Brit|ain /'brɪtən/ n Gran Bretaña f. ~**ish** /'brɪtɪʃ/ adj británico. ● npl **the** ~**ish** los británicos. ~**on** /'brɪtən/ n británico m

Brittany /'brɪtənɪ/ n Bretaña f

brittle /'brɪtl/ adj quebradizo

broach /brəʊtʃ/ vt abordar

broad /brɔːd/ adj (-er, -est) ancho. **in** ~ **daylight** a plena luz del día. ~**band** n banda f ancha. ~ **bean** n haba f. ~**cast** n emisión f. ● vt (pt broadcast) emitir. ● vi hablar por la radio. ~**caster** n locutor m. ~**casting** n radio-difusión f. ~**en** vt ensanchar. ● vi ensancharse. ~**ly** adv en general. ~**-minded** /-'maɪndɪd/ adj de miras amplias, tolerante

broccoli /'brɒkəli/ n invar brécol m

brochure /'brəʊʃə(r)/ n folleto m

broil /brɔɪl/ vt (Amer) asar a la parrilla. **~er** n (Amer) parrilla f

broke /brəʊk/ see BREAK. ● adj 🗉 sin blanca, en la ruina

broken /'brəʊkən/ see BREAK. ● adj roto

broker /'brəʊkə(r)/ n corredor m

brolly /'brɒli/ n 🗉 paraguas m

bronchitis /brɒŋ'kaɪtɪs/ n bronquitis f

bronze /brɒnz/ n bronce m. ● adj de bronce

brooch /brəʊtʃ/ n broche m

brood /bruːd/ n cría f; (humorous) prole m. ● vi empollar; (fig) meditar

brook /brʊk/ n arroyo m. ● vt soportar

broom /bruːm/ n escoba f. **~stick** n palo m de escoba

broth /brɒθ/ n caldo m

brothel /'brɒθl/ n burdel m

brother /'brʌðə(r)/ n hermano m. **~hood** n fraternidad f. **~-in-law** (pl **~s-in-law**) n cuñado m. **~ly** adj fraternal

brought /brɔːt/ see BRING

brow /braʊ/ n frente f; (of hill) cima f. **~beat** n (pt **-beaten**, pp **-beat**) intimidar

brown /braʊn/ adj (-er, -est) marrón, café (Mex); (hair) castaño; (skin) moreno; (tanned) bronceado. ● n marrón m, café m (Mex). ● vt poner moreno; (Culin) dorar. **~ bread** n pan m integral. **~ sugar** /braʊn 'ʃʊgə(r)/ n azúcar m moreno, azúcar f morena

browse /braʊz/ vi (in a shop) curiosear; (animal) pacer; (Comp) navegar. **~r** (Comp) browser m,

navegador m

bruise /bruːz/ n magulladura f. ● vt magullar; machucar (fruit)

brunch /brʌntʃ/ n 🗉 desayuno m tardío

brunette /bruː'net/ n morena f

brunt /brʌnt/ n. bear o take the **~** of sth sufrir algo

brush /brʌʃ/ n cepillo m; (large) escoba; (for decorating) brocha f; (artist's) pincel; (skirmish) escaramuza f. ● vt cepillar. □ **~ against** vt rozar. □ **~ aside** vt rechazar. □ **~ off** vt (rebuff) desairar. □ **~ up (on)** vt refrescar

brusque /bruːsk/ adj brusco. **~ly** adv bruscamente

Brussels /'brʌslz/ n Bruselas f. **~ sprout** n col f de Bruselas

brutal /'bruːtl/ adj brutal. **~ity** /-'tælətɪ/ n brutalidad f. **~ly** adv brutalmente

brute /bruːt/ n bestia f. **~ force** fuerza f bruta

BSc abbr see BACHELOR

BSE abbr (bovine spongiform encephalopathy) EBE f

bubbl|e /'bʌbl/ n burbuja f. ● vi burbujear. □ **~ over** vi desbordarse. **~ly** adj burbujeante

buck /bʌk/ adj macho. ● n (deer) ciervo m; (Amer fam) dólar m. **pass the ~** pasar la pelota

bucket /'bʌkɪt/ n balde m, cubo m, cubeta f (Mex)

buckle /'bʌkl/ n hebilla f. ● vt abrochar. ● vi torcerse

bud /bʌd/ n brote m. ● vi (pt budded) brotar

Buddhis|m /'bʊdɪzəm/ n budismo m. **~t** adj & n budista (m & f)

budding /'bʌdɪŋ/ adj (fig) en ciernes

buddy /'bʌdɪ/ n 🔲 amigo m, cuate m (Mex)

budge /bʌdʒ/ vt mover. ● vi moverse

budgerigar /'bʌdʒərɪgaː(r)/ n periquito m

budget /'bʌdʒɪt/ n presupuesto m

buffalo /'bʌfələʊ/ n (pl -oes or -o) búfalo m

buffer /'bʌfə(r)/ n parachoques m

buffet[1] /'bʊfeɪ/ n (meal) buffet m; (in train) bar m

buffet[2] /'bʌfɪt/ n golpe m.

bug /bʌg/ n bicho m; 🔲 (germ) microbio m; (fam, device) micrófono m oculto. ● vt (pt bugged) 🔲 ocultar un micrófono en; (bother) molestar

buggy /'bʌgɪ/ n. baby ~ sillita f de paseo (plegable); (Amer) cochecito m

bugle /'bjuːgl/ n corneta f

build /bɪld/ vt/i (pt built) construir. ● n (of person) figura f, tipo m. □ ~ up vt/i fortalecer; (increase) aumentar. ~er n (contractor) contratista m & f; (labourer) albañil m. ~ing n edificio m; (construction) construcción f. ~up n aumento m; (of gas etc) acumulación f

built /bɪlt/ see BUILD. ~-in adj empotrado. ~-up area n zona f urbanizada

bulb /bʌlb/ n bulbo m; (Elec) bombilla f, foco m (Mex)

Bulgaria /bʌl'geərɪə/ n Bulgaria f. ~n adj & n búlgaro (m)

bulge /bʌldʒ/ n protuberancia f. ● vi pandearse. ~ing adj abultado; (eyes) saltón

bulk /bʌlk/ n bulto m, volumen m. in ~ a granel; (loose) suelto. the ~ of la mayor parte de. ~y adj voluminoso

bull /bʊl/ n toro m. ~dog n bulldog m. ~dozer /-dəʊzə(r)/ n bulldozer m

bullet /'bʊlɪt/ n bala f

bulletin /'bʊlətɪn/ n anuncio m; (journal) boletín m. ~ board n (Amer) tablón m de anuncios, tablero m de anuncios (LAm)

bulletproof /'bʊlɪtpruːf/ adj a prueba de balas

bullfight /'bʊlfaɪt/ n corrida f (de toros). ~er n torero m. ~ing n (deporte m de) los toros

bull: ~ring n plaza f de toros. ~'s-eye n diana f. ~shit n (vulgar) sandeces fpl 🔲, gillipolleces fpl ⊠

bully /'bʊlɪ/ n matón m. ● vt intimidar. ~ing n intimidación f

bum /bʌm/ n (fam, backside) trasero m; (Amer fam, tramp) holgazán m

bumblebee /'bʌmblbiː/ n abejorro m

bump /bʌmp/ vt chocar contra. ● vi dar sacudidas. ● n (blow) golpe m; (jolt) sacudida f. □ ~ into vt chocar contra; (meet) encontrar.

bumper /'bʌmpə(r)/ n parachoques m. ● adj récord. ~ edition n edición f especial

bun /bʌn/ n bollo m; (bread roll) panecillo m, bolillo m (Mex); (hair) moño m, chongo m (Mex)

bunch /bʌntʃ/ n (of people) grupo m; (of bananas, grapes) racimo m; (of flowers) ramo m

bundle /'bʌndl/ n bulto m; (of papers) legajo m. □ ~ up vt atar

bungalow /'bʌŋgələʊ/ n casa f de un solo piso

bungle /'bʌŋgl/ vt echar a perder

bunk /bʌŋk/ n litera f

bunker /'bʌŋkə(r)/ n carbonera f;

(*Golf, Mil*) búnker *m*

bunny /'bʌnɪ/ *n* conejito *m*

buoy /bɔɪ/ *n* boya *f*. □ ~ **up** *vt* hacer flotar; (*fig*) animar

buoyant /'bɔɪənt/ *adj* flotante; (*fig*) optimista

burden /'bɜːdn/ *n* carga *f*. ●*vt* cargar (with de)

bureau /'bjʊərəʊ/ *n* (*pl* -eaux /-əʊz/) agencia *f*; (*desk*) escritorio *m*; (*Amer, chest of drawers*) cómoda *f*

bureaucra|cy /bjʊə'rɒkrəsɪ/ *n* burocracia *f*. ~**t** /'bjʊərəkræt/ *n* burócrata *m & f*. ~**tic** /-'krætɪk/ *adj* burocrático

burger /'bɜːgə(r)/ *n* hamburguesa *f*

burgl|ar /'bɜːglə(r)/ *n* ladrón *m*. ~**ar alarm** *n* alarma *f* antirrobo. ~**ary** *n* robo *m* (*en casa o edificio*). ~**e** /'bɜːgl/ *vt* entrar a robar en. **we were** ~**ed** nos entraron a robar

burial /'berɪəl/ *n* entierro *m*

burly /'bɜːlɪ/ *adj* (-ier, -iest) corpulento

burn /bɜːn/ *vt* (*pt* burned *or* burnt) quemar. ●*vi* quemarse. ●*n* quemadura *f*. ~**er** *n* quemador *m*. □ ~ **down** *vt* incendiar. ●*vi* incendiarse

burnt /bɜːnt/ *see* BURN

burp /bɜːp/ *n* 🔢 eructo *m*. ●*vi* 🔢 eructar

burrow /'bʌrəʊ/ *n* madriguera *f*. ●*vt* excavar

burst /bɜːst/ *vt* (*pt* burst) reventar. ●*vi* reventarse. ~ **into tears** echarse a llorar. ~ **out laughing** echarse a reír. ●*n* (*Mil*) ráfaga *f*; (*of activity*) arrebato *m*; (*of applause*) salva *f*

bury /'berɪ/ *vt* enterrar; (*hide*) ocultar

bus /bʌs/ *n* (*pl* buses) autobús *m*, camión *m* (*Mex*)

bush /bʊʃ/ *n* arbusto *m*; (*land*) monte *m*. ~**y** *adj* espeso

business /'bɪznɪs/ *n* negocio *m*; (*Com*) negocios *mpl*; (*profession*) ocupación *f*; (*fig*) asunto *m*. **mind one's own** ~ ocuparse de sus propios asuntos. ~**like** *adj* práctico, serio. ~**man** /-mæn/ *n* hombre *m* de negocios. ~**woman** *n* mujer *f* de negocios

busker /'bʌskə(r)/ *n* músico *m* ambulante

bus stop *n* parada *f* de autobús, paradero *m* de autobús (*LAm*)

bust /bʌst/ *n* busto *m*; (*chest*) pecho *m*. ●*vt* (*pt* busted *or* bust) 🔢 romper. ●*vi* romperse. ●*adj* roto. **go** ~ 🔢 quebrar

bust-up /'bʌstʌp/ *n* 🔢 riña *f*

busy /'bɪzɪ/ *adj* (-ier, -iest) ocupado; (*street*) concurrido. **be** ~ (*Amer*) (*phone*) estar comunicando, estar ocupado (*LAm*). ●*vt.* ~ **o.s. with** ocuparse de. ~**body** *n* entrometido *m*

but /bʌt/ *conj* pero; (*after negative*) sino. ●*prep* menos. ~ **for** si no fuera por. **last** ~ **one** penúltimo

butcher /'bʊtʃə(r)/ *n* carnicero *m*. ●*vt* matar; (*fig*) hacer una carnicería con

butler /'bʌtlə(r)/ *n* mayordomo *m*

butt /bʌt/ *n* (*of gun*) culata *f*; (*of cigarette*) colilla *f*; (*target*) blanco *m*; (*Amer fam, backside*) trasero *m*. ●*vi* topar. □ ~ **in** *vi* interrumpir

butter /'bʌtə(r)/ *n* mantequilla *f*. ●*vt* untar con mantequilla. ~**cup** *n* ranúnculo *m*. ~**fingers** *n* manazas *m*, torpe *m*. ~**fly** *n* mariposa *f*; (*swimming*) estilo *m* mariposa

buttock /'bʌtək/ *n* nalga *f*

button /'bʌtn/ n botón m. ● vt abotonar. ● vi abotonarse. ~hole n ojal m. ● vt (fig) detener

buy /baɪ/ vt/i (pt bought) comprar. ● n compra f. ~er n comprador m

buzz /bʌz/ n zumbido m. ● vi zumbar. □ ~ off vi ⊠ largarse. ~er n timbre m

by /baɪ/ prep por; (near) cerca de; (before) antes de; (according to) según. ~ and large en conjunto, en general. ~ car en coche. ~ oneself por sí solo

bye /baɪ/, **bye-bye** /'baɪbaɪ/ int 🗓 ¡adiós!

by: ~**-election** n elección f parcial. ~**-law** n reglamento m (local). ~**pass** n carretera f de circunvalación. ● vt eludir; (road) circunvalar. ~**-product** n subproducto m. ~**stander** /-stændə(r)/ n espectador m

byte /baɪt/ n (Comp) byte m, octeto m

....

Cc

....

cab /kæb/ n taxi m; (of lorry, train) cabina f

cabaret /'kæbəreɪ/ n cabaret m

cabbage /'kæbɪdʒ/ n col f, repollo m

cabin /'kæbɪn/ n (house) cabaña f; (in ship) camarote m; (in plane) cabina f

cabinet /'kæbɪnɪt/ n (cupboard) armario m; (for display) vitrina f. C~ (Pol) gabinete m

cable /'keɪbl/ n cable m. ~ car n teleférico m. ~ TV n televisión f por cable, cablevisión f (LAm)

cackle /'kækl/ n (of hen) cacareo m; (laugh) risotada f. ● vi cacarear; (laugh) reírse a carcajadas

cactus /'kæktəs/ n (pl -ti /-taɪ/ or -tuses) cacto m

caddie, caddy /'kædɪ/ n (golf) portador m de palos

cadet /kə'det/ n cadete m

cadge /kædʒ/ vt/i gorronear

café /'kæfeɪ/ n cafetería f

cafeteria /kæfɪ'tɪərɪə/ n restaurante m autoservicio

caffeine /'kæfiːn/ n cafeína f

cage /keɪdʒ/ n jaula f. ● vt enjaular

cake /keɪk/ n pastel m, tarta f; (sponge) bizcocho m. ~ of soap pastilla f de jabón

calamity /kə'læmətɪ/ n calamidad f

calcium /'kælsɪəm/ n calcio m

calculat|e /'kælkjʊleɪt/ vt/i calcular. ~ion /-'leɪʃn/ n cálculo m. ~or n calculadora f

calculus /'kælkjʊləs/ n (Math) cálculo m

calendar /'kælɪndə(r)/ n calendario m

calf /kɑːf/ n (pl calves) (animal) ternero m; (of leg) pantorrilla f

calibre /'kælɪbə(r)/ n calibre m

call /kɔːl/ vt/i llamar. ● n llamada f; (shout) grito m; (visit) visita f. be on ~ estar de guardia. long-distance ~ llamada f de larga distancia, conferencia f. □ ~ back vt hacer volver; (on phone) volver a llamar. vi volver; (on phone) volver a llamar. □ ~ for vt pedir; (fetch) ir a buscar. □ ~ off vt suspender. □ ~ on vt pasar a visitar. □ ~ out vi dar voces. □ ~ together vt convocar. □ ~ up vt (Mil) llamar al servicio militar; (phone) llamar. ~

box n cabina f telefónica. ~ **centre** n centro m de llamadas. ~**er** n visita f; (phone) persona que llama m. ~**ing** n vocación f

callous /'kæləs/ adj insensible, cruel

calm /kɑːm/ adj (-er, -est) tranquilo; (sea) en calma. ● n tranquilidad f, calma f. ● vt calmar. ● vi calmarse. ~ **down** vi tranquilizarse. vt calmar. ~**ly** adv con calma

calorie /'kælərɪ/ n caloría f

calves /kɑːvz/ npl see CALF

camcorder /'kæmkɔːdə(r)/ n videocámara f, camcórder m

came /keɪm/ see COME

camel /'kæml/ n camello m

camera /'kæmərə/ n cámara f, máquina f fotográfica. ~**man** /-mən/ n camarógrafo m, cámara m

camouflage /'kæməflɑːʒ/ n camuflaje m. ● vt camuflar

camp /kæmp/ n campamento m. ● vi acampar. go ~**ing** hacer camping

campaign /kæm'peɪn/ n campaña f. ● vi hacer campaña

camp: ~**bed** n catre m de tijera. ~**er** n campista m & f; (vehicle) cámper m. ~**ground** n (Amer) see ~**SITE**. ~**ing** n camping m. ~**site** n camping m

campus /'kæmpəs/ n (pl -puses) campus m, ciudad f universitaria

---

can¹ /kæn//kən/

negative **can't, cannot** (formal); past **could**

auxiliary verb

····▸ (be able to) poder. I ~'t lift it no lo puedo levantar. she

says she ~ come dice que puede venir

····▸ (be allowed to) poder. ~ I smoke? ¿puedo fumar?

····▸ (know how to) saber. ~ you swim? ¿sabes nadar?

····▸ (with verbs of perception) not translated. I ~'t see you no te veo. I ~ hear you better now ahora te oigo mejor

····▸ (in requests) ~ I have a glass of water, please? ¿me trae un vaso de agua, por favor?. ~ I have a kilo of cheese, please? ¿me da un kilo de queso, por favor?

····▸ (in offers) ~ I help you? ¿te ayudo?; (in shop) ¿lo/la atienden?

---

can² /kæn/ n lata f, bote m. ● vt (pt canned) enlatar. ~**ned music** música f grabada

Canad|a /'kænədə/ n (el) Canadá m. ~**ian** /kə'neɪdɪən/ adj & n canadiense (m & f)

canal /kə'næl/ n canal m

Canaries /kə'neərɪz/ npl = CANARY ISLANDS

canary /kə'neərɪ/ n canario m. C~ **Islands** npl. the C~ Islands las Islas Canarias

cancel /'kænsl/ vt (pt cancelled) cancelar; anular (command, cheque); (delete) tachar. ~**lation** /-'leɪʃn/ n cancelación f

cancer /'kænsə(r)/ n cáncer m. C~ n (in astrology) Cáncer m. ~**ous** adj canceroso

candid /'kændɪd/ adj franco

candidate /'kændɪdeɪt/ n candidato m

candle /'kændl/ n vela f. ~**stick** n candelero m

candour /'kændə(r)/ n franqueza f

candy /'kændɪ/ n (Amer) caramelo m, dulce f (LAm). ~floss /-flɒs/ n algodón m de azúcar

cane /keɪn/ n caña f; (for baskets) mimbre m; (stick) bastón m; (for punishment) palmeta f. • vt castigar con palmeta

canister /'kænɪstə(r)/ n bote m

cannabis /'kænəbɪs/ n cáñamo m índico, hachís m, cannabis m

cannibal /'kænɪbl/ n caníbal m. ~ism n canibalismo m

cannon /'kænən/ n invar cañón m. ~ ball n bala f de cañón

cannot /'kænɒt/ see CAN¹

canoe /kə'nu:/ n canoa f, piragua f. • vi ir en canoa

canon /'kænən/ n canon m; (person) canónigo m. ~ize vt canonizar

can opener n abrelatas m

canopy /'kænəpɪ/ n dosel m

can't /kɑːnt/ see CAN¹

cantankerous /kæn'tæŋkərəs/ adj mal humorado

canteen /kæn'ti:n/ n cantina f; (of cutlery) juego m de cubiertos

canter /'kæntə(r)/ n medio galope m. • vi ir a medio galope

canvas /'kænvəs/ n lona f; (artist's) lienzo m

canvass /'kænvəs/ vi hacer campaña, solicitar votos. ~ing n solicitación f (de votos)

canyon /'kænjən/ n cañón m

cap /kæp/ n gorra f; (lid) tapa f; (of cartridge) cápsula f; (of pen) capuchón m. • vt (pt capped) tapar, poner cápsula a; (outdo) superar

capab|ility /keɪpə'bɪlətɪ/ n capacidad f. ~le /-'keɪpəbl/ adj capaz

capacity /kə'pæsɪtɪ/ n capacidad

f; (function) calidad f

cape /keɪp/ n (cloak) capa f; (headland) cabo m

capital /'kæpɪtl/ adj capital. ~ letter mayúscula f. • n (town) capital f; (money) capital m. ~ism n capitalismo m. ~ist adj & n capitalista (m & f.). ~ize vt capitalizar; escribir con mayúsculas (word). • vi. ~ize on aprovechar

capitulat|e /kə'pɪtʃʊleɪt/ vi capitular. ~ion /-'leɪʃn/ n capitulación f

> **Capitol** El Capitolio o sede del Congreso (Congress) de EE.UU., en Washington DC. Situado en Capitol Hill, a menudo la prensa emplea este nombre para hacer referencia al Congreso de EE.UU. *i*

Capricorn /'kæprɪkɔːn/ n Capricornio m

capsize /kæp'saɪz/ vt hacer volcar. • vi volcarse

capsule /'kæpsjuːl/ n cápsula f

captain /'kæptɪn/ n capitán m; (of plane) comandante m & f. • vt capitanear

caption /'kæpʃn/ n (heading) título m; (of cartoon etc) leyenda f

captivate /'kæptɪveɪt/ vt encantar

captiv|e /'kæptɪv/ adj & n cautivo (m). ~ity /-'tɪvətɪ/ n cautiverio m, cautividad f

capture /'kæptʃə(r)/ vt capturar; atraer (attention); (Mil) tomar. • n apresamiento m; (Mil) toma f

car /kɑː(r)/ n coche m, carro m (LAm), (Amer, of train) vagón m

caramel /'kærəmel/ n azúcar m quemado; (sweet) caramelo m, dulce m (LAm)

caravan /ˈkærəvæn/ n caravana f

carbohydrate /kɑːbəʊˈhaɪdreɪt/ n hidrato m de carbono

carbon /ˈkɑːbən/ n carbono m; (paper) carbón m. ~ **copy** n copia f al carbón. ~ **dioxide** /daɪˈɒksaɪd/ n anhídrido m carbónico. ~ **footprint** n huella f de carbono. ~ **monoxide** /məˈnɒksaɪd/ n monóxido de carbono

carburettor /kɑːbjʊˈretə(r)/ n carburador m

carcass /ˈkɑːkəs/ n cuerpo m de animal muerto; (for meat) res f muerta

card /kɑːd/ n tarjeta f; (for games) carta f; (membership) carnet m; (records) ficha f. ~**board** n cartón m

cardigan /ˈkɑːdɪɡən/ n chaqueta f de punto, rebeca f

cardinal /ˈkɑːdɪnl/ adj cardinal. ●n cardenal m

care /keə(r)/ n cuidado m; (worry) preocupación f; (protection) cargo m. ~ **of** a cuidado de, en casa de. take ~ tener cuidado. take ~ **of** cuidar de (person); ocuparse de (matter). ● vi interesarse. I don't ~ me da igual. □ ~ **about** vt preocuparse por. □ ~ **for** vt cuidar de; (like) querer

career /kəˈrɪə(r)/ n carrera f. ● vi correr a toda velocidad

care: ~**free** adj despreocupado. ~**ful** adj cuidadoso; (cautious) prudente. be ~**ful** tener cuidado. ~**fully** adv con cuidado. ~**less** adj negligente; (not worried) indiferente. ~**lessly** adv descuidadamente. ~**lessness** n descuido m. ~**r** n persona f que cuida de un discapacitado

caress /kəˈres/ n caricia f. ● vt acariciar

caretaker /ˈkeəteɪkə(r)/ n vigilante m; (of flats etc) portero m

car ferry n transbordador m de coches

cargo /ˈkɑːɡəʊ/ n (pl -oes) carga f

Caribbean /kærɪˈbiːən/ adj caribeño. the ~ (Sea) n el mar Caribe

caricature /ˈkærɪkətʃʊə(r)/ n caricatura f. ● vt caricaturizar

carnage /ˈkɑːnɪdʒ/ n carnicería f, matanza f

carnation /kɑːˈneɪʃn/ n clavel m

carnival /ˈkɑːnɪvl/ n carnaval m

carol /ˈkærəl/ n villancico m

carousel /kærəˈsel/ n tiovivo m, carrusel m (LAm); (for baggage) cinta f transportadora

carp /kɑːp/ n invar carpa f. □ ~ **at** vi quejarse de

car park n aparcamiento m, estacionamiento m

carpent|er /ˈkɑːpɪntə(r)/ n carpintero m. ~**ry** /-trɪ/ n carpintería f

carpet /ˈkɑːpɪt/ n alfombra f. ~ **sweeper** n cepillo m mecánico

carriage /ˈkærɪdʒ/ n coche m; (Mec) carro m; (transport) transporte m; (cost, bearing) porte m; (of train) vagón m. ~**way** n calzada f

carrier /ˈkærɪə(r)/ n transportista m & f; (company) empresa f de transportes; (Med) portador m. ~ **bag** n bolsa f

carrot /ˈkærət/ n zanahoria f

carry /ˈkærɪ/ vt llevar; transportar (goods); (involve) llevar consigo, implicar. ● vi (sounds) llegar, oírse. □ ~ **off** vt llevarse. □ ~ **on** vi seguir, continuar. □ ~ **out** vt realizar; cumplir (promise, threat). ~ **cot** n cuna f portátil

carsick /ˈkɑːsɪk/ adj mareado (por viajar en coche)

cart /kɑːt/ n carro m; (Amer, in supermarket, airport) carrito m. ● vt acarrear; (fam, carry) llevar

carton /'kɑːtən/ n caja f de cartón

cartoon /kɑː'tuːn/ n caricatura f, chiste m; (strip) historieta f; (film) dibujos mpl animados

cartridge /'kɑːtrɪdʒ/ n cartucho m

carve /kɑːv/ vt tallar; trinchar (meat)

cascade /kæs'keɪd/ n cascada f. ● vi caer en cascadas

case /keɪs/ n caso m; (Jurid) proceso m; (crate) cajón m; (box) caja f; (suitcase) maleta f, petaca f (Mex). in any ~ en todo caso. in ~ he comes por si viene. in ~ of en caso de

cash /kæʃ/ n dinero m efectivo. pay (in) ~ pagar al contado. ● vt cobrar. ~ in (on) aprovecharse de. ~ desk n caja f. ~ dispenser n cajero m automático

cashier /kæ'ʃɪə(r)/ n cajero m

cashpoint /'kæʃpɔɪnt/ n cajero m automático

casino /kə'siːnəʊ/ n (pl -os) casino m

cask /kɑːsk/ n barril m

casket /'kɑːskɪt/ n cajita f; (Amer) ataúd m, cajón m (LAm)

casserole /'kæsərəʊl/ n cacerola f; (stew) guiso m, guisado m (Mex)

cassette /kə'set/ n cassette m & f

cast /kɑːst/ vt (pt cast) arrojar; fundir (metal); emitir (vote). ● n lanzamiento m; (in play) reparto m; (mould) molde m

castanets /kæstə'nets/ npl castañuelas fpl

castaway /'kɑːstəweɪ/ n náufrago m

caster /'kɑːstə(r)/ n ruedecita f. ~ sugar n azúcar m extrafino

Castille /kæ'stiːl/ n Castilla f. ~ian /kæ'stɪlɪən/ adj & n castellano (m)

cast: ~ iron n hierro m fundido. ~-iron adj (fig) sólido

castle /'kɑːsl/ n castillo m; (Chess) torre f

cast-offs /'kɑːstɒfs/ npl desechos mpl

castrate /kæ'streɪt/ vt castrar. ~ion /-ʃn/ n castración f

casual /'kæʒʊəl/ adj casual; (meeting) fortuito; (work) ocasional; (attitude) despreocupado; (clothes) informal, de sport. ~ly adv de paso

casualty /'kæʒʊəltɪ/ n (injured) herido m; (dead) víctima f; (in hospital) urgencias fpl. ~ies npl (Mil) bajas fpl

cat /kæt/ n gato m

Catalan /'kætəlæn/ adj & n catalán (m)

catalogue /'kætəlɒg/ n catálogo m. ● vt catalogar

Catalonia /kætə'ləʊnɪə/ n Cataluña f

catalyst /'kætəlɪst/ n catalizador m

catamaran /kætəmə'ræn/ n catamarán m

catapult /'kætəpʌlt/ n catapulta f; (child's) tirachinas f, resortera f (Mex)

catarrh /kə'tɑː(r)/ n catarro m

catastrophe /kə'tæstrəfɪ/ n catástrofe m. ~ic /kætə'strɒfɪk/ adj catastrófico

catch /kætʃ/ vt (pt caught) coger (esp Spain), agarrar; tomar (train, bus); (unawares) sorprender; (understand) entender; contagiarse de (disease). ~ a cold resfriarse.

~ **sight of** avistar. ● vi (get stuck) engancharse; (fire) prenderse. ● n (by goalkeeper) parada f; (of fish) pesca f; (on door) pestillo m; (of window) cerradura f. □ ~ **on** vi 🔲 hacerse popular. □ ~ **up** vi poner al día. ~ **up with** alcanzar; ponerse al corriente de (news etc). ~**ing** adj contagioso. ~**phrase** n eslogan m. ~**y** adj pegadizo

categor|ical /kætɪ'gɒrɪkl/ adj categórico. ~**y** /'kætɪgərɪ/ n categoría f

cater /'keɪtə(r)/ vi encargarse del servicio de comida. ~ **for** proveer a (needs). ~**er** n proveedor m

caterpillar /'kætəpɪlə(r)/ n oruga f, azotador m (Mex)

cathedral /kə'θiːdrəl/ n catedral f

catholic /'kæθəlɪk/ adj universal. **C~** adj & n católico (m). **C~ism** /kə'θɒlɪsɪzəm/ n catolicismo m

cat: ~**nap** n sueñecito m. **C~seyes** npl (®) catafaros mpl

cattle /'kætl/ npl ganado m

catwalk /'kætwɔːk/ n pasarela f

Caucasian /kɔː'keɪʒən/ n. a male ~ (Amer) un hombre de raza blanca

caught /kɔːt/ see CATCH

cauliflower /'kɒlɪflaʊə(r)/ n coliflor f

cause /kɔːz/ n causa f, motivo m. ● vt causar

cautio|n /'kɔːʃn/ n cautela f; (warning) advertencia f. ● vt advertir; (Jurid) amonestar. ~**us** /-ʃəs/ adj cauteloso, prudente

cavalry /'kævəlrɪ/ n caballería f

cave /keɪv/ n cueva f. □ ~ **in** vi hundirse. ~**man** n troglodita m

cavern /'kævən/ n caverna f

caviare /'kævɪɑː(r)/ n caviar m

cavity /'kævətɪ/ n cavidad f; (in tooth) caries f

CCTV abbr (closed circuit television) CCTV m

CD abbr (= compact disc) CD m. ~ **player** (reproductor m de) compact-disc m. ~**-ROM** n CD-ROM m

cease /siːs/ vt/i cesar. ~**fire** n alto m el fuego

cedar /'siːdə(r)/ n cedro m

ceiling /'siːlɪŋ/ n techo m

celebrat|e /'selɪbreɪt/ vt celebrar. ● vi divertirse. ~**ed** adj célebre. ~**ion** /-'breɪʃn/ n celebración f; (party) fiesta f

celebrity /sɪ'lebrətɪ/ n celebridad f

celery /'selərɪ/ n apio m

cell /sel/ n celda f; (in plants, electricity) célula f

cellar /'selə(r)/ n sótano m; (for wine) bodega f

cello /'tʃeləʊ/ n (pl -os) violonc(h)elo m, chelo m

Cellophane /'seləfeɪn/ n (®) celofán m (®)

cellphone /'selfəʊn/ n celular m (LAm), móvil m (Esp)

cellul|ar /'seljʊlə(r)/ adj celular. ~**phone** n teléfono celular m (LAm), teléfono móvil m (Esp). ~**oid** n celuloide m

Celsius /'selsɪəs/ adj. 20 degrees ~ 20 grados centígrados or Celsio(s)

cement /sɪ'ment/ n cemento m. ● vt cementar

cemetery /'semətrɪ/ n cementerio m

cens|or /'sensə(r)/ n censor m. ● vt censurar. ~**ship** n censura f. ~**ure** /'senʃə(r)/ vt censurar

census /'sensəs/ n censo m

cent /sent/ n ($) centavo m; (€) céntimo m

centenary /sen'ti:nəri/ n centenario m

centi|grade /'sentɪɡreɪd/ adj centígrado. ~**litre** n centilitro m. ~**metre** n centímetro m. ~**pede** /-pi:d/ n ciempiés m

central /'sentrəl/ adj central; (of town) céntrico. ~ **heating** n calefacción f central. ~**ize** vt centralizar

centre /'sentə(r)/ n centro m. ●vt (pt centred) centrar. ●vi centrarse (on en)

century /'sentʃərɪ/ n siglo m

cereal /'sɪərɪəl/ n cereal m

ceremon|ial /serɪ'məʊnɪəl/ adj & n ceremonial (m). ~**y** /'serɪmənɪ/ n ceremonia f

certain /'sɜ:tn/ adj cierto. for ~ seguro. make ~ of asegurarse de. ~**ly** adv desde luego

certificate /sə'tɪfɪkət/ n certificado m; (of birth, death etc) partida f

certify /'sɜ:tɪfaɪ/ vt certificar

chafe /tʃeɪf/ vt rozar. ●vi rozarse

chaffinch /'tʃæfɪntʃ/ n pinzón m

chagrin /'ʃæɡrɪn/ n disgusto m

chain /tʃeɪn/ n cadena f. ●vt encadenar. ~ **reaction** n reacción f en cadena. ~-**smoker** n fumador m que siempre tiene un cigarrillo encendido. ~ **store** n tienda f de una cadena

chair /tʃeə(r)/ n silla f; (Univ) cátedra f. ●vt presidir. ~-**lift** n telesquí m, telesilla m (LAm). ~-**man** /-mən/ n presidente m

chalet /'ʃæleɪ/ n chalé m

chalk /tʃɔ:k/ n (in geology) creta f; (stick) tiza f, gis m (Mex)

challeng|e /'tʃælɪndʒ/ n desafío

m; (fig) reto m. ●vt desafiar; (question) poner en duda. ~**ing** adj estimulante

chamber /'tʃeɪmbə(r)/ n (old use) cámara f. ~**maid** n camarera f. ~**pot** n orinal m

champagne /ʃæm'peɪn/ n champaña m, champán m

champion /'tʃæmpɪən/ n campeón m. ●vt defender. ~**ship** n campeonato m

chance /tʃɑ:ns/ n casualidad f; (likelihood) posibilidad f; (opportunity) oportunidad f; (risk) riesgo m. by ~ por casualidad. ●adj fortuito

chancellor /'tʃɑ:nsələ(r)/ n canciller m; (Univ) rector m. **C~ of the Exchequer** Ministro m de Hacienda

chandelier /ʃændə'lɪə(r)/ n araña f (de luces)

chang|e /tʃeɪndʒ/ vt cambiar; (substitute) reemplazar. ~ one's mind cambiar de idea. ●vi cambiarse. ●n cambio m; (coins) cambio m, sencillo m (LAm), feria f (Mex); (money returned) cambio m, vuelta f, vuelto m (LAm). ~**eable** adj cambiable; (weather) variable. ~ **room** n (Sport) vestuario m, vestidor m (Mex); (in shop) probador m

channel /'tʃænl/ n canal m; (fig) medio m. ●vt (pt channelled) acanalar; (fig) encauzar. **the (English) C~** el Canal de la Mancha. **the C~ Islands** las islas Anglonormandas. **C~ Tunnel** n. the C~ **Tunnel** el Eurotúnel

chant /tʃɑ:nt/ n canto m. ●vt/i cantar

chao|s /'keɪɒs/ n caos m. ~**tic** /-'ɒtɪk/ adj caótico

chap /tʃæp/ n [1] tipo m, tío m [1]. ●vt (pt chapped) agrietar. ●vi agrietarse

chapel /'tʃæpl/ n capilla f

chaperon /'ʃæpərəʊn/ n acompañante f

chapter /'tʃæptə(r)/ n capítulo m

char /tʃɑː(r)/ vt (pt charred) carbonizar

character /'kærəktə(r)/ n carácter m; (in book, play) personaje m. **in ~** característico. **~istic** /-'rɪstɪk/ adj típico. ● n característica f. **~ize** vt caracterizar

charade /ʃə'rɑːd/ n farsa f. **~s** npl (game) charada f

charcoal /'tʃɑːkəʊl/ n carbón m vegetal; (for drawing) carboncillo m

charge /tʃɑːdʒ/ n precio m; (Elec, Mil) carga f; (Jurid) acusación f; (task, custody) encargo m; (responsibility) responsabilidad f. **in ~ of** responsable de, encargado de. **the person in ~** la persona responsable. **take ~ of** encargarse de. ● vt pedir; (Elec, Mil) cargar; (Jurid) acusar. ● vi cargar; (animal) embestir (at contra)

charit|able /'tʃærɪtəbl/ adj caritativo. **~y** /'tʃærɪtɪ/ n caridad f; (society) institución f benéfica

charm /tʃɑːm/ n encanto m; (spell) hechizo m; (on bracelet) dije m, amuleto m. ● vt encantar. **~ing** adj encantador

chart /tʃɑːt/ n (for navigation) carta f de navegación; (table) tabla f

charter /'tʃɑːtə(r)/ n carta f. ● vt alquilar (bus, train); fletar (plane, ship). **~ flight** n vuelo m chárter

chase /tʃeɪs/ vt perseguir. ● vi correr (after tras). ● n persecución f. □ **~ away**, □ **~ off** vt ahuyentar

chassis /'ʃæsɪ/ n chasis m

chastise /tʃæs'taɪz/ vt castigar

chastity /'tʃæstɪtɪ/ n castidad f

chat /tʃæt/ n charla f, conversación f (LAm), plática f (Mex). ● vi (pt chatted) charlar, conversar (LAm), platicar (Mex)

chatter /'tʃætə(r)/ n charla f. ● vi charlar. **his teeth are ~ing** le castañetean los dientes. **~box** n parlanchín m

chauffeur /'ʃəʊfə(r)/ n chófer m

chauvinis|m /'ʃəʊvɪnɪzəm/ n patriotería f; (male) machismo m. **~t** n patriotero m; (male) machista m

cheap /tʃiːp/ adj (-er, -est) barato; (poor quality) de baja calidad; (rate) económico. **~(ly)** adv barato, a bajo precio

cheat /tʃiːt/ vt defraudar; (deceive) engañar. ● vi (at cards) hacer trampas. ● n trampa f; (person) tramposo m

check /tʃek/ vt comprobar; (examine) inspeccionar; (curb) frenar. ● vi comprobar. ● n comprobación f; (of tickets) control m; (curb) freno m; (Chess) jaque m; (pattern) cuadro m; (Amer, bill) cuenta f; (Amer, cheque) cheque m. □ **~ in** vi registrarse; (at airport) facturar el equipaje, chequear el equipaje (LAm), registrar el equipaje (Mex). □ **~ out** vi pagar la cuenta y marcharse. □ **~ up** vi confirmar. □ **~ up on** vt investigar. **~book** n (Amer) see CHEQUEBOOK. **~ered** /'tʃekəd/ adj (Amer) see CHEQUERED

checkers /'tʃekəz/ n (Amer) damas fpl

check: **~mate** n jaque m mate. ● vt dar mate a. **~out** n caja f. **~point** control m. **~up** n chequeo m, revisión f

cheek /tʃiːk/ n mejilla f; (fig) descaro m. **~bone** n pómulo m. **~y** adj descarado

cheep /tʃiːp/ vi piar

cheer /tʃɪə(r)/ n alegría f; (*applause*) viva m. ~s! ¡salud!.• vt alegrar; (*applaud*) aplaudir. • vi alegrarse; (*applaud*) aplaudir. ~ up! ¡anímate! ~ful adj alegre

cheerio /tʃɪərɪˈəʊ/ int 🔊 ¡adiós!, ¡hasta luego!

cheerless /ˈtʃɪəlɪs/ adj triste

cheese /tʃiːz/ n queso m

cheetah /ˈtʃiːtə/ n guepardo m

chef /ʃef/ n jefe m de cocina

chemical /ˈkemɪkl/ adj químico. • n producto m químico

chemist /ˈkemɪst/ n farmacéutico m; (*scientist*) químico m. ~ry n química f. ~'s (shop) n farmacia f

cheque /tʃek/ n cheque m, talón m. ~book n chequera f, talonario m

cherish /ˈtʃerɪʃ/ vt cuidar; (*love*) querer; abrigar (hope)

cherry /ˈtʃerɪ/ n cereza f. ~ tree n cerezo m

chess /tʃes/ n ajedrez m. ~board n tablero m de ajedrez

chest /tʃest/ n pecho m; (box) cofre m, cajón m

chestnut /ˈtʃesnʌt/ n castaña f. • adj castaño. ~ tree n castaño m

chest of drawers n cómoda f

chew /tʃuː/ vt masticar. ~ing gum n chicle m

chic /ʃiːk/ adj elegante

chick /tʃɪk/ n polluelo m. ~en /ˈtʃɪkɪn/ n pollo m. • adj 🔊 cobarde. □ ~en out vi 🔊 acobardarse. ~enpox n /ˈtʃɪkɪmpɒks/ n varicela f. ~pea n garbanzo m

chicory /ˈtʃɪkərɪ/ n (in coffee) achicoria f; (in salad) escarola f

chief /tʃiːf/ n jefe m. • adj principal. ~ly adv principalmente

chilblain /ˈtʃɪlbleɪn/ n sabañón m

child /tʃaɪld/ n (pl children /ˈtʃɪldrən/) niño m; (offspring) hijo m. ~birth n parto m. ~hood n niñez f. ~ish adj infantil. ~less adj sin hijos. ~like adj ingenuo, de niño

Chile /ˈtʃɪlɪ/ n Chile m. ~an adj & n chileno (m)

chill /tʃɪl/ n frío m; (illness) resfriado m. • adj frío. • vt enfriar; refrigerar (food)

chilli /ˈtʃɪlɪ/ n (pl -ies) chile m

chilly /ˈtʃɪlɪ/ adj frío

chime /tʃaɪm/ n carillón m. • vt tocar (bells); dar (hours). • vi repicar

chimney /ˈtʃɪmnɪ/ n (pl -eys) chimenea f. ~ sweep n deshollinador m

chimpanzee /tʃɪmpænˈziː/ n chimpancé m

chin /tʃɪn/ n barbilla f

china /ˈtʃaɪnə/ n porcelana f

China /ˈtʃaɪnə/ n China f. ~ese /-ˈniːz/ adj & n chino (m)

chink /tʃɪŋk/ n (crack) grieta f; (sound) tintín m. • vi tintinear

chip /tʃɪp/ n pedacito m; (splinter) astilla f; (Culin) patata f frita, papa f frita (LAm); (in gambling) ficha f; (Comp) chip m. have a ~ on one's shoulder guardar rencor. • vt (pt chipped) desportillar. □ ~ in vi 🔊 interrumpir; (with money) contribuir

chiropodist /kɪˈrɒpədɪst/ n callista m & f, pedicuro m

chirp /tʃɜːp/ n pío m. • vi piar. ~y adj alegre

chisel /ˈtʃɪzl/ n formón m. • vt (pt chiselled) cincelar

chivalr|ous /ˈʃɪvəlrəs/ adj caballeroso. ~y /-rɪ/ n caballerosidad f

chlorine /ˈklɔːriːn/ n cloro m

chock /tʃɒk/ n cuña f. ~-**a-block** adj, ~-**full** adj atestado

chocolate /'tʃɒklət/ n chocolate m; (*individual sweet*) bombón m, chocolate m (*LAm*)

choice /tʃɔɪs/ n elección f; (*preference*) preferencia f. ● adj escogido

choir /'kwaɪə(r)/ n coro m

choke /tʃəʊk/ vt sofocar. ● vi sofocarse. ● n (*Auto*) choke m, estárter m, ahogador m (*Mex*)

cholera /'kɒlərə/ n cólera m

cholesterol /kə'lestərɒl/ n colesterol m

choose /tʃuːz/ vt/i (*pt* chose, *pp* chosen) elegir, escoger. ~y adj �† exigente

chop /tʃɒp/ vt (*pt* chopped) cortar. ● n (*Culin*) chuleta f. □ ~ **down** vt talar. □ ~ **off** vt cortar. ~**per** n hacha f; (*butcher's*) cuchilla f. ~**py** adj picado

chord /kɔːd/ n (*Mus*) acorde m

chore /tʃɔː(r)/ n tarea f, faena f. **household** ~**s** npl quehaceres mpl domésticos

chorus /'kɔːrəs/ n coro m; (*of song*) estribillo m

chose/tʃəʊz/, **chosen** /'tʃəʊzn/ *see* CHOOSE

Christ /kraɪst/ n Cristo m

christen /'krɪsn/ vt bautizar. ~**ing** n bautizo m

Christian /'krɪstjən/ adj & n cristiano (m). ~**ity** /krɪstɪ'ænətɪ/ n cristianismo m. ~ **name** n nombre m de pila

Christmas /'krɪsməs/ n Navidad f. Merry ~! ¡Feliz Navidad!, ¡Felices Pascuas! Father ~ Papá m Noel. ● adj de Navidad, navideño. ~ **card** n tarjeta f de Navidad f. ~ **day** n día m de Navidad. ~ **Eve** n Nochebuena f. ~ **tree** n árbol m de

Navidad

chrome /krəʊm/ n cromo m.

~ium /'krəʊmɪəm/ n cromo m

chromosome /'krəʊməsəʊm/ n cromosoma m

chronic /'krɒnɪk/ adj crónico; (*fam, bad*) terrible

chronicle /'krɒnɪkl/ n crónica f. ● vt historiar

chronological /krɒnə'lɒdʒɪkl/ adj cronológico

chubby /'tʃʌbɪ/ adj (-ier, -iest) regordete; (*person*) gordinflón ⚐

chuck /tʃʌk/ vt ⚐ tirar. □ ~ **out** vt tirar

chuckle /'tʃʌkl/ n risa f ahogada. ● vi reírse entre dientes

chug /tʃʌg/ vi (*pt* chugged) (*of motor*) traquetear

chum /tʃʌm/ n amigo m, compinche m, cuate m (*Mex*)

chunk /tʃʌŋk/ n trozo m grueso. ~y adj macizo

church /tʃɜːtʃ/ n iglesia f. ~**yard** n cementerio m

churn /tʃɜːn/ n (*for milk*) lechera f, cántara f; (*for making butter*) mantequera f. ● vt agitar. □ ~ **out** vt producir en profusión

chute /ʃuːt/ n tobogán m

cider /'saɪdə(r)/ n sidra f

cigar /sɪ'gɑː(r)/ n puro m

cigarette /sɪgə'ret/ n cigarrillo m. ~ **end** n colilla f. ~ **holder** n boquilla f. ~ **lighter** n mechero m, encendedor m

cinecamera /'sɪnɪkæmərə/ n tomavistas m, filmadora f (*LAm*)

cinema /'sɪnəmə/ n cine m

cipher /'saɪfə(r)/ n (*Math, fig*) cero m; (*code*) clave f

circle /'sɜːkl/ n círculo m; (*in theatre*) anfiteatro m. ● vt girar alrededor de. ● vi dar vueltas

circuit /'sɜːkɪt/ n circuito m

circular /'sɜːkjʊlə(r)/ adj & n circular (f)

circulat|e /'sɜːkjʊleɪt/ vt hacer circular. ● vi circular. ~ion /-'leɪʃn/ n circulación f; (number of copies) tirada f

circumcise /'sɜːkəmsaɪz/ vt circuncidar

circumference /sə'kʌmfərəns/ n circunferencia f

circumstance /'sɜːkəmstəns/ n circunstancia f. ~s (means) npl situación f económica

circus /'sɜːkəs/ n circo m

cistern /'sɪstən/ n cisterna f

cite /saɪt/ vt citar

citizen /'sɪtɪzn/ n ciudadano m; (inhabitant) habitante m & f

citrus /'sɪtrəs/ n. ~ fruits cítricos mpl

city /'sɪtɪ/ n ciudad f; the C~ el centro m financiero de Londres

---

> ### City - the
> *i*
> Área ubicada dentro de los límites de la antigua ciudad de Londres. Actualmente es el centro financiero de la capital donde tienen sus sedes centrales muchas instituciones financieras. A menudo, cuando se habla de *The City*, se está refiriendo a ésas y no a la zona propiamente dicha.

---

civic /'sɪvɪk/ adj cívico

civil /'sɪvl/ adj civil; (polite) cortés

civilian /sɪ'vɪlɪən/ adj & n civil (m & f)

civiliz|ation /sɪvɪlaɪ'zeɪʃn/ n civilización f. ~ed /'sɪvɪlaɪzd/ adj civilizado.

civil: ~ **partnership** n matrimonio m de homosexuales. ~

servant n funcionario m (del Estado), burócrata m f (Mex). ~ **service** n administración f pública. ~ **war** n guerra f civil

clad /klæd/ see **CLOTHE**

claim /kleɪm/ vt reclamar; (assert) pretender. ● n reclamación f; (right) derecho m; (Jurid) demanda f

clairvoyant /kleə'vɔɪənt/ n clarividente m & f

clam /klæm/ n almeja f. ● vi (pt clammed). ~ **up** ① ponerse muy poco comunicativo

clamber /'klæmbə(r)/ vi trepar a gatas

clammy /'klæmɪ/ adj (-ier, -iest) húmedo

clamour /'klæmə(r)/ n clamor m. ● vi. ~ **for** pedir a gritos

clamp /klæmp/ n abrazadera f; (Auto) cepo m. ● vt sujetar con abrazadera; poner cepo a (car). □ ~ **down on** vt reprimir

clan /klæn/ n clan m

clang /klæŋ/ n sonido m metálico

clap /klæp/ vt (pt clapped) aplaudir; batir (hands). ● n aplauso m; palmada f; (of thunder) trueno m

clarif|ication /klærɪfɪ'keɪʃn/ n aclaración f. ~**y** /'klærɪfaɪ/ vt aclarar. ● vi aclararse

clarinet /klærɪ'net/ n clarinete m

clarity /'klærətɪ/ n claridad f

clash /klæʃ/ n choque m; (noise) estruendo m; (contrast) contraste m; (fig) conflicto m. ● vt golpear. ● vi encontrarse; (colours) desentonar

clasp /klɑːsp/ n cierre m. ● vt agarrar; apretar (hand)

class /klɑːs/ n clase f. **evening** ~ n clase nocturna. ● vt clasificar

classic /'klæsɪk/ adj & n clásico (m). ~**al** adj clásico. ~**s** npl estudios mpl clásicos

classif|ication /klæsɪfɪˈkeɪʃn/ n clasificación f. **~y** /ˈklæsɪfaɪ/ vt clasificar

class: **~room** n aula f, clase f. **~y** adj 🄵 elegante

clatter /ˈklætə(r)/ n ruido m; (of train) traqueteo m. ●vi hacer ruido

clause /klɔːz/ n cláusula f; (Gram) oración f

claustrophobia /ˌklɔːstrə ˈfəʊbɪə/ n claustrofobia f

claw /klɔː/ n garra f; (of cat) uña f; (of crab) pinza f. ●vt arañar

clay /kleɪ/ n arcilla f

clean /kliːn/ adj (-er, -est) limpio; (stroke) bien definido. ●adv completamente. ●vt limpiar. ●vi limpiar. □ **~ up** vt hacer la limpieza. **~er** n persona f que hace la limpieza. **~liness** /ˈklenlɪnɪs/ n limpieza f

cleans|e /klenz/ vt limpiar. **~er** n producto m de limpieza; (for skin) crema f de limpieza. **~ing cream** n crema f de limpieza

clear /klɪə(r)/ adj (-er, -est) claro; (transparent) transparente; (without obstacles) libre; (profit) neto; (sky) despejado. **keep ~ of** evitar. ●adv claramente. ●vt despejar; liquidar (goods); (Jurid) absolver; (jump over) saltar por encima de; quitar, levantar (LAm) (table). □ **~ off** vi 🄴, **~ out** vi (🄵, go away) largarse. □ **~ up** vt (tidy) ordenar; aclarar (mystery). vi (weather) despejarse. **~ance** n (removal of obstructions) despeje m; (authorization) permiso m; (by security) acreditación f. **~ing** n claro m. **~ly** adv evidentemente. **~way** n carretera f en la que no se permite parar

cleavage /ˈkliːvɪdʒ/ n escote m

clef /klef/ n (Mus) clave f

clench /klentʃ/ vt apretar

clergy /ˈklɜːdʒɪ/ n clero m. **~man** /-mən/ n clérigo m

cleric /ˈklerɪk/ n clérigo m. **~al** adj clerical; (of clerks) de oficina

clerk /klɑːk/ n empleado m; (Amer, salesclerk) vendedor m

clever /ˈklevə(r)/ adj (-er, -est) inteligente; (skilful) hábil. **~ly** adv inteligentemente; (with skill) hábilmente. **~ness** n inteligencia f

cliché /ˈkliːʃeɪ/ n lugar m común m, cliché m

click /klɪk/ n golpecito m. ●vi chascar; 🄵 llevarse bien. **~ on sth** hacer clic en algo. ●vt chasquear

client /ˈklaɪənt/ n cliente m

cliff /klɪf/ n acantilado m

climat|e /ˈklaɪmət/ n clima m. **~e change** n cambio m climático. **~ic** /-ˈmætɪk/ adj climático

climax /ˈklaɪmæks/ n clímax m; (orgasm) orgasmo m

climb /klaɪm/ vt subir (stairs); trepar (tree); escalar (mountain). ●vi subir. ●n subida f. □ **~ down** vi bajar; (fig) ceder. **~er** n (Sport) alpinista m & f, andinista m & f (LAm); (plant) trepadora f

clinch /klɪntʃ/ vt cerrar (deal)

cling /klɪŋ/ vi (pt clung) agarrarse; (stick) pegarse

clinic /ˈklɪnɪk/ n centro m médico; (private hospital) clínica f. **~al** adj clínico

clink /klɪŋk/ n tintineo m. ●vt hacer tintinear. ●vi tintinear

clip /klɪp/ n (fastener) clip m; (for paper) sujetapapeles m; (for hair) horquilla f. ●vt (pt clipped) (cut) cortar; (join) sujetar. **~pers** /ˈklɪpəz/ npl (for hair) maquinilla f para cortar el pelo; (for nails) cortauñas *m*. ~**ping** *n* recorte *m*

cloak /kləʊk/ *n* capa *f*. ~**room** *n* guardarropa *m*; (*toilet*) lavabo *m*, baño *m* (*LAm*)

clock /klɒk/ *n* reloj *m*. ~**wise** *a/adv* en el sentido de las agujas del reloj. ~**work** *n* mecanismo *m* de relojería. like ~**work** con precisión

clog /klɒg/ *n* zueco *m*. ● *vt* (*pt* clogged) atascar

cloister /'klɔɪstə(r)/ *n* claustro *m*

clone /kləʊn/ *n* clon *m*

close[1] /kləʊs/ *adj* (-er, -est) cercano; (*together*) apretado; (*friend*) íntimo; (*weather*) bochornoso; (*link etc*) estrecho; (*game, battle*) reñido. have a ~ **shave** (*fig*) escaparse de milagro. ● *adv* cerca

close[2] /kləʊz/ *vt* cerrar. ● *vi* cerrarse; (*end*) terminar. ~ **down** *vt/i* cerrar. ● *n* fin *m*. ~**d** *adj* cerrado

closely /'kləʊslɪ/ *adv* estrechamente; (*at a short distance*) de cerca; (*with attention*) detenidamente; (*precisely*) rigurosamente

closet /'klɒzɪt/ *n* (*Amer*) armario *m*; (*for clothes*) armario *m*, closet *m* (*LAm*)

close-up /'kləʊsʌp/ *n* (*Cinema etc*) primer plano *m*

closure /'kləʊʒə(r)/ *n* cierre *m*

clot /klɒt/ *n* (*Med*) coágulo *m*; 🄸 tonto *m*. ● *vi* (*pt* clotted) cuajarse; (*blood*) coagularse

cloth /klɒθ/ *n* tela *f*; (*duster*) trapo *m*; (*tablecloth*) mantel *m*

cloth|e /kləʊð/ *vt* (*pt* clothed or clad) vestir. ~**es** /kləʊðz/ *npl* ropa. ~**espin**, ~**espeg** (*Amer*) *n* pinza *f* (para tender la ropa). ~**ing** *n* ropa *f*

cloud /klaʊd/ *n* nube *f*. ● ~ **over** *vi* nublarse. ~**y** *adj* (-ier, -iest) nu-

blado; (*liquid*) turbio

clout /klaʊt/ *n* bofetada *f*. ● *vt* abofetear

clove /kləʊv/ *n* clavo *m*. ~ **of garlic** *n* diente *m* de ajo

clover /'kləʊvə(r)/ *n* trébol *m*

clown /klaʊn/ *n* payaso *m*. ● *vi* hacer el payaso

club /klʌb/ *n* club *m*; (*weapon*) porra *f*; (*golf club*) palo *m* de golf; (*at cards*) trébol *m*. ● *vt* (*pt* clubbed) aporrear. □ ~ **together** *vi* contribuir con dinero (to para)

cluck /klʌk/ *vi* cloquear

clue /kluː/ *n* pista *f*; (*in crosswords*) indicación *f*. not to have a ~ no tener la menor idea

clump /klʌmp/ *n* grupo *m*. ● *vt* agrupar

clums|iness /'klʌmzɪnɪs/ *n* torpeza *f*. ~**y** /'klʌmzɪ/ *adj* (-ier, -iest) torpe

clung /klʌŋ/ *see* CLING

cluster /'klʌstə(r)/ *n* grupo *m*. ● *vi* agruparse

clutch /klʌtʃ/ *vt* agarrar. ● *n* (*Auto*) embrague *m*

clutter /'klʌtə(r)/ *n* desorden *m*. ● *vt*. ~ (**up**) amontonar. ~**ed** /'klʌtəd/ *adj* abarrotado de cosas

coach /kəʊtʃ/ *n* autocar *m*, autobús *m*; (*of train*) vagón *m*; (*horse-drawn*) coche *m*; (*Sport*) entrenador *m*. ● *vt* (*Sport*) entrenar

coal /kəʊl/ *n* carbón *m*

coalition /kəʊə'lɪʃn/ *n* coalición *f*

coarse /kɔːs/ *adj* (-er, -est) grueso; (*material*) basto; (*person, language*) ordinario

coast /kəʊst/ *n* costa *f*. ● *vi* (*with cycle*) deslizarse sin pedalear; (*with car*) ir en punto muerto. ~**al** *adj* costero. ~**guard** *n* guardacostas *m*. ~**line** *n* litoral *m*

coat /kəʊt/ n abrigo m; (jacket) chaqueta f; (of animal) pelo m; (of paint) mano f. ● vt cubrir, revestir. **~hanger** n percha f, gancho m (LAm). **~ing** n capa f. **~ of arms** n escudo m de armas

coax /kəʊks/ vt engatusar

cobbler /'kɒblə(r)/ n zapatero m (remendón)

cobblestone /'kɒbəlstəʊn/ n adoquín m

cobweb /'kɒbweb/ n telaraña f

cocaine /kə'keɪn/ n cocaína f

cock /kɒk/ n (cockerel) gallo m; (male bird) macho m. ● vt amartillar (gun); aguzar (ears). **~erel** /'kɒkərəl/ n gallo m. **~eyed** /-aɪd/ adj 🄸 torcido

cockney /'kɒknɪ/ adj & n (pl -eys) londinense (m & f) (del este de Londres)

cockpit /'kɒkpɪt/ n (in aircraft) cabina f del piloto

cockroach /'kɒkrəʊtʃ/ n cucaracha f

cocktail /'kɒkteɪl/ n cóctel m

cock-up /'kɒkʌp/ n 🄻 lío m

cocky /'kɒkɪ/ adj (-ier, -iest) engreído

cocoa /'kəʊkəʊ/ n cacao m; (drink) chocolate m, cocoa f (LAm)

coconut /'kəʊkənʌt/ n coco m

cocoon /kə'ku:n/ n capullo m

cod /kɒd/ n invar bacalao m

code /kəʊd/ n código m; (secret) clave f; **in ~** en clave

coeducational /kəʊedʒʊ'keɪʃənl/ adj mixto

coerc|e /kəʊ'ɜːs/ vt coaccionar. **~ion** /-ʃn/ n coacción f

coffee /'kɒfɪ/ n café m. **~ bean** n grano m de café. **~ maker** n cafetera f. **~pot** n cafetera f

coffin /'kɒfɪn/ n ataúd m, cajón m (LAm)

cog /kɒg/ n diente m; (fig) pieza f

coherent /kəʊ'hɪərənt/ adj coherente

coil /kɔɪl/ vt enrollar. ● n rollo m; (one ring) vuelta f

coin /kɔɪn/ n moneda f. ● vt acuñar

coincide /kəʊɪn'saɪd/ vi coincidir. **~nce** /kəʊ'ɪnsɪdəns/ n casualidad f. **~ntal** /kəʊɪnsɪ'dentl/ adj casual

coke /kəʊk/ n (coal) coque m. **C~** (®) Coca-Cola f (®)

colander /'kʌləndə(r)/ n colador m

cold /kəʊld/ adj (-er, -est) frío m. be **~** (person) tener frío. **it is ~** (weather) hace frío. ● n frío m; (Med) resfriado m. **have a ~** estar resfriado. **~-blooded** /-'blʌdɪd/ adj (animal) de sangre fría; (murder) a sangre fría. **~-shoulder** /-'ʃəʊldə(r)/ vt tratar con frialdad. **~ sore** n herpes m labial. **~ storage** n conservación f en frigorífico

coleslaw /'kəʊlslɔ:/ n ensalada f de col

collaborat|e /kə'læbəreɪt/ vi colaborar. **~ion** /-'reɪʃn/ n colaboración f. **~or** n colaborador m

collaps|e /kə'læps/ vi derrumbarse; (Med) sufrir un colapso. ● n derrumbamiento m; (Med) colapso m. **~ible** /-əbl/ adj plegable

collar /'kɒlə(r)/ n cuello m; (for animals) collar m. ● vt 🄸 hurtar. **~bone** n clavícula f

colleague /'kɒli:g/ n colega m & f

collect /kə'lekt/ vt reunir; (hobby) coleccionar, juntar (LAm); (pick up) recoger; cobrar (rent). ● vi (people) reunirse; (things) acumularse. **~ion** /-ʃn/ n colección f; (in church) colecta f; (of post) recogida

f. ~**or** n coleccionista m & f

college /'kɒlɪdʒ/ n colegio m; (of
art, music etc) escuela f; (Amer) uni-
versidad f

colli|de /kə'laɪd/ vi chocar. ~**sion**
/-'lɪʒn/ n choque m

colloquial /kə'ləʊkwɪəl/ adj colo-
quial

Colombia /kə'lʌmbɪə/ n Colom-
bia f. ~**n** adj & n colombiano (m)

colon /'kəʊlən/ n (Gram) dos pun-
tos mpl; (Med) colon m

colonel /'kɜːnl/ n coronel m

colon|ial /kə'ləʊnɪəl/ adj colonial.
~**ize** /'kɒlənaɪz/ vt colonizar. ~**y**
/'kɒlənɪ/ n colonia f

colossal /kə'lɒsl/ adj colosal

colour /'kʌlə(r)/ n color m. **off** ~
(fig) indispuesto. ●adj de color(es),
en color(es) ●vt colorear; (dye)
teñir. ~**-blind** adj daltónico. ~**ed**
/'kʌləd/ adj de color. ~**ful** adj lleno
de color; (fig) pintoresco. ~**ing** n
color; (food colouring) colorante m.
~**less** adj incoloro

column /'kɒləm/ n columna f.
~**ist** n columnista m & f

coma /'kəʊmə/ n coma m

comb /kəʊm/ n peine m. ●vt
(search) registrar. ~ **one's hair**
peinarse

combat /'kɒmbæt/ n combate m.
●vt (pt combated) combatir

combination /kɒmbɪ'neɪʃn/ n
combinación f

combine /kəm'baɪn/ vt combinar.
●vi combinarse. ●/'kɒmbaɪn/ n
asociación f. ~ **harvester** n cose-
chadora f

combustion /kəm'bʌstʃən/ n
combustión f

come /kʌm/ vi (pt came, pp come)
venir; (occur) pasar. □ ~ **across** vt
encontrarse con (person); encon-

trar (object). □ ~ **apart** vi desha-
cerse. □ ~ **away** vi (leave) salir;
(become detached) salirse. □ ~
back vi volver. □ ~ **by** vt obtener.
□ ~ **down** vi bajar. □ ~ **in** vi en-
trar; (arrive) llegar. □ ~ **into** vt en-
trar en; heredar (money). □ ~ **off**
vi desprenderse; (succeed) tener
éxito. vt. ~ **off it!** 🗈 ¡no me ven-
gas con eso! □ ~ **on** vi (start to
work) encenderse. ~ **on, hurry**
up! ¡vamos, date prisa! □ ~ **out** vi
salir. □ ~ **round** vi (after fainting)
volver en sí; (be converted) cambiar
de idea; (visit) venir. □ ~ **to** vt lle-
gar a (decision etc). □ ~ **up** vi
subir; (fig) surgir. □ ~ **up with** vt
proponer (idea). ~**back** n retorno
m; (retort) réplica f

comedian /kə'miːdɪən/ n có-
mico m

comedy /'kɒmədɪ/ n comedia f

comet /'kɒmɪt/ n cometa m

comfort /'kʌmfət/ n comodidad f;
(consolation) consuelo m. ●vt con-
solar. ~**able** adj cómodo. ~**er** n
(for baby) chupete m, chupón m
(LAm); (Amer, for bed) edredón m

comic /'kɒmɪk/ adj cómico. ●n có-
mico m; (periodical) revista f de
historietas, tebeo m. ~**al** adj có-
mico. ~ **strip** n tira f cómica

coming /'kʌmɪŋ/ n llegada f. ~**s**
and goings idas fpl y venidas. ●adj
próximo; (week, month etc) que
viene

comma /'kɒmə/ n coma f

command /kə'mɑːnd/ n orden f;
(mastery) dominio m. ●vt ordenar;
imponer (respect)

commandeer /kɒmən'dɪə(r)/ vt
requisar

command: ~**er** n comandante
m. ~**ing** adj imponente. ~**ment**
n mandamiento m

commando /kəˈmɑːndəʊ/ n (pl -os) comando m

commemorat|e /kəˈmeməreɪt/ vt conmemorar. ~ion /-ˈreɪʃn/ n conmemoración f. ~ive /-ətɪv/ adj conmemorativo

commence /kəˈmens/ vt dar comienzo a. ●vi iniciarse

commend /kəˈmend/ vt alabar. ~able adj loable. ~ation /kɒmenˈdeɪʃn/ n elogio m

comment /ˈkɒment/ n observación f. ●vi hacer observaciones (on sobre)

commentary /ˈkɒməntrɪ/ n comentario m; (Radio, TV) reportaje m

commentat|e /ˈkɒmənteɪt/ vi narrar. ~or n (Radio, TV) locutor m

commerc|e /ˈkɒmɜːs/ n comercio m. ~ial /kəˈmɜːʃl/ adj comercial. ●n anuncio m; aviso m (LAm). ~ialize vt comercializar

commiserat|e /kəˈmɪzəreɪt/ vi compadecerse (with de). ~ion /-ˈreɪʃn/ n conmiseración f

commission /kəˈmɪʃn/ n comisión f. out of ~ fuera de servicio. ●vt encargar; (Mil) nombrar oficial

commissionaire /kəmɪʃəˈneə(r)/ n portero m

commit /kəˈmɪt/ vt (pt committed) cometer; (entrust) confiar. ~ o.s. comprometerse. ~ment n compromiso m

committee /kəˈmɪtɪ/ n comité m

commodity /kəˈmɒdətɪ/ n producto m, artículo m

common /ˈkɒmən/ adj (-er, -est) común; (usual) corriente; (vulgar) ordinario. ●n. in ~ en común. ~er n plebeyo m. ~ law n derecho m consuetudinario. ~ly adv comúnmente. C~ Market n Mercado m Común. ~place adj banal.

●n banalidad f. ~ room n sala f común, salón m común. C~s n. the (House of) C~s la Cámara de los Comunes. ~sense n sentido m común. C~wealth n. the C~wealth la Mancomunidad f Británica

commotion /kəˈməʊʃn/ n confusión f

> **Commonwealth** La Commonwealth es una asociación de las antiguas colonias y territorios que conformaban el Imperio Británico. Cada dos años se celebra una reunión de sus jefes de gobierno. Entre los países miembros existen muchos vínculos culturales, educativos y deportivos. En EE.UU., es el término oficial para referirse a cuatro estados: Kentucky, Massachussets, Pensilvania y Virginia.

commune /ˈkɒmjuːn/ n comuna f

communicat|e /kəˈmjuːnɪkeɪt/ vt comunicar. ●vi comunicarse. ~ion /-ˈkeɪʃn/ n comunicación f. ~ive /-ɪv/ adj comunicativo

communion /kəˈmjuːnɪən/ n comunión f

communis|m /ˈkɒmjʊnɪsəm/ n comunismo m. ~t n comunista m & f

community /kəˈmjuːnətɪ/ n comunidad f. ~ centre n centro m social

commute /kəˈmjuːt/ vi viajar diariamente (entre el lugar de residencia y el trabajo). ●vt (Jurid) conmutar. ~r n viajero m diario

compact /kəmˈpækt/ adj compacto. ●/ˈkɒmpækt/ n (for powder) polvera f. ~ disc, ~ disk /ˈkɒmpækt/ n disco m compacto, compact-disc *m*. **~ disc player** *n* (reproductor *m* de) compact-disc

companion /kəm'pænɪən/ *n* compañero *m*. **~ship** *n* compañía *f*

company /'kʌmpənɪ/ *n* compañía *f*; (*guests*) visita *f*; (*Com*) sociedad *f*

compar|able /'kɒmpərəbl/ *adj* comparable. **~ative** /kəm'pærətɪv/ *adj* comparativo; (*fig*) relativo. ● *n* (*Gram*) comparativo *m*. **~e** /kəm'peə(r)/ *vt* comparar. **~ison** /kəm'pærɪsn/ *n* comparación *f*

compartment /kəm'pɑːtmənt/ *n* compartim(i)ento *m*

compass /'kʌmpəs/ *n* brújula *f*. **~es** *npl* compás *m*

compassion /kəm'pæʃn/ *n* compasión *f*. **~ate** /-ət/ *adj* compasivo

compatible /kəm'pætəbl/ *adj* compatible

compel /kəm'pel/ *vt* (*pt* compelled) obligar. **~ling** *adj* irresistible

compensat|e /'kɒmpənseɪt/ *vt* compensar; (*for loss*) indemnizar. ● *vi*. **~e for sth** compensar algo. **~ion** /-'seɪʃn/ *n* compensación *f*; (*financial*) indemnización *f*

compère /'kɒmpeə(r)/ *n* presentador *m*. ● *vt* presentar

compete /kəm'piːt/ *vi* competir

competen|ce /'kɒmpətəns/ *n* competencia *f*. **~t** *adj* competente

competit|ion /kɒmpə'tɪʃn/ *n* (*contest*) concurso *m*; (*Sport*) competición *f*, competencia *f* (*LAm*); (*Com*) competencia *f*. **~ive** /kəm'petɪtɪv/ *adj* competidor; (*price*) competitivo. **~or** /kəm'petɪtə(r)/ *n* competidor *m*; (*in contest*) concursante *m* & *f*

compile /kəm'paɪl/ *vt* compilar

complacen|cy /kəm'pleɪsənsɪ/ *n* autosuficiencia *f*. **~t** *adj* satisfecho de sí mismo

complain /kəm'pleɪn/ *vi*. **~ (about)** quejarse (de). ● *vt*. **~ that** quejarse de que. **~t** *n* queja *f*; (*Med*) enfermedad *f*

complement /'kɒmplɪmənt/ *n* complemento *m*. ● *vt* complementar. **~ary** /-'mentrɪ/ *adj* complementario

complet|e /kəm'pliːt/ *adj* completo; (*finished*) acabado; (*downright*) total. ● *vt* acabar; llenar (a form). **~ely** *adv* completamente. **~ion** /-ʃn/ *n* finalización *f*

complex /'kɒmpleks/ *adj* complejo. ● *n* complejo *m*

complexion /kəm'plekʃn/ *n* tez *f*; (*fig*) aspecto *m*

complexity /kəm'pleksətɪ/ *n* complejidad *f*

complicat|e /'kɒmplɪkeɪt/ *vt* complicar. **~ed** *adj* complicado. **~ion** /-'keɪʃn/ *n* complicación *f*

compliment /'kɒmplɪmənt/ *n* cumplido *m*; (*amorous*) piropo *m*. ● *vt* felicitar. **~ary** /-'mentrɪ/ *adj* halagador; (*given free*) de regalo. **~s** *npl* saludos *mpl*

comply /kəm'plaɪ/ *vi*. **~ with** conformarse con

component /kəm'pəʊnənt/ *adj* & *n* componente (*m*)

compos|e /kəm'pəʊz/ *vt* componer. **be ~ed of** estar compuesto de. **~er** *n* compositor *m*. **~ition** /kɒmpə'zɪʃn/ *n* composición *f*

compost /'kɒmpɒst/ *n* abono *m*

composure /kəm'pəʊʒə(r)/ *n* serenidad *f*

compound /'kɒmpaʊnd/ *n* compuesto *m*; (*enclosure*) recinto *m*. ● *adj* compuesto; (*fracture*) complicado

comprehen|d /kɒmprɪ'hend/ vt comprender. **~sion** /kɒmprɪ'henʃn/ n comprensión f **~sive** /kɒmprɪ'hensɪv/ adj extenso; (insurance) contra todo riesgo. **~sive (school)** n instituto m de enseñanza secundaria

compress /'kɒmpres/ n (Med) compresa f. ● /kəm'pres/ vt comprimir. **~ion** /-'preʃn/ n compresión f

comprise /kəm'praɪz/ vt comprender

compromise /'kɒmprəmaɪz/ n acuerdo m, compromiso m, arreglo m. ● vt comprometer. ● vi llegar a un acuerdo. **~ing** adj (situation) comprometido

compuls|ion /kəm'pʌlʃn/ n (force) coacción f; (obsession) compulsión f. **~ive** /kəm'pʌlsɪv/ adj compulsivo. **~ory** /kəm'pʌlsərɪ/ adj obligatorio

comput|e /kəm'pjuːt/ vb calcular. **~er** n ordenador m, computadora f (LAm). **~erize** vt computarizar, computerizar. **~er studies** n, **~ing** n informática f, computación f

comrade /'kɒmreɪd/ n camarada m & f

con /kɒn/ vt (pt conned) 🔲 estafar. ● n (fraud) estafa f; (objection) see PRO

concave /'kɒnkeɪv/ adj cóncavo

conceal /kən'siːl/ vt ocultar

concede /kən'siːd/ vt conceder

conceit /kən'siːt/ n vanidad f. **~ed** adj engreído

conceiv|able /kən'siːvəbl/ adj concebible. **~e** /kən'siːv/ vt/i concebir

concentrat|e /'kɒnsəntreɪt/ vt

concentrar. ● vi concentrarse (on en). **~ion** /-'treɪʃn/ n concentración f

concept /'kɒnsept/ n concepto m

conception /kən'sepʃn/ n concepción f

concern /kən'sɜːn/ n asunto m; (worry) preocupación f; (Com) empresa f. ● vt tener que ver con; (deal with) tratar de. as far as I'm **~ed** en cuanto a mí. be **~ed about** preocuparse por. **~ing** prep acerca de

concert /'kɒnsət/ n concierto m. **~ed** /kən'sɜːtɪd/ adj concertado

concertina /kɒnsə'tiːnə/ n concertina f

concerto /kən'tʃɜːtəʊ/ n (pl -os or -ti /-tɪ/) concierto m

concession /kən'seʃn/ n concesión f

concise /kən'saɪs/ adj conciso

conclu|de /kən'kluːd/ vt/i concluir. **~ding** adj final. **~sion** /-ʃn/ n conclusión f. **~sive** /-sɪv/ adj decisivo. **~sively** adv concluyentemente

concoct /kən'kɒkt/ vt confeccionar; (fig) inventar. **~ion** /-ʃn/ n mezcla f; (drink) brebaje m

concrete /'kɒŋkriːt/ n hormigón m, concreto m (LAm). ● adj concreto

concussion /kən'kʌʃn/ n conmoción f cerebral

condemn /kən'dem/ vt condenar. **~ation** /kɒndem'neɪʃn/ n condena f

condens|ation /kɒnden'seɪʃn/ n condensación f. **~e** /kən'dens/ vt condensar. ● vi condensarse

condescend /kɒndɪ'send/ vi dignarse (to a). **~ing** adj superior

condition /kən'dɪʃn/ n condición

f. on ~ that a condición de que.
●*vt* condicionar. ~al *adj* condicional. ~er *n* (*for hair*) suavizante *m*, enjuague *m* (*LAm*)

condo /'kɒndəʊ/ *n* (*pl* -os) (*Amer fam*) see CONDOMINIUM

condolences /kən'dəʊlənsɪz/ *npl* pésame *m*

condom /'kɒndɒm/ *n* condón *m*

condominium /kɒndə'mɪnɪəm/ *n* (*Amer*) apartamento *m*, piso *m* (en régimen de propiedad horizontal)

condone /kən'dəʊn/ *vt* condonar

conduct /kən'dʌkt/ *vt* llevar a cabo (*business, experiment*); conducir (*electricity*); dirigir (*orchestra*). ●/'kɒndʌkt/ *n* conducta *f*. ~or /kən'dʌktə(r)/ *n* director *m*; (*of bus*) cobrador *m*. ~ress /kən'dʌktrɪs/ *n* cobradora *f*

cone /kəʊn/ *n* cono *m*; (*for ice cream*) cucurucho *m*, barquillo *m* (*Mex*)

confectionery /kən'fekʃənrɪ/ *n* productos *mpl* de confitería

confederation /kənfedə'reɪʃn/ *n* confederación *f*

conference /'kɒnfərəns/ *n* congreso *m*; an international ~ on ... un congreso internacional sobre ...

confess /kən'fes/ *vt* confesar. ●*vi* confesarse. ~ion /-ʃn/ *n* confesión *f*

confetti /kən'fetɪ/ *n* confeti *m*

confide /kən'faɪd/ *vt/i* confiar

confiden|ce /'kɒnfɪdəns/ *n* confianza *f*; (*self-confidence*) confianza *f* en sí mismo; (*secret*) confidencia *f*. ~ce trick *n* estafa *f*, timo *m*. ~t /'kɒnfɪdənt/ *adj* seguro de sí mismo. be ~t of confiar en

confidential /kɒnfɪ'denʃl/ *adj* confidencial. ~ity /-denʃɪ'ælətɪ/ *n*

confidencialidad *f*

configur|ation /kənfɪgə'reɪʃn/ *n* configuración *f*. ~e /kən'fɪgə(r)/ *vt* configurar

confine /kən'faɪn/ *vt* confinar; (*limit*) limitar. ~ment *n* (*imprisonment*) prisión *f*

confirm /kən'fɜːm/ *vt* confirmar. ~ation /kɒnfə'meɪʃn/ *n* confirmación *f*. ~ed *adj* inveterado

confiscat|e /'kɒnfɪskeɪt/ *vt* confiscar. ~ion /-'keɪʃn/ *n* confiscación *f*

conflict /'kɒnflɪkt/ *n* conflicto *m*. ●/kən'flɪkt/ *vi* chocar. ~ing /kən'flɪktɪŋ/ *adj* contradictorio

conform /kən'fɔːm/ *vi* conformarse. ~ist *n* conformista *m & f*

confound /kən'faʊnd/ *vt* confundir. ~ed *adj* 🅴 maldito

confront /kən'frʌnt/ *vt* hacer frente a; (*face*) enfrentarse con. ~ation /kɒnfrʌn'teɪʃn/ *n* confrontación *f*

confus|e /kən'fjuːz/ *vt* confundir. ~ed *adj* confundido. get ~ed confundirse. ~ing *adj* confuso. ~ion /-ʒn/ *n* confusión *f*

congeal /kən'dʒiːl/ *vi* coagularse

congest|ed /kən'dʒestɪd/ *adj* congestionado. ~ion /-tʃən/ *n* congestión *f*

congratulat|e /kən'grætjʊleɪt/ *vt* felicitar. ~ions /-'leɪʃnz/ *npl* enhorabuena *f*, felicitaciones *fpl* (*LAm*)

congregat|e /'kɒŋgrɪgeɪt/ *vi* congregarse. ~ion /-'geɪʃn/ *n* asamblea *f*; (*Relig*) fieles *mpl*, feligreses *mpl*

congress /'kɒŋgres/ *n* congreso *m*. C~ (*Amer*) el Congreso. ~man /-mən/ *n* (*Amer*) miembro *m* del Congreso. ~woman *n* (*Amer*) miembro *f* del Congreso.

Congress El Congreso es el organismo legislativo de EE.UU. Se reúne en el Capitolio (*Capitol*) y está compuesto por dos cámaras: El Senado y la Cámara de Representantes. Se renueva cada dos años y su función es elaborar leyes que deben ser aprobadas, primero, por las dos cámaras y posteriormente por el Presidente. *i*

conifer /'kɒnɪfə(r)/ n conifera f

conjugat|e /'kɒndʒʊgeɪt/ vt conjugar. ~**ion** /-'geɪʃn/ n conjugación f

conjunction /kən'dʒʌŋkʃn/ n conjunción f

conjur|e /'kʌndʒə(r)/ vi hacer juegos de manos. ●vt. □ ~ **e up** vt evocar. ~**er**, ~**or** n prestidigitador m

conk /kɒŋk/ vi. ~ **out** 🔢 fallar; (*person*) desmayarse

conker /'kɒŋkə(r)/ n 🔢 castaña f de Indias

conman /'kɒnmæn/ n (*pl* -men) 🔢 estafador m, timador m

connect /kə'nekt/ vt conectar; (*associate*) relacionar. ●vi (*be fitted*) estar conectado (to a). □ ~ **with** vt (train) enlazar con. ~**ed** adj unido; (*related*) relacionado. be ~**ed with** tener que ver con, estar emparentado con. ~**ion** /-ʃn/ n conexión f; (*Rail*) enlace m; (*fig*) relación f. **in** ~**ion with** a propósito de, con respecto a

connive /kə'naɪv/ vi. ~**e at** ser cómplice en

connoisseur /kɒnə'sɜː(r)/ n experto m

connotation /kɒnə'teɪʃn/ n connotación f

conquer /'kɒŋkə(r)/ vt conquistar; (*fig*) vencer. ~**or** n conquistador m

conquest /'kɒŋkwest/ n conquista f

conscience /'kɒnʃəns/ n conciencia f

conscientious /kɒnʃɪ'enʃəs/ adj concienzudo

conscious /'kɒnʃəs/ adj consciente; (*deliberate*) intencional. ~**ly** adv a sabiendas. ~**ness** n consciencia f; (*Med*) conocimiento m

conscript /'kɒnskrɪpt/ n recluta m & f, conscripto m (LAm). ●/kən'skrɪpt/ vt reclutar. ~**ion** /kən'skrɪpʃn/ n reclutamiento m, conscripción f (LAm)

consecrate /'kɒnsɪkreɪt/ vt consagrar

consecutive /kən'sekjʊtɪv/ adj sucesivo

consensus /kən'sensəs/ n consenso m

consent /kən'sent/ vi consentir. ●n consentimiento m

consequen|ce /'kɒnsɪkwəns/ n consecuencia f. ~**t** adj consiguiente. ~**tly** adv por consiguiente

conservation /kɒnsə'veɪʃn/ n conservación f, preservación f. ~**ist** n conservacionista m & f

conservative /kən'sɜːvətɪv/ adj conservador; (*modest*) prudente, moderado. **C**~ adj & n conservador (m)

conservatory /kən'sɜːvətrɪ/ n invernadero m

conserve /kən'sɜːv/ vt conservar

consider /kən'sɪdə(r)/ vt considerar; (*take into account*) tomar en cuenta. ~**able** adj considerable. ~**ably** adv considerablemente

considerat|e /kən'sɪdərət/ adj

considerado. **~ion** /-'reɪʃn/ n consideración f. **take sth into ~ion** tomar algo en cuenta

considering /kən'sɪdərɪŋ/ prep teniendo en cuenta. ● conj. ~ **(that)** teniendo en cuenta que

consign /kən'saɪn/ vt consignar; (send) enviar. **~ment** n envío m

consist /kən'sɪst/ vi. ~ **of** consistir en. **~ency** n consistencia f; (fig) coherencia f. **~ent** adj coherente; (unchanging) constante. **~ent with** compatible con. **~ently** adv constantemente

consolation /kɒnsə'leɪʃn/ n consuelo m

console /kən'səʊl/ vt consolar. ● /'kɒnsəʊl/ n consola f

consolidate /kən'sɒlɪdeɪt/ vt consolidar

consonant /'kɒnsənənt/ n consonante f

conspicuous /kən'spɪkjʊəs/ adj (easily seen) visible; (showy) llamativo; (noteworthy) notable

conspir|acy /kən'spɪrəsɪ/ n conspiración f. **~ator** /kən'spɪrətə(r)/ n conspirador m. **~e** /kən'spaɪə(r)/ vi conspirar

constable /'kʌnstəbl/ n agente m & f de policía

constant /'kɒnstənt/ adj constante. **~ly** adv constantemente

constellation /kɒnstə'leɪʃn/ n constelación f

consternation /kɒnstə'neɪʃn/ n consternación f

constipat|ed /'kɒnstɪpeɪtɪd/ adj estreñido. **~ion** /-'peɪʃn/ n estreñimiento m

constituen|cy /kən'stɪtjuənsɪ/ n distrito m electoral. **~t** n (Pol) elector m. ● adj constituyente, constitutivo

constitut|e /'kɒnstɪtjuːt/ vt constituir. **~ion** /-'tjuːʃn/ n constitución f. **~ional** /-'tjuːʃənl/ adj constitucional. ● n paseo m

constrict /kən'strɪkt/ vt apretar. **~ion** /-ʃn/ n constricción f

construct /kən'strʌkt/ vt construir. **~ion** /-ʃn/ n construcción f. **~ive** adj constructivo

consul /'kɒnsl/ n cónsul m & f. **~ate** /'kɒnsjʊlət/ n consulado m

consult /kən'sʌlt/ vt/i consultar. **~ancy** n asesoría. **~ant** n asesor m; (Med) especialista m & f; (Tec) consejero m técnico. **~ation** /kɒnsl'teɪʃn/ n consulta f

consume /kən'sjuːm/ vt consumir. **~r** n consumidor m. ● adj de consumo

consummate /'kɒnsəmət/ adj consumado. ● /'kɒnsəmeɪt/ vt consumar

consumption /kən'sʌmpʃn/ n consumo m

contact /'kɒntækt/ n contacto m. ● vt ponerse en contacto con. **~ lens** n lentilla f, lente f de contacto (LAm)

contagious /kən'teɪdʒəs/ adj contagioso

contain /kən'teɪn/ vt contener. **~ o.s.** contenerse. **~er** n recipiente m; (Com) contenedor m

contaminat|e /kən'tæmɪneɪt/ vt contaminar. **~ion** /-'neɪʃn/ n contaminación f

contemplate /'kɒntəmpleɪt/ vt contemplar; (consider) considerar

contemporary /kən'tempərərɪ/ adj & n contemporáneo (m)

contempt /kən'tempt/ n desprecio m. **~ible** adj despreciable. **~uous** /-tjʊəs/ adj desdeñoso

contend /kən'tend/ vt competir.

~er n aspirante m & f (for a)

content /'kɒntent/ adj satisfecho. ● /'kɒntent/ n contenido m. ● /kən'tent/ vt contentar. **~ed** /kən'tentɪd/ adj satisfecho. **~ment** /kən'tentmənt/ n satisfacción f. **~s** /'kɒntents/ n contenido m; (of book) índice m de materias

contest /'kɒntest/ n (competition) concurso m; (Sport) competición f, competencia f (LAm). ● /kən'test/ vt disputar. **~ant** /kən'testənt/ n concursante m & f

context /'kɒntekst/ n contexto m

continent /'kɒntɪnənt/ n continente m. the C~ Europa f. **~al** /-'nentl/ adj continental. **~al quilt** n edredón m

contingen|cy /kən'tɪndʒənsɪ/ n contingencia f. **~t** adj & n contingente (m)

continu|al /kən'tɪnjʊəl/ adj continuo. **~ally** adv continuamente. **~ation** /-'eɪʃn/ n continuación f. **~e** /kən'tɪnjuː/ vt/i continuar, seguir. **~ed** adj continuo. **~ity** /kɒntɪ'njuːətɪ/ n continuidad f. **~ous** /kən'tɪnjʊəs/ adj continuo. **~ously** adv continuamente

contort /kən'tɔːt/ vt retorcer. **~ion** /-ʃn/ n contorsión f. **~ionist** /-ʃənɪst/ n contorsionista m & f

contour /'kɒntʊə(r)/ n contorno m

contraband /'kɒntrəbænd/ n contrabando m

contracepti|on /kɒntrə'sepʃn/ n anticoncepción f. **~ve** /-tɪv/ adj & n anticonceptivo (m)

contract /'kɒntrækt/ n contrato m. ● /kən'trækt/ vt contraer. ● vi contraerse. **~ion** /kən'trækʃn/ n contracción f. **~or** /kən'træktə(r)/ n contratista m & f

contradict /kɒntrə'dɪkt/ vt contradecir. **~ion** /-ʃn/ n contradicción f. **~ory** adj contradictorio

contraption /kən'træpʃn/ n 🔲 artilugio m

contrary /'kɒntrərɪ/ adj contrario. the ~ lo contrario. on the ~ al contrario. ● adv. ~ to contrariamente a. ● /kən'treərɪ/ adj (obstinate) terco

contrast /'kɒntrɑːst/ n contraste m. ● /kən'trɑːst/ vt/i contrastar. **~ing** adj contrastante

contravene /kɒntrə'viːn/ vt contravenir

contribut|e /kən'trɪbjuːt/ vt contribuir con. ● vi contribuir. **~e to** escribir para (newspaper). **~ion** /kɒntrɪ'bjuːʃn/ n contribución f. **~or** n contribuyente m & f; (to newspaper) colaborador m

contrite /'kɒntraɪt/ adj arrepentido, pesaroso

contriv|e /kən'traɪv/ vt idear. **~e to** conseguir. **~ed** adj artificioso

control /kən'trəʊl/ vt (pt controlled) controlar. ● n control m. **~ler** n director m. **~s** npl (Mec) mandos mpl

controvers|ial /kɒntrə'vɜːʃl/ adj controvertido. **~y** /'kɒntrəvɜːsɪ/ n controversia f

conundrum /kə'nʌndrəm/ n adivinanza f

convalesce /kɒnvə'les/ vi convalecer. **~nce** n convalecencia f

convector /kən'vektə(r)/ n estufa f de convección

convene /kən'viːn/ vt convocar. ● vi reunirse

convenien|ce /kən'viːnɪəns/ n conveniencia f, comodidad f. all modern ~ces todas las comodidades. at your ~ce según le convenga. ~ces npl servicios mpl, baños mpl (LAm). ~t adj conveniente; (place) bien situado; (time) oportuno. be ~t convenir. ~tly adv convenientemente

convent /'kɒnvənt/ n convento m

convention /kən'venʃn/ n convención f. ~al adj convencional

converge /kən'vɜːdʒ/ vi converger

conversation /kɒnvə'seɪʃn/ n conversación f. ~al adj familiar, coloquial.

converse /kən'vɜːs/ vi conversar. ●/'kɒnvɜːs/ adj inverso. ●n lo contrario. ~ly adv a la inversa

conver|sion /kən'vɜːʃn/ n conversión f. ~t /kən'vɜːt/ vt convertir. ●/'kɒnvɜːt/ n converso m. ~tible /kən'vɜːtɪbl/ adj convertible. ●n (Auto) descapotable m, convertible m (LAm)

convex /'kɒnveks/ adj convexo

convey /kən'veɪ/ vt transportar (goods, people); comunicar (idea, feeling). ~or belt n cinta f transportadora, banda f transportadora (LAm)

convict /kən'vɪkt/ vt condenar. ●/'kɒnvɪkt/ n presidiario m. ~ion /kən'vɪkʃn/ n condena f; (belief) creencia f

convinc|e /kən'vɪns/ vt convencer. ~ing adj convincente

convoluted /'kɒnvəluːtɪd/ adj (argument) intrincado

convoy /'kɒnvɔɪ/ n convoy m

convuls|e /kən'vʌls/ vt convulsionar. be ~ed with laughter desternillarse de risa. ~ion /-ʃn/ n convulsión f

coo /kuː/ vi arrullar

cook /kʊk/ vt hacer, preparar. ●vi cocinar; (food) hacerse. ●n coci-

nero m. □ ~ **up** vt 🔢 inventar. ~**book** n libro m de cocina. ~**er** n cocina f, estufa f (Mex). ~**ery** n cocina f

cookie /'kʊkɪ/ n (Amer) galleta f

cool /kuːl/ adj (-er, -est) fresco; (calm) tranquilo; (unfriendly) frío. ●n fresco m; 🗶 calma f. ●vt enfriar. ●vi enfriarse. □ ~ **down** vi (person) calmarse. ~**ly** adv tranquilamente

coop /kuːp/ n gallinero m. □ ~ **up** vt encerrar

co-op /'kəʊɒp/ n cooperativa f

cooperat|e /kəʊ'ɒpəreɪt/ vi cooperar. ~**ion** /-'reɪʃn/ n cooperación f. ~**ive** /kəʊ'ɒpərətɪv/ adj cooperativo. ●n cooperativa f

co-opt /kəʊ'ɒpt/ vt cooptar

co-ordinat|e /kəʊ'ɔːdɪneɪt/ vt coordinar. ●/kəʊ'ɔːdɪnət/ n (Math) coordenada f. ~**es** npl prendas fpl para combinar. ~**ion** /kəʊɔːdɪ'neɪʃn/ n coordinación f

cop /kɒp/ n 🔢 poli m & f 🔢, tira m & f (Mex, fam)

cope /kəʊp/ vi arreglárselas. ~ **with** hacer frente a

copious /'kəʊpɪəs/ adj abundante

copper /'kɒpə(r)/ n cobre m; (coin) perra f; 🔢 poli m & f 🔢, tira m & f (Mex, fam). ●adj de cobre

copy /'kɒpɪ/ n copia f; (of book, newspaper) ejemplar m. ●vt copiar. ~**right** n derechos mpl de reproducción

coral /'kɒrəl/ n coral m

cord /kɔːd/ n cuerda f; (fabric) pana f; (Amer, Elec) cordón m, cable m

cordial /'kɔːdɪəl/ adj cordial. ●n refresco m (concentrado)

cordon /'kɔːdn/ n cordón m. □ ~ **off** vt acordonar

core /kɔː(r)/ n (of apple) corazón m; (of Earth) centro m; (of problem) meollo m

cork /kɔːk/ n corcho m. **~screw** n sacacorchos m

corn /kɔːn/ n (wheat) trigo m; (Amer) maíz m; (hard skin) callo m

corned beef /kɔːnd 'biːf/ n carne f de vaca en lata

corner /'kɔːnə(r)/ n ángulo m; (inside) rincón m; (outside) esquina f; (football) córner m. ● vt arrinconar; (Com) acaparar

cornet /'kɔːnɪt/ n (Mus) corneta f; (for ice cream) cucurucho m, barquillo m (Mex)

corn: **~flakes** npl copos mpl de maíz. **~flour** n maizena f (®)

Cornish /'kɔːnɪʃ/ adj de Cornualles

cornstarch /'kɔːnstɑːtʃ/ n (Amer) maizena f (®)

corny /'kɔːnɪ/ adj (fam, trite) gastado

coronation /kɒrə'neɪʃn/ n coronación f

coroner /'kɒrənə(r)/ n juez m de primera instancia

corporal /'kɔːpərəl/ n cabo m. ● adj corporal

corporate /'kɔːpərət/ adj corporativo

corporation /kɔːpə'reɪʃn/ n corporación f; (Amer) sociedad f anónima

corps /kɔː(r)/ n (pl corps /kɔːz/) cuerpo m

corpse /kɔːps/ n cadáver m

corpulent /'kɔːpjʊlənt/ adj corpulento

corral /kə'rɑːl/ n (Amer) corral m

correct /kə'rekt/ adj correcto; (time) exacto. ● vt corregir. **~ion** /-ʃn/ n corrección f

correspond /kɒrɪ'spɒnd/ vi corresponder; (write) escribirse. **~ence** n correspondencia f. **~ent** n corresponsal m & f

corridor /'kɒrɪdɔː(r)/ n pasillo m

corro|de /kə'rəʊd/ vt corroer. ● vi corroerse. **~sion** /-ʒn/ n corrosión f. **~sive** /-sɪv/ adj corrosivo

corrugated /'kɒrəgeɪtɪd/ adj ondulado. **~ iron** n chapa f de zinc

corrupt /kə'rʌpt/ adj corrompido. ● vt corromper. **~ion** /-ʃn/ n corrupción f

corset /'kɔːsɪt/ n corsé m

cosmetic /kɒz'metɪk/ adj & n cosmético (m)

cosmic /'kɒzmɪk/ adj cósmico

cosmopolitan /kɒzmə'pɒlɪtən/ adj & n cosmopolita (m & f)

cosmos /'kɒzmɒs/ n cosmos m

cosset /'kɒsɪt/ vt (pt cosseted) mimar

cost /kɒst/ vt (pt cost) costar; (pt costed) calcular el coste de, calcular el costo de (LAm). ● n coste m, costo m (LAm). **at all ~s** cueste lo que cueste. **to one's ~** a sus expensas. **~s** npl (Jurid) costas fpl

Costa Rica /kɒstə'riːkə/ n Costa f Rica. **~n** adj & n costarricense (m & f), costarriqueño (m & f)

cost: **~-effective** adj rentable. **~ly** adj (-ier, -iest) costoso

costume /'kɒstjuːm/ n traje m; (for party, disguise) disfraz m

cosy /'kəʊzɪ/ adj (-ier, -iest) acogedor. ● n cubreteras fpl

cot /kɒt/ n cuna f

cottage /'kɒtɪdʒ/ n casita f. **~ cheese** n requesón m. **~ pie** n pastel m de carne cubierta con puré

cotton /'kɒtn/ n algodón m; (thread) hilo m; (Amer) see **~**

WOOL. □~ **on** vi 🔲 comprender.
~ **bud** n bastoncillo m, cotonete m (Mex). ~ **candy** n (Amer) algodón m de azúcar. ~ **swab** n (Amer) see ~ **BUD**. ~ **wool** n algodón m hidrófilo

couch /kaʊtʃ/ n sofá m

cough /kɒf/ vi toser. • n tos f. ~ **up** vt 🔲 pagar. ~ **mixture** n jarabe m para la tos

could /kʊd/ pt of CAN¹

couldn't /'kʊdnt/ = could not

council /'kaʊnsl/ n consejo m; (of town) ayuntamiento m. ~ **house** n vivienda f subvencionada. ~lor n concejal m

counsel /'kaʊnsl/ n consejo m; (pl invar) (Jurid) abogado m. • vt (pt counselled) aconsejar. ~ling n terapia f de apoyo. ~lor n consejero m

count /kaʊnt/ n recuento m; (nobleman) conde m. • vt/i contar. □~ **on** vt contar. ~down n cuenta f atrás

counter /'kaʊntə(r)/ n (in shop) mostrador m; (in bank, post office) ventanilla f; (token) ficha f. • adv. ~ **to** en contra de. • adj opuesto. • vt oponerse a; parar (blow)

counter... /'kaʊntə(r)/ pref contra.... ~act /-'ækt/ vt contrarrestar. ~-attack n contraataque m. • vt/i contraatacar. ~balance n contrapeso m. • vt/i contrapesar. ~clockwise /-'klɒkwaɪz/ a/adv (Amer) en sentido contrario a las agujas del reloj

counterfeit /'kaʊntəfɪt/ adj falsificado. • n falsificación f. • vt falsificar

counterfoil /'kaʊntəfɔɪl/ n matriz f, talón m (LAm)

counter-productive /kaʊntəprə'dʌktɪv/ adj contraproducente

countess /'kaʊntɪs/ n condesa f

countless /'kaʊntlɪs/ adj innumerable

country /'kʌntrɪ/ n (native land) país m; (countryside) campo m; (Mus) (música f) country m. ~-and-western /-en'westən/ (música f) country m. ~man /-mən/ n (of one's own country) compatriota m. ~side n campo m; (landscape) paisaje m

county /'kaʊntɪ/ n condado m

coup /kuː/ n golpe m

couple /'kʌpl/ n (of things) par m; (of people) pareja f; (married) matrimonio m. a ~ of un par de

coupon /'kuːpɒn/ n cupón m

courage /'kʌrɪdʒ/ n valor m. ~ous /kə'reɪdʒəs/ adj valiente

courgette /kʊə'ʒet/ n calabacín m

courier /'kʊrɪə(r)/ n mensajero m; (for tourists) guía m & f

course /kɔːs/ n curso m; (behaviour) conducta f; (in navigation) rumbo m; (Culin) plato m; (for golf) campo m. in due ~ a su debido tiempo. in the ~ of en el transcurso de, durante. of ~ claro, por supuesto. of ~ not claro que no, por supuesto que no

court /kɔːt/ n corte f; (tennis) pista f; cancha f (LAm); (Jurid) tribunal m. • vt cortejar; buscar (danger)

courteous /'kɜːtɪəs/ adj cortés

courtesy /'kɜːtəsɪ/ n cortesía f

courtier /'kɔːtɪə(r)/ n (old use) cortesano m

court:: ~ **martial** n (pl ~s martial) consejo m de guerra. **-martial** vt (pt ~-martialled) juzgar en consejo de guerra. ~ship n cortejo m. ~yard n patio m

cousin /'kʌzn/ n primo m. first ~ primo carnal. second ~ primo segundo

cove /kəʊv/ n ensenada f, cala f

Coventry /'kɒvntri/ n. send s.o. to ~ hacer el vacío a uno

cover /'kʌvə(r)/ vt cubrir. ● n cubierta f; (shelter) abrigo m; (lid) tapa f; (for furniture) funda f; (pretext) pretexto m; (of magazine) portada f. □ ~ **up** vt cubrir; (fig) ocultar. **~age** n cobertura f. **~ charge** n precio m del cubierto. **~ing** n cubierta f. **~ing letter** n carta f adjunta

covet /'kʌvɪt/ vt codiciar

cow /kaʊ/ n vaca f

coward /'kaʊəd/ n cobarde m. **~ice** /'kaʊədɪs/ n cobardía f. **~ly** adj cobarde

cowboy /'kaʊbɔɪ/ n vaquero m

cower /'kaʊə(r)/ vi encogerse, acobardarse

coxswain /'kɒksn/ n timonel m

coy /kɔɪ/ adj (-er, -est) (shy) tímido; (evasive) evasivo

crab /kræb/ n cangrejo m, jaiba f (LAm)

crack /kræk/ n grieta f; (noise) crujido m; (of whip) chasquido m; (drug) crack m. ● adj 🗓 de primera. ● vt agrietar; chasquear (whip, fingers); cascar (nut); gastar (joke); resolver (problem). ● vi agrietarse. get **~ing** 🗓 darse prisa. □ ~ **down on** vt 🗓 tomar medidas enérgicas contra

cracker /'krækə(r)/ n (Culin) cracker f, galleta f (salada); (Christmas cracker) sorpresa f (que estalla al abrirla)

crackle /'krækl/ vi crepitar. ● n crepitación f, crujido m

crackpot /'krækpɒt/ n 🗓 chiflado m

cradle /'kreɪdl/ n cuna f. ● vt acunar

craft /krɑːft/ n destreza f; (technique) arte f; (cunning) astucia f. ● n invar (boat) barco m

craftsman /'krɑːftsmən/ n (pl -men) artesano m. **~ship** n artesanía f

crafty /'krɑːftɪ/ adj (-ier, -iest) astuto

cram /kræm/ vt (pt crammed) rellenar. ~ **with** llenar de. ● vi (for exams) memorizar, empollar 🗓, zambutir (Mex)

cramp /kræmp/ n calambre m

cramped /kræmpt/ adj apretado

crane /kreɪn/ n grúa f. ● vt estirar (neck)

crank /kræŋk/ n manivela f; (person) excéntrico m. **~y** adj excéntrico

cranny /'krænɪ/ n grieta f

crash /kræʃ/ n accidente m; (noise) estruendo m; (collision) choque m; (Com) quiebra f. ● vt estrellar. ● vi quebrar con estrépito; (have accident) tener un accidente; (car etc) estrellarse, chocar; (fail) fracasar. ~ **course** n curso m intensivo. ~ **helmet** n casco m protector. **~land** vi hacer un aterrizaje forzoso

crass /kræs/ adj craso, burdo

crate /kreɪt/ n cajón m. ● vt embalar

crater /'kreɪtə(r)/ n cráter m

crav|e /kreɪv/ vt ansiar. **~ing** n ansia f

crawl /krɔːl/ vi (baby) gatear; (move slowly) avanzar lentamente; (drag o.s.) arrastrarse. ~ **to** humillarse ante. ~ **with** hervir de. ● n (*swimming*) crol *m*. at a ~ a paso lento

crayon /'kreɪən/ *n* lápiz *m* de color; (*made of wax*) lápiz *m* de cera, crayola *f* (®), crayón *m* (*Mex*)

craz|e /kreɪz/ *n* manía *f*. ~**y** /'kreɪzɪ/ *adj* (-**ier**, -**iest**) loco. be ~**y** about estar loco por

creak /kriːk/ *n* crujido *m*; (*of hinge*) chirrido *m*. ●*vi* crujir; (*hinge*) chirriar

cream /kriːm/ *n* crema *f*; (*fresh*) nata *f*, crema *f* (*LAm*). ●*adj* (*colour*) color crema. ●*vt* (*beat*) batir. ~ **cheese** *n* queso *m* para untar, queso *m* crema (*LAm*). ~**y** *adj* cremoso

crease /kriːs/ *n* raya *f*, pliegue *m* (*Mex*); (*crumple*) arruga *f*. ●*vt* plegar; (*wrinkle*) arrugar. ●*vi* arrugarse

creat|e /kriː'eɪt/ *vt* crear. ~**ion** /-ʃn/ *n* creación *f*. ~**ive** *adj* creativo. ~**or** *n* creador *m*

creature /'kriːtʃə(r)/ *n* criatura *f*

crèche /kreʃ/ *n* guardería *f* (infantil)

credib|ility /kredə'bɪlətɪ/ *n* credibilidad *f*. ~**le** /'kredəbl/ *adj* creíble

credit /'kredɪt/ *n* crédito *m*; (*honour*) mérito *m*. take the ~ for atribuirse el mérito de. ●*vt* (*pt* credited) acreditar; (*believe*) creer. ~ **s.o. with** atribuir a uno. ~ **card** *n* tarjeta *f* de crédito. ~**or** *n* acreedor *m*

creed /kriːd/ *n* credo *m*

creek /kriːk/ *n* ensenada *f*. up the ~ ⊠ en apuros

creep /kriːp/ *vi* (*pt* crept) arrastrarse; (*plant*) trepar. ●*n* 🄳 adulador. ~**s** *mpl/npl*. give s.o. the ~**s** poner los pelos de punta a uno. ~**er** *n* enredadera *f*

cremat|e /krɪ'meɪt/ *vt* incinerar. ~**ion** /-ʃn/ *n* cremación *f*. ~**orium** /kremə'tɔːrɪəm/ *n* (*pl* -**ia** /-ɪə/) crematorio *m*

crept /krept/ *see* CREEP

crescendo /krɪ'ʃendəʊ/ *n* (*pl* -os) crescendo *m*

crescent /'kresnt/ *n* media luna *f*; (*street*) calle *f* en forma de media luna

crest /krest/ *n* cresta *f*; (*on coat of arms*) emblema *m*

crevice /'krevɪs/ *n* grieta *f*

crew /kruː/ *n* tripulación *f*; (*gang*) pandilla *f*. ~ **cut** *n* corte *m* al rape

crib /krɪb/ *n* (*Amer*) cuna *f*; (*Relig*) belén *m*. ●*vt/i* (*pt* cribbed) copiar

crick /krɪk/ *n* calambre *m*; (*in neck*) tortícolis *f*

cricket /'krɪkɪt/ *n* (*Sport*) críquet *m*; (*insect*) grillo *m*

crim|e /kraɪm/ *n* delito *m*; (*murder*) crimen *m*; (*acts*) delincuencia *f*. ~**inal** /'krɪmɪnl/ *adj* & *n* criminal (*m & f*)

crimson /'krɪmzn/ *adj* & *n* carmesí (*m*)

cringe /krɪndʒ/ *vi* encogerse; (*fig*) humillarse

crinkle /'krɪŋkl/ *vt* arrugar. ●*vi* arrugarse. ●*n* arruga *f*

cripple /'krɪpl/ *n* lisiado *m*. ●*vt* lisiar; (*fig*) paralizar

crisis /'kraɪsɪs/ *n* (*pl* crises /-siːz/) crisis *f*

crisp /krɪsp/ *adj* (-**er**, -**est**) (*Culin*) crujiente; (*air*) vigorizador. ~**s** *npl* patatas *fpl* fritas, papas *fpl* fritas (*LAm*) (*de bolsa*)

crisscross /'krɪskrɒs/ *adj* entrecruzado. ●*vt* entrecruzar. ●*vi* entrecruzarse

criterion /kraɪ'tɪərɪən/ *n* (*pl* -**ia** /-ɪə/) criterio *m*

critic /'krɪtɪk/ n crítico m. ~**al** adj crítico. ~**ally** adv críticamente; (ill) gravemente

critici|sm /'krɪtɪsɪzəm/ n crítica f. ~**ze** /'krɪtɪsaɪz/ vt/i criticar

croak /krəʊk/ n (of person) gruñido m; (of frog) canto m. ●vi gruñir; (frog) croar

Croat /'krəʊæt/ n croata m & f. ~**ia** /krəʊ'eɪʃə/ n Croacia f. ~**ian** adj croata

crochet /'krəʊʃeɪ/ n crochet m, ganchillo m. ●vt tejer a crochet or a ganchillo

crockery /'krɒkərɪ/ n loza f

crocodile /'krɒkədaɪl/ n cocodrilo m. ~ **tears** npl lágrimas fpl de cocodrilo

crocus /'krəʊkəs/ n (pl -es) azafrán m de primavera

crook /krʊk/ n 🄸 sinvergüenza m & f. ~**ed** /'krʊkɪd/ adj torcido, chueco (LAm); (winding) tortuoso; (dishonest) deshonesto

crop /krɒp/ n cosecha f; (haircut) corte m de pelo muy corto. ●vt (pt cropped) cortar. □ ~ **up** vi surgir

croquet /'krəʊkeɪ/ n croquet m

cross /krɒs/ n cruz f; (of animals) cruce m. ●vt cruzar; (oppose) contrariar. ~ **s.o.'s mind** ocurrírsele a uno. ●vi cruzar. ~ **o.s.** santiguarse. ●adj enfadado, enojado (esp LAm) □ ~ **out** vt tachar. ~**bar** n travesaño m. ~**-examine** /-ɪg'zæmɪn/ vt interrogar. ~**-eyed** adj bizco. ~**fire** n fuego m cruzado. ~**ing** n (by boat) travesía f; (on road) cruce m peatonal. ~**ly** adv con enfado, con enojo (esp LAm). ~**purposes** /-'pɜːpəsɪz/ npl. talk at ~**purposes** hablar sin entenderse. ~**reference** /-'refrəns/ n remisión f. ~**roads** n invar cruce m.

~**-section** /-'sekʃn/ n sección f transversal; (fig) muestra f representativa. ~**walk** n (Amer) paso de peatones. ~**word** n ~**word** (puzzle) crucigrama m

crotch /krɒtʃ/ n entrepiernas fpl

crouch /kraʊtʃ/ vi agacharse

crow /krəʊ/ n cuervo m. **as the** ~ **flies** en línea recta. ●vi cacarear. ~**bar** n palanca f

crowd /kraʊd/ n muchedumbre f. ●vt amontonar; (fill) llenar. ●vi amontonarse; (gather) reunirse. ~**ed** adj atestado

crown /kraʊn/ n corona f; (of hill) cumbre f; (of head) coronilla f. ●vt coronar

crucial /'kruːʃl/ adj crucial

crucifix /'kruːsɪfɪks/ n crucifijo m. ~**ion** /-'fɪkʃn/ n crucifixión f

crucify /'kruːsɪfaɪ/ vt crucificar

crude /kruːd/ adj (-er, -est) (raw) crudo; (rough) tosco; (vulgar) ordinario

cruel /'kruːəl/ adj (crueller, cruellest) cruel. ~**ty** n crueldad f

cruet /'kruːɪt/ n vinagrera f

cruise /kruːz/ n crucero m. ●vi hacer un crucero; (of car) circular lentamente. ~**r** n crucero m

crumb /krʌm/ n miga f

crumble /'krʌmbl/ vt desmenuzar. ●vi desmenuzarse; (collapse) derrumbarse

crummy /'krʌmɪ/ adj (-ier, -iest) 🄳 miserable

crumpet /'krʌmpɪt/ n bollo m blando

crumple /'krʌmpl/ vt arrugar. ●vi arrugarse

crunch /krʌntʃ/ vt hacer crujir; (bite) masticar. ~**y** adj crujiente

crusade /kruː'seɪd/ n cruzada f

~r n cruzado m

crush /krʌʃ/ vt aplastar; arrugar (clothes). ● n (crowd) aglomeración f. have a ~ on Ⓣ estar chiflado por

crust /krʌst/ n corteza f. ~y adj (bread) de corteza dura

crutch /krʌtʃ/ n muleta f; (between legs) entrepiernas fpl

crux /krʌks/ n (pl cruxes). the ~ (of the matter) el quid (de la cuestión)

cry /kraɪ/ n grito m. be a far ~ from (fig) distar mucho de. ● vi llorar; (call out) gritar. ▫ ~ **off** vi echarse atrás, rajarse. ~**baby** n llorón m

crypt /krɪpt/ n cripta f

cryptic /krɪptɪk/ adj enigmático

crystal /krɪstl/ n cristal m. ~**lize** vi cristalizarse

cub /kʌb/ n cachorro m. C~ (Scout) n lobato m

Cuba /kjuːbə/ n Cuba f. ~**n** adj & n cubano (m)

cubbyhole /kʌbɪhəʊl/ n cuchitril m

cub|**e** /kjuːb/ n cubo m. ~**ic** adj cúbico

cubicle /kjuːbɪkl/ n cubículo m; (changing room) probador m

cuckoo /kʊkuː/ n cuco m, cuclillo m

cucumber /kjuːkʌmbə(r)/ n pepino m

cuddl|**e** /kʌdl/ vt abrazar. ● vi abrazarse. ● n abrazo m. ~**y** adj adorable

cue /kjuː/ n (Mus) entrada f; (in theatre) pie m; (in snooker) taco m

cuff /kʌf/ n puño m; (Amer, of trousers) vuelta f, dobladillo m; (blow) bofetada f. speak off the ~ hablar de improviso. ● vt abofetear. ~**link** n gemelo m, mancuerna f (Mex)

cul-de-sac /kʌldəsæk/ n callejón m sin salida

culinary /kʌlɪnərɪ/ adj culinario

cull /kʌl/ vt sacrificar en forma selectiva (animals)

culminat|**e** /kʌlmɪneɪt/ vi culminar. ~**ion** /-ˈneɪʃn/ n culminación f

culprit /kʌlprɪt/ n culpable m & f

cult /kʌlt/ n culto m

cultivat|**e** /kʌltɪveɪt/ vt cultivar. ~**ion** /-ˈveɪʃn/ n cultivo m

cultur|**al** /kʌltʃərəl/ adj cultural. ~**e** /kʌltʃə(r)/ n cultura f; (Bot etc) cultivo m. ~**ed** adj cultivado; (person) culto

cumbersome /kʌmbəsəm/ adj incómodo; (heavy) pesado

cunning /kʌnɪŋ/ adj astuto. ● n astucia f

cup /kʌp/ n taza f; (trophy) copa f

cupboard /kʌbəd/ n armario m

curator /kjʊəˈreɪtə(r)/ n (of museum) conservador m

curb /kɜːb/ n freno m; (Amer) bordillo m (de la acera), borde m de la banqueta (Mex). ● vt refrenar

curdle /kɜːdl/ vt cuajar. ● vi cuajarse; (go bad) cortarse

cure /kjʊə/(r)/ vt curar. ● n cura f

curfew /kɜːfjuː/ n toque m de queda

curio|**sity** /kjʊərɪˈɒsɪtɪ/ n curiosidad f. ~**us** /kjʊərɪəs/ adj curioso

curl /kɜːl/ vt rizar, enchinar (Mex). ~ **o.s. up** acurrucarse. ● vi (hair) rizarse, enchinarse (Mex); (paper) ondularse. ● n rizo m, chino m (Mex). ~**er** n rulo m, chino m (Mex). ~**y** adj (-ier, -iest) rizado, chino (Mex)

currant /kʌrənt/ n pasa f de Corinto

currency /'kʌrənsɪ/ n moneda f

current /'kʌrənt/ adj & n corriente (f); (existing) actual. ~ **affairs** npl sucesos de actualidad. ~**ly** adv actualmente

curriculum /kə'rɪkjʊləm/ n (pl -la) programa m de estudios. ~ **vitae** n currículum m vitae

curry /'kʌrɪ/ n curry m. ● vt preparar al curry

curse /kɜːs/ n maldición f; (oath) palabrota f. ● vt maldecir. ● vi decir palabrotas

cursory /'kɜːsərɪ/ adj superficial

curt /kɜːt/ adj brusco

curtain /'kɜːtn/ n cortina f; (in theatre) telón m

curtsey, curtsy /'kɜːtsɪ/ n reverencia f. ● vi hacer una reverencia

curve /kɜːv/ n curva f. ● vi estar curvado; (road) torcerse

cushion /'kʊʃn/ n cojín m, almohadón m

cushy /'kʊʃɪ/ adj (-ier, -iest) 🔲 fácil

custard /'kʌstəd/ n natillas fpl

custody /'kʌstədɪ/ n custodia f; be in ~ Jurid estar detenido

custom /'kʌstəm/ n costumbre f; (Com) clientela f. ~**ary** /-arɪ/ adj acostumbrado. ~**er** n cliente m. ~**s** npl aduana f. ~**s officer** n aduanero m

cut /kʌt/ vt/i (pt cut, pres p cutting) cortar; reducir (prices). ● n corte m; (reduction) reducción f. □ ~ **across** vt cortar camino por. □ ~ **back**, □ ~ **down** vt reducir. □ ~ **in** vi interrumpir. □ ~ **off** vt cortar; (phone) desconectar; (fig) aislar. □ ~ **out** vt recortar; (omit) suprimir. □ ~ **through** vt cortar camino por. □ ~ **up** vt cortar en pedazos

cute /kjuːt/ adj (-er, -est) 🔲

mono, amoroso (LAm); (Amer, attractive) guapo, buen mozo (LAm)

cutlery /'kʌtlərɪ/ n cubiertos mpl

cutlet /'kʌtlɪt/ n chuleta f

cut: ~**-price**, (Amer) ~**-rate** adj a precio reducido. ~**-throat** adj despiadado. ~**ting** adj cortante; (remark) mordaz. ● n (from newspaper) recorte m; (of plant) esqueje m

CV n (= **curriculum vitae**) currículum m (vitae)

cyberspace /'saɪbəspeɪs/ cibrespacio m

cycl|e /'saɪkl/ n ciclo m; (bicycle) bicicleta f. ● vi ir en bicicleta. ~**ing** n ciclismo m. ~**ist** n ciclista m & f

cylind|er /'sɪlɪndə(r)/ n cilindro m. ~**er head** (Auto) n culata f. ~**rical** /-'lɪndrɪkl/ adj cilíndrico

cymbal /'sɪmbl/ n címbalo m

cynic /'sɪnɪk/ n cínico m. ~**al** adj cínico. ~**ism** /-sɪzəm/ n cinismo m

Czech /tʃek/ adj & n checo (m). ~**oslovakia** /-əslə'vækɪə/ n (History) Checoslovaquia f. ~ **Republic** n. the ~ **Republic** n la República Checa

Dd

dab /dæb/ vt (pt dabbed) tocar ligeramente. ● n toque m suave. a ~ of un poquito de

dad /dæd/ n 🔲 papá m. ~**dy** n papi m. ~**dy-long-legs** n invar (cranefly) típula f; (Amer, harvestman) segador m, falangio f

daffodil /'dæfədɪl/ n narciso m

daft /dɑːft/ adj (-er, -est) ⚑ tonto

dagger /'dægə(r)/ n daga f, puñal m

daily /'deɪli/ adj diario. ● adv diariamente, cada día

ⓘ **Dáil Éireann** Es el nombre de la cámara baja del Parlamento de la República de Irlanda. Se pronuncia /dɔɪl/ y consta de 166 representantes o diputados, comúnmente llamados *TDs*, que representan 41 circunscripciones. Se eligen por medio del sistema de representación proporcional. Según la Constitución debe haber un diputado por cada 20.000 a 30.000 personas.

---

dainty /'deɪntɪ/ adj (-ier, -iest) delicado

dairy /'deərɪ/ n vaquería f; (shop) lechería f

daisy /'deɪzɪ/ n margarita f

dam /dæm/ n presa f, represa f (LAm)

damag|e /'dæmɪdʒ/ n daño m; ~s (npl, Jurid) daños mpl y perjuicios mpl. ● vt (a)dañar, estropear. ~ing adj perjudicial

dame /deɪm/ n (old use) dama f; (Amer, sl) chica f

damn /dæm/ vt condenar; (curse) maldecir. ● int ⚑ ¡caray! ⚑. ● adj maldito. ● n **I don't give a ~** (no) me importa un comino

damp /dæmp/ n humedad f. ● adj (-er, -est) húmedo. ● vt mojar. ~ness n humedad f

danc|e /dɑːns/ vt/i bailar. ● n baile m. ~e **hall** n salón m de baile. ~er n bailador m; (professional) bailarín m. ~ing n baile m

dandelion /'dændɪlaɪən/ n diente m de león

dandruff /'dændrʌf/ n caspa f

dandy /'dændɪ/ n petimetre m

Dane /deɪn/ n danés m

danger /'deɪndʒə(r)/ n peligro m; (risk) riesgo m. ~ous adj peligroso

dangle /'dæŋgl/ vt balancear. ● vi suspender, colgar

Danish /'deɪnɪʃ/ adj danés. ● m (language) danés m

dar|e /deə(r)/ vt desafiar. ● vi atreverse a. **I ~ say** probablemente. ● n desafío m. ~edevil n atrevido m. ~ing adj atrevido

dark /dɑːk/ adj (-er, -est) oscuro; (skin, hair) moreno. ● n oscuridad f; (nightfall) atardecer m. **in the ~** a oscuras. ~**en** vt oscurecer. ● vi oscurecerse. ~**ness** n oscuridad f. ~**room** n cámara f oscura

darling /'dɑːlɪŋ/ adj querido. ● n cariño m

darn /dɑːn/ vt zurcir

dart /dɑːt/ n dardo m. ● vi lanzarse; (run) precipitarse. ~**board** n diana f. ~s npl los dardos mpl

dash /dæʃ/ vi precipitarse. ● vt tirar; (break) romper; defraudar (hopes). ● n (small amount) poquito m; (punctuation mark) guión m. □ ~ **off** vi marcharse apresuradamente. □ ~ **out** vi salir corriendo. ~**board** n tablero m de mandos

data /'deɪtə/ npl datos mpl. ~**base** n base f de datos. ~ **processing** n proceso m de datos

date /deɪt/ n fecha f; (appointment) cita f; (fruit) dátil m. **to ~** hasta la fecha. ● vt fechar. ● vi datar; datar (remains); (be old-fashioned) quedar anticuado. ~**d** adj pasado de moda

daub /dɔːb/ vt embadurnar

daughter /'dɔːtə(r)/ n hija f.
~-in-law n nuera f
dawdle /'dɔːdl/ vi andar despacio;
(waste time) perder el tiempo
dawn /dɔːn/ n amanecer m. ● vi
amanecer; (fig) nacer. it ~ed on
me that caí en la cuenta de que
day /deɪ/ n día m; (whole day) jor-
nada f; (period) época f. **~break** n
amanecer m. **~ care center** n
(Amer) guardería f infantil. **~dream**
n ensueño m. ● vi soñar despierto.
~light n luz f del día. **~time** n
día m
daze /deɪz/ vt aturdir. ● n aturdi-
miento m. **in a ~** aturdido. **~d** adj
aturdido
dazzle /'dæzl/ vt deslumbrar
dead /ded/ adj muerto; (numb)
dormido. ● adv justo; (🆎, com-
pletely) completamente. ● **beat** adj
rendido. **~ slow** muy lento. **stop
~** parar en seco. **~en** vt amorti-
guar (sound, blow); calmar (pain).
~ end n callejón m sin salida.
~line n fecha f tope, plazo m de
entrega. **~lock** n punto m muerto.
~ly adj (-ier, -iest) mortal
deaf /def/ adj (-er, -est) sordo.
~en vt ensordecer. **~ness** n sor-
dera f
deal /diːl/ n (agreement) acuerdo
m; (treatment) trato m. **a good ~**
bastante. **a great ~ (of)** muchí-
simo. ● vt (pt dealt) dar (a blow,
cards). ● vi (cards) dar, repartir.
□ ~ **in** vt comerciar en. □ ~ **out** vt
repartir, distribuir. □ ~ **with** vt tra-
tar con (person); tratar de (sub-
ject); ocuparse de (problem). **~er**
n comerciante m. **drug ~er** trafi-
cante m & f de drogas
dean /diːn/ n deán m; (Univ) de-
cano m
dear /dɪə(r)/ adj (-er, -est) querido;

(expensive) caro. ● n querido m.
● adv caro. oh ~! ¡ay, oh ~! ¡ay por
Dios! ~ **me!** ¡Dios mío! **~ly** adv
(pay) caro; (very much) muchísimo
death /deθ/ n muerte f. ● **sen-
tence** n pena f de muerte. ~ **trap**
n lugar m peligroso.
debatable /dɪ'beɪtəbl/ adj discu-
tible. **~e** /dɪ'beɪt/ n debate m. ● vt
debatir, discutir
debauchery /dɪ'bɔːtʃərɪ/ vt liber-
tinaje m
debit /'debɪt/ n débito m. ● vt debi-
tar, cargar. ~ **card** n tarjeta f de
cobro automático
debris /'debriː/ n escombros mpl
debt /det/ n deuda f. **be in ~**
tener deudas. **~or** n deudor m
debut /'debjuː/ n debut m
decade /'dekeɪd/ n década f
decadence /'dekədəns/ n deca-
dencia f. **~t** adj decadente
decay /dɪ'keɪ/ vi descomponerse;
(tooth) cariarse. ● n descomposición
f; (of tooth) caries f
deceased /dɪ'siːst/ adj difunto
deceit /dɪ'siːt/ n engaño m. **~ful**
adj falso. **~fully** adv falsamente
deceive /dɪ'siːv/ vt engañar
December /dɪ'sembə(r)/ n di-
ciembre m
decency /'diːsənsɪ/ n decencia f.
~t adj decente; (fam, good)
bueno; (fam, kind) amable. **~tly**
adv decentemente
deception /dɪ'sepʃn/ n engaño
m. **~ve** /-tɪv/ adj engañoso
decibel /'desɪbel/ n decibel(io)
decide /dɪ'saɪd/ vt/i decidir. **~d**
adj resuelto; (unquestionable) indu-
dable
decimal /'desɪml/ adj & n decimal
(m). ~ **point** n coma f (decimal),

punto m decimal

decipher /dɪˈsaɪfə(r)/ vt descifrar

decis|ion /dɪˈsɪʒn/ n decisión f.
~**ive** /dɪˈsaɪsɪv/ adj decisivo; (manner) decidido

deck /dek/ n (Naut) cubierta f;
(Amer, of cards) baraja f; (of bus)
piso m. ● vt adornar. ~**chair** n
tumbona f, silla f de playa

declar|ation /dekləˈreɪʃn/ n declaración f. ~**e** /dɪˈkleə(r)/ vt declarar

decline /dɪˈklaɪn/ vt rehusar;
(Gram) declinar. ● vi disminuir; (deteriorate) deteriorarse. ● n decadencia f; (decrease) disminución f

decode /diːˈkəʊd/ vt descifrar

decompose /diːkəmˈpəʊz/ vi
descomponerse

décor /ˈdeɪkɔː(r)/ n decoración f

decorat|e /ˈdekəreɪt/ vt adornar,
decorar (LAm); empapelar y pintar
(room). ~**ion** /-ˈreɪʃn/ n (act) decoración f; (ornament) adorno m.
~**ive** /-ətɪv/ adj decorativo. ~**or** n
pintor m decorador

decoy /ˈdiːkɔɪ/ n señuelo m. ● /dɪˈkɔɪ/ vt atraer con señuelo

decrease /dɪˈkriːs/ vt/i disminuir.
● /ˈdiːkriːs/ n disminución f

decree /dɪˈkriː/ n decreto m. ● vt
decretar

decrepit /dɪˈkrepɪt/ adj decrépito

decriminalize /diːˈkrɪmɪnəlaɪz/
vt despenalizar

dedicat|e /ˈdedɪkeɪt/ vt dedicar.
~**ion** /-ˈkeɪʃn/ n dedicación f

deduce /dɪˈdjuːs/ vt deducir

deduct /dɪˈdʌkt/ vt deducir. ~**ion**
/-ʃn/ n deducción f

deed /diːd/ n hecho m; (Jurid) escritura f

deem /diːm/ vt juzgar, considerar

deep /diːp/ adj (-er, -est) adv profundo. ● adv profundamente. be ~
in thought estar absorto en sus
pensamientos. ~**en** vt hacer más
profundo. ● vi hacerse más profundo. ~**freeze** n congelador m,
freezer m (LAm). ~**ly** adv profundamente

deer /dɪə(r)/ n invar ciervo m

deface /dɪˈfeɪs/ vt desfigurar

default /dɪˈfɔːlt/ vi faltar. ● n opción por defecto. by ~ en rebeldía

defeat /dɪˈfiːt/ vt vencer; (frustrate) frustrar. ● n derrota f. ~**ism**
n derrotismo m. ~**ist** n derrotista a
& (m & f)

defect /ˈdiːfekt/ n defecto m. ● /dɪ
ˈfekt/ vi desertar. ~ **to** pasar a.
~**ion** /dɪˈfekʃn/ n (Pol) defección f.
~**ive** /dɪˈfektɪv/ adj defectuoso

defence /dɪˈfens/ n defensa f.
~**less** adj indefenso

defen|d /dɪˈfend/ vt defender.
~**dant** n (Jurid) acusado m. ~**sive**
/-sɪv/ adj defensivo. ● n defensiva f

defer /dɪˈfɜː(r)/ vt (pt deferred)
aplazar. ~**ence** /ˈdefərəns/ n deferencia f. ~**ential** /defəˈrenʃl/ adj
deferente

defian|ce /dɪˈfaɪəns/ n desafío m.
in ~**ce** of a despecho de. ~**t** adj
desafiante. ~**tly** adv con actitud
desafiante

deficien|cy /dɪˈfɪʃənsɪ/ n falta f.
~**t** adj deficiente. be ~**t in** carecer de

deficit /ˈdefɪsɪt/ n déficit m

define /dɪˈfaɪn/ vt definir

definite /ˈdefɪnɪt/ adj (final) definitivo; (certain) seguro; (clear)
claro; (firm) firme. ~**ly** adv seguramente; (definitively) definitivamente

definition /defɪˈnɪʃn/ n definición f

definitive /dɪˈfɪnətɪv/ adj definitivo

deflate /dɪˈfleɪt/ vt desinflar. • vi desinflarse

deflect /dɪˈflekt/ vt desviar

deform /dɪˈfɔːm/ vt deformar. ~**ed** adj deforme. ~**ity** n deformidad f

defrost /diːˈfrɒst/ vt descongelar. • vi descongelarse

deft /deft/ adj (-er, -est) hábil. ~**ly** adv hábilmente f

defuse /diːˈfjuːz/ vt desactivar (bomb); (fig) calmar

defy /dɪˈfaɪ/ vt desafiar

degenerate /dɪˈdʒenəreɪt/ vi degenerar. • /dɪˈdʒenərət/ adj & n degenerado (m)

degrad|ation /degrəˈdeɪʃn/ n degradación f. ~**e** /dɪˈɡreɪd/ vt degradar

degree /dɪˈgriː/ n grado m; (Univ) licenciatura f; (rank) rango m. **to a certain** ~ hasta cierto punto

deign /deɪn/ vi. ~ **to** dignarse

deity /ˈdiːɪtɪ/ n deidad f

deject|ed /dɪˈdʒektɪd/ adj desanimado. ~**ion** /-ʃn/ n abatimiento m

delay /dɪˈleɪ/ vt retrasar, demorar (LAm). • vi tardar, demorar (LAm). • n retraso m, demora f (LAm)

delegat|e /ˈdelɪgeɪt/ vt/i delegar. • /ˈdelɪgət/ n delegado m. ~**ion** /-ˈgeɪʃn/ n delegación f

delet|e /dɪˈliːt/ vt tachar. ~**ion** /-ʃn/ n supresión f

deliberat|e /dɪˈlɪbəreɪt/ vt/i deliberar. • /dɪˈlɪbərət/ adj intencionado; (steps etc) pausado. ~**ely** adv a propósito. ~**ion** /-ˈreɪʃn/ n deliberación f

delica|cy /ˈdelɪkəsɪ/ n delicadeza f; (food) manjar m. ~**te** /ˈdelɪkət/ adj delicado

delicatessen /delɪkəˈtesn/ n charcutería f, salchichonería f (Mex)

delicious /dɪˈlɪʃəs/ adj delicioso

delight /dɪˈlaɪt/ n placer m. • vt encantar. • vi deleitarse. ~**ed** adj encantado. ~**ful** adj delicioso

deliri|ous /dɪˈlɪrɪəs/ adj delirante. ~**um** /-əm/ n delirio m

deliver /dɪˈlɪvə(r)/ vt entregar; (distribute) repartir; (aim) lanzar; (Med) **he** ~**ed the baby** la asistió en el parto. ~**ance** n liberación f. ~**y** n entrega f; (of post) reparto m; (Med) parto m

delta /ˈdeltə/ n (of river) delta m

delude /dɪˈluːd/ vt engañar. ~ **o.s.** engañarse

deluge /ˈdeljuːdʒ/ n diluvio m

delusion /dɪˈluːʒn/ n ilusión f

deluxe /dɪˈlʌks/ adj de lujo

delve /delv/ vi hurgar. ~ **into** (investigate) ahondar en

demand /dɪˈmɑːnd/ vt exigir. • n petición f, pedido m (LAm); (claim) exigencia f; (Com) demanda f. **in** ~ muy popular, muy solicitado. **on** ~ a solicitud. ~**ing** adj exigente. ~**s** npl exigencias fpl

demean /dɪˈmiːn/ vt. ~ **o.s.** rebajarse

demeanour /dɪˈmiːnə(r)/, (Amer) **demeanor** n comportamiento m

demented /dɪˈmentɪd/ adj demente

demo /ˈdeməʊ/ n (pl -os) 🔲 manifestación f

democra|cy /dɪˈmɒkrəsɪ/ n democracia f. ~**t** /ˈdeməkræt/ n demócrata m & f; **D**~**t a** & n (in US) demócrata (m & f). ~**tic** /demə
ˈkrætɪk/ adj democrático

demoli|sh /dɪˈmɒlɪʃ/ vt derribar. ~**tion** /deməˈlɪʃn/ n demolición f

demon /ˈdiːmən/ n demonio m

demonstrat|e /ˈdemənstreɪt/ vt demostrar. • vi manifestarse, hacer una manifestación. ~**ion** /-ˈstreɪʃn/ n demostración f; (Pol) manifestación f. ~or /'demənstreɪtə(r)/n (Pol) manifestante m & f; (marketing) demostrador m

demoralize /dɪ'mɒrəlaɪz/ vt desmoralizar

demote /dɪ'məʊt/ vt bajar de categoría

demure /dɪ'mjʊə(r)/ adj recatado

den /den/ n (of animal) guarida f, madriguera f

denial /dɪ'naɪəl/ n denegación f; (statement) desmentimiento m

denim /'denɪm/ n tela f vaquera or de jeans, mezclilla (Mex) f. ~s npl vaqueros mpl, jeans mpl, tejanos mpl, pantalones mpl de mezclilla (Mex)

Denmark /'denmɑːk/ n Dinamarca f

denote /dɪ'nəʊt/ vt denotar

denounce /dɪ'naʊns/ vt denunciar

dens|e /dens/ adj (-er, -est) espeso; (person) torpe. ~ely adv densamente. ~ity n densidad f

dent /dent/ n abolladura f. •vt abollar

dental /'dentl/ adj dental. ~ floss /flɒs/ n hilo m or seda f dental. ~ surgeon n dentista m & f

dentist /'dentɪst/ n dentista m & f. ~ry n odontología f

dentures /'dentʃəz/ npl dentadura f postiza

deny /dɪ'naɪ/ vt negar; desmentir (rumour); denegar (request)

deodorant /diː'əʊdərənt/ adj & n desodorante f

depart /dɪ'pɑːt/ vi partir, salir. ~ from (deviate from) apartarse de

department /dɪ'pɑːtmənt/ n departamento m; (Pol) ministerio m, secretaría f (Mex). ~ store n grandes almacenes mpl, tienda f de departamentos (Mex)

departure /dɪ'pɑːtʃə(r)/ n partida f; (of train etc) salida f

depend /dɪ'pend/ vi depender. ~ on depender de. ~able adj digno de confianza. ~ant /dɪ'pendənt/ n familiar m & f dependiente. ~ence n dependencia f. ~ent adj dependiente. be ~ent on depender de

depict /dɪ'pɪkt/ vt representar; (in words) describir

deplete /dɪ'pliːt/ vt agotar

deplor|able /dɪ'plɔːrəbl/ adj deplorable. ~e /dɪ'plɔː(r)/ vt deplorar

deploy /dɪ'plɔɪ/ vt desplegar

deport /dɪ'pɔːt/ vt deportar. ~ation /-'teɪʃn/ n deportación f

depose /dɪ'pəʊz/ vt deponer

deposit /dɪ'pɒzɪt/ vt (pt deposited) depositar. •n depósito m

depot /'depəʊ/ n depósito m; (Amer) estación f de autobuses

deprav|ed /dɪ'preɪvd/ adj depravado. ~ity /dɪ'prævəti/ n depravación f

depress /dɪ'pres/ vt deprimir; (press down) apretar. ~ed adj deprimido. ~ing adj deprimente. ~ion /-ʃn/ n depresión f

depriv|ation /deprɪ'veɪʃn/ n privación f. ~e /dɪ'praɪv/ vt. ~e of privar de. ~d adj carenciado

depth /depθ/ n profundidad f. be out of one's ~ perder pie; (fig) meterse en honduras. in ~ a fondo

deput|ize /'depjutaɪz/ vi. ~ize for sustituir a. ~y /'depjuti/ n sustituto m. ~y chairman n vicepresidente m

derail /dɪ'reɪl/ vt hacer descarrilar. ~ment n descarrilamiento m

derelict /'derəlɪkt/ adj abandonado y en ruinas

deri|de /dɪ'raɪd/ vt mofarse de.

~sion /dɪˈrɪʒn/ n mofa f. ~sive /dɪˈraɪsɪv/ adj burlón. ~sory /dɪˈraɪsərɪ/ adj (offer etc) irrisorio

deriv|ation /derɪˈveɪʃn/ n derivación f. ~ative /dɪˈrɪvətɪv/ n derivado m. ~e /dɪˈraɪv/ vt/i derivar

derogatory /dɪˈrɒgətrɪ/ adj despectivo

descen|d /dɪˈsend/ vt/i descender, bajar. ~dant n descendiente m & f. ~t n descenso m, bajada f; (lineage) ascendencia f

descri|be /dɪsˈkraɪb/ vt describir. ~ption /-ˈkrɪpʃn/ n descripción f. ~ptive /-ˈkrɪptɪv/ adj descriptivo

desecrate /ˈdesɪkreɪt/ vt profanar

desert¹ /dɪˈzɜːt/ vt abandonar. ● vi (Mil) desertar. ~er /dɪˈzɜːtə(r)/ n desertor m

desert² /ˈdezət/ adj & n desierto (m)

deserts /dɪˈzɜːts/ npl lo merecido. get one's just ~ llevarse su merecido

deserv|e /dɪˈzɜːv/ vt merecer. ~ing adj (cause) meritorio

design /dɪˈzaɪn/ n diseño m; (plan) plan m. ~s (intentions) propósitos mpl. ● vt diseñar; (plan) planear

designate /ˈdezɪgneɪt/ vt designar

designer /dɪˈzaɪnə(r)/ n diseñador m; (fashion ~) diseñador m de modas. ● adj (clothes) de diseño exclusivo

desirable /dɪˈzaɪərəbl/ adj deseable

desire /dɪˈzaɪə(r)/ n deseo m. ● vt desear

desk /desk/ n escritorio m; (at school) pupitre m; (in hotel) recepción f; (Com) caja f. ~top publishing n autoedición f, edición f electrónica

desolat|e /ˈdesələt/ adj desolado; (uninhabited) deshabitado. ~ion /-ˈleɪʃn/ n desolación f

despair /dɪˈspeə(r)/ n desesperación f. be in ~ estar desesperado. ● vi. ~ of desesperarse de

despatch /dɪˈspætʃ/ vt, n see DISPATCH

desperat|e /ˈdespərət/ adj desesperado. ~ely adv desesperadamente. ~ion /-ˈreɪʃn/ n desesperación f

despicable /dɪˈspɪkəbl/ adj despreciable

despise /dɪˈspaɪz/ vt despreciar

despite /dɪˈspaɪt/ prep a pesar de

despondent /dɪˈspɒndənt/ adj abatido

despot /ˈdespɒt/ n déspota m

dessert /dɪˈzɜːt/ n postre m. ~spoon n cuchara f de postre

destination /destɪˈneɪʃn/ n destino m

destiny /ˈdestɪnɪ/ n destino m

destitute /ˈdestɪtjuːt/ adj indigente

destroy /dɪˈstrɔɪ/ vt destruir. ~er n destructor m

destruct|ion /dɪˈstrʌkʃn/ n destrucción f. ~ve /-ɪv/ adj destructivo

desultory /ˈdesəltrɪ/ adj desganado

detach /dɪˈtætʃ/ vt separar. ~able adj separable. ~ed adj (aloof) distante; (house) no adosado. ~ment n desprendimiento m; (Mil) destacamento m; (aloofness) indiferencia f

detail /ˈdiːteɪl/ n detalle m. explain sth in ~ explicar algo detalladamente. ● vt detallar; (Mil) destacar. ~ed adj detallado

detain /dɪˈteɪn/ vt detener; (delay) retener. ~ee /diːteɪˈniː/ n detenido m

detect /dɪˈtekt/ vt percibir; (*discover*) descubrir. **~ive** n (*private*) detective m; (*in police*) agente m & f. **~or** n detector m

detention /dɪˈtenʃn/ n detención f

deter /dɪˈtɜː(r)/ vt (*pt* deterred) disuadir; (*prevent*) impedir

detergent /dɪˈtɜːdʒənt/ adj & n detergente (m)

deteriorat|e /dɪˈtɪəriəreɪt/ vi deteriorarse. **~ion** /-ˈreɪʃn/ n deterioro m

determin|ation /dɪtɜːmɪˈneɪʃn/ n determinación f. **~e** /dɪˈtɜːmɪn/ vt determinar; (*decide*) decidir. **~ed** adj determinado; (*resolute*) decidido

deterrent /dɪˈterənt/ n elemento m de disuasión

detest /dɪˈtest/ vt aborrecer. **~able** adj odioso

detonat|e /ˈdetəneɪt/ vt hacer detonar. • vi detonar. **~ion** /-ˈneɪʃn/ n detonación f. **~or** n detonador m

detour /ˈdiːtʊə(r)/ n rodeo m, (*Amer, of transport*) desvío m, desviación f. • vt (*Amer*) desviar

detract /dɪˈtrækt/ vi. **~ from** disminuir

detriment /ˈdetrɪmənt/ n. to the **~ of** en perjuicio de. **~al** /-ˈmentl/ adj perjudicial

devalue /diːˈvæljuː/ vt desvalorizar

devastat|e /ˈdevəsteɪt/ vt devastar. **~ing** adj devastador; (*fig*) arrollador. **~ion** /-ˈsteɪʃn/ n devastación f

develop /dɪˈveləp/ vt desarrollar; contraer (*illness*); urbanizar (*land*). • vi desarrollarse; (*appear*) surgir. **~ing** adj (*country*) en vías de desarrollo. **~ment** n desarrollo m. (*new*) **~ment** novedad f

deviant /ˈdiːviənt/ adj desviado

deviat|e /ˈdiːvieɪt/ vi desviarse. **~ion** /-ˈeɪʃn/ n desviación f

device /dɪˈvaɪs/ n dispositivo m; (*scheme*) estratagema f

devil /ˈdevl/ n diablo m

devious /ˈdiːviəs/ adj taimado

devise /dɪˈvaɪz/ vt idear

devoid /dɪˈvɔɪd/ adj. be **~ of** carecer de

devolution /diːvəˈluːʃn/ n descentralización f; (*of power*) delegación f

devot|e /dɪˈvəʊt/ vt dedicar. **~ed** adj (*couple*) unido; (*service*) leal. **~ee** /devəˈtiː/ n partidario m. **~ion** /-ʃn/ n devoción f

devour /dɪˈvaʊə(r)/ vt devorar

devout /dɪˈvaʊt/ adj devoto

dew /djuː/ n rocío m

dexterity /dekˈsterəti/ n destreza f

diabet|es /daɪəˈbiːtiːz/ n diabetes f. **~ic** /-ˈbetɪk/ adj & n diabético (m)

diabolical /daɪəˈbɒlɪkl/ adj diabólico

diagnos|e /ˈdaɪəgnəʊz/ vt diagnosticar. **~is** /-ˈnəʊsɪs/ n (*pl* -oses/-siːz/) diagnóstico m

diagonal /daɪˈægənl/ adj & n diagonal (f)

diagram /ˈdaɪəgræm/ n diagrama m

dial /ˈdaɪəl/ n cuadrante m; (*on clock, watch*) esfera f; (*on phone*) disco m. • vt (*pt* dialled) marcar, discar (LAm)

dialect /ˈdaɪəlekt/ n dialecto m

dialling:. ~ code n prefijo m, código m de la zona (LAm). **~ tone** n tono m de marcar, tono m de discado (LAm)

dialogue /ˈdaɪəlɒg/ n diálogo m

dial tone n (Amer) see DIALLING TONE

diameter /daɪˈæmɪtə(r)/ n diámetro m

diamond /ˈdaɪəmənd/ n diamante m; (shape) rombo m. ~s npl (Cards) diamantes mpl

diaper /ˈdaɪəpə(r)/ n (Amer) pañal m

diaphragm /ˈdaɪəfræm/ n diafragma m

diarrhoea /daɪəˈrɪə/ n diarrea f

diary /ˈdaɪərɪ/ n diario m; (book) agenda f

dice /daɪs/ n invar dado m. ● vt (Culin) cortar en cubitos

dictat|e /dɪkˈteɪt/ vt/i dictar. ~ion /dɪkˈteɪʃn/ n dictado m. ~or n dictador m. ~orship n dictadura f

dictionary /ˈdɪkʃənərɪ/ n diccionario m

did /dɪd/ see DO

didn't /ˈdɪdnt/ = did not

die /daɪ/ vi (pres p dying) morir. be dying to morirse por. □ ~ **down** vi irse apagando. □ ~ **out** vi extinguirse

diesel /ˈdiːzl/ n (fuel) gasóleo m. ~ **engine** n motor m diésel

diet /ˈdaɪət/ n alimentación f; (restricted) régimen m. be on a ~ estar a régimen. ● vi estar a régimen

differ /ˈdɪfə(r)/ vi ser distinto; (disagree) no estar de acuerdo. ~ence /ˈdɪfrəns/ n diferencia f; (disagreement) desacuerdo m. ~ent /ˈdɪfrənt/ adj distinto, diferente. ~ently adv de otra manera

difficult /ˈdɪfɪkəlt/ adj difícil. ~y n dificultad f

diffus|e /dɪˈfjuːs/ adj difuso. ● /dɪˈfjuːz/ vt difundir. ● vi difundirse. ~ion /-ʒn/ n difusión f

dig /dɪg/ n (poke) empujón m; (poke with elbow) codazo m; (remark) indirecta f. ~s npl 🛈 alojamiento m ● vt (pt dug, pres p digging) cavar; (thrust) empujar. ● vi cavar. □ ~ **out** vt extraer. □ ~ **up** vt desenterrar

digest /ˈdaɪdʒest/ n resumen m. ● /daɪˈdʒest/ vt digerir. ~ion /-ˈdʒestʃn/ n digestión f. ~ive /-ˈdʒestɪv/ adj digestivo

digger /ˈdɪgə(r)/ n (Mec) excavadora f

digit /ˈdɪdʒɪt/ n dígito m; (finger) dedo m. ~al /ˈdɪdʒɪtl/ adj digital

dignified /ˈdɪgnɪfaɪd/ adj solemne

dignitary /ˈdɪgnɪtərɪ/ n dignatario m

dignity /ˈdɪgnətɪ/ n dignidad f

digress /daɪˈgres/ vi divagar. ~ from apartarse de. ~ion /-ˈʃn/ n digresión f

dike /daɪk/ n dique m

dilapidated /dɪˈlæpɪdeɪtɪd/ adj ruinoso

dilate /daɪˈleɪt/ vt dilatar. ● vi dilatarse

dilemma /daɪˈlemə/ n dilema m

diligent /ˈdɪlɪdʒənt/ adj diligente

dilute /daɪˈljuːt/ vt diluir

dim /dɪm/ adj (dimmer, dimmest) (light) débil; (room) oscuro; (fam, stupid) torpe. ● vt (pt dimmed) atenuar. ~ one's headlights (Amer) poner las (luces) cortas or de cruce, poner las (luces) bajas (LAm). ● vi (light) irse atenuando

dime /daɪm/ n (Amer) moneda de diez centavos

dimension /daɪˈmenʃn/ n dimensión f

diminish /dɪˈmɪnɪʃ/ vt/i disminuir

dimple /ˈdɪmpl/ n hoyuelo m

d

din /dɪn/ n jaleo m

dine /daɪn/ vi cenar. **∼r** n comensal m & f; (*Amer, restaurant*) cafetería f

dinghy /'dɪŋɡɪ/ n bote m; (*inflatable*) bote m neumático

dingy /'dɪndʒɪ/ adj (-ier, -iest) miserable, sucio

dinner /'dɪnə(r)/ n cena f, comida f (*LAm*). **have ∼** cenar, comer (*LAm*). **∼ party** n cena f, comida f (*LAm*)

dinosaur /'daɪnəsɔː(r)/ n dinosaurio m

dint /dɪnt/ n. **by ∼ of** a fuerza de

dip /dɪp/ vt (*pt* dipped) meter; (*in liquid*) mojar. **∼ one's headlights** poner las (luces) cortas or de cruce, poner las (luces) bajas (*LAm*). • vi bajar. • n (*slope*) inclinación f; (*in sea*) baño m. ◻ **∼ into** vt hojear (*book*)

diphthong /'dɪfθɒŋ/ n diptongo m

diploma /dɪ'pləʊmə/ n diploma m

diploma|cy /dɪ'pləʊməsɪ/ n diplomacia f. **∼t** /'dɪpləmæt/ n diplomático m. **∼tic** /-'mætɪk/ adj diplomático

dipstick /'dɪpstɪk/ n (*Auto*) varilla f del nivel de aceite

dire /daɪə(r)/ adj (-er, -est) terrible; (*need, poverty*) extremo

direct /dɪ'rekt/ adj directo. • adv directamente. • vt dirigir; (*show the way*) indicar. **∼ion** /-ʃn/ n dirección f. **∼ions** npl instrucciones fpl. **∼ly** adv directamente; (*at once*) en seguida. • conj 🅴 en cuanto. **∼or** n director m; (*of company*) directivo m

directory /dɪ'rektərɪ/ n guía f; (*Comp*) directorio m

dirt /dɜːt/ n suciedad f. **∼y** adj

(-ier, -iest) sucio. • vt ensuciar

disab|ility /dɪsə'bɪlətɪ/ n invalidez f. **∼le** /dɪs'eɪbl/ vt incapacitar. **∼led** adj minusválido

disadvantage /dɪsəd'vɑːntɪdʒ/ n desventaja f. **∼d** adj desfavorecido

disagree /dɪsə'griː/ vi no estar de acuerdo (**with** con). **∼ with** (*food, climate*) sentarle mal a. **∼able** adj desagradable. **∼ment** n desacuerdo m; (*quarrel*) riña f

disappear /dɪsə'pɪə(r)/ vi desaparecer. **∼ance** n desaparición f

disappoint /dɪsə'pɔɪnt/ vt decepcionar. **∼ing** adj decepcionante. **∼ment** n decepción f

disapprov|al /dɪsə'pruːvl/ n desaprobación f. **∼e** /dɪsə'pruːv/ vi. **∼e of** desaprobar. **∼ing** adj de reproche

disarm /dɪs'ɑːm/ vt desarmar. • vi desarmarse. **∼ament** n desarme m

disarray /dɪsə'reɪ/ n desorden m

disast|er /dɪ'zɑːstə(r)/ n desastre m. **∼rous** /-strəs/ adj catastrófico

disband /dɪs'bænd/ vt disolver. • vi disolverse

disbelief /dɪsbɪ'liːf/ n incredulidad f

disc /dɪsk/ n disco m

discard /dɪs'kɑːd/ vt descartar; abandonar (*beliefs etc*)

discern /dɪ'sɜːn/ vt percibir. **∼ing** adj exigente; (*ear, eye*) educado

discharge /dɪs'tʃɑːdʒ/ vt descargar; cumplir (*duty*); (*Mil*) licenciar. • /'dɪstʃɑːdʒ/ n descarga f; (*Med*) secreción f; (*Mil*) licenciamiento m

disciple /dɪ'saɪpl/ n discípulo m

disciplin|ary /dɪsə'plɪnərɪ/ adj disciplinario. **∼e** /'dɪsɪplɪn/ n disciplina f. • vt disciplinar; (*punish*) sancionar

disc jockey /'dɪskdʒɒkɪ/ n pinchadiscos *m* & *f*

disclaim /dɪsˈkleɪm/ *vt* desconocer. **~er** *n* (*Jurid*) descargo *m* de responsabilidad

disclos|e /dɪsˈkləʊz/ *vt* revelar. **~ure** /-ʒə(r)/ *n* revelación *f*

disco /ˈdɪskəʊ/ *n* (*pl* -os) ① discoteca *f*

discolour /dɪsˈkʌlə(r)/ *vt* decolorar. ● *vi* decolorarse

discomfort /dɪsˈkʌmfət/ *n* malestar *m*; (*lack of comfort*) incomodidad *f*

disconcert /dɪskənˈsɜːt/ *vt* desconcertar

disconnect /dɪskəˈnekt/ *vt* separar; (*Elec*) desconectar

disconsolate /dɪsˈkɒnsələt/ *adj* desconsolado

discontent /dɪskənˈtent/ *n* descontento *m*. **~ed** *adj* descontento

discontinue /dɪskənˈtɪnjuː/ *vt* interrumpir

discord /ˈdɪskɔːd/ *n* discordia *f*; (*Mus*) disonancia *f*. **~ant** /-ˈskɔːdənt/ *adj* discorde; (*Mus*) disonante

discotheque /ˈdɪskətek/ *n* discoteca *f*

discount /ˈdɪskaʊnt/ *n* descuento *m*. ● /dɪsˈkaʊnt/ *vt* hacer caso omiso de; (*Com*) descontar

discourag|e /dɪsˈkʌrɪdʒ/ *vt* desanimar; (*dissuade*) disuadir. **~ing** *adj* desalentador

discourteous /dɪsˈkɜːtɪəs/ *adj* descortés

discover /dɪsˈkʌvə(r)/ *vt* descubrir. **~y** *n* descubrimiento *m*

discredit /dɪsˈkredɪt/ *vt* (*pt* discredited) desacreditar. ● *n* descrédito *m*

discreet /dɪsˈkriːt/ *adj* discreto. **~ly** *adv* discretamente

discrepancy /dɪsˈkrepənsɪ/ *n* discrepancia *f*

discretion /dɪsˈkreʃn/ *n* discreción *f*

discriminat|e /dɪsˈkrɪmɪneɪt/ *vt* discriminar. **~e between** distinguir entre. **~ing** *adj* perspicaz. **~ion** /-ˈneɪʃn/ *n* discernimiento *m*; (*bias*) discriminación *f*

discus /ˈdɪskəs/ *n* disco *m*

discuss /dɪsˈkʌs/ *vt* discutir. **~ion** /-ʃn/ *n* discusión *f*

disdain /dɪsˈdeɪn/ *n* desdén *m*. **~ful** *adj* desdeñoso

disease /dɪˈziːz/ *n* enfermedad *f*

disembark /dɪsɪmˈbɑːk/ *vi* desembarcar

disenchant|ed /dɪsɪnˈtʃɑːntɪd/ *adj* desilusionado. **~ment** *n* desencanto *m*

disentangle /dɪsɪnˈtæŋgl/ *vt* desenredar

disfigure /dɪsˈfɪgə(r)/ *vt* desfigurar

disgrace /dɪsˈgreɪs/ *n* vergüenza *f*. ● *vt* deshonrar. **~ful** *adj* vergonzoso

disgruntled /dɪsˈgrʌntld/ *adj* descontento

disguise /dɪsˈgaɪz/ *vt* disfrazar. ● *n* disfraz *m*. **in ~** disfrazado

disgust /dɪsˈgʌst/ *n* repugnancia *f*, asco *m*. ● *vt* dar asco a. **~ed** *adj* indignado; (*stronger*) asqueado. **~ing** *adj* repugnante, asqueroso

dish /dɪʃ/ *n* plato *m*. **wash** o **do the ~es** fregar los platos, lavar los trastes (*Mex*). **□ ~ up** *vt/i* servir. **~cloth** *n* bayeta *f*

disheartening /dɪsˈhɑːtnɪŋ/ *adj* desalentador

dishonest /dɪsˈɒnɪst/ *adj* deshonesto. **~y** *n* falta *f* de honradez

dishonour /dɪsˈɒnə(r)/ *n* deshonra *f*

dish: ~ **soap** n (Amer) lavavajillas m. ~ **towel** n paño m de cocina. ~**washer** n lavaplatos m, lavavajillas m. ~**washing liquid** n (Amer) see ~ **SOAP**

disillusion /dɪsɪ'lu:ʒn/ vt desilusionar. ~**ment** n desilusión f

disinfect /dɪsɪn'fekt/ vt desinfectar. ~**ant** n desinfectante m

disintegrate /dɪs'ɪntɪgreɪt/ vt desintegrar. ● vi desintegrarse

disinterested /dɪs'ɪntrəstɪd/ adj desinteresado

disjointed /dɪs'dʒɔɪntɪd/ adj inconexo

disk /dɪsk/ n disco m. ~ **drive** (Comp) unidad f de discos. ~**ette** /dɪs'ket/ n disquete m

dislike /dɪs'laɪk/ n aversión f. ● vt. I ~ dogs no me gustan los perros

dislocate /'dɪsləkeɪt/ vt dislocar(se) (limb)

dislodge /dɪs'lɒdʒ/ vt sacar

disloyal /dɪs'lɔɪəl/ adj desleal. ~**ty** n deslealtad f

dismal /'dɪzməl/ adj triste; (bad) fatal

dismantle /dɪs'mæntl/ vt desmontar

dismay /dɪs'meɪ/ n consternación f. ● vt consternar

dismiss /dɪs'mɪs/ vt despedir; (reject) rechazar. ~**al** n despido m; (of idea) rechazo m

dismount /dɪs'maʊnt/ vi desmontar

disobe|dience /dɪsə'bi:dɪəns/ n desobediencia f. ~**dient** adj desobediente. ~**y** /dɪsə'beɪ/ vt/i desobedecer

disorder /dɪs'ɔ:də(r)/ n desorden m; (ailment) afección f. ~**ly** adj desordenado

disorganized /dɪs'ɔ:gənaɪzd/ adj

desorganizado

disorientate /dɪs'ɔ:rɪənteɪt/ vt desorientar

disown /dɪs'əʊn/ vt repudiar

disparaging /dɪs'pærɪdʒɪŋ/ adj despreciativo

dispatch /dɪs'pætʃ/ vt despachar. ● n despacho m. ~ **rider** n mensajero m

dispel /dɪs'pel/ vt (pt **dispelled**) disipar

dispens|able /dɪs'pensəbl/ adj prescindible. ~**e** vt distribuir; (Med) preparar. □ ~ **with** vt prescindir de

dispers|al /dɪs'pɜ:sl/ n dispersión f. ~**e** /dɪs'pɜ:s/ vt dispersar. ● vi dispersarse

dispirited /dɪs'pɪrɪtɪd/ adj desanimado

display /dɪs'pleɪ/ vt exponer (goods); demostrar (feelings). ● n exposición f; (of feelings) demostración f

displeas|e /dɪs'pli:z/ vt desagradar. be ~**ed with** estar disgustado con. ~**ure** /-'pleʒə(r)/ n desagrado m

dispos|able /dɪs'pəʊzəbl/ adj desechable. ~**al** /dɪs'pəʊzl/ n (of waste) eliminación f. at s.o.'s ~**al** a la disposición de uno. ~**e** of /dɪs'pəʊz/ vt deshacerse de

disproportionate /dɪsprə'pɔ:ʃənət/ adj desproporcionado

disprove /dɪs'pru:v/ vt desmentir (claim); refutar (theory)

dispute /dɪs'pju:t/ vt discutir. ● n disputa f. **in** ~ disputado

disqualif|ication /dɪskwɒlɪfɪ'keɪʃn/ n descalificación f. ~**y** /dɪs'kwɒlɪfaɪ/ vt incapacitar; (Sport) descalificar

disregard /dɪsrɪ'gɑ:d/ vt no hacer caso de. ● n indiferencia f (for a)

disreputable /dɪs'repjʊtəbl/ adj de mala fama

disrespect /dɪsrɪ'spekt/ n falta f de respeto

disrupt /dɪs'rʌpt/ vt interrumpir; trastorno (plans). **∼ion** /-ʃn/ n trastorno m. **∼ive** adj (influence) perjudicial, negativo

dissatis|faction /dɪsætɪs'fækʃn/ n descontento m. **∼fied** /dɪ'sætɪsfaɪd/ adj descontento

dissect /dɪ'sekt/ vt disecar

dissent /dɪ'sent/ vi disentir. ● n disentimiento m

dissertation /dɪsə'teɪʃn/ n (Univ) tesis f

dissident /'dɪsɪdənt/ adj & n disidente (m & f)

dissimilar /dɪ'sɪmɪlə(r)/ adj distinto

dissolute /'dɪsəluːt/ adj disoluto

dissolve /dɪ'zɒlv/ vt disolver. ● vi disolverse

dissuade /dɪ'sweɪd/ vt disuadir

distan|ce /'dɪstəns/ n distancia f. from a **∼ce** desde lejos. in the **∼ce** a lo lejos. **∼t** adj distante, lejano; (aloof) distante

distaste /dɪs'teɪst/ n desagrado m. **∼ful** adj desagradable

distil /dɪs'tɪl/ vt (pt distilled) destilar. **∼lery** /dɪs'tɪləri/ n destilería f

distinct /dɪs'tɪŋkt/ adj distinto; (clear) claro; (marked) marcado. **∼ion** /-ʃn/ n distinción f; (in exam) sobresaliente m. **∼ive** adj distintivo

distinguish /dɪs'tɪŋgwɪʃ/ vt/i distinguir. **∼ed** adj distinguido

distort /dɪs'tɔːt/ vt torcer. **∼ion** /-ʃn/ n deformación f

distract /dɪs'trækt/ vt distraer. **∼ed** adj distraído. **∼ion** /-ʃn/ n distracción f; (confusion) aturdimiento m

distraught /dɪs'trɔːt/ adj consternado, angustiado

distress /dɪs'tres/ n angustia f. ● vt afligir. **∼ed** adj afligido. **∼ing** adj penoso

distribut|e /dɪ'strɪbjuːt/ vt repartir, distribuir. **∼ion** /-'bjuːʃn/ n distribución f. **∼or** n distribuidor m; (Auto) distribuidor m (del encendido)

district /'dɪstrɪkt/ n zona f, región f; (of town) barrio m

distrust /dɪs'trʌst/ n desconfianza f. ● vt desconfiar de

disturb /dɪs'tɜːb/ vt molestar; (perturb) inquietar; (move) desordenar; (interrupt) interrumpir. **∼ance** n disturbio m; (tumult) alboroto m. **∼ed** adj trastornado. **∼ing** adj inquietante

disused /dɪs'juːzd/ adj fuera de uso

ditch /dɪtʃ/ n zanja f; (for irrigation) acequia f. ● vt [X] abandonar

dither /'dɪðə(r)/ vi vacilar

ditto /'dɪtəʊ/ adv ídem

divan /dɪ'væn/ n diván m

dive /daɪv/ vi tirarse (al agua), zambullirse; (rush) meterse (precipitadamente). ● n (into water) zambullida f; (Sport) salto m (de trampolín); (of plane) descenso m en picado, descenso m en picada (LAm); ([X], place) antro m. **∼r** n saltador m; (underwater) buzo m

diverge /daɪ'vɜːdʒ/ vi divergir. **∼nt** adj divergente

diverse /daɪ'vɜːs/ adj diverso. **∼ify** vt diversificar. **∼ity** n diversidad f

diver|sion /daɪ'vɜːʃn/ n desvío m; (distraction) diversión f. **∼t** /daɪ'vɜːt/ vt desviar; (entertain) divertir

divide | dock

divide /dɪˈvaɪd/ vt dividir. ● vi dividirse. ~**d highway** n (Amer) autovía f, carretera f de doble pista

dividend /ˈdɪvɪdend/ n dividendo m

divine /dɪˈvaɪn/ adj divino

division /dɪˈvɪʒn/ n división f

divorce /dɪˈvɔːs/ n divorcio m. ● vt divorciarse de. **get** ~**d** divorciarse. ● vi divorciarse. ~**e** /dɪvɔːˈsiː/ n divorciado m

divulge /daɪˈvʌldʒ/ vt divulgar

DIY abbr see **DO-IT-YOURSELF**

dizz|iness /ˈdɪzɪnɪs/ n vértigo m. ~**y** adj (-ier, -iest) mareado. **be** or **feel** ~**y** marearse

DJ abbr see **DISC JOCKEY**

do /duː//dʊ, də/

3rd person singular present **does**; past **did**; past participle **done**

● transitive verb

····▸ hacer. **he does what he wants** hace lo que quiere. **to do one's homework** hacer los deberes. **to do the cooking** preparar la comida, cocinar. **well done!** ¡muy bien!

····▸ (clean) lavar (dishes). limpiar (windows)

····▸ (as job) **what does he do?** ¿en qué trabaja?

····▸ (swindle) estafar. **I've been done!** ¡me han estafado!

····▸ (achieve) **she's done it!** ¡lo ha logrado!

● intransitive verb

····▸ hacer. **do as you're told!** ¡haz lo que se te dice!

····▸ (fare) **how are you doing?**

(with a task) ¿qué tal te va? **how do you do?**, (as greeting) mucho gusto, encantado

····▸ (perform) **she did well/badly** le fue bien/mal

····▸ (be suitable) **will this do?** ¿esto sirve?

····▸ (be enough) ser suficiente, bastar. **one box will do** con una caja basta, con una caja es suficiente

● auxiliary verb

····▸ (to form interrogative and negative) **do you speak Spanish?** ¿hablas español?. **I don't want to** no quiero. **don't shut the door** no cierres la puerta

····▸ (in tag questions) **you eat meat, don't you?** ¿comes carne, ¿verdad? or ¿no? **he lives in London, doesn't he?** vive en Londres, ¿no? or ¿verdad? or ¿no es cierto?

····▸ (in short answers) **do you like it? - yes, I do** ¿te gusta? - sí. **who wrote it? - I did** ¿quién lo escribió? - yo

····▸ (emphasizing) **do come in!** ¡pase Ud!. **you do exaggerate!** ¡cómo exageras! □ **do away with** vt abolir. □ **do in** vt (sl, kill) eliminar. □ **do up** vt abrochar (coat etc); arreglar (house). □ **do with** vt (need) (with can, could) necesitar; (expressing connection) **it has nothing to do with that** no tiene nada que ver con eso. □ **do without** vt prescindir de

docile /ˈdəʊsaɪl/ adj dócil

dock /dɒk/ n (Naut) dársena f; (wharf, quay) muelle m; (Jurid) banquillo m de los acusados. ~**s** npl (port) puerto m. ● vt cortar (tail);

atracar (ship). ● *vi* (ship) atracar. ~**er** *n* estibador *m*. ~**yard** *n* astillero *m*

doctor /ˈdɒktə(r)/ *n* médico *m*, doctor *m*

doctrine /ˈdɒktrɪn/ *n* doctrina *f*

document /ˈdɒkjʊmənt/ *n* documento *m*. ~**ary** /-ˈmentrɪ/ *adj* & *n* documental (*m*)

dodge /dɒdʒ/ *vt* esquivar. ● *vi* esquivarse. ● *n* treta *f*. ~**ems** /ˈdɒdʒəmz/ *npl* autos *mpl* de choque. ~**y** *adj* (-**ier**, -**iest**) (*awkward*) difícil

doe /dəʊ/ *n* (*rabbit*) coneja *f*; (*hare*) liebre *f* hembra; (*deer*) cierva *f*

does /dʌz/ *see* **DO**

doesn't /ˈdʌznt/ = **does not**

dog /dɒg/ *n* perro *m*. ● *vt* (*pt* dogged) perseguir

dogged /ˈdɒgɪd/ *adj* obstinado

doghouse /ˈdɒghaʊs/ *n* (*Amer*) casa *f* del perro. in the ~ 🄳 en desgracia

dogma /ˈdɒgmə/ *n* dogma *m*. ~**tic** /-ˈmætɪk/ *adj* dogmático

doings *npl* actividades *fpl*. ~**it-yourself** /dʊˈɪtjɔːˈself/ *n* bricolaje *m*

dole /dəʊl/ 🄳 subsidio *m* de paro, subsidio *m* de desempleo. on the ~ 🄳 parado, desempleado. □ ~ **out** *vt* distribuir

doleful /ˈdəʊlfl/ *adj* triste

doll /dɒl/ *n* muñeca *f*

dollar /ˈdɒlə(r)/ *n* dólar *m*

dollarization /dɒləraɪˈzeɪʃn/ *n* dolarización *f*

dollop /ˈdɒləp/ *n* 🄳 porción *f*

dolphin /ˈdɒlfɪn/ *n* delfín *m*

domain /dəʊˈmeɪn/ *n* dominio *m*

dome /dəʊm/ *n* cúpula *f*

domestic /dəˈmestɪk/ *adj* doméstico; (*trade, flights, etc*) nacional.

~**ated** /dəˈmestɪkeɪtɪd/ *adj* (animal) domesticado. ~ **science** *n* economía *f* doméstica

dominance /ˈdɒmɪnəns/ *n* dominio *m*. ~**ant** *adj* dominante. ~**ate** /-eɪt/ *vt/i* dominar. ~**ation** /-ˈneɪʃn/ *n* dominación *f*. ~**eering** *adj* dominante

Dominican Republic /də ˈmɪnɪkən/ *n* República *f* Dominicana

dominion /dəˈmɪnjən/ *n* dominio *m*

domino /ˈdɒmɪnəʊ/ *n* (*pl* -**oes**) ficha *f* de dominó. ~**es** *npl* (*game*) dominó *m*

donate /dəʊˈneɪt/ *vt* donar. ~**ion** /-ʃn/ *n* donativo *m*, donación *f*

done /dʌn/ *see* **DO**

donkey /ˈdɒŋkɪ/ *n* burro *m*, asno *m*. ~**'s years** 🄳 siglos *mpl*

donor /ˈdəʊnə(r)/ *n* donante *m* & *f*

don't /dəʊnt/ = **do not**

doodle /ˈduːdl/ *vi/t* garrapatear

doom /duːm/ *n* destino *m*; (*death*) muerte *f*. ● *vt*. be ~**ed** to estar condenado a

door /dɔː(r)/ *n* puerta *f*. ~**bell** *n* timbre *m*. ~ **knob** *n* pomo *m* (de la puerta). ~**mat** *n* felpudo *m*. ~**step** *n* peldaño *m*. ~**way** *n* entrada *f*

dope /dəʊp/ *n* 🄳 droga *f*; (*sl, idiot*) imbécil *m*. ● *vt* 🄳 drogar

dormant /ˈdɔːmənt/ *adj* aletargado, (volcano) inactivo

dormice /ˈdɔːmaɪs/ *see* **DOR-MOUSE**

dormitory /ˈdɔːmɪtrɪ/ *n* dormitorio *m*

dormouse /ˈdɔːmaʊs/ *n* (*pl* -**mice**) lirón *m*

DOS /dɒs/ *abbr* (= disc-operating system) DOS *m*

dos|age /'dəʊsɪdʒ/ n dosis f. **~e** /dəʊs/ n dosis f

dot /dɒt/ n punto m. on the ~ en punto. **~-com** n punto m com. **~-com company** empresa f punto com

dote /dəʊt/ vi. ~ on adorar

dotty /'dɒtɪ/ adj (-ier, -iest) 🛈 chiflado

double /'dʌbl/ adj doble. ● adv el doble. ● n doble m; (person) doble m & f. at the ~ corriendo. ● vt doblar; redoblar (efforts etc). ● vi doblarse. ~ bass /beɪs/ n contrabajo m. ~ bed n cama f de matrimonio, cama f de doa plazas (LAm). ~ chin n papada f. ~ click vt hacer doble clic en. ~-cross /-'krɒs/ vt traicionar. ~-decker /-'dekə(r)/ n autobús m de dos pisos. ~ Dutch n 🛈 chino m. ~ glazing /-'gleɪzɪŋ/ n doble ventana f. ~s npl (tennis) dobles mpl

doubly /'dʌblɪ/ adv doblemente

doubt /daʊt/ n duda f. ● vt dudar; (distrust) dudar de. ~ful adj dudoso. ~less adv sin duda

dough /dəʊ/ n masa f; (sl, money) pasta f 🛈, lana f (LAm fam). ~nut n donut m, dona f (Mex)

dove /dʌv/ n paloma f

down /daʊn/ adv abajo. ~ with abajo. come ~ bajar. go ~ bajar; (sun) ponerse. ● prep abajo. ● adj 🛈 deprimido. ● vt derribar; (fam, drink) beber. ● n (feathers) plumón m. ~ and out adj en la miseria. ~cast adj abatido. ~fall n perdición f; (of king, dictator) caída f. ~-hearted /-'hɑːtɪd/ adj abatido. ~hill /-'hɪl/ adv cuesta abajo. ~load /-'ləʊd/ vt (Comp) bajar. ~market /-'mɑːkɪt/ adj (newspaper) popular; (store) barato. ~payment n depósito m. ~pour n

aguacero m. ~right adj completo. ● adv completamente. ~s npl colinas fpl. ~stairs /-'steəz/ adv abajo. ● /-steəz/ adj de abajo. ~stream adv río abajo. ~-to-earth /-tʊ:ɜ:θ/ adj práctico. ~town /-'taʊn/ n centro m (de la ciudad). ● adv. go ~town ir al centro. ● under adv en las antípodas; (in Australia) en Australia. ~ward /-wəd/ adj & adv, ~wards adv hacia abajo

dowry /'daʊərɪ/ n dote f

Downing Street Es una calle en el barrio londinense de Westminster. El número 10 es la residencia oficial del Primer Ministro y el 11, la del *Chancellor of the Exchequer* (Ministro de Economía y Hacienda). Los periodistas suelen utilizar las expresiones *Downing Street* o *Number 10* para referirse al Primer Ministro y al Gobierno.

doze /dəʊz/ vi dormitar

dozen /'dʌzn/ n docena f. a ~ eggs una docena de huevos. ~s of 🛈 miles de, muchos

Dr /'dɒktə(r)/ abbr (**Doctor**)

drab /dræb/ adj monótono

draft /drɑːft/ n borrador m; (Com) letra f de cambio; (Amer, Mil) reclutamiento m; (Amer, of air) corriente f de aire. ● vt redactar el borrador de; (Amer, conscript) reclutar

drag /dræg/ vt (pt dragged) arrastrar. ● n 🛈 lata f

dragon /'drægən/ n dragón m. ~fly n libélula f

drain /dreɪn/ vt vaciar (tank, glass); drenar (land); (fig) agotar. ● vi escurrirse. ● n (pipe) sumidero m, resumidero m (LAm); (plughole) desagüe m. ~board (Amer), ~ing

board n escurridero m

drama /'drɑːmə/ n drama m; (art) arte m teatral. **~tic** /drə'mætɪk/ adj dramático. **~tist** /'dræmətɪst/ n dramaturgo m. **~tize** /'dræmətaɪz/ vt adaptar al teatro; (fig) dramatizar

drank /dræŋk/ see **DRINK**

drape /dreɪp/ vt cubrir; (hang) colgar. **~s** npl (Amer) cortinas fpl

drastic /'dræstɪk/ adj drástico

draught /drɑːft/ n corriente f de aire. **~ beer** n cerveza f de barril. **~s** npl (game) juego m de damas fpl. **~y** adj lleno de corrientes de aire

draw /drɔː/ vt (pt drew, pp drawn) tirar; (attract) atraer; dibujar (picture); trazar (line). **~ the line** trazar el límite. ● vi (Art) dibujar; (Sport) empatar; **~ near** acercarse. ● n (Sport) empate m; (in lottery) sorteo m. □ **~ in** vi (days) acortarse. □ **~ out** vt sacar (money). □ **~ up** vi pararse. vt redactar (document); acercar (chair). **~back** n desventaja f. **~bridge** n puente m levadizo

drawer /drɔː(r)/ n cajón m, gaveta f (Mex). **~s** npl calzones mpl

drawing /'drɔːɪŋ/ n dibujo m. **~pin** n tachuela f, chincheta f, chinche f. **~ room** n salón m

drawl /drɔːl/ n habla f lenta

drawn /drɔːn/ see **DRAW**

dread /dred/ n terror m. ● vt temer. **~ful** adj terrible. **~fully** adv terriblemente

dream /driːm/ n sueño m. ● vt/i (pt dreamed or dreamt /dremt/) soñar. □ **~ up** vt idear. adj ideal. **~er** n soñador m

dreary /'drɪərɪ/ adj (-ier, -iest) triste; (boring) monótono

dredge /dredʒ/ n draga f. ● vt dragar. **~r** n draga f

dregs /dregz/ npl posos mpl, heces fpl; (fig) hez f

drench /drentʃ/ vt empapar

dress /dres/ n vestido m; (clothing) ropa f. ● vt vestir; (decorate) adornar; (Med) vendar. ● vi vestirse. □ **~ up** vi ponerse elegante. **~ up as** disfrazarse de. **~ circle** n primer palco m

dressing /'dresɪŋ/ n (sauce) aliño m; (bandage) vendaje m. **~-down** /-'daʊn/ n rapapolvo m, reprensión f. **~ gown** n bata f. **~ room** n vestidor m; (in theatre) camarín m. **~ table** n tocador m

dress: ~maker n modista m & f. **~making** n costura f. **~ rehearsal** n ensayo m general

drew /druː/ see **DRAW**

dribble /'drɪbl/ vi (baby) babear; (in football) driblar, driblear

drie|d /draɪd/ adj (food) seco; (milk) en polvo. **~r** /'draɪə(r)/ n secador m

drift /drɪft/ vi ir a la deriva; (snow) amontonarse. ● n (movement) dirección f; (of snow) montón m

drill /drɪl/ n (tool) taladro m; (of dentist) torno m; (training) ejercicio m. ● vt taladrar, perforar; (train) entrenar. ● vi entrenarse

drink /drɪŋk/ vt/i (pt drank, pp drunk) beber, tomar (LAm). ● n bebida f. **~able** adj bebible; (water) potable. **~er** n bebedor m. **~ing water** n agua f potable

drip /drɪp/ vi (pt dripped) gotear. ● n gota f; (Med) goteo m intravenoso; (fam, person) soso m. **~-dry** /-'draɪ/ adj de lava y pon. **~ping** adj. be **~ping** wet estar chorreando

drive /draɪv/ vt (pt drove, pp

driven) conducir, manejar (LAm) (car etc). ~ **s.o. mad** volver loco a uno. ~ **s.o. to do sth** llevar a uno a hacer algo. ● n paseo m; (road) calle f; (private road) camino m de entrada; (fig) empuje m. ~r n conductor m, chofer m (LAm). ~**r's license** n (Amer) see **DRIVING LICENSE**

drivel /'drɪvl/ n tonterías fpl

driving /'draɪvɪŋ/ n conducción f. ~ **licence** n permiso m de conducir, licencia f de conducción (LAm), licencia f (de manejar) (Mex). ~ **test** n examen m de conducir, examen m de manejar (LAm)

drizzle /'drɪzl/ n llovizna f. ● vi lloviznar

drone /drəʊn/ n zumbido m. ● vi zumbar

drool /druːl/ vi babear

droop /druːp/ vi inclinarse; (flowers) marchitarse

drop /drɒp/ n gota f; (fall) caída f; (decrease) descenso m. ● vt (pt dropped) dejar caer; (lower) bajar. ● vi caer. □ ~ **off** vi (sleep) dormirse. □ ~ **out** vi retirarse; (student) abandonar los estudios. ~**out** n marginado m

drought /draʊt/ n sequía f

drove /drəʊv/ see **DRIVE**. ● n manada f

drown /draʊn/ vt ahogar. ● vi ahogarse

drowsy /'draʊzɪ/ adj soñoliento

drudgery /'drʌdʒərɪ/ n trabajo m pesado

drug /drʌg/ n droga f; (Med) medicamento m. ● vt (pt drugged) drogar. ~ **addict** n drogadicto m.

~**gist** n (Amer) farmacéutico m. ~**store** n (Amer) farmacia f (que vende otros artículos también)

drum /drʌm/ n tambor m; (for oil) bidón m. ● vi (pt drummed) tocar el tambor. ● vt. ~ **sth into s.o.** hacerle aprender algo a uno a fuerza de repetírselo. ~**mer** n tambor m; (in group) batería f. ~**s** npl batería f. ~**stick** n baqueta f; (Culin) muslo m

drunk /drʌŋk/ see **DRINK**. ● adj borracho. **get** ~ emborracharse. ● n borracho m. ~**ard** /-ad/ n borracho m. ~**en** adj borracho

dry /draɪ/ adj (drier, driest) seco. ● vt secar. ● vi secarse. □ ~ **up** vi (stream) secarse; (funds) agotarse. ~**-clean** vt limpiar en seco. ~**-cleaner's** tintorería f. ~**er** n see **DRIER**

DTD abbrev **Document Type Definition** DTD m

dual /'djuːəl/ adj doble. ~ **carriageway** n autovía f, carretera f de doble pista

dub /dʌb/ vt (pt dubbed) doblar (film)

dubious /'djuːbɪəs/ adj dudoso; (person) sospechoso

duchess /'dʌtʃɪs/ n duquesa f

duck /dʌk/ n pato m. ● vt sumergir; bajar (head). ● vi agacharse. ~**ling** /'dʌklɪŋ/ n patito m

duct /dʌkt/ n conducto m

dud /dʌd/ adj inútil; (cheque) sin fondos

due /djuː/ adj debido; (expected) esperado. ~ **to** debido a. ● adv. ~ **north** derecho hacia el norte. ~**s** npl derechos mpl

duel /'djuːəl/ n duelo m

duet /dju'et/ n dúo m

duffel, duffle /'dʌfl/: ~ **bag** n bolsa f de lona. ~ **coat** n trenca f

dug /dʌg/ *see* DIG

duke /dju:k/ *n* duque *m*

dull /dʌl/ *adj* (-er, -est) (weather) gris; (colour) apagado; (person, play, etc) pesado; (sound) sordo

dumb /dʌm/ *adj* (-er, -est) mudo; Ⓣ estúpido. □ ~ **down** *vt* reducir el valor intelectual de. ~**found** /dʌmˈfaʊnd/ *vt* pasmar

dummy /ˈdʌmɪ/ *n* muñeco *m*; (of tailor) maniquí *m*; (for baby) chupete *m*. ● *adj* falso. ~ **run** prueba *f*

dump /dʌmp/ *vt* tirar, botar (LAm). ● *n* vertedero *m*; (Mil) depósito *m*; Ⓣ lugar *m* desagradable. **be down in the ~s** estar deprimido

dumpling /ˈdʌmplɪŋ/ *n* bola *f* de masa hervida

Dumpster /ˈdʌmpstə(r)/ *n* (Amer, ®) contenedor *m* (para escombros)

dumpy /ˈdʌmpɪ/ *adj* (-ier, -iest) regordete

dunce /dʌns/ *n* burro *m*

dung /dʌŋ/ *n* (manure) estiércol *m*

dungarees /dʌŋgəˈriːz/ *npl* mono *m*, peto *m*

dungeon /ˈdʌndʒən/ *n* calabozo *m*

dunk /dʌŋk/ *vt* remojar

dupe /dju:p/ *vt* engañar. ● *n* inocentón *m*

duplicat|e /ˈdju:plɪkət/ *adj* & *n* duplicado (*m*). ● /ˈdju:plɪkeɪt/ *vt* duplicar; (on machine) reproducir. ~**ing machine**, ~**or** *n* multicopista *f*

durable /ˈdjʊərəbl/ *adj* durable

duration /djʊˈreɪʃn/ *n* duración *f*

duress /djʊˈres/ *n*. **under ~** bajo coacción

during /ˈdjʊərɪŋ/ *prep* durante

dusk /dʌsk/ *n* anochecer *m*

dust /dʌst/ *n* polvo *m*. ● *vt* quitar el polvo a; (sprinkle) espolvorear

(with con). ~**bin** *n* cubo *m* de la basura, bote *m* de la basura (Mex). ~ **cloth** (Amer), ~**er** *n* trapo *m*. ~**jacket** *n* sobrecubierta *f*. ~**man** /-mən/ *n* basurero *m*. ~**pan** *n* recogedor *m*. ~**y** *adj* (-ier, -iest) polvoriento

Dutch /dʌtʃ/ *adj* holandés. ● *n* (language) holandés *m*. **the ~** (people) los holandeses. ~**man** /-mən/ *m* holandés *m*. ~**woman** *n* holandesa *f*

duty /ˈdju:tɪ/ *n* deber *m*; (tax) derechos *mpl* de aduana. **on ~** de servicio. ~**-free** /-ˈfri:/ *adj* libre de impuestos

duvet /ˈdju:veɪ/ *n* edredón *m*

DVD *abbr* (= digital video disc) DVD *m*

dwarf /dwɔ:f/ *n* (*pl* -s or dwarves) enano *m*

dwell /dwel/ *vi* (*pt* dwelt or dwelled) morar. □ ~ **on** *vt* detenerse en. ~**ing** *n* morada *f*

dwindle /ˈdwɪndl/ *vi* disminuir

dye /daɪ/ *vt* (*pres p* dyeing) teñir. ● *n* tinte *m*

dying /ˈdaɪɪŋ/ *see* DIE

dynamic /daɪˈnæmɪk/ *adj* dinámico. ~**s** *npl* dinámica *f*

dynamite /ˈdaɪnəmaɪt/ *n* dinamita *f*. ● *vt* dinamitar

dynamo /ˈdaɪnəməʊ/ *n* (*pl* -os) dínamo *f*, dínamo *f*, dinamo *m* (LAm), dínamo *m* (LAm)

dynasty /ˈdɪnəstɪ/ *n* dinastía *f*

d

Ee

E abbr (= East) E

each /iːtʃ/ adj cada. ●pron cada uno. ~ **one** cada uno. ~ **other** uno a otro, el uno al otro. **they love** ~ **other** se aman

eager /'iːgə(r)/ adj impaciente; (enthusiastic) ávido. ~**ness** n impaciencia f; (enthusiasm) entusiasmo m

eagle /'iːgl/ n águila f

ear /ɪə(r)/ n oído m; (outer) oreja f; (of corn) espiga f. ~**ache** n dolor m de oído. ~**drum** n tímpano m

earl /ɜːl/ n conde m

early /'ɜːlɪ/ adj (-ier, -iest) temprano; (before expected time) prematuro. ●adv temprano; (ahead of time) con anticipación

earn /ɜːn/ vt ganar; (deserve) merecer

earnest /'ɜːnɪst/ adj serio. **in** ~ **serio**

earnings /'ɜːnɪŋz/ npl ingresos mpl; (Com) ganancias fpl

ear: ~**phone** n audífono m. ~**ring** n pendiente m, arete m (LAm). ~**shot** n. **within** ~**shot** al alcance del oído

earth /ɜːθ/ n tierra f. **the E**~ (planet) la Tierra. ●vt (Elec) conectar a tierra. ~**quake** n terremoto m

earwig /'ɪəwɪg/ n tijereta f

ease /iːz/ n facilidad f; (comfort) tranquilidad f. **at** ~ a gusto; (Mil) en posición de descanso. **ill at** ~ molesto. **with** ~ fácilmente. ●vt calmar; aliviar (pain). ●vi calmarse;

(lessen) disminuir

easel /'iːzl/ n caballete m

easily /'iːzɪlɪ/ adv fácilmente

east /iːst/ n este m. ●adj este, oriental; (wind) del este. ●adv hacia el este.

Easter /'iːstə(r)/ n Semana f Santa; (Relig) Pascua f de Resurrección. ~ **egg** n huevo m de Pascua

east: ~**erly** /-əlɪ/ adj (wind) del este. ~**ern** /-ən/ adj este, oriental. ~**ward** /-wəd/, ~**wards** adv hacia el este

easy /'iːzɪ/ adj (-ier, -iest) fácil. ●adv. **go** ~ **on sth** 🄸 no pasarse con algo. **take it** ~ tomarse las cosas con calma. ●int ¡despacio! ~**chair** n sillón m. ~**going** /-'gəʊɪŋ/ adj acomodadizo

eat /iːt/ vt/i (pt **ate**, pp **eaten**) comer. □ ~ **into** vt corroer. ~**er** n comedor m

eaves /iːvz/ npl alero m. ~**drop** vi (pt -**dropped**). ~**drop (on)** escuchar a escondidas

ebb /eb/ n reflujo m. ●vi bajar; (fig) decaer

ebola /iː'bəʊlə/ n Ébola f

ebony /'ebənɪ/ n ébano m

EC /iː'siː/ abbr (= **European Community**) CE f (Comunidad f Europea)

eccentric /ɪk'sentrɪk/ adj & n excéntrico (m). ~**ity** /eksen'trɪsətɪ/ n excentricidad f

echo /'ekəʊ/ n (pl -**oes**) eco m. ●vi hacer eco

eclipse /ɪ'klɪps/ n eclipse m. ●vt eclipsar

ecolog|ical /iːkə'lɒdʒɪkl/ adj ecológico. ~**y** n ecología f

e-commerce /iː'kɒmɜːs/ n comercio m electrónico

econom|ic /iːkə'nɒmɪk/ adj eco-

nómico; ~ **refugee** refugiado *m*
económico. ~**ical** *adj* económico.
~**ics** /ı/ *n* economía *f*. ~**ist** /ı
'kɒnəmɪst/ *n* economista *m* & *f*.
~**ize** /ı'kɒnəmaɪz/ *vt* economizar.
~**ize on sth** economizar algo. ~**y**
/ı'kɒnəmɪ/ *n* economía *f*

ecsta|sy /'ekstəsɪ/ *n* éxtasis *f*.
~**tic** /ık'stætık/ *adj* extático

Ecuador /'ekwədɔː(r)/ *n* Ecuador
m. ~**ean** /ekwə'dɔːrɪən/ *adj* & *n*
ecuatoriano (*m*)

edge /edʒ/ *n* borde *m*; (*of knife*)
filo *m*; (*of town*) afueras *fpl*. **have
the** ~**e on** 🔲 llevar la ventaja a.
on ~**e** nervioso. ● *vt* ribetear. ● *vi*
avanzar cautelosamente. ~**eways**
adv de lado. ~**y** *adj* nervioso

edible /'edɪbl/ *adj* comestible

edit /'edɪt/ *vt* dirigir (*newspaper*);
preparar una edición de (text);
editar (film). ~**ion** /ı'dɪʃn/ *n* edición *f*.
~**or** *n* (*of newspaper*) director *m*;
(*of text*) redactor *m*. ~**orial** /edɪ
'tɔːrɪəl/ *adj* editorial. ● *n* artículo *m*
de fondo

Edinburgh Festival Es el
principal acontecimiento
cultural británico que, desde
1947, se celebra en agosto, en la
capital de Escocia. El festival atrae
a un gran número de visitantes y
un aspecto muy importante del
mismo son los espectáculos que
no forman parte del programa
oficial, que se conocen como the
Fringe.

educat|e /'edʒʊkeıt/ *vt* educar.
~**ed** *adj* culto. ~**ion** /-'keıʃn/ *n*
educación *f*; (*knowledge, culture*)
cultura *f*. ~**ional** /-'keıʃənl/ *adj* instructivo

EC /i:'si:/ *abbr* (= **European Com-**

mission) CE *f* (Comisión *f* Europea)

eel /i:l/ *n* anguila *f*

eerie /'ɪərɪ/ *adj* (**-ier, -iest**) misterioso

effect /ı'fekt/ *n* efecto *m*. **in** ~
efectivamente. **take** ~ entrar en
vigor. ~**ive** *adj* eficaz; (*striking*) impresionante; (*real*) efectivo.
~**ively** *adv* eficazmente. ~**iveness**
n eficacia *f*

effeminate /ı'femınət/ *adj* afeminado

efficien|cy /ı'fıʃənsɪ/ *n* eficiencia
f; (*Mec*) rendimiento *m*. ~**t** *adj* eficiente. ~**tly** *adv* eficientemente

effort /'efət/ *n* esfuerzo *m*. ~**less**
adj fácil

e.g. /i:'dʒi:/ *abbr* (= **exempli gratia**) p.ej., por ejemplo

egg /eg/ *n* huevo *m*. □ ~ **on** *vt* 🔲
incitar. ~**cup** *n* huevera *f*. ~**plant**
n (*Amer*) berenjena *f*. ~**shell** *n* cáscara *f* de huevo

ego /'i:gəʊ/ *n* (*pl* -**os**) yo *m*. ~**ism**
n egoísmo *m*. ~**ist** *n* egoísta *m* & *f*.
~**centric** /i:gəʊ'sentrık/ *adj* egocéntrico. ~**tism** *n* egoísmo *m*.
~**tist** *n* egotista *m* & *f*

eh /eı/ *int* 🔲 ¡eh!

eiderdown /'aɪdədaʊn/ *n* edredón *m*

eight /eıt/ *adj* & *n* ocho (*m*). ~**een**
/eı'ti:n/ *adj* & *n* dieciocho (*m*).
~**eenth** *adj* decimoctavo. ● *n* dieciochavo *m*. ~**h** /eıtθ/ *adj* & *n* octavo (*m*) ~**ieth** /'eıtıəθ/ *adj* octogésimo. ● *n* ochentavo *m*. ~**y** /'eıtı/
adj & *n* ochenta (*m*)

either /'aɪðə(r)/ *adj* cualquiera de
los dos; (*negative*) ninguno de los
dos; (*each*) cada. ● *pron* uno u otro;
(*with negative*) ni uno ni otro. ● *adv*
(*negative*) tampoco. ● *conj* o. ~

Tuesday or Wednesday o el martes o el miércoles; (with negative) ni el martes ni el miércoles
eject /ɪ'dʒekt/ vt expulsar
eke /iːk/ vt. ~ **out** hacer alcanzar (resources). ~ **out a living** ganarse la vida a duras penas
elaborate /ɪ'læbərət/ adj complicado. • /ɪ'læbəreɪt/ vt elaborar. • /ɪ'læbəreɪt/ vi explicarse
elapse /ɪ'læps/ vi transcurrir
elastic /ɪ'læstɪk/ adj & n elástico (m). ~ **band** n goma f (elástica), liga f (Mex)
elated /ɪ'leɪtɪd/ adj regocijado. ~**ion** /-ʃn/ n regocijo m
elbow /'elbəʊ/ n codo m. • vt dar un codazo a
elder /'eldə(r)/ adj mayor. • n mayor m & f; (tree) saúco m. ~**ly** /'eldəlɪ/ adj mayor, anciano
eldest /'eldɪst/ adj & n mayor (m & f)
elect /ɪ'lekt/ vt elegir. ~ **to do** decidir hacer. • adj electo. ~**ion** /-ʃn/ n elección f. ~**or** n elector m. ~**oral** adj electoral. ~**orate** /-ət/ n electorado m
electric /ɪ'lektrɪk/ adj eléctrico. ~**al** adj eléctrico. ~ **blanket** n manta f eléctrica. ~**ian** /ɪlek'trɪʃn/ n electricista m & f. ~**ity** /ɪlek 'trɪsətɪ/ n electricidad f
electrify /ɪ'lektrɪfaɪ/ vt electrificar; (fig) electrizar
electrocute /ɪ'lektrəkjuːt/ vt electrocutar
electrode /ɪ'lektrəʊd/ n electrodo m
electron /ɪ'lektrɒn/ n electrón m
electronic /ɪlek'trɒnɪk/ adj electrónico. ~ **mail** n correo m electrónico. ~**s** n electrónica f
elegan|ce /'elɪgəns/ n elegancia f.

~**t** adj elegante. ~**tly** adv elegantemente
element /'elɪmənt/ n elemento m. ~**ary** /-'mentrɪ/ adj elemental. ~**ary school** n (Amer) escuela f primaria
elephant /'elɪfənt/ n elefante m
elevat|e /'elɪveɪt/ vt elevar. ~**ion** /-'veɪʃn/ n elevación f. ~**or** n (Amer) ascensor m
eleven /ɪ'levn/ adj & n once (m). ~**th** adj undécimo. • n onceavo m
elf /elf/ n (pl **elves**) duende m
eligible /'elɪdʒəbl/ adj elegible. be ~ **for** tener derecho a
eliminat|e /ɪ'lɪmɪneɪt/ vt eliminar. ~**ion** /-'neɪʃn/ n eliminación f
élite /eɪ'liːt/ n elite f, élite f
ellip|se /ɪ'lɪps/ n elipse f. ~**tical** adj elíptico
elm /elm/ n olmo m
elope /ɪ'ləʊp/ vi fugarse con el amante
eloquen|ce /'eləkwəns/ n elocuencia f. ~**t** adj elocuente
El Salvador /el'sælvədɔː(r)/ n El Salvador
else /els/ adv. **somebody** ~ otra persona. **everybody** ~ todos los demás. **nobody** ~ ningún otro, nadie más. **nothing** ~ nada más. **or** ~ o bien. **somewhere** ~ en otra parte. ~**where** adv en otra parte
elu|de /ɪ'luːd/ vt eludir. ~**sive** /-sɪv/ adj esquivo
elves /elvz/ see ELF
emaciated /ɪ'meɪʃɪeɪtɪd/ adj consumido
email, e-mail /'iːmeɪl/ n correo m electrónico, correo-e m. • vt mandar por correo electrónico, emailear. ~ **address** n casilla f electrónica, dirección f de correo

electrónico

emancipat|e /ɪˈmænsɪpeɪt/ vt emancipar. **~ion** /-ˈpeɪʃn/ n emancipación f

embankment /ɪmˈbæŋkmənt/ n terraplén m; (of river) dique m

embargo /ɪmˈbɑːɡəʊ/ n (pl -oes) embargo m

embark /ɪmˈbɑːk/ vi embarcarse. **~ on** (fig) emprender. **~ation** /emba:ˈkeɪʃn/ n embarque m

embarrass /ɪmˈbærəs/ vt avergonzar. **~ed** adj avergonzado. **~ing** adj embarazoso. **~ment** n vergüenza f

embassy /ˈembəsɪ/ n embajada f

embellish /ɪmˈbelɪʃ/ vt adornar. **~ment** n adorno m

embers /ˈembəz/ npl ascuas fpl

embezzle /ɪmˈbezl/ vt desfalcar. **~ment** n desfalco m

emblem /ˈembləm/ n emblema m

embrace /ɪmˈbreɪs/ vt abrazar; (fig) abarcar. ● vi abrazarse. ● n abrazo m

embroider /ɪmˈbrɔɪdə(r)/ vt bordar. **~y** n bordado m

embroil /ɪmˈbrɔɪl/ vt enredar

embryo /ˈembrɪəʊ/ n (pl -os) embrión m. **~nic** /-ˈɒnɪk/ adj embrionario

emend /ɪˈmend/ vt enmendar

emerald /ˈemərəld/ n esmeralda f

emerge /ɪˈmɜːdʒ/ vi salir. **~nce** /-əns/ n aparición f

emergency /ɪˈmɜːdʒənsɪ/ n emergencia f; (Med) urgencia f. **in an ~** en caso de emergencia. **~ exit** n salida f de emergencia. **~ room** n urgencias fpl

emigra|nt /ˈemɪɡrənt/ n emigrante m & f. **~te** /ˈemɪɡreɪt/ vi emigrar. **~tion** /-ˈɡreɪʃn/ n

emigración f

eminen|ce /ˈemɪnəns/ n eminencia f. **~t** adj eminente.

emi|ssion /ɪˈmɪʃn/ n emisión f. **~t** vt (pt emitted) emitir

emotio|n /ɪˈməʊʃn/ n emoción f. **~onal** adj emocional; (person) emotivo; (moving) conmovedor. **~ve** /ɪˈməʊtɪv/ adj emotivo

empathy /ˈempəθɪ/ n empatía f

emperor /ˈempərə(r)/ n emperador m

empha|sis /ˈemfəsɪs/ n (pl ~ses /-siːz/) énfasis m. **~size** /ˈemfəsaɪz/ vt enfatizar. **~tic** /ɪmˈfætɪk/ adj (gesture) enfático; (assertion) categórico

empire /ˈempaɪə(r)/ n imperio m

empirical /ɪmˈpɪrɪkl/ adj empírico

employ /ɪmˈplɔɪ/ vt emplear. **~ee** /emplɔɪˈiː/ n empleado m. **~er** n patrón m. **~ment** n empleo m. **~ment agency** n agencia f de trabajo

empower /ɪmˈpaʊə(r)/ vt autorizar (to do a hacer)

empress /ˈempris/ n emperatriz f

empty /ˈemptɪ/ adj vacío; (promise) vano. **on an ~y stomach** con el estómago vacío. ● n 🇬🇧 envase m (vacío). ● vt vaciar. ● vi vaciarse

emulate /ˈemjʊleɪt/ vt emular

emulsion /ɪˈmʌlʃn/ n emulsión f

enable /ɪˈneɪbl/ vt. **~s.o. to do sth** permitir a uno hacer algo

enact /ɪˈnækt/ vt (Jurid) decretar; (in theatre) representar

enamel /ɪˈnæml/ n esmalte m. ● vt (pt enamelled) esmaltar

enchant /ɪnˈtʃɑːnt/ vt encantar. **~ing** adj encantador. **~ment** n encanto m

encircle /ɪnˈsɜːkl/ vt rodear

enclave /'enkleɪv/ n enclave m

enclos|e /ɪn'kləʊz/ vt cercar (land); (Com) adjuntar. ~ed adj (space) cerrado; (Com) adjunto. ~ure /ɪn'kləʊʒə(r)/ n cercamiento m

encode /ɪn'kəʊd/ vt codificar, cifrar

encore /'ɒŋkɔː(r)/ int ¡otra! ● n bis m, repetición f

encounter /ɪn'kaʊntə(r)/ vt encontrar. ● n encuentro m

encourag|e /ɪn'kʌrɪdʒ/ vt animar; (stimulate) fomentar. ~ement n ánimo m. ~ing adj alentador

encroach /ɪn'krəʊtʃ/ vi. ~ on invadir (land); quitar (time)

encyclopaedi|a /ɪnsaɪklə'piːdɪə/ n enciclopedia f. ~c adj enciclopédico

end /end/ n fin m; (furthest point) extremo m. in the ~ por fin. make ~s meet poder llegar a fin de mes. put an ~ to poner fin a. no ~ of muchísimos. on ~ de pie; (consecutive) seguido. ● vt/i terminar, acabar

endanger /ɪn'deɪndʒə(r)/ vt poner en peligro. ~ed adj (species) en peligro

endearing /ɪn'dɪərɪŋ/ adj simpático

endeavour /ɪn'devə(r)/ n esfuerzo m, intento m. ● vi. ~ to esforzarse por

ending /'endɪŋ/ n fin m

endless /'endlɪs/ adj interminable

endorse /ɪn'dɔːs/ vt endosar; (fig) aprobar. ~ment n endoso m; (fig) aprobación f; (Auto) nota f de inhabilitación

endur|ance /ɪn'djʊərəns/ n resistencia f. ~e /ɪn'djʊə(r)/ vt aguantar. ~ing adj perdurable

enemy /'enəmɪ/ n & a enemigo (m)

energ|etic /enə'dʒetɪk/ adj enérgico. ~y /'enədʒɪ/ n energía f. ~y-efficient adj energéticamente eficiente

enforce /ɪn'fɔːs/ vt hacer cumplir (law); hacer valer (claim). ~d adj forzado

engag|e /ɪn'geɪdʒ/ vt emplear (staff); captar (attention); (Mec) hacer engranar. ● vi (Mec) engranar. ~e in dedicarse a. ~ed adj prometido, comprometido (LAm); (busy) ocupado. be ~ed (of phone) estar comunicando, estar ocupado (LAm). get ~ed prometerse, comprometerse (LAm). ~ement n compromiso m

engine /'endʒɪn/ n motor m; (of train) locomotora f. ~ driver n maquinista m

engineer /endʒɪ'nɪə(r)/ n ingeniero m; (mechanic) mecánico m; (Amer, Rail) maquinista m. ● vt (contrive) fraguar. ~ing n ingeniería f

England /'ɪŋglənd/ n Inglaterra f

English /'ɪŋglɪʃ/ adj inglés. ● n (language) inglés m. ● npl. the ~ los ingleses. ~man /-mən/ n inglés m. ~woman n inglesa f

engrav|e /ɪn'greɪv/ vt grabar. ~ing n grabado m

engrossed /ɪn'grəʊst/ adj absorto

engulf /ɪn'gʌlf/ vt envolver

enhance /ɪn'hɑːns/ vt realzar; aumentar (value)

enigma /ɪ'nɪgmə/ n enigma m. ~tic /enɪg'mætɪk/ adj enigmático

enjoy /ɪn'dʒɔɪ/ vt. I ~ reading me gusta la lectura. ~ o.s. divertirse. ~able adj agradable. ~ment n placer m

enlarge /ɪn'lɑːdʒ/ vt agrandar;

(*Photo*) ampliar. ● *vi* agrandarse. ~ upon extenderse sobre. ~ment *n.* (*Photo*) ampliación *f*

enlighten /ɪnˈlaɪtn/ *vt* ilustrar. ~ment *n.* the E~ment el siglo de la luces

enlist /ɪnˈlɪst/ *vt* alistar; conseguir (support). ● *vi* alistarse

enliven /ɪnˈlaɪvn/ *vt* animar

enorm|ity /ɪˈnɔːmətɪ/ *n* enormidad *f.* ~ous /ɪˈnɔːməs/ *adj* enorme. ~ously *adv* enormemente

enough /ɪˈnʌf/ *adj* & *adv* bastante. ● *n* bastante *m*, suficiente *m.* ● *int* ¡basta!

enquir|e /ɪnˈkwaɪə(r)/ *vt/i* preguntar. ~e about informarse de. ~y pregunta *f*; (*investigation*) investigación *f*

enrage /ɪnˈreɪdʒ/ *vt* enfurecer

enrol /ɪnˈrəʊl/ *vt* (*pt* enrolled) inscribir, matricular (student). ● *vi* inscribirse, matricularse

ensue /ɪnˈsjuː/ *vi* seguir

ensure /ɪnˈʃʊə(r)/ *vt* asegurar

entail /ɪnˈteɪl/ *vt* suponer; acarrear (expense)

entangle /ɪnˈtæŋgl/ *vt* enredar. ~ment *n* enredo *m*

enter /ˈentə(r)/ *vt* entrar en, entrar a (*esp LAm*); presentarse a (competition); inscribir en (race); (*write*) escribir. ● *vi* entrar

enterpris|e /ˈentəpraɪz/ *n* empresa *f*; (*fig*) iniciativa *f.* ~ing *adj* emprendedor

entertain /entəˈteɪn/ *vt* entretener; recibir (guests); abrigar (ideas, hopes); (*consider*) considerar. ~ing *adj* entretenido. ~ment *n* entretenimiento *m*; (*show*) espectáculo *m*

enthral /ɪnˈθrɔːl/ *vt* (*pt* enthralled) cautivar

enthuse /ɪnˈθjuːz/ *vi.* ~ over entusiasmarse por

enthusias|m /ɪnˈθjuːzɪæzəm/ *n* entusiasmo *m.* ~t *n* entusiasta *m* & *f.* ~tic /-ˈæstɪk/ *adj* entusiasta. ~tically *adv* con entusiasmo

entice /ɪnˈtaɪs/ *vt* atraer

entire /ɪnˈtaɪə(r)/ *adj* entero. ~ly *adv* completamente. ~ty /ɪnˈtaɪərətɪ/ *n.* in its ~ty en su totalidad

entitle /ɪnˈtaɪtl/ *vt* titular; (*give a right*) dar derecho a. be ~d to tener derecho a. ~ment *n* derecho *m*

entity /ˈentətɪ/ *n* entidad *f*

entrails /ˈentreɪlz/ *npl* entrañas *fpl*

entrance /ˈentrəns/ *n* entrada *f.* ● /ɪnˈtrɑːns/ *vt* encantar

entrant /ˈentrənt/ *n* participante *m* & *f*; (*in exam*) candidato *m*

entreat /ɪnˈtriːt/ *vt* suplicar. ~y *n* súplica *f*

entrenched /ɪnˈtrentʃt/ *adj* (position) afianzado

entrust /ɪnˈtrʌst/ *vt* confiar

entry /ˈentrɪ/ *n* entrada *f*

entwine /ɪnˈtwaɪn/ *vt* entrelazar

enumerate /ɪˈnjuːməreɪt/ *vt* enumerar

envelop /ɪnˈveləp/ *vt* envolver

envelope /ˈenvələʊp/ *n* sobre *m*

enviable /ˈenvɪəbl/ *adj* envidiable

envious /ˈenvɪəs/ *adj* envidioso

environment /ɪnˈvaɪərənmənt/ *n* medio *m* ambiente. ~al /-ˈmentl/ *adj* ambiental

envisage /ɪnˈvɪzɪdʒ/ *vt* prever; (*imagine*) imaginar

envision /ɪnˈvɪʒn/ *vt* (*Amer*) prever

envoy /ˈenvɔɪ/ *n* enviado *m*

envy /ˈenvɪ/ *n* envidia *f.* ● *vt* envidiar

enzyme /ˈenzaɪm/ *n* enzima *f*

ephemeral /ɪˈfemərəl/ *adj*

e

efímero

epic /'epɪk/ n épica f. ● adj épico

epidemic /epɪ'demɪk/ n epidemia f. ● adj epidémico

epilep|sy /'epɪlepsɪ/ n epilepsia f. ~**tic** /-'leptɪk/ adj & n epiléptico (m)

epilogue /'epɪlɒg/ n epílogo m

episode /'epɪsəʊd/ n episodio m

epitaph /'epɪtɑːf/ n epitafio m

epitom|e /ɪ'pɪtəmɪ/ n personificación f, epítome m. ~**ize** vt ser la personificación de

epoch /'iːpɒk/ n época f

equal /'iːkwəl/ adj & n igual (m & f). ~ **to** (a task) a la altura de. ● vt (pt **equalled**) ser igual a; (Math) ser. ~**ity** /ɪ'kwɒlətɪ/ n igualdad f. ~**ize** vt igualar. ● vi (Sport) empatar. ~**izer** n (Sport) gol m del empate. ~**ly** adv igualmente; (share) por igual

equation /ɪ'kweɪʒn/ n ecuación f

equator /ɪ'kweɪtə(r)/ n ecuador m. ~**ial** /ekwə'tɔːrɪəl/ adj ecuatorial

equilibrium /iːkwɪ'lɪbrɪəm/ n equilibrio m

equinox /'iːkwɪnɒks/ n equinoccio m

equip /ɪ'kwɪp/ vt (pt **equipped**) equipar. ~ **sth with** proveer algo de. ~**ment** n equipo m

equivalen|ce /ɪ'kwɪvələns/ n equivalencia f. ~**t** adj & n equivalente (m). be ~**t to** equivaler

equivocal /ɪ'kwɪvəkl/ adj equívoco

era /'ɪərə/ n era f

eradicate /ɪ'rædɪkeɪt/ vt erradicar, extirpar

erase /ɪ'reɪz/ vt borrar. ~**r** n goma f (de borrar)

erect /ɪ'rekt/ adj erguido. ● vt levantar. ~**ion** /-ʃn/ n construcción

f; (physiology) erección f

ero|de /ɪ'rəʊd/ vt erosionar. ~**sion** /-ʒn/ n erosión f

erotic /ɪ'rɒtɪk/ adj erótico

err /ɜː(r)/ vi errar; (sin) pecar

errand /'erənd/ n recado m, mandado m (LAm)

erratic /ɪ'rætɪk/ adj desigual; (person) voluble

erroneous /ɪ'rəʊnɪəs/ adj erróneo

error /'erə(r)/ n error m

erudit|e /'eruːdaɪt/ adj erudito. ~**ion** /-'dɪʃn/ n erudición f

erupt /ɪ'rʌpt/ vi entrar en erupción; (fig) estallar. ~**ion** /-ʃn/ n erupción f

escalat|e /'eskəleɪt/ vt intensificar. ● vi intensificarse. ~**ion** /-'leɪʃn/ n intensificación f. ~**or** n escalera f mecánica

escapade /eskə'peɪd/ n aventura f

escap|e /ɪ'skeɪp/ vi escaparse. ● vt evitar. ● n fuga f; (of gas, water) escape m. **have a narrow** ~**e** escapar por un pelo. ~**ism** /-ɪzəm/ n escapismo m

escort /'eskɔːt/ n acompañante m; (Mil) escolta f ● /ɪ'skɔːt/ vt acompañar; (Mil) escoltar

Eskimo /'eskɪməʊ/ n (pl -**os** or invar) esquimal m & f

especial /ɪ'speʃl/ adj especial. ~**ly** adv especialmente

espionage /'espɪənɑːʒ/ n espionaje m

Esq. /ɪ'skwaɪə(r)/ abbr (= Esquire) (in address) E. Ashton, ~ Sr. Don E. Ashton

essay /'eseɪ/ n ensayo m; (at school) composición f

essence /'esns/ n esencia f. **in** ~ esencialmente

essential /ɪ'senʃl/ adj esencial. ● n elemento m esencial. **~ly** adv esencialmente

establish /ɪ'stæblɪʃ/ vt establecer. **~ment** n establecimiento m. **the E~ment** los que mandan

estate /ɪ'steɪt/ n finca f; (housing estate) complejo m habitacional, urbanización f, fraccionamiento m (Mex); (possessions) bienes mpl. **~ agent** n agente m inmobiliario. **~ car** n ranchera f, (coche m) familiar m, camioneta f (LAm)

esteem /ɪ'stiːm/ n estima f

estimat|e /'estɪmət/ n cálculo m; (Com) presupuesto m. ● /'estɪmeɪt/ vt calcular. **~ion** /-'meɪʃn/ n estimación f; (opinion) opinión f

estranged /ɪs'treɪndʒd/ adj alejado

estuary /'estʃʊərɪ/ n estuario m

etc /et'setrə/ abbr (= et cetera) etc.

etching /'etʃɪŋ/ n aguafuerte m

etern|al /ɪ'tɜːnl/ adj eterno. **~ity** /-ətɪ/ n eternidad f

ether /'iːθə(r)/ n éter m

ethic /'eθɪk/ n ética f. **~al** adj ético. **~s** npl ética f

ethnic /'eθnɪk/ adj étnico

etiquette /'etɪket/ n etiqueta f

etymology /etɪ'mɒlədʒɪ/ n etimología f

EU /iː'juː/ abbr (**European Union**) UE (Unión Europea)

euphemism /'juːfəmɪzəm/ n eufemismo m

euphoria /juː'fɔːrɪə/ n euforia f

euro /'jʊərəʊ/ n euro m

Europe /'jʊərəp/ n Europa f. **~an** /-'pɪən/ adj & n europeo (m). **~an Health Insurance Card** n Tarjeta f Sanitaria Europea. **~an Union** n Unión f Europea

euthanasia /juːθə'neɪzɪə/ n eutanasia f

evacuat|e /ɪ'vækjʊeɪt/ vt evacuar; desocupar (building). **~ion** /-'eɪʃn/ n evacuación f

evade /ɪ'veɪd/ vt evadir

evaluat|e /ɪ'væljʊeɪt/ vt evaluar. **~tion** /-'eɪʃn/ vt evaluación f

evangelical /iːvæn'dʒelɪkl/ adj evangélico

evaporat|e /ɪ'væpəreɪt/ vi evaporarse. **~ion** /-'reɪʃn/ n evaporación f

evasi|on /ɪ'veɪʒn/ n evasión f. **~ve** /ɪ'veɪsɪv/ adj evasivo

eve /iːv/ n víspera f

even /'iːvn/ adj (flat, smooth) plano; (colour) uniforme; (distribution) equitativo; (number) par. **get ~ with** desquitarse con. **~ vt** nivelar. □ **~ up** vt equilibrar. ● adv aun, hasta, incluso. **~ if** aunque. **~ so** aun así. **not ~** ni siquiera

evening /'iːvnɪŋ/ n tarde f; (after dark) noche f. **~ class** n clase f nocturna

event /ɪ'vent/ n acontecimiento m; (Sport) prueba f. **in the ~ of** en caso de. **~ful** adj lleno de acontecimientos

eventual /ɪ'ventʃʊəl/ adj final, definitivo. **~ity** /-'ælətɪ/ n eventualidad f. **~ly** adv finalmente

ever /'evə(r)/ adv (negative) nunca, jamás; (at all times) siempre. **have you ~ been to Greece?** ¿has estado (alguna vez) en Grecia?, **~ after** desde entonces. **~ since** desde entonces. **~ so** 🔲 muy. **for ~** para siempre. **hardly ~** casi nunca. **~green** adj de hoja perenne. ● n árbol m de hoja perenne. **~lasting** adj eterno.

every /'evrɪ/ adj cada, todo. **~**

child todos los niños. ~ one cada uno. ~ other day un día sí y otro no. ~body pron todos, todo el mundo. ~day adj de todos los días. ~one pron todos, todo el mundo. ~thing pron todo. ~where adv (be) en todas partes, (go) a todos lados

evict /ɪˈvɪkt/ vt desahuciar. ~ion /-ʃn/ n desahucio m

eviden|ce /ˈevɪdəns/ n evidencia f; (proof) pruebas fpl; (Jurid) testimonio m; give ~ce prestar declaración. ~ce of señales de. in ~ce visible. ~t adj evidente. ~tly adv evidentemente

evil /ˈiːvl/ adj malvado. ●n mal m

evo|cative /ɪˈvɒkətɪv/ adj evocador. ~ke /ɪˈvəʊk/ vt evocar

evolution /iːvəˈluːʃn/ n evolución f

evolve /ɪˈvɒlv/ vt desarrollar. ●vi evolucionar

ewe /juː/ n oveja f

exact /ɪɡˈzækt/ adj exacto. ●vt exigir (from a). ~ing adj exigente. ~ly adv exactamente

exaggerat|e /ɪɡˈzædʒəreɪt/ vt exagerar. ~ion /-ˈreɪʃn/ n exageración f

exam /ɪɡˈzæm/ n examen m. ~ination /ɪɡzæmɪˈneɪʃn/ n examen m. ~ine /ɪɡˈzæmɪn/ vt examinar; interrogar (witness). ~iner n examinador m

example /ɪɡˈzɑːmpl/ n ejemplo m. for ~ por ejemplo. make an ~ of s.o. darle un castigo ejemplar a uno

exasperat|e /ɪɡˈzæspəreɪt/ vt exasperar. ~ing adj exasperante. ~ion /-ˈreɪʃn/ n exasperación f

excavat|e /ˈekskəveɪt/ vt excavar. ~ion /-ˈveɪʃn/ n excavación f

exceed /ɪkˈsiːd/ vt exceder. ~ingly adv sumamente

excel /ɪkˈsel/ vi (pt excelled) sobresalir. ●vt. ~ o.s. lucirse. ~lence /ˈeksələns/ n excelencia f. ~lent adj excelente

except /ɪkˈsept/ prep menos, excepto. ~ for si no fuera por. ●vt exceptuar. ~ing prep con excepción de

exception /ɪkˈsepʃən/ n excepción f. take ~ to ofenderse por. ~al adj excepcional. ~ally adv excepcionalmente

excerpt /ˈeksɜːpt/ n extracto m

excess /ɪkˈses/ n exceso m. ●/ˈekses/ adj excedente. ~ fare suplemento m. ~ luggage exceso m de equipaje. ~ive adj excesivo

exchange /ɪksˈtʃeɪndʒ/ vt cambiar. ●n intercambio m; (of money) cambio m. (telephone) ~ central f telefónica

excise /ˈeksaɪz/ n impuestos mpl interos. ●/ekˈsaɪz/ vt quitar

excit|able /ɪkˈsaɪtəbl/ adj excitable. ~e /ɪkˈsaɪt/ vt emocionar; (stimulate) excitar. ~ed adj entusiasmado. get ~ed entusiasmarse. ~ement n emoción f; (enthusiasm) entusiasmo m. ~ing adj emocionante

excla|im /ɪkˈskleɪm/ vi/t exclamar. ~mation /ekskləˈmeɪʃn/ n exclamación f. ~mation mark n signo m de admiración f

exclu|de /ɪkˈskluːd/ vt excluir. ~sion /-ʒən/ n exclusión f. ~sive /ɪkˈskluːsɪv/ adj exclusivo; (club) selecto. ~sively adv exclusivamente

excruciating /ɪkˈskruːʃieɪtɪŋ/ adj atroz, insoportable

excursion /ɪkˈskɜːʃn/ n excursión f

excus|able /ɪkˈskjuːzəbl/ adj perdonable. **~e** /ɪkˈskjuːz/ vt perdonar.**~e** from dispensar de. **~e** me! ¡perdón! ● /ɪkˈskjuːs/ n excusa f

ex-directory /eksdɪˈrektərɪ/ adj que no figura en la guía telefónica, privado (Mex)

execut|e /ˈeksɪkjuːt/ vt ejecutar. **~ion** /eksɪˈkjuːʃn/ n ejecución f. **~ioner** n verdugo m

executive /ɪgˈzekjʊtɪv/ adj & n ejecutivo (m)

exempt /ɪgˈzempt/ adj exento (from de). ● vt dispensar. **~ion** /-ʃn/ n exención f

exercise /ˈeksəsaɪz/ n ejercicio m. ● vt ejercer. ● vi hacer ejercicio. **~ book** n cuaderno m

exert /ɪgˈzɜːt/ vt ejercer. **~ o.s.** hacer un gran esfuerzo. **~ion** /-ʃn/ n esfuerzo m

exhale /eksˈheɪl/ vt/i exhalar

exhaust /ɪgˈzɔːst/ vt agotar. ● n (Auto) tubo m de escape. **~ed** adj agotado. **~ion** /-stʃən/ n agotamiento m. **~ive** adj exhaustivo

exhibit /ɪgˈzɪbɪt/ vt exponer; (fig) mostrar. ● n objeto m expuesto; (Jurid) documento m. **~ion** /eksɪˈbɪʃn/ n exposición f. **~ionist** n exhibicionista m & f. **~or** /ɪgˈzɪbɪtə(r)/ n expositor m

exhilarat|ing /ɪgˈzɪləreɪtɪŋ/ adj excitante. **~ion** /-ˈreɪʃn/ n regocijo m

exhort /ɪgˈzɔːt/ vt exhortar

exile /ˈeksaɪl/ n exilio m; (person) exiliado m. ● vt desterrar

exist /ɪgˈzɪst/ vi existir. **~ence** n existencia f. in **~ence** existente

exit /ˈeksɪt/ n salida f

exorbitant /ɪgˈzɔːbɪtənt/ adj exorbitante

exorcis|e /ˈeksɔːsaɪz/ vt exorcizar. **~m** /-sɪzəm/ n exorcismo m. **~t** n exorcista m & f

exotic /ɪgˈzɒtɪk/ adj exótico

expand /ɪkˈspænd/ vt expandir; (develop) desarrollar. ● vi expandirse

expanse /ɪkˈspæns/ n extensión f

expansion /ɪkˈspænʃn/ n expansión f

expatriate /eksˈpætrɪət/ adj & n expatriado (m)

expect /ɪkˈspekt/ vt esperar; (suppose) suponer; (demand) contar con. I **~** so supongo que sí. **~ancy** n esperanza f. life **~ancy** esperanza f de vida. **~ant** adj expectante. **~ant mother** n futura madre f

expectation /ekspekˈteɪʃn/ n expectativa f

expedient /ɪkˈspiːdɪənt/ adj conveniente. ● n expediente m

expedition /ekspɪˈdɪʃn/ n expedición f

expel /ɪkˈspel/ vt (pt expelled) expulsar

expend /ɪkˈspend/ vt gastar. **~able** adj prescindible. **~iture** /-ɪtʃə(r)/ n gastos mpl

expens|e /ɪkˈspens/ n gasto m. at s.o.'s **~e** a costa de uno. **~es** npl (Com) gastos mpl. **~ive** adj caro

experience /ɪkˈspɪərɪəns/ n experiencia f. ● vt experimentar. **~d** adj con experiencia; (driver) experimentado

experiment /ɪkˈsperɪmənt/ n experimento m. ● vi experimentar. **~al** /-ˈmentl/ adj experimental

expert /ˈekspɜːt/ adj & n experto (m). **~ise** /ekspɜːˈtiːz/ n pericia f. **~ly** adv hábilmente

expir|e /ik'spaiǝ(r)/ vi (passport, ticket) caducar; (contract) vencer. **∼y** n vencimiento m, caducidad f

expla|in /ik'splein/ vt explicar. **∼nation** /eksplǝ'neiʃn/ n explicación f. **∼natory** /iks'plænǝtǝri/ adj explicativo

explicit /ik'splisit/ adj explícito

explode /ik'splǝud/ vt hacer explotar. ● vi estallar

exploit /'eksplɔit/ n hazaña f. ● /ik'splɔit/ vt explotar. **∼ation** /eksplɔi'teiʃn/ n explotación f

explor|ation /eksplǝ'reiʃn/ n exploración f. **∼atory** /ik'splɔrǝtri/ adj exploratorio. **∼e** /ik'splɔ:(r)/ vt explorar. **∼er** n explorador m

explosi|on /ik'splǝuʒn/ n explosión f. **∼ve** /-siv/ adj & n explosivo (m)

export /ik'spɔ:t/ vt exportar. ● /'ekspɔ:t/ n exportación f; (item) artículo m de exportación. **∼er** /iks'pɔ:tǝ(r)/ n exportador m

expos|e /ik'spǝuz/ vt exponer; (reveal) descubrir. **∼ure** /-ʒǝ(r)/ n exposición f, die of **∼ure** morir de frío

express /ik'spres/ vt expresar. ● adj expreso; (letter) urgente. ● adv (by express post) por correo urgente. ● n (train) rápido m, expreso m. **∼ion** n expresión f. **∼ive** adj expresivo. **∼ly** adv expresadamente. **∼way** n (Amer) autopista f

expulsion /ik'spʌlʃn/ n expulsión f

exquisite /'ekskwizit/ adj exquisito

exten|d /ik'stend/ vt extender; (prolong) prolongar; ampliar (house). ● vi extenderse. **∼sion** /-ʃn/ n extensión f; (of road, time) prolongación f; (building) anejo m.

∼sive /-siv/ adj extenso. **∼sively** adv extensamente. **∼t** n extensión f; (fig) alcance m. to a certain **∼t** hasta cierto punto

exterior /ik'stiǝriǝ(r)/ adj & n exterior (m)

exterminat|e /ik'stɜ:mineit/ vt exterminar. **∼ion** /-'neiʃn/ n exterminio m

external /ik'stɜ:nl/ adj externo

extinct /ik'stiŋkt/ adj extinto. **∼ion** /-ʃn/ n extinción f

extinguish /ik'stiŋgwiʃ/ vt extinguir. **∼er** n extintor m, extinguidor m (LAm)

extol /ik'stǝul/ vt (pt extolled) alabar

extort /ik'stɔ:t/ vt sacar por la fuerza. **∼ion** /-ʃn/ n exacción f. **∼ionate** /-ǝnat/ adj exorbitante

extra /'ekstrǝ/ adj de más. ● adv extraordinariamente. ● n suplemento m; (Cinema) extra m & f

extract /'ekstrækt/ n extracto m. ● /ik'strækt/ vt extraer. **∼ion** /ik 'strækʃn/ n extracción f

extradit|e /'ekstrǝdait/ vt extraditar. **∼ion** /-'diʃn/ n extradición f

extra:∼ordinary /ik'strɔ:dnri/ adj extraordinario. **∼sensory** /ekstrǝ'sensǝri/ adj extrasensorial

extravagan|ce /ik'strævǝgǝns/ n prodigalidad f; (of gestures, dress) extravagancia f. **∼t** adj pródigo; (behaviour) extravagante. **∼za** n gran espectáculo m

extrem|e /ik'stri:m/ adj & n extremo (m). **∼ely** adv extremadamente. **∼ist** n extremista m & f

extricate /'ekstrikeit/ vt desenredar, librar

extrovert /'ekstrǝvɜ:t/ n extrovertido m

exuberan|ce /ig'zju:bǝrǝns/ n

exude | fair

exuberancia f. ~t adj exuberante

exude /ɪgˈzjuːd/ vt rezumar

exult /ɪgˈzʌlt/ vi exultar. ~ation /egzʌlˈteɪʃn/ n exultación f

eye /aɪ/ n ojo m. keep an ~ on no perder de vista. see ~ to ~ with s.o. estar de acuerdo con uno. ● vt (pt eyed, pres p eyeing) mirar. ~ball n globo m ocular. ~brow n ceja f. ~drops npl colirio m. ~lash n pestaña f. ~lid n párpado m. ~opener n revelación f. ~shadow n sombra f de ojos. ~sight n vista f. ~sore n (fig, fam) monstruosidad f, adefesio m. ~witness n testigo m ocular

Ff

fable /ˈfeɪbl/ n fábula f

fabric /ˈfæbrɪk/ n tejido m, tela f

fabricate /ˈfæbrɪkeɪt/ vt inventar. ~ation /-ˈkeɪʃn/ n invención f

fabulous /ˈfæbjʊləs/ adj fabuloso

facade /fəˈsɑːd/ n fachada f

face /feɪs/ n cara f, rostro m; (of watch) esfera f, carátula f (Mex); (aspect) aspecto m. ~ down(wards) boca abajo. ~ up(wards) boca arriba. in the ~ of frente a. lose ~ quedar mal. pull ~s hacer muecas. ● vt mirar hacia; (house) dar a; (confront) enfrentarse con. ● vi volverse. □ ~ up to vt enfrentarse con. ~ flannel n paño m (para lavarse la cara). ~less adj anónimo. ~ lift n cirugía f estética en la cara

facetious /fəˈsiːʃəs/ adj burlón

facial /ˈfeɪʃl/ adj facial

facile /ˈfæsaɪl/ adj superficial, simplista

facilitate /fəˈsɪlɪteɪt/ vt facilitar

facility /fəˈsɪlɪtɪ/ n facilidad f

fact /fækt/ n hecho m. as a matter of ~, in ~ en realidad, de hecho

faction /ˈfækʃn/ n facción f

factor /ˈfæktə(r)/ n factor m

factory /ˈfæktərɪ/ n fábrica f

factual /ˈfæktʃʊəl/ adj basado en hechos, factual

faculty /ˈfækəltɪ/ n facultad f

fad /fæd/ n manía f, capricho m

fade /feɪd/ vi (colour) desteñirse; (flowers) marchitarse; (light) apagarse; (memory, sound) desvanecerse

fag /fæg/ n (fam, chore) faena f; (sl, cigarette) cigarrillo m, pitillo m

Fahrenheit /ˈfærənhaɪt/ adj Fahrenheit

fail /feɪl/ vi fracasar; (brakes) fallar; (in an exam) suspender, ser reprobado (LAm). he ~ed to arrive no llegó. ● vt suspender, ser reprobado en (LAm) (exam); suspender, reprobar (LAm) (candidate). ● n. without ~ sin falta. ~ing n defecto m. ● prep. ~ing that, ... si eso no resulta.... ~ure /ˈfeɪljə(r)/ n fracaso m

faint /feɪnt/ adj (-er, -est) (weak) débil; (indistinct) indistinto. feel ~ estar mareado. the ~est idea la más remota idea. ● vi desmayarse. ● n desmayo m. ~hearted /-ˈhɑːtɪd/ adj pusilánime, cobarde. ~ly adv (weakly) débilmente; (indistinctly) indistintamente; (slightly) ligeramente

fair /feə(r)/ adj (-er, -est) (just) justo; (weather) bueno; (amount) razonable; (hair) rubio, güero (Mex fam); (skin) blanco. ● adv limpio. ● n feria f. **~-haired** /-'heəd/ adj rubio, güero (Mex fam). **~ly** adv (justly) justamente; (rather) bastante. **~ness** n justicia f. **in all ~ness** sinceramente. **~ play** n juego m limpio. **~ trade** n comercio m justo

fairy /'feərɪ/ n hada f. **~ story**, **~ tale** n cuento m de hadas

faith /feɪθ/ n (trust) confianza f; (Relig) fe f. **~ful** adj fiel. **~fully** adv fielmente. yours **~fully** (in letters) (le saluda) atentamente

fake /feɪk/ n falsificación f; (person) farsante m. ● adj falso. ● vt falsificar

falcon /'fɔːlkən/ n halcón m

Falkland Islands /'fɔːlklənd/ npl. **the Falkland Islands**, **the Falklands** las (Islas) Malvinas

fall /fɔːl/ vi (pt fell, pp fallen) caer; (decrease) bajar. ● n caída f; (Amer, autumn) otoño m; (in price) bajada f. □ **~ apart** vi deshacerse. □ **~ back on** vt recurrir a. □ **~ down** vi (fall) caerse. □ **~ for** vt ▣ enamorarse de (person); dejarse engañar por (trick). □ **~ in** vi (Mil) formar filas. □ **~ off** vi caerse; (diminish) disminuir. □ **~ out** vi (quarrel) reñir (with con); (drop out) caerse; (Mil) romper filas. □ **~ over** vi caerse. vt tropezar con. □ **~ through** vi no salir adelante

fallacy /'fæləsɪ/ n falacia f

fallible /'fælɪbl/ adj falible

fallout /'fɔːlaʊt/ n lluvia f radiactiva. **~ shelter** n refugio m antinuclear

fallow /'fæləʊ/ adj en barbecho

false /fɔːls/ adj falso. **~ alarm** n falsa alarma. **~hood** n mentira f. **~ly** adv falsamente. **~ teeth** npl dentadura f postiza

falsify /'fɔːlsɪfaɪ/ vt falsificar

falter /'fɔːltə(r)/ vi vacilar

fame /feɪm/ n fama f. **~d** adj famoso

familiar /fə'mɪlɪə(r)/ adj familiar. **the name sounds ~** el nombre me suena. **be ~ with** conocer. **~ity** /-'ærætɪ/ n familiaridad f. **~ize** vt familiarizar

family /'fæməlɪ/ n familia f. ● adj de (la) familia, familiar. **~ tree** n árbol m genealógico

famine /'fæmɪn/ n hambre f, hambruna f

famished /'fæmɪʃt/ adj hambriento

famous /'feɪməs/ adj famoso

fan /fæn/ n abanico m; (Mec) ventilador m; (enthusiast) aficionado m; (of group, actor) fan m & f; (of sport, team) hincha m & f. ● vt (pt fanned) abanicar; avivar (interest). □ **~ out** vi desparramarse en forma de abanico

fanatic /fə'nætɪk/ n fanático m. **~al** adj fanático. **~ism** /-sɪzəm/ n fanatismo m

fan belt n correa f de ventilador, banda f del ventilador (Mex)

fanciful /'fænsɪfl/ adj (imaginative) imaginativo; (impractical) extravagante

fancy /'fænsɪ/ n imaginación f; (liking) gusto m. **take a ~ to** tomar cariño a (person); aficionarse a (thing). ● adj de lujo. ● vt (imagine) imaginar; (believe) creer; (fam, want) apetecer a. **~ dress** n disfraz m

fanfare /'fænfeə(r)/ n fanfarria f

fang /fæŋ/ n (of animal) colmillo m; (of snake) diente m

fantasize /'fæntəsaɪz/ vi fantasear

fantastic /fæn'tæstɪk/ adj fantástico

fantasy /'fæntəsɪ/ n fantasía f

far /fɑ:(r)/ adv lejos; (much) mucho. **as ~ as** hasta. **as ~ as I know** que yo sepa. **by ~** con mucho. ● adj (further, furthest or farther, farthest) lejano. **~ away** lejano

farce /fɑ:s/ n farsa f. **~ical** adj ridículo

fare /feə(r)/ n (on bus) precio m del billete, precio m del boleto (LAm); (on train, plane) precio m del billete, precio m del pasaje (LAm); (food) comida f

Far East /fɑ:'ri:st/ n Extremo or Lejano Oriente m

farewell /feə'wel/ int & n adiós (m)

far-fetched /fɑ:'fetʃt/ adj improbable

farm /fɑ:m/ n granja f. ● vt cultivar. □ **~ out** vt encargar (a terceros). ● vi ser agricultor. **~er** n agricultor m, granjero m. **~house** n granja f. **~ing** n agricultura f. **~yard** n corral m

far: **~off** adj lejano. **~-reaching** /fɑ:'ri:tʃɪŋ/ adj trascendental. **~-sighted** /fɑ:'saɪtɪd/ adj (on vision of the future); (Med, Amer) hipermétrope

farther, farthest /'fɑ:ðə(r), 'fɑ:ðəst/ see FAR

fascinat|e /'fæsɪneɪt/ vt fascinar. **~ed** adj fascinado. **~ing** adj fascinante. **~ion** /-'neɪʃn/ n fascinación f

fascis|m /'fæʃɪzəm/ n fascismo m. **~t** adj & n fascista (m & f)

fashion /'fæʃn/ n (manner) manera f; (vogue) moda f. **be in/out of ~** estar de moda/estar pasado de moda. **~able** adj de moda

fast /fɑ:st/ adj (-er, -est) rápido; (clock) adelantado; (secure) fijo; (colours) sólido. ● adv rápidamente; (securely) firmemente. **~ asleep** profundamente dormido. ● vi ayunar. ● n ayuno m

fasten /'fɑ:sn/ vt sujetar; cerrar (case); abrochar (belt etc). ● vi (case) cerrar; (belt etc) cerrarse. **~er**, **~ing** (on box, window) cierre m; (on door) cerrojo m

fat /fæt/ n grasa f. ● adj (fatter, fattest) gordo; (meat) que tiene mucha grasa; (thick) grueso. **get ~** engordar

fatal /'feɪtl/ adj mortal; (fateful) fatídico. **~ity** /fə'tælətɪ/ n muerto m. **~ly** adv mortalmente

fate /feɪt/ n destino m; (one's lot) suerte f. **~d** adj predestinado. **~ful** adj fatídico

father /'fɑ:ðə(r)/ n padre m. **~hood** n paternidad f. **~-in-law** m (pl **~s-in-law**) n suegro m. **~ly** adj paternal

fathom /'fæðəm/ n braza f. ● vt. (out) comprender

fatigue /fə'ti:g/ n fatiga f. ● vt fatigar

fat|ten vt. **~ten (up)** cebar (animal). **~tening** adj que engorda. **~ty** adj graso, grasoso (LAm). ● n 🄵 gordinflón m

fatuous /'fætjʊəs/ adj fatuo

faucet /'fɔ:sɪt/ n (Amer) grifo m, llave f (LAm)

fault /fɔ:lt/ n defecto m; (blame) culpa f; (tennis) falta f; (in geology) falla f. **at ~** culpable. ● vt encontrarle defectos a. **~less** adj impecable. **~y** adj defectuoso

favour /'feɪvə(r)/ n favor m. ● vt favorecer; (support) estar a favor de; (prefer) preferir. **~able** adj favorable. **~ably** adv favorablemente. **~ite** adj & n preferido (m). **~itism** n favoritismo m

fawn /fɔːn/ n cervato m. ● adj beige, beis. ● vi. ~ on adular

fax /fæks/ n fax m. ● vt faxear

fear /fɪə(r)/ n miedo m. ● vt temer. ~ful adj (frightening) espantoso; (frightened) temeroso. ~less adj intrépido. ~some /-səm/ adj espantoso

feasib|ility /fiːzə'bɪlətɪ/ n viabilidad f. ~le /'fiːzəbl/ adj factible; (likely) posible

feast /fiːst/ n (Relig) fiesta f; (meal) banquete m

feat /fiːt/ n hazaña f

feather /'feðə(r)/ n pluma f. ~weight n peso m pluma

feature /'fiːtʃə(r)/ n (on face) rasgo m; (characteristic) característica f; (in newspaper) artículo m; ~ (film) película f principal, largometraje m. ● vt presentar; (give prominence to) destacar

February /'februərɪ/ n febrero m

fed /fed/ see **FEED**

feder|al /'fedərəl/ adj federal. ~ation /-'reɪʃn/ n federación f

fed up adj 🔟 harto (with de)

fee /fiː/ n (professional) honorarios mpl; (enrolment) derechos mpl; (club) cuota f

feeble /'fiːbl/ adj (-er, -est) débil

feed /fiːd/ vt (pt fed) dar de comer a; (supply) alimentar. ● vi comer. ● n (for animals) pienso m; (for babies) comida f. ~back n reacción f

feel /fiːl/ vt (pt felt) sentir; (touch) tocar; (think) considerar. do you ~ it's a good idea? ¿te parece buena idea? ~ as if tener la impresión de que. ~ hot/hungry tener calor/hambre. ~ like (fam, want) tener ganas de. ● n sensación f. get the ~ of sth acostumbrarse a algo. ~er n (of insect) antena f. ~ing n

sentimiento m; (physical) sensación f

feet /fiːt/ see **FOOT**

feign /feɪn/ vt fingir

feint /feɪnt/ n finta f

fell /fel/ see **FALL**. ● vt derribar; talar (tree)

fellow /'feləʊ/ n 🔢 tipo m; (comrade) compañero m; (of society) socio m. ~ countryman n compatriota m. ~ passenger/traveller n compañero m de viaje

felony /'felənɪ/ n delito m grave

felt /felt/ see **FEEL**. ● n fieltro m

female /'fiːmeɪl/ adj hembra; (voice, sex etc) femenino. ● n mujer f; (animal) hembra f

femini|ne /'femənɪn/ adj & n femenino (m). ~nity /-'nɪnətɪ/ n feminidad f. ~st adj & n feminista m & f

fenc|e /fens/ n cerca f, cerco m (LAm). ● vt. ~e (in) encerrar, cercar. ● vi (Sport) practicar la esgrima. ~er n esgrimidor m. ~ing n (Sport) esgrima f

fend /fend/ vi. ~ for o.s. valerse por sí mismo. □ ~ off vt defenderse de

fender /'fendə(r)/ n rejilla f; (Amer, Auto) guardabarros m, salpicadera f (Mex)

ferment /fə'ment/ vt/i fermentar. ~ation /-'teɪʃn/ n fermentación f

fern /fɜːn/ n helecho m

feroci|ous /fə'rəʊʃəs/ adj feroz. ~ty /fə'rɒsətɪ/ n ferocidad f

ferret /'ferɪt/ n hurón m. ● vi (pt ferreted) ~ about husmear. ● vt. ~ out descubrir

ferry /'ferɪ/ n ferry m. ● vt transportar

fertile /'fɜːtaɪl/ adj fértil. ~ity /-'tɪlətɪ/ n fertilidad f. ~ize

fervent | figure

/ˈfɜːtəlaɪz/ vt fecundar, abonar (soil). **~izer** n fertilizante m

ferv|ent /ˈfɜːvənt/ adj ferviente. **~our** /-və(r)/ n fervor m

fester /ˈfestə(r)/ vi enconarse

festival /ˈfestəvl/ n fiesta f; (of arts) festival m

festive /ˈfestɪv/ adj festivo. **the ~e season** n las Navidades. **~ity** /feˈstɪvəti/ n festividad f

fetch /fetʃ/ vt (go for) ir a buscar; (bring) traer; (be sold for) venderse en. **~ing** adj atractivo

fête /feɪt/ n fiesta f. ● vt festejar

fetish /ˈfetɪʃ/ n fetiche m

fetter /ˈfetə(r)/ vt encadenar

feud /fjuːd/ n contienda f

feudal /ˈfjuːdl/ adj feudal. **~ism** n feudalismo m

fever /ˈfiːvə(r)/ n fiebre f. **~ish** adj febril

few /fjuː/ adj pocos. **a ~ houses** algunas casas. ● n pocos mpl. **a ~ unos** (pocos). **a good ~**, **quite a ~** ① muchos. **~er** adj & n menos. **~est** adj el menor número de

fiancé /fiˈɒnseɪ/ n novio m. **~e** /fiˈɒnseɪ/ n novia f

fiasco /fiˈæskəʊ/ n (pl -os) fiasco m

fib /fɪb/ n ① mentirilla f. ● vi ① mentir, decir mentirillas

fibre /ˈfaɪbə(r)/ n fibra f. **~glass** n fibra f de vidrio

fickle /ˈfɪkl/ adj inconstante

ficti|on /ˈfɪkʃn/ n ficción f. (works of) **~** novelas fpl. **~onal** adj novelesco. **~tious** /fɪkˈtɪʃəs/ adj ficticio

fiddle /ˈfɪdl/ n ① violín m; (fam, swindle) trampa f. ● vt falsificar. **~ with** juguetear con

fidget /ˈfɪdʒɪt/ vi (pt fidgeted) moverse, ponerse nervioso. **~ with** juguetear con. ● n persona f inquieta. **~y** adj inquieto

field /fiːld/ n campo m. **~ day** n. have a **~ day** hacer su agosto. **~ glasses** npl gemelos mpl. **F~ Marshal** n mariscal m de campo. **~ trip** n viaje m de estudio. **~work** n investigaciones fpl en el terreno

fiend /fiːnd/ n demonio m. **~ish** adj diabólico

fierce /fɪəs/ adj (-er, -est) feroz; (attack) violento. **~ly** adv (growl) con ferocidad; (fight) con fiereza

fiery /ˈfaɪərɪ/ adj (-ier, -iest) ardiente; (temper) exaltado

fifteen /fɪfˈtiːn/ adj & n quince (m). **~th** adj decimoquinto. ● n quinceavo m

fifth /fɪfθ/ adj & n quinto (m)

fift|ieth /ˈfɪftɪəθ/ adj quincuagésimo. ● n cincuentavo m. **~y** adj & n cincuenta (m). **~y-~y** adv mitad y mitad, a medias. ● adj. **a ~y-~y chance** una posibilidad que de cada dos

fig /fɪg/ n higo m

fight /faɪt/ vi (pt fought) luchar; (quarrel) disputar. ● vt luchar contra. ● n pelea m; (struggle) lucha f; (quarrel) disputa f; (Mil) combate m. **□ ~ back** vi defenderse. **□ ~ off** vt rechazar (attack); luchar contra (illness). **~er** n luchador m; (aircraft) avión m de caza. **~ing** n luchas fpl

figment /ˈfɪgmənt/ n. **~ of the imagination** producto m de la imaginación

figurative /ˈfɪgjʊrətɪv/ adj figurado

figure /ˈfɪgə(r)/ n (number) cifra f; (person) figura f; (shape) forma f; (of woman) tipo m. ● vt imaginar

f

(*Amer fam*, reckon) calcular. • *vi* figurar. that ~s (*fam*) es lógico. □ ~ out *vt* entender. ~head *n* testaferro *m*, mascarón *m* de proa. ~ of speech *n* figura *f* retórica

filch /fɪltʃ/ *vt* [1] hurtar

file /faɪl/ *n* (*tool*, for nails) lima *f*; (*folder*) carpeta *f*; (*set of papers*) expediente *m*; (*Comp*) archivo *m*; (*row*) fila *f*. in single ~ en fila india. • *vt* archivar (papers); limar (metal, nails). • ~ in *vi* entrar en fila. ~ past *vt* desfilar ante

filing cabinet /'faɪlɪŋ/ *n* archivador *m*

fill /fɪl/ *vt* llenar. • *vi* llenarse. • *n*. eat one's ~ hartarse de comer. have had one's ~ of estar harto de. □ ~ in *vt* rellenar (form, hole). □ ~ out *vt* rellenar (form). *vi* (*get fatter*) engordar. □ ~ up *vt* llenar. *vi* llenarse

fillet /'fɪlɪt/ *n* filete *m*. • *vt* (*pt* filleted) cortar en filetes (meat); quitar la espina a (fish)

filling /'fɪlɪŋ/ *n* (in tooth) empaste *m*, tapadura *f* (*Mex*). ~ station *n* gasolinera *f*

film /fɪlm/ *n* película *f*. • *vt* filmar. ~ star *n* estrella *f* de cine

filter /'fɪltə(r)/ *n* filtro *m*. • *vt* filtrar. • *vi* filtrarse. ~-tipped *adj* con filtro

filth /fɪlθ/ *n* mugre *f*. ~y *adj* mugriento

fin /fɪn/ *n* aleta *f*

final /'faɪnl/ *adj* último; (*conclusive*) decisivo. • *n* (*in Sport*) final *f*. ~s *npl* (*Schol*) exámenes *mpl* de fin de curso

finale /fɪ'nɑːlɪ/ *n* final *m*

final|ist *n* finalista *m* & *f*. ~ize *vt* ultimar. ~ly *adv* (*lastly*) finalmente, por fin

financ|e /'faɪnæns/ *n* finanzas *fpl*. • *vt* financiar. ~ial /faɪ'nænʃl/ *adj* financiero; (*difficulties*) económico

find /faɪnd/ *vt* (*pt* found) encontrar. ~ out *vt* descubrir. • *vi* (*learn*) enterarse. ~ings *npl* conclusiones *fpl*

fine /faɪn/ *adj* (-er, -est) (*delicate*) fino; (*excellent*) excelente. • *adv* muy bien. • *n* multa *f*. • *vt* multar. ~ arts *npl* bellas artes *fpl*. ~ly *adv* (*cut*) en trozos pequeños; (*adjust*) con precisión

finger /'fɪŋgə(r)/ *n* dedo *m*. • *vt* tocar. ~nail *n* uña *f*. ~print *n* huella *f* digital. ~tip *n* punta *f* del dedo

finish /'fɪnɪʃ/ *vt/i* terminar, acabar. ~ doing terminar de hacer. • *n* fin *m*; (*of race*) llegada *f*

finite /'faɪnaɪt/ *adj* finito

Fin|land /'fɪnlənd/ *n* Finlandia *f*. ~n *n* finlandés *m*. ~nish *adj* & *n* finlandés (*m*)

fiord /fjɔːd/ *n* fiordo *m*

fir /fɜː(r)/ *n* abeto *m*

fire /faɪə(r)/ *n* fuego *m*; (*conflagration*) incendio *m*. • *vt* disparar (gun); (*dismiss*) despedir; avivar (imagination). • *vi* disparar. ~ alarm *n* alarma *f* contra incendios. ~arm *n* arma *f* de fuego. ~ brigade, ~ department (*Amer*) *n* cuerpo *m* de bomberos. ~ engine *n* coche *m* de bomberos, carro *m* de bomberos (*Mex*). ~escape *n* escalera *f* de incendios. ~ extinguisher *n* extintor *m*, extinguidor *m* (*LAm*). ~fighter *n* bombero *m*. ~man /-mən/ *n* bombero *m*. ~place *n* chimenea *f*. ~side *n* hogar *m*. ~ truck *n* (*Amer*) see ENGINE. ~wood *n* leña *f*. ~work *n* fuego *m* artificial

firm /fɜːm/ *n* empresa *f*. • *adj* (-er,

first | flare

-est) firme. ~ly adv firmemente

first /fɜːst/ adj primero, (before masculine singular noun) primer. at ~ hand directamente. ● n primero m. ● adv primero; (first time) por primera vez. ~ of all primero. ~ aid n primeros auxilios mpl. ~ aid kit n botiquín m. ~ class /-'klɑːs/ adv (travel) en primera clase. ~-class adj de primera clase. ~ floor n primer piso m; (Amer) planta f baja. F~ Lady n (Amer) Primera Dama f. ~ly adv en primer lugar. ~ name n nombre m de pila. ~-rate /-'reɪt/ adj excelente

fish /fɪʃ/ n (pl invar or -es) pez m; (as food) pescado m. ● vi pescar. go ~ing ir de pesca. □ ~ out vt sacar. ~erman n pescador m. ~ing n pesca f. ~ing pole n (Amer), ~ing rod n caña f de pesca. ~monger n pescadero m. ~ shop n pescadería f. ~y adj (smell) a pescado; (fam, questionable) sospechoso

fission /'fɪʃn/ n fisión f

fist /fɪst/ n puño m

fit /fɪt/ adj (fitter, fittest) (healthy) en forma; (good enough) adecuado; (able) capaz. ● n (attack) ataque; (of clothes) corte m. ● vt (pt fitted) (adapt) adaptar; (be the right size for) quedarle bien a; (install) colocar. ● vi encajar. (in certain space) caber; (clothes) quedarle bien a uno. □ ~ in vi caber. ~ful adj irregular. ~ness n salud f; (Sport) (buena) forma f física. ~ting adj apropiado. ● n (of clothes) prueba f. ~ting room n probador m

five /faɪv/ adj & n cinco (m)

fix /fɪks/ vt fijar; (mend, deal with) arreglar. ● n. in a ~ en un aprieto. ~ed adj fijo. ~ture /'fɪkstʃə(r)/ n

(Sport) partido m

fizz /fɪz/ vi burbujear. ● n efervescencia f. ~le /fɪzl/ vi. ~le out fracasar. ~y adj efervescente; (water) con gas

fjord /fjɔːd/ n fiordo m

flabbergasted /'flæbəgɑːstɪd/ adj estupefacto

flabby /'flæbɪ/ adj flojo

flag /flæg/ n bandera f. ● vi (pt flagged) (weaken) flaquear; (conversation) languidecer

flagon /'flægən/ n botella f grande, jarro m

flagpole /'flægpəʊl/ n asta f de bandera

flagrant /'fleɪgrənt/ adj flagrante

flair /fleə(r)/ n don m (for de)

flak|e /fleɪk/ n copo m; (of plant, metal) escama f. ● vi desconcharse. ~y adj escamoso

flamboyant /flæm'bɔɪənt/ adj (clothes) vistoso; (manner) extravagante

flame /fleɪm/ n llama f. go up in ~s incendiarse

flamingo /flə'mɪŋgəʊ/ n (pl -o(e)s) flamenco m

flammable /'flæməbl/ adj inflamable

flan /flæn/ n tartaleta f

flank /flæŋk/ n (of animal) ijada f; (of person) costado m; (Mil, Sport) flanco m

flannel /'flænl/ n franela f; (for face) paño m (para lavarse la cara).

flap /flæp/ vi (pt flapped) ondear; (wings) aletear. ● vt batir (wings); agitar (arms). ● n (cover) tapa f; (of pocket) cartera f; (of table) ala f get into a ~ 🔢 ponerse nervioso

flare /fleə(r)/ n llamarada f; (Mil)

f

bengala f; (in skirt) vuelo m. □ ~ up vi llamear; (fighting) estallar; (person) encolerizarse

flash /flæʃ/ • vi destellar. • vt (aim torch) dirigir; (flaunt) hacer ostentación de. ~ past pasar como un rayo. • n destello m, (Photo) flash m. ~back n escena f retrospectiva. ~light n (Amer, torch) linterna f. ~y adj ostentoso

flask /flɑːsk/ n frasco m; (vacuum flask) termo m

flat /flæt/ adj (flatter, flattest) plano; (tyre) desinflado; (refusal) categórico; (fare, rate) fijo; (Mus) bemol. • adv (Mus) demasiado bajo. ~ out (at top speed) a toda velocidad. • n (rooms) apartamento m, piso m; 🔲 pinchazo m; (Mus) (Auto, esp Amer) bemol m. ~ly adv categóricamente. ~ten vt allanar, aplanar

flatter /ˈflætə(r)/ vt adular. ~ing adj (person) lisonjero; (clothes) favorecedor. ~y n adulación f

flaunt /flɔːnt/ vt hacer ostentación de

flavour /ˈfleɪvə(r)/ n sabor m. • vt sazonar. ~ing n condimento m

flaw /flɔː/ n defecto m. ~less adj perfecto

flea /fliː/ n pulga f

fleck /flek/ n mancha f, pinta f

fled /fled/ see FLEE

flee /fliː/ vi (pt fled) huir. • vt huir de

fleece /fliːs/ n vellón m. • vt 🔲 desplumar

fleet /fliːt/ n flota f; (of cars) parque m móvil

fleeting /ˈfliːtɪŋ/ adj fugaz

Flemish /ˈflemɪʃ/ adj & n flamenco (m)

flesh /fleʃ/ n carne f. in the ~ en persona

flew /fluː/ see FLY

flex /fleks/ vt doblar; flexionar (muscle). • n (Elec) cable m

flexibility /fleksəˈbɪlətɪ/ n flexibilidad f. ~le /ˈfleksəbl/ adj flexible

flexitime /ˈfleksɪtaɪm/, (Amer) **flextime** /ˈflekstaɪm/ n horario m flexible

flick /flɪk/ n golpecito m. • vt dar un golpecito a. □ ~ through vt hojear

flicker /ˈflɪkə(r)/ vi parpadear. • n parpadeo m; (of hope) resquicio m

flies /flaɪz/ npl (on trousers) bragueta f

flight /flaɪt/ n vuelo m; (fleeing) huida f; (of stairs) tramo m de escalera f. take (to) ~ darse a la fuga. ~ attendant n (male) sobrecargo m, aeromozo m (LAm); (female) azafata f, aeromoza f (LAm). ~-deck n cubierta f de vuelo

flimsy /ˈflɪmzɪ/ adj (-ier, -iest) flojo, débil, poco sólido

flinch /flɪntʃ/ vi retroceder (from ante)

fling /flɪŋ/ vt (pt flung) arrojar. • n (love affair) aventura f; (wild time) juerga f

flint /flɪnt/ n pedernal m; (for lighter) piedra f

flip /flɪp/ vt (pt flipped) dar un golpecito a. • n golpecito m. □ ~ through vt hojear

flippant /ˈflɪpənt/ adj poco serio

flipper /ˈflɪpə(r)/ n aleta f

flirt /flɜːt/ vi coquetear. • n (woman) coqueta f; (man) coqueto m

flit /flɪt/ vi (pt flitted) revolotear

float /fləʊt/ vi flotar. • vt hacer flotar; introducir en Bolsa (company).

flock | focus

● n flotador m; (cash) caja f chica

flock /flɒk/ n (of birds) bandada f; (of sheep) rebaño m. ● vi congregarse

flog /flɒg/ vt (pt **flogged**) (beat) azotar; (fam, sell) vender

flood /flʌd/ n inundación f; (fig) avalancha f. ● vt inundar. ● vi (building etc) inundarse; (river) desbordar. ~**light** n foco m. ● vt (pt -**lit**) iluminar (con focos)

floor /flɔː(r)/ n suelo m; (storey) piso m; (for dancing) pista f. ● vt derribar; (baffle) confundir

flop /flɒp/ vi (pt **flopped**) dejarse caer pesadamente; (fam, fail) fracasar. ● n 🖳 fracaso m. ~**py** adj flojo. ● n see ▸**PY DISK**. ~**py disk** n disquete m, floppy (disk) m

floral /ˈflɔːrəl/ adj floral

florid /ˈflɒrɪd/ adj florido

florist /ˈflɒrɪst/ n florista m & f

flounder /ˈflaʊndə(r)/ vi (in water) luchar para mantenerse a flote; (speaker) quedar sin saber qué decir

flour /ˈflaʊə(r)/ n harina f

flourish /ˈflʌrɪʃ/ vi florecer; (business) prosperar. ● vt blandir. ● n ademán m elegante; (in handwriting) rasgo m. ~**ing** adj próspero

flout /flaʊt/ vt burlarse de

flow /fləʊ/ vi fluir; (blood) correr; (hang loosely) caer. ● n flujo m; (stream) corriente f; (of traffic, information) circulación f. ~ **chart** n organigrama m

flower /ˈflaʊə(r)/ n flor f. ● vi florecer, florear (Mex). ~ **bed** n macizo m de flores. ~**y** adj florido

flown /fləʊn/ see **FLY**

flu /fluː/ n gripe f

fluctuat|e /ˈflʌktjʊeɪt/ vi fluctuar. ~**ion** /-ˈeɪʃn/ n fluctuación f

flue /fluː/ n tiro m

fluen|cy /ˈfluːənsɪ/ n fluidez f. ~**t** adj (style) fluido; (speaker) elocuente. be ~**t in** a language hablar un idioma con fluidez. ~**tly** adv con fluidez

fluff /flʌf/ n pelusa f. ~**y** adj (-ier, -iest) velloso

fluid /ˈfluːɪd/ adj & n fluido (m)

flung /flʌŋ/ see **FLING**

fluorescent /flʊəˈresnt/ adj fluorescente

flush /flʌʃ/ vi ruborizarse. ● vt. ~ **the toilet** tirar de la cadena, jalarle a la cadena (LAm). ● n (blush) rubor m

fluster /ˈflʌstə(r)/ vt poner nervioso

flute /fluːt/ n flauta f

flutter /ˈflʌtə(r)/ vi ondear; (bird) revolotear. ● n (of wings) revoloteo m; (fig) agitación f

flux /flʌks/ n flujo m. be in a state of ~ estar siempre cambiando

fly /flaɪ/ vi (pt **flew**, pp **flown**) volar; (passenger) ir en avión; (flag) flotar; (rush) correr. ● vt pilotar, pilotear (LAm) (aircraft); transportar en avión (passengers, goods); izar (flag). ● n mosca f; (of trousers) see **FLIES**. ~**ing** adj volante. ~**ing visit** visita f relámpago. ● n (activity) aviación f. ~**leaf** n guarda f. ~**over** n paso m elevado

foal /fəʊl/ n potro m

foam /fəʊm/ n espuma f. ● vi espumar. ~ **rubber** n goma f espuma, hule m espuma (Mex)

fob /fɒb/ vt (pt **fobbed**). ~ **sth off onto s.o.** (palm off) encajarle algo a uno

focal /ˈfəʊkl/ adj focal

focus /ˈfəʊkəs/ n (pl -**cuses** or -**ci** /-saɪ/) foco m; (fig) centro m. **in ~**

enfocado. **out of ~** desenfocado.
• **vt** (**pt focused**) enfocar (**fig**) concentrar. • **vi** enfocar; (**fig**) concentrarse (**on en**)

fodder /'fɒdə(r)/ **n** forraje **m**

foe /fəʊ/ **n** enemigo **m**

foetus /'fiːtəs/ **n** (**pl -tuses**) feto **m**

fog /fɒg/ **n** niebla **f**

fog|gy **adj** (**-ier, -iest**) nebuloso. **it is ~gy** hay niebla. **~horn** **n** sirena **f** de niebla

foible /'fɔɪbl/ **n** punto **m** débil

foil /fɔɪl/ **vt** (**thwart**) frustrar. • **n** papel **m** de plata

foist /fɔɪst/ **vt** encajar (**on a**)

fold /fəʊld/ **vt** doblar; cruzar (**arms**). • **vi** doblarse; (**fail**) fracasar. • **n** pliegue **m**. (**for sheep**) redil **m**. **~er** **n** carpeta **f**. **~ing** **adj** plegable

foliage /'fəʊlɪɪdʒ/ **n** follaje **m**

folk /fəʊk/ **n** gente **f**. • **adj** popular. **~lore** /-lɔː(r)/ **n** folklore **m**. **~ music** **n** música **f** folklórica. (**modern**) música **f** folk. **~s** **npl** (**one's relatives**) familia **f**

follow /'fɒləʊ/ **vt**/**i** seguir. □ **~ up** **vt** seguir. **~er** **n** seguidor **m**. **~ing** **n** partidarios **mpl**. • **adj** siguiente. • **prep** después de

folly /'fɒlɪ/ **n** locura **f**

fond /fɒnd/ **adj** (**-er, -est**) (**loving**) cariñoso; (**hope**) vivo. **be ~ of s.o.** tener(le) cariño a uno. **be ~ of sth** ser aficionado a algo

fondle /'fɒndl/ **vt** acariciar

fondness /'fɒndnɪs/ **n** cariño **m**; (**for things**) afición **f**

font /fɒnt/ **n** pila **f** bautismal

food /fuːd/ **n** comida **f**. **~ processor** **n** robot **m** de cocina

fool /fuːl/ **n** idiota **m** & **f**. • **vt** engañar. □ **~ about** **vi** hacer payasadas.

~hardy **adj** temerario. **~ish** **adj** tonto. **~ishly** **adv** tontamente. **~ishness** **n** tontería **f**. **~proof** **adj** infalible

foot /fʊt/ **n** (**pl feet**) pie **m**; (**measure**) pie **m** (= 30,48cm); (**of animal, furniture**) pata **f**. **get under s.o.'s feet** estorbar a uno. **on ~** a pie. **on/to one's feet** de pie. **put one's ~ in it** meter la pata. • **vt** pagar (**bill**). **~age** /-ɪdʒ/ **n** (**of film**) secuencia **f**. **~-and-mouth disease** **n** fiebre **f** aftosa. **~ball** **n** (**ball**) balón **m**; (**game**) fútbol **m**; (**American ~ball**) fútbol **m** americano. **~baller** **n** futbolista **m** & **f**. **~bridge** **n** puente **m** para peatones. **~hills** **npl** estribaciones **fpl**. **~hold** **n** punto **m** de apoyo. **~ing** **n** pie **m**. **on an equal ~ing** en igualdad de condiciones. **~lights** **npl** candilejas **fpl**. **~man** /-mən/ **n** lacayo **m**. **~note** **n** nota **f** (**al pie de la página**). **~path** **n** (**in country**) senda **f**; (**in town**) acera **f**, banqueta **f** (**Mex**). **~print** **n** huella **f**. **~step** **n** paso **m**. **~wear** **n** calzado **m**

for /fɔː(r)/**/fə(r)/**
• **preposition**
····▸ (**intended for**) para. **it's ~ my mother** es para mi madre. **she works ~ a multinational** trabaja para una multinacional
····▸ (**on behalf of**) por. **I did it ~ you** lo hice por ti

➡ See entries **para** and **por** for further information

····▸ (**expressing purpose**) para. **I use it ~ washing the car** lo uso para limpiar el coche. **what ~?** ¿para qué? **to go out ~ a meal** salir a comer fuera

····▸ (*in favour of*) a favor de. are you ~ or against the idea? ¿estás a favor o en contra de la idea?

····▸ (*indicating cost, in exchange for*) por. I bought it ~ 30 pounds lo compré por 30 libras. she left him ~ another man lo dejó por otro. thanks ~ everything gracias por todo. what's the Spanish ~ toad? ¿cómo se dice toad' en español?

····▸ (*expressing duration*) he read ~ two hours leyó durante dos horas. how long are you going ~? ¿por cuánto tiempo vas? I've been waiting ~ three hours hace tres horas que estoy esperando, llevo tres horas esperando

····▸ (*in the direction of*) para. the train ~ Santiago el tren para Santiago

● conjunction (*because*) porque, pues (*literary usage*). she left at once, ~ it was getting late se fue en seguida, porque o pues se hacía tarde

forage /ˈfɒrɪdʒ/ vi forrajear. ● n forraje m

forbade /fəˈbæd/ see **FORBID**

forbearance /fɔːˈbeərəns/ n paciencia f

forbid /fəˈbɪd/ vt (pt forbade, pp forbidden) prohibir (s.o. to do a uno hacer). ~ s.o. sth prohibir algo a uno. ~**ding** adj imponente

force /fɔːs/ n fuerza f. by ~ a la fuerza. come into ~ entrar en vigor. the ~s las fuerzas fpl armadas. ● vt forzar; (*compel*) obligar (s.o. to do sth a uno a hacer

algo). ~ on imponer a. ~ open forzar. ~**d** adj forzado. ~**feed** vt alimentar a la fuerza. ~**ful** adj enérgico

forceps /ˈfɔːseps/ n fórceps m

forcibl|e /ˈfɔːsəbl/ adj a la fuerza. ~**y** adv a la fuerza

ford /fɔːd/ n vado m ● vt vadear

fore /fɔː(r)/ adj anterior. ● n. come to the ~ hacerse evidente

forearm /ˈfɔːrɑːm/ n antebrazo m

foreboding /fɔːˈbəʊdɪŋ/ n presentimiento m

forecast /ˈfɔːkɑːst/ vt (pt forecast) pronosticar (weather); prever (result). ● n pronóstico m. weather ~ pronóstico m del tiempo

forecourt /ˈfɔːkɔːt/ n patio m delantero

forefinger /ˈfɔːfɪŋgə(r)/ n (dedo m) índice m

forefront /ˈfɔːfrʌnt/ n vanguardia f. in the ~ a la vanguardia

forego /fɔːˈgəʊ/ vt (pt forewent, pp foregone) see **FORGO**

foregone /ˈfɔːgɒn/ adj. ~ conclusion resultado m previsto

foreground /ˈfɔːgraʊnd/ n. in the ~ en primer plano

forehead /ˈfɒrɪd/ n frente f

foreign /ˈfɒrən/ adj extranjero; (*trade*) exterior; (*travel*) al extranjero, en el extranjero. ~**er** n extranjero m

foreman /ˈfɔːmən/ (pl -men /-mən/) n capataz m

foremost /ˈfɔːməʊst/ adj primero. ● adv. first and ~ ante todo

forerunner /ˈfɔːrʌnə(r)/ n precursor m

foresee /fɔːˈsiː/ vt (pt -saw, pp -seen) prever. ~**able** adj previsible

foresight /ˈfɔːsaɪt/ n previsión f

forest /'fɒrɪst/ n bosque m

forestall /fɔː'stɔːl/ vt (prevent) prevenir; (preempt) anticiparse a

forestry /'fɒrɪstrɪ/ n silvicultura f

foretaste /'fɔːteɪst/ n anticipo m

foretell /fɔː'tel/ vt (pt foretold) predecir

forever /fə'revə(r)/ adv para siempre; (always) siempre

forewarn /fɔː'wɔːn/ vt advertir

forewent /fɔː'went/ see FOREGO

foreword /'fɔːwɜːd/ n prefacio m

forfeit /'fɔːfɪt/ n (penalty) pena f; (in game) prenda f. ● vt perder; perder el derecho a (property)

forgave /fə'geɪv/ see FORGIVE

forge /fɔːdʒ/ n fragua f. ● vt fraguar; (copy) falsificar. □~ ahead vi adelantarse rápidamente. ~r n falsificador m. ~ry n falsificación f

forget /fə'get/ vt (pt forgot, pp forgotten) olvidar, olvidarse de. ● vi olvidarse (about de). I forgot se me olvidó. ~ful adj olvidadizo

forgive /fə'gɪv/ vt (pt forgave, pp forgiven) perdonar. ~ s.o. for sth perdonar algo a uno. ~ness n perdón m

forgo /fɔː'gəʊ/ vt (pt forwent, pp forgone) renunciar a

fork /fɔːk/ n tenedor m; (for digging) horca f; (in road) bifurcación f. ● vi (road) bifurcarse. □~ out vt 🄐 desembolsar, aflojar 🄐. ~lift truck n carretilla f elevadora

forlorn /fə'lɔːn/ adj (hope, attempt) desesperado; (smile) triste

form /fɔːm/ n forma f; (document) formulario m; (Schol) clase f. ● vt formar. ● vi formarse

formal /'fɔːml/ adj formal; (person) formalista; (dress) de etiqueta. ~ity /-'mælətɪ/ n formalidad f ~ly adv oficialmente

format /'fɔːmæt/ n formato m. ● vt (pt formatted) (Comp) formatear

formation /fɔː'meɪʃn/ n formación f

former /'fɔːmə(r)/ adj anterior; (first of two) primero. ● n. the ~ el primero m, la primera f, los primeros mpl, las primeras fpl. ~ly adv antes

formidable /'fɔːmɪdəbl/ adj formidable

formula /'fɔːmjʊlə/ n (pl -ae /-iː/ or -as) fórmula f. ~te /-leɪt/ vt formular

forsake /fə'seɪk/ vt (pt forsook, pp forsaken) abandonar

fort /fɔːt/ n fuerte m

forth /fɔːθ/ adv. and so ~ y así sucesivamente. ~coming /-'kʌmɪŋ/ adj próximo, venidero; (sociable) comunicativo. ~right adj directo. ~with /-'wɪθ/ adv inmediatamente

fortieth /'fɔːtɪɪθ/ adj cuadragésimo. ● n cuadragésima parte f

fortnight /'fɔːtnaɪt/ n quince días mpl, quincena f. ~ly adj bimensual. ● adv cada quince días

fortress /'fɔːtrɪs/ n fortaleza f

fortunate /'fɔːtʃənət/ adj afortunado. be ~ tener suerte. ~ly adv afortunadamente

fortune /'fɔːtʃuːn/ n fortuna f. ~-teller n adivino m

forty /'fɔːtɪ/ adj & n cuarenta (m). ~ winks un sueñecito

forum /'fɔːrəm/ n foro m

forward /'fɔːwəd/ adj (movement) hacia adelante; (advanced) precoz; (pert) impertinente. ● n (Sport) delantero m. ● adv adelante. go ~ avanzar. ● vt hacer seguir (letter); enviar (goods). ~s adv adelante

forwent /fɔː'went/ see FORGO

fossil /'fɒsl/ adj & n fósil (m)

foster | free

foster /'fɒstə(r)/ vt (promote) fomentar; criar (child). ~ **child** n hijo m adoptivo

fought /fɔːt/ see **FIGHT**

foul /faʊl/ adj (-er, -est) (smell) nauseabundo; (weather) pésimo; (person) asqueroso; (dirty) sucio; (language) obsceno. ●n (Sport) falta f. ●vt contaminar; (entangle) enredar. ~ **play** n (Sport) jugada f sucia; (crime) delito m

found /faʊnd/ see **FIND**. ●vt fundar.

foundation /faʊn'deɪʃn/ n fundación f; (basis) fundamento. (cosmetic) base f (de maquillaje). ~**s** npl (of building) cimientos mpl

founder /'faʊndə(r)/ n fundador m. ●vi (ship) hundirse

fountain /'faʊntɪn/ n fuente f. ~ **pen** n pluma f (estilográfica) f, estilográfica f

four /fɔː(r)/ adj & n cuatro (m). ~**fold** adj cuádruple. ●adv cuatro veces. ~**some** /-səm/ n grupo m de cuatro personas ~**teen** /'fɔːtiːn/ adj & n catorce (m). ~**teenth** adj & n decimocuarto (m). ~**th** /fɔːθ/ adj & n cuarto (m). ~**-wheel drive** n tracción f integral

fowl /faʊl/ n ave f

fox /fɒks/ n zorro m, zorra f. ●vt ⚠ confundir

foyer /'fɔɪeɪ/ n (of theatre) foyer m; (of hotel) vestíbulo m

fraction /'frækʃn/ n fracción f,

fracture /'fræktʃə(r)/ n fractura f. ●vt fracturar. ●vi fracturarse

fragile /'frædʒaɪl/ adj frágil

fragment /'frægmənt/ n fragmento m. ~**ary** /-ərɪ/ adj fragmentario

fragran|ce /'freɪɡrəns/ n fragan-

cia f. ~**t** adj fragante

frail /freɪl/ adj (-er, -est) frágil

frame /freɪm/ n (of picture, door, window) marco m; (of spectacles) montura f; (fig, structure) estructura f. ●vt enmarcar (picture); formular (plan, question); (fam, incriminate unjustly) incriminar falsamente. ~**work** n estructura f; (context) marco m

France /frɑːns/ n Francia f

frank /fræŋk/ adj franco. ●vt franquear. ~**ly** adv francamente

frantic /'fræntɪk/ adj frenético. ~ **with** loco de

fratern|al /frə'tɜːnl/ adj fraternal. ~**ity** /frə'tɜːnɪtɪ/ n fraternidad f; (club) asociación f. ~**ize** /'frætənaɪz/ vi fraternizar

fraud /frɔːd/ n fraude m; (person) impostor m. ~**ulent** /-jʊlənt/ adj fraudulento

fraught /frɔːt/ adj (tense) tenso. ~ **with** cargado de

fray /freɪ/ n riña f

freak /friːk/ n fenómeno m; (monster) monstruo m. ●adj anormal. ~**ish** adj anormal

freckle /'frekl/ n peca f. ~**d** adj pecoso

free /friː/ adj (freer /'friːə(r)/, freest /'friːɪst/) libre; (gratis) gratuito. ~ **of charge** gratis. ●vt (pt freed) (set at liberty) poner en libertad; (relieve from) liberar (from/ of de); (untangle) desenredar. ~**dom** n libertad f. ~**hold** n propiedad f absoluta. ~ **kick** n tiro m libre. ~**lance** adj & adv por cuenta propia. ~**ly** adv libremente. ~**mason** n masón m. ~**-range** adj (eggs) de granja. ~ **speech** n libertad f de expresión. ~**style** n estilo m libre. ~**way** n (Amer) autopista f

freeze /friːz/ vt (pt **froze**, pp **frozen**) helar; congelar (food, wages). • vi helarse; (become motionless) quedarse inmóvil. • n (on wages, prices) congelación f. ~**er** n congelador m. ~**ing** adj glacial. • n. ~**ing** (point) punto m de congelación f. below ~**ing** bajo cero

freight /freɪt/ n (goods) mercancías fpl. ~**er** n buque m de carga

French /frentʃ/ adj francés. • n (language) francés m. • npl. the ~ (people) los franceses. ~ **fries** npl patatas fpl fritas, papas fpl fritas (LAm). ~**man** /-mən/ n francés m. ~ **window** n puerta f ventana. ~**woman** n francesa f

frenz|ied /frenzɪd/ adj frenético. ~**y** n frenesí m

frequency /friːkwənsɪ/ n frecuencia f

frequent /frɪˈkwent/ vt frecuentar. • /friːkwənt/ adj frecuente. ~**ly** adv frecuentemente

fresh /freʃ/ adj (-er, -est) fresco; (different, additional) nuevo; (water) dulce. ~**en** vi refrescar. □ ~**en up** vi (person) refrescarse. ~**er** n ⇒**MAN**. ~**ly** adv recientemente. ~**man** /-mən/ estudiante m de primer año. ~**ness** n frescura f

fret /fret/ vi (pt **fretted**) preocuparse. ~**ful** adj (discontented) quejoso; (irritable) irritable

friction /frɪkʃn/ n fricción f

Friday /ˈfraɪdeɪ/ n viernes m

fridge /frɪdʒ/ n ⇒ frigorífico m, nevera f, refrigerador m (LAm)

fried /fraɪd/ see **FRY**. • adj frito

friend /frend/ n amigo m. ~**liness** n simpatía f. ~**ly** adj (-ier, -iest) simpático. ~**ship** n amistad f

fries /fraɪz/ npl see **FRENCH FRIES**

frieze /friːz/ n friso m

frigate /ˈfrɪɡət/ n fragata f

fright /fraɪt/ n miedo m; (shock) susto m. ~**en** vt asustar. □ ~ **off** vt ahuyentar. ~**ened** adj asustado. be ~**ened** tener miedo (of de.) ~**ful** adj espantoso, horrible. ~**fully** adv terriblemente

frigid /ˈfrɪdʒɪd/ adj frígido

frill /frɪl/ n volante m, olán m (Mex). ~**s** npl (fig) adornos mpl. with no ~**s** sencillo

fringe /frɪndʒ/ n (sewing) fleco m; (ornamental border) franja f; (of hair) flequillo m, cerquillo m (LAm), fleco m (Mex); (of area) periferia f; (of society) margen m

fritter /ˈfrɪtə(r)/ vt. □ ~ **away** vt desperdiciar (time); malgastar (money)

frivol|ity /frɪˈvɒlətɪ/ n frivolidad f. ~**ous** /ˈfrɪvələs/ adj frívolo

fro /frəʊ/ see **TO AND FRO**

frock /frɒk/ n vestido m

frog /frɒg/ n rana f. have a ~ in one's throat tener carraspera. ~**man** /-mən/ n hombre m rana. ~**spawn** n huevos mpl de rana

frolic /ˈfrɒlɪk/ vi (pt **frolicked**) retozar

from /frɒm/ /frəm/ prep de; (indicating starting point) desde; (habit, conviction) por; ~ **then on** a partir de ahí

front /frʌnt/ n parte f delantera; (of building) fachada f; (of clothes) delantera f; (Mil, Pol) frente f; (of book) principio m; (fig, appearance) apariencia f; (seafront) paseo m marítimo, malecón m (LAm). in ~ of delante de. • adj delantero; (first) primero. ~**al** adj frontal; (attack) de frente. ~ **door** n puerta f principal

frontier /ˈfrʌntɪə(r)/ n frontera f

front page n (of newspaper) primera plana f

frost /frɒst/ n (freezing) helada f; (frozen dew) escarcha f. ~**bite** n congelación f. ~**bitten** adj congelado. ~**ed** adj (glass) esmerilado. ~**ing** n (Amer) glaseado m. ~**y** adj (weather) helado; (night) de helada; (fig) glacial

froth /frɒθ/ n espuma f. • vi espumar. ~**y** adj espumoso

frown /fraʊn/ vi fruncir el entrecejo • n ceño m. □ ~ **on** vt desaprobar.

froze /frəʊz/ see FREEZE. ~**n** /'frəʊzn/ see FREEZE. • adj congelado; (region) helado

frugal /'fruːɡl/ adj frugal

fruit /fruːt/ n (in botany) fruto m; (as food) fruta f. ~**ful** /'fruːtfl/ adj fértil; (fig) fructífero. ~**ion** /fruː'ɪʃn/ n. come to ~ verse realizarse. ~**less** adj infructuoso. ~ **salad** n macedonia f de frutas. ~**y** adj que sabe a fruta

frustrat|e /frʌ'streɪt/ vt frustrar. ~**ion** /-ʃn/ n frustración f. ~**ed** adj frustrado. ~**ing** adj frustrante

fry /fraɪ/ vt (pt fried) freír. • vi freírse. ~**ing pan** n sartén f, sartén m (LAm)

fudge /fʌdʒ/ n dulce m de azúcar

fuel /'fjuːəl/ n combustible m

fugitive /'fjuːdʒɪtɪv/ adj & n fugitivo (m)

fulfil /fʊl'fɪl/ vt (pt fulfilled) cumplir (con) (promise, obligation); satisfacer (condition); hacer realidad (ambition). ~**ment** n (of promise, obligation) cumplimiento m; (of conditions) satisfacción f; (of hopes, plans) realización f

full /fʊl/ adj (-er, -est) lleno; (bus, hotel) completo; (account) deta-

llado. at ~ speed a máxima velocidad. be ~ (up) (with food) no poder más. • n. in ~ sin quitar nada. to the ~ completamente. write in ~ escribir con todas las letras. ~**back** n (Sport) defensa m & f. ~**-blown** /fʊl'bləʊn/ adj verdadero. ~**-fledged** /-'fledʒd/ adj (Amer) see FULLY-FLEDGED. ~ **moon** n luna f llena. ~**-scale** /-'skeɪl/ adj (drawing) de tamaño natural; (fig) amplio. ~ **stop** n punto m. ~**-time** adj (employment) de jornada completa. • /-'taɪm/ adv a tiempo completo. ~**y** adv completamente. ~**-fledged** /-'fledʒd/ adj (chick) capaz de volar; (lawyer, nurse) hecho y derecho

fulsome /'fʊlsəm/ adj excesivo

fumble /'fʌmbl/ vi buscar (a tientas)

fume /fjuːm/ vi despedir gases; (fig, be furious) estar furioso. ~**s** npl gases mpl

fumigate /'fjuːmɪgeɪt/ vt fumigar

fun /fʌn/ n (amusement) diversión f; (merriment) alegría f. for ~ en broma. have ~ divertirse. make ~ of burlarse de

function /'fʌŋkʃn/ n (purpose, duty) función f; (reception) recepción f • vi funcionar. ~**al** adj funcional

fund /fʌnd/ n fondo m. • vt financiar

fundamental /fʌndə'mentl/ adj fundamental. ~**ist** adj & n fundamentalista (m & f)

funeral /'fjuːnərəl/ n entierro m, funerales mpl. ~ **director** n director m de pompas fúnebres

funfair /'fʌnfeə(r)/ n feria f; (permanent) parque m de atracciones, parque m de diversiones (LAm)

fungus /'fʌŋgəs/ n (pl -gi/-gaɪ/) hongo m

funnel /'fʌnl/ n (for pouring) embudo m; (of ship) chimenea f

funn|ily /'fʌnɪlɪ/ adv (oddly) curiosamente. ~y adj (-ier, -iest) divertido, gracioso; (odd) curioso, raro

fur /fɜ:(r)/ n pelo m; (pelt) piel f

furious /'fjʊərɪəs/ adj furioso. ~ly adv furiosamente

furlough /'fɜːləʊ/ n (Amer) permiso m. on ~ de permiso

furnace /'fɜːnɪs/ n horno m

furnish /'fɜːnɪʃ/ vt amueblar, amoblar (LAm); (supply) proveer. ~ings npl muebles mpl, mobiliario m

furniture /'fɜːnɪtʃə(r)/ n muebles mpl, mobiliario m. a piece of ~ un mueble

furrow /'fʌrəʊ/ n surco m

furry /'fɜːrɪ/ adj peludo

furthe|r /'fɜːðə(r)/ adj más lejano; (additional) nuevo. ● adv más lejos; (more) además. ● vt fomentar. ~rmore adv además. ~st adj más lejano. ● adv más lejos

furtive /'fɜːtɪv/ adj furtivo

fury /'fjʊərɪ/ n furia f

fuse /fju:z/ vt (melt) fundir; (fig, unite) fusionar. ~ the lights fundir los plomos. ● vi fundirse; (fig) fusionarse. ● n fusible m, plomo m; (of bomb) mecha f. ~box n caja f de fusibles

fuselage /'fju:zəlɑ:ʒ/ n fuselaje m

fusion /'fju:ʒn/ n fusión f

fuss /fʌs/ n (commotion) jaleo m. kick up a ~ armar un lío, armar una bronca. make a ~ of tratar con mucha atención. ● vi preocuparse. ~y adj (-ier, -iest) (finicky) remilgado; (demanding) exigente

futile /'fju:taɪl/ adj inútil, vano. ~ity /fju:'tɪlətɪ/ n inutilidad f

futur|e /'fju:tʃə(r)/ adj futuro. ● n futuro m. in ~e de ahora en adelante. ~istic /fju:tʃə'rɪstɪk/ adj futurista

fuzz /fʌz/ n pelusa f. ~y adj (hair) crespo; (photograph) borroso

Gg

gab /gæb/ n. have the gift of the ~ tener un pico de oro

gabardine /gæbə'di:n/ n gabardina f

gabble /'gæbl/ vi hablar atropelladamente

gable /'geɪbl/ n aguilón m

gad /gæd/ vi (pt gadded). ~ about callejear

gadget /'gædʒɪt/ n chisme m

Gaelic /'geɪlɪk/ adj & n gaélico (m)

gaffe /gæf/ n plancha f, metedura f de pata, metida f de pata (LAm)

gag /gæg/ n mordaza f; (joke) chiste m. ● vt (pt gagged) amordazar. ● vi hacer arcadas

gaiety /'geɪətɪ/ n alegría f

gaily /'geɪlɪ/ adv alegremente

gain /geɪn/ vt ganar; (acquire) adquirir; (obtain) conseguir. ● vi (clock) adelantar. ● n ganancia f; (increase) aumento m

gait /geɪt/ n modo m de andar

gala /'gɑ:lə/ n fiesta f. ~ performance (función f de) gala f

galaxy /'gæləksɪ/ n galaxia f

gale /geɪl/ n vendaval m

gall /gɔ:l/ n bilis f; (fig) hiel f; (impudence) descaro m

gallant /'gælənt/ adj (brave) va-

gall bladder | garish

liente; (*chivalrous*) galante. ~**ry** n valor m

gall bladder /'gɔːlblædə(r)/ n vesícula f biliar

gallery /'gælərɪ/ n galería f

galley /'gælɪ/ n (*ship*) galera f; (*ship's kitchen*) cocina f ~ (**proof**) n galerada f

gallivant /'gælɪvænt/ vi 🄸 callejear

gallon /'gælən/ n galón m (*imperial* = 4,546l; *Amer* = 3,785l)

gallop /'gæləp/ n galope m. ●vi (pt galloped) galopar

gallows /'gæləʊz/ n horca f

galore /gə'lɔː(r)/ adj en abundancia

galvanize /'gælvənaɪz/ vt galvanizar

gambl|e /'gæmbl/ vi jugar. ~**e on** contar con. ●vt jugarse. ●n (*venture*) empresa f arriesgada; (*bet*) apuesta f; (*risk*) riesgo m. ~**er** n jugador m. ~**ing** n juego m

game /geɪm/ n juego m; (*match*) partido m; (*animals, birds*) caza f. ●adj valiente. ~ **for** listo para. ~**keeper** n guardabosque m. ~**s** n (*in school*) deportes mpl

gammon /'gæmən/ n jamón m fresco

gamut /'gæmət/ n gama f

gander /'gændə(r)/ n ganso m

gang /gæŋ/ n pandilla f; (*of workmen*) equipo m. ~**master** n contratista de mano de obra indocumentada. □ ~ **up** vi unirse (on contra)

gangling /'gæŋglɪŋ/ adj larguirucho

gangrene /'gæŋgriːn/ n gangrena f

gangster /'gæŋstə(r)/ n bandido m, gángster m & f

gangway /'gæŋweɪ/ n pasillo m; (*of ship*) pasarela f

gaol /dʒeɪl/ n cárcel f. ~**er** n carcelero m

gap /gæp/ n espacio m; (*in fence, hedge*) hueco m; (*in time*) intervalo m; (*in knowledge*) laguna f; (*difference*) diferencia f

---

gap year En Gran Bretaña, es el periodo, entre el final de los estudios secundarios y el ingreso a la universidad, que muchos estudiantes destinan a obtener experiencia laboral relacionada con sus futuras carreras. Otros emprenden actividades no relacionadas con los estudios y para algunos es la oportunidad para ahorrar dinero o viajar.

i

g

---

gap|e /geɪp/ vi quedarse boquiabierto; (*be wide open*) estar muy abierto. ~**ing** adj abierto; (*person*) boquiabierto

garage /'gærɑːʒ/ n garaje m, garage m (LAm), cochera f (Mex); (*petrol station*) gasolinera f; (*for repairs, sales*) taller m, garage m (LAm)

garbage /'gɑːbɪdʒ/ n basura f. ~ **can** n (*Amer*) cubo m de la basura, bote m de la basura (Mex). ~ **collector**, ~ **man** n (*Amer*) basurero m

garble /'gɑːbl/ vt tergiversar, embrollar

garden /'gɑːdn/ n (*of flowers*) jardín m; (*of vegetables/fruit*) huerto m. ●vi trabajar en el jardín. ~**er** /'gɑːdnə(r)/ n jardinero m. ~**ing** n jardinería f; (*vegetable growing*) horticultura f

gargle /'gɑːgl/ vi hacer gárgaras

gargoyle /'gɑːgɔɪl/ n gárgola f

garish /'geərɪʃ/ adj chillón

garland /'gɑːlənd/ n guirnalda f

garlic /'gɑːlɪk/ n ajo m

garment /'gɑːmənt/ n prenda f (de vestir)

garnish /'gɑːnɪʃ/ vt adornar, decorar. ● n adorno m

garret /'gærət/ n buhardilla f

garrison /'gærɪsn/ n guarnición f

garrulous /'gærələs/ adj hablador

garter /'gɑːtə(r)/ n liga f

gas /gæs/ n (pl gases) gas m; (anaesthetic) anestésico m; (Amer, petrol) gasolina f. ● vt (pt gassed) asfixiar con gas

gash /gæʃ/ n tajo m. ● vt hacer un tajo de

gasket /'gæskɪt/ n junta f

gas: ~ **mask** n careta f antigás. ~ **meter** n contador m de gas

gasoline /'gæsəliːn/ n (Amer) gasolina f

gasp /gɑːsp/ vi jadear; (with surprise) dar un grito ahogado. ● n exclamación f, grito m

gas: ~ **ring** n hornillo m de gas. ~ **station** n (Amer) gasolinera f

gastric /'gæstrɪk/ adj gástrico

gate /geɪt/ n puerta f; (of metal) verja f; (barrier) barrera f

gate: ~**crash** vt colarse en. ~**crasher** n intruso m (que ha entrado sin ser invitado). ~**way** n puerta f

gather /'gæðə(r)/ vt reunir (people, things); (accumulate) acumular; (pick up) recoger; recoger (flowers); (fig, infer) deducir; (sewing) fruncir. ~ **speed** acelerar. ● vi (people) reunirse; (things) acumularse. ~**ing** n reunión f

gaudy /'gɔːdɪ/ adj (-ier, -iest) chillón

gauge /geɪdʒ/ n (measurement)

medida f; (Rail) entrevía f; (instrument) indicador m. ● vt medir; (fig) estimar

gaunt /gɔːnt/ adj descarnado; (from illness) demacrado

gauntlet /'gɔːntlɪt/ n. run the ~ of aguantar el acoso de

gauze /gɔːz/ n gasa f

gave /geɪv/ see GIVE

gawky /'gɔːkɪ/ adj (-ier, -iest) torpe

gawp /gɔːp/ vi. ~ at mirar como un tonto

gay /geɪ/ adj (-er, -est) (fam, homosexual) homosexual, gay 🄵; (dated, joyful) alegre

gaze /geɪz/ vi. ~ (at) mirar (fijamente). ● n mirada f (fija)

gazelle /gə'zel/ n (pl invar or -s) gacela f

GB abbr see GREAT BRITAIN

gear /gɪə(r)/ n equipo m; (Tec) engranaje m; (Auto) marcha f, cambio m. in ~ engranado. out of ~ desengranado. change ~, shift ~ (Amer) cambiar de marcha. ● vt adaptar. ~**box** n (Auto) caja f de cambios

geese /giːs/ see GOOSE

gel /dʒel/ n gel m

gelatine /'dʒelətiːn/ n gelatina f

gelignite /'dʒelɪgnaɪt/ n gelignita f

gem /dʒem/ n piedra f preciosa

Gemini /'dʒemɪnaɪ/ n Géminis mpl

gender /'dʒendə(r)/ n género m

gene /dʒiːn/ n gen m, gene m

genealogy /dʒiːnɪ'ærlədʒɪ/ n genealogía f

general /'dʒenərəl/ adj general. ● n general m. in ~ en general. ~ **election** n elecciones fpl generales. ~**ization** /-'zeɪʃn/ n generalización

f. ~**ize** *vt/i* generalizar. ~ **knowledge** *n* cultura *f* general. ~**ly** *adv* generalmente. ~ **practitioner** *n* médico *m* de cabecera

generat|e /'dʒenəreɪt/ *vt* generar. ~**ion** /-'reɪʃn/ *n* generación *f*. ~**ion gap** *n* brecha *f* generacional. ~**or** *n* generador *m*

genero|sity /dʒenə'rɒsəti/ *n* generosidad *f*. ~**us** /'dʒenərəs/ *adj* generoso; (*plentiful*) abundante

genetic /dʒɪ'netɪk/ *adj* genético. ~**s** *n* genética *f*

Geneva /dʒɪ'niːvə/ *n* Ginebra *f*

genial /'dʒiːnɪəl/ *adj* simpático, afable

genital /'dʒenɪtl/ *adj* genital. ~**s** *npl* genitales *mpl*

genitive /'dʒenɪtɪv/ *adj & n* genitivo (*m*)

genius /'dʒiːnɪəs/ *n* (*pl* -**uses**) genio *m*

genocide /'dʒenəsaɪd/ *n* genocidio *m*

genome /'dʒiːnəʊm/ *n* genoma *m*

genre /ʒɑ:ŋr/ *n* género *m*

gent /dʒent/ *n* 🅸 señor *m*. ~**s** *n* aseo *m* de caballeros

genteel /dʒen'tiːl/ *adj* distinguido

gentl|e /'dʒentl/ *adj* (-**er**, -**est**) (person) dulce; (murmur, breeze) suave; (hint) discreto. ~**eman** *n* señor *m*; (*well-bred*) caballero *m*. ~**eness** *n* amabilidad *f*

genuine /'dʒenjʊɪn/ *adj* verdadero; (person) sincero

geograph|er /dʒɪ'ɒgrəfə(r)/ *n* geógrafo *m*. ~**ical** /dʒɪə'græfɪkl/ *adj* geográfico. ~**y** /dʒɪ'ɒgrəfɪ/ *n* geografía *f*

geolog|ical /dʒɪə'lɒdʒɪkl/ *adj* geológico. ~**ist** /dʒɪ'ɒlədʒɪst/ *n* geólogo *m*. ~**y** /dʒɪ'ɒlədʒɪ/ *n* geología *f*

geometr|ic(al) /dʒɪə'metrɪk(l)/ *adj* geométrico. ~**y** /dʒɪ'ɒmətrɪ/ *n* geometría *f*

geranium /dʒə'reɪnɪəm/ *n* geranio *m*

geriatric /dʒerɪ'ætrɪk/ *adj* (patient) anciano; (ward) de geriatría. ~**s** *n* geriatría *f*

germ /dʒɜːm/ *n* microbio *m*, germen *m*

German /'dʒɜːmən/ *adj & n* alemán (*m*). ~**ic** /dʒɜː'mænɪk/ *adj* germánico. ~ **measles** *n* rubéola *f*. ~**y** /'dʒɜːmənɪ/ *n* Alemania *f*

germinate /'dʒɜːmɪneɪt/ *vi* germinar

gesticulate /dʒe'stɪkjʊleɪt/ *vi* hacer ademanes, gesticular

gesture /'dʒestʃə(r)/ *n* gesto *m*, ademán *m*; (*fig*) gesto *m*. ● *vi* hacer gestos

---

get /get/

past **got**; past participle **got**, **gotten** (*Amer*); present participle **getting**

● *transitive verb*

···▸ (*obtain*) conseguir, obtener. did you get the job? ¿conseguiste el trabajo?

···▸ (*buy*) comprar. I got it in the sales lo compré en las rebajas

···▸ (*achieve, win*) sacar. she got very good marks sacó muy buenas notas

···▸ (*receive*) recibir. I got a letter from Alex recibí una carta de Alex

···▸ (*fetch*) ir a buscar. ~ your coat vete a buscar tu abrigo

····▸ (*experience*) llevarse. I got a terrible shock me llevé un shock espantoso

····▸ (*fam, understand*) entender. I don't ~ what you mean no entiendo lo que quieres decir

····▸ (*ask or persuade*) to ~ s.o. to do sth hacer que uno haga algo

Note that *hacer que* is followed by the subjunctive form of the verb

····▸ (*cause to be done or happen*) I must ~ this watch fixed tengo que llevar a arreglar este reloj. they got the roof mended hicieron arreglar el techo

● *intransitive verb*

····▸ (*arrive, reach*) llegar. I got there late llegué tarde. how do you ~ to Paddington? ¿cómo se llega a Paddington?

····▸ (*become*) to ~ tired cansarse. she got very angry se puso furiosa. it's ~ting late se está haciendo tarde

➡️ For translations of expressions such as **get better, get old** see entries **better, old** etc. See also **got**

····▸ to get to do sth (*manage to*) llegar a. did you get to see him? ¿llegaste a verlo? □ **get along** vi (*manage*) arreglárselas; (*progress*) hacer progresos. □ **get along with** vt llevarse bien con. □ **get at** vt (*reach*) llegar a; (*imply*) querer decir. □ **get away** vi salir; (*escape*) escaparse. □ **get back** vi

volver. vt (*recover*) recobrar.
□ **get by** vi (*manage*) arreglárselas; (*pass*) pasar. □ **get down** vi bajar. vt (*make depressed*) deprimir. □ **get in** vi entrar. □ **get into** vt entrar en; subir a (*car*) □ **get off** vt bajar(se) de (train etc). vi (*from train etc*) bajarse; (*Jurid*) salir absuelto. □ **get on** vi (*progress*) hacer progresos; (*succeed*) tener éxito. vt subirse a (train etc). □ **get on with** vt (*be on good terms with*) llevarse bien con; (*continue*) seguir con. □ **get out** vi salir. vt (*take out*) sacar. □ **get out of** vt (*fig*) librarse de. □ **get over** vt reponerse de (illness). □ **get round** vt soslayar (difficulty etc); engatusar (person). □ **get through** vi pasar; (*on phone*) comunicarse (to con). □ **get together** vi (*meet up*) reunirse. vt (*assemble*) reunir.
□ **get up** vi levantarse; (*climb*) subir

geyser /ˈgiːzə(r)/ n géiser m

ghastly /ˈgɑːstlɪ/ adj (-ier, -iest) horrible

gherkin /ˈgɜːkɪn/ n pepinillo m

ghetto /ˈgetəʊ/ n (pl -os) gueto m

ghost /gəʊst/ n fantasma m. ~ly adj espectral

giant /ˈdʒaɪənt/ n gigante m. ● adj gigantesco

gibberish /ˈdʒɪbərɪʃ/ n jerigonza f

gibe /dʒaɪb/ n pulla f

giblets /ˈdʒɪblɪts/ npl menudillos mpl

gidd|iness /ˈgɪdɪnɪs/ n vértigo m. ~y adj (-ier, -iest) mareado. be/feel ~y estar/sentirse mareado

gift /gɪft/ n regalo m; (*ability*) don

m. **~ed** *adj* dotado de talento.
~-wrap *vt* envolver para regalo
gigantic /dʒaɪˈɡæntɪk/ *adj* gigantesco

giggle /ˈɡɪɡl/ *vi* reírse tontamente. ●*n* risita *f*
gild /ɡɪld/ *vt* dorar
gills /ɡɪlz/ *npl* agallas *fpl*
gilt /ɡɪlt/ *n* dorado *m*. ●*adj* dorado
gimmick /ˈɡɪmɪk/ *n* truco *m*
gin /dʒɪn/ *n* ginebra *f*
ginger /ˈdʒɪndʒə(r)/ *n* jengibre *m*. ●*adj* rojizo. **he has ~ hair** es pelirrojo. **~bread** *n* pan *m* de jengibre
gipsy /ˈdʒɪpsɪ/ *n* gitano *m*
giraffe /dʒɪˈrɑːf/ *n* jirafa *f*
girder /ˈɡɜːdə(r)/ *n* viga *f*
girdle /ˈɡɜːdl/ *n* (belt) cinturón *m*; (corset) corsé *m*
girl /ɡɜːl/ *n* chica *f*, muchacha *f*; (child) niña *f*. **~ band** *n* grupo *m* pop de chicas. **~friend** *n* amiga *f*; (of boy) novia *f*. **~ish** *adj* de niña; (boy) afeminado. **~ scout** *n* (Amer) exploradora *f*, guía *f*
giro /ˈdʒaɪrəʊ/ *n* (pl -os) giro *m* (bancario)
girth /ɡɜːθ/ *n* circunferencia *f*
gist /dʒɪst/ *n* lo esencial
give /ɡɪv/ *vt* (pt gave, pp given) dar; (deliver) entregar; regalar (present); prestar (aid, attention). **~ o.s. to** darse a. ●*vi* dar; (yield) ceder; (stretch) dar de sí. ●*n* elasticidad *f*. □ **~ away** *vt* regalar; revelar (secret). □ **~ back** *vt* devolver. □ **~ in** *vi* ceder. □ **~ off** *vt* emitir. □ **~ out** *vt* distribuir. (become used up) agotarse. □ **~ up** *vt* renunciar a; (yield) ceder. **~ up doing sth** dejar de hacer algo. **~ o.s. up** entregarse (to a). *vi* rendirse. **~n** /ˈɡɪvn/ see **GIVE**. ●*adj* dado. **~n name** *n* nombre *m* de pila

glacier /ˈɡlæsɪə(r)/ *n* glaciar *m*
glad /ɡlæd/ *adj* contento. **be ~** alegrarse (about de). **~den** *vt* alegrar
gladly /ˈɡlædlɪ/ *adv* alegremente; (willingly) con mucho gusto
glamo|rous /ˈɡlæmərəs/ *adj* glamoroso. **~ur** /ˈɡlæmə(r)/ *n* glamour *m*
glance /ɡlɑːns/ *n* ojeada *f*. ●*vi*. **~ at** dar un vistazo a
gland /ɡlænd/ *n* glándula *f*
glar|e /ɡleə(r)/ *vi* (light) deslumbrar; (stare angrily) mirar airadamente. ●*n* resplandor *m*; (stare) mirada *f* airada. **~ing** *adj* deslumbrante; (obvious) manifiesto
glass /ɡlɑːs/ *n* (material) cristal *m*, vidrio *m*; (without stem or for wine) vaso *m*; (with stem) copa *f*; (for beer) caña *f*; (mirror) espejo *m*. **~es** *npl* (spectacles) gafas *fpl*, lentes *fpl* (LAm), anteojos *mpl* (LAm). **~y** *adj* vítreo
glaze /ɡleɪz/ *vt* poner cristal(es) or vidrio(s) a (windows, doors); vidriar (pottery). ●*vi*. **~ (over)** (eyes) vidriarse. ●*n* barniz *m*; (for pottery) esmalte *m*
gleam /ɡliːm/ *n* destello *m*. ●*vi* destellar
glean /ɡliːn/ *vt* espigar; recoger (information)
glee /ɡliː/ *n* regocijo *m*
glib /ɡlɪb/ *adj* de mucha labia; (reply) fácil
glid|e /ɡlaɪd/ *vi* deslizarse; (plane) planear. **~er** *n* planeador *m*. **~ing** *n* planeo *m*
glimmer /ˈɡlɪmə(r)/ *n* destello *m*. ●*vi* destellar
glimpse /ɡlɪmps/ *n*. **catch a ~ of** vislumbrar, ver brevemente. ●*vt* vislumbrar

glint /glɪnt/ n destello m. • vi destellar

glisten /ˈglɪsn/ vi brillar

glitter /ˈglɪtə(r)/ vi brillar. • n brillo m

gloat /gləʊt/ vi. ~ on/over regodearse sobre

glob|al /ˈgləʊbl/ adj (worldwide) mundial; (all-embracing) global. ~alization n globalización f. ~al warming n calentamiento m global. ~e /gləʊb/ n globo m

gloom /gluːm/ n oscuridad f; (sadness, fig) tristeza f ~y adj (-ier, -iest) triste; (pessimistic) pesimista

glor|ify /ˈglɔːrɪfaɪ/ vt glorificar. ~ious /ˈglɔːrɪəs/ adj espléndido; (deed, hero etc) glorioso. ~y /ˈglɔːrɪ/ n gloria f

gloss /glɒs/ n lustre m. ~ (paint) (pintura f al or de) esmalte m. □ ~ over vt (make light of) minimizar; (cover up) encubrir

glossary /ˈglɒsərɪ/ n glosario m

glossy /ˈglɒsɪ/ adj brillante

glove /glʌv/ n guante m. ~ compartment n (Auto) guantera f

glow /gləʊ/ vi brillar. • n brillo m. ~ing /ˈgləʊɪŋ/ adj incandescente; (account) entusiasta; (complexion) rojo

glucose /ˈgluːkəʊs/ n glucosa f

glue /gluː/ n cola f, goma f de pegar. • vt (pres p gluing) pegar

glum /glʌm/ adj (glummer, glummest) triste

glutton /ˈglʌtn/ n glotón m

gnarled /nɑːld/ adj nudoso

gnash /næʃ/ vt. ~ one's teeth rechinar los dientes

gnat /næt/ n jején m, mosquito m

gnaw /nɔː/ vt roer. • vi. ~ at roer

gnome /nəʊm/ n gnomo m

---

go /gəʊ/

3rd pers sing present **goes**; past **went**; past participle **gone**

● *intransitive verb*

····▸ ir. I'm going to France voy a Francia. to go shopping ir de compras. to go swimming ir a nadar

····▸ (leave) irse. we're going on Friday nos vamos el viernes

····▸ (work, function) (engine, clock) funcionar

····▸ (become) to go deaf quedarse sordo. to go mad volverse loco. his face went red se puso colorado

····▸ (stop) (headache, pain) irse (+ me/te/le). the pain's gone se me ha ido el dolor

····▸ (turn out, progress) ir. everything's going very well todo va muy bien. how did the exam go? ¿qué tal te fue en el examen?

····▸ (match, suit) combinar. the jacket and the trousers go well together la chaqueta y los pantalones combinan bien.

····▸ (cease to function) (bulb, fuse) fundirse. the brakes have gone los frenos no funcionan

● *auxiliary verb* to be going to + infinitive ir a + infinitivo. it's going to rain va a llover. she's going to win! ¡va a ganar!

● *noun* (pl goes)

····▸ (turn) turno m. you have three goes tienes tres turnos. it's your go te toca a ti

····▸ (attempt) to have a go at

doing sth intentar hacer algo.
have another go inténtalo de
nuevo

···▸ (energy, drive) empuje m. she
has a lot of go tiene mucho
empuje

···▸ (in phrases) I've been on the
go all day no he parado en
todo el día. to make a go of
sth sacar algo adelante □ **go
across** vt/vi cruzar. □ **go after** vi
perseguir. □ **go away** vi irse.
□ **go back** vi volver. □ **go back
on** vt faltar a (promise etc).
□ **go by** vi pasar. □ **go down** vi
bajar; (sun) ponerse. □ **go for** vt
(fam, attack) atacar. □ **go in** vi
entrar. □ **go in for** vt presen-
tarse para (exam); participar en
(competition). □ **go off** vi
(leave) irse; (milk, go bad) pasarse;
(explode) estallar; (lights) apa-
garse. □ **go on** vi seguir; (hap-
pen) pasar; (be switched on) en-
cenderse, prenderse (LAm). □ **go
out** vi salir; (fire, light) apa-
garse. □ **go over** vt (check) revi-
sar; (revise) repasar. □ **go
through** vt pasar por; (search)
registrar; (check) examinar.
□ **go up** vi subir. □ **go with-
out** vt pasar sin

goad /gəʊd/ vt aguijonear

go-ahead /ˈɡəʊəhed/ n luz f
verde. ● adj dinámico

goal /ɡəʊl/ n (Sport) gol m; (objec-
tive) meta f. ~ie /ˈɡəʊliː/ n 🔢,
~keeper n portero m, arquero m
(LAm). ~post n poste m de la porte-
ría, poste m del arco (LAm)

goat /ɡəʊt/ n cabra f

gobble /ˈɡɒbl/ vt engullir

goblin /ˈɡɒblɪn/ n duende m

god /ɡɒd/ n dios m. **G~** n Dios m.

~child n ahijado m. ~daughter
n ahijada f. ~dess /ˈɡɒdes/ n diosa
f. ~father n padrino m. ~for-
saken adj olvidado de Dios.
~mother n madrina f. ~send n
beneficio m inesperado. ~son n
ahijado m

going /ˈɡəʊɪŋ/ n camino m; (ra-
cing) (estado m del) terreno m. it is
slow/hard ~ es lento/difícil. ● adj
(price) actual; (concern) en funcio-
namiento

gold /ɡəʊld/ n oro m. ● adj de oro.
~en adj de oro; (in colour) dorado;
(opportunity) único. ~en wed-
ding n bodas fpl de oro. ~fish n
invar pez m de colores. ~mine n
mina f de oro; (fig) fuente f de
gran riqueza. ~plated /-ˈpleɪtɪd/
adj chapado en oro. ~smith n or-
febre m

golf /ɡɒlf/ n golf m. ~ ball n pe-
lota f de golf. ~ club n palo m de
golf; (place) club m de golf.
~course n campo m de golf. ~er
n jugador m de golf

gondola /ˈɡɒndələ/ n góndola f

gone /ɡɒn/ see **go**. ● adj pasado. ~
six o'clock después de las seis

gong /ɡɒŋ/ n gong(o) m

good /ɡʊd/ adj (better, best)
bueno, (before masculine singular noun)
buen. ~ afternoon buenas tardes.
~ evening (before dark) buenas
tardes; (after dark) buenas noches.
~ morning buenos días. ~ night
buenas noches. as ~ as (almost)
casi. feel ~ sentirse bien. have a
~ time divertirse. ● n bien m. for
~ para siempre. it is no ~ shout-
ing es inútil gritar etc. ~bye /-ˈbaɪ/
int ¡adiós! ● n adiós m. say ~bye to
despedirse de. ~-for-nothing
/-ˈfʌnəθɪŋ/ adj & n inútil (m). **G~ Fri-
day** n Viernes m Santo. ~-looking

/-'lʊkɪŋ/ adj guapo, buen mozo m (LAm), buena moza f (LAm). **~ness** n bondad f. **~ness!**, **~ness gracious!**, **~ness me!**, **my ~ness!** ¡Dios mío! **~s** npl mercancías fpl. **~will** /-'wɪl/ n buena voluntad f. **~y** n (Culin, fam) golosina f; (in film) bueno m

gooey /'guːɪ/ adj (gooier, gooiest) 🄸 pegajoso; (fig) sentimental

goofy /'guːfɪ/ adj (Amer) necio

google (®) /'guːgl/ vt, vi 🄸 googlear 🄸

goose /guːs/ n (pl geese) oca f, ganso m. **~berry** /'guzbarɪ/ n uva f espina, grosella f espinosa. **~flesh** n, **~pimples** npl carne f de gallina

gore /gɔː(r)/ n sangre f ● vt cornear

gorge /gɔːdʒ/ n (of river) garganta f ● vt. **~ o.s.** hartarse (on de)

gorgeous /'gɔːdʒəs/ adj precioso; (splendid) magnífico

gorilla /gə'rɪlə/ n gorila m

gorse /gɔːs/ n aulaga f

gory /'gɔːrɪ/ adj (-ier, -iest) 🄸 sangriento

gosh /gɒʃ/ int ¡caramba!

go-slow /gəʊ'sləʊ/ n huelga f de celo, huelga f pasiva

gospel /'gɒspl/ n evangelio m

gossip /'gɒsɪp/ n (chatter) chismorreo m; (person) chismoso m. ● vi (pt gossiped) (chatter) chismorrear; (repeat scandal) contar chismes

got /gɒt/ see GET. **have ~** tener. **I've ~ to do it** tengo que hacerlo.

gotten /'gɒtn/ see GET

gouge /gaʊdʒ/ vt abrir (hole). □ **~ out** vt sacar

gourmet /'gʊəmeɪ/ n gastrónomo m

govern /'gʌvən/ vt/i gobernar.

~ess n institutriz f. **~ment** n gobierno m. **~or** n gobernador m

gown /gaʊn/ n vestido m; (of judge, teacher) toga f

GP abbr see GENERAL PRACTITIONER

GPS abbrev Global Positioning System GPS m

grab /græb/ vt (pt grabbed) agarrar

grace /greɪs/ n gracia f. **~ful** adj elegante

gracious /'greɪʃəs/ adj (kind) amable; (elegant) elegante

grade /greɪd/ n clase f, categoría f; (of goods) clase f, calidad f; (on scale) grado m; (school mark) nota f; (Amer, class) curso m, año m

gradient /'greɪdɪənt/ n pendiente f, gradiente f (LAm)

gradual /'grædʒʊəl/ adj gradual. **~ly** adv gradualmente, poco a poco

graduat|e /'grædʒʊət/ n (Univ) licenciado. ● /'grædʒʊeɪt/ vi licenciarse. **~ion** /-'eɪʃn/ n graduación f

graffiti /grə'fiːtɪ/ npl graffiti mpl, pintadas fpl

graft /grɑːft/ n (Med, Bot) injerto m; (Amer fam, bribery) chanchullos mpl. ● vt injertar

grain /greɪn/ n grano m

gram /græm/ n gramo m

gramma|r /'græmə(r)/ n gramática f. **~tical** /grə'mætɪkl/ adj gramatical

gramme /græm/ n gramo m

grand /grænd/ adj (-er, -est) magnífico; (fam, excellent) estupendo. **~child** n nieto m. **~daughter** n nieta f. **~eur** /'grændʒə(r)/ n grandiosidad f. **~father** n abuelo m. **~father clock** n reloj m de caja. **~iose** /'grændɪəʊs/ adj grandioso

~**mother** n abuela f. ~**parents** npl abuelos mpl. ~ **piano** n piano m de cola. ~**son** n nieto m. ~**stand** /'grænstænd/ n tribuna f

granite /'grænɪt/ n granito m

granny /'grænɪ/ n 🔢 abuela f

grant /grɑːnt/ vt conceder; (give) donar; (admit) admitir (that que). **take for** ~**ed** dar por sentado. ●n concesión f; (Univ) beca f

granule /'grænuːl/ n gránulo m

grape /greɪp/ n uva f. ~**fruit** n invar pomelo m, toronja f (LAm)

graph /grɑːf/ n gráfica f

graphic /'græfɪk/ adj gráfico. ~**s** npl diseño m gráfico; (Comp) gráficos mpl

grapple /'græpl/ vi. ~ **with** forcejear con; (mentally) lidiar con

grasp /grɑːsp/ vt agarrar. ●n (hold) agarro m; (fig) comprensión f. ~**ing** adj avaro

grass /grɑːs/ n hierba f. ~**hopper** n saltamontes m. ~ **roots** npl base f popular. ●adj de las bases. ~**y** adj cubierto de hierba

grate /greɪt/ n rejilla f; (fireplace) chimenea f. ●vt rallar. ●vi rechinar; (be irritating) ser crispante

grateful /'greɪtfl/ adj agradecido. ~**ly** adv con gratitud

grater /'greɪtə(r)/ n rallador m

gratif|ied /'grætɪfaɪd/ adj contento. ~**y** /'grætɪfaɪ/ vt satisfacer; (please) agradar a. ~**ying** adj agradable

grating /'greɪtɪŋ/ n reja f

gratitude /'grætɪtjuːd/ n gratitud f

gratuitous /grə'tjuːɪtəs/ adj gratuito

gratuity /grə'tjuːətɪ/ n (tip) propina f

grave /greɪv/ n sepultura f. ●adj (-er, -est) (serious) grave

gravel /'grævl/ n grava f

gravely /'greɪvlɪ/ adv (seriously) seriamente; (solemnly) con gravedad

grave: ~**stone** n lápida f. ~**yard** n cementerio m

gravitate /'grævɪteɪt/ vi gravitar

gravity /'grævətɪ/ n gravedad f

gravy /'greɪvɪ/ n salsa f

gray /greɪ/ adj & n (Amer) see GREY

graze /greɪz/ vi (eat) pacer. ●vt (touch) rozar; (scrape) raspar. ●n rasguño m

greas|e /griːs/ n grasa f. ●vt engrasar. ~**eproof paper** n papel m encerado or de cera. ~**y** adj (hands) grasiento; (food) graso; (hair, skin) graso, grasoso (LAm)

great /greɪt/ adj (-er, -est) grande; (before singular noun) gran; (fam, very good) estupendo. G~ **Britain** n Gran Bretaña f. ~**grandfather** /-'grænfɑːðə(r)/ n bisabuelo m. ~**grandmother** /-'grænmʌðə(r)/ n bisabuela f. ~**ly** adv (very) muy; (much) mucho

Greece /griːs/ n Grecia f

greed /griːd/ n avaricia f; (for food) glotonería f. ~**y** adj avaro; (for food) glotón

Greek /griːk/ adj & n griego (m)

green /griːn/ adj (-er, -est) verde. ●n verde m; (grass) césped m. ~ **belt** n zona f verde. ~ **card** n (Amer) permiso m de residencia y trabajo. ~**ery** n verdor m. ~**gage** /-geɪdʒ/ n claudia f. ~**grocer** n verdulero m. ~**house** n invernadero m. the ~**house** effect el efecto invernadero. ~ **light** n luz f verde. ~**s** npl verduras fpl

Green Card En EE.UU., *i* documento oficial que toda persona que no sea ciudadana norteamericana debe obtener para residir y trabajar en este país. En el Reino Unido, es el documento que se debe obtener de la compañía de seguros, cuando se lleva un automóvil al extranjero, a fin de que siga vigente la cobertura de la póliza.

greet /griːt/ *vt* saludar; (*receive*) recibir. ~**ing** *n* saludo *m*

gregarious /grɪˈɡeərɪəs/ *adj* gregario; (*person*) sociable

grenade /grɪˈneɪd/ *n* granada *f*

grew /gruː/ *see* GROW

grey /greɪ/ *adj* (**-er, -est**) gris. have ~ **hair** ser canoso. ● *n* gris *m*. ~**hound** *n* galgo *m*

grid /grɪd/ *n* reja *f*; (*Elec, network*) red *f*; (*on map*) cuadriculado *m*

grief /griːf/ *n* dolor *m*. come to ~ (*person*) acabar mal; (*fail*) fracasar

grievance /ˈgriːvns/ *n* queja *f* formal

grieve /griːv/ *vt* apenar. ● *vi* afligirse. ~ **for** llorar

grievous /ˈgriːvəs/ *adj* doloroso; (*serious*) grave. ~ **bodily harm** (*Jurid*) lesiones *fpl* (corporales) graves

grill /grɪl/ *n* parrilla *f*. ● *vt* asar a la parrilla; (🗆, *interrogate*) interrogar

grille /grɪl/ *n* rejilla *f*

grim /grɪm/ *adj* (**grimmer, grimmest**) severo

grimace /ˈɡrɪməs/ *n* mueca *f*. ● *vi* hacer muecas

grim|e /graɪm/ *n* mugre *f* ~**y** *adj* mugriento

grin /grɪn/ *vt* (*pt* grinned) sonreír. ● *n* sonrisa *f* (abierta)

grind /graɪnd/ *vt* (*pt* ground) moler (coffee, corn etc); (*pulverize*) pulverizar; (*sharpen*) afilar; (*Amer*) picar, moler (meat)

grip /grɪp/ *vt* (*pt* gripped) agarrar; (*interest*) captar. ● *n* (*hold*) agarro *m*; (*strength of hand*) apretón *m*; (*hairgrip*) horquilla *f*, pasador *m* (*Mex*). come to ~**s with** entender (subject)

grisly /ˈgrɪzlɪ/ *adj* (**-ier, -iest**) horrible

gristle /ˈgrɪsl/ *n* cartílago *m*

grit /grɪt/ *n* arenilla *f*; (*fig*) agallas *fpl*. ● *vt* (*pt* gritted) echar arena en (road). ~ **one's teeth** (*fig*) acorazarse

groan /grəʊn/ *vi* gemir. ● *n* gemido *m*

grocer /ˈgrəʊsə(r)/ *n* tendero *m*, abarrotero *m* (*Mex*). ~**ies** *npl* comestibles *mpl*. ~**y** *n* tienda *f* de comestibles, tienda *f* de abarrotes (*Mex*)

groggy /ˈgrɒgɪ/ *adj* (*weak*) débil; (*unsteady*) inseguro; (*ill*) malucho

groin /grɔɪn/ *n* ingle *f*

groom /gruːm/ *n* mozo *m* de caballos; (*bridegroom*) novio *m*. ● *vt* almohazar (horses); (*fig*) preparar

groove /gruːv/ *n* ranura *f*; (*in record*) surco *m*

grope /grəʊp/ *vi* (*find one's way*) moverse a tientas. ~ **for** buscar a tientas

gross /grəʊs/ *adj* (**-er, -est**) (*coarse*) grosero; (*Com*) bruto; (*fat*) grueso; (*flagrant*) flagrante. ● *n invar* gruesa *f*. ~**ly** *adv* (*very*) enormemente

grotesque /grəʊˈtesk/ *adj* grotesco

ground /graʊnd/ *see* GRIND. ● *n* suelo *m*; (*area*) terreno *m*; (*reason*) razón f; (*Amer, Elec*) toma f de tierra. • vt fundar (theory); retirar del servicio (aircraft). ~s npl jardines mpl; (*sediment*) poso m. ~ **beef** n (*Amer*) carne f picada, carne f molida. ~ **cloth** n (*Amer*) see ~**SHEET**. ~ **floor** n planta f baja. ~ing n base f, conocimientos mpl (in de). ~**less** adj infundado. ~**sheet** n suelo m impermeable (de una tienda de campaña). ~**work** n trabajo m preparatorio

group /gruːp/ n grupo m. • vt agrupar. • vi agruparse

grouse /graʊs/ n invar (*bird*) urogallo m. • vi 🔟 rezongar

grovel /ˈɡrɒvl/ vi (pt grovelled) postrarse; (*fig*) arrastrarse

grow /ɡrəʊ/ vi (pt grew, pp grown) crecer; (*become*) volverse, ponerse. • vt cultivar. ~ **a beard** dejarse (crecer) la barba. □ ~ **up** vi hacerse mayor. ~**ing** adj (quantity) cada vez mayor; (influence) creciente

growl /ɡraʊl/ vi gruñir. • n gruñido m

grown /ɡrəʊn/ see **GROW**. • adj adulto. ~-**up** adj & n adulto (m)

growth /ɡrəʊθ/ n crecimiento m; (increase) aumento m; (development) desarrollo m; (*Med*) bulto m, tumor m

grub /ɡrʌb/ n (larva) larva f; (fam, food) comida f

grubby /ˈɡrʌbɪ/ adj (-ier, -iest) mugriento

grudge /ɡrʌdʒ/ vt see **BEGRUDGE**. • n rencilla f. **bear/have a ~e against** s.o. guardarle rencor a uno. ~**ingly** adv de mala gana

gruelling /ˈɡruːəlɪŋ/ adj agotador

gruesome /ˈɡruːsəm/ adj horrible

gruff /ɡrʌf/ adj (-er, -est) (man-

ners) brusco; (voice) ronco

grumble /ˈɡrʌmbl/ vi rezongar

grumpy /ˈɡrʌmpɪ/ adj (-ier, -iest) malhumorado

grunt /ɡrʌnt/ vi gruñir. • n gruñido m

guarantee /ɡærənˈtiː/ n garantía f. • vt garantizar. ~**or** n garante m & f

guard /ɡɑːd/ vt proteger; (watch) vigilar. • n (vigilance, Mil group) guardia f; (person) guardia m; (on train) jefe m de tren. □ ~ **against** vt evitar; protegerse contra (risk). ~**ed** adj cauteloso. ~**ian** /-ɪən/ n guardián m; (of orphan) tutor m

Guatemala /ɡwɑːtəˈmɑːlə/ n Guatemala f. ~**n** adj & n guatemalteco (m)

guer(r)illa /ɡəˈrɪlə/ n guerrillero m. ~ **warfare** n guerrilla f

guess /ɡes/ vt adivinar; (*Amer, suppose*) suponer. • n conjetura f. ~**work** n conjeturas fpl

guest /ɡest/ n invitado m; (in hotel) huésped m. ~**house** n casa f de huéspedes

guffaw /ɡʌˈfɔː/ n carcajada f. • vi reírse a carcajadas

guidance /ˈɡaɪdəns/ n (advice) consejos mpl; (information) información f

guide /ɡaɪd/ n (person) guía m & f; (book) guía f. **Girl G~** exploradora f, guía f. • vt guiar. ~**book** n guía f. ~ **dog** n perro m guía, perro m lazarillo. ~**d missile** n proyectil m teledirigido. ~**lines** npl pauta f

guild /ɡɪld/ n gremio m

guile /ɡaɪl/ n astucia f

guillotine /ˈɡɪlətiːn/ n guillotina f

guilt /ɡɪlt/ n culpa f; (*Jurid*) culpabilidad f. ~**y** adj culpable

guinea pig /ˈɡɪnɪ/ n conejillo m

de Indias, cobaya f

guitar /gɪˈtɑː(r)/ n guitarra f. **~ist** n guitarrista m & f

gulf /gʌlf/ n (part of sea) golfo m; (gap) abismo m

gull /gʌl/ n gaviota f

gullet /ˈgʌlɪt/ n garganta f, gaznate m ⊞

gullible /ˈgʌləbl/ adj crédulo

gully /ˈgʌlɪ/ n (ravine) barranco m

gulp /gʌlp/ vt. □ ~ (**down**) tragarse de prisa. ● vi tragar saliva. ● n trago m

gum /gʌm/ n (in mouth) encía f; (glue) goma f de pegar; (for chewing) chicle m. ● vt (pt gummed) engomar

gun /gʌn/ n (pistol) pistola f; (rifle) fusil m, escopeta f; (artillery piece) cañón m. ● vt (pt gunned). □ ~ **down** vt abatir a tiros. **~fire** n tiros mpl

gun: **~man** /-mən/ n pistolero m, gatillero m (Mex). **~powder** n pólvora f. **~shot** n disparo m

gurgle /ˈgɜːgl/ vi (liquid) gorgotear; (baby) gorjear

gush /gʌʃ/ vi. □ ~ (**out**) salir a borbotones. ● n (of liquid) chorro m; (fig) torrente m

gusset /ˈgʌsɪt/ n entretela f

gust /gʌst/ n ráfaga f

gusto /ˈgʌstəʊ/ n entusiasmo m

gusty /ˈgʌstɪ/ adj borrascoso

gut /gʌt/ n intestino m. ● vt (pt gutted) destripar; (fire) destruir. **~s** npl tripas fpl; (fam, courage) agallas fpl

gutter /ˈgʌtə(r)/ n (on roof) canalón m, canaleta f; (in street) cuneta f; (fig, slum) arroyo m

guttural /ˈgʌtərəl/ adj gutural

guy /gaɪ/ n (fam, man) tipo m ⊞.

tío m ⊞

guzzle /ˈgʌzl/ vt (drink) chupar ⊞; (eat) tragarse

gym /dʒɪm/ n ⊞ (gymnasium) gimnasio m; (gymnastics) gimnasia f

gymnasium /dʒɪmˈneɪzɪəm/ n gimnasio m

gymnast /ˈdʒɪmnæst/ n gimnasta m & f. **~ics** /dʒɪmˈnæstɪks/ npl gimnasia f

gymslip /ˈdʒɪmslɪp/ n túnica f (de gimnasia)

gynaecolog|ist /gaɪnɪ ˈkɒlədʒɪst/ n ginecólogo m. **~y** n ginecología f

gypsy /ˈdʒɪpsɪ/ n gitano m

gyrate /dʒaɪəˈreɪt/ vi girar

Hh

haberdashery /ˈhæbədæʃərɪ/ n mercería f; (Amer, clothes) ropa f y accesorios mpl para caballeros

habit /ˈhæbɪt/ n costumbre f; (Relig, costume) hábito m. be in the ~ of (+ gerund) tener la costumbre de (+ infinitivo), soler (+ infinitivo). get into the ~ of (+ gerund) acostumbrarse a (+ infinitivo)

habitable /ˈhæbɪtəbl/ adj habitable

habitat /ˈhæbɪtæt/ n hábitat m

habitation /hæbɪˈteɪʃn/ n habitación f

habitual /həˈbɪtjʊəl/ adj habitual; (liar) inveterado. **~ly** adv de costumbre

hack /hæk/ n (old horse) jamelgo

m; (*writer*) escritorzuelo *m*. ●*vt* cortar. ~**er** *n* (*Comp*) pirata *m* informático

hackneyed /ˈhæknɪd/ *adj* manido

had /hæd/ *see* HAVE

haddock /ˈhædək/ *n invar* eglefino *m*

haemorrhage /ˈhemərɪdʒ/ *n* hemorragia *f*

haemorrhoids /ˈhemərɔɪdz/ *npl* hemorroides *fpl*

hag /hæɡ/ *n* bruja *f*

haggard /ˈhæɡəd/ *adj* demacrado

hail /heɪl/ *n* granizo *m*. ●*vi* granizar. ●*vt* (*greet*) saludar; llamar (*taxi*). □ ~ **from** *vt* venir de. ~**stone** *n* grano *m* de granizo

hair /heə(r)/ *n* pelo *m*. ~**band** *n* cinta *f*, banda *f* (*Mex*). ~**brush** *n* cepillo *m* (para el pelo). ~**cut** *n* corte *m* de pelo. have a ~cut cortarse el pelo. ~**do** *n* ⊞ peinado *m*. ~**dresser** *n* peluquero *m*. ~**dresser's (shop)** *n* peluquería *f*. ~**dryer** *n* secador *m*, secadora *f* (*Mex*). ~**grip** *n* horquilla *f*, pasador *m* (*Mex*). ~**pin** *n* horquilla *f*. ~**pin bend** *n* curva *f* cerrada. ~**raising** *adj* espeluznante. ~**spray** *n* laca *f*, fijador *m* (para el pelo). ~**style** *n* peinado *m*. ~**y** *adj* (-ier, -iest) peludo

half /hɑːf/ *n* (*pl* halves) mitad *f*. ●*adj* medio. a ~ a dozen media docena *f*. a ~ an hour media hora *f*. ●*adv* medio, a medias. ~**-hearted** /ˈhɑːtɪd/ *adj* poco entusiasta. ~**-mast** /ˈmɑːst/ *n*. at ~-mast a media asta. ~ **term** *n* vacaciones *fpl* de medio trimestre. ~**-time** *n* (*Sport*) descanso *m*, medio tiempo *m* (*LAm*). ~**way** *adj* medio. ●*adv* a medio camino

hall /hɔːl/ *n* (*entrance*) vestíbulo *m*;

(*for public events*) sala *f*, salón *m*. ~ **of residence** residencia *f* universitaria, colegio *m* mayor. ~**mark** /ˈmɑːk/ *n* (*on gold, silver*) contraste *m*; (*fig*) sello *m* (distintivo)

hallo /həˈləʊ/ *int see* HELLO

Hallowe'en /ˈhæləʊˈiːn/ *n* víspera *f* de Todos los Santos

hallucination /həluːsɪˈneɪʃn/ *n* alucinación *f*

halo /ˈheɪləʊ/ *n* (*pl* -oes) aureola *f*

halt /hɔːlt/ *n*. come to a ~ pararse. ●*vt* parar. ●*vi* pararse

halve /hɑːv/ *vt* reducir a la mitad; (*divide into halves*) partir por la mitad

halves /hɑːvz/ *see* HALF

ham /hæm/ *n* jamón *m*

hamburger /ˈhæmbɜːɡə(r)/ *n* hamburguesa *f*

hammer /ˈhæmə(r)/ *n* martillo *m*. ●*vt* martill(e)ar

hammock /ˈhæmək/ *n* hamaca *f*

hamper /ˈhæmpə(r)/ *n* cesta *f*. ●*vt* estorbar

hamster /ˈhæmstə(r)/ *n* hámster *m*

hand /hænd/ *n* mano *f*; (*of clock, watch*) manecilla *f*; (*worker*) obrero *m*. by ~ a mano. lend a ~ echar una mano. on ~ a mano. on the one ~... on the other ~ por un lado... por otro. out of ~ fuera de control. to ~ a mano. ●*vt* pasar. □ ~ **down** *vt* pasar. □ ~ **in** *vt* entregar. □ ~ **over** *vt* entregar. □ ~ **out** *vt* distribuir. ~**bag** *n* bolso *m*, cartera *f* (*LAm*), bolsa *f* (*Mex*). ~**brake** *n* (*in car*) freno *m* de mano. ~**cuffs** *npl* esposas *fpl*. ~**ful** *n* puñado *m*; (*fam, person*) persona *f* difícil

handicap /ˈhændɪkæp/ *n* desventaja *f*; (*Sport*) hándicap *m*. ~**ped** *adj* minusválido

handicraft /'hændɪkrɑːft/ n artesanía f

handkerchief /'hæŋkətʃɪf/ n (pl -fs or -chieves /-'tʃiːvz/) pañuelo m

handle /'hændl/ n (of door) picaporte m; (of drawer) tirador m; (of implement) mango m; (of cup, bag, jug) asa f. ● vt manejar; (touch) tocar. **~bars** npl manillar m, manubrio m (LAm).

hand: ~out n folleto m; (of money, food) dádiva f. **~shake** n apretón m de manos

handsome /'hænsəm/ adj (good-looking) guapo, buen mozo, buena moza (LAm); (generous) generoso

handwriting /'hændraɪtɪŋ/ n letra f

handy /'hændɪ/ adj (-ier, -iest) (useful) práctico; (person) diestro; (near) a mano. come in **~** venir muy bien. **~man** n hombre m habilidoso

hang /hæŋ/ vt (pt hung) colgar; (pt hanged) (capital punishment) ahorcar. ● vi colgar; (clothing) caer. ● n. get the **~** of sth coger el truco de algo. □ **~ about**, **~ around** vi holgazanear. □ **~ on** vi (wait) esperar. □ **~ out** vt tender (washing). □ **~ up** vi (also telephone) colgar

hangar /'hæŋə(r)/ n hangar m

hang: ~er n (for clothes) percha f. **~glider** n ala f delta, deslizador m (Mex). **~over** n (after drinking) resaca f. **~up** n 🔲 complejo m

hankie, hanky /'hæŋkɪ/ n 🔲 pañuelo m

haphazard /hæp'hæzəd/ adj fortuito. **~ly** adv al azar

happen /'hæpən/ vi pasar, suce-

der, ocurrir. if he **~s** to come si acaso viene. **~ing** n acontecimiento m

happ|ily /'hæpɪlɪ/ adv alegremente; (fortunately) afortunadamente. **~iness** n felicidad f. **~y** adj (-ier, -iest) feliz; (satisfied) contento

harass /'hærəs/ vt acosar. **~ment** n acoso m

harbour /'hɑːbə(r)/ n puerto m

hard /hɑːd/ adj (-er, -est) duro; (difficult) difícil. **~** adv mucho; (pull) con fuerza. **~** done by tratado injustamente. **~boiled egg** /-'bɔɪld/ n huevo m duro. **~en** vt endurecer. ● vi endurecerse. **~headed** /-'hedɪd/ adj realista

hardly /'hɑːdlɪ/ adv apenas. **~** ever casi nunca

hard: ~ness n dureza f. **~ship** n apuro m. **~ shoulder** n arcén m, acotamiento m (Mex). **~ware** /-'weə(r)/ n ferretería f; (Comp) hardware m. **~ware store** n (Amer) ferretería f. **~working** /-'wɜːkɪŋ/ adj trabajador

hardy /'hɑːdɪ/ adj (-ier, -iest) fuerte; (plants) resistente

hare /heə(r)/ n liebre f

hark /hɑːk/ vi escuchar. □ **~ back to** vt volver a

harm /hɑːm/ n daño m. there is no **~** in asking con preguntar no se pierde nada. ● vt hacer daño a (person); dañar (thing); perjudicar (interests). **~ful** adj perjudicial. **~less** adj inofensivo

harmonica /hɑː'mɒnɪkə/ n armónica f

harmon|ious /hɑː'məʊnɪəs/ adj armonioso. **~y** /'hɑːmənɪ/ n armonía f

harness /'hɑːnɪs/ n arnés m. ● vt poner el arnés a (horse); (fig) aprovechar

harp /hɑːp/ n arpa f. ● vi. ~ on (about) machacar (con)

harpoon /hɑːˈpuːn/ n arpón m

harpsichord /'hɑːpsɪkɔːd/ n clavicémbalo m, clave m

harrowing / 'hærəʊɪŋ/ adj desgarrador

harsh /hɑːʃ/ adj (-er, -est) duro, severo; (light) fuerte; (climate) riguroso. ~ly adv severamente. ~ness n severidad f

harvest /'hɑːvɪst/ n cosecha f. ● vt cosechar

has /hæz/ see HAVE

hassle /'hæsl/ n 🔟 lío m 🔟, rollo m 🔟. ● vt (harass) fastidiar

hast|e /heɪst/ n prisa f, apuro m (LAm). make ~e darse prisa. ~ily /'heɪstɪlɪ/ adv de prisa. ~y /'heɪstɪ/ adj (-ier, -iest) rápido; (rash) precipitado

hat /hæt/ n sombrero m

hatch /hætʃ/ n (for food) ventanilla f; (Naut) escotilla f. ● vt empollar (eggs); tramar (plot). ● vi salir del cascarón. ~back n coche m con tres/cinco puertas; (door) puerta f trasera

hatchet /'hætʃɪt/ n hacha f

hat|e /heɪt/ n odio m. ● vt odiar. ~eful adj odioso. ~red /'heɪtrɪd/ n odio m

haughty /'hɔːtɪ/ adj (-ier, -iest) altivo

haul /hɔːl/ vt arrastrar; transportar (goods). ● n (catch) redada f; (stolen goods) botín m; (journey) recorrido m. ~age /-ɪdʒ/ n transporte m. ~er (Amer), ~ier n transportista m & f

haunt /hɔːnt/ vt frecuentar; (ghost) rondar. ● n sitio m preferido. ~ed adj (house) embrujado; (look) angustiado

---

have /hæv//həv, əv/

3rd person singular present **has**, past **had**

● transitive verb

····▸ tener. I ~ three sisters tengo tres hermanas. do you ~ a credit card? ¿tiene una tarjeta de crédito?

····▸ (in requests) can I ~ a kilo of apples, please? ¿me da un kilo de manzanas, por favor?

····▸ (eat) comer. I had a pizza comí una pizza

····▸ (drink) tomar. come and ~ a drink ven a tomar una copa

····▸ (smoke) fumar (cigarette)

····▸ (hold, organize) hacer (party, meeting)

····▸ (get, receive) I had a letter from Tony yesterday recibí una carta de Tony ayer. we've had no news of her no hemos tenido noticias suyas

····▸ (illness) tener (flu, headache). to ~ a cold estar resfriado, tener catarro

····▸ to have sth done: we had it painted lo hicimos pintar. I had my hair cut me corté el pelo

····▸ to have it in for s.o. tenerle manía a uno

● auxiliary verb

····▸ haber. I've seen her already ya la he visto, ya la vi (LAm)

····▸ to have just done sth acabar de hacer algo. I've just

seen her acabo de verla

....> to have to do sth tener que hacer algo. I ~ to or I've got to go to the bank tengo que ir al banco

....> (in tag questions) you've met her, ~n't you? ya la conoces, ¿no? or ¿verdad? or ¿no es cierto?

....> (in short answers) you've forgotten something - have I? has olvidado algo - ¿sí?

haven /'heɪvn/ n puerto m; (refuge) refugio m

haversack /'hævəsæk/ n mochila f

havoc /'hævək/ n estragos mpl

hawk /hɔːk/ n halcón m

hawthorn /'hɔːθɔːn/ n espino m

hay /heɪ/ n heno m. ~ **fever** n fiebre f del heno. ~**stack** n almiar m. ~**wire** adj. go ~**wire** (plans) desorganizarse; (machine) estropearse

hazard /'hæzəd/ n riesgo m. ~**ous** adj arriesgado

haze /heɪz/ n neblina f

hazel /'heɪzl/ n avellano m. ~**nut** n avellana f

hazy /'heɪzɪ/ adj (-ier, -iest) nebuloso

he /hiː/ pron él

head /hed/ n cabeza f; (of family, government) jefe m; (of organization) director m; (of beer) espuma f. ~**s or tails** cara o cruz. • adj principal. • vt encabezar, cabecear (ball). □ **for** vt dirigirse a. ~**ache** n dolor m de cabeza. ~**er** n (football) cabezazo m. ~**first** /-'fɜːst/ adv & adj de cabeza. ~**ing** n título m, encabezamiento m. ~**lamp** n faro m, foco m (LAm). ~**land** /-lənd/ n promontorio m. ~**line** n

titular m. the news ~**lines** el resumen informativo. ~**long** adv de cabeza; (precipitately) precipitadamente. ~**master** n director m. ~**mistress** n directora f. ~**on** /-'ɒn/ adj & adv de frente. ~**phones** npl auriculares mpl, cascos mpl. ~**quarters** /-'kwɔːtəz/ n (of business) oficina f central; (Mil) cuartel m general. ~**strong** adj testarudo. ~**teacher** /-'tiːtʃə(r)/ n director m. ~**y** adj (-ier, -iest) (scent) embriagador

heal /hiːl/ vt curar. • vi cicatrizarse

health /helθ/ n salud f. ~**y** adj sano

heap /hiːp/ n montón m. • vt amontonar

hear /hɪə(r)/ vt/i (pt heard /hɜːd/) oír. ~, ~! ¡bravo! ~ **about** oír hablar de. ~ **from** recibir noticias de. ~**ing** n oído m; (Jurid) vista f. ~**ing-aid** n audífono m. ~**say** n rumores mpl

hearse /hɜːs/ n coche m fúnebre

heart /hɑːt/ n corazón m. at ~ en el fondo. by ~ de memoria. lose ~ descorazonarse. ~**ache** n congoja f. ~ **attack** n ataque m al corazón, infarto m. ~**break** n congoja f. ~**breaking** adj desgarrador. ~**burn** n ardor m de estómago. ~**felt** adj sincero

hearth /hɑːθ/ n hogar m

heart: ~**ily** adv de buena gana. ~**less** adj cruel. ~**y** adj (welcome) caluroso; (meal) abundante

heat /hiːt/ n calor m; (contest) (prueba f) eliminatoria f. • vt calentar. • vi calentarse. ~**ed** adj (fig) acalorado. ~**er** n calentador m

heath /hiːθ/ n brezal m, monte m

heathen /'hiːðn/ n & a pagano (m)

heather /'heðə(r)/ n brezo m

heat: ~**ing** n calefacción f. ~**stroke** n insolación f. ~**wave** n ola f de calor

heave /hiːv/ vt (lift) levantar; exhalar (sigh); (fam, throw) tirar. ●vi (pull) tirar, jalar (LAm); (🎼, retch) dar arcadas

heaven /ˈhevn/ n cielo m. ~**ly** adj celestial; (astronomy) celeste; (fam, excellent) divino

heav|ily /ˈhevɪlɪ/ adv pesadamente; (smoke, drink) mucho. ~**y** adj (-ier, -iest) pesado; (rain) fuerte; (traffic) denso. ~**yweight** n peso m pesado

heckle /ˈhekl/ vt interrumpir

hectic /ˈhektɪk/ adj febril

he'd /hiːd/ = he had, he would

hedge /hedʒ/ n seto m (vivo). ●vi escaparse por la tangente. ~**hog** n erizo m

heed /hiːd/ vt hacer caso de. ●n. take ~ tener cuidado

heel /hiːl/ n talón m; (of shoe) tacón m

hefty /ˈheftɪ/ adj (-ier, -iest) (sturdy) fuerte; (heavy) pesado

heifer /ˈhefə(r)/ n novilla f

height /haɪt/ n altura f; (of person) estatura f; (of fame, glory) cumbre f. ~**en** vt elevar; (fig) aumentar

heir /eə(r)/ n heredero m. ~**ess** n heredera f. ~**loom** n reliquia f heredada

held /held/ see HOLD

helicopter /ˈhelɪkɒptə(r)/ n helicóptero m

hell /hel/ n infierno m

he'll /hiːl/ = he will

hello /həˈləʊ/ int ¡hola!; (Telephone, caller) ¡oigal, ¡bueno! (Mex); (Telephone, person answering) ¡diga!, ¡bueno! (Mex). **say** ~ to saludar

helm /helm/ n (Naut) timón m

helmet /ˈhelmɪt/ n casco m

help /help/ vt/i ayudar. he cannot ~ laughing no puede menos de reír. ~ **o.s.** to servirse. it cannot be ~ed no hay más remedio. ●n ayuda f. ●int ¡socorro! ~**er** n ayudante m. ~**ful** adj útil; (person) amable. ~**ing** n porción f. ~**less** adj (unable to manage) incapaz; (defenceless) indefenso

hem /hem/ n dobladillo m

hemisphere /ˈhemɪsfɪə(r)/ n hemisferio m

hen /hen/ n (chicken) gallina f; (female bird) hembra f

hence /hens/ adv de aquí. ~**forth** adv de ahora en adelante

henpecked /ˈhenpekt/ adj dominado por su mujer

her /hɜː(r)/ pron (direct object) la; (indirect object) le; (after prep) ella. I know ~ la conozco. ●adj su, sus pl

herb /hɜːb/ n hierba f. ~**al** adj de hierbas

herd /hɜːd/ n (of cattle, pigs) manada f; (of goats) rebaño m. ●vt arrear. ~ **together** reunir

here /hɪə(r)/ adv aquí, acá (esp LAm). ~! (take this) ¡tenga! ~**abouts** /-əˈbaʊts/ adv por aquí. ~**after** /-ˈɑːftə(r)/ adv en el futuro. ~**by** /-ˈbaɪ/ adv por este medio

heredit|ary /hɪˈredɪtərɪ/ adj hereditario

here|sy /ˈherəsɪ/ n herejía f. ~**tic** n hereje m & f

herewith /hɪəˈwɪθ/ adv adjunto

heritage /ˈherɪtɪdʒ/ n herencia f; (fig) patrimonio m. ~ **tourism** n turismo m cultural, turismo m patrimonial (LAm)

hermetically /hɜːˈmetɪklɪ/ adv. ~ **sealed** herméticamente cerrado

h

hermit /'hɜːmɪt/ n ermitaño m, eremita m

hernia /'hɜːnɪə/ n hernia f

hero /'hɪərəʊ/ n (pl -oes) héroe m. **~ic** /hɪ'rəʊɪk/ adj heroico

heroin /'herəʊɪn/ n heroína f

hero: **~ine** /'herəʊɪn/ n heroína f. **~ism** /'herəʊɪzm/ n heroísmo m

heron /'herən/ n garza f (real)

herring /'herɪŋ/ n arenque m

hers /hɜːz/ poss pron (el) suyo m, (la) suya f, (los) suyos mpl, (las) suyas fpl

herself /hɜː'self/ pron ella misma; (reflexive) se; (after prep) sí misma

he's /hiːz/ = **he is, he has**

hesit|ant /'hezɪtənt/ adj vacilante. **~ate** /-teɪt/ vi vacilar. **~ation** /-'teɪʃn/ n vacilación f

heterosexual /hetərəʊ'seksjʊəl/ adj & n heterosexual (m & f)

het up /het'ʌp/ adj 🅃 nervioso

hew /hjuː/ vt (pp hewed or hewn) cortar; (cut into shape) tallar

hexagon /'heksəgən/ n hexágono m. **~al** /-'ægənl/ adj hexagonal

hey /heɪ/ int ¡eh!; (expressing dismay, protest) ¡oye!

heyday /'heɪdeɪ/ n apogeo m

hi /haɪ/ int 🅃 ¡hola!

hibernat|e /'haɪbəneɪt/ vi hibernar. **~ion** /-'neɪʃn/ n hibernación f

hiccough, hiccup /'hɪkʌp/ n hipo m. **have (the) ~s** tener hipo. ● vi hipar

hide /haɪd/ vt (pt hid, pp hidden) esconder. ● vi esconderse. ● n piel f; (tanned) cuero m. **~-and-seek** /'haɪdnsɪk/ n. **play ~-and-seek** jugar al escondite, jugar a las escondidas (LAm)

hideous /'hɪdɪəs/ adj (dreadful) horrible; (ugly) feo

hideout /'haɪdaʊt/ n escondrijo m

hiding /'haɪdɪŋ/ n (🅃, thrashing) paliza f. **go into ~** esconderse. **~ place** n escondite m, escondrijo m

hierarchy /'haɪərɑːkɪ/ n jerarquía f

hieroglyphics /haɪərə'glɪfɪks/ n jeroglíficos mpl

hi-fi /'haɪfaɪ/ adj de alta fidelidad. ● n equipo m de alta fidelidad, hi-fi m

high /haɪ/ adj (-er, -est) alto; (ideals) elevado; (wind) fuerte; (fam, drugged) drogado, colocado 🅃; (voice) agudo; (meat) pasado. ● n alto nivel m. **a (new) ~** un récord. ● adv alto. **~er education** n enseñanza f superior. **~-handed** /-'hændɪd/ adj prepotente. **~ heels** npl zapatos mpl de tacón alto. **~lands** /-ləndz/ npl tierras fpl altas. **~-level** adj de alto nivel. **~light** n punto m culminante. ● vt destacar; (Art) realzar. **~ly** adv muy; (paid) muy bien. **~ly strung** adj nervioso. **H~ness** n (title) alteza f. **~-rise** adj (building) alto. **~ school** n (Amer) instituto m, colegio m secundario. **~ street** n calle f principal. **~-strung** adj (Amer) nervioso. **~way** n carretera f

> **High School** En EE.UU., el último ciclo del colegio secundario, generalmente para alumnos de edades comprendidas entre los 14 y los 18 años. En Gran Bretaña, algunos colegios secundarios también reciben el nombre de high schools. *i*

hijack /'haɪdʒæk/ vt secuestrar. ● n secuestro m. **~er** n secuestrador

hike /haɪk/ n caminata f. ● vi ir de

caminata. ~**r** n excursionista m & f

hilarious /hɪˈleərɪəs/ adj muy divertido

hill /hɪl/ n colina f; (slope) cuesta f. ~**side** n ladera f. ~**y** adj accidentado

hilt /hɪlt/ n (of sword) puño m. **to the** ~ (fig) totalmente

him /hɪm/ pron (direct object) lo, le (only Spain); (indirect object) le; (after prep) él. **I know** ~ lo/le conozco. ~**self** pron él mismo; (reflexive) se; (after prep) sí mismo

hind|er /ˈhɪndə(r)/ vt estorbar. ~**rance** /ˈhɪndrəns/ n obstáculo m

hindsight /ˈhaɪnsaɪt/ n. **with** ~ retrospectivamente

Hindu /ˈhɪnduː/ n & a hindú (m & f). ~**ism** n hinduismo m

hinge /hɪndʒ/ n bisagra f

hint /hɪnt/ n indirecta f; (advice) consejo m. ● vi soltar una indirecta. ~ **at** dar a entender

hip /hɪp/ n cadera f

hippie /ˈhɪpɪ/ n hippy m & f

hippopotamus /hɪpəˈpɒtəməs/ n (pl -muses or -mi /-maɪ/) hipopótamo m

hire /haɪə(r)/ vt alquilar (thing); contratar (person). ● n alquiler m. ~**car** ~ alquiler m de coches. ~ **purchase** n compra f a plazos

his /hɪz/ adj su, sus pl. ● poss pron (el) suyo m, (la) suya f, (los) suyos mpl, (las) suyas fpl

Hispan|ic /hɪˈspænɪk/ adj hispánico. ● n (Amer) hispano m. ~**ist** /ˈhɪspənɪst/ n hispanista m & f

hiss /hɪs/ n silbido. ● vt/i silbar

histor|ian /hɪˈstɔːrɪən/ n historiador m. ~**ic(al)** /hɪˈstɒrɪk(l)/ adj histórico. ~**y** /ˈhɪstərɪ/ n historia f.

hit /hɪt/ vt (pt hit, pres p hitting) golpear (object); pegarle a (per-

son); (collide with) chocar con; (affect) afectar. ~ **it off with** hacer buenas migas con. □ ~ **on** vt dar con. ● n (blow) golpe m; (success) éxito m. (Internet) visita f

hitch /hɪtʃ/ vt (fasten) enganchar. ● n (snag) problema m. ~ **a lift**, ~ **a ride** (Amer) see ~HIKE. ~**hike** vi hacer autostop, hacer dedo, ir de aventón (Mex). ~**hiker** n autoestopista m & f

hither /ˈhɪðə(r)/ adv aquí, acá. ~ **and thither** acá y allá. ~**to** adv hasta ahora

hit-or-miss /hɪtɔːˈmɪs/ adj (approach) poco científico

hive /haɪv/ n colmena f

hoard /hɔːd/ vt acumular. ● n provisión f; (of money) tesoro m

hoarding /ˈhɔːdɪŋ/ n valla f publicitaria

hoarse /hɔːs/ adj (-er, -est) ronco. ~**ly** adv con voz ronca

hoax /həʊks/ n engaño m. ● vt engañar

hob /hɒb/ n (of cooker) hornillos mpl, hornillas fpl (LAm)

hobble /ˈhɒbl/ vi cojear, renguear (LAm)

hobby /ˈhɒbɪ/ n pasatiempo m. ~**horse** n (toy) caballito m (de niño); (fixation) caballo m de batalla

hockey /ˈhɒkɪ/ n hockey m; (Amer) hockey m sobre hielo

hoe /həʊ/ n azada f. ● vt (pres p hoeing) azadonar

hog /hɒg/ n (Amer) cerdo m. ● vt (pt hogged) 🔢 acaparar

hoist /hɔɪst/ vt levantar; izar (flag). ● n montacargas m

hold /həʊld/ vt (pt held) tener; (grasp) coger (esp Spain), agarrar (LAm); (contain) contener; mantener

hole | hooligan

(interest); (believe) creer. ● vi mantenerse. ● n (influence) influencia f; (Naut, Aviat) bodega f. get ~ of agarrar; (fig, acquire) adquirir. □ ~ back vt (contain) contener. □ ~ on vi (stand firm) resistir; (wait) esperar. □ ~ on to vt (keep) guardar; (cling to) agarrarse a. □ ~ out vt (offer) ofrecer. vi (resist) resistir. □ ~ up vt (raise) levantar; (support) sostener; (delay) retrasar; (rob) atracar. ~all n bolsa f (de viaje). ~er n tenedor m; (of post) titular m; (wallet) funda f. ~up atraco m

hole /həʊl/ n agujero m; (in ground) hoyo m; (in road) bache m. ● vt agujerear

holiday /ˈhɒlɪdeɪ/ n vacaciones fpl; (public) fiesta f. go on ~ ir de vacaciones. ~maker n veraneante m & f

holiness /ˈhəʊlɪnɪs/ n santidad f

Holland /ˈhɒlənd/ n Holanda f

hollow /ˈhɒləʊ/ adj & n hueco (m)

holly /ˈhɒlɪ/ n acebo m

holocaust /ˈhɒləkɔːst/ n holocausto m

holster /ˈhəʊlstə(r)/ n pistolera f

holy /ˈhəʊlɪ/ adj (-ier, -iest) santo, sagrado. H~ Ghost n, H~ Spirit n Espíritu m Santo. ~ water n agua f bendita

homage /ˈhɒmɪdʒ/ n homenaje m. pay ~ to rendir homenaje a

home /həʊm/ n casa f; (for old people) residencia f de ancianos; (native land) patria f. ● adj (cooking) casero; (address) particular; (background) familiar; (Pol) interior; (match) de casa. ● adv. (at) ~ en casa. ~land n patria f. ~ land security seguridad f nacional. ~less adj sin hogar. ~ly adj (-ier, -iest) casero; (Amer, ugly) feo. ~-made

adj hecho en casa. ~ **page** n (Comp) página f frontal. ~**sick** adj. be ~sick echar de menos a su familia/su país, extrañar a su familia/su país (LAm). ~ **town** n ciudad f natal. ~**work** n deberes mpl

homicide /ˈhɒmɪsaɪd/ n homicidio m

homoeopathic /həʊmɪəʊˈpæθɪk/ adj homeopático

homogeneous /hɒməʊˈdʒiːnɪəs/ adj homogéneo

homosexual /həʊməʊˈseksjʊəl/ adj & n homosexual (m)

honest /ˈɒnɪst/ adj honrado; (frank) sincero. ~ly adv honradamente. ~y n honradez f

honey /ˈhʌnɪ/ n miel f. ~**comb** n panal m. ~**moon** n luna f de miel. ~**suckle** n madreselva f

honorary /ˈɒnərərɪ/ adj honorario

honour /ˈɒnə(r)/ n honor m. ● vt honrar; cumplir (con) (promise). ~**able** adj honorable

hood /hʊd/ n capucha f; (car roof) capota f; (Amer, car bonnet) capó m, capote m (Mex)

hoodwink /ˈhʊdwɪŋk/ vt engañar

hoof /huːf/ n (pl hoofs or hooves) (of horse) casco m, pezuña f (Mex); (of cow) pezuña f

hook /hʊk/ n gancho m; (on garment) corchete m; (for fishing) anzuelo m. let s.o. off the ~ dejar salir a uno del atolladero. off the ~ (telephone) descolgado. ● vt. ~ed on 𝕋 adicto a. □ ~ up vt enganchar. ~ed (tool) en forma de gancho; (nose) aguileño

hookey /ˈhʊkɪ/ n. play ~ (Amer fam) faltar a clase, hacer novillos

hooligan /ˈhuːlɪɡən/ n vándalo m, gamberro m

hoop /hu:p/ n aro m

hooray /hʊˈreɪ/ int & n ¡viva! (m)

hoot /hu:t/ n (of horn) bocinazo m; (of owl) ululato m. ●vi tocar la bocina; (owl) ulular

Hoover /ˈhu:və(r)/ n (®) aspiradora f. ●vt pasar la aspiradora por, aspirar (LAm)

hooves /hu:vz/ see HOOF

hop /hɒp/ vi (pt hopped) saltar a la pata coja; (frog, rabbit) brincar, saltar; (bird) dar saltitos. ●n salto m; (flight) etapa f. ~(s) (plant) lúpulo m

hope /həʊp/ n esperanza f. ●vt/i esperar. ~ for esperar. ~ful adj (optimistic) esperanzado; (promising) esperanzador. ~fully adv con optimismo; (it is hoped) se espera. ~less adj desesperado

horde /hɔ:d/ n horda f

horizon /həˈraɪzn/ n horizonte m

horizontal /hɒrɪˈzɒntl/ adj horizontal. ~ly adv horizontalmente

hormone /ˈhɔ:məʊn/ n hormona f

horn /hɔ:n/ n cuerno m, asta f, cacho m (LAm); (of car) bocina f; (Mus) trompa f. ~ed adj con cuernos

hornet /ˈhɔ:nɪt/ n avispón m

horoscope /ˈhɒrəskəʊp/ n horóscopo m

horrible /ˈhɒrəbl/ adj horrible

horrid /ˈhɒrɪd/ adj horrible

horrific /həˈrɪfɪk/ adj horroroso

horrify /ˈhɒrɪfaɪ/ vt horrorizar

horror /ˈhɒrə(r)/ n horror m

hors-d'oeuvre /ɔːˈdɜːvr/ n (pl ~s /-ˈdɜːvr/) entremés m, botana f (Mex)

horse /hɔ:s/ n caballo m. ~back n. on ~back a caballo. ~power n (unit) caballo m (de fuerza). ~ra-

cing n carreras fpl de caballos. ~shoe n herradura f

horticultural /hɔːtɪˈkʌltʃərəl/ adj hortícola. ~e /ˈhɔːtɪkʌltʃə(r)/ n horticultura f

hose /həʊz/ n manguera f, manga f. ●vt. ~ down lavar (con manguera). ~pipe n manga f

hosiery /ˈhəʊzɪərɪ/ n calcetería f

hospice /ˈhɒspɪs/ n residencia f para enfermos desahuciados

hospitable /hɒˈspɪtəbl/ adj hospitalario

hospital /ˈhɒspɪtl/ n hospital m

hospitality /hɒspɪˈtælɪtɪ/ n hospitalidad f

host /həʊst/ n (master of house) anfitrión m; (Radio, TV) presentador m; (multitude) gran cantidad f; (Relig) hostia f

hostage /ˈhɒstɪdʒ/ n rehén m

hostel /ˈhɒstl/ n (for students) residencia f; (for homeless people) hogar m

hostess /ˈhəʊstɪs/ n anfitriona f

hostile /ˈhɒstaɪl/ adj hostil. ~ity /-ˈtɪlətɪ/ n hostilidad f

hot /hɒt/ adj (hotter, hottest) caliente; (weather, day) caluroso; (climate) cálido; (Culin) picante; (news) de última hora. be/feel ~ tener calor. get ~ calentarse. it is ~ hace calor. ~bed n (fig) semillero m

hotchpotch /ˈhɒtʃpɒtʃ/ n mezcolanza f

hot dog n perrito m caliente

hotel /həʊˈtel/ n hotel m. ~ier /-ɪeɪ/ n hotelero m

hot: ~house n invernadero m. ~plate n placa f, hornilla f (LAm). ~-water bottle /-ˈwɔːtə(r)/ n bolsa f de agua caliente

hound /haʊnd/ n perro m de caza.

● vt perseguir

hour /aʊə(r)/ n hora f. ~**ly** adj (rate) por hora. ● adv (every hour) cada hora; (by the hour) por hora

house /haʊs/ n (pl -s /ˈhaʊzɪz/) casa f; (Pol) cámara f. ● /haʊz/ vt alojar; (keep) guardar. ~**hold** n casa f. ~**holder** n dueño m de una casa. ~**keeper** n ama f de llaves. ~**maid** n criada f, mucama f (LAm). ~**proud** adj meticuloso. ~**warming** (party) n fiesta de inauguración de una casa. ~**wife** n ama f de casa. ~**work** n tareas fpl domésticas

housing /ˈhaʊzɪŋ/ n alojamiento m. ~ **development** (Amer), ~ **estate** n complejo m habitacional, urbanización f

hovel /ˈhɒvl/ n casucha f

hover /ˈhɒvə(r)/ vi (bird, threat etc) cernerse; (loiter) rondar. ~**craft** n (pl invar or -crafts) aerodeslizador m

how /haʊ/ adv cómo. ~ about a walk? ¿qué te parece si damos un paseo? ~ are you? ¿cómo está Vd? ~ do you do? (in introduction) mucho gusto. ~ long? (in time) ¿cuánto tiempo? ~ long is the room? ¿cuánto mide de largo el cuarto? ~ often? ¿cuántas veces?

however /haʊˈevə(r)/ adv (nevertheless) no obstante, sin embargo; (with verb) de cualquier manera que (+ subjunctive); (with adjective or adverb) por... que (+ subjunctive). ~ much it rains por mucho que llueva

howl /haʊl/ n aullido. ● vi aullar

hp abbr see **HORSEPOWER**

HP abbr see **HIRE-PURCHASE**

hub /hʌb/ n (of wheel) cubo m;

(fig) centro m

hubcap /ˈhʌbkæp/ n tapacubos m

huddle /ˈhʌdl/ vi apiñarse

hue /hjuː/ n (colour) color m

huff /hʌf/ n. be in a ~ estar enfurruñado

hug /hʌg/ vt (pt hugged) abrazar. ● n abrazo m

huge /hjuːdʒ/ adj enorme. ~**ly** adv enormemente

hulk /hʌlk/ n (of ship) barco m viejo

hull /hʌl/ n (of ship) casco m

hullo /həˈləʊ/ int see **HELLO**

hum /hʌm/ vt/i (pt hummed) (person) canturrear; (insect, engine) zumbar. ● n zumbido m

human /ˈhjuːmən/ adj & n humano (m). ~ **being** n ser m humano. ~**e** /hjuːˈmeɪn/ adj humano. ~**itarian** /hjuːmænɪˈteərɪən/ adj humanitario. ~**ity** /hjuːˈmænətɪ/ n humanidad f

humbl|e /ˈhʌmbl/ adj (-er, -est) humilde. ● vt humillar. ~**y** adv humildemente

humdrum /ˈhʌmdrʌm/ adj monótono

humid /ˈhjuːmɪd/ adj húmedo. ~**ity** /hjuːˈmɪdətɪ/ n humedad f

humiliat|e /hjuːˈmɪlɪeɪt/ vt humillar. ~**ion** /-ˈeɪʃn/ n humillación f

humility /hjuːˈmɪlətɪ/ n humildad f

humongous /hjuːˈmʌŋgəs/ adj 🅴 de primera

humo|rist /ˈhjuːmərɪst/ n humorista m & f. ~**rous** /-rəs/ adj humorístico. ~**rously** adv con gracia. ~**ur** /ˈhjuːmə(r)/ n humor m. sense of ~**ur** sentido m del humor

hump /hʌmp/ n (of person, camel) joroba f; (in ground) montículo m

hunch /hʌntʃ/ *vt* encorvar. ● *n* presentimiento *m*; (*lump*) joroba *f*. ~**back** *n* jorobado *m*

hundred /ˈhʌndrəd/ *adj* ciento, (*before noun*) cien. **one** ~ **and ninety-eight** ciento noventa y ocho. **two** ~ doscientos. **three** ~ **pages** trescientas páginas. **four** ~ cuatrocientos. **five** ~ quinientos. ● *n* ciento *m*. ~**s of** centenares de. ~**th** *adj* & *n* centésimo (*m*). ~**weight** *n* 50,8kg; (*Amer*) 45,36kg

hung /hʌŋ/ *see* HANG

Hungar|ian /hʌŋˈgeəriən/ *adj* & *n* húngaro (*m*). ~**y** /ˈhʌŋgəri/ *n* Hungría *f*

hung|er /ˈhʌŋgə(r)/ *n* hambre *f*. ● *vi*. ~**er for** tener hambre de. ~**rily** /ˈhʌŋgrəli/ *adv* ávidamente. ~**ry** *adj* (**-ier, -iest**) hambriento. **be** ~**ry** tener hambre

hunk /hʌŋk/ *n* (buen) pedazo *m*

hunt /hʌnt/ *vt* cazar. ● *vi* cazar. ~ **for** buscar. ● *n* caza *f*. ~**er** *n* cazador *m*. ~**ing** *n* caza *f*. **go** ~**ing** ir de caza

hurl /hɜːl/ *vt* lanzar

hurrah /huˈrɑː/, **hurray** /huˈreɪ/ *int* & *n* ¡viva! (*m*)

hurricane /ˈhʌrɪkən/ *n* huracán *m*

hurr|ied /ˈhʌrɪd/ *adj* apresurado. ~**iedly** *adv* apresuradamente. ~**y** *vi* darse prisa, apurarse (*LAm*). ● *vt* meter prisa a, apurar (*LAm*). ● *n* prisa *f*. **be in a** ~**y** tener prisa, estar apurado (*LAm*)

hurt /hɜːt/ *vt* (*pt* **hurt**) hacer daño a, lastimar (*LAm*). ~ **s.o.'s feelings** ofender a uno. ● *vi* doler. **my head** ~**s** me duele la cabeza. ~**ful** *adj* hiriente

hurtle /ˈhɜːtl/ *vt* ir volando. ● *vi*. ~ **along** mover rápidamente

husband /ˈhʌzbənd/ *n* marido *m*, esposo *m*

hush /hʌʃ/ *vt* acallar. ● *n* silencio *m*. □ ~ **up** *vt* acallar (*affair*). ~**-hush** *adj* 🄻 super secreto

husk /hʌsk/ *n* cáscara *f*

husky /ˈhʌski/ *adj* (**-ier, -iest**) (*hoarse*) ronco

hustle /ˈhʌsl/ *vt* (*jostle*) empujar. ● *vi* (*hurry*) darse prisa, apurarse (*LAm*). ● *n* empuje *m*

hut /hʌt/ *n* cabaña *f*

hutch /hʌtʃ/ *n* conejera *f*

hybrid /ˈhaɪbrɪd/ *adj* & *n* híbrido (*m*)

hydrangea /haɪˈdreɪndʒə/ *n* hortensia *f*

hydrant /ˈhaɪdrənt/ *n*. (**fire**) ~ *n* boca *f* de riego, boca *f* de incendios (*LAm*)

hydraulic /haɪˈdrɔːlɪk/ *adj* hidráulico

hydroelectric /haɪdrəʊˈlektrɪk/ *adj* hidroeléctrico

hydrofoil /ˈhaɪdrəfɔɪl/ *n* hidrodeslizador *m*

hydrogen /ˈhaɪdrədʒən/ *n* hidrógeno *m*

hyena /haɪˈiːnə/ *n* hiena *f*

hygien|e /ˈhaɪdʒiːn/ *n* higiene *f*. ~**ic** /haɪˈdʒiːnɪk/ *adj* higiénico

hymn /hɪm/ *n* himno *m*

hyper... /ˈhaɪpə(r)/ *pref* hiper...

hyphen /ˈhaɪfn/ *n* guión *m*. ~**ate** /-eɪt/ *vt* escribir con guión

hypno|sis /hɪpˈnəʊsɪs/ *n* hipnosis *f*. ~**tic** /-ˈnɒtɪk/ *adj* hipnótico. ~**tism** /ˈhɪpnətɪzəm/ *n* hipnotismo *m*. ~**tist** /ˈhɪpnətɪst/ *n* hipnotista *m* & *f*. ~**tize** /ˈhɪpnətaɪz/ *vt* hipnotizar

hypochondriac /haɪpəˈkɒndriæk/ *n* hipocondríaco *m*

hypocri|sy /hɪˈpɒkrəsɪ/ *n* hipo-

h

cresía f. **~te** /'hɪpəkrɪt/ n hipócrita m & f. **~tical** /hɪpə'krɪtɪkl/ adj hipócrita

hypodermic /haɪpə'dɜːmɪk/ adj hipodérmico. ●n hipodérmica f

hypothe|sis /haɪ'pɒθəsɪs/ n (pl -theses/-siːz/) hipótesis f. **~tical** /-ə'θetɪkl/ adj hipotético

hysteri|a /hɪ'stɪərɪə/ n histerismo m. **~cal** /-'terɪkl/ adj histérico. **~cs** /hɪ'sterɪks/ npl histerismo m. have **~cs** ponerse histérico; (laugh) morir de risa

Ii

I /aɪ/ pron yo

ice /aɪs/ n hielo m. ●vt helar; glasear (cake). ●vi. **~ (up)** helarse, congelarse. **~berg** /-bɜːg/ n iceberg m. **~ box** n (compartment) congelador m (Amer fam, refrigerator) frigorífico m, refrigerador m (LAm). **~cream** n helado m. **~ cube** n cubito m de hielo

Iceland /'aɪslənd/ n Islandia f

ice: **~ lolly** polo m, paleta f helada (LAm). **~ rink** n pista f de hielo. **~ skating** n patinaje m sobre hielo

icicle /'aɪsɪkl/ n carámbano m

icing /'aɪsɪŋ/ n glaseado m

icon /'aɪkɒn/ n icono m

icy /'aɪsɪ/ adj (-ier, -iest) helado; (fig) glacial

I'd /aɪd/ = I had, I would

idea /aɪ'dɪə/ n idea f

ideal /aɪ'dɪəl/ adj & n ideal (m). **~ism** n idealismo m. **~ist** n idea-

lista m & f. **~istic** /-'lɪstɪk/ adj idealista. **~ize** vt idealizar. **~ly** adv idealmente

identical /aɪ'dentɪkl/ adj idéntico. **~ twins** npl gemelos mpl idénticos, gemelos mpl (LAm)

identif|ication /aɪdentɪfɪ'keɪʃn/ n identificación f. **~y** /aɪ'dentɪfaɪ/ vt identificar. ●vi. **~y with** identificarse con

identity /aɪ'dentɪtɪ/ n identidad f. **~ card** n carné m de identidad. **~ theft** n robo m de identidad

ideolog|ical /aɪdɪə'lɒdʒɪkl/ adj ideológico. **~y** /aɪdɪ'ɒlədʒɪ/ n ideología f

idiocy /'ɪdɪəsɪ/ n idiotez f

idiom /'ɪdɪəm/ n locución f. **~atic** /-'mætɪk/ adj idiomático

idiot /'ɪdɪət/ n idiota m & f. **~ic** /-'ɒtɪk/ adj idiota

idle /'aɪdl/ adj (-er, -est) ocioso; (lazy) holgazán; (out of work) desocupado; (machine) parado. ●vi (engine) andar al ralentí. **~ness** n ociosidad f; (laziness) holgazanería f

idol /'aɪdl/ n ídolo m. **~ize** vt idolatrar

idyllic /ɪ'dɪlɪk/ adj idílico

i.e. abbr (= id est) es decir

if /ɪf/ conj si

igloo /'ɪgluː/ n iglú m

ignit|e /ɪg'naɪt/ vt encender. ●vi encenderse. **~ion** /-'nɪʃn/ n ignición f; (Auto) encendido m. **~ion key** n llave f de contacto

ignoramus /ɪgnə'reɪməs/ n (pl -muses) ignorante

ignoran|ce /'ɪgnərəns/ n ignorancia f. **~t** adj ignorante

ignore /ɪg'nɔː(r)/ vt no hacer caso de; hacer caso omiso de (warning)

ill /ɪl/ adj enfermo. ●adv mal. ●n mal m

I'll /aɪl/ = I will

ill: ~**-advised** /-əd'vaɪzd/ adj imprudente. ~ **at ease** /-ət'i:z/ adj incómodo. ~**-bred** /-'bred/ adj mal educado

illegal /ɪ'li:gl/ adj ilegal

illegible /ɪ'ledʒəbl/ adj ilegible

illegitima|cy /ɪlɪ'dʒɪtɪməsɪ/ n ilegitimidad f. ~**te** /-ət/ adj ilegítimo

illitera|cy /ɪ'lɪtərəsɪ/ n analfabetismo m. ~**te** /-ət/ adj analfabeto

illness /'ɪlnɪs/ n enfermedad f

illogical /ɪ'lɒdʒɪkl/ adj ilógico

illuminat|e /ɪ'lu:mɪneɪt/ vt iluminar. ~**ion** /-'neɪʃn/ n iluminación f

illus|ion /ɪ'lu:ʒn/ n ilusión f. ~**sory** /-sərɪ/ adj ilusorio

illustrat|e /'ɪləstreɪt/ vt ilustrar. ~**ion** /-'streɪʃn/ n ilustración f; (example) ejemplo m

illustrious /ɪ'lʌstrɪəs/ adj ilustre

ill will /ɪl'wɪl/ n mala voluntad f

I'm /aɪm/ = I am

image /'ɪmɪdʒ/ n imagen f. ~**ry** n imágenes fpl

imagin|able /ɪ'mædʒɪnəbl/ adj imaginable. ~**ary** adj imaginario. ~**ation** /-'neɪʃn/ n imaginación f. ~**ative** adj imaginativo. ~**e** /ɪ'mædʒɪn/ vt imaginar(se)

imbalance /ɪm'bæləns/ n desequilibrio m

imbecile /'ɪmbəsi:l/ n imbécil m & f

imitat|e /'ɪmɪteɪt/ vt imitar. ~**ion** /-'teɪʃn/ n imitación f. ●adj de imitación. ~**or** n imitador m

immaculate /ɪ'mækjʊlət/ adj inmaculado

immatur|e /ɪmə'tjʊə(r)/ adj inmaduro. ~**ity** n inmadurez f

immediate /ɪ'mi:dɪət/ adj inmediato. ~**ly** adv inmediatamente

● conj en cuanto (+ subjunctive)

immens|e /ɪ'mens/ adj inmenso. ~**ely** adv inmensamente; (fam, very much) muchísimo

immers|e /ɪ'mɜ:s/ vt sumergir. ~**ion** /-ʃn/ n inmersión f. ~**ion heater** n calentador m de inmersión

immigra|nt /'ɪmɪgrənt/ adj & n inmigrante (m & f). ~**tion** /-'greɪʃn/ n inmigración f

imminent /'ɪmɪnənt/ adj inminente

immobil|e /ɪ'məʊbaɪl/ adj inmóvil. ~**ize** /-bɪlaɪz/ vt inmovilizar. ~**izer** /-bɪlaɪzə(r)/ n inmovilizador m

immoderate /ɪ'mɒdərət/ adj inmoderado

immodest /ɪ'mɒdɪst/ adj inmodesto

immoral /ɪ'mɒrəl/ adj inmoral. ~**ity** /ɪmə'rælətɪ/ n inmoralidad f

immortal /ɪ'mɔ:tl/ adj inmortal. ~**ity** /-'tælətɪ/ n inmortalidad f. ~**ize** vt inmortalizar

immun|e /ɪ'mju:n/ adj inmune (to a). ~**ity** n inmunidad f. ~**ization** /ɪmjʊnaɪ'zeɪʃn/ n inmunización f. ~**ize** /'ɪmjʊnaɪz/ vt inmunizar

imp /ɪmp/ n diablillo m

impact /'ɪmpækt/ n impacto m

impair /ɪm'peə(r)/ vt perjudicar

impale /ɪm'peɪl/ vt atravesar (on con)

impart /ɪm'pɑ:t/ vt comunicar (news); impartir (knowledge)

impartial /ɪm'pɑ:ʃl/ adj imparcial. ~**ity** /-ʃɪ'ælətɪ/ n imparcialidad f

impassable /ɪm'pɑ:səbl/ adj (road) intransitable

impassive /ɪm'pæsɪv/ adj impasible

impatien|ce /ɪmˈpeɪʃəns/ n impaciencia f. ∼t adj impaciente. get ∼t impacientarse. ∼tly adv con impaciencia

impeccable /ɪmˈpekəbl/ adj impecable

impede /ɪmˈpiːd/ vt estorbar

impediment /ɪmˈpedɪmənt/ n obstáculo m. (speech) ∼ n defecto m del habla

impending /ɪmˈpendɪŋ/ adj inminente

impenetrable /ɪmˈpenɪtrəbl/ adj impenetrable

imperative /ɪmˈperətɪv/ adj imprescindible. ● n (Gram) imperativo m

imperceptible /ɪmpəˈseptəbl/ adj imperceptible

imperfect /ɪmˈpɜːfɪkt/ adj imperfecto. ∼ion /ɪmpəˈfekʃn/ n imperfección f

imperial /ɪmˈpɪərɪəl/ adj imperial. ∼ism n imperialismo m

impersonal /ɪmˈpɜːsənl/ adj impersonal

impersonat|e /ɪmˈpɜːsəneɪt/ vt hacerse pasar por; (mimic) imitar. ∼ion /-ˈneɪʃn/ n imitación f. ∼or n imitador m

impertinen|ce /ɪmˈpɜːtɪnəns/ n impertinencia f. ∼t adj impertinente

impervious /ɪmˈpɜːvɪəs/ adj. ∼ to impermeable a

impetuous /ɪmˈpetjʊəs/ adj impetuoso

impetus /ˈɪmpɪtəs/ n ímpetu m

implacable /ɪmˈplækəbl/ adj implacable

implant /ɪmˈplɑːnt/ vt implantar

implement /ˈɪmplɪmənt/ n instrumento m, implemento m (LAm). ● /ˈɪmplɪment/ vt implementar

implementation /ˌɪmplɪmenˈteɪʃn/ n implementación f

implicat|e /ˈɪmplɪkeɪt/ vt implicar. ∼ion /ˌɪmplɪˈkeɪʃn/ n implicación f

implicit /ɪmˈplɪsɪt/ adj (implied) implícito; (unquestioning) absoluto

implore /ɪmˈplɔː(r)/ vt implorar

imply /ɪmˈplaɪ/ vt (involve) implicar; (insinuate) dar a entender, insinuar

impolite /ˌɪmpəˈlaɪt/ adj mal educado

import /ɪmˈpɔːt/ vt importar. ● /ˈɪmpɔːt/ n importación f; (item) artículo m de importación; (meaning) significación f

importan|ce /ɪmˈpɔːtəns/ n importancia f. ∼t adj importante

importer /ɪmˈpɔːtə(r)/ n importador m

impos|e /ɪmˈpəʊz/ vt imponer. ● vi. ∼e on abusar de la amabilidad de. ∼ing adj imponente. ∼ition /ˌɪmpəˈzɪʃn/ n imposición f; (fig) abuso m

impossib|ility /ɪmˌpɒsəˈbɪlətɪ/ n imposibilidad f. ∼le /ɪmˈpɒsəbl/ adj imposible

impostor /ɪmˈpɒstə(r)/ n impostor m

impoten|ce /ˈɪmpətəns/ n impotencia f. ∼t adj impotente

impound /ɪmˈpaʊnd/ vt confiscar

impoverished /ɪmˈpɒvərɪʃt/ adj empobrecido

impractical /ɪmˈpræktɪkl/ adj poco práctico

impregnable /ɪmˈpregnəbl/ adj inexpugnable

impregnate /ˈɪmpregneɪt/ vt impregnar (with con, de)

impress /ɪmˈpres/ vt impresionar; (make good impression) causar una buena impresión a. ● vi impresionar

impression /ɪmˈpreʃn/ n impresión f. **~able** adj impresionable. **~ism** n impresionismo m

impressive /ɪmˈpresɪv/ adj impresionante

imprint /ˈɪmprɪnt/ n impresión f. •/ɪmˈprɪnt/ vt imprimir

imprison /ɪmˈprɪzn/ vt encarcelar. **~ment** n encarcelamiento m

improbab|ility /ɪmprɒbəˈbɪlɪtɪ/ n improbabilidad f. **~le** /ɪmˈprɒbəbl/ adj improbable

impromptu /ɪmˈprɒmptjuː/ adj improvisado. • adv de improviso

improper /ɪmˈprɒpə(r)/ adj impropio; (incorrect) incorrecto

improve /ɪmˈpruːv/ vt mejorar. • vi mejorar. **~ment** n mejora f

improvis|ation /ɪmprəvaɪˈzeɪʃn/ n improvisación f. **~e** /ˈɪmprəvaɪz/ vt/i improvisar

impuden|ce /ˈɪmpjʊdəns/ n insolencia f. **~t** adj insolente

impuls|e /ˈɪmpʌls/ n impulso m. on **~e** sin reflexionar. **~ive** adj irreflexivo

impur|e /ɪmˈpjʊə(r)/ adj impuro. **~ity** n impureza f

in /ɪn/ prep en; (within) dentro de. **~** a firm manner de una manera terminante. **~** an hour's (time) dentro de una hora. **~** doing al hacer. **~** so far as en la medida en que. **~** the evening por la tarde. **~** the rain bajo la lluvia. **~** the sun al sol. one **~** ten uno de cada diez. the best **~** the world el mejor del mundo. • adv (inside) dentro; (at home) en casa. come **~** entrar. • n. the **~s** and outs of los detalles de

inability /ɪnəˈbɪlɪtɪ/ n incapacidad f

inaccessible /mækˈsesəbl/ adj inaccesible

inaccura|cy /ɪnˈækjʊrəsɪ/ n inexactitud f. **~te** /-ət/ adj inexacto

inactive /ɪnˈæktɪv/ adj inactivo. **~ity** /-ˈtɪvətɪ/ n inactividad f

inadequa|cy /ɪnˈædɪkwəsɪ/ adj insuficiencia f. **~te** /-ət/ adj insuficiente

inadvertently /ɪnədˈvɜːtəntlɪ/ adv sin querer

inadvisable /ɪnədˈvaɪzəbl/ adj desaconsejable

inane /ɪˈneɪn/ adj estúpido

inanimate /ɪnˈænɪmət/ adj inanimado

inappropriate /ɪnəˈprəʊprɪət/ adj inoportuno

inarticulate /ɪnɑːˈtɪkjʊlət/ adj incapaz de expresarse claramente

inattentive /ɪnəˈtentɪv/ adj desatento

inaudible /ɪnˈɔːdəbl/ adj inaudible

inaugurate /ɪˈnɔːgjʊreɪt/ vt inaugurar

inborn /ˈɪnbɔːn/ adj innato

inbred /ɪnˈbred/ adj (inborn) innato; (social group) endogámico

Inc /ɪŋk/ abbr (Amer) (= Incorporated) S.A., Sociedad Anónima

incalculable /ɪnˈkælkjʊləbl/ adj incalculable

incapable /ɪnˈkeɪpəbl/ adj incapaz

incapacit|ate /ɪnkəˈpæsɪteɪt/ vt incapacitar. **~y** n incapacidad f

incarcerate /ɪnˈkɑːsəreɪt/ vt encarcelar

incarnat|e /ɪnˈkɑːnət/ adj encarnado. **~ion** /-ˈneɪʃn/ n encarnación f

incendiary /ɪnˈsendɪərɪ/ adj incendiario. **~ bomb** bomba f incendiaria

incense /'ɪnsens/ n incienso m.
● /ɪn'sens/ vt enfurecer

incentive /ɪn'sentɪv/ n incentivo m

incessant /ɪn'sesnt/ adj incesante. ~ly adv sin cesar

incest /'ɪnsest/ n incesto m. ~uous /ɪn'sestjʊəs/ adj incestuoso

inch /ɪntʃ/ n pulgada f; (= 2,54cm). ● vi. ~ forward avanzar lentamente

incidence /'ɪnsɪdəns/ n frecuencia f

incident /'ɪnsɪdənt/ n incidente m

incidental /ɪnsɪ'dentl/ adj (effect) secundario; (minor) incidental. ~ly adv a propósito

incinerat|e /ɪn'sɪnəreɪt/ vt incinerar. ~or n incinerador m

incision /ɪn'sɪʒn/ n incisión f

incite /ɪn'saɪt/ vt incitar. ~ment n incitación f

inclination /ɪnklɪ'neɪʃn/ n inclinación f. have no ~ to no tener deseos de

incline /ɪn'klaɪn/ vt inclinar. be ~d to tener tendencia a. ● vi inclinarse. ● /'ɪnklaɪn/ n pendiente f

inclu|de /ɪn'kluːd/ vt incluir. ~ding prep incluso. ~sion /-ʒn/ n inclusión f. ~sive /-sɪv/ adj inclusivo

incognito /ɪnkɒg'niːtəʊ/ adv de incógnito

incoherent /ɪnkəʊ'hɪərənt/ adj incoherente

incom|e /'ɪnkʌm/ n ingresos mpl. ~e tax n impuesto m sobre la renta. ~ing adj (tide) ascendente

incomparable /ɪn'kɒmpərəbl/ adj incomparable

incompatible /ɪnkəm'pætəbl/ adj incompatible

incompeten|ce /ɪn'kɒmpɪtəns/ n incompetencia f. ~t adj incompetente

incomplete /ɪnkəm'pliːt/ adj incompleto

incomprehensible /ɪnkɒmprɪ'hensəbl/ adj incomprensible

inconceivable /ɪnkən'siːvəbl/ adj inconcebible

inconclusive /ɪnkən'kluːsɪv/ adj no concluyente

incongruous /ɪn'kɒŋgrʊəs/ adj incongruente

inconsiderate /ɪnkən'sɪdərət/ adj desconsiderado

inconsisten|cy /ɪnkən'sɪstənsɪ/ n inconsecuencia f. ~t adj inconsecuente. be ~t with no concordar con

inconspicuous /ɪnkən'spɪkjʊəs/ adj que no llama la atención. ~ly adv sin llamar la atención

incontinent /ɪn'kɒntɪnənt/ adj incontinente

inconvenien|ce /ɪnkən'viːnɪəns/ adj inconveniencia f; (drawback) inconveniente m. ~t adj inconveniente

incorporate /ɪn'kɔːpəreɪt/ vt incorporar; (include) incluir; (Com) constituir (en sociedad)

incorrect /ɪnkə'rekt/ adj incorrecto

increas|e /'ɪnkriːs/ n aumento m (in de). ● /ɪn'kriːs/ vt/i aumentar. ~ing /ɪn'kriːsɪŋ/ adj creciente. ~ingly adv cada vez más

incredible /ɪn'kredəbl/ adj increíble

incredulous /ɪn'kredjʊləs/ adj incrédulo

incriminat|e /ɪn'krɪmɪneɪt/ vt incriminar. ~ing adj comprometedor

incubat|e /ˈɪŋkjʊbeɪt/ vt incubar. **~ion** /-ˈbeɪʃn/ n incubación f. **~or** n incubadora f

incur /ɪnˈkɜː(r)/ vt (pt incurred) incurrir en; contraer (debts)

incurable /ɪnˈkjʊərəbl/ adj (disease) incurable; (romantic) empedernido

indebted /ɪnˈdetɪd/ adj. be ~ to s.o. estar en deuda con uno

indecen|cy /ɪnˈdiːsnsɪ/ n indecencia f. **~t** adj indecente

indecisi|on /ɪndɪˈsɪʒn/ n indecisión f. **~ve** /-ˈsaɪsɪv/ adj indeciso

indeed /ɪnˈdiːd/ adv en efecto; (really?) ¿de veras?

indefinable /ɪndɪˈfaɪnəbl/ adj indefinible

indefinite /ɪnˈdefɪnət/ adj indefinido. **~ly** adv indefinidamente

indelible /ɪnˈdelɪbl/ adj indeleble

indemni|fy /ɪnˈdemnɪfaɪ/ vt (insure) asegurar; (compensate) indemnizar. **~ty** /-ətɪ/ n (insurance) indemnidad f; (payment) indemnización f

indent /ɪnˈdent/ vt sangrar (text). **~ation** /-ˈteɪʃn/ n mella f

independen|ce /ɪndɪˈpendəns/ n independencia f. **~t** adj independiente. **~tly** adv independientemente

in-depth /ɪnˈdepθ/ adj a fondo

indescribable /ɪndɪˈskraɪbəbl/ adj indescriptible

indestructible /ɪndɪˈstrʌktəbl/ adj indestructible

indeterminate /ɪndɪˈtɜːmɪnət/ adj indeterminado

index /ˈɪndeks/ n (pl indexes) (in book) índice m; (pl indexes or indices) (Com, Math) índice m. ● vt poner índice a; (enter in index) poner en un índice. **~ finger** n

(dedo m) índice m. **~-linked** /-ˈlɪŋkt/ adj indexado

India /ˈɪndɪə/ n la India. **~n** adj & n indio (m)

indicat|e /ˈɪndɪkeɪt/ vt indicar. **~ion** /-ˈkeɪʃn/ n indicación f. **~ive** /ɪnˈdɪkətɪv/ adj & n indicativo (m). **~or** /ˈɪndɪkeɪtə(r)/ n indicador m; (Auto) intermitente m

indices /ˈɪndɪsiːz/ see **INDEX**

indict /ɪnˈdaɪt/ vt acusar. **~ment** n acusación f

indifferen|ce /ɪnˈdɪfrəns/ n indiferencia f. **~t** adj indiferente; (not good) mediocre

indigesti|ble /ɪndɪˈdʒestəbl/ adj indigesto. **~on** /-tʃən/ n indigestión f

indigna|nt /ɪnˈdɪgnənt/ adj indignado. **~tion** /-ˈneɪʃn/ n indignación f

indirect /ɪndɪˈrekt/ adj indirecto. **~ly** adv indirectamente

indiscre|et /ɪndɪˈskriːt/ adj indiscreto. **~tion** /-ˈkreʃn/ n indiscreción f

indiscriminate /ɪndɪˈskrɪmɪnət/ adj indistinto. **~ly** adv indistintamente

indispensable /ɪndɪˈspensəbl/ adj indispensable, imprescindible

indisposed /ɪndɪˈspəʊzd/ adj indispuesto

indisputable /ɪndɪˈspjuːtəbl/ adj indiscutible

indistinguishable /ɪndɪˈstɪŋgwɪʃəbl/ adj indistinguible (from de)

individual /ɪndɪˈvɪdjʊəl/ adj individual. ● n individuo m. **~ly** adv individualmente

indoctrinat|e /ɪnˈdɒktrɪneɪt/ vt adoctrinar. **~ion** /-ˈneɪʃn/ n adoctrinamiento m

indolen|ce /ˈɪndələns/ n indolencia f. ~t adj indolente

indomitable /ɪnˈdɒmɪtəbl/ adj indómito

indoor /ˈɪndɔː(r)/ adj interior; (clothes etc) de casa; (covered) cubierto. ~s adv dentro, adentro (LAm)

induc|e /ɪnˈdjuːs/ vt inducir. ~ement n incentivo m.

indulge /ɪnˈdʌldʒ/ vt satisfacer (desires); complacer (person). • vi. ~ in permitirse. ~nce /-əns/ n (of desires) satisfacción f; (extravagance) lujo m. ~nt adj indulgente

industrial /ɪnˈdʌstrɪəl/ adj industrial; (unrest) laboral. ~ist n industrial m & f. ~ized adj industrializado

industrious /ɪnˈdʌstrɪəs/ adj trabajador

industry /ˈɪndəstrɪ/ n industria f; (zeal) aplicación f

inebriated /ɪˈniːbrɪeɪtɪd/ adj beodo, ebrio

inedible /ɪnˈedɪbl/ adj incomible

ineffective /ɪnɪˈfektɪv/ adj ineficaz; (person) incompetente

ineffectual /ɪnɪˈfektjʊəl/ adj ineficaz

inefficien|cy /ɪnɪˈfɪʃnsɪ/ n ineficacia f; (of person) incompetencia f. ~t adj ineficaz; (person) incompetente

ineligible /ɪnˈelɪdʒəbl/ adj inelegible. be ~ for no tener derecho a

inept /ɪˈnept/ adj inepto

inequality /ɪnɪˈkwɒlətɪ/ n desigualdad f

inert /ɪˈnɜːt/ adj inerte. ~ia /-ʃə/ n inercia f

inescapable /ɪnɪˈskeɪpəbl/ adj ineludible

inevitable /ɪnˈevɪtəbl/ adj inevitable. • n. the ~e lo inevitable. ~y adv inevitablemente

inexact /ɪnɪɡˈzækt/ adj inexacto

inexcusable /ɪnɪkˈskjuːsəbl/ adj imperdonable

inexpensive /ɪnɪkˈspensɪv/ adj económico, barato

inexperience /ɪnɪkˈspɪərɪəns/ n falta f de experiencia. ~d adj inexperto

inexplicable /ɪnɪkˈsplɪkəbl/ adj inexplicable

infalli|bility /ɪnfælə'bɪlətɪ/ n infalibilidad f. ~le /ɪnˈfæləbl/ adj infalible

infam|ous /ˈɪnfəməs/ adj infame. ~y n infamia f

infan|cy /ˈɪnfənsɪ/ n infancia f. ~t n niño m. ~tile /ˈɪnfəntaɪl/ adj infantil

infantry /ˈɪnfəntrɪ/ n infantería f

infatuat|ed /ɪnˈfætjʊeɪtɪd/ adj. be ~ed with estar encaprichado con. ~ion /-ˈeɪʃn/ n encaprichamiento m

infect /ɪnˈfekt/ vt infectar; (fig) contagiar. ~ s.o. with sth contagiarle algo a uno. ~ion /-ʃn/ n infección f. ~ious /-ʃəs/ adj contagioso

infer /ɪnˈfɜː(r)/ vt (pt inferred) deducir

inferior /ɪnˈfɪərɪə(r)/ adj & n inferior (m & f). ~ity /-ˈɒrətɪ/ n inferioridad f

inferno /ɪnˈfɜːnəʊ/ n (pl -os) infierno m

infertil|e /ɪnˈfɜːtaɪl/ adj estéril. ~ity /-ˈtɪlətɪ/ n infertilidad f

infest /ɪnˈfest/ vt infestar

infidelity /ɪnfɪˈdelətɪ/ n infidelidad f

infiltrat|e /ˈɪnfɪltreɪt/ vt infiltrarse en. • vi infiltrarse. ~or n infiltrado m

infinite /ˈɪnfɪnət/ adj infinito. ~ly

adv infinitamente

infinitesimal /ˌmfɪnɪˈtesɪml/ *adj* infinitesimal

infinitive /ɪnˈfɪnətɪv/ *n* infinitivo *m*

infinity /ɪnˈfɪnətɪ/ *n* (*infinite distance*) infinito *m*; (*infinite quantity*) infinidad *f*

infirm /ɪnˈfɜːm/ *adj* enfermizo. ~**ity** *n* enfermedad *f*

inflam|e /ɪnˈfleɪm/ *vt* inflamar. ~**mable** /ɪnˈflæməbl/ *adj* inflamable. ~**mation** /-əˈmeɪʃn/ *n* inflamación *f*

inflat|e /ɪnˈfleɪt/ *vt* inflar. ~**ion** /-ʃn/ *n* inflación *f* ~**ionary** *adj* inflacionario

inflection /ɪnˈflekʃn/ *n* inflexión *f*

inflexible /ɪnˈfleksəbl/ *adj* inflexible

inflict /ɪnˈflɪkt/ *vt* infligir (on a)

influen|ce /ˈɪnfluəns/ *n* influencia *f* under the ~**ce** (*fam*, *drunk*) borracho. • *vt* influir (en). ~**tial** /-ˈenʃl/ *adj* influyente

influenza /ˌɪnfluˈenzə/ *n* gripe *f*

influx /ˈɪnflʌks/ *n* afluencia *f*

inform /ɪnˈfɔːm/ *vt* informar. keep ~**ed** tener al corriente. • *vi*. ~ **on** s.o. delatar a uno

informal /ɪnˈfɔːml/ *adj* informal; (*language*) familiar. ~**ity** /-ˈmælətɪ/ *n* falta *f* de ceremonia. ~**ly** *adv* (*casually*) de manera informal; (*unofficially*) informalmente

inform|ation /ˌɪnfəˈmeɪʃn/ *n* información *f* ~**ation technology** *n* informática *f*. ~**ative** *adj* /ɪnˈfɔːmətɪv/ informativo. ~**er** /ɪbˈfɔːmə(r)/ *n* informador

infrared /ˌɪnfrəˈred/ *adj* infrarrojo

infrequent /ɪnˈfriːkwənt/ *adj* poco frecuente. ~**ly** *adv* raramente

infringe /ɪnˈfrɪndʒ/ *vt* infringir. ~

on violar. ~**ment** *n* violación *f*

infuriat|e /ɪnˈfjuərɪeɪt/ *vt* enfurecer. ~**ing** *adj* exasperante

ingen|ious /ɪnˈdʒiːnɪəs/ *adj* ingenioso. ~**uity** /ˌɪndʒɪˈnjuːətɪ/ *n* ingeniosidad *f*

ingot /ˈɪŋgət/ *n* lingote *m*

ingrained /ɪnˈgreɪnd/ *adj* (*belief*) arraigado

ingratiate /ɪnˈgreɪʃɪeɪt/ *vt*. ~ **o.s. with** congraciarse con

ingratitude /ɪnˈgrætɪtjuːd/ *n* ingratitud *f*

ingredient /ɪnˈgriːdɪənt/ *n* ingrediente *m*

ingrowing /ˈɪngrəʊɪŋ/, **ingrown** /ˈɪngrəʊn/ *adj*. ~ **nail** uñero *m*, uña *f* encarnada

inhabit /ɪnˈhæbɪt/ *vt* habitar. ~**able** *adj* habitable. ~**ant** *n* habitante *m*

inhale /ɪnˈheɪl/ *vt* aspirar. • *vi* (*when smoking*) aspirar el humo. ~**r** *n* inhalador *m*

inherent /ɪnˈhɪərənt/ *adj* inherente. ~**ly** *adv* intrínsecamente

inherit /ɪnˈherɪt/ *vt* heredar. ~**ance** /-əns/ *n* herencia *f*

inhibit /ɪnˈhɪbɪt/ *vt* inhibir. ~**ed** *adj* inhibido. ~**ion** /-ˈbɪʃn/ *n* inhibición *f*

inhospitable /ˌɪnhəˈspɪtəbl/ *adj* (*place*) inhóspito; (*person*) inhospitalario

inhuman /ɪnˈhjuːmən/ *adj* inhumano. ~**e** /ɪnhjuːˈmeɪn/ *adj* inhumano. ~**ity** /ɪnhjuːˈmænətɪ/ *n* inhumanidad *f*

initial /ɪˈnɪʃl/ *n* inicial *f*. • *vt* (*pt* **tialled**) firmar con iniciales. • *adj* inicial. ~**ly** *adv* al principio

initiat|e /ɪˈnɪʃɪeɪt/ *vt* iniciar; promover (*scheme* etc). ~**ion** /-ˈeɪʃn/ *n* iniciación *f*

initiative /ɪˈnɪʃətɪv/ n iniciativa f. on one's own ~ por iniciativa propia. take the ~ tomar la iniciativa

inject /ɪnˈdʒekt/ vt inyectar. ~**ion** /-ʃn/ n inyección f

injure /ˈɪndʒə(r)/ vt herir. ~**y** n herida f

injustice /ɪnˈdʒʌstɪs/ n injusticia f

ink /ɪŋk/ n tinta f. ~**well** n tintero m. ~**y** adj manchado de tinta

inland /ˈɪnlənd/ adj interior. ● /ɪn ˈlænd/ adv tierra adentro. **I~ Revenue** /ˈɪnlənd/ n Hacienda f

in-laws /ˈɪnlɔːz/ npl parientes mpl políticos

inlay /ɪnˈleɪ/ vt (pt inlaid) taracear, incrustar. ● /ˈɪnleɪ/ n taracea f, incrustación f

inlet /ˈɪnlet/ n (in coastline) ensenada f; (of river, sea) brazo m

inmate /ˈɪnmeɪt/ n (of asylum) interno m; (of prison) preso m

inn /ɪn/ n posada f

innate /ɪˈneɪt/ adj innato

inner /ˈɪnə(r)/ adj interior; (fig) íntimo. ~**most** adj más íntimo. ~**tube** n cámara f

innocen|ce /ˈɪnəsns/ n inocencia f. ~**t** adj & n inocente (m & f)

innocuous /ɪˈnɒkjuəs/ adj inocuo

innovat|e /ˈɪnəveɪt/ vi innovar. ~**ion** /-ˈveɪʃn/ n innovación f. ~**ive** /ˈɪnəvətɪv/ adj innovador. ~**or** n innovador m

innuendo /ɪnjuːˈendəʊ/ n (pl -oes) insinuación f

innumerable /ɪˈnjuːmərəbl/ adj innumerable

inoculat|e /ɪˈnɒkjuleɪt/ vt inocular. ~**ion** /-ˈleɪʃn/ n inoculación f

inoffensive /ɪnəˈfensɪv/ adj inofensivo

inopportune /ɪnˈɒpətjuːn/ adj inoportuno

input /ˈɪnpʊt/ n aportación f, aporte m (LAm); (Comp) entrada f. ● vt (pt input, pres p inputting) entrar (data)

inquest /ˈɪnkwest/ n investigación f judicial

inquir|e /ɪnˈkwaɪə(r)/ vt/i preguntar. ~**e about** informarse de. ~**y** n pregunta f; (investigation) investigación f

inquisition /ɪnkwɪˈzɪʃn/ n inquisición f

inquisitive /ɪnˈkwɪzətɪv/ adj inquisitivo

insane /ɪnˈseɪn/ adj loco. ~**ity** /ɪnˈsænəti/ n locura f

insatiable /ɪnˈseɪʃəbl/ adj insaciable

inscri|be /ɪnˈskraɪb/ vt inscribir (letters); grabar (design). ~**ption** /-ɪpʃn/ n inscripción f

inscrutable /ɪnˈskruːtəbl/ adj inescrutable

insect /ˈɪnsekt/ n insecto m. ~**icide** /ɪnˈsektɪsaɪd/ n insecticida f

insecur|e /ɪnsɪˈkjʊə(r)/ adj inseguro. ~**ity** n inseguridad f

insensitive /ɪnˈsensətɪv/ adj insensible

inseparable /ɪnˈsepərəbl/ adj inseparable

insert /ˈɪnsɜːt/ n materia f insertada. ● /ɪnˈsɜːt/ vt insertar. ~**ion** /ɪnˈsɜːʃn/ n inserción f

inside /ɪnˈsaɪd/ n interior m. ~ **out** al revés; (thoroughly) a fondo. ● adj interior. ● adv dentro, adentro (LAm). ● prep dentro de. ~**s** npl tripas fpl

insight /ˈɪnsaɪt/ n perspicacia f. gain an ~ into llegar a comprender bien

insignificant /ɪnsɪg'nɪfɪkənt/ adj insignificante

insincer|e /ɪnsɪn'sɪə(r)/ adj poco sincero. **~ity** /-'serətɪ/ n falta f de sinceridad

insinuat|e /ɪn'sɪnjueɪt/ vt insinuar. **~ion** /-'eɪʃn/ n insinuación f

insipid /ɪn'sɪpɪd/ adj insípido

insist /ɪn'sɪst/ vt insistir (that en que). ● vi insistir. **~ on** insistir en. **~ence** /-əns/ n insistencia f. **~ent** adj insistente. **~ently** adv con insistencia

insolen|ce /'ɪnsələns/ n insolencia f. **~t** adj insolente

insoluble /ɪn'sɒljʊbl/ adj insoluble

insolvent /ɪn'sɒlvənt/ adj insolvente

insomnia /ɪn'sɒmnɪə/ n insomnio m. **~c** /-ɪæk/ n insomne m & f

inspect /ɪn'spekt/ vt (officially) inspeccionar; (look at closely) revisar, examinar. **~ion** /-ʃn/ n inspección f. **~or** n inspector m; (on train, bus) revisor m, inspector m (LAm)

inspir|ation /ɪnspə'reɪʃn/ n inspiración f. **~e** /ɪn'spaɪə(r)/ vt inspirar. **~ing** adj inspirador

instability /ɪnstə'bɪlətɪ/ n inestabilidad f

install /ɪn'stɔːl/ vt instalar. **~ation** /-ə'leɪʃn/ n instalación f

instalment /ɪn'stɔːlmənt/ n (payment) plazo m; (of publication) entrega f; (of radio, TV serial) episodio m

instance /'ɪnstəns/ n ejemplo m; (case) caso m. **for ~** por ejemplo. **in the first ~** en primer lugar

instant /'ɪnstənt/ adj instantáneo. ● n instante m. **~aneous** /ɪnstən 'teɪnɪəs/ adj instantáneo

instead /ɪn'sted/ adv en cambio.

~ of en vez de, en lugar de

instigat|e /'ɪnstɪgeɪt/ vt instigar. **~ion** /-'geɪʃn/ n instigación f

instinct /'ɪnstɪŋkt/ n instinto m. **~ive** adj instintivo

institut|e /'ɪnstɪtjuːt/ n instituto m. ● vt instituir; iniciar (enquiry etc). **~ion** /-'tjuːʃn/ n institución f. **~ional** adj institucional

instruct /ɪn'strʌkt/ vt instruir; (order) mandar. **~ s.o. in sth** enseñar algo a uno. **~ion** /-ʃn/ n instrucción f. **~ions** npl (for use) modo m de empleo. **~ive** adj instructivo. **~or** n instructor m

instrument /'ɪnstrəmənt/ n instrumento m. **~al** /ɪnstrə'mentl/ adj instrumental. **be ~al in** jugar un papel decisivo en

insubordinat|e /ɪnsə'bɔːdɪnət/ adj insubordinado. **~ion** /-'neɪʃn/ n insubordinación f

insufferable /ɪn'sʌfərəbl/ adj (person) insufrible; (heat) insoportable

insufficient /ɪnsə'fɪʃnt/ adj insuficiente

insular /'ɪnsjʊlə(r)/ adj insular; (narrow-minded) estrecho de miras

insulat|e /'ɪnsjʊleɪt/ vt aislar. **~ion** /-'leɪʃn/ n aislamiento m

insulin /'ɪnsjʊlɪn/ n insulina f

insult /ɪn'sʌlt/ vt insultar. ● /'ɪnsʌlt/ n insulto m. **~ing** /ɪn 'sʌltɪŋ/ adj insultante

insur|ance /ɪn'ʃʊərəns/ n seguro m. **~e** /ɪn'ʃʊə(r)/ vt (Com) asegurar; (Amer) see ENSURE

insurmountable /ɪnsə 'maʊntəbl/ adj insuperable

intact /ɪn'tækt/ adj intacto

integral /'ɪntɪgrəl/ adj integral

integrat|e /'ɪntɪgreɪt/ vt integrar. ● vi integrarse. **~ion** /-'greɪʃn/ n integración f

integrity /ɪnˈtegrɪtɪ/ n integridad f

intellect /ˈɪntəlekt/ n intelecto m. ~**ual** /ɪntəˈlektʃʊəl/ adj & n intelectual (m)

intelligen|ce /ɪnˈtelɪdʒəns/ n inteligencia f. ~**t** adj inteligente. ~**tly** adv inteligentemente

intelligible /ɪnˈtelɪdʒəbl/ adj inteligible

intend /ɪnˈtend/ vt. ~ **to do** pensar hacer

intens|e /ɪnˈtens/ adj intenso; (person) apasionado. ~**ely** adv intensamente; (very) sumamente. ~**ify** /-ɪfaɪ/ vt intensificar. • vi intensificarse. ~**ity** /-ɪtɪ/ n intensidad f

intensive /ɪnˈtensɪv/ adj intensivo. ~ **care** n cuidados mpl intensivos

intent /ɪnˈtent/ n propósito m. • adj atento. ~ **on** absorto en. ~ **on doing** resuelto a hacer

intention /ɪnˈtenʃn/ n intención f. ~**al** adj intencional

intently /ɪnˈtentlɪ/ adv atentamente

interact /ɪntərˈækt/ vi relacionarse. ~**ion** /-ʃn/ n interacción f

intercept /ɪntəˈsept/ vt interceptar. ~**ion** /-ʃn/ n interceptación f

interchange /ˈɪntətʃeɪndʒ/ vt intercambiar. • /ɪntəˈtʃeɪndʒ/ n intercambio m; (road junction) cruce m. ~**able** /-ˈtʃeɪndʒəbl/ adj intercambiable

intercity /ɪntəˈsɪtɪ/ adj rápido interurbano m

intercourse /ˈɪntəkɔːs/ n trato m; (sexual) acto m sexual

interest /ˈɪntrest/ n interés m. • vt interesar. ~**ed** adj interesado. be

~**ed in** interesarse por. ~**ing** adj interesante

interface /ˈɪntəfeɪs/ n interfaz m & f; (interaction) interrelación f

interfere /ɪntəˈfɪə(r)/ vi entrometerse. ~ **in** entrometerse en. ~ **with** afectar (a); interferir (radio). ~**nce** /-rəns/ n intromisión f; (Radio) interferencia f

interior /ɪnˈtɪərɪə(r)/ adj & n interior (m)

interjection /ɪntəˈdʒekʃn/ n interjección f

interlude /ˈɪntəluːd/ n intervalo m; (theatre, music) interludio m

intermediary /ɪntəˈmiːdɪərɪ/ adj & n intermediario (m)

interminable /ɪnˈtɜːmɪnəbl/ adj interminable

intermittent /ɪntəˈmɪtnt/ adj intermitente. ~**ly** adv con discontinuidad

intern /ɪnˈtɜːn/ vt internar. • /ˈɪntɜːn/ n (Amer, doctor) interno m

internal /ɪnˈtɜːnl/ adj interno. ~**ly** adv internamente. I~ **Revenue Service** n (Amer) Hacienda f

international /ɪntəˈnæʃənl/ adj internacional

Internet /ˈɪntənet/ n. the ~ el Internet

interpret /ɪnˈtɜːprɪt/ vt/i interpretar. ~**ation** /-ˈteɪʃn/ n interpretación f. ~**er** n intérprete m & f

interrogat|e /ɪnˈterəgeɪt/ vt interrogar. ~**ion** /-ˈgeɪʃn/ n interrogatorio m. ~**ive** /-ˈrɒgətɪv/ adj interrogativo

interrupt /ɪntəˈrʌpt/ vt/i interrumpir. ~**ion** /-ʃn/ n interrupción f

intersect /ɪntəˈsekt/ vt cruzar. • vi (roads) cruzarse; (geometry) intersecarse. ~ion /-ʃn/ n (roads) cruce m; (geometry) intersección f

intersperse /ɪntəˈspɜːs/ vt intercalar

interstate (highway) /ˈɪntəsteɪt/ n (Amer) carretera f interestatal

intertwine /ɪntəˈtwaɪn/ vt entrelazar. ● vi entrelazarse

interval /ˈɪntəvl/ n intervalo m; (theatre) descanso m. at ~s a intervalos

interven|e /ɪntəˈviːn/ vi intervenir. ~tion /-ˈvenʃn/ n intervención f

interview /ˈɪntəvjuː/ n entrevista f. ● vt entrevistar. ~ee /-ˈiː/ n entrevistado m. ~er n entrevistador m

intestine /ɪnˈtestɪn/ n intestino m

intimacy /ˈɪntɪməsɪ/ n intimidad f

intimate /ˈɪntɪmət/ adj íntimo. ● /ˈɪntɪmeɪt/ vt (state) anunciar; (imply) dar a entender. ~ly /ˈɪntɪmətlɪ/ adv íntimamente

intimidat|e /ɪnˈtɪmɪdeɪt/ vt intimidar. ~ion /-ˈdeɪʃn/ n intimidación f

into /ˈɪntʊ//ˈɪntə/ prep en; (translate) a

intolerable /ɪnˈtɒlərəbl/ adj intolerable

intoleran|ce /ɪnˈtɒlərəns/ n intolerancia f. ~t adj intolerante

intoxicat|e /ɪnˈtɒksɪkeɪt/ vt embriagar; (Med) intoxicar. ~ed adj ebrio. ~ing adj (substance) estupefaciente. ~ion /-ˈkeɪʃn/ n embriaguez f; (Med) intoxicación f

intransitive /ɪnˈtrænsɪtɪv/ adj intransitivo

intravenous /ɪntrəˈviːnəs/ adj intravenoso

intrepid /ɪnˈtrepɪd/ adj intrépido

intrica|cy /ˈɪntrɪkəsɪ/ n complejidad f. ~te /-at/ adj complejo

intrigue /ɪnˈtriːɡ/ vt intrigar. ● /ˈɪntriːɡ/ n intriga f. ~ing /ɪnˈtriːɡɪŋ/ adj intrigante

intrinsic /ɪnˈtrɪnsɪk/ adj intrínseco. ~ally adv intrínsecamente

introduc|e /ɪntrəˈdjuːs/ vt introducir; presentar (person). ~tion /ɪntrəˈdʌkʃn/ n introducción f; (to person) presentación f. ~tory /ɪntrəˈdʌktərɪ/ adj preliminar; (course) de introducción

introvert /ˈɪntrəvɜːt/ n introvertido m

intru|de /ɪnˈtruːd/ vi entrometerse; (disturb) importunar. ~der n intruso m. ~sion /-ʒn/ n intrusión f. ~sive /-sɪv/ adj impertinente

intuiti|on /ɪntjuːˈɪʃn/ n intuición f. ~ve /ɪnˈtjuːɪtɪv/ adj intuitivo

inundat|e /ˈɪnʌndeɪt/ vt inundar. ~ion /-ˈdeɪʃn/ n inundación f

invade /ɪnˈveɪd/ vt invadir. ~r n invasor m

invalid /ˈɪnvəlɪd/ n inválido m. ● /ɪnˈvælɪd/ adj inválido. ~ate /ɪnˈvælɪdeɪt/ vt invalidar

invaluable /ɪnˈvæljʊəbl/ adj inestimable, invalorable (LAm)

invariabl|e /ɪnˈveərɪəbl/ adj invariable. ~y adv invariablemente

invasion /ɪnˈveɪʒn/ n invasión f

invent /ɪnˈvent/ vt inventar. ~ion /-ˈvenʃn/ n invención f. ~ive adj inventivo. ~or n inventor m

inventory /ˈɪnvəntrɪ/ n inventario m

invertebrate /ɪnˈvɜːtɪbrət/ n invertebrado m

inverted commas /ɪnvɜːtɪd ˈkɒmaz/npl comillas fpl

invest /ɪnˈvest/ vt invertir. ● vi. ~ in invertir en

investigate /ɪnˈvestɪgeɪt/ vt investigar. ~**ion** /-ˈgeɪʃn/ n investigación f. under ~**ion** sometido a examen. ~**or** n investigador m

investment /ɪnˈvestmənt/ n inversión f

investor /ɪnˈvestə(r)/ n inversionista m & f

inveterate /ɪnˈvetərət/ adj inveterado

invidious /ɪnˈvɪdɪəs/ adj (hateful) odioso; (unfair) injusto

invigorating /ɪnˈvɪgəreɪtɪŋ/ adj vigorizante; (stimulating) estimulante

invincible /ɪnˈvɪnsɪbl/ adj invencible

invisible /ɪnˈvɪzəbl/ adj invisible

invitation /ɪnvɪˈteɪʃn/ n invitación f. ~**e** /ɪnˈvaɪt/ vt invitar; (ask for) pedir. ● /ˈɪnvaɪt/ n 🔢 invitación f. ~**ing** /ɪnˈvaɪtɪŋ/ adj atrayente

invoice /ˈɪnvɔɪs/ n factura f. ● vt. ~ **s.o.** (for sth) pasarle a uno factura (por algo)

involuntary /ɪnˈvɒləntərɪ/ adj involuntario

involve /ɪnˈvɒlv/ vt (entail) suponer; (implicate) implicar. ~**d** in envuelto en. ~**d** adj (complex) complicado. ~**ment** n participación f; (relationship) enredo m

inward /ˈɪnwəd/ adj interior. ● adv hacia adentro. ~**s** adv hacia dentro

iodine /ˈaɪədiːn/ n yodo m

ion /ˈaɪən/ n ion m

iota /aɪˈəʊtə/ n (amount) pizca f

IOU /aɪəʊˈjuː/ abbr (= I owe you) pagaré m

IQ abbr (= intelligence quotient) CI m, cociente m intelectual

Iran /ɪˈrɑːn/ n Irán m. ~**ian** /ɪˈreɪnɪən/ adj & n iraní (m)

Iraq /ɪˈrɑːk/ n Irak m. ~**i** adj & n iraquí (m & f)

irate /aɪˈreɪt/ adj colérico

Ireland /ˈaɪələnd/ n Irlanda f

iris /ˈaɪərɪs/ n (of eye) iris m; (flower) lirio m

Irish /ˈaɪərɪʃ/ adj irlandés. ● n (language) irlandés m. npl. the ~ (people) los irlandeses. ~**man** n irlandés m. ~**woman** n irlandesa f

iron /ˈaɪən/ n hierro m; (appliance) plancha f. ● adj de hierro. ● vt planchar. □ ~ **out** vt allanar

ironic /aɪˈrɒnɪk/ adj irónico. ~**ally** adv irónicamente

ironing board /ˈaɪənɪŋ/ n tabla f de planchar, burro m de planchar (Mex)

iron: ~**monger** /-mʌŋgə(r)/ n ferretero m. ~**monger's** n ferretería f

irony /ˈaɪərənɪ/ n ironía f

irrational /ɪˈræʃənl/ adj irracional

irrefutable /ɪˈrɪfjuːtəbl/ adj irrefutable

irregular /ɪˈregjʊlə(r)/ adj irregular. ~**ity** /-ˈlærəti/ n irregularidad f

irrelevan|ce /ɪˈreləvəns/ n irrelevancia f. ~**t** adj irrelevante

irreparable /ɪˈrepərəbl/ adj irreparable

irreplaceable /ɪrɪˈpleɪsəbl/ adj irreemplazable

irresistible /ɪrɪˈzɪstəbl/ adj irresistible

irrespective /ɪrɪˈspektɪv/ adj. ~ **of** sin tomar en cuenta

irresponsible /ɪrɪˈspɒnsəbl/ adj irresponsable

irretrievable /ɪrɪˈtriːvəbl/ adj irrecuperable

irreverent /ɪˈrevərənt/ adj irreverente

irrevocable /ɪˈrevəkəbl/ adj irrevocable

irrigat|e /ˈɪrɪgeɪt/ vt regar, irrigar. **~ion** /-ˈgeɪʃn/ n riego m, irrigación f

irritable /ˈɪrɪtəbl/ adj irritable

irritat|e /ˈɪrɪteɪt/ vt irritar. **~ed** adj irritado. **~ing** adj irritante. **~ion** /-ˈteɪʃn/ n irritación f

IRS abbr (Amer) see **INTERNAL REVENUE SERVICE**

is /ɪz/ see **BE**

ISDN abbr (Integrated Services Digital Network) RDSI

Islam /ˈɪzlɑːm/ n el Islam. **~ic** /ɪzˈlæmɪk/ adj islámico

island /ˈaɪlənd/ n isla f. **~er** n isleño m

isolat|e /ˈaɪsəleɪt/ vt aislar. **~ion** /-ˈleɪʃn/ n aislamiento m

Israel /ˈɪzreɪl/ n Israel m. **~i** /ɪzˈreɪlɪ/ adj & n israelí (m)

issue /ˈɪʃuː/ n tema m, asunto m; (of magazine etc) número m; (of stamps, bank notes) emisión f; (of documents) expedición f. be at ~ with discrepar de. ● vt hacer público (statement); expedir (documents); emitir (stamps etc); prestar (library book)

it /ɪt/ pronoun

→ (as subject) generally not translated. it's huge es enorme. where is it? ¿dónde está?. it's all lies son todas mentiras

→ (as direct object) lo (m), la (f). he read it to me me lo/la leyó. give it to me dámelo/ dámela

→ (as indirect object) le. I gave it another coat of paint le di otra mano de pintura

→ (after a preposition) generally not translated. there's nothing behind it no hay nada detrás

! Note, however, that in some cases él or ella must be used e.g. he picked up the spoon and hit me with it agarró la cuchara y me golpeó con ella

→ (at door) who is it? ¿quién es?. it's me soy yo; (on telephone) who is it, please? ¿quién habla, por favor?; (before passing on to sb else) ¿de parte de quién, por favor? it's Carol soy Carol (Spain), habla Carol

→ (in impersonal constructions) it is well known that ... bien se sabe que ... it's five o'clock son las cinco. so it seems así parece

→ that's it (that's right) eso es; (that's enough, that's finished) ya está

Italian /ɪˈtæljən/ adj & n italiano (m)

italics /ɪˈtælɪks/ npl (letra f) cursiva f

Italy /ˈɪtəlɪ/ n Italia f

itch /ɪtʃ/ n picazón f. ● vi picar. I'm ~ing to estoy que me muero por. my arm ~es me pica el brazo. ~y adj que pica. I've got an ~y nose me pica la nariz

it'd /ɪtəd/ = it had, it would

item /ˈaɪtəm/ n artículo m; (on agenda) punto m. news ~ n noticia f. ~ize vt detallar

itinerary /aɪˈtɪnərərɪ/ n itinerario m

it'll /ɪtl/ = it will

its /ɪts/ adj su, sus (pl). ● pron (el)

suyo *m*, (la) suya *f*, (los) suyos *mpl*, (las) suyas *fpl*

it's /ɪts/ = **it is**, **it has**

itself /ɪt'self/ *pron* él mismo, ella misma, ello mismo; (*reflexive*) se; (*after prep*) sí mismo, sí misma

I've /aɪv/ = **I have**

ivory /'aɪvərɪ/ *n* marfil *m*. ~ **tower** *n* torre *f* de marfil

ivy /'aɪvɪ/ *n* hiedra *f*

Ivy League - the El grupo de universidades más antiguas y respetadas de EE.UU. Situadas al noreste del país, son: Harvard, Yale, Columbia, Cornell, Dartmouth College, Brown, Princeton y Pensylvania. El término proviene de la hiedra que crece en los antiguos edificios de estos establecimientos.

Jj

jab /dʒæb/ *vt* (*pt* jabbed) pinchar; (*thrust*) hurgonear. ● *n* pinchazo *m*

jack /dʒæk/ *n* (*Mec*) gato *m*; (*socket*) enchufe *m* hembra; (*Cards*) sota *f*. □ ~ **up** *vt* alzar con gato

jackal /'dʒækl/ *n* chacal *m*

jackdaw /'dʒækdɔː/ *n* grajilla *f*

jacket /'dʒækɪt/ *n* chaqueta *f*; (*casual*) americana *f*, saco *m* (*LAm*); (*Amer, of book*) sobrecubierta *f*; (*of record*) funda *f*, carátula *f*

jack: ~ **knife** *vi* (lorry) plegarse. ~ **pot** *n* premio *m* gordo. **hit the** ~ **pot** sacar el premio gordo

jade /dʒeɪd/ *n* (*stone*) jade *m*

jagged /dʒægɪd/ *adj* (edge, cut) irregular; (rock) recortado

jaguar /'dʒægjʊə(r)/ *n* jaguar *m*

jail /dʒeɪl/ *n* cárcel *m*, prisión *f*. ● *vt* encarcelar. ~**er** *n* carcelero *m*. ~**house** (*Amer*) cárcel *f*

jam /dʒæm/ *vt* (*pt* jammed) interferir con (radio); atestar (road). ~ **sth into sth** meter algo a la fuerza en algo. ● *vi* bloquearse; (machine) trancarse. ● *n* mermelada *f*; (*fam, situation*) apuro *m*

jangle /'dʒæŋgl/ *n* sonido *m* metálico (y áspero). ● *vi* hacer ruido (metálico)

janitor /'dʒænɪtə(r)/ *n* portero *m*

January /'dʒænjʊərɪ/ *n* enero *m*

Japan /dʒə'pæn/ *n* (el) Japón *m*. ~**ese** /dʒæpə'niːz/ *adj & n invar* japonés (*m*)

jar /dʒɑː(r)/ *n* tarro *m*, bote *m*. ● *vi* (*pt* jarred) (clash) desentonar. ● *vt* sacudir

jargon /'dʒɑːgən/ *n* jerga *f*

jaundice /'dʒɔːndɪs/ *n* icteria *f*

jaunt /dʒɔːnt/ *n* excursión *f*

jaunty /'dʒɔːntɪ/ *adj* (-ier, -iest) garboso

jaw /dʒɔː/ *n* mandíbula *f*. ~**s** *npl* fauces *fpl*. ~**bone** *n* mandíbula *f*, maxilar *m*; (*of animal*) quijada *f*

jay /dʒeɪ/ *n* arrendajo *m*. ~**walk** *vi* cruzar la calle descuidadamente. ~**walker** *n* peatón *m* imprudente

jazz /dʒæz/ *n* jazz *m*. □ ~ **up** *vt* animar. ~**y** *adj* chillón

jealous /'dʒeləs/ *adj* celoso; (*envious*) envidioso. ~**y** *n* celos *mpl*

jeans /dʒiːnz/ *npl* vaqueros *mpl*, jeans *mpl*, tejanos *mpl*, pantalones *mpl* de mezclilla (*Mex*)

Jeep (P), **jeep** /dʒiːp/ *n* Jeep *m* (P)

jeer /dʒɪə(r)/ *vi*. ~ **at** mofarse de;

(boo) abuchear. ● n burla f; (boo) abucheo m

Jell-O /'dʒeləʊ/ n (P) (Amer) gelatina f (con sabor a frutas)

jelly /'dʒelɪ/ n (clear jam) jalea f; (pudding) see JELL-O; (substance) gelatina f. ~fish n (pl invar or -es) medusa f

jeopardize /'dʒepədaɪz/ vt arriesgar

jerk /dʒɜːk/ n sacudida f; (sl, fool) idiota m & f. ● vt sacudir

jersey /'dʒɜːzɪ/ n (pl -eys) jersey m, suéter m, pulóver m

jest /dʒest/ n broma f. ● vi bromear

Jesus /'dʒiːzəs/ n Jesús m

jet /dʒet/ n (stream) chorro m; (plane) avión m (con motor a reacción); (mineral) azabache m. ~-**black** /-'blæk/ adj azabache negro a invar. ~ **lag** n jet lag m, desfase f horario. have ~ **lag** estar desfasado. ~-**propelled** /-prə'peld/ adj (de propulsión) a reacción

jettison /'dʒetɪsn/ vt echar al mar; (fig, discard) deshacerse de

jetty /'dʒetɪ/ n muelle m

Jew /dʒuː/ n judío m

jewel /'dʒuːəl/ n joya f. ~**ler** n joyero m. ~**lery** n joyas fpl

Jewish /'dʒuːɪʃ/ adj judío

jiffy /'dʒɪfɪ/ n momentito m. do sth in a ~ hacer algo en un santiamén

jig /dʒɪg/ n (dance) giga f

jigsaw /'dʒɪgsɔː/ n. ~ (puzzle) rompecabezas m

jilt /dʒɪlt/ vt dejar plantado

jingle /'dʒɪŋgl/ vt hacer sonar. ● vi tintinear. ● n (sound) tintineo m; (advert) jingle m (publicitario)

job /dʒɒb/ n empleo m, trabajo m; (piece of work) trabajo m. **it is a**

good ~ that menos mal que. ~**less** adj desempleado

jockey /'dʒɒkɪ/ n jockey m

jocular /'dʒɒkjʊlə(r)/ adj jocoso

jog /dʒɒg/ vt (pt jogged) empujar; refrescar (memory). ● vi hacer footing, hacer jogging. ~**er** n persona f que hace footing. ~**ging** n footing m, jogging m. go ~**ging** salir a hacer footing or jogging

join /dʒɔɪn/ vt (link) unir; hacerse socio de (club); hacerse miembro de (political group); alistarse en (army); reunirse con (another person). ● n juntura f. ● vi. ~ **together** (parts) unirse; (roads etc) empalmar; (rivers) confluir. □ ~ **in** vi participar (en). □ ~ **up** vi (Mil) alistarse. ~**er** n carpintero m

joint /dʒɔɪnt/ adj conjunto. ● n (join) unión f, junta f; (in limbs) articulación f. (Culin) trozo m de carne (para asar). **out of** ~ descoyuntado. ~ **account** n cuenta f conjunta. ~**ly** adv conjuntamente. ~ **owner** n copropietario m.

joist /dʒɔɪst/ n viga f

joke /dʒəʊk/ n (story) chiste m; (practical joke) broma f. ● vi bromear. ~**er** n bromista m & f; (Cards) comodín m. ~**y** adj jocoso

jolly /'dʒɒlɪ/ adj (-ier, -iest) alegre. ● adv Ⓔ muy

jolt /dʒɒlt/ vt sacudir. ● vi (vehicle) dar una sacudida. ● n sacudida f

jostle /'dʒɒsl/ vt empujar. ● vi empujarse

jot /dʒɒt/ n pizca f. ● vt (pt jotted). □ ~ **down** vt apuntar (rápidamente). ~**ter** n bloc m

journal /'dʒɜːnl/ n (diary) diario m; (newspaper) periódico m; (magazine) revista f. ~**ism** n periodismo m. ~**ist** n periodista m f

journey /'dʒɜːnɪ/ n viaje m. go on a ~ hacer un viaje. •vi viajar

jovial /'dʒəʊvɪəl/ adj jovial

joy /dʒɔɪ/ n alegría f. ~**ful** adj feliz. ~**ous** adj feliz. ~**rider** n joven m que roba un coche para dar una vuelta. ~**stick** n (in aircraft) palanca f de mando; (Comp) mando m, joystick m

jubila|nt /'dʒuːbɪlənt/ adj jubiloso. ~**tion** /-'leɪʃn/ n júbilo m

jubilee /'dʒuːbɪliː/ n aniversario m especial

Judaism /'dʒuːdeɪɪzəm/ n judaísmo m

judge /dʒʌdʒ/ n juez m. •vt juzgar. ~**ment** n juicio m

judicial /dʒuː'dɪʃl/ adj judicial. ~**ry** /-ərɪ/ n judicatura f

judo /'dʒuːdəʊ/ n judo m

jug /dʒʌg/ n jarra f

juggernaut /'dʒʌgənɔːt/ n camión m grande

juggle /'dʒʌgl/ vi hacer malabarismos. •vt hacer malabarismos con. ~**r** n malabarista m & f

juic|e /dʒuːs/ n jugo m, zumo m. ~**y** adj jugoso, zumoso; (story etc) 𝕀 picante

jukebox /'dʒuːkbɒks/ n máquina f de discos, rocola f (LAm)

July /dʒuː'laɪ/ n julio m

jumble /'dʒʌmbl/ vt. ~ (up) mezclar. •n (muddle) revoltijo m. ~ **sale** n venta f de objetos usados m

jumbo /'dʒʌmbəʊ/ adj gigante. ~ **jet** n jumbo m

jump /dʒʌmp/ vt saltar. ~ **rope** (Amer) saltar a la comba, saltar a la cuerda. ~ **the gun** obrar prematuramente. ~ **the queue** colarse. •vi saltar; (start) sobresaltarse; (prices) alzarse. ~ **at** aprovechar una oportunidad. •n salto m; (start) susto m; (increase) aumento m. ~**er** n jersey m, suéter m, pulóver m; (Amer, dress) pichi m, jumper m & f (LAm). ~**er cables** (Amer), ~ **leads** npl cables mpl de arranque. ~ **rope** (Amer) comba f, cuerda f, reata f (Mex). ~**suit** n mono m. ~**y** adj nervioso

junction /'dʒʌŋkʃn/ n (of roads, rails) cruce m; (Elec) empalme m

June /dʒuːn/ n junio m

jungle /'dʒʌŋgl/ n selva f, jungla f

junior /'dʒuːnɪə(r)/ adj (in age) más joven (to que); (in rank) subalterno. •n menor m

junk /dʒʌŋk/ n trastos mpl viejos; (worthless stuff) basura f. •vt 𝕀 tirar. ~ **food** n comida f basura, alimento m chatarra (Mex). ~**ie** /'dʒʌŋkɪ/ n 𝕀 drogadicto m, yonqui m & f 𝕀. ~ **mail** n propaganda f que se recibe por correo. ~ **shop** n tienda f de trastos viejos

junta /'dʒʌntə/ n junta f militar

Jupiter /'dʒuːpɪtə(r)/ n Júpiter m

jurisdiction /dʒʊərɪs'dɪkʃn/ n jurisdicción f

jur|or /'dʒʊərə(r)/ n (miembro m de un) jurado m. ~**y** n jurado m

just /dʒʌst/ adj (fair) justo. •adv exactamente, justo; (barely) justo; (only) sólo, solamente. ~ **as tall** tan alto (as como). ~ **listen!** ¡escucha! **he has ~ arrived** acaba de llegar, recién llegó (LAm)

justice /'dʒʌstɪs/ n justicia f. **J~ of the Peace** juez m de paz

justif|iable /dʒʌstɪ'faɪəbl/ adj justificable. ~**iably** adv con razón. ~**ication** /dʒʌstɪfɪ'keɪʃn/ n justificación f. ~**y** /'dʒʌstɪfaɪ/ vt justificar

jut /dʒʌt/ vi (pt jutted). ~ **(out)**

sobresalir

juvenile /'dʒuːvənaɪl/ *adj* juvenil; (*childish*) infantil. ● *n* (*Jurid*) menor *m* & *f*

. . . .

Kk

. . . .

kaleidoscope /kə'laɪdəskəʊp/ *n* caleidoscopio *m*

kangaroo /kæŋgə'ruː/ *n* canguro *m*

karate /kə'rɑːtɪ/ *n* kárate *m*, karate *m* (*LAm*)

keel /kiːl/ *n* (*of ship*) quilla *f*. □ ~ **over** *vi* volcar(se)

keen /kiːn/ *adj* (-er, -est) (*interest, feeling*) vivo; (*wind, mind, analysis*) penetrante; (*eyesight*) agudo; (*eager*) entusiasta. I'm ~ **on golf** me encanta el golf. **he's** ~ **on Shostakovich** le gusta Shostakovich. **~ly** *adv* vivamente; (*enthusiastically*) con entusiasmo. **~ness** *n* intensidad *f*; (*enthusiasm*) entusiasmo *m*.

keep /kiːp/ *vt* (*pt* kept) guardar; cumplir (*promise*); tener (*shop, animals*); mantener (*family*); observar (*rule*); (*celebrate*) celebrar; (*delay*) detener; (*prevent*) impedir. ● *vi* (*food*) conservarse; (*remain*) quedarse; (*continue*) seguir. ~ **doing** seguir haciendo. ● *n* subsistencia *f*; (*of castle*) torreón *m*. **for** ~**s** 🔲 para siempre. □ ~ **back** *vt* retener. ● *vi* no acercarse. □ ~ **in** *vt* no dejar salir. □ ~ **off** *vt* mantenerse alejado de (*land*). '~ **off the grass**' 'prohibido pisar el césped'. □ ~ **on** *vi* seguir. ~ **on doing sth**

seguir haciendo. □ ~ **out** *vt* no dejar entrar. □ ~ **up** *vt* mantener. □ ~ **up with** *vt* estar al día en

kennel /'kenl/ *n* casa *f* del perro; (*Amer, for boarding*) residencia *f* canina. ~**s** *n invar* residencia *f* canina

kept /kept/ *see* KEEP

kerb /kɜːb/ *n* bordillo *m* (de la acera), borde *m* de la banqueta (Mex)

kerosene /'kerəsiːn/ *n* queroseno *m*

ketchup /'ketʃʌp/ *n* salsa *f* de tomate

kettle /'ketl/ *n* pava *f*, tetera *f* (para calentar agua)

key /kiː/ *n* llave *f*; (*of computer, piano*) tecla *f*; (*Mus*) tono *m*. **be off** ~ no estar en el tono. ● *adj* clave. □ ~ **in** *vt* teclear. **~board** *n* teclado *m*. **~hole** *n* ojo *m* de la cerradura. **~ring** *n* llavero *m*

khaki /'kɑːkɪ/ *adj* caqui

kick /kɪk/ *vt* dar una patada a (person); patear (ball). ● *vi* dar patadas; (*horse*) cocear. ● *n* patada *f*; (*of horse*) coz *f*; (*fam, thrill*) placer *m*. □ ~ **out** *vt* 🔲 echar. □ ~ **up** *vt* armar (fuss etc). ~**off** *n* (*Sport*) saque *m* inicial. ~ **start** *vt* arrancar (con el pedal de arranque) (engine)

kid /kɪd/ *n* (*young goat*) cabrito *m*; (*fam, child*) niño *m*, chaval *m*, escuincle *m* (Mex). ● *vt* (*pt* kidded) tomar el pelo a. ● *vi* bromear

kidnap /'kɪdnæp/ *vt* (*pt* kidnapped) secuestrar. **~per** *n* secuestrador *m*. **~ping** *n* secuestro *m*

kidney /'kɪdnɪ/ *n* riñón *m*

kill /kɪl/ *vt* matar; (*fig*) acabar con. ● *n* matanza *f*. □ ~ **off** *vt* matar. **~er** *n* asesino *m*. **~ing** *n* matanza *f*; (*murder*) asesinato *m*. **make a**

~**ing** (*fig*) hacer un gran negocio
kiln /kɪln/ n horno m
kilo /ˈkiːləʊ/ n (*pl* -os) kilo m.
~**gram(me)** /ˈkɪləɡræm/ n kilogramo m. ~**metre** /ˈkɪləmiːtə(r)/, /kɪˈlɒmɪtə(r)/ n kilómetro m.
~**watt** /ˈkɪləwɒt/ n kilovatio m
kilt /kɪlt/ n falda f escocesa
kin /kɪn/ n familiares mpl
kind /kaɪnd/ n tipo m, clase f. ~ **of** (*fam, somewhat*) un poco. **in** ~ en especie. **be two of a** ~ ser tal para cual. ● adj amable
kindergarten /ˈkɪndəɡɑːtn/ n jardín m de infancia
kind-hearted /kaɪndˈhɑːtɪd/ adj bondadoso
kindle /ˈkɪndl/ vt encender
kind|ly adj (-ier, -iest) bondadoso. ● adv amablemente; (*please*) haga el favor de. ~**ness** n bondad f; (*act*) favor m
king /kɪŋ/ n rey m. ~**dom** n reino m. ~**fisher** n martín m pescador. ~**-size(d)** adj extragrande
kink /kɪŋk/ n (*in rope*) vuelta f, curva f; (*in hair*) onda f. ~**y** adj 🄵 pervertido
kiosk /ˈkiːɒsk/ n quiosco m
kipper /ˈkɪpə(r)/ n arenque m ahumado
kiss /kɪs/ n beso m. ● vt besar. ● vi besarse
kit /kɪt/ n avíos mpl. **tool** ~ caja f de herramientas. □ ~ **out** vt (*pt kitted*) equipar
kitchen /ˈkɪtʃɪn/ n cocina f
kite /kaɪt/ n cometa f, papalote m (Mex)
kitten /ˈkɪtn/ n gatito m
knack /næk/ n truco m
knapsack /ˈnæpsæk/ n mochila f
knead /niːd/ vt amasar

knee /niː/ n rodilla f. ~**cap** n rótula f
kneel /niːl/ vi (*pt kneeled or knelt*). ~ (**down**) arrodillarse; (*be on one's knees*) estar arrodillado
knelt /nelt/ *see* KNEEL
knew /njuː/ *see* KNOW
knickers /ˈnɪkəz/ npl bragas fpl, calzones mpl (LAm), pantaletas fpl (Mex)
knife /naɪf/ n (*pl knives*) cuchillo m. ● vt acuchillar
knight /naɪt/ n caballero m; (Chess) caballo m. ● vt conceder el título de Sir a. ~**hood** n título m de Sir
knit /nɪt/ vt (*pt knitted or knit*) hacer, tejer (LAm). ~, hacer punto. ~ **one's brow** fruncir el ceño. ~**ting** n tejido m, punto m. ~**ting needle** n aguja f de hacer punto, aguja f de tejer
knives /naɪvz/ *see* KNIFE
knob /nɒb/ n botón m; (*of door, drawer etc*) tirador m. ~**bly** adj nudoso
knock /nɒk/ vt golpear; (*criticize*) criticar. ● vi golpear; (*at door*) llamar, golpear (LAm). ● n golpe m. □ ~ **about** vt maltratar. □ ~ **down** vt derribar; atropellar (person). □ ~ **off** vt hacer caer. ● vi (*fam, finish work*) terminar, salir del trabajo. □ ~ **out** vt (*by blow*) dejar sin sentido; (*eliminate*) eliminar. ● vt atropellar; (*eliminate*) eliminar. □ ~ **over** vt tirar; atropellar (person). ~**er** n aldaba f. ~**-kneed** /ˈniːd/ adj patizambo. ~**out** n (Boxing) nocaut m
knot /nɒt/ n nudo m. ● vt (*pt knotted*) anudar
know /nəʊ/ vt (*pt knew*) saber; (*be acquainted with*) conocer. **let s.o.** ~ **sth** decirle algo a uno;

(*warn*) avisarle algo a uno. ● *vi* saber. ~ how to do sth saber hacer algo. ~ about entender de (cars etc). ~ of saber de. ● he be in the ~ estar enterado. ~-all *n* *in* sabelotodo *m* & *f*. ~-how *n* know-how *m*, conocimientos *mpl* y experiencia. ~ingly *adv* a sabiendas. ~-it-all *n* (*Amer*) see ~-ALL

knowledge /'nɒlɪdʒ/ *n* saber *m*; (*awareness*) conocimiento *m*; (*learning*) conocimientos *mpl*. ~able *adj* informado

known /nəʊn/ see KNOW. ● *adj* conocido

knuckle /'nʌkl/ *n* nudillo *m*. □ ~ **under** *vi* someterse

Korea /kə'rɪə/ *n* Corea *f*. ~n *adj* & *n* coreano (*m*)

kudos /'kju:dɒs/ *n* prestigio *m*

....

Ll

....

lab /læb/ *n* 🄵 laboratorio *m*

label /'leɪbl/ *n* etiqueta *f*. ● *vt* (*pt* labelled) poner etiqueta a; (*fig, describe as*) tachar de

laboratory /lə'bɒrətərɪ/ *n* laboratorio *m*

laborious /lə'bɔ:rɪəs/ *adj* penoso

labour /'leɪbə(r)/ *n* trabajo *m*; (*workers*) mano *f* de obra; (*Med*) parto *m*. **in** ~ de parto. ● *vi* trabajar. ● *vt* insistir en. **L**~ *n* el partido *m* laborista. ● *adj* laborista. ~er *n* peón *m*

lace /leɪs/ *n* encaje *m*; (*of shoe*) cordón *m*, agujeta *f* (*Mex*). ● *vt* (*fasten*) atar

lacerate /'læsəreɪt/ *vt* lacerar

lack /læk/ *n* falta *f*. for ~ of por falta de. ● *vt* faltarle a uno. he ~s confidence le falta confianza en sí mismo. ~ing be ~ing faltar. be ~ing in no tener

lad /læd/ *n* muchacho *m*

ladder /'lædə(r)/ *n* escalera *f* (de mano); (*in stocking*) carrera *f*. ● *vt* hacerse una carrera en. ● *vi* hacérsele una carrera a

laden /'leɪdn/ *adj* cargado (with de)

ladle /'leɪdl/ *n* cucharón *m*

lady /'leɪdɪ/ *n* señora *f*, young ~ señorita *f*. ~bird *n*, ~bug *n* (*Amer*) mariquita *f*, catarina *f* (*Mex*). ~-in-waiting *n* dama *f* de honor. ~like *adj* fino

lag /læg/ *vi* (*pt* lagged) ~ (behind) retrasarse. ● *vt* revestir (*pipes*). ● *n* (*interval*) intervalo *m*

lager /'lɑ:gə(r)/ *n* cerveza *f* (rubia)

lagging /'lægɪŋ/ *n* revestimiento *m*

lagoon /lə'gu:n/ *n* laguna *f*

laid /leɪd/ see LAY

lain /leɪn/ see LIE¹

lair /leə(r)/ *n* guarida *f*

lake /leɪk/ *n* lago *m*

lamb /læm/ *n* cordero *m*

lame /leɪm/ *adj* (-er, -est) cojo, rengo (*LAm*); (*excuse*) pobre, malo

lament /lə'ment/ *n* lamento *m*. ● *vt* lamentar. ~able /'læməntəbl/ *adj* lamentable

lamp /læmp/ *n* lámpara *f*

lamp: ~post *n* farol *m*. ~shade *n* pantalla *f*

lance /lɑ:ns/ *n* lanza *f*

land /lænd/ *n* tierra *f*; (*country*) país *m*; (*plot*) terreno *m*. ● *vt* desembarcar; (*obtain*) conseguir; dar (*blow*). ● *vi* (*from ship*) desembar-

k
l

car; (aircraft) aterrizar. □ ~ **up** vi ir a parar. ~**ing** n desembarque m; (by aircraft) aterrizaje m; (top of stairs) descanso m. ~**lady** n casera f; (of inn) dueña f. ~**lord** n casero m, dueño m; (of inn) dueño m. ~**mark** n punto m destacado. ~**scape** /-skeɪp/ n paisaje m. ~**slide** n desprendimiento m de tierras; (Pol) victoria f arrolladora

lane /leɪn/ n (path, road) camino m, sendero m; (strip of road) carril m

language /'læŋgwɪdʒ/ n idioma m; (speech, style) lenguaje m

lank /læŋk/ adj (hair) lacio. ~**y** adj (-ier, -iest) larguirucho

lantern /'læntən/ n linterna f

lap /læp/ n (of body) rodillas fpl; (Sport) vuelta f. □ ~ **up** vt (pt lapped) beber a lengüetazos; (fig) aceptar con entusiasmo. ● vi (waves) chapotear

lapel /lə'pel/ n solapa f

lapse /læps/ vi (decline) degradarse; (expire) caducar; (time) transcurrir. ~ **into silence** callarse. ● n error m; (of time) intervalo m

laptop /'læptop/ n. ~ (computer) laptop m, portátil m

lard /lɑːd/ n manteca f de cerdo

larder /'lɑːdə(r)/ n despensa f

large /lɑːdʒ/ adj (-er, -est) grande; (before singular noun) gran. at ~ en libertad. ~**ly** adv en gran parte

lark /lɑːk/ n (bird) alondra f; (joke) broma f; (bit of fun) travesura f. □ ~ **about** vt hacer el tonto 🔟

larva /'lɑːvə/ n (pl -vae /-viː/) larva f

laser /'leɪzə(r)/ n láser m. ~ **beam** n rayo m láser. ~ **printer** n impresora f láser

lash /læʃ/ vt azotar. □ ~ **out** vi atacar. ~ **out against** vt atacar. ● n latigazo m; (eyelash) pestaña f; (whip) látigo m

lashings /'læʃɪŋz/ npl. ~ **of** (fam, cream etc) montones de

lass /læs/ n muchacha f

lasso /læ'suː/ n (pl -os) lazo m

last /lɑːst/ adj último; (week etc) pasado. ~ **Monday** el lunes pasado. ~ **night** anoche. ● adv por último; (most recently) la última vez. he came ~ llegó el último. ● n último m; (remainder) lo que queda. ~ **but one** penúltimo. at (long) ~ por fin. ● vi/t durar. □ ~ **out** vi sobrevivir. ~**ing** adj duradero. ~**ly** adv por último

latch /lætʃ/ n pestillo m

late /leɪt/ adj (-er, -est) (not on time) tarde; (recent) reciente; (former) antiguo, ex. be ~ llegar tarde. in ~ **July** a fines de julio. the ~ **Dr Phillips** el difunto Dr. Phillips. ● adv tarde. ~**ly** adv últimamente

latent /'leɪtnt/ adj latente

later /'leɪtə(r)/ adv más tarde

lateral /'lætərəl/ adj lateral

latest /'leɪtɪst/ adj último. ● n. at the ~ a más tardar

lathe /leɪð/ n torno m

lather /'lɑːðə(r)/ n espuma f

Latin /'lætɪn/ n (language) latín m. ● adj latino. ~ **America** n América f Latina, Latinoamérica f. ~ **American** adj & n latinoamericano f

latitude /'lætɪtjuːd/ n latitud m

latter /'lætə(r)/ adj último; (of two) segundo. ● n. the ~ éste m, ésta f, éstos mpl, éstas fpl

laugh /lɑːf/ vi reír(se). ~ **at** reírse de. ● n risa f. ~**able** adj ridículo. ~**ing stock** n hazmerreír m. ~**ter**

n risas fpl

launch /lɔːntʃ/ vt lanzar; botar (new vessel). ● n lanzamiento m; (of new vessel) botadura; (boat) lancha f (a motor). ~**ing pad**, ~ **pad** n plataforma f de lanzamiento

laund|er /'lɔːndə(r)/ vt lavar (y planchar). ~**erette** /-et/, **L~romat** /'lɔːndrəmæt/ (Amer) (P) n lavandería f automática. ~**ry** n (place) lavandería f; (dirty clothes) ropa f sucia; (clean clothes) ropa f limpia

lava /'lɑːvə/ n lava f

lavatory /'lævətərɪ/ n (cuarto m de) baño m. **public** ~ servicios mpl, baños mpl (LAm)

lavish /'lævɪʃ/ adj (lifestyle) de derroche; (meal) espléndido; (production) fastuoso. ● vt prodigar (on a)

law /lɔː/ n ley f; (profession, subject of study) derecho m. ~ **and order** n orden m público. ~ **court** n tribunal m

lawn /lɔːn/ n césped m, pasto m (LAm). ~**mower** n cortacésped f, cortadora f de pasto (LAm)

lawsuit /'lɔːsuːt/ n juicio m

lawyer /'lɔːjə(r)/ n abogado m

lax /læks/ adj descuidado; (morals etc) laxo

laxative /'læksətɪv/ n laxante m

lay /leɪ/ see **LIE**. ● vt (pt laid) poner (also table, eggs); tender (trap); formar (plan). ~ **hands on echar** mano a. ~ **hold of** agarrar. ● adj (non-clerical) laico; (opinion etc) profano. □ ~ **down** vt dejar a un lado; imponer (condition). □ ~ **into** vt 🔊 dar una paliza a. □ ~ **off** vt despedir (worker). vi 🔢 terminar. □ ~ **on** vt (provide) proveer. □ ~ **out** vt (design) disponer; (display) exponer; gastar (money). □ ~**about**

n holgazán. ~**by** n área f de reposo

layer /'leɪə(r)/ n capa f

layette /leɪ'et/ n canastilla f

layman /'leɪmən/ n (pl -men) lego m

layout /'leɪaʊt/ n disposición f

laz|e /leɪz/ vi holgazanear; (relax) descansar. ~**iness** n pereza f. ~**y** adj perezoso. ~**ybones** n holgazán m

lead[1] /liːd/ vt (pt led) conducir; dirigir (team); llevar (life); encabezar (parade, attack). **be led to believe that** ... me dieron a entender que .... ● vi (go first) ir delante; (in race) aventajar. ● n mando m; (clue) pista f; (leash) correa f; (wire) cable m. **be in the** ~ llevar la delantera

lead[2] /led/ n plomo m; (of pencil) mina f. ~**ed** adj (fuel) con plomo

lead|er /'liːdə(r)/ ~**er** n jefe m; (Pol) líder m & f; (of gang) cabecilla m. ~**ership** n dirección f. ~**ing** adj principal; (in front) delantero

leaf /liːf/ n (pl **leaves**) hoja f. □ ~ **through** vt hojear (book). ~**let** /'liːflɪt/ n folleto m. ~**y** adj frondoso

league /liːg/ n liga f. **be in** ~ **with** estar aliado con

leak /liːk/ n (hole) agujero m; (of gas, liquid) escape m; (of information) filtración f; (in roof) gotera f; (in boat) vía f de agua. ● vi gotear; (liquid) salirse; (boat) hacer agua. ● vt perder; filtrar (information). ~**y** adj (receptacle) agujereado; (roof) que tiene goteras

lean /liːn/ (pt **leaned** or **leant** /lent/) vt apoyar. ● vi inclinarse. □ ~ **against** vt apoyarse en. □ ~ **on** vt apoyarse en. □ ~ **out** vt asomarse (of a). □ ~ **over** vi inclinarse. ● adj (-er, -est) (person) delgado;

leap | lens

(animal) flaco; (meat) magro. **~ing** adj inclinado. **~-to** n colgadizo m

leap /liːp/ vi (pt **leaped** or **leapt** /lept/) saltar. ● n salto m. **~frog** n. play **~frog** saltar al potro, jugar a la pídola, brincar al burro (Mex). ● vi (pt **-frogged**) saltar. **~ year** n año m bisiesto

learn /lɜːn/ vt/i (pt **learned** or **learnt**) aprender (to do a hacer). **~ed** /-ɪd/ adj culto. **~er** n principiante m & f; (apprentice) aprendiz m. **~ing** n saber m. **~ing curve** n curva f del aprendizaje

lease /liːs/ n arriendo m. ● vt arrendar

leash /liːʃ/ n correa f

least /liːst/ adj (smallest amount of) mínimo; (slightest) menor; (smallest) más pequeño. ● n. the **~** lo menos. at **~** por lo menos. not in the **~** en absoluto. ● adv menos

leather /ˈleðə(r)/ n piel f, cuero m

leave /liːv/ vt (pt **left**) dejar; (depart from) salir de. **~ alone** dejar de tocar (thing); dejar en paz (person). ● vi marcharse; (train) salir. ● n permiso m. □ **~ behind** vt dejar. □ **~ out** vt omitir. □ **~ over** vt. be left over quedar. on **~** (Mil) de permiso

leaves /liːvz/ see **LEAF**

lecture /ˈlektʃə(r)/ n conferencia f; (Univ) clase f; (rebuke) sermón m. ● vi dar clase. ● vt (scold) sermonear. **~r** n conferenciante m & f, conferencista m & f (LAm); (Univ) profesor m universitario

led /led/ see **LEAD**[1]

ledge /ledʒ/ n cornisa f; (of window) alféizar m

leek /liːk/ n puerro m

leer /ˈlɪə(r)/ vi. **~ at** mirar impúdicamente. ● n mirada impúdica f

left /left/ see **LEAVE**. adj izquierdo. ● adv a la izquierda f. ● n izquierda f. **~-handed** /-ˈhændɪd/ adj zurdo. **luggage** n consigna f. **~overs** npl restos mpl. **~-wing** /-ˈwɪŋ/ adj izquierdista

leg /leg/ n pierna f; (of animal, furniture) pata f; (of pork) pernil m; (of lamb) pierna f; (of journey) etapa f. on its last **~s** en las últimas. pull s.o.'s **~** 🛈 tomarle el pelo a uno

legacy /ˈlegəsɪ/ n herencia f

legal /ˈliːgl/ adj (permitted by law) lícito; (recognized by law) legítimo; (system etc) jurídico. **~ity** /liːˈgælətɪ/ n legalidad f. **~ize** vt legalizar. **~ly** adv legalmente

legend /ˈledʒənd/ n leyenda f. **~ary** adj legendario

legible /ˈledʒəbl/ adj legible

legislat|**e** /ˈledʒɪsleɪt/ vi legislar. **~ion** /-ˈleɪʃn/ n legislación f.

legitimate /lɪˈdʒɪtɪmət/ adj legítimo

leisure /ˈleʒə(r)/ n ocio m. at your **~** cuando le venga bien. **~ly** adj lento, pausado

lemon /ˈlemən/ n limón m. **~ade** /-ˈneɪd/ n (fizzy) gaseosa f (de limón); (still) limonada f

lend /lend/ vt (pt **lent**) prestar. **~ing** n préstamo m.

length /leŋθ/ n largo m; (of time) duración f; (of cloth) largo m. at **~** (at last) por fin. at (great) **~** detalladamente. **~en** /ˈleŋθən/ vt alargar. ● vi alargarse. **~ways** adv a lo largo. **~y** adj largo

lenient /ˈliːnɪənt/ adj indulgente

lens /lenz/ n lente f; (of camera) objetivo m. (contact) **~es** npl (optics) lentillas fpl, lentes mpl de contacto (*LAm*)

lent /lent/ *see* LEND

Lent /lent/ *n* cuaresma *f*

Leo /'li:əʊ/ *n* Leo *m*

leopard /'lepəd/ *n* leopardo *m*

leotard /'li:ətɑ:d/ *n* malla *f*

lesbian /'lezbɪən/ *n* lesbiana *f*.
● *adj* lesbiano

less /les/ *adj* & *n* & *adv* & *prep*
menos. ~ **than** menos que; (*with
numbers*) menos de. ~ **and** ~
cada vez menos. **none the** ~ sin
embargo. ~**en** *vt/i* disminuir

lesson /'lesn/ *n* clase *f*

lest /lest/ *conj* no sea que (+ *sub-
junctive*)

let /let/ *vt* (*pt* let, *pres p* letting)
dejar; (*lease*) alquilar. ~ **me do it**
déjame hacerlo. ● *modal verb*. ~'s
go! ¡vamos!, ¡vámonos! ~'s **see**
(vamos) a ver. ~'s **talk/drink**
hablemos/bebamos. □ ~ **down** *vt*
bajar; (*deflate*) desinflar; (*fig*) de-
fraudar. □ ~ **go** *vt* soltar. □ ~ **in** *vt*
dejar entrar. □ ~ **off** *vt* disparar
(*gun*); (*cause to explode*) hacer ex-
plotar; hacer estallar (*firework*);
(*excuse*) perdonar. □ ~ **out** *vt* dejar
salir. □ ~ **through** *vt* dejar pasar.
□ ~ **up** *vi* disminuir. ~**down** *n*
desilusión *f*

lethal /'li:θl/ *adj* (*dose, wound*)
mortal; (*weapon*) mortífero

letharg|ic /lɪ'θɑ:dʒɪk/ *adj* letár-
gico. ~**y** /'leθədʒi/ *n* letargo *m*

letter /'letə(r)/ *n* (*of alphabet*)
letra *f*; (*written message*) carta *f*. ~
bomb *n* carta *f* bomba. ~**box** *n*
buzón *m*. ~**ing** *n* letras *fpl*

lettuce /'letɪs/ *n* lechuga *f*

let-up /'letʌp/ *n* interrupción *f*

leukaemia /lu:'ki:mɪə/ *n* leuce-
mia *f*

level /'levl/ *adj* (*flat, even*) plano,

parejo (*LAm*); (*spoonful*) raso. ~
with (*at same height*) al nivel de.
● *n* nivel *m*. ● *vt* (*pt* levelled) nive-
lar; (*aim*) apuntar. ~ **crossing** *n*
paso *m* a nivel, crucero *m* (*Mex*)

lever /'li:və(r)/ *n* palanca *f*. ● *vt*
apalancar. ~ **open** abrir haciendo
palanca. ~**age** /-ɪdʒ/ *n* apalanca-
miento *m*

levy /'levi/ *vt* imponer (tax). ● *n*
impuesto *m*

lewd /lu:d/ *adj* (-**er**, -**est**) lascivo

liab|ility /laɪə'bɪlətɪ/ *n* responsa-
bilidad *f*; (*fam, disadvantage*) lastre
m. ~**ilities** *npl* (*debts*) deudas *fpl*.
~**le** /'laɪəbl/ *adj*. **be** ~**le to do**
tener tendencia a hacer. ~**le for**
responsable de. ~**le to** susceptible
de; expuesto a (*a fine*)

liais|e /lɪ'eɪz/ *vi* actuar de enlace
(**with** con). ~**on** /-ɒn/ *n* enlace *m*

liar /'laɪə(r)/ *n* mentiroso *m*

libel /'laɪbl/ *n* difamación *f*. ● *vt* (*pt*
libelled) difamar (por escrito)

liberal /'lɪbərəl/ *adj* liberal; (*gener-
ous*) generoso. **L**~ (*Pol*) del Partido
Liberal. ● *n* liberal *m* & *f*. ~**ly** *adv* li-
beralmente; (*generously*) generosa-
mente

liberat|e /'lɪbəreɪt/ *vt* liberar.
~**ion** /-'reɪʃn/ *n* liberación *f*

liberty /'lɪbətɪ/ *n* libertad *f*. **take
liberties** tomarse libertades. **take
the** ~ **of** tomarse la libertad de

Libra /'li:brə/ *n* Libra *f*

librar|ian /laɪ'breərɪən/ *n* biblio-
tecario *m*. ~**y** /'laɪbrərɪ/ *n* biblio-
teca *f*

Library of Congress La
biblioteca nacional de
EEUU, situada en Washington DC.
Fundada por el Congreso *Con-
gress*, alberga más de ochenta

millones de libros en 470 idiomas, y otros objetos.

lice /laɪs/ see LOUSE

licence /'laɪsns/ n licencia f, permiso m

license /'laɪsns/ vt autorizar. ●n (Amer) see LICENCE. ~ **number** n (Amer) (número m de) matrícula f. ~ **plate** n (Amer) matrícula f, placa f (LAm)

lick /lɪk/ vt lamer; (sl, defeat) dar una paliza a. ●n lametón m

licorice /'lɪkərɪs/ n (Amer) regaliz m

lid /lɪd/ n tapa f; (eyelid) párpado m

lie[1] /laɪ/ vi (pt lay, pp lain, pres p lying) echarse, tenderse; (be in lying position) estar tendido; (be) estar, encontrarse. ~ **low** quedarse escondido. □ ~ **down** vi echarse, tenderse

lie[2] /laɪ/ n mentira f. ●vi (pt lied, pres p lying) mentir

lie-in /laɪˈɪn/ n. have a ~ quedarse en la cama

lieutenant /lefˈtenənt/ n (Mil) teniente m

life /laɪf/ n (pl lives) vida f. ~ **belt** n salvavidas m. ~**boat** n lancha f de salvamento; (on ship) bote m salvavidas. ~**buoy** n boya f salvavidas. ~ **coach** n coach m & f personal. ~**guard** n salvavidas m & f, socorrista m & f. ~ **jacket** n chaleco m salvavidas. ~**less** adj sin vida. ~**like** adj verosímil. ~**line** n cuerda f de salvamento; (fig) tabla f de salvación. ~**long** adj de toda la vida. ~ **preserver** n (Amer, buoy) see ~BUOY; (jacket) see ~JACKET. ~ **ring** n (Amer) see ~ BELT. ~**saver** n (person) salvavidas m & f; (fig) salvación f. ~**size(d)** adj (de)

tamaño natural. ~**time** n vida f. ~ **vest** n (Amer) see ~ JACKET

lift /lɪft/ vt levantar. ●vi (fog) disiparse. ●n ascensor m. give a ~ to s.o. llevar a uno en su coche, dar aventón a uno (Mex). □ ~ **up** vt levantar. ~**off** n despegue m

light /laɪt/ n luz f; (lamp) lámpara f, luz f; (flame) fuego m. come to ~ salir a la luz. have you got a ~? ¿tienes fuego? the ~s npl (traffic signals) el semáforo; (on vehicle) las luces. ●adj (-er, -est) (in colour) claro; (not heavy) ligero. ●vt (pt lit or lighted) encender, prender (LAm); (illuminate) iluminar. ●vi encenderse, prenderse (LAm). ~ **up** vt iluminar. ●vi iluminarse. ~ **bulb** n bombilla f, foco m (Mex). ~**en** vt (make less heavy) aligerar, aliviar (LAm); (give light to) iluminar; (make brighter) aclarar. ~**er** n (for cigarettes) mechero m, encendedor m. ~**hearted** /-'hɑːtɪd/ adj alegre. ~**house** n faro m. ~**ly** adv ligeramente

lightning /'laɪtnɪŋ/ n. flash of ~ relámpago m. ●adj relámpago

lightweight adj ligero, liviano (LAm)

like /laɪk/ adj parecido. ●prep como. ●conj 🄳 como. ●vt. I ~ chocolate me gusta el chocolate. they ~ swimming (a ellos) les gusta nadar. would you ~ a coffee? ¿quieres un café?. ~**able** adj simpático.

like|lihood /'laɪklɪhʊd/ n probabilidad f. ~**ly** adj (-ier, -iest) probable. he is ~**ly** to come es probable que venga. ●adv probablemente. not ~**ly!** ¡ni hablar! ~**n** vt comparar (to con, a). ~**ness** n parecido m. be a good ~**ness** parecerse mucho. ~**wise**

adv (*also*) también; (*the same way*) lo mismo

liking /'laɪkɪŋ/ *n* (*for thing*) afición *f*; (*for person*) simpatía *f*

lilac /'laɪlək/ *adj* lila. ●*n* lila *f*; (*color*) lila *m*

lily /'lɪlɪ/ *n* lirio *m*; (*white*) azucena *f*

limb /lɪm/ *n* miembro *m*. **out on a** ~ aislado

lime /laɪm/ *n* (*white substance*) cal *f*; (*fruit*) lima *f*. ~**light** *n*. **be in the** ~**light** ser el centro de atención

limerick /'lɪmərɪk/ *n* quintilla *f* humorística

limit /'lɪmɪt/ *n* límite *m*. ●*vt* limitar. ~**ation** /-'teɪʃn/ *n* limitación *f*. ~**ed** *adj* limitado. ~**ed company** *n* sociedad *f* anónima

limousine /'lɪməziːn/ *n* limusina *f*

limp /lɪmp/ *vi* cojear, renguear (*LAm*). ●*n* cojera *f*, renguera *f* (*LAm*). **have a** ~ cojear. ●*adj* (*-er*, *-est*) flojo

linden /'lɪndn/ *n* (*Amer*) tilo *m*

line /laɪn/ *n* línea *f*; (*track*) vía *f*; (*wrinkle*) arruga *f*; (*row*) fila *f*; (*of poem*) verso *m*; (*rope*) cuerda *f*; (*of goods*) surtido *m*; (*Amer*, *queue*) cola *f*. **stand in** ~ (*Amer*) hacer cola. **get in** ~ (*Amer*) ponerse en la cola.. **cut in** ~ (*Amer*) colarse. **in** ~ **with** de acuerdo con. ●*vt* forrar (*skirt*, *box*); bordear (*streets* etc). □ ~ **up** *vi* alinearse; (*in queue*) hacer cola. *vt* (*form into line*) poner en fila; (*align*) alinear. ~**d** /laɪnd/ *adj* (*paper*) con renglones; (*with fabric*) forrado

linen /'lɪnɪn/ *n* (*sheets* etc) ropa *f* blanca; (*material*) lino *m*

liner /'laɪnə(r)/ *n* (*ship*) transatlántico *m*

linger /'lɪŋɡə(r)/ *vi* tardar en mar-

charse. ~ (**on**) (smells etc) persistir. □ ~ **over** *vt* dilatarse en

lingerie /'lænʒəri/ *n* lencería *f*

linguist /'lɪŋɡwɪst/ *n* políglota *m* & *f*; lingüista *m* & *f*. ~**ic** /lɪŋ 'ɡwɪstɪk/ *adj* lingüístico. ~**ics** *n* lingüística *f*

lining /'laɪnɪŋ/ *n* forro *m*

link /lɪŋk/ *n* (*of chain*) eslabón *m*; (*connection*) conexión *f*; (*bond*) vínculo *m*; (*transport*, *telecommunications*) conexión *f*, enlace *m*. ●*vt* conectar; relacionar (*facts*, *events*). □ ~ **up** *vt/i* conectar

lino /'laɪnəʊ/ *n* (*pl* -**os**) linóleo *m*

lint /lɪnt/ *n* (*Med*) hilas *fpl*

lion /'laɪən/ *n* león *m*. ~**ess** /-nɪs/ *n* leona *f*

lip /lɪp/ *n* labio *m*; (*edge*) borde *m*. ~**read** *vi* leer los labios. ~**salve** *n* crema *f* para los labios. ~**service** *n*. **pay** ~ **service** to aprobar de boquilla, aprobar de los dientes para afuera (*Mex*). ~**stick** *n* lápiz *m* de labios

liqueur /lɪ'kjʊə(r)/ *n* licor *m*

liquid /'lɪkwɪd/ *adj* & *n* líquido (*m*)

liquidate /'lɪkwɪdeɪt/ *vt* liquidar

liquidize /'lɪkwɪdaɪz/ *vt* licuar. ~**r** *n* licuadora *f*

liquor /'lɪkə(r)/ *n* bebidas *fpl* alcohólicas

liquorice /'lɪkərɪs/ *n* regaliz *m*

liquor store *n* (*Amer*) tienda *f* de bebidas alcohólicas

lisp /lɪsp/ *n* ceceo *m*. **speak with a** ~ cecear. ●*vi* cecear

list /lɪst/ *n* lista *f*. ●*vt* hacer una lista de; (*enter in a list*) inscribir. ●*vi* (*ship*) escorar

listen /'lɪsn/ *vi* escuchar. ~ **in (to)** escuchar. ~ **to** escuchar. ~**er** *n* oyente *m* & *f*

listless /'lɪstlɪs/ adj apático

lit /lɪt/ see LIGHT

literacy /'lɪtərəsɪ/ n alfabetismo m

literal /'lɪtərəl/ adj literal. **~ly** adv literalmente

literary /'lɪtərərɪ/ adj literario

literate /'lɪtərət/ adj alfabetizado

literature /'lɪtərətʃə(r)/ n literatura f; (fig) folletos mpl

lithe /laɪð/ adj ágil

litre /'liːtə(r)/ n litro m

litter /'lɪtə(r)/ n basura f; (of animals) camada f. • vt ensuciar; (scatter) esparcir. **~ed with** lleno de. **~ bin** n papelera f. **~bug, ~lout** n persona f que tira basura en lugares públicos

little /'lɪtl/ adj pequeño; (not much) poco. a **~** water un poco de agua. • pron poco, poca. a **~** un poco. • adv poco. **by ~** poco a poco. **~ finger** n (dedo m) meñique m

live /lɪv/ vt/i vivir. □ **~ down** vt lograr borrar. □ **~ off** vt vivir a costa de (family, friends); (feed on) alimentarse de. □ **~ on** vt (feed o.s. on) vivir de. vi (memory) seguir presente; (tradition) seguir existiendo. □ **~ up** vt. **~ it up** 🔢 darse la gran vida. □ **~ up to** vt vivir de acuerdo con; cumplir (promise). • /laɪv/ adj vivo; (wire) con corriente; (broadcast) en directo

livelihood /'laɪvlɪhʊd/ n sustento m

lively /'laɪvlɪ/ adj (-ier, -iest) vivo

liven up /laɪvn/ vt animar. • vi animar(se)

liver /'lɪvə(r)/ n hígado m

lives /laɪvz/ see LIFE

livestock /'laɪvstɒk/ n animales mpl (de cría); (cattle) ganado m

livid /'lɪvɪd/ adj lívido; (fam, angry) furioso

living /'lɪvɪŋ/ adj vivo. • n vida f. make a **~** ganarse la vida. **~ room** n salón m, sala f (de estar), living m (LAm)

lizard /'lɪzəd/ n lagartija f; (big) lagarto m

load /ləʊd/ n (also Elec) carga f; (quantity) cantidad f; (weight, strain) peso m. **~s of** 🔢 montones de. • vt cargar. **~ed** adj cargado

loaf /ləʊf/ n (pl loaves) pan m; (stick of bread) barra f de pan. • vi. (**~ around**) holgazanear

loan /ləʊn/ n préstamo m. **on ~** prestado. • vt prestar

loath|e /ləʊð/ vt odiar. **~ing** n odio m (of a). **~esome** /-səm/ adj repugnante

lobby /'lɒbɪ/ n vestíbulo m; (Pol) grupo m de presión. • vt ejercer presión sobre. • vi. **for sth** ejercer presión para obtener algo

lobe /ləʊb/ n lóbulo m

lobster /'lɒbstə(r)/ n langosta f, bogavante m

local /'ləʊkl/ adj local. **~ (phone) call** llamada f urbana. • n (fam, pub) **the ~s** los vecinos mpl. **~ government** n administración f municipal. **~ity** /-'kælətɪ/ n localidad f. **~ization** n localización f. **~ly** adv (live, work) en la zona

locat|e /ləʊ'keɪt/ vt (situate) situar, ubicar (LAm); (find) localizar, ubicar (LAm). **~ion** /-ʃn/ n situación f, ubicación f (LAm). **on ~ion** fuera del estudio. **to film on ~ion in** Andalusia rodar en Andalusia

lock /lɒk/ n (of door etc) cerradura f; (on canal) esclusa f; (of hair) mechón m. • vt cerrar con llave. • vi cerrarse con llave. □ ~ **in** vt encerrar. □ ~ **out** vt cerrar la puerta a. □ ~ **up** vt encerrar (person); cerrar con llave (building)

locker /'lɒkə(r)/ n armario m, locker m (LAm). ~ **room** n (Amer) vestuario m, vestidor m (Mex)

locket /'lɒkɪt/ n medallón m

lock: ~**out** /'lɒkaʊt/ n cierre m patronal, paro m patronal (LAm). ~**smith** n cerrajero m

locomotive /ləʊkə'məʊtɪv/ n locomotora f

lodg|e /lɒdʒ/ n (of porter) portería f. ● vt alojar; presentar (complaint). ~**er** n huésped m. ~**ings** n alojamiento m; (room) habitación f alquilada

loft /lɒft/ n desván m, altillo m (LAm)

lofty /'lɒftɪ/ adj (-ier, -iest) elevado; (haughty) altanero

log /lɒg/ n (of wood) tronco m; (as fuel) leño m; (record) diario m. sleep like a ~ dormir como un tronco. ● vt (pt logged) registrar. □ ~ **in**, ~ **on** vi (Comp) entrar (al sistema). □ ~ **off**, ~ **out** vi (Comp) salir (del sistema)

logarithm /'lɒgərɪðəm/ n logaritmo m

loggerheads /'lɒgəhedz/ npl. be at ~ with estar a matar con

logic /'lɒdʒɪk/ adj lógica f. ~**al** adj lógico. ~**ally** adv lógicamente

logistics /lə'dʒɪstɪks/ n logística f. ● npl (practicalities) problemas mpl logísticos

logo /'ləʊgəʊ/ n (pl -os) logo m

loin /lɔɪn/ n (Culin) lomo m. ~**s** npl entrañas fpl

loiter /'lɔɪtə(r)/ vi perder el tiempo

loll /lɒl/ vi repantigarse

loll|ipop /'lɒlɪpɒp/ n piruli m. ~**y** n polo m, paleta f (helada) (LAm)

London /'lʌndən/ n Londres m. ● adj londinense. ~**er** n londinense m & f

lone /ləʊn/ adj solitario. ~**ly** adj (-ier, -iest) solitario. feel ~**ly** sentirse muy solo. ~ n solitario m. ~**some** /-səm/ adj solitario

long /lɒŋ/ adj (-er, -est) largo. a ~ time mucho tiempo. how ~ is it? ¿cuánto tiene de largo? ● adv largo/mucho tiempo. as ~ as (while) mientras; (provided that) con tal que (+ subjunctive). before ~ dentro de poco. so ~! ¡hasta luego! so as ~ as (provided that) con tal que (+ subjunctive). □ ~ **for** vi anhelar. ~ to do estar deseando hacer. ~**-distance** /-'dɪstəns/ adj de larga distancia. ~**-distance** **phone call** llamada f de larga distancia, conferencia f. ~**er** adv. no ~**er** ya no. ~**-haul** /-'hɔːl/ adj de larga distancia. ~**ing** n anhelo m, ansia f

longitude /'lɒŋgɪtjuːd/ n longitud f

long: ~ **jump** n salto m de longitud. ~**-playing record** n elepé m. ~**-range** adj de largo alcance. ~**-sighted** /-'saɪtɪd/ adj hipermétrope. ~**-term** adj a largo plazo. ~**-winded** /-'wɪndɪd/ adj prolijo

loo /luː/ n 🔲 váter m, baño m (LAm)

look /lʊk/ vt mirar; representar (age). ● vi mirar; (seem) parecer; (search) buscar. ● n mirada f; (appearance) aspecto m. good ~**s** belleza f. □ ~ **after** vt cuidar (person); (be responsible for) encargarse de. □ ~ **at** vt mirar; (consider) considerar. □ ~ **down on** vt despreciar. □~ **for** vt buscar. □~ **forward to** vt esperar con ansia. □~ **into** vt investigar. □~ **like** vt parecerse a. □~ **on** vi mirar. □~ **out** vi tener cuidado. □~ **out for** vt buscar; (watch) tener cuidado con. □~ **round** vi volver la cabeza. □~ **through** vt hojear. □~ **up** vt buscar (word); (visit) ir a ver. □~ **up to** vt admirar. **~alike** a 🔲 doble m & f. **~out** n (Mil, person) vigía m. be on the ~out for andar a la caza de. **~s** npl belleza f

loom /luːm/ n telar m. ● vi aparecerse

looney /ˈluːnɪ/ adj & n 🔲 chiflado (m) 🔲, loco (m)

loop /luːp/ n (shape) curva f; (in string) lazada f. ● vt hacer una lazada con. **~hole** n (in rule) escapatoria f

loose /luːs/ adj (-er, -est) suelto; (garment, thread, hair) flojo; (inexact) vago; (not packed) suelto. be at a ~ end no tener nada que hacer. **~ly** adv sueltamente; (roughly) aproximadamente. **~n** vt aflojar

loot /luːt/ n botín m. ● vt/i saquear. **~er** n saqueador m

lop /lɒp/ vt (pt lopped). ~ **off** cortar

lop-sided /-ˈsaɪdɪd/ adj ladeado

lord /lɔːd/ n señor m; (British title) lord m. (good) L~! ¡Dios mío! the L~ el Señor. (the House of) L~s la Cámara de los Lores

lorry /ˈlɒrɪ/ n camión m. ~ **driver** n camionero m

lose /luːz/ vt/i (pt lost) perder. **~r** n perdedor m

loss /lɒs/ n pérdida f. be at a ~ estar perplejo. be at a ~ for words no encontrar palabras

lost /lɒst/ see **LOSE**. ● adj perdido. get ~ perderse. ~ **property** n, ~ **and found** (Amer) oficina f de objetos perdidos

lot /lɒt/ n (fate) suerte f; (at auction) lote m; (land) solar m. a ~ (of) mucho. quite a ~ of 🔲 bastante. **~s** (of) 🔲 muchos. they ate the ~ se lo comieron todo

lotion /ˈləʊʃn/ n loción f

lottery /ˈlɒtərɪ/ n lotería f

loud /laʊd/ adj (-er, -est) fuerte; (noisy) ruidoso; (gaudy) chillón. out ~ en voz alta. **~hailer** /-ˈheɪlə(r)/ n megáfono m. **~ly** adv (speak) en voz alta; (shout) fuerte; (complain) a voz en grito. **~speaker** /-ˈspiːkə(r)/ n altavoz m, altoparlante m (LAm)

lounge /laʊndʒ/ vi repantigarse. ● n salón m, sala f (de estar), living m (LAm)

louse /laʊs/ n (pl lice) piojo m. **~y** /ˈlaʊzɪ/ adj (-ier, -iest) (sl, bad) malísimo

lout /laʊt/ n patán m

lov|able /ˈlʌvəbl/ adj adorable. **~e** /lʌv/ n amor m; (tennis) cero m. be in ~e (with) estar enamorado (de). fall in ~e (with) enamorarse (de). ● vt querer, amar (person). I ~e milk me encanta la leche. **~e affair** n aventura f, amorío m

lovely /ˈlʌvlɪ/ adj (-ier, -iest) (appearance) precioso, lindo (LAm); (person) encantador, amoroso (LAm)

lover /ˈlʌvə(r)/ n amante m & f

loving /ˈlʌvɪŋ/ adj cariñoso

low /ləʊ/ adj & adv (-er, -est) bajo. ● vi (cattle) mugir. **~er** vt bajar. **~er o.s.** envilecerse. **~level** adj a bajo nivel. **~ly** adj (-ier, -iest) humilde

loyal /'lɔɪəl/ adj leal, fiel. ~ty n lealtad f. ~ty card tarjeta f de fidelidad

lozenge /'lɒzɪndʒ/ n (shape) rombo m; (tablet) pastilla f

LP abbr (= **long-playing record**) elepé m

Ltd /'lɪmɪtɪd/ abbr (= **Limited**) S.A., Sociedad Anónima

lubricate /'luːbrɪkeɪt/ vt lubricar

lucid /'luːsɪd/ adj lúcido

luck /lʌk/ n suerte f. ~ good ~! ¡(buena) suerte! ~ily adv por suerte. ~y adj (-ier, -iest) (person) con suerte. be ~y tener suerte. ~y number número m de la suerte

lucrative /'luːkrətɪv/ adj lucrativo

ludicrous /'luːdɪkrəs/ adj ridículo

lug /lʌɡ/ vt (pt lugged) 🔢 arrastrar

luggage /'lʌɡɪdʒ/ n equipaje m. ~ rack n rejilla f

lukewarm /'luːkwɔːm/ adj tibio; (fig) poco entusiasta

lull /lʌl/ vt (soothe, send to sleep) adormecer; (calm) calmar. ● n periodo m de calma

lullaby /'lʌləbaɪ/ n canción f de cuna

lumber /'lʌmbə(r)/ n trastos mpl viejos; (wood) maderos mpl. ● vt. s.o. with sth 🔢 endilgar algo a uno. ~jack n leñador m

luminous /'luːmɪnəs/ adj luminoso

lump /lʌmp/ n (swelling) bulto m; (as result of knock) chichón m; (in liquid) grumo m; (of sugar) terrón m. ● vt. ~ together agrupar. ~ it 🔢 aguantarse. ~ sum n suma f global. ~y adj (sauce) grumoso; (mattress, cushions) lleno de protuberancias

lunacy /'luːnəsɪ/ n locura f

lunar /'luːnə(r)/ adj lunar

lunatic /'luːnətɪk/ n loco m

lunch /lʌntʃ/ n comida f, almuerzo m. have ~ comer, almorzar

luncheon /'lʌntʃən/ n comida f, almuerzo m. ~ voucher n vale m de comida

lung /lʌŋ/ n pulmón m

lunge /lʌndʒ/ n arremetida f. ● vi. ~ at arremeter contra

lurch /lɜːtʃ/ vi tambalearse. ● n. leave in the ~ dejar plantado

lure /ljʊə(r)/ vt atraer

lurid /'ljʊərɪd/ adj (colour) chillón; (shocking) morboso

lurk /lɜːk/ vi merodear; (in ambush) estar al acecho

luscious /'lʌʃəs/ adj delicioso

lush /lʌʃ/ adj exuberante

lust /lʌst/ n lujuria f; (craving) deseo m. ● vi. ~ after codiciar

lute /luːt/ n laúd m

Luxembourg, Luxemburg /'lʌksəmbɜːɡ/ n Luxemburgo m

luxuriant /lʌɡ'zjʊərɪənt/ adj exuberante

luxurious /lʌɡ'zjʊərɪəs/ adj lujoso. ~y /'lʌkʃərɪ/ n lujo m. ● adj de lujo

lying /'laɪɪŋ/ see LIE¹, LIE². ● n mentiras fpl. ● adj mentiroso

lynch /lɪntʃ/ vt linchar

lyric /'lɪrɪk/ adj lírico. ~al adj lírico. ~s npl letra f

Mm

MA /em'eɪ/ abbr see **MASTER**

mac /mæk/ n ① impermeable m

macabre /məˈkɑːbrə/ adj macabro

macaroni /mækəˈrəʊnɪ/ n macarrones mpl

mace /meɪs/ n (staff) maza f; (spice) macis f. M~ (P) (Amer) gas m para defensa personal

machine /məˈʃiːn/ n máquina f. ~ **gun** n ametralladora f. ~**ry** n maquinaria f; (working parts, fig) mecanismo m

mackintosh /ˈmækɪntɒʃ/ n impermeable m

macro /ˈmækrəʊ/ n (pl -os) (Comp) macro m

macrobiotic /mækrəʊbaɪˈɒtɪk/ adj macrobiótico

mad /mæd/ adj (madder, maddest) loco; (fam, angry) furioso. be ~ **about** estar loco por

madam /ˈmædəm/ n señora f

mad: ~**cap** adj atolondrado. ~ **cow disease** f enfermedad f de las vacas locas. ~**den** vt (make mad) enloquecer; (make angry) enfurecer

made /meɪd/ see **MAKE**. ~-**to-measure** hecho a (la) medida

mad: ~**house** n manicomio m. ~**ly** adv (interested, in love etc) locamente; (frantically) como un loco. ~**man** /-mən/ n loco m. ~**ness** n locura f

Madonna /məˈdɒnə/ n. **the** ~ (Relig) la Virgen

maestro /ˈmaɪstrəʊ/ n (pl maestri /-striː/ or -os) maestro m

Mafia /ˈmæfɪə/ n mafia f

magazine /mægəˈziːn/ n revista f; (of gun) recámara f

magenta /məˈdʒentə/ adj magenta, morado

maggot /ˈmægət/ n gusano m

magic /ˈmædʒɪk/ n magia f. ● adj mágico. ~**al** adj mágico. ~**ian** /məˈdʒɪʃn/ n mago m

magistrate /ˈmædʒɪstreɪt/ n juez m que conoce de faltas y asuntos civiles de menor importancia

magnet /ˈmægnɪt/ n imán m. ~**ic** /-ˈnetɪk/ adj magnético; (fig) lleno de magnetismo. ~**ism** n magnetismo m. ~**ize** vt imantar, magnetizar

magnif|ication /mægnɪfɪˈkeɪʃn/ n aumento m. ~**y** /ˈmægnɪfaɪ/ vt aumentar. ~**ying glass** n lupa f

magnificen|ce /mægˈnɪfɪsns/ adj magnificencia f. ~**t** adj magnífico

magnitude /ˈmægnɪtjuːd/ n magnitud f

magpie /ˈmægpaɪ/ n urraca f

mahogany /məˈhɒgənɪ/ n caoba f

maid /meɪd/ n (servant) criada f, sirvienta f; (girl, old use) doncella f. **old** ~ solterona f

maiden /ˈmeɪdn/ n doncella f. ● adj (voyage) inaugural. ~ **name** n apellido m de soltera

mail /meɪl/ n correo m; (armour) (cota f de) malla f. ● adj correo. ● vt echar al correo (letter); (send) enviar por correo. ~**box** n (Amer) buzón m. ~**ing list** n lista f de direcciones. ~**man** /-mən/ n (Amer) cartero m. ~ **order** n venta f por correo

maim /meɪm/ vt mutilar

main /meɪn/ n. **(water/gas)** ~ cañería f principal. **in the** ~ en su mayor parte. **the** ~**s** npl (Elec) la red f de suministro. ● adj principal. ~ **course** n plato m principal, plato m fuerte. ~ **frame** n (Comp) unidad f central. ~**land** n. **the** ~ la masa territorial de un país excluyendo sus islas. ● adj. ~**land** China (la) China continental. ~**ly** adv principalmente. ~ **road** n carretera f principal. ~**stream** adj (culture) establecido. ~ **street** n calle f principal

maint|ain /meɪnˈteɪn/ vt mantener. ~**enance** /ˈmeɪntənəns/ n mantenimiento m

maisonette /meɪzəˈnet/ n (small house) casita f; (part of house) dúplex m

maize /meɪz/ n maíz m

majestic /məˈdʒestɪk/ adj majestuoso

majesty /ˈmædʒəsti/ n majestad f

major /ˈmeɪdʒə(r)/ adj (important) muy importante; (Mus) mayor. a ~ road una calle prioritaria. ● n comandante m & f, mayor m & f (LAm). ● vi. ~ **in** (Amer, Univ) especializarse en

Majorca /məˈjɔːkə/ n Mallorca f

majority /məˈdʒɒrəti/ n mayoría f. ● adj mayoritario

make /meɪk/ vt (pt made) hacer; (manufacture) fabricar; ganar (money); tomar (decision); llegar a (destination). ~ **s.o. do sth** obligar a uno a hacer algo. **be made of** estar hecho de. I ~ **it two o'clock** yo tengo las dos. ~ **believe** fingir. ~ **do** (manage) arreglarse. ~ **do with** (content o.s.) contentarse con. ~ **it** llegar; (succeed) tener éxito. ● n marca f. ~ **for** vt dirigirse a. ~ **good** vt compensar; (repair) reparar. □ ~ **off** vi

escaparse (with con). □ ~ **out** vt distinguir; (understand) entender; (write out) hacer; (assert) dar a entender. vi (cope) arreglárselas. □ ~ **up** vt (constitute) formar; (prepare) preparar; inventar (story); ~ **it up** (become reconciled) hacer las paces. ~ **up** (one's face) maquillarse. □ ~ **up for** vt compensar. ~**believe** adj fingido, simulado. n ficción f (Amer) maquillaje m. ~ **r** n fabricante m & f. ~**shift** adj (temporary) provisional, provisorio (LAm); (improvised) improvisado. ~**up** n maquillaje m. put on ~**up** maquillarse.

making /ˈmeɪkɪŋ/ n. he has the ~**s** of tiene madera de. **in the** ~ en vías de formación

maladjusted /mælæˈdʒʌstɪd/ adj inadaptado

malaria /məˈleərɪə/ n malaria f, paludismo m

Malaysia /məˈleɪzɪə/ n Malasia f. ~**n** adj & n malaisio (m)

male /meɪl/ adj macho; (voice, attitude) masculino. ● n macho m; (man) varón m

malevolent /məˈlevələnt/ adj malévolo

malfunction /mælˈfʌŋkʃn/ vi fallar, funcionar mal

malic|e /ˈmælɪs/ n mala intención f, maldad f. bear s.o. ~**e** guardar rencor a uno. ~**ious** /məˈlɪʃəs/ adj malintencionado. ~**iously** adv con malevolencia

malignant /məˈlɪɡnənt/ adj maligno

mallet /ˈmælɪt/ n mazo m

malnutrition /mælnjuːˈtrɪʃn/ n desnutrición f

malpractice /mælˈpræktɪs/ n mala práctica f (en el ejercicio de

m

una profesión)

malt /mɔ:lt/ n malta f

Malt|a /ˈmɔ:ltə/ n Malta f. **~ese**
/-ˈti:z/ adj & n maltés (m)

mammal /ˈmæml/ n mamífero m

mammoth /ˈmæməθ/ n mamut
m. ●adj gigantesco

man /mæn/ n (pl men /men/)
hombre m; (Chess) pieza f. **~ in
the street** hombre m de la calle.
●vt (pt **manned**) encargarse de
(switchboard); tripular (ship); servir
(guns)

manacles /ˈmænəklz/ n (for
wrists) esposas fpl; (for legs) grillos
mpl

manag|e /ˈmænɪdʒ/ vt dirigir; ad-
ministrar (land, finances); (handle)
manejar. ●vi (Com) dirigir; (cope)
arreglárselas. **~e to** do lograr
hacer. **~eable** adj (task) posible de
alcanzar; (size) razonable.
~ement n dirección f. **~er** n di-
rector m; (of shop) encargado m; (of
soccer team) entrenador m, director
m técnico (LAm). **~eress** /-ˈres/ n
encargada f. **~erial** /-ˈdʒɪərɪəl/ adj
directivo, gerencial (LAm). **~ing
director** n director m ejecutivo

mandate /ˈmændeɪt/ n man-
dato m

mandatory /ˈmændətərɪ/ adj
obligatorio

mane /meɪn/ n (of horse) crin(es)
f(pl); (of lion) melena f

mangle /ˈmæŋɡl/ n rodillo m (es-
curridor). ●vt destrozar

man: ~handle vt mover a
pulso; (treat roughly) maltratar.
~hole n registro m. **~hood** n
madurez f; (quality) virilidad f.
~hour n hora f hombre.
~hunt n persecución f

mania /ˈmeɪnɪə/ n manía f. **~c**

/-ɪæk/ n maníaco m

manicure /ˈmænɪkjʊə(r)/ n ma-
nicura f, manicure f (LAm)

manifest /ˈmænɪfest/ adj mani-
fiesto. ●vt manifestar. **~ation**
/-ˈsteɪʃn/ n manifestación f

manifesto /mænɪˈfestəʊ/ n (pl
-os) manifiesto m

manipulat|e /məˈnɪpjʊleɪt/ vt
manipular. **~ion** /-ˈleɪʃn/ n mani-
pulación f. **~ive** /-lətɪv/ adj mani-
pulador

man: ~kind n humanidad f.
~ly adj viril. **~-made** adj artifi-
cial

manner /ˈmænə(r)/ n manera f;
(demeanour) actitud f; (kind) clase
f. **~ed** adj amanerado. **~s** npl mo-
dales mpl, educación f. **bad ~s**
mala educación

manoeuvre /məˈnu:və(r)/ n ma-
niobra f. ●vt/i maniobrar

manor /ˈmænə(r)/ n. **~ house**
casa f solariega

manpower n mano f de obra

mansion /ˈmænʃn/ n mansión f

man: ~-size(d) adj grande.
~slaughter n homicidio m sin
premeditación

mantelpiece /ˈmæntlpi:s/ n re-
pisa f de la chimenea

manual /ˈmænjʊəl/ adj manual.
●n (handbook) manual m

manufacture /mænjʊ
ˈfæktʃə(r)/ vt fabricar. ●n fabrica-
ción f. **~r** n fabricante m & f

manure /məˈnjʊə(r)/ n estiércol m

manuscript /ˈmænjʊskrɪpt/ n
manuscrito m

many /ˈmenɪ/ adj & pron muchos,
muchas. **~ people** mucha gente.
a great/good ~ muchísimos. **how
~?** ¿cuántos? **so ~** tantos. **too ~**
demasiados

map /mæp/ n mapa m; (of streets etc) plano m

mar /mɑː(r)/ vt (pt marred) estropear

marathon /ˈmærəθən/ n maratón m & f

marble /ˈmɑːbl/ n mármol m; (for game) canica f

march /mɑːtʃ/ vi (Mil) marchar. ~ **off** vi irse. ●n marcha f

March /mɑːtʃ/ n marzo m

march-past /ˈmɑːtʃpɑːst/ n desfile m

mare /meə(r)/ n yegua f

margarine /mɑːdʒəˈriːn/ n margarina f

margin /ˈmɑːdʒɪn/ n margen f. ~al adj marginal

marijuana /mærɪˈhwɑːnə/ n marihuana f

marina /məˈriːnə/ n puerto m deportivo

marine /məˈriːn/ adj marino. ●n (sailor) infante m de marina

marionette /mærɪəˈnet/ n marioneta f

marital status /mærɪtl ˈsteɪtəs/ n estado m civil

mark /mɑːk/ n marca f; (stain) mancha f; (Schol) nota f; (target) blanco m. ●vt (indicate) señalar, marcar; (stain) manchar; corregir (exam). ~ **time** marcar el paso. □ ~ **out** vt (select) señalar; (distinguish) distinguir. ●vt adj marcado. ~**edly** /-kɪdlɪ/ adv marcadamente. ~**er** n marcador m. ~**er (pen)** n rotulador m, marcador m (LAm)

market /ˈmɑːkɪt/ n mercado m. **on the** ~ en venta. ●vt comercializar. ~ **garden** n huerta f. ~**ing** n marketing m

marking /ˈmɑːkɪŋ/ n marcas fpl; (on animal, plant) mancha f

marksman /ˈmɑːksmən/ n (pl -men) tirador m. ~**ship** n puntería f

marmalade /ˈmɑːməleɪd/ n mermelada f (de cítricos)

maroon /məˈruːn/ adj & n granate (m). ●vt abandonar (en una isla desierta)

marquee /mɑːˈkiː/ n toldo m, entoldado m; (Amer, awning) marquesina f

marriage /ˈmærɪdʒ/ n matrimonio m; (ceremony) casamiento m

married /ˈmærɪd/ adj casado; (life) conyugal

marrow /ˈmærəʊ/ n (of bone) tuétano m; (vegetable) calabaza f verde alargada. ~ **squash** n (Amer) calabaza f verde alargada

marry /ˈmærɪ/ vt casarse con; (give or unite in marriage) casar. ●vi casarse. **get married** casarse (to con)

Mars /mɑːz/ n Marte m

marsh /mɑːʃ/ n pantano m

marshal /ˈmɑːʃl/ n (Mil) mariscal m; (Amer, police chief) jefe m de policía. ●vt (pt marshalled) reunir; poner en orden (thoughts)

marsh: ~**mallow** /-ˈmæləʊ/ n malvavisco m, bombón m (LAm). ~**y** adj pantanoso

martial /ˈmɑːʃl/ adj marcial. ~ **arts** npl artes fpl marciales. ~ **law** n ley f marcial

martyr /ˈmɑːtə(r)/ n mártir m & f

marvel /ˈmɑːvl/ n maravilla f. ●vi (pt marvelled) maravillarse (at de). ~**lous** adj maravilloso

Marxis|m /ˈmɑːksɪzəm/ n marxismo m. ~**t** adj & n marxista (m & f)

marzipan /ˈmɑːzɪpæn/ n mazapán m

mascara /mæˈskɑːrə/ n rímel® m

mascot /'mæskɒt/ n mascota f

masculin|e /'mæskjulın/ adj & n masculino (m). ~**ity** /-'lınıtı/ n masculinidad f

mash /mæʃ/ n (Brit 🔢, potatoes) puré m de patatas, puré m de papas (LAm). ● vt hacer puré de, moler (Mex). ~**ed potatoes** n puré m de patatas, puré m de papas (LAm)

mask /mɑːsk/ n máscara f; (Sport) careta f. ● vt ocultar

masochis|m /'mæsəkızəm/ n masoquismo m. ~**t** n masoquista m & f. ~**tic** /-'kıstık/ adj masoquista

mason /'meısn/ n (stone ~) mampostero m. **M**~ (freemason) masón m. ~**ry** /'meısnrı/ n albañilería f

masquerade /mɑːskə'reıd/ n mascarada f. ● vi. ~ **as** hacerse pasar por

mass /mæs/ n masa f; (Relig) misa f; (large quantity) montón m. **the** ~**es** las masas. ● vi concentrarse

massacre /'mæsəkə(r)/ n masacre f, matanza f. ● vt masacrar

mass|age /'mæsɑːʒ/ n masaje m. ● vt masajear. ~**eur** /mæ'sɜː(r)/ n masajista m. ~**euse** /mæ'sɜːz/ n masajista f

massive /'mæsıv/ adj masivo; (heavy) macizo; (huge) enorme

mass: ~ **media** n medios mpl de comunicación. ~**-produce** /-prə'djuːs/ vt fabricar en serie

mast /mɑːst/ n mástil m; (for radio, TV) antena f repetidora

master /'mɑːstə(r)/ n amo m; (expert) maestro m; (in secondary school) profesor m; (of ship) capitán m; (master copy) original m. ~'s degree master m, maestría f. **M**~ **of**

Arts (MA) poseedor m de una maestría en filosofía y letras. **M**~ **of Science** (MSc) poseedor m de una maestría en ciencias. ● vt llegar a dominar. ~ **key** n llave f maestra. ~**mind** n cerebro m. ● vt dirigir. ~**piece** n obra f maestra. ~**stroke** n golpe m de maestro. ~**y** n dominio m; (skill) maestría f

masturbat|e /'mæstəbeıt/ vi masturbarse. ~**ion** /-'beıʃn/ n masturbación f

mat /mæt/ n estera f; (at door) felpudo m. ● adj (Amer) see **MATT**

match /mætʃ/ n (Sport) partido m; (for fire) cerilla f, fósforo m (LAm), cerillo m (Mex); (equal) igual m. ● vt emparejar; (equal) igualar; (clothes, colours) hacer juego con. ● vi hacer juego. ~**box** n caja f de cerillas, caja f de fósforos (LAm), caja f de cerillos (Mex). ~**ing** adj que hace juego. ~**stick** n cerilla f, fósforo m (LAm), cerillo m (Mex)

mate /meıt/ n (of person) pareja f; (of animals, male) macho m; (of animals, female) hembra f; (assistant) ayudante m; (🔢, friend) amigo m, cuate m (Mex); (Chess) (jaque) m mate m. ● vi aparearse

material /mə'tıərıəl/ n material m; (cloth) tela f. ● adj material. ~**istic** /-'lıstık/ adj materialista. ~**ize** vi materializarse. ~**s** npl materiales mpl

matern|al /mə'tɜːnl/ adj maternal. ~**ity** /-ətı/ n maternidad f. ● adj (ward) de obstetricia; (clothes) premamá, de embarazada

math /mæθ/ n (Amer) see **MATHS**

mathematic|ian /mæθəmə'tıʃn/ n matemático m. ~**al** /-'mætıkl/ adj matemático. ~**s** /-'mætıks/ n matemática(s) f(pl)

maths /mæθs/ *n* matemática(s) *f(pl)*

matinée, matinee /ˈmætɪneɪ/ *n* (*Theatre*) función *f* de tarde; (*Cinema*) primera sesión *f* (de la tarde)

matrices /ˈmeɪtrɪsiːz/ *see* MATRIX

matriculat|e /məˈtrɪkjʊleɪt/ *vi* matricularse. ~**ion** /-ˈleɪʃn/ *n* matrícula *f*

matrimon|ial /mætrɪˈməʊnɪəl/ *adj* matrimonial. ~**y** /ˈmætrɪməni/ *n* matrimonio *m*

matrix /ˈmeɪtrɪks/ *n* (*pl* matrices) matriz *f*

matron /ˈmeɪtrən/ *n* (married, elderly) matrona *f*; (in school) ama *f* de llaves; (former use, in hospital) enfermera *f* jefe

matt, matte (*Amer*) /mæt/ *adj* mate

matted /ˈmætɪd/ *adj* enmarañado y apelmazado

matter /ˈmætə(r)/ *n* (substance) materia *f*; (affair) asunto *m*; (pus) pus *m*. **as a ~ of fact** en realidad. **no ~** no importa. **what is the ~?** ¿qué pasa? **to make ~s worse** para colmo (de males). ● *vi* importar. **it doesn't ~** no importa. ~**-of-fact** /-əvˈfækt/ *adj* (person) práctico

mattress /ˈmætrɪs/ *n* colchón *m*

matur|e /məˈtjʊə(r)/ *adj* maduro. ● *vi* madurar. ~**ity** *n* madurez *f*

maudlin /ˈmɔːdlɪn/ *adj* llorón

maul /mɔːl/ *vt* atacar (y herir)

mauve /məʊv/ *adj* & *n* malva (*m*)

maverick /ˈmævərɪk/ *n* inconformista *m* & *f*

maxim /ˈmæksɪm/ *n* máxima *f*

maxim|ize /ˈmæksɪmaɪz/ *vt* maximizar. ~**um** /-əm/ *adj* & *n* máximo (*m*)

---

may /meɪ/,

past **might**

auxiliary verb

····▸ (*expressing possibility*) **he ~ come** puede que venga, es posible que venga. **it ~ be true** puede ser verdad. **she ~ not have seen him** es posible que or puede que no lo haya visto

····▸ (*asking for or giving permission*) **~ I smoke?** ¿puedo fumar?, ¿se puede fumar? **~ I have your name and address, please?** ¿quiere darme su nombre y dirección, por favor?

····▸ (*expressing a wish*) **~ he be happy** que sea feliz

····▸ (*conceding*) **he ~ not have much experience, but he's very hardworking** no tendrá mucha experiencia, pero es muy trabajador. **that's as ~ be** puede ser

····▸ **I ~ as well stay** más vale quedarme

May /meɪ/ *n* mayo *m*

maybe /ˈmeɪbɪ/ *adv* quizá(s), tal vez, a lo mejor

May Day *n* el primero de mayo

mayhem /ˈmeɪhem/ *n* caos *m*

mayonnaise /meɪəˈneɪz/ *n* mayonesa *f*, mahonesa *f*

mayor /meə(r)/ *n* alcalde *m*, alcaldesa *f*. ~**ess** /-ɪs/ *n* alcaldesa *f*

maze /meɪz/ *n* laberinto *m*

me /miː/ *pron* me; (after prep) mí. **he knows ~** me conoce. **it's ~** soy yo

meadow /ˈmedəʊ/ *n* prado *m*, pradera *f*

meagre /ˈmiːgə(r)/ *adj* escaso

meal /miːl/ n comida f. ~time n hora f de comer

mean /miːn/ vt (pt meant) (intend) tener la intención de, querer; (signify) querer decir, significar. ~ to do tener la intención de hacer. ~ well tener buenas intenciones. be meant for estar destinado a. ● adj (-er, -est) (miserly) tacaño; (unkind) malo; (Math) medio. ● n media f; (average) promedio m

meander /mɪˈændə(r)/ vi (river) serpentear

meaning /ˈmiːnɪŋ/ n sentido m. ~ful adj significativo. ~less adj sin sentido

meanness /ˈmiːnnɪs/ n (miserliness) tacañería f; (unkindness) maldad f

means /miːnz/ n medio m. by ~ of por medio de, mediante. by all ~ por supuesto. by no ~ de ninguna manera. ● npl (wealth) medios mpl, recursos mpl. ~ test n investigación f de ingresos

meant /ment/ see MEAN

meantime /ˈmiːntaɪm/ adv mientras tanto, entretanto. ● n. in the ~ mientras tanto, entretanto

meanwhile /ˈmiːnwaɪl/ adv mientras tanto, entretanto

measles /ˈmiːzlz/ n sarampión m. ~y /ˈmiːzlɪ/ ① miserable

measure /ˈmeʒə(r)/ n medida f; (ruler) regla f. ● vt/i medir. □ ~ up to vt estar a la altura de. ~ment n medida f

meat /miːt/ n carne f. ~ball n albóndiga f. ~y adj (taste, smell) a carne; (soup, stew) con mucha carne

mechanic /mɪˈkænɪk/ n mecánico m. ~ical adj mecánico. ~ics n mecánica f. ~ism /ˈmekənɪzəm/ n

mecanismo m. ~ize /ˈmekənaɪz/ vt mecanizar

medal /ˈmedl/ n medalla f. ~list /ˈmedəlɪst/ n medallista m & f. be a gold ~list ganar una medalla de oro

meddle /ˈmedl/ vi meterse, entrometerse (in en). ~ with (tinker) toquetear

media /ˈmiːdɪə/ see MEDIUM. ● npl. the ~ los medios de comunicación

mediate /ˈmiːdɪeɪt/ vi mediar. ~ion /-ˈeɪʃn/ n mediación f ~or n mediador m

medical /ˈmedɪkl/ adj médico; (student) de medicina. ● n revisión f médica

medicated /ˈmedɪkeɪtɪd/ adj medicinal. ~ion /-ˈkeɪʃn/ n medicación f

medicinal /mɪˈdɪsɪnl/ adj medicinal. ~e /ˈmedsɪn/ n medicina f

medieval /medɪˈiːvl/ adj medieval

mediocre /miːdɪˈəʊkə(r)/ adj mediocre

meditate /ˈmedɪteɪt/ vi meditar. ~ion /-ˈteɪʃn/ n meditación f

Mediterranean /medɪtəˈreɪnɪən/ adj mediterráneo. ● n. the ~ el Mediterráneo

medium /ˈmiːdɪəm/ n (pl media) medio m. happy ~ término m medio. ● adj mediano. ~-size(d) /-saɪz(d)/ adj de tamaño mediano

medley /ˈmedlɪ/ n (Mus) popurrí m; (mixture) mezcla f

meek /miːk/ adj (-er, -est) dócil

meet /miːt/ vt (pt met) encontrar; (bump into s.o.) encontrarse con; (fetch) ir a buscar; (get to know, be introduced to) conocer. ● vi encontrarse; (get to know) conocerse; (have meeting) reunirse. ~ up vi

encontrarse (with con). □ ~ **with**
vt ser recibido con (Amer, meet) encontrarse con. ~**ing** n reunión f; (accidental between two people) encuentro m

megabyte /ˈmegəbaɪt/ n (Comp) megabyte m, megaocteto m

megaphone /ˈmegəfəʊn/ n megáfono m

melanchol|ic /melənˈkɒlɪk/ adj melancólico. ~**y** /ˈmelənkɒlɪ/ n melancolía f. ●adj melancólico

mellow /ˈmeləʊ/ adj (-er, -est) (fruit) maduro; (sound) dulce; (colour) tenue; (person) apacible

melodrama /ˈmelədrɑːmə/ n melodrama m. ~**tic** /melədrəˈmætɪk/ adj melodramático

melody /ˈmelədɪ/ n melodía f

melon /ˈmelən/ n melón m

melt /melt/ vt (make liquid) derretir; fundir (metals). ● vi (become liquid) derretirse; (metals) fundirse. □ ~ **down** vt fundir

member /ˈmembə(r)/ n miembro m & f; (of club) socio m. ~ **of staff** empleado m. M~ **of Congress** n (Amer) miembro m & f del Congreso. M~ **of Parliament** n diputado m. ~**ship** n calidad f de socio; (members) socios mpl, membresía f (LAm)

membrane /ˈmembreɪn/ n membrana f

memento /mɪˈmentəʊ/ n (pl -os or -oes) recuerdo m

memo /ˈmeməʊ/ n (pl -os) memorándum m, memo m

memoir /ˈmemwɑː(r)/ n memoria f

memorable /ˈmemərəbl/ adj memorable

memorandum /meməˈrændəm/ n (pl -ums or -da /-də/) memorándum m

memorial /mɪˈmɔːrɪəl/ n monumento m. ● adj conmemorativo

memor|ize /ˈmeməraɪz/ vt aprender de memoria. ~**y** /ˈmemərɪ/ n (faculty) memoria f; (thing remembered) recuerdo m. from ~**y** de memoria. in ~**y** of a la memoria de

men /men/ see MAN

menac|e /ˈmenəs/ n amenaza f; (fam, nuisance) peligro m público. ● vt amenazar. ~**ing** adj amenazador

mend /mend/ vt reparar; arreglar (garment). ~ **one's ways** enmendarse. □ ~ remiendo m. be on the ~ ir mejorando

menfolk /ˈmenfəʊk/ n hombres mpl

menial /ˈmiːnɪəl/ adj servil

meningitis /menɪnˈdʒaɪtɪs/ n meningitis f

menopause /ˈmenəpɔːz/ n menopausia f

menstruat|e /ˈmenstrʊeɪt/ vi menstruar. ~**ion** /-ˈeɪʃn/ n menstruación f

mental /ˈmentl/ adj mental; (hospital) psiquiátrico. ~**ity** /-ˈtælətɪ/ n mentalidad f. ~**ly** adv mentalmente. be ~**ly** ill ser un enfermo mental

mention /ˈmenʃn/ vt mencionar. don't ~ it! ¡no hay de qué! ● n mención f

mentor /ˈmentɔː(r)/ n mentor m

menu /ˈmenjuː/ n menú m

meow /mɪˈaʊ/ n & vi see MEW

mercenary /ˈmɜːsɪnərɪ/ adj & n mercenario (m)

merchandise /ˈmɜːtʃəndaɪz/ n mercancías fpl, mercadería f (LAm)

merchant /ˈmɜːtʃənt/ n comerciante m. ● adj (ship, navy) mer-

m

cante. ~ **bank** n banco m mercantil

merci|ful /'mɜːsɪfl/ adj misericordioso. ~**less** adj despiadado

mercury /'mɜːkjʊrɪ/ n mercurio m. M~ (planet) Mercurio m

mercy /'mɜːsɪ/ n compasión f. at the ~ of a merced de

mere /mɪə(r)/ adj simple. ~**ly** adv simplemente

merge /mɜːdʒ/ vt unir; fusionar (companies). • vi unirse; (companies) fusionarse. ~**r** n fusión f

meridian /mə'rɪdɪən/ n meridiano m

meringue /mə'ræŋ/ n merengue m

merit /'merɪt/ n mérito m. • vt (pt merited) merecer

mermaid /'mɜːmeɪd/ n sirena f

merr|ily /'merɪlɪ/ adv alegremente. ~**iment** /'merɪmənt/ n alegría f. ~**y** /'merɪ/ adj (-ier, -iest) alegre. make ~ divertirse. ~**y-go-round** n tiovivo m, carrusel m (LAm). ~**y-making** n jolgorio m

mesh /meʃ/ n malla f

mesmerize /'mezməraɪz/ vt hipnotizar; (fascinate) cautivar

mess /mes/ n desorden m; (dirt) suciedad f; (Mil) rancho m. make a ~ of estropear. □ ~ **up** vt desordenar; (dirty) ensuciar; estropear (plans). □ ~ **about** vi tontear. □ ~ **with** vt (tinker with) manosear

mess|age /'mesɪdʒ/ n mensaje m; (when phoning) recado m. ~**enger** /'mesɪndʒə(r)/ n mensajero m

Messiah /mɪ'saɪə/ n Mesías m

Messrs /'mesəz/ npl. ~ Smith los señores Smith, los Sres. Smith

messy /'mesɪ/ adj (-ier, -iest) en desorden; (dirty) sucio

met /met/ see **MEET**

metabolism /mɪ'tæbəlɪzəm/ n metabolismo m

metal /'metl/ n metal. • adj de metal. ~**lic** /mɪ'tælɪk/ adj metálico

metaphor /'metəfə(r)/ n metáfora f. ~**ical** /-'fɒrɪkl/ adj metafórico

mete /miːt/ vt. ~ **out** repartir; dar (punishment)

meteor /'miːtɪə(r)/ n meteoro m. ~**ic** /-'ɒrɪk/ adj meteórico. ~**ite** /'miːtɪəraɪt/ n meteorito m

meteorolog|ical /miːtɪərə'lɒdʒɪkl/ adj meteorológico. ~**ist** /-'rɒlədʒɪst/ n meteorólogo m. ~**y** /-'rɒlədʒɪ/ n meteorología f

meter /'miːtə(r)/ n contador m, medidor m (LAm); (Amer) see **METRE**

method /'meθəd/ n método m. ~**ical** /mɪ'θɒdɪkl/ adj metódico. M~**ist** /'meθədɪst/ adj & n metodista (m & f)

methylated /'meθɪleɪtɪd/ adj. ~ **spirit(s)** n alcohol m desnaturalizado

meticulous /mɪ'tɪkjʊləs/ adj meticuloso

metre /'miːtə(r)/ n metro m

metric /'metrɪk/ adj métrico

metropoli|s /mɪ'trɒpəlɪs/ n metrópoli(s) f

mettle /'metl/ n. be on one's ~ (fig) estar dispuesto a dar lo mejor de sí

mew /mjuː/ n maullido m. • vi maullar

Mexic|an /'meksɪkən/ adj & n mejicano (m), mexicano (m). ~**o** /-kəʊ/ n Méjico m, México m

miaow /miː'aʊ/ n & vi see **MEW**

mice /maɪs/ see **MOUSE**

mickey /'mɪkɪ/ n. take the ~ out of 🔢 tomar el pelo a

micro... /'maɪkrəʊ/ *pref* micro...

microbe /'maɪkrəʊb/ *n* microbio *m*

micro: **~chip** *n* pastilla *f*. **~film** *n* microfilme *m*. **~light** *n* aeroligero *m*. **~phone** *n* micrófono *m*. **~processor** /-'prəʊsesə(r)/ *n* microprocesador *m*. **~scope** /-skəʊp/ *n* microscopio *m*. **~scopic** /-'skɒpɪk/ *adj* microscópico. **~wave** *n* microonda *f*. **~wave oven** *n* horno *m* de microondas

mid- /mɪd/ *pref.* **in ~ air** en pleno aire. **in ~ March** a mediados de marzo

midday /mɪd'deɪ/ *n* mediodía *m*

middle /'mɪdl/ *adj* de en medio. ●*n* medio *m*. **in the ~** en el medio de. **~-aged** /-'eɪdʒd/ *adj* de mediana edad. **M~e Ages** *npl* Edad *f* Media. **~e class** *n* clase *f* media. **~e-class** *adj* de la clase media. **M~e East** *n* Oriente *m* Medio. **~eman** *n* intermediario *m*. **~e name** *n* segundo nombre *m*. **~ing** *adj* regular

midge /mɪdʒ/ *n* mosquito *m*

midget /'mɪdʒɪt/ *n* enano *m*. ●*adj* minúsculo

Midlands /'mɪdləndz/ *npl* región *f* central de Inglaterra

midnight /'mɪdnaɪt/ *n* medianoche *f*

midriff /'mɪdrɪf/ *n* diafragma *m*

midst /mɪdst/ *n*. **in our ~** entre nosotros. **in the ~ of** en medio de

midsummer /mɪd'sʌmə(r)/ *n* pleno verano *m*; (*solstice*) solsticio *m* de verano

midway /mɪd'weɪ/ *adv* a mitad de camino

Midwest /mɪd'west/ región *f* central de los EE.UU.

midwife /'mɪdwaɪf/ *n* comadrona *f*, partera *f*

midwinter /mɪd'wɪntə(r)/ *n* pleno invierno *m*

might /maɪt/ *see* MAY. ●*n* (*strength*) fuerza *f*; (*power*) poder *m*. **~y** *adj* (*strong*) fuerte; (*powerful*) poderoso. ●*adv* Ⓔ muy

migraine /'miːgreɪn/ *n* jaqueca *f*

migra|nt /'maɪgrənt/ *adj* migratorio. ●*n* (*person*) emigrante *m & f*. **~te** /maɪ'greɪt/ *vi* emigrar. **~tion** /-'greɪʃn/ *n* migración *f*

mild /maɪld/ *adj* (-er, -est) (*person*) afable; (*climate*) templado; (*slight*) ligero; (*taste, manner*) suave

mildew /'mɪldjuː/ *n* moho *m*; (*on plants*) mildeu *m*, mildiu *m*

mildly /'maɪldlɪ/ *adv* (*gently*) suavemente; (*slightly*) ligeramente Ⓔ

mile /maɪl/ *n* milla *f*. **~s better** Ⓔ mucho mejor. **~s too big** Ⓔ demasiado grande. **~age** /-ɪdʒ/ *n* (*loosely*) kilometraje *m*. **~ometer** /maɪ'lɒmɪtə(r)/ *n* (*loosely*) cuentakilómetros *m*. **~stone** *n* mojón *m*; (*event, stage, fig*) hito *m*

militant /'mɪlɪtənt/ *adj & n* militante (*m & f*)

military /'mɪlɪtərɪ/ *adj* militar

militia /mɪ'lɪʃə/ *n* milicia *f*

milk /mɪlk/ *n* leche *f*. ●*adj* (*product*) lácteo; (*chocolate*) con leche. ●*vt* ordeñar (*cow*). **~man** /-mən/ *n* lechero *m*. **~ shake** *n* batido *m*, (*leche f*) malteada *f* (*LAm*), licuado *m* con leche (*LAm*). **~y** *adj* lechoso. **M~y Way** *n* Vía *f* Láctea

mill /mɪl/ *n* molino *m*; (*for coffee, pepper*) molinillo *m*; (*factory*) fábrica *f* de tejidos de algodón. ●*vt* moler. □ **~ about, mill around** *vi* dar vueltas

m

millennium /mɪˈlenɪəm/ n (pl -ia /-ɪə/ or -iums) milenio m

miller /ˈmɪlə(r)/ n molinero m

milli... /ˈmɪlɪ/ pref mili...
~**gram(me)** n miligramo m.
~**metre** n milímetro m

milliner /ˈmɪlɪnə(r)/ n sombrerero m

million /ˈmɪljən/ n millón m. a ~ pounds un millón de libras. ~**aire** /-ˈeə(r)/ n millonario m

millstone /ˈmɪlstəʊn/ n muela f (de molino); (fig, burden) carga f

mime /maɪm/ n mímica f. ● vt imitar, hacer la mímica de. ● vi hacer la mímica

mimic /ˈmɪmɪk/ vt (pt mimicked) imitar. ● n imitador m. ~**ry** n imitación f

mince /mɪns/ vt picar, moler (LAm) (meat). not to ~ matters/words no andar(se) con rodeos. ● n carne f picada, carne f molida (LAm). ~**pie** n pastelito m de Navidad (pastelito relleno de picadillo de frutos secos). ~**r** n máquina f de picar carne, máquina f de moler carne (LAm)

mind /maɪnd/ n mente f; (sanity) juicio m. to my ~ a mi parecer. be on one's mind preocuparle a uno. make up one's ~ decidirse. ● vt (look after) cuidar (de); atender (shop). ~ the steps! ¡cuidado con las escaleras! never ~ him no le hagas caso. I don't ~ the noise no me molesta el ruido. would you ~ closing the door? ¿le importaría cerrar la puerta? ● vi. never ~ no importa, no te preocupes. I don't ~ (don't object) me da igual. do you ~ if I smoke? ¿le importa si fumo? ~**ful** adj atento (of a). ~**less** adj (activity) mecánico; (violence) ciego

mine¹ /maɪn/ poss pron (sing) mío, mía; (pl) míos, mías. it is ~ es mío. ~ are blue los míos/las mías son azules. a friend of ~ un amigo mío/una amiga mía

mine² /maɪn/ n mina f; (Mil) mina f. ● vt extraer. ~**field** n campo m de minas. ~**r** n minero m

mineral /ˈmɪnərəl/ adj & n mineral (m). ~ **water** n agua f mineral

mingle /ˈmɪŋɡl/ vi mezclarse

mini... /ˈmɪnɪ/ pref mini...

miniature /ˈmɪnɪtʃə(r)/ n miniatura f. ● adj en miniatura

mini: ~**bus** n microbús m. ~**cab** n taxi m (que se pide por teléfono)

minim|al /ˈmɪnɪml/ adj mínimo. ~**ize** vt reducir al mínimo. ~**um** /-məm/ adj & n (pl -ima /-mə/) mínimo (m)

mining /ˈmaɪnɪŋ/ n minería f. ● adj minero

miniskirt /ˈmɪnɪskɜːt/ n minifalda f

minist|er /ˈmɪnɪstə(r)/ n ministro m, secretario m (Mex); (Relig) pastor m. ~**erial** /-ˈstɪərɪəl/ adj ministerial. ~**ry** n ministerio m, secretaría f (Mex)

mink /mɪŋk/ n visón m

minor /ˈmaɪnə(r)/ adj (also Mus) menor; (injury) leve; (change) pequeño; (operation) de poca importancia. ● n menor m & f de edad. ~**ity** /maɪˈnɒrətɪ/ n minoría f. ● adj minoritario

minstrel /ˈmɪnstrəl/ n juglar m

mint /mɪnt/ n (plant) menta f; (sweet) pastilla f de menta; (Finance) casa f de la moneda. in ~ condition como nuevo. ● vt acuñar

minus /ˈmaɪnəs/ prep menos; (fam, without) sin. ● n (sign) menos *m*. five ~ three is two cinco menos tres is igual a dos. ~ **sign** *n* (signo *m* de) menos *f*

minute[1] /'mɪnɪt/ *n* minuto *m*. **the ~s** *npl* (*of meeting*) el acta *f*

minute[2] /maɪ'njuːt/ *adj* diminuto; (*detailed*) minucioso

mirac|le /'mɪrəkl/ *n* milagro *m*. **~ulous** /mɪ'rækjʊləs/ *adj* milagroso

mirage /'mɪrɑːʒ/ *n* espejismo *m*

mirror /'mɪrə(r)/ *n* espejo *m*; (*driving ~*) (espejo *m*) retrovisor *m*. ● *vt* reflejar

mirth /mɜːθ/ *n* regocijo *m*; (*laughter*) risas *fpl*

misapprehension /mɪsæprɪ'henʃn/ *n* malentendido *m*

misbehav|e /mɪsbɪ'heɪv/ *vi* portarse mal. **~iour** *n* mala conducta

miscalculat|e /mɪs'kælkjʊleɪt/ *vt/i* calcular mal. **~ion** /-'leɪʃn/ *n* error *m* de cálculo

miscarr|iage /'mɪskærɪdʒ/ *n* aborto *m* espontáneo. **~iage of justice** *n* injusticia *f*. **~y** *vi* abortar

miscellaneous /mɪsə'leɪnɪəs/ *adj* heterogéneo

mischie|f /'mɪstʃɪf/ *n* (*foolish conduct*) travesura *f*; (*harm*) daño *m*. **get into ~f** hacer travesuras. **make ~f** causar daños. **~vous** /'mɪstʃɪvəs/ *adj* travieso; (*grin*) pícaro

misconception /mɪskən'sepʃn/ *n* equivocación *f*

misconduct /mɪs'kɒndʌkt/ *n* mala conducta *f*

misdeed /mɪs'diːd/ *n* fechoría *f*

misdemeanour /mɪsdɪ'miːnə(r)/ *n* delito *m* menor, falta *f*

miser /'maɪzə(r)/ *n* avaro *m*

miserable /'mɪzərəbl/ *adj* (*sad*) triste; (*in low spirits*) abatido;

(*wretched, poor*) mísero; (*weather*) pésimo

miserly /'maɪzəlɪ/ *adj* avariento

misery /'mɪzərɪ/ *n* (*unhappiness*) tristeza *f*; (*pain*) sufrimiento *m*

misfire /mɪs'faɪə(r)/ *vi* fallar

misfit /'mɪsfɪt/ *n* inadaptado *m*

misfortune /mɪs'fɔːtʃuːn/ *n* desgracia *f*

misgiving /mɪs'gɪvɪŋ/ *n* recelo *m*

misguided /mɪs'gaɪdɪd/ *adj* equivocado

mishap /'mɪshæp/ *n* percance *m*

misinform /mɪsɪn'fɔːm/ *vt* informar mal

misinterpret /mɪsɪn'tɜːprɪt/ *vt* interpretar mal

misjudge /mɪs'dʒʌdʒ/ *vt* juzgar mal; (*miscalculate*) calcular mal

mislay /mɪs'leɪ/ *vt* (*pt* **mislaid**) extraviar, perder

mislead /mɪs'liːd/ *vt* (*pt* **misled** /mɪs'led/) engañar. **~ing** *adj* engañoso

mismanage /mɪs'mænɪdʒ/ *vt* administrar mal. **~ment** *n* mala administración *f*

misplace /mɪs'pleɪs/ *vt* (*lose*) extraviar, perder

misprint /'mɪsprɪnt/ *n* errata *f*

miss /mɪs/ *vt* (*fail to hit*) no dar en; (*regret absence of*) echar de menos, extrañar (*LAm*); perder (*train, party*); perder (*chance*). **the point** no comprender. ● *vi* errar el tiro, fallar; (*bullet*) no dar en el blanco. ● *n* fallo *m*, falla *f* (*LAm*); (*title*) señorita *f*. □ ~ **out** *vt* saltarse (*line*). **~out on sth** perderse algo

misshapen /mɪs'ʃeɪpən/ *adj* deforme

missile /'mɪsaɪl/ *n* (*Mil*) misil *m*

m

missing /'mɪsɪŋ/ adj (lost) perdido. **be ~** faltar. **go ~** desaparecer. **~ person** desaparecido m

mission /'mɪʃn/ n misión f. **~ary** /'mɪʃənərɪ/ n misionero m

mist /mɪst/ n neblina f; (at sea) bruma f. □ **~ up** vi empañarse

mistake /mɪ'steɪk/ n error m. **make a ~** cometer un error. **by ~** por error. ● vt (pt **mistook**, pp **mistaken**) confundir. **~ for** confundir con. **~n** /-ən/ adj equivocado. **be ~n** equivocarse

mistletoe /'mɪsltəʊ/ n muérdago m

mistreat /mɪs'triːt/ vt maltratar

mistress /'mɪstrɪs/ n (of house) señora f; (lover) amante f

mistrust /mɪs'trʌst/ vt desconfiar de. ● n desconfianza f. **~ful** adj desconfiado

misty /'mɪstɪ/ adj (-ier, -iest) neblinoso; (day) de neblina. **it's ~** hay neblina

misunderstand /mɪsʌndə'stænd/ vt (pt **-stood**) entender mal. **~ing** n malentendido m

misuse /mɪs'juːz/ vt emplear mal; malversar (funds). ● /mɪs'juːs/ n mal uso m; (unfair use) abuso m; (of funds) malversación f

mite /maɪt/ n (insect) ácaro m

mitten /'mɪtn/ n mitón m

mix /mɪks/ vt mezclar. ● vi mezclarse; (go together) combinar. **~ with** tratarse con (people). ● n mezcla f. □ **~ up** vt mezclar; (confuse) confundir. **~ed** adj (school etc) mixto; (assorted) mezclado. **be ~ed up** estar confuso. **~er** n (Culin) batidora f (TV, machine) mezcladora f. **~ture** /'mɪkstʃə(r)/ n mezcla f. **~-up** n lío m

moan /məʊn/ n gemido m. ● vi

gemir; (complain) quejarse (about de)

moat /məʊt/ n foso m

mob /mɒb/ n turba f. ● vt (pt mobbed) acosar

mobil|e /'məʊbaɪl/ adj móvil. **~e home** n caravana f fija, trailer m (LAm). **~e (phone)** n (teléfono m) móvil m, (teléfono m) celular m (LAm). **~ize** /'məʊbɪlaɪz/ vt movilizar. ● vi movilizarse

mock /mɒk/ vt burlarse de. ● adj (anger) fingido; (exam) de práctica. **~ery** /'mɒkərɪ/ n burla f. **make a ~ery of sth** ridiculizar algo

model /'mɒdl/ n (example) modelo m; (mock-up) maqueta f; (person) modelo m. ● adj (exemplary) modelo; (car etc) en miniatura. ● vt (pt **modelled**) modelar. **~ s.o. on** s.o. tomar a uno como modelo

modem /'məʊdem/ n (Comp) módem m

moderat|e /'mɒdərət/ adj & n moderado (m). ● /'mɒdəreɪt/ vt moderar. **~ely** /'mɒdərətlɪ/ adv (fairly) medianamente. **~ion** /-'reɪʃn/ n moderación f. **in ~ion** con moderación

modern /'mɒdn/ adj moderno. **~ize** vt modernizar

modest /'mɒdɪst/ adj modesto. **~y** n modestia f

modif|ication /mɒdɪfɪ'keɪʃn/ n modificación f. **~y** /-faɪ/ vt modificar

module /'mɒdjuːl/ n módulo m

moist /mɔɪst/ adj (-er, -est) húmedo. **~en** /'mɔɪsn/ vt humedecer

moistur|e /'mɔɪstʃə(r)/ n humedad f. **~ize** vt hidratar. **~izer**, **~izing cream** n crema f hidratante

mole | moped

mole /məʊl/ n (animal) topo m; (on skin) lunar m

molecule /'mɒlɪkjuːl/ n molécula f

molest /mə'lest/ vt abusar (sexualmente) de

mollify /'mɒlɪfaɪ/ vt aplacar

mollusc /'mɒləsk/ n molusco m

mollycoddle /'mɒlɪkɒdl/ vt mimar

molten /'məʊltən/ adj fundido; (lava) líquido

mom /mɒm/ n (Amer, 🔟) mamá f 🔟

moment /'məʊmənt/ n momento m. **at the ~** en este momento. **for the ~** de momento. **~ary** /'məʊməntərɪ/ adj momentáneo

momentous /mə'mentəs/ adj trascendental

momentum /mə'mentəm/ n momento m; (speed) velocidad f

mommy /'mɒmɪ/ n (Amer, fam) mamá m 🔟

monarch /'mɒnək/ n monarca m. **~y** n monarquía f

monastery /'mɒnəstərɪ/ n monasterio m

Monday /'mʌndeɪ/ n lunes m

money /'mʌnɪ/ n dinero m, plata f (LAm). **~box** n hucha f, alcancía f (LAm). **~ order** n giro m postal

mongrel /'mʌŋgrəl/ n perro m mestizo, chucho m 🔟

monitor /'mɒnɪtə(r)/ n (Tec) monitor m. • vt observar (elections); seguir (progress); (electronically) monitorizar, escuchar

monk /mʌŋk/ n monje m. **~fish** n rape m

monkey /'mʌŋkɪ/ n mono m. **~-nut** n cacahuete m, cacahuate m (Mex), maní m (LAm). **~wrench** n

llave f inglesa

mono /'mɒnəʊ/ n monofonía f

monologue /'mɒnəlɒg/ n monólogo m

monopol|ize /mə'nɒpəlaɪz/ vt monopolizar; acaparar (conversation). **~y** n monopolio m

monoton|e /'mɒnətəʊn/ n tono m monocorde. **~ous** /mə'nɒtənəs/ adj monótono. **~y** n monotonía f

monsoon /mɒn'suːn/ n monzón m

monst|er /'mɒnstə(r)/ n monstruo m. **~rous** /-strəs/ adj monstruoso

month /mʌnθ/ n mes m. **£200 a ~** 200 libras mensuales or al mes. **~ly** adj mensual. **~ly payment** mensualidad f, cuota f mensual (LAm). • adv mensualmente

monument /'mɒnjʊmənt/ n monumento m. **~al** /-'mentl/ adj monumental

moo /muː/ n mugido m. • vi mugir

mood /muːd/ n humor m. **be in a good/bad ~** estar de buen/mal humor. **~y** adj (-ier, -iest) temperamental; (bad-tempered) malhumorado

moon /muːn/ n luna f. **~light** n luz f de la luna. **~lighting** n pluriempleo m. **~lit** adj iluminado por la luna; (night) de luna

moor /mʊə(r)/ n páramo m; (of heather) brezal m. • vt amarrar. **~ing** n (place) amarradero m. **~ings** npl (ropes) amarras fpl

moose /muːs/ n invar alce m americano

mop /mɒp/ n fregona f, trapeador m (LAm). **~ of hair** pelambrera f. • vt (pt mopped). **~ (up)** limpiar

mope /məʊp/ vi estar abatido

moped /'məʊped/ n ciclomotor m

m

moral /ˈmɒrəl/ adj moral. ● n (of tale) moraleja f

morale /məˈrɑːl/ n moral f

moral|ity /məˈrælətɪ/ n moralidad f. **~ly** adv moralmente. **~s** npl moralidad f

morbid /ˈmɔːbɪd/ adj morboso

more /mɔː(r)/ adj más. two ~ bottles dos botellas más. ● pron más. you ate ~ than me comiste más que yo. some ~ más. ~ than six más de seis. the ~ he has, the ~ he wants cuánto más tiene, más quiere. ● adv más. ~ and ~ cada vez más. ~ or less más o menos. once ~ una vez más. she doesn't live here any ~ ya no vive aquí. **~over** /mɔːˈrəʊvə(r)/ adv además

morgue /mɔːg/ n depósito m de cadáveres, morgue f (LAm)

morning /ˈmɔːnɪŋ/ n mañana f; (early hours) madrugada f. at 11 o'clock in the ~ a las once de la mañana. in the ~ por la mañana, en la mañana (LAm). tomorrow/ yesterday ~ mañana/ayer por la mañana or (LAm) en la mañana. (good) ~! ¡buenos días!

Moroccan /məˈrɒkən/ adj & n marroquí (m & f). **~o** /-kəʊ/ n Marruecos m

moron /ˈmɔːrɒn/ n imbécil m & f

morose /məˈrəʊs/ adj taciturno

Morse /mɔːs/ n Morse m. in ~ (code) n en (código) morse

morsel /ˈmɔːsl/ n bocado m

mortal /ˈmɔːtl/ adj & n mortal (m). **~ity** /-ˈtælətɪ/ n mortalidad f

mortar /ˈmɔːtə(r)/ n (all senses) mortero m

mortgage /ˈmɔːgɪdʒ/ n hipoteca f. ● vt hipotecar

mortify /ˈmɔːtɪfaɪ/ vt darle mucha vergüenza a

mortuary /ˈmɔːtjʊərɪ/ n depósito m de cadáveres, morgue f (LAm)

mosaic /məʊˈzeɪk/ n mosaico m

mosque /mɒsk/ n mezquita f

mosquito /mɒsˈkiːtəʊ/ n (pl -oes) mosquito m, zancudo m (LAm)

moss /mɒs/ n musgo m

most /məʊst/ adj la mayoría de, la mayor parte de. ~ days casi todos los días. ● pron la mayoría, la mayor parte. at ~ como máximo. make the ~ of aprovechar al máximo. ● adv más; (very) muy; (Amer, almost) casi. **~ly** adv principalmente

MOT n. ~ (test) ITV f, inspección f técnica de vehículos

motel /məʊˈtel/ n motel m

moth /mɒθ/ n mariposa f de la luz, palomilla f; (in clothes) polilla f

mother /ˈmʌðə(r)/ n madre f. ● vt mimar. **~-in-law** (pl **~s-in-law**) suegra f. **~land** n patria f. **~ly** adj maternal. **~-of-pearl** n nácar m, madreperla f. **M~'s Day** n el día m de la Madre. **~-to-be** n futura madre f. **~ tongue** n lengua f materna

motif /məʊˈtiːf/ n motivo m

motion /ˈməʊʃn/ n movimiento m; (proposal) moción f. put or set in ~ poner algo en marcha. ● vt/i. ~ (to) s.o. to hacerle señas a uno para que. **~less** adj inmóvil

motiv|ate /ˈməʊtɪveɪt/ vt motivar. **~ation** /-ˈveɪʃn/ n motivación f. **~e** /ˈməʊtɪv/ n motivo m

motley /ˈmɒtlɪ/ adj variopinto

motor /ˈməʊtə(r)/ n motor m. ● adj motor; (fem) motora, motriz. **~ bike** n [1] motocicleta f, moto f [1]. **~ boat** n lancha f a motor. **~ car** n automóvil m. **~ cycle** n motocicleta f. **~cyclist** n motociclista m & f. **~ing** n automovilismo m. **~ist** n automovilista m & f. **~way** n autopista f

motto /ˈmɒtəʊ/ n (pl **-oes**) lema m

mould /məʊld/ n molde m; (fungus) moho m. ●vt moldear; formar (character). **~ing** n (on wall etc) moldura f. **~y** adj mohoso

moult /məʊlt/ vi mudar de pelo/piel/plumas

mound /maʊnd/ n montículo m; (pile, fig) montón m

mount /maʊnt/ vt montar (horse); engarzar (gem); preparar (attack). ●vi subir, crecer. ●n. montura f; (mountain) monte m. □ **~ up** vi irse acumulando

mountain /ˈmaʊntɪn/ n montaña f. **~eer** /maʊntɪˈnɪə(r)/ n alpinista m & f. **~eering** n alpinismo m. **~ous** adj montañoso

mourn /mɔːn/ vt llorar. ●vi lamentarse. **~ for** s.o. llorar a uno. **~er** n doliente m & f. **~ful** adj triste. **~ing** n duelo m, luto m. **be in ~ing** estar de duelo

mouse /maʊs/ n (pl **mice**) ratón m. **~trap** n ratonera f

mousse /muːs/ n (Culin) mousse f or m; (for hair) mousse f

moustache /məˈstɑːʃ/ n bigote m

mouth /maʊθ/ n boca f; (of cave) entrada f; (of river) desembocadura f. **~ful** n bocado m. **~organ** n armónica f. **~wash** n enjuague m bucal

move /muːv/ vt mover; (relocate) trasladar; (with emotion) conmover; (propose) proponer. **~ the television** cambiar de lugar la televisión. ●vi moverse; (be in motion) estar en movimiento; (take action) tomar medidas. ●n movimiento m; (in

game) jugada f; (player's turn) turno m; (removal) mudanza f. □ **~ away** vi alejarse. □ **~ in** vi instalarse. □ **~ in with** s.o. ir a vivir con uno. □ **~ over** vi correrse. **~ment** n movimiento m

movie /ˈmuːvɪ/ n (Amer) película f. **the ~s** npl el cine. **~ camera** n (Amer) tomavistas m, filmadora f (LAm)

moving /ˈmuːvɪŋ/ adj en movimiento; (touching) conmovedor

mow /məʊ/ vt (pt mowed or mown /məʊn/) cortar (lawn); segar (hay). □ **~ down** vt acribillar. **~er** n (for lawn) cortacésped m

MP abbr see MEMBER OF PARLIAMENT

Mr /ˈmɪstə(r)/ abbr (pl **Messrs**) (= Mister) Sr. **~ Coldbeck** Sr. Coldbeck

Mrs /ˈmɪsɪz/ abbr (pl **Mrs**) (= Missis) Sra. **~ Andrews** Sra. Andrews

Ms /mɪz/ abbr (title of married or unmarried woman)

MSc abbr see MASTER

much /mʌtʃ/ adj & pron mucho, mucha. ●adv mucho; (before pp) muy. **~ as** por mucho que. **~ the same** más o menos lo mismo. **how ~?** ¿cuánto? **so ~** tanto. **too ~** demasiado

muck /mʌk/ n estiércol m; (fam, dirt) mugre f. □ **~ about** vi 🚹 tontear

mud /mʌd/ n barro m, lodo m

muddle /ˈmʌdl/ vt embrollar. ●n desorden m; (mix-up) lío m. □ **~ through** vi salir del paso

muddy adj lodoso; (hands etc) cubierto de lodo. **~guard** n guardabarros m, salpicadera f (Mex)

muffle /ˈmʌfl/ vt amortiguar (sound). **~r** n (scarf) bufanda f;

(*Amer, Auto*) silenciador *m*

mug /mʌg/ *n* taza *f* (*alta y sin platillo*), tarro *m* (*Mex*); (*for beer*) jarra *f*; (*fam, face*) cara *f*, jeta *f* 🖻; (*fam, fool*) idiota *m & f* ● *vt* (*pt* mugged) asaltar. ~**ger** *n* asaltante *m & f*. ~**ging** *n* asalto *m*

muggy /ˈmʌgɪ/ *adj* bochornoso

mule /mjuːl/ *n* mula *f*

mull /mʌl/ (*Amer*), ~ **over** *vt* reflexionar sobre

multi|coloured /mʌltɪˈkʌləd/ *adj* multicolor. ~**national** /-ˈnæʃənl/ *adj & n* multinacional (*f*)

multipl|e /ˈmʌltɪpl/ *adj* múltiple. ● *n* múltiplo *m*. ~**ication** /mʌltɪplɪˈkeɪʃn/ *n* multiplicación *f* ~**y** /ˈmʌltɪplaɪ/ *vt* multiplicar. ● *vi* (*Math*) multiplicar; (*increase*) multiplicarse

multitude /ˈmʌltɪtjuːd/ *n*. a ~ of problems múltiples problemas

mum /mʌm/ *n* 🖻 mamá *f* 🖻

mumble /ˈmʌmbl/ *vt* mascullar. ● *vi* hablar entre dientes

mummy /ˈmʌmɪ/ *n* (*fam, mother*) mamá *f* 🖻; (*archaeology*) momia *f*

mumps /mʌmps/ *n* paperas *fpl*

munch /mʌntʃ/ *vt/i* mascar

mundane /mʌnˈdeɪn/ *adj* mundano

municipal /mjuːˈnɪsɪpl/ *adj* municipal

mural /ˈmjʊərəl/ *adj & n* mural (*f*)

murder /ˈmɜːdə(r)/ *n* asesinato *m*. ● *vt* asesinar. ~**er** *n* asesino *m*

murky /ˈmɜːkɪ/ *adj* (*-ier, -iest*) turbio

murmur /ˈmɜːmə(r)/ *n* murmullo *m*. ● *vt/i* murmurar

musc|le /ˈmʌsl/ *n* músculo *m*. ~**ular** /ˈmʌskjʊlə(r)/ *adj* muscular; (*arm, body*) musculoso

muse /mjuːz/ *vi* meditar (on sobre)

museum /mjuːˈzɪəm/ *n* museo *m*

mush /mʌʃ/ *n* papilla *f*

mushroom /ˈmʌʃrʊm/ *n* champiñón *m*; (*in botany*) seta *f*. ● *vi* aparecer como hongos

mushy /ˈmʌʃɪ/ *adj* blando

music /ˈmjuːzɪk/ *n* música *f*. ~**al** *adj* musical. be ~ tener sentido musical. ● *n* musical *m*. ~**ian** /mjuːˈzɪʃn/ *n* músico *m*

Muslim /ˈmʊzlɪm/ *adj & n* musulmán (*m*)

mussel /ˈmʌsl/ *n* mejillón *m*

must /mʌst/ *modal verb* deber, tener que; (*expressing supposition*) deber (de). he ~ be old debe (de) ser viejo. I ~ have done it debo (de) haberlo hecho. ● *n*. be a ~ ser imprescindible

mustache /ˈmʌstæʃ/ *n* (*Amer*) bigote *m*

mustard /ˈmʌstəd/ *n* mostaza *f*

muster /ˈmʌstə(r)/ *vt* reunir

musty /ˈmʌstɪ/ *adj* (*-ier, -iest*) que huele a humedad

mutation /mjuːˈteɪʃn/ *n* mutación *f*

mute /mjuːt/ *adj* mudo

mutilate /ˈmjuːtɪleɪt/ *vt* mutilar

mutiny /ˈmjuːtɪnɪ/ *n* motín *m*. ● *vi* amotinarse

mutter /ˈmʌtə(r)/ *vt/i* murmurar

mutton /ˈmʌtn/ *n* carne *f* de ovino

mutual /ˈmjuːtʃʊəl/ *adj* mutuo; (*fam, common*) común

muzzle /ˈmʌzl/ *n* (*snout*) hocico *m*; (*device*) bozal *m*

my /maɪ/ *adj* (*sing*) mi; (*pl*) mis

myself /maɪˈself/ *pron* (*reflexive*) me; (*used for emphasis*) yo mismo *m*, yo misma *f*. I cut ~ me corté. I made it ~ lo hice yo mismo/misma. I was by ~ estaba solo/sola

mysterious /mɪs'tɪərɪəs/ *adj* misterioso. ~**y** /'mɪstərɪ/ *n* misterio *m*

mystical /'mɪstɪkl/ *adj* místico

mystify /'mɪstɪfaɪ/ *vt* dejar perplejo

mystique /mɪs'tiːk/ *n* mística *f*

myth /mɪθ/ *n* mito *m*. ~**ical** *adj* mítico. ~**ology** /mɪ'θɒlədʒɪ/ *n* mitología *f*

Nn

N *abbr* (= north) N

nab /næb/ *vt* (*pt* nabbed) (*sl, arrest*) pescar; (*snatch*) agarrar

nag /næg/ *vt* (*pt* nagged) fastidiar; (*scold*) estarle encima a. ● *vi* criticar

nail /neɪl/ *n* clavo *m*; (*of finger, toe*) uña *f*. ~ **polish** esmalte *m* para las uñas. ● *vt*. ~ clavar

naive /naɪ'iːv/ *adj* ingenuo

naked /'neɪkɪd/ *adj* desnudo. to the ~ **eye** a simple vista

name /neɪm/ *n* nombre *m*; (*of book, film*) título *m*; (*fig*) fama *f*. my ~ **is Chris** me llamo Chris. good ~ buena reputación. ● *vt* ponerle nombre a; (*appoint*) nombrar. a man ~**d Jones** un hombre llamado Jones. she was ~**d after** *or* (*Amer*) for her grandmother le pusieron el nombre de su abuela. ~**less** *adj* anónimo. ~**ly** *adv* a saber. ~**sake** *n* (*person*) tocayo *m*

nanny /'nænɪ/ *n* niñera *f*

nap /næp/ *n* (*sleep*) sueñecito *m*; (*after lunch*) siesta *f*. have a ~ echarse un sueño

napkin /'næpkɪn/ *n* servilleta *f*

nappy /'næpɪ/ *n* pañal *m*

narcotic /nɑː'kɒtɪk/ *adj & n* narcótico (*m*)

narrate /nə'reɪt/ *vt* narrar. ~**ive** /'nærətɪv/ *n* narración *f*. ~**or** /nə'reɪtə(r)/ *n* narrador *m*

narrow /'nærəʊ/ *adj* (-er, -est) estrecho, angosto (*LAm*). have a ~ **escape** salvarse de milagro. ● *vt* estrechar; (*limit*) limitar. ● *vi* estrecharse. ~**ly** *adv* (*just*) por poco. ~-**minded** /-'maɪndɪd/ *adj* de miras estrechas

nasal /'neɪzl/ *adj* nasal; (*voice*) gangoso

nasty /'nɑːstɪ/ *adj* (-ier, -iest) desagradable; (*spiteful*) malo (to con); (*taste, smell*) asqueroso; (*cut*) feo

nation /'neɪʃn/ *n* nación *f*

national /'næʃənl/ *adj* nacional. ● *n* ciudadano *m*. ~ **anthem** *n* himno *m* nacional. ~**ism** *n* nacionalismo *m*. ~**ity** /næʃə'nælətɪ/ *n* nacionalidad *f*. ~**ize** *vt* nacionalizar. ~**ly** *adv* a escala nacional

> **National Trust** Fundación *i* británica cuyo objetivo es la conservación de lugares de interés histórico o de belleza natural. Se financia mediante legados y subvenciones privadas. Es la mayor propietaria de tierras de Gran Bretaña. En Escocia, es independiente y recibe el nombre de *National Trust for Scotland*.

nationwide /'neɪʃnwaɪd/ *adj & adv* a escala nacional

native /'neɪtɪv/ *n* natural *m & f*. be

a ~ de ser natural de. ● *adj* nativo;
(country, town) natal; (language)
materno; (plant, animal) autóc-
tono. N~ American indio *m* ame-
ricano

nativity /nə'tɪvətɪ/ *n*. the N~ la
Natividad *f*

NATO /'neɪtəʊ/ *abbr* (= North At-
lantic Treaty Organization)
OTAN *f*

natter /'nætə(r)/ 🔒 *vi* charlar. ● *n*
charla *f*

natural /'nætʃərəl/ *adj* natural. ~
history *n* historia *f* natural. ~ist
n naturalista *m* & *f*. ~ized *adj* (citizen)
naturalizado. ~ly *adv* (of course)
naturalmente; (by nature) por natu-
raleza

nature /'neɪtʃə(r)/ *n* naturaleza *f*;
(of person) carácter *m*; (of things)
naturaleza *f*

naught /nɔ:t/ *n* cero *m*

naughty /'nɔ:tɪ/ *adj* (-ier, -iest)
malo, travieso

nause|a /'nɔ:zɪə/ *n* náuseas *fpl*.
~ous /-ɪəs/ *adj* nauseabundo

nautical /'nɔ:tɪkl/ *adj* náutico. ~
mile *n* milla *f* marina

naval /'neɪvl/ *adj* naval; (officer) de
marina

nave /neɪv/ *n* nave *f*

navel /'neɪvl/ *n* ombligo *m*

naviga|ble /'nævɪɡəbl/ *adj* nave-
gable. ~te /'nævɪɡeɪt/ *vt* navegar
por (sea etc); gobernar (ship). ● *vi*
navegar. ~tion /-'ɡeɪʃn/ *n* navega-
ción *f*. ~tor *n* oficial *m* & *f* de de-
rrota

navy /'neɪvɪ/ *n* marina *f* de guerra.
~ (blue) *a* & *n* azul (*m*) marino

NE *abbr* (= north-east) NE

near /nɪə(r)/ *adv* cerca. draw ~
acercarse. ● *prep*. ~ (to) cerca de.
go ~ (to) sth acercarse a algo.

● *adj* cercano. ● *vt* acercarse a. ~by
adj cercano. ~ly *adv* casi. he ~ly
died por poco se muere, casi se
muere. not ~ly ni con mucho.
~sighted /-'saɪtɪd/ *adj* miope,
corto de vista

neat /ni:t/ *adj* (-er, -est) (person)
pulcro; (room etc) bien arreglado;
(ingenious) hábil; (whisky, gin) solo;
; (Amer fam, great) fantástico 🔒.
~ly *adv* pulcramente; (organized)
cuidadosamente

necessar|ily /nesə'serɪlɪ/ *adv* ne-
cesariamente. ~y /'nesəserɪ/ *adj*
necesario

necessit|ate /nə'sesɪteɪt/ *vt* exi-
gir. ~y /nɪ'sesətɪ/ *n* necesidad *f*.
the bare ~ies lo indispensable

neck /nek/ *n* (of person, bottle,
dress) cuello *m*; (of animal) pes-
cuezo *m*. ~ and ~ a la par, pare-
jos (LAm). ~lace /'neklas/ *n* collar
m. ~line *n* escote *m*

nectar /'nektə(r)/ *n* néctar *m*

nectarine /'nektərɪn/ *n* necta-
rina *f*

née /neɪ/ *adj* de soltera

need /ni:d/ *n* necesidad *f* (for de).
● *vt* necesitar; (demand) exigir. you
~ not speak no tienes que hablar

needle /'ni:dl/ *n* aguja *f*. ● *vt* (fam,
annoy) pinchar

needless /'ni:dlɪs/ *adj* innecesario

needlework /'ni:dlwɜ:k/ *n* labo-
res *fpl* de aguja; (embroidery) bor-
dado *m*

needy /'ni:dɪ/ *adj* (-ier, -iest) ne-
cesitado

negative /'neɡətɪv/ *adj* negativo.
● *n* (of photograph) negativo *m*;
(no) negativa *f*

neglect /nɪ'ɡlekt/ *vt* descuidar
(house); desatender (children); no
cumplir con (duty). ● *n* negligencia

_f._ (state of) ~ abandono _m._ ~**ful** _adj_ negligente

negligen|ce /'neglɪdʒəns/ _n_ negligencia _f,_ descuido _m._ ~**ent** _adj_ negligente. ~**ible** /neglɪdʒəbl/ _adj_ insignificante

negotia|ble /nɪ'gəʊʃəbl/ _adj_ negociable. ~**te** /nɪ'gəʊʃɪeɪt/ _vt/i_ negociar. ~**tion** /-'eɪʃn/ _n_ negociación _f._ ~**tor** _n_ negociador _m_

neigh /neɪ/ _vi_ relinchar

neighbour /'neɪbə(r)/ _n_ vecino _m._ ~**hood** _n_ vecindad _f,_ barrio _m._ **in the** ~**hood of** alrededor de. ~**ing** _adj_ vecino

neither /'naɪðə(r)/ _adj._ ~ **book** ninguno de los libros. ● _pron_ ninguno, -na. ● _conj._ **neither...nor** ni...ni. ~ **do I** yo tampoco

neon /'niːɒn/ _n_ neón _m._ ● _adj_ (lamp etc) de neón

nephew /'nevju:/ _n_ sobrino _m._

Neptune /'neptju:n/ _n_ Neptuno _m_

nerv|e /nɜːv/ _n_ nervio _m;_ (courage) valor _m;_ (calm) sangre _f_ fría; (_fam, impudence_) descaro _m._ ~**es** _npl_ (before exams etc) nervios _mpl._ **get on s.o.'s** ~**es** crispar los nervios de a uno. ~**e-racking** _adj_ exasperante. ~**ous** /'nɜːvəs/ _adj_ nervioso. **be/feel** ~**ous** estar nervioso. ~**ousness** _n_ nerviosismo _m._ ~**y** /'nɜːvɪ/ _adj_ nervioso; (Amer fam) descarado

nest /nest/ _n_ nido _m._ ● _vi_ anidar

nestle /'nesl/ _vi_ acurrucarse

net /net/ _n_ red _f._ **the N**~ (Comp) la Red. ● _vt_ (pt netted) pescar (con red) (fish). ● _adj_ neto. ~**ball** _n_ especie de baloncesto

Netherlands /'neðələndz/ _npl._ **the** ~ los Países Bajos

netting /'netɪŋ/ _n_ redes _fpl._ **wire** ~ tela _f_ metálica

nettle /'netl/ _n_ ortiga _f_

network /'netwɜːk/ _n_ red _f;_ (TV) cadena _f_

neuro|sis /njʊə'rəʊsɪs/ _n_ (pl -oses /-siːz/) neurosis _f._ ~**tic** /-'rɒtɪk/ _adj_ & _n_ neurótico (m)

neuter /'njuːtə(r)/ _adj_ & _n_ neutro (m). ● _vt_ castrar (animals)

neutral /'njuːtrəl/ _adj_ neutral; (colour) neutro; (Elec) neutro. ~ **(gear)** (Auto) punto _m_ muerto. ~**ize** _vt_ neutralizar

neutron /'njuːtrɒn/ _n_ neutrón _m_

never /'nevə(r)/ _adv_ nunca; (more emphatic) jamás; (_fam, not_) no. ~ **again** nunca más. **he** ~ **smiles** no sonríe nunca, nunca sonríe. **I** ~ **saw him** 🇬🇧 no lo vi. ~**-ending** _adj_ interminable. ~**theless** /-ðə'les/ _adv_ sin embargo, no obstante

new /njuː/ _adj_ (-er, -est) nuevo. ~**born** _adj_ recién nacido. ~**comer** _n_ recién llegado _m._ ~**fangled** /-'fæŋgld/ _adj_ (pej) moderno. ~**ly** _adv_ recién. ~**ly-weds** _npl_ recién casados _mpl_

news /njuːz/ _n._ **a piece of** ~ una noticia. **good/bad** ~ buenas/malas noticias. **the** ~ (TV, Radio) las noticias. ~**agent** _n_ vendedor _m_ de periódicos. ~**caster** _n_ locutor _m._ ~**dealer** _n_ (Amer) see ~**AGENT**. ~**flash** _n_ información _f_ de última hora. ~**letter** _n_ boletín _m,_ informativo _m._ ~**paper** _n_ periódico _m,_ diario _m._ ~**reader** _n_ locutor _m_

newt /njuːt/ _n_ tritón _m_

New Year /njuː'jɪə(r)/ _n_ Año _m_ Nuevo. **N**~'**s Day** _n_ día _m_ de Año Nuevo. **N**~'**s Eve** _n_ noche _f_ vieja, noche _f_ de fin de Año

New Zealand /njuː'ziːlənd/ _n_ Nueva Zeland(i)a _f_

next /nekst/ _adj_ próximo; (week,

n

month etc) que viene, próximo; (*adjoining*) vecino; (*following*) siguiente. ● *adv* luego, después. ~ to al lado de. **when you see me** ~ la próxima vez que me veas. ~ **to nothing** casi nada. ~ **door** al lado (to de). ~**-door** *adj* de al lado. ~ **of kin** *n* familiar(es) *m(pl)* más cercano(s)

nib /nɪb/ *n* plumilla *f*

nibble /'nɪbl/ *vt/i* mordisquear. ● *n* mordisco *m*

Nicaragua /nɪkə'ræɡjʊə/ *n* Nicaragua *f*. ~**n** *adj* & *n* nicaragüense (*m* & *f*)

nice /naɪs/ *adj* (-er, -est) agradable; (*likeable*) simpático; (*kind*) amable; (*weather, food*) bueno. **we had a** ~ **time** lo pasamos bien. ~**ly** *adv* (*kindly*) amablemente; (*politely*) con buenos modales

niche /nɪtʃ, niːʃ/ *n* nicho *m*

nick /nɪk/ *n* corte *m* pequeño. **in the** ~ **of time** justo a tiempo. ● *vt* (*sl, steal*) afanar 🄳

nickel /'nɪkl/ *n* (*metal*) níquel *m*; (*Amer*) moneda *f* de cinco centavos

nickname /'nɪkneɪm/ *n* apodo *m*. ● *vt* apodar

nicotine /'nɪkətiːn/ *n* nicotina *f*

niece /niːs/ *n* sobrina *f*

niggling /'nɪɡlɪŋ/ *adj* (*doubt*) constante

night /naɪt/ *n* noche *f*; (*evening*) tarde *f*. **at** ~ por la noche, de noche. **good** ~ ¡buenas noches! ● *adj* nocturno, de noche. ~**cap** *n* (*drink*) bebida *f* (tomada antes de acostarse). ~**club** *n* club *m* nocturno. ~**dress** *n* camisón *m*. ~**fall** *n* anochecer *m*. ~**gown** *n*, ~**ie** /'naɪtɪ/ 🄳 *n* camisón *m*. ~**life** *n* vida *f* nocturna. ~**ly** *adj* de todas

las noches. ~**mare** *n* pesadilla *f*. ~ **school** *n* escuela *f* nocturna. ~**time** *n* noche *f*. ~**watchman** *n* sereno *m*

nil /nɪl/ *n* nada *f*; (*Sport*) cero *m*

nimble /'nɪmbl/ *adj* (-er, -est) ágil

nine /naɪn/ *adj* & *n* nueve (*m*). ~**teen** /naɪn'tiːn/ *adj* & *n* diecinueve (*m*). ~**teenth** *adj* decimonoveno. ● *n* diecinueveavo *m*. ~**tieth** /'naɪntɪəθ/ *adj* nonagésimo. ● *n* noventavo *m*. ~**ty** *adj* & *n* noventa (*m*)

ninth /naɪnθ/ *adj* & *n* noveno (*m*)

nip /nɪp/ *vt* (*pt* nipped) (*pinch*) pellizcar; (*bite*) mordisquear. ● *vi* (*fam, rush*) correr

nipple /'nɪpl/ *n* (*of woman*) pezón *m*; (*of man*) tetilla *f*; (*of baby's bottle*) tetina *f*, chupón *m* (*Mex*)

nippy /'nɪpɪ/ *adj* (-ier, -iest) (*fam, chilly*) fresquito

nitrogen /'naɪtrədʒən/ *n* nitrógeno *m*

no /nəʊ/ *adj* ninguno, (*before masculine singular noun*) ningún. **I have** ~ **money** no tengo dinero. **there's** ~ **food left** no queda nada de comida. **it has** ~ **windows** no tiene ventanas. **I'm** ~ **expert** no soy ningún experto. ~ **smoking** prohibido fumar. ~ **way!** 🄸 ¡ni hablar! ● *adv* & *int* no. ● *n* (*pl* noes) no *m*

noble /'nəʊbl/ *adj* (-er, -est). noble. ~**man** /-mən/ *n* noble *m*

nobody /'nəʊbədɪ/ *pron* nadie. **there's** ~ **there** no hay nadie

nocturnal /nɒk'tɜːnl/ *adj* nocturno

nod /nɒd/ *vt* (*pt* nodded). ~ **one's head** asentir con la cabeza. ● *vi* (*in agreement*) asentir con la cabeza; (*in greeting*) saludar con la cabeza.

□ ~ off *vi* dormirse

nois|e /nɔɪz/ *n* ruido *m*. ~**ily** *adv* ruidosamente. ~**y** *adj* (-ier, -iest) ruidoso. it's too ~y here hay demasiado ruido aquí

nomad /ˈnəʊmæd/ *n* nómada *m* & *f*. ~**ic** /-ˈmædɪk/ *adj* nómada

no man's land *n* tierra *f* de nadie

nominat|e /ˈnɒmɪneɪt/ *vt* (*put forward*) proponer; postular (*LAm*); (*appoint*) nombrar. ~**ion** /-ˈneɪʃn/ *n* nombramiento *m*; (*Amer, Pol*) proclamación *f*

non-... /nɒn/ *pref* no ...

nonchalant /ˈnɒnʃələnt/ *adj* despreocupado

non-committal /nɒnkəˈmɪtl/ *adj* evasivo

nondescript /ˈnɒndɪskrɪpt/ *adj* anodino

none /nʌn/ *pron* ninguno, ninguna. there were ~ left no quedaba ninguno/ninguna. ~ of us ninguno de nosotros. ~ *adv* no, de ninguna manera. he is ~ the happier no está más contento

nonentity /nɒˈnentəti/ *n* persona *f* insignificante

non-existent /nɒnɪgˈzɪstənt/ *adj* inexistente

nonplussed /nɒnˈplʌst/ *adj* perplejo

nonsens|e /ˈnɒnsns/ *n* tonterías *fpl*, disparates *mpl*. ~**ical** /-ˈsensɪkl/ *adj* disparatado

non-smoker /nɒnˈsməʊkə(r)/ *n* no fumador *m*. I'm a ~ no fumo

non-stop /nɒnˈstɒp/ *adj* (train) directo; (flight) sin escalas. ● *adv* sin parar; (by train) directamente; (by air) sin escalas

noodles /ˈnuːdlz/ *npl* fideos *mpl*

nook /nʊk/ *n* rincón *m*

noon /nuːn/ *n* mediodía *m*

no-one /ˈnəʊwʌn/ *pron* nadie

noose /nuːs/ *n* soga *f*

nor /nɔː(r)/ *conj* ni, tampoco. neither blue ~ red ni azul ni rojo. he doesn't play the piano ~ do I no sabe tocar el piano, ni yo tampoco

norm /nɔːm/ *n* norma *f*

normal /ˈnɔːml/ *adj* normal. ~**cy** *n* (Amer) normalidad *f*. ~**ity** /-ˈmælətɪ/ *n* normalidad *f*. ~**ly** *adv* normalmente

north /nɔːθ/ *n* norte *m*. ● *adj* norte. ● *adv* hacia el norte. N~ **America** *n* América *f* del Norte, Norteamérica *f*. N~ **American** *adj* & *n* norteamericano (*m*). ~**east** *n* nor(d)este *m*. ● *adj* nor(d)este. ● *adv* (go) hacia el nor(d)este. it's ~east of Leeds está al nor(d)este de Leeds. ~**erly** /ˈnɔːðəlɪ/ *adj* (wind) del norte. ~**ern** /ˈnɔːðən/ *adj* del norte. ~**erner** *n* norteño *m*. N~**ern Ireland** *n* Irlanda *f* del Norte. N~ **Sea** *n* mar *m* del Norte. ~**ward** /ˈnɔːθwəd/, ~**wards** *adv* hacia el norte. ~**west** *n* noroeste *m*. ● *adj* noroeste. ● *adv* hacia el noroeste

Norw|ay /ˈnɔːweɪ/ *n* Noruega *f*. ~**egian** /-ˈwiːdʒən/ *adj* & *n* noruego (*m*)

nose /nəʊz/ *n* nariz *f*. ~**bleed** *n* hemorragia *f* nasal. ~**dive** *vi* descender en picado, descender en picada (*LAm*)

nostalgi|a /nɒˈstældʒə/ *n* nostalgia *f*. ~**c** *adj* nostálgico

nostril /ˈnɒstrɪl/ *n* ventana *f* de la nariz *f*

nosy /ˈnəʊzɪ/ *adj* (-ier, -iest) 🄸 entrometido, metiche (*LAm*)

n

not /nɒt/

Cuando **not** va precedido del verbo auxiliar **do** or **have** o de un verbo modal como **should** etc, se suele emplear la forma contraída **don't, haven't, shouldn't** etc

adverb

····▸ no. I don't know no sé. ~ yet todavía no. ~ me yo no

····▸ (*replacing a clause*) I suppose ~ supongo que no. of course ~ por supuesto que no. are you going to help me or ~? ¿me vas a ayudar o no?

····▸ (*emphatic*) ni. ~ a penny more! ¡ni un penique más!

····▸ (*in phrases*) certainly ~ de ninguna manera. ~ you again! ¡tú otra vez!

notabl|e /ˈnəʊtəbl/ *adj* notable; (*author*) distinguido. ~**y** /ˈnəʊtəblɪ/ *adv* notablemente. (*in particular*) particularmente

notch /nɒtʃ/ *n* muesca *f*. □ ~ **up** *vt* apuntarse

note /nəʊt/ *n* (*incl Mus*) nota *f*; (*banknote*) billete *m*. take ~**s** tomar apuntes. ● *vt* (*notice*) observar; (*record*) anotar. □ ~ **down** *vt* apuntar. ~**book** *n* cuaderno *m*. ~**d** *adj* célebre. ~**paper** *n* papel *m* de carta(s)

nothing /ˈnʌθɪŋ/ *pron* nada. he eats ~ no come nada. for ~ (*free*) gratis; (*in vain*) en vano. ~ else nada más. ~ much happened no pasó gran cosa. he does ~ but complain no hace más que quejarse

notice /ˈnəʊtɪs/ *n* (*sign*) letrero *m*;

(*item of information*) anuncio *m*; (*notification*) aviso *m*; (*of termination of employment*) preaviso *m*; ~ (*of dismissal*) despido *m*. take ~ of hacer caso a (a person). ● *vt* notar. ● *vi* darse cuenta. ~**able** *adj* perceptible. ~**ably** *adv* perceptiblemente. ~**board** *n* tablón *m* de anuncios, tablero *m* de anuncios (*LAm*)

notif|ication /nəʊtɪfɪˈkeɪʃn/ *n* notificación *f*. ~**y** /ˈnəʊtɪfaɪ/ *vt* informar; (*in writing*) notificar. ~**y** s.o. of sth comunicarle algo a uno

notion /ˈnəʊʃn/ *n* (*concept*) concepto *m*; (*idea*) idea *f*

notorious /nəʊˈtɔːrɪəs/ *adj* notorio

notwithstanding /nɒtwɪð-ˈstændɪŋ/ *prep* a pesar de. ● *adv* no obstante

nougat /ˈnuːgɑː/ *n* turrón *m*

nought /nɔːt/ *n* cero *m*

noun /naʊn/ *n* sustantivo *m*, nombre *m*

nourish /ˈnʌrɪʃ/ *vt* alimentar. ~**ment** *n* alimento *m*

novel /ˈnɒvl/ *n* novela *f*. ● *adj* original, novedoso. ~**ist** *n* novelista *m* & *f*. ~**ty** *n* novedad *f*

November /nəʊˈvembə(r)/ *n* noviembre *m*

novice /ˈnɒvɪs/ *n* principiante *m* & *f*

now /naʊ/ *adv* ahora. ~ and again, ~ and then de vez en cuando. right ~ ahora mismo. from ~ on a partir de ahora. ● *conj*. ~ (that) ahora que. ~**adays** /ˈnaʊədeɪz/ *adv* hoy (en) día

nowhere /ˈnəʊweə(r)/ *adv* por ninguna parte, por ningún lado; (*after motion towards*) a ninguna parte, a ningún lado

nozzle /ˈnɒzl/ n (on hose) boca f; (on fire extinguisher) boquilla f

nuance /ˈnjuːɑːns/ n matiz m

nuclear /ˈnjuːklɪə(r)/ adj nuclear

nucleus /ˈnjuːklɪəs/ n (pl -lei /-lɪaɪ/) núcleo m

nude /njuːd/ adj & n desnudo (m). in the ~ desnudo

nudge /nʌdʒ/ vt codear (ligeramente). ●n golpe m (suave) con el codo

nudi|st /ˈnjuːdɪst/ n nudista m & f. ~ty /ˈnjuːdəti/ n desnudez f

nuisance /ˈnjuːsns/ n (thing, event) molestia f, fastidio m; (person) pesado m

null /nʌl/ adj nulo

numb /nʌm/ adj entumecido. go ~ entumecerse ●vt entumecer

number /ˈnʌmbə(r)/ n número m; (telephone number) número m de teléfono. a ~ of people varias personas. ●vt numerar; (count, include) contar. ~plate n matrícula f, placa f (LAm)

numer|al /ˈnjuːmərəl/ n número m. ~ical /njuːˈmerɪkl/ adj numérico. ~ous /ˈnjuːmərəs/ adj numeroso

nun /nʌn/ n monja f

nurse /nɜːs/ n enfermero m, enfermera f; (nanny) niñera f. ●vt cuidar; abrigar (hope etc)

nursery /ˈnɜːsəri/ n (for plants) vivero m; (day ~) guardería f. ~ rhyme n canción f infantil. ~ school n jardín m de infancia, jardín m infantil (LAm)

nursing home /ˈnɜːsɪŋ/ n (for older people) residencia f de ancianos (con mayor nivel de asistencia médica)

nut /nʌt/ n fruto m seco (nuez, almendra, avellana etc); (Tec) tuerca f. ~case n 🅃 chiflado m. ~crackers npl cascanueces m. ~meg /-meg/ n nuez f moscada

nutri|ent /ˈnjuːtrɪənt/ n nutriente m. ~tion /njuːˈtrɪʃn/ n nutrición f. ~tious /njuːˈtrɪʃəs/ adj nutritivo

nuts /nʌts/ adj (fam, crazy) chiflado

nutshell /ˈnʌtʃel/ n cáscara f de nuez. in a ~ en pocas palabras

NW abbr (= north-west) NO

nylon /ˈnaɪlɒn/ n nylon m

Oo

oaf /əʊf/ n zoquete m

oak /əʊk/ n roble m

OAP /əʊeɪˈpiː/ abbr (= old-age pensioner) n pensionista m & f, pensionado m

oar /ɔː(r)/ n remo m

oasis /əʊˈeɪsɪs/ n (pl oases /-siːz/) oasis m

oath /əʊθ/ n juramento m

oat|meal /ˈəʊtmiːl/ n harina f de avena; (Amer, flakes) avena f (en copos). ~s /əʊts/ npl avena f

obedien|ce /əʊˈbiːdɪəns/ n obediencia f. ~t adj obediente. ~tly adv obedientemente

obes|e /əʊˈbiːs/ adj obeso. ~ity n obesidad f

obey /əʊˈbeɪ/ vt/i obedecer

obituary /əˈbɪtʃʊəri/ n nota f necrológica, obituario m

object /ˈɒbdʒɪkt/ n objeto m; (aim) objetivo m. ●/əbˈdʒekt/ vi oponerse (to a). ~ion /əbˈdʒekʃn/ n objeción f. ~ionable adj censurable; (unpleasant) desagradable. ~ive /ə'dʒektɪv/ adj & n objetivo (m)

oblig|ation /ɒblɪ'ɡeɪʃn/ n obligación f. be under an ~ation to estar obligado a. ~atory /ə 'blɪɡətrɪ/ adj obligatorio. ~e /ə 'blaɪdʒ/ vt obligar. I'd be much ~ed if you could help me le quedaría muy agradecido si pudiera ayudarme. ● vi hacer un favor. ~ing adj atento

oblique /ə'bliːk/ adj oblicuo

obliterate /ə'blɪtəreɪt/ vt arrasar; (erase) borrar

oblivio|n /ə'blɪvɪən/ n olvido m. ~us /-vɪəs/ adj (unaware) inconsciente (to, of de)

oblong /'ɒblɒŋ/ adj oblongo. ● n rectángulo m

obnoxious /əb'nɒkʃəs/ adj odioso

oboe /'əʊbəʊ/ n oboe m

obscen|e /əb'siːn/ adj obsceno. ~ity /əb'senətɪ/ n obscenidad f

obscur|e /əb'skjʊə(r)/ adj oscuro. ● vt ocultar; impedir ver claramente (issue). ~ity n oscuridad f

obsequious /əb'siːkwɪəs/ adj servil

observ|ant /əb'zɜːvənt/ adj observador. ~ation /ɒbzə'veɪʃn/ n observación f. ~atory /əb'zɜːvətrɪ/ n observatorio m. ~e /əb'zɜːv/ vt observar. ~er n observador m

obsess /əb'ses/ vt obsesionar. ~ed /əb'sest/ adj obsesionado. ~ion /-ʃn/ n obsesión f. ~ive adj obsesivo

obsolete /'ɒbsəliːt/ adj obsoleto

obstacle /'ɒbstəkl/ n obstáculo m

obstina|cy /'ɒbstɪnəsɪ/ n obstinación f. ~te /-ət/ adj obstinado. ~tely adv obstinadamente

obstruct /əb'strʌkt/ vt obstruir; bloquear (traffic). ~ion /-ʃn/ n obstrucción f

obtain /əb'teɪn/ vt conseguir, obtener. ~able adj asequible

obtrusive /əb'truːsɪv/ adj (presence) demasiado prominente; (noise) molesto

obtuse /əb'tjuːs/ adj obtuso

obvious /'ɒbvɪəs/ adj obvio. ~ly adv obviamente

occasion /ə'keɪʒn/ n ocasión f. ~al adj esporádico. ~ally adv de vez en cuando

occult /ə'kʌlt/ adj oculto

occup|ant /'ɒkjʊpənt/ n ocupante m & f. ~ation /ɒkjʊ'peɪʃn/ n ocupación f. ~ier /'ɒkjʊpaɪə(r)/ n ocupante m & f. ~y /'ɒkjʊpaɪ/ vt ocupar. keep o.s. ~ied entretenerse

occur /ə'kɜː(r)/ vi (pt occurred) tener lugar, ocurrir; (change) producirse; (exist) encontrarse. It ~red to me that se me ocurrió que. ~rence /ə'kʌrəns/ n (incidence) incidencia f. it is a rare ~rence no es algo frecuente

ocean /'əʊʃn/ n océano m

o'clock /ə'klɒk/ adv. it is 7 ~ son las siete. it's one ~ es la una

octagon /'ɒktəgən/ n octágono m

octave /'ɒktɪv/ n octava f

October /ɒk'təʊbə(r)/ n octubre m

octopus /'ɒktəpəs/ n (pl -puses) pulpo m

odd /ɒd/ adj (-er, -est) extraño, raro; (number) impar; (one of pair) desparejado. smoke the ~ cigarette fumarse algún que otro cigarrillo. fifty-~ unos cincuenta, cincuenta y pico. the ~ one out la excepción. ~ity n (thing) rareza f;

(*person*) bicho *m* raro. ~ly *adv* de una manera extraña. ~ly **enough** por extraño que parezca. ~**ment** *n* retazo *m*. ~**s** *npl* probabilidades *fpl*; (*in betting*) apuesta *f*. **be at** ~**s** estar en desacuerdo. ~**s and ends** *mpl* ⊡ cosas *fpl* sueltas

odious /ˈəʊdɪəs/ *adj* odioso

odometer /ɒˈdɒmətə(r)/ *n* (*Amer*) cuentakilómetros *m*

odour /ˈəʊdə(r)/ *n* olor *m*

---

of /ɒv/ /əv/ *preposition*

····▸ de. a pound of cheese una libra de queso. it's made of wood es de madera. a girl of ten una niña de diez años

····▸ (*in dates*) de. the fifth of November el cinco de noviembre

····▸ (*Amer, when telling the time*) it's ten (minutes) of five son las cinco menos diez, son diez para las cinco (*LAm*)

! **of** is not translated in cases such as the following: **a colleague of mine** un colega mío; **there were six of us** éramos seis; **that's very kind of you** es Ud muy amable

---

off /ɒf/ *prep* (*from*) de. he picked it up ~ the floor lo recogió del suelo; (*distant from*) just ~ the coast of Texas a poca distancia de la costa de Tejas. 2 ft ~ the ground a dos pies del suelo; (*absent from*) I've been ~ work for a week hace una semana que no voy a trabajar. ● *adv* (*removed*) the lid was ~ la tapa no estaba puesta; (*distant*) some way ~ a cierta distancia; (*leaving*) I'm ~ me voy; (*switched off*) (light, TV) apa-

gado; (water) cortado; (*cancelled*) (match) cancelado; (*not on duty*) (day) libre. ● *adj*. **be** ~ (meat) estar malo, estar pasado; (milk) estar cortado. ~**beat** *adj* poco convencional. ~**chance** *n*. **on the** ~ **chance** por si acaso

---

off-licence En el Reino Unido, es una tienda que tiene licencia para vender bebidas alcohólicas que se deben consumir fuera del local. Abren cuando los bares y *pubs* están cerrados y también suelen vender bebidas no alcohólicas, tabaco, golosinas etc. A menudo alquilan vasos y copas para fiestas, etc. *i*

---

offen|ce /əˈfens/ *n* (*breach of law*) infracción *f*; (*criminal* ~ce) delito *m*; (*cause of outrage*) atentado *m*; (*Amer, attack*) ataque *m*. **take** ~**ce** ofenderse. ~**d** *vt* ofender. ~**der** *n* delincuente *m & f*. ~**sive** /-sɪv/ *adj* ofensivo; (*disgusting*) desagradable

offer /ˈɒfə(r)/ *vt* ofrecer. ~ **to do** sth ofrecerse a hacer algo. ● *n* oferta *f*. **on** ~ de oferta

offhand /ɒfˈhænd/ *adj* (*brusque*) brusco. say sth in an ~ way decir algo a la ligera. ● *adv* de improviso

office /ˈɒfɪs/ *n* oficina *f*; (*post*) cargo *m*. doctor's ~ (*Amer*) consultorio *m*, consulta *m*. ~ **block** *n* edificio *m* de oficinas. ~**r** *n* oficial *m & f*; (*police* ~**r**) policía *m & f*; (*as form of address*) agente

offic|ial /əˈfɪʃl/ *adj* oficial. ● *n* funcionario *m* del Estado; (*of party, union*) dirigente *m & f*. ~**ally** *adv* oficialmente. ~**ous** /əˈfɪʃəs/ *adj* oficioso

offing /ˈɒfɪŋ/ *n*. **in the** ~ en perspectiva

o

off: ~-**licence** n tienda f de vinos y licores. ~-**putting** adj (disconcerting) desconcertante; (disagreeable) desagradable. ~**set** vt (pt -set, pres p -setting) compensar. ~**shore** adj (breeze) que sopla desde la tierra; (drilling) off-shore; (well) submarino. ● adv a un lugar de mano de obra barata. ~**side** /ɒfˈsaɪd/ adj (Sport) fuera de juego. ~**spring** n invar prole f. ~-**stage** /-ˈsteɪdʒ/ adv fuera del escenario. ~-**white** adj color hueso

often /ˈɒfn/ adv a menudo, con frecuencia. how ~? ¿con qué frecuencia? more ~ con más frecuencia

ogle /ˈəʊgl/ vt comerse con los ojos

ogre /ˈəʊgə(r)/ n ogro m

oh /əʊ/ int ¡ah!; (expressing dismay) ¡ay!

oil /ɔɪl/ n aceite m; (petroleum) petróleo m. ● vt lubricar. ~**field** n yacimiento m petrolífero. ~-**painting** n pintura f al óleo; (picture) óleo m. ~ **rig** n plataforma f petrolífera. ~**y** adj (substance) oleaginoso; (food) aceitoso

ointment /ˈɔɪntmənt/ n ungüento m

OK /əʊˈkeɪ/ int ¡vale!, ¡de acuerdo!, ¡bueno! (LAm). ● adj ~, thanks bien, gracias. the job's ~ el trabajo no está mal

old /əʊld/ adj (-er, -est) viejo; (not modern) antiguo; (former) antiguo; an ~ friend un viejo amigo. how ~ is she? ¿cuántos años tiene? she is ten years ~ tiene diez años. his ~er sister su hermana mayor. ~ **age** n vejez f. ~-**fashioned** /-ˈfæʃənd/ adj anticuado

olive /ˈɒlɪv/ n aceituna f.

Olympic /əˈlɪmpɪk/ adj olímpico. the ~ npl, the ~ **Games** npl los Juegos Olímpicos

omelette /ˈɒmlɪt/ n tortilla f francesa, omelette m (LAm)

omen /ˈəʊmen/ n agüero m

omi|ssion /əˈmɪʃn/ n omisión f. ~t /əˈmɪt/ vt (pt omitted) omitir

on /ɒn/ prep en, sobre; (about) sobre. ~ foot a pie. ~ Monday el lunes. ~ seeing al ver. I heard it ~ the radio lo oí por la radio. ● adv (light etc) encendido, prendido (LAm); (machine) en marcha; (tap) abierto. ~ and ~ sin cesar. and so ~ y así sucesivamente. have a hat ~ llevar (puesto) un sombrero. further ~ un poco más allá. what's ~ at the Odeon? ¿qué dan en el Odeon? go ~ continuar. later ~ más tarde

once /wʌns/ adv una vez; (formerly) antes. at ~ inmediatamente. ~ upon a time there was... érase una vez.... ~ and for all de una vez por todas. ● conj una vez que

one /wʌn/ adj uno, (before masculine singular noun) un. the ~ person I trusted la única persona en la que confiaba. ● n uno m. ~ by ~ uno a uno. ● pron uno (m), una (f). the blue ~ el/la azul. this ~ éste/ésta. ~ another el uno al otro

onerous /ˈɒnərəs/ adj (task) pesado

one: ~**self** /-ˈself/ pron (reflexive) se; (after prep) sí (mismo); (emphatic use) uno mismo, una misma. by ~**self** solo. ~-**way** adj (street) de sentido único; (ticket) de ida, sencillo

onion /ˈʌnɪən/ n cebolla f

online /ɒnˈlaɪn/ adj en línea

onlooker /'ɒnlʊkə(r)/ n espectador m

only /'əʊnli/ adj único. she's an ~ child es hija única. ● adv sólo, solamente. ~ just (barely) apenas. I've ~ just arrived acabo de llegar. ● conj pero, sólo que

onset /'ɒnset/ n comienzo m; (of disease) aparición f

onshore /'ɒnʃɔ:(r)/ adj (breeze) que sopla desde el mar; (oil field) en tierra

onslaught /'ɒnslɔ:t/ n ataque m

onus /'əʊnəs/ n responsabilidad f

onward(s) /'ɒnwəd(z)/ adj & adv hacia adelante

ooze /u:z/ vt/i rezumar

opaque /əʊ'peɪk/ adj opaco

open /'əʊpən/ adj abierto; (question) discutible. in the ~ al aire libre. ● vt/i abrir. ~ing n abertura f; (beginning) principio m. ~ly adv abiertamente. ~-minded /-'maɪndɪd/ adj de actitud abierta

---

Open University La universidad a distancia británica, fundada en 1969. La enseñanza se imparte fundamentalmente por correspondencia, mediante materiales impresos, material enviado por internet y programas de televisión emitidos por la BBC. También hay cursos de verano a los que los alumnos deben asistir. No se exigen calificaciones académicas para su ingreso.

---

opera /'ɒprə/ n ópera f

operate /'ɒpəreɪt/ vt manejar, operar, (Mex) (machine). ● vi funcionar; (company) operar. ~ (on) (Med) operar (a)

operatic /ɒpə'rætɪk/ adj operístico

operation /ɒpə'reɪʃn/ n operación f; (Mec) funcionamiento m; (using of machine) manejo m. he had an ~ lo operaron. in ~ en vigor. ~al adj operacional

operative /'ɒpərətɪv/ adj. be ~ estar en vigor

operator n operador m

opinion /ə'pɪnɪən/ n opinión f. in my ~ en mi opinión, a mi parecer

opponent /ə'pəʊnənt/ n adversario m; (in sport) contrincante m & f

opportun|e /'ɒpətju:n/ adj oportuno. ~ist /ɒpə'tju:nɪst/ n oportunista m & f. ~ity /ɒpə'tju:nəti/ n oportunidad f

oppos|e /ə'pəʊz/ vt oponerse a. be ~ed to oponerse a, estar en contra de. ~ed to al opuesto. ~ite /'ɒpəzɪt/ adj (contrary) opuesto; (facing) de enfrente. ● n. the ~ite lo contrario. quite the ~ite al contrario. ● adv enfrente. ● prep enfrente de. ~ite number n homólogo m. ~ition /ɒpə'zɪʃn/ n oposición f; (resistance) resistencia f

oppress /ə'pres/ vt oprimir. ~ion /-ʃn/ n opresión f. ~ive adj (cruel) opresivo; (heat) sofocante

opt /ɒpt/ vi. ~ to optar por. □ ~ out vi decidir no tomar parte

optic|al /'ɒptɪkl/ adj óptico. ~ian /ɒp'tɪʃn/ n óptico m

optimis|m /'ɒptɪmɪzəm/ n optimismo m. ~t n optimista m & f. ~tic /-'mɪstɪk/ adj optimista

option /'ɒpʃn/ n opción f. ~al adj facultativo

or /ɔ:(r)/ conj o; (before o- and ho-) u; (after negative) ni. ~ else si no, o bien

oral /'ɔ:rəl/ adj oral. ● n 🄴 examen m oral

orange /'ɒrɪndʒ/ n naranja f; (colour) naranja m. • adj naranja. ~**ade** /-'eɪd/ n naranjada f

orbit /'ɔːbɪt/ n órbita f. • vt orbitar

orchard /'ɔːtʃəd/ n huerto m

orchestra /'ɔːkɪstrə/ n orquesta f; (Amer, in theatre) platea f. ~**l** /-'kestrəl/ adj orquestal. ~**te** /-eɪt/ vt orquestar

orchid /'ɔːkɪd/ n orquídea f

ordain /ɔː'deɪn/ vt (Relig) ordenar; (decree) decretar

ordeal /ɔː'diːl/ n dura prueba f

order /'ɔːdə(r)/ n orden m; (Com) pedido m; (command) orden f. in ~ that para que. in ~ to para. • vt (command) ordenar, mandar; (Com) pedir; (in restaurant) pedir, ordenar (LAm); encargar (book); llamar, ordenar (LAm) (taxi). ~**ly** adj ordenado. • n camillero m

ordinary /'ɔːdɪnrɪ/ adj corriente; (average) medio; (mediocre) ordinario

ore /ɔː(r)/ n mena f

organ /'ɔːgən/ n órgano m

organic /ɔː'gænɪk/ adj orgánico. ~**ism** /'ɔːgənɪzəm/ n organismo m. ~**ist** /'ɔːgənɪst/ n organista m & f. ~**ization** /ɔːgənaɪ'zeɪʃn/ n organización f. ~**ize** /'ɔːgənaɪz/ vt organizar. ~**izer** n organizador m

orgasm /'ɔːgæzəm/ n orgasmo m

orgy /'ɔːdʒɪ/ n orgía f

Orient /'ɔːrɪənt/ n Oriente m. ~**al** /-'entl/ adj oriental

orientate /'ɔːrɪənteɪt/ vt orientar. ~**ion** /-'teɪʃn/ n orientación f

origin /'ɒrɪdʒɪn/ n origen m. ~**al** /ə'rɪdʒənl/ adj original. ~**ally** adv originariamente. ~**ate** /ə'rɪdʒɪneɪt/ vi. ~**ate from** provenir de

ornament /'ɔːnəmənt/ n adorno m. ~**al** /-'mentl/ adj de adorno

ornate /ɔː'neɪt/ adj ornamentado; (style) recargado

ornithology /ɔːnɪ'θɒlədʒɪ/ n ornitología f

orphan /'ɔːfn/ n huérfano m. • vt. be ~**ed** quedar huérfano. ~**age** /-ɪdʒ/ n orfanato m

orthodox /'ɔːθədɒks/ adj ortodoxo

oscillate /'ɒsɪleɪt/ vi oscilar

ostentatious /ɒsten'teɪʃəs/ adj ostentoso

osteopath /'ɒstɪəpæθ/ n osteópata m & f

ostracize /'ɒstrəsaɪz/ vt hacerle vacío a

ostrich /'ɒstrɪtʃ/ n avestruz m

other /'ʌðə(r)/ adj & pron otro. ~ than aparte de. the ~ one el otro. ~**wise** adv de lo contrario, si no

otter /'ɒtə(r)/ n nutria f

ouch /aʊtʃ/ int ¡ay!

ought /ɔːt/ modal verb. I ~ to see it debería verlo. he ~ to have done it debería haberlo hecho

ounce /aʊns/ n onza f (= 28.35 gr.)

our /'aʊə(r)/ adj (sing) nuestro, nuestra, (pl) nuestros, nuestras. ~**s** /'aʊəz/ poss pron (sing) nuestro, nuestra; (pl) nuestros, nuestras. ~**s** is red es nuestro es rojo. a friend of ~**s** un amigo nuestro. ~**selves** /-'selvz/ pron (reflexive) nos; (used for emphasis and after prepositions) nosotros mismos, nosotras mismas. we behaved ~**selves** nos portamos bien. we did it ~**selves** lo hicimos nosotros mismos/nosotras mismas

oust /aʊst/ vt desbancar; derrocar (government)

out /aʊt/ adv (outside) fuera, afuera

(LAm). (not lighted, not on) apagado; (in blossom) en flor; (in error) equivocado. he's ~ (not at home) no está; be ~ to estar resuelto a. ~ of prep (from inside) de; (outside) fuera, afuera (LAm). five ~ of six cinco de cada seis. made ~ of hecho de. we're ~ of bread nos hemos quedado sin pan. ~**break** n (of war) estallido m; (of disease) brote m. ~**burst** n arrebato m. ~**cast** n paria m & f. ~**come** n resultado m. ~**cry** n protesta f. ~**dated** /-'deɪtɪd/ adj anticuado. ~**do** /-'duː/ vt (pt -did, pp -done) superar. ~**door** adj (clothes) de calle; (pool) descubierto. ~**doors** /-'dɔːz/ adv al aire libre

outer /'aʊtə(r)/ adj exterior

out: ~**fit** n equipo m; (clothes) conjunto m. ~**going** adj (minister etc) saliente; (sociable) abierto. ~**goings** npl gastos mpl. ~**grow** /-'ɡrəʊ/ vt (pt -grew, pp -grown) crecer más que (person). he's ~grown his new shoes le han quedado pequeños los zapatos nuevos. ~**ing** n excursión f

outlandish /aʊt'lændɪʃ/ adj extravagante

out: ~**law** n forajido m. ● vt proscribir. ~**lay** n gastos mpl. ~**let** n salida f; (Com) punto m de venta; (Amer, Elec) toma f de corriente. ~**line** n contorno m; (summary) resumen m; (plan of project) esquema m. ● vt trazar; (summarize) esbozar. ~**live** /-'lɪv/ vt sobrevivir a. ~**look** n perspectivas fpl; (attitude) punto m de vista. ~**lying** adj alejado. ~**number** /-'nʌmbə(r)/ vt superar en número. ~**-of-date** adj (ideas) desfasado; (clothes) pasado de moda. ~**patient** n paciente m externo.

~**post** n avanzada f. ~**put** n producción f; (of machine, worker) rendimiento m. ~**right** adv completamente; (frankly) abiertamente; (kill) en el acto. ● adj completo; (refusal) rotundo. ~**set** n principio m. at the ~ como máximo. ● prep fuera de. ~**size** adj de talla gigante. ~**skirts** npl afueras fpl. ~**spoken** /-'spəʊkn/ adj directo, franco. ~**standing** /-'stændɪŋ/ adj excepcional; (debt) pendiente. ~**stretched** /aʊt'stretʃt/ adj extendido. ~**strip** /-'strɪp/ vt (pt -stripped) (run faster than) tomarle la delantera a; (exceed) sobrepasar. ~**ward** /-wəd/ adj (appearance) exterior; (sign) externo; (journey) de ida. ~**wardly** adv hacia fuera, exteriormente. ~(**s**) adv hacia afuera. ~**weigh** /-'weɪ/ vt ser mayor que. ~**wit** /-'wɪt/ vt (pt -witted) burlar

oval /'əʊvl/ adj ovalado, oval. ● n óvalo m

Oval Office El Despacho Oval es el despacho oficial del Presidente de los Estados Unidos, ubicado en el ala oeste de la Casa Blanca. La forma oval fue determinada por George Washington, lo que le permitiría tener contacto visual con todos durante las reuniones. Originariamente, quería que todas las habitaciones de la Casa Blanca fueran ovales, pero pronto comprendió que este diseño era poco práctico.

ovary /'əʊvəri/ n ovario m

ovation /əʊ'veɪʃn/ n ovación f

oven /'ʌvn/ n horno m

over /ˈəʊvə(r)/ *prep* por encima de; (*across*) al otro lado de; (*during*) durante; (*more than*) más de. ~ **and above** por encima de. ● *adv* (*ended*) terminado; (*more*) más; (*in excess*) de sobra. ~ **again** otra vez. ~ **and** una y otra vez. ~ **here** por aquí. ~ **there** por allí. **all** ~ (*finished*) acabado; (*everywhere*) por todas partes

over... /ˈəʊvə(r)/ *pref* excesivamente, demasiado

over: ~**all** /ˈɔːl/ *adj* global; (*length, cost*) total. ● *adv* en conjunto. ~ /ˈəʊvərɔːl/ *n*, ~**alls** *npl* mono *m*, overol *m* (*LAm*); (*Amer, dungarees*) peto *m*, overol *m*. ~**awe** /ˈɔː/ *vt* intimidar. ~**balance** /ˈbæləns/ *vi* perder el equilibrio. ~**bearing** /ˈbeərɪŋ/ *adj* dominante. ~**board** *adv* (*throw*) por la borda. ~**cast** /ˈkɑːst/ *adj* (*day*) nublado; (*sky*) cubierto. ~**charge** /ˈtʃɑːdʒ/ *vt* cobrarle de más a. ~**coat** *n* abrigo *m*. ~**come** /ˈkʌm/ *vt* (*pt* -**came**, *pp* -**come**) superar, vencer. ~**crowded** /ˈkraʊdɪd/ *adj* abarrotado (de gente). ~**do** /ˈduː/ *vt* (*pt* -**did**, *pp* -**done**) exagerar; (*Culin*) recocer. ~**dose** *n* sobredosis *f*. ~**draft** *n* descubierto *m*. ~**draw** /ˈdrɔː/ *vt* (*pt* -**drew**, *pp* -**drawn**) girar en descubierto. **be** ~**drawn** tener un descubierto. ~**due** /ˈdjuː/ *adj*. **the book is a month** ~ **due** el plazo de devolución del libro venció hace un mes. ~**estimate** /ˈestɪmeɪt/ *vt* sobreestimar. ~**flow** /ˈfləʊ/ *vi* desbordarse. ● *n* /ˈfləʊ/ (*excess*) exceso *m*; (*outlet*) rebosadero *m*. ~**flow car park** *n* estacionamiento *m* extra (*LAm*), aparcamiento *m* extra (*Esp*). ~**grown** /ˈɡrəʊn/ *adj* de-

masiado grande; (*garden*) lleno de maleza. ~**haul** /ˈhɔːl/ *vt* revisar. ● /ˈhɔːl/ *n* revisión *f*. ~**head** /ˈhed/ *adv* por encima. ● /ˈhed/ *adj* de arriba. ● /ˈhed/ *adj* de arriba. ~**heads** /ˈhedz/ *npl*. ~**head** *n* (*Amer*) gastos *mpl* indirectos. ~**hear** /ˈhɪə(r)/ *vt* (*pt* -**heard**) oír por casualidad. ~**joyed** /ˈdʒɔɪd/ *adj* encantado. ~**land** a/*adv* por tierra. ~**lap** /ˈlæp/ *vi* (*pt* -**lapped**) traslaparse. ~**leaf** /ˈliːf/ *adv* al dorso. ~**load** /ˈləʊd/ *vt* sobrecargar. ~**look** /ˈlʊk/ *vt* (*room*) dar a; (*not notice*) pasar por alto; (*disregard*) disculpar. ~**night** /ˈnaɪt/ *adv* durante la noche. **stay** ~**night** quedarse a pasar la noche. ● *adj* (*journey*) de noche; (*stay*) de una noche. ~**pass** *n* paso *m* elevado, paso *m* a desnivel (*Mex*). ~**pay** /ˈpeɪ/ *vt* (*pt* -**paid**) pagar demasiado. ~**power** /ˈpaʊə(r)/ *vt* dominar (*opponent*); (*emotion*) abrumar. ~**powering** /ˈpaʊərɪŋ/ *adj* (*smell*) muy fuerte; (*desire*) irresistible. ~**priced** /ˈpraɪst/ *adj* demasiado caro. ~**rated** /ˈreɪtɪd/ *adj* sobrevalorado. ~**react** /ˈrɪækt/ *vi* reaccionar en forma exagerada. ~**ride** /ˈraɪd/ *vt* (*pt* -**rode**, *pp* -**ridden**) invalidar. ~**riding** /ˈraɪdɪŋ/ *adj* dominante. ~**rule** /ˈruːl/ *vt* anular; rechazar (*objection*). ~**run** /ˈrʌn/ *vt* (*pt* -**ran**, *pp* -**run**, *pres p* -**running**) invadir; exceder (*limit*). ~**seas** /ˈsiːz/ *adj* (*trade*) exterior; (*investments*) en el exterior; (*visitor*) extranjero. ● *adv* al extranjero. ~**see** /ˈsiː/ *vt* (*pt* -**saw**, *pp* -**seen**) supervisar. ~**seer** /ˈsɪə(r)/ *n* capataz *m* & *f*, supervisor *m*. ~**shadow** /ˈʃædəʊ/ *vt* eclipsar. ~**shoot** /ˈʃuːt/ *vt* (*pt* -**shot**) excederse. ~**sight** /ˈsaɪt/ *n* descuido *m*. ~**sleep** /ˈsliːp/ *vi* (*pt*

~slept) quedarse dormido. ~step /ˈstep/ vt (pt -stepped) sobrepasar. ~step the mark pasarse de la raya

overt /ˈəʊvɜːt/ adj manifiesto

over: ~**take** /-ˈteɪk/ vt/i (pt -took, pp -taken) sobrepasar; (Auto) adelantar, rebasar (Mex). ~**throw** /-ˈθrəʊ/ vt (pt -threw, pp -thrown) derrocar. ~**time** n horas fpl extra

overture /ˈəʊvətjʊə(r)/ n obertura f

over: ~**turn** /-ˈtɜːn/ vt darle la vuelta a. ●vi volcar. ~**weight** /-ˈweɪt/ adj demasiado gordo. be ~weight pesar demasiado. ~**whelm** /-ˈwelm/ vt aplastar; (with emotion) abrumar. ~**whelming** adj aplastante; (fig) abrumador. ~**work** /-ˈwɜːk/ vt hacer trabajar demasiado. ●vi trabajar demasiado. ●n agotamiento m

owe /əʊ/ vt deber. ~**ing** to debido a

owl /aʊl/ n búho m

own /əʊn/ adj propio. my ~ house mi propia casa. ●pron. it's my ~ es mío (propio)/mía (propia). on one's ~ solo. get one's ~ back 🄸 desquitarse. ●vt tener. □~ up vi. 🄸 confesarse culpable. ~**er** n propietario, dueño m. ~**ership** n propiedad f

oxygen /ˈɒksɪdʒən/ n oxígeno m

oyster /ˈɔɪstə(r)/ n ostra f

Pp

p abbr (= pence, penny) penique(s) (m(pl))

p. (pl pp.) (= page) pág., p.

pace /peɪs/ n paso m. keep with s.o. seguirle el ritmo a uno. ●vi. ~ up and down andar de un lado para otro. ~**maker** n (runner) liebre f; (Med) marcapasos m

Pacific /pəˈsɪfɪk/ n. the ~ (Ocean) el (Océano) Pacífico m

pacif|ist /ˈpæsɪfɪst/ n pacifista m & f. ~**y** /ˈpæsɪfaɪ/ vt apaciguar

pack /pæk/ n fardo m; (of cigarettes) paquete m, cajetilla f; (of cards) baraja f; (of hounds) jauría f; (of wolves) manada f. a ~ of lies una sarta de mentiras. ●vt empaquetar; hacer (suitcase); (press down) apisonar. ●vi hacer la maleta, empacar (LAm). ~**age** /-ɪdʒ/ n paquete m. ~ **holiday** n vacaciones fpl organizadas. ~**ed** /pækt/ adj lleno (de gente). ~**et** /ˈpækɪt/ n paquete m

pact /pækt/ n pacto m, acuerdo m

pad /pæd/ n (for writing) bloc m. shoulder ~s hombreras fpl. ●vt (pt padded) rellenar

paddle /ˈpædl/ n pala f. ●vi mojarse los pies; (in canoe) remar (con pala)

paddock /ˈpædək/ n prado m

padlock /'pædlɒk/ n candado m.
● vt cerrar con candado

paed|iatrician /ˌpiːdɪəˈtrɪʃn/ n pediatra m & f. **~ophile** /'piːdəfaɪl/ n pedófilo m

pagan /'peɪɡən/ adj & n pagano (m)

page /peɪdʒ/ n página f; (attendant) paje m; (in hotel) botones m.
● vt llamar por megafonía/por buscapersonas, vocear (LAm)

paid /peɪd/ see PAY. ● adj. put ~ to ⊞ acabar con

pail /peɪl/ n balde m, cubo m

pain /peɪn/ n dolor m. I have a ~ in my back me duele la espalda. ~ m. be in ~ tener dolores. be a ~ in the neck ⊞ ser un pesado; (thing) ser una lata. ● vt doler. ~ful adj doloroso. it's very ~ful duele mucho. ~killer n analgésico m. ~less adj indoloro. ~staking /ˈpeɪnzteɪkɪŋ/ adj concienzudo

paint /peɪnt/ n pintura f. ● vt/i pintar. ~er n pintor m. ~ing n (medium) pintura f; (picture) cuadro m

pair /peə(r)/ n par m; (of people) pareja f. a ~ of trousers unos pantalones. □ ~off, ~ up vi formar parejas

pajamas /pəˈdʒɑːməz/ npl (Amer) pijama m

Pakistan /pɑːkɪˈstɑːn/ n Pakistán m. ~i adj & n paquistaní (m & f)

pal /pæl/ n ⊞ amigo m

palace /'pælɪs/ n palacio m

palat|able /'pælətəbl/ adj agradable. ~e /'pælət/ n paladar m

pale /peɪl/ adj (-er, -est) pálido. go ~, turn ~ palidecer. ~ness n palidez f

Palestin|e /'pælɪstaɪn/ n Palestina f. ~ian /-'stɪnɪən/ adj & n palestino (m)

palette /'pælɪt/ n paleta f

palm /pɑːm/ n palma f. □ ~ off vt encajar (on a). P~ Sunday n Domingo m de Ramos

palpable /'pælpəbl/ adj palpable

palpitat|e /'pælpɪteɪt/ vi palpitar. ~ion /-'teɪʃn/ n palpitación f

pamper /'pæmpə(r)/ vt mimar

pamphlet /'pæmflɪt/ n folleto m

pan /pæn/ n cacerola f; (for frying) sartén f

panacea /pænəˈsɪə/ n panacea f

Panama /'pænəmɑː/ n Panamá m. ~nian /-'meɪnɪən/ adj & n panameño (m)

pancake /'pænkeɪk/ n crep(e) m, panqueque m (LAm)

panda /'pændə/ n panda m

pandemonium /pændɪˈməʊnɪəm/ n pandemonio m

pander /'pændə(r)/ vi. ~ to s.o. consentir los caprichos a uno

pane /peɪn/ n vidrio m, cristal m

panel /'pænl/ n panel m; (group of people) jurado m. ~ling n paneles mpl

pang /pæŋ/ n punzada f

panic /'pænɪk/ n pánico m. ● vi (pt panicked) dejarse llevar por el pánico. ~-stricken adj aterrorizado

panoram|a /pænəˈrɑːmə/ n panorama m. ~ic /-'ræmɪk/ adj panorámico

pansy /'pænzɪ/ n (flower) pensamiento m

pant /pænt/ vi jadear

panther /'pænθə(r)/ n pantera f

panties /'pæntɪz/ npl bragas fpl, calzones mpl (LAm), pantaletas fpl (Mex)

pantihose /'pæntɪhəʊz/ npl see PANTYHOSE

pantomime /'pæntəmaɪm/ n pantomima f

pantry /'pæntri/ n despensa f

pants /pænts/ npl (man's) calzoncillos mpl; (woman's) bragas fpl, calzones npl (LAm), pantaletas fpl (Mex); (Amer, trousers) pantalones mpl

pantyhose /'pæntihəuz/ npl (Amer) panty m, medias fpl, pantimedias fpl (Mex)

paper /'peɪpə(r)/ n papel m; (newspaper) diario m, periódico m; (exam) examen m; (document) documento m. ●vt empapelar, tapizar (Mex). **~back** n libro m en rústica. **~ clip** n sujetapapeles m, clip m. **~weight** n pisapapeles m. **~work** n papeleo m, trabajo m administrativo

parable /'pærəbl/ n parábola f

parachut|e /'pærəʃuːt/ n paracaídas m. ●vi saltar en paracaídas. **~ist** n paracaidista m & f

parade /pə'reɪd/ n desfile m; (Mil) formación f. ●vi desfilar. ●vt hacer alarde de

paradise /'pærədaɪs/ n paraíso m

paraffin /'pærəfɪn/ n queroseno m

paragraph /'pærəgrɑːf/ n párrafo m

Paraguay /'pærəgwaɪ/ n Paraguay m. **~an** adj & n paraguayo (m)

parallel /'pærəlel/ adj paralelo. ●n paralelo m; (line) paralela f

paraly|se /'pærəlaɪz/ vt paralizar. **~sis** /pə'ræləsɪs/ n (pl -ses /-siːz/) parálisis f

parameter /pə'ræmɪtə(r)/ n parámetro m

paranoia /pærə'nɔɪə/ n paranoia f

parapet /'pærəpɪt/ n parapeto m

paraphernalia /pærəfə'neɪlɪə/ n trastos mpl

parasite /'pærəsaɪt/ n parásito m

paratrooper /'pærətruːpə(r)/ n paracaidista m (del ejército)

parcel /'pɑːsl/ n paquete m

parch /pɑːtʃ/ vt resecar. be **~ed** 🄸 estar muerto de sed

parchment /'pɑːtʃmənt/ n pergamino m

pardon /'pɑːdn/ n perdón m; (Jurid) indulto m. I beg your **~** perdón. (I beg your) **~**? ¿cómo?, ¿mande? (Mex). ●vt perdonar; (Jurid) indultar. **~** me? (Amer) ¿cómo?

parent /'peərənt/ n (father) padre m; (mother) madre f. my **~s** mis padres. **~al** /pə'rentl/ adj de los padres

parenthesis /pə'renθəsɪs/ n (pl -theses /-siːz/) paréntesis m

parenthood /'peərənthʊd/ n el ser padre/madre

Paris /'pærɪs/ n París m

parish /'pærɪʃ/ n parroquia f; (municipal) distrito m. **~ioner** /pə'rɪʃənə(r)/ n feligrés m

park /pɑːk/ n parque m. **~-and-ride** estacionamiento m disuasorio (LAm), aparcamiento m disuasorio (Esp). ●vt/i aparcar, estacionar (LAm)

parking: /'pɑːkɪŋ/ n: **~ lot** n (Amer) aparcamiento m, estacionamiento m (LAm). **~ meter** n parquímetro m

parkway /'pɑːkweɪ/ n (Amer) carretera f ajardinada

parliament /'pɑːləmənt/ n parlamento m. **~ary** /-'mentri/ adj parlamentario

---

Parliament El Parlamento británico, el más alto organismo legislativo. Está formado por la Cámara de los Lores y la Cámara de los Comunes. La primera, consta de 703 miembros, en la mayoría nombrados, con un número de cargos hereditarios, lo que es objeto de reforma en la actualidad. La Cámara de los Comunes consta de 659 miembros elegidos por el pueblo. Ver ▷ DÁIL ÉIREANN, ▷ SCOTTISH PARLIAMENT, ▷ WELSH ASSEMBLY.

parlour /'pɑːlə(r)/ n salón m

parochial /pə'rəʊkɪəl/ adj (fig) provinciano

parody /'pærədɪ/ n parodia f. ● vt parodiar

parole /pə'rəʊl/ n libertad f condicional

parrot /'pærət/ n loro m, papagayo m

parsley /'pɑːslɪ/ n perejil m

parsnip /'pɑːsnɪp/ n pastinaca f

part /pɑːt/ n parte f; (of machine) pieza f; (of serial) episodio m; (in play) papel m; (Amer, in hair) raya f take ∼ in tomar parte en, participar en. for the most ∼ en su mayor parte. ● adv en parte. ● vt separar. ● vi separarse. □ ∼ with vt desprenderse de

partial /'pɑːʃl/ adj parcial. be ∼ to tener debilidad por. ∼ly adv parcialmente

participa|nt /pɑː'tɪsɪpənt/ n participante m & f. ∼te /-'peɪt/ vi participar. ∼tion /-'peɪʃn/ n participación f

particle /'pɑːtɪkl/ n partícula f

particular /pə'tɪkjʊlə(r)/ adj particular; (precise) meticuloso; (fastidious) quisquilloso. in ∼ en particular. ● n detalle m. ∼ly adv particularmente; (specifically) específicamente

parting /'pɑːtɪŋ/ n despedida f; (in hair) raya f. ● adj de despedida

partition /pɑː'tɪʃn/ n partición f; (wall) tabique m. ● vt dividir

partly /'pɑːtlɪ/ adv en parte

partner /'pɑːtnə(r)/ n socio m; (Sport) pareja f. ∼ship n asociación f; (Com) sociedad f

partridge /'pɑːtrɪdʒ/ n perdiz f

part-time /pɑːt'taɪm/ adj & adv a tiempo parcial, de medio tiempo (LAm)

party /'pɑːtɪ/ n reunión f, fiesta f; (group) grupo m; (Pol) partido m; (Jurid) parte f

pass /pɑːs/ vt (hand, convey) pasar; (go past) pasar por delante de; (overtake) adelantar, rebasar (Mex); (approve) aprobar (exam, bill, law); pronunciar (judgement). ● vi (pain) pasarse; (Sport) pasar la pelota. □ ∼ away vi fallecer. □ ∼ down vt transmitir. □ ∼ out vi desmayarse. □ ∼ round vt distribuir. □ ∼ up vt 🔢 dejar pasar. ● n (permit) pase m; (ticket) abono m; (in mountains) puerto m, desfiladero m; (Sport) pase m; (in exam) aprobado m. make a ∼ at 🔢 intentar besar. ∼able adj pasable; (road) transitable

passage /'pæsɪdʒ/ (voyage) travesía f; (corridor) pasillo m; (alleyway) pasaje m; (in book) pasaje m

passenger /'pæsɪndʒə(r)/ n pasajero m

passer-by /pɑːsə'baɪ/ n (pl passers-by) transeúnte m & f

passion /'pæʃn/ n pasión f. ∼ate /-ət/ adj apasionado. ∼ately adv apasionadamente

passive /'pæsɪv/ adj pasivo

Passover /'pɑːsəʊvə(r)/ n Pascua f de los hebreos

pass: ~**port** n pasaporte m.
~**word** n contraseña f

past /pɑːst/ adj anterior; (life) pasado; (week, year) último. in time ~ en tiempos pasados. ●n pasado m. in the ~ (formerly) antes, antiguamente. ●prep por delante de; (beyond) más allá de. it's twenty ~ four son las cuatro y veinte. ●adv. drive ~ pasar en coche. go ~ pasar

paste /peɪst/ n pasta f; (glue) engrudo m; (wallpaper ~) pegamento m; (jewellery) estrás m

pastel /ˈpæstl/ adj & n pastel (m)

pasteurize /ˈpɑːstʃəraɪz/ vt pasteurizar

pastime /ˈpɑːstaɪm/ n pasatiempo m

pastry /ˈpeɪstrɪ/ n masa f; (cake) pastelito m

pasture /ˈpɑːstʃə(r)/ n pasto(s) mpl

pasty /ˈpæstɪ/ n empanadilla f, empanada f (LAm)

pat /pæt/ vt (pt patted) darle palmaditas. ●n palmadita f; (of butter) porción f

patch /pætʃ/ n (on clothes) remiendo m, parche m; (over eye) parche m. a bad ~ una mala racha. ●vt remendar. □ ~ up vt hacerle un arreglo a

patent /ˈpeɪtnt/ adj patente. ●n patente f. ●vt patentar. ~ **leather** n charol m. ~**ly** adv. it's ~ly obvious that... está clarísimo que...

patern|al /pəˈtɜːnl/ adj paterno. ~**ity** /-ətɪ/ n paternidad f

path /pɑːθ/ n (pl ~s /-s/pɑːðz/) sendero m; (Sport) pista f; (of rocket) trayectoria f; (fig) camino m

pathetic /pəˈθetɪk/ adj (pitiful) patético; (excuse) pobre. don't be so

~ no seas tan pusilánime

patien|ce /ˈpeɪʃns/ n paciencia f. ~**t** adj & n paciente (m & f). be ~**t** with s.o. tener paciencia con uno. ~**tly** adv pacientemente

patio /ˈpætɪəʊ/ n (pl -os) patio m

patriot /ˈpætrɪət/ n patriota m & f. ~**ic** /-ˈɒtɪk/ adj patriótico. ~**ism** n patriotismo m

patrol /pəˈtrəʊl/ n patrulla f. ●vt/i patrullar

patron /ˈpeɪtrən/ n (of the arts) mecenas m & f; (of charity) patrocinador m; (customer) cliente m & f. ~**age** /ˈpætrənɪdʒ/ n (sponsorship) patrocinio m; (of the arts) mecenazgo m. ~**ize** /ˈpætrənaɪz/ vt ser cliente de; (fig) tratar con condescendencia. ~**izing** adj condescendiente

pattern /ˈpætn/ n diseño m; (sample) muestra f; (in dressmaking) patrón m

paunch /pɔːntʃ/ n panza f

pause /pɔːz/ n pausa f. ●vi hacer una pausa

pave /peɪv/ vt pavimentar; (with flagstones) enlosar. ~**ment** n pavimento m; (at side of road) acera f, banqueta f (Mex)

paving stone /ˈpeɪvɪŋstəʊn/ n losa f

paw /pɔː/ n pata f

pawn /pɔːn/ n (Chess) peón m; (fig) títere m. ●vt empeñar. ~**broker** n prestamista m & f

pay /peɪ/ vt (pt paid) pagar; prestar (attention); hacer (compliment, visit). ~ cash pagar al contado. ●vi (be profitable) rendir. ●n paga f. in the ~ of al servicio de. □ ~ **back** vt devolver; pagar (loan). □ ~ **in** vt ingresar, depositar (LAm). □ ~ **off** vt cancelar, saldar (debt). vi

valer la pena. □ ~ **up** vi pagar.
~**able** adj pagadero. ~**ment** n
pago m. ~**roll** n nómina f.

pea /piː/ n guisante m, arveja f
(LAm), chícharo m (Mex)

peace /piːs/ n paz f. ~ **of mind**
tranquilidad f. ~**ful** adj tranquilo.
~**maker** n conciliador m

peach /piːtʃ/ n melocotón m, durazno m (LAm)

peacock /ˈpiːkɒk/ n pavo m real

peak /piːk/ n cumbre f; (of career)
apogeo m; (maximum) máximo m.
~ **hours** npl horas fpl de mayor demanda (o consumo etc)

peal /piːl/ n repique m. ~**s of
laughter** risotadas fpl

peanut /ˈpiːnʌt/ n cacahuete m,
maní m (LAm), cacahuate m (Mex)

pear /peə(r)/ n pera f. ~ **(tree)**
peral m

pearl /pɜːl/ n perla f

peasant /ˈpeznt/ n campesino m

peat /piːt/ n turba f

pebble /ˈpebl/ n guijarro m

peck /pek/ vt picotear. ● n picotazo
m; (kiss) besito m

peculiar /prˈkjuːlɪə(r)/ adj raro;
(special) especial. ~**ity** /-ˈærətɪ/ n
rareza f; (feature) particularidad f

pedal /ˈpedl/ n pedal m. ● vi pedalear

pedantic /prˈdæntɪk/ adj pedante

peddle /ˈpedl/ vt vender por las
calles

pedestal /ˈpedɪstl/ n pedestal m

pedestrian /prˈdestrɪən/ n peatón m. ~ **crossing** paso m de peatones. ● adj pedestre; (dull) prosaico

pedigree /ˈpedɪɡriː/ n linaje m; (of
animal) pedigrí m. ● adj (animal) de
raza

peek /piːk/ vi mirar a hurtadillas

peel /piːl/ n piel f, cáscara f. ● vt
pelar (fruit, vegetables). ● vi pelarse

peep /piːp/ vi. ~ **at** echarle un vistazo a. ● n (look) vistazo m; (bird
sound) pío m

peer /pɪə(r)/ vi mirar. ~ **at** escudriñar. ● n (equal) par m & f; (contemporary) coetáneo m; (lord) par
m. ~**age** /-ɪdʒ/ n nobleza f

peg /peɡ/ n (in ground) estaca f;
(on violin) clavija f; (for washing)
pinza f; (hook) gancho m; (for tent)
estaquilla f. **off the** ~ de confección. ● vt (pt pegged) sujetar (con
estacas, etc); fijar (precios)

pejorative /prˈdʒɒrətɪv/ adj peyorativo, despectivo

pelican /ˈpelɪkən/ n pelícano m

pellet /ˈpelɪt/ n bolita f; (for gun)
perdigón m

pelt /pelt/ n pellejo m. ● vt. ~ **s.o.
with sth** lanzarle algo a uno. ● vi.
~ **with rain**, ~ **down** llover a
cántaros

pelvis /ˈpelvɪs/ n pelvis f

pen /pen/ (for writing) pluma f;
(ballpoint) bolígrafo m; (sheep ~)
redil m; (cattle ~) corral m

penal /ˈpiːnl/ adj penal. ~**ize** vt
sancionar. ~**ty** /ˈpenltɪ/ n pena f;
(fine) multa f; (in soccer) penalty
m; (in US football) castigo m. ~**ty
kick** n (in soccer) penalty m

penance /ˈpenəns/ n penitencia f

pence /pens/ see PENNY

pencil /ˈpensl/ n lápiz m. ● vt (pt
pencilled) escribir con lápiz.
~**-sharpener** n sacapuntas m

pendulum /ˈpendjʊləm/ n péndulo m

penetrat|e /ˈpenɪtreɪt/ vt/i penetrar. ~**ing** adj penetrante. ~**ion**

penguin | period

/-'treɪʃn/ n penetración f

penguin /'peŋgwɪn/ n pingüino m

penicillin /penɪ'sɪlɪn/ n penicilina f

peninsula /pə'nɪnsjʊlə/ n península f

penis /'piːnɪs/ n pene m

pen: ~**knife** /'pennaɪf/ n (pl pen-knives) navaja f. ~**name** n seudónimo m

penniless /'penɪlɪs/ adj sin un céntimo. ~**y** /'penɪ/ n (pl pennies or pence) penique m

pension /'penʃn/ n pensión f; (for retirement) pensión f de jubilación. ~**er** n jubilado m

pensive /'pensɪv/ adj pensativo

Pentecost /'pentɪkɒst/ n Pentecostés m

penthouse /'penthaʊs/ n penthouse m

pent-up /'pent'ʌp/ adj reprimido; (confined) encerrado

penultimate /pen'ʌltɪmət/ adj penúltimo

people /'piːpl/ npl gente f; (citizens) pueblo m. ~ say (that) se dice que, dicen que. English ~ (nation) el pueblo. • vt poblar

pepper /'pepə(r)/ n pimienta f; (vegetable) pimiento m. • vt (intersperse) salpicar (with de). ~**box** n (Amer) pimentero m. ~**corn** n grano m de pimienta. ten miles ~**mint** n (Bot) menta f; (sweet) caramelo m de menta. ~**pot** n pimentero m

per /pɜː(r)/ prep por. ~ annum al año. ~ cent see **PERCENT**. ~ head por cabeza, por persona. ten miles ~ hour diez millas por hora

perceive /pə'siːv/ vt percibir; (notice) darse cuenta de

percent, per cent /pə'sent/ n

(no pl) porcentaje m. • adv por ciento. ~**age** /-ɪdʒ/ n porcentaje m

perceptible /pə'septəbl/ adj perceptible. ~**on** /-ʃn/ n percepción f. ~**ve** /-tɪv/ adj perspicaz

perch /pɜːtʃ/ n (of bird) percha f; (fish) perca f. • vi (bird) posarse. ~ on (person) sentarse en el borde de

percolate /'pɜːkəleɪt/ vi filtrarse. ~**or** n cafetera f eléctrica

percussion /pə'kʌʃn/ n percusión f

perfect /'pɜːfɪkt/ adj perfecto; (place, day) ideal. • /pə'fekt/ vt perfeccionar. ~**ion** /pə'fekʃn/ n perfección f. to ~**ion** a la perfección. ~**ly** /'pɜːfɪktlɪ/ adv perfectamente

perform /pə'fɔːm/ vt desempeñar (function, role); ejecutar (task); realizar (experiment); representar (play); (Mus) interpretar. ~ an operation (Med) operar. • vi (actor) actuar; (musician) tocar; (produce results) (vehicle) responder; (company) rendir. ~**ance** /-əns/ n ejecución f; (of play) representación f; (of actor, musician) interpretación f; (of team) actuación f; (of car) rendimiento m. ~**er** n (actor) actor m; (entertainer) artista m & f

perfume /'pɜːfjuːm/ n perfume m

perhaps /pə'hæps/ adv quizá(s), tal vez, a lo mejor

peril /'perəl/ n peligro m. ~**ous** adj arriesgado, peligroso

perimeter /pə'rɪmɪtə(r)/ n perímetro m

period /'pɪərɪəd/ n período m; (in history) época f; (lesson) clase f; (Amer, Gram) punto m; (menstruation) período m, regla f. • adj de (la) época. ~**ic** /-'ɒdɪk/ adj periódico. ~**ical** /pɪərɪ'ɒdɪkl/ n revista f.

~ically adv periódico

peripher|al /pəˈrɪfərəl/ adj secundario; (Comp) periférico. ~y n periferia f

perish /ˈperɪʃ/ vi perecer; (rot) deteriorarse. ~able adj perecedero. ~ing adj 🄸 glacial

perjur|e /ˈpɜːdʒə(r)/ vr. ~e o.s. perjurarse. ~y n perjurio m

perk /pɜːk/ n gaje m. □ ~ up vt reanimar. vi reanimarse

perm /pɜːm/ n permanente f. ● vt. have one's hair ~ed hacerse la permanente

permanen|ce /ˈpɜːmənəns/ n permanencia f. ~t adj permanente. ~tly adv permanentemente

permissible /pəˈmɪsəbl/ adj permisible

permission /pəˈmɪʃn/ n permiso m

permit /pəˈmɪt/ vt (pt permitted) permitir. ● /ˈpɜːmɪt/ n permiso m

peroxide /pəˈrɒksaɪd/ n peróxido m

perpendicular /pɜːpənˈdɪkjʊlə(r)/ adj & n perpendicular (f)

perpetrat|e /ˈpɜːpɪtreɪt/ vt cometer. ~or n autor m

perpetua|l /pəˈpetʃʊəl/ adj perpetuo. ~te /pəˈpetʃʊeɪt/ vt perpetuar

perplex /pəˈpleks/ vt dejar perplejo. ~ed adj perplejo

persecut|e /ˈpɜːsɪkjuːt/ vt perseguir. ~ion /-ˈkjuːʃn/ n persecución f

persever|ance /pɜːsɪˈvɪərəns/ n perseverancia f. ~e /pɜːsɪˈvɪə(r)/ vi perseverar, persistir

Persian /ˈpɜːʃn/ adj persa. the ~ Gulf n el golfo Pérsico

persist /pəˈsɪst/ vi persistir.

~ence /-əns/ n persistencia f.
~ent adj persistente; (continual) continuo

person /ˈpɜːsn/ n persona f. in ~ en persona. ~al adj personal; (call) particular; (property) privado. ~al assistant n secretario m personal. ~ality /-ˈnælətɪ/ n personalidad f. ~ally adv personalmente. ~nel /pɜːsəˈnel/ n personal m. P~ (department) sección f de personal

perspective /pəˈspektɪv/ n perspectiva f

perspir|ation /pɜːspəˈreɪʃn/ n transpiración f. ~e /pəsˈpaɪə(r)/ vi transpirar

persua|de /pəˈsweɪd/ vt convencer, persuadir. ~e s.o. to do sth convencer a uno para que haga algo. ~sion n /-ʃn/ persuasión f. ~sive /-sɪv/ adj persuasivo

pertinent /ˈpɜːtɪnənt/ adj pertinente. ~ly adv pertinentemente

perturb /pəˈtɜːb/ vt perturbar

Peru /pəˈruː/ n el Perú m

peruse /pəˈruːz/ vt leer cuidadosamente

Peruvian /pəˈruːvɪən/ adj & n peruano (m)

perver|se /pəˈvɜːs/ adj retorcido; (stubborn) obstinado. ~sion n perversión f. ~t /pəˈvɜːt/ vt pervertir. ● /ˈpɜːvɜːt/ n pervertido m

pessimis|m /ˈpesɪmɪzəm/ n pesimismo m. ~t n pesimista m & f. ~tic /-ˈmɪstɪk/ adj pesimista

pest /pest/ n plaga f; (🄸, person, thing) peste f

pester /ˈpestə(r)/ vt importunar

pesticide /ˈpestɪsaɪd/ n pesticida f

pet /pet/ n animal m doméstico; (favourite) favorito m. ● adj preferido. my ~ hate lo que más odio. ● vt (pt petted) acariciar

petal /ˈpetl/ n pétalo m

petition /pɪˈtɪʃn/ n petición f

pet name n apodo m

petrified /ˈpetrɪfaɪd/ adj (terrified) muerto de miedo; (rock) petrificado

petrol /ˈpetrəl/ n gasolina f. ~ **pump** n surtidor m. ~ **station** n gasolinera f. ~ **tank** n depósito m de gasolina ~**eum** /pɪˈtrəʊlɪəm/ n petróleo m.

petticoat /ˈpetɪkəʊt/ n enagua f; (slip) combinación f

petty /ˈpeti/ adj (-ier, -iest) insignificante; (mean) mezquino. ~**y cash** n dinero m para gastos menores

petulant /ˈpetjʊlənt/ adj irritable

pew /pjuː/ n banco m (de iglesia)

phantom /ˈfæntəm/ n fantasma m

pharma|ceutical /ˌfɑːmə-ˈsjuːtɪkl/ adj farmacéutico. ~**cist** /ˈfɑːməsɪst/ n farmacéutico m. ~**cy** /ˈfɑːməsi/ n farmacia f

phase /feɪz/ n etapa f. □ ~ **out** vt retirar progresivamente

PhD abbr (= Doctor of Philosophy) n doctorado m; (person) Dr., Dra.

pheasant /ˈfeznt/ n faisán m

phenomen|al /fɪˈnɒmɪnl/ adj fenomenal. ~**on** /-mən/ n (pl -ena /-inə/) fenómeno m

philistine /ˈfɪlɪstaɪn/ adj & n filisteo (m)

philosoph|er /fɪˈlɒsəfə(r)/ n filósofo m. ~**ical** /-əˈsɒfɪkl/ adj filosófico. ~**y** /fɪˈlɒsəfi/ n filosofía f

phlegm /flem/ n flema f. ~**atic** /fleɡˈmætɪk/ adj flemático

phobia /ˈfəʊbɪə/ n fobia f

phone /fəʊn/ n 🕮 teléfono m. ●vt/i llamar (por teléfono). ~ **back** (call again) volver a llamar; (return

call) llamar (más tarde). ~ **book** n guía f telefónica, directorio m (LAm). ~ **booth**, ~ **box** n cabina f telefónica. ~ **call** n llamada f (telefónica). ~ **card** n tarjeta f telefónica. ~ **number** n número m de teléfono

phonetic /fəˈnetɪk/ adj fonético. ~**s** n fonética f

phoney /ˈfəʊni/ adj (-ier, -iest) 🕮 falso

phosph|ate /ˈfɒsfeɪt/ n fosfato m. ~**orus** /ˈfɒsfərəs/ n fósforo m

photo /ˈfəʊtəʊ/ n (pl -os) 🕮 foto f. take a ~ sacar una foto. ~**copier** /-kɒpɪə(r)/ n fotocopiadora f. ~**copy** n fotocopia f. ●vt fotocopiar. ~**genic** /-ˈdʒenɪk/ adj fotogénico. ~**graph** /-ɡrɑːf/ n fotografía f. ●vt fotografiar, sacarle una foto a. ~**grapher** /fəˈtɒɡrəfə(r)/ n fotógrafo m. ~**graphic** /-ˈɡræfɪk/ adj fotográfico. ~**graphy** /fəˈtɒɡrəfi/ n fotografía f

phrase /freɪz/ n frase f. ●vt expresar. ~ **book** n manual m de conversación

physi|cal /ˈfɪzɪkl/ adj físico. ~**cian** /fɪˈzɪʃn/ n médico m. ~**cist** /ˈfɪzɪsɪst/ n físico m. ~**cs** /ˈfɪzɪks/ n física f. ~**ology** /fɪzɪˈɒlədʒɪ/ n fisiología f. ~**otherapist** /fɪzɪəʊˈθerəpɪst/ n fisioterapeuta m & f. ~**otherapy** /fɪzɪəʊˈθerəpɪ/ n fisioterapia f. ~**que** /fɪˈziːk/ n físico m

pian|ist /ˈpɪənɪst/ n pianista m & f. ~**o** /pɪˈænəʊ/ n (pl -os) piano m

pick /pɪk/ (tool) pico m. ●vt escoger; cortar (flowers); recoger (fruit, cotton); abrir con una ganzúa (lock). ~ a quarrel buscar camorra. ~ **holes** in criticar. □ ~ **on** vt meterse con. □ ~ **out** vt escoger; (identify) reconocer. □ ~ **up** vt recoger; (*lift*) levantar; (*learn*) aprender; adquirir (habit, etc); contagiarse de (illness). • vi mejorar; (sales) subir. ~**axe** n pico m

picket /'pɪkɪt/ n (group) piquete m. ~ **line** n piquete m. • vt formar un piquete frente a

pickle /'pɪkl/ n (in vinegar) encurtido m; (Amer, gherkin) pepinillo m; (relish) salsa f (a base de encurtidos). • vt encurtir

pick: ~**pocket** n carterista m & f. ~**-up** n (truck) camioneta f

picnic /'pɪknɪk/ n picnic m

picture /'pɪktʃə(r)/ n (painting) cuadro m; (photo) foto f; (drawing) dibujo m; (illustration) ilustración f; (film) película f; (fig) descripción f. • vt imaginarse. □~**sque** /-'resk/ adj pintoresco

pie /paɪ/ n empanada f; (sweet) pastel m, tarta f

piece /piːs/ n pedazo m, trozo m; (part of machine) pieza f; (coin) moneda f; (in chess) figura f. a ~ of advice un consejo. a ~ of furniture un mueble. a ~ of news una noticia. take to ~s desmontar. □~ **together** vt juntar. ~**meal** adj gradual; (unsystematic) poco sistemático. • adv poco a poco

pier /pɪə(r)/ n muelle m; (with amusements) paseo con atracciones sobre un muelle

pierc|e /pɪəs/ vt perforar. ~**ing** adj penetrante

piety /'paɪətɪ/ n piedad f

pig /pɪg/ n cerdo m, chancho m (LAm)

pigeon /'pɪdʒɪn/ n paloma f; (Culin) pichón m. ~**-hole** n casillero m; (fig) casilla f

piggy /'pɪgɪ/ n cerdito m. ~**back**

n. give s.o. a ~**back** llevar a uno a cuestas. ~ **bank** n hucha f

pig-headed /-'hedɪd/ adj terco

pigment /'pɪgmənt/ n pigmento m

pig|sty /'pɪgstaɪ/ n pocilga f. ~**tail** n (plait) trenza f; (bunch) coleta f

pike /paɪk/ n invar (fish) lucio m

pilchard /'pɪltʃəd/ n sardina f

pile /paɪl/ n (heap) montón m; (of fabric) pelo m. • vt amontonar. ~ **it on** exagerar. • vi amontonarse. □ ~ **up** vt amontonar. • vi amontonarse. ~**s** /paɪlz/ npl (Med) almorranas fpl. ~**-up** n choque m múltiple

pilgrim /'pɪlgrɪm/ n peregrino. ~**age** /-ɪdʒ/ n peregrinación f

pill /pɪl/ n pastilla f

pillar /'pɪlə(r)/ n columna f. ~ **box** n buzón m

pillow /'pɪləʊ/ n almohada f. ~**case** n funda f de almohada

pilot /'paɪlət/ n piloto m. • vt pilotar. ~ **light** n fuego m piloto

pimple /'pɪmpl/ n grano m, espinilla f (LAm)

pin /pɪn/ n alfiler m; (Mec) perno m. ~**s and needles** hormigueo m. • vt (pt pinned) prender con alfileres; (fix) sujetar

PIN /pɪn/ n (= **personal identification number**) NIP m

pinafore /'pɪnəfɔː(r)/ n delantal m. ~ **dress** n pichi m, jumper m & f (LAm)

pincers /'pɪnsəz/ npl tenazas fpl

pinch /pɪntʃ/ vt pellizcar; (fam, steal) hurtar. • vi (shoe) apretar. • n pellizco m; (small amount) pizca f. at a ~ si fuera necesario

pine /paɪn/ n pino m. • vi. ~ **for** sth suspirar por algo. □ ~ **away** vi

languidecer de añoranza. ~apple
/'paɪnæpl/ n piña f

ping-pong /'pɪŋpɒŋ/ n ping-
pong m

pink /pɪŋk/ adj & n rosa (m), rosado
(m)

pinnacle /'pɪnəkl/ n pináculo m

pin: ~**point** vt determinar con
precisión f. ~**stripe** n raya f fina

pint /paɪnt/ n pinta f (= 0.57 litros)

pioneer /paɪə'nɪə(r)/ n pionero m

pious /'paɪəs/ adj piadoso

pip /pɪp/ n (seed) pepita f; (time
signal) señal f

pipe /paɪp/ n tubo m; (Mus) carami-
llo m; (for smoking) pipa f. ● vt lle-
var por tuberías. ~**dream** n ilu-
sión f. ~**line** n conducto m; (for
oil) oleoducto m. in the ~line en
preparación f

piping /'paɪpɪŋ/ n tubería f. ● adv.
~ hot muy caliente, hirviendo

pira|cy /'paɪərəsɪ/ n piratería f.
~**te** /'paɪərət/ n pirata m

Pisces /'paɪsiːz/ n Piscis m

piss /pɪs/ vi 🆇 mear. ~ **off** vi 🆇.
~ off! ¡vete a la mierda! ~**ed**
/pɪst/ adj (🆇, drunk) como una
cuba; (Amer, fed up) cabreado

pistol /'pɪstl/ n pistola f

piston /'pɪstən/ n pistón m

pit /pɪt/ n hoyo m; (mine) mina f;
(Amer, in fruit) hueso m

pitch /pɪtʃ/ n (substance) brea f;
(degree) grado m; (Mus) tono m;
(Sport) campo m. ● vt (throw) lanzar;
armar (tent). ● vi (ship) cabecear.
~-**black** /-'blæk/ adj oscuro como
boca de lobo. ~**er** n jarra f

pitfall /'pɪtfɔːl/ n trampa f

pith /pɪθ/ n (of orange, lemon) mé-
dula f; (fig) meollo m

pitiful /'pɪtɪfl/ adj lastimoso

pittance /'pɪtns/ n miseria f

pity /'pɪtɪ/ n lástima f, pena f;
(compassion) piedad f. it's a ~ you
can't come es una lástima que no
puedas venir. ● vt tenerle lástima a

pivot /'pɪvət/ n pivote m. ● vi pivo-
tar; (fig) depender (on de)

placard /'plækɑːd/ n pancarta f;
(sign) letrero m

placate /plə'keɪt/ vt apaciguar

place /pleɪs/ n lugar m; (seat)
asiento m; (in firm, team) puesto m;
(fam, house) casa f. feel out of ~
sentirse fuera de lugar. take ~
tener lugar. ● vt poner, colocar;
(identify) identificar. be ~d (in
race) colocarse. ~-**mat** n mantel m
individual

placid /'plæsɪd/ adj plácido

plague /pleɪg/ n peste f; (fig)
plaga f. ● vt atormentar

plaice /pleɪs/ n invar platija f

plain /pleɪn/ adj (-er, -est) (clear)
claro; (simple) sencillo; (candid)
franco; (ugly) feo. in ~ clothes de
civil. ● adv totalmente. ● n llanura f.
~**ly** adv claramente; (frankly) fran-
camente; (simply) con sencillez

plaintiff /'pleɪntɪf/ n demandante
m & f

plait /plæt/ vt trenzar. ● n trenza f

plan /plæn/ n plan m; (map) plano
m; (of book, essay) esquema f. ● vt
(pt planned) planear; planificar
(strategies). I'm ~ning to go to
Greece pienso ir a Grecia

plane /pleɪn/ n (tree) plátano m;
(level) nivel m; (aircraft) avión m;
(tool) cepillo m. ● vt cepillar

planet /'plænɪt/ n planeta m.
~**ary** adj planetario

plank /plæŋk/ n tabla f

planning /'plænɪŋ/ n planifica-
ción f. family ~ planificación fami-

liar. town ~ urbanismo *m*

plant /plɑːnt/ *n* planta *f*; (*Mec*) maquinaria *f*; (*factory*) fábrica *f*. ● *vt* plantar; (*place in position*) colocar. ~**ation** /plæn'teɪʃn/ *n* plantación *f*

plaque /plæk/ *n* placa *f*

plasma /'plæzmə/ *n* plasma *m*

plaster /'plɑːstə(r)/ *n* yeso *m*; (*on walls*) revoque *m*; (*sticking plaster*) tirita *f* (®), curita *f* (®) (*LAm*); (*for setting bones*) yeso *m*, escayola *f*. ● *vt* revocar; rellenar con yeso (*cracks*)

plastic /'plæstɪk/ *adj & n* plástico (*m*)

Plasticine /'plæstisiːn/ *n* (®) plastilina *f* (®)

plastic surgery /plæstɪk 'sɜːdʒərɪ/ *n* cirugía *f* estética

plate /pleɪt/ *n* plato *m*; (*of metal*) chapa *f*; (*silverware*) vajilla *f* de plata; (*in book*) lámina *f*. ● *vt* recubrir (with de)

platform /'plætfɔːm/ *n* plataforma *f*; (*Rail*) andén *m*

platinum /'plætɪnəm/ *n* platino *m*

platitude /'plætɪtjuːd/ *n* lugar *m* común

platonic /plə'tɒnɪk/ *adj* platónico

plausible /'plɔːzəbl/ *adj* verosímil; (*person*) convincente

play /pleɪ/ *vt* jugar a (*game, cards*); jugar a, jugar (*LAm*) (*football, chess*); tocar (*instrument*); (*act role*) representar el papel de. ● *vi* jugar. ● *n* juego *m*; (*drama*) obra *f* de teatro. □ ~ **down** *vt* minimizar. □ ~ **up** *vi* 🅸 (*child*) dar guerra; (*car, TV*) no funcionar bien. ~**er** *n* jugador *m*; (*Mus*) músico *m*. ~**ful** *adj* juguetón. ~**ground** *n* parque *m* de juegos infantiles; (*in school*) patio *m* de recreo. ~**group** *n* jardín *m* de la infancia. ~**ing**

card *n* naipe *m*. ~**ing field** *n* campo *m* de deportes. ~**pen** *n* corralito *m*. ~**wright** /-raɪt/ *n* dramaturgo *m*

plc *abbr* (= public limited company) S.A.

plea /pliː/ *n* súplica *f*; (*excuse*) excusa *f*; (*Jurid*) defensa *f*

plead /pliːd/ *vt* (*Jurid*) alegar; (*as excuse*) pretextar. ● *vi* suplicar. ~ **with** suplicarle a. ~ **guilty** declararse culpable

pleasant /'pleznt/ *adj* agradable

pleas|e /pliːz/ *int* por favor. ● *vt* complacer; (*satisfy*) contentar. ● *vi* agradar; (*wish*) querer. ~**ed** *adj* (*satisfied*) satisfecho; (*happy*) contento. ~**ed with** satisfecho de. ~**ing** *adj* agradable; (*news*) grato. ~**ure** /'pleʒə(r)/ *n* placer *m*

pleat /pliːt/ *n* pliegue *m*

pledge /pledʒ/ *n* cantidad *f* prometida

plent|iful /'plentɪfl/ *adj* abundante. ~**y** /'plentɪ/ *n* abundancia *f*. ● *pron.* ~**y of** muchos, -chas; (*of sth uncountable*) mucho, -cha

pliable /'plaɪəbl/ *adj* flexible

pliers /'plaɪəz/ *npl* alicates *mpl*

plight /plaɪt/ *n* situación *f* difícil

plimsolls /'plɪmsɒlz/ *npl* zapatillas *fpl* de lona

plod /plɒd/ *vi* (*pt* plodded) caminar con paso pesado

plot /plɒt/ *n* complot *m*; (*of novel etc*) argumento *m*; (*piece of land*) parcela *f*. ● *vt* (*pt* plotted) tramar; (*mark out*) trazar. ● *vi* conspirar

plough /plaʊ/ *n* arado *m*. ● *vt/i* arar. □ ~ **into** *vt* estrellarse contra. □ ~ **through** *vt* avanzar laboriosamente por

ploy /plɔɪ/ *n* treta *f*

pluck /plʌk/ *vt* arrancar; depilarse

(eyebrows); desplumar (bird). ~ up courage to armarse de valor para. ●n valor m. ~y adj (-ier, -iest) valiente

plug /plʌg/ n (in bath) tapón m; (Elec) enchufe m; (spark ~) bujía f ●vt (pt plugged) tapar; (fam, advertise) hacerle propaganda a. □~ in vt (Elec) enchufar. ~hole n desagüe m

plum /plʌm/ n ciruela f

plumage /ˈpluːmɪdʒ/ n plumaje m

plumb|er /ˈplʌmə(r)/ n fontanero m, plomero m (LAm). ~ing n instalación f sanitaria, instalación f de cañerías

plume /pluːm/ n pluma f

plump /plʌmp/ adj (-er, -est) rechoncho

plunge /plʌndʒ/ vt hundir (knife); (in water) sumergir; (into state, condition) sumir. ●vi zambullirse; (fall) caer. ●n zambullida f

plural /ˈplʊərəl/ n plural m. ●adj en plural

plus /plʌs/ prep más. ●adj positivo. ●n signo m de más. (fig) ventaja f

plush /plʌʃ/ adj lujoso

Pluto /ˈpluːtəʊ/ n Plutón m

plutonium /pluːˈtəʊnɪəm/ n plutonio m

ply /plaɪ/ vt manejar (tool); ejercer (trade). ~ s.o. with drink dar continuamente de beber a uno. ~wood n contrachapado m

p.m. abbr (= post meridiem) de la tarde

pneumatic drill /njuːˈmætɪk/ adj martillo m neumático

pneumonia /njuːˈməʊnjə/ n pulmonía f

poach /pəʊtʃ/ vt escalfar (egg); cocer (fish etc); (steal) cazar furtivamente. ~er n cazador m furtivo

PO box /piːˈəʊ/ n Apdo. postal

pocket /ˈpɒkɪt/ n bolsillo m; (of air, resistance) bolsa f. ●vt poner en el bolsillo. ~book n (notebook) libro m de bolsillo; (Amer, wallet) cartera f; (Amer, handbag) bolso m, cartera f (LAm), bolsa f (Mex). ~money n dinero m de bolsillo, mesada f (LAm)

pod /pɒd/ n vaina f

poem /ˈpəʊɪm/ n poema m

poet /ˈpəʊɪt/ n poeta m. ~ic /-ˈetɪk/ adj poético. ~ry /ˈpəʊɪtrɪ/ n poesía f

poignant /ˈpɔɪnjənt/ adj conmovedor

point /pɔɪnt/ n (dot, on scale) punto m; (sharp end) punta f; (in time) momento m; (statement) observación f; (on agenda, in discussion) punto m; (Elec) toma f de corriente. to the ~ pertinente. up to a ~ hasta cierto punto. be on the ~ of estar a punto de. get to the ~ ir al grano. there's no ~ (in) arguing no sirve de nada discutir. ●vt (aim) apuntar; (show) indicar. ●vi señalar. ~ at/to sth señalar algo. □~ out vt señalar. ~blank adj & adv a quemarropa. ~ed adj (chin, nose) puntiagudo; (fig) mordaz. ~less adj inútil

poise /pɔɪz/ n porte m; (composure) desenvoltura f

poison /ˈpɔɪzn/ n veneno m. ●vt envenenar. ~ous adj venenoso; (chemical etc) tóxico

poke /pəʊk/ vt empujar; atizar (fire). ●vi hurgar; (pry) meterse. ●n golpe m. □~ about vi fisgonear. ~r /ˈpəʊkə(r)/ n atizador m; (Cards) póquer m

poky /ˈpəʊkɪ/ adj (-ier, -iest) diminuto

Poland /ˈpəʊlənd/ n Polonia f
polar /ˈpəʊlə(r)/ adj polar. ~ **bear** n oso m blanco
pole /pəʊl/ n palo m; (fixed) poste m; (for flag) mástil m; (in geography) polo m
police /pəˈliːs/ n policía f. ~**man** /-mən/ n policía m, agente m. ~ **station** n comisaría f. ~**woman** n policía f, agente f
policy /ˈpɒlɪsɪ/ n política f; (insurance) póliza f (de seguros)
polish /ˈpɒlɪʃ/ n (for shoes) betún m; (furniture ~) cera f para muebles; (floor ~) abrillantador m de suelos; (shine) brillo m; (fig) finura f. ● vt darle brillo a; limpiar (shoes); (refine) pulir. ◻ ~ **off** vt despachar. ~**ed** adj pulido
Polish /ˈpəʊlɪʃ/ adj & n polaco (m)
polite /pəˈlaɪt/ adj cortés. ~**ly** adv cortésmente. ~**ness** n cortesía f
politic|al /pəˈlɪtɪkl/ adj político. ~**ian** /pɒlɪˈtɪʃn/ n político m. ~**s** /ˈpɒlɪtɪks/ n política f
poll /pəʊl/ n elección f; (survey) encuesta f. ● vt obtener (votes)
pollack /ˈpɒlæk/ n abadejo m
pollen /ˈpɒlən/ n polen m
polling booth n cabina f de votar
pollut|e /pəˈluːt/ vt contaminar. ~**ion** /-ʃn/ n contaminación f
polo /ˈpəʊləʊ/ n polo m. ~ **neck** n cuello m vuelto
poly|styrene /pɒlɪˈstaɪriːn/ n poliestireno m. ~**thene** /ˈpɒlɪθiːn/ n plástico, polietileno m
pomp /pɒmp/ n pompa f. ~**ous** adj pomposa
pond /pɒnd/ n (natural) laguna f; (artificial) estanque m
ponder /ˈpɒndə(r)/ vt considerar. ~**ous** adj pesado

pony /ˈpəʊnɪ/ n poni m. ~-**tail** n cola f de caballo
poodle /ˈpuːdl/ n caniche m
pool /puːl/ n charca f; (artificial) estanque m; (puddle) charco m, (common fund) fondos mpl comunes; (snooker) billar m americano. (swimming) ~ n piscina f, alberca f (Mex). ~**s** npl quinielas fpl. ● vt aunar
poor /pʊə(r)/ adj (-er, -est) pobre; (quality, diet) malo. be in ~ health estar mal de salud. ~**ly** adj 🄴 malito. ● adv mal
pop /pɒp/ n (Mus) música f pop; (Amer fam, father) papá m. ● vt (pt popped) hacer reventar; (put) poner. ◻ ~ **in** vi (visit) pasar por. ◻ ~ **out** vi saltar; (person) salir un rato. ◻ ~ **up** vi surgir, aparecer
popcorn /ˈpɒpkɔːn/ n palomitas fpl
pope /pəʊp/ n papa m
poplar /ˈpɒplə(r)/ n álamo m (blanco)
poppy /ˈpɒpɪ/ n amapola f
popular /ˈpɒpjʊlə(r)/ adj popular. ~**ity** /-ˈlærətɪ/ n popularidad f. ~**ize** vt popularizar
populat|e /ˈpɒpjʊleɪt/ vt poblar. ~**ion** /-ˈleɪʃn/ n población f
pop-up /ˈpɒpʌp/ n ventana f emergente, pop-up m
porcelain /ˈpɔːsəlɪn/ n porcelana f
porch /pɔːtʃ/ n porche m
porcupine /ˈpɔːkjʊpaɪn/ n puerco m espín
pore /pɔː(r)/ n poro m
pork /pɔːk/ n carne f de cerdo m, carne f de puerco m (Mex)
porn /pɔːn/ n 🄴 pornografía f. ~**ographic** /-əˈɡræfɪk/ adj pornográfico. ~**ography** /pɔːˈnɒɡrəfɪ/ n pornografía f

porpoise /'pɔːpəs/ n marsopa f

porridge /'pɒrɪdʒ/ n avena f (cocida)

port /pɔːt/ n puerto m; (Naut) babor m; (Comp) puerto m; (Culin) oporto m

portable /'pɔːtəbl/ adj portátil

porter /'pɔːtə(r)/ n (for luggage) maletero m; (concierge) portero m

porthole /'pɔːthəʊl/ n portilla f

portion /'pɔːʃn/ n porción f; (part) parte f

portrait /'pɔːtrɪt/ n retrato m

portray /pɔːˈtreɪ/ vt representar. ~al n representación f

Portug|al /'pɔːtjʊgl/ n Portugal m. ~uese /-ˈɡiːz/ adj & n portugués (m)

pose /pəʊz/ n pose f, postura f. • vt representar (threat); plantear (problem, question). • vi posar. ~ as hacerse pasar por

posh /pɒʃ/ adj 🅸 elegante

position /pəˈzɪʃn/ n posición f; (job) puesto m; (situation) situación f. • vt colocar

positive /'pɒzətɪv/ adj positivo; (real) auténtico; (certain) seguro. • n (Photo) positiva f. ~ly adv positivamente

possess /pəˈzes/ vt poseer. ~ion /-ʃn/ n posesión f; (Jurid) bien m. ~ive adj posesivo

possib|ility /pɒsəˈbɪlətɪ/ n posibilidad f. ~le /'pɒsəbl/ adj posible. ~ly adv posiblemente

post /pəʊst/ n (pole) poste m; (job) puesto m; (mail) correo m. • vt echar al correo (letter); (send) enviar por correo. keep s.o. ~ed mantener a uno al corriente

post... /pəʊst/ pref post, pos

post: ~age /-ɪdʒ/ /-ɪdʒ/ n franqueo m. ~al adj postal. ~al

order n giro m postal. ~ box n buzón m. ~card n (tarjeta f) postal f. ~code n código m postal

poster /'pəʊstə(r)/ n cartel m, póster m

posterity /pɒsˈterətɪ/ n posteridad f

posthumous /'pɒstjʊməs/ adj póstumo

post: ~man /-mən/ n cartero m. ~mark n matasellos m

post mortem /pəʊstˈmɔːtəm/ n autopsia f

post office n oficina f de correos, correos mpl, correo m (LAm)

postpone /pəʊstˈpəʊn/ vt aplazar, posponer. ~ment n aplazamiento m

postscript /'pəʊstskrɪpt/ n posdata f

posture /'pɒstʃə(r)/ n postura f

posy /'pəʊzɪ/ n ramillete m

pot /pɒt/ n (for cooking) olla f; (for jam, honey) tarro m; (for flowers) tiesto m; (in pottery) vasija f. ~s and pans cacharros mpl

potato /pəˈteɪtəʊ/ n (pl -oes) patata f, papa f (LAm)

potent /'pəʊtnt/ adj potente; (drink) fuerte

potential /pəˈtenʃl/ adj & n potencial (m). ~ly adv potencialmente

pot: ~hole n cueva f subterránea; (in road) bache m. ~holing n espeleología f

potion /'pəʊʃn/ n poción f

pot-shot n tiro m al azar

potter /'pɒtə(r)/ n alfarero m. • vi hacer pequeños trabajos agradables. ~y n (pots) cerámica f; (workshop, craft) alfarería f

potty /'pɒtɪ/ adj (-ier, -iest) 🅸

P

chiflado. ●n orinal m

pouch /paʊtʃ/ n bolsa f pequeña; (for correspondence) valija f

poultry /ˈpəʊltrɪ/ n aves fpl de corral

pounce /paʊns/ vi saltar. ~ on abalanzarse sobre

pound /paʊnd/ n (weight) libra f (= 454g); (money) libra f (esterlina); (for cars) depósito m. ●vt (crush) machacar. ●vi aporrear; (heart) palpitar; (sound) retumbar

pour /pɔː(r)/ vt verter; echar (salt). ~ (out) servir (drink). ●vi (blood) manar; (water) salir; (rain) llover a cántaros. □ ~ out vi (people) salir en tropel. ~ing adj. ~ing rain lluvia f torrencial

pout /paʊt/ vi hacer pucheros

poverty /ˈpɒvətɪ/ n pobreza f

powder /ˈpaʊdə(r)/ n polvo m; (cosmetic) polvos mpl. ●vt empolvar. ~ one's face ponerse polvos en la cara. ~y adj como polvo

power /ˈpaʊə(r)/ n poder m; (energy) energía f; (electricity) electricidad f; (nation) potencia f. ●vt. ~ed by impulsado by. ~ cut n apagón m. ~ed adj con motor. ~ful adj poderoso. ~less adj impotente. ~ plant, ~-station n central f eléctrica

PR = **public relations**

practicable /ˈpræktɪkəbl/ adj practicable

practical /ˈpræktɪkl/ adj práctico. ~ joke n broma f. ~ly adv prácticamente

practi|ce /ˈpræktɪs/ n práctica f; (custom) costumbre f; (exercise) ejercicio m; (Sport) entrenamiento m; (clients) clientela f. he's out of ~ce le falta práctica. in ~ce (in fact) en la práctica. ~se /ˈpræktɪs/

vt practicar; ensayar (act); ejercer (profession). ●vi practicar; (professional) ejercer. ~tioner /-ˈtɪʃənə(r)/ n médico m

prairie /ˈpreərɪ/ n pradera f

praise /preɪz/ vt (Relig) alabar; (compliment) elogiar. ●n (credit) elogios mpl. ~worthy adj loable

pram /præm/ n cochecito m

prank /præŋk/ n travesura f

prawn /prɔːn/ n gamba f, camarón m (LAm)

pray /preɪ/ vi rezar (for por). ~er /preə(r)/ n oración f

pre... /priː/ pref pre...

preach /priːtʃ/ vt/i predicar. ~er n predicador m; (Amer, minister) pastor m

pre-arrange /priːəˈreɪndʒ/ vt concertar de antemano

precarious /prɪˈkeərɪəs/ adj precario. ~ly adv precariamente

precaution /prɪˈkɔːʃn/ n precaución f

precede /prɪˈsiːd/ vt preceder. ~nce /ˈpresədəns/ n precedencia f. ~nt /ˈpresədənt/ n precedente m

preceding /prɪˈsiːdɪŋ/ adj anterior

precept /ˈpriːsept/ n precepto m

precinct /ˈpriːsɪŋkt/ n recinto m; (Amer, police district) distrito m policial; (Amer, voting district) circunscripción f. **pedestrian** ~ zona f peatonal. ~s (of city) límites mpl

precious /ˈpreʃəs/ adj precioso. ●adv 🔲 muy

precipice /ˈpresɪpɪs/ n precipicio m

precipitate /prɪˈsɪpɪteɪt/ vt precipitar. ●/prɪˈsɪpɪtət/ n precipitado m. ●/prɪˈsɪpɪtət/ adj precipitado

precis|e /prɪˈsaɪs/ adj (accurate)

exacto; (*specific*) preciso; (*meticulous*) minucioso. **~ely** *adv* con precisión. **~!** ¡exacto! **~ion** /-'sɪʒn/ n precisión f

preclude /prɪ'kluːd/ vt excluir

precocious /prɪ'kəʊʃəs/ adj precoz. **~ly** *adv* precozmente

preconce|ived /priːkən'siːvd/ adj preconcebido. **~ption** /-'sepʃn/ n preconcepción f

precursor /priː'kɜːsə(r)/ n precursor m

predator /'predətə(r)/ n depredador m. **~y** adj predador

predecessor /'priːdɪsesə(r)/ n predecesor m, antecesor m

predicament /prɪ'dɪkəmənt/ n aprieto m

predict /prɪ'dɪkt/ vt predecir. **~ion** /-ʃn/ n predicción f

preen /priːn/ vt arreglar. **~ o.s.** atildarse

prefab /'priːfæb/ n 🔲 casa f prefabricada. **~ricated** /-'fæbrɪkeɪtɪd/ adj prefabricado

preface /'prefəs/ n prefacio m; (*to event*) prólogo m

prefect /'priːfekt/ n (*Schol*) monitor m; (*official*) prefecto m

prefer /prɪ'fɜː(r)/ vt (pt **preferred**) preferir. **~ sth to sth** preferir algo a algo. **~able** /'prefrəbl/ adj preferible. **~ence** /'prefrəns/ n preferencia f. **~ential** /-ə'renʃl/ adj preferente

pregnan|cy /'pregnənsi/ n embarazo m. **~t** adj embarazada

prehistoric /priːhɪ'stɒrɪk/ adj prehistórico

prejudge /priː'dʒʌdʒ/ vt prejuzgar

prejudice /'predʒʊdɪs/ n prejuicio m. ●vt predisponer; (*harm*) perjudicar. **~d** adj lleno de prejuicios

preliminary /prɪ'lɪmɪnəri/ adj

preliminar

prelude /'preljuːd/ n preludio m

premature /'premətjʊə(r)/ adj prematuro

premeditated /priː'medɪteɪtɪd/ adj premeditado

premier /'premɪə(r)/ n (*Pol*) primer ministro m

première /'premɪeə(r)/ n estreno m

premise /'premɪs/ n premisa f. **~s** /'premɪsɪz/ npl local m. **on the ~s** en el local

premium /'priːmɪəm/ n (*insurance* **~**) prima f de seguro. **be at a ~** escasear

premonition /priːmə'nɪʃn/ n premonición f, presentimiento m

preoccup|ation /priːɒkjʊ'peɪʃn/ n (*obsession*) obsesión f; (*concern*) preocupación f. **~ied** /-'ɒkjʊpaɪd/ adj absorto; (*worried*) preocupado

preparat|ion /prepə'reɪʃn/ n preparación f. **~ions** npl preparativos mpl. **~ory** /prɪ'pærətrɪ/ adj preparatorio

prepare /prɪ'peə(r)/ vt preparar. ●vi prepararse. ●adj preparado (*willing*). **be ~d to** estar dispuesto a

preposition /prepə'zɪʃn/ n preposición f

preposterous /prɪ'pɒstərəs/ adj absurdo

prerequisite /priː'rekwɪzɪt/ n requisito m esencial

prerogative /prɪ'rɒgətɪv/ n prerrogativa f

Presbyterian /prezbɪ'tɪərɪən/ adj & n presbiteriano (m)

prescri|be /prɪ'skraɪb/ vt prescribir; (*Med*) recetar. **~ption** /-'ɪpʃn/ n (*Med*) receta f

p

presence /'prezns/ n presencia f. ~ of mind presencia f de ánimo

present /'preznt/ n (gift) regalo m; (current time) presente m. at ~ actualmente. for the ~ por ahora. ● adj presente. ● /prɪ'zent/ vt presentar; (give) obsequiar. ~ s.o. with obsequiar a uno con. ~able /prɪ'zentəbl/ adj presentable. ~ation /prezn'teɪʃn/ n presentación f; (ceremony) ceremonia f de entrega. ~er /prɪ'zentə(r)/ n presentador m. ~ly /'prezntlɪ/ adv dentro de poco

preserv|ation /preza'veɪʃn/ n conservación f. ~ative /prɪ'zɜːvətɪv/ n conservante m. ~e /prɪ'zɜːv/ vt conservar; (maintain) mantener; (Culin) hacer conserva de. ● n coto m; (jam) confitura f. wildlife ~e (Amer) reserva f de animales

preside /prɪ'zaɪd/ vi presidir. ~ over presidir

presiden|cy /'prezɪdənsɪ/ n presidencia f. ~t n presidente m. ~tial /-'denʃl/ adj presidencial

press /pres/ vt apretar; prensar (grapes); (put pressure on) presionar; (iron) planchar. be ~ed for time andar escaso de tiempo. ● vi apretar; (time) apremiar; (fig) urgir. ● n (Mec, newspapers) prensa f; (printing) imprenta f. □ ~ on vi seguir adelante (with con). ~ conference n rueda f de prensa. ~ cutting n recorte m de periódico. ~ing adj urgente. ~-up n flexión f, fondo m

pressur|e /'preʃə(r)/ n presión f. ● vt presionar. ~e-cooker n olla f a presión. ~ize vt presionar

prestig|e /pre'stiːʒ/ n prestigio m. ~ious /-'stɪdʒəs/ adj prestigioso

presum|ably /prɪ'zjuːməblɪ/ adv. ~... supongo que..., me imagino

que... ~e /prɪ'zjuːm/ vt suponer. ~ptuous /prɪ'zʌmptʃʊəs/ adj impertinente

presuppose /priːsə'pəʊz/ vt presuponer

preten|ce /prɪ'tens/ n fingimiento m; (claim) pretensión f; (pretext) pretexto m. ~d /-'tend/ vt/i fingir. ~sion /-'tenʃn/ n pretensión f. ~tious /-'tenʃəs/ adj pretencioso

pretext /'priːtekst/ n pretexto m

pretty /'prɪtɪ/ adj (-ier, -iest) adv bonito, lindo (esp LAm)

prevail /prɪ'veɪl/ vi predominar; (win) prevalecer. □ ~ on vt persuadir

prevalen|ce /'prevələns/ n (occurrence) preponderancia f; (predominance) predominio m. ~t adj extendido

prevent /prɪ'vent/ vt (hinder) impedir; (forestall) prevenir, evitar. ~ion /-ʃn/ n prevención f. ~ive adj preventivo

preview /'priːvjuː/ n preestreno m; (trailer) avance m

previous /'priːvɪəs/ adj anterior. ~ to antes de. ~ly adv antes

prey /preɪ/ n presa f. bird of ~ ave f de rapiña

price /praɪs/ n precio m. ● vt fijar el precio de. ~less adj inestimable; (fam, amusing) muy divertido. ~y adj 🔲 carito

prick /prɪk/ vt/i pinchar. ● n pinchazo m

prickl|e /'prɪkl/ n (thorn) espina f; (of animal) púa f; (sensation) picor m. ~y adj espinoso; (animal) con púas; (touchy) quisquilloso

pride /praɪd/ n orgullo m. ● vr. ~ o.s. enorgullecerse de

priest /priːst/ n sacerdote m. ~hood n sacerdocio m

prim /prɪm/ adj (primmer, primmest) mojigato; (affected) remilgado

primar|ily /'praɪmərɪli/ adv en primer lugar. **~y** /'praɪmərɪ/ adj (principal) primordial; (first, basic) primario. **~ school** n escuela f primaria

prime /praɪm/ vt cebar (gun); (prepare) preparar; aprestar (surface). ● adj principal; (first rate) excelente. **~ minister** n primer ministro m. ● n. **be in one's ~** estar en la flor de la vida. **~r** n (paint) imprimación f

primeval /praɪ'miːvl/ adj primigenio

primitive /'prɪmɪtɪv/ adj primitivo

primrose /'prɪmrəʊz/ n primavera f

prince /prɪns/ n príncipe m. **~ss** /prɪn'ses/ n princesa f

principal /'prɪnsəpl/ adj principal. ● n (of school) director m; (of university) rector m. **~ly** /'prɪnsɪpəlɪ/ adv principalmente

principle /'prɪnsəpl/ n principio m. **in ~** en principio. **on ~** por principio

print /prɪnt/ vt imprimir; (write in capitals) escribir con letras de molde. **~ed matter** impresos mpl. ● n (characters) letra f; (picture) grabado m; (Photo) copia f; (fabric) estampado m. in ~ (published) publicado; (available) a la venta. out of ~ agotado. **~er** /'prɪntə(r)/ n impresor m; (machine) impresora f. **~ing** n impresión f; (trade) imprenta f. **~out** n listado m

prion /'praɪɒn/ n prión m

prior /'praɪə(r)/ n prior m. ● adj previo. **~ to** antes de. **~ity** /praɪ'ɒrətɪ/ n prioridad f. **~y** n priorato m

prise /praɪz/ vt. **~ open** abrir haciendo palanca

prison /'prɪzn/ n cárcel m. **~er** n prisionero m; (in prison) preso m; (under arrest) detenido m. **~ officer** n funcionario m de prisiones

priva|cy /'prɪvəsɪ/ n privacidad f. **~te** /'praɪvət/ adj privado; (confidential) personal; (lessons, house) particular. **in ~te** en privado; (secretly) en secreto. ● n soldado m raso. **~te detective** n detective m & f privado. **~tely** adv en privado. **~tion** /praɪ'veɪʃn/ n privación f

privilege /'prɪvəlɪdʒ/ n privilegio m. **~d** adj privilegiado. **be ~d to** tener el privilegio de

prize /praɪz/ n premio m. ● adj (idiot etc) de remate. ● vt estimar

pro /prəʊ/ n. **~s and cons** los pros m y los contras

probab|ility /prɒbə'bɪlətɪ/ n probabilidad f. **~le** /'prɒbəbl/ adj probable. **~ly** adv probablemente

probation /prə'beɪʃn/ n período m de prueba; (Jurid) libertad f condicional

probe /prəʊb/ n sonda f; (fig) investigación f. ● vt sondar. ● vi. **~ into** investigar

problem /'prɒbləm/ n problema m. ● adj difícil. **~atic** /-'mætɪk/ adj problemático

procedure /prə'siːdʒə(r)/ n procedimiento m

proceed /prə'siːd/ vi proceder; (move forward) avanzar. **~ings** npl (report) actas fpl; (Jurid) proceso m. **~s** /'prəʊsiːdz/ npl. **the ~s** lo recaudado

process /'prəʊses/ n proceso m. **in the ~ of** en vías de. ● vt tratar; revelar (photo); tramitar (order).

P

proclaim | prom

~**ion** /prəˈseʃn/ n desfile m; (Relig) procesión f. ~**or** n procesador m. food ~ procesador m de alimentos

proclaim /prəˈkleɪm/ vt proclamar. ~**mation** /prɒkləˈmeɪʃn/ n proclamación f

procure /prəˈkjʊə(r)/ vt obtener

prod /prɒd/ vt (pt prodded) (with sth sharp) pinchar; (with elbow) darle un codazo a. ●n (with sth sharp) pinchazo m; (with elbow) codazo m

produc|e /prəˈdjuːs/ vt producir; surtir (effect); sacar (gun); producir (film); poner en escena (play). ●/ˈprɒdjuːs/ n productos mpl. ~**er** /prəˈdjuːsə(r)/ n (TV, Cinema) productor m; (in theatre) director m; (manufacturer) fabricante m & f. ~**t** /ˈprɒdʌkt/ n producto m. ~**tion** /prəˈdʌkʃn/ n (manufacture) fabricación f; (output) producción f; (of play) producción f. ~**tive** /prəˈdʌktɪv/ adj productivo. ~**tivity** /prɒdʌkˈtɪvətɪ/ n productividad f

profess /prəˈfes/ vt profesar; (pretend) pretender. ~**ion** /-ˈfeʃn/ n profesión f. ~**ional** adj & n profesional (m & f). ~**or** /-ˈfesə(r)/ n catedrático m; (Amer) profesor m

proficien|cy /prəˈfɪʃənsɪ/ n competencia f. ~**t** adj competente

profile /ˈprəʊfaɪl/ n perfil m

profit /ˈprɒfɪt/ n (Com) ganancia f; (fig) provecho m. ●vi. ~ **from** sacar provecho de. ~**able** adj provechoso

profound /prəˈfaʊnd/ adj profundo. ~**ly** adv profundamente

profus|e /prəˈfjuːs/ adj profuso. ~**ely** adv profusamente

prognosis /prɒgˈnəʊsɪs/ n (pl -oses) pronóstico n

program /ˈprəʊgræm/ n (Comp)

programa m; (Amer, course) curso m. ~**me** /ˈprəʊgræm/ n programa m. ●vt (pt -med) programar. ~**mer** n programador m

progress /ˈprəʊgres/ n progreso m; (development) desarrollo m. make ~ hacer progresos. in ~ en curso. ●/prəˈgres/ vi hacer progresos; (develop) desarrollarse. ~**ion** /prəˈgreʃn/ n progresión f; (advance) evolución f. ~**ive** /prəˈgresɪv/ adj progresivo; (reforming) progresista. ~**ively** adv progresivamente

prohibit /prəˈhɪbɪt/ vt prohibir; (prevent) impedir. ~**ive** adj prohibitivo

project /prəˈdʒekt/ vt proyectar. ●vi (stick out) sobresalir. ●/ˈprɒdʒekt/ n proyecto m; (Schol) trabajo m; (Amer, housing ~) complejo m de viviendas subvencionadas. ~**or** /prəˈdʒektə(r)/ n proyector m

prolific /prəˈlɪfɪk/ adj prolífico

prologue /ˈprəʊlɒg/ n prólogo m

prolong /prəˈlɒŋ/ vt prolongar

prom /prɒm/ n (Amer) baile m de fin de colegio. ~**enade** /prɒməˈnɑːd/ n paseo m marítimo. ●vi pasearse.

Prom En EE.UU. un *prom* es un baile que se celebra para los estudiantes que terminan el *High School*. En Londres los *Proms* son una serie de conciertos de música clásica, durante los cuales una gran parte del público permanece de pie. Tienen lugar en el *Albert Hall* en el verano, durante ocho semanas. Oficialmente, son conocidos como los *Henry Wood Promenade Concerts*, en memoria de su fundador.

prominen|ce /'prɒmɪnəns/ n prominencia f; (fig) importancia f. **~t** adj prominente; (important) importante; (conspicuous) destacado

promiscu|ity /prɒmɪ'skju:ətɪ/ n promiscuidad f. **~ous** /prə'mɪskjʊəs/ adj promiscuo

promis|e /'prɒmɪs/ n promesa f. ●vt/i prometer. **~ing** adj prometedor; (future) halagüeño

promot|e /prə'məʊt/ vt promover; promocionar (product); (in rank) ascender. **~ion** /-'məʊʃn/ n promoción f; (in rank) ascenso m

prompt /prɒmpt/ adj rápido; (punctual) puntual. ●adv en punto. ●n (Comp) presto m. ●vt incitar; apuntar (actor). **~ly** adv puntualmente

prone /prəʊn/ adj (tendido) boca abajo. **be ~ to** ser propenso a

pronoun /'prəʊnaʊn/ n pronombre m

pronounc|e /prə'naʊns/ vt pronunciar; (declare) declarar. **~ement** n declaración f. **~ed** adj pronunciado; (noticeable) marcado

pronunciation /prənʌnsɪ'eɪʃn/ n pronunciación f

proof /pru:f/ n prueba f, pruebas fpl; (of alcohol) graduación f normal. ●adj. **~ against** a prueba de. **~-reading** n corrección f de pruebas

propaganda /prɒpə'gændə/ n propaganda f

propagate /'prɒpəgeɪt/ vt propagar. ●vi propagarse

propel /prə'pel/ vt (pt propelled) propulsar. **~ler** n hélice f

proper /'prɒpə(r)/ adj correcto; (suitable) apropiado; (Gram) propio; (fam, real) verdadero. **~ly** adv correctamente; (eat, work) bien

property /'prɒpətɪ/ n propiedad f; (things owned) bienes mpl. ●adj inmobiliario

prophe|cy /'prɒfəsɪ/ n profecía f. **~sy** /'prɒfəsaɪ/ vt/i profetizar. **~t** /'prɒfɪt/ n profeta m. **~tic** /prə'fetɪk/ adj profético

proportion /prə'pɔ:ʃn/ n proporción f. **~al** adj, **~ate** /-ət/ adj proporcional

propos|al /prə'pəʊzl/ n propuesta f; (of marriage) proposición f matrimonial. **~e** /prə'pəʊz/ vt proponer. ●vi. **~e to s.o.** hacerle una oferta de matrimonio a una. **~ition** /prɒpə'zɪʃn/ n propuesta f; (offer) oferta f

proprietor /prə'praɪətə(r)/ n propietario m

pro rata /prəʊ'rɑ:tə/ adv a prorrata

prose /prəʊz/ n prosa f

prosecut|e /'prɒsɪkju:t/ vt procesar (for por); (carry on) proseguir. **~ion** /-'kju:ʃn/ n proceso m. **the ~** (side) la acusación. **~or** n fiscal m & f; (in private prosecutions) abogado m de la acusación

prospect /'prɒspekt/ n (possibility) posibilidad f (of de); (situation envisaged) perspectiva f. **~s** (chances) perspectivas fpl. **~ive** /prə'spektɪv/ adj posible; (future) futuro. **~or** /prə'spektə(r)/ n prospector m. **~us** /prə'spektəs/ n folleto m informativo

prosper /'prɒspə(r)/ vi prosperar. **~ity** /-'sperɪtɪ/ n prosperidad f. **~ous** adj próspero

prostitut|e /'prɒstɪtju:t/ n prostituta f. **~ion** /-'tju:ʃn/ n prostitución f

prostrate /'prɒstreɪt/ adj postrado

P

protagonist /prə'tægənɪst/ n protagonista m & f

protect /prə'tekt/ vt proteger. **~ion** /-ʃn/ n protección f. **~ive** adj protector. **~or** n protector m

protein /'prəʊtiːn/ n proteína f

protest /'prəʊtest/ n protesta f. in ~ (against) en señal de protesta (contra). under ~ bajo protesta. ● /prə'test/ vt/i protestar

Protestant /'prɒtɪstənt/ adj & n protestante (m & f)

protester /prə'testə(r)/ n manifestante m & f

protocol /'prəʊtəkɒl/ n protocolo m

protrud|e /prə'truːd/ vi sobresalir. **~ing** adj (chin) prominente. **~ing eyes** ojos saltones

proud /praʊd/ adj orgulloso. **~ly** adv con orgullo; (arrogantly) orgullosamente

prove /pruːv/ vt probar; demostrar (loyalty). ● vi resultar. **~n** adj probado

proverb /'prɒvɜːb/ n refrán m, proverbio m

provide /prə'vaɪd/ vt proporcionar; dar (accommodation). ~ s.o. with sth proveer a uno de algo. ● vi. ~ for (allow for) prever; mantener (person). **~d** conj. ~d (that) con tal de que, siempre que

providen|ce /'prɒvɪdəns/ n providencia f. **~tial** /-'denʃl/ adj providencial

providing /prə'vaɪdɪŋ/ conj. ~ that con tal de que, siempre que

provinc|e /'prɒvɪns/ n provincia f; (fig) competencia f. **~ial** /prə'vɪnʃl/ adj provincial

provision /prə'vɪʒn/ n provisión f; (supply) suministro m; (stipulation) disposición f. **~s** npl provisiones fpl, víveres mpl. **~al** adj provisional

provo|cation /prɒvə'keɪʃn/ n provocación f. **~cative** /-'vɒkətɪv/ adj provocador. **~ke** /prə'vəʊk/ vt provocar

prow /praʊ/ n proa f

prowess /'praʊɪs/ n destreza f; (valour) valor m

prowl /praʊl/ vi merodear. **~er** n merodeador m

proximity /prɒk'sɪmətɪ/ n proximidad f

prude /pruːd/ n mojigato m

pruden|ce /'pruːdəns/ n prudencia f. **~t** adj prudente. **~tly** adv prudentemente

prudish /'pruːdɪʃ/ adj mojigato

prune /pruːn/ n ciruela f pasa. ● vt podar

pry /praɪ/ vi curiosear. ~ into sth entrometerse en algo. vt (Amer) see **PRISE**

PS n (postscript) P.D.

psalm /sɑːm/ n salmo m

psychiatr|ic /saɪkɪ'ætrɪk/ adj psiquiátrico. **~ist** /saɪ'kaɪətrɪst/ n psiquiatra m & f. **~y** /saɪ'kaɪətrɪ/ n psiquiatría f

psychic /'saɪkɪk/ adj para(p)sicológico

psycho|analysis /saɪkəʊə'næləsɪs/ n (p)sicoanálisis m. **~logical** /saɪkə'lɒdʒɪkl/ adj (p)sicológico. **~logist** /saɪ'kɒlədʒɪst/ n (p)sicólogo m. **~logy** /saɪ'kɒlədʒɪ/ n (p)sicología f. **~therapy** /-'θerəpɪ/ n (p)sicoterapia f

pub /pʌb/ n bar m

pub En Gran Bretaña, establecimiento donde se vende cerveza y otras bebidas

(alcohólicas y no alcohólicas) para consumir en el local. *Pub* es la forma abreviada de *public house*. Suelen ofrecer comidas y una variedad de juegos, especialmente dardos, billar etc. Recientemente, las horas en que pueden abrir dependen de la licencia, siendo lo normal de 11 - 23 horas.

puberty /'pjuːbətɪ/ *n* pubertad *f*

pubic /'pjuːbɪk/ *adj* pubiano, púbico

public /'pʌblɪk/ *adj* público. ~**an** *n* tabernero *m*. ~**ation** /-'keɪʃn/ *n* publicación *f*. ~ **holiday** *n* día *m* festivo, día *m* feriado (*LAm*). ~ **house** *n* bar *m*. ~**ity** /pʌb'lɪsətɪ/ *n* publicidad *f*. ~**ize** /'pʌblɪsaɪz/ *vt* hacer público. ~**ly** *adv* públicamente. ~ **school** *n* colegio *m* privado; (*Amer*) instituto *m*, escuela *f* pública

publish /'pʌblɪʃ/ *vt* publicar. ~**er** *n* editor *m*. ~**ing** *n* publicación *f*. ~**ing house** editorial *f*

pudding /'pʊdɪŋ/ *n* postre *m*; (*steamed*) budín *m*

puddle /'pʌdl/ *n* charco *m*

Puerto Ric|an /pwɜːtəʊ'riːkən/ *adj & n* portorriqueño (*m*), puertorriqueño (*m*). ~**o** /-əʊ/ *n* Puerto Rico *m*

puff /pʌf/ *n* (*of wind*) ráfaga *f*; (*of smoke*) nube *f*; (*action*) soplo *m*; (*on cigarette*) chupada *f*, calada *f*. ● *vt/i* soplar. ~ **at** dar chupadas a (*pipe*). □ ~ **out** (*swell up*) inflar, hinchar. ~**ed** *adj* (*out of breath*) sin aliento. ~ **paste** (*Amer*), ~ **pastry** *n* hojaldre *m*. ~**y** *adj* hinchado

pull /pʊl/ *vt* tirar de, jalar (*LAm*); desgarrarse (*muscle*). ~ **a face** hacer una mueca. ~ **a fast one** hacer una mala jugada. ● *vi* tirar, jalar (*LAm*). ~ **at** tirar de, jalar (*LAm*). ● *n* tirón *m*, jalón *m* (*LAm*); (*pulling force*) fuerza *f*; (*influence*) influencia *f*. □ ~ **away** *vi* (*Auto*) alejarse. □ ~ **back** *vi* retirarse. □ ~ **down** *vt* echar abajo (*building*); (*lower*) bajar. □ ~ **in** *vi* (*Auto*) parar. □ ~ **off** *vt* (*remove*) quitar; (*achieve*) conseguir. □ ~ **out** *vt* sacar; retirar (*team*). *vi* (*Auto*) salirse. □ ~ **through** *vi* recobrar la salud. □ ~ **up** *vi* (*Auto*) parar. *vt* (*uproot*) arrancar; (*reprimand*) regañar

pullover /'pʊləʊvə(r)/ *n* suéter *m*, pulóver *m*, jersey *m*

pulp /pʌlp/ *n* pulpa *f*; (*for paper*) pasta *f*

pulpit /'pʊlpɪt/ *n* púlpito *m*

pulse /pʌls/ *n* (*Med*) pulso *m*; (*Culin*) legumbre *f*

pummel /'pʌml/ *vt* (*pt* pummelled) aporrear

pump /pʌmp/ *n* bomba *f*; (*for petrol*) surtidor *m*. ● *vt* sacar con una bomba. □ ~ **up** *vt* inflar

pumpkin /'pʌmpkɪn/ *n* calabaza *f*

pun /pʌn/ *n* juego *m* de palabras

punch /pʌntʃ/ *vt* darle un puñetazo a; (*perforate*) perforar; hacer (*hole*). ● *n* puñetazo *m*; (*vigour*) fuerza *f*; (*device*) perforadora *f*; (*drink*) ponche *m*. □ ~ **in** *vi* (*Amer*) fichar (*al entrar al trabajo*). ~ **out** *vi* (*Amer*) fichar (*al salir del trabajo*)

p

punctual /ˈpʌŋktʃʊəl/ adj puntual. ~ity /-ˈælɪtɪ/ n puntualidad f. ~ly adv puntualmente

punctuat|e /ˈpʌŋktʃʊeɪt/ vt puntuar. ~ion /-ˈeɪʃn/ n puntuación f

puncture /ˈpʌŋktʃə(r)/ n (in tyre) pinchazo m. have a ~ pinchar. ● vt pinchar. ● vi pincharse

punish /ˈpʌnɪʃ/ vt castigar. ~ment n castigo m

punk /pʌŋk/ n punk m & f, punki m & f; (Music) punk m; (Amer, hoodlum) vándalo m

punt /pʌnt/ n (boat) batea f. ~er n apostante m & f

puny /ˈpjuːnɪ/ adj (-ier, -iest) enclenque

pup /pʌp/ n cachorro m

pupil /ˈpjuːpl/ n alumno m; (of eye) pupila f

puppet /ˈpʌpɪt/ n marioneta f, títere m; (glove ~) títere m

puppy /ˈpʌpɪ/ n cachorro m

purchase /ˈpɜːtʃəs/ vt adquirir. ● n adquisición f. ~r n comprador m

pur|e /ˈpjʊə(r)/ adj (-er, -est) puro. ~ity n pureza f

purgatory /ˈpɜːɡətrɪ/ n purgatorio m

purge /pɜːdʒ/ vt purgar. ● n purga f

purif|ication /pjʊərɪfɪˈkeɪʃn/ n purificación f. ~y /ˈpjʊərɪfaɪ/ vt purificar

purist /ˈpjʊərɪst/ n purista m & f

puritan /ˈpjʊərɪtən/ n puritano m. ~ical /-ˈtænɪkl/ adj puritano

purple /ˈpɜːpl/ adj morado. ● n morado m, púrpura f

purport /pəˈpɔːt/ vt. ~ to be pretender ser

purpose /ˈpɜːpəs/ n propósito m; (determination) resolución f. on ~

a propósito. serve a ~ servir de algo. ~ful adj (resolute) resuelto. ~ly adv a propósito

purr /pɜː(r)/ vi ronronear

purse /pɜːs/ n monedero m; (Amer) bolso m, cartera f (LAm), bolsa f (Mex)

pursu|e /pəˈsjuː/ vt perseguir, continuar con (course of action). ~it /pəˈsjuːt/ n persecución f; (pastime) actividad f

pus /pʌs/ n pus m

push /pʊʃ/ vt empujar; apretar (button). ● n empujón m; (effort) esfuerzo m. □ ~ back vt hacer retroceder. □ ~ off vi 🗙 largarse. ~chair n sillita f de paseo, carreola f (Mex). ~y adj (pej) ambicioso

pussy /ˈpʊsɪ/ (pl -sies), **pussycat** /ˈpʊsɪkæt/ n 🔟 minino m

put /pʊt/ vt (pt **put**, pres p **putting**) poner; (with care, precision) colocar; (inside sth) meter; (express) decir. □ ~ across vt comunicar. □ ~ away vt guardar. □ ~ back vt volver a poner; retrasar (clock). □ ~ by vt guardar; ahorrar (money). □ ~ down vt (on a surface) dejar; colgar (phone); (suppress) sofocar; (write) apuntar; (kill) sacrificar. □ ~ forward vt presentar (plan); proponer (candidate); adelantar (clocks); adelantar (meeting). □ ~ in vt (instal) poner; presentar (claim). □ ~ in for vt solicitar. □ ~ off vt aplazar, posponer; (disconcert) desconcertar. □ ~ on vt (wear) ponerse; poner (CD, music); encender (light). □ ~ out vt (extinguish) apagar; (inconvenience) incomodar; extender (hand); (disconcert) desconcertar. □ ~ through vt (phone) poner, pasar (to con). □ ~ up vt levantar; aumentar (rent); subir (price); poner (sign); alojar (guest). □ ~ **up with** vt aguantar, soportar

putrid /ˈpjuːtrɪd/ adj putrefacto

putt /pʌt/ n (golf) golpe m suave

puzzle /ˈpʌzl/ n misterio m; (game) rompecabezas m. ● vt dejar perplejo. ~**ed** adj (expression) de desconcierto. I'm ~**ed** about it me tiene perplejo. ~**ing** adj incomprensible; (odd) curioso

pygmy /ˈpɪɡmɪ/ n pigmeo m

pyjamas /pəˈdʒɑːməz/ npl pijama m, piyama m or f (LAm)

pylon /ˈpaɪlɒn/ n pilón m

pyramid /ˈpɪrəmɪd/ n pirámide f

python /ˈpaɪθn/ n pitón m

Qq

quack /kwæk/ n (of duck) graznido m; (person) charlatán m. ~ **doctor** n curandero m

quadrangle /ˈkwɒdræŋɡl/ n cuadrilátero m

quadruped /ˈkwɒdruped/ n cuadrúpedo m

quadruple /ˈkwɒdrʊpl/ adj & n cuádruplo (m). ● vt cuadruplicar

quagmire /ˈkwæɡmaɪə(r)/ n lodazal m

quail /kweɪl/ n codorniz f

quaint /kweɪnt/ adj (-er, -est) pintoresco; (odd) curioso

quake /kweɪk/ vi temblar. ● n 🄸 terremoto m

qualification /kwɒlɪfɪˈkeɪʃn/ n título m; (requirement) requisito m; (ability) capacidad f; (Sport) clasifica-

ción f; (fig) reserva f. ~**ied** /ˈkwɒlɪfaɪd/ adj cualificado; (with degree, diploma) titulado; (competent) capacitado. ~**y** /ˈkwɒlɪfaɪ/ vt calificar; (limit) limitar. ● vi titularse; (Sport) clasificarse. ~**y for sth** (be entitled to) tener derecho a algo

qualitative /ˈkwɒlɪtətɪv/ adj cualitativo. ~**y** /ˈkwɒlɪtɪ/ n calidad f; (attribute) cualidad f

qualm /kwɑːm/ n reparo m

quandary /ˈkwɒndrɪ/ n dilema m

quantify /ˈkwɒntɪfaɪ/ vt cuantificar. ~**ty** /-tɪ/ n cantidad f

quarantine /ˈkwɒrəntiːn/ n cuarentena f. ● vt poner en cuarentena

quarrel /ˈkwɒrəl/ n pelea f. ● vi (pt quarrelled) pelearse, discutir. ~**some** /-səm/ adj pendenciero

quarry /ˈkwɒrɪ/ n (excavation) cantera f; (prey) presa f

quart /kwɔːt/ n cuarto m de galón

quarter /ˈkwɔːtə(r)/ n cuarto m; (of year) trimestre m; (district) barrio m. a ~ **of an hour** un cuarto de hora. ● vt dividir en cuartos; (Mil) acuartelar. ~**-final** n cuarto m de final. ~**ly** adj trimestral. ● adv trimestralmente

quartz /kwɔːts/ n cuarzo m

quay /kiː/ n muelle m

queasy /ˈkwiːzɪ/ adj mareado

queen /kwiːn/ n reina f. ~ **mother** n reina f madre

queer /kwɪə(r)/ adj (-er, -est) extraño

quench /kwentʃ/ vt quitar (thirst); sofocar (desire)

query /ˈkwɪərɪ/ n pregunta f. ● vt preguntar; (doubt) poner en duda

quest /kwest/ n busca f

question /ˈkwestʃən/ n pregunta f; (for discussion) cuestión f. **in ~** en cuestión. **out of the ~** imposi-

ble. without ~ sin duda. ● vt
hacer preguntas a; (police etc) in-
terrogar; (doubt) poner en duda.
~able adj discutible. ~ mark n
signo m de interrogación. ~naire
/-'neə(r)/ n cuestionario m

queue /kju:/ n cola f. ● vi (pres p
queuing) hacer cola

quibble /'kwɪbl/ vi discutir; (split
hairs) sutilizar

quick /kwɪk/ adj (-er, -est) rápido.
be ~! ¡date prisa! ● adv rápido.
~en vt acelerar. ● vi acelerarse.
~ly adv rápido. ~sand n arena f
movediza. ~-tempered /-'tempəd/
adj irascible

quid /kwɪd/ n invar £ libra f (ester-
lina)

quiet /'kwaɪət/ adj (-er, -est) tran-
quilo; (silent) callado; (discreet) dis-
creto. ● n tranquilidad f. ● vt/i
(Amer) see QUIETEN. ~en vt calmar.
● n calmarse. ~ly adv tranquila-
mente; (silently) silenciosamente;
(discreetly) discretamente. ~ness n
tranquilidad f

quilt /kwɪlt/ n edredón m. ~ed adj
acolchado

quintet /kwɪn'tet/ n quinteto m

quirk /kwɜ:k/ n peculiaridad f

quit /kwɪt/ vt (pt quitted) dejar. ~
doing (Amer, cease) dejar de hacer.
● vi (give in) abandonar; (stop)
parar; (resign) dimitir

quite /kwaɪt/ adv bastante; (com-
pletely) totalmente; (really) verda-
deramente. ~ (so)! ¡claro! ~ a
few bastante

quits /kwɪts/ adj. be ~ estar en
paz. call it ~ darlo por terminado

quiver /'kwɪvə(r)/ vi temblar

quiz /kwɪz/ n (pl quizzes) serie f
de preguntas; (game) concurso m.
● vt (pt quizzed) interrogar. ~zical
/ adj burlón

quota /'kwəʊtə/ n cuota f

quot|ation /kwəʊ'teɪʃn/ n cita f;
(price) presupuesto m. ~ation
marks npl comillas fpl. ~e /kwəʊt/
vt citar; (Com) cotizar. ● n 🄳 cita f;
(price) presupuesto m. in ~es npl
entre comillas

. . . .

Rr

. . . .

rabbi /'ræbaɪ/ n rabino m

rabbit /'ræbɪt/ n conejo m

rabi|d /'ræbɪd/ adj feroz; (dog) ra-
bioso. ~es /'reɪbiːz/ n rabia f

race /reɪs/ n (in sport) carrera f;
(ethnic group) raza f. ● vt hacer co-
rrer (horse). ● vi (run) correr, ir co-
rriendo; (rush) ir de prisa.
~course n hipódromo m. ~horse
n caballo m de carreras. ~ rela-
tions npl relaciones fpl raciales.
~track n hipódromo m

racial /'reɪʃl/ adj racial

racing /'reɪsɪŋ/ n carreras fpl. ~
car n coche m de carreras

racis|m /'reɪsɪzəm/ n racismo m.
~t adj & n racista (m & f)

rack¹ /ræk/ n (shelf) estante m;
(for luggage) rejilla f; (for plates)
escurreplatos m. ● vt. ~ one's
brains devanarse los sesos

rack² /ræk/ n. go to ~ and ruin
quedarse en la ruina

racket /'rækɪt/ n (for sports) ra-
queta f; (din) alboroto m; (swindle)
estafa f. ~eer /-ə'tɪə(r)/ n estafa-
dor m

racy /'reɪsɪ/ adj (-ier, -iest) vivo

radar /ˈreɪdɑː(r)/ n radar m

radian|ce /ˈreɪdɪəns/ n resplandor m. **~t** adj radiante

radiat|e /ˈreɪdɪeɪt/ vt irradiar. • vi divergir. **~ion** /-ˈeɪʃn/ n radiación f. **~or** n radiador m

radical /ˈrædɪkl/ adj & n radical (m)

radio /ˈreɪdɪəʊ/ n (pl -os) radio f or m. • vt transmitir por radio. **~active** /ˈreɪdɪəʊˈæktɪv/ adj radiactivo. **~activity** /-ˈtɪvɪtɪ/ n radiactividad f

radish /ˈrædɪʃ/ n rábano m

radius /ˈreɪdɪəs/ n (pl -dii /-dɪaɪ/) radio m

raffle /ˈræfl/ n rifa f

raft /rɑːft/ n balsa f

rafter /ˈrɑːftə(r)/ n cabrio m

rag /ræg/ n andrajo m; (for wiping) trapo m. in **~s** (person) andrajoso

rage /reɪdʒ/ n rabia f; (fashion) moda f. • vi estar furioso; (storm) bramar

ragged /ˈrægɪd/ adj (person) andrajoso; (clothes) hecho jirones

raid /reɪd/ n (Mil) incursión f; (by police etc) redada f; (by thieves) asalto m. • vt (Mil) atacar; (police) hacer una redada en; (thieves) asaltar. **~er** n invasor m; (thief) ladrón m

rail /reɪl/ n barandilla f; (for train) riel m; (rod) barra f. by **~** por ferrocarril. **~ing** n barandilla f. (fence) verja f. **~road** n (Amer), **~way** n ferrocarril m. **~way station** n estación f de ferrocarril

rain /reɪn/ n lluvia f. • vi llover. **~bow** /-bəʊ/ n arco m iris. **~coat** n impermeable m. **~fall** n precipitación f. **~y** adj (-ier, -iest) lluvioso

raise /reɪz/ vt levantar; (breed) criar; obtener (money etc); formular (question); plantear (problem);

subir (price). • n (Amer) aumento m

raisin /ˈreɪzn/ n (uva f) pasa f

rake /reɪk/ n rastrillo m. • vt rastrillar; (search) buscar en. □ **~ up** vt remover

rally /ˈrælɪ/ vt reunir; (revive) reanimar. • n reunión f; (Auto) rally m

ram /ræm/ n carnero m. • vt (pt rammed) (thrust) meter por la fuerza; (crash into) chocar con

RAM /ræm/ n (Comp) RAM f

ramble /ˈræmbl/ n excursión f a pie. • vi ir de paseo; (in speech) divagar. □ **~ on** vi divagar. **~er** n excursionista m & f. **~ing** adj (speech) divagador

ramp /ræmp/ n rampa f

rampage /ræmˈpeɪdʒ/ vi alborotarse. • /ˈræmpeɪdʒ/ n. go on the **~** alborotarse

ramshackle /ˈræmʃækl/ adj desvencijado

ran /ræn/ see RUN

ranch /rɑːntʃ/ n hacienda f

random /ˈrændəm/ adj hecho al azar; (chance) fortuito. • n. at **~** al azar

rang /ræŋ/ see RING²

range /reɪndʒ/ n alcance m; (distance) distancia f; (series) serie f; (of mountains) cordillera f; (extent) extensión f; (Com) surtido m; (stove) cocina f económica. • vi extenderse; (vary) variar. **~r** n guardabosque m

rank /ræŋk/ n posición f, categoría f; (row) fila f; (for taxis) parada f. the **~ and file** la masa f. **~s** npl soldados mpl rasos. • adj (-er, -est) (smell) fétido; (fig) completo. • vt clasificar. • vi clasificarse

ransack /ˈrænsæk/ vt registrar; (pillage) saquear

ransom /ˈrænsəm/ n rescate m.

r

hold s.o. to ~ exigir rescate por uno. ●vt rescatar; (redeem) redimir

rant /rænt/ vi despotricar

rap /ræp/ n golpe m seco. ●vt/i (pt rapped) golpear

rape /reɪp/ vt violar. ●n violación f

rapid /'ræpɪd/ adj rápido. ~s npl rápidos mpl

rapist /'reɪpɪst/ n violador m

raptur|e /'ræptʃə(r)/ n éxtasis m. ~ous /-rəs/ adj extático

rare /reə(r)/ adj (-er, -est) raro; (Culin) poco hecho. ~fied /'reərɪfaɪd/ adj enrarecido. ~ly adv raramente

raring /'reərɪŋ/ adj 🆃. ~ to impaciente por

rarity /'reərətɪ/ n rareza f

rascal /'rɑːskl/ n granuja m & f

rash /ræʃ/ adj (-er, -est) precipitado, imprudente. ●n erupción f

rasher /'ræʃə(r)/ n loncha f

rashly /'ræʃlɪ/ adv precipitadamente, imprudentemente

rasp /rɑːsp/ n (file) escofina f

raspberry /'rɑːzbrɪ/ n frambuesa f

rat /ræt/ n rata f

rate /reɪt/ n (ratio) proporción f; (speed) velocidad f; (price) precio m; (of interest) tipo m. at any ~ de todas formas. at this ~ así. ~s npl (taxes) impuestos mpl municipales. ●vt valorar; (consider) considerar; (Amer, deserve) merecer. ●vi ser considerado

rather /'rɑːðə(r)/ adv mejor dicho; (fairly) bastante; (a little) un poco. ●int claro. I would ~ not prefiero no

rating /'reɪtɪŋ/ n clasificación f; (sailor) marinero m; (number, TV) índice m

ratio /'reɪʃɪəʊ/ n (pl -os) proporción f

ration /'ræʃn/ n ración f. ~s npl (provisions) víveres mpl. ●vt racionar

rational /'ræʃənəl/ adj racional. ~ize vt racionalizar

rattle /'rætl/ vi traquetear. ●vt (shake) agitar; 🆃 desconcertar. ●n traqueteo m; (toy) sonajero m. □ ~ off vt (fig) decir de corrida

raucous /'rɔːkəs/ adj estridente

ravage /'rævɪdʒ/ vt estragar

rave /reɪv/ vi delirar; (in anger) despotricar. ~ about sth poner a algo por las nubes

raven /'reɪvn/ n cuervo m

ravenous /'rævənəs/ adj voraz; (person) hambriento. be ~ morirse de hambre

ravine /rə'viːn/ n barranco m

raving /'reɪvɪŋ/ adj. ~ mad loco de atar

ravishing /'rævɪʃɪŋ/ adj (enchanting) encantador

raw /rɔː/ adj (-er, -est) crudo; (sugar) sin refinar; (inexperienced) inexperto. ~ deal n tratamiento m injusto, injusticia f. ~ materials npl materias fpl primas

ray /reɪ/ n rayo m

raze /reɪz/ vt arrasar

razor /'reɪzə(r)/ n navaja f de afeitar; (electric) maquinilla f de afeitar

Rd /rəʊd/ abbr (= Road) C/, Calle f

re /riː/ prep con referencia a. ●pref re.

reach /riːtʃ/ vt alcanzar; (extend) extender; (arrive at) llegar a; (achieve) lograr; (hand over) pasar, dar. ●vi extenderse. ●n alcance m. within ~ of al alcance de; (close to) a corta distancia de. □ ~ out vt alargar la mano

react /rɪ'ækt/ vt reaccionar. ∼ion /rɪ'ækʃn/ n reacción f. ∼ionary adj & n reaccionario (m). ∼or /rɪ'æktə(r)/ n reactor m

read /riːd/ vt (pt read /red/) leer; (study) estudiar; (interpret) interpretar. ● vi leer; (instrument) indicar. □ ∼ **out** vt leer en voz alta. ∼able adj (clear) legible. ∼er n lector m

readily /'redɪlɪ/ adv (willingly) de buena gana; (easily) fácilmente

reading /'riːdɪŋ/ n lectura f

readjust /riːə'dʒʌst/ vt reajustar. ● vi readaptarse (to a)

ready /'redɪ/ adj (-ier, -iest) listo, preparado. **get** ∼ prepararse. ∼**-made** adj confeccionado

real /rɪəl/ adj verdadero. ● adv (Amer fam) verdaderamente. ∼ estate n bienes mpl raíces, propiedad f inmobiliaria. ∼ estate agent see REALTOR. ∼ism n realismo m. ∼ist n realista m & f. ∼istic /-'lɪstɪk/ adj realista. ∼ity /rɪ'ælətɪ/ n realidad f. ∼ization /rɪəlaɪ'zeɪʃn/ n comprensión f. ∼ize /'rɪəlaɪz/ vt darse cuenta de; (fulfil, Com) realizar. ∼ly /'rɪəlɪ/ adv verdaderamente

realm /relm/ n reino m

realtor /'rɪːəltə(r)/ n (Amer) agente m inmobiliario

reap /riːp/ vt segar; (fig) cosechar

reappear /riːə'pɪə(r)/ vi reaparecer

rear /rɪə(r)/ n parte f de atrás. ● adj posterior, trasero. ● vt (bring up, breed) criar. ● vi ∼ (up) (horse) encabritarse

rearguard /'rɪəɡɑːd/ n retaguardia f

rearrange /riːə'reɪndʒ/ vt arreglar de otra manera

reason /'riːzn/ n razón f, motivo m. **within** ∼ dentro de lo razona-

ble. ● vi razonar. ∼able adj razonable. ∼ing n razonamiento m

reassur|ance /riːə'ʃʊərəns/ n promesa f tranquilizadora; (guarantee) garantía f. ∼e /riːə'ʃʊə(r)/ vt tranquilizar

rebate /'riːbeɪt/ n (discount) rebaja f

rebel /'rebl/ n rebelde m & f. ●/rɪ'bel/ vi (pt rebelled) rebelarse. ∼lion /rɪ'belɪən/ n rebelión f. ∼lious adj rebelde

rebound /rɪ'baʊnd/ vi rebotar; (fig) recaer. ● /'riːbaʊnd/ n rebote m

rebuff /rɪ'bʌf/ vt rechazar. ●n desaire m

rebuild /riː'bɪld/ vt (pt rebuilt) reconstruir

rebuke /rɪ'bjuːk/ vt reprender. ●n reprimenda f

recall /rɪ'kɔːl/ vt (call s.o. back) llamar; (remember) recordar. ●n /'riːkɔːl/ (of goods, ambassador) retirada f; (memory) memoria f

recap /'riːkæp/ vt/i (pt recapped) 🄵 resumir

recapitulate /riːkə'pɪtʃʊleɪt/ vt/i resumir

recapture /riː'kæptʃə(r)/ vt recobrar; (recall) hacer revivir

recede /rɪ'siːd/ vi retroceder

receipt /rɪ'siːt/ n recibo m. ∼s npl (Com) ingresos mpl

receive /rɪ'siːv/ vt recibir. ∼r n (of stolen goods) perista m & f; (part of phone) auricular m

recent /'riːsnt/ adj reciente. ∼ly adv recientemente

recept|ion /rɪ'sepʃn/ n recepción f; (welcome) acogida f. ∼ionist n recepcionista m & f. ∼ive /-tɪv/ adj receptivo

recess /rɪ'ses/ n hueco m; (holiday)

vacaciones *fpl.* ∼**ion** /rɪ'seʃn/ *n* recesión *f*

recharge /riːˈtʃɑːdʒ/ *vt* cargar de nuevo, recargar

recipe /'resəpɪ/ *n* receta *f.* ∼ **book** *n* libro *m* de cocina

recipient /rɪ'sɪpɪənt/ *n* recipiente *m* & *f;* (of letter) destinatario *m*

recit|al /rɪ'saɪtl/ *n* (Mus) recital *m.* ∼**e** /rɪ'saɪt/ *vt* recitar; (list) enumerar

reckless /'reklɪs/ *adj* imprudente. ∼**ly** *adv* imprudentemente

reckon /'rekən/ *vt/i* calcular; (consider) considerar; (think) pensar. □ ∼ **on** *vt* (rely) contar con

reclaim /rɪ'kleɪm/ *vt* reclamar; recuperar (land)

reclin|e /rɪ'klaɪn/ *vi* recostarse. ∼**ing** *adj* acostado; (seat) reclinable

recluse /rɪ'kluːs/ *n* ermitaño *m*

recogni|tion /rekəg'nɪʃn/ *n* reconocimiento *m.* beyond ∼**tion** irreconocible. ∼**ze** /'rekəgnaɪz/ *vt* reconocer

recoil /rɪ'kɔɪl/ *vi* retroceder. ● /'riːkɔɪl/ *n* (of gun) culatazo *m*

recollect /rekə'lekt/ *vt* recordar. ∼**ion** /-ʃn/ *n* recuerdo *m*

recommend /rekə'mend/ *vt* recomendar. ∼**ation** /-'deɪʃn/ *n* recomendación *f*

reconcil|e /'rekənsaɪl/ *vt* reconciliar (people); conciliar (facts). ∼**e o.s.** resignarse (to a). ∼**iation** /-sɪlɪ'eɪʃn/ *n* reconciliación *f*

reconnaissance /rɪ'kɒnɪsns/ *n* reconocimiento *m*

reconnoitre /rekə'nɔɪtə(r)/ *vt* (pres p ∼**tring**) (Mil) reconocer

re: ∼**consider** /riːkən'sɪdə(r)/ *vt* volver a considerar. ∼**construct** /riːkən'strʌkt/ *vt* reconstruir

record /rɪ'kɔːd/ *vt* (in register) registrar; (in diary) apuntar; (Mus) grabar. ● /'rekɔːd/ *n* (document) documento *m*; (of events) registro *m*; (Mus) disco *m*; (Sport) récord *m.* off the ∼ en confianza. ∼**er** /rɪ'kɔːdə(r)/ *n* registrador *m*; (Mus) flauta *f* dulce. ∼**ing** /rɪ'kɔːdɪŋ/ *n* grabación *f.* ∼**-player** /'rekɔːd-/ *n* tocadiscos *m invar*

recount /rɪ'kaʊnt/ *vt* contar, relatar

re-count /'riːkaʊnt/ *vt* volver a contar; recontar (votes). ● /'riːkaʊnt/ *n* (Pol) recuento *m*

recover /rɪ'kʌvə(r)/ *vt* recuperar. ● *vi* reponerse. ∼**y** *n* recuperación *f*

recreation /rekrɪ'eɪʃn/ *n* recreo *m.* ∼**al** *adj* de recreo

recruit /rɪ'kruːt/ *n* recluta *m.* ● *vt* reclutar; contratar (staff). ∼**ment** *n* reclutamiento *m*

rectang|le /'rektæŋgl/ *n* rectángulo *m.* ∼**ular** /-'tæŋgjʊlə(r)/ *adj* rectangular

rectify /'rektɪfaɪ/ *vt* rectificar

rector /'rektə(r)/ *n* párroco *m*; (of college) rector *m.* ∼**y** *n* rectoría *f*

recuperat|e /rɪ'kuːpəreɪt/ *vt* recuperar. ● *vi* reponerse. ∼**ion** /-'reɪʃn/ *n* recuperación *f*

recur /rɪ'kɜː(r)/ *vi* (pt recurred) repetirse. ∼**rence** /rɪ'kʌrəns/ *n* repetición *f.* ∼**rent** /rɪ'kʌrənt/ *adj* repetido

recycle /riː'saɪkl/ *vt* reciclar

red /red/ *adj* (redder, reddest) rojo. ● *n* rojo. **be in the ∼** estar en números rojos. ∼**den** *vi* enrojecerse. ∼**dish** *adj* rojizo

redecorate /riː'dekəreɪt/ *vt* pintar de nuevo

rede|em /rɪ'diːm/ *vt* redimir. ∼**mption** /-'dempʃn/ *n* redención *f*

red: ~**-handed** /-'hændɪd/ adj.
catch s.o. ~**handed** agarrar a uno
con las manos en la masa. ~
herring n (fig) pista f falsa.
~**-hot** adj al rojo vivo. ~ **light** n
luz f roja

redo /ri:'du:/ vt (pt **redid,** pp **re-**
done) rehacer

redouble /ri'dʌbl/ vt redoblar

red tape /red'teɪp/ n (fig) pape-
leo m

reduc|e /rɪ'dju:s/ vt reducir; aliviar
(pain). ● vi (Amer, slim) adelgazar.
~**tion** /rɪ'dʌkʃn/ n reducción f

redundan|cy /rɪ'dʌndənsɪ/ n su-
perfluidad f; (unemployment) des-
pido m. ~**t** superfluo. she was
made ~**t** la despidieron por re-
ducción de plantilla

reed /ri:d/ n caña f; (Mus) len-
güeta f

reef /ri:f/ n arrecife m

reek /ri:k/ n mal olor m. ● vi. ~
(of) apestar a

reel /ri:l/ n carrete m. ● vi dar vuel-
tas; (stagger) tambalearse. □ ~ **off**
vt (fig) enumerar

refectory /rɪ'fektərɪ/ n refecto-
rio m

refer /rɪ'fɜ:(r)/ vt (pt **referred**) re-
mitir. ● vi referirse. ~ **to** referirse
a; (consult) consultar. ~**ee** /refə
'ri:/ n árbitro m; (for job) referencia
f. ● vi (pt **refereed**) arbitrar. ~**ence**
/'refrəns/ n referencia f. ~**ence**
book n libro m de consulta. **in** ~
to, with ~ **to** con referencia a;
(Com) respecto a. ~**endum** /refə
'rendəm/ n (pl **-ums** or **-da**) refe-
réndum m

refill /ri:'fɪl/ vt volver a llenar.
● /'ri:fɪl/ n recambio m

refine /rɪ'faɪn/ vt refinar. ~**d** adj
refinado. ~**ry** /-ərɪ/ n refinería f

reflect /rɪ'flekt/ vt reflejar. ● vi re-
flejarse; (think) reflexionar. □ ~
badly upon perjudicar. ~**ion** /-ʃn/
n reflexión f; (image) reflejo m.
~**or** n reflector m

reflex /'ri:fleks/ adj & n reflejo (m).
~**ive** /rɪ'fleksɪv/ adj (Gram) refle-
xivo

reform /rɪ'fɔ:m/ vt reformar. ● vi
reformarse. ● n reforma f

refrain /rɪ'freɪn/ n estribillo m. ● vi
abstenerse (from de)

refresh /rɪ'freʃ/ vt refrescar. ~**ing**
adj refrescante. ~**ments** npl (food
and drink) refrigerio m

refrigerat|e /rɪ'frɪdʒəreɪt/ vt re-
frigerar. ~**or** n frigorífico m, refri-
gerador m (LAm)

refuel /ri:'fju:əl/ vt/i (pt **refuelled**)
repostar

refuge /'refju:dʒ/ n refugio m.
take ~ refugiarse. ~**e** /refjʊ'dʒi:/
n refugiado m

refund /rɪ'fʌnd/ vt reembolsar.
● /'ri:fʌnd/ n reembolso m

refusal /rɪ'fju:zl/ n negativa f

refuse /rɪ'fju:z/ vt rehusar. ● vi ne-
garse. ● /'refju:s/ n residuos mpl

refute /rɪ'fju:t/ vt refutar

regain /rɪ'geɪn/ vt recobrar

regal /'ri:gl/ adj real

regard /rɪ'gɑ:d/ vt considerar;
(look at) contemplar. **as** ~**s** en lo
que se refiere a. ● n (consideration)
consideración f; (esteem) estima f.
~**s** npl saludos mpl. **kind** ~**s** recu-
erdos. ~**ing** prep en lo que se
refiere a. ~**less** adv a pesar de
todo. ~**less of** sin tener en cuenta

regatta /rɪ'gætə/ n regata f

regime /reɪ'ʒi:m/ n régimen m

regiment /'redʒɪmənt/ n regi-
miento m. ~**al** /-'mentl/ adj del re-
gimiento

region /ˈriːdʒən/ n región f. in the ~ of alrededor de. ~**al** adj regional

register /ˈredʒɪstə(r)/ n registro m. • vt registrar; matricular (vehicle); declarar (birth); certificar (letter); facturar (luggage). • vi (enrol) inscribirse; (fig) producir impresión

registrar /redʒɪˈstrɑː(r)/ n secretario m del registro civil; (Univ) secretario m general

registration /redʒɪˈstreɪʃn/ n registro m; (in register) inscripción f. ~ **number** n (Auto) (número de) matrícula f

registry /ˈredʒɪstrɪ/ n. ~ **office** n registro m civil

regret /rɪˈɡret/ n pesar m; (remorse) arrepentimiento m. • vt (pt regretted) lamentar. I ~ that siento (que). ~**table** adj lamentable

regula|r /ˈreɡjʊlə(r)/ adj regular; (usual) habitual. • n 🔲 cliente m habitual. ~**rity** /-ˈlærətɪ/ n regularidad f. ~**rly** adv con regularidad. ~**te** /ˈreɡjʊleɪt/ vt regular. ~**tion** /-ˈleɪʃn/ n regulación f; (rule) regla f

rehears|al /rɪˈhɜːsl/ n ensayo m. ~**e** /rɪˈhɜːs/ vt ensayar

reign /reɪn/ n reinado m. • vi reinar

reindeer /ˈreɪndɪə(r)/ n invar reno m

reinforce /riːɪnˈfɔːs/ vt reforzar. ~**ment** n refuerzo m

reins /reɪnz/ npl riendas fpl

reiterate /riːˈɪtəreɪt/ vt reiterar

reject /rɪˈdʒekt/ vt rechazar. • /ˈriːdʒekt/ n producto m defectuoso. ~**ion** /rɪˈdʒekʃn/ n rechazo m; (after job application) respuesta f negativa

rejoice /rɪˈdʒɔɪs/ vi regocijarse

rejoin /rɪˈdʒɔɪn/ vt reunirse con

rejuvenate /rɪˈdʒuːvəneɪt/ vt rejuvenecer

relapse /rɪˈlæps/ n recaída f. • vi recaer; (into crime) reincidir

relat|e /rɪˈleɪt/ vt contar; (connect) relacionar. • vi relacionarse (to con). ~**ed** adj emparentado; (ideas etc) relacionado. ~**ion** /rɪˈleɪʃn/ n relación f; (person) pariente m & f. ~**ionship** n relación f; (blood ties) parentesco m; (affair) relaciones fpl. ~**ive** /ˈrelətɪv/ n pariente m & f. • adj relativo. ~**ively** adv relativamente

relax /rɪˈlæks/ vt relajar. • vi relajarse. ~**ation** /-ˈseɪʃn/ n relajación f; (rest) descanso m; (recreation) recreo m. ~**ing** adj relajante

relay /ˈriːleɪ/ n relevo m. ~ (race) n carrera f de relevos. • /rɪˈleɪ/ vt transmitir

release /rɪˈliːs/ vt soltar; poner en libertad (prisoner); estrenar (film); (Mec) soltar; publicar (news). • n liberación f; (of film) estreno m; (record) disco m nuevo

relent /rɪˈlent/ vi ceder. ~**less** adj implacable; (continuous) incesante

relevan|ce /ˈreləvəns/ n pertinencia f. ~**t** adj pertinente

relia|bility /rɪlaɪəˈbɪlətɪ/ n fiabilidad f. ~**ble** /rɪˈlaɪəbl/ adj (person) de confianza; (car) fiable. ~**nce** /rɪˈlaɪəns/ n dependencia f; (trust) confianza f. ~**nt** /rɪˈlaɪənt/ adj confiado

relic /ˈrelɪk/ n reliquia f

relie|f /rɪˈliːf/ n alivio m; (assistance) socorro m. be on ~ f (Amer) recibir prestaciones de la seguridad social. ~**ve** /rɪˈliːv/ vt aliviar; (take over from) relevar. ~**ved** adj aliviado. feel ～ved sentir un gran alivio

religio|n /rɪˈlɪdʒən/ n religión f. ～**us** /rɪˈlɪdʒəs/ adj religioso

relinquish /rɪˈlɪŋkwɪʃ/ vt abandonar, renunciar

relish /ˈrelɪʃ/ n gusto m; (Culin) salsa f. ● vt saborear

reluctan|ce /rɪˈlʌktəns/ n desgana f. ～**t** adj mal dispuesto. be ～**t to** no tener ganas de. ～**tly** adv de mala gana

rely /rɪˈlaɪ/ vi. ～ **on** contar con; (trust) fiarse de; (depend) depender

remain /rɪˈmeɪn/ vi (be left) quedar; (stay) quedarse; (continue to be) seguir. ～**der** n resto m. ～**s** npl (left-overs) sobras fpl

remand /rɪˈmɑːnd/ vt. ～ **in custody** mantener bajo custodia. ● n. **on** ～ en prisión preventiva

remark /rɪˈmɑːk/ n observación f. ● vt observar. ～**able** adj notable

remarry /riːˈmærɪ/ vi volver a casarse

remedy /ˈremədɪ/ n remedio m. ● vt remediar

remember /rɪˈmembə(r)/ vt acordarse de, recordar. ● vi acordarse

remind /rɪˈmaɪnd/ vt recordar. ～**er** n recordatorio m

reminisce /remɪˈnɪs/ vi rememorar los viejos tiempos. ～**nces** /-ənsɪz/ npl recuerdos mpl. ～**nt** /-ˈnɪsnt/ adj. be ～**nt of** recordar

remnant /ˈremnənt/ n resto m; (of cloth) retazo m; (trace) vestigio m

remorse /rɪˈmɔːs/ n remordimiento m. ～**ful** adj arrepentido. ～**less** adj implacable

remote /rɪˈməʊt/ adj remoto. ～ **control** n mando m a distancia.

～**ly** adv remotamente

remov|able /rɪˈmuːvəbl/ adj (detachable) de quita y pon; (handle) desmontable. ～**al** n eliminación f; (from house) mudanza f. ～**e** /rɪˈmuːv/ vt quitar; (dismiss) destituir; (get rid of) eliminar

render /ˈrendə(r)/ vt rendir (homage); prestar (help etc). ～ **sth useless** hacer que algo resulte inútil

rendezvous /ˈrɒndɪvuː/ n (pl -vous/-vuːz/) cita f

renegade /ˈrenɪgeɪd/ n renegado

renew /rɪˈnjuː/ vt renovar; (resume) reanudar. ～**al** n renovación f

renounce /rɪˈnaʊns/ vt renunciar a

renovat|e /ˈrenəveɪt/ vt renovar. ～**ion** /-ˈveɪʃn/ n renovación f

renown /rɪˈnaʊn/ n renombre m. ～**ed** adj de renombre

rent /rent/ n alquiler m. ● vt alquilar. ～**al** n alquiler m. **car** ～ (Amer) alquiler m de coche

renunciation /rɪnʌnsɪˈeɪʃn/ n renuncia f

reopen /riːˈəʊpən/ vt volver a abrir. ● vi reabrirse

reorganize /riːˈɔːgənaɪz/ vt reorganizar

rep /rep/ n (Com) representante m & f

repair /rɪˈpeə(r)/ vt arreglar, reparar; arreglar (clothes, shoes). ● n reparación f; (patch) remiendo m. **in good** ～ en buen estado. **it's beyond** ～ ya no tiene arreglo

repatriat|e /riːˈpætrɪeɪt/ vt repatriar

repay /riːˈpeɪ/ vt (pt repaid) reembolsar; pagar (debt); corresponder a (kindness). ～**ment** n pago m

repeal /rɪˈpiːl/ vt revocar. ● n revo-

r

cación f

repeat /rɪˈpiːt/ vt repetir. • vi repetir(se). • n repetición f. **~edly** adv repetidas veces

repel /rɪˈpel/ vt (pt repelled) repeler. **~lent** adj repelente

repent /rɪˈpent/ vi arrepentirse. **~ant** adj arrepentido

repercussion /riːpəˈkʌʃn/ n repercusión f

repertoire /ˈrepətwɑː(r)/ n repertorio m

repetit|ion /repɪˈtɪʃn/ n repetición f. **~ious** /-ˈtɪʃəs/ adj, **~ive** /rɪˈpetɪtɪv/ adj repetitivo

replace /rɪˈpleɪs/ vt reponer; cambiar (battery); (take the place of) sustituir. **~ment** n sustitución f; (person) sustituto m

replay /ˈriːpleɪ/ n (Sport) repetición f del partido; (recording) repetición f inmediata

replenish /rɪˈplenɪʃ/ vt reponer

replica /ˈreplɪkə/ n réplica f

reply /rɪˈplaɪ/ vt/i responder, contestar. **~ to sth** responder a algo, contestar algo. • n respuesta f

report /rɪˈpɔːt/ vt (reporter) informar sobre; informar de (accident); (denounce) denunciar. • vi informar; (present o.s.) presentarse. • n informe m; (Schol) boletín m de notas; (rumour) rumor m; (in newspaper) reportaje m. **~ card** (Amer) n boletín m de calificaciones. **~edly** adv según se dice. **~er** n periodista m & f, reportero m

reprehensible /reprɪˈhensəbl/ adj reprensible

represent /reprɪˈzent/ vt representar. **~ation** /-ˈteɪʃn/ n representación f. **~ative** adj representativo. • n representante m & f; (Amer, in government) diputado m

repress /rɪˈpres/ vt reprimir. **~ion** /-ʃn/ n represión f. **~ive** adj represivo

reprieve /rɪˈpriːv/ n indulto m; (fig) respiro m. • vt indultar

reprimand /ˈreprɪmɑːnd/ vt reprender. • n reprensión f

reprisal /rɪˈpraɪzl/ n represalia f

reproach /rɪˈprəʊtʃ/ vt reprochar. • n reproche m. **~ful** adj de reproche

reproduc|e /riːprəˈdjuːs/ vt reproducir. • vi reproducirse. **~tion** /-ˈdʌkʃn/ n reproducción f. **~tive** /-ˈdʌktɪv/ adj reproductor

reprove /rɪˈpruːv/ vt reprender

reptile /ˈreptaɪl/ n reptil m

republic /rɪˈpʌblɪk/ n república f. **~an** adj & n republicano (m). R**~** a & n (in US) republicano (m)

repugnan|ce /rɪˈpʌɡnəns/ n repugnancia f. **~t** adj repugnante

repuls|e /rɪˈpʌls/ vt rechazar, repulsar. **~ion** /-ʃn/ n repulsión f. **~ive** adj repulsivo

reput|able /ˈrepjʊtəbl/ adj acreditado, reputado. **~ation** /repjʊˈteɪʃn/ n reputación f

request /rɪˈkwest/ n petición f. • vt pedir

require /rɪˈkwaɪə(r)/ vt requerir; (need) necesitar; (demand) exigir. **~d** adj necesario. **~ment** n requisito m

rescue /ˈreskjuː/ vt rescatar, salvar. • n rescate m. **~r** n salvador m

research /rɪˈsɜːtʃ/ n investigación f. • vt investigar. **~er** n investigador m

resembl|ance /rɪˈzembləns/ n parecido m. **~e** /rɪˈzembl/ vt parecerse a

resent /rɪˈzent/ vt guardarle rencor a (person). she **~ed** his success le molestaba que él tuviera éxito. ~**ful** adj resentido. ~**ment** n resentimiento m

reserv|ation /rezə'veɪʃn/ n reserva f; (booking) reserva f. ~**e** /rɪ'zɜːv/ vt reservar. • n reserva f; (in sports) suplente m & f. ~**ed** adj reservado. ~**oir** /'rezəvwɑː(r)/ n embalse m

reshuffle /riːˈʃʌfl/ n (Pol) reorganización f

residen|ce /'rezɪdəns/ n residencia f. ~**t** adj & n residente (m & f). ~**tial** /rezɪ'denʃl/ adj residencial

residue /'rezɪdjuː/ n residuo m

resign /rɪ'zaɪn/ vt/i dimitir. ~ **o.s.** to resignarse a. ~**ation** /rezɪg 'neɪʃn/ n resignación f; (from job) dimisión f. ~**ed** adj resignado

resilien|ce /rɪ'zɪliəns/ n elasticidad f; (of person) resistencia f. ~**t** adj elástico; (person) resistente

resin /'rezɪn/ n resina f

resist /rɪ'zɪst/ vt resistir. • vi resistirse. ~**ance** n resistencia f. ~**ant** adj resistente

resolut|e /'rezəluːt/ adj resuelto. ~**ion** /-'luːʃn/ n resolución f

resolve /rɪ'zɒlv/ vt resolver. ~ **to do** resolver a hacer. • n resolución f

resort /rɪ'zɔːt/ n recurso m; (place) lugar m turístico. **in the last** ~ como último recurso. □ ~ **to** vt recurrir a.

resource /rɪ'sɔːs/ n recurso m. ~**ful** adj ingenioso

respect /rɪ'spekt/ n (esteem) respeto m; (aspect) respecto m. **with** ~ **to** con respecto a. • vt respetar. ~**able** adj respetable. ~**ful** adj respetuoso. ~**ive** adj respectivo. ~**ively** adv respectivamente

respiration /respə'reɪʃn/ n respiración f

respite /'respaɪt/ n respiro m

respon|d /rɪ'spɒnd/ vi responder. ~**se** /rɪ'spɒns/ n respuesta f; (reaction) reacción f

responsib|ility /rɪspɒnsə'bɪləti/ n responsabilidad f. ~**le** /rɪ'spɒnsəbl/ adj responsable; (job) de responsabilidad. ~**ly** adv con formalidad

responsive /rɪ'spɒnsɪv/ adj que reacciona bien. ~ **to** sensible a

rest /rest/ vt descansar; (lean) apoyar. • vi descansar; (lean) apoyarse. • n descanso m; (Mus) pausa f; (remainder) resto m, lo demás; (people) los demás, los otros mpl. **to have a** ~ tomarse un descanso. □ ~ **up** vi (Amer) descansar

restaurant /'restərɒnt/ n restaurante m

rest: ~ful adj sosegado. ~**ive** adj impaciente. ~**less** adj inquieto

restor|ation /restə'reɪʃn/ n restablecimiento m; (of building, monarch) restauración f. ~**e** /rɪ'stɔː(r)/ vt restablecer; restaurar (building); devolver (confidence, health)

restrain /rɪ'streɪn/ vt contener. ~ **o.s.** contenerse. ~**ed** adj (moderate) moderado; (in control of self) comedido. ~**t** n restricción f; (moderation) compostura f

restrict /rɪ'strɪkt/ vt restringir. ~**ion** /-ʃn/ n restricción f. ~**ive** adj restrictivo

rest room n (Amer) baño m, servicio m

result /rɪ'zʌlt/ n resultado m. **as a** ~ **of** como consecuencia de. • vi. ~ **from** resultar de. ~ **in** dar como resultado

resume /rɪ'zjuːm/ vt reanudar. • vi reanudarse

résumé /'rezjuːmeɪ/ n resumen m;

(*Amer, CV*) currículum *m*, historial *m* personal

resurrect /rezə'rekt/ *vt* resucitar. **~ion** /-ʃn/ *n* resurrección *f*

resuscitat|e /rɪ'sʌsɪteɪt/ *vt* resucitar. **~ion** /-'teɪʃn/ *n* resucitación *f*

retail /'riːteɪl/ *n* venta *f* al por menor. ● *adj* & *adv* al por menor. ● *vt* vender al por menor. ● *vi* venderse al por menor. **~er** *n* minorista *m* & *f*

retain /rɪ'teɪn/ *vt* retener; conservar (heat)

retaliat|e /rɪ'tælɪeɪt/ *vi* desquitarse; (*Mil*) tomar represalias. **~ion** /-'eɪʃn/ *n* represalias *fpl*

retarded /rɪ'tɑːdɪd/ *adj* retrasado

rethink /riː'θɪŋk/ *vt* (*pt* rethought) reconsiderar

reticen|ce /'retɪsns/ *n* reticencia *f*. **~t** *adj* reticente

retina /'retɪnə/ *n* retina *f*

retinue /'retɪnjuː/ *n* séquito *m*

retir|e /rɪ'taɪə(r)/ *vi* (*from work*) jubilarse; (*withdraw*) retirarse; (*go to bed*) acostarse. **~ed** *adj* jubilado. **~ement** *n* jubilación *f*. **~ing** *adj* retraído

retort /rɪ'tɔːt/ *vt/i* replicar. ● *n* réplica *f*

retrace /riː'treɪs/ *vt*. **~** one's steps volver sobre sus pasos

retract /rɪ'trækt/ *vt* retirar (statement). ● *vi* retractarse

retrain /riː'treɪn/ *vi* hacer un curso de reciclaje

retreat /rɪ'triːt/ *vi* retirarse. ● *n* retirada *f*; (*place*) refugio *m*

retrial /riː'traɪəl/ *n* nuevo juicio *m*

retriev|al /rɪ'triːvl/ *n* recuperación *f*. **~e** /rɪ'triːv/ *vt* recuperar. **~er** *n* (*dog*) perro *m* cobrador

retro|grade /'retrəgreɪd/ *adj* re-

trógrado. **~spect** /-spekt/ *n*. in **~** en retrospectiva. **~spective** /-'spektɪv/ *adj* retrospectivo

return /rɪ'tɜːn/ *vi* volver, regresar; (*symptom*) reaparecer. ● *vt* devolver; corresponder a (affection). ● *n* regreso *m*, vuelta *f*; (*Com*) rendimiento *m*; (*to owner*) devolución *f*. in **~** for a cambio de. many happy **~s!** ¡feliz cumpleaños! **~ ticket** *n* billete *m* or (*LAm*) boleto *m* de ida y vuelta, boleto *m* redondo (*Mex*). **~s** *npl* (*Com*) ingresos *mpl*

reun|ion /riː'juːnɪən/ *n* reunión *f*. **~ite** /riːjuː'naɪt/ *vt* reunir

rev /rev/ *n* (*Auto, fam*) revolución *f*. ● *vt/i*. **~ (up)** (*Auto, fam*) acelerar(se)

reveal /rɪ'viːl/ *vt* revelar. **~ing** *adj* revelador

revel /'revl/ *vi* (*pt* revelled) tener un jolgorio. **~ in** deleitarse en. **~ry** *n* jolgorio *m*

revelation /revə'leɪʃn/ *n* revelación *f*

revenge /rɪ'vendʒ/ *n* venganza *f*. take **~** vengarse. ● *vt* vengar

revenue /'revənjuː/ *n* ingresos *mpl*

revere /rɪ'vɪə(r)/ *vt* venerar. **~nce** /'revərəns/ *n* reverencia *f*

Reverend /'revərənd/ *adj* reverendo

reverent /'revərənt/ *adj* reverente

reverie /'revərɪ/ *n* ensueño *m*

revers|al /rɪ'vɜːsl/ *n* inversión *f*. **~e** /rɪ'vɜːs/ *adj* inverso. ● *n* contrario *m*; (*back*) revés *m*; (*Auto*) marcha *f* atrás. ● *vt* invertir; anular (decision); (*Auto*) dar marcha atrás a. ● *vi* (*Auto*) dar marcha atrás

revert /rɪ'vɜːt/ *vi*. **~ to** volver a; (*Jurid*) revertir a

review /rɪ'vjuː/ *n* revisión *f*; (*Mil*)

revista f; (of book, play, etc) crítica f. ● vt examinar (situation); reseñar (book, play, etc); (Amer, for exam) repasar

revis|e /rɪ'vaɪz/ vt revisar; (Schol) repasar. **~ion** /rɪ'vɪʒn/ n revisión f; (Schol) repaso m

revive /rɪ'vaɪv/ vt resucitar (person)

revolt /rɪ'vəʊlt/ vi sublevarse. ● n revuelta f. **~ing** adj asqueroso

revolution /revə'luːʃn/ n revolución f. **~ary** adj & n revolucionario (m). **~ize** vt revolucionar

revolv|e /rɪ'vɒlv/ vi girar. **~er** n revólver m. **~ing** /rɪ'vɒlvɪŋ/ adj giratorio

revue /rɪ'vjuː/ n revista f

revulsion /rɪ'vʌlʃn/ n asco m

reward /rɪ'wɔːd/ n recompensa f. ● vt recompensar. **~ing** adj gratificante

rewrite /riː'raɪt/ vt (pt rewrote, pp rewritten) volver a escribir or redactar; (copy out) escribir otra vez

rhetoric /'retərɪk/ n retórica f. **~al** /rɪ'tɒrɪkl/ adj retórico

rheumatism /'ruːmətɪzəm/ n reumatismo m

rhinoceros /raɪ'nɒsərəs/ n (pl -oses or invar) rinoceronte m

rhubarb /'ruːbɑːb/ n ruibarbo m

rhyme /raɪm/ n rima f; (poem) poesía f. ● vt/i rimar

rhythm /'rɪðəm/ n ritmo m. **~ic(al)** /'rɪðmɪk(l)/ adj rítmico

rib /rɪb/ n costilla f

ribbon /'rɪbən/ n cinta f

rice /raɪs/ n arroz m. **~ pudding** n arroz con leche

rich /rɪtʃ/ adj (-er, -est) rico. ● n ricos mpl. **~es** npl riquezas fpl

ricochet /'rɪkəʃeɪ/ vi rebotar

rid /rɪd/ vt (pt rid, pres p ridding) librar (of de). **get ~ of** deshacerse de. **~dance** /'rɪdns/ n. **good ~dance!** ¡adiós y buen viaje!

ridden /'rɪdn/ see RIDE

riddle /'rɪdl/ n acertijo m. ● vt acribillar. **be ~d with** estar lleno de

ride /raɪd/ vi (pt rode, pp ridden) (on horseback) montar a caballo; (go) ir (en bicicleta, a caballo etc). ● vt montar a (horse); ir en (bicycle); (Amer) ir en (bus, train); recorrer (distance). ● n (on horse) cabalgata f; (in car) paseo m en coche. **take s.o. for a** T engañarle a uno. **~r** n (on horse) jinete m; (cyclist) ciclista m & f

ridge /rɪdʒ/ n (of hills) cadena f; (hilltop) cresta f

ridicul|e /'rɪdɪkjuːl/ n burlas fpl. ● vt ridiculizar. **~ous** /rɪ'dɪkjələs/ adj ridículo

rife /raɪf/ adj difundido

rifle /'raɪfl/ n fusil m

rift /rɪft/ n grieta f; (fig) ruptura f

rig /rɪg/ vt (pt rigged) (pej) amañar. ● n (at sea) plataforma f de perforación. **□ ~ up** vt improvisar

right /raɪt/ adj (answer) correcto; (morally) bueno; (not left) derecho; (suitable) adecuado. **be ~** (person) tener razón; (clock) estar bien. **it is ~** (just, moral) es justo. **put ~** rectificar. **the ~ person for the job** la persona indicada para el puesto. ● n (entitlement) derecho m; (not left) derecha f; (not evil) bien m. **~ of way** (Auto) prioridad f. **be in the ~** tener razón. **on the ~** a la derecha. **on the ~** a la derecha, (fig) reparar. ● adv a la derecha; (directly) derecho; (completely) completamente. **~ angle** n ángulo m recto.

r

~ away adv inmediatamente. **~eous** /'raɪtʃəs/ adj recto; (cause) justo. **~ful** /'raɪtfl/ adj legítimo. **~-handed** /-'hændɪd/ adj diestro. **~-hand man** n brazo m derecho. **~ly** adv justamente. **~ wing** adj (Pol) derechista

rigid /'rɪdʒɪd/ adj rígido

rig|orous /'rɪgərəs/ adj riguroso. **~our** /'rɪgə(r)/ n rigor m

rim /rɪm/ n borde m; (of wheel) llanta f; (of glasses) montura f

rind /raɪnd/ n corteza f; (of fruit) cáscara f

ring[1] /rɪŋ/ n (circle) círculo m; (circle of metal etc) aro m; (on finger) anillo m; (on finger with stone) sortija f; (Boxing) cuadrilátero m; (bullring) ruedo m; (for circus) pista f; ● vt cercar

ring[2] /rɪŋ/ n (of bell) toque m; (tinkle) tintineo m; (telephone call) llamada f. ● vt (pt rang, pp rung) hacer sonar; (telephone) llamar por teléfono. **~ the bell** tocar el timbre. ● vi sonar. **~ back** vt/i volver a llamar. □ **~ up** vt llamar por teléfono

ring:: **~leader** /'rɪŋliːdə(r)/ n cabecilla m & f. **~ road** n carretera f de circunvalación

rink /rɪŋk/ n pista f

rinse /rɪns/ vt enjuagar. ● n aclarado m; (of dishes) enjuague m; (for hair) tintura f (no permanente)

riot /'raɪət/ n disturbio m; (of colours) profusión f. **run ~** desenfrenarse. ● vi causar disturbios

rip /rɪp/ vt (pt ripped) rasgar. ● vi rasgarse. ● n rasgón m. □ **~ off** vt (pull off) arrancar; (🛈, cheat) robar

ripe /raɪp/ adj (-er, -est) maduro. **~n** /'raɪpn/ vt/i madurar

rip-off /'rɪpɒf/ n 🛈 timo m

ripple /'rɪpl/ n (on water) onda f

ris|e /raɪz/ vi (pt rose, pp risen) subir; (sun) salir; (river) crecer; (prices) subir; (land) elevarse; (get up) levantarse. ● n subida f; (land) altura f; (increase) aumento m; (to power) ascenso m. **give ~e to** ocasionar. **~er** n. **early ~er** n madrugador m. **~ing** n. ● adj (sun) naciente; (number) creciente; (prices) en alza

risk /rɪsk/ n riesgo m. ● vt arriesgar. **~y** adj (-ier, -iest) arriesgado

rite /raɪt/ n rito m

ritual /'rɪtʃʊəl/ adj & n ritual (m)

rival /'raɪvl/ adj & n rival (m). **~ry** n rivalidad f

river /'rɪvə(r)/ n río m

rivet /'rɪvɪt/ n remache m. **~ing** adj fascinante

road /rəʊd/ n (in town) calle f; (between towns) carretera f; (route, way) camino m. **~ map** n mapa m de carreteras. **~side** n borde m de la carretera. **~works** npl obras fpl. **~worthy** adj (vehicle) apto para circular

roam /rəʊm/ vi vagar

roar /rɔː(r)/ n rugido m; (laughter) carcajada f. ● vt/i rugir. **~ past** (vehicles) pasar con estruendo. **~ with laughter** reírse a carcajadas. **~ing** adj (trade etc) activo

roast /rəʊst/ vt asar; tostar (coffee). ● adj & n asado (m). **~ beef** n rosbif m

rob /rɒb/ vt (pt robbed) atracar, asaltar (bank); robarle a (person). **~ of** (deprive of) privar de. **~ber** n ladrón m; (of bank) atracador m. **~bery** n robo m; (of bank) atraco m

robe /rəʊb/ n bata f; (Univ etc)

toga f

robin /'rɒbɪn/ n petirrojo m

robot /'rəʊbɒt/ n robot m

robust /rəʊ'bʌst/ adj robusto

rock /rɒk/ n roca f; (crag, cliff) peñasco m. ● vt mecer; (shake) sacudir. ● vi mecerse; (shake) sacudirse. ● n (Mus) música f rock. ~**-bottom** /-'bɒtəm/ adj 🄵 bajísimo

rocket /'rɒkɪt/ n cohete m

rock: ~**ing-chair** n mecedora f. ~**y** adj (-ier, -iest) rocoso; (fig, shaky) bamboleante

rod /rɒd/ n vara f; (for fishing) caña f; (metal) barra f

rode /rəʊd/ see RIDE

rodent /'rəʊdnt/ n roedor m

rogue /rəʊg/ n pícaro m

role /rəʊl/ n papel m

roll /rəʊl/ vt hacer rodar; (roll up) enrollar; allanar (lawn); aplanar (pastry). ● vi rodar; (ship) balancearse; (on floor) revolcarse. be ~**ing** in money 🄵 nadar en dinero. ● n rollo m; (of ship) balanceo m; (of drum) redoble m; (of thunder) retumbo m; (bread) panecillo m, bolillo m (Mex). □ ~ **over** vi (turn over) dar una vuelta. □ ~ **up** vt enrollar; arremangar (sleeve). vi 🄵 llegar. ~**-call** n lista f

roller /'rəʊlə(r)/ n rodillo m; (wheel) rueda f; (for hair) rulo m. R~ **blades** npl (P) patines mpl en línea. ~**-coaster** n montaña f rusa. ~**-skate** n patín m de ruedas. ~**-skating** patinaje m (sobre ruedas)

rolling /'rəʊlɪŋ/ adj ondulado. ~**-pin** n rodillo m

ROM /rɒm/ n (= read-only memory) ROM f

Roman /'rəʊmən/ adj & n romano (m). ~ **Catholic** adj & n católico (m) (romano)

romance /rəʊ'mæns/ n novela f romántica; (love) amor m; (affair) aventura f

Romania /ru:'meɪnɪə/ n Rumania f. Rumanía f. ~**n** adj & n rumano (m)

romantic /rəʊ'mæntɪk/ adj romántico

Rome /'rəʊm/ n Roma f

romp /rɒmp/ vi retozar

roof /ru:f/ n techo m, tejado m; (of mouth) paladar m. ● vt techar. ~**rack** n baca f. ~**top** n tejado m

rook /rʊk/ n grajo m; (in chess) torre f

room /ru:m/ n cuarto m, habitación f; (bedroom) dormitorio m; (space) espacio m; (large hall) sala f. ~**y** adj espacioso

roost /ru:st/ vi posarse. ~**er** n gallo m

root /ru:t/ n raíz f. take ~ echar raíces; (idea) arraigarse. ● vi echar raíces. □ ~ **about** vi hurgar. □ ~ **for** vt 🄵 alentar. □ ~ **out** vt extirpar

rope /rəʊp/ n cuerda f. know the ~s estar al corriente. ● vt atar; (Amer, lasso) enlazar. □ ~ **in** vt agarrar

rose[1] /rəʊz/ n rosa f; (nozzle) roseta f

rose[2] /rəʊz/ see RISE

rosé /'rəʊzeɪ/ n (vino m) rosado m

rot /rɒt/ vt (pt rotted) pudrir. ● vi pudrirse. ● n putrefacción f

rota /'rəʊtə/ n lista f (de turnos)

rotary /'rəʊtərɪ/ adj rotatorio

rotat|e /rəʊ'teɪt/ vt girar; (change round) alternar. ● vi (change round) alternarse. ~**ion** /-ʃn/ n rotación f

rote /rəʊt/ n. by ~ de memoria

rotten /'rɒtn/ adj podrido; 🄵 pésimo 🔲; (weather) horrible

rough /rʌf/ adj (-er, -est) áspero; (person) tosco; (bad) malo; (ground) accidentado; (violent) brutal; (approximate) aproximado; (diamond) bruto. ● adv duro. ~ copy, ~ draft borrador m. ● vt. ~ it vivir sin comodidades. **~age** /'rʌfɪdʒ/ n fibra f. **~-and-ready** adj improvisado. **~ly** adv bruscamente; (more or less) aproximadamente

roulette /ruː'let/ n ruleta f

round /raʊnd/ adj (-er, -est) redondo. ● n círculo m; (of visits, drinks) ronda f; (of competition) vuelta f; (Boxing) asalto m. ● prep alrededor de. ● adv alrededor. ~ **about** (approximately) aproximadamente. come ~ to, go ~ to (a friend etc) pasar por casa de. ● vt doblar (corner). □ ~ **off** vt terminar; redondear (number). □ ~ **up** vt rodear (cattle); hacer una redada de (suspects). **~about** n tiovivo m, carrusel m (LAm); (for traffic) glorieta f, rotonda f. ● adj in directo. ~ **trip** n viaje m de ida y vuelta. **~-up** n resumen m; (of suspects) redada f

rous|e /raʊz/ vt despertar. **~ing** adj enardecedor

route /ruːt/ n ruta f; (Naut, Aviat) rumbo m; (of bus) línea f

routine /ruː'tiːn/ n rutina f. ● adj rutinario

row[1] /rəʊ/ n fila f. ● vi remar

row[2] /raʊ/ n (fam, noise) bulla f 🔲; (quarrel) pelea f. ● vi 🔲 pelearse

rowboat /'rəʊbəʊt/ (Amer) n bote m de remos

rowdy /'raʊdɪ/ adj (-ier, -iest) n escandaloso, alborotador

rowing /'rəʊɪŋ/ n remo m. ~

boat n bote m de remos

royal /'rɔɪəl/ adj real. **~ist** adj & n monárquico (m). **~ly** adv magníficamente. **~ty** n realeza f

rub /rʌb/ vt (pt rubbed) frotar. □ ~ **out** vt borrar

rubber /'rʌbə(r)/ n goma f, caucho m, hule m (Mex); (eraser) goma f (de borrar). ~ **band** n goma f (elástica). **~-stamp** vt (fig) autorizar. **~y** adj parecido al caucho

rubbish /'rʌbɪʃ/ n basura f; (junk) trastos mpl; (fig) tonterías fpl. ~ **bin** n cubo m de la basura, bote m de la basura (Mex). **~y** adj sin valor

rubble /'rʌbl/ n escombros mpl

ruby /'ruːbɪ/ n rubí m

rucksack /'rʌksæk/ n mochila f

rudder /'rʌdə(r)/ n timón m

rude /ruːd/ adj (-er, -est) grosero, mal educado; (improper) indecente; (brusque) brusco. **~ly** adv groseramente. **~ness** n mala educación f

rudimentary /ruːdɪ'mentrɪ/ adj rudimentario

ruffian /'rʌfɪən/ n rufián m

ruffle /'rʌfl/ vt despeinar (hair); arrugar (clothes)

rug /rʌɡ/ n alfombra f, tapete m (Mex); (blanket) manta f de viaje

rugged /'rʌɡɪd/ adj (coast) escarpado; (landscape) escabroso

ruin /'ruːɪn/ n ruina f. ● vt arruinar; (spoil) estropear

rul|e /ruːl/ n regla f; (Pol) dominio m. as a ~ por regla general. ● vt gobernar; (master) dominar; (Jurid) dictaminar. **~e out** vt descartar. **~ed paper** n papel m rayado. **~er** n (sovereign) soberano m; (leader) gobernante m & f; (measure) regla f. **~ing** adj (class) dirigente. ● n decisión f

rum /rʌm/ n ron m

rumble /'rʌmbl/ vi retumbar; (stomach) hacer ruidos

rummage /'rʌmɪdʒ/ vi hurgar

rumour /'ruːmə(r)/ n rumor m. ● vt. it is ~ed that se rumorea que

rump steak /rʌmpsteɪk/ n filete m de cadera

run /rʌn/ vi (pt ran, pp run, pres p running) correr; (water) correr; (function) funcionar; (melt) derretirse; (makeup) correrse; (colour) desteñir; (bus etc) circular; (in election) presentarse. ● vt correr (race); dirigir (business); correr (risk); (move, pass) pasar; tender (wire); preparar (bath). ~ a temperature tener fiebre. ● n corrida f, carrera f; (outing) paseo m (en coche); (ski) pista f. in the long ~ a la larga. be on the ~ estar prófugo. □ ~ away vi huir, escaparse. □ ~ down vi bajar corriendo; (battery) descargarse. vt (Auto) atropellar; (belittle) denigrar. □ ~ in vi entrar corriendo. □ ~ into vt toparse con (friend); (hit) chocar con. □ ~ off vt sacar (copies). □ ~ out vi salir corriendo; (liquid) salirse; (fig) agotarse. □ ~ out of vt quedarse sin. □ ~ over vt (Auto) atropellar. □ ~ through vt (review) ensayar; (rehearse) repasar. □ ~ up vt ir acumulando (bill). vi subir corriendo. ~away n fugitivo m. ~ down adj (person) agotado

rung[1] /rʌŋ/ n (of ladder) peldaño m

rung[2] /rʌŋ/ see RING

run: ~ner /'rʌnə(r)/ n corredor m; (on sledge) patín m. ~ner bean n judía f escarlata. ~ner-up n. be ~er-up quedar en segundo lugar. ~ning n. be in the ~ning tener posibilidades de

ganar. ● adj (water) corriente; (commentary) en directo. four times ~ning cuatro veces seguidas. ~ny /'rʌnɪ/ adj líquido; (nose) que moquea. ~way n pista f de aterrizaje

rupture /'rʌptʃə(r)/ n ruptura f. ● vt romper

rural /'rʊərəl/ adj rural

ruse /ruːz/ n ardid m

rush /rʌʃ/ n (haste) prisa f; (crush) bullicio m; (plant) junco m. ● vi precipitarse. ● vt apresurar; (Mil) asaltar. ~-hour n hora f punta, hora f pico (LAm)

Russia /'rʌʃə/ n Rusia f. ~n adj & n ruso (m)

rust /rʌst/ n orín m. ● vt oxidar. ● vi oxidarse

rustle /'rʌsl/ vt hacer susurrar; (Amer) robar. ● vi susurrar □ ~ up vt □ preparar.

rust: ~proof adj inoxidable. ~y (-ier, -iest) oxidado

rut /rʌt/ n surco m. be in a ~ estar anquilosado

ruthless /'ruːθlɪs/ adj despiadado

rye /raɪ/ n centeno m

....

Ss

....

S abbr (= south) S

sabot|age /'sæbətɑːʒ/ n sabotaje m. ● vt sabotear. ~eur /-'tɜː(r)/ n saboteador m

saccharin /'sækərɪn/ n sacarina f

sachet /'sæʃeɪ/ n bolsita f

sack /sæk/ n saco m. get the ~ 🄳 ser despedido. ● vt 🄳 despedir, echar

sacrament /'sækrəmənt/ n sacramento m

sacred /'seɪkrɪd/ adj sagrado

sacrifice /'sækrɪfaɪs/ n sacrificio m. ● vt sacrificar

sacrileg|e /'sækrɪlɪdʒ/ n sacrilegio m. ~ious /-'lɪdʒəs/ adj sacrílego

sad /sæd/ adj (sadder, saddest) triste. ~den vt entristecer

saddle /'sædl/ n silla f de montar. ● vt ensillar (horse). ~ s.o. with sth (fig) endilgarle algo a uno

sadist /'seɪdɪst/ n sádico m. ~tic /sə'dɪstɪk/ adj sádico

sadly /'sædlɪ/ adv tristemente; (fig) desgraciadamente. ~ness n tristeza f

safe /seɪf/ adj (-er, -est) seguro; (out of danger) salvo; (cautious) prudente. ~ and sound sano y salvo. ● n caja f fuerte. ~ deposit n caja f de seguridad. ~guard n salvaguardia f ● vt salvaguardar. ~ly adv sin peligro; (in safe place) en lugar seguro. ~ty n seguridad f. ~ty belt n cinturón m de seguridad. ~ty pin n imperdible m

sag /sæg/ vi (pt sagged) (ceiling) combarse; (bed) hundirse

saga /'sɑːgə/ n saga f

Sagittarius /sædʒɪ'teərɪəs/ n Sagitario m

said /sed/ see SAY

sail /seɪl/ n vela f; (trip) paseo m (en barco). set ~ zarpar. ● vi navegar; (leave) partir; (Sport) practicar la vela; (fig) deslizarse. go ~ing salir a navegar. vt gobernar (boat). ~boat n (Amer) barco m de vela. ~ing n (Sport) vela f ~ing boat n, ~ing ship n barco m de vela. ~or n marinero m

saint /seɪnt//sənt/ n santo m. ~ly

adj santo

sake /seɪk/ n. for the ~ of por. for God's ~ por el amor de Dios

salad /'sæləd/ n ensalada f. ~ bowl n ensaladera f. ~ dressing n aliño m

salary /'sælərɪ/ n sueldo m

sale /seɪl/ n venta f; (at reduced prices) liquidación f. for ~ (sign) se vende. be for ~ estar a la venta. be on ~ (Amer, reduced) estar en liquidación. ~able adj vendible. (for sale) estar a la venta. ~s clerk n (Amer) dependiente m, dependienta f. ~sman /-mən/ n vendedor m; (in shop) dependiente m. ~swoman n vendedora f; (in shop) dependienta f

saliva /sə'laɪvə/ n saliva f

salmon /'sæmən/ n invar salmón m

saloon /sə'luːn/ n (on ship) salón m; (Amer, bar) bar m; (Auto) turismo m

salt /sɔːlt/ n sal f. ● vt salar. ~cellar n salero m. ~y adj salado

salute /sə'luːt/ n saludo m. ● vt saludar. ● vi hacer un saludo

Salvadorean, Salvadorian /sælvə'dɔːrɪən/ adj & n salvadoreño (m)

salvage /'sælvɪdʒ/ vt salvar

salvation /sæl'veɪʃn/ n salvación f

same /seɪm/ adj igual (as que); (before noun) mismo (as que). at the ~ time al mismo tiempo. ● pron. the ~ lo mismo. all the ~ de todas formas. ● adv. the ~ igual

sample /'sɑːmpl/ n muestra f. ● vt degustar (food)

sanct|ify /'sæŋktɪfaɪ/ vt santificar. ~ion /'sæŋkʃn/ n sanción f. ● vt sancionar. ~uary /'sæŋktʃʊərɪ/ n (Relig) santuario m; (for wildlife) re-

serva f; (*refuge*) asilo m
sand /sænd/ n arena f ● vt pulir
(floor). □ **~ down** vt lijar (wood)
sandal /ˈsændl/ n sandalia f
sand: **~castle** n castillo m de
arena. **~paper** n papel m de lija.
● vt lijar. **~storm** n tormenta f de
arena
sandwich /ˈsænwɪdʒ/ n bocadillo
m, sandwich m. ● vt. be **~ed be-
tween** (person) estar apretujado
entre
sandy /ˈsændɪ/ adj arenoso
sane /seɪn/ adj (-er, -est) (person)
cuerdo; (*sensible*) sensato
sang /sæŋ/ see SING
sanitary /ˈsænɪtrɪ/ adj higiénico;
(system etc) sanitario. **~ towel**,
~ napkin n (Amer) compresa f (hi-
giénica)
sanitation /sænɪˈteɪʃn/ n higiene
f; (drainage) sistema m sanitario
sanity /ˈsænɪtɪ/ n cordura f
sank /sæŋk/ see SINK
Santa (Claus) /ˈsæntə(klɔːz)/ n
Papá m Noel
sap /sæp/ n (in plants) savia f. ● (pt
sapped) minar
sapling /ˈsæplɪŋ/ n árbol m joven
sapphire /ˈsæfaɪə(r)/ n zafiro m
sarcas|m /ˈsɑːkæzəm/ n sarcasmo
m. **~tic** /-ˈkæstɪk/ adj sarcástico
sardine /sɑːˈdiːn/ n sardina f
sash /sæʃ/ n (over shoulder) banda
f; (round waist) fajín m.
sat /sæt/ see SIT
SAT abbr (Amer) (**Scholastic Apti-
tude Test**); (Brit) (**Standard As-
sessment Task**)
satchel /ˈsætʃl/ n cartera f
satellite /ˈsætəlaɪt/ n & a satélite
(m). **~ TV** n televisión f por satélite
satin /ˈsætɪn/ n raso m. ● adj de

raso
satir|e /ˈsætaɪə(r)/ n sátira f. **~ical**
/səˈtɪrɪkl/ adj satírico. **~ize**
/ˈsætəraɪz/ vt satirizar
satis|faction /sætɪsˈfækʃn/ n sa-
tisfacción f. **~factorily**
/-ˈfæktərɪlɪ/ adv satisfactoriamente.
~factory /-ˈfæktərɪ/ adj satisfacto-
rio. **~fy** /ˈsætɪsfaɪ/ vt satisfacer;
(convince) convencer. **~fying** adj
satisfactorio
satphone /ˈsætfəʊn/ n teléfono m
satélite
saturat|e /ˈsætʃəreɪt/ vt saturar.
~ed adj saturado; (drenched) em-
papado
Saturday /ˈsætədeɪ/ n sábado m
Saturn /ˈsætən/ n Saturno m
sauce /sɔːs/ n salsa f; (cheek) des-
caro m. **~pan** /ˈsɔːspən/ n cazo m,
cacerola f. **~r** /ˈsɔːsə(r)/ n plati-
llo m
saucy /ˈsɔːsɪ/ adj (-ier, -iest) des-
carado
Saudi /ˈsaʊdɪ/ adj & n saudita (m &
f). **~ Arabia** /-əˈreɪbɪə/ n Arabia f
Saudí
sauna /ˈsɔːnə/ n sauna f
saunter /ˈsɔːntə(r)/ vi pasearse
sausage /ˈsɒsɪdʒ/ n salchicha f
savage /ˈsævɪdʒ/ adj salvaje;
(fierce) feroz. ● n salvaje m & f. ● vt
atacar. **~ry** n ferocidad f
sav|e /seɪv/ vt (rescue) salvar; aho-
rrar (money, time); (prevent) evi-
tar; (Comp) guardar. ● n (football)
parada f. ● prep salvo, excepto.
□ **~ up** vi/t ahorrar. **~er** n aho-
rrador m. **~ing** n ahorro m. **~ings**
npl ahorros mpl
saviour /ˈseɪvɪə(r)/ n salvador m
savour /ˈseɪvə(r)/ vt saborear. **~y**
adj (appetizing) sabroso; (not sweet)
no dulce

s

saw[1] /sɔ:/ *see* SEE[1]

saw[2] /sɔ:/ n sierra f. ●vt (pt sawed, pp sawn) serrar. ~**dust** n serrín m. ~**n** /sɔ:n/ *see* SAW[2]

saxophone /ˈsæksəfəʊn/ n saxofón m, saxófono m

say /seɪ/ vt/i (pt said /sed/) decir; rezar (prayer). ●n. have a ~ expresar una opinión; (in decision) tener voz en capítulo. have no ~ no tener ni voz ni voto. ~**ing** n refrán m

scab /skæb/ n costra f; (fam, blackleg) esquirol m

scaffolding /ˈskæfəldɪŋ/ n andamios mpl

scald /skɔ:ld/ vt escaldar

scale /skeɪl/ n (also Mus) escala f; (of fish) escama f. ~ **down** vt (climb) escalar. ~ **down** vt reducir (a escala) (drawing); recortar (operation). ~**s** npl (for weighing) balanza f, peso m

scallion /ˈskæljən/ n (Amer) cebolleta f

scalp /skælp/ vt quitar el cuero cabelludo a. ●n cuero m cabelludo

scamper /ˈskæmpə(r)/ vi. ~ away irse correteando

scan /skæn/ vt (pt scanned) escudriñar; (quickly) echar un vistazo a; (radar) explorar

scandal /ˈskændl/ n escándalo m; (gossip) chismorreo m. ~**ize** vt escandalizar. ~**ous** adj escandaloso

Scandinavia /skændɪˈneɪvɪə/ n Escandinavia f. ~**n** adj & n escandinavo (m)

scant /skænt/ adj escaso. ~**y** adj (-ier, -iest) escaso

scapegoat /ˈskeɪpgəʊt/ n cabeza f de turco

scar /skɑ:(r)/ n cicatriz f

scarc|e /skeəs/ adj (-er, -est) escaso. be ~**e** escasear. make o.s.

~**e** 🔲 mantenerse lejos. ~**ely** adv apenas. ~**ity** n escasez f

scare /skeə(r)/ vt asustar. be ~**d** tener miedo. be ~**d** of sth tenerle miedo a algo. ●n susto m. ~**crow** n espantapájaros m

scarf /skɑ:f/ n (pl scarves) bufanda f; (over head) pañuelo m

scarlet /ˈskɑ:lət/ adj escarlata f. ~ **fever** n escarlatina f

scarves /skɑ:vz/ *see* SCARF

scary /ˈskeərɪ/ adj (-ier, -iest) que da miedo

scathing /ˈskeɪðɪŋ/ adj mordaz

scatter /ˈskætə(r)/ vt (throw) esparcir; (disperse) dispersar. ●vi dispersarse. ~**ed** /ˈskætəd/ adj disperso; (occasional) esporádico

scavenge /ˈskævɪndʒ/ vi escarbar (en la basura)

scenario /sɪˈnɑ:rɪəʊ/ n (pl -os) perspectiva f; (of film) guión m

scen|e /si:n/ n escena f; (sight) vista f; (fuss) lío m. **behind the** ~**es** entre bastidores. ~**ery** /ˈsi:nərɪ/ n paisaje m; (in theatre) decorado m. ~**ic** /ˈsi:nɪk/ adj pintoresco

scent /sent/ n olor m; (perfume) perfume m; (trail) pista f. ●vt intuir; (make fragrant) perfumar

sceptic /ˈskeptɪk/ n escéptico m. ~**al** adj escéptico. ~**ism** /-sɪzəm/ n escepticismo m

sceptre /ˈseptə(r)/ n cetro m

schedule /ˈʃedju:l, ˈskedʒu:l/ n programa f; (timetable) horario m. **behind** ~ atrasado. **it's on** ~ va de acuerdo a lo previsto. ●vt proyectar. ~**d flight** n vuelo m regular

scheme /ski:m/ n proyecto m; (plot) intriga f. ●vi (pej) intrigar

schizophrenic /skɪtsəˈfrenɪk/ adj & n esquizofrénico (m)

scholar /ˈskɒlə(r)/ n erudito m.

school | scrape

~ly adj erudito. **~ship** n erudición f; (grant) beca f

school /skuːl/ n escuela f; (Univ) facultad f. ● adj (age, holidays, year) escolar. ● vt instruir; (train) capacitar. **~boy** n colegial m. **~girl** n colegiala f. **~ing** n instrucción f. **~master** n (primary) maestro m; (secondary) profesor m. **~mistress** n (primary) maestra f; (secondary) profesora f. **~teacher** n (primary) maestro m; (secondary) profesor m

scien|ce /'saɪəns/ n ciencia f. **study ~ce** estudiar ciencias. **~ce fiction** n ciencia f ficción. **~tific** /-'tɪfɪk/ adj científico. **~tist** /'saɪəntɪst/ n científico m

scissors /'sɪsəz/ npl tijeras fpl

scoff /skɒf/ vt 🗊 zamparse. ● vi. **~ at** mofarse de

scold /skəʊld/ vt regañar

scoop /skuːp/ n pala f; (news) primicia f. □ **~ out** vt sacar; excavar (hole)

scooter /'skuːtə(r)/ n escúter m; (for child) patinete m

scope /skəʊp/ n alcance m; (opportunity) oportunidad f

scorch /skɔːtʃ/ vt chamuscar. **~ing** adj 🗊 de mucho calor

score /skɔː(r)/ n tanteo m; (Mus) partitura f; (twenty) veintena f. on that **~** 🗊 en cuanto a eso. know the **~** 🗊 saber cómo son las cosas. ● vt marcar (goal); anotarse (points); (cut, mark) rayar; conseguir (success). ● vi marcar

scorn /skɔːn/ n desdén m. ● vt desdeñar. **~ful** adj desdeñoso

Scorpio /'skɔːpɪəʊ/ n Escorpio m, Escorpión m

scorpion /'skɔːpɪən/ n escorpión m

Scot /skɒt/ n escocés m. **~ch**

~tch /skɒtʃ/ n whisky m, güisqui m

scotch /skɒtʃ/ vt frustrar; acallar (rumours)

Scotch tape n (Amer) celo m, cinta f Scotch

Scot|land /'skɒtlənd/ n Escocia f. **~s** adj escocés. **~tish** adj escocés

scoundrel /'skaʊndrəl/ n canalla f

scour /'skaʊə(r)/ vt fregar; (search) registrar. **~er** n estropajo m

scourge /skɜːdʒ/ n azote m

scout /skaʊt/ n explorador m. Boy S**~** explorador m

scowl /skaʊl/ n ceño m fruncido. ● vi fruncir el ceño

scram /skræm/ vi 🗊 largarse

scramble /'skræmbl/ vi (clamber) gatear. ● n (difficult climb) subida f difícil; (struggle) rebatiña f. **~d egg** n huevos mpl revueltos

scrap /skræp/ n pedacito m; (fam, fight) pelea f. ● vt (pt scrapped) desechar. **~book** n álbum m de recortes. **~s** npl sobras fpl

scrape /skreɪp/ n (fig) apuro m. ● vt raspar; (graze) rasparse; (rub) rascar. □ **~ through** vi/t aprobar por los pelos (exam). □ **~ together** vt reunir. **~r** n rasqueta f

scrap: ~**heap** n montón m de deshechos. ~ **yard** n chatarrería f

scratch /skrætʃ/ vt rayar (furniture, record); (with nail etc) arañar; rascarse (itch). ● vi arañar. ● n rayón m; (from nail etc) arañazo m. **start from** ~ empezar desde cero. **be up to** ~ dar la talla

scrawl /skrɔːl/ n garabato m. ● vt/i garabatear

scream /skriːm/ vt/i gritar. ● n grito m

screech /skriːtʃ/ vi chillar; (brakes etc) chirriar. ● n chillido m; (of brakes etc) chirrido m

screen /skriːn/ n pantalla f; (folding) biombo m. ● vt (hide) ocultar; (protect) proteger; proyectar (film)

screw /skruː/ n tornillo m. ● vt atornillar. □ ~ **up** vt atornillar; entornar (eyes); torcer (face); (sl, ruin) fastidiar. ~**driver** n destornillador m

scribble /ˈskrɪbl/ vt/i garabatear. ● n garabato m

script /skrɪpt/ n escritura f; (of film etc) guión m

scroll /skrəʊl/ n rollo m (de pergamino). □ ~ **down** vi retroceder la pantalla. □ ~ **up** vi avanzar la pantalla

scrounge /skraʊndʒ/ vt/i gorronear. ~**r** n gorrón m

scrub /skrʌb/ n (land) maleza f. ● vt/i (pt **scrubbed**) fregar

scruff /skrʌf/ n. **by the** ~ **of the neck** por el pescuezo. ~**y** adj (-ier, -iest) desaliñado

scrup|le /ˈskruːpl/ n escrúpulo m. ~**ulous** /-jʊləs/ adj escrupuloso

scrutin|ize /ˈskruːtɪnaɪz/ vt escudriñar; inspeccionar (document). ~**y** /ˈskruːtɪni/ n examen m minucioso

scuffle /ˈskʌfl/ n refriega f

sculpt /skʌlpt/ vt/i esculpir. ~**or** n escultor m. ~**ure** /-tʃə(r)/ n escultura f ● vt/i esculpir

scum /skʌm/ n espuma f; (people, pej) escoria f

scupper /ˈskʌpə(r)/ vt echar por tierra (plans)

scurry /ˈskʌri/ vi corretear

scuttle /ˈskʌtl/ n cubo m del carbón. ● vt barrenar (ship). ● vi. ~ **away** escabullirse rápidamente

scythe /saɪð/ n guadaña f

SE abbr (= **south-east**) SE

sea /siː/ n mar m. **at** ~ en el mar; (fig) confuso. **by** ~ por mar. ~**food** n mariscos mpl. ~ **front** n paseo m marítimo, malecón m (LAm). ~**gull** n gaviota f. ~**horse** n caballito m de mar

seal /siːl/ n sello m; (animal) foca f. ● vt sellar

sea level n nivel m del mar

sea lion n león m marino

seam /siːm/ n costura f; (of coal) veta f

seaman /ˈsiːmən/ n (pl **-men**) marinero m

seamy /ˈsiːmi/ adj sórdido

seance /ˈseɪɑːns/ n sesión f de espiritismo

search /sɜːtʃ/ vt registrar; buscar en (records). ● vi buscar. ● n (for sth) búsqueda f; (of sth) registro m; (Comp) búsqueda f. **in** ~ **of** en busca de. □ ~ **for** vt buscar. ~ **engine** n buscador m. ~**ing** adj penetrante. ~**light** n reflector m. ~ **party** n partida f de rescate

sea: ~**shore** n orilla f del mar. ~**sick** adj mareado. **be** ~**sick** marearse. ~**side** n playa f

season /ˈsiːzn/ n estación f; (period) temporada f. **high/low** ntemporada *f* alta/baja. ● *vt* (*Culin*) sazonar. ~**al** *adj* estacional; (demand) de estación. ~**ed** *adj* (*fig*) avezado. ~**ing** *n* condimento *m*. ~ **ticket** *n* abono *m* (de temporada)

seat /siːt/ *n* asiento *m*; (*place*) lugar *m*; (*in cinema, theatre*) localidad *f*; (*of trousers*) fondillos *mpl*. take a ~ sentarse. ● *vt* sentar; (*have seats for*) (auditorium) tener capacidad para; (bus) tener asientos para. ~**belt** *n* cinturón *m* de seguridad

sea: ~ **trout** *n* reo *m*. ~-**urchin** *n* erizo *m* de mar. ~**weed** *n* alga *f* marina. ~**worthy** *adj* en condiciones de navegar

seclu|ded /sɪˈkluːdɪd/ *adj* aislado. ~**ing** *n* condición *f*

second /ˈsekənd/ *adj & n* segundo (*m*). on ~ **thoughts** pensándolo bien. ● *adv* (*in race etc*) en segundo lugar. ● *vt* secundar. ~**s** *npl* (*goods*) artículos *mpl* de segunda calidad; (*fam, more food*) **have** ~ repetir. ● /sɪˈkɒnd/ *vt* (*transfer*) trasladar temporalmente. ~**ary** /ˈsekəndrɪ/ *adj* secundario. ~**ary school** *n* instituto *m* (de enseñanza secundaria)

second: ~-**class** *adj* de segunda (clase). ~-**hand** *adj* de segunda mano. ~**ly** *adv* en segundo lugar. ~-**rate** *adj* mediocre

secre|cy /ˈsiːkrəsɪ/ *n* secreto *m*. ~**t** *adj & n* secreto (*m*). **in** ~**t** en secreto

secretar|ial /sekrəˈteərɪəl/ *adj* de secretario; (course) de secretariado. ~**y** /ˈsekrətrɪ/ *n* secretario *m*. **S**~**y of State** (*in UK*) ministro *m*; (*in US*) secretario *m* de Estado

secretive /ˈsiːkrɪtɪv/ *adj* reservado

sect /sekt/ *n* secta *f*. ~**arian** /-ˈteərɪən/ *adj* sectario

section /ˈsekʃn/ *n* sección *f*; (*part*) parte *f*

sector /ˈsektə(r)/ *n* sector *m*

secular /ˈsekjʊlə(r)/ *adj* secular

secur|e /sɪˈkjʊə(r)/ *adj* seguro; (shelf) firme. ● *vt* asegurar; (*obtain*) obtener. ~**ely** *adv* seguramente. ~**ity** *n* seguridad *f*; (*for loan*) garantía *f*

sedat|e /sɪˈdeɪt/ *adj* reposado. ● *vt* sedar. ~**ion** /sɪˈdeɪʃn/ *n* sedación *f*. ~**ive** /ˈsedətɪv/ *adj & n* sedante (*m*)

sediment /ˈsedɪmənt/ *n* sedimento *m*

seduc|e /sɪˈdjuːs/ *vt* seducir. ~**er** *n* seductor *m*. ~**tion** /sɪˈdʌkʃn/ *n* seducción *f*. ~**tive** /sɪˈdʌktɪv/ *adj* seductor

see /siː/ ● *vt* (*pt* saw, *pp* seen) ver; (*understand*) comprender; (*escort*) acompañar. ~**ing that** visto que lo. ~ **you later!** ¡hasta luego! ● *vi* ver. □ ~ **off** *vt* (*say goodbye to*) despedirse de. □ ~ **through** *vt* llevar a cabo; calar (person). □ ~ **to** *vt* ocuparse de

seed /siːd/ *n* semilla *f*; (*fig*) germen *m*; (*Amer, pip*) pepita *f*. **go to** ~ granar; (*fig*) echarse a perder. ~**ling** *n* planta *f* de semillero. ~**y** *adj* (-ier, -iest) sórdido

seek /siːk/ *vt* (*pt* sought) buscar; pedir (approval). □ ~ **out** *vt* buscar

seem /siːm/ *vi* parecer

seen /siːn/ *see* SEE

seep /siːp/ *vi* filtrarse

see-saw /ˈsiːsɔː/ *n* balancín *m*

seethe /siːð/ *vi* (*fig*) estar furioso. I was seething with anger me hervía la sangre

see-through /ˈsiːθruː/ *adj* transparente

segment /ˈsegmənt/ *n* segmento

m; (of orange) gajo m

segregat|e /'segrɪgeɪt/ vt segregar. **∼ion** /-'geɪʃn/ n segregación f

seiz|e /siːz/ vt agarrar; (Jurid) incautar. **∼e on** vt aprovechar (chance). **∼e up** vi (Tec) agarrotarse. **∼ure** /'siːʒə(r)/ n incautación f; (Med) ataque m

seldom /'seldəm/ adv rara vez

select /sɪ'lekt/ vt escoger; (Sport) seleccionar. ● adj selecto; (exclusive) exclusivo. **∼ion** /-ʃn/ n selección f. **∼ive** adj selectivo

self /self/ n (pl selves). he's his old **∼** again vuelve a ser el de antes. **∼-addressed** adj con el nombre y la dirección del remitente. **∼-catering** adj con facilidades para cocinar. **∼-centred** adj egocéntrico. **∼-confidence** n confianza f en sí mismo. **∼-confident** adj seguro de sí mismo. **∼-conscious** adj cohibido. **∼-contained** adj independiente. **∼-control** n dominio m de sí mismo. **∼-defence** n defensa f propia. **∼-employed** adj que trabaja por cuenta propia. **∼-evident** adj evidente. **∼-important** adj presumido. **∼-indulgent** adj inmoderado. **∼-interest** n interés m (personal). **∼-ish** adj egoísta. **∼-ishness** n egoísmo m. **∼-pity** n autocompasión. **∼-portrait** n autorretrato m. **∼-respect** n amor m propio. **∼-righteous** adj santurrón. **∼-sacrifice** n abnegación f. **∼-satisfied** adj satisfecho de sí mismo. **∼-serve** (Amer), **∼-service** adj & n autoservicio (m). **∼-sufficient** adj independiente

sell /sel/ vt (pt sold) vender. ● vi venderse. **∼ off** vt liquidar. **∼ out** vi. we've sold out of gloves los guantes están agotados. **∼-by**

date n fecha f límite de venta. **∼er** n vendedor m

Sellotape /'seləteɪp/ n (®) celo m, cinta f Scotch

sell-out /'selaʊt/ n (performance) éxito m de taquilla; (fam, betrayal) capitulación f

semblance /'sembləns/ n apariencia f

semester /sɪ'mestə(r)/ n (Amer) semestre m

semi... /'semɪ/ pref semi...

semi|breve /-briːv/ n redonda f. **∼circle** n semicírculo m. **∼colon** /-'kəʊlən/ n punto m y coma. **∼detached** /-dɪ'tætʃt/ adj (house) adosado. **∼final** /-'faɪnl/ n semifinal f

seminar /'semɪnɑː(r)/ n seminario m

senat|e /'senɪt/ n senado m. the S∼e (Amer) el Senado. **∼or** /-ətə(r)/ n senador m

send /send/ vt/i (pt sent) mandar, enviar. □ **∼ away** vt despedir. □ **∼ away for** vt pedir (por correo). □ **∼ for** vt enviar a buscar. □ **∼ off for** vt pedir (por correo). □ **∼ up** vt 🇬🇧 parodiar. **∼er** n remitente m. **∼-off** n despedida f

senile /'siːnaɪl/ adj senil

senior /'siːnɪə(r)/ adj mayor; (in rank) superior; (partner etc) principal. ● n mayor m & f. **∼ citizen** n jubilado m. **∼ high school** n (Amer) colegio m secundario. **∼ity** /-'ɒrətɪ/ n antigüedad f

sensation /sen'seɪʃn/ n sensación f. **∼al** adj sensacional

sens|e /sens/ n sentido m; (common sense) juicio m; (feeling) sensación f. **make ∼e** vt tener sentido. **make ∼e of sth** entender algo. **∼eless** adj sin sentido. **∼ible**

/ˈsensəbl/ adj sensato; (clothing) práctico. ~itive /ˈsensɪtɪv/ adj sensible; (touchy) susceptible. ~itivity /-ˈtɪvɪtɪ/ n sensibilidad f. ~ual /ˈsenʃʊəl/ adj sensual. ~uous /ˈsensʊəs/ adj sensual

sent /sent/ see SEND

sentence /ˈsentəns/ n frase f; (judgment) sentencia f; (punishment) condena f. ● vt. ~ to condenar a

sentiment /ˈsentɪmənt/ n sentimiento m; (opinion) opinión f. ~al /-ˈmentl/ adj sentimental. ~ality /-ˈtælətɪ/ n sentimentalismo m

sentry /ˈsentrɪ/ n centinela f

separa|ble /ˈsepərəbl/ adj separable. ~te /ˈseprət/ adj separado; (independent) independiente. ● vt /ˈsepəreɪt/ separar. ● vi separarse. ~tely /ˈseprətlɪ/ adv por separado. ~tion /-ˈreɪʃn/ n separación f. ~tist /ˈsepərətɪst/ n separatista m & f

September /sepˈtembə(r)/ n se(p)tiembre m

septic /ˈseptɪk/ adj séptico

sequel /ˈsiːkwəl/ n continuación f; (later events) secuela f

sequence /ˈsiːkwəns/ n sucesión f; (of film) secuencia f

Serb /sɜːb/ adj & n see SERBIAN. ~ia /ˈsɜːbɪə/ n Serbia f ~ian adj & n serbio (m)

serenade /serəˈneɪd/ n serenata f. ● vt dar serenata a

serene /sɪˈriːn/ adj sereno

sergeant /ˈsɑːdʒənt/ n sargento m

serial /ˈsɪərɪəl/ n serie f. ~ize vt serializar

series /ˈsɪərɪːz/ n serie f

serious /ˈsɪərɪəs/ adj serio. ~ly adv seriamente; (ill) gravemente. take ~ly tomar en serio

sermon /ˈsɜːmən/ n sermón m

serum /ˈsɪərəm/ n (pl -a) suero m

servant /ˈsɜːvənt/ n criado m

serve /sɜːv/ vt servir; servir a (country); cumplir (sentence). ~ as servir de. it ~s you right ¡bien te lo mereces! ● vi servir; (in tennis) sacar. ● n (in tennis) saque m. ~r n (Comp) servidor m

service /ˈsɜːvɪs/ n servicio m; (of car etc) revisión f. ● vt revisar (car etc). ~ charge n (in restaurant) servicio m. ~s npl (Mil) fuerzas fpl armadas. ~ station n estación f de servicio

serviette /sɜːvɪˈet/ n servilleta f

servile /ˈsɜːvaɪl/ adj servil

session /ˈseʃn/ n sesión f

set /set/ vt (pt set, pres p setting) poner; poner en hora (clock etc); fijar (limit etc); (typeset) componer. ~ fire to prender fuego a. ~ free vt poner en libertad. ● vi (sun) ponerse; (jelly) cuajarse. ● n serie f; (of cutlery etc) juego m; (tennis) set m; (TV, Radio) aparato m; (in theatre) decorado m; (of people) círculo m. ● adj fijo. be ~ on estar resuelto a. □ ~ back vt (delay) retardar; (fam, cost) costar. □ ~ off vi salir, vt hacer sonar (alarm); hacer explotar (bomb). □ ~ out vt exponer (argument). vi (leave) salir. □ ~ up vt establecer. ~back n revés m

settee /seˈtiː/ n sofá m

setting /ˈsetɪŋ/ n (of dial, switch) posición f

settle /ˈsetl/ vt (arrange) acordar; arreglar (matter); resolver (dispute); pagar (bill); saldar (debt). ● vi (live) establecerse. □ ~ down vi calmarse; (become more responsible) sentar (la) cabeza. □ ~ for vt aceptar. □ ~ up vi arreglar cuentas. ~ment n establecimiento m; (agreement) acuerdo m; (of debt) liquidación f; (colony) colonia f. ~r n colono m

set: ~to n pelea f. ~up n ⊞ sistema m; (con) tinglado m

seven /'sevn/ adj & n siete (m). ~teen /'sevn'ti:n/ adj & n diecisiete (m). ~teenth adj decimoséptimo. ●n diecisietavo m. ~th adj & n séptimo (m). ~tieth /'sevntnθ/ adj septuagésimo. ●n setentavo m. ~ty /'sevnti/ adj & n setenta (m)

sever /'sevə(r)/ vt cortar; (fig) romper

several /'sevrəl/ adj & pron varios

sever|e /sɪ'vɪə(r)/ adj (-er, -est) severo; (serious) grave; (weather) riguroso. ~ely adv severamente. ~ity /sɪ'verəti/ n severidad f; (seriousness) gravedad f

sew /səʊ/ vt/i (pt sewed, pp sewn, or sewed) coser. □ ~ up vt coser

sew|age /'su:ɪdʒ/ n aguas fpl residuales. ~er /'su:ə(r)/ n cloaca f

sewing /'səʊɪŋ/ n costura f. ~machine n máquina f de coser

sewn /səʊn/ see SEW

sex /seks/ n sexo m. have ~ tener relaciones sexuales. ●adj sexual. ~ist adj & n sexista (m & f). ~ual /'sekʃʊəl/ adj sexual. ~ual intercourse n relaciones fpl sexuales. ~uality /-'ælətɪ/ n sexualidad f. ~y adj (-ier, -iest) excitante, sexy, provocativo

shabby /'ʃæbɪ/ adj (-ier, -iest) (clothes) gastado; (person) pobremente vestido

shack /ʃæk/ n choza f

shade /ʃeɪd/ n sombra f; (of colour) tono m; (for lamp) pantalla f; (nuance) matiz m; (Amer, over window) persiana f

shadow /'ʃædəʊ/ n sombra f. ●vt (follow) seguir de cerca a. ~y adj (fig) vago

shady /'ʃeɪdɪ/ adj (-ier, -iest) sombreado; (fig) turbio; (character) sospechoso

shaft /ʃɑːft/ n (of arrow) astil m; (Mec) eje m; (of light) rayo m; (of lift, mine) pozo m

shaggy /'ʃægɪ/ adj (-ier, -iest) peludo

shake /ʃeɪk/ vt (pt shook, pp shaken) sacudir; agitar (bottle); (shock) desconcertar. ~ hands with estrechar la mano a. ~ one's head negar con la cabeza; (Amer, meaning yes) asentir con la cabeza. ●vi temblar. □ ~ off vt deshacerse de. ●n sacudida f

shaky /'ʃeɪkɪ/ adj (-ier, -iest) tembloroso; (table etc) inestable

shall /ʃæl/ modal verb. we ~ see veremos. ~ we go to the cinema? ¿vamos al cine?

shallow /'ʃæləʊ/ adj (-er, -est) poco profundo; (fig) superficial

sham /ʃæm/ n farsa f. ●adj fingido

shambles /'ʃæmblz/ npl (fam, mess) caos m

shame /ʃeɪm/ n (feeling) vergüenza f. what a ~! ¡qué lástima! ●vt avergonzar. ~ful adj vergonzoso. ~less adj desvergonzado

shampoo /ʃæm'puː/ n champú m. ●vt lavar

shan't /ʃɑːnt/ = shall not

shape /ʃeɪp/ n forma f. ●vt formar; determinar (future). ●vi tomar forma. ~less adj informe

share /ʃeə(r)/ n porción f; (Com) acción f. ●vt compartir; (divide) dividir. ●vi compartir. ~ in sth participar en algo. □ ~ out vt repartir. ~holder n accionista m & f. ~out n reparto m

shark /ʃɑːk/ n tiburón m

sharp /ʃɑːp/ adj (-er, -est) (knife etc) afilado; (pin etc) puntiagudo; (pain, sound) agudo; (taste) ácido; (bend) cerrado; (contrast) marcado; (clever) listo; (Mus) sostenido. ● adv en punto. at seven o'clock ~ a las siete en punto. ● n (Mus) sostenido m. ~en vt afilar; sacar punta a (pencil). ~ener n (Mec) afilador m; (for pencils) sacapuntas m. ~ly adv bruscamente

shatter /ˈʃætə(r)/ vt hacer añicos. he was ~ed by the news la noticia lo dejó destrozado. ● vi hacerse añicos. ~ed /ˈʃætəd/adj (exhausted) agotado

shav|e /ʃeɪv/ vt afeitar, rasurar (Mex). ● vi afeitarse, rasurarse (Mex). ● n afeitada f, rasurada f (Mex). have a ~e afeitarse. ~er n maquinilla f (de afeitar). ~ing brush n brocha f de afeitar. ~ing cream n crema f de afeitar

shawl /ʃɔːl/ n chal m

she /ʃiː/ pron ella

sheaf /ʃiːf/ n (pl sheaves /ʃiːvz/) gavilla f

shear /ʃɪə(r)/ vt (pp shorn or sheared) esquilar. ~s /ʃɪəz/ npl tijeras fpl grandes

shed /ʃed/ n cobertizo m. ● vt (pt shed, pres p shedding) perder; derramar (tears); despojarse de (clothes). ~ light on arrojar luz sobre

she'd /ʃiː(ə)d/ = she had, she would

sheep /ʃiːp/ n invar oveja f. ~dog n perro m pastor. ~ish adj avergonzado

sheer /ʃɪə(r)/ adj (as intensifier) puro; (steep) perpendicular

sheet /ʃiːt/ n sábana f; (of paper) hoja f; (of glass) lámina f; (of ice) capa f

shelf /ʃelf/ n (pl shelves) estante m. a set of shelves unos estantes

shell /ʃel/ n concha f; (of egg) cáscara f; (of crab, snail, tortoise) caparazón m or f; (explosive) proyectil m, obús m. ● vt pelar (peas etc); (Mil) bombardear

she'll /ʃiː(ə)l/ = she had, she would

shellfish /ˈʃelfɪʃ/ n invar marisco m; (collectively) mariscos mpl

shelter /ˈʃeltə(r)/ n refugio m. take ~ refugiarse. ● vt darle cobijo a (fugitive); (protect from weather) resguardar. ● vi refugiarse. ~ed /ˈʃeltəd/ adj (spot) abrigado; (life) protegido

shelv|e /ʃelv/ vt (fig) dar carpetazo a. ~ing n estantería f

shepherd /ˈʃepəd/ n pastor m. ~ess /-ˈdes/ n pastora f

sherbet /ˈʃɜːbət/ n (Amer, water ice) sorbete m

sheriff /ˈʃerɪf/ n (in US) sheriff m

sherry /ˈʃerɪ/ n (vino m de) jerez m

she's /ʃiːz/ = she is, she has

shield /ʃiːld/ n escudo m. ● vt proteger

shift /ʃɪft/ vt cambiar; correr (furniture etc). ● vi (wind) cambiar; (attention, opinion) pasar a; (Amer, change gear) cambiar de velocidad. ● n cambio m; (work) turno m; (workers) tanda f. ~y adj (adj (-ier, -iest) furtivo

shilling /ˈʃɪlɪŋ/ n chelín m

shimmer /ˈʃɪmə(r)/ vi rielar, relucir

shin /ʃɪn/ n espinilla f

shine /ʃaɪn/ vi (pt shone) brillar.

shingle /ˈʃɪŋgl/ n (pebbles) guijarros mpl.

shin|ing /ˈʃaɪnɪŋ/ adj brillante. ~y /ˈʃaɪnɪ/ adj (-ier, -iest) brillante.

ship /ʃɪp/ n barco m, buque m. ●vt (pt shipped) transportar; (send) enviar; (load) embarcar. ~building n construcción f naval. ~ment n envío m. ~ping n transporte m; (ships) barcos mpl. ~shape adj limpio y ordenado. ~wreck n naufragio m. ~wrecked adj naufragado. be ~wrecked naufragar. ~yard n astillero m.

shirk /ʃɜːk/ vt esquivar

shirt /ʃɜːt/ n camisa f. in ~sleeves en mangas de camisa

shit /ʃɪt/ n & int (vulgar) mierda f. ●vi (vulgar) (pt shat, pres p shitting) cagar

shiver /ˈʃɪvə(r)/ vi temblar. ●n escalofrío m

shoal /ʃəʊl/ n banco m

shock /ʃɒk/ n (of impact) choque m; (of earthquake) sacudida f; (surprise) shock m; (scare) susto m; (Elec) descarga f; (Med) shock m. get a ~ llevarse un shock. ●vt escandalizar; (appal) horrorizar. ~ing adj escandaloso. ● espantoso

shod /ʃɒd/ see SHOE

shoddy /ˈʃɒdɪ/ adj (-ier, -iest) mal hecho, de pacotilla

shoe /ʃuː/ n zapato m; (of horse) herradura f. ●vt (pt shod, pres p shoeing) herrar (horse). ~horn n calzador m. ~lace n cordón m (de zapato). ~polish n betún m.

shone /ʃɒn/ see SHINE

shoo /ʃuː/ vt ahuyentar

shook /ʃʊk/ see SHAKE

shoot /ʃuːt/ vt (pt shot) disparar; rodar (film). ●vi (hunt) cazar. ■ n (of plant) retoño m. ■ ~ down vt derribar. ■ ~ out vi (rush) salir disparado. ■ ~ up vi (prices) dispararse; (grow) crecer mucho

shop /ʃɒp/ n tienda f. go to the ~s ir de compras. talk ~ hablar del trabajo. ●vi (pt shopping) hacer compras. go ~ping ir de compras. ■ ~ around vi buscar el mejor precio. ~assistant n dependiente m, dependienta f, empleado m, empleada f (LAm). ~keeper n comerciante m, tendero m. ~lifter n ladrón m (que roba en las tiendas). ~lifting n hurto m (en las tiendas). ~per n comprador m. ~ping n (purchases) compras fpl. do the ~ping hacer la compra, hacer el mandado (Mex). ~ping bag n bolsa f de la compra. ~ping cart n (Amer) carrito m (de la compra). ~ping centre, ~ping mall (Amer) n centro m comercial. ~ping trolley n carrito m de la compra. ~ steward n enlace m sindical. ~ window n escaparate m, vidriera f (LAm), aparador m (Mex)

shore /ʃɔː(r)/ n orilla f

shorn /ʃɔːn/ see SHEAR

short /ʃɔːt/ adj (-er, -est) corto; (not lasting) breve; (person) bajo; (curt) brusco. a ~ time ago hace poco. be ~ of time/money andar corto de tiempo/dinero. Mick is ~ for Michael Mick es el diminutivo de Michael. ●adv (stop) en seco. we never went ~ of food nunca nos faltó comida. ●n. in ~ en resumen. ~age /-ɪdʒ/ n escasez f, falta f. ~bread n galleta f (de mantequilla). ~ circuit n cortocircuito m. ~coming n defecto m. ~cut n atajo m. ~en vt acortar.

~hand n taquigrafía f. **~ly** adv (soon) dentro de poco. **~ly before midnight** poco antes de la medianoche. **~s** npl pantalones m cortos, shorts mpl; (Amer, underwear) calzoncillos mpl. **~-sighted** /-ˈsaɪtɪd/ adj miope

shot /ʃɒt/ see **SHOOT**. ● n (from gun) disparo m; tiro m; (in soccer) tiro m, disparo m; (in other sports) tiro m; (Photo) foto f. **be a good/poor ~** ser un buen/mal tirador. **be off like a ~** salir disparado. **~gun** n escopeta f

should /ʃʊd, ʃəd/ modal verb. **I ~ go** debería ir. **you ~n't have said that** no deberías haber dicho eso. **I ~ like to see her** me gustaría verla. **if he ~ come** si viniese

shoulder /ˈʃəʊldə(r)/ n hombro m. ● vt cargar con (responsibility); ponerse al hombro (burden). **~blade** n omóplato m

shout /ʃaʊt/ n grito m. ● vt/i gritar. **~ at s.o.** gritarle a uno

shove /ʃʌv/ n empujón m. ● vt empujar; (fam, put) poner. ● vi empujar. □ **~ off** vi 🔢 largarse

shovel /ˈʃʌvl/ n pala f. ● vt (pt shovelled) palear (coal); espalar (snow)

show /ʃəʊ/ vt (pt showed, pp shown) mostrar; (put on display) exponer; poner (film). **I'll ~ you to your room** lo acompaño a su cuarto. ● vi (be visible) verse. ● n muestra f; (exhibition) exposición f; (in theatre) espectáculo m; (on TV, radio) programa m; (ostentation) pompa f. **be on ~** estar expuesto. □ **~ off** vt (pej) lucir, presumir de. vi presumir, lucirse. □ **~ up** vi (be visible) notarse; (arrive) aparecer. vt (reveal) poner de manifiesto; (embarrass) hacer quedar mal. **~case**

n vitrina f. **~down** n confrontación f

shower /ˈʃaʊə(r)/ n (of rain) chaparrón m; (for washing) ducha f. **have a ~, take a ~** ducharse. ● vi ducharse

showjumping n concursos mpl hípicos.

shown /ʃəʊn/ see **SHOW**.

show: **~off** n fanfarrón m. **~room** n sala f de exposición f. **~y** adj (-ier, -iest) llamativo; (attractive) ostentoso

shrank /ʃræŋk/ see **SHRINK**

shred /ʃred/ n pedazo m; (fig) pizca f. ● vt (pt shredded) hacer tiras; destruir, triturar (documents). **~der** n (for paper) trituradora f; (for vegetables) cortadora f

shrewd /ʃruːd/ adj (-er, -est) astuto

shriek /ʃriːk/ n chillido m; (of pain) alarido m. ● vt/i chillar

shrift /ʃrɪft/ n. **give s.o. short ~** despachar a uno con brusquedad. **give sth short ~** desestimar algo de plano

shrill /ʃrɪl/ adj agudo

shrimp /ʃrɪmp/ n gamba f, camarón m (LAm); (Amer, large) langostino m

shrine /ʃraɪn/ n (place) santuario m; (tomb) sepulcro m

shrink /ʃrɪŋk/ vt (pt shrank, pp shrunk) encoger. ● vi encogerse; (amount) reducirse; retroceder (recoil)

shrivel /ˈʃrɪvl/ vi (pt shrivelled). **~ (up)** (plant) marchitarse; (fruit) resecarse y arrugarse

shroud /ʃraʊd/ n mortaja f; (fig) velo m. ● vt envolver

Shrove /ʃrəʊv/ n. **~ Tuesday** n martes m de carnaval

shrub /ʃrʌb/ n arbusto m

shrug /ʃrʌg/ vt (pt shrugged) encogerse de hombros

shrunk /ʃrʌŋk/ see SHRINK. **~en** adj encogido

shudder /'ʃʌdə(r)/ vi estremecerse. ● n estremecimiento m

shuffle /'ʃʌfl/ vi andar arrastrando los pies. ● vt barajar (cards). ~ one's feet arrastrar los pies

shun /ʃʌn/ vt (pt shunned) evitar

shunt /ʃʌnt/ vt cambiar de vía

shush /ʃʊʃ/ int ¡chitón!

shut /ʃʌt/ vt (pt shut, pres p shutting) cerrar. ● vi cerrarse. ● adj. be ~ estar cerrado. □ ~ **down** vt/i cerrar. □ ~ **up** vt cerrar; 🄸 hacer callar. vi callarse. **~ter** n contraventana f; (Photo) obturador m

shuttle /'ʃʌtl/ n lanzadera f; (by air) puente m aéreo; (space ~) transbordador m espacial. ● vi. ~ (back and forth) ir y venir. **~cock** n volante m. **~ service** n servicio m de enlace

shy /ʃaɪ/ adj (-er, -est) tímido. ● vi (pt shied) asustarse. **~ness** n timidez f

sick /sɪk/ adj enfermo; (humour) negro; (fam, fed up) harto. be ~ estar enfermo; (vomit) vomitar. be ~ of (fig) estar harto de. feel ~ sentir náuseas. get ~ (Amer) caer enfermo, enfermarse (LAm). ~ **leave** n permiso m por enfermedad, baja f por enfermedad. **~ly** /'sɪklɪ/ adj (-lier, -liest) enfermizo; (taste, smell etc) nauseabundo. **~ness** /'sɪknɪs / n enfermedad f

side /saɪd/ n lado m; (of hill) ladera f; (of person) costado m; (team) equipo m; (fig) parte f. ~ **by** ~ uno al lado del otro. take ~s tomar partido. ● adj lateral. □ ~

with vt ponerse de parte de. **~board** n aparador m. **~ dish** n acompañamiento m. **~effect** n efecto m secundario; (fig) consecuencia f indirecta. **~line** n actividad f suplementaria. ~ **road** n calle f secundaria. **~step** vt eludir. **~track** vt desviar del tema. **~walk** n (Amer) acera f, vereda f (LAm), banqueta f (Mex). **~ways** adj & adv de lado

siding /'saɪdɪŋ/ n apartadero m

sidle /'saɪdl/ vi. ~ **up to s.o.** acercarse furtivamente a uno

siege /siːdʒ/ n sitio m

sieve /sɪv/ n tamiz m. ● vt tamizar, cernir

sift /sɪft/ vt tamizar, cernir. ● vi. ~ **through sth** pasar algo por el tamiz

sigh /saɪ/ n suspiro. ● vi suspirar

sight /saɪt/ n vista f; (spectacle) espectáculo m; (on gun) mira f. **at first** ~ a primera vista. **catch** ~ **of** ver; (in distance) avistar. **lose** ~ **of** perder de vista. **see the** ~s visitar los lugares de interés. **within** ~ **of** (near) cerca de. ● vt ver; divisar (land). **~-seeing** n. **go** ~ ir a visitar los lugares de interés. **~seer** /-siːə(r)/ n turista m & f

sign /saɪn/ n (indication) señal f, indicio m; (gesture) señal f, seña f; (notice) letrero m; (astrological) signo m. ● vt firmar. □ ~ **on** vi (for unemployment benefit) anotarse para recibir el seguro de desempleo

signal /'sɪgnəl/ n señal f. ● vt (pt signalled) señalar. ● vi. ~ (**to s.o.**) hacer señas (a uno); (Auto) poner el intermitente, señalizar

signature /'sɪgnətʃə(r)/ n firma f. ~ **tune** n sintonía f

significan|ce /sɪɡˈnɪfɪkəns/ n importancia f. **~t** adj (*important*) importante; (*fact*) significativo

signify /ˈsɪɡnɪfaɪ/ vt significar

signpost /ˈsaɪmpəʊst/ n señal f, poste m indicador

silen|ce /ˈsaɪləns/ n silencio m. ● vt hacer callar. **~cer** n (*on gun and on car*) silenciador m. **~t** adj silencioso; (*film*) mudo. **remain ~t** quedarse callado. **~tly** adv silenciosamente

silhouette /ˌsɪluːˈet/ n silueta f. ● vt. **be ~d** perfilarse (*against* contra)

silicon /ˈsɪlɪkən/ n silicio m. **~ chip** n pastilla f de silicio

silk /sɪlk/ n seda f. **~y** adj (*of silk*) de seda; (*like silk*) sedoso

silly /ˈsɪlɪ/ adj (-ier, -iest) tonto

silt /sɪlt/ n cieno m

silver /ˈsɪlvə(r)/ n plata f. ● adj de plata. **~-plated** adj bañado en plata, plateado. **~ware** /-weə(r)/ n platería f

SIM card n tarjeta f SIM

simil|ar /ˈsɪmɪlə(r)/ adj parecido, similar. **~arity** /-ˈlærətɪ/ n parecido m. **~arly** adv de igual manera. **~e** /ˈsɪmɪlɪ/ n símil m ()

simmer /ˈsɪmə(r)/ vt/i hervir a fuego lento. □ **~ down** vi calmarse

simpl|e /ˈsɪmpl/ adj (-er, -est) sencillo, simple; (*person*) (*humble*) simple; (*backward*) simple. **~e-minded** /-ˈmaɪndɪd/ adj ingenuo. **~icity** /-ˈplɪsetɪ/ n simplicidad f, sencillez f. **~ify** /ˈsɪmplɪfaɪ/ vt simplificar. **~y** adv sencillamente, simplemente; (*absolutely*) realmente

simulate /ˈsɪmjʊleɪt/ vt simular

simultaneous /ˌsɪmlˈteɪnɪəs/ adj simultáneo. **~ly** adv simultáneamente

sin /sɪn/ n pecado m. ● vi (pt sinned) pecar

since /sɪns/

● **preposition** desde. **he's been living here ~ 1991** vive aquí desde 1991. **~ Christmas** desde Navidad. **~ then** desde entonces. **I haven't been feeling well ~ Sunday** desde el domingo que no me siento bien. **how long is it ~ your interview?** ¿cuánto (tiempo) hace de la entrevista?

● **adverb** desde entonces. **I haven't spoken to her ~** no he hablado con ella desde entonces

● **conjunction**

····▸ desde que. **I haven't seen her ~** she left no la he visto desde que se fue. **~ coming to Manchester** desde que vine (*or* vino *etc*) a Manchester. **it's ten years ~** he died hace diez años que se murió

····▸ (*because*) como, ya que. **~ it was quite late, I decided to stay** como *or* ya que era bastante tarde, decidí quedarme

sincer|e /sɪnˈsɪə(r)/ adj sincero. **~ely** adv sinceramente. **yours ~ely, ~ely (yours)** (*in letters*) (saluda) a usted atentamente. **~ity** /-ˈserətɪ/ n sinceridad f

sinful /ˈsɪnfl/ adj (*person*) pecador; (*act*) pecaminoso

sing /sɪŋ/ vt/i (pt sang, pp sung) cantar

singe /sɪndʒ/ vt (pres p singeing) chamuscar

singer /ˈsɪŋə(r)/ n cantante m & f

single /ˈsɪŋɡl/ adj solo; (*not*

s

double) sencillo; (*unmarried*) soltero; (bed, room) individual, de una plaza (*LAm*); (ticket) de ida, sencillo. not a ~ house ni una sola casa. every ~ day todos los días sin excepción. ● n (*ticket*) billete m sencillo, boleto m de ida (*LAm*). □~ **out** vt escoger; (*distinguish*) distinguir. ~**s** npl (*Sport*) individuales mpl

singular /'sɪŋɡjʊlə(r)/ n singular f. ● adj singular; (*unusual*) raro; (noun) en singular

sinister /'sɪnɪstə(r)/ adj siniestro

sink /sɪŋk/ vt (pt sank, pp sunk) hundir. ● vi hundirse. ● n fregadero m (Amer, in bathroom) lavabo m, lavamanos m. □~ **in** vi penetrar

sinner /'sɪnə(r)/ n pecador m

sip /sɪp/ n sorbo m. ● vt (pt sipped) sorber

siphon /'saɪfən/ n sifón m. ~ (out) sacar con sifón. □~ **off** vt desviar (money).

sir /sɜː(r)/ n señor m. **S~** n (title) sir m. Dear S~, (in letters) De mi mayor consideración.

siren /'saɪərən/ n sirena f

sister /'sɪstə(r)/ n hermana f; (nurse) enfermera f jefe. ~**-in-law** n (pl ~**s-in-law**) cuñada f

sit /sɪt/ vi (pt sat, pres p sitting) sentarse; (committee etc) reunirse en sesión. be ~**ting** estar sentado. ● vt sentar; hacer (exam). □~ **back** vi (fig) relajarse. □~ **down** vi sentarse. be ~**ting down** estar sentado. □~ **up** vi (from lying) incorporarse; (straighten back) ponerse derecho. ~**-in** n (strike) encierro m, ocupación f

site /saɪt/ n emplazamiento m; (piece of land) terreno m; (archaeo-

logical) yacimiento m. **building** ~ n solar m. ● vt situar

sit: ~**ting** n sesión f; (in restaurant) turno m. ~**ting room** n sala f de estar, living m

situat|e /'sɪtjʊeɪt/ vt situar. ~**ion** /-'eɪʃn/ n situación f

six /sɪks/ adj & n seis (m). ~**teen** /sɪk'stiːn/ adj & n dieciséis (m). ~**teenth** adj decimosexto. ● n dieciseisavo m. ~**th** adj & n sexto (m). ~**tieth** /'sɪkstɪɪθ/ adj sexagésimo. ● n sesentavo m. ~**ty** /'sɪkstɪ/ adj & n sesenta (m)

size /saɪz/ n tamaño m; (of clothes) talla f; (of shoes) número m; (of problem, operation) magnitud f. what ~ do you take? (clothes) ¿qué talla tiene?; (shoes) ¿qué número calza?. □~ **up** vt 🛈 evaluar (problem); calar (person)

sizzle /'sɪzl/ vi crepitar

skat|e /skeɪt/ n patín m.● vi patinar. ~**eboard** n monopatín m, patineta f (Mex). ~**er** n patinador m. ~**ing** n patinaje m. ~**ing-rink** n pista f de patinaje

skeleton /'skelɪtn/ n esqueleto m. ~ **key** n llave f maestra

sketch /sketʃ/ n (drawing) dibujo m; (rougher) esbozo m; (TV, Theatre) sketch m. ● vt esbozar. ● vi dibujar. ~**y** adj (-ier, -iest) incompleto

ski /skiː/ n (pl skis) esquí m. ● vi (pt skied, pres p skiing) esquiar. go ~**ing** ir a esquiar

skid /skɪd/ vi (pt skidded) patinar. ● n patinazo m

ski: ~**er** n esquiador m. ~**ing** n esquí m

skilful /'skɪlfl/ adj diestro

ski-lift /'skiːlɪft/ n telesquí m

skill /skɪl/ n habilidad f; (technical) destreza f. ~**ed** adj hábil; (worker) cualificado

skim /skɪm/ vt (pt skimmed) espumar (soup); desnatar, descremar (milk); (glide over) pasar casi rozando. ~ **milk** (Amer), ~**med milk** n leche f desnatada, leche f descremada. ~ **through** vt leer por encima

skimp /skɪmp/ vi. ~ **on** sth escatimar algo. ~**y** adj (-ier, -iest) escaso; (skirt, dress) brevísimo

skin /skɪn/ n piel f. • vt (pt skinned) despellejar. ~**-deep** adj superficial. ~**-diving** n submarinismo m. ~**ny** adj (-ier, -iest) flaco

skip /skɪp/ vi (pt skipped) vi saltar; (with rope) saltar a la comba, saltar a la cuerda. • vt saltarse (chapter); faltar a (class). • n brinco m; (container) contenedor m (para escombros). ~**per** n capitán m. ~**ping-rope**, ~**rope** (Amer) n comba f, cuerda f de saltar, reata f (Mex)

skirmish /'skɜːmɪʃ/ n escaramuza f

skirt /skɜːt/ n falda f. • vt bordear; (go round) ladear. ~**ing-board** n rodapié m, zócalo m

skittle /'skɪtl/ n bolo m

skive off /skaɪv/ (vi 🄵, disappear) escurrir el bulto; (stay away from work) no ir a trabajar

skulk /skʌlk/ vi (hide) esconderse. ~ **around** vi merodear

skull /skʌl/ n cráneo m; (remains) calavera f

sky /skaɪ/ n cielo m. ~**lark** n alondra f. ~**light** n tragaluz m. ~ **marshal** n guardia m armado a bordo. ~**scraper** n rascacielos m

slab /slæb/ n (of concrete) bloque m; (of stone) losa f

slack /slæk/ adj (-er, -est) flojo;

---

skim | sledge-hammer

(person) poco aplicado; (period) de poca actividad. • vi flojear. ~**en** vt aflojar. • vi (person) descansar. □ ~ **off** vt/i aflojar

slain /sleɪn/ see SLAY

slake /sleɪk/ vt apagar

slam /slæm/ vt (pt slammed). ~ **the door** dar un portazo. ~ **the door shut** cerrar de un portazo. ~ **on the brakes** pegar un frenazo; (sl, criticize) atacar violentamente. • vi cerrarse de un portazo

slander /'slɑːndə(r)/ n calumnia f. • vt difamar

slang /slæŋ/ n argot m

slant /slɑːnt/ vt inclinar. • n inclinación f

slap /slæp/ vt (pt slapped) (on face) pegarle una bofetada a; (put) tirar. ~ **s.o. on the back** darle una palmada a uno en la espalda. • n bofetada f; (on back) palmada f. • adv de lleno. ~**dash** adj descuidado; (work) chapucero

slash /slæʃ/ vt acuchillar; (fig) rebajar drásticamente. • n cuchillada f

slat /slæt/ n tablilla f

slate /sleɪt/ n pizarra f. • vt 🄵 poner por los suelos

slaughter /'slɔːtə(r)/ vt matar salvajemente; matar (animal). • n carnicería f; (of animals) matanza f

slave /sleɪv/ n esclavo m. • vi ~ (away) trabajar como un negro. ~**-driver** n 🄵 negrero m. ~**ry** /-əri/ n esclavitud f

slay /sleɪ/ vt (pt slew, pp slain) dar muerte a

sleazy /'sliːzi/ adj (-ier, -iest) 🄵 sórdido

sled /sled/ (Amer), **sledge** /sledʒ/ n trineo m

sledge-hammer n mazo m, almádena f

S

sleek /sliːk/ adj (-er, -est) liso, brillante

sleep /sliːp/ n sueño m. go to ~ dormirse. • vi (pt slept) dormir. ~er n (on track) traviesa f, durmiente m. be a light/heavy ~er tener el sueño ligero/pesado. ~ing bag n saco m de dormir. ~ing pill n somnífero m. ~less adj. have a ~less night pasar la noche en blanco. ~walk vi caminar dormido. ~y adj (-ier, -iest) soñoliento. be/feel ~y tener sueño

sleet /sliːt/ n aguanieve f

sleeve /sliːv/ n manga f; (for record) funda f, carátula f. up one's ~ en reserva. ~less adj sin mangas

sleigh /sleɪ/ n trineo m

slender /'slendə(r)/ adj delgado; (fig) escaso

slept /slept/ see SLEEP

slew /sluː/ see SLAY

slice /slaɪs/ n (of ham) lonja f; (of bread) rebanada f; (of meat) tajada f; (of cheese) trozo m; (of sth round) rodaja f. • vt cortar (en rebanadas, tajadas etc)

slick /slɪk/ adj (performance) muy pulido. • n. (oil) ~ marea f negra

slide /slaɪd/ vt (pt slid) deslizar. • vi (intentionally) deslizarse; (unintentionally) resbalarse. • n resbalón m; (in playground) tobogán m, resbaladilla f (Mex); (for hair) pasador m, broche m (Mex); (Photo) diapositiva f. ~ing scale n escala f móvil

slight /slaɪt/ adj (-er, -est) ligero; (slender) delgado. • vt desairar. • n desaire m. ~est adj mínimo. not in the ~est en absoluto. ~ly adv un poco, ligeramente

slim /slɪm/ adj (slimmer, slim-

mest) delgado. • vi (pt slimmed) (become slimmer) adelgazar; (diet) hacer régimen

slim|**e** /slaɪm/ n limo m; (of snail, slug) baba f. ~y adj viscoso; (fig) excesivamente obsequioso

sling /slɪŋ/ n (Med) cabestrillo m. • vt (pt slung) lanzar

slip /slɪp/ vt (pt slipped) deslizar. ~ s.o.'s mind olvidársele a uno. • vi resbalarse. it ~ped out of my hands se me resbaló de las manos. he ~ped out the back door se deslizó por la puerta trasera • n resbalón m; (mistake) error m; (petticoat) combinación f; (paper) trozo m. give s.o. the ~ lograr zafarse de uno. ~ of the tongue n lapsus m linguae. ~ away vi escabullirse. □ ~ up vi 🄸 equivocarse

slipper /'slɪpə(r)/ n zapatilla f

slippery /'slɪpərɪ/ adj resbaladizo

slip: ~ **road** n rampa f de acceso. ~**shod** /'slɪpʃɒd/ adj descuidado. ~**-up** n 🄸 error m

slit /slɪt/ n raja f; (cut) corte m. • vt (pt slit, pres p slitting) rajar; (cut) cortar

slither /'slɪðə(r)/ vi deslizarse

slobber /'slɒbə(r)/ vi babear

slog /slɒɡ/ vt (pt slogged) golpear. • vi caminar trabajosamente. • n golpetazo m; (hard work) trabajo m penoso. □ ~ **away** vi sudar tinta 🄸

slogan /'sləʊɡən/ n eslogan m

slop /slɒp/ vt (pt slopped) derramar. • vi derramarse

slop|**e** /sləʊp/ vi inclinarse. • vt inclinar. • n declive m, pendiente f. ~**ing** adj inclinado

sloppy /'slɒpɪ/ adj (-ier, -iest) (work) descuidado; (person) desaliñado

slosh /slɒʃ/ vi 🔢 chapotear

slot /slɒt/ n ranura f. ● vt (pt slotted) encajar

slot-machine n distribuidor m automático; (for gambling) máquina f tragamonedas

slouch /slautʃ/ vi andar cargado de espaldas; (in chair) repanchigarse

Slovak /ˈsləʊvæk/ adj & n eslovaco (m). ~**ia** n Eslovaquia f

slovenly /ˈslʌvnlɪ/ adj (work) descuidado; (person) desaliñado

slow /sləʊ/ adj (-er, -est) lento. be ~ (clock) estar atrasado. in ~ motion a cámara lenta. ● adv despacio. ● vt retardar. vi ir más despacio. □ ~ **down**, ~ **up** retardar. vi ir más despacio. ~**ly** adv despacio, lentamente

sludge /slʌdʒ/ n fango m

slug /slʌg/ n babosa f. ~**gish** adj lento

slum /slʌm/ n barrio m bajo

slumber /ˈslʌmbə(r)/ vi dormir

slump /slʌmp/ n baja f repentina; (in business) depresión f. ● vi desplomarse

slung /slʌŋ/ see SLING

slur /slɜː(r)/ vt (pt slurred). ~ one's words arrastrar las palabras. ● n. a racist ~ un comentario racista

slush /slʌʃ/ n nieve f medio derretida. ~ **fund** n fondo m de reptiles

sly /slaɪ/ adj (slyer, slyest) (crafty) astuto. ● n. on the ~ a hurtadillas. ~**ly** adv astutamente

smack /smæk/ n manotazo m. ● adv 🔢 ~ **in** the middle justo en el medio. he went ~ **into** a tree se dio contra un árbol. ● vt pegarle a (con la mano)

small /smɔːl/ adj (-er, -est) pequeño, chico (LAm). ● n. the ~ of the back la región lumbar. ~ **ads** npl anuncios mpl (clasificados), avisos mpl (clasificados) (LAm). ~-**change** n suelto m. ~**pox** /-pɒks/ n viruela f. ~ **talk** n charla f sobre temas triviales

smart /smɑːt/ adj (-er, -est) elegante; (clever) listo; (brisk) rápido. ● vi escocer. □ ~**en up** vt arreglar. vi (person) mejorar su aspecto, arreglarse. ~**ly** adv elegantemente; (quickly) rápidamente

smash /smæʃ/ vt romper; (into little pieces) hacer pedazos; batir (record). ● vi romperse; (collide) chocar (into con). ● n (noise) estrépito m; (collision) choque m; (in sport) smash m. □ ~ **up** vt destrozar. ~**ing** adj 🔢 estupendo

smattering /ˈsmætərɪŋ/ n nociones fpl

smear /smɪə(r)/ vt untar (with de); (stain) manchar (with de); (fig) difamar. ● n mancha f

smell /smel/ n olor m; (sense) olfato m. ● vt (pt smelt) oler; (animal) olfatear. ● vi oler. ~ **of** sth oler a algo. ~**y** adj maloliente. be ~**y** oler mal

smelt /smelt/ see SMELL. ● vt fundir

smile /smaɪl/ n sonrisa f. ● vi sonreír. ~ **at** s.o. sonreírle a uno

smirk /smɜːk/ n sonrisita f (de suficiencia etc)

smith /smɪθ/ n herrero m

smithereens /smɪðəˈriːnz/ npl. smash sth to ~ hacer algo añicos

smock /smɒk/ n blusa f, bata f

smog /smɒg/ n smog m

smoke /sməʊk/ n humo m. ● vt fumar (tobacco); ahumar (food).

● vi fumar. ~**eless** adj que arde sin humo. ~**er** n fumador m. ~**y** adj (room) lleno de humo

smooth /smuːð/ adj (-er, -est) (texture/stone) liso; (skin) suave; (movement) suave; (sea) tranquilo. ● vt alisar. □ ~ **out** vt allanar (problems). ~**ly** adv suavemente; (without problems) sin problemas

smother /ˈsmʌðə(r)/ vt asfixiar (person). ~ **s.o. with kisses** cubrir a uno de besos

smoulder /ˈsməʊldə(r)/ vi arder sin llama

smudge /smʌdʒ/ n borrón m. ● vi tiznarse

smug /smʌɡ/ adj (smugger, smuggest) pagado de sí mismo; (expression) de suficiencia

smuggl|e /ˈsmʌɡl/ vt pasar de contrabando. ~**er** n contrabandista m & f. ~**ing** n contrabando m

snack /snæk/ n tentempié m. ~ **bar** n cafetería f

snag /snæɡ/ n problema m

snail /sneɪl/ n caracol m. at a ~'s **pace** a paso de tortuga

snake /sneɪk/ n culebra f, serpiente f

snap /snæp/ vt (pt snapped) (break) romper. ~ **one's fingers** chasquear los dedos. ● vi romperse; (dog) intentar morder; (say) contestar bruscamente. ~ **at** (dog) intentar morder; (say) contestar bruscamente. ● n chasquido m; (Photo) foto f. ● adj instantáneo. □ ~ **up** vt no dejar escapar (offer). ~**py** adj (-ier, -iest) 🔲 rápido. **make it ~py!** ¡date prisa! ~**shot** n foto f

snare /sneə(r)/ n trampa f

snarl /snɑːl/ vi gruñir

snatch /snætʃ/ vt. ~ **sth from s.o.** arrebatarle algo a uno; (steal)

robar. ● n (short part) fragmento m

sneak /sniːk/ n soplón m. ● vi (past & pp sneaked or 🔲 snuck) □ ~ **in** entrar a hurtadillas. ~ **off** escabullirse. ~**ers** /ˈsniːkəz/ npl zapatillas fpl de deporte. ~**y** adj artero

sneer /snɪə(r)/ n expresión f desdeñosa. ● vi hacer una mueca de desprecio. ~ **at** hablar con desprecio a

sneeze /sniːz/ n estornudo m. ● vi estornudar

snide /snaɪd/ adj insidioso

sniff /snɪf/ vt oler. ● vi sorberse la nariz

snigger /ˈsnɪɡə(r)/ n risilla f. ● vi reírse (por lo bajo)

snip /snɪp/ vt (pt snipped) dar un tijeretazo a. ● n tijeretazo m

sniper /ˈsnaɪpə(r)/ n francotirador m

snippet /ˈsnɪpɪt/ n (of conversation) trozo m. ~**s of information** datos mpl aislados

snivel /ˈsnɪvl/ vi (pt snivelled) lloriquear

snob /snɒb/ n esnob m & f. ~**bery** n esnobismo m. ~**bish** adj esnob

snooker /ˈsnuːkə(r)/ n snooker m

snoop /snuːp/ vi 🔲 husmear

snooze /snuːz/ n sueñecito m. ● vi dormitar

snore /snɔː(r)/ n ronquido m. ● vi roncar

snorkel /ˈsnɔːkl/ n esnórkel m

snort /snɔːt/ n bufido m. ● vi bufar

snout /snaʊt/ n hocico m

snow /snəʊ/ n nieve f. ● vi nevar. **be ~ed in** estar aislado por la nieve. **be ~ed under with work** estar agobiado de trabajo. ~**ball** n bola f de nieve. ~**drift** n nieve f amontonada. ~**fall** n nevada f.

~**flake** n copo m de nieve. ~**man** n muñeco m de nieve. ~**plough** n quitanieves m. ~**storm** n tormenta f de nieve. ~**y** adj (day, weather) nevoso; (landscape) nevado

snub /snʌb/ vt (pt snubbed) desairar. ● n desaire m. ~-**nosed** adj chato

snuck /snʌk/ see SNEAK

snuff out /snʌf/ vt apagar (candle)

snug /snʌg/ adj (snugger, snuggest) cómodo; (tight) ajustado

snuggle (up) /ˈsnʌgl/ vi acurrucarse

so /səʊ/ adv (before a or adv) tan; (thus) así; and ~ on, and ~ forth etcétera (etcétera). I **think** ~ creo que sí. or ~ más o menos. ~ **long!** ¡hasta luego! ● conj (therefore) así que. ~ **am I** yo también. ~ **as to** para. ~ **far** adv (time) hasta ahora. ~ **far as I know** que yo sepa. ~ **that** conj para que.

soak /səʊk/ vt remojar. ● vi empaparse. □ ~ **in** vi penetrar. □ ~ **up** vt absorber. ~**ing** adj empapado

so-and-so /ˈsəʊənsəʊ/ n fulano m

soap /səʊp/ n jabón m. ● vt enjabonar. ~ **opera** n telenovela f, culebrón m. ~ **powder** n jabón m en polvo. ~**y** adj jabonoso

soar /sɔː(r)/ vi (bird/plane) planear; (rise) elevarse; (price) dispararse. ~**ing** adj (inflation) galopante

sob /sɒb/ n sollozo m. ● vi (pt sobbed) sollozar

sober /ˈsəʊbə(r)/ adj (not drunk) sobrio

so-called /ˈsəʊkɔːld/ adj denominado; (expert) supuesto

soccer /ˈsɒkə(r)/ n fútbol m, futbol m (Mex)

sociable /ˈsəʊʃəbl/ adj sociable

social /ˈsəʊʃl/ adj social; (sociable) sociable. ~**ism** n socialismo m. ~**ist** adj & n socialista (m & f). ~**ize** vt socializar. ~ **security** n seguridad f social. ~ **worker** n asistente m social

society /səˈsaɪətɪ/ n sociedad f

sociological /ˌsəʊsɪəˈlɒdʒɪkl/ adj sociológico. ~**ist** /-ˈɒlədʒɪst/ n sociólogo m. ~**y** /-ˈɒlədʒɪ/ n sociología f

sock /sɒk/ n calcetín m

socket /ˈsɒkɪt/ n (of joint) hueco m; (of eye) cuenca f; (wall plug) enchufe m; (for bulb) portalámparas m

soda /ˈsəʊdə/ n soda f. ~-**water** n soda f

sodium /ˈsəʊdɪəm/ n sodio m

sofa /ˈsəʊfə/ n sofá m

soft /sɒft/ adj (-er, -est) blando; (light, colour) suave; (gentle) dulce, tierno; (not strict) blando. ~ **drink** n refresco m. ~**en** /ˈsɒfn/ vt ablandar; suavizar (skin). ● vi ablandarse. ~**ly** adv dulcemente; (speak) bajito. ~**ware** /-weə(r)/ n software m

soggy /ˈsɒgɪ/ adj (-ier, -iest) empapado

soil /sɔɪl/ n tierra f; (Amer, dirt) suciedad f. ● vt ensuciar

solar /ˈsəʊlə(r)/ adj solar

sold /səʊld/ see SELL

solder /ˈsɒldə(r)/ vt soldar

soldier /ˈsəʊldʒə(r)/ n soldado m. □ ~ **on** vi 🄸 seguir al pie del cañon

sole /səʊl/ n (of foot) planta f; (of shoe) suela f. ● adj único, solo. ~**ly** adv únicamente

solemn /ˈsɒləm/ adj solemne

solicitor /səˈlɪsɪtə(r)/ n abogado m; (notary) notario m

solid /ˈsɒlɪd/ adj sólido; (gold etc)

macizo; (*unanimous*) unánime; (*meal*) sustancioso. ● *n* sólido *m*. **~s** *npl* alimentos *mpl* sólidos.
~arity /ˌsɒlɪˈdærəti/ *n* solidaridad *f*. **~ify** /səˈlɪdɪfaɪ/ *vi* solidificarse

solitary /ˈsɒlɪtri/ *adj* solitario

solitude /ˈsɒlɪtjuːd/ *n* soledad *f*

solo /ˈsəʊləʊ/ *n* (*pl* -os) (*Mus*) solo *m*. **~ist** *n* solista *m* & *f*

solstice /ˈsɒlstɪs/ *n* solsticio *m*

solu|ble /ˈsɒljʊbl/ *adj* soluble. **~tion** /səˈluːʃn/ *n* solución *f*

solve /sɒlv/ *vt* solucionar (problem); resolver (mystery). **~nt** /-vənt/ *adj & n* solvente (*m*)

sombre /ˈsɒmbə(r)/ *adj* sombrío

---

some /sʌm/səm/

● *adjective*

····▸ (*unspecified number*) unos, unas. he ate ~ olives comió unas aceitunas

····▸ (*unspecified amount*) *not translated*. I have to buy ~ bread tengo que comprar pan. would you like ~ coffee? ¿quieres café?

····▸ (*certain, not all*) algunos, -nas. I like ~ modern writers algunos escritores modernos me gustan

····▸ (*a little*) algo de. I eat ~ meat, but not much como algo de carne, pero no mucho

····▸ (*considerable amount of*) we've known each other for ~ time ya hace tiempo que nos conocemos

····▸ (*expressing admiration*) that's ~ car you've got! ¡vaya coche que tienes!

● *pronoun*

····▸ (*a number of things or*

people) algunos, -nas, unos, unas. ~ are mine and ~ aren't algunos *or* unos son míos y otros no. aren't there any apples? we bought ~ yesterday ¿no hay manzanas? compramos algunas ayer

····▸ (*part of an amount*) he wants ~ quiere un poco. ~ of what he said parte *or* algo de lo que dijo

····▸ (*certain people*) algunos, -nas. ~ say that... algunos dicen que...

● *adverb*

····▸ (*approximately*) unos, unas, alrededor de. there were ~ fifty people there había unas cincuenta personas, había alrededor de cincuenta personas

---

some: ~body /-bɒdi/ *pron* alguien. **~how** *adv* de algún modo. **~how** *or* other de una manera u otra. **~one** *pron* alguien

somersault /ˈsʌməsɔːlt/ *n* salto *m* mortal. ● *vi* dar un salto mortal

some: ~thing *pron* algo *m*. **~thing like** (*approximately*) alrededor de. **~time** *adj* ex. ● *adv* algún día. **~time next week** un día de la semana que viene. **~times** *adv* a veces. **~what** *adv* un tanto. **~where** *adv* en alguna parte, en algún lado

son /sʌn/ *n* hijo *m*

sonata /səˈnɑːtə/ *n* sonata *f*

song /sɒŋ/ *n* canción *f*

sonic /ˈsɒnɪk/ *adj* sónico

son-in-law /ˈsʌnɪnlɔː/ *n* (*pl* sons-in-law) yerno *m*

sonnet /ˈsɒnɪt/ *n* soneto *m*

son of a bitch *n* (*pl* sons of bitches) (*esp Amer sl*) hijo *m* de puta

soon /suːn/ adv (-er, -est) pronto; (in a short time) dentro de poco. ~ after poco después. ~er or later tarde o temprano. as ~ as en cuanto; as ~ as possible lo antes posible. the ~er the better cuanto antes mejor

soot /sut/ n hollín m

sooth|e /suːð/ vt calmar; aliviar (pain). ~ing adj (medicine) calmante; (words) tranquilizador

sooty /'suti/ adj cubierto de hollín

sophisticated /sə'fɪstɪkeɪtɪd/ adj sofisticado; (complex) complejo

sophomore /'sɒfəmɔː(r)/ n (Amer) estudiante m & f de segundo curso (en la universidad)

sopping /'sɒpɪŋ/ adj. ~ (wet) empapado

soppy /'sɒpɪ/ adj (-ier, -iest) 🄸 sentimental

soprano /sə'prɑːnəʊ/ n (pl -os) soprano f

sordid /'sɔːdɪd/ adj sórdido

sore /sɔː(r)/ adj (-r, -est) dolorido; (Amer fam, angry) be ~ at s.o. estar picado con uno. ~ throat n dolor m de garganta. I've got a ~ throat me duele la garganta. ● n llaga f

sorrow /'sɒrəʊ/ n pena f, pesar m

sorry /'sɒrɪ/ adj (-ier, -ier) arrepentido; (wretched) lamentable. I'm ~ lo siento. be ~ for s.o. (pity) compadecer a uno. I'm ~ you can't come siento que no puedas venir. say ~ pedir perdón. ~! (apologizing) ¡lo siento! ¡perdón!. ~? (asking s.o. to repeat) ¿cómo?

sort /sɔːt/ n tipo m, clase f; (fam, person) tipo m. a ~ of una especie de. ● vt clasificar. □ ~ out vt (or-

ganize) ordenar; organizar (finances); (separate out) separar; solucionar (problem)

so-so /'səʊsəʊ/ adj regular

soufflé /'suːfleɪ/ n suflé m

sought /sɔːt/ see SEEK

soul /səʊl/ n alma f

sound /saʊnd/ n sonido m; (noise) ruido m. ● vt tocar. ● vi sonar; (seem) parecer (as if que). it ~s interesting suena interesante.. ● adj (-er, -est) sano; (argument) lógico; (secure) seguro. ● adv. ~ asleep profundamente dormido. ~ barrier n barrera f del sonido. ~ly adv sólidamente; (asleep) profundamente. ~proof adj insonorizado. ~track n banda f sonora

soup /suːp/ n sopa f

sour /saʊə(r)/ adj (-er, -est) agrio; (milk) cortado

source /sɔːs/ n fuente f

south /saʊθ/ n sur m. ● adj sur a invar; (wind) del sur. ● adv (go) hacia el sur. it's ~ of está al sur de. S~ Africa n Sudáfrica f. S~ America n América f (del Sur), Sudamérica f. S~ American adj & n sudamericano (m). ~-east n sudeste m, sureste m. ~erly /'sʌðəlɪ/ (wind) del sur. ~ern /'sʌðən/ adj del sur, meridional. ~erner n sureño m. ~ward /səʊθ/, ~wards adv hacia el sur. ~-west n sudoeste m, suroeste m

souvenir /suːvə'nɪə(r)/ n recuerdo m

sovereign /'sɒvrɪn/ n & a soberano (m)

Soviet /'səʊvɪət/ adj (History) soviético. the ~ Union n la Unión f Soviética

sow[1] /saʊ/ vt (pt sowed, pp sowed or sown /səʊn/) sembrar

sow² /saʊ/ n cerda f

soy (esp Amer), **soya** /'sɔɪə/ n. ~ **bean** n soja f

spa /spɑː/ n balneario m

space /speɪs/ n espacio m; (room) espacio m, lugar m. • adj (research etc) espacial. • vt espaciar. □ ~ **out** vt espaciar. ~**craft**, ~**ship** n nave f espacial

spade /speɪd/ n pala f. ~**s** npl (Cards) picas fpl

spaghetti /spə'getɪ/ n espaguetis mpl

Spain /speɪn/ n España f

spam /spæm/ n (Comp) correo m basura

span /spæn/ n (of arch) luz f; (of time) espacio m; (of wings) envergadura f. • vt (pt spanned) extenderse sobre. • adj see **SPICK**

Spaniard /'spænjəd/ n español m

spaniel /'spænjəl/ n spaniel m

Spanish /'spænɪʃ/ adj español; (language) castellano, español. • n (language) castellano m, español m. npl. the ~ (people) los españoles

spank /spæŋk/ vt pegarle a (en las nalgas)

spanner /'spænə(r)/ n llave f

spare /speə(r)/ vt. if you can ~ the time si tienes tiempo. can you ~ me a pound? ¿tienes una libra que me des? ~ no effort no escatimar esfuerzos. have money to ~ tener dinero de sobra. • adj (not in use) de más; (replacement) de repuesto; (free) libre. • n (part) n repuesto m. ~ **room** n cuarto m de huéspedes. ~ **time** n tiempo m libre. ~ **tyre** n neumático m de repuesto

sparingly /'speərɪŋlɪ/ adv (use) con moderación

spark /spɑːk/ n chispa f. • vt pro-

vocar (criticism); suscitar (interest). ~**ing plug** n (Auto) bujía f

sparkl|e /'spɑːkl/ vi centellear. • n destello m. ~**ing** adj centelleante; (wine) espumoso

spark plug n (Auto) bujía f

sparrow /'spærəʊ/ n gorrión m

sparse /spɑːs/ adj escaso. ~**ly** adv escasamente

spasm /'spæzəm/ n espasmo m; (of cough) acceso m. ~**odic** /-'mɒdɪk/ adj espasmódico; (Med) irregular

spat /spæt/ see **SPIT**

spate /speɪt/ n racha f

spatial /'speɪʃl/ adj espacial

spatter /'spætə(r)/ vt salpicar (with de)

spawn /spɔːn/ n huevas fpl. • vt generar. • vi desovar

speak /spiːk/ vt/i (pt spoke, pp spoken) hablar. ~ **for s.o.** hablar en nombre de uno. □ ~ **up** vi hablar más fuerte. ~**er** n (in public) orador m; (loudspeaker) altavoz m; (of language) hablante m f

spear /spɪə(r)/ n lanza f. ~**head** vt (lead) encabezar

special /'speʃl/ adj especial. ~**ist** /'speʃəlɪst/ n especialista m & f. ~**ity** /-ɪ'ælətɪ/ n especialidad f. ~**ization** /-əlaɪ'zeɪʃn/ n especialización f. ~**ize** /-əlaɪz/ vi especializarse. ~**ized** adj especializado. ~**ly** adv especialmente. ~**ty** n (Amer) especialidad f

species /'spiːʃiːz/ n especie f

specif|ic /spə'sɪfɪk/ adj específico. ~**ically** adv específicamente; (state) explícitamente. ~**ication** /-ɪ'keɪʃn/ n especificación f. ~**y** /'spesɪfaɪ/ vt especificar

specimen /'spesɪmɪn/ n muestra f

speck /spek/ n (of dust) mota f; (in distance) punto m

specs /speks/ npl 🗓 see SPECTACLES

spectac|le /'spektəkl/ n espectáculo m. ~les npl gafas fpl, lentes fpl (LAm), anteojos mpl (LAm). ~ular /-'tækjʊlə(r)/ adj espectacular

spectator /spek'teɪtə(r)/ n espectador m

spectr|e /'spektə(r)/ n espectro m. ~um /'spektrəm/ n (pl -tra /-trə/) espectro m; (of views) gama f

speculat|e /'spekjʊleɪt/ vi especular. ~ion /-'leɪʃn/ n especulación f. ~or n especulador m

sped /sped/ see SPEED

speech /spiːtʃ/ n (faculty) habla f; (address) discurso m. ~less adj mudo

speed /spiːd/ n velocidad f; (rapidity) rapidez f. ● vi (pt speeded) (drive too fast) ir a exceso de velocidad. □ ~ off, ~ away (pt sped) vi alejarse a toda velocidad. □ ~ by (pt speed) vi (time) pasar volando. □ ~ up (pt speeded) vt acelerar. vi acelerarse. ~boat n lancha f motora. ~ camera n cámara f de control de velocidad. ~ dating n cita f flash, speed dating m. ~ limit n velocidad f máxima. ~ometer /spiː'dɒmɪtə(r)/ n velocímetro m. ~way n (Amer) autopista f. ~y adj (-ier, -iest) rápido

spell /spel/ n (magic) hechizo m; (of weather, activity) período m. go through a bad ~ pasar por una mala racha. ● vt/i (pt spelled or spelt) escribir. □ ~ out vt deletrear; (fig) explicar. ~ checker n corrector m ortográfico. ~ing n ortografía f

spellbound /'spelbaʊnd/ adj embelesado

spelt /spelt/ see SPELL

spend /spend/ vt (pt spent /spent/) gastar (money); pasar (time); dedicar (care). ● vi gastar dinero

sperm /spɜːm/ n (pl sperms or sperm) esperma f; (individual) espermatozoide m

spew /spjuː/ vt/i vomitar

spher|e /sfɪə(r)/ n esfera f. ~ical /'sferɪkl/ adj esférico

spice /spaɪs/ n especia f

spick /spɪk/ adj. ~ and span limpio y ordenado

spicy /'spaɪsɪ/ adj picante

spider /'spaɪdə(r)/ n araña f

spik|e /spaɪk/ n (of metal etc) punta f. ~y adj puntiagudo

spill /spɪl/ vt (pt spilled or spilt) derramar. ● vi derramarse. □ ~ over vi (container) desbordarse; (liquid) rebosar

spin /spɪn/ vt (pt spun, pres p spinning) hacer girar; hilar (wool); centrifugar (washing). ● vi girar. ● n. give sth a ~ hacer girar algo. go for a ~ (Auto) ir a dar un paseo en coche

spinach /'spɪnɪdʒ/ n espinacas fpl

spindly /'spɪndlɪ/ adj larguirucho

spin-drier /spɪn'draɪə(r)/ n centrifugadora f (de ropa)

spine /spaɪn/ n columna f vertebral; (of book) lomo m; (on animal) púa f. ~less adj (fig) sin carácter

spinning wheel /'spɪnɪŋ/ n rueca f

spin-off /'spɪnɒf/ n resultado m indirecto; (by-product) producto m derivado

spinster /'spɪnstə(r)/ n soltera f

spiral /'spaɪərəl/ adj espiral;

s

(shape) de espiral. • n espiral f. • vi (pt **spiralled**) (unemployment) escalar; (prices) disparrarse. ~ **staircase** n escalera f de caracol

spire /'spaɪə(r)/ n aguja f

spirit /'spɪrɪt/ n espíritu m. be in good ~s estar animado. in low ~s abatido. ~**ed** adj animado, fogoso. ~s npl (drinks) bebidas fpl alcohólicas (de alta graduación). ~**ual** /'spɪrɪtʃuəl/ adj espiritual

spit /spɪt/ vt (pt **spat** or (Amer) **spit**, pres p **spitting**) escupir. • vi escupir. it's ~ting caen algunas gotas. • n saliva f; (for roasting) asador m

spite /spaɪt/ n rencor m. in ~ of a pesar de. • vt fastidiar. ~**ful** adj rencoroso

spittle /'spɪtl/ n baba f

splash /splæʃ/ vt salpicar. • vi (person) chapotear. □ ~ n salpicadura f. a ~ of paint un poco de pintura. □ ~ **about** vi chapotear. □ ~ **down** vi (spacecraft) amerizar. □ ~ **out** vi gastarse un dineral (on en)

splend|id /'splendɪd/ adj espléndido. ~**our** /-ə(r)/ n esplendor m

splint /splɪnt/ n tablilla f

splinter /'splɪntə(r)/ n astilla f. • vi astillarse

split /splɪt/ vt (pt **split**, pres p **splitting**) partir; fisionar (atom); reventar (trousers); (divide) dividir. • vi partirse; (divide) dividirse. a ~**ting headache** un dolor de cabeza espantoso. • n (in garment) descosido m; (in wood, glass) rajadura f. □ ~ **up** vi separarse. ~ **second** n fracción f de segundo

splutter /'splʌtə(r)/ vi chisporrotear; (person) farfullar

spoil /spɔɪl/ vt (pt **spoilt** or **spoiled**) estropear, echar a perder; (indulge) consentir, malcriar. ~**s** npl

botín m. ~-**sport** n aguafiestas m & f

spoke¹ /spəʊk/ see **SPEAK**

spoke² /spəʊk/ n (of wheel) rayo m

spoken /spəʊkən/ see **SPEAK**

spokesman /'spəʊksmən/ n (pl -men) portavoz m

sponge /spʌndʒ/ n esponja f. • vt limpiar con una esponja. □ ~ **off**, ~ **on** vi vivir a costillas de. ~ **cake** n bizcocho m

sponsor /'spɒnsə(r)/ n patrocinador m; (of the arts) mecenas m & f; (surety) garante m. • vt patrocinar. ~**ship** n patrocinio m; (of the arts) mecenazgo m

spontaneous /spɒn'teɪnɪəs/ adj espontáneo. ~**ously** adv espontáneamente

spoof /spuːf/ n 🔢 parodia f

spooky /'spuːkɪ/ adj (-ier, -iest) 🔢 espeluznante

spool /spuːl/ n carrete m

spoon /spuːn/ n cuchara f. ~**ful** n cucharada f

sporadic /spə'rædɪk/ adj esporádico

sport /spɔːt/ n deporte m. ~**s car** n coche m deportivo. ~**s centre** n centro m deportivo. ~**sman** /-mən/ n, (pl -men), ~**swoman** n deportista m & f

spot /spɒt/ n mancha f; (pimple) grano m; (place) lugar m; (in pattern) lunar m. be in a ~ 🔢 estar en apuros. on the ~ allí mismo; (decide) en ese mismo momento. • vt (pt **spotted**) manchar; (fam, notice) ver, divisar; descubrir (mistake). ~ **check** n control m hecho al azar. ~-**less** adj (clothes) impecable; (house) limpísimo. ~**light** n reflector m; (in theatre) foco m.

∼ted adj moteado; (material) de lunares. **∼ty** adj (-ier, -iest) (skin) lleno de granos; (youth) con la cara llena de granos

spouse /spauz/ n cónyuge m & f

spout /spaut/ n pico m; (jet) chorro m

sprain /sprein/ vt hacerse un esguince en. ●n esguince m

sprang /spræŋ/ see SPRING

spray /sprei/ n (of flowers) ramillete m; (from sea) espuma f; (liquid in spray form) espray m; (device) rociador m. ●vt rociar

spread /spred/ vt (pt spread) (stretch, extend) extender; desplegar (wings); difundir (idea, news). ∼ butter on a piece of toast untar una tostada con mantequilla. ●vi extenderse; (disease) propagarse; (idea, news) difundirse. ●n (of ideas) difusión f; (of disease, fire) propagación f; (fam, feast) festín m. □∼ **out** vi (move apart) desplegarse

spree /spri:/ n. go on a shopping ∼ ir de expedición a las tiendas

sprightly /spraitli/ adj (-ier, -iest) vivo

spring /spriŋ/ n (season) primavera f; (device) resorte m; (in mattress) muelle m, resorte m (LAm); (elasticity) elasticidad f; (water) manantial m. ●adj primaveral. ●vi (pt sprang, pp sprung) saltar; (issue) brotar. ∼ **from sth** (problem) provenir de algo. □∼ **up** vi surgir. **∼board** n trampolín m. **∼-clean** /-'kli:n/ vi hacer una limpieza general. ∼ **onion** n cebolleta f. **∼time** n primavera f **∼y** adj (-ier, -iest) (mattress, grass) mullido

sprinkle /spriŋkl/ vt salpicar; (with liquid) rociar. ●n salpicadura f; (of liquid) rociada f. **∼r** n regadera f

sprint /sprint/ n carrera f corta. ●vi (Sport) esprintar; (run fast) correr. **∼er** n corredor m

sprout /spraut/ vi brotar. ●n brote m. (Brussels) **∼s** npl coles fpl de Bruselas

sprung /sprʌŋ/ see SPRING

spud /spʌd/ n 🅔 patata f, papa f (LAm)

spun /spʌn/ see SPIN

spur /spɜ:(r)/ n espuela f; (stimulus) acicate m. **on the** ∼ **of the moment** sin pensarlo. ●vt (pt spurred). ∼ **(on)** espolear; (fig) estimular

spurn /spɜ:n/ vt desdeñar; (reject) rechazar

spurt /spɜ:t/ vi (liquid) salir a chorros. ●n chorro m; (of activity) racha f

spy /spai/ n espía m & f. ●vt descubrir, ver. ●vi espiar. ∼ **on s.o.** espiar a uno

squabble /skwɒbl/ vi reñir

squad /skwɒd/ n (Mil) pelotón m; (of police) brigada f; (Sport) equipo m. ∼ **car** n coche m patrulla. **∼ron** /skwɒdrən/ n (Mil, Aviat) escuadrón m; (Naut) escuadra f

squalid /skwɒlid/ adj miserable

squall /skwɔ:l/ n turbión m

squalor /skwɒlə(r)/ n miseria f

squander /skwɒndə(r)/ vt derrochar; desaprovechar (opportunity)

square /skweə(r)/ n cuadrado m; (in town) plaza f. ●adj cuadrado; (meal) decente; (fam, old-fashioned) chapado a la antigua. ●vt (settle) arreglar; (Math) elevar al cuadrado. ●vi (agree) cuadrar. □∼ **up** vi arreglar cuentas (with con). **∼ly** adv directamente

squash /skwɒʃ/ vt aplastar; (sup-

press) acallar. ● **n**. it was a terrible ~ íbamos (or iban) terriblemente apretujados; *(drink)* orange ~ naranjada *f*; *(Sport)* squash *m*; *(vegetable)* calabaza *f*. ~**y** *adj* blando

squat /skwɒt/ *vi (pt* **squatted)** ponerse en cuclillas; *(occupy illegally)* ocupar sin autorización. ● *adj* rechoncho y bajo. ~**ter** *n* ocupante *m* & *f* ilegal, okupa *m* & *f*

squawk /skwɔːk/ *n* graznido m. ● *vi* graznar

squeak /skwiːk/ *n* chillido *m*; *(of door)* chirrido *m*. ● *vi* chillar; (door) chirriar; (shoes) crujir. ~**y** *adj* chirriante

squeal /skwiːl/ *n* chillido *m* ● *vi* chillar

squeamish /ˈskwiːmɪʃ/ *adj* impresionable, delicado

squeeze /skwiːz/ *vt* apretar; exprimir (lemon etc). ● *vi*. ~ **in** meterse. ● *n* estrujón *m*; *(of hand)* apretón *m*

squid /skwɪd/ *n* calamar *m*

squiggle /ˈskwɪɡl/ *n* garabato *m*

squint /skwɪnt/ *vi* bizquear; *(trying to see)* entrecerrar los ojos. ● *n* estrabismo *m*

squirm /skwɜːm/ *vi* retorcerse

squirrel /ˈskwɪrəl/ *n* ardilla *f*

squirt /skwɜːt/ *vt* (liquid) echar un chorro de. ● *vi* salir a chorros. ● *n* chorrito *m*

St /sənt/ *abbr* (= **saint**) /sənt/ S, San(to); (= **street**) C/, Calle *f*

stab /stæb/ *vt (pt* **stabbed)** apuñalar. ● *n* puñalada *f*; *(pain)* punzada *f*. have a ~ **at** sth intentar algo

stability /stəˈbɪlətɪ/ *n* estabilidad *f*. ~**ze** /ˈsteɪbɪlaɪz/ *vt/i* estabilizar

stable /ˈsteɪbl/ *adj* (-er, -est) estable. ● *n* caballeriza *f*, cuadra *f*

stack /stæk/ *n* montón *m*. ● *vt*. ~

(up) amontonar

stadium /ˈsteɪdɪəm/ *n (pl* -**diums** or -**dia** /-dɪə/) estadio *m*

staff /stɑːf/ *n* (stick) palo *m*; *(employees)* personal *m*. teaching ~ personal *m* docente. a member of ~ un empleado

stag /stæɡ/ *n* ciervo *m*. ~-**night**, ~-**party** *n (before wedding)* fiesta *f* de despedida de soltero; *(men-only party)* fiesta *f* para hombres

stage /steɪdʒ/ *n (in theatre)* escenario *m*; *(platform)* plataforma *f*; *(phase)* etapa *f*. the ~ *(profession, medium)* el teatro. ● *vt* poner en escena (play); *(arrange)* organizar; *(pej)* orquestar. ~**coach** *n* diligencia *f*

stagger /ˈstæɡə(r)/ *vi* tambalearse. ● *vt* dejar estupefacto; escalonar (holidays etc). ~**ing** *adj* asombroso

stagnant /ˈstæɡnənt/ *adj* estancado. ~**te** /stæɡˈneɪt/ *vi* estancarse

staid /steɪd/ *adj* serio, formal

stain /steɪn/ *vt* manchar; (colour) teñir. ● *n* mancha *f*; (dye) tintura *f*. ~**ed glass window** *n* vidriera *f* de colores. ~**less steel** *n* acero *m* inoxidable. ~ **remover** *n* quitamanchas *m*

stair /steə(r)/ *n* escalón *m*. ~**s** *npl* escalera *f*. ~**case**, ~**way** *n* escalera *f*

stake /steɪk/ *n* estaca *f*; (wager) apuesta *f*; *(Com)* intereses *mpl*. be at ~ estar en juego. ● *vt* estacar; jugarse (reputation). ~ **a claim** reclamar

stalactite /ˈstæləktaɪt/ *n* estalactita *f*. ~**gmite** /ˈstæləɡmaɪt/ *n* estalagmita *f*

stale /steɪl/ *adj* (-er, -est) no fresco; (bread) duro; (smell) viciado. ~mate n (Chess) ahogado m; (deadlock) punto m muerto

stalk /stɔːk/ n tallo m. ● vt acechar. ● vi irse indignado

stall /stɔːl/ n (in stable) compartimiento m; (in market) puesto m. ~s npl (in theatre) platea f, patio m de butacas. ● vt parar (engine). ● vi (engine) pararse; (fig) andar con rodeos

stallion /ˈstæljən/ n semental m

stalwart /ˈstɔːlwət/ adj (supporter) leal, incondicional

stamina /ˈstæmɪnə/ n resistencia f

stammer /ˈstæmə(r)/ vi tartamudear. ● n tartamudeo m

stamp /stæmp/ vt (with feet) patear; (press) estampar; (with rubber stamp) sellar; (fig) señalar. ● vi dar patadas en el suelo. ● n sello m, estampilla f (LAm), timbre m (Mex); (on passport) sello m; (with foot) patada f; (mark) marca f, señal f. □ ~ out vt (fig) erradicar. ~ed addressed envelope n sobre m franqueado con su dirección

stampede /stæmˈpiːd/ n estampida f. ● vi salir en estampida

stance /stɑːns/ n postura f

stand /stænd/ vi (pt stood) estar de pie, estar parado (LAm); (rise) ponerse de pie, pararse; (be) encontrarse; (Pol) presentarse como candidato (for en). the offer ~s la oferta sigue en pie. to ~ to reason ser lógico. ● vt (endure) soportar; (place) colocar. ~ a chance tener una posibilidad. ● n posición f, postura f; (for lamp etc) pie m, sostén m; (at market) puesto m; (booth) quiosco m; (Sport) tribuna f. make a ~ against sth oponer resistencia a algo. □ ~ back vi apartarse. □ ~ by vi estar preparado. vt (support) apoyar. □ ~ down vi retirarse. □ ~ for vt significar. □ ~ in for vt suplir a. □ ~ out vi destacarse. □ ~ up vi ponerse de pie, pararse (LAm). □ ~ up for vt defender. ~ up for oneself defenderse. □ ~ up to vt resistir a

standard /ˈstændəd/ n norma f; (level) nivel m; (flag) estandarte m. ● adj estándar a invar, normal. ~ize vt estandarizar. ~ lamp n lámpara f de pie. ~s npl principios mpl

stand: ~-by n (at airport) standby m. be on ~-by (police) estar en estado de alerta. ~-in n suplente m & f. ~-ing adj de pie, parado (LAm); (permanent) permanente f. ● n posición f; (prestige) prestigio m. ~off m (Amer, draw) empate m; (deadlock) callejón m sin salida. ~point n punto m de vista. ~still n. be at a ~still estar paralizado. come to a ~still (vehicle) parar; (city) quedar paralizado

stank /stæŋk/ see STINK

staple /ˈsteɪpl/ adj principal. ● n grapa f. ● vt sujetar con una grapa. ~r n grapadora f

star /stɑː(r)/ n (incl Cinema, Theatre) estrella f; (asterisk) asterisco m. ● vi (pt starred) ~ in a film protagonizar una película. ~board n estribor m.

starch /stɑːtʃ/ n almidón m; (in food) fécula f. ● vt almidonar. ~y (food) adj a base de féculas

stardom /ˈstɑːdəm/ n estrellato m

stare /steə(r)/ n mirada f fija. ● vi. ~ (at) mirar fijamente

starfish /ˈstɑːfɪʃ/ n estrella f de mar

stark /stɑːk/ adj (-er, -est) escueto. ● adv completamente

starling /ˈstɑːlɪŋ/ n estornino m

starry /'stɑːrɪ/ adj estrellado

start /stɑːt/ vt empezar, comenzar; encender (engine); arrancar (car); (cause) provocar; abrir (business). ● vi empezar; (car etc) arrancar; (jump) dar un respingo. to ~ with (as linker) para empezar. ~ off by doing sth empezar por hacer algo. ● n principio m; (Sport) ventaja f; (jump) susto m. **make an early** ~ (on journey) salir temprano. ~er n (Auto) motor m de arranque; (Culin) primer plato m. ~ing-point n punto m de partida

startle /'stɑːtl/ vt asustar

starv|ation /stɑːˈveɪʃn/ n hambre f, inanición f. ~e /stɑːv/ vt hacer morir de hambre. ● vi morirse de hambre. I'm ~ing me muero de hambre.

state /steɪt/ n estado m. **be in a** ~ estar agitado. **the S**~ los Estados mpl Unidos. ● vt declarar; expresar (views); (fix) fijar. ● adj del Estado; (Schol) público; (with ceremony) de gala. ~ly adj (-ier, -iest) majestuoso. ~ly home n casa f solariega. ~ment n declaración f; (account) informe m. ~sman /-mən/ n estadista m

static /'stætɪk/ adj estacionario. ● n (interference) estática f.

station /'steɪʃn/ n estación f; (on radio) emisora f; (TV) canal m. ● vt colocar; (Mil) estacionar. ~ary adj estacionario. ~er's (shop) n papelería f. ~ery n artículos mpl de papelería. ~ wagon n (Amer) ranchera f, (coche m) familiar m, camioneta f (LAm)

statistic /stəˈtɪstɪk/ n estadística f. ~al adj estadístico. ~s n (science) estadística f

statue /'stætʃuː/ n estatua f

stature /'stætʃə(r)/ n talla f, estatura f

status /'steɪtəs/ n posición f social; (prestige) categoría f; (Jurid) estado m

statut|e /'stætʃuːt/ n estatuto m. ~ory /-ʊtrɪ/ adj estatutario

staunch /stɔːnʃ/ adj (-er, -est) leal

stave /steɪv/ n (Mus) pentagrama m. □ ~ **off** vt evitar

stay /steɪ/ n (of time) estancia f, estadía f (LAm); (Jurid) suspensión f. ● vi quedarse; (reside) alojarse. I'm ~ing in a hotel estoy en un hotel. □ ~ **in** vi quedarse en casa. □ ~ **up** vi quedarse levantado

stead /sted/ n. in s.o.'s ~ en lugar de uno. **stand s.o. in good** ~ resultarle muy útil a uno. ~ily adv firmemente; (regularly) regularmente. ~y adj (-ier, -iest) firme; (regular) regular; (flow) continuo; (worker) serio

steak /steɪk/ n. a ~ un filete. some ~ carne para guisar

steal /stiːl/ vt (pt stole, pp stolen) robar. □ ~ **in** vi entrar a hurtadillas

stealth /stelθ/ n. **by** ~ sigilosamente. ~y adj sigiloso

steam /stiːm/ n vapor m. let off ~ (fig) desahogarse. ● vt (cook) cocer al vapor. ● vi echar vapor. □ ~ **up** vi empañarse. ~ **engine** n máquina f de vapor. ~er n (ship) barco m de vapor. ~roller n apisonadora f. **~y** adj lleno de vapor

steel /stiːl/ n acero m. • vt **~ o.s.** armarse de valor. **~ industry** n industria f siderúrgica

steep /stiːp/ ● adj (-er, -est) empinado; (increase) considerable; (price) 🛈 excesivo

steeple /'stiːpl/ n aguja f, campanario m

steeply /'stiːpl/ adv abruptamente; (increase) considerablemente

steer /stɪə(r)/ vt dirigir; gobernar (ship). ● vi (in ship) estar al timón. **~ clear of** evitar. **~ing** /-ɪŋ/ n (Auto) dirección f. **~ing wheel** n volante m

stem /stem/ n (of plant) tallo m; (of glass) pie m; (of word) raíz f. ● vt (pt stemmed) contener (bleeding). ● vi. **~ from** provenir de

stench /stentʃ/ n hedor m

stencil /'stensl/ n plantilla f

stenographer /ste'nɒɡrəfə(r)/ n estenógrafo m

step /step/ vi (pt stepped). **~ in** sth pisar algo. **~ aside** vi hacerse a un lado. □ **~ down** vi retirarse. □ **~ in** vi (fig) intervenir. □ **~ up** vt intensificar; redoblar (security). ● n paso m; (stair) escalón m; (fig) medida f. **take a ~** tomar medidas. **be in ~** llevar el paso. **be out of ~** no llevar el paso. **~brother** n hermanastro m. **~daughter** n hijastra f. **~father** n padrastro m. **~ladder** n escalera f de tijera. **~mother** n madrastra f. **~ping-stone** n peldaño m. **~sister** n hermanastra f. **~son** n hijastro m

stereo /'steriəʊ/ n (pl -os estéreo m. ● adj estéreo a invar. **~type** n estereotipo m

sterile /'steraɪl/ adj estéril. **~ize**

/'sterɪlaɪz/ vt esterilizar

sterling /'stɜːlɪŋ/ n libras fpl esterlinas. ● adj (pound) esterlina

stern /stɜːn/ n (of boat) popa f. ● adj (-er, -est) severo

stethoscope /'steθəskəʊp/ n estetoscopio m

stew /stjuː/ vt/i guisar. ● n estofado m, guiso m

steward /'stjuːəd/ n administrador m; (on ship) camarero m; (air steward) sobrecargo m, aeromozo m (LAm). **~ess** /-'des/ n camarera f; (on aircraft) auxiliar f de vuelo, azafata f

stick /stɪk/ n palo m; (for walking) bastón m; (of celery etc) tallo m. ● vt (pt stuck) (glue) pegar; (fam, put) poner; (thrust) clavar; (fam, endure) soportar. ● vi pegarse; (jam) atascarse. □ **~ out** vi sobresalir. □ **~ to** vt ceñirse a. □ **~ up for** vt 🛈 defender. **~er** n pegatina f. **~ing plaster** n esparadrapo m; (individual) tirita f, curita f (LAm). **~ler** /'stɪklə(r)/. n. be a **~ler for** insistir en. **~y** /'stɪki/ adj (-ier, -iest) (surface) pegajoso; (label) engomado

stiff /stɪf/ adj (-er, -est) rígido; (joint, fabric) tieso; (muscle) entumecido; (difficult) difícil; (manner) estirado; (drink) fuerte. **have a ~** neck tener torticolis. **~en** vi (become rigid) agarrotarse; (become firm) endurecerse. **~ly** adv rígidamente

stifle /'staɪfl/ vt sofocar. **~ing** adj sofocante

stiletto (heel) /stɪ'letəʊ/ n (pl -os) tacón m de aguja

still /stɪl/ adj inmóvil; (peaceful) tranquilo; (drink) sin gas. **sit ~, stand ~** quedarse tranquilo. ● adv todavía, aún; (nevertheless) sin embargo. **~born** adj nacido muerto. **~ life** n (pl ~s) bodegón m. **~ness** n tranquilidad f

stilted /'stɪltɪd/ adj rebuscado; (conversation) forzado

stilts /stɪlts/ npl zancos mpl

stimul|ant /'stɪmjʊlənt/ n estimulante m. **~ate** /-leɪt/ vt estimular. **~ation** /-'leɪʃn/ n estímulo m. **~us** /-əs/ n (pl -li /-laɪ/) estímulo m

sting /stɪŋ/ n picadura f; (organ) aguijón m. ● vt/i (pt stung) picar

stingy /'stɪndʒɪ/ adj (-ier, -iest) tacaño

stink /stɪŋk/ n hedor m. ● vi (pt stank or stunk, pp stunk) apestar, oler mal

stipulat|e /'stɪpjʊleɪt/ vt/i estipular. **~ion** /-'leɪʃn/ n estipulación f

stir /stɜː(r)/ vt (pt stirred) remover, revolver; (move) agitar; estimular (imagination). ● vi moverse. **~ up** trouble armar lío 🄵. ● n revuelo m, conmoción f

stirrup /'stɪrəp/ n estribo m

stitch /stɪtʃ/ n (in sewing) puntada f; (in knitting) punto m; (pain) dolor m costado. be in ~es 🄵 desternillarse de risa. ● vt coser

stock /stɒk/ n (com, supplies) existencias fpl; (Com, variety) surtido m; (livestock) ganado m; (Culin) caldo m. **~s and shares, ~s and bonds** (Amer) acciones fpl. **out of ~** agotado. **take ~ of sth** (fig) hacer un balance de algo. ● adj estándar a invar; (fig) trillado. ● vt surtir, abastecer (with de). □ **~ up** vi abastecerse (with de). **~broker** /-brəʊkə(r)/ n corredor m de bolsa. **S~ Exchange** n bolsa f. **~ing** n media f. **~pile** n reservas fpl. ● vt almacenar. **~-still** adj inmóvil.

~-taking n (Com) inventario m. **~y** adj (-ier, -iest) bajo y fornido

stodgy /'stɒdʒɪ/ (-dgier, -dgiest) adj pesado

stoke /stəʊk/ vt echarle carbón (or leña) a

stole /stəʊl/ see STEAL

stolen /'stəʊlən/ see STEAL

stomach /'stʌmək/ n estómago m. ● vt soportar. **~ache** n dolor m de estómago

ston|e /stəʊn/ n piedra f; (in fruit) hueso m; (weight, pl stone) unidad de peso equivalente a 14 libras o 6,35 kg. ● adj de piedra. ● vt apedrear. **~-deaf** adj sordo como una tapia. **~y** adj (silence) sepulcral

stood /stʊd/ see STAND

stool /stuːl/ n taburete m

stoop /stuːp/ vi agacharse; (fig) rebajarse. ● n. **have a ~** ser cargado de espaldas

stop /stɒp/ vt (pt stopped) (halt, switch off) parar; (cease) terminar; (prevent) impedir; (interrupt) interrumpir. **~ doing sth** dejar de hacer algo. **~ it!** ¡basta ya! ● vi (bus) parar, detenerse; (clock) pararse. **it's ~ped raining** ha dejado de llover. ● n (bus etc) parada f; (break on journey) parada f. **put a ~ to sth** poner fin a algo. **come to a ~** detenerse. **~gap** n parada m provisional. **~over** n escala f. **~page** /'stɒpɪdʒ/ n suspensión f; paradero m (LAm); (of work) huelga f, paro m (LAm); (interruption) interrupción f. **~per** n tapón m. **~watch** n cronómetro m

storage /'stɔːrɪdʒ/ n almacenamiento m

store /stɔː(r)/ n provisión f; (depot) almacén m; (Amer, shop)

tienda f; (fig) reserva f. **in** ~ en reserva. ●vt (for future) poner en reserva; (in warehouse) almacenar. □ ~ **up** vt ir acumulando.
~**keeper** n (Amer) tendero m, comerciante m & f. ~**room** n almacén m; (for food) despensa f

storey /'stɔːrɪ/ n (pl -eys) piso m, planta f

stork /stɔːk/ n cigüeña f

storm /stɔːm/ n tempestad f. ●vi rabiar. ●vt (Mil) asaltar. ~**y** adj tormentoso; (sea, relationship) tempestuoso

story /'stɔːrɪ/ n historia f; (in newspaper) artículo m; (rumour) rumor m; (🇺🇸, lie) mentira f, cuento m. ~**teller** n cuentista m & f

stout /staʊt/ adj (-er, -est) robusto, corpulento. ●n cerveza f negra

stove /stəʊv/ n estufa f

stow /stəʊ/ vt guardar; (hide) esconder. □ ~ **away** vi viajar de polizón. ~**away** n polizón m & f

straggl|e /'stræɡl/ vi rezagarse. ~**y** adj desordenado

straight /streɪt/ adj (-er, -est) recto; (tidy) en orden; (frank) franco; (hair) lacio; (🇺🇸, conventional) convencional. **be** ~ estar derecho. ●adv (sit up) derecho; (direct) directamente; (without delay) inmediatamente. ~ **away** en seguida, inmediatamente. ~ **on** todo recto. ~ **out** sin rodeos. ●n recta f. ~**en** vt enderezar. □ ~ **up** vt ordenar. ~**forward** /-'fɔːwəd/ adj franco; (easy) sencillo

strain /streɪn/ n (tension) tensión f; (injury) torcedura f. ●vt forzar (voice, eyesight); someter a demasiada tensión (relations); (sieve) colar. ~ **one's back** hacerse daño en la espalda. ~ **a muscle** hacerse

un esguince. ~**ed** adj forzado; (relations) tirante. ~**er** n colador m. ~**s** npl (Mus) acordes mpl

strait /streɪt/ n estrecho m. **be in dire** ~**s** estar en grandes apuros. ~**jacket** n camisa f de fuerza

strand /strænd/ n (thread) hebra f. **a** ~ **of hair** un pelo. ●vt. **be** ~**ed** (ship) quedar encallado. **I was left** ~**ed** me abandonaron a mi suerte

strange /streɪndʒ/ adj (-er, -est) raro, extraño; (not known) desconocido. ~**ly** adv de una manera rara. ~**ly enough** aunque parezca mentira. ~**r** n desconocido m; (from another place) forastero m

strangle /'stræŋɡl/ vt estrangular

strap /stræp/ n correa f; (of garment) tirante m. ●vt (pt strapped) atar con una correa

strateg|ic /strə'tiːdʒɪk/ adj estratégico. ~**y** /'strætədʒɪ/ n estrategia f

straw /strɔː/ n paja f; (drinking ~) pajita f, paja f, popote m (Mex). **the last** ~ el colmo. ~**berry** /-bərɪ/ n fresa f; (large) fresón m

stray /streɪ/ vi (wander away) apartarse; (get lost) extraviarse; (deviate) desviarse (from de). ●adj (animal) (without owner) callejero; (lost) perdido. ●n (without owner) perro m/gato m callejero; (lost) perro m/gato m perdido

streak /striːk/ n lista f, raya f; (in hair) reflejo m; (in personality) veta f

stream /striːm/ n arroyo m; (current) corriente f. **a** ~ **of abuse** una sarta de insultos. ●vi correr. □ ~ **out** vi (people) salir en tropel. ~**er** n (paper) serpentina f; (banner) banderín m. ~**line** vt dar línea aerodinámica a; (simplify) racionalizar. ~**lined** adj aerodinámico

street /striːt/ n calle f. ~**car** n
(Amer) tranvía m. ~ **lamp** n farol m.
~ **map**, ~ **plan** n plano m

strength /streŋθ/ n fuerza f. (of
wall etc) solidez f. ~**en** vt reforzar
(wall); fortalecer (muscle)

strenuous /'strenjʊəs/ adj enér-
gico; (arduous) arduo; (tiring) fati-
goso

stress /stres/ n énfasis f; (Gram)
acento m; (Mec, Med, tension) ten-
sión f. • vt insistir en

stretch /stretʃ/ vt estirar; (extend)
extender; forzar (truth); estirar (re-
sources). • vi estirarse; (when
sleepy) desperezarse; (extend) ex-
tenderse; (be elastic) estirarse. • n
(period) período m; (of road) tramo
m. at a ~ sin parar. □ ~ **out** vi
(person) tenderse. ~**er** n camilla f

strict /strɪkt/ adj (-er, -est) es-
tricto; (secrecy) absoluto. ~**ly** adv
con severidad; (rigorously) termi-
nantemente. ~**ly speaking** en
rigor

stridden /strɪdn/ see **STRIDE**

stride /straɪd/ vi (pt strode, pp
stridden) andar a zancadas. • n
zancada f. **take sth in one's** ~ to-
marse algo con calma. ~**nt**
/'straɪdnt/ adj estridente

strife /straɪf/ n conflicto m

strike /straɪk/ vt (pt struck) gol-
pear; encender (match); encontrar
(gold, oil); (clock) dar. it ~**s me as**
odd me parece raro. • vi golpear;
(go on strike) declararse en huelga;
(be on strike) estar en huelga; (at-
tack) atacar; (clock) dar la hora. • n
(of workers) huelga f, paro m; (at-
tack) ataque m. **come out on** ~ ir
a la huelga. □ ~ **off**, ~ **out** vt ta-
char. ~ **up a friendship** trabar
amistad. ~**r** n huelguista m & f;
(Sport) artillero f

striking /'straɪkɪŋ/ adj (resem-
blance) sorprendente; (colour) lla-
mativo

string /strɪŋ/ n cordel m, mecate
m (Mex); (Mus) cuerda f; (of lies,
pearls) sarta f; (of people) sucesión
f. □ ~ **along** vt 🆃 engañar

stringent /'strɪndʒənt/ adj rigu-
roso

strip /strɪp/ vt (pt stripped) desnu-
dar (person); deshacer (bed). • vi
desnudarse. • n tira f; (of land)
franja f. ~ **cartoon** n historieta f

stripe /straɪp/ n raya f. ~**d** adj a
rayas, rayado

strip lighting n luz f fluores-
cente

strive /straɪv/ vi (pt strove, pp
striven) ~ **to** esforzarse por

strode /strəʊd/ see **STRIDE**

stroke /strəʊk/ n golpe m; (in
swimming) brazada f; (Med) ataque
m de apoplejía; (of pen etc) trazo m;
(of clock) campanada f; (caress) ca-
ricia f. a ~ **of luck** un golpe de
suerte. • vt acariciar

stroll /strəʊl/ vi pasearse. • n
paseo m. ~**er** n (Amer) sillita f de
paseo, cochecito m

strong /strɒŋ/ adj (-er, -est)
fuerte. ~**hold** n fortaleza f.; (fig)
baluarte m. ~**ly** adv (greatly) fuer-
temente; (protest) enérgicamente;
(deeply) profundamente. ~**room** n
cámara f acorazada

strove /strəʊv/ see **STRIVE**

struck /strʌk/ see **STRIKE**

structur|al /'strʌktʃərəl/ adj es-
tructural. ~**e** /'strʌktʃə(r)/ n es-
tructura f

struggle /'strʌgl/ vi luchar;
(thrash around) forcejear. • n
lucha f

strum /strʌm/ vt (pt strummed)

rasguear

strung /strʌŋ/ *see* STRING

strut /strʌt/ *n* (*in building*) puntal *m.* ● *vi* (*pt* strutted) pavonearse

stub /stʌb/ *n* (*of pencil, candle*) cabo *m*; (*counterfoil*) talón *m*; (*of cigarette*) colilla. □ **~ out** (*pt* stubbed) *vt* apagar

stubble /'stʌbl/ *n* rastrojo *m*; (*beard*) barba *f* de varios días

stubborn /'stʌbən/ *adj* terco

stuck /stʌk/ *see* STICK. ● *adj*. **the drawer is ~** el cajón se ha atascado. **the door is ~** la puerta se ha atrancado. **~-up** *adj* [T] estirado

stud /stʌd/ *n* tachuela *f*; (*for collar*) gemelo *m.*

student /'stju:dənt/ *n* estudiante *m & f*; (*at school*) alumno *m.* **~ driver** *n* (*Amer*) persona que está aprendiendo a conducir

studio /'stju:dɪəʊ/ *n* (*pl* -os) estudio *m.* **~ apartment**, **~ flat** *n* estudio *m*

studious /'stju:dɪəs/ *adj* estudioso

study /'stʌdɪ/ *n* estudio *m.* ● *vt/i* estudiar

stuff /stʌf/ *n* [T] cosas *fpl*. **what's this ~ called?** ¿cómo se llama esta cosa?. ● *vt* rellenar; disecar (*animal*); (*cram*) atiborrar; (*put*) meter de prisa. **~ o.s.** [T] darse un atracón. **~ing** *n* relleno *m.* **~y** *adj* (-ier, -iest) mal ventilado; (*old-fashioned*) acartonado. **it's ~y in here** el ambiente está muy cargado en aquí

stumble /'stʌmbl/ *vi* tropezar. **~e across**, **~e on** *vt* dar con. **~ing-block** *n* tropiezo *m*, impedimento *m*

stump /stʌmp/ *n* (*of limb*) muñón *m*; (*of tree*) tocón *m*

stun /stʌn/ *vt* (*pt* stunned) (*daze*)

aturdir; (*bewilder*) dejar atónito. **~ning** *adj* sensacional

stung /stʌŋ/ *see* STING

stunk /stʌŋk/ *see* STINK

stunt /stʌnt/ *n* [T] ardid *m* publicitario. ● *vt* detener, atrofiar. **~ed** *adj* (*growth*) atrofiado; (*body*) raquítico. **~man** *n* especialista *m.* **~woman** *n* especialista *f*

stupendous /stju:'pendəs/ *adj* estupendo

stupid /'stju:pɪd/ *adj* (*foolish*) tonto; (*unintelligent*) estúpido. **~ity** /-'pɪdətɪ/ *n* estupidez *f* **~ly** *adv* estúpidamente

stupor /'stju:pə(r)/ *n* estupor *m*

sturdy /'stɜ:dɪ/ *adj* (-ier, -iest) robusto

stutter /'stʌtə(r)/ *vi* tartamudear. ● *n* tartamudeo *m*

sty /staɪ/ *n* (*pl* sties) pocilga *f*; (*Med*) orzuelo *m*

style /staɪl/ *n* estilo *m*; (*fashion*) moda *f*; (*design, type*) diseño *m.* **in ~** a lo grande. ● *vt* diseñar. **~ish** *adj* elegante. **~ist** *n* estilista *m & f.* **hair ~ist** *n* estilista *m & f*

stylus /'staɪləs/ *n* (*pl* -uses) aguja *f* (de tocadiscos)

suave /swɑ:v/ *adj* elegante y desenvuelto

subconscious /sʌb'kɒnʃəs/ *adj & n* subconsciente (*m*)

subdivide /sʌbdɪ'vaɪd/ *vt* subdividir

subdued /səb'dju:d/ *adj* apagado

subject /'sʌbdʒɪkt/ *adj* sometido. **~ to** sujeto a. ● *n* (*theme*) tema *m*; (*Schol*) asignatura *f*, materia *f* (*LAm*); (*Gram*) sujeto *m*; (*Pol*) súbdito *m.* /səb'dʒekt/ *vt* someter. **~ive** /səb'dʒektɪv/ *adj* subjetivo

subjunctive /səb'dʒʌŋktɪv/ *adj &*

n subjuntivo (m)

sublime /sə'blaɪm/ adj sublime

submarine /sʌbmə'riːn/ n submarino m

submerge /səb'mɜːdʒ/ vt sumergir. • vi sumergirse

submi|ssion /səb'mɪʃn/ n sumisión f. ~**t** /səb'mɪt/ vt (pt submitted) (subject) someter; presentar (application). • vi rendirse

subordinate /sə'bɔːdɪmət/ adj & n subordinado (m). • /sə'bɔːdɪneɪt/ vt subordinar

subscri|be /səb'skraɪb/ vi suscribir. ~**be to** suscribirse a (magazine). ~**ber** n suscriptor m. ~**ption** /-rɪpʃn/ n (to magazine) suscripción f

subsequent /'sʌbsɪkwənt/ adj posterior, subsiguiente. ~**ly** adv posteriormente

subside /səb'saɪd/ vi (land) hundirse; (flood) bajar; (storm, wind) amainar. ~**nce** /'sʌbsɪdəns/ n hundimiento m

subsidiary /səb'sɪdɪərɪ/ adj secundario; (subject) complementario. • n (Com) filial

subsid|ize /'sʌbsɪdaɪz/ vt subvencionar, subsidiar (LAm). ~**y** /'sʌbsədɪ/ n subvención f, subsidio m

substance /'sʌbstəns/ n sustancia f

substandard /sʌb'stændəd/ adj de calidad inferior

substantial /səb'stænʃl/ adj (sturdy) sólido; (meal) sustancioso; (considerable) considerable

substitut|e /'sʌbstɪtjuːt/ n (person) substituto m; (thing) sucedáneo m. • vt/i sustituir. ~**ion** /-'tjuːʃn/ n sustitución f

subterranean /sʌbtə'reɪnjən/

adj subterráneo

subtitle /'sʌbtaɪtl/ n subtítulo m

subtle /'sʌtl/ adj (-er, -est) sutil; (tactful) discreto. ~**ty** n sutileza f

subtract /səb'trækt/ vt restar. ~**ion** /-ʃn/ n resta f

suburb /'sʌbɜːb/ n barrio m residencial de las afueras, colonia f. the ~**s** las afueras fpl. ~**an** /sə'bɜːbən/ adj suburbano. ~**ia** /sə'bɜːbɪə/ n zonas residenciales de las afueras de una ciudad

subversive /səb'vɜːsɪv/ adj subversivo

subway /'sʌbweɪ/ n paso m subterráneo; (Amer) metro m

succeed /sək'siːd/ vi (plan) dar resultado; (person) tener éxito. ~ **in doing** lograr hacer. • vt suceder

success /sək'ses/ n éxito m. ~**ful** adj (person) de éxito, exitoso (LAm). the ~**ful** applicant el candidato que obtenga el puesto. ~**fully** adv satisfactoriamente. ~**ion** /-ʃn/ n sucesión f. for 3 years in ~**ion** durante tres años consecutivos. in rapid ~**ion** uno tras otro. ~**ive** adj sucesivo. ~**or** n sucesor m

succulent /'sʌkjʊlənt/ adj suculento

succumb /sə'kʌm/ vi sucumbir

such /sʌtʃ/ adj tal (+ noun), tan (+ adj). ~ a big house una casa tan grande. • pron tal. ~ and ~ tal o cual. ~ as como. ~ as it is tal como es

suck /sʌk/ vt chupar (sweet, thumb); sorber (liquid). □~ **up** vt (vacuum cleaner) aspirar; (pump) succionar. □~ **up to** vt 🔟 dar coba a. ~**er** n (plant) chupón m; (fam, person) imbécil m

suckle /'sʌkl/ vt amamantar

suction /'sʌkʃn/ n succión f

sudden /'sʌdn/ adj repentino. **all of a ~** de repente. **~ly** adv de repente

suds /sʌds/ npl espuma f de jabón

sue /suː/ vt (pres p **suing**) demandar (**for** por)

suede /sweɪd/ n ante m

suet /'suːɪt/ n sebo m

suffer /'sʌfə(r)/ vt sufrir; (tolerate) aguantar. ● vi sufrir; (be affected) resentirse

suffic|e /sə'faɪs/ vi bastar. **~ient** /sə'fɪʃnt/ adj suficiente, bastante. **~iently** adv (lo) suficientemente

suffix /'sʌfɪks/ n (pl **-ixes**) sufijo m

suffocat|e /'sʌfəkeɪt/ vt asfixiar. ● vi asfixiarse. **~ion** /-'keɪʃn/ n asfixia f

sugar /'ʃʊgə(r)/ n azúcar m & f. **~ bowl** n azucarero m. **~y** adj azucarado.

suggest /sə'dʒest/ vt sugerir. **~ion** /-tʃən/ n sugerencia f

suicid|al /suːɪ'saɪdl/ adj suicida. **~e** /'suːɪsaɪd/ n suicidio m. **commit ~e** suicidarse

suit /suːt/ n traje m; (woman's) traje m de chaqueta; (Cards) palo m; (Jurid) pleito m. ● vt venirle bien a, convenirle a; (clothes) quedarle bien a; (adapt) adaptar. **be ~ed to** (thing) ser apropiado para. **I'm not ~ed to this kind of work** no sirvo para este tipo de trabajo. **~able** adj apropiado, adecuado. **~ably** adv (dressed) apropiadamente; (qualified) adecuadamente. **~case** n maleta f, valija f (LAm)

suite /swiːt/ n (of furniture) juego m; (of rooms) suite f

sulk /sʌlk/ vi enfurruñarse

sullen /'sʌlən/ adj hosco

sulphur /'sʌlfə(r)/ n azufre m. **~ic acid** /sʌl'fjʊərɪk/ n ácido m

sulfúrico

sultan /'sʌltən/ n sultán m

sultana /sʌl'tɑːnə/ n pasa f de Esmirna

sultry /'sʌltrɪ/ adj (**-ier, -iest**) (weather) bochornoso; (fig) sensual

sum /sʌm/ n (of money) suma f, cantidad f; (Math) suma f. **● □ ~ up** (pt **summed**) vt resumir. ● vi recapitular

summar|ily /'sʌmərɪlɪ/ adv sumariamente. **~ize** vt resumir. **~y** n resumen m

summer /'sʌmə(r)/ n verano m. **~ camp** n (in US) colonia f de vacaciones. **~time** n verano m. **~y** adj veraniego

summer camp En EE.UU., *i*
es el campamento de verano, aspecto muy importante en la vida de muchos niños. Las actividades al aire libre se practican en un ambiente natural entre las que se incluyen natación, montañismo, supervivencia al aire libre. En estos campamentos trabajan miles de estudiantes como supervisores.

summit /'sʌmɪt/ n (of mountain) cumbre f. **~ conference** n conferencia f cumbre

summon /'sʌmən/ vt llamar; convocar (meeting, s.o. to meeting); (Jurid) citar. □ **~ up** vt armarse de. **~s** n (Jurid) citación f. ● vt citar

sumptuous /'sʌmptjʊəs/ adj suntuoso

sun /sʌn/ n sol m. **~bathe** vi tomar el sol, asolearse (LAm). **~beam** n rayo m de sol. **~burn** n quemadura f de sol. **~burnt** adj quemado por el sol

Sunday /'sʌndeɪ/ n domingo m

sunflower /'sʌnflaʊə(r)/ n gira-sol m

sung /sʌŋ/ see SING

sunglasses /'sʌnglɑːsɪz/ npl gafas fpl de sol, lentes mpl de sol (LAm)

sunk /sʌŋk/ see SINK. **~en** /'sʌŋkən/ ● adj hundido

sun: **~light** n luz f del sol. **~ny** adj (-ier, -iest) (day) de sol; (place) soleado. it is **~ny** hace sol. **~rise** n. at **~rise** al amanecer. salida f del sol. **~roof** n techo m corredizo. **~set** n puesta f del sol. **~shine** n sol m. **~stroke** n insolación f. **~tan** n bronceado m. get a **~tan** broncearse. **~tan lotion** n bronceador m

super /'suːpə(r)/ adj [I] genial, super a invar

superb /suː'pɜːb/ adj espléndido

supercilious /suːpə'sɪliəs/ adj desdeñoso

superficial /suːpə'fɪʃl/ adj superficial

superfluous /suː'pɜːfluəs/ adj superfluo

superhighway /'suːpəhaɪweɪ/ n (Amer, Auto) autopista f. (Comp) information **~** autopista f de la comunicación

superhuman /suːpə'hjuːmən/ adj sobrehumano

superintendent /suːpərɪn'tendənt/ n director m; (Amer, of building) portero m; (of police) comisario m; (in US) superintendente m & f

superior /suː'pɪərɪə(r)/ adj & n superior (m). **~ity** /-'ɒrətɪ/ n superioridad f

superlative /suː'pɜːlətɪv/ adj inigualable. ● n superlativo m

supermarket /'suːpəmɑːkɪt/ n supermercado m

supernatural /suːpə'nætʃrəl/ adj sobrenatural

superpower /'suːpəpaʊə(r)/ n superpotencia f

supersede /suːpə'siːd/ vt reemplazar, sustituir

supersonic /suːpə'sɒnɪk/ adj supersónico

superstitio|n /suːpə'stɪʃn/ n superstición f. **~us** adj /-əs/ supersticioso

supervis|e /'suːpəvaɪz/ vt supervisar. **~ion** /-'vɪʒn/ n supervisión f. **~or** n supervisor m

supper /'sʌpə(r)/ n cena f (ligera), comida f (ligera) (LAm)

supple /sʌpl/ adj flexible

supplement /'sʌplɪmənt/ n suplemento m; (to diet, income) complemento m. ● vt complementar (diet, income). **~ary** /-'mentrɪ/ adj suplementario

suppl|ier /sə'plaɪə(r)/ n (Com) proveedor m. **~y** /sə'plaɪ/ vt suministrar; proporcionar (information). **~y s.o. with sth** (equipment) proveer a uno de algo; (in business) abastecer a uno de algo. ● n suministro m. **~y and demand** oferta f y demanda. **~ies** npl provisiones mpl, víveres mpl; (Mil) pertrechos mpl. **office ~ies** artículos mpl de oficina

support /sə'pɔːt/ vt (hold up) sostener; (back) apoyar; mantener (family). ● n apoyo m; (Tec) soporte m. **~er** n partidario m, (Sport) hincha m & f

suppos|e /sə'pəʊz/ vt suponer, imaginarse; (think) creer. I'm **~ed to start work at nine** se supone que tengo que empezar a trabajar a las nueve. **~edly** adv supuestamente. **~ition** /sʌpə'zɪʃn/ n suposición f

suppress /sə'pres/ vt reprimir (feelings); sofocar (rebellion). **~ion** /-ʃn/ n represión f

suprem|acy /suː'preməsɪ/ n supremacía f. **~e** /suː'priːm/ adj supremo

sure /ʃʊə(r)/ adj (-er, -est) seguro. make ~ that asegurarse de que. • adv ¡claro!. **~ly** adv (undoubtedly) seguramente; (gladly) desde luego. ~ly you don't believe that! ¡no te creerás eso! **~ty** /-ətɪ/ n garantía f

surf /sɜːf/ n oleaje m; (foam) espuma f. • vi hacer surf. • vt (Comp) surfear, navegar

surface /'sɜːfɪs/ n superficie f. • adj superficial. • vt recubrir (with de). • vi salir a la superficie; (problems) aflorar

surfboard /'sɜːfbɔːd/ n tabla f de surf

surfeit /'sɜːfɪt/ n exceso m

surf: ~er n surfista m & f; (Internet) navegador m. **~ing** n surf m

surge /sɜːdʒ/ vi (crowd) moverse en tropel; (sea) hincharse. • n oleada f; (in demand, sales) aumento m

surg|eon /'sɜːdʒən/ n cirujano m. **~ery** n cirugía f; (consulting room) consultorio m; (consulting hours) consulta f. **~ical** adj quirúrgico

surly /'sɜːlɪ/ adj (-ier, -iest) hosco

surmise /sə'maɪz/ vt conjeturar

surmount /sə'maʊnt/ vt superar

surname /'sɜːneɪm/ n apellido m

surpass /sə'pɑːs/ vt superar

surplus /'sɜːpləs/ adj & n excedente (m)

surprise /sə'praɪz/ n sorpresa f. • vt sorprender. **~ed** adj sorpren-

dido. **~ing** adj sorprendente. **~ingly** adv sorprendentemente

surrender /sə'rendə(r)/ vt entregar. • vi rendirse. • n rendición f

surreptitious /sʌrəp'tɪʃəs/ adj furtivo

surround /sə'raʊnd/ vt rodear; (Mil) rodear, cercar. **~ing** adj circundante. **~ings** npl alrededores mpl; (environment) ambiente m

surveillance /sɜː'veɪləns/ n vigilancia f

survey /'sɜːveɪ/ n inspección f; (report) informe m; (general view) vista f general. • /sə'veɪ/ vt inspeccionar; (measure) medir; (look at) contemplar. **~or** n topógrafo m, agrimensor m; (of building) perito m

surviv|al /sə'vaɪvl/ n supervivencia f. **~e** /sə'vaɪv/ vt/i sobrevivir. **~or** n superviviente m & f

susceptible /sə'septəbl/ adj. ~ to propenso a

suspect /sə'spekt/ vt sospechar; sospechar de (person). • /'sʌspekt/ adj & n sospechoso (m)

suspen|d /sə'spend/ vt suspender. **~ders** npl (Amer, braces) tirantes mpl. **~se** /-s/ n (in film etc) suspense m, suspenso m (LAm). keep s.o. in ~se mantener a uno sobre ascuas. **~sion** /-ʃn/ n suspensión f. **~sion bridge** n puente m colgante

suspici|on /sə'spɪʃn/ n (belief) sospecha f; (mistrust) desconfianza f. **~ous** /-ʃəs/ adj desconfiado; (causing suspicion) sospechoso

sustain /sə'steɪn/ vt sostener; mantener (conversation, interest); (suffer) sufrir

SW abbr (= south-west) SO

swab /swɒb/ n (specimen) muestra f, frotis m

swagger /'swægə(r)/ vi pavonearse

swallow /'swɒləʊ/ vt/i tragar. ● n trago m; (bird) golondrina f

swam /swæm/ see **SWIM**

swamp /swɒmp/ n pantano m, ciénaga f. ● vt inundar. ~y adj pantanoso

swan /swɒn/ n cisne m

swap /swɒp/ vt/i (pt swapped) intercambiar. ~ sth for sth cambiar algo por algo. ● n cambio m

swarm /swɔːm/ n enjambre m. ● vi (bees) enjambrar; (fig) hormiguear

swarthy /'swɔːðɪ/ adj (-ier, -iest) moreno

swat /swɒt/ vt (pt swatted) matar (con matamoscas etc)

sway /sweɪ/ vi balancearse; (gently) mecerse. ● vt (influence) influir en

swear /sweə(r)/ vt/i (pt swore, pp sworn) jurar. ~word n palabrota f

sweat /swet/ n sudor m, transpiración f. ● vi sudar

sweat|er /'swetə(r)/ n jersey m, suéter m. ~shirt n sudadera f. ~suit n (Amer) chándal m, equipo m de deportes

swede /swiːd/ n nabo m sueco

Swede /swiːd/ n sueco m. ~n /'swiːdn/ n Suecia f. ~ish adj sueco. ● n (language) sueco m. ● npl. the ~ (people) los suecos

sweep /swiːp/ vt (pt swept) barrer; deshollinar (chimney). ● vi barrer. ● n barrido m. ~ away vt (carry away) arrastrar; (abolish) erradicar. ~er n barrendero m. ~ing adj (gesture) amplio; (changes) radical; (statement) demasiado general

sweet /swiːt/ adj (-er, -est) dulce; (fragrant) fragante; (pleasant) agradable; (kind, gentle) dulce; (cute) rico. ~ a **tooth** ser dulcero. ● n caramelo m, dulce m (Mex); (dish) postre m. ~en vt endulzar. ~heart n enamorado m; (as form of address) amor m. ~ly adv dulcemente. ~ potato n boniato m, batata f, camote m LAm

swell /swel/ vt (pt swelled, pp swollen or swelled) hinchar; (increase) aumentar. ● vi hincharse; (increase) aumentar. ● adj (Amer fam) fenomenal. ● n (of sea) oleaje m. ~ing n hinchazón m

sweltering /'sweltərɪŋ/ vi sofocante

swept /swept/ see **SWEEP**

swerve /swɜːv/ vi virar bruscamente

swift /swɪft/ adj (-er, -est) veloz, rápido; (reply) rápido. ● n (bird) vencejo m. ~ly adv rápidamente

swig /swɪg/ vt (pt swigged) 🔢 beber a grandes tragos. ● n 🔢 trago m

swim /swɪm/ vi (pt swam, pp swum) nadar. ● n baño m. ~mer n nadador m. ~ming n natación f. ~ming bath(s) n(pl) piscina f cubierta, alberca f techada (Mex). ~ming pool n piscina f, alberca f (Mex). ~ming trunks npl bañador m, traje m de baño ~suit n traje m de baño, bañador m

swindle /'swɪndl/ vt estafar. ● n estafa f. ~r n estafador m

swine /swaɪn/ npl cerdos mpl. ● n (pl swine) (fam, person) canalla m & f. ~ fever n fiebre f porcina

swing /swɪŋ/ vt (pt swung) balancear; (object on rope) hacer oscilar. ● vi (dangle) balancearse; (swing on a swing) columpiarse; (pendulum)

oscilar. ~ **open/shut** abrirse/
cerrarse. ●**n** oscilación f, vaivén m;
(seat) columpio m; (in opinion)
cambio m. **in full** ~ en plena acti-
vidad

swipe /swaɪp/ vt darle un golpe a;
(fam, snatch) birlar. ●**n** golpe m

Swiss /swɪs/ adj suizo (m). ●npl.
the ~ los suizos

switch /swɪtʃ/ n (Elec) interruptor
m; (exchange) intercambio m; (Amer,
Rail) agujas fpl. ●vt cambiar; (devi-
ate) desviar. □ ~ **off** vt (Elec) apa-
gar (light, TV, heating); desconec-
tar (electricity). □ ~ **on** vt
encender, prender (LAm); arrancar
(engine). ~**board** n centralita f

Switzerland /ˈswɪtsələnd/ n
Suiza f

swivel /ˈswɪvl/ vi (pt swivelled)
girar. ●vt hacer girar

swollen /ˈswəʊlən/ see **SWELL**
●adj hinchado

swoop /swuːp/ vi (bird) abatirse;
(police) llevar a cabo una redada.
●n (of bird) descenso m en picado
or (LAm) en picada; (by police) re-
dada f

sword /sɔːd/ n espada f

swore /swɔː(r)/ see **SWEAR**

sworn /swɔːn/ see **SWEAR**. ●adj
(enemy) declarado; (statement) ju-
rado

swot /swɒt/ vt/i (pt swotted)
(Schol, fam) empollar, estudiar como
loco. ●n (Schol, fam) empollón m,
matado m (Mex)

swum /swʌm/ see **SWIM**

swung /swʌŋ/ see **SWING**

syllable /ˈsɪləbl/ n sílaba f

syllabus /ˈsɪləbəs/ n (pl -buses)
plan m de estudios; (of a particular
subject) programa m

symbol /ˈsɪmbl/ n símbolo m.
~**ic(al)** /-ˈbɒlɪk(l)/ adj simbólico.
~**ism** n simbolismo m. ~**ize** vt
simbolizar

symmetr|ical /sɪˈmetrɪkl/ adj si-
métrico. ~**y** /ˈsɪmətri/ n simetría f

sympath|etic /sɪmpəˈθetɪk/ adj
comprensivo; (showing pity) com-
pasivo. ~**ize** /ˈsɪmpəθaɪz/ vi com-
prender; (commiserate) ~**ize with**
s.o. compadecer a uno. ~**y**
/ˈsɪmpəθi/ n comprensión f; (pity)
compasión f; (condolences) el pé-
same m

symphony /ˈsɪmfəni/ n sinfonía f

symptom /ˈsɪmptəm/ n síntoma
m. ~**atic** /-ˈmætɪk/ adj sintomático

synagogue /ˈsɪnəgɒg/ n sina-
goga f

synchronize /ˈsɪŋkrənaɪz/ vt sin-
cronizar

syndicate /ˈsɪndɪkət/ n agrupa-
ción f; (Amer, TV) agencia f de distri-
bución periodística

synonym /ˈsɪnənɪm/ n sinónimo
m. ~**ous** /-ˈnɒnɪməs/ adj sinónimo

syntax /ˈsɪntæks/ n sintaxis f

synthesi|s /ˈsɪnθəsɪs/ n (pl
-theses /-siːz/) síntesis f. ~**ze** /-aɪz/
vt sintetizar

synthetic /sɪnˈθetɪk/ adj sintético

syringe /ˈsɪrɪndʒ/ n jeringa f, je-
ringuilla f

syrup /ˈsɪrəp/ n (sugar solution) al-
míbar m; (with other ingredients) ja-
rabe m; (medicine) jarabe m

system /ˈsɪstəm/ n sistema m, mé-
todo m; (Tec, Med, Comp) sistema m.
the digestive ~ el aparato diges-
tivo. ~**atic** /-əˈmætɪk/ adj sistemá-
tico. ~**atically** /-əˈmætɪklɪ/ adv sis-
temáticamente. ~**s analyst** n
analista m & f de sistemas

Tt

tab /tæb/ n (flap) lengüeta f; (label) etiqueta f

table /'teɪbl/ n mesa f; (list) tabla f; ~**cloth** n mantel m. ~ **mat** n salvamanteles m. ~**spoon** n cuchara f grande; (measure) cucharada f (grande)

tablet /'tæblɪt/ n pastilla f; (pill) comprimido m

table tennis n tenis m de mesa, ping-pong m

tabloid /'tæblɔɪd/ n tabloide m

taboo /təˈbuː/ adj & n tabú (m)

tacit /'tæsɪt/ adj tácito

taciturn /'tæsɪtɜːn/ adj taciturno

tack /tæk/ n tachuela f; (stitch) hilván m. ● vt clavar con tachuelas; (sew) hilvanar. ● vi (Naut) virar □ ~ **on** vt añadir.

tackle /'tækl/ n (equipment) equipo m; (soccer) entrada f fuerte; (US football, Rugby) placaje m. **fishing** ~ aparejo m de pesca. ● vt abordar (problem); (in soccer) entrarle a; (in US football, Rugby) placar

tacky /'tækɪ/ adj pegajoso

tact /tækt/ n tacto m. ~**ful** adj diplomático

tactic|al /'tæktɪkl/ adj táctico. ~**s** npl táctica f

tactless /'tæktləs/ adj indiscreto

tadpole /'tædpəʊl/ n renacuajo m

tag /tæg/ n (label) etiqueta f. □ ~ **along** (pt tagged) vt 🔢 seguir

tail /teɪl/ n (of horse, fish, bird) cola f; (of dog, pig) rabo m. ~**s** npl (tailcoat) frac m; (of coin) cruz f. ● vt seguir. □ ~ **off** vi disminuir.

tailor /'teɪlə(r)/ n sastre m. ~**ed** /'teɪləd/ adj entallado. ~-**made** n hecho a (la) medida

taint /teɪnt/ vt contaminar

take /teɪk/ vt (pt took, pp taken) tomar, coger (esp Spain), agarrar (esp LAm); (capture) capturar; (endure) aguantar; (require) requerir; llevar (time); tomar (bath); tomar (medicine); (carry) llevar; aceptar (cheque). I ~ a size 10 uso la talla 14. □ ~ **after** vt parecerse a. □ ~ **away** vt llevarse; (confiscate) quitar. □ ~ **back** vt retirar (statement etc). □ ~ **in** vt achicar (garment); (understand) asimilar; (deceive) engañar. □ ~ **off** vt (remove) quitar, sacar; quitarse (shoes, jacket); (mimic) imitar. vi (aircraft) despegar. □ ~ **on** vt contratar (employee). □ ~ **out** vt sacar. □ ~ **over** vt tomar posesión de; hacerse cargo de (job). vi (assume control) asumir el poder. □ ~ **up** vt empezar a hacer (hobby); aceptar (challenge); subir (hem); llevar (time); ocupar (space). ● n (Cinema) toma f. ~-**off** n despegue m. ~-**over** n (Com) absorción f

takings /'teɪkɪŋz/ npl recaudación f; (at box office) taquilla f

talcum powder /'tælkəm/ n polvos mpl de talco, talco m (LAm)

tale /teɪl/ n cuento m

talent /'tælənt/ n talento m. ~**ed** adj talentoso

talk /tɔːk/ vt/i hablar. ~ **to s.o.** hablar con uno. ~ **about** hablar de. ● n conversación f; (lecture) charla f. □ ~ **over** vt discutir. ~**ative** /-ətɪv/ adj hablador

tall /tɔːl/ adj (-er, -est) alto. ~ **story** n 🔢 cuento m chino

tally /'tælɪ/ vi coincidir (with con)

talon /'tælən/ n garra f

tambourine /tæmbəˈriːn/ n pandereta f

tame /teɪm/ adj (-er, -est) (animal) (by nature) manso; (tamed) domado. • vt domar (wild animal)

tamper /ˈtæmpə(r)/ vi. ~ with tocar; (alter) alterar, falsificar

tampon /ˈtæmpɒn/ n tampón m

tan /tæn/ vi (pt tanned) broncearse. • n bronceado m. get a ~ broncearse. • adj habano

tang /tæŋ/ n sabor m fuerte

tangent /ˈtændʒənt/ n tangente f

tangerine /tændʒəˈriːn/ n mandarina f

tangible /ˈtændʒəbl/ adj tangible

tangle /ˈtæŋgl/ vt enredar. get ~d (up) enredarse. • n enredo m, maraña f

tango /ˈtæŋgəʊ/ n (pl -os) tango m

tank /tæŋk/ n depósito m; (Auto) tanque m; (Mil) tanque m

tanker /ˈtæŋkə(r)/ n (ship) buque m cisterna; (truck) camión m cisterna

tantrum /ˈtæntrəm/ n berrinche m, rabieta f

tap /tæp/ n grifo m, llave f (LAm); (knock) golpecito m. • vt (pt tapped) (knock) dar un golpecito en; interceptar (phone). • vi dar golpecitos (en en). ~ dancing n claqué m

tape /teɪp/ n cinta f; (Med) esparadrapo m. • vt (record) grabar. ~measure n cinta f métrica

taper /ˈteɪpə(r)/ vt afilar. • vi afilarse. □ ~ off vi disminuir

tape recorder n magnetófon m, magnetófono m

tapestry /ˈtæpɪstrɪ/ n tapiz m

tar /tɑː(r)/ n alquitrán m. • vt (pt

tarred) alquitranar

target /ˈtɑːgɪt/ n blanco m; (fig) objetivo m

tarmac /ˈtɑːmæk/ n pista f. T~ n (Amer, ®) asfalto m

tarnish /ˈtɑːnɪʃ/ vt deslustrar; empañar (reputation)

tart /tɑːt/ n pastel m; (individual) pastelillo m; (sl, woman) prostituta f, fulana f 🔁. • vt. ~ o.s. up 🔁 engalanarse. • adj (-er, -est) ácido

tartan /ˈtɑːtn/ n tartán m, tela f escocesa

task /tɑːsk/ n tarea f. take to ~ reprender

tassel /ˈtæsl/ n borla f

taste /teɪst/ n sabor m, gusto m; (liking) gusto m. • vt probar. • vi. ~e of saber a. ~eful adj de buen gusto. ~eless adj soso; (fig) de mal gusto. ~y adj (-ier, -iest) sabroso

tat /tæt/ see TIT FOR TAT

tattered /ˈtætəd/ adj hecho jirones. ~s /ˈtætəz/ npl andrajos mpl

tattoo /tæˈtuː/ n (on body) tatuaje m. • vt tatuar

tatty /ˈtætɪ/ adj (-ier, -iest) gastado, estropeado

taught /tɔːt/ see TEACH

taunt /tɔːnt/ vt provocar mediante burlas. • n pulla f

Taurus /ˈtɔːrəs/ n Tauro m

taut /tɔːt/ adj tenso

tavern /ˈtævən/ n taberna f

tax /tæks/ n impuesto m. • vt imponer contribuciones a (person); gravar (thing); (strain) poner a prueba. ~able adj imponible. ~ation /-ˈseɪʃn/ n impuestos mpl; (system) sistema m tributario. ~ collector n recaudador m de impuestos. ~-free adj libre de impuestos

taxi /'tæksɪ/ n (pl **-is**) taxi m. ● vi (pt **taxied**, pres p **taxiing**) (aircraft) rodar por la pista

taxpayer /'tæksˌpeɪə(r)/ n contribuyente m & f

tea /tiː/ n té m; (afternoon tea) merienda f. ~ **bag** n bolsita f de té

teach /tiːtʃ/ vt (pt **taught**) dar clases de, enseñar (subject); dar clase a (person). ~ **school** (Amer) dar clase(s) en un colegio. ● vi dar clase(s). ~**er** n profesor m; (primary) maestro m. ~**ing** n enseñanza f. ● adj docente

tea: ~**cup** n taza f de té. ~ **leaf** n hoja f de té

team /tiːm/ n equipo m. □ ~ **up** vi asociarse (with con). ~ **work** n trabajo m de equipo

teapot /'tiːpɒt/ n tetera f

tear¹ /teə(r)/ vt (pt **tore**, pp **torn**) romper, rasgar. ● vi romperse, rasgarse. ● n rotura f; (rip) desgarrón m. □ ~ **along** vi ir a toda velocidad. □ ~ **apart** vt desgarrar. □ ~ **off**, ~ **out** vt arrancar. □ ~ **up** vt romper

tear² /tɪə(r)/ n lágrima f. be in ~s estar llorando. ~**ful** adj lloroso (farewell) triste. ~ **gas** n gas m lacrimógeno

tease /tiːz/ vt tomarle el pelo a

tea: ~ **set** n juego m de té. ~**spoon** n cucharita f, cucharilla f; (amount) cucharadita f

teat /tiːt/ n (of animal) tetilla f; (for bottle) tetina f

tea towel /'tiːtaʊəl/ n paño m de cocina

techni|cal /'teknɪkl/ adj técnico. ~**cality** n /-'kælətɪ/ n detalle m técnico. ~**cally** adv técnicamente. ~**cian** /tek'nɪʃn/ n técnico m.

~**que** /tek'niːk/ n técnica f

technolog|ical /teknə'lɒdʒɪkl/ adj tecnológico. ~**y** /tek'nɒlədʒɪ/ n tecnología f

teddy bear /'tedɪ/ n osito m de peluche

tedi|ous /'tiːdɪəs/ adj tedioso. ~**um** /'tiːdɪəm/ n tedio m

teem /tiːm/ vi abundar (with en), estar repleto (with de)

teen|age /'tiːneɪdʒ/ adj adolescente; (for teenagers) para jóvenes. ~**ager** n adolescente m & f. ~**s** /tiːnz/ npl adolescencia f

teeny /'tiːnɪ/ adj (-ier, -iest) 🅸 chiquito

teeter /'tiːtə(r)/ vi balancearse

teeth /tiːθ/ see **TOOTH**. ~**e** /tiːð/ vi. he's ~**ing** le están saliendo los dientes. ~**ing troubles** npl (fig) problemas mpl iniciales

tele|communications /telɪkəmjuːnɪ'keɪʃnz/ npl telecomunicaciones fpl. ~**gram** /'telɪɡræm/ n telegrama m. ~**pathic** /telɪ'pæθɪk/ adj telepático. ~**pathy** /tə'lepəθɪ/ n telepatía f

telephon|e /'telɪfəʊn/ n teléfono m. ● vt llamar por teléfono. ~**booth**, ~**e box** n cabina f telefónica. ~**e call** n llamada f telefónica. ~**e card** n tarjeta f telefónica. ~**e directory** n guía f telefónica. ~**e exchange** n central f telefónica. ~**ist** /tɪ'lefənɪst/ n telefonista m & f

tele|sales /'telɪseɪlz/ npl televentas fpl. ~**scope** n telescopio m. ~**scopic** /-'skɒpɪk/ adj telescópico. ~**text** n teletex(to) m. ~**working** n teletrabajo m

televis|e /'telɪvaɪz/ vt televisar. ~**ion** /'telɪvɪʒn/ n (medium) televisión f. ~**ion (set)** n televisor m

telex /'teleks/ n télex m

tell /tel/ vt (pt told) decir; contar (story, joke); (distinguish) distinguir. ~ the difference notar la diferencia. ~ the time decir la hora. • vi (produce an effect) tener efecto; (know) saber. □ ~ off vt regañar. ~ing adj revelador. ~tale n soplón m. • adj revelador

telly /'teli/ n 🖵 tele f

temp /temp/ n empleado m eventual or temporal

temper /'tempə(r)/ n (mood) humor m; (disposition) carácter m; (fit of anger) cólera f. be in a ~ estar furioso. lose one's ~ perder los estribos. ~ament /'temprəmənt/ n temperamento m. ~amental /-'mentl/ adj temperamental. ~ate /'tempərət/ adj templado. ~ature /'temprɪtʃə(r)/ n temperatura f. have a ~ature tener fiebre

tempestuous /tem'pestjʊəs/ adj tempestuoso

temple /'templ/ n templo m; (of head) sien f

tempo /'tempəʊ/ n (pl -os or tempi) ritmo m

temporar|ily /'tempərərəlɪ/ adv temporalmente, temporariamente (LAm). ~y /'tempərərɪ/ adj temporal, provisional; (job) eventual, temporal

tempt /tempt/ vt tentar. ~ation /-'teɪʃn/ n tentación f. ~ing adj tentador

ten /ten/ adj & n diez (m)

tenacious /tɪ'neɪʃəs/ adj tenaz. ~ty /tɪ'næsətɪ/ n tenacidad f

tenancy /'tenənsɪ/ n inquilinato m. ~t n inquilino m, arrendatario m

tend /tend/ vi. ~ to tender a. • vt cuidar (de). ~ency /'tendənsɪ/ n

tendencia f

tender /'tendə(r)/ adj tierno; (painful) sensible. • n (Com) oferta f. **legal** ~ n moneda f de curso legal. • vt ofrecer, presentar. ~ly adv tiernamente

tendon /'tendən/ n tendón m

tennis /'tenɪs/ n tenis m

tenor /'tenə(r)/ n tenor m

tens|e /tens/ adj (-er, -est) (taut) tenso, tirante; (person) tenso. • n (Gram) tiempo m. ~ion /'tenʃn/ n tensión f; (between two parties) conflicto m

tent /tent/ n tienda f (de campaña), carpa f (LAm)

tentacle /'tentəkl/ n tentáculo m

tentative /'tentətɪv/ adj (plan) provisional; (offer) tentativo; (person) indeciso

tenterhooks /'tentəhʊks/ npl. be on ~ estar en ascuas

tenth /tenθ/ adj & n décimo (m)

tenuous /'tenjʊəs/ adj (claim) poco fundado; (link) indirecto

tenure /'tenjʊə(r)/ n tenencia f; (period of office) ejercicio m

tepid /'tepɪd/ adj tibio

term /tɜːm/ n (of time) período m; (Schol) trimestre m; (word etc) término m. ~s npl condiciones fpl; (Com) precio m. on good/bad ~s en buenas/malas relaciones. • vt calificar de

termin|al /'tɜːmɪnl/ adj terminal. • n (transport) terminal f; (Comp, Elec) terminal m. ~ate /-eɪt/ vt poner fin a; poner término a (contract); (Amer, fire) despedir. • vi terminarse. ~ology /-'nɒlədʒɪ/ n terminología f

terrace /'terəs/ n terraza f; (houses) hilera f de casas

terrain /tə'reɪn/ n terreno m

terrestrial /tɪˈrestrɪəl/ *adj* terrestre

terribl|e /ˈterəbl/ *adj* espantoso. **~y** *adv* terriblemente

terrific /təˈrɪfɪk/ *adj* (*fam, excellent*) estupendo. (*fam, huge*) enorme. **~ied** /ˈterɪfaɪd/ *adj* aterrorizado. **~y** /ˈterɪfaɪ/ *vt* aterrorizar. **~ying** *adj* aterrador

territor|ial /terɪˈtɔːrɪəl/ *adj* territorial. **~y** /ˈterɪtrɪ/ *n* territorio *m*

terror /ˈterə(r)/ *n* terror *m*. **~ism** *n* terrorismo *m*. **~ist** *n* terrorista *m* & *f*. **~ize** *vt* aterrorizar

terse /tɜːs/ *adj* seco, lacónico

test /test/ *n* (*of machine, drug*) prueba *f*; (*exam*) prueba *f*, test *m*; (*of blood*) análisis *m*; (*for eyes, hearing*) examen *m*. ● *vt* probar, poner a prueba (product); hacerle una prueba a (student); evaluar (knowledge); examinar (sight)

testament /ˈtestəmənt/ *n* (*will*) testamento *m*. **Old/New T~** Antiguo/Nuevo Testamento

testicle /ˈtestɪkl/ *n* testículo *m*

testify /ˈtestɪfaɪ/ *vt* atestiguar. ● *vi* declarar

testimon|ial /testɪˈməʊnɪəl/ *n* recomendación *f*. **~y** /ˈtestɪmənɪ/ *n* testimonio *m*

test: **~ match** *n* partido *m* internacional. **~ tube** *n* tubo *m* de ensayo, probeta *f*

tether /ˈteðə(r)/ *n* atar. ● *n*. be at the end of one's **~** no poder más

text /tekst/ *n* texto *m*. ● *vt* mandar un mensaje a. **~book** *n* libro *m* de texto

textile /ˈtekstaɪl/ *adj* & *n* textil (*m*)

texture /ˈtekstʃə(r)/ *n* textura *f*

Thames /temz/ *n* Támesis *m*

than /ðæn, ðən/ *conj* que; (*with quantity*) de

thank /θæŋk/ *vt* darle las gracias a, agradecer. **~ you** gracias. **~ful** *adj* agradecido. **~fully** *adv* (*happily*) gracias a Dios. **~less** *adj* ingrato. **~s** *npl* agradecimiento *m*. **~s!** 🔢 ¡gracias!. **~s to** gracias a

Thanksgiving (Day) /θæŋks ˈɡɪvɪŋ/ *n* (*in US*) el día de Acción de Gracias

that /ðæt, ðət/ *adj* (*pl* those) ese, aquel, esa, aquella. ● *pron* (*pl* those) ése, aquél, ésa, aquélla. **~** is es decir. **~'s not true** eso no es cierto. **~'s why** por eso. **is ~ you?** ¿eres tú? **like ~** así. ● *adv* tan. ● *rel pron* que; (*with prep*) el que, la que, el cual, la cual. ● *conj* que

thatched /θætʃt/ *adj* (roof) de paja; (cottage) con techo de paja

thaw /θɔː/ *vt* descongelar. ● *vi* descongelarse; (snow) derretirse. ● *n* deshielo *m*

---

the *definite article*

····▸ el (*m*), la (*f*), los (*mpl*), las (*fpl*). **~ building** el edificio. **~ windows** las ventanas

❗ Feminine singular nouns beginning with a stressed or accented a or ha take the article el instead of la, e.g. **~ soul** el alma; **~ axe** el hacha; **~ eagle** el águila

Note that when el follows the prepositions de and a, it combines to form del and al, e.g. **of ~ group** del grupo. **I went to ~ bank** fui al banco

····▸ (before an ordinal number in

names, titles) not translated.
Henry ~ Eighth Enrique Octavo. Elizabeth ~ Second Isabel Segunda
····▸ *(in abstractions)* lo. ~ impossible lo imposible

theatr|e /'θɪətə(r)/ n teatro m; *(Amer, movie theater)* cine m. ~**ical** /-'ætrɪkl/ adj teatral

theft /θeft/ n hurto m

their /ðeə(r)/ adj su, sus pl. ~**s** /ðeəz/ poss pron (el) suyo m, (la) suya f, (los) suyos mpl, (las) suyas fpl

them /ðem, ðəm/ pron *(accusative)* los m, las f; *(dative)* les; *(after prep)* ellos m, ellas f

theme /θi:m/ n tema m. ~ **park** n parque m temático. ~ **song** n motivo m principal

themselves /ðəm'selvz/ pron ellos mismos m, ellas mismas f; *(reflexive)* se; *(after prep)* sí mismos m, sí mismas f

then /ðen/ adv entonces; *(next)* luego, después. **by** ~ para entonces. **now and** ~ de vez en cuando. **since** ~ desde entonces. ● adj entonces

theology /θɪ'ɒlədʒɪ/ n teología f

theor|etical /θɪə'retɪkl/ adj teórico. ~**y** /'θɪərɪ/ n teoría f

therap|eutic /θerə'pju:tɪk/ adj terapéutico. ~**ist** /'θerəpɪst/ n terapeuta m & f. ~**y** /'θerəpɪ/ n terapia f

there /ðeə(r)/ adv ahí; *(further away)* allí, ahí; *(less precise, further)* allá. ~ **is**, ~ **are** hay. ~ **it is** ahí está. **down** ~ ahí abajo. **up** ~ ahí arriba. ● int. ~! that's the last box ¡listo! ésa es la última caja. ~, ~, don't cry! vamos, no llores. ~**abouts** adv por ahí. ~**fore** /-fɔ:(r)/ adv por lo tanto.

---

thermometer /θə'mɒmɪtə(r)/ n termómetro m

Thermos /'θɜ:məs/ n (®) termo m

thermostat /'θɜ:məstæt/ n termostato m

thesaurus /θɪ'sɔ:rəs/ n *(pl -ri/-raɪ/)* diccionario m de sinónimos

these /ði:z/ adj estos, estas. ● pron éstos, éstas

thesis /'θi:sɪs/ n *(pl theses/-si:z/)* tesis f

they /ðeɪ/ pron ellos m, ellas f. ~ **say** that dicen o se dice que

they'd /ðeɪ(ə)d/ = **they had**, **they would**

they'll /ðeɪl/ = **they will**

they're /ðeɪə(r)/ = **they are**

they've /ðeɪv/ = **they have**

thick /θɪk/ adj (-er, -est) *(layer, sweater)* grueso, gordo; *(sauce)* espeso; *(fog, smoke)* espeso, denso; *(fur)* tupido; *(fam, stupid)* burro. ● adv espesamente, densamente. ● n. **in the** ~ **of** en medio de. ~**en** vt espesar. ● vi espesarse. ~**et** /-ɪt/ n matorral m. ~**ness** *(of fabric)* grosor m; *(of paper, wood, wall)* espesor m

thief /θi:f/ n *(pl thieves* /θi:vz/) ladrón m

thigh /θaɪ/ n muslo m

thimble /'θɪmbl/ n dedal m

thin /θɪn/ adj (thinner, thinnest) *(person)* delgado, flaco; *(layer, slice)* fino; *(hair)* ralo

thing /θɪŋ/ n cosa f. **it's a good** ~ *(that)...* menos mal que.... **just the** ~ exactamente lo que se necesita. **poor** ~! ¡pobrecito!

think /θɪŋk/ vt *(pt thought)* pensar, creer. ● vi pensar *(about on)*. *(carefully)* reflexionar; *(imagine)* imaginarse. **I** ~ **so** creo que sí. ~ **of s.o.** pensar en uno. **I hadn't**

t

thought of that eso no se me ha ocurrido. ~ **over** vt pensar bien. ~ **up** vt idear, inventar. ~**er** n pensador m. ~**tank** n gabinete m estratégico

third /θɜːd/ adj tercero, (before masculine singular noun) tercer. ●n tercio m, tercera parte f. ~ (**gear**) n (Auto) tercera f. ~**rate** adj muy inferior. **T~ World** n Tercer Mundo m

thirst /θɜːst/ n sed f. ~**y** adj sediento. **be** ~**y** tener sed

thirt|een /θɜːˈtiːn/ adj & n trece (m). ~**teenth** adj decimotercero. ●n treceavo m. ~**ieth** /ˈθɜːtɪəθ/ adj trigésimo. ●n treintavo m. ~**y** /ˈθɜːtɪ/ adj & n treinta (m)

this /ðɪs/ adj (pl these) este, esta. ~ **one** éste, ésta. ●pron (pl these) éste, ésta, esto. **like** ~ así

thistle /ˈθɪsl/ n cardo m

thong /θɒŋ/ n correa f; (Amer, sandal) chancla f

thorn /θɔːn/ n espina f. ~**y** adj espinoso

thorough /ˈθʌrə/ adj (investigation) riguroso; (cleaning etc) a fondo; (person) concienzudo. ~**bred** /-bred/ adj de pura sangre. ~**fare** n vía f pública; (street) calle f. **no** ~**fare** prohibido el paso. ~**ly** adv (clean) a fondo; (examine) minuciosamente; (completely) perfectamente

those /ðəʊz/ adj esos, esas, aquellos, aquellas. ●pron ésos, ésas, aquéllos, aquéllas

though /ðəʊ/ conj aunque. ●adv sin embargo. **as** ~ como si

thought /θɔːt/ see **THINK.** ●n pensamiento m; (idea) idea f. ~**ful** adj pensativo; (considerate) atento. ~**fully** adv pensativamente; (con-siderately) atentamente. ~**less** adj desconsiderado

thousand /ˈθaʊznd/ adj & n mil (m). ~**th** adj & n milésimo (m)

thrash /θræʃ/ vt azotar; (defeat) derrotar

thread /θred/ n hilo m; (of screw) rosca f. ●vt enhebrar (needle); ensartar (beads). ~**bare** adj gastado, raído

threat /θret/ n amenaza f. ~**en** vt/i amenazar. ~**ening** adj amenazador

three /θriː/ adj & n tres (m). ~**fold** adj triple. ●adv tres veces

threshold /ˈθreʃhəʊld/ n umbral m

threw /θruː/ see **THROW**

thrift /θrɪft/ n economía f, ahorro m. ~**y** adj frugal

thrill /θrɪl/ n emoción f. ●vt emocionar. ~**ed** adj contentísimo (with con). ~**er** n (book) libro m de suspense or (LAm) suspenso; (film) película f de suspense or (LAm) suspenso. ~**ing** adj emocionante

thrive /θraɪv/ vi prosperar. ~**ing** adj próspero

throat /θrəʊt/ n garganta f

throb /θrɒb/ vi (pt throbbed) palpitar; (with pain) dar punzadas; (engine) vibrar. ~**bing** adj (pain) punzante

throes /θrəʊz/ npl. **be in one's death** ~ estar agonizando

throne /θrəʊn/ n trono m

throng /θrɒŋ/ n multitud f

throttle /ˈθrɒtl/ n (Auto) acelerador m (que se acciona con la mano). ●vt estrangular

through /θruː/ prep por, a través de; (during) durante; (by means of) a través de; (Amer, until and including) **Monday** ~ **Friday** de lunes a viernes. ●adv de parte a parte, de un lado a otro; (entirely) completamente; (to the end) hasta el final. be ~ (finished) haber terminado. ●adj (train etc) directo. no ~ road calle sin salida. ~out /-'aʊt/ prep por todo; (time) durante todo. ~out his career a lo largo de su carrera

throve /θrəʊv/ see THRIVE

throw /θrəʊ/ vt (pt threw, pp thrown) tirar, aventar (Mex); lanzar (grenade, javelin); (disconcert) desconcertar; Ⓣ hacer, dar (party). ●n (of ball) tiro m; (of dice) tirada f. □ ~ away vt tirar. □ ~ up vi (vomit) vomitar.

thrush /θrʌʃ/ n tordo m

thrust /θrʌst/ vt (pt thrust) empujar; (push in) clavar. ●n empujón m; (of sword) estocada f

thud /θʌd/ n ruido m sordo

thug /θʌɡ/ n matón m

thumb /θʌm/ n pulgar m. ●vt. ~ a lift ir a dedo. ~tack n (Amer) chincheta f, tachuela f, chinche f (Mex)

thump /θʌmp/ vt golpear. ●vi (heart) latir fuertemente. ●n golpazo m

thunder /'θʌndə(r)/ n truenos mpl, (of traffic) estruendo m. ●vi tronar. ~bolt n rayo m. ~storm n tormenta f eléctrica. ~y adj con truenos

Thursday /'θɜːzdeɪ/ n jueves m

thus /ðʌs/ adv así

thwart /θwɔːt/ vt frustrar

tic /tɪk/ n tic m

tick /tɪk/ n (sound) tic m; (insect) garrapata f, (mark) marca f, visto m, palomita f (Mex); (fam, instant) momentito m. ●vi hacer tictac. ●vt. ~ (off) marcar

ticket /'tɪkɪt/ n (for bus, train) billete m, boleto m (LAm); (for plane) pasaje m, billete m; (for theatre, museum) entrada f; (for baggage, coat) ticket m; (fine) multa f. ~ collector n revisor m. ~ office n (transport) mostrador m de venta de billetes or (LAm) boletos; (in theatre) taquilla f, boletería f (LAm)

tickle /'tɪkl/ vt hacerle cosquillas a. ●n cosquilleo m. ~ish /'tɪklɪʃ/ adj. be ~ish tener cosquillas

tidal wave /'taɪdl/ n maremoto m

tide /taɪd/ n marea f. high/low ~ marea alta/baja. □ ~ over vt ayudar a salir de un apuro

tidily /'taɪdɪlɪ/ adv ordenadamente. ~iness n orden m. ~y adj (-ier, -iest) ordenado. ●vt/i ~y (up) ordenar, arreglar

tie /taɪ/ vt (pres p tying) atar, amarrar (LAm); hacer (knot). ●vi (Sport) empatar. ●n (constraint) atadura f; (bond) lazo m; (necktie) corbata f; (Sport) empate m. ~ in with vt concordar con. □ ~ up vt atar. be ~d up (busy) estar ocupado

tier /tɪə(r)/ n hilera f superpuesta; (in stadium etc) grada f; (of cake) piso m

tiger /'taɪɡə(r)/ n tigre m

tight /taɪt/ adj (-er, -est) (clothes) ajustado, ceñido; (taut) tieso; (control) estricto; (knot, nut) apretado; (fam, drunk) borracho. ~en vt apretar. □ ~en up vt hacer más estricto. ~fisted /-'fɪstɪd/ adj tacaño. ~ly adv bien, fuerte; (fastened) fuertemente. ~rope n cuerda f floja. ~s npl (for ballet etc) leotardo(s) m(pl); (pantyhose) medias fpl

tile /taɪl/ n (decorative) azulejo m; (on roof) teja f; (on floor) baldosa f

t

till /tɪl/ prep hasta. ● conj hasta que. ● n caja f. ● vt cultivar

tilt /tɪlt/ vt inclinar. ● vi inclinarse. ● n inclinación f

timber /'tɪmbə(r)/ n madera f (para construcción)

time /taɪm/ n tiempo m; (moment) momento m; (occasion) ocasión f; (by clock) hora f; (epoch) época f; (rhythm) compás m. at ~s a veces. for the ~ being por el momento. from ~ to ~ de vez en cuando. have a good ~ divertirse, pasarlo bien. in a year's ~ dentro de un año. in no ~ en un abrir y cerrar de ojos. in ~ a tiempo; (eventually) con el tiempo. arrive on ~ llegar a tiempo. it's ~ we left es hora de irnos. ● vt elegir el momento; cronometrar (race). ~ bomb n bomba f de tiempo. ~ly adj oportuno. ~r n cronómetro m; (Culin) avisador m; (with sand) reloj m de arena; (Elec) interruptor m de reloj. ~s /taɪmz/ prep. 2 ~s 4 is 8 2 (multiplicado) por 4 son 8. ~table n horario m

timid /'tɪmɪd/ adj tímido; (fearful) miedoso

tin /tɪn/ n estaño m; (container) lata f. ~ foil n papel m de estaño

tinge /tɪndʒ/ vt. be ~d with sth estar matizado de algo. ● n matiz m

tingle /'tɪŋgl/ vi sentir un hormigueo

tinker /'tɪŋkə(r)/ vi. ~ with juguetear con

tinkle /'tɪŋkl/ vi tintinear

tinned /tɪnd/ adj en lata, enlatado

tin opener n abrelatas m

tint /tɪnt/ n matiz m

tiny /'taɪnɪ/ adj (-ier, -iest) minúsculo, diminuto

tip /tɪp/ n punta f. ● vt (pt tipped) (tilt) inclinar; (overturn) volcar; (pour) verter; (give gratuity to) darle (una) propina a. □ ~ off vt avisar. □ ~ out vt verter. □ ~ over vi caerse. n propina f; (advice) consejo m (práctico); (for rubbish) vertedero m. ~ped adj (cigarette) con filtro

tipsy /'tɪpsɪ/ adj achispado

tiptoe /'tɪptəʊ/ n. on ~ de puntillas

tiptop /'tɪptɒp/ adj 🄸 de primera. in ~ condition en excelente estado

tire /taɪə(r)/ n (Amer) see TYRE. ● vt cansar. ● vi cansarse. ~d /taɪəd/ adj cansado. get ~d cansarse. ~d out agotado. ~less adj incansable; (efforts) inagotable. ~some /-səm/ adj (person) pesado; (task) tedioso

tiring /'taɪərɪŋ/ adj cansado, cansador (LAm)

tissue /'tɪʃuː/ n (of bones, plants) tejido m; (paper handkerchief) pañuelo m de papel. ~ paper n papel m de seda

tit /tɪt/ n (bird) paro m; (🄱, breast) teta f

titbit /'tɪtbɪt/ n exquisitez f

tit for tat n: it was ~ fue ojo por ojo, diente por diente

title /'taɪtl/ n título m

to /tuː, tə/ prep a; (towards) hacia; (in order to) para; (as far as) hasta; (of) de. give it ~ me dámelo. what did you say ~ him? ¿qué le dijiste? I don't want ~ no quiero. it's twenty ~ seven (by clock) son las siete menos veinte, son veinte para las siete (LAm). ● adv. pull ~

cerrar. ~ **and fro** adv de un lado a otro

toad /təʊd/ n sapo m. ~**stool** n hongo m (no comestible)

toast /təʊst/ n pan m tostado, tostadas fpl. (drink) brindis m. **a piece of** ~ una tostada, un pan tostado (Mex). **drink a** ~ **to** brindar por. ● vt (Culin) tostar; (drink: to) brindar por. ~**er** n tostadora f (eléctrica), tostador m

tobacco /təˈbækəʊ/ n tabaco m. ~**nist** /-ˈənɪst/ n estanquero m

toboggan /təˈbɒgən/ n tobogán m

today /təˈdeɪ/ n & adv hoy (m)

toddler /ˈtɒdlə(r)/ n niño m pequeño (entre un año y dos años y medio de edad)

toe /təʊ/ n dedo m (del pie); (of shoe) punta f. **big** ~ dedo m gordo (del pie). **on one's** ~**s** (fig) alerta. ● vt. ~ **the line** acatar la disciplina

toffee /ˈtɒfɪ/ n toffee m (golosina hecha con azúcar y mantequilla)

together /təˈgeðə(r)/ adv juntos; (at same time) a la vez. ~ **with** junto con

toil /tɔɪl/ vi afanarse. ● n trabajo m duro

toilet /ˈtɔɪlɪt/ n servicio m, baño m (LAm). ~ **paper** n papel m higiénico. ~**ries** /ˈtɔɪlɪtrɪz/ npl artículos mpl de tocador. ~ **roll** n rollo m de papel higiénico

token /ˈtəʊkən/ n muestra f; (voucher) vale m; (coin) ficha f. ● adj simbólico

told /təʊld/ see **TELL**

tolera|ble /ˈtɒlərəbl/ adj tolerable; (not bad) pasable. ~**nce** /ˈtɒlərəns/ n tolerancia f. ~**nt** adj tolerante. ~**te** /-reɪt/ vt tolerar. ~**tion** /-ˈreɪʃən/ n tolerancia f

toll /təʊl/ n (on road) peaje m, cuota f (Mex). **death** ~ número m de muertos. ~ **call** n (Amer) llamada f interurbana, conferencia f. ● vi doblar, tocar a muerto

tomato /təˈmɑːtəʊ/ n (pl -oes) tomate m, jitomate m (Mex)

tomb /tuːm/ n tumba f, sepulcro m. ~**stone** n lápida f

tomorrow /təˈmɒrəʊ/ n & adv mañana (f). **see you** ~! ¡hasta mañana!

ton /tʌn/ n tonelada f (= 1,016kg). ~**s of** 🔢 montones de. **metric** ~ tonelada f (métrica) (= 1,000kg)

tone /təʊn/ n tono m. ○ ~ **down** vt atenuar; moderar (language). ~**-deaf** adj que no tiene oído (musical)

tongs /tɒŋz/ npl tenacillas fpl

tongue /tʌŋ/ n lengua f. **say sth** ~ **in cheek** decir algo medio burlándose. ~**-tied** adj cohibido. ~**-twister** n trabalenguas m

tonic /ˈtɒnɪk/ adj tónico. ● n (Med, fig) tónico m. ~ **(water)** n tónica f

tonight /təˈnaɪt/ adv & n esta noche (f); (evening) esta tarde (f)

tonne /tʌn/ n tonelada f (métrica)

tonsil /ˈtɒnsl/ n amígdala f. ~**litis** /-ˈlaɪtɪs/ n amigdalitis f

too /tuː/ adv (excessively) demasiado; (also) también. **I'm not** ~ **sure** no estoy muy seguro. ~ **many** demasiados. ~ **much**

demasiado

took /tʊk/ see TAKE

tool /tuːl/ n herramienta f

tooth /tuːθ/ n (pl teeth) diente m; (molar) muela f. ~ache n dolor m de muelas. ~brush n cepillo m de dientes. ~paste n pasta f dentífrica, pasta f de dientes. ~pick n palillo m (de dientes)

top /tɒp/ n parte f superior, parte f de arriba; (of mountain) cima f; (of tree) copa f; (of page) parte f superior; (lid, of bottle) tapa f; (of pen) capuchón m; (spinning ~) trompo m, peonza f. be ~ of the class ser el primero de la clase. from ~ to bottom de arriba abajo. on ~ of encima de; (besides) además de. ● adj más alto; (shelf) superior; (speed) máximo; (in rank) superior; (leading) más destacado. ● vt (pt topped) cubrir; (exceed) exceder. ~ floor n último piso m. □ ~ up vt llenar; (mobile phone) recargar el saldo. ~ hat n chistera f. ~-heavy /-ˈhevɪ/ adj inestable (por ser más pesado en su parte superior)

topic /ˈtɒpɪk/ n tema m. ~al adj de actualidad

topless /ˈtɒpləs/ adj topless

topple /ˈtɒpl/ vi (Pol) derribar; (overturn) volcar. ● vi caerse

top secret /tɒpˈsiːkrɪt/ adj secreto, reservado

torch /tɔːtʃ/ n linterna f; (flaming) antorcha f

tore /tɔː(r)/ see TEAR¹

torment /ˈtɔːment/ n tormento m. ● /tɔːˈment/ vt atormentar

torn /tɔːn/ see TEAR¹

tornado /tɔːˈneɪdəʊ/ n (pl -oes) tornado m

torpedo /tɔːˈpiːdəʊ/ n (pl -oes) torpedo m. ● vt torpedear

torrent /ˈtɒrənt/ n torrente m. ~ial /təˈrenʃl/ adj torrencial

torrid /ˈtɒrɪd/ adj tórrido; (affair) apasionado

tortoise /ˈtɔːtəs/ n tortuga f. ~shell n carey m

tortuous /ˈtɔːtjʊəs/ adj tortuoso

torture /ˈtɔːtʃə(r)/ n tortura f. ● vt torturar

toss /tɒs/ vt tirar, lanzar (ball); (shake) sacudir. ● vi. ~ and turn (in bed) dar vueltas

tot /tɒt/ n pequeño m; (fam, of liquor) trago m. ● vt (pt totted). ~ up 🗊 sumar

total /ˈtəʊtl/ adj & n total (m). ● vt (pt totalled) ascender a un total de; (add up) totalizar. ~itarian /təʊtælɪˈteərɪən/ adj totalitario. ~ly adv totalmente

totter /ˈtɒtə(r)/ vi tambalearse

touch /tʌtʃ/ vt tocar; (move) conmover; (concern) afectar. ● vi tocar; (wires) tocarse. ● n toque m; (sense) tacto m; (contact) contacto m. be/get/stay in ~ with estar/ponerse/mantenerse en contacto con. □ ~ down vi (aircraft) aterrizar. □ ~ up vt retocar. ~ing adj enternecedor. ~y adj quisquilloso

tough /tʌf/ adj (-er, -est) duro; (strong) fuerte, resistente; (difficult) difícil; (severe) severo. ~en. ~ (up) vt endurecer; hacer más fuerte (person)

tour /tʊə(r)/ n viaje m, (visit) visita f; (excursion) excursión f; (by team etc) gira f. be on ~ estar de gira. ● vt recorrer; (visit) visitar. ~ guide n guía de turismo

tourism /ˈtʊərɪzəm/ n turismo m. ~t /ˈtʊərɪst/ n turista m & f. ● adj turístico. ~t office n oficina f de turismo

tournament /'tɔːnəmənt/ n torneo m

tousle /'taʊzl/ vt despeinar

tout /taʊt/ vi. ~ (for) solicitar

tow /təʊ/ vt remolcar. ●n remolque m

toward(s) /tə'wɔːd(z)/ prep hacia. his attitude ~ her su actitud para con ella

towel /'taʊəl/ n toalla f

tower /'taʊə(r)/ n torre f. ●vi. ~ above (building) descollar sobre; (person) destacar sobre. ~ block n edificio m or bloque m de apartamentos. ~ing adj altísimo; (rage) violento

town /taʊn/ n ciudad f; (pueblo m. go to ~ 🄘 no escatimar dinero. ~ hall n ayuntamiento m

toxic /'tɒksɪk/ adj tóxico

toy /tɔɪ/ n juguete m. ●a ~ with vt juguetear con (object); darle vueltas a (idea). ~shop n juguetería f

trac|e /treɪs/ n señal f, rastro m. ●vt trazar; (draw) dibujar; (with tracing paper) calcar; (track down) localizar. ~ing paper n papel m de calcar

track /træk/ n pista f, huellas fpl; (path) sendero m, (Sport) pista f. the ~(s) la vía férrea; (Rail) vía f. keep ~ of seguir la pista a (person). ●vt seguirle la pista a. □ ~ down vt localizar. ~ suit n equipo m (de deportes) chándal m

tract /trækt/ n (land) extensión f; (pamphlet) tratado m breve

traction /'trækʃn/ n tracción f

tractor /'træktə(r)/ n tractor m

trade /treɪd/ n comercio m; (occupation) oficio m; (exchange) cambio m; (industry) industria f. ●vt. ~ sth for sth cambiar algo por algo. ●vi comerciar. □ ~ in vt (give in part-exchange) entregar como parte del pago. ~ mark n marca f (de fábrica). ~r n comerciante m & f. ~ union n sindicato m

tradition /trə'dɪʃn/ n tradición f. ~al adj tradicional

traffic /'træfɪk/ n tráfico m. ●vi (pt trafficked) comerciar (in en). ~ circle n (Amer) glorieta f, rotonda f. ~ island n isla f peatonal. ~ jam n embotellamiento m, atasco m. ~ lights npl semáforo m. ~ warden n guardia m, controlador m de tráfico

trag|edy /'trædʒɪdɪ/ n tragedia f. ~ic /'trædʒɪk/ adj trágico

trail /treɪl/ vi arrastrarse; (lag) rezagarse. ●vt (track) seguir la pista de. ●n (left by animal, person) huellas fpl; (path) sendero m. be on the ~ of s.o./sth seguir la pista de uno/algo. ~er n remolque m; (Amer, caravan) caravana f, rulot m; (film) avance m

train /treɪn/ n (Rail) tren m; (of events) serie f; (of dress) cola f. ●vt capacitar (employee); (Sport) entrenar (soldier); educar (voice); guiar (plant); amaestrar (animal). ●vi estudiar; (Sport) entrenarse. ~ed adj (skilled) cualificado, calificado; (doctor) diplomado. ~ee /treɪ'niː/ n aprendiz m; (Amer, Mil) recluta m/f. ~er n (Sport) entrenador m; (of animals) amaestrador m. ~ers mpl zapatillas fpl de deporte. ~ing n capacitación f; (Sport) entrenamiento m

trait /treɪt/ n rasgo m

traitor /'treɪtə(r)/ n traidor m

tram /træm/ n tranvía m

tramp /træmp/ vi. ~ (along) caminar pesadamente. ●n vagabundo m

trample /'træmpl/ vt pisotear.
● vi. ~ **on** pisotear

trampoline /'træmpəli:n/ n
trampolín m

trance /trɑ:ns/ n trance m

tranquil /'træŋkwɪl/ adj tranquilo.
~**lity** /-'kwɪlətɪ/ n tranquilidad f;
(of person) serenidad f. ~**lize**
/'træŋkwɪlaɪz/ vt sedar, dar un se-
dante a. ~**lizer** n sedante m, tran-
quilizante m

transaction /træn'zækʃn/ n
transacción f, operación f

transatlantic /trænzət'læntɪk/
adj transatlántico

transcend /træn'send/ vt (go be-
yond) exceder

transcript /'trænskrɪpt/ n trans-
cripción f

transfer /træns'fɜ:(r)/ vt (pt
transferred) trasladar; traspasar
(player); transferir (funds, prop-
erty); pasar (call). ● vi trasladarse.
● /'trænsfɜ:(r)/ n traslado m; (of
player) traspaso m; (of funds, prop-
erty) transferencia f; (paper) calco-
manía f

transform /træns'fɔ:m/ vt trans-
formar. ~**ation** /-ə'meɪʃn/ n trans-
formación f. ~**er** n transforma-
dor m

transfusion /træns'fju:ʒn/ n
transfusión f

transient /'trænzɪənt/ adj pasa-
jero

transistor /træn'zɪstə(r)/ n tran-
sistor m

transit /'trænsɪt/ n tránsito m.
~**ion** /træn'zɪʒn/ n transición f.
~**ive** /'trænsɪtɪv/ adj transitivo

translat|e /trænz'leɪt/ vt traducir.
~**ion** /-ʃn/ n traducción f. ~**or** n
traductor m

transmission /træns'mɪʃn/ n

transmisión f

transmit /trænz'mɪt/ vt (pt trans-
mitted) transmitir. ~**ter** n trans-
misor m

transparen|cy /træns'pærənsɪ/
n transparencia f; (Photo) diapositiva
f. ~**t** adj transparente

transplant /træns'plɑ:nt/ vt tras-
plantar. ● /'trænsplɑ:nt/ n tras-
plante m

transport /træns'pɔ:t/ vt trans-
portar. ● /'trænspɔ:t/ n transporte
m. ~**ation** /-'teɪʃn/ n transporte m

trap /træp/ n trampa f. ● vt (pt
trapped) atrapar; (jam) atascar;
(cut off) bloquear. ~**door** n tram-
pilla f

trapeze /trə'pi:z/ n trapecio m

trash /træʃ/ n basura f; (Amer,
worthless people) escoria f. ~ **can** n
(Amer) cubo m de la basura, bote m
de la basura (Mex). ~**y** adj (sou-
venir) de porquería; (magazine)
malo

travel /'trævl/ vi (pt travelled) via-
jar; (vehicle) desplazarse. ● vt reco-
rrer. ● n viajes mpl. ~ **agency** n
agencia f de viajes. ~**ler** n viajero
m. ~**ler's cheque** n cheque m de
viaje or viajero. ~**ling expenses**
npl gastos mpl de viaje

trawler /'trɔ:lə(r)/ n barca f pes-
quera

tray /treɪ/ n bandeja f

treacher|ous /'tretʃərəs/ adj traidor; (decep-
tive) engañoso. ~**y** n traición f

treacle /'tri:kl/ n melaza f

tread /tred/ vi (pt trod, pp trod-
den) pisar. ~ **on sth** pisar algo. ~
carefully andarse con cuidado. ● n
(step) paso m; (of tyre) banda f de
rodamiento

treason /'tri:zn/ n traición f

treasur|e /'treʒə(r)/ n tesoro m.

~ed /'treʒəd/ *adj* (possession) preciado. **~er** /'treʒərə(r)/ *n* tesorero *m*. **~y** *n* erario *m*, tesoro *m*. the T**~y** el fisco, la hacienda pública. Department of the T**~y** (*in US*) Departamento *m* del Tesoro

treat /triːt/ *vt* tratar; (*Med*) tratar. **~ s.o.** (to *meal etc*) invitar a uno. ● *n* placer *m*; (*present*) regalo *m*

treatise /'triːtɪz/ *n* tratado *m*

treatment /'triːtmənt/ *n* tratamiento *m*

treaty /'triːtɪ/ *n* tratado *m*

treble /'trebl/ *adj* triple; (clef) de sol; (voice) de tiple. ● *vt* triplicar. ● *vi* triplicarse. ● *n* tiple *m* & *f*

tree /triː/ *n* árbol *m*

trek /trek/ *n* caminata *f*. ● *vi* (*pt* trekked) caminar

trellis /'trelɪs/ *n* enrejado *m*

tremble /'trembl/ *vi* temblar

tremendous /trɪ'mendəs/ *adj* formidable; (*fam, huge*) tremendo. **~ly** *adv* tremendamente

tremor /'tremə(r)/ *n* temblor *m*

trench /trentʃ/ *n* zanja *f*; (*Mil*) trinchera *f*

trend /trend/ *n* tendencia *f*; (*fashion*) moda *f*. **~y** *adj* (**-ier, -iest**) Ⓘ moderno

trepidation /trepɪ'deɪʃn/ *n* inquietud *f*

trespass /'trespəs/ *vi*. **~ on** entrar sin autorización (en propiedad ajena). **~er** *n* intruso *m*

trial /'traɪəl/ *n* prueba *f*; (*Jurid*) proceso *m*, juicio *m*; (*ordeal*) prueba *f* dura. by **~** and error por ensayo y error. be on **~** estar a prueba; (*Jurid*) estar siendo procesado

triang|le /'traɪæŋgl/ *n* triángulo *m*. **~ular** /-'æŋgjʊlə(r)/ *adj* triangular

trib|al /'traɪbl/ *adj* tribal. **~e** /traɪb/ *n* tribu *f*

tribulation /trɪbjʊ'leɪʃn/ *n* tribulación *f*

tribunal /traɪ'bjuːnl/ *n* tribunal *m*

tributary /'trɪbjʊtrɪ/ *n* (*of river*) afluente *m*

tribute /'trɪbjuːt/ *n* tributo *m*; (*acknowledgement*) homenaje *m*. pay **~** to rendir homenaje a

trick /trɪk/ *n* trampa *f*, ardid *m*; (*joke*) broma *f*; (*feat*) truco *m*; (*in card games*) baza *f*. play a **~** on gastar una broma a. ● *vt* engañar. **~ery** *n* engaño *m*

trickle /'trɪkl/ *vi* gotear. **~ in** (*fig*) entrar poco a poco

trickster /'trɪkstə(r)/ *n* estafador *m*

tricky /'trɪkɪ/ *adj* delicado, difícil

tricycle /'traɪsɪkl/ *n* triciclo *m*

tried /traɪd/ *see* TRY

trifl|e /'traɪfl/ *n* nimiedad *f*; (*Culin*) postre de bizcocho, jerez, frutas y nata. ● *vi*. **~e with** *vt* jugar con. **~ing** *adj* insignificante

trigger /'trɪgə(r)/ *n* (*of gun*) gatillo *m*. ● *vt*. **~ (off)** desencadenar

trim /trɪm/ *adj* (trimmer, trimmest) (*slim*) esbelto; (*neat*) elegante. ● *vt* (*pt* trimmed) (*cut*) recortar; (*adorn*) adornar. ● *n* (*cut*) recorte *m*. in **~** en buen estado. **~mings** *npl* recortes *mpl*

trinity /'trɪnɪtɪ/ *n*. the (Holy) T**~** la (Santísima) Trinidad

trinket /'trɪŋkɪt/ *n* chuchería *f*

trio /'triːəʊ/ *n* (*pl* **-os**) trío *m*

trip /trɪp/ *n* (*pt* tripped) *vt* **~ (up)** hacerle una zancadilla a, hacer tropezar a; *vi* tropezar. ● *n* (*journey*) viaje *m*; (*outing*) excursión *f*; (*stumble*) traspié *m*

tripe /traɪp/ *n* callos *mpl*, mon-

t

dongo m (LAm), pancita f (Mex); (fam, nonsense) paparruchas fpl

triple /'trɪpl/ adj triple. •vt triplicar. •vi triplicarse. ~t /'trɪplɪt/ n trillizo m

triplicate /'trɪplɪkət/ adj triplicado. in ~ por triplicado

tripod /'traɪpɒd/ n trípode m

trite /traɪt/ adj trillado

triumph /'traɪʌmf/ n triunfo m. •vi triunfar (over sobre). ~al /-'ʌmfl/ adj triunfal. ~ant /-'ʌmfnt/ adj (triumphant) triunfador; (moment) triunfal; (smile) de triunfo

trivial /'trɪvɪəl/ adj insignificante; (concerns) trivial. ~ity /-'ælətɪ/ n trivialidad f

trod, trodden /trɒd, trɒdn/ see TREAD

trolley /'trɒlɪ/ n (pl -eys) carretón m; (in supermarket, airport) carrito m; (for food, drink) carrito m, mesa f rodante. ~ car n (Amer) tranvía f

trombone /trɒm'bəʊn/ n trombón m

troop /tru:p/ n compañía f; (of cavalry) escuadrón m. •vi. ~ in entrar en tropel. ~ out salir en tropel. ~er n soldado m de caballería; (Amer, state police officer) agente m & f. ~s npl (Mil) tropas fpl

trophy /'trəʊfɪ/ n trofeo m

tropic /'trɒpɪk/ n trópico m. ~al adj tropical. ~s npl trópicos mpl

trot /trɒt/ n trote m. •vi (pt trotted) trotar

trouble /'trʌbl/ n problemas mpl; (awkward situation) apuro m; (inconvenience) molestia f. be in ~ estar en apuros. get into ~ meterse en problemas. look for ~ buscar camorra. take the ~ to do sth molestarse en hacer algo. •vt (bother) molestar; (worry) preocu-

par. ~-maker n alborotador m. ~some /-səm/ adj problemático. ~ spot n punto m conflictivo

trough /trɒf/ n (for drinking) abrevadero m; (for feeding) comedero m

troupe /tru:p/ n compañía f teatral

trousers /'traʊzəz/ npl pantalón m, pantalones mpl

trout /traʊt/ n (pl trout) trucha f

trowel /'traʊəl/ n (garden) desplantador m; (for mortar) paleta f

truant /'tru:ənt/ n. play ~ hacer novillos

truce /tru:s/ n tregua f

truck /trʌk/ n camión m; (Rail) vagón m, furgón m; (Amer, vegetables, fruit) productos mpl de la huerta. ~ driver, ~er (Amer) n camionero m. ~ing n transporte m por carretera

trudge /trʌdʒ/ vi andar penosamente

true /tru:/ adj (-er, -est) verdadero; (story, account) verídico; (friend) auténtico, de verdad. ~ to sth/ s.o. fiel a algo/uno. be ~ cierto. come ~ hacerse realidad

truffle /'trʌfl/ n trufa f; (chocolate) trufa f de chocolate

truly /'tru:lɪ/ adv verdaderamente; (sincerely) sinceramente. yours ~ (in letters) cordiales saludos

trump /trʌmp/ n (Cards) triunfo m; (fig) baza f

trumpet /'trʌmpɪt/ n trompeta f. ~er n trompetista m & f, trompeta m & f

truncheon /'trʌntʃən/ n porra f

trunk /trʌŋk/ n (of tree) tronco m; (box) baúl m; (of elephant) trompa f; (Amer, Auto) maletero m, cajuela f (Mex). ~s npl bañador m, traje m de baño

truss /trʌs/ vt. truss (up) vt atar

trust /trʌst/ n confianza f; (money, property) fondo m de inversiones; (institution) fundación f. **on** ~ a ojos cerrados; (Com) al fiado. ●vi. ~ **in** s.o./sth confiar en uno/algo. ●vt confiar en; (in negative sentences) fiarse; (hope) esperar. ~**ed** adj leal. ~**ee** /trʌ'stiː/ n fideicomisario m. ~**ful** adj confiado. ~**ing** adj confiado. ~**worthy** adj digno de confianza

truth /truːθ/ n (pl ~**s** /truːðz/) verdad f; (of account, story) veracidad f. ~**ful** adj veraz.

try /traɪ/ vt (pt **tried**) intentar; probar (food, product); (be a strain on) poner a prueba; (Jurid) procesar. ~ **to do sth** tratar de hacer algo, intentar hacer algo. ~ **not to forget** procura no olvidarte. ●n tentativa f, prueba f; (Rugby) ensayo m. □ ~ **on** vt desprecio (garment). □ ~ **out** vt probar. ~**ing** adj duro; (annoying) molesto

tsar /zɑː(r)/ n zar m

T-shirt /'tiːʃɜːt/ n camiseta f

tub /tʌb/ n cuba f; (for washing clothes) tina f; (bathtub) bañera f; (for ice cream) envase m, tarrina f

tuba /'tjuːbə/ n tuba f

tubby /'tʌbɪ/ adj (-ier, -iest) rechoncho

tube /tjuːb/ n tubo m; (fam, Rail) metro m; (Amer fam, television) tele f. **inner** ~ n cámara f de aire

tuberculosis /tjuːbɜːkjʊ'ləʊsɪs/ n tuberculosis f

tub|ing /'tjuːbɪŋ/ n tubería f. ~**ular** /-jʊlə(r)/ adj tubular

tuck /tʌk/ n (fold) jareta f. ●vt plegar; (put) meter. □ ~ **in(to)** vi (fam, eat) ponerse a comer. □ ~

up vt arropar (child)

Tuesday /'tjuːzdeɪ/ n martes m

tuft /tʌft/ n (of hair) mechón m; (of feathers) penacho m; (of grass) mata f

tug /tʌg/ vt (pt **tugged**) tirar de. ●vi. ~ **at sth** tirar de algo. ●n tirón m; (Naut) remolcador m. ~**of-war** n juego de tira y afloja

tuition /tjuː'ɪʃn/ n clases fpl

tulip /'tjuːlɪp/ n tulipán m

tumble /'tʌmbl/ vi caerse. ●n caída f. □ ~**down** adj en ruinas. ~**drier** n secadora f. ~**r** n (glass) vaso m (de lados rectos)

tummy /'tʌmɪ/ n 🄳 barriga f

tumour /'tjuːmə(r)/ n tumor m

tumult /'tjuːmʌlt/ n tumulto m. ~**uous** /-'mʌltjʊəs/ adj (applause) apoteósico

tuna /'tjuːnə/ n (pl **tuna**) atún m

tune /tjuːn/ n melodía f; (piece) tonada f. **be in** ~ estar afinado. **be out of** ~ estar desafinado. ●vt afinar, sintonizar (radio, TV); (Mec) poner a punto. ●vi. ~ **in (to)** sintonizar (con). □ ~ **up** vt/i afinar. ~**ful** adj melodioso. ~**r** n afinador m; (Radio) sintonizador m

tunic /'tjuːnɪk/ n túnica f

tunnel /'tʌnl/ n túnel m. ●vi (pt **tunnelled**) abrir un túnel

turban /'tɜːbən/ n turbante m

turbine /'tɜːbaɪn/ n turbina f

turbo /'tɜːbəʊ/ n (pl -**os**) turbo (compresor) m

turbulen|ce /'tɜːbjʊləns/ n turbulencia f. ~**t** adj turbulento

turf /tɜːf/ n (pl **turfs** or **turves**) césped m; (segment of grass) tepe m. □ ~ **out** vt echar

turgid /'tɜːdʒɪd/ adj (language) ampuloso

turkey /'tɜːkɪ/ n (pl -eys) pavo m

Turk|ey /'tɜːkɪ/ f Turquía f. **~ish** adj & n turco (m)

turmoil /'tɜːmɔɪl/ n confusión f

turn /tɜːn/ vt hacer girar; volver (head, page); doblar (corner); (change) cambiar; (deflect) desviar. **~ sth into sth** convertir or transformar algo en algo. • vi (handle) girar, dar vueltas; (person) volverse, darse la vuelta. **~ right** girar or doblar or torcer a la derecha. **~ red** ponerse rojo. **~ into sth** convertirse en algo. • n vuelta f; (in road) curva f; (change) giro m; (sequence) turno m; (fam, of illness) ataque m. **good ~** favor m. **in ~** a su vez. □ **~ down** vt (fold) doblar; (reduce) bajar; (reject) rechazar. □ **~ off** vt cerrar (tap); apagar (light, TV, etc). vi (from road) doblar. □ **~ on** vt abrir (tap); encender, prender (LAm) (light etc). □ **~ out** vt apagar (light etc). vi (result) resultar. □ **~ round** vi darse la vuelta. □ **~ up** vi aparecer. vt (find) encontrar; levantar (collar); subir (hem); acortar (trousers); poner más fuerte (gas). **~ed-up** adj (nose) respingón. **~ing** n (in town) bocacalle f. **we've missed the ~ing** nos hemos pasado la calle (or carretera). **~ing-point** n momento m decisivo.

turnip /'tɜːnɪp/ n nabo m

turn: **~over** n (Com) facturación f; (of staff) movimiento m. **~pike** n (Amer) autopista f de peaje. **~stile** n torniquete m. **~table** n platina f. **~-up** n (of trousers) vuelta f, valenciana f (Mex)

turquoise /'tɜːkwɔɪz/ adj & n turquesa (f)

turret /'tʌrɪt/ n torrecilla f

turtle /'tɜːtl/ n tortuga f de mar; (Amer, tortoise) tortuga f

turves /tɜːvz/ see TURF

tusk /tʌsk/ n colmillo m

tussle /'tʌsl/ n lucha f

tutor /'tjuːtə(r)/ n profesor m particular

tuxedo /tʌk'siːdəʊ/ n (pl -os) (Amer) esmoquin m, smoking m

TV /tiː'viː/ n televisión f, tele f Ⓣ

twang /twæŋ/ n tañido m; (in voice) gangueo m

tweet /twiːt/ n piada f. • vi piar

tweezers /'twiːzəz/ npl pinzas fpl

twel|fth /twelfθ/ adj duodécimo. • n doceavo m. **~ve** /twelv/ adj & n doce (m)

twent|ieth /'twentɪəθ/ adj vigésimo. • n veinteavo m. **~y** /'twentɪ/ adj & n veinte (m)

twice /twaɪs/ adv dos veces. **~ as many people** el doble de gente

twiddle /'twɪdl/ vt (hacer) girar

twig /twɪg/ n ramita f. • vi (pt twigged) Ⓣ caer, darse cuenta

twilight /'twaɪlaɪt/ n crepúsculo m

twin /twɪn/ adj & n gemelo (m), mellizo (m) (LAm)

twine /twaɪn/ n cordel m, bramante m

twinge /twɪndʒ/ n punzada f; (of remorse) punzada f

twinkle /'twɪŋkl/ vi centellear. • n centelleo m; (in eye) brillo m

twirl /twɜːl/ vt (hacer) girar. • vi girar. • n vuelta f

twist /twɪst/ vt retorcer; (roll) enrollar; girar (knob); tergiversar (words); (distort) retorcer. **~ one's ankle** torcerse el tobillo. • vi (rope, wire) enrollarse; (road, river) serpentear. • n torsión f; (curve) vuelta f

twit /twɪt/ n 🔲 imbécil m

twitch /twɪtʃ/ vi moverse. ● n tic m

twitter /'twɪtə(r)/ vi gorjear

two /tuː/ adj & n dos (m). ~**-bit** adj (Amer) de tres al cuarto. ~**-faced** adj falso, insincero. ~**fold** adj doble. ● adv dos veces. ~**pence** /'tʌpəns/ n dos peniques mpl. ~**-piece** (suit) n traje m de dos piezas. ~**-way** adj (traffic) de doble sentido

tycoon /taɪ'kuːn/ n magnate m

tying /'taɪɪŋ/ see TIE

type /taɪp/ n tipo m. ● vt/i escribir a máquina. ~**-cast** adj (actor) encasillado. ~**script** n texto m mecanografiado, manuscrito m (de una obra, novela etc). ~**writer** n máquina f de escribir. ~**written** adj escrito a máquina, mecanografiado

typhoon /taɪ'fuːn/ n tifón m

typical /'tɪpɪkl/ adj típico. ~**ly** adv típicamente

typify /'tɪpɪfaɪ/ vt tipificar

typi|ng /'taɪpɪŋ/ n mecanografía f. ~**st** n mecanógrafo m

tyran|nical /tɪ'rænɪkl/ adj tiránico. ~**ny** /'tɪrənɪ/ n tiranía f. ~**t** /'taɪərənt/ n tirano m

tyre /'taɪə(r)/ n neumático m, llanta f (LAm)

Uu

udder /'ʌdə(r)/ n ubre f

UFO /'juːfəʊ/ abbr (= **unidentified flying object**) OVNI m (objeto volante no identificado)

ugly /'ʌglɪ/ adj (-ier, -iest) feo

UK /juː'keɪ/ abbr (= **United Kingdom**) Reino m Unido

Ukraine /juː'kreɪn/ n Ucrania f

ulcer /'ʌlsə(r)/ n úlcera f; (external) llaga f

ultimate /'ʌltɪmət/ adj (eventual) final; (utmost) máximo. ~**ly** adv en última instancia; (in the long run) a la larga

ultimatum /ʌltɪ'meɪtəm/ n (pl -ums) ultimátum m

ultra... /'ʌltrə/ pref ultra... ~**violet** /-'vaɪələt/ adj ultravioleta

umbilical cord /ʌm'bɪlɪkl/ n cordón m umbilical

umbrella /ʌm'brelə/ n paraguas m

umpire /'ʌmpaɪə(r)/ n árbitro m. ● vt arbitrar

umpteen /'ʌmptiːn/ adj 🔲 tropecientos 🔲. ~**th** adj 🔲 enésimo

un... /ʌn/ pref in..., des..., no, poco, sin

UN /juː'en/ abbr (= **United Nations**) ONU f (Organización de las Naciones Unidas)

unable /ʌn'eɪbl/ adj. be ~ to no poder; (be incapable of) ser incapaz de

unacceptable /ʌnək'septəbl/ adj (behaviour) inaceptable; (terms) inadmisible

unaccompanied /ˌʌnə
ˈkʌmpənid/ adj (luggage) no acom-
pañado; (person, instrument) solo;
(singing) sin acompañamiento

unaccustomed /ˌʌnəˈkʌstəmd/
adj desacostumbrado. **be ~ to** adj
no estar acostumbrado a

unaffected /ˌʌnəˈfektɪd/ adj natu-
ral

unaided /ˌʌnˈeɪdɪd/ adj sin ayuda

unanimous /juːˈnænɪməs/ adj
unánime. **~ly** adv unánimemente;
(elect) por unanimidad

unarmed /ˌʌnˈɑːmd/ adj desar-
mado

unattended /ˌʌnəˈtendɪd/ adj sin
vigilar

unattractive /ˌʌnəˈtræktɪv/ adj
poco atractivo

unavoidabl|e /ˌʌnəˈvɔɪdəbl/ adj
inevitable. **~y** adv. **I was ~y** de-
layed no pude evitar llegar tarde

unaware /ˌʌnəˈweə(r)/ adj. **be ~
of** ignorar, no ser consciente de.
~s /-eəz/ adv desprevenido

unbearabl|e /ˌʌnˈbeərəbl/ adj in-
soportable, inaguantable. **~y** adv
inaguantablemente

unbeat|able /ˌʌnˈbiːtəbl/ adj
(quality) insuperable; (team) inven-
cible. **~en** adj no vencido; (record)
insuperado

unbelievabl|e /ˌʌnbɪˈliːvəbl/ adj
increíble. **~y** adv increíblemente

unbiased /ˌʌnˈbaɪəst/ adj impar-
cial

unblock /ˌʌnˈblɒk/ vt desatascar

unbolt /ˌʌnˈbəʊlt/ vt descorrer el
pestillo de

unborn /ˌʌnˈbɔːn/ adj que todavía
no ha nacido

unbreakable /ˌʌnˈbreɪkəbl/ adj
irrompible

unbroken /ˌʌnˈbrəʊkən/ adj (in-

tact) intacto; *(continuous)* ininte-
rrumpido

unbutton /ˌʌnˈbʌtn/ vt desaboto-
nar, desabrochar

uncalled-for /ˌʌnˈkɔːldfɔː(r)/ adj
fuera de lugar

uncanny /ˌʌnˈkænɪ/ adj (-ier,
-iest) raro, extraño

uncertain /ˌʌnˈsɜːtn/ adj incierto;
(hesitant) vacilante. **be ~ of/about**
sth no estar seguro de algo. **~ty** n
incertidumbre f

uncharitable /ˌʌnˈtʃærɪtəbl/ adj
severo

uncivilized /ˌʌnˈsɪvɪlaɪzd/ adj in-
civilizado

uncle /ˈʌŋkl/ n tío m

Uncle Sam Es la típica ⓘ
personificación de EE.UU.,
en que éste es representado por
un hombre de barba blanca, ves-
tido con los colores nacionales y
con un sombrero de copa adorna-
do con estrellas. Es posible que
la imagen se haya extraído del
cartel de reclutamiento, en 1917,
que llevaba la leyenda: "A Ud. lo
necesito".

---

unclean /ˌʌnˈkliːn/ adj impuro

unclear /ˌʌnˈklɪə(r)/ adj poco claro

uncomfortable /ˌʌnˈkʌmfətəbl/
adj incómodo

uncommon /ˌʌnˈkɒmən/ adj poco
común

uncompromising /ˌʌn
ˈkɒmprəmaɪzɪŋ/ adj intransigente

unconcerned /ˌʌnkənˈsɜːnd/ adj
indiferente

unconditional /ˌʌnkənˈdɪʃənl/
adj incondicional

unconnected /ˌʌnkəˈnektɪd/ adj
(unrelated) sin conexión. **the**

events are ~ estos acontecimientos no guardan ninguna relación (entre sí)

unconscious /ʌnˈkɒnʃəs/ adj (Med) inconsciente. **~ly** adv inconscientemente

unconventional /ʌnkən-ˈvenʃənl/ adj poco convencional

uncork /ʌnˈkɔːk/ vt descorchar

uncouth /ʌnˈkuːθ/ adj zafio

uncover /ʌnˈkʌvə(r)/ vt destapar; revelar (plot, scandal)

undaunted /ʌnˈdɔːntɪd/ adj impertérrito

undecided /ʌndɪˈsaɪdɪd/ adj indeciso

undeniabl|e /ʌndɪˈnaɪəbl/ adj innegable. **~y** adv sin lugar a dudas

under /ˈʌndə(r)/ prep debajo de; (less than) menos de; (heading) bajo; (according to) según; (expressing movement) por debajo de. ● adv debajo, abajo

under... pref sub...

under: **~carriage** n tren m de aterrizaje. **~charge** vt /-ˈtʃɑːdʒ/ cobrarle de menos a. **~clothes** npl ropa f interior. **~coat**, **~coating** (Amer) n (paint) pintura f base; (first coat) primera mano f de pintura. **~cover** /-ˈkʌvə(r)/ secreto. **~current** n corriente f submarina. **~dog** n. **the ~dog** el que tiene menos posibilidades. **the ~dogs** npl los de abajo. **~done** adj /-ˈdʌn/ (meat) poco hecho. **~estimate** /-ˈestɪmeɪt/ vt (underrate) subestimar. **~fed** /-ˈfed/ adj subalimentado. **~foot** /-ˈfʊt/ adv debajo de los pies. **~go** vt (pt -went, pp -gone) sufrir. **~graduate** /-ˈɡrædjʊət/ n estudiante m universitario (no licenciado). **~ground**

/-ˈɡraʊnd/ adv bajo tierra; (in secret) clandestinamente. ● /-ˈɡraʊnd/ adj subterráneo; (secret) clandestino. ● n metro m. **~growth** n maleza f. **~hand** /-ˈhænd/ adj (secret) clandestino; (deceptive) fraudulento. **~lie** /-ˈlaɪ/ vt (pt -lay, pp -lain, pres p -lying) subyacer a. **~line** /-ˈlaɪn/ vt subrayar. **~lying** /-ˈlaɪɪŋ/ adj subyacente. **~mine** /-ˈmaɪn/ vt socavar. **~neath** /-ˈniːθ/ prep debajo de, abajo de (LAm). ● adv por debajo. **~paid** /-ˈpeɪd/ adj mal pagado. **~pants** npl calzoncillos mpl. **~pass** n paso m subterráneo; (for traffic) paso m inferior. **~privileged** /-ˈprɪvɪlɪdʒd/ adj desfavorecido. **~rate** /-ˈreɪt/ vt subestimar. **~rated** /-ˈreɪtɪd/ adj no debidamente apreciado. **~shirt** n (Amer) camiseta f (interior).

understand /ʌndəˈstænd/ vt (pt -stood) entender; (empathize with) comprender, entender. ● vi entender, comprender. **~able** adj comprensible. **~ing** adj comprensivo. ● n (grasp) entendimiento m; (sympathy) comprensión f; (agreement) acuerdo m

under: **~statement** n subestimación f. **~take** /-ˈteɪk/ vt (pt -took, pp -taken) emprender (task); asumir (responsibility). **~taker** n director m de pompas fúnebres. **~taking** /-ˈteɪkɪŋ/ n empresa f; (promise) promesa f. **~tone** n. **in an ~tone** en voz baja. **~value** /-ˈvælju:/ vt subvalorar. **~water** /-ˈwɔːtə(r)/ adj submarino. ● adv debajo del agua. **~wear** n ropa f interior. **~weight** /-ˈweɪt/ adj de peso más bajo que el normal.

~went /-ˈwent/ see UNDERGO.

~world n (criminals) hampa f.

~write /-'raɪt/ vt (pt -wrote, pp -written) (Com) asegurar; (guarantee financially) financiar

undeserved /ʌndɪ'zɜːvd/ adj inmerecido

undesirable /ʌndɪ'zaɪərəbl/ adj indeseable

undignified /ʌn'dɪgnɪfaɪd/ adj indecoroso

undisputed /ʌndɪs'pjuːtɪd/ adj (champion) indiscutido; (facts) innegable

undo /ʌn'duː/ vt (pt -did, pp -done) desabrochar (button, jacket); abrir (zip); desatar (knot, laces)

undoubted /ʌn'daʊtɪd/ adj indudable. **~ly** adv indudablemente, sin duda

undress /ʌn'dres/ vt desvestir, desnudar. • vi desvestirse, desnudarse

undue /ʌn'djuː/ adj excesivo

undulate /'ʌndjʊleɪt/ vi ondular

unduly /ʌn'djuːlɪ/ adv excesivamente

unearth /ʌn'ɜːθ/ vt desenterrar; descubrir (document)

unearthly /ʌn'ɜːθlɪ/ adj sobrenatural. at an **~** hour a estas horas intempestivas

uneasy /ʌn'iːzɪ/ adj incómodo

uneconomic /ʌniːkə'nɒmɪk/ adj poco económico

uneducated /ʌn'edjʊkertɪd/ adj sin educación

unemploy|ed /ʌnɪm'plɔɪd/ adj desempleado, parado. **~ment** n desempleo m, paro m

unending /ʌn'endɪŋ/ adj interminable, sin fin

unequal /ʌn'iːkwəl/ adj desigual

unequivocal /ʌnɪ'kwɪvəkl/ adj inequívoco

unethical /ʌn'eθɪkl/ adj poco ético, inmoral

uneven /ʌn'iːvn/ adj desigual

unexpected /ʌnɪk'spektɪd/ adj inesperado; (result) imprevisto. **~ly** adv (arrive) de improviso; (happen) de forma imprevista

unfair /ʌn'feə(r)/ adj injusto; procedente (dismissal). **~ly** adv injustamente

unfaithful /ʌn'feɪθfl/ adj infiel

unfamiliar /ʌnfə'mɪlɪə(r)/ adj desconocido. be **~** with desconocer

unfasten /ʌn'fɑːsn/ vt desabrochar (clothes); (untie) desatar

unfavourable /ʌn'feɪvərəbl/ adj desfavorable

unfeeling /ʌn'fiːlɪŋ/ adj insensible

unfit /ʌn'fɪt/ adj. I'm **~** no estoy en forma. **~** for human consumption no apto para el consumo

unfold /ʌn'fəʊld/ vt desdoblar; desplegar (wings); (fig) revelar. • vi (leaf) abrirse; (events) desarrollarse

unforeseen /ʌnfɔː'siːn/ adj imprevisto

unforgettable /ʌnfə'getəbl/ adj inolvidable

unforgivable /ʌnfə'gɪvəbl/ adj imperdonable

unfortunate /ʌn'fɔːtʃənət/ adj desafortunado; (regrettable) lamentable. **~ly** adv desafortunadamente; (stronger) por desgracia, desgraciadamente

unfounded /ʌn'faʊndɪd/ adj infundado

unfriendly /ʌn'frendlɪ/ adj poco amistoso; (stronger) antipático

unfurl | unmarried

unfurl /ʌnˈfɜːl/ vt desplegar

ungainly /ʌnˈgeɪnlɪ/ adj desgarbado

ungrateful /ʌnˈgreɪtfʊl/ adj desagradecido, ingrato

unhapp|iness /ʌnˈhæpɪnəs/ n infelicidad f, tristeza f. **~y** adj (**-ier**, **-iest**) infeliz, triste; (unsuitable) inoportuno. **be ~y about sth** no estar contento con algo

unharmed /ʌnˈhɑːmd/ adj (person) ileso

unhealthy /ʌnˈhelθɪ/ adj (**-ier**, **-iest**) (person) de mala salud; (complexion) enfermizo; (conditions) poco saludable

unhurt /ʌnˈhɜːt/ adj ileso

unification /juːnɪfɪˈkeɪʃn/ n unificación f

uniform /ˈjuːnɪfɔːm/ adj & n uniforme (m). **~ity** /-ˈfɔːmətɪ/ n uniformidad f

unify /ˈjuːnɪfaɪ/ vt unir

unilateral /juːnɪˈlætərəl/ adj unilateral

unimaginable /ʌnɪˈmædʒɪnəbl/ adj inimaginable

unimaginative /ʌnɪˈmædʒɪnətɪv/ adj (person) poco imaginativo

unimportant /ʌnɪmˈpɔːtnt/ adj sin importancia

uninhabited /ʌnɪnˈhæbɪtɪd/ adj deshabitado; (island) despoblado

unintelligible /ʌnɪnˈtelɪdʒəbl/ adj ininteligible

unintentional /ʌnɪnˈtenʃənl/ adj involuntario

union /ˈjuːnjən/ n unión f; (trade union) sindicato m; (student ~) asociación f de estudiantes. **U~ Jack** n bandera f del Reino Unido

unique /juːˈniːk/ adj único

unison /ˈjuːnɪsn/ n. **in ~** al unísono

unit /ˈjuːnɪt/ n unidad f; (of furniture etc) módulo m; (in course) módulo m

unite /juːˈnaɪt/ vt unir. • vi unirse. **U~d Kingdom** n Reino m Unido. **U~d Nations** n Organización f de las Naciones Unidas (ONU). **U~d States (of America)** n Estados mpl Unidos (de América)

unity /ˈjuːnɪtɪ/ n unidad f

univers|al /juːnɪˈvɜːsl/ adj universal. **~e** /ˈjuːnɪvɜːs/ n universo m

university /juːnɪˈvɜːsətɪ/ n universidad f. • adj universitario

unjust /ʌnˈdʒʌst/ adj injusto. **~ified** /-ɪfaɪd/ adj injustificado

unkind /ʌnˈkaɪnd/ adj poco amable; (cruel) cruel; (remark) hiriente

unknown /ʌnˈnəʊn/ adj desconocido

unlawful /ʌnˈlɔːfl/ adj ilegal

unleaded /ʌnˈledɪd/ adj (fuel) sin plomo

unleash /ʌnˈliːʃ/ vt soltar

unless /ʌnˈles, ənˈles/ conj a menos que, a no ser que

unlike /ʌnˈlaɪk/ prep diferente de. (in contrast to) a diferencia de. **~ly** adj improbable

unlimited /ʌnˈlɪmɪtɪd/ adj ilimitado

unlisted /ʌnˈlɪstɪd/ adj (Amer) que no figura en la guía telefónica, privado (Mex)

unload /ʌnˈləʊd/ vt descargar

unlock /ʌnˈlɒk/ vt abrir (con llave)

unluck|ily /ʌnˈlʌkɪlɪ/ adv desgraciadamente. **~y** adj (**-ier**, **-iest**) (person) sin suerte, desafortunado. **be ~y** tener mala suerte; (bring bad luck) traer mala suerte

unmarried /ʌnˈmærɪd/ adj

u

soltero

unmask /ʌnˈmɑːsk/ vt desenmascarar

unmentionable /ʌnˈmenʃənəbl/ adj inmencionable

unmistakable /ʌnmɪˈsteɪkəbl/ adj inconfundible

unnatural /ʌnˈnætʃərəl/ adj poco natural; (not normal) anormal

unnecessarily /ʌnˈnesəsərɪli/ adv innecesariamente. **~y** adj innecesario

unnerve /ʌnˈnɜːv/ vt desconcertar

unnoticed /ʌnˈnəʊtɪst/ adj inadvertido

unobtainable /ʌnəbˈteɪnəbl/ adj imposible de conseguir

unobtrusive /ʌnəbˈtruːsɪv/ adj discreto

unofficial /ʌnəˈfɪʃl/ adj no oficial. **~ly** adv extraoficialmente

unpack /ʌnˈpæk/ vt sacar las cosas de (bags); deshacer, desempacar (LAm) (suitcase). ●vi deshacer las maletas, desempacar (LAm)

unpaid /ʌnˈpeɪd/ adj (work) no retribuido, no remunerado; (leave) sin sueldo

unperturbed /ʌnpəˈtɜːbd/ adj impasible. he carried on ~ siguió sin inmutarse

unpleasant /ʌnˈpleznt/ adj desagradable

unplug /ʌnˈplʌg/ vt desenchufar

unpopular /ʌnˈpɒpjələ(r)/ adj impopular

unprecedented /ʌnˈpresɪdentɪd/ adj sin precedentes

unpredictable /ʌnprɪˈdɪktəbl/ adj imprevisible

unprepared /ʌnprɪˈpeəd/ adj no preparado; (unready) desprevenido

unprofessional /ʌnprəˈfeʃənəl/ adj poco profesional

unprofitable /ʌnˈprɒfɪtəbl/ adj no rentable

unprotected /ʌnprəˈtektɪd/ adj sin protección; (sex) sin el uso de preservativos

unqualified /ʌnˈkwɒlɪfaɪd/ adj sin título; (fig) absoluto

unquestion|able /ʌnˈkwestʃənəbl/ adj incuestionable, innegable. **~ing** adj (obedience) ciego; (loyalty) incondicional

unravel /ʌnˈrævl/ vt (pt unravelled) desenredar; desentrañar (mystery)

unreal /ʌnˈrɪəl/ adj irreal. **~istic** /-ˈlɪstɪk/ adj poco realista

unreasonable /ʌnˈriːzənəbl/ adj irrazonable

unrecognizable /ʌnrekəɡˈnaɪzəbl/ adj irreconocible

unrelated /ʌnrɪˈleɪtɪd/ adj (facts) no relacionados (entre sí); (people) no emparentado

unreliable /ʌnrɪˈlaɪəbl/ adj (person) informal; (machine) poco fiable; (information) poco fidedigno

unrepentant /ʌnrɪˈpentənt/ adj impenitente

unrest /ʌnˈrest/ n (discontent) descontento m; (disturbances) disturbios mpl

unrivalled /ʌnˈraɪvld/ adj incomparable

unroll /ʌnˈrəʊl/ vt desenrollar. ●vi desenrollarse

unruffled /ʌnˈrʌfld/ (person) sereno

unruly /ʌnˈruːli/ adj (class) indisciplinado; (child) revoltoso

unsafe /ʌnˈseɪf/ adj inseguro

unsatisfactory /ʌnsætɪsˈfæktəri/ adj insatisfactorio

unsavoury /ʌnˈseɪvərɪ/ adj desagradable

unscathed /ʌnˈskeɪðd/ adj ileso

unscheduled /ʌnˈʃedjuːld/ adj no programado, no previsto

unscrew /ʌnˈskruː/ vt destornillar; desenroscar (lid)

unscrupulous /ʌnˈskruːpjələs/ adj inescrupuloso

unseemly /ʌnˈsiːmlɪ/ adj indecoroso

unseen /ʌnˈsiːn/ adj (danger) oculto; (unnoticed) sin ser visto

unselfish /ʌnˈselfɪʃ/ adj (act) desinteresado; (person) nada egoísta

unsettle /ʌnˈsetl/ vt desestabilizar (situation); alterar (plans). ~d adj agitado; (weather) inestable; (undecided) pendiente (de resolución)

unshakeable /ʌnˈʃeɪkəbl/ adj inquebrantable

unshaven /ʌnˈʃeɪvn/ adj sin afeitar, sin rasurar (Mex)

unsightly /ʌnˈsaɪtlɪ/ adj feo

unskilled /ʌnˈskɪld/ adj (work) no especializado; (worker) no cualificado, no calificado

unsociable /ʌnˈsəʊʃəbl/ adj insociable

unsolved /ʌnˈsɒlvd/ adj no resuelto; (murder) sin esclarecerse

unsophisticated /ʌnsəˈfɪstɪkeɪtɪd/ adj sencillo

unsound /ʌnˈsaʊnd/ adj poco sólido

unspecified /ʌnˈspesɪfaɪd/ adj no especificado

unstable /ʌnˈsteɪbl/ adj inestable

unsteady /ʌnˈstedɪ/ adj inestable, poco firme

unstuck /ʌnˈstʌk/ adj despegado. come ~ despegarse; (fail) fracasar

unsuccessful /ʌnsəkˈsesfʊl/ adj

(attempt) infructuoso. be ~ no tener éxito, fracasar

unsuitable /ʌnˈsuːtəbl/ adj (clothing) poco apropiado, poco adecuado; (time) inconveniente. she is ~ for the job no es la persona indicada para el trabajo

unsure /ʌnˈʃʊə(r)/ adj inseguro

unthinkable /ʌnˈθɪŋkəbl/ adj inconcebible

untid|iness /ʌnˈtaɪdɪnəs/ n desorden m. ~y adj (-ier, -iest) desordenado; (appearance, writing) descuidado

untie /ʌnˈtaɪ/ vt desatar, desamarrar (LAm)

until /ənˈtɪl, ʌnˈtɪl/ prep hasta.
● conj hasta que

untold /ʌnˈtəʊld/ adj incalculable

untouched /ʌnˈtʌtʃt/ adj intacto

untried /ʌnˈtraɪd/ adj no probado

untrue /ʌnˈtruː/ adj falso

unused /ʌnˈjuːzd/ adj nuevo.
● /ʌnˈjuːst/ adj. ~ to no acostumbrado a

unusual /ʌnˈjuːʒʊəl/ adj poco común, poco corriente. it's ~ to see so many people es raro ver a tanta gente. ~ly adv excepcionalmente, inusitadamente

unveil /ʌnˈveɪl/ vt descubrir

unwanted /ʌnˈwɒntɪd/ adj superfluo; (child) no deseado

unwelcome /ʌnˈwelkəm/ adj (news) poco grato; (guest) inoportuno

unwell /ʌnˈwel/ adj indispuesto

unwieldy /ʌnˈwiːldɪ/ adj pesado y difícil de manejar

unwilling /ʌnˈwɪlɪŋ/ adj mal dispuesto. be ~ no querer

unwind /ʌnˈwaɪnd/ vt (pt unwound) desenrollar. ● vi (fam,

u

relax) relajarse

unwise /ʌnˈwaɪz/ *adj* poco sensato

unworthy /ʌnˈwɜːðɪ/ *adj* indigno

unwrap /ʌnˈræp/ *vt* (*pt* unwrapped) desenvolver

unwritten /ʌnˈrɪtn/ *adj* no escrito; (*agreement*) verbal

up /ʌp/ *adv* arriba; (*upwards*) hacia arriba; (*higher*) más arriba. ~ **here** aquí arriba. ~ **there** allí arriba. ~ **to** hasta. he's not ~ **yet** todavía no se ha levantado. be ~ **against** enfrentarse con. come ~ subir. go ~ subir. he's not ~ **to the job** no tiene las condiciones necesarias para el trabajo. it's ~ **to you** depende de ti. what's ~? ¿qué pasa? ● *prep*. go ~ **the stairs** subir la escalera. it's just ~ **the road** está un poco más allá. ● *vt* (*pt* upped) aumentar. ● *n*. ~**s and downs** *npl* altibajos *mpl*; (*of life*) vicisitudes *fpl*. ~**bringing** /ˈʌpbrɪŋɪŋ/ *n* educación *f*. ~**date** /ʌpˈdeɪt/ *vt* poner al día. ~**grade** /ʌpˈɡreɪd/ *vt* elevar de categoría (*person*); mejorar (*equipment*). ~**heaval** /ʌpˈhiːvl/ *n* trastorno *m*. ~**hill** /ʌpˈhɪl/ *adv* cuesta arriba. ~**hold** /ʌpˈhəʊld/ *vt* (*pt* upheld) mantener (*principle*); confirmar (*decision*). ~**holster** /ʌpˈhəʊlstə(r)/ *vt* tapizar. ~**holstery** *n* tapicería *f*. ~**keep** *n* mantenimiento *m*. ~**market** /ʌpˈmɑːkɪt/ *adj* de categoría

upon /əˈpɒn/ *prep* sobre. once ~ **a time** érase una vez

upper /ˈʌpə(r)/ *adj* superior. ~ **class** *n* clase *f* alta

up:: ~**right** *adj* vertical; (*citizen*) recto. **place sth** ~**right** poner algo de pie. ~**rising** /ˈʌpraɪzɪŋ/ *n* levantamiento *m*. ~**roar** *n* tu-

multo *m*

upset /ʌpˈset/ *vt* (*pt* upset, *pres p* upsetting) (*hurt*) disgustar; (*offend*) ofender; (*distress*) alterar; desbaratar (plans). ● *adj* (*hurt*) disgustado; (*distressed*) alterado; (*offended*) ofendido; (*disappointed*) desilusionado. ● /ˈʌpset/ *n* trastorno *m*. **have a stomach** ~ estar mal del estómago

up:: ~**shot** *n* resultado *m*. ~**side down** /ʌpsaɪdˈdaʊn/ *adv* al revés (con la parte de arriba abajo); (in disorder) patas arriba. **turn sth** ~**side down** poner algo boca abajo. ~**stairs** /ʌpˈsteəz/ *adv* arriba. go ~**stairs** subir. ● /ˈʌpsteəz/ *adj* de arriba. ~**start** *n* advenedizo *m*. ~**state** *adj* (Amer). **I live** ~**state** vivo en el norte del estado. ~**stream** /ʌpˈstriːm/ *adv* río arriba. ~**take** *n*. **be quick on the** ~**take** agarrar las cosas al vuelo. ~**-to-date** /ʌptəˈdeɪt/ *adj* al día; (*news*) de última hora. ~**turn** *n* repunte *m*, mejora *f*. ~**ward** /ˈʌpwəd/ *adj* (*movement*) ascendente; (*direction*) hacia arriba. ● *adv* hacia arriba. ~**wards** *adv* hacia arriba

uranium /jʊˈreɪnɪəm/ *n* uranio *m*

Uranus /ˈjʊərənəs/jʊəˈreɪnəs/ *n* Urano *m*

urban /ˈɜːbən/ *adj* urbano

urchin /ˈɜːtʃɪn/ *n* pilluelo *m*

urge /ɜːdʒ/ *vt* instar. ~ **s.o. to do sth** instar a uno a que haga algo. ● *n* impulso *m*; (*wish, whim*) ganas *fpl*. ~ **on** *vt* animar

urgen|cy /ˈɜːdʒənsɪ/ *n* urgencia *f*. ~**t** *adj* urgente. ~**tly** *adv* urgentemente, con urgencia

urin|ate /ˈjʊərɪneɪt/ *vi* orinar. ~**e** /ˈjʊərɪn/ *n* orina *f*

Uruguay /ˈjʊərəɡwaɪ/ *n* Uruguay

m. **~an** *adj & n* uruguayo (*m*)

us /ʌs, əs/ *pron* nos; (*after prep*) nosotros *m*, nosotras *f*

US(A) /juːesˈeɪ/ *abbr* (= **United States (of America)**) EE.UU. (*only written*), Estados *mpl* Unidos

usage /ˈjuːzɪdʒ/ *n* uso *m*

use /juːz/ *vt* usar; utilizar (service, facilities); consumir (fuel). ● /juːs/ *n* uso *m*, empleo *m*. **be of** ~ servir. **it is no** ~ es inútil. □ ~ **up** *vt* agotar, consumir. **~d** /juːzd/ *adj* usado. ● /juːst/ *v mod* ~ **to**. **he** ~**d to say** decía, solía decir. **there** ~**d to be** antes había. ● *adj* /juːst/. **be** ~**d to** estar acostumbrado a. **~ful** /ˈjuːsfl/ *adj* útil. **~fully** *adv* útilmente. **~less** *adj* inútil. (person) incompetente. ~**r** /-zə(r)/ *n* usuario *m*. **drug** ~ consumidor *m* de drogas

usher /ˈʌʃə(r)/ *n* (*in theatre etc*) acomodador *m*. □ ~ **in** *vt* hacer pasar; marcar el comienzo de (new era). ~**ette** /-ˈret/ *n* acomodadora *f*

USSR *abbr* (*History*) (= **Union of Soviet Socialist Republics**) URSS

usual /ˈjuːʒʊəl/ *adj* usual; (*habitual*) acostumbrado, habitual; (place, route) de siempre. **as** ~ como de costumbre, como siempre. ~**ly** *adv* normalmente. **he** ~**ly wakes up early** suele despertarse temprano

utensil /juːˈtensl/ *n* utensilio *m*

utilize /ˈjuːtɪlaɪz/ *vt* utilizar

utmost /ˈʌtməʊst/ *adj* sumo. ● *n*. **do one's** ~ hacer todo lo posible (to para)

utter /ˈʌtə(r)/ *adj* completo. ● *vt* pronunciar (word); dar (cry). ~**ly** *adv* totalmente

U-turn /ˈjuːtɜːn/ *n* cambio *m* de sentido

Vv

vacan|cy /ˈveɪkənsɪ/ *n* (*job*) vacante *f*; (room) habitación *f* libre. ~**t** *adj* (building) desocupado; (seat) libre; (post) vacante; (look) ausente

vacate /vəˈkeɪt/ *vt* dejar

vacation /vəˈkeɪʃn/ *n* (*Amer*) vacaciones *fpl*. **go on** ~ ir de vacaciones. ~**er** *n* (*Amer*) veraneante *m & f*

vaccin|ate /ˈvæksɪneɪt/ *vt* vacunar. ~**ation** /-ˈneɪʃn/ *n* vacunación *f*. ~**e** /ˈvæksiːn/ *n* vacuna *f*

vacuum /ˈvækjʊəm/ *n* vacío *m*. ~ **cleaner** *n* aspiradora *f*

vagina /vəˈdʒaɪnə/ *n* vagina *f*

vague /veɪg/ *adj* (-**er**, -**est**) vago; (outline) borroso; (person, expression) despistado. ~**ly** *adv* vagamente

vain /veɪn/ *adj* (-**er**, -**est**) vanidoso; (useless) vano. **in** ~ en vano

Valentine's Day /ˈvæləntaɪnz/ *n* el día de San Valentín

valiant /ˈvælɪənt/ *adj* valeroso

valid /ˈvælɪd/ *adj* válido. ~**ate** /-eɪt/ *vt* dar validez a; validar (contract). ~**ity** /-ˈɪdətɪ/ *n* validez *f*

valley /ˈvælɪ/ *n* (*pl* -**eys**) valle *m*

valour /ˈvælə(r)/ *n* valor *m*

valu|able /ˈvæljʊəbl/ *adj* valioso. ~**ables** *npl* objetos *mpl* de valor. ~**ation** /-ˈeɪʃn/ *n* valoración *f*. ~**e** /ˈvæljuː/ *n* valor *m*. ● *vt* valorar; tasar, valorar, avaluar (*Lam*) (property). ~**e added tax** *n* impuesto *m* sobre el valor añadido

valve /vælv/ *n* válvula *f*

vampire /ˈvæmpaɪə(r)/ *n*

van | verb

vampiro m

van /væn/ n furgoneta f, camioneta f; (Rail) furgón m

vandal /'vændl/ n vándalo m. ~**ism** n vandalismo m. ~**ize** vt destruir

vanilla /və'nɪlə/ n vainilla f

vanish /'vænɪʃ/ vi desaparecer

vanity /'vænɪtɪ/ n vanidad f. ~ **case** n neceser m

vapour /'veɪpə(r)/ n vapor m

varia|ble /'veərɪəbl/ adj variable. ~**nce** /-əns/ n. **at** ~**ce** en desacuerdo. ~**nt** n variante f. ~**tion** /-'eɪʃn/ n variación f

vari|ed /'veərɪd/ adj variado. ~**ety** /və'raɪətɪ/ n variedad f. ~**ety show** n espectáculo m de variedades. ~**ous** /'veərɪəs/ adj (several) varios; (different) diversos

varnish /'vɑːnɪʃ/ n barniz m; (for nails) esmalte m. ●vt barnizar; pintar (nails)

vary /'veərɪ/ vt/i variar

vase /vɑːz/, (Amer) /veɪs/ n (for flowers) florero m; (ornamental) jarrón m

vast /vɑːst/ adj vasto, extenso; (size) inmenso. ~**ly** adv infinitamente

vat /væt/ n cuba f

VAT /viːeɪˈtiː/ abbr (= value added tax) IVA m

vault /vɔːlt/ n (roof) bóveda f; (in bank) cámara f acorazada; (tomb) cripta f. ●vt/i saltar

VCR n = videocassette recorder

VDU n = visual display unit

veal /viːl/ n ternera f

veer /vɪə(r)/ vi dar un viraje, virar

vegeta|ble /'vedʒɪtəbl/ adj vegetal. ●n verdura f. ~**rian** /vedʒɪ

'teərɪən/ adj & n vegetariano (m). ~**tion** /vedʒɪ'teɪʃn/ n vegetación f

vehemen|ce /'viːəmənt/ adj vehemente. ~**tly** adv con vehemencia

vehicle /'viːɪkl/ n vehículo m

veil /veɪl/ n velo m

vein /veɪn/ n vena f; (in marble) veta f

velocity /vɪ'lɒsɪtɪ/ n velocidad f

velvet /'velvɪt/ n terciopelo m

vendetta /ven'detə/ n vendetta f

vend|ing machine /'vendɪŋ/ n distribuidor m automático. ~**or** /'vendə(r)/ n vendedor m

veneer /və'nɪə(r)/ n chapa f, enchapado m; (fig) barniz m, apariencia f

venerate /'venəreɪt/ vt venerar

venereal /və'nɪərɪəl/ adj venéreo

Venetian blind /vəˈniːʃn/ n persiana f veneciana

Venezuela /venə'zweɪlə/ n Venezuela f. ~**n** adj & n venezolano (m)

vengeance /'vendʒəns/ n venganza f. **with a** ~ (fig) con ganas

venom /'venəm/ n veneno m. ~**ous** adj venenoso

vent /vent/ n (conducto m de) ventilación f; (air ~) respiradero m. **give** ~ **to** dar rienda suelta a. ●vt descargar

ventilat|e /'ventɪleɪt/ vt ventilar. ~**ion** /-'leɪʃn/ n ventilación f

ventriloquist /ven'trɪləkwɪst/ n ventrílocuo m

venture /'ventʃə(r)/ n empresa f. ●vt aventurar. ●vi atreverse

venue /'venjuː/ n (for concert) lugar m de actuación

Venus /'viːnəs/ n Venus m

veranda /və'rændə/ n galería f

verb /vɜːb/ n verbo m. ~**al** adj

verbal

verdict /'vɜːdɪkt/ n veredicto m; (*opinion*) opinión f

verge /vɜːdʒ/ n borde m. □ ~ **on** vt rayar en

verify /'verɪfaɪ/ vt (*confirm*) confirmar; (*check*) verificar

vermin /'vɜːmɪn/ n alimañas fpl

versatile /'vɜːsətaɪl/ adj versátil. ~**ity** /-'tɪlətɪ/ n versatilidad f

verse /vɜːs/ n estrofa f; (*poetry*) poesías fpl. ~**d** /vɜːst/ adj. be well-~**ed** in ser muy versado en. ~**ion** /'vɜːʃn/ n versión f

versus /'vɜːsəs/ prep contra

vertebra /'vɜːtɪbrə/ n (pl -**brae** /-briː/) vértebra f. ~**te** /-brət/ n vertebrado m

vertical /'vɜːtɪkl/ adj & n vertical (f). ~**ly** adv verticalmente

vertigo /'vɜːtɪgəʊ/ n vértigo m

verve /vɜːv/ n brío m

very /'verɪ/ adv muy. ~ **much** muchísimo. ~ **well** muy bien. the ~ first el primero de todos. ● adj mismo. the ~ **thing** exactamente lo que hace falta

vessel /'vesl/ n (*receptacle*) recipiente m; (*ship*) navío m, nave f

vest /vest/ n camiseta f; (*Amer*) chaleco m.

vestige /'vestɪdʒ/ n vestigio m

vet /vet/ n veterinario m; (*Amer fam, veteran*) veterano m. ● vt (pt **vetted**) someter a investigación (*applicant*)

veteran /'vetərən/ n veterano m

veterinary /'vetərɪnərɪ/ adj veterinario. ~ **surgeon** n veterinario m & f

veto /'viːtəʊ/ n (pl -**oes**) veto m. ● vt vetar

vex /veks/ vt fastidiar

via /'vaɪə/ prep por, por vía de

viable /'vaɪəbl/ adj viable

viaduct /'vaɪədʌkt/ n viaducto m

vibrate /vaɪ'breɪt/ vt/i vibrar. ~**ion** /-ʃn/ n vibración f

vicar /'vɪkə(r)/ n párroco m. ~**age** /-rɪdʒ/ n casa f del párroco

vice /vaɪs/ n vicio m; (*Tec*) torno m de banco

vice versa /vaɪsɪ'vɜːsə/ adv viceversa

vicinity /vɪ'sɪnɪtɪ/ n vecindad f. in the ~ **of** cerca de

vicious /'vɪʃəs/ adj (*attack*) feroz; (*dog*) fiero; (*rumour*) malicioso. ~ **circle** n círculo m vicioso

victim /'vɪktɪm/ n víctima f. ~**ize** vt victimizar

victor /'vɪktə(r)/ n vencedor m

Victorian /vɪk'tɔːrɪən/ adj victoriano

victorious /vɪk'tɔːrɪəs/ adj (*army*) victorioso; (*team*) vencedor. ~**y** /'vɪktərɪ/ n victoria f

video /'vɪdɪəʊ/ n (pl -**os**) vídeo m, video m (*LAm*). ~ **camera** n videocámara f. ~ **(cassette) recorder** n magnetoscopio m. ~ **tape** n videocassette f

vie /vaɪ/ vi (pres p **vying**) rivalizar

Vietnam /vjet'næm/ n Vietnam m. ~**ese** adj & n vietnamita (m & f)

view /vjuː/ n vista f; (*mental survey*) visión f de conjunto; (*opinion*) opinión f. in my ~ a mi juicio. in ~ **of** en vista de. on ~ expuesto. ● vt ver (*scene, property*); (*consider*) considerar. ~**er** n (TV) televidente m & f. ~**finder** n visor m. ~**point** n punto m de vista

vigilance n vigilancia f. ~**ant** adj vigilante

vigorous /'vɪgərəs/ adj enérgico;

v

(growth) vigoroso. ~**ur** /'vɪɡə(r)/ n vigor m

vile /vaɪl/ adj (base) vil; (food) asqueroso; (weather, temper) horrible

village /'vɪlɪdʒ/ n pueblo m; (small) aldea f. ~**r** n vecino m del pueblo; (of small village) aldeano m

villain /'vɪlən/ n maleante m & f; (in story etc) villano m

vindicate /'vɪndɪkeɪt/ vt justificar

vindictive /vɪn'dɪktɪv/ adj vengativo

vine /vaɪn/ n (on ground) vid f; (climbing) parra f

vinegar /'vɪnɪɡə(r)/ n vinagre m

vineyard /'vɪnjəd/ n viña f

vintage /'vɪntɪdʒ/ n (year) cosecha f. ● adj (wine) añejo; (car) de época

vinyl /'vaɪnɪl/ n vinilo m

viola /vɪ'əʊlə/ n viola f

violate /'vaɪəleɪt/ vt violar. ~**ion** /-'leɪʃn/ n violación f

violen|ce /'vaɪələns/ n violencia f. ~**t** adj violento. ~**tly** adv violentamente

violet /'vaɪələt/ adj & n violeta (f); (colour) violeta (m)

violin /'vaɪəlɪn/ n violín m. ~**ist** n violinista m & f

VIP /viːaɪ'piː/ abbr (= very important person) VIP m

viper /'vaɪpə(r)/ n víbora f

virgin /'vɜːdʒɪn/ adj & n virgen (f)

Virgo /'vɜːɡəʊ/ n Virgo m

virile /'vɪraɪl/ adj viril

virtual /'vɜːtʃʊəl/ adj. traffic is at a ~ standstill el tráfico está prácticamente paralizado. ~ **reality** n realidad f virtual. ~**ly** adv prácticamente

virtue /'vɜːtʃuː/ n virtud f. by ~ of en virtud de

virtuous /'vɜːtʃʊəs/ adj virtuoso

virulent /'vɪrʊlənt/ adj virulento

virus /'vaɪərəs/ n (pl -uses) virus m

visa /'viːzə/ n visado m, visa f (LAm)

vise /vaɪs/ n (Amer) torno m de banco

visib|ility /vɪzɪ'bɪlətɪ/ n visibilidad f. ~**le** /'vɪzɪbl/ adj visible; (sign, improvement) evidente

vision /'vɪʒn/ n visión f; (sight) vista f

visit /'vɪzɪt/ vt visitar; hacer una visita a (person). ● vi hacer visitas. ~ **with s.o.** (Amer) ir a ver a uno. ● n visita f. **pay s.o. a** ~ hacerle una visita a uno. ~**or** n visitante m & f; (guest) visita f

visor /'vaɪzə(r)/ n visera f

visual /'vɪʒʊəl/ adj visual. ~**ize** vt imaginar(se); (foresee) prever

vital /'vaɪtl/ adj (essential) esencial; (factor) de vital importancia; (organ) vital. ~**ity** /vaɪ'tælətɪ/ n vitalidad f

vitamin /'vɪtəmɪn/ n vitamina f.

vivacious /vɪ'veɪʃəs/ adj vivaz

vivid /'vɪvɪd/ adj vivo. ~**ly** adv intensamente; (describe) gráficamente

vivisection /vɪvɪ'sekʃn/ n vivisección f

vocabulary /və'kæbjʊlərɪ/ n vocabulario m

vocal /'vəʊkl/ adj vocal. ~**ist** n cantante m & f

vocation /və'keɪʃn/ n vocación f. ~**al** adj profesional

vociferous /və'sɪfərəs/ adj vociferador

vogue /vəʊɡ/ n moda f, boga f

voice /vɔɪs/ n voz f. ● vt expresar

void /vɔɪd/ adj (not valid) nulo. ● n vacío m

volatile /ˈvɒlətaɪl/ adj volátil; (person) imprevisible

volcan|ic /vɒlˈkænɪk/ adj volcánico. **~o** /vɒlˈkeɪnəʊ/ n (pl -oes) volcán m

volley /ˈvɒlɪ/ n (pl -eys) (of gunfire) descarga f cerrada; (sport) volea f. **~ball** n vóleibol m

volt /vəʊlt/ n voltio m. **~age** /-ɪdʒ/ n voltaje m

volume /ˈvɒljuːm/ n volumen m; (book) tomo m

voluntar|ily /ˈvɒləntərəlɪ/ adv voluntariamente. **~y** adj voluntario; (organization) de beneficencia

volunteer /vɒlənˈtɪə(r)/ n voluntario m. ● vt ofrecer. ● vi. **~ (to)** ofrecerse (a)

vomit /ˈvɒmɪt/ vt/i vomitar. ● n vómito m

voracious /vəˈreɪʃəs/ adj voraz

vot|e /vəʊt/ n voto m; (right) derecho m al voto; (act) votación f. ● vi votar. **~er** n votante m & f. **~ing** n votación f

vouch /vaʊtʃ/ vi. **~ for s.o.** responder por uno. **~er** /-ə(r)/ n vale m

vow /vaʊ/ n voto m. ● vi jurar

vowel /ˈvaʊəl/ n vocal f

voyage /ˈvɔɪɪdʒ/ n viaje m; (by sea) travesía f

vulgar /ˈvʌlɡə(r)/ adj (coarse) grosero, vulgar; (tasteless) de mal gusto. **~ity** /-ˈɡærətɪ/ n vulgaridad f

vulnerable /ˈvʌlnərəbl/ adj vulnerable

vulture /ˈvʌltʃə(r)/ n buitre m

vying /ˈvaɪɪŋ/ see VIE

Ww

W abbr (= West) O

wad /wɒd/ n (of notes) fajo m; (tied together) lío m; (papers) montón m

waddle /ˈwɒdl/ vi contonearse

wade /weɪd/ vi caminar (por el agua etc)

wafer /ˈweɪfə(r)/ n galleta f de barquillo

waffle /ˈwɒfl/ n 🅱 palabrería f. ● vi 🅱 divagar; (in essay, exam) meter paja 🅱. ● n (Culin) gofre m, wafle m (LAm)

waft /wɒft/ vi flotar

wag /wæɡ/ vt (pt wagged) menear. ● vi menearse

wage /weɪdʒ/ n sueldo m. **~s** npl salario m, sueldo m. **~r** n apuesta f

waggle /ˈwæɡl/ vt menear. ● vi menearse

wagon /ˈwæɡən/ n carro m; (Rail) vagón m; (Amer, delivery truck) furgoneta f de reparto

wail /weɪl/ vi llorar

waist /weɪst/ n cintura f. **~coat** n chaleco m. **~line** n cintura f

wait /weɪt/ vi esperar; (at table) servir. **~ for** esperar. **~ on s.o.** atender a uno. ● vt (await) esperar (chance, turn). **~ table** (Amer) servir a la mesa. **I can't ~** me muero de ganas de verlo. ● n espera f. **lie in ~** acechar

waiter /ˈweɪtə(r)/ n camarero m, mesero m (LAm)

wait: ~ing-list n lista f de espera. **~ing-room** n sala f de espera

waitress /ˈweɪtrɪs/ n camarera f,

mesera f (LAm)

waive /weɪv/ vt renunciar a

wake /weɪk/ vt (pt woke, pp woken) despertar. • vi despertarse. • n (Naut) estela f. **in the ~ of** como resultado de. □ ~ **up** vt despertar. vi despertarse

Wales /weɪlz/ n (el país de) Gales

walk /wɔːk/ vi andar, caminar; (not ride) ir a pie; (stroll) pasear. • vt andar or (streets); llevar de paseo (dog). • n paseo m; (long) caminata f; (gait) manera f de andar. □ ~ **out** vi salir; (workers) declararse en huelga. □ ~ **out on** vt abandonar. **~er** n excursionista m & f

walkie-talkie /wɔːkɪˈtɔːkɪ/ n walkie-talkie m

walk: ~ing-stick n bastón m. **W~man** /-mən/ n Walkman m (P). **~-out** n retirada en señal de protesta; (strike) abandono m del trabajo

wall /wɔːl/ n (interior) pared f; (exterior) muro m

Wall Street Una calle en Manhattan, Nueva York, donde se encuentran la Bolsa neoyorquina y las sedes de muchas instituciones financieras. Cuando se habla de Wall Street, a menudo se está refiriendo a esas instituciones.

wallet /ˈwɒlɪt/ n cartera f, billetera f

wallop /ˈwɒləp/ vt (pt walloped) 🔲 darle un golpazo a.

wallow /ˈwɒləʊ/ vi revolcarse

wallpaper /ˈwɔːlpeɪpə(r)/ n papel m pintado

walnut /ˈwɔːlnʌt/ n nuez f; (tree) nogal m

walrus /ˈwɔːlrəs/ n morsa f

waltz /wɔːls/ n vals m. • vi valsar

wand /wɒnd/ n varita f (mágica)

wander /ˈwɒndə(r)/ vi vagar; (stroll) pasear; (digress) divagar. • n vuelta f, paseo m. **~er** n trotamundos m

wane /weɪn/ vi (moon) menguar; (interest) decaer. • n. **be on the ~** (popularity) estar decayendo

wangle /ˈwæŋɡl/ vt 🔲 agenciarse

want /wɒnt/ vt querer; (need) necesitar. • vi. **for carecer de.** • n necesidad f; (lack) falta f. **~ed** adj (criminal) buscado

war /wɔː(r)/ n guerra f. **at ~** en guerra

warble /ˈwɔːbl/ vi trinar, gorjear

ward /wɔːd/ n (in hospital) sala f; (child) pupilo m. □ ~ **off** vt conjurar (danger); rechazar (attack)

warden /ˈwɔːdn/ n guarda m

warder /ˈwɔːdə(r)/ n celador m (de una cárcel)

wardrobe /ˈwɔːdrəʊb/ n armario m; (clothes) guardarropa f, vestuario m

warehouse /ˈweəhaʊs/ n depósito m, almacén m

wares /weəz/ npl mercancía(s) f(pl)

war: ~fare n guerra f. **~head** n cabeza f, ojiva f

warm /wɔːm/ adj (-er, -est) (water, day) tibio, templado; (room) caliente; (climate, wind) cálido; (clothes) de abrigo; (welcome) caluroso. **be ~** (person) tener calor. **it's ~ today** hoy hace calor. • vt. □ ~ **(up)** calentar (room); recalentar (food); (fig) animar. • vi. □ ~ **(up)** calentarse; (fig) animarse. **~-blooded** /-ˈblʌdɪd/ adj de sangre caliente. **~ly** adv (heartily) ca-

warn | wave

lurosamente. ~th n calor m; (of colour, atmosphere) calidez f

warn /wɔːn/ vt advertir. ~ing n advertencia f; (notice) aviso m

warp /wɔːp/ vt alabear; ~ed /'wɔːpt/ adj (wood) alabeado; (mind) retorcido

warrant /'wɒrənt/ n orden f judicial; (search ~) orden f de registro; (for arrest) orden f de arresto. ● vt justificar. ~y n garantía f

warrior /'wɒrɪə(r)/ n guerrero m

warship /'wɔːʃɪp/ n buque m de guerra

wart /wɔːt/ n verruga f

wartime /'wɔːtaɪm/ n tiempo m de guerra

wary /'weərɪ/ adj (-ier, -iest) cauteloso. be ~ of recelar de

was /wəz, wɒz/ see BE

wash /wɒʃ/ vt lavar; fregar, lavar (LAm) (floor). ~ one's face lavarse la cara. ● vi lavarse. ● n (in washing machine) lavado m. have a ~ lavarse. I gave the car a ~ lavé el coche. □ ~ out vt (clean) lavar; (rinse) enjuagar. □ ~ up vi fregar los platos, lavar los trastes (Mex); (Amer, wash face and hands) lavarse. ~able adj lavable. ~basin, ~bowl (Amer) n lavabo m. ~er n arandela f. ~ing n lavado m; (dirty clothes) ropa f para lavar; (wet clothes) ropa f lavada. do the ~ing lavar la ropa, hacer la colada. ~ing-machine n máquina f de lavar, lavadora f. ~ing-powder n jabón m en polvo. ~ing-up n do the ~ing-up lavar los platos, fregar (los platos). ~ing-up liquid n lavavajillas m. ~out n 🄴 desastre m. ~room n (Amer) baños mpl, servicios mpl

wasp /wɒsp/ n avispa f

waste /weɪst/ ● adj (matter) de desecho; (land) (barren) yermo; (uncultivated) baldío. ● n (of materials) desperdicio m; (of time) pérdida f; (refuse) residuos mpl. ● vt despilfarrar (electricity, money); desperdiciar (talent, effort); perder (time). ● vi. ~disposal unit n trituradora f de desperdicios. ~ful adj poco económico; (person) despilfarrador. ~-paper basket n papelera f

watch /wɒtʃ/ vt mirar; observar (person, expression); ver (TV); (keep an eye on) vigilar; (take heed) tener cuidado con. ● vi mirar. ● n (observation) vigilancia f; (period of duty) guardia f; (timepiece) reloj m. ~ out vi (be careful) tener cuidado; (look carefully) estarse atento. ~dog n perro m guardián. ~man /-mən/ n (pl -men) vigilante m.

water /'wɔːtə(r)/ n agua f. ● vt regar (plants etc). ● vi (eyes) llorar. make s.o.'s mouth ~ hacérsele la boca agua, hacérsele agua la boca (LAm). □ ~ down vt diluir; aguar (wine). ~-colour n acuarela f. ~cress n berro m. ~fall n cascada f; (large) catarata f. ~ing-can n regadera f. ~ lily n nenúfar m. ~logged /-lɒgd/ adj anegado; (shoes) empapado. ~proof adj impermeable; (watch) sumergible. ~-skiing n esquí m acuático. ~tight adj hermético; (boat) estanco; (argument) irrebatible. ~way n canal m navegable. ~y adj acuoso; (eyes) lloroso

watt /wɒt/ n vatio m

wave /weɪv/ n ola f; (of hand) señal f; (fig) oleada f. ● vt agitar; (curl) ondular (hair). ● vi (signal) hacer señales con la mano; ondear (flag). ~band n banda f de fre-

w

cuencia. ~**length** n longitud f de onda

waver /'weɪvə(r)/ vi (be indecisive) vacilar; (falter) flaquear

wavy /'weɪvɪ/ adj (-ier, -iest) ondulado

wax /wæks/ n cera f. ●vi (moon) crecer. ~**work** n figura f de cera. ~**works** npl museo m de cera

way /weɪ/ n (route) camino m; (manner) manera f, forma f, modo m; (direction) dirección f; (habit) costumbre f. it's a long ~ from here queda muy lejos de aquí. be in the ~ estorbar. by the ~ a propósito. either ~ de cualquier manera. give ~ (collapse) ceder, romperse; (Auto) ceder el paso. in a ~ en cierta manera. in some ~s en ciertos modos. make ~ dejar paso a. no ~! ¡ni hablar! on my ~ to de camino a. out of the ~ remoto; (extraordinary) fuera de lo común. that ~ por allí. this ~ por aquí. ~ in entrada f. ~**lay** /weɪ'leɪ/ vt (pt -laid) abordar. ~ **out** n salida f. ~**out** adj ultramoderno, original. ~s npl costumbres fpl

we /wiː/ pron nosotros m, nosotras f

weak /wiːk/ adj (-er, -est) débil; (structure) poco sólido; (performance, student) flojo; (coffee) poco cargado; (solution) diluido; (beer) suave; (pej) aguado. ~**en** vt debilitar. ●vi (resolve) flaquear. ~**ling** n alfeñique m. ~**ness** n debilidad f

wealth /welθ/ n riqueza f. ~**y** adj (-ier, -iest) rico

weapon /'wepən/ n arma f. ~**s of mass destruction** armas de destrucción masiva

wear /weə(r)/ vt (pt wore, pp worn) llevar; vestirse de (black, red, etc); (usually) usar. I've got

nothing to ~ no tengo nada que ponerme. ●vi (through use) gastarse; (last) durar. ●n uso m; (damage) desgaste m; ~ and tear desgaste m natural. □ ~ **out** vt gastar; (tire) agotar. vi gastarse

weary /'wɪərɪ/ adj (-ier, -iest) cansado. ●vt cansar. ●vi cansarse. ~ **of** cansarse de

weather /'weðə(r)/ n tiempo m. what's the ~ like? ¿qué tiempo hace? the ~ was bad hizo mal tiempo. be under the ~ □ no andar muy bien □. ●vt (survive) sobrellevar. ~**-beaten** adj curtido. ~ **forecast** n pronóstico m del tiempo. ~**-vane** n veleta f

weave /wiːv/ vt (pt wove, pp woven) tejer; entretejer (threads). ~ one's way abrirse paso. ●vi (person) zigzaguear; (road) serpentear. ~ r n tejedor m

web /web/ n (of spider) telaraña f; (of intrigue) enredo m. ~ **page** n página web. ~ **site** n sitio web m

wed /wed/ vt (pt wedded) casarse con. ●vi casarse.

we'd /wiːd//wɪəd/ = **we had**, **we would**

wedding /'wedɪŋ/ n boda f, casamiento m. ~**-cake** n pastel m de boda. ~**-ring** n anillo m de boda

wedge /wedʒ/ n cuña f

Wednesday /'wenzdeɪ/ n miércoles m

wee /wiː/ adj □ pequeñito. ●n. have a ~ □ hacer pis □

weed /wiːd/ n mala hierba f. ●vt desherbar. □ ~ **out** vt eliminar. ~**killer** n herbicida m. ~**y** adj (person) enclenque; (Amer, lanky) larguirucho □

week /wiːk/ n semana f. ~**day** n día m de semana. ~**end** n fin m de semana. ~**ly** adj semanal. ●n semanario m. ● adv semanalmente

weep /wiːp/ vi (pt **wept**) llorar

weigh /weɪ/ vt/i pesar. □ **~ anchor** levar anclas. □ **~ down** vt (fig) oprimir. □ **~ up** vt pesar; (fig) considerar

weight /weɪt/ n peso m; (sport) pesa f. **put on ~** engordar. **lose ~** adelgazar. **~-lifting** n halterofilia f, levantamiento m de pesos

weir /wɪə(r)/ n presa f.

weird /wɪəd/ adj (-er, -est) raro, extraño; (unearthly) misterioso

welcome /ˈwelkəm/ adj bienvenido. **you're ~!** (after thank you) ¡de nada! ● n bienvenida f; (reception) acogida f. ● vt dar la bienvenida a; (appreciate) alegrarse de. **~ing** adj acogedor

weld /weld/ vt soldar. ● n soldadura f. **~er** n soldador m

welfare /ˈwelfeə(r)/ n bienestar m; (aid) asistencia f social. **W~ State** n estado m benefactor

well /wel/ adv (better, best) bien. **~ done!** ¡muy bien!, ¡bravo! as ~ también. as **~ as** además de. **we may as ~ go** tomorrow más vale que vayamos mañana. **do ~** (succeed) tener éxito. **very ~** muy bien. ● adj bien. **I'm very ~** estoy muy bien. ● int (introducing, continuing sentence) bueno; (surprise) ¡vaya!; (indignation, resignation) bueno. **~ I never!** ¡no me digas! ● n pozo m

we'll /wiːl/wɪəl/ = **we will**

well: ~-behaved /-bɪˈheɪvd/ adj que se porta bien. **~-educated** /-ˈedjʊkeɪtɪd/ adj culto.

wellington (boot) /ˈwelɪŋtən/ n bota f de goma or de agua; (Amer, short boot) botín m

well: ~-known /-ˈnəʊn/ adj conocido. **~ off** adj adinerado. **~-stocked** /-ˈstɒkt/ adj bien provisto. **~-to-do** /-təˈduː/ adj adinerado

Welsh /welʃ/ adj & n galés (m). **the ~** los galeses

went /went/ see **GO**

wept /wept/ see **WEEP**

were /wɜː(r), wə(r)/ see **BE**

we're /wɪə(r)/ = **we are**

west /west/ n oeste m. **the W~** el Occidente m. ● adj oeste; (wind) del oeste. ● adv (go) hacia el oeste, al oeste. **it's ~** of York está al oeste de York. **~erly** /-əlɪ/ adj (wind) del oeste. **~ern** /-ən/ adj occidental. ● n (film) película f del Oeste. **~erner** n occidental m & f. **W~ Indian** adj & n antillano (m). **W~ Indies** npl Antillas fpl. **~ward(s)** /-wəd(z)/

wet /wet/ adj (wetter, wettest) mojado; (rainy) lluvioso; (fam, person) soso. **~ paint** 'pintura fresca'. **get ~** mojarse. **he got his feet ~** se mojó los pies. ● vt (pt wetted) mojar; (dampen) humedecer. **~ o.s.** orinarse. **~-back** n espalda f mojada. **~ blanket** n aguafiestas m & f. **~ suit** n traje m de neopreno

w

we've /wiːv/ = we have

whack /wæk/ vt 🔊 golpear. ●n 🔊 golpe m.

whale /weɪl/ n ballena f. we had a ~ of a time 🔊 lo pasamos bomba 🔊

wham /wæm/ int ¡zas!

wharf /wɔːf/ n (pl wharves or wharfs) muelle m

what /wɒt/

● adjective

····▶ (in questions) qué. ~ perfume are you wearing? ¿qué perfume llevas?. ~ colour are the walls? ¿de qué color son las paredes?

····▶ (in exclamations) qué. ~ a beautiful house! ¡qué casa más linda!. ~ a lot of people! ¡cuánta gente!

····▶ (in indirect speech) qué. I'll ask him ~ bus to take le preguntaré qué autobús hay que tomar. do you know ~ time it leaves? ¿sabes a qué hora sale?

● pronoun

····▶ (in questions) qué. ~ is it? ¿qué es? ~ for? ¿para qué? ~'s the problem? ¿cuál es el problema? ~'s he like? ¿cómo es? what? (say that again) ¿cómo?, ¿qué?

····▶ (in indirect questions) qué. I didn't know ~ to do no sabía qué hacer

····▶ (relative) lo que. I did ~ I could hice lo que pude. ~ I need is a new car lo que necesito es un coche nuevo

····▶ (in phrases) ~ about me? ¿y yo qué? ~ if he doesn't come? ¿y si no viene?

whatever /wɒtˈevə(r)/ adj cualquiera. ●pron (todo) lo que, cualquier cosa que

whatsoever /wɒtsəʊˈevə(r)/ adj & pron = whatever

wheat /wiːt/ n trigo m

wheel /wiːl/ n rueda f. at the ~ al volante. ●vt empujar (bicycle etc); llevar (en silla de ruedas etc) (person). ~barrow n carretilla f. ~chair n silla f de ruedas

wheeze /wiːz/ vi respirar con dificultad

when /wen/ adv cuándo. ●conj cuando. ●ever /-'evə(r)/ adv (every time that) cada vez que, siempre que; (at whatever time) we'll go ~ever you're ready saldremos cuando estés listo

where /weə(r)/ adv & conj donde; (interrogative) dónde. ~ are you going? ¿adónde vas? ~ are you from? ¿de dónde eres? ~abouts /-əbaʊts/ adv en qué parte. ●n paradero m. ~as /-'æz/ conj por cuanto; (in contrast) mientras (que). ~ver /weər'evə(r)/ adv (in questions) dónde; (no matter where) en cualquier parte. ●conj donde (+ subjunctive), dondequiera (+ subjunctive)

whet /wet/ vt (pt whetted) abrir (appetite)

whether /'weðə(r)/ conj si. I don't know ~ she will like it no sé si le gustará. ~ you like it or not te guste o no te guste

which /wɪtʃ/ adj (in questions) (sing) qué, cuál; (pl) qué, cuáles. ~ one cuál. ~ one of you cuál de ustedes. ●pron (in questions) (sing) cuál; (pl) cuáles; (relative) que; (object) el cual, la cual, lo cual, los cuales, las cuales. ~ever /-'evə(r)

while | wicker

adj cualquier. ● *pron* cualquiera que, el que, la que; (*in questions*) cuál; (*pl*) cuáles

while /waɪl/ *n* rato m. a ~ **ago** hace un rato. ● *conj* mientras; (*although*) aunque. □ ~ **away** *vt* pasar (time)

whilst /waɪlst/ *conj* see **WHILE**

whim /wɪm/ *n* capricho m

whimper /ˈwɪmpə(r)/ *vi* gimotear. ● *n* quejido m

whine /waɪn/ *vi* (person) gemir; (child) lloriquear; (dog) aullar

whip /wɪp/ *n* látigo m; (for punishment) azote m. ● *vt* (pt **whipped** /wɪpt/) fustigar, pegarle a (con la fusta) (horse); azotar (person); (Culin) batir

whirl /wɜːl/ *vi* girar rápidamente. ~**pool** *n* remolino m. ~**wind** *n* torbellino m

whirr /wɜː(r)/ *n* zumbido m. ● *vi* zumbar

whisk /wɪsk/ *vt* (Culin) batir. ● *n* (Culin) batidor m. ~ **away** llevarse

whisker /ˈwɪskə(r)/ *n* pelo m. ~**s** *npl* (of cat etc) bigotes mpl

whisky /ˈwɪskɪ/ *n* whisky m, güisqui m

whisper /ˈwɪspə(r)/ *vt* susurrar. ● *vi* cuchichear. ● *n* susurro m

whistle /ˈwɪsl/ *n* silbido m; (loud) chiflado m; (instrument) silbato m, pito m. ● *vi* silbar; (loudly) chiflar

white /waɪt/ *adj* (-er, -est) blanco. go ~ ponerse pálido. in blanco; (of egg) clara f. ~ **coffee** *n* café m con leche. ~-**collar worker** *n* empleado m de oficina. ~ **elephant** *n* objeto m inútil y costoso. ~-**hot** *adj* (metal) al rojo blanco. ~ **lie** *n* mentirijilla f. ~**n** *vt/i* blanquear. ~**wash** *n* cal f; (cover-up) tapadera

f ⬚. ● *vt* blanquear, encalar

Whitsun /ˈwɪtsn/ *n* Pentecostés *m*

whiz /wɪz/ *vi* (pt **whizzed**) ~ **by**, ~ **past** pasar zumbando. ~-**kid** *n* ⬚ lince m

who /huː/ *pron* (in questions) quién; (*pl*) quiénes; (as relative) que; the girl ~ **lives** there la chica que vive allí. those ~ **can't** come tomorrow los que no puedan venir mañana. ~**ever** /huːˈevə(r)/ *pron* quienquiera que; (interrogative) quién

whole /həʊl/ adj. the ~ **country** todo el país. there's a ~ **bottle** left queda una botella entera. in todo m, conjunto m; (total) total m. on the ~ en general. ~-**hearted** /-ˈhɑːtɪd/ adj (support) incondicional; (approval) sin reservar. ~**meal** adj integral. ~**sale** *n* venta f al por mayor. ● adj & adv al por mayor. ~**some** /-səm/ adj sano

wholly /ˈhəʊlɪ/ adv completamente

whom /huːm/ *pron* que, a quien; (in questions) a quién

whooping cough /ˈhuːpɪŋ/ *n* tos f convulsa

whore /hɔː(r)/ *n* puta f

whose /huːz/ *pron* de quién; (pl) de quiénes; (in questions) de quién; (pl) de quiénes; (relative) cuyo; (pl) cuyos

why /waɪ/ *adv* por qué. ~ **not**? ¿por qué no? that's ~ I couldn't go por eso no fue. ● *int* ¡vaya!

wick /wɪk/ *n* mecha f

wicked /ˈwɪkɪd/ *adj* malo; (mischievous) travieso m; (fam, very bad) malísimo

wicker /ˈwɪkə(r)/ *n* mimbre m & f. ● adj de mimbre. ~**work** *n* artículos *mpl* de mimbre

wicket /ˈwɪkɪt/ *n* (*cricket*) rastri-
llo *m*

wide /waɪd/ *adj* (-er, -est) ancho;
(*range, experience*) amplio; (*off
target*) desviado. it's four metres
~ tiene cuatro metros de ancho.
● *adv.* open ~ abra bien la boca.
~ **awake** *adj* completamente des-
pierto; (*fig*) despabilado. I left the
door ~ open dejé la puerta
abierta de par en par. ~**ly** *adv* ex-
tensamente; (*believed*) general-
mente; (*different*) muy. ~**n** *vt* en-
sanchar. ● *vi* ensancharse.
~**spread** *adj* extendido; (*fig*) difun-
dido

widow /ˈwɪdəʊ/ *n* viuda *f*. ~**er** *n*
viudo *m*.

width /wɪdθ/ *n* anchura *f*. in ~ de
ancho

wield /wiːld/ *vt* manejar; ejercer
(*power*)

wife /waɪf/ *n* (*pl* wives) mujer *f*,
esposa *f*

wig /wɪg/ *n* peluca *f*

wiggle /ˈwɪgl/ *vt* menear. ● *vi* me-
nearse

wild /waɪld/ *adj* (-er, -est) (*animal*)
salvaje; (*flower*) silvestre; (*country*)
agreste; (*enraged*) furioso; (*idea*)
extravagante; (*with joy*) loco. a ~
guess una conjetura hecha total-
mente al azar. I'm not ~ about
the idea la idea no me enloquece.
● *adv* en estado salvaje. run ~
(*children*) criarse como salvajes.
~**s** *npl* regiones *fpl* salvajes.
~**erness** /ˈwɪldənɪs/ *n* páramo *m*.
~**fire** *n*. spread like ~**fire** correr
como un reguero de pólvora.
~**-goose chase** *n* empresa *f* inútil.
~**life** *n* fauna *f*. ~**ly** *adv* violenta-
mente; (*fig*) locamente

will /wɪl/
● *auxiliary verb*

past **would**; contracted forms
I'll, you'll, etc = I will, you
will, etc.; **won't** = will not

····▶ (*talking about the future*)

❗ The Spanish future tense is
not always the first option
for translating the English fu-
ture tense. The present tense of
ir + a + verb is commonly
used instead, particularly in
Latin American countries. **he'll
be here on Tuesday** estará el
martes, va a estar el martes;
she won't agree no va a
aceptar, no aceptará

····▶ (*in invitations and requests*)
~ **you have some wine?**
¿quieres (un poco de) vino?
**you'll stay for dinner, won't
you?** te quedas a cenar, ¿no?

····▶ (*in tag questions*) **you** ~ **be
back soon, won't you?** vas a
volver pronto, ¿no?

····▶ (*in short answers*) **will it be
ready by Monday?** - yes, it
~ ¿estará listo para el lunes? -
sí

● *noun*

····▶ (*mental power*) voluntad *f*

····▶ (*document*) testamento *m*

willing /ˈwɪlɪŋ/ *adj* complaciente.
~ **to** dispuesto a. ~**ly** *adv* de
buena gana

willow /ˈwɪləʊ/ *n* sauce *m*

will-power /ˈwɪlpaʊə(r)/ *n*
fuerza *f* de voluntad

wilt /wɪlt/ *vi* marchitarse

win /wɪn/ vt (pt **won**, pres p **winning**) ganar; (achieve, obtain) conseguir. • vi ganar. • n victoria f. □ **~ over** vt ganarse a

wince /wɪns/ vi hacer una mueca de dolor

winch /wɪntʃ/ n cabrestante m. • vt levantar con un cabrestante

wind¹ /wɪnd/ n viento m; (in stomach) gases mpl. **~ instrument** n instrumento m de viento. • vt dejar sin aliento

wind² /waɪnd/ vt (pt **wound**) (wrap around) enrollar; dar cuerda a (clock etc). • vi (road etc) serpentear. □ **~ up** vt dar cuerda a (watch, clock); (fig) terminar, concluir

winding /ˈwaɪndɪŋ/ adj tortuoso

windmill /ˈwɪndmɪl/ n molino m (de viento)

window /ˈwɪndəʊ/ n ventana f; (in shop) escaparate m, vitrina f (LAm), vidriera f (LAm), aparador m (Mex); (of vehicle, booking-office) ventanilla f; (Comp) ventana f, window m. **~ box** n jardinera f. **~shop** vi mirar los escaparates. **~sill** n alféizar m o repisa f de la ventana

wine /waɪn/ n vino m. **~cellar** n bodega f. **~glass** n copa f de vino. **~growing** n vinicultura f. • adj vinícola. **~ list** n lista f de vinos. **~tasting** n cata f de vinos

wing /wɪŋ/ n ala f; (Auto) aleta f. **under one's ~** bajo la protección de uno. **~er** n (Sport) ala m & f. **~s** npl (in theatre) bastidores mpl

wink /wɪŋk/ vi guiñar el ojo; (light etc) centellear. • n guiño m. **not to sleep a ~** no pegar ojo

win: **~ner** n ganador m. **~ning-post** n poste m de llegada. **~nings** npl ganancias fpl

wint|er /ˈwɪntə(r)/ n invierno m. • vi invernar. **~ry** adj invernal

wipe /waɪp/ vt limpiar, pasarle un trapo a; (dry) secar. **~ one's nose** limpiarse la nariz. • n. **give sth a ~** limpiar algo, pasarle un trapo a algo. □ **~ out** vt (cancel) cancelar; (destroy) destruir; (obliterate) borrar. □ **~ up** vt limpiar

wir|e /ˈwaɪə(r)/ n alambre m; (Elec) cable m. **~ing** n instalación f eléctrica

wisdom /ˈwɪzdəm/ n sabiduría f. **~ tooth** n muela f del juicio

wise /waɪz/ adj (-er, -est) sabio; (sensible) prudente; (decision, choice) acertado. **~ly** adv sabiamente; (sensibly) prudentemente

wish /wɪʃ/ n deseo m; (greeting) saludo m. **make a ~** pedir un deseo. **best ~es, John** (in letters) saludos de John, un abrazo de John. • vt desear. **~ s.o. well** desear buena suerte a uno. **I ~ I were rich** ¡ojalá fuera rico! **he ~ed he hadn't told her** lamentó habérselo dicho. **~ful thinking** n ilusiones fpl

wistful /ˈwɪstfl/ adj melancólico

wit /wɪt/ n gracia f; (intelligence) ingenio m. **be at one's ~s' end** no saber más qué hacer

witch /wɪtʃ/ n bruja f. **~craft** n brujería f.

with /wɪð/ prep con; (cause, having) de. **come ~ me** ven conmigo. **take it ~ you** llévalo contigo; (formal) llévelo consigo. **the man ~ the beard** el hombre de la barba. **trembling ~ fear** temblando de miedo

withdraw /wɪðˈdrɔː/ vt (pt withdrew, pp withdrawn) retirar. • vi apartarse. **~al** n retirada f. **~n** adj (person) retraído

wither /ˈwɪðə(r)/ vi marchitarse

withhold /wɪðˈhəʊld/ vt (pt withheld) retener; (conceal) ocultar (from a)

within /wɪðˈɪn/ prep dentro de. ● adv dentro. **~ sight** a la vista

without /wɪðˈaʊt/ prep sin. **~ paying** sin pagar

withstand /wɪðˈstænd/ vt (pt -stood) resistir

witness /ˈwɪtnɪs/ n testigo m; (proof) testimonio m. ● vt presenciar; atestiguar (signature). **~-box** n tribuna f de los testigos

witt|icism /ˈwɪtɪsɪzəm/ n ocurrencia f. **~y** /ˈwɪtɪ/ adj (-ier, -iest) gracioso

wives /waɪvz/ see **WIFE**

wizard /ˈwɪzəd/ n hechicero m

wizened /ˈwɪznd/ adj arrugado

wobbl|e /ˈwɒbl/ vi (chair) tambalearse; (bicycle) bambolearse; (voice, jelly, hand) temblar. **~y** adj (chair etc) cojo

woe /wəʊ/ n aflicción f

woke/wəʊk/, **woken** /ˈwəʊkən/ see **WAKE**

wolf /wʊlf/ n (pl **wolves** /wʊlvz/) lobo m

woman /ˈwʊmən/ n (pl **women**) mujer f

womb /wuːm/ n matriz f

women /ˈwɪmɪn/ npl see **WOMAN**

won /wʌn/ see **WIN**

wonder /ˈwʌndə(r)/ n maravilla f; (bewilderment) asombro m. no **~** no es de extrañarse (that que). ● vt (ask oneself) preguntarse. I **~ whose book this is** me pregunto de quién será este libro; (in polite requests) I **~ if you could help** me? ¿me podría ayudar? **~ful** adj maravilloso. **~fully** adv maravillosamente

won't /wəʊnt/ = **will not**

wood /wʊd/ n madera f; (for burning) leña f; (area) bosque m. **~ed** adj poblado de árboles, boscoso. **~en** adj de madera. **~land** n bosque m. **~wind** /-wɪnd/ n instrumentos mpl de viento de madera. **~work** n carpintería f; (in room etc) maderaje m. **~worm** n carcoma f. **~y** adj leñoso

wool /wʊl/ n lana f. **pull the ~ over s.o.'s eyes** engañar a uno. **~len** adj de lana. **~ly** adj (-ier, -iest) de lana; (unclear) vago. ● n jersey m

word /wɜːd/ n palabra f; (news) noticia f. **by ~ of mouth** de palabra. **I didn't say a ~** yo no dije nada. **in other ~s** es decir. ● vt expresar. **~ing** n redacción f; (of question) formulación f. **~ processor** n procesador m de textos. **~y** adj prolijo

wore /wɔː(r)/ see **WEAR**

work /wɜːk/ n trabajo m; (arts) obra f. **be out of ~** estar sin trabajo, estar desocupado. ● vt hacer trabajar; manejar (machine). ● vi trabajar; (machine) funcionar; (student) estudiar; (drug etc) surtir efecto. □ **~ off** vt desahogar. □ **~ out** vt resolver (problem); (calculate) calcular; (understand) entender. ● vi (succeed) salir bien; (Sport) entrenarse. □ **~ up** vt. **get ~ed up** exaltarse. **~able** adj (project, solution) factible. **~er** n trabajador m; (manual) obrero m; (in office, bank) empleado m. **~ing** adj (day) laborable; (clothes etc) de trabajo. **in ~ing order** en estado de funcionamiento. **~ing class** n clase f obrera. ~**ing-class** adj de la clase obrera. ~**man** /-mæn/ n (pl -men) obrero m. ~**manship** n destreza f. ~**s** npl (building) fábrica f. (Mec) mecanismo m. ~**shop** n taller m

world /wɜːld/ n mundo m. out of this ~ maravilloso. ● adj mundial. **W~ Cup** n. the **W~ Cup** la Copa del Mundo. ~**ly** adj mundano. ~**wide** adj universal. **W~ Wide Web** n World Wide Web m

worm /wɜːm/ n gusano m, lombriz f

worn /wɔːn/ see WEAR. ● adj gastado. ~**out** adj gastado; (person) rendido

worr|ied /ˈwʌrɪd/ adj preocupado. ~**y** /ˈwʌrɪ/ vt preocupar; (annoy) molestar. ● vi preocuparse. ● n preocupación f. ~**ying** adj inquietante

worse /wɜːs/ adj peor. get ~ empeorar. ● adv peor; (more) más. ~**n** vt/i empeorar

worship /ˈwɜːʃɪp/ n culto m; (title) Su Señoría. ● vt (pt worshipped) adorar

worst /wɜːst/ adj peor. he's the ~ in the class es el peor de la clase. ● adv peor. ● n. the ~ lo peor

worth /wɜːθ/ n valor m. ● adj. be ~ valer. it's ~ trying vale la pena probarlo. it was ~ my while (me) valió la pena. ~**less** adj sin valor. ~**while** /-ˈwaɪl/ adj que vale la pena. ~**y** /ˈwɜːðɪ/ adj meritorio; (respectable) respetable; (laudable) loable

would /wʊd/ modal verb. (in conditional sentences) ~ you go? ¿irías tú? he ~ come if he could vendría si pudiera; (in reported speech) I thought you'd forget pensé que te olvidarías; (in requests, invita-

tions) ~ you come here, please? ¿quieres venir aquí? ~ you switch the television off? ¿podrías apagar la televisión?; (be prepared to) he ~n't listen to me no me quería escuchar

wound[1] /wuːnd/ n herida f. ● vt herir

wound[2] /waʊnd/ see WIND[2]

wove, woven /wəʊv, ˈwəʊvn/ see WEAVE

wow /waʊ/ int ¡ah!

wrangle /ˈræŋgl/ vi reñir. ● n riña f

wrap /ræp/ vt (pt wrapped) envolver. ~ **per** n, ~**ping** envoltura f

wrath /rɒθ/ n ira f

wreak /riːk/ vt sembrar. ~ havoc causar estragos

wreath /riːθ/ n (pl -ths /-ðz/) corona f

wreck /rek/ n (ship) restos mpl de un naufragio; (vehicle) restos mpl de un avión siniestrado. be a nervous ~ tener los nervios destrozados. ● vt provocar el naufragio de (ship); destrozar (car); (Amer, demolish) demoler; (fig) destrozar. ~**age** /-ɪdʒ/ n restos mpl; (of building) ruinas fpl

wrench /rentʃ/ vt arrancar; (sprain) desgarrarse; dislocarse (joint). ● n tirón m; (emotional) dolor m (causado por una separación); (tool) llave f inglesa

wrestl|e /ˈresl/ vi luchar. ~**er** n luchador m. ~**ing** n lucha f

wretch /retʃ/ n (despicable person) desgraciado m; (unfortunate person) desdichado m & f. ~**ed** /-ɪd/ adj desdichado; (weather) horrible

wriggle /ˈrɪgl/ vi retorcerse. ~

out of escaparse de

wring /rɪŋ/ vt (pt **wrung**) retorcer (neck). ~ **out of** (obtain from) arrancar. □ ~ **out** vt retorcer

wrinkl|e /'rɪŋkl/ n arruga f. ● vt arrugar. ● vi arrugarse. ~y adj arrugado

wrist /rɪst/ n muñeca f. ~**watch** n reloj m de pulsera

writ /rɪt/ n orden m judicial

write /raɪt/ vt/i (pt **wrote**, pp **written**, pres p **writing**) escribir. □ ~ **down** vt anotar. □ ~ **off** vt cancelar (debt). ~**off** n. the car was a ~**off** el coche fue declarado un siniestro total. ~**r** n escritor m

writhe /raɪð/ vi retorcerse

writing /'raɪtɪŋ/ n (script) escritura f; (handwriting) letra f. in ~ por escrito. ~**s** npl obra f, escritos mpl. ~ **desk** n escritorio m. ~ **pad** n bloc m. ~ **paper** n papel m de escribir

written /'rɪtn/ see WRITE

wrong /rɒŋ/ adj equivocado, incorrecto; (not just) injusto; (mistaken) equivocado. be ~ no tener razón; (be mistaken) equivocarse. what's ~? ¿qué pasa? it's ~ to steal robar está mal. what's ~ with that? ¿qué hay de malo en eso?. ● adv mal. go ~ equivocarse; (plan) salir mal. ● n injusticia f; (evil) mal m. in the ~ equivocado. ● vt ser injusto con. ~**ful** adj injusto. ~**ly** adv mal; (unfairly) injustamente

wrote /rəʊt/ see WRITE

wrought iron /rɔːt/ n hierro m forjado

wrung /rʌŋ/ see WRING

wry /raɪ/ adj (wryer, wryest) irónico. make a ~ face torcer el gesto

Xx

xerox /'zɪərɒks/ vt fotocopiar, xerografiar

Xmas /'krɪsməs/ n abbr (**Christmas**) Navidad f

X-ray /'eksreɪ/ n (ray) rayo m X; (photograph) radiografía f. ~**s** npl rayos mpl. ● vt hacer una radiografía de

xylophone /'zaɪləfəʊn/ n xilófon m, xilófono m

Yy

yacht /jɒt/ n yate m. ~**ing** n navegación f a vela

yank /jæŋk/ vt 🔢 tirar de (violentamente)

Yankee /'jæŋkɪ/ n 🔢 yanqui m & f

yap /jæp/ vi (pt yapped) (dog) ladrar (con ladridos agudos)

yard /jɑːd/ n patio m; (Amer, garden) jardín m; (measurement) yarda f (= 0.9144 metre)

yarn /jɑːn/ n hilo m; (fam, tale) cuento m

yawn /jɔːn/ vi bostezar. ● n bostezo m

yeah /jeə/ adv 🔢 sí

year /jɪə(r)/ n año m. be three ~s old tener tres años. ~**ly** adj anual. ● adv cada año

yearn /'jɜːn/ vi. ~ **to do sth** anhelar hacer algo. ~ **for sth** añorar algo. **~ing** n anhelo m, ansia f

yeast /jiːst/ n levadura f

yell /jel/ vi gritar. ● n grito m

yellow /ˈjeləʊ/ adj & n amarillo (m)

yelp /jelp/ n gañido m. ● vi gañir

yes /jes/ int & n sí (m)

yesterday /ˈjestədeɪ/ adv & n ayer (m). **the day before ~** anteayer m. **~ morning** ayer por la mañana, ayer en la mañana (LAm)

yet /jet/ adv todavía, aún; (already) ya. **as ~** hasta ahora; (as a linker) sin embargo. ● conj pero

Yiddish /ˈjɪdɪʃ/ n yidish m

yield /jiːld/ vt (surrender) ceder; producir (crop/mineral); dar (results). ● vi ceder. **'yield'** (Amer, traffic sign) ceda el paso. ● n rendimiento m

yoga /ˈjəʊɡə/ n yoga m

yoghurt /ˈjɒɡət/ n yogur m

yoke /jəʊk/ n (fig also) yugo m

yokel /ˈjəʊkl/ n palurdo m

yolk /jəʊk/ n yema f (de huevo)

you /juː/ pronoun

····▸ (as the subject) (familiar form) (sing) tú, vos (River Plate and parts of Central America); (pl) vosotros, -tras (Spain), ustedes (LAm); (formal) (sing) usted; (pl) ustedes

❗ In Spanish the subject pronoun is usually only used to give emphasis or mark contrast.

····▸ (as the direct object) (familiar form) (sing) te; (pl) os (Spain), los, las (LAm); (formal) (sing) lo or (Spain) le, la; (pl) los or (Spain) les, las. **I love ~** te quiero

····▸ (as the indirect object) (familiar form) (sing) te; (pl) os (Spain), les (LAm); (formal) (sing) le; (pl) les. **I sent ~ the book yesterday** te mandé el libro ayer

❗ The pronoun se replaces the indirect object pronoun le or les when the latter is used with the direct object pronoun (lo, la etc), e.g. **I gave it to ~** se lo di

····▸ (when used after a preposition) (familiar form) (sing) ti, vos (River Plate and parts of Central America); (pl) vosotros, -tras (Spain), ustedes (LAm); (formal) (sing) usted; (pl) ustedes

····▸ (generalizing) uno, tú (esp Spain). **~ feel very proud** uno se siente muy orgulloso, te sientes muy orgulloso (esp Spain). **~ have to be patient** hay que tener paciencia

you'd /juːd/, /jʊəd/ = **you had**, **you would**

you'll /juːl/, /jʊəl/ = **you will**

young /jʌŋ/ adj (-er, -est) joven. **my ~er sister** mi hermana menor. **he's a year ~er than me** tiene un año menos que yo. **~ lady** n señorita f. **~ man** n joven m. **~ster** /-stə(r)/ n joven m

your /jɔː(r)/ adj (belonging to one person) (sing, familiar) tu; (pl, familiar) tus; (sing, formal) su; (belonging to more than one person) (sing, familiar) vuestro, -tra, su (LAm); (pl, familiar) vuestros, -tras, sus (LAm); (sing, formal) su; (pl, formal) sus

you're /jʊə(r)/, /jɔː(r)/ = **you are**

yours /jɔːz/ *poss pron* (*belonging to one person*) (*sing, familiar*) tuyo, -ya; (*pl, familiar*) tuyos, -yas; (*sing, formal*) suyo, -ya; (*pl, formal*) suyos, -yas. (*belonging to more than one person*) (*sing, familiar*) vuestro, -tra; (*pl, familiar*) vuestros, -tras, suyos, -ya (LAm); (*sing, formal*) suyo, -ya; (*pl, formal*) suyos, -yas. **an aunt of** ∼ una tía tuya/suya; ∼ **is here** el tuyo/la tuya/el suyo/la suya está aquí

yourself /jɔːˈself/ *pron* (*reflexive*). (*emphatic use*) Ⓤ tú mismo, tú misma; (*formal*) usted mismo, usted misma. **describe** ∼f descríbete; (*Ud form*) descríbase. **stop thinking about** ∼f Ⓤ deja de pensar en ti mismo; (*formal*) deje de pensar en sí mismo. **by** ∼f solo, sola. ∼**ves** /jɔːˈselvz/ *pron* vosotros mismos, vosotras mismas (*familiar*), ustedes mismos, ustedes mismas (LAm familiar), ustedes mismos, ustedes mismas (*formal*); (*reflexive*). **behave** ∼**ves** ¡portaos bien! (*familiar*), ¡pórtense bien! (*formal, LAm familiar*). **by** ∼**ves** solos, solas

youth /juːθ/ *n* (*pl* **youths** /juːðz/) (*early life*) juventud *f*; (*boy*) joven *m*; (*young people*) juventud *f*. ∼**ful** *adj* joven, juvenil. ∼ **hostel** *n* albergue *m* juvenil

you've /juːv/ = **you have**

Yugoslav /ˈjuːgəslaːv/ *adj & n* yugoslavo (*m*). ∼**ia** /-ˈslɑːvɪə/ *n* Yugoslavia *f*

Zz

zeal /ziːl/ *n* fervor *m*, celo *m*

zeal|ot /ˈzelət/ *n* fanático *m*. ∼**ous** /-əs/ *adj* ferviente; (*worker*) que pone gran celo en su trabajo

zebra /ˈzebrə/ *n* cebra *f*. ∼ **crossing** *n* paso *m* de cebra

zenith /ˈzenɪθ/ *n* cenit *m*

zero /ˈzɪərəʊ/ *n* (*pl* -os) cero *m*

zest /zest/ *n* entusiasmo *m*; (*peel*) cáscara *f*

zigzag /ˈzɪgzæg/ *n* zigzag *m*. ● *vi* (*pt* zigzagged) zigzaguear

zilch /zɪltʃ/ *n* Ⓧ nada de nada

zinc /zɪŋk/ *n* cinc *m*

zip /zɪp/ *n* cremallera *f*, cierre *m* (LAm), zíper *m* (Mex). ● *vt*. ∼ (**up**) cerrar (la cremallera). **Z**∼ **code** *n* (Amer) código *m* postal. ∼ **fastener** *n* cremallera *f*. ∼**per** *n*/*vt* see **ZIP**

zodiac /ˈzəʊdɪæk/ *n* zodíaco *m*, zodiaco *m*

zombie /ˈzɒmbɪ/ *n* zombi *m & f*

zone /zəʊn/ *n* zona *f*. **time** ∼ *n* huso *m* horario

zoo /zuː/ *n* zoo *m*, zoológico *m*. ∼**logical** /zuːəˈlɒdʒɪkl/ *adj* zoológico. ∼**logist** /zuːˈɒlədʒɪst/ *n* zoólogo *m*. ∼**logy** /zuːˈɒlədʒɪ/ *n* zoología *f*

zoom /zuːm/. □ ∼ **in** *vi* (Photo) hacer un zoom in (**on** sobre). □ ∼ **past** *vi*/*t* pasar zumbando. ∼ **lens** *n* teleobjetivo *m*, zoom *m*

zucchini /zʊˈkiːnɪ/ *n* (*invar* or ∼s) (Amer) calabacín *m*

Numbers/números

English		Spanish
zero	0	cero
one (first)	1	uno (primero)
two (second)	2	dos (segundo)
three (third)	3	tres (tercero)
four (fourth)	4	cuatro (cuarto)
five (fifth)	5	cinco (quinto)
six (sixth)	6	seis (sexto)
seven (seventh)	7	siete (séptimo)
eight (eighth)	8	ocho (octavo)
nine (ninth)	9	nueve (noveno)
ten (tenth)	10	diez (décimo)
eleven (eleventh)	11	once (undécimo)
twelve (twelfth)	12	doce (duodécimo)
thirteen (thirteenth)	13	trece (decimotercero)
fourteen (fourteenth)	14	catorce (decimocuarto)
fifteen (fifteenth)	15	quince (decimoquinto)
sixteen (sixteenth)	16	dieciséis (decimosexto)
seventeen (seventeenth)	17	diecisiete (decimoséptimo)
eighteen (eighteenth)	18	dieciocho (decimoctavo)
nineteen (nineteenth)	19	diecinueve (decimonoveno)
twenty (twentieth)	20	veinte (vigésimo)
twenty-one (twenty-first)	21	veintiuno (vigésimo primero)
twenty-two (twenty-second)	22	veintidós (vigésimo segundo)
twenty-three (twenty-third)	23	veintitrés (vigésimo tercero)
twenty-four (twenty-fourth)	24	veinticuatro (vigésimo cuarto)
twenty-five (twenty-fifth)	25	veinticinco (vigésimo quinto)
twenty-six (twenty-sixth)	26	veintiséis (vigésimo sexto)
thirty (thirtieth)	30	treinta (trigésimo)

Numbers

thirty-one (thirty-first)	**31**	treinta y uno (trigésimo primero)
forty (fortieth)	**40**	cuarenta (cuadragésimo)
fifty (fiftieth)	**50**	cincuenta (quincuagésimo)
sixty (sixtieth)	**60**	sesenta (sexagésimo)
seventy (seventieth)	**70**	setenta (septuagésimo)
eighty (eightieth)	**80**	ochenta (octogésimo)
ninety (ninetieth)	**90**	noventa (nonagésimo)
a/one hundred (hundredth)	**100**	cien (centésimo)
a/one hundred and one (hundred and first)	**101**	ciento uno (centésimo primero)
two hundred (two hundredth)	**200**	doscientos (ducentésimo)
three hundred (three hundredth)	**300**	trescientos (tricentésimo)
four hundred (four hundredth)	**400**	cuatrocientos (cuadringentésimo)
five hundred (five hundredth)	**500**	quinientos (quingentésimo)
six hundred (six hundredth)	**600**	seiscientos (sexcentésimo)
seven hundred (seven hundredth)	**700**	setecientos (septingentésimo)
eight hundred (eight hundredth)	**800**	ochocientos (octingentésimo)
nine hundred (nine hundredth)	**900**	novecientos (noningentésimo)
a/one thousand (thousandth)	**1000**	mil (milésimo)
two thousand (two thousandth)	**2000**	dos mil (dos milésimo)
a/one million (millionth)	**1,000,000**	un millón (millonésimo)

Verbos irregulares ingleses

Infinitivo	Pretérito	Participio pasado	Infinitivo	Pretérito	Participio pasado
be	was	been	**drive**	drove	driven
bear	bore	borne	**eat**	ate	eaten
beat	beat	beaten	**fall**	fell	fallen
become	became	become	**feed**	fed	fed
begin	began	begun	**feel**	felt	felt
bend	bent	bent	**fight**	fought	fought
bet	bet, betted	bet, betted	**find**	found	found
			flee	fled	fled
bid	bade, bid	bidden, bid	**fly**	flew	flown
bind	bound	bound	**freeze**	froze	frozen
bite	bit	bitten	**get**	got	got, gotten *US*
bleed	bled	bled	**give**	gave	given
blow	blew	blown	**go**	went	gone
break	broke	broken	**grow**	grew	grown
breed	bred	bred	**hang**	hung, hanged	hung, hanged
bring	brought	brought			
build	built	built	**have**	had	had
burn	burnt, burned	burnt, burned	**hear**	heard	heard
			hide	hid	hidden
burst	burst	burst	**hit**	hit	hit
buy	bought	bought	**hold**	held	held
catch	caught	caught	**hurt**	hurt	hurt
choose	chose	chosen	**keep**	kept	kept
cling	clung	clung	**kneel**	knelt	knelt
come	came	come	**know**	knew	known
cost	cost, costed (vt)	cost, costed	**lay**	laid	laid
			lead	led	led
cut	cut	cut	**lean**	leaned, leant	leaned, leant
deal	dealt	dealt			
dig	dug	dug	**learn**	learnt, learned	learnt, learned
do	did	done			
draw	drew	drawn	**leave**	left	left
dream	dreamt, dreamed	dreamt, dreamed	**lend**	lent	lent
			let	let	let
drink	drank	drunk	**lie**	lay	lain

Infinitivo	Pretérito	Participio pasado	Infinitivo	Pretérito	Participio pasado
lose	lost	lost	**spend**	spent	spent
make	made	made	**spit**	spat	spat
mean	meant	meant	**spoil**	spoilt,	spoilt,
meet	met	met		spoiled	spoiled
pay	paid	paid	**spread**	spread	spread
put	put	put	**spring**	sprang	sprung
read	read	read	**stand**	stood	stood
ride	rode	ridden	**steal**	stole	stolen
ring	rang	rung	**stick**	stuck	stuck
rise	rose	risen	**sting**	stung	stung
run	ran	run	**stride**	strode	stridden
say	said	said	**strike**	struck	struck
see	saw	seen	**swear**	swore	sworn
seek	sought	sought	**sweep**	swept	swept
sell	sold	sold	**swell**	swelled	swollen,
send	sent	sent			swelled
set	set	set	**swim**	swam	swum
sew	sewed	sewn, sewed	**swing**	swung	swung
shake	shook	shaken	**take**	took	taken
shine	shone	shone	**teach**	taught	taught
shoe	shod	shod	**tear**	tore	torn
shoot	shot	shot	**tell**	told	told
show	showed	shown	**think**	thought	thought
shut	shut	shut	**throw**	threw	thrown
sing	sang	sung	**thrust**	thrust	thrust
sink	sank	sunk	**tread**	trod	trodden
sit	sat	sat	**under-**	under-	understood
sleep	slept	slept	**stand**	stood	
sling	slung	slung	**wake**	woke	woken
smell	smelt,	smelt,	**wear**	wore	worn
	smelled	smelled	**win**	won	won
speak	spoke	spoken	**write**	wrote	written
spell	spelled,	spelled,			
	spelt	spelt			

Spanish verbs

Regular verbs:

● in **-ar** (e.g. **comprar**)

Present; compr|o, ~as, ~a, ~amos, ~áis, ~an

Future: comprar|é, ~ás, ~á, ~emos, ~éis, ~án

Imperfect: compr|aba, ~abas, ~aba, ~ábamos, ~abais, ~aban

Preterite: compr|é, ~aste, ~ó, ~amos, ~asteis, ~aron

Present subjunctive: compr|e, ~es, ~e, ~emos, ~éis, ~en

Imperfect subjunctive: compr|ara, ~aras, ~ara, ~áramos, ~arais, ~aran

compr|ase, ~ases, ~ase, ~ásemos, ~aseis, ~asen

Conditional: comprar|ía, ~ías, ~ía, ~íamos, ~íais, ~ían

Present participle: comprando

Past participle: comprado

Imperative: compra, comprad

● in **-er** (e.g. **beber**)

Present: beb|o, ~es, ~e, ~emos, ~éis, ~en

Future: beber|é, ~ás, ~á, ~emos, ~éis, ~án

Imperfect: beb|ía, ~ías, ~ía, ~íamos, ~íais, ~ían

Preterite: beb|í, ~iste, ~ió, ~imos, ~isteis, ~ieron

Present subjunctive: beb|a, ~as, ~a, ~amos, ~áis, ~an

Imperfect subjunctive: beb|iera, ~ieras, ~iera, ~iéramos, ~ierais, ~ieran

beb|iese, ~ieses, ~iese, ~iésemos, ~ieseis, ~iesen

Conditional: beber|ía, ~ías, ~ía, ~íamos, ~íais, ~ían

Present participle: bebiendo

Past participle: bebido

Imperative: bebe, bebed

● in **-ir** (e.g. **vivir**)

Present: viv|o, ~es, ~e, ~imos, ~is, ~en

Future: vivir|é, ~ás, ~á, ~emos, ~éis, ~án

Imperfect: viv|ía, ~ías, ~ía, ~íamos, ~íais, ~ían

Preterite: viv|í, ~iste, ~ió, ~imos, ~isteis, ~ieron

Present subjunctive: viv|a, ~as, ~a, ~amos, ~áis, ~an

Imperfect subjunctive: viv|iera, ~ieras, ~iera, ~iéramos, ~ierais, ~ieran

viv|iese, ~ieses, ~iese, ~iésemos, ~ieseis, ~iesen

Conditional: vivir|ía, ~ías, ~ía, ~íamos, ~íais, ~ían

Present participle: viviendo

Past participle: vivido

Imperative: vive, vivid

Irregular verbs:

[1] cerrar

Present: cierro, cierras, cierra, cerramos, cerráis, cierran

Present subjunctive: cierre, cierres, cierre, cerremos, cerréis, cierren

Imperative: cierra, cerrad

[2] contar, mover

Present: cuento, cuentas, cuenta,
contamos, contáis, cuentan
muevo, mueves, mueve,
movemos, movéis, mueven
Present subjunctive: cuente, cuentes,
cuente, contemos, contéis,
cuenten
mueva, muevas, mueva,
movamos, mováis, muevan
Imperative: cuenta, contad
mueve, moved

[3] jugar

Present: juego, juegas, juega,
jugamos, jugáis, juegan
Preterite: jugué, jugaste, jugó,
jugamos, jugasteis, jugaron
Present subjunctive: juegue, juegues,
juegue, juguemos, juguéis,
jueguen

[4] sentir

Present: siento, sientes, siente,
sentimos, sentís, sienten
Preterite: sentí, sentiste, sintió,
sentimos, sentisteis, sintieron
Present subjunctive: sienta, sientas,
sienta, sintamos, sintáis, sientan
Imperfect subjunctive: sint|iera,
~ieras, ~iera, ~iéramos, ~ierais, ~ieran
sint|iese, ~ieses, ~iese, ~iésemos,
~ieseis, ~iesen
Present participle: sintiendo
Imperative: siente, sentid

[5] pedir

Present: pido, pides, pide, pedimos,
pedís, piden
Preterite: pedí, pediste, pidió,
pedimos, pedisteis, pidieron

Present subjunctive: pid|a, ~as, ~a,
~amos, ~áis, ~an
Imperfect subjunctive: pid|iera, ~ieras,
~iera, ~iéramos, ~ierais, ~ieran
pid|iese, ~ieses, ~iese, ~iésemos,
~ieseis, ~iesen
Present participle: pidiendo
Imperative: pide, pedid

[6] dormir

Present: duermo, duermes, duerme,
dormimos, dormís, duermen
Preterite: dormí, dormiste, durmió,
dormimos, dormisteis, durmieron
Present subjunctive: duerma, duermas,
duerma, durmamos, durmáis,
duerman
Imperfect subjunctive: durm|iera,
~ieras, ~iera, ~iéramos, ~ierais,
~ieran
durm|iese, ~ieses, ~iese,
~iésemos, ~ieseis, ~iesen
Present participle: durmiendo
Imperative: duerme, dormid

[7] dedicar

Preterite: dediqué, dedicaste, dedicó,
dedicamos, dedicasteis, dedicaron
Present subjunctive: dediqu|e, ~es,
~e, ~emos, ~éis, ~en

[8] delinquir

Present: delinco, delinques, delinque,
delinquimos, delinquís, delinquen
Present subjunctive: delinc|a, ~as, ~a,
~amos, ~áis, ~an

[9] vencer, esparcir

Present: venzo, vences, vence,
vencemos, vencéis, vencen
esparzo, esparces, esparce,
esparcimos, esparcís, esparcen

Present subjunctive: venz|a, ~as, ~a, ~amos, ~áis, ~an

esparz|a, ~as, ~a, ~amos, ~áis, ~an

[10] rechazar

Preterite: rechacé, rechazaste, rechazó, rechazamos, rechazasteis, rechazaron

Present subjunctive: rechac|e, ~es, ~e, ~emos, ~éis, ~en

[11] conocer, lucir

Present: conozco, conoces, conoce, conocemos, conocéis, conocen

luzco, luces, luce, lucimos, lucís, lucen

Present subjunctive: conozc|a, ~as, ~a, ~amos, ~áis, ~an

luzc|a, ~as, ~a, ~amos, ~áis, ~an

[12] pagar

Preterite: pagué, pagaste, pagó, pagamos, pagasteis, pagaron

Present subjunctive: pagu|e, ~es, ~e, ~emos, ~éis, ~en

[13] distinguir

Present: distingo, distingues, distingue, distinguimos, distinguís, distinguen

Present subjunctive: disting|a, ~as, ~a, ~amos, ~áis, ~an

[14] acoger, afligir

Present: acojo, acoges, acoge, acogemos, acogéis, acogen

aflijo, afliges, aflige, afligimos, afligís, afligen

Present subjunctive: acoj|a, ~as, ~a, ~amos, ~áis, ~an

aflij|a, ~as, ~a, ~amos, ~áis, ~an

[15] averiguar

Preterite: averigüé, averiguaste, averiguó, averiguamos, averiguasteis, averiguaron

Present subjunctive: averigü|e, ~es, ~e, ~emos, ~éis, ~en

[16] agorar

Present: agüero, agüeras, agüera, agoramos, agoráis, agüeran

Present subjunctive: agüere, agüeres, agüere, agoremos, agoréis, agüeren

Imperative: agüera, agorad

[17] huir

Present: huyo, huyes, huye, huimos, huís, huyen

Preterite: huí, huiste, huyó, huimos, huisteis, huyeron

Present subjunctive: huy|a, ~as, ~a, ~amos, ~áis, ~an

Imperfect subjunctive: huy|era, ~eras, ~era, ~éramos, ~erais, ~eran

huy|ese, ~eses, ~ese, ~ésemos, ~eseis, ~esen

Present participle: huyendo
Imperative: huye, huid

[18] creer

Preterite: creí, creíste, creyó, creímos, creísteis, creyeron

Imperfect subjunctive: crey|era, ~eras, ~era, ~éramos, ~erais, ~eran

crey|ese, ~eses, ~ese, ~ésemos, ~eseis, ~esen

Present participle: creyendo
Past participle: creído

[19] argüir

Present: arguyo, arguyes, arguye, argüimos, argüís, arguyen
Preterite: argüí, argüiste, arguyó, argüimos, argüisteis, arguyeron
Present subjunctive: arguy|a, ~as, ~a, ~amos, ~áis, ~an
Imperfect subjunctive: arguy|era, ~eras, ~era, ~éramos, ~erais, ~eran
arguy|ese, ~eses, ~ese, ~ésemos, ~eseis, ~esen
Present participle: arguyendo
Imperative: arguye, argüid

[20] vaciar

Present: vacío, vacías, vacía, vaciamos, vaciáis, vacían
Present subjunctive: vacíe, vacíes, vacíe, vaciemos, vaciéis, vacíen
Imperative: vacía, vaciad

[21] acentuar

Present: acentúo, acentúas, acentúa, acentuamos, acentuáis, acentúan
Present subjunctive: acentúe, acentúes, acentúe, acentuemos, acentuéis, acentúen
Imperative: acentúa, acentuad

[22] atañer, engullir

Preterite: atañ|í, ~iste, ~ó, ~imos, ~isteis, ~eron
engull|í ~iste, ~ó, ~imos, ~isteis, ~eron
Imperfect subjunctive: atañera, ~eras, ~era, ~éramos, ~erais, ~eran
atañese, ~eses, ~ese, ~ésemos, ~eseis, ~esen
engull|era, ~eras, ~era, ~éramos, ~erais, ~eran

engull|ese, ~eses, ~ese, ~ésemos, ~eseis, ~esen
Present participle: atañendo
engullendo

[23] aislar, aullar

Present: aíslo, aíslas, aísla, aislamos, aisláis, aíslan
aúllo, aúllas, aúlla, aullamos, aulláis, aúllan
Present subjunctive: aísle, aísles, aísle, aislemos, aisléis, aíslen
aúlle, aúlles, aúlle, aullemos, aulléis, aúllen
Imperative: aísla, aislad
aúlla, aullad

[24] abolir

Present: abolimos, abolís
Present subjunctive: not used
Imperative: abolid

[25] andar

Preterite: anduv|e, ~iste, ~o, ~imos, ~isteis, ~ieron
Imperfect subjunctive: anduv|iera, ~ieras, ~iera, ~iéramos, ~ierais, ~ieran
anduv|iese, ~ieses, ~iese, ~iésemos, ~ieseis, ~iesen

[26] dar

Present: doy, das, da, damos, dais, dan
Preterite: di, diste, dio, dimos, disteis, dieron
Present subjunctive: dé, des, dé, demos, deis, den
Imperfect subjunctive: diera, dieras, diera, diéramos, dierais, dieran
diese, dieses, diese, diésemos, dieseis, diesen

[27] estar

Present: estoy, estás, está, estamos,
estáis, están
Preterite: estuv|e, ~iste, ~o, ~imos,
~isteis, ~ieron
Present subjunctive: esté, estés, esté,
estemos, estéis, estén
Imperfect subjunctive: estuv|iera,
~ieras, ~iera, ~iéramos, ~ierais,
~ieran
estuv|iese, ~ieses, ~iese,
~iésemos, ~ieseis, ~iesen
Imperative: está, estad

[28] caber

Present: quepo, cabes, cabe,
cabemos, cabéis, caben
Future: cabr|é, ~ás, ~á, ~emos,
~éis, ~án
Preterite: cup|e, ~iste, ~o, ~imos,
~isteis, ~ieron
Present subjunctive: quep|a, ~as, ~a,
~amos, ~áis, ~an
Imperfect subjunctive: cup|iera, ~ieras,
~iera, ~iéramos, ~ierais, ~ieran
cup|iese, ~ieses, ~iese, ~iésemos,
~ieseis, ~iesen
Conditional: cabr|ía, ~ías, ~ía,
~íamos, ~íais, ~ían

[29] caer

Present: caigo, caes, cae, caemos,
caéis, caen
Preterite: caí, caiste, cayó, caímos,
caísteis, cayeron
Present subjunctive: caig|a, ~as, ~a,
~amos, ~áis, ~an
Imperfect subjunctive: cay|era, ~eras,
~era, ~éramos, ~erais, ~eran
cay|ese, ~eses, ~ese, ~ésemos,
~eseis, ~esen
Present participle: cayendo

Past participle: caído

[30] haber

Present: he, has, ha, hemos, habéis,
han
Future: habr|é, ~ás, ~á, ~emos,
~éis, ~án
Preterite: hub|e, ~iste, ~o, ~imos,
~isteis, ~ieron
Present subjunctive: hay|a, ~as, ~a,
~amos, ~áis, ~an
Imperfect subjunctive: hub|iera,
~ieras, ~iera, ~iéramos, ~ierais,
~ieran
hub|iese, ~ieses, ~iese, ~iésemos,
~ieseis, ~iesen
Conditional: habr|ía, ~ías, ~ía,
~íamos, ~íais, ~ían
Imperative: he, habed

[31] hacer

Present: hago, haces, hace, hacemos,
hacéis, hacen
Future: har|é, ~ás, ~á, ~emos, ~éis,
~án
Preterite: hice, hiciste, hizo, hicimos,
hicisteis, hicieron
Present subjunctive: hag|a, ~as, ~a,
~amos, ~áis, ~an
Imperfect subjunctive: hic|iera, ~ieras,
~iera, ~iéramos, ~ierais, ~ieran
hic|iese, ~ieses, ~iese, ~iésemos,
~ieseis, ~iesen
Conditional: har|ía, ~ías, ~ía,
~íamos, ~íais, ~ían
Past participle: hecho
Imperative: haz, haced

[32] placer

Present subjunctive: plazca
Imperfect subjunctive: placiera,
placiese

[33] poder

Present: puedo, puedes, puede,
podemos, podéis, pueden
Future: podr|é, ~ás, ~á, ~emos,
~éis, ~án
Preterite: pud|e, ~iste, ~o, ~imos,
~isteis, ~ieron
Present subjunctive: pueda, puedas,
pueda, podamos, podáis, puedan
Imperfect subjunctive: pud|iera,
~ieras, ~iera, ~iéramos, ~ierais,
~ieran
pud|iese, ~ieses, ~iese, ~iésemos,
~ieseis, ~iesen
Conditional: podr|ía, ~ías, ~ía,
~íamos, ~íais, ~ían
Past participle: pudiendo

[34] poner

Present: pongo, pones, pone,
ponemos, ponéis, ponen
Future: pondr|é, ~ás, ~á, ~emos,
~éis, ~án
Preterite: pus|e, ~iste, ~o, ~imos,
~isteis, ~ieron
Present subjunctive: pong|a, ~as, ~a,
~amos, ~áis, ~an
Imperfect subjunctive: pus|iera, ~ieras,
~iera, ~iéramos, ~ierais, ~ieran
pus|iese, ~ieses, ~iese, ~iésemos,
~ieseis, ~iesen
Conditional: pondr|ía, ~ías, ~ía,
~íamos, ~íais, ~ían
Past participle: puesto
Imperative: pon, poned

[35] querer

Present: quiero, quieres, quiere,
queremos, queréis, quieren
Future: querr|é, ~ás, ~á, ~emos,
~éis, ~án

Preterite: quis|e, ~iste, ~o, ~imos,
~isteis, ~ieron
Present subjunctive: quiera, quieras,
quiera, queramos, queráis,
quieran
Imperfect subjunctive: quis|iera,
~ieras, ~iera, ~iéramos, ~ierais,
~ieran
quis|iese, ~ieses, ~iese,
~iésemos, ~ieseis, ~iesen
Conditional: querr|ía, ~ías, ~ía,
~íamos, ~íais, ~ían
Imperative: quiere, quered

[36] raer

Present: raigo/rayo, raes, rae, raemos,
raéis, raen
Preterite: raí, raíste, rayó, raímos,
raísteis, rayeron
Present subjunctive: raig|a, ~as, ~a,
~amos, ~áis, ~an ray|a, ~as, ~a,
~amos, ~áis, ~an
Imperfect subjunctive: ray|era, ~eras,
~era, ~éramos, ~erais, ~eran
ray|ese, ~eses, ~ese, ~ésemos,
~eseis, ~esen
Present participle: rayendo
Past participle: raído

[37] roer

Present: roo, roes, roe, roemos, roéis,
roen
Preterite: roí, roíste, royó, roímos,
roísteis, royeron
Present subjunctive: ro|a, ~as, ~a,
~amos, ~áis, ~an
Imperfect subjunctive: roy|era, ~eras,
~era, ~éramos, ~erais, ~eran
roy|ese, ~eses, ~ese, ~ésemos,
~eseis, ~esen
Present participle: royendo
Past participle: roído

[38] saber

Present: sé, sabes, sabe, sabemos, sabéis, saben
Future: sabr|é, ~ás, ~á, ~emos, ~éis, ~án
Preterite: sup|e, ~iste, ~o, ~imos, ~isteis, ~ieron
Present subjunctive: sep|a, ~as, ~a, ~amos, ~áis, ~an
Imperfect subjunctive: sup|iera, ~ieras, ~iera, ~iéramos, ~ierais, ~ieran
sup|iese, ~ieses, ~iese, ~iésemos, ~ieseis, ~iesen
Conditional: sabr|ía, ~ías, ~ía, ~íamos, ~íais, ~ían

[39] ser

Present: soy, eres, es, somos, sois, son
Imperfect: era, eras, era, éramos, erais, eran
Preterite: fui, fuiste, fue, fuimos, fuisteis, fueron
Present subjunctive: se|a, ~as, ~a, ~amos, ~áis, ~an
Imperfect subjunctive: fu|era, ~eras, ~era, ~éramos, ~erais, ~eran
fu|ese, ~eses, ~ese, ~ésemos, ~eseis, ~esen
Imperative: sé, sed

[40] tener

Present: tengo, tienes, tiene, tenemos, tenéis, tienen
Future: tendr|é, ~ás, ~á, ~emos, ~éis, ~án
Preterite: tuv|e, ~iste, ~o, ~imos, ~isteis, ~ieron
Present subjunctive: teng|a, ~as, ~a, ~amos, ~áis, ~an
Imperfect subjunctive: tuv|iera, ~ieras, ~iera, ~iéramos, ~ierais, ~ieran
tuv|iese, ~ieses, ~iese, ~iésemos, ~ieseis, ~iesen
Conditional: tendr|ía, ~ías, ~ía, ~íamos, ~íais, ~ían
Imperative: ten, tened

[41] traer

Present: traigo, traes, trae, traemos, traéis, traen
Preterite: traj|e, ~iste, ~o, ~imos, ~isteis, ~eron
Present subjunctive: traig|a, ~as, ~a, ~amos, ~áis, ~an
Imperfect subjunctive: traj|era, ~eras, ~era, ~éramos, ~erais, ~eran
traj|ese, ~eses, ~ese, ~ésemos, ~eseis, ~esen
Present participle: trayendo
Past participle: traído

[42] valer

Present: valgo, vales, vale, valemos, valéis, valen
Future: valdr|é, ~ás, ~á, ~emos, ~éis, ~án
Present subjunctive: valg|a, ~as, ~a, ~amos, ~áis, ~an
Conditional: valdr|ía, ~ías, ~ía, ~íamos, ~íais, ~ían
Imperative: vale, valed

[43] ver

Present: veo, ves, ve, vemos, veis, ven
Imperfect: ve|ía, ~ías, ~ía, ~íamos, ~íais, ~ían
Preterite: vi, viste, vio, vimos, visteis, vieron
Present subjunctive: ve|a, ~as, ~a, ~amos, ~áis, ~an
Past participle: visto

[44] yacer

Present: yazco, yaces, yace, yacemos, yacéis, yacen
Present subjunctive: yazc|a, ~as, ~a, ~amos, ~áis, ~an
Imperative: yace, yaced

[45] asir

Present: asgo, ases, ase, asimos, asís, asen
Present subjunctive: asg|a, ~as, ~a, ~amos, ~áis, ~an

[46] decir

Present: digo, dices, dice, decimos, decís, dicen
Future: dir|é, ~ás, ~á, ~emos, ~éis, ~án
Preterite: dij|e, ~iste, ~o, ~imos, ~isteis, ~eron
Present subjunctive: dig|a, ~as, ~a, ~amos, ~áis, ~an
Imperfect subjunctive: dij|era, ~eras, ~era, ~éramos, ~erais, ~eran
dij|ese, ~eses, ~ese, ~ésemos, ~eseis, ~esen
Conditional: dir|ía, ~ías, ~ía, ~íamos, ~íais, ~ían
Present participle: dicho
Imperative: di, decid

[47] reducir

Present: reduzco, reduces, reduce, reducimos, reducís, reducen
Preterite: reduj|e, ~iste, ~o, ~imos, ~isteis, ~eron
Present subjunctive: reduzc|a, ~a, ~amos, ~áis, ~an
Imperfect subjunctive: reduj|era, ~eras, ~era, ~éramos, ~erais, ~eran

reduj|ese, ~eses, ~ese, ~ésemos, ~eseis, ~esen

[48] erguir

Present: yergo, yergues, yergue, erguimos, erguís, yerguen
Preterite: erguí, erguiste, irguió, erguimos, erguisteis, irguieron
Present subjunctive: yerg|a, ~as, ~a, ~amos, ~áis, ~an
Imperfect subjunctive: irgu|iera, ~ieras, ~iera, ~iéramos, ~ierais, ~ieran
irgu|iese, ~ieses, ~iese, ~iésemos, ~ieseis, ~iesen
Present participle: irguiendo
Imperative: yergue, erguid

[49] ir

Present: voy, vas, va, vamos, vais, van
Imperfect: iba, ibas, iba, íbamos, ibais, iban
Preterite: fui, fuiste, fue, fuimos, fuisteis, fueron
Present subjunctive: vay|a, ~as, ~a, ~amos, ~áis, ~an
Imperfect subjunctive: fu|era, ~eras, ~era, ~éramos, ~erais, ~eran
fu|ese, ~eses, ~ese, ~ésemos, ~eseis, ~esen
Present participle: yendo
Imperative: ve, id

[50] oír

Present: oigo, oyes, oye, oímos, oís, oyen
Preterite: oí, oíste, oyó, oímos, oísteis, oyeron
Present subjunctive: oig|a, ~as, ~a, ~amos, ~áis, ~an
Imperfect subjunctive: oy|era, ~eras, ~era, ~éramos, ~erais, ~eran

Spanish verbs

oy|ese, ∼eses, ∼ese, ∼ésemos,
∼eseis, ∼esen
Present participle: oyendo
Past participle: oído
Imperative: oye, oíd

[51] reír

Present: río, ríes, ríe, reímos, reís,
ríen
Preterite: reí, reíste, rió, reímos,
reísteis, rieron
Present subjunctive: ría, rías, ría,
riamos, riáis, rían
Present participle: riendo
Past participle: reído
Imperative: ríe, reíd

[52] salir

Present: salgo, sales, sale, salimos,
salís, salen
Future: saldr|é, ∼ás, ∼á, ∼emos,
∼éis, ∼án
Present subjunctive: salg|a, ∼as, ∼a,
∼amos, ∼áis, ∼an

Conditional: saldr|ía, ∼ías, ∼ía,
∼íamos, ∼íais, ∼ían
Imperative: sal, salid

[53] venir

Present: vengo, vienes, viene,
venimos, venís, vienen
Future: vendr|é, ∼ás, ∼á, ∼emos,
∼éis, ∼án
Preterite: vin|e, ∼iste, ∼o, ∼imos,
∼isteis, ∼ieron
Present subjunctive: veng|a, ∼as, ∼a,
∼amos, ∼áis, ∼an
Imperfect subjunctive: vin|iera,
∼ieras, ∼iera, ∼iéramos, ∼ierais, ∼ieran
vin|iese, ∼ieses, ∼iese, ∼iésemos,
∼ieseis, ∼iesen
Conditional: vendr|ía, ∼ías, ∼ía,
∼íamos, ∼íais, ∼ían
Present participle: viniendo
Imperative: ven, venid